D0661997

HarperCollins Publishers
Westerhill Road
Bishopbriggs
Glasgow
G64 2QT
Great Britain

Fifth Edition 2007

Previously published as
Collins Express Italian Dictionary
© HarperCollins Publishers 2007

Reprint 10 9 8 7 6 5 4 3 2 1

© William Collins Sons & Co. Ltd 1990
© HarperCollins Publishers 1996,
1999, 2002, 2007

ISBN 978-0-00-725345-6

Collins® and Bank of English® are
registered trademarks of
HarperCollins Publishers Limited

www.collins.co.uk

A catalogue record for this book is
available from the British Library

HarperCollins Publishers,
10 East 53rd Street,
New York, NY 10022

COLLINS POCKET ITALIAN DICTIONARY.
Third US Edition 2007

ISBN-13 978-0-06-114187-4
ISBN-10 0-06-114187-9

www.harpercollins.com

HarperCollins books may be
purchased for educational, business,
or sales promotional use. For
information, please write to:
Special Markets Department,
HarperCollins Publishers,
10 East 53rd Street,
New York, NY 10022

Dictionary text typeset by
Thomas Callan

Supplement text typeset by
Davidson Pre-Press, Glasgow

Printed in Italy by
Rotolito Lombarda S.p.A.

Acknowledgements
We would like to thank those authors
and publishers who kindly gave
permission for copyright material to
be used in the Collins Word Web. We
would also like to thank Times
Newspapers Ltd for providing
valuable data.

All rights reserved.

Entered words that we have reason to
believe constitute trademarks have
been designated as such. However,
neither the presence nor absence of
such designation should be regarded
as affecting the legal status of any
trademark.

GENERAL EDITOR
Maree Airlie

CONTRIBUTORS
Gabriella Bacchelli
Daphne Day

EDITORIAL COORDINATION
Susie Beattie

SERIES EDITOR
Lorna Knight

This book is set in Collins Fedra, a
typeface specially created for Collins
Dictionaries by Peter Bil'ak

Collins

Collins
Italian
Dictionary

William Collins' dream of knowledge for all began with the publication of his first book in 1819. A self-educated mill worker, he not only enriched millions of lives, but also founded a flourising publishing house. Today, staying true to this spirit, Collins books are packed with inspiration, innovation, and practical expertise. They place you at the centre of a world of possibility and give you exactly what you need to explore it.

Language is the key to this exploration, and at the heart of Collins Dictionaries is language as it is really used. New words, phrases, and meanings spring up every day, and all of them are captured and analysed by the Collins Word Web. Constantly updated, and with over 2.5 billion entries, this living language resource is unique to our dictionaries.

Words are tools for life. And a Collins Dictionary makes them work for you.

Collins. Do more.

INDICE

CONTENTS

I marchi registrati
I termini che a nostro parere costituiscono un marchio registrato sono stati designati come tali. In ogni caso, né la presenza né l'assenza di tale designazione implicano alcuna valutazione del loro reale stato giuridico.

Note on trademarks
Entered words that we have reason to believe constitute trademarks have been designated as such. However, neither the presence nor the absence of such designation should be regarded as affecting the legal status of any trademark.

INTRODUZIONE

Vi ringraziamo di aver scelto questo dizionario inglese e ci auguriamo che esso si riveli uno strumento utile e piacevole da usare nello studio, in vacanza e sul lavoro.

In questa introduzione troverete alcuni suggerimenti per aiutarvi a trarre il massimo beneficio dal vostro nuovo dizionario, ricco non solo per il suo ampio lemmario ma anche per il gran numero di informazioni contenute in ciascuna voce.

All'inizio del dizionario troverete l'elenco delle abbreviazioni usate nel testo e una guida alla pronuncia. Troverete inoltre un utile elenco delle forme dei verbi irregolari inglesi e italiani, seguito da una sezione finale con i numeri, l'ora e la data.

Come usare il dizionario

Per imparare ad usare in modo efficace il dizionario è importante comprendere la funzione delle differenziazioni tipografiche, dei simboli e delle abbreviazioni usati nel testo. Vi forniamo pertanto qui di seguito alcuni chiarimenti in merito a tali convenzioni.

I lemmi

Sono le parole in **neretto** elencate in ordine alfabetico. Il primo e l'ultimo lemma di ciascuna pagina appaiono al margine superiore.

Dove opportuno, informazioni sull'ambito d'uso o il livello di formalità di certe parole vengono fornite tra parentesi in corsivo e spesso in forma abbreviata dopo l'indicazione della categoria grammaticale (es. (*Comm*), (*inf*)).

In certi casi più parole con radice comune sono raggruppate sotto lo stesso lemma. Tali parole appaiono in neretto ma in un carattere leggermente ridotto (es. **acceptance**).

Esempi d'uso del lemma sono a loro volta in neretto ma in un carattere diverso dal lemma (es. **to be cold**).

La trascrizione fonetica

La trascrizione fonetica che illustra la corretta pronuncia del lemma è tra parentesi quadre e segue immediatamente il lemma (es. **knee** [ni:]). L'elenco dei simboli fonetici è alle pagine xii-xiii.

Le traduzioni

Le traduzioni sono in carattere tondo e, quando il lemma ha più di un significato, le traduzioni sono separate da un punto e virgola. Spesso diverse traduzioni di un lemma sono introdotte da una o più parole in corsivo tra parentesi tonde: la loro funzione è di chiarire a quale significato del lemma si riferisce la traduzione. Possono essere sinonimi, indicazioni di ambito d'uso o di registro del lemma (es. **party** *(Pol)*, *(team)*, *(celebration)*; **laid back** *(inf)* ecc.).

Le 'parole chiave' ⬤

Un trattamento particolare è stato riservato a quelle parole che, per frequenza d'uso o complessità, necessitano una strutturazione più chiara ed esauriente (es. **da, di, avere** in italiano, **at, to, be, this** in inglese). Frecce e numeri vi guidano attraverso le varie distinzioni grammaticali e di significato; ulteriori informazioni sono fornite in corsivo tra parentesi.

Informazioni grammaticali

Le parti del discorso (noun, adjective ecc.) sono espresse da abbreviazioni convenzionali in corsivo *(n, adj* ecc.) e seguono la trascrizione fonetica del lemma.

Eventuali ulteriori informazioni grammaticali, come ad esempio le forme di un verbo irregolare o il plurale irregolare di un sostantivo, precedono tra parentesi la parte del discorso (es. **give** *(pt* **gave**, *pp* **given**) *vt;* **man** [...] *(pl* **men**) *n*).

INTRODUCTION

We are delighted that you have decided to buy this Italian Dictionary and hope you will enjoy and benefit from using it at school, at home, on holiday or at work.

This introduction gives you a few tips on how to get the most out of your dictionary – not simply from its comprehensive wordlist but also from the information provided in each entry. This will help you to read and understand modern Italian, as well as communicate and express yourself in the language.

The dictionary begins by listing the abbreviations used in the text and illustrating the sounds shown by the phonetic symbols. You will also find Italian and English verb tables, followed by a section on numbers and time expressions.

Using your dictionary

A wealth of information is presented in the dictionary, using various typefaces, sizes of type, symbols, abbreviations and brackets. The various conventions and symbols used are explained in the following sections.

Headwords

The words you look up in a dictionary – "headwords" – are listed alphabetically. They are printed in **bold type** for rapid identification. The two headwords appearing at the top of each page indicate the first and last word dealt with on the page in question.

Information about the usage or form of certain headwords is given in brackets after the part of speech. This usually appears in abbreviated form and in italics (e.g. (*fam*), (*Comm*)).

Where appropriate, words related to headwords are grouped in the same entry (e.g. **illustrare, illustrazione**) in a slightly smaller bold type than the headword.

Common expressions in which the headword appears are shown in a different bold roman type (e.g. **aver freddo**).

Phonetic spellings

Where the phonetic spelling of headwords (indicating their pronunciation) is given, it will appear in square brackets immediately after the headword (e.g. **calza** ['kaltsa]). A list of these symbols is given on pages xii-xiii.

Translations

Headword translations are given in ordinary type and, where more than one meaning or usage exists, these are separated by a semi-colon. You will often find other words in italics in brackets before the translations. These offer suggested contexts in which the headword might appear (e.g. **duro** (*pietra*) or (*lavoro*)) or provide synonyms (e.g. **duro** (*ostinato*)).

"Key" words ⬤

Special status is given to certain Italian and English words which are considered as "key" words in each language. They may, for example, occur very frequently or have several types of usage (e.g. **da, di, avere** in Italian, **at, to, be, this** in English). A combination of arrows and numbers helps you to distinguish different parts of speech and different meanings. Further helpful information is provided in brackets and italics.

Grammatical information

Parts of speech are given in abbreviated form in italics after the phonetic spellings of headwords (e.g. *vt*, *av*, *cong*).

Genders of Italian nouns are indicated as follows: *sm* for a masculine and *sf* for a feminine noun. Feminine and irregular plural forms of nouns are also shown (e.g. **uovo**, (*pl(f)* **uova**); **dottore**, **essa**).

Feminine adjective endings are given, as are plural forms (e.g. **opaco**, **a**, **chi**, **che**).

ABBREVIAZIONI		ABBREVIATIONS
abbreviazione	*abbr*	abbreviation
aggettivo	*adj*	adjective
amministrazione	*Admin*	administration
avverbio	*adv*	adverb
aeronautica, viaggi aerei	*Aer*	flying, air travel
aggettivo	*ag*	adjective
agricoltura	*Agr*	agriculture
amministrazione	*Amm*	administration
anatomia	*Anat*	anatomy
architettura	*Archit*	architecture
articolo determinativo	*art def*	definite article
articolo indeterminativo	*art indef*	indefinite article
attributivo	*attrib*	attributive
ausiliare	*aus, aux*	auxiliary
automobile	*Aut*	motor car and motoring
avverbio	*av*	adverb
aeronautica, viaggi aerei	*Aviat*	flying, air travel
biologia	*Biol*	biology
botanica	*Bot*	botany
inglese britannico	*BRIT*	British English
consonante	C	consonant
chimica	*Chim, Chem*	chemistry
commercio, finanza	*Comm*	commerce, finance
comparativo	*compar*	comparative
informatica	*Comput*	computing
congiunzione	*cong, conj*	conjunction
edilizia	*Constr*	building
sostantivo usato come aggettivo, ma mai con funzione predicativa	*cpd*	compound element: noun used as adjective and which cannot follow the noun it qualifies
cucina	*Cuc, Culin*	cookery
davanti a	*dav*	before

ABBREVIAZIONI		ABBREVIATIONS
articolo determinativo	*def art*	definite article
determinativo; articolo, aggettivo dimostrativo o indefinito ecc	*det*	determiner: article, demonstrative etc
diminutivo	*dimin*	diminutive
diritto	*Dir*	law
economia	*Econ*	economics
edilizia	*Edil*	building
elettricità, elettronica	*Elettr, Elec*	electricity, electronics
esclamazione	*escl, excl*	exclamation
femminile	*f*	feminine
familiare (! da evitare)	*fam(!)*	colloquial usage (! particularly offensive)
ferrovia	*Ferr*	railways
senso figurato	*fig*	figurative use
fisiologia	*Fisiol*	physiology
fotografia	*Fot*	photography
verbo inglese la cui particella è inseparabile dal verbo	*fus*	(phrasal verb) where the particle cannot be separated from the main verb
nella maggior parte dei sensi; generalmente	*gen*	in most or all senses; generally
geografia, geologia	*Geo*	geography, geology
geometria	*Geom*	geometry
storia, storico	*Hist*	history, historical
impersonale	*impers*	impersonal
articolo indeterminativo	*indef art*	indefinite article
familiare (! da evitare)	*inf(!)*	colloquial usage (! particularly offensive)
infinito	*infin*	infinitive
informatica	*Inform*	computing

ABBREVIAZIONI		ABBREVIATIONS
insegnamento, sistema scolastico e universitario	*Ins*	schooling, schools and universities
invariabile	*inv*	invariable
irregolare	*irreg*	irregular
grammatica, linguistica	*Ling*	grammar, linguistics
maschile	*m*	masculine
matematica	*Mat(h)*	mathematics
termine medico, medicina	*Med*	medical term, medicine
il tempo, meteorologia	*Meteor*	the weather, meteorology
maschile o femminile	*m/f*	masculine or feminine
esercito, linguaggio militare	*Mil*	military matters
musica	*Mus*	music
sostantivo	*n*	noun
nautica	*Naut*	sailing, navigation
numerale (aggettivo, sostantivo)	*num*	numeral adjective or noun
	o.s.	oneself
peggiorativo	*peg, pej*	derogatory, pejorative
fotografia	*Phot*	photography
fisiologia	*Physiol*	physiology
plurale	*pl*	plural
politica	*Pol*	politics
participio passato	*pp*	past participle
preposizione	*prep*	preposition
pronome	*pron*	pronoun
psicologia, psichiatria	*Psic, Psych*	psychology, psychiatry
tempo passato	*pt*	past tense
qualcosa	*qc*	
qualcuno	*qn*	
religione, liturgia	*Rel*	religions, church service
sostantivo	*s*	noun
	sb	somebody

ABBREVIAZIONI		ABBREVIATIONS
insegnamento, sistema scolastico e universitario	*Scol*	schooling, schools and universities
singolare	*sg*	singular
soggetto (grammaticale)	*sog*	(grammatical) subject
	sth	something
congiuntivo	*sub*	subjunctive
soggetto (grammaticale)	*subj*	(grammatical) subject
superlativo	*superl*	superlative
termine tecnico, tecnologia	*Tecn, Tech*	technical term, technology
telecomunicazioni	*Tel*	telecommunications
tipografia	*Tip*	typography, printing
televisione	*TV*	television
tipografia	*Typ*	typography, printing
università	*Univ*	university
inglese americano	*US*	American English
vocale	*V*	vowel
verbo	*vb*	verb
verbo o gruppo verbale con funzione intransitiva	*vi*	verb or phrasal verb used intransitively
verbo pronominale o riflessivo	*vpr*	pronominal or reflexive verb
verbo o gruppo verbale con funzione transitiva	*vt*	verb or phrasal verb used transitively
zoologia	*Zool*	zoology
marchio registrato	®	registered trademark
introduce un'equivalenza culturale	≈	introduces a cultural equivalent

TRASCRIZIONE FONETICA

Consonanti		Consonants

NB **p, b, t, d, k, g** sono seguite da un'aspirazione in inglese.

NB **p, b, t, d, k, g** are not aspirated in Italian.

padre	p	**p**up**p**y
bam**b**ino	b	**b**a**b**y
tu**tt**o	t	**t**en**t**
da**d**o	d	**d**a**dd**y
cane **ch**e	k	**c**ork **k**iss **ch**ord
gola **gh**iro	g	**g**a**g** **g**uess
sano	s	**s**o ri**c**e ki**ss**
sva**g**o e**s**ame	z	cou**s**in buz**z**
scena	ʃ	**sh**eep **s**ugar
	ʒ	plea**s**ure bei**ge**
pe**c**e lan**c**iare	tʃ	**ch**ur**ch**
giro **g**ioco	dʒ	**j**ud**ge** **g**eneral
a**f**a **f**aro	f	**f**arm ra**ff**le
vero bra**v**o	v	**v**ery re**v**
	θ	**th**in ma**th**s
	ð	**th**at o**th**er
le**tt**o a**l**a	l	**l**itt**l**e ba**ll**
g**l**i	ʎ	mi**lli**on
rete a**r**co	r	**r**at **r**a**r**e
ramo ma**d**re	m	**m**u**mm**y co**mb**
no fu**m**ante	n	**n**o ra**n**
gnomo	ɲ	ca**ny**on
	ŋ	si**ng**i**ng** ba**n**k
	h	**h**at re**h**eat
bu**i**o p**i**acere	j	**y**et
uomo g**u**aio	w	**w**all be**w**ail
	x	lo**ch**

Varie		Miscellaneous

per l'inglese: la "r" finale viene pronunciata se seguita da una vocale	r	
precede la sillaba accentata	'	precedes the stressed syllable

PHONETIC TRANSCRIPTION

Vocali		Vowels
NB La messa in equivalenza di certi suoni indica solo una rassomiglianza approssimativa.		NB The pairing of some vowel sounds only indicates approximate equivalence.

Vocali		Vowels
vino idea	i iː	heel bead
	ɪ	hit pity
stella edera	e	
epoca eccetto	ɛ	set tent
mamma amore	a æ	bat apple
	ɑː	after car calm
	ɑ̃	fiancé
	ʌ	fun cousin
müsli	y	
	ə	over above
	əː	urn fern work
rosa occhio	ɔ	wash pot
	ɔː	born cork
ponte ognuno	o	
föhn	ø	
utile zucca	u	full soot
	uː	boon lewd

Dittonghi		Diphthongs
	ɪə	beer tier
	ɛə	tear fair there
	eɪ	date plaice day
	aɪ	life buy cry
	au	owl foul now
	əu	low no
	ɔɪ	boil boy oily
	uə	poor tour

ITALIAN PRONUNCIATION

Vowels

Where the vowel **e** or the vowel **o** appears in a stressed syllable it can be either open [ɛ], [ɔ] or closed [e], [o]. As the open or closed pronunciation of these vowels is subject to regional variation, the distinction is of little importance to the user of this dictionary. Phonetic transcription for headwords containing these vowels will therefore only appear where other pronunciation difficulties are present.

Consonants

c before "e" or "i" is pronounced like the "*tch*" in match.
ch is pronounced like the "*k*" in "kit".
g before "e" or "i" is pronounced like the "*j*" in "jet".
gh is pronounced like the "*g*" in "get".
gl before "e" or "i" is normally pronounced like the "*lli*" in "million", and in a few cases only like the "*gl*" in "glove".
gn is pronounced like the "*ny*" in "canyon"
sc before "e" or "i" is pronounced "*sh*".
z is pronounced like the "*ts*" in "stetson", or like the "*d's*" in "bird's-eye".

Headwords containing the above consonants and consonantal groups have been given full phonetic transcription in this dictionary.

NB All double written consonants in Italian are fully sounded: e.g. the *tt* in "tutto" is pronounced as in "hat trick".

ITALIAN VERB FORMS

1 Gerundio 2 Participio passato 3 Presente 4 Imperfetto 5 Passato remoto
6 Futuro 7 Condizionale 8 Congiuntivo presente 9 Congiuntivo passato
10 Imperativo

andare 3 vado, vai, va, andiamo, andate, vanno 6 andrò ecc. 8 vada 10 va'!, vada!, andate!, vadano!

apparire 2 apparso 3 appaio, appari o apparisci, appare o apparisce, appaiono o appariscono 5 apparvi o apparsi, apparisti, apparve o apparì o apparse, apparvero o apparirono o apparsero 8 appaia o apparisca

aprire 2 aperto 3 apro 5 aprii, apristi 8 apra

AVERE 3 ho, hai, ha, abbiamo, avete, hanno 5 ebbi, avesti, ebbe, avemmo, aveste, ebbero 6 avrò ecc. 8 abbia ecc. 10 abbi!, abbia!, abbiate!, abbiano!

bere 1 bevendo 2 bevuto 3 bevo ecc. 4 bevevo ecc. 5 bevvi o bevetti, bevesti 6 berrò ecc. 8 beva ecc. 9 bevessi ecc.

cadere 5 caddi, cadesti 6 cadrò ecc.

cogliere 2 colto 3 colgo, colgono 5 colsi, cogliesti 8 colga

correre 2 corso 5 corsi, corresti

cuocere 2 cotto 3 cuocio, cociamo, cuociono 5 cossi, cocesti

dare 3 do, dai, dà, diamo, date, danno 5 diedi o detti, desti 6 darò ecc. 8 dia ecc. 9 dessi ecc. 10 da'!, dai!, date!, diano!

dire 1 dicendo 2 detto 3 dico, dici, dice, diciamo, dite, dicono 4 dicevo ecc. 5 dissi, dicesti 6 dirò ecc. 8 dica, diciamo, diciate, dicano 9 dicessi ecc. 10 di'!, dica!, dite!, dicano!

dolere 3 dolgo, duoli, duole, dolgono 5 dolsi, dolesti 6 dorrò ecc. 8 dolga

dovere 3 devo o debbo, devi, deve, dobbiamo, dovete, devono o debbono 6 dovrò ecc. 8 debba, dobbiamo, dobbiate, devano o debbano

ESSERE 2 stato 3 sono, sei, è, siamo, siete, sono 4 ero, eri, era, eravamo, eravate, erano 5 fui, fosti, fu, fummo, foste, furono 6 sarò ecc. 8 sia ecc. 9 fossi, fossi, fosse, fossimo, foste, fossero 10 sii!, sia!, siate!, siano!

fare 1 facendo 2 fatto 3 faccio, fai, fa, facciamo, fate, fanno 4 facevo ecc. 5 feci, facesti 6 farò ecc. 8 faccia ecc. 9 facessi ecc. 10 fa'!, faccia!, fate!, facciano!

FINIRE 1 finendo 2 finito 3 finisco, finisci, finisce, finiamo, finite, finiscono 4 finivo, finivi, finiva, finivamo, finivate, finivano 5 finii, finisti, finì, finimmo, finiste, finirono 6 finirò, finirai, finirà, finiremo, finirete, finiranno 7 finirei, finiresti, finirebbe, finiremmo, finireste, finirebbero 8 finisca, finisca, finisca, finiamo, finiate, finiscano 9 finissi, finissi, finisse, finissimo, finiste, finissero 10 finisci!, finisca!, finite!, finiscano!

giungere 2 giunto 5 giunsi, giungesti

leggere 2 letto 5 lessi, leggesti

mettere 2 messo 5 misi, mettesti

morire 2 morto 3 muoio, muori, muore, moriamo, morite, muoiono 6 morirò o morrò ecc. 8 muoia

muovere 2 mosso 5 mossi, movesti

nascere 2 nato 5 nacqui, nascesti

nuocere 2 nuociuto 3 nuoccio, nuoci, nuoce, nociamo o nuociamo, nuocete, nuocciono 4 nuocevo ecc. 5 nocqui, nuocesti 6 nuocerò ecc. 7 nuoccia

offrire 2 offerto 3 offro 5 offersi o offrii, offristi 8 offra

parere 2 parso 3 paio, paiamo, paiono 5 parvi o parsi, paresti 6 parrò ecc. 8 paia, paiamo, paiate, paiano

PARLARE 1 parlando **2** parlato **3** parlo, parli, parla, parliamo, parlate, parlano **4** parlavo, parlavi, parlava, parlavamo, parlavate, parlavano **5** parlai, parlasti, parlò, parlammo, parlaste, parlarono **6** parlerò, parlerai, parlerà, parleremo, parlerete, parleranno **7** parlerei, parleresti, parlerebbe, parleremmo, parlereste, parlerebbero **8** parli, parli, parli, parliamo, parliate, parlino **9** parlassi, parlassi, parlasse, parlassimo, parlaste, parlassero **10** parla!, parli!, parlate!, parlino!

piacere 2 piaciuto **3** piaccio, piacciamo, piacciono **5** piacqui, piacesti **8** piacci *ecc.*

porre 1 ponendo **2** posto **3** pongo, poni, pone, poniamo, ponete, pongono **4** ponevo *ecc.* **5** posi, ponesti **6** porrò *ecc.* **8** ponga, poniamo, poniate, pongano **9** ponessi *ecc.*

potere 3 posso, puoi, può, possiamo, potete, possono **6** potrò *ecc.* **8** possa, possiamo, possiate, possano

prendere 2 preso **5** presi, prendesti

ridurre 1 riducendo **2** ridotto **3** riduco *ecc.* **4** riducevo *ecc.* **5** ridussi, riducesti **6** ridurrò *ecc.* **8** riduca *ecc.* **9** riducessi *ecc.*

riempire 1 riempiendo **3** riempio, riempi, riempie, riempiono

rimanere 2 rimasto **3** rimango, rimangono **5** rimasi, rimanesti **6** rimarrò *ecc.* **8** rimanga

rispondere 2 risposto **5** risposi, rispondesti

salire 3 salgo, sali, salgono **8** salga

sapere 3 so, sai, sa, sappiamo, sapete, sanno **5** seppi, sapesti **6** saprò *ecc.* **8** sappia *ecc.* **10** sappi!, sappia!, sappiate!, sappiano!

scrivere 2 scritto **5** scrissi, scrivesti

sedere 3 siedo, siedi, siede, siedono **8** sieda

spegnere 2 spento **3** spengo, spengono **5** spensi, spegnesti **8** spenga

stare 2 stato **3** sto, stai, sta, stiamo, state, stanno **5** stetti, stesti **6** starò *ecc.* **8** stia *ecc.* **9** stessi *ecc.* **10** sta'!, stia!, state!, stiano!

tacere 2 taciuto **3** taccio, tacciono **5** tacqui, tacesti **8** taccia

tenere 3 tengo, tieni, tiene, tengono **5** tenni, tenesti **6** terrò *ecc.* **8** tenga

trarre 1 traendo **2** tratto **3** traggo, trai, trae, traiamo, traete, traggono **4** traevo *ecc.* **5** trassi, traesti **6** trarrò *ecc.* **8** tragga **9** traessi *ecc.*

udire 3 odo, odi, ode, odono **8** oda

uscire 3 esco, esci, esce, escono **8** esca

valere 2 valso **3** valgo, valgono **5** valsi, valesti **6** varrò *ecc.* **8** valga

vedere 2 visto *o* veduto **5** vidi, vedesti **6** vedrò *ecc.*

VENDERE 1 vendendo **2** venduto **3** vendo, vendi, vende, vendiamo, vendete, vendono **4** vendevo, vendevi, vendeva, vendevamo, vendevate, vendevano **5** vendei *o* vendetti, vendesti, vendé *o* vendette, vendemmo, vendeste, venderono *o* vendettero **6** venderò, venderai, venderà, venderemo, venderete, venderanno **7** venderei, venderesti, venderebbe, venderemmo, vendereste, venderebbero **8** venda, venda, venda, vendiamo, vendiate, vendano **9** vendessi, vendessi, vendesse, vendessimo, vendeste, vendessero **10** vendi!, venda!, vendete!, vendano!

venire 2 venuto **3** vengo, vieni, viene, vengono **5** venni, venisti **6** verrò *ecc.* **8** venga

vivere 2 vissuto **5** vissi, vivesti

volere 3 voglio, vuoi, vuole, vogliamo, volete, vogliono **5** volli, volesti **6** vorrò *ecc.* **8** voglia *ecc.* **10** vogli!, voglia!, vogliate!, vogliano!

ENGLISH VERB FORMS

present	pt	pp	present	pt	pp
arise	arose	arisen	**feed**	fed	fed
awake	awoke	awoken	**feel**	felt	felt
be(am,is,	was,were	been	**fight**	fought	fought
are; being)			**find**	found	found
bear	bore	born(e)	**flee**	fled	fled
beat	beat	beaten	**fling**	flung	flung
become	became	become	**fly**	flew	flown
begin	began	begun	**forbid**	forbade	forbidden
bend	bent	bent	**forecast**	forecast	forecast
bet	bet,	bet,	**forget**	forgot	forgotten
	betted	betted	**forgive**	forgave	forgiven
bid (at auction,	bid	bid	**forsake**	forsook	forsaken
cards)			**freeze**	froze	frozen
bid (say)	bade	bidden	**get**	got	got, (US)
bind	bound	bound			gotten
bite	bit	bitten	**give**	gave	given
bleed	bled	bled	**go** (goes)	went	gone
blow	blew	blown	**grind**	ground	ground
break	broke	broken	**grow**	grew	grown
breed	bred	bred	**hang**	hung	hung
bring	brought	brought	**hang** (execute)	hanged	hanged
build	built	built	**have** (has;	had	had
burn	burnt,	burnt,	having)		
	burned	burned	**hear**	heard	heard
burst	burst	burst	**hide**	hid	hidden
buy	bought	bought	**hit**	hit	hit
can	could	(been able)	**hold**	held	held
cast	cast	cast	**hurt**	hurt	hurt
catch	caught	caught	**keep**	kept	kept
choose	chose	chosen	**kneel**	knelt,	knelt,
cling	clung	clung		kneeled	kneeled
come	came	come	**know**	knew	known
cost	cost	cost	**lay**	laid	laid
cost (work	costed	costed	**lead**	led	led
out price of)			**lean**	leant,	leant,
creep	crept	crept		leaned	leaned
cut	cut	cut	**leap**	leapt,	leapt,
deal	dealt	dealt		leaped	leaped
dig	dug	dug	**learn**	learnt,	learnt,
do (does)	did	done		learned	learned
draw	drew	drawn	**leave**	left	left
dream	dreamed,	dreamed,	**lend**	lent	lent
	dreamt	dreamt	**let**	let	let
drink	drank	drunk	**lie** (lying)	lay	lain
drive	drove	driven	**light**	lit,	lit,
dwell	dwelt	dwelt		lighted	lighted
eat	ate	eaten	**lose**	lost	lost
fall	fell	fallen	**make**	made	made

present	pt	pp	present	pt	pp
may	might	—	spell	spelt, spelled	spelt, spelled
mean	meant	meant			
meet	met	met	spend	spent	spent
mistake	mistook	mistaken	spill	spilt, spilled	spilt, spilled
mow	mowed	mown, mowed			
			spin	spun	spun
must	(had to)	(had to)	spit	spat	spat
pay	paid	paid	split	split	split
put	put	put	spoil	spoiled, spoilt	spoiled, spoilt
quit	quit, quitted	quit, quitted			
read	read	read	spread	spread	spread
rid	rid	rid	spring	sprang	sprung
ride	rode	ridden	stand	stood	stood
ring	rang	rung	steal	stole	stolen
rise	rose	risen	stick	stuck	stuck
run	ran	run	sting	stung	stung
saw	sawed	sawed, sawn	stink	stank	stunk
			stride	strode	stridden
say	said	said	strike	struck	struck, stricken
see	saw	seen			
seek	sought	sought	strive	strove	striven
sell	sold	sold	swear	swore	sworn
send	sent	sent	sweep	swept	swept
set	set	set	swell	swelled	swollen, swelled
sew	sewed	sewn			
shake	shook	shaken	swim	swam	swum
shear	sheared	shorn, sheared	swing	swung	swung
			take	took	taken
shed	shed	shed	teach	taught	taught
shine	shone	shone	tear	tore	torn
shoot	shot	shot	tell	told	told
show	showed	shown	think	thought	thought
shrink	shrank	shrunk	throw	threw	thrown
shut	shut	shut	thrust	thrust	thrust
sing	sang	sung	tread	trod	trodden
sink	sank	sunk	wake	woke, waked	woken, waked
sit	sat	sat			
slay	slew	slain	wear	wore	worn
sleep	slept	slept	weave	wove, weaved	woven, weaved
slide	slid	slid			
sling	slung	slung	wed	wedded, wed	wedded, wed
slit	slit	slit			
smell	smelt, smelled	smelt, smelled	weep	wept	wept
			win	won	won
sow	sowed	sown, sowed	wind	wound	wound
			wring	wrung	wrung
speak	spoke	spoken	write	wrote	written
speed	sped, speeded	sped, speeded			

I NUMERI		NUMBERS
uno(a)	1	one
due	2	two
tre	3	three
quattro	4	four
cinque	5	five
sei	6	six
sette	7	seven
otto	8	eight
nove	9	nine
dieci	10	ten
undici	11	eleven
dodici	12	twelve
tredici	13	thirteen
quattordici	14	fourteen
quindici	15	fifteen
sedici	16	sixteen
diciassette	17	seventeen
diciotto	18	eighteen
diciannove	19	nineteen
venti	20	twenty
ventuno	21	twenty-one
ventidue	22	twenty-two
ventitré	23	twenty-three
ventotto	28	twenty-eight
trenta	30	thirty
quaranta	40	forty
cinquanta	50	fifty
sessanta	60	sixty
settanta	70	seventy
ottanta	80	eighty
novanta	90	ninety
cento	100	a hundred
cento uno	101	a hundred and one
duecento	200	two hundred
mille	1000	a thousand
milleduecentodue	1202	one thousand two hundred and two
cinquemila	5000	five thousand
un milione	1000000	a million

I NUMERI

primo(a)
secondo(a)
terzo(a)
quarto(a)
quinto(a)
sesto(a)
settimo(a)
ottavo(a)
nono(a)
decimo(a)
undicesimo(a)
dodicesimo(a)
tredicesimo(a)
quattordicesimo(a)
quindicesimo(a)
sedicesimo(a)
diciassettesimo(a)
diciottesimo(a)
diciannovesimo(a)
ventesimo(a)
ventunesimo(a)
ventiduesimo(a)
ventitreesimo(a)
ventottesimo(a)
trentesimo(a)
centesimo(a)
centunesimo(a)
millesimo(a)
milionesimo(a)

NUMBERS

first, 1st
second, 2nd
third, 3rd
fourth, 4th
fifth, 5th
sixth, 6th
seventh
eighth
ninth
tenth
eleventh
twelfth
thirteenth
fourteenth
fifteenth
sixteenth
seventeenth
eighteenth
nineteenth
twentieth
twenty-first
twenty-second
twenty-third
twenty-eighth
thirtieth
hundredth
hundred-and-first
thousandth
millionth

Frazioni

mezzo
terzo
due terzi
quarto
quinto
zero virgola cinque, 0,5
tre virgola quattro, 3,4
dieci per cento
cento per cento

Esempi

abita al numero dieci
si trova nel capitolo sette,
  a pagina sette
abita al terzo piano
arrivò quarto
scala uno a venticinquemila

Fractions

half
third
two thirds
quarter
fifth
(nought) point five, 0.5
three point four, 3.4
ten per cent
a hundred per cent

Examples

he lives at number 10
it's in chapter 7, on page 7

he lives on the 3rd floor
he came in 4th
scale 1:25,000

L'ORA

che ora è?, che ore sono?

è ..., sono ...

mezzanotte
l'una (di notte)

le tre del mattino

l'una e cinque
l'una e dieci
l'una e un quarto, l'una e quindici

l'una e venticinque

l'una e mezzo *or* mezza, l'una e
 trenta
le due meno venticinque, l'una
 e trentacinque
le due meno venti, l'una e
 quaranta
le due meno un quarto, l'una e
 tre quarti
le due meno dieci, l'una e cinquanta
le dodici, mezzogiorno

l'una, le tredici

le sette (di sera), le diciannove

a che ora?

a mezzanotte
all'una, alle tredici
fra venti minuti
venti minuti fa

THE TIME

what time is it?

it's ...

midnight
one o'clock (in the
 morning), one (a.m.)
three o'clock (in the
 morning), three (a.m.)
five past one
ten past one
a quarter past one,
 one fifteen
twenty-five past one,
 one twenty-five
half past one, one thirty

twenty-five to two,
 one thirty-five
twenty to two, one forty

a quarter to two, one
 forty-five
ten to two, one fifty
twelve o'clock, midday,
 noon
one o'clock (in the
 afternoon), one (p.m.)
seven o'clock (in the
 evening), seven (p.m.)

at what time?

at midnight
at one o'clock
in twenty minutes
twenty minutes ago

LA DATA

oggi	today
ogni giorno, tutti i giorni	every day
ieri	yesterday
stamattina	this morning
domani notte; domani sera	tomorrow night
l'altroieri notte; l'altroieri sera	the night before last
l'altroieri	the day before yesterday
ieri notte; ieri sera	last night
due giorni/sei anni fa	two days/six years ago
domani pomeriggio	tomorrow afternoon
dopodomani	the day after tomorrow
tutti i giovedì, di *or* il giovedì	every Thursday, on Thursdays
ci va di *or* il venerdì	he goes on Fridays
"chiuso il mercoledì"	"closed on Wednesdays"
dal lunedì al venerdì	from Monday to Friday
per giovedì, entro giovedì	by Thursday
un sabato di marzo	one Saturday in March
tra una settimana	in a week's time
martedì a otto	a week next *or* on Tuesday
questa/la prossima/la scorsa settimana	this/next/last week
tra due settimane, tra quindici giorni	in two weeks *or* a fortnight
lunedì a quindici	two weeks on Monday
il primo/l'ultimo venerdì del mese	the first/last Friday of the month
il mese prossimo	next month
l'anno scorso	last year
il primo giugno	the 1st of June, June first
il due ottobre	the 2nd of October *or* October 2nd
sono nato nel 1987	I was born in 1987
il suo compleano è il 5 giugno	his birthday is on June 5th (*BRIT*) *or* 5th June (*US*)
il 18 agosto	on 18th August (*BRIT*) *or* August 18 (*US*)
nel '96	in '96
nella primavera del '94	in the Spring of '94
dal 19 al 3	from the 19th to the 3rd
quanti ne abbiamo oggi?	what's the date? *or* what date is it today?

DATES

xxiii

oggi è il 15	today's date is the 15th *or* today is the 15th
1988 - millenovecentottantotto	1988 - nineteen eighty-eight
2005 - duemilacinque	2005 - two thousand and five
10 anni esatti	10 years to the day
alla fine del mese	at the end of the month
la settimana del 30/7	week ending 30/7
giornalmente *or* al giorno	daily
settimanalmente *or* alla settimana	weekly
mensilmente, al mese	monthly
annualmente *or* all'anno	annually
due volte alla settimana/al mese/ all'anno	twice a week/month/year
bimestralmente	bi-monthly
nel 4 a.C.	in 4 B.C. *or* B.C. 4
nel 79 d.C.	in 79 A.D *or* A.D. 79
nel tredicesimo secolo	in the 13th century
negli anni '80	in *or* during the 80s
nel 1990 e rotti	in 1990 something

La data nelle lettere
9 ottobre 2004

Headings of letters
9th October 2004 *or* 9 October 2004

PAROLA CHIAVE

a (*a + il* = **al**, *a + lo* = **allo**, *a + l'* = **all'**, *a + la* = **alla**, *a + i* = **ai**, *a + gli* = **agli**, *a + le* = **alle**) *prep* **1** (*stato in luogo*) at; (: *in*) in; **essere alla stazione** to be at the station; **essere a casa/a scuola/a Roma** to be at home/at school/in Rome; **è a 10 km da qui** it's 10 km from here, it's 10 km away
2 (*moto a luogo*) to; **andare a casa/a scuola** to go home/to school
3 (*tempo*) at; (*epoca, stagione*) in; **alle cinque** at five (o'clock); **a mezzanotte/Natale** at midnight/Christmas; **al mattino** in the morning; **a maggio/primavera** in May/spring; **a cinquant'anni** at fifty (years of age); **a domani!** see you tomorrow!
4 (*complemento di termine*) to; **dare qc a qn** to give sth to sb

5 (*mezzo, modo*) with, by; **a piedi/cavallo** on foot/horseback; **fatto a mano** made by hand, handmade; **una barca a motore** a motorboat; **a uno a uno** one by one; **all'italiana** the Italian way, in the Italian fashion
6 (*rapporto*) a, per; (: *con prezzi*) at; **prendo 850 euro al mese** I get 850 euros a *o* per month; **pagato a ore** paid by the hour; **vendere qc a 2 euro il chilo** to sell sth at 2 euros a *o* per kilo

abbagli'ante [abbaʎˈʎante] *ag* dazzling; **abbaglianti** *smpl* (*Aut*): **accendere gli abbaglianti** to put one's headlights on full (BRIT) *o* high (US) beam
abbagli'are [abbaʎˈʎare] *vt* to dazzle; (*illudere*) to delude
abbai'are *vi* to bark
abbando'nare *vt* to leave, abandon, desert; (*trascurare*) to neglect; (*rinunciare a*) to abandon, give up; **abbandonarsi** *vpr* to let o.s. go; **abbandonarsi a** (*ricordi, vizio*) to give o.s. up to
abbas'sare *vt* to lower; (*radio*) to turn down; **abbassarsi** *vpr* (*chinarsi*) to stoop; (*livello, sole*) to go down; (*fig: umiliarsi*) to demean o.s.; **~ i fari** (*Aut*) to dip *o* dim (US) one's lights
ab'basso *escl*: **~ il re!** down with the king!
abbas'tanza [abbasˈtantsa] *av* (*a sufficienza*) enough; (*alquanto*) quite, rather, fairly; **non è ~ furbo** he's not shrewd enough; **un vino ~ dolce** quite a sweet wine; **averne ~ di qn/qc** to have had enough of sb/sth
ab'battere *vt* (*muro, casa*) to pull down; (*ostacolo*) to knock down; (*albero*) to fell; (: *vento*) to bring down; (*bestie da macello*) to slaughter; (*cane, cavallo*) to destroy, put down; (*selvaggina, aereo*) to shoot down; (*fig: malattia, disgrazia*) to lay low; **abbattersi** *vpr* (*avvilirsi*) to lose heart;

A *abbr* (= *autostrada*) ≈ M (*motorway*)

abbat'tuto, -a *ag* (*fig*) depressed

abba'zia [abbat'tsia] *sf* abbey

'abbia *vb vedi* **avere**

abbi'ente *ag* well-to-do, well-off; **abbienti** *smpl* **gli abbienti** the well-to-do

abbiglia'mento [abbiλλa'mento] *sm* dress *no pl*; (*indumenti*) clothes *pl*; (*industria*) clothing industry

abbi'nare *vt*: **~ (a)** to combine (with)

abboc'care *vi* (*pesce*) to bite; (*tubi*) to join; **~ (all'amo)** (*fig*) to swallow the bait

abbona'mento *sm* subscription; (*alle ferrovie ecc*) season ticket; **fare l'~** to take out a subscription (*o* season ticket)

abbo'narsi *vpr*: **~ a un giornale** to take out a subscription to a newspaper; **~ al teatro/alle ferrovie** to take out a season ticket for the theatre/the train

abbon'dante *ag* abundant, plentiful; (*giacca*) roomy

abbon'danza [abbon'dantsa] *sf* abundance; plenty

abbor'dabile *ag* (*persona*) approachable; (*prezzo*) reasonable

abbotto'nare *vt* to button up, do up

abbracci'are [abbrat'tʃare] *vt* to embrace; (*persona*) to hug, embrace; (*professione*) to take up; (*contenere*) to include; **abbracciarsi** *vpr* to hug *o* embrace (one another); **ab'braccio** *sm* hug, embrace

abbrevi'are *vt* to shorten; (*parola*) to abbreviate

abbreviazi'one [abbrevjat'tsjone] *sf* abbreviation

abbron'zante [abbron'dzante] *ag* tanning, sun *cpd*

abbronzarsi *vpr* to tan, get a tan

abbron'zato, -a [abbron'dzato] *ag* (sun)tanned

abbrusto'lire *vt* (*pane*) to toast; (*caffè*) to roast; **abbrustolirsi** *vpr* to toast; (*fig: al sole*) to soak up the sun

abbuf'farsi *vpr* (*fam*): **~ (di qc)** to stuff o.s. (with sth)

abdi'care *vi* to abdicate; **~ a** to give up, renounce

a'bete *sm* fir (tree); **abete rosso** spruce

'abile *ag* (*idoneo*): **~ (a qc/a fare qc)** fit (for sth/to do sth); (*capace*) able; (*astuto*) clever; (*accorto*) skilful; **~ al servizio militare** fit for military service; **abilità** *sf inv* ability; cleverness; skill

a'bisso *sm* abyss, gulf

abi'tante *sm/f* inhabitant

abi'tare *vt* to live in, dwell in ▷ *vi* **~ in campagna/a Roma** to live in the country/in Rome; **dove abita?** where do you live?; **abitazi'one** *sf* residence; house

'abito *sm* dress *no pl*; (*da uomo*) suit; (*da donna*) dress; (*abitudine, disposizione, Rel*) habit; **abiti** *smpl* (*vestiti*) clothes; **in ~ da sera** in evening dress

abitu'ale *ag* usual, habitual; (*cliente*) regular

abitual'mente *av* usually, normally

abitu'are *vt*: **~ qn a** to get sb used *o* accustomed to; **abituarsi a** to get used to, accustom o.s. to

abitudi'nario, -a *ag* of fixed habits ▷ *sm/f* regular customer

abi'tudine *sf* habit; **aver l'~ di fare qc** to be in the habit of doing sth; **d'~** usually; **per ~** from *o* out of habit

abo'lire *vt* to abolish; (*Dir*) to repeal

abor'tire *vi* (*Med*) to miscarry, have a miscarriage; (*: deliberatamente*) to have an abortion; (*fig*) to miscarry, fail; **a'borto** *sm* miscarriage; abortion

ABS [abiεse] *sigla m* (= *Anti-Blockier System*) ABS

'abside *sf* apse

abu'sare *vi*: **~ di** to abuse, misuse; (*alcool*) to take to excess; (*approfittare, violare*) to take advantage of

abu'sivo, -a *ag* unauthorized,

unlawful; **(occupante)** ~ *(di una casa)* squatter

> Attenzione! In inglese esiste la parola *abusive* che però vuol dire *ingiurioso*.

a.C. *av abbr* (= *avanti Cristo*) B.C.

a'cacia, -cie [a'katʃa] *sf* (*Bot*) acacia

ac'cadde *vb vedi* **accadere**

acca'demia *sf* (*società*) learned society; (*scuola: d'arte, militare*) academy

acca'dere *vb impers* to happen, occur

accal'dato *ag* hot

accalo'rarsi *vpr* (*fig*) to get excited

accampa'mento *sm* camp

accamparsi *vpr* to camp

acca'nirsi *vpr* (*infierire*) to rage; (*ostinarsi*) to persist; **acca'nito, -a** *ag* (*odio, gelosia*) fierce, bitter; (*lavoratore*) assiduous, dogged; (*fumatore*) inveterate

ac'canto *av* near, nearby; ~ **a** *prep* near, beside, close to

accanto'nare *vt* (*problema*) to shelve; (*somma*) to set aside

accappa'toio *sm* bathrobe

accarez'zare [akkaret'tsare] *vt* to caress, stroke, fondle; (*fig*) to toy with

acca'sarsi *vpr* to set up house; to get married

accasci'arsi [akkaʃ'ʃarsi] *vpr* to collapse; (*fig*) to lose heart

accat'tone, -a *sm/f* beggar

accaval'lare *vt* (*gambe*) to cross

acce'care [attʃe'kare] *vt* to blind ▷ *vi* to go blind

ac'cedere [at'tʃedere] *vi*: ~ **a** to enter; (*richiesta*) to grant, accede to

accele'rare [attʃele'rare] *vt* to speed up ▷ *vi* (*Aut*) to accelerate; ~ **il passo** to quicken one's pace; **accelera'tore** *sm* (*Aut*) accelerator

ac'cendere [at'tʃendere] *vt* (*fuoco, sigaretta*) to light; (*luce, televisione*) to put on, switch on, turn on; (*Aut: motore*) to switch on; (*Comm: conto*) to open; (*fig: suscitare*) to inflame, stir

up; **ha da ~?** have you got a light?; **non riesco ad ~ il riscaldamento** I can't turn the heating on; **accen'dino, accendi'sigaro** *sm* (*cigarette*) lighter

accen'nare [attʃen'nare] *vt* (*Mus*) to pick out the notes of; to hum ▷ *vi* ~ **a** (*fig: alludere a*) to hint at; (: *far atto di*) to make as if; ~ **un saluto** (*con la mano*) to make as if to wave; (*col capo*) to half nod; **accenna a piovere** it looks as if it's going to rain

ac'cenno [at'tʃenno] *sm* (*cenno*) sign; nod; (*allusione*) hint

accensi'one [attʃen'sjone] *sf* (*vedi verbo*) lighting; switching on; opening; (*Aut*) ignition

ac'cento [at'tʃento] *sm* accent; (*Fonetica, fig*) stress; (*inflessione*) tone (of voice)

accentu'are [attʃentu'are] *vt* to stress, emphasize; **accentuarsi** *vpr* to become more noticeable

accerchi'are [attʃer'kjare] *vt* to surround, encircle

accerta'mento [attʃerta'mento] *sm* check; assessment

accer'tare [attʃer'tare] *vt* to ascertain; (*verificare*) to check; (*reddito*) to assess; **accertarsi** *vpr* **accertarsi (di)** to make sure (of)

ac'ceso, -a [at'tʃeso] *pp di* **accendere** ▷ *ag* lit; on; open; (*colore*) bright

acces'sibile [attʃes'sibile] *ag* (*luogo*) accessible; (*persona*) approachable; (*prezzo*) reasonable

ac'cesso [at'tʃesso] *sm* (*anche Inform*) access; (*Med*) attack, fit; (*impulso violento*) fit, outburst

accessori *smpl* accessories

ac'cetta [at'tʃetta] *sf* hatchet

accet'tabile [attʃet'tabile] *ag* acceptable

accet'tare [attʃet'tare] *vt* to accept; **accettate carte di credito?** do you accept credit cards?; ~ **di fare qc** to agree to do sth; **accettazi'one** *sf* acceptance; (*locale di servizio pubblico*)

reception; **accettazione bagagli**
(*Aer*) check-in (desk)
acchiap'pare [akkjap'pare] *vt* to
catch
acciaie'ria [attʃaje'ria] *sf*
steelworks *sg*
acci'aio [at'tʃajo] *sm* steel
acciden'tato, -a [attʃiden'tato] *ag*
(*terreno ecc*) uneven
accigli'ato, -a [attʃiʎ'ʎato] *ag*
frowning
ac'cingersi [at'tʃindʒersi] *vpr*: **~ a
fare qc** to be about to do sth
acciuf'fare [attʃuf'fare] *vt* to seize,
catch
acci'uga, -ghe [at'tʃuga] *sf* anchovy
ac'cludere *vt* to enclose
accocco'larsi *vpr* to crouch
accogli'ente [akkoʎ'ʎɛnte] *ag*
welcoming, friendly
ac'cogliere [ak'kɔʎʎere] *vt* (*ricevere*)
to receive; (*dare il benvenuto*) to
welcome; (*approvare*) to agree
to, accept; (*contenere*) to hold,
accommodate
ac'colgo *ecc vb vedi* **accogliere**
ac'colsi *ecc vb vedi* **accogliere**
accoltel'lare *vt* to knife, stab
accomoda'mento *sm* agreement,
settlement
accomo'dante *ag* accommodating
accomo'darsi *vpr* (*sedersi*) to
sit down; (*entrare*) to come in;
s'accomodi! (*venga avanti*) come in!;
(*si sieda*) take a seat!
accompagna'mento
[akkompaɲɲa'mento] *sm* (*Mus*)
accompaniment
accompa'gnare [akkompaɲ'ɲare]
vt to accompany, come *o* go with;
(*Mus*) to accompany; (*unire*) to couple;
~ la porta to close the door gently
accompagna'tore, -trice *sm/f*
companion; **~ turistico** courier
acconcia'tura [akkontʃa'tura] *sf*
hairstyle
accondiscen'dente

[akkondiʃʃen'dɛnte] *ag* affable
acconsen'tire *vi*: **~ (a)** to agree *o*
consent (to)
acconten'tare *vt* to satisfy;
accontentarsi *vpr* **accontentarsi di**
to be satisfied with, content o.s. with
ac'conto *sm* part payment; **pagare
una somma in ~** to pay a sum of
money as a deposit
acco'rato, -a *ag* heartfelt
accorci'are [akkor'tʃare] *vt* to ∴
shorten; **accorciarsi** *vpr* to become
shorter
accor'dare *vt* to reconcile; (*colori*) to
match; (*Mus*) to tune; (*Ling*): **~ qc con
qc** to make sth agree with sth; (*Dir*)
to grant; **accordarsi** *vpr* to agree, come
to an agreement; (*colori*) to match
ac'cordo *sm* agreement; (*armonia*)
harmony; (*Mus*) chord; **essere d'~**
to agree; **andare d'~** to get on well
together; **d'~!** all right!, agreed!;
accordo commerciale trade
agreement
ac'corgersi [ak'kordʒersi] *vpr*: **~ di** to
notice; (*fig*) to realize
ac'correre *vi* to run up
ac'corto, -a *pp di* **accorgersi** ▷ *ag*
shrewd; **stare ~** to be on one's guard
accos'tare *vt* (*avvicinare*): **~ qc a**
to bring sth near to, put sth near
to; (*avvicinarsi a*) to approach;
(*socchiudere: imposte*) to half-close;
(*: porta*) to leave ajar ▷ *vi* (*Naut*) to
come alongside; **accostarsi** *vpr*
accostarsi a to draw near, approach;
(*fig*) to support
accredi'tare *vt* (*notizia*) to confirm
the truth of; (*Comm*) to credit;
(*diplomatico*) to accredit
ac'credito *sm* (*Comm: atto*) crediting;
(*: effetto*) credit
accucci'arsi [akkut'tʃarsi] *vpr* (*cane*)
to lie down
accu'dire *vt* (*anche: vi*: **~ a**) to attend to
accumu'lare *vt* to accumulate;
accumularsi *vpr* to accumulate;

(Finanza) to accrue

accu'rato, -a *ag* (*diligente*) careful; (*preciso*) accurate

ac'cusa *sf* accusation; (*Dir*) charge; **la pubblica ~** the prosecution

accu'sare *vt*: **~ qn di qc** to accuse sb of sth; (*Dir*) to charge sb with sth; **~ ricevuta di** (*Comm*) to acknowledge receipt of

accusa'tore, -'trice *sm/f* accuser ▷ *sm* (*Dir*) prosecutor

a'cerbo, -a [a'tʃerbo] *ag* bitter; (*frutta*) sour, unripe; (*persona*) immature

'acero ['atʃero] *sm* maple

a'cerrimo, -a [a'tʃerrimo] *ag* very fierce

a'ceto [a'tʃeto] *sm* vinegar

ace'tone [atʃe'tone] *sm* nail varnish remover

A.C.I. ['atʃi] *sigla m* = **Automobile Club d'Italia**

'acido, -a ['atʃido] *ag* (*sapore*) acid, sour; (*Chim*) acid ▷ *sm* (*Chim*) acid

'acino ['atʃino] *sm* berry; **acino d'uva** grape

'acne *sf* acne

'acqua *sf* water; (*pioggia*) rain; **acque** *sfpl* (*di mare, fiume ecc*) waters; **fare ~** (*Naut*) to leak, take in water; **~ in bocca!** mum's the word!; **acqua corrente** running water; **acqua dolce/salata** fresh/salt water; **acqua minerale/potabile/tonica** mineral/drinking/tonic water; **acque termali** thermal waters

a'cquaio *sm* sink

acqua'ragia [akkwa'radʒa] *sf* turpentine

a'cquario *sm* aquarium; (*dello zodiaco*): **A~** Aquarius

acquascooter [akkwas'kuter] *sm inv* Jet Ski®

ac'quatico, -a, -ci, -che *ag* aquatic; (*Sport, Scienza*) water *cpd*

acqua'vite *sf* brandy

acquaz'zone [akkwat'tsone] *sm* cloudburst, heavy shower

acque'dotto *sm* aqueduct; waterworks *pl*, water system

acque'rello *sm* watercolour

acqui'rente *sm/f* purchaser, buyer

acquis'tare *vt* to purchase, buy; (*fig*) to gain; **a'cquisto** *sm* purchase; **fare acquisti** to go shopping

acquo'lina *sf*: **far venire l'~ in bocca a qn** to make sb's mouth water

a'crobata, -i, -e *sm/f* acrobat

a'culeo *sm* (*Zool*) sting; (*Bot*) prickle

a'cume *sm* acumen, perspicacity

a'custico, -a, ci, che *ag* acoustic ▷ *sf* (*scienza*) acoustics *sg*; (*di una sala*) acoustics *pl*; **cornetto ~** ear trumpet; **apparecchio ~** hearing aid

a'cuto, -a *ag* (*appuntito*) sharp, pointed; (*suono, voce*) shrill, piercing; (*Mat, Ling, Med*) acute; (*Mus*) high-pitched; (*fig: dolore, desiderio*) intense; (: *perspicace*) acute, keen

a'dagio [a'dadʒo] *av* slowly ▷ *sm* (*Mus*) adagio; (*proverbio*) adage, saying

adatta'mento *sm* adaptation

adat'tare *vt* to adapt; (*sistemare*) to fit; **adattarsi** *vpr* **adattarsi (a)** (*ambiente, tempi*) to adapt (to); (*essere adatto*) to be suitable (for)

a'datto, -a *ag* **~ (a)** suitable (for), right (for)

addebi'tare *vt*: **~ qc a qn** to debit sb with sth

ad'debito *sm* (*Comm*) debit

adden'tare *vt* to bite into

adden'trarsi *vpr* **~ in** to penetrate, go into

addestra'mento *sm* training

addes'trare *vt* to train

ad'detto, -a *ag* **~ a** (*persona*) assigned to; (*oggetto*) intended for ▷ *sm* employee; (*funzionario*) attaché; **gli addetti ai lavori** authorized personnel; (*fig*) those in the know; **addetto commerciale** commercial attaché; **addetto stampa** press attaché

ad'dio *sm, escl* goodbye, farewell

addirit'tura av (veramente)
really, absolutely; (perfino) even;
(direttamente) directly, right away
addi'tare vt to point out; (fig) to
expose
addi'tivo sm additive
addizi'one sf addition
addob'bare vt to decorate; **ad'dobbo**
sm decoration
addolo'rare vt to pain, grieve;
addolorarsi (per) to be distressed
(by)
addolo'rato, -a ag distressed,
upset; **l'Addolorata** (Rel) Our Lady of
Sorrows
ad'dome sm abdomen
addomesti'care vt to tame
addomi'nale ag abdominal;
(muscoli mpl**) addominali** stomach
muscles
addormen'tare vt to put to sleep;
addormentarsi vpr to fall asleep, go
to sleep
ad'dosso av on; **mettersi ~ il**
cappotto to put one's coat on; **~ a**
(sopra) on; (molto vicino) right next to;
stare ~ a qn (fig) to breathe down sb's
neck; **dare ~ a qn** (fig) to attack sb
adeguarsi vpr to adapt
adegu'ato, -a ag adequate;
(conveniente) suitable; (equo) fair
a'dempiere vt to fulfil, carry out
ade'rente ag adhesive; (vestito) close-
fitting ▷ sm/f follower
ade'rire vi (stare attaccato) to adhere,
stick; **~ a** to adhere to, stick to; (fig:
società, partito) to join; (: opinione) to
support; (richiesta) to agree to
adesi'one sf adhesion; (fig)
agreement, acceptance; **ade'sivo, -a**
ag, sm adhesive
a'desso av (ora) now; (or ora, poco fa)
just now; (tra poco) any moment now
adia'cente [adja'tʃɛnte] ag adjacent
adi'bire vt (usare): **~ qc a** to turn sth
into
adole'scente [adoleʃʃɛnte] ag, sm/f

adolescent
adope'rare vt to use
ado'rare vt to adore; (Rel) to adore,
worship
adot'tare vt to adopt; (decisione,
provvedimenti) to pass; **adot'tivo,**
-a ag (genitori) adoptive; (figlio,
patria) adopted; **adozi'one** sf
adoption; **adozione a distanza** child
sponsorship
adri'atico, -a, -ci, -che ag Adriatic
▷ sm **l'A~, il mare A~** the Adriatic, the
Adriatic Sea
adu'lare vt to adulate, flatter
a'dultero, -a ag adulterous ▷ sm/f
adulterer (adulteress)
a'dulto, -a ag adult; (fig) mature ▷ sm
adult, grown-up
a'ereo, -a ag air cpd; (radice) aerial
▷ sm aerial; (aeroplano) plane; **aereo**
da caccia fighter (plane); **aereo di**
linea airliner; **aereo a reazione** jet
(plane); **ae'robica** sf aerobics sg;
aero'nautica sf (scienza) aeronautics
sg; **aeronautica militare** air force
aero'porto sm airport; **all'~ per**
favore to the airport, please
aero'sol sm inv aerosol
'afa sf sultriness
af'fabile ag affable
affaccen'dato, -a [affattʃen'dato]
ag (persona) busy
affacci'arsi [affat'tʃarsi] vpr **~ (a)** to
appear (at)
affa'mato, -a ag starving; (fig): **~ (di)**
eager (for)
affan'noso, -a ag (respiro) difficult;
(fig) troubled, anxious
af'fare sm (faccenda) matter, affair;
(Comm) piece of business, (business)
deal; (occasione) bargain; (Dir) case;
(fam: cosa) thing; **affari** smpl (Comm)
business sg; **Ministro degli Affari**
esteri Foreign Secretary (BRIT),
Secretary of State (US)
affasci'nante [affaʃʃi'nante] ag
fascinating

affasci'nare [affaʃʃiˈnare] *vt* to bewitch; (*fig*) to charm, fascinate

affati'care *vt* to tire; **affaticarsi** *vpr* (*durar fatica*) to tire o.s. out; **affati'cato, -a** *ag* tired

af'fatto *av* completely; **non ... ~** not ... at all; **niente ~** not at all

affer'mare *vt* (*dichiarare*) to maintain, affirm; **affermarsi** *vpr* to assert o.s., make one's name known; **affer'mato, -a** *ag* established, well-known; **affermazi'one** *sf* affirmation, assertion; (*successo*) achievement

affer'rare *vt* to seize, grasp; (*fig: idea*) to grasp; **afferrarsi** *vpr* **afferrarsi a** to cling to

affet'tare *vt* (*tagliare a fette*) to slice; (*ostentare*) to affect

affetta'trice [affetta'tritʃe] *sf* meat slicer

affet'tivo, -a *ag* emotional, affective

af'fetto *sm* affection; **affettu'oso, -a** *ag* affectionate

affezio'narsi [affettsjoˈnarsi] *vpr* **~ a** to grow fond of

affezio'nato, -a [affettsjoˈnato] *ag* **~ a qn/qc** fond of sb/sth; (*attaccato*) attached to sb/sth

affia'tato, -a *ag* **essere molto affiatati** to get on very well

affibbi'are *vt* (*fig: dare*) to give

affi'dabile *ag* reliable

affida'mento *sm* (*Dir: di bambino*) custody; (*fiducia*): **fare ~ su qn** to rely on sb; **non dà nessun ~** he's not to be trusted

affi'dare *vt*: **~ qc o qn a qn** to entrust sth o sb to sb; **affidarsi** *vpr* **affidarsi a** to place one's trust in

affi'lare *vt* to sharpen

affi'lato, -a *ag* (*gen*) sharp; (*volto, naso*) thin

affinché [affinˈke] *cong* in order that, so that

affit'tare *vt* (*dare in affitto*) to let, rent (out); (*prendere in affitto*) to rent;

af'fitto *sm* rent; (*contratto*) lease

af'fliggere [afˈfliddʒere] *vt* to torment; **affliggersi** *vpr* to grieve

af'flissi *ecc vb vedi* **affliggere**

afflosci'arsi [affloʃˈʃarsi] *vpr* to go limp

afflu'ente *sm* tributary

affo'gare *vt, vi* to drown

affol'lare *vt* to crowd; **affollarsi** *vpr* to crowd; **affol'lato, -a** *ag* crowded

affon'dare *vt* to sink

affran'care *vt* to free, liberate; (*Amm*) to redeem; (*lettera*) to stamp; (*: meccanicamente*) to frank (BRIT), meter (US)

af'fresco, -schi *sm* fresco

affrettarsi *vpr* to hurry; **~ a fare qc** to hurry o hasten to do sth

affret'tato, -a *ag* (*veloce: passo, ritmo*) quick, fast; (*frettoloso: decisione*) hurried, hasty; (*: lavoro*) rushed

affron'tare *vt* (*pericolo ecc*) to face; (*nemico*) to confront; **affrontarsi** *vpr* (*reciproco*) to come to blows

affumi'cato, -a *ag* (*prosciutto, aringa ecc*) smoked

affuso'lato, -a *ag* tapering

Af'ganistan *sm* **l'~** Afghanistan

a'foso, -a *ag* sultry, close

'Africa *sf* **l'~** Africa; **afri'cano, -a** *ag, sm/f* African

a'genda [aˈdʒɛnda] *sf* diary

> Attenzione! In inglese esiste la parola *agenda* che però vuol dire *ordine del giorno*.

a'gente [aˈdʒɛnte] *sm* agent; **agente di cambio** stockbroker; **agente di polizia** police officer; **agente segreto** secret agent; **agen'zia** *sf* agency; (*succursale*) branch; **agenzia immobiliare** estate agent's (office) (BRIT), real estate office (US); **agenzia di collocamento/stampa** employment/press agency; **agenzia viaggi** travel agency

agevo'lare [adʒevo'lare] vt to facilitate, make easy

agevolazi'one [adʒevolat'tsjone] sf (facilitazione economica) facility; **agevolazione di pagamento** payment on easy terms; **agevolazioni creditizie** credit facilities; **agevolazioni fiscali** tax concessions

a'gevole [a'dʒevole] ag easy; (strada) smooth

agganci'are [aggan'tʃare] vt to hook up; (Ferr) to couple

ag'geggio [ad'dʒeddʒo] sm gadget, contraption

agget'tivo [addʒet'tivo] sm adjective

agghiacci'ante [aggjat'tʃante] ag chilling

aggior'nare [addʒor'nare] vt (opera, manuale) to bring up-to-date; (seduta ecc) to postpone; **aggiornarsi** vpr to bring (o keep) o.s. up-to-date; **aggior'nato, -a** ag up-to-date

aggi'rare [addʒi'rare] vt to go round; (fig: ingannare) to trick; **aggirarsi** vpr to wander about; **il prezzo s'aggira sul milione** the price is around the million mark

aggi'ungere [ad'dʒundʒere] vt to add

aggi'unsi ecc [ad'dʒunsi] vb vedi **aggiungere**

aggius'tare [addʒus'tare] vt (accomodare) to mend, repair; (riassettare) to adjust; (fig: lite) to settle

aggrap'parsi vpr ~ **a** to cling to

aggra'vare vt (aumentare) to increase; (appesantire: anche fig) to weigh down, make heavy; (pena) to make worse; **aggravarsi** vpr to worsen, become worse

aggre'dire vt to attack, assault

aggressi'one sf aggression; (atto) attack, assault

aggres'sivo, -a ag aggressive

aggres'sore sm aggressor, attacker

aggrot'tare vt: ~ **le sopracciglia** to frown

aggrovigli'arsi vpr (fig) to become complicated

aggu'ato sm trap; (imboscata) ambush; **tendere un ~ a qn** to set a trap for sb

agguer'rito, -a ag fierce

agi'ato, -a [a'dʒato] ag (vita) easy; (persona) well-off, well-to-do

'agile ['adʒile] ag agile, nimble

'agio ['adʒo] sm ease, comfort; **mettersi a proprio ~** to make o.s. at home o comfortable; **agi** smpl comforts; **mettersi a proprio ~** to make o.s. at home o comfortable; **dare ~ a qn di fare qc** to give sb the chance of doing sth

a'gire [a'dʒire] vi to act; (esercitare un'azione) to take effect; (Tecn) to work, function; **~ contro qn** (Dir) to take action against sb

agi'tare [adʒi'tare] vt (bottiglia) to shake; (mano, fazzoletto) to wave; (fig: turbare) to disturb; (: incitare) to stir (up); (: dibattere) to discuss; **agitarsi** vpr (mare) to be rough; (malato, dormitore) to toss and turn; (bambino) to fidget; (emozionarsi) to get upset; (Pol) to agitate; **agi'tato, -a** ag rough; restless; fidgety; upset, perturbed

'aglio ['aʎʎo] sm garlic

a'gnello [aɲ'ɲɛllo] sm lamb

'ago (pl **'aghi**) sm needle

ago'nistico, -a, -ci, -che ag athletic; (fig) competitive

agopun'tura sf acupuncture

a'gosto sm August

a'grario, -a ag agrarian, agricultural; (riforma) land cpd

a'gricolo, -a ag agricultural, farm cpd; **agricol'tore** sm farmer; **agricol'tura** sf agriculture, farming

agri'foglio [agri'fɔʎʎo] sm holly

agritu'rismo sm farm holidays pl

agrodolce ag bittersweet; (salsa) sweet and sour

a'grume *sm* (*spesso al pl: pianta*)
citrus; (: *frutto*) citrus fruit

a'guzzo, -a [a'guttso] *ag* sharp

'ahi *escl* (*dolore*) ouch!

'Aia *sf* l'~ the Hague

'aids *abbr m* of Aids

airbag *sm inv* air bag

ai'rone *sm* heron

aiu'ola *sf* flower bed

aiu'tante *sm/f* assistant ▷ *sm* (*Mil*)
adjutant; (*Naut*) master-at-arms;
aiutante di campo aide-de-camp

aiu'tare *vt* to help; **~ qn (a fare)** to
help sb (to do); **aiutarsi** *vpr* to help
each other; **~ qn in qc/a fare qc**
to help sb with sth/to do sth; **può
aiutarmi?** can you help me?

ai'uto *sm* help, assistance, aid;
(*aiutante*) assistant; **venire in ~ di qn**
to come to sb's aid; **aiuto chirurgo**
assistant surgeon

'ala (*pl* **'ali**) *sf* wing; **fare ~** to fall back,
make way; **ala destra/sinistra**
(*Sport*) right/left wing

ala'bastro *sm* alabaster

a'lano *sm* Great Dane

'alba *sf* dawn

alba'nese *ag, sm/f, sm* Albanian

Alba'nia *sf* l'~ Albania

albe'rato, -a *ag* (*viale, piazza*) lined
with trees, tree-lined

al'bergo, -ghi *sm* hotel; **albergo
della gioventù** youth hostel

'albero *sm* tree; (*Naut*) mast; (*Tecn*)
shaft; **albero genealogico** family
tree; **albero a gomiti** crankshaft;
albero maestro mainmast; **albero
di Natale** Christmas tree; **albero di
trasmissione** transmission shaft

albi'cocca, -che *sf* apricot

'album *sm* album; **album da disegno**
sketch book

al'bume *sm* albumen

'alce [altʃe] *sm* elk

'alcol *sm inv* = **alcool**

al'colico, -a, -ci, -che *ag* alcoholic
▷ *sm* alcoholic drink

alcoliz'zato, -a [alcolid'dzato] *sm/f*
alcoholic

'alcool *sm inv* alcohol

al'cuno, -a (*det: dav sm:* **alcun** + *C, V,*
alcuno + *s impura, gn, pn, ps, x, z; dav sf:*
alcuna + *C,* **alcun'** +*V*) *det* (*nessuno*):
non ... ~ no, not any; **alcuni, e** *det pl*
some, a few; **non c'è alcuna fretta**
there's no hurry, there isn't any hurry;
senza alcun riguardo without any
consideration ▷ *pron pl* **alcuni, e**
some, a few

alfa'betico, -a, ci, che *ag*
alphabetical

alfa'beto *sm* alphabet

'alga, -ghe *sf* seaweed *no pl*, alga

'algebra ['aldʒebra] *sf* algebra

Alge'ria [aldʒe'ria] *sf* l'~ Algeria

alge'rino, -a [aldʒe'rino] *ag, sm/f*
Algerian

ali'ante *sm* (*Aer*) glider

'alibi *sm inv* alibi

a'lice [a'litʃe] *sf* anchovy

ali'eno, -a *ag* (*avverso*): **~ (da)**
opposed (to), averse (to) ▷ *sm/f* alien

alimen'tare *vt* to feed; (*Tecn*) to feed;
to supply; (*fig*) to sustain ▷ *ag* food
cpd; **alimentari** *smpl* foodstuffs;
(*anche:* **negozio di alimentari**)
grocer's shop; **alimentazi'one** *sf*
feeding; supplying; sustaining; (*gli
alimenti*) diet

a'liquota *sf* share; (*d'imposta*) rate;
aliquota d'imposta tax rate

alis'cafo *sm* hydrofoil

'alito *sm* breath

all. *abbr* (= *allegato*) encl.

allaccia'mento [allattʃa'mento] *sm*
(*Tecn*) connection

allacci'are [allat'tʃare] *vt* (*scarpe*) to
tie, lace (up); (*cintura*) to do up, fasten;
(*luce, gas*) to connect; (*amicizia*) to
form

allacci'atura [allattʃa'tura] *sf*
fastening

alla'gare *vt* to flood; **allagarsi** *vpr*
to flood

allar'gare vt to widen; (vestito) to let out; (aprire) to open; (fig: dilatare) to extend; **allargarsi** vpr (gen) to widen; (scarpe, pantaloni) to stretch; (fig: problema, fenomeno) to spread

allar'mare vt to alarm

al'larme sm alarm; **allarme aereo** air-raid warning

allat'tare vt to feed

alle'anza [alle'antsa] sf alliance

alle'arsi vpr to form an alliance; **alle'ato, -a** ag allied ▷ sm/f ally

alle'gare vt (accludere) to enclose; (Dir: citare) to cite, adduce; (denti) to set on edge; **alle'gato, -a** ag enclosed ▷ sm enclosure; (di e-mail) attachment; **in allegato** enclosed

allegge'rire [alledd͡ʒe'rire] vt to lighten, make lighter; (fig: lavoro, tasse) to reduce

alle'gria sf gaiety, cheerfulness

al'legro, -a ag cheerful, merry; (un po' brillo) merry, tipsy; (vivace: colore) bright ▷ sm (Mus) allegro

allena'mento sm training

alle'nare vt to train; **allenarsi** vpr to train; **allena'tore** sm (Sport) trainer, coach

allen'tare vt to slacken; (disciplina) to relax; **allentarsi** vpr to become slack; (ingranaggio) to work loose

aller'gia, -'gie [aller'd͡ʒia] sf allergy; **al'lergico, -a, -ci, -che** ag allergic; **sono allergico alla penicillina** I'm allergic to penicillin

alles'tire vt (cena) to prepare; (esercito, nave) to equip, fit out; (spettacolo) to stage

allet'tante ag attractive, alluring

alle'vare vt (animale) to breed, rear; (bambino) to bring up

allevi'are vt to alleviate

alli'bito, -a ag astounded

alli'evo sm pupil; (apprendista) apprentice; (Mil) cadet

alliga'tore sm alligator

alline'are vt (persone, cose) to line up; (Tip) to align; (fig: economia, salari) to adjust, align; **allinearsi** vpr to line up; (fig: a idee): **allinearsi a** to come into line with

al'lodola sf (sky)lark

alloggi'are [allod͡ʒ'd͡ʒare] vt to accommodate ▷ vi to live; **al'loggio** sm lodging, accommodation (BRIT), accommodations (US)

allonta'nare vt to send away, send off; (impiegato) to dismiss; (pericolo) to avert, remove; (estraniare) to alienate; **allontanarsi** vpr **allontanarsi (da)** to go away (from); (estraniarsi) to become estranged (from)

al'lora av (in quel momento) then ▷ cong (in questo caso) well then; (dunque) well then, so; **la gente d'~** people then o in those days; **da ~ in poi** from then on

al'loro sm laurel

'alluce ['allut͡ʃe] sm big toe

alluci'nante [allut͡ʃi'nante] ag awful; (fam) amazing

allucinazi'one [allut͡ʃinat'tsjone] sf hallucination

al'ludere vi: **~ a** to allude to, hint at

allu'minio sm aluminium (BRIT), aluminum (US)

allun'gare vt to lengthen; (distendere) to prolong, extend; (diluire) to water down; **allungarsi** vpr to lengthen; (ragazzo) to stretch, grow taller; (sdraiarsi) to lie down, stretch out

al'lusi ecc vb vedi **alludere**

allusi'one sf hint, allusion

alluvi'one sf flood

al'meno av at least ▷ cong **(se) ~** if only; **(se) ~ piovesse!** if only it would rain!

a'logeno, -a [a'lɔd͡ʒeno] ag **lampada alogena** halogen lamp

a'lone sm halo

'Alpi sfpl **le ~** the Alps

alpi'nismo sm mountaineering, climbing; **alpi'nista, -i, -e** sm/f

mountaineer, climber
al'pino, -a *ag* Alpine; mountain *cpd*;
alpini *smpl* (*Mil*) Italian Alpine troops
alt *escl* halt!, stop!
alta'lena *sf* (*a funi*) swing; (*in bilico*)
seesaw
al'tare *sm* altar
alter'nare *vt* to alternate; **alternarsi**
vpr to alternate; **alterna'tiva** *sf*
alternative; **alterna'tivo, -a** *ag*
alternative
al'terno, -a *ag* alternate; **a giorni
alterni** on alternate days, every other
day
al'tero, -a *ag* proud
al'tezza [al'tettsa] *sf* height; width,
breadth; depth; pitch; (*Geo*) latitude;
(*titolo*) highness; (*fig: nobiltà*)
greatness; **essere all'~ di** to be on a
level with; (*fig*) to be up to *o* equal to
al'ticcio, -a, -ci, -ce [al'tittʃo] *ag*
tipsy
alti'tudine *sf* altitude
'alto, -a *ag* high; (*persona*) tall;
(*tessuto*) wide, broad; (*sonno, acque*)
deep; (*suono*) high(-pitched); (*Geo*)
upper; (*settentrionale*) northern ▷ *sm*
top (part) ▷ *av* high; (*parlare*) aloud,
loudly; **il palazzo è ~ 20 metri** the
building is 20 metres high; **ad alta
voce** aloud; **a notte alta** in the dead
of night; **in ~** up, upwards; at the top;
dall'~ in *o* **al basso** up and down;
degli alti e bassi (*fig*) ups and downs;
alta definizione (*TV*) high definition;
alta fedeltà high fidelity, hi-fi; **alta
finanza/società** high finance/
society; **alta moda** haute couture;
alta velocità (*Ferr*) high speed rail
system
altopar'lante *sm* loudspeaker
altopi'ano (*pl* **altipi'ani**) *sm* plateau,
upland plain
altret'tanto, -a *ag, pron* as much; (*pl*)
as many *o* equally; **tanti auguri!
— grazie, ~** all the best! — thank you,
the same to you

altri'menti *av* otherwise

⭕ **PAROLA CHIAVE**

'altro, -a *det* **1** (*diverso*) other,
different; **questa è un'altra cosa**
that's another *o* a different thing
2 (*supplementare*) other; **prendi un
altro cioccolatino** have another
chocolate; **hai avuto altre notizie?**
have you had any more *o* any other
news?
3 (*nel tempo*): **l'altro giorno** the other
day; **l'altr'anno** last year; **l'altro ieri**
the day before yesterday; **domani
l'altro** the day after tomorrow;
quest'altro mese next month
4: **d'altra parte** on the other hand
▷ *pron* **1** (*persona, cosa diversa o
supplementare*): **un altro, un'altra**
another (one); **lo farà un altro**
someone else will do it; **altri, e**
others; **gli altri** (*la gente*) others,
other people; **l'uno e l'altro** both (of
them); **aiutarsi l'un l'altro** to help
one another; **da un giorno all'altro**
from day to day; (*nel giro di 24 ore*) from
one day to the next; (*da un momento
all'altro*) any day now
2 (*sostantivato: solo maschile*) è
something else; (: *in espressioni
interrogative*) anything else; **non ho
altro da dire** I have nothing else *o* I
don't have anything else to say; **più
che altro** above all; **se non altro** at
least; **tra l'altro** among other things;
ci mancherebbe altro! that's all we
need!; **non faccio altro che lavorare**
I do nothing but work; **contento?
— altro che!** are you pleased? — and
how!; *vedi* **senza**; **noialtri**; **voialtri**;
tutto

al'trove *av* elsewhere, somewhere
else
altru'ista, -i, -e *ag* altruistic
a'lunno, -a *sm/f* pupil

alve'are *sm* hive

al'zare [al'tsare] *vt* to raise, lift; (*issare*) to hoist; (*costruire*) to build, erect; **alzarsi** *vpr* to rise; (*dal letto*) to get up; (*crescere*) to grow tall (*o taller*); **~ le spalle** to shrug one's shoulders; **alzarsi in piedi** to stand up, get to one's feet

a'maca, -che *sf* hammock

amalga'mare *vt* to amalgamate; **amalgamarsi** *vpr* to amalgamate

a'mante *ag*: **~ di** (*musica ecc*) fond of ▷ *sm/f* lover/mistress

a'mare *vt* to love; (*amico, musica, sport*) to like; **amarsi** *vpr* to love each other

amareggi'ato, -a [amared'dʒato] *ag* upset, saddened

ama'rena *sf* sour black cherry

ama'rezza [ama'rettsa] *sf* bitterness

a'maro, -a *ag* bitter ▷ *sm* bitterness; (*liquore*) bitters *pl*

amaz'zonico, -a, ci, che [amad'dzoniko] *ag* Amazonian; Amazon *cpd*

ambasci'ata [ambaʃ'ʃata] *sf* embassy; (*messaggio*) message; **ambascia'tore, -'trice** *sm/f* ambassador/ambassadress

ambe'due *ag inv*: **~ i ragazzi** both boys ▷ *pron inv* both

ambienta'lista, -i, e *ag* environmental ▷ *sm/f* environmentalist

ambien'tare *vt* to acclimatize; (*romanzo, film*) to set; **ambientarsi** *vpr* to get used to one's surroundings

ambi'ente *sm* environment; (*fig: insieme di persone*) milieu; (*stanza*) room

am'biguo, -a *ag* ambiguous

ambizi'one [ambit'tsjone] *sf* ambition; **ambizi'oso, -a** *ag* ambitious

'ambo *ag inv* both ▷ *sm* (*al gioco*) double

'ambra *sf* amber; **ambra grigia** ambergris

ambu'lante *ag* itinerant ▷ *sm* peddler

ambu'lanza [ambu'lantsa] *sf* ambulance; **chiamate un ~** call an ambulance

ambula'torio *sm* (*studio medico*) surgery

A'merica *sf* l'~ America; l'~ **latina** Latin America; **ameri'cano, -a** *ag*, *sm/f* American

ami'anto *sm* asbestos

ami'chevole [ami'kevole] *ag* friendly

ami'cizia [ami'tʃittsja] *sf* friendship; **amicizie** *sfpl* (*amici*) friends

a'mico, -a, -ci, -che *sm/f* friend; (*fidanzato*) boyfriend/girlfriend; **amico del cuore** bosom friend

'amido *sm* starch

ammac'care *vt* (*pentola*) to dent; (*persona*) to bruise

ammac'catura *sf* dent; bruise

ammaes'trare *vt* (*animale*) to train

ammai'nare *vt* to lower, haul down

amma'larsi *vpr* to fall ill; **amma'lato, -a** *ag* ill, sick ▷ *sm/f* sick person; (*paziente*) patient

ammanet'tare *vt* to handcuff

ammas'sare *vt* (*ammucchiare*) to amass; (*raccogliere*) to gather together; **ammassarsi** *vpr* to pile up; to gather

ammat'tire *vi* to go mad

ammaz'zare [ammat'tsare] *vt* to kill; **ammazzarsi** *vpr* (*uccidersi*) to kill o.s.; (*rimanere ucciso*) to be killed; **ammazzarsi di lavoro** to work o.s. to death

am'mettere *vt* to admit; (*riconoscere: fatto*) to acknowledge, admit; (*permettere*) to allow, accept; (*supporre*) to suppose

amminis'trare *vt* to run, manage; (*Rel, Dir*) to administer; **amministra'tore** *sm* administrator; (*di condominio*) flats manager; **amministratore**

delegato managing director;
amministrazi'one sf management;
administration

ammi'raglio [ammi'raʎʎo] sm
admiral

ammi'rare vt to admire;
ammirazi'one sf admiration

am'misi ecc vb vedi **ammettere**

ammobili'ato, -a ag furnished

am'mollo sm: **lasciare in ~** to leave
to soak

ammo'niaca sf ammonia

ammo'nire vt (avvertire) to warn;
(rimproverare) to admonish; (Dir) to
caution

ammonizi'one [ammonit'tsjone]
sf (monito: anche Sport) warning;
(rimprovero) reprimand; (Dir) caution

ammon'tare vi: **~ a** to amount to
▷ sm (total) amount

ammorbi'dente sm fabric
conditioner

ammorbi'dire vt to soften

ammortizza'tore sm (Aut, Tecn)
shock-absorber

ammucchi'are [ammuk'kjare] vt to
pile up, accumulate

ammuf'fire vi to go mouldy (BRIT) o
moldy (US)

ammuto'lire vi to be struck dumb

amne'sia sf amnesia

amnis'tia sf amnesty

'amo sm (Pesca) hook; (fig) bait

a'more sm love; **amori** smpl love
affairs; **il tuo bambino è un ~** your
baby's a darling; **fare l'~** o **all'~** to
make love; **per ~** o **per forza** by
hook or by crook; **amor proprio** self-
esteem, pride

amo'roso, -a ag (affettuoso) loving,
affectionate; (d'amore: sguardo)
amorous; (: poesia, relazione) love cpd

'ampio, -a ag wide, broad; (spazioso)
spacious; (abbondante: vestito) loose;
(: gonna) full; (: spiegazione) ample, full

am'plesso sm intercourse

ampli'are vt (ingrandire) to enlarge;

(allargare) to widen; **ampliarsi** vpr to
grow, increase

amplifica'tore sm (Tecn, Mus)
amplifier

ampu'tare vt (Med) to amputate

A.N. sigla f (= Alleanza Nazionale) Italian
right-wing party

anabbaglianti smpl dipped (BRIT) o
dimmed (US) headlights

anaboliz'zante ag anabolic ▷ sm
anabolic steroid

anal'colico, -a, -ci, -che ag non-
alcoholic ▷ sm soft drink

analfa'beta, -i, -e ag, sm/f illiterate

anal'gesico, -a, -ci, -che
[anal'dʒeziko] ag, sm analgesic

a'nalisi sf inv analysis; (Med: esame)
test; **analisi del sangue** blood test sg

analiz'zare [analid'dzare] vt to
analyse; (Med) to test

a'nalogo, -a, -ghi, -ghe ag
analogous

'ananas sm inv pineapple

anar'chia [anar'kia] sf anarchy;
a'narchico, -a, -ci, -che ag
anarchic(al) ▷ sm/f anarchist

anarco-insurreziona'lista ag
anarcho-revolutionary

'A.N.A.S. sigla f (= Azienda Nazionale
Autonoma delle Strade) national roads
department

anato'mia sf anatomy

'anatra sf duck

'anca, -che sf (Anat) hip

'anche ['anke] cong (inoltre, pure) also,
too; (perfino) even; **vengo anch'io** I'm
coming too; **~ se** even if

an'cora av still; (di nuovo) again; (di
più) some more; (persino): **~ più forte**
even stronger; **non ~** not yet; **~ una
volta** once more, once again; **~ un po'**
a little more; (di tempo) a little longer

an'dare sm: **a lungo ~** in the long run
▷ vi to go; (essere adatto): **~ a** to suit;
(piacere): **il suo comportamento non
mi va** I don't like the way he behaves;
ti va di ~ al cinema? do you feel like

going to the cinema?; **andarsene** to go away; **questa camicia va lavata** this shirt needs a wash o should be washed; **~ a cavallo** to ride; **~ in macchina/aereo** to go by car/plane; **~ a fare qc** to go and do sth; **~ a pescare/sciare** to go fishing/skiing; **~ a male** to go bad; **come va?** (lavoro, progetto) how are things?; **come va? — bene, grazie!** how are you? — fine, thanks!; **va fatto entro oggi** it's got to be done today; **ne va della nostra vita** our lives are at stake; **an'data** sf going; (viaggio) outward journey; **biglietto di sola andata** single (BRIT) o one-way ticket; **biglietto di andata e ritorno** return (BRIT) o round-trip (US) ticket

andrò ecc vb vedi **andare**

a'neddoto sm anecdote

a'nello sm ring; (di catena) link; **anelli** smpl (Ginnastica) rings

a'nemico, -a, -ci, -che ag anaemic

aneste'sia sf anaesthesia

'angelo ['andʒelo] sm angel; **angelo custode** guardian angel

anghe'ria [ange'ria] sf vexation

angli'cano, -a ag Anglican

anglo'sassone ag Anglo-Saxon

'angolo sm corner; (Mat) angle; **angolo cottura** (di appartamento ecc) cooking area

an'goscia, -sce [an'goʃʃa] sf deep anxiety, anguish no pl

angu'illa sf eel

an'guria sf watermelon

'anice ['anitʃe] sm (Cuc) aniseed; (Bot) anise

'anima sf soul; (abitante) inhabitant; **non c'era ~ viva** there wasn't a living soul; **anima gemella** soul mate

ani'male sm, ag animal; **animale domestico** pet

anna'cquare vt to water down, dilute

annaffi'are vt to water; **annaffia'toio** sm watering can

an'nata sf year; (importo annuo) annual amount; **vino d'~** vintage wine

anne'gare vt, vi to drown

anne'rire vt to blacken ▷ vi to become black

annien'tare vt to annihilate, destroy

anniver'sario sm anniversary; **anniversario di matrimonio** wedding anniversary

'anno sm year; **ha 8 anni** he's 8 (years old)

anno'dare vt to knot, tie; (fig: rapporto) to form

annoi'are vt to bore; **annoiarsi** vpr to be bored

⚠ Attenzione! In inglese esiste il verbo to annoy che però vuol dire dare fastidio a.

anno'tare vt (registrare) to note, note down; (commentare) to annotate

annu'ale ag annual

annu'ire vi to nod; (acconsentire) to agree

annul'lare vt to annihilate, destroy; (contratto, francobollo) to cancel; (matrimonio) to annul; (sentenza) to quash; (risultati) to declare void

annunci'are [annun'tʃare] vt to announce; (dar segni rivelatori) to herald

an'nuncio [an'nuntʃo] sm announcement; (fig) sign; **annunci economici** classified advertisements, small ads; **annunci mortuari** (colonna) obituary column; **annuncio pubblicitario** advertisement

'annuo, -a ag annual, yearly

annu'sare vt to sniff, smell; **~ tabacco** to take snuff

a'nomalo, -a ag anomalous

a'nonimo, -a ag anonymous ▷ sm (autore) anonymous writer (o painter ecc); **società anonima** (Comm) joint stock company

anores'sia sf anorexia

ano'ressico, -a, ci, che ag anorexic

anor'male ag abnormal ▷ sm/f
subnormal person

ANSA sigla f (= Agenzia Nazionale
Stampa Associata) press agency

'ansia sf anxiety

ansi'mare vi to pant

ansi'oso, -a ag anxious

'anta sf (di finestra) shutter; (di
armadio) door

An'tartide sf: **l'~** Antarctica

an'tenna sf (Radio, TV) aerial; (Zool)
antenna, feeler; (Naut) yard; **antenna
parabolica** satellite dish

ante'prima sf preview; **anteprima
di stampa** (Inform) print preview

anteri'ore ag (ruota, zampa) front;
(fatti) previous, preceding

antiade'rente ag non-stick

antibi'otico, -a, -ci, -che ag, sm
antibiotic

anti'camera sf anteroom; **fare ~** to
wait (for an audience)

antici'pare [antitʃi'pare] vt
(consegna, visita) to bring forward,
anticipate; (somma di denaro) to pay
in advance; (notizia) to disclose ▷ vi
to be ahead of time; **an'ticipo** sm
anticipation; (di denaro) advance; **in
anticipo** early, in advance; **occorre
che prenoti in anticipo?** do I need to
book in advance?

an'tico, -a, -chi, -che ag (quadro,
mobili) antique; (dell'antichità) ancient;
all'antica old-fashioned

anticoncezio'nale
[antikontʃettsjo'nale] sm
contraceptive

anticonfor'mista, -i, -e ag, sm/f
nonconformist

anti'corpo sm antibody

antidolo'rifico, -ci sm painkiller

anti'doping sm drug testing ▷ ag inv
test ~ drugs (BRIT) o drug (US) test

an'tifona sf (Mus, Rel) antiphon;
capire l'~ (fig) to take the hint

anti'forfora ag inv anti-dandruff

anti'furto sm anti-theft device

anti'gelo [anti'dʒɛlo] ag inv **(liquido)
~** (per motore) antifreeze; (per cristalli)
de-icer

antiglobalizzazione [antigloba-
liddzat'tsjone] ag inv **movimento ~**
anti-globalization movement

An'tille sfpl: **le ~** the West Indies

antin'cendio [antin'tʃɛndjo] ag inv
fire cpd

anti'nebbia sm inv (anche: **faro ~**:
Aut) fog lamp

antinfiamma'torio, -a ag, sm anti-
inflammatory

antio'rario [antio'rarjo] ag: **in senso
~** anticlockwise

anti'pasto sm hors d'œuvre

antipa'tia sf antipathy, dislike;
anti'patico, -a, -ci, -che ag
unpleasant, disagreeable

antiproi'ettile ag inv bulletproof

antiquari'ato sm antique trade; **un
oggetto d'~** an antique

anti'quario sm antique dealer

anti'quato, -a ag antiquated, old-
fashioned

anti'rughe ag inv (crema, prodotto)
anti-wrinkle

antitraspi'rante ag antiperspirant

anti'vipera ag inv: **siero ~** remedy for
snake bites

antivirus [anti'virus] sm inv antivirus
software no pl ▷ ag inv antivirus

antolo'gia, -'gie [antolo'dʒia] sf
anthology

anu'lare ag ring cpd ▷ sm third finger

'anzi ['antsi] av (invece) on the
contrary; (o meglio) or rather, or better
still

anzi'ano, -a [an'tsjano] ag old;
(Amm) senior ▷ sm/f old person;
senior member

anziché [antsi'ke] cong rather than

a'patico, -a, -ci, -che ag apathetic

'ape sf bee

aperi'tivo sm apéritif

aperta'mente av openly

a'perto, -a pp di **aprire** ▷ ag open;

all'~ in the open (air); **è ~ al pubblico?** is it open to the public?; **quando è ~ il museo?** when is the museum open?

aper'tura *sf* opening; (*ampiezza*) width; (*Fot*) aperture; **apertura alare** wing span; **apertura mentale** open-mindedness

ap'nea *sf*: **immergersi in ~** to dive without breathing apparatus

a'postrofo *sm* apostrophe

ap'paio *ecc vb vedi* **apparire**

ap'palto *sm* (*Comm*) contract; **dare/prendere in ~ un lavoro** to let out/undertake a job on contract

appannarsi *vpr* to mist over; to grow dim

apparecchi'are [apparek'kjare] *vt* to prepare; (*tavola*) to set ▷ *vi* to set the table

appa'recchio [appa'rekkjo] *sm* piece of apparatus, device; (*aeroplano*) aircraft *inv*; **apparecchio acustico** hearing aid; **apparecchio telefonico** telephone; **apparecchio televisivo** television set

appa'rente *ag* apparent

appa'rire *vi* to appear; (*sembrare*) to seem, appear

apparta'mento *sm* flat (*BRIT*), apartment (*US*)

appar'tarsi *vpr* to withdraw

apparte'nere *vi* **~ a** to belong to

ap'parvi *ecc vb vedi* **apparire**

appassio'nare *vt* to thrill; (*commuovere*) to move; **appassionarsi** *vpr* **appassionarsi a qc** to take a great interest in sth; **appassio'nato, -a** *ag* passionate; (*entusiasta*): **appassionato (di)** keen (on)

appas'sire *vi* to wither

appas'sito, -a *ag* dead

ap'pello *sm* roll-call; (*implorazione, Dir*) appeal; **fare ~ a** to appeal to

ap'pena *av* (*a stento*) hardly, scarcely; (*solamente, da poco*) just ▷ *cong* as soon as; **(non) ~ furono arrivati ...** as soon as they had arrived ...; **~ ... che** o

quando no sooner ... than

ap'pendere *vt* to hang (up)

appen'dice [appen'ditʃe] *sf* appendix; **romanzo d'~** popular serial

appendi'cite [appendi'tʃite] *sf* appendicitis

Appen'nini *smpl*: **gli ~** the Apennines

appesan'tire *vt* to make heavy; **appesantirsi** *vpr* to grow stout

appe'tito *sm* appetite

appic'care *vt*: **~ il fuoco a** to set fire to, set on fire

appicci'care [appittʃi'kare] *vt* to stick; **appiccicarsi** *vpr* to stick; (*fig: persona*) to cling

appiso'larsi *vpr* to doze off

applau'dire *vt, vi* to applaud; **ap'plauso** *sm* applause

appli'care *vt* to apply; (*regolamento*) to enforce; **applicarsi** *vpr* to apply o.s.

appoggi'are [appod'dʒare] *vt* (*mettere contro*): **~ qc a qc** to lean o rest sth against sth; (*fig: sostenere*) to support; **appoggiarsi** *vpr* **appoggiarsi a** to lean against; (*fig*) to rely upon; **ap'poggio** *sm* support

apposita'mente *av* specially; (*apposta*) on purpose

ap'posito, -a *ag* appropriate

ap'posta *av* on purpose, deliberately

appos'tarsi *vpr* to lie in wait

ap'prendere *vt* (*imparare*) to learn

appren'dista, -i, -e *sm/f* apprentice

apprensi'one *sf* apprehension

apprez'zare [appret'tsare] *vt* to appreciate

appro'dare *vi* (*Naut*) to land; (*fig*): **non ~ a nulla** to come to nothing

approfit'tare *vi* **~ di** to make the most of; (*peg*) to take advantage of

approfon'dire *vt* to deepen; (*fig*) to study in depth

appropri'ato, -a *ag* appropriate

approssima'tivo, -a *ag* approximate, rough; (*impreciso*) inexact, imprecise

appro'vare vt (condotta, azione) to approve of; (candidato) to pass; (progetto di legge) to approve

appunta'mento sm appointment; (amoroso) date; **darsi ~** to arrange to meet (one another); **ho un ~ con...** I have an appointment with ...; **vorrei prendere un ~** I'd like to make an appointment

ap'punto sm note; (rimprovero) reproach ▷ av (proprio) exactly, just; **per l'~!, ~!** exactly!

apribot'tiglie [apribot'tiʎʎe] sm inv bottle opener

a'prile sm April

a'prire vt to open; (via, cadavere) to open up; (gas, luce, acqua) to turn on ▷ vi to open; **aprirsi** vpr to open; **aprirsi a qn** to confide in sb, open one's heart to sb; **a che ora aprite?** what time do you open?

apris'catole sm inv tin (BRIT) o can opener

APT sigla f (= Azienda di Promozione) ≈ tourist board

aquagym [akkwa'dʒim] sf aquaerobics

'aquila sf (Zool) eagle; (fig) genius

aqui'lone sm (giocattolo) kite; (vento) North wind

A/R abbr = **andata e ritorno** (biglietto) return ticket (BRIT), round-trip ticket (US)

A'rabia Sau'dita sf l'~ Saudi Arabia

'arabo, -a ag, sm/f Arab ▷ sm (Ling) Arabic

a'rachide [a'rakide] sf peanut

ara'gosta sf crayfish; lobster

a'rancia, -ce [a'rantʃa] sf orange; **aranci'ata** sf orangeade; **aranci'one** ag inv **(color) arancione** bright orange

a'rare vt to plough (BRIT), plow (US)

a'ratro sm plough (BRIT), plow (US)

a'razzo [a'rattso] sm tapestry

arbi'trare vt (Sport) to referee; to umpire; (Dir) to arbitrate

arbi'trario, -a ag arbitrary

'arbitro sm arbiter, judge; (Dir) arbitrator; (Sport) referee; (: Tennis, Cricket) umpire

ar'busto sm shrub

archeolo'gia [arkeolo'dʒia] sf arch(a)eology; **arche'ologo, -a, -gi, -ghe** sm/f arch(a)eologist

architet'tare [arkitet'tare] vt (fig: ideare) to devise; (: macchinare) to plan, concoct

archi'tetto [arki'tetto] sm architect; **architet'tura** sf architecture

ar'chivio [ar'kivjo] sm archives pl; (Inform) file

'arco sm (arma, Mus) bow; (Archit) arch; (Mat) arc

arcoba'leno sm rainbow

arcu'ato, -a ag curved, bent

'ardere vt, vi to burn

ar'desia sf slate

'area sf area; (Edil) land, ground; **area di rigore** (Sport) penalty area; **area di servizio** (Aut) service area

a'rena sf arena; (per corride) bullring; (sabbia) sand

are'narsi vpr to run aground

argente'ria [ardʒente'ria] sf silverware, silver

Argen'tina [ardʒen'tina] sf: l'~ Argentina; **argen'tino, -a** ag, sm/f Argentinian

ar'gento [ar'dʒento] sm silver; **argento vivo** quicksilver

ar'gilla [ar'dʒilla] sf clay

'argine ['ardʒine] sm embankment, bank; (diga) dyke, dike

argo'mento sm argument; (motivo) motive; (materia, tema) subject

'aria sf air; (espressione, aspetto) air, look; (Mus: melodia) tune; (di opera) aria; **mandare all'~ qc** to ruin o upset sth; **all'~ aperta** in the open (air)

'arido, -a ag arid

arieggi'are [arjed'dʒare] vt (cambiare aria) to air; (imitare) to imitate

ari'ete sm ram; (Mil) battering ram;

(dello zodiaco): **A~** Aries
a'ringa, -ghe sf herring inv
arit'metica sf arithmetic
'arma, -i sf weapon, arm; (parte dell'esercito) arm; **chiamare alle armi** to call up (BRIT), draft (US); **sotto le armi** in the army (o forces); **alle armi!** to arms!; **arma atomica/nucleare** atomic/nuclear weapon; **arma da fuoco** firearm; **armi di distruzione di massa** weapons of mass destruction
arma'dietto sm (di medicinali) medicine cabinet; (in palestra ecc) locker; (in cucina) (kitchen) cupboard
ar'madio sm cupboard; (per abiti) wardrobe; **armadio a muro** built-in cupboard
ar'mato, -a ag: **~ (di)** (anche fig) armed (with) ▷ sf (Mil) army; (Naut) fleet; **rapina a mano armata** armed robbery
arma'tura sf (struttura di sostegno) framework; (impalcatura) scaffolding; (Storia) armour no pl, suit of armour
armis'tizio [armis'tittsjo] sm armistice
armo'nia sf harmony
ar'nese sm tool, implement; (oggetto indeterminato) thing, contraption; **male in ~** (malvestito) badly dressed; (di salute malferma) in poor health; (povero) down-at-heel
'arnia sf hive
a'roma, -i sm aroma; fragrance; **aromi** smpl (Cuc) herbs and spices; **aromatera'pia** sf aromatherapy
'arpa sf (Mus) harp
arrabbi'are vi (cane) to be affected with rabies; **arrabbiarsi** vpr (essere preso dall'ira) to get angry, fly into a rage; **arrabbi'ato, -a** ag rabid, with rabies; furious, angry
arrampi'carsi vpr to climb (up)
arrangiarsi vpr to manage, do the best one can
arreda'mento sm (studio) interior design; (mobili ecc) furnishings pl

arre'dare vt to furnish
ar'rendersi vpr to surrender
arres'tare vt (fermare) to stop, halt; (catturare) to arrest; **arrestarsi** vpr (fermarsi) to stop; **ar'resto** sm (cessazione) stopping; (fermata) stop; (cattura, Med) arrest; **subire un arresto** to come to a stop o standstill; **mettere agli arresti** to place under arrest; **arresti domiciliari** house arrest sg
arre'trare vt, vi to withdraw; **arre'trato, -a** ag (lavoro) behind schedule; (paese, bambino) backward; (numero di giornale) back cpd; **arretrati** smpl arrears
arric'chire [arrik'kire] vt to enrich; **arricchirsi** vpr to become rich
arri'vare vi to arrive; (accadere) to happen, occur; **~ a** (livello, grado ecc) to reach; **a che ora arriva il treno da Londra?** what time does the train from London arrive?; **non ci arrivo** I can't reach it; (fig: non capisco) I can't understand it
arrive'derci [arrive'dertʃi] escl goodbye!
arri'vista, -i, -e sm/f go-getter
ar'rivo sm arrival; (Sport) finish, finishing line
arro'gante ag arrogant
arros'sire vi (per vergogna, timidezza) to blush, flush; (per gioia, rabbia) to flush
arros'tire vt to roast; (pane) to toast; (ai ferri) to grill
ar'rosto sm, ag inv roast
arroto'lare vt to roll up
arroton'dare vt (forma, oggetto) to round; (stipendio) to add to; (somma) to round off
arruggi'nito, -a [arruddʒin'nito] ag rusty
'arsi vb vedi **ardere**
'arte sf art; (abilità) skill
ar'teria sf artery; **arteria stradale** main road

'artico, -a, -ci, -che *ag* Arctic

articolazi'one *sf* articulation; (*Anat, Tecn*) joint

ar'ticolo *sm* article; **articolo di fondo** (*Stampa*) leader, leading article

artifici'ale [artifi'tʃale] *ag* artificial

artigia'nato [artidʒa'nato] *sm* craftsmanship; craftsmen *pl*

artigi'ano, -a [arti'dʒano] *sm/f* craftsman/woman

ar'tista, -i, -e *sm/f* artist; **ar'tistico, -a, -ci, -che** *ag* artistic

ar'trite *sf* (*Med*) arthritis

a'scella [aʃʃella] *sf* (*Anat*) armpit

ascen'dente [aʃʃen'dɛnte] *sm* ancestor; (*fig*) ascendancy; (*Astr*) ascendant

ascen'sore [aʃʃen'sore] *sm* lift

a'scesso [aʃʃɛsso] *sm* (*Med*) abscess

asciuga'pelli [aʃʃugaka'pelli] *sm* hair-drier

asciuga'mano [aʃʃuga'mano] *sm* towel

asciu'gare [aʃʃu'gare] *vt* to dry; **asciugarsi** *vpr* to dry o.s.; (*diventare asciutto*) to dry

asci'utto, -a [aʃʃutto] *ag* dry; (*fig: magro*) lean; (: *burbero*) curt; **restare a bocca asciutta** (*fig*) to be disappointed

ascol'tare *vt* to listen to

as'falto *sm* asphalt

'Asia *sf* l'~ Asia; **asi'atico, -a, -ci, -che** *ag, sm/f* Asiatic, Asian

a'silo *sm* refuge, sanctuary; ~ **(d'infanzia)** nursery(-school); **asilo nido** crèche; **asilo politico** political asylum

'asino *sm* donkey, ass

ASL *sigla f* (= *Azienda Sanitaria Locale*) local health centre

'asma *sf* asthma

as'parago, -gi *sm* asparagus *no pl*

aspet'tare *vt* to wait for; (*anche Comm*) to await; (*aspettarsi*) to expect ▷ *vi* to wait; **aspettami, per favore** wait for me, please

as'petto *sm* (*apparenza*) aspect, appearance, look; (*punto di vista*) point of view; **di bell'~** good-looking

aspira'polvere *sm inv* vacuum cleaner

aspi'rare *vt* (*respirare*) to breathe in, inhale; (*apparecchi*) to suck (up) ▷ *vi* ~ **a** to aspire to

aspi'rina *sf* aspirin

'aspro, -a *ag* (*sapore*) sour, tart; (*odore*) acrid, pungent; (*voce, clima, fig*) harsh; (*superficie*) rough; (*paesaggio*) rugged

assaggi'are [assad'dʒare] *vt* to taste; **posso assaggiarlo?** can I have a taste?; **assaggino** [assad'dʒino] *sm* **assaggini** (*Cuc*) selection of first courses; **solo un assaggino** just a little

as'sai *av* (*molto*) a lot, much; (: *con ag*) very; (*a sufficienza*) enough ▷ *ag inv* (*quantità*) a lot of, much; (*numero*) a lot of, many; ~ **contento** very pleased

as'salgo *ecc vb vedi* **assalire**

assa'lire *vt* to attack, assail

assal'tare *vt* (*Mil*) to storm; (*banca*) to raid; (*treno, diligenza*) to hold up

as'salto *sm* attack, assault

assassi'nare *vt* to murder; to assassinate; (*fig*) to ruin; **assas'sino, -a** *ag* murderous ▷ *sm/f* murderer; assassin

'asse *sm* (*Tecn*) axle; (*Mat*) axis ▷ *sf* board; **asse da stiro** ironing board

assedi'are *vt* to besiege

asse'gnare [assen'ɲare] *vt* to assign, allot; (*premio*) to award

as'segno [as'seɲɲo] *sm* allowance; (*anche*: ~ **bancario**) cheque (BRIT), check (US); **contro ~** cash on delivery; **posso pagare con un ~?** can I pay by cheque?; **assegno circolare** bank draft; **assegni familiari** ≈ child benefit *no pl*; **assegno sbarrato** crossed cheque; **assegno di viaggio** traveller's cheque; **assegno a vuoto** dud cheque; **assegno di malattia/di invalidità** sick pay/disability benefit

assem'blea *sf* assembly

assen'tarsi vpr to go out
as'sente ag absent; (fig) faraway,
vacant; **as'senza** sf absence
asse'tato, -a ag thirsty, parched
assicu'rare vt (accertare) to ensure;
(infondere certezza) to assure; (fermare,
legare) to make fast, secure; (fare
un contratto di assicurazione) to
insure; **assicurarsi** vpr (accertarsi):
assicurarsi (di) to make sure (of);
(contro il furto ecc): **assicurarsi
(contro)** to insure o.s. (against);
assicurazi'one sf assurance;
insurance
assi'eme av (insieme) together; **~ a**
(together) with
assil'lare vt to pester, torment
assis'tente sm/f assistant;
assistente sociale social worker;
assistente di volo (Aer) steward/
stewardess
assis'tenza [assis'tɛntsa] sf
assistance; **~ ospedaliera** free
hospital treatment; **~ sociale** welfare
services pl; **assistenza sanitaria**
health service
as'sistere vt (aiutare) to assist, help;
(curare) to treat ▷ vi **~ (a qc)** (essere
presente) to be present (at sth), to
attend (sth)
'asso sm ace; **piantare qn in ~** to
leave sb in the lurch
associ'are [asso'tʃare] vt to
associate; **associarsi** vpr to enter
into partnership; **associarsi a** to
become a member of, join; (dolori,
gioie) to share in; **~ qn alle carceri** to
take sb to prison
associazi'one [assotʃat'tsjone] sf
association; (Comm) association,
society; **~ a delinquere** (Dir) criminal
association
as'solsi ecc vb vedi **assolvere**
assoluta'mente av absolutely
asso'luto, -a ag absolute
assoluzi'one [assolut'tsjone] sf (Dir)
acquittal; (Rel) absolution

as'solvere vt (Dir) to acquit; (Rel)
to absolve; (adempiere) to carry out,
perform
assomigli'are [assomiʎ'ʎare] vi **~ a**
to resemble, look like; **assomigliarsi**
vpr to look alike; (nel carattere) to be
alike
asson'nato, -a ag sleepy
asso'pirsi vpr to doze off
assor'bente ag absorbent ▷ sm:
assorbente interno tampon;
assorbente esterno/igienico
sanitary towel
assor'bire vt to absorb
assor'dare vt to deafen
assorti'mento sm assortment
assor'tito, -a ag assorted; matched,
matching
assuefazi'one [assuefat'tsjone] sf
(Med) addiction
as'sumere vt (impiegato) to take on,
engage; (responsabilità) to assume,
take upon o.s.; (contegno, espressione)
to assume, put on; (droga) to consume
as'sunsi ecc vb vedi **assumere**
assurdità sf inv absurdity; **dire delle
~** to talk nonsense
as'surdo, -a ag absurd
'asta sf pole; (vendita) auction
as'temio, -a ag teetotal ▷ sm/f
teetotaller

> Attenzione! In inglese esiste la
> parola abstemious che però vuol
> dire moderato.

aste'nersi vpr: **~ (da)** to abstain
(from), refrain (from); (Pol) to abstain
(from)
aste'risco, -schi sm asterisk
'astice ['astitʃe] sm lobster
astig'matico, -a, ci, che ag
astigmatic
asti'nenza [asti'nɛntsa] sf
abstinence; **essere in crisi di ~** to
suffer from withdrawal symptoms
as'tratto, -a ag abstract
'astro... prefisso; **astrolo'gia**
[astrolo'dʒia] sf astrology;

astro'nauta, -i, -e *sm/f* astronaut;
astro'nave *sf* space ship;
astrono'mia *sf* astronomy;
astro'nomico, -a, -ci, -che *ag*
astronomic(al)
as'tuccio [as'tuttʃo] *sm* case, box,
holder
as'tuto, -a *ag* astute, cunning,
shrewd
A'tene *sf* Athens
'ateo, -a *ag, sm/f* atheist
at'lante *sm* atlas
at'lantico, -a, -ci, -che *ag* Atlantic
▷ *sm* **l'A~, l'Oceano A~** the Atlantic,
the Atlantic Ocean
at'leta, -i, -e *sm/f* athlete; **at'letica**
sf athletics *sg*; **atletica leggera** track
and field events *pl*; **atletica pesante**
weightlifting and wrestling
atmos'fera *sf* atmosphere
a'tomico, -a, -ci, -che *ag* atomic;
(*nucleare*) atomic, atom *cpd*, nuclear
'atomo *sm* atom
'atrio *sm* entrance hall, lobby
a'troce [a'trotʃe] *ag* (*che provoca orrore*)
dreadful; (*terribile*) atrocious
attac'cante *sm/f* (*Sport*) forward
attacca'panni *sm* hook, peg;
(*mobile*) hall stand
attac'care *vt* (*unire*) to attach;
(*cucendo*) to sew on; (*far aderire*) to
stick (on); (*appendere*) to hang (up);
(*assalire: anche fig*) to attack; (*iniziare*)
to begin, start; (*fig: contagiare*) to pass
on ▷ *vi* to stick, adhere; **attaccarsi**
vpr to stick, adhere; (*trasmettersi per
contagio*) to be contagious; (*afferrarsi*):
attaccarsi (a) to cling (to); (*fig:
affezionarsi*): **attaccarsi (a)** to become
attached (to); **~ discorso** to start
a conversation; **at'tacco, -chi** *sm*
(*azione offensiva: anche fig*) attack;
(*Med*) attack, fit; (*Sci*) binding; (*Elettr*)
socket
atteggia'mento [atteddʒa'mento]
sm attitude
at'tendere *vt* to wait for, await ▷ *vi* ~

a to attend to
atten'dibile *ag* (*storia*) credible;
(*testimone*) reliable
atten'tato *sm* attack; **~ alla vita di
qn** attempt on sb's life
attenta'tore, -trice *sm/f* bomber;
attentatore suicida suicide bomber
at'tento, -a *ag* attentive; (*accurato*)
careful, thorough; **stare ~ a qc** to pay
attention to sth; **~!** be careful!
attenzi'one [atten'tsjone] *sf*
attention; **~!** watch out!, be careful!;
attenzioni *sfpl* (*premure*) attentions;
fare ~ a to watch out for; **coprire qn
di attenzioni** to lavish attentions
on sb
atter'raggio [atter'raddʒo] *sm*
landing
atter'rare *vt* to bring down ▷ *vi* to
land
at'tesa *sf* waiting; (*tempo trascorso
aspettando*) wait; **essere in ~ di qc** to
be waiting for sth
at'tesi *ecc vb vedi* **attendere**
at'teso, -a *pp di* **attendere**
'attico, -ci *sm* attic
attil'lato, -a *ag* (*vestito*) close-fitting
'attimo *sm* moment; **in un ~** in a
moment
atti'rare *vt* to attract
atti'tudine *sf* (*disposizione*) aptitude;
(*atteggiamento*) attitude
attività *sf inv* activity; (*Comm*) assets
pl
at'tivo, -a *ag* active; (*Comm*) profit-
making, credit *cpd* ▷ *sm* (*Comm*) assets
pl; **in ~** in credit
'atto *sm* act; (*azione, gesto*) action,
act, deed; (*Dir: documento*) deed,
document; **atti** *smpl* (*di congressi ecc*)
proceedings; **mettere in ~** to put into
action; **fare ~ di fare qc** to make as if
to do sth; **atto di morte/di nascita**
death/birth certificate
at'tore, -'trice *sm/f* actor/actress
at'torno *av* round, around, about; **~ a**
round, around, about

attrac'care vt, vi (Naut) to dock, berth
at'tracco, -chi sm (Naut) docking no
  pl; berth
at'trae ecc vb vedi **attrarre**
attra'ente ag attractive
at'traggo ecc vb vedi **attrarre**
at'trarre vt to attract
at'trassi ecc vb vedi **attrarre**
attraver'sare vt to cross; (città,
  bosco, fig: periodo) to go through;
  (fiume) to run through
attra'verso prep through; (da una
  parte all'altra) across
attrazi'one [attrat'tsjone] sf
  attraction
at'trezzo sm tool, instrument; (Sport)
  piece of equipment
at'trice [at'tritʃe] sf vedi **attore**
attu'ale ag (presente) present; (di
  attualità) topical
  > Attenzione! In inglese esiste la
  parola actual che però vuol dire
  effettivo.
attualità sf inv topicality;
  (avvenimento) current event
attual'mente av at the moment, at
  present
  > Attenzione! In inglese esiste la
  parola actually che però vuol dire
  effettivamente oppure veramente.
attu'are vt to carry out
attu'tire vt to deaden, reduce
'audio sm (TV, Radio, Cine) sound
audiovi'sivo, -a ag audiovisual
audizi'one [audit'tsjone] sf hearing;
  (Mus) audition
augu'rare vt to wish; **augurarsi qc**
  to hope for sth
au'guri smpl best wishes; **fare gli
  ~ a qn** to give sb one's best wishes;
  tanti ~! best wishes!; (per compleanno)
  happy birthday!
'aula sf (scolastica) classroom;
  (universitaria) lecture theatre; (di
  edificio pubblico) hall
aumen'tare vt, vi to increase;
  au'mento sm increase

au'rora sf dawn
ausili'are ag, sm, sm/f auxiliary
Aus'tralia sf l'~ Australia;
  australi'ano, -a ag, sm/f Australian
'Austria sf l'~ Austria; **aus'triaco, -a,
  -ci, -che** ag, sm/f Austrian
au'tentico, -a, -ci, -che ag
  authentic, genuine
au'tista, -i sm driver
'auto sf inv car
autoabbron'zante sm, ag self-tan
autoade'sivo, -a ag self-adhesive
  ▷ sm sticker
autobio'grafico, -a, ci, che ag
  autobiographic(al)
'autobus sm inv bus
auto'carro sm lorry (BRIT), truck
autocertificazi'one [autotʃertifi-
  kat'tsjone] sf self-declaration
autodistrut'tivo, -a ag self-
  destructive
auto'gol sm inv own goal
au'tografo, -a ag, sm autograph
auto'grill® sm inv motorway
  restaurant
auto'matico, -a, -ci, -che ag
  automatic ▷ sm (bottone) snap
  fastener; (fucile) automatic
auto'mobile sf (motor) car
automobi'lista, -i, -e sm/f motorist
autono'leggio sm car hire
autono'mia sf autonomy; (di volo)
  range
au'tonomo, -a ag autonomous,
  independent
autop'sia sf post-mortem, autopsy
auto'radio sf inv (apparecchio) car
  radio; (autoveicolo) radio car
au'tore, -'trice sm/f author
autoreggente [autored'dʒɛnte] ag
  calze autoreggenti hold ups
auto'revole ag authoritative;
  (persona) influential
autoricari'cabile ag **scheda ~**
  top-up card
autori'messa sf garage
autorità sf inv authority

autoriz'zare [autorid'dzare] *vt*
(*permettere*) to authorize; (*giustificare*)
to allow, sanction
autos'contro *sm* dodgem car (BRIT),
bumper car (US)
autoscu'ola *sf* driving school
autos'tima *sf* self-esteem
autos'top *sm* hitchhiking;
autostop'pista, -i, -e *sm/f* hitchhiker
autos'trada *sf* motorway
(BRIT), highway (US); **autostrada
informatica** information
superhighway

● **AUTOSTRADE**
●
● You have to pay to use Italian
● motorways. They are indicated
● by an "A" followed by a number on
● a green sign. The speed limit on
● Italian motorways is 130 kph.

auto'velox® *sm inv* (police) speed
camera
autovet'tura *sf* (motor) car
au'tunno *sm* autumn
avam'braccio [avam'bratt∫o] (*pl (f)*)
-cla) *sm* forearm
avangu'ardia *sf* vanguard
a'vanti *av* (*stato in luogo*) in front;
(*moto: andare, venire*) forward; (*tempo:
prima*) before ▷ *prep* (*luogo*): **~ a**
before, in front of; (*tempo*): **~ Cristo**
before Christ ▷ *escl* (*entrare*) come
(*o go*) in!; (*Mil*) forward!; (*coraggio*)
come on! ▷ *sm inv* (*Sport*) forward; **~
e indietro** backwards and forwards;
andare ~ to go forward; (*continuare*)
to go on; (*precedere*) to go (on) ahead;
(*orologio*) to be fast; **essere ~ negli
studi** to be well advanced with one's
studies
avan'zare [avan'tsare] *vt* (*spostare
in avanti*) to move forward, advance;
(*domanda*) to put forward; (*promuovere*)
to promote; (*essere creditore*): **~ qc da
qn** to be owed sth by sb ▷ *vi* (*andare*

avanti) to move forward, advance;
(*progredire*) to make progress; (*essere
d'avanzo*) to be left, remain
ava'ria *sf* (*guasto*) damage;
(: *meccanico*) breakdown
a'varo, -a *ag* avaricious, miserly ▷ *sm*
miser

 PAROLA CHIAVE

a'vere *sm* (Comm) credit; **gli averi**
(*ricchezze*) wealth *sg*
▷ *vt* **1** (*possedere*) to have; **ha due
bambini/una bella casa** she has
(got) two children/a lovely house; **ha
i capelli lunghi** he has (got) long hair;
non ho da mangiare/bere I've (got)
nothing to eat/drink, I don't have
anything to eat/drink
2 (*indossare*) to wear, have on; **aveva
una maglietta rossa** he was wearing
o he had on a red tee-shirt; **ha gli
occhiali** he wears *o* has glasses
3 (*ricevere*) to get; **hai avuto
l'assegno?** did you get *o* have you had
the cheque?
4 (*età, dimensione*) to be; **ha 9 anni** he
is 9 (years old); **la stanza ha 3 metri
di lunghezza** the room is 3 metres in
length; *vedi* **fame**; **paura** *ecc*
5 (*tempo*): **quanti ne abbiamo oggi?**
what's the date today?; **ne hai per
molto?** will you be long?
6 (*fraseologia*): **avercela con qn** to be
angry with sb; **cos'hai?** what's wrong
o what's the matter with you?; **non
ha niente a che vedere** *o* **fare con
me** it's got nothing to do with me
▷ *vb aus* **1** to have; **aver bevuto/
mangiato** to have drunk/eaten
2 (+ *da* + *infinito*): **avere da fare qc**
to have to do sth; **non hai che da
chiederlo** you only have to ask him

avi'ario, -a *agg*: **influenza aviaria**
bird flu
aviazi'one [avjat'tsjone] *sf* aviation;

(Mil) air force

'avido, -a ag eager; (peg) greedy

avo'cado sm avocado

a'vorio sm ivory

Avv. abbr = **avvocato**

avvantaggi'are [avvantad'dʒare] vt to favour; **avvantaggiarsi** vpr **avvantaggiarsi negli affari/sui concorrenti** to get ahead in business/ of one's competitors

avvele'nare vt to poison

av'vengo ecc vb vedi **avvenire**

avveni'mento sm event

avve'nire vi, vb impers to happen, occur ▷ sm future

av'venni ecc vb vedi **avvenire**

avven'tato, -a ag rash, reckless

avven'tura sf adventure; (amorosa) affair

avventu'rarsi vpr to venture

avventu'roso, -a ag adventurous

avve'rarsi vpr to come true

av'verbio sm adverb

avverrò ecc vb vedi **avvenire**

avver'sario, -a ag opposing ▷ sm opponent, adversary

avver'tenza [avver'tɛntsa] sf (ammonimento) warning; (cautela) care; (premessa) foreword; **avvertenze** sfpl (istruzioni per l'uso) instructions

avverti'mento sm warning

avver'tire vt (avvisare) to warn; (rendere consapevole) to inform, notify; (percepire) to feel

avvi'are vt (mettere sul cammino) to direct; (impresa, trattative) to begin, start; (motore) to start; **avviarsi** vpr to set off, set out

avvici'nare [avvitʃi'nare] vt to bring near; (trattare con: persona) to approach; **avvicinarsi** vpr **avvicinarsi (a qn/qc)** to approach (sb/sth), draw near (to sb/sth)

avvi'lito, -a ag discouraged

avvin'cente ag captivating

avvi'sare vt (far sapere) to inform;

(mettere in guardia) to warn;

av'viso sm warning; (annuncio) announcement; (: affisso) notice; (inserzione pubblicitaria) advertisement; **a mio avviso** in my opinion; **avviso di chiamata** (servizio) call waiting; (segnale) call waiting signal; **avviso di garanzia** (Dir) notification (of impending investigation and of the right to name a defence lawyer)

> Attenzione! In inglese esiste la parola *advice* che però vuol dire *consiglio*.

avvis'tare vt to sight

avvi'tare vt to screw down (o in)

avvo'cato, -'essa sm/f (Dir) barrister (BRIT), lawyer; (fig) defender, advocate

av'volgere [av'voldʒere] vt to roll up; (avviluppare) to wrap up; **avvolgersi** vpr (avvilupparsi) to wrap o.s. up; **avvol'gibile** sm roller blind (BRIT), blind

av'volsi ecc vb vedi **avvolgere**

avvol'toio sm vulture

aza'lea [addza'lea] sf azalea

azi'enda [ad'dzjɛnda] sf business, firm, concern; **azienda agricola** farm

azi'one [at'tsjone] sf action; (Comm) share

a'zoto [ad'dzɔto] sm nitrogen

azzar'dare [addzar'dare] vt (soldi, vita) to risk, hazard; (domanda, ipotesi) to hazard, venture; **azzardarsi** vpr **azzardarsi a fare** to dare (to) do

az'zardo [ad'dzardo] sm risk

azzec'care [attsek'kare] vt (risposta ecc) to get right

azzuf'farsi [attsuf'farsi] vpr to come to blows

az'zurro, -a [ad'dzurro] ag blue ▷ sm (colore) blue; **gli azzurri** (Sport) the Italian national team

b

'babbo *sm* (*fam*) dad, daddy; **Babbo Natale** Father Christmas

baby'sitter ['beɪbɪsɪtəʳ] *sm/f inv* baby-sitter

'bacca, -che *sf* berry

baccalà *sm* dried salted cod; (*fig: peg*) dummy

bac'chetta [bak'ketta] *sf* (*verga*) stick, rod; (*di direttore d'orchestra*) baton; (*di tamburo*) drumstick; **~ magica** magic wand

ba'checa, -che [ba'kɛka] *sf* (*mobile*) showcase, display case; (*Univ, in ufficio*) notice board (*BRIT*), bulletin board (*US*)

baci'are [ba'tʃare] *vt* to kiss; **baciarsi** *vpr* to kiss (one another)

baci'nella [batʃi'nɛlla] *sf* basin

ba'cino [ba'tʃino] *sm* basin; (*Mineralogia*) field, bed; (*Anat*) pelvis; (*Naut*) dock

'bacio ['batʃo] *sm* kiss

'baco, -chi *sm* worm; **baco da seta** silkworm

ba'dante *sm/f* care worker

ba'dare *vi* (*fare attenzione*) to take care, be careful; (*occuparsi di*): **~ a** to look after, take care of; (*dar ascolto*): **~ a** to pay attention to; **bada ai fatti tuoi!** mind your own business!

'baffi *smpl* moustache *sg*; (*di animale*) whiskers; **ridere sotto i ~** to laugh up one's sleeve; **leccarsi i ~** to lick one's lips

bagagli'aio [bagaʎ'ʎajo] *sm* luggage van (*BRIT*) o car (*US*); (*Aut*) boot (*BRIT*), trunk (*US*)

ba'gaglio [ba'gaʎʎo] *sm* luggage *no pl*, baggage *no pl*; **fare/disfare i bagagli** to pack/unpack; **i nostri bagagli non sono arrivati** our luggage has not arrived; **può mandare qualcuno a prendere i nostri bagagli?** could you send someone to collect our luggage?; **bagaglio a mano** hand luggage

bagli'ore [baʎ'ʎore] *sm* flash, dazzling light; **un ~ di speranza** a ray of hope

ba'gnante [baɲ'ɲante] *sm/f* bather

ba'gnare [baɲ'ɲare] *vt* to wet; (*inzuppare*) to soak; (*innaffiare*) to water; (*fiume*) to flow through; (: *mare*) to wash, bathe; **bagnarsi** *vpr* to get wet; (*al mare*) to go swimming o bathing; (*in vasca*) to have a bath

ba'gnato, -a [baɲ'ɲato] *ag* wet

ba'gnino [baɲ'ɲino] *sm* lifeguard

'bagno ['baɲɲo] *sm* bath; (*stanza*) bathroom; (*toilette*) toilet; **bagni** *smpl* (*stabilimento*) baths; **fare il ~** to have a bath; (*nel mare*) to go swimming o bathing; **dov'è il ~?** where's the toilet?; **fare il ~ a qn** to give sb a bath; **mettere a ~** to soak; **~ schiuma** bubble bath

bagnoma'ria [baɲɲoma'ria] *sm* **cuocere a ~** to cook in a double saucepan

bagnoschi'uma [baɲɲoskj'uma] *sm inv* bubble bath

'baia *sf* bay

balbet'tare *vi* to stutter, stammer; (*bimbo*) to babble ▷ *vt* to stammer out

bal'canico, -a, ci, che *ag* Balkan

bal'cone *sm* balcony; **avete una camera con ~?** do you have a room with a balcony?

bal'doria *sf* **fare ~** to have a riotous time

ba'lena *sf* whale

ba'leno *sm* flash of lightning; **in un ~** in a flash

bal'lare *vt, vi* to dance

balle'rina *sf* dancer; ballet dancer; (*scarpa*) ballet shoe

balle'rino *sm* dancer; ballet dancer

bal'letto *sm* ballet

'ballo *sm* dance; (*azione*) dancing *no pl*; **essere in ~** (*fig: persona*) to be involved; (: *cosa*) to be at stake

balne'are *ag* seaside *cpd*; (*stagione*) bathing

'balsamo *sm* (*aroma*) balsam; (*lenimento, fig*) balm

bal'zare [bal'tsare] *vi* to bounce; (*lanciarsi*) to jump, leap; **'balzo** *sm* bounce; jump, leap; (*del terreno*) crag

bam'bina *ag, sf vedi* **bambino**

bam'bino, -a *sm/f* child

'bambola *sf* doll

bambù *sm* bamboo

ba'nale *ag* banal, commonplace

ba'nana *sf* banana

'banca, -che *sf* bank; **banca dati** data bank

banca'rella *sf* stall

banca'rotta *sf* bankruptcy; **fare ~** to go bankrupt

ban'chetto [ban'ketto] *sm* banquet

banchi'ere [ban'kjɛre] *sm* banker

ban'china [ban'kina] *sf* (*di porto*) quay; (*per pedoni, ciclisti*) path; (*di stazione*) platform; **~ cedevole** (*Aut*) soft verge (*BRIT*) *o* shoulder (*US*)

'banco, -chi *sm* bench; (*di negozio*) counter; (*di mercato*) stall; (*di officina*) (work-)bench; (*Geo, banca*) bank; **banco di corallo** coral reef; **banco**

degli imputati dock; **banco di prova** (*fig*) testing ground; **banco dei testimoni** witness box; **banco dei pegni** pawnshop; **banco di nebbia** bank of fog

'Bancomat® *sm inv* automated banking; (*tessera*) cash card

banco'nota *sf* banknote

'banda *sf* band; (*di stoffa*) band, stripe; (*lato, parte*) side; **~ perforata** punch tape

bandi'era *sf* flag, banner

ban'dito *sm* outlaw, bandit

'bando *sm* proclamation; (*esilio*) exile, banishment; **~ alle chiacchiere!** that's enough talk!; **bando di concorso** announcement of a competition

bar *sm inv* bar

'bara *sf* coffin

ba'racca, -che *sf* shed, hut; (*peg*) hovel; **mandare avanti la ~** to keep things going

ba'rare *vi* to cheat

'baratro *sm* abyss

ba'ratto *sm* barter

ba'rattolo *sm* (*di latta*) tin; (*di vetro*) jar; (*di coccio*) pot

'barba *sf* beard; **farsi la ~** to shave; **farla in ~ a qn** (*fig*) to do sth to sb's face; **che ~!** what a bore!

barbabi'etola *sf* beetroot (*BRIT*), beet (*US*); **barbabietola da zucchero** sugar beet

barbi'ere *sm* barber

bar'bone *sm* (*cane*) poodle; (*vagabondo*) tramp

'barca, -che *sf* boat; **barca a motore** motorboat; **barca a remi** rowing boat; **barca a vela** sail(ing) boat

barcol'lare *vi* to stagger

ba'rella *sf* (*lettiga*) stretcher

ba'rile *sm* barrel, cask

ba'rista, -i, -e *sm/f* barman/maid; (*proprietario*) bar owner

ba'rocco, -a, -chi, -che *ag, sm* baroque

ba'rometro *sm* barometer
ba'rone *sm* baron; **baro'nessa** *sf* baroness
'barra *sf* bar; (*Naut*) helm; (*linea grafica*) line, stroke
bar'rare *vt* to bar
barri'carsi *vpr* to barricade o.s.
barri'era *sf* barrier; (*Geo*) reef
ba'ruffa *sf* scuffle
barzel'letta [bardzel'letta] *sf* joke, funny story
ba'sare *vt* to base, found; **basarsi** *vpr* **basarsi su** (*fatti, prove*) to be based o founded on; (: *persona*) to base one's arguments on
'basco, -a, -schi, -sche *ag* Basque ▷ *sm* (*copricapo*) beret
'base *sf* base; (*fig: fondamento*) basis; (*Pol*) rank and file; **di ~** basic; **in ~ a** on the basis of, according to; **a ~ di caffè** coffee-based
'baseball ['beisbɔːl] *sm* baseball
ba'sette *sfpl* sideburns
ba'silica, -che *sf* basilica
ba'silico *sm* basil
basket ['basket] *sm* basketball
bas'sista, -i, -e *sm/f* bass player
'basso, -a *ag* low; (*di statura*) short; (*meridionale*) southern ▷ *sm* bottom, lower part; (*Mus*) bass; **la bassa Italia** southern Italy
bassorili'evo *sm* bas-relief
bas'sotto, -a *ag* squat ▷ *sm* (*cane*) dachshund
'basta *escl* (that's) enough!, that will do!
bas'tardo, -a *ag* (*animale, pianta*) hybrid, crossbreed; (*persona*) illegitimate, bastard; (*peg*) ▷ *sm/f* illegitimate child, bastard (*peg*)
bas'tare *vi, vb impers* to be enough, be sufficient; **~ a qn** to be enough for sb; **basta chiedere** *o* **che chieda a un vigile** you have only to o need only ask a policeman; **basta così, grazie** that's enough, thanks
basto'nare *vt* to beat, thrash

baston'cino [baston't∫ino] *sm* (*Sci*) ski pole; **bastoncini di pesce** fish fingers
bas'tone *sm* stick; **~ da passeggio** walking stick
bat'taglia [bat'taʎʎa] *sf* battle; fight
bat'tello *sm* boat
bat'tente *sm* (*imposta: di porta*) wing, flap; (: *di finestra*) shutter; (*batacchio: di porta*) knocker; (: *di orologio*) hammer; **chiudere i battenti** (*fig*) to shut up shop
'battere *vt* to beat; (*grano*) to thresh; (*percorrere*) to scour ▷ *vi* (*bussare*) to knock; (*urtare*): **~ contro** to hit o strike against; (*pioggia, sole*) to beat down; (*cuore*) to beat; (*Tennis*) to serve; **battersi** *vpr* to fight; **~ le mani** to clap; **~ i piedi** to stamp one's feet; **~ a macchina** to type; **~ bandiera italiana** to fly the Italian flag; **~ in testa** (*Aut*) to knock; **in un batter d'occhio** in the twinkling of an eye
batte'ria *sf* battery; (*Mus*) drums *pl*
bat'terio *sm* bacterium
batte'rista, -i, -e *sm/f* drummer
bat'tesimo *sm* (*rito*) baptism; christening
battez'zare [batted'dzare] *vt* to baptize; to christen
batti'panni *sm inv* carpet-beater
battis'trada *sm inv* (*di pneumatico*) tread; (*di gara*) pacemaker
'battito *sm* beat, throb; **battito cardiaco** heartbeat
bat'tuta *sf* blow; (*di macchina da scrivere*) stroke; (*Mus*) bar; beat; (*Teatro*) cue; (*frase spiritosa*) witty remark; (*di caccia*) beating; (*Polizia*) combing, scouring; (*Tennis*) service
ba'tuffolo *sm* wad
ba'ule *sm* trunk; (*Aut*) boot (*BRIT*), trunk (*US*)
'bava *sf* (*di animale*) slaver, slobber; (*di lumaca*) slime; (*di vento*) breath
bava'glino [bavaʎ'ʎino] *sm* bib
ba'vaglio [ba'vaʎʎo] *sm* gag

'bavero *sm* collar

ba'zar [bad'dzar] *sm inv* bazaar

BCE *sigla f* (= *Banca centrale europea*) ECB

be'ato, -a *ag* blessed; (*fig*) happy; **~ te!** lucky you!

bec'care *vt* to peck; (*fig: raffreddore*) to catch; **beccarsi** *vpr* (*fig*) to squabble; **beccarsi qc** to catch sth

beccherò *ecc* [bekke'rɔ] *vb vedi* **beccare**

'becco, -chi *sm* beak, bill; (*di caffettiera ecc*) spout; lip

be'fana *sf* hag, witch; **la B~** old woman who, according to legend, brings children their presents at the Epiphany; (*Epifania*) Epiphany

○ **BEFANA**
○
○
○ The **Befana** is a national holiday on
○ the feast of the Epiphany. It takes
○ its name from **la Befana**, the old
○ woman who, according to Italian
○ legend comes down the chimney
○ during the night leaving gifts for
○ children who have been good, and
○ coal for those who have not.

bef'fardo, -a *ag* scornful, mocking

'begli ['beʎʎi] *ag vedi* **bello**

'bei *ag vedi* **bello**

beige [bɛʒ] *ag inv* beige

bel *ag vedi* **bello**

be'lare *vi* to bleat

'belga, -gi, -ghe *ag, sm/f* Belgian

'Belgio ['bɛldʒo] *sm* **il ~** Belgium

'bella *sf* (*Sport*) decider; *vedi anche* **bello**

bel'lezza [bel'lettsa] *sf* beauty

 PAROLA CHIAVE

'bello, -a (*ag*: *dav sm* **bel** + C, **bell'** + V, **bello** + *s impura, gn, pn, ps, x, z, pl* **bei** + C, **begli** + *s impura ecc o* V) *ag* **1** (*oggetto, donna, paesaggio*) beautiful, lovely;

(*uomo*) handsome; (*tempo*) beautiful, fine, lovely; **le belle arti** fine arts

2 (*quantità*): **una bella cifra** a considerable sum of money; **un bel niente** absolutely nothing

3 (*rafforzativo*): **è una truffa bella e buona!** it's a real fraud!; **è bell'e finito** it's already finished

▷ *sm* **1** (*bellezza*) beauty; (*tempo*) fine weather

2: **adesso viene il bello** now comes the best bit; **sul più bello** at the crucial point; **cosa fai di bello?** are you doing anything interesting?

▷ *av* **fa bello** the weather is fine, it's fine

'belva *sf* wild animal

belve'dere *sm inv* panoramic viewpoint

benché [ben'ke] *cong* although

'benda *sf* bandage; (*per gli occhi*) blindfold; **ben'dare** *vt* to bandage; to blindfold

'bene *av* well; (*completamente, affatto*): **è ben difficile** it's very difficult ▷ *ag inv* **gente ~** well-to-do people ▷ *sm* good; **beni** *smpl* (*averi*) property *sg*, estate *sg*; **io sto ~/poco ~** I'm well/ not very well; **va ~** all right; **volere un ~ dell'anima a qn** to love sb very much; **un uomo per ~** a respectable man; **fare ~** to do the right thing; **fare ~ a** (*salute*) to be good for; **fare del ~ a qn** to do sb a good turn; **beni di consumo** consumer goods

bene'detto, -a *pp di* **benedire** ▷ *ag* blessed, holy

bene'dire *vt* to bless; to consecrate

benedu'cato, -a *ag* well-mannered

benefi'cenza [benefi'tʃentsa] *sf* charity

bene'ficio [bene'fitʃo] *sm* benefit; **con ~ d'inventario** (*fig*) with reservations

be'nessere *sm* well-being

benes'tante *ag* well-to-do

be'nigno, -a [be'niɲɲo] *ag* kind, kindly; (*critica ecc*) favourable; (*Med*) benign

benve'nuto, -a *ag, sm* welcome; **dare il ~ a qn** to welcome sb

ben'zina [ben'dzina] *sf* petrol (*BRIT*), gas (*US*); **fare ~** to get petrol (*BRIT*) o gas (*US*); **sono rimasto senza ~** I have run out of petrol (*BRIT*) o gas (*US*); **benzina verde** unleaded (petrol); **benzi'naio** *sm* petrol (*BRIT*) o gas (*US*) pump attendant

'bere *vt* to drink; **darla a ~ a qn** (*fig*) to fool sb; **vuoi qualcosa da ~?** would you like a drink?

ber'lina *sf* (*Aut*) saloon (car) (*BRIT*), sedan (*US*)

Ber'lino *sf* Berlin

ber'muda *smpl* (*calzoncini*) Bermuda shorts

ber'noccolo *sm* bump; (*inclinazione*) flair

ber'retto *sm* cap

berrò *ecc vb vedi* **bere**

ber'saglio [ber'saʎʎo] *sm* target

besciamella [beʃʃa'mɛlla] *sf* béchamel sauce

bes'temmia *sf* curse; (*Rel*) blasphemy

bestemmi'are *vi* to curse, swear; to blaspheme ▷ *vt* to curse, swear at; to blaspheme

'bestia *sf* animal; **andare in ~** (*fig*) to fly into a rage; **besti'ale** *ag* beastly; animal *cpd*; (*fam*): **fa un freddo bestiale** it's bitterly cold; **besti'ame** *sm* livestock; (*bovino*) cattle *pl*

be'tulla *sf* birch

be'vanda *sf* drink, beverage

'bevo *ecc vb vedi* **bere**

be'vuto, -a *pp di* **bere**

'bevvi *ecc vb vedi* **bere**

bianche'ria [bjanke'ria] *sf* linen; **~ da donna** ladies' underwear, lingerie; **biancheria femminile** lingerie; **biancheria intima** underwear

bi'anco, -a, -chi, -che *ag* white; (*non scritto*) blank ▷ *sm* white; (*intonaco*) whitewash ▷ *sm/f* white, white man/ woman; **in ~** (*foglio, assegno*) blank; (*notte*) sleepless; **in ~ e nero** (*TV, Fot*) black and white; **mangiare in ~** to follow a bland diet; **pesce in ~** boiled fish; **andare in ~** (*non riuscire*) to fail; **bianco dell'uovo** egg-white

biasi'mare *vt* to disapprove of, censure

'Bibbia *sf* (*anche fig*) bible

bibe'ron *sm inv* feeding bottle

'bibita *sf* (soft) drink

biblio'teca, -che *sf* library; (*mobile*) bookcase

bicarbo'nato *sm*: **~ (di sodio)** bicarbonate (of soda)

bicchi'ere [bik'kjɛre] *sm* glass

bici'cletta [bitʃi'kletta] *sf* bicycle; **andare in ~** to cycle

bidè *sm inv* bidet

bi'dello, -a *sm/f* (*Ins*) janitor

bi'done *sm* drum, can; (*anche*: **~ dell'immondizia**) (dust)bin; (*fam*: *truffa*) swindle; **fare un ~ a qn** (*fam*) to let sb down; to cheat sb

bien'nale *ag* biennial

● **BIENNALE DI VENEZIA**
●
● The **Biennale di Venezia** is an
● international contemporary art
● festival, which takes place every
● two years at Giardini in Venice. In
● its current form, it includes exhibits
● by artists from the many countries
● taking part, a thematic exhibition
● and a section for young artists.

bifamili'are *sf* ≈ semi-detached house

bifor'carsi *vpr* to fork

bigiotte'ria [bidʒotte'ria] *sf* costume jewellery; (*negozio*) jeweller's (*selling only costume jewellery*)

bigliet'taio, -a *sm/f* (*in treno*) ticket inspector; (*in autobus*) conductor

bigliette'ria [biʎʎette'ria] *sf* (*di stazione*) ticket office; booking office; (*di teatro*) box office

bigli'etto [biʎ'ʎetto] *sm* (*per viaggi, spettacoli ecc*) ticket; (*cartoncino*) card; (*anche: ~ di banca*) (bank)note; **biglietto d'auguri** greetings card; **biglietto da visita** visiting card; **biglietto d'andata e ritorno** return (ticket), round-trip ticket (*us*); **biglietto di sola andata** single (ticket); **biglietto elettronico** e-ticket

bignè [biɲ'ɲe] *sm inv* cream puff

bigo'dino *sm* roller, curler

bi'gotto, -a *ag* over-pious ▷ *sm/f* church fiend

bi'kini *sm inv* bikini

bi'lancia, -ce [bi'lantʃa] *sf* (*pesa*) scales *pl*; (: *di precisione*) balance; (*dello zodiaco*): **B~** Libra; **bilancia commerciale** balance of trade; **bilancia dei pagamenti** balance of payments

bi'lancio [bi'lantʃo] *sm* (*Comm*) balance(-sheet); (*statale*) budget; **fare il ~ di** (*fig*) to assess; **bilancio consuntivo** (final) balance; **bilancio preventivo** budget

bili'ardo *sm* billiards *sg*; billiard table

bi'lingue *ag* bilingual

bilo'cale *sm* two-room flat (*Brit*) *o* apartment (*us*)

bi'nario, -a *ag* (*sistema*) binary ▷ *sm* (*railway*) track *o* line; (*piattaforma*) platform; **da che ~ parte il treno per Londra?** which platform does the train for London go from?; **binario morto** dead-end track

bi'nocolo *sm* binoculars *pl*

bio... *prefisso*: **biodegra'dabile** *ag* biodegradable; **biodi'namico, -a, -ci, -che** *ag* biodynamic; **biogra'fia** *sf* biography; **biolo'gia** *sf* biology

bio'logico, -a, -ci, -che *ag* (*scienze, fenomeni ecc*) biological; (*agricoltura, prodotti*) organic; **guerra biologica** biological warfare

bi'ondo, -a *ag* blond, fair

biotecnologia [bioteknolo'dʒia] *sf* biotechnology

biri'chino, -a [biri'kino] *ag* mischievous ▷ *sm/f* scamp, little rascal

bi'rillo *sm* skittle (*BRIT*), pin (*US*)

'biro® *sf inv* biro®

'birra *sf* beer; **a tutta ~** (*fig*) at top speed; **birra chiara/scura** ≈ lager/stout; **birre'ria** *sf* ≈ bierkeller

bis *escl, sm inv* encore

bis'betico, -a, -ci, -che *ag* ill-tempered, crabby

bisbigli'are [bisbiʎ'ʎare] *vt, vi* to whisper

'bisca, -sche *sf* gambling-house

'biscia, -sce ['biʃʃa] *sf* snake; **biscia d'acqua** grass snake

biscot'tato, -a *ag* crisp; **fette biscottate** rusks

bis'cotto *sm* biscuit

bisessu'ale *ag, sm/f* bisexual

bises'tile *ag* **anno ~** leap year

bis'nonno, -a *sm/f* great grandfather/grandmother

biso'gnare [bizoɲ'ɲare] *vb impers*: **bisogna che tu parta/lo faccia** you'll have to go/do it; **bisogna parlargli** we'll (*o* I'll) have to talk to him

bi'sogno [bi'zoɲɲo] *sm* need; **ha ~ di qualcosa?** do you need anything?

bis'tecca, -che *sf* steak, beefsteak

bisticci'are [bistit'tʃare] *vi* to quarrel, bicker; **bisticciarsi** *vpr* to quarrel, bicker

'bisturi *sm* scalpel

'bivio *sm* fork; (*fig*) dilemma

biz'zarro, -a [bid'dzarro] *ag* bizarre, strange

blate'rare *vi* to chatter

blin'dato, -a *ag* armoured

bloc'care *vt* to block; (*isolare*) to isolate, cut off; (*porto*) to blockade; (*prezzi, beni*) to freeze; (*meccanismo*) to jam; **bloccarsi** *vpr* (*motore*) to stall;

(freni, porta) to jam, stick; (ascensore) to stop, get stuck

blocchero ecc [blokke'rɔ] vb vedi **bloccare**

bloc'chetto [blok'ketto] sm notebook; (di biglietti) book

'blocco, -chi sm block; (Mil) blockade; (dei fitti) restriction; (quadernetto) pad; (fig: unione) coalition; (il bloccare) blocking; isolating, cutting-off; blockading; freezing; jamming; **in ~** (nell'insieme) as a whole; (Comm) in bulk; **blocco cardiaco** cardiac arrest; **blocco stradale** road block

blu ag inv, sm dark blue

'blusa sf (camiciotto) smock; (camicetta) blouse

'boa sm inv (Zool) boa constrictor; (sciarpa) feather boa ▷ sf buoy

bo'ato sm rumble, roar

bob [bɔb] sm inv bobsleigh

'bocca, -che sf mouth; **in ~ al lupo!** good luck!

boc'caccia, -ce [bok'kattʃa] sf (malalingua) gossip; **fare le boccacce** to pull faces

boc'cale sm jug; **boccale da birra** tankard

boc'cetta [bot'tʃetta] sf small bottle

'boccia, -ce ['bottʃa] sf bottle; (da vino) decanter, carafe; (palla) bowl; **gioco delle bocce** bowls sg

bocci'are [bot'tʃare] vt (proposta, progetto) to reject; (Ins) to fail; (Bocce) to hit

bocci'olo [bot'tʃɔlo] sm bud

boc'cone sm mouthful, morsel

boicot'tare vt to boycott

'bolla sf bubble; (Med) blister; **bolla di consegna** (Comm) delivery note; **bolla papale** papal bull

bol'lente ag boiling; boiling hot

bol'letta sf bill; (ricevuta) receipt; **essere in ~** to be hard up

bollet'tino sm bulletin; (Comm) note; **bollettino meteorologico** weather report; **bollettino di spedizione**

consignment note

bollicina [bolli'tʃina] sf bubble

bol'lire vt, vi to boil

bolli'tore sm (Cuc) kettle; (per riscaldamento) boiler

'bollo sm stamp; **bollo per patente** driving licence tax; **bollo postale** postmark

'bomba sf bomb; **bomba atomica** atom bomb; **bomba a mano** hand grenade; **bomba ad orologeria** time bomb

bombarda'mento sm bombardment; bombing

bombar'dare vt to bombard; (da aereo) to bomb

'bombola sf cylinder

bombo'letta sf aerosol

bomboni'era sf box of sweets (as souvenir at weddings, first communions etc)

bo'nifico, -ci sm (riduzione, abbuono) discount; (versamento a terzi) credit transfer

bontà sf goodness; (cortesia) kindness; **aver la ~ di fare qc** to be good o kind enough to do sth

borbot'tare vi to mumble

'borchia ['borkja] sf stud

bor'deaux [bor'dɔ] ag inv, sm inv maroon

'bordo sm (Naut) ship's side; (orlo) edge; (striscia di guarnizione) border, trim; **a ~ di** (nave, aereo) aboard, on board; (macchina) in

bor'ghese [bor'geze] ag (spesso peg) middle-class; bourgeois; **abito ~** civilian dress

'borgo, -ghi sm (paesino) village; (quartiere) district; (sobborgo) suburb

boro'talco sm talcum powder

bor'raccia, -ce [bor'rattʃa] sf canteen, water-bottle

'borsa sf bag; (anche: **~ da signora**) handbag; (Econ) the Stock Exchange; **la B~ (valori)** the Stock Exchange; **borsa dell'acqua calda** hot-water bottle; **borsa nera**

black market; **borsa della spesa**
shopping bag; **borsa di studio** grant;
borsel'lino sm purse; **bor'setta** sf
handbag
'bosco, -schi sm wood
bos'niaco, -a, ci, che ag, sm/f
Bosnian
'Bosnia Erze'govina ['bɔsnja
erdze'govina] sf **la ~** Bosnia
Herzegovina
Bot, bot sigla m inv (= buono ordinario
del Tesoro) short-term Treasury bond
bo'tanica sf botany
bo'tanico, -a, -ci, -che ag botanical
▷ sm botanist
'botola sf trap door
'botta sf blow; (rumore) bang
'botte sf barrel, cask
bot'tega, -ghe sf shop; (officina)
workshop
bot'tiglia [bot'tiʎʎa] sf bottle;
bottiglie'ria sf wine shop
bot'tino sm (di guerra) booty; (di
rapina, furto) loot
'botto sm bang; crash; **di ~** suddenly
bot'tone sm button; **attaccare ~ a
qn** (fig) to buttonhole sb
bo'vino, -a ag bovine; **bovini** smpl
cattle
box [bɔks] sm inv (per cavalli) horsebox;
(per macchina) lock-up; (per macchina da
corsa) pit; (per bambini) playpen
boxe [bɔks] sf boxing
'boxer ['bɔkser] sm inv (cane) boxer
▷ smpl (mutande): **un paio di ~** a pair
of boxer shorts
BR sigla fpl = **Brigate Rosse**
brac'cetto [brat'tʃetto] sm: **a ~** arm
in arm
braccia'letto sm bracelet, bangle
bracci'ata [brat'tʃata] sf (nel nuoto)
stroke
'braccio ['brattʃo] (pl(f) **braccia**)
sm (Anat) arm; (pl(m) bracci: di gru,
fiume) arm; (: di edificio) wing; **braccio
di mare** sound; **bracci'olo** sm
(appoggio) arm

'bracco, -chi sm hound
'brace ['bratʃe] sf embers pl
braci'ola [bra'tʃɔla] sf (Cuc) chop
'branca, -che sf branch
'branchia ['brankja] sf (Zool) gill
'branco, -chi sm (di cani, lupi) pack;
(di pecore) flock; (peg: di persone) gang,
pack
bran'dina sf camp bed (BRIT), cot (US)
'brano sm piece; (di libro) passage
Bra'sile sm **il ~** Brazil; **brasili'ano, -a**
ag, sm/f Brazilian
'bravo, -a ag (abile) clever, capable,
skilful; (buono) good, honest;
(: bambino) good; (coraggioso) brave; **~!**
well done!; (a teatro) bravo!
bra'vura sf cleverness, skill
Bre'tagna [bre'taɲɲa] sf: **la ~** Brittany
bre'tella sf (Aut) link; **bretelle** sfpl (di
calzoni) braces
bretone ag, sm/f Breton
'breve ag brief, short; **in ~** in short
brevet'tare vt to patent
bre'vetto sm patent; **brevetto di
pilotaggio** pilot's licence (BRIT) o
license (US)
'bricco, -chi sm jug; **bricco del caffè**
coffeepot
briciola ['britʃola] sf crumb
bri'ciolo ['britʃolo] sm (specie fig) bit
'briga, -ghe sf (fastidio) trouble,
bother; **pigliarsi la ~ di fare qc** to
take the trouble to do sth
bri'gata sf (Mil) brigade; (gruppo)
group, party; **Brigate Rosse** (Pol) Red
Brigades
'briglia ['briʎʎa] sf rein; **a ~ sciolta** at
full gallop; (fig) at full speed
bril'lante ag bright; (anche fig)
brilliant; (che luccica) shining ▷ sm
diamond
bril'lare vi to shine; (mina) to blow up
▷ vt (mina) to set off
'brillo, -a ag merry, tipsy
'brina sf hoarfrost
brin'dare vi: **~ a qn/qc** to drink to o
toast sb/sth

'brindisi *sm inv* toast

bri'oche [bri'ɔʃ] *sf inv* brioche

bri'tannico, -a, -ci, -che *ag* British

'brivido *sm* shiver; (*di ribrezzo*) shudder; (*fig*) thrill

brizzo'lato, -a [brittso'lato] *ag* (*persona*) going grey; (*barba, capelli*) greying

'brocca, -che *sf* jug

'broccoli *smpl* broccoli *sg*

'brodo *sm* broth; (*per cucinare*) stock; **brodo ristretto** consommé

bron'chite [bron'kite] *sf* (*Med*) bronchitis

bronto'lare *vi* to grumble; (*tuono, stomaco*) to rumble

'bronzo ['brondzo] *sm* bronze

'browser ['brauzer] *sm inv* (*Inform*) browser

brucia'pelo [brutʃa'pelo]: **a ~** *av* point-blank

bruci'are [bru'tʃare] *vt* to burn; (*scottare*) to scald ▷ *vi* to burn; **bruciarsi** *vpr* to burn o.s.; (*fallire*) to ruin one's chances; **~ le tappe** (*fig*) to shoot ahead; **bruciarsi la carriera** to ruin one's career

'bruco, -chi *sm* caterpillar; grub

'brufolo *sm* pimple, spot

'brullo, -a *ag* bare, bleak

'bruno, -a *ag* brown, dark; (*persona*) dark(-haired)

'brusco, -a, -schi, -sche *ag* (*sapore*) sharp; (*modi, persona*) brusque, abrupt; (*movimento*) abrupt, sudden

bru'sio *sm* buzz, buzzing

bru'tale *ag* brutal

'brutto, -a *ag* ugly; (*cattivo*) bad; (*malattia, strada, affare*) nasty, bad; **~ tempo** bad weather

Bru'xelles [bry'sɛl] *sf* Brussels

BSE [biɛsse'e] *sigla f* (= *encefalopatia spongiforme bovina*) BSE

'buca, -che *sf* hole; (*avvallamento*) hollow; **buca delle lettere** letterbox

buca'neve *sm inv* snowdrop

bu'care *vt* (*forare*) to make a hole (o

holes) in; (*pungere*) to pierce; (*biglietto*) to punch; **bucarsi** *vpr* (*di eroina*) to mainline; **~ una gomma** to have a puncture

bu'cato *sm* (*operazione*) washing; (*panni*) wash, washing

'buccia, -ce ['buttʃa] *sf* skin, peel

bucherò *ecc* [buke'rɔ] *vb vedi* **bucare**

'buco, -chi *sm* hole

bud'dismo *sm* Buddhism

bu'dino *sm* pudding

'bue *sm* ox; **carne di ~** beef

bu'fera *sf* storm

'buffo, -a *ag* funny; (*Teatro*) comic

bu'gia, -gie [bu'dʒia] *sf* lie; **dire una ~** to tell a lie; **bugi'ardo, -a** *ag* lying, deceitful ▷ *sm/f* liar

'buio, -a *ag* dark ▷ *sm* dark, darkness

'bulbo *sm* (*Bot*) bulb; **bulbo oculare** eyeball

Bulga'ria *sf* **la ~** Bulgaria

'bulgaro, -a *ag, sm/f, sm* Bulgarian

buli'mia *sf* bulimia; **bu'limico, -a, -ci, -che** *ag* bulimic

bul'lone *sm* bolt

buona'notte *escl* good night! ▷ *sf* **dare la ~ a** to say good night to

buona'sera *escl* good evening!

buongi'orno [bwon'dʒorno] *escl* good morning (o afternoon)!

buongus'taio, -a *sm/f* gourmet

⊙ **PAROLA CHIAVE**

bu'ono, -a (*ag: dav sm* **buon** + C o V, **buono** + *s impura, gn, pn, ps, x, z; dav sf* **buon'** + V) *ag* **1** (*gen*) good; **un buon pranzo/ristorante** a good lunch/ restaurant; **(stai) buono!** behave!

2 (*benevolo*): **buono (con)** good (to), kind (to)

3 (*giusto, valido*) right; **al momento buono** at the right moment

4 (*adatto*): **buono a/da** fit for/to; **essere buono a nulla** to be no good o use at anything

5 (*auguri*): **buon anno!** happy New

Year!; **buon appetito!** enjoy your meal!; **buon compleanno!** happy birthday!; **buon divertimento!** have a nice time!; **buona fortuna!** good luck!; **buon riposo!** sleep well!; **buon viaggio!** bon voyage!, have a good trip!

6: **a buon mercato** cheap; **di buon'ora** early; **buon senso** common sense; **alla buona** *ag* simple ▷ *av* in a simple way, without any fuss ▷ *sm* 1 (*bontà*) goodness, good 2 (*Comm*) voucher, coupon; **buono di cassa** cash voucher; **buono di consegna** delivery note; **buono del Tesoro** Treasury bill

buon'senso *sm* = **buon senso**
burat'tino *sm* puppet
'burbero, -a *ag* surly, gruff
buro'cratico, -a, ci, che *ag* bureaucratic
burocra'zia [burokrat'tsia] *sf* bureaucracy
bur'rasca, -sche *sf* storm
'burro *sm* butter
bur'rone *sm* ravine
bus'sare *vi* to knock
'bussola *sf* compass
'busta *sf* (*da lettera*) envelope; (*astuccio*) case; **in ~ aperta/chiusa** in an unsealed/sealed envelope; **busta paga** pay packet
busta'rella *sf* bribe, backhander
bus'tina *sf* (*piccola busta*) envelope; (*di cibi, farmaci*) sachet; (*Mil*) forage cap; **bustina di tè** tea bag
'busto *sm* bust; (*indumento*) corset, girdle; **a mezzo ~** (*foto*) half-length
but'tare *vt* to throw; (*anche: ~ via*) to throw away; **~ giù** (*scritto*) to scribble down; (*cibo*) to gulp down; (*edificio*) to pull down, demolish; (*pasta, verdura*) to put into boiling water; **buttarsi** *vpr* (*saltare*) to jump; **buttarsi dalla finestra** to jump out of the window
byte ['bait] *sm inv* byte

C

ca'bina *sf* (*di nave*) cabin; (*da spiaggia*) beach hut; (*di autocarro, treno*) cab; (*di aereo*) cockpit; (*di ascensore*) cage; **cabi'nato** *sm* cabin cruiser; **cabina di pilotaggio** cockpit; **cabina telefonica** call o (tele)phone box
ca'cao *sm* cocoa
'caccia ['kattʃa] *sf* hunting; (*con fucile*) shooting; (*inseguimento*) chase; (*cacciagione*) game ▷ *sm inv* (*aereo*) fighter; (*nave*) destroyer; **caccia grossa** big-game hunting; **caccia all'uomo** manhunt
cacci'are [kat'tʃare] *vt* to hunt; (*mandar via*) to chase away; (*ficcare*) to shove, stick ▷ *vi* to hunt; **cacciarsi** *vpr* **dove s'è cacciata la mia borsa?** where has my bag got to?; **cacciarsi nei guai** to get into trouble; **~ fuori qc** to whip o pull sth out; **~ un urlo** to let out a yell; **caccia'tore** *sm* hunter; **cacciatore di frodo** poacher
caccia'vite [kattʃa'vite] *sm inv* screwdriver

'cactus sm inv cactus
ca'davere sm (dead) body, corpse
'caddi ecc vb vedi **cadere**
ca'denza [ka'dɛntsa] sf cadence; (ritmo) rhythm; (Mus) cadenza
ca'dere vi to fall; (denti, capelli) to fall out; (tetto) to fall in; **questa gonna cade bene** this skirt hangs well; **lasciar ~** (anche fig) to drop; (anche: **~ dal sonno**) to be falling asleep on one's feet; **~ dalle nuvole** (fig) to be taken aback
cadrò ecc vb vedi **cadere**
ca'duta sf fall; **la ~ dei capelli** hair loss
caffè sm inv coffee; (locale) café; **caffè corretto** espresso coffee with a shot of spirits; **caffè macchiato** coffee with a dash of milk; **caffè macinato** ground coffee
caffel'latte sm inv white coffee
caffetti'era sf coffeepot
'cagna ['kaɲɲa] sf (Zool, peg) bitch
CAI sigla m = **Club Alpino Italiano**
cala'brone sm hornet
cala'maro sm squid
cala'mita sf magnet
calamità sf inv calamity, disaster
ca'lare vt (far discendere) to lower; (Maglia) to decrease ▷ vi (discendere) to go (o come) down; (tramontare) to set, go down; **~ di peso** to lose weight
cal'cagno [kal'kaɲɲo] sm heel
cal'care sm (incrostazione) (lime)scale
'calce ['kaltʃe] sm **in ~** at the foot of the page ▷ sf lime; **calce viva** quicklime
calci'are [kal'tʃare] vt, vi to kick; **calcia'tore** sm footballer
'calcio ['kaltʃo] sm (pedata) kick; (sport) football, soccer; (di pistola, fucile) butt; (Chim) calcium; **calcio d'angolo** (Sport) corner (kick); **calcio di punizione** (Sport) free kick; **calcio di rigore** penalty
calco'lare vt to calculate, work out, reckon; (ponderare) to weigh (up);

calcola'tore, -'trice ag calculating ▷ sm calculator; (fig) calculating person; **calcolatore elettronico** computer; **calcola'trice** sf calculator
'calcolo sm (anche Mat) calculation; (infinitesimale ecc) calculus; (Med) stone; **fare i propri calcoli** (fig) to weigh the pros and cons; **per ~** out of self-interest
cal'daia sf boiler
'caldo, -a ag warm; (molto caldo) hot; (fig: appassionato) keen; hearty ▷ sm heat; **ho ~** I'm warm; I'm hot; **fa ~** it's warm; it's hot
caleidos'copio sm kaleidoscope
calen'dario sm calendar
'calibro sm (di arma) calibre, bore; (Tecn) callipers pl; (fig) calibre; **di grosso ~** (fig) prominent
'calice ['kalitʃe] sm goblet; (Rel) chalice
Cali'fornia sf California
californi'ano, -a ag Californian
calligra'fia sf (scrittura) handwriting; (arte) calligraphy
'callo sm callus; (ai piedi) corn
'calma sf calm
cal'mante sm tranquillizer
cal'mare vt to calm; (lenire) to soothe; **calmarsi** vpr to grow calm, calm down; (vento) to abate; (dolori) to ease
'calmo, -a ag calm, quiet
'calo sm (Comm: di prezzi) fall; (: di volume) shrinkage; (: di peso) loss
ca'lore sm warmth; heat; **in ~** (Zool) on heat
calo'ria sf calorie
calo'rifero sm radiator
calo'roso, -a ag warm
calpes'tare vt to tread on, trample on; **"è vietato ~ l'erba"** "keep off the grass"
ca'lunnia sf slander; (scritta) libel
cal'vizie [kal'vittsje] sf baldness
'calvo, -a ag bald
'calza ['kaltsa] sf (da donna) stocking; (da uomo) sock; **fare la ~** to knit; **calze**

di nailon nylons, (nylon) stockings

calza'maglia [kaltsa'maʎʎa] *sf*
tights *pl*; (*per danza, ginnastica*) leotard

calzet'tone [kaltset'tone] *sm* heavy
knee-length sock

cal'zino [kal'tsino] *sm* sock

calzo'laio [kaltso'lajo] *sm*
shoemaker; (*che ripara scarpe*) cobbler

calzon'cini [kaltson'tʃini] *smpl*
shorts; **calzoncini da bagno**
(swimming) trunks

cal'zone [kal'tsone] *sm* trouser
leg; (*Cuc*) savoury turnover made with
pizza dough; **calzoni** *smpl* (*pantaloni*)
trousers (*BRIT*), pants (*US*)

camale'onte *sm* chameleon

cambia'mento *sm* change;
cambiamenti climatici climate
change *sg*

cambi'are *vt* to change; (*modificare*)
to alter, change; (*barattare*): **~ (qc con
qn/qc)** to exchange (sth with sb/for
sth) ▷ *vi* to change, alter; **cambiarsi**
vpr (*d'abito*) to change; **~ casa** to
move (house); **~ idea** to change one's
mind; **~ treno** to change trains; **dove
posso ~ dei soldi?** where can I change
some money?; **ha da ~?** have you got
any change?; **posso cambiarlo, per
favore?** could I exchange this, please?

cambiava'lute *sm inv* exchange
office

'cambio *sm* change; (*modifica*)
alteration, change; (*scambio, Comm*)
exchange; (*corso dei cambi*) rate (of
exchange); (*Tecn, Aut*) gears *pl*; **in ~ di**
in exchange for; **dare il ~ a qn** to take
over from sb

'camera *sf* room; (*anche: ~ da letto*)
bedroom; (*Pol*) chamber, house;
camera ardente mortuary chapel;
camera d'aria inner tube; (*di pallone*)
bladder; **camera di commercio**
Chamber of Commerce; **Camera
dei Deputati** Chamber of Deputies,
≈ House of Commons (*BRIT*), ≈ House
of Representatives (*US*); **camera**

a gas gas chamber; **camera a un
letto/due letti** single/twin-bedded
room; **camera matrimoniale** double
room; **camera oscura** (*Fot*) dark room

> Attenzione! In inglese esiste la
> parola *camera*, che però significa
> *macchina fotografica*.

came'rata, -i, -e *sm/f* companion,
mate ▷ *sf* dormitory

cameri'era *sf* (*domestica*) maid;
(*che serve a tavola*) waitress; (*che fa le
camere*) chambermaid

cameri'ere *sm* (man)servant; (*di
ristorante*) waiter

came'rino *sm* (*Teatro*) dressing room

'camice ['kamitʃe] *sm* (*Rel*) alb; (*per
medici ecc*) white coat

cami'cetta [kami'tʃetta] *sf* blouse

ca'micia, -cie [ka'mitʃa] *sf* (*da uomo*)
shirt; (*da donna*) blouse; **camicia di
forza** straitjacket; **camicia da notte**
(*da donna*) nightdress; (*da uomo*)
nightshirt

cami'netto *sm* hearth, fireplace

ca'mino *sm* chimney; (*focolare*)
fireplace, hearth

'camion *sm inv* lorry (*BRIT*), truck (*US*)

camio'nista, -i *sm* lorry driver (*BRIT*),
truck driver (*US*)

cam'mello *sm* (*Zool*) camel; (*tessuto*)
camel hair

cammi'nare *vi* to walk; (*funzionare*)
to work, go

cam'mino *sm* walk; (*sentiero*) path;
(*itinerario, direzione, tragitto*) way;
mettersi in ~ to set *o* start off

camo'milla *sf* camomile; (*infuso*)
camomile tea

ca'moscio [ka'moʃʃo] *sm* chamois; **di
~** (*scarpe, borsa*) suede *cpd*

cam'pagna [kam'paɲɲa] *sf*
country, countryside; (*Pol, Comm, Mil*)
campaign; **in ~** in the country; **andare
in ~** to go to the country; **fare una ~** to
campaign; **campagna pubblicitaria**
advertising campaign

cam'pana *sf* bell; (*anche: ~ di vetro*)

bell jar; **campana (per la raccolta del vetro)** bottle bank; **campa'nello** sm (all'uscio, da tavola) bell

campa'nile sm bell tower, belfry

cam'peggio sm camping; (terreno) camp site; **fare (del) ~** to go camping

camper ['kamper] sm inv motor caravan (BRIT), motor home (US)

campio'nario, -a ag **fiera campionaria** trade fair ▷ sm collection of samples

campio'nato sm championship

campi'one, -'essa sm/f (Sport) champion ▷ sm (Comm) sample

'**campo** sm field; (Mil) field; (accampamento) camp; (spazio delimitato: sportivo ecc) ground; field; (di quadro) background; **i campi** (campagna) the countryside; **campo da aviazione** airfield; **campo di battaglia** (Mil, fig) battlefield; **campo di concentramento** concentration camp; **campo da golf** golf course; **campo profughi** refugee camp; **campo sportivo** sports ground; **campo da tennis** tennis court; **campo visivo** field of vision

'**Canada** sm: **il ~** Canada; **cana'dese** ag, sm/f Canadian ▷ sf (anche: **tenda canadese**) ridge tent

ca'naglia [ka'naʎʎa] sf rabble, mob; (persona) scoundrel, rogue

ca'nale sm (anche fig) channel; (artificiale) canal

'**canapa** sf hemp; **canapa indiana** (droga) cannabis

cana'rino sm canary

cancel'lare [kantʃel'lare] vt (con la gomma) to rub out, erase; (con la penna) to strike out; (annullare) to annul, cancel; (disdire) to cancel

cancelle'ria [kantʃelle'ria] sf chancery; (materiale per scrivere) stationery

can'cello [kan'tʃello] sm gate

'**cancro** sm (Med) cancer; (dello zodiaco): **C~** Cancer

candeg'gina [kanded'dʒina] sf bleach

can'dela sf candle; **candela (di accensione)** (Aut) spark(ing) plug

cande'labro sm candelabra

candeli'ere sm candlestick

candi'dare vt to present as candidate; **candidarsi** vpr to present o.s. as candidate

candi'dato, -a sm/f candidate; (aspirante a una carica) applicant

'**candido, -a** ag white as snow; (puro) pure; (sincero) sincere, candid

can'dito, -a ag candied

'**cane** sm dog; (di pistola, fucile) cock; **fa un freddo ~** it's bitterly cold; **non c'era un ~** there wasn't a soul; **cane da caccia/da guardia** hunting/guard dog; **cane lupo** Alsatian, **cane pastore** sheepdog

ca'nestro sm basket

can'guro sm kangaroo

ca'nile sm kennel; (di allevamento) kennels pl; **canile municipale** dog pound

'**canna** sf (pianta) reed; (: indica, da zucchero) cane; (bastone) stick, cane; (di fucile) barrel; (di organo) pipe; (fam: droga) joint; **canna fumaria** chimney flue; **canna da pesca** (fishing) rod; **canna da zucchero** sugar cane

cannel'loni smpl pasta tubes stuffed with sauce and baked

cannocchi'ale [kannok'kjale] sm telescope

can'none sm (Mil) gun; (Storia) cannon; (tubo) pipe, tube; (piega) box pleat; (fig) ace •

can'nuccia, -ce [kan'nuttʃa] sf (drinking) straw

ca'noa sf canoe

'**canone** sm canon, criterion; (mensile, annuo) rent; fee

canot'taggio [kanot'taddʒo] sm rowing

canotti'era sf vest

ca'notto sm small boat, dinghy;

canoe

can'tante *sm/f* singer

can'tare *vt, vi* to sing; **cantau'tore, -'trice** *sm/f* singer-composer

canti'ere *sm* (*Edil*) (building) site; (*cantiere navale*) shipyard

can'tina *sf* cellar; (*bottega*) wine shop; **cantina sociale** cooperative winegrowers' association

> Attenzione! In inglese esiste la parola *canteen*, che però significa *mensa*.

'canto *sm* song; (*arte*) singing; (*Rel*) chant; chanting; (*poesia*) poem, lyric; (*parte di una poesia*) canto; (*parte, lato*): **da un ~** on the one hand; **d'altro ~** on the other hand

canzo'nare [kantso'nare] *vt* to tease

can'zone [kan'tsone] *sf* song; (*Poesia*) canzone

'caos *sm inv* chaos; **ca'otico, -a, -ci, -che** *ag* chaotic

CAP *sigla m* = **codice di avviamento postale**

ca'pace [ka'patʃe] *ag* able, capable; (*ampio, vasto*) large, capacious; **sei ~ di farlo?** can you *o* are you able to do it?; **capacità** *sf inv* ability; (*Dir, di recipiente*) capacity

ca'panna *sf* hut

capan'none *sm* (*Agr*) barn; (*fabbricato industriale*) (factory) shed

ca'parbio, -a *ag* stubborn

ca'parra *sf* deposit, down payment

ca'pello *sm* hair; **capelli** *smpl* (*capigliatura*) hair *sg*

ca'pezzolo [ka'pettsolo] *sm* nipple

ca'pire *vt* to understand; **non capisco** I don't understand

capi'tale *ag* (*mortale*) capital; (*fondamentale*) main, chief ▷ *sf* (*città*) capital ▷ *sm* (*Econ*) capital

capi'tano *sm* captain

capi'tare *vi* (*giungere casualmente*) to happen to go, find o.s.; (*accadere*) to happen; (*presentarsi: cosa*) to turn up, present itself ▷ *vb impers* to happen;

mi è capitato un guaio I've had a spot of trouble

capi'tello *sm* (*Archit*) capital

ca'pitolo *sm* chapter

capi'tombolo *sm* headlong fall, tumble

'capo *sm* head; (*persona*) head, leader; (: *in ufficio*) head, boss; (: *in tribù*) chief; (*di oggetti*) head; top; end; (*Geo*) cape; **andare a ~** to start a new paragraph; **da ~** over again; **capo di bestiame** head *inv* of cattle; **capo di vestiario** item of clothing; **Capo'danno** *sm* New Year; **capo'giro** *sm* dizziness *no pl*; **capola'voro, -i** *sm* masterpiece; **capo'linea** (*pl* **capi'linea**) *sm* terminus; **capostazi'one** (*pl* **capistazi'one**) *sm* station master

capo'tavola (*pl(m)* **capi'tavola**) *pl(f) inv sm/f* (*persona*) head of the table; **sedere a ~** to sit at the head of the table

capo'volgere [kapo'voldʒere] *vt* to overturn; (*fig*) to reverse; **capovolgersi** *vpr* to overturn; (*barca*) to capsize; (*fig*) to be reversed

'cappa *sf* (*mantello*) cape, cloak; (*del camino*) hood

cap'pella *sf* (*Rel*) chapel

cap'pello *sm* hat

'cappero *sm* caper

cap'pone *sm* capon

cap'potto *sm* (over)coat

cappuc'cino [kapput'tʃino] *sm* (*frate*) Capuchin monk; (*bevanda*) cappuccino, *frothy white coffee*

cap'puccio [kap'puttʃo] *sm* (*copricapo*) hood; (*della biro*) cap

'capra *sf* (she-)goat

ca'priccio [ka'prittʃo] *sm* caprice, whim; (*bizza*) tantrum; **fare i capricci** to be very naughty; **capricci'oso, -a** *ag* capricious, whimsical; naughty

Capri'corno *sm* Capricorn

capri'ola *sf* somersault

capri'olo *sm* roe deer

'capro *sm*: **~ espiatorio** scapegoat

ca'prone *sm* billy-goat

'capsula *sf* capsule; (*di arma, per bottiglie*) cap

cap'tare *vt* (*Radio, TV*) to pick up; (*cattivarsi*) to gain, win

carabini'ere *sm* member of Italian military police force

● **CARABINIERI**
●
● Originally part of the armed forces,
● the **carabinieri** are police who
● perform both military and civil
● duties. They include paratroopers
● and mounted divisions.

ca'raffa *sf* carafe

Ca'raibi *smpl*: **il mar dei ~** the Caribbean (Sea)

cara'mella *sf* sweet

ca'rattere *sm* character; (*caratteristica*) characteristic, trait; **avere un buon ~** to be good-natured; **carattere jolly** wild card; **caratte'ristica, -che** *sf* characteristic, trait, peculiarity; **caratte'ristico, -a, -ci, -che** *ag* characteristic

car'bone *sm* coal

carbu'rante *sm* (*motor*) fuel

carbura'tore *sm* carburettor

carce'rato, -a [kartʃe'rato] *sm/f* prisoner

'carcere ['kartʃere] *sm* prison; (*pena*) imprisonment

carci'ofo [kar'tʃɔfo] *sm* artichoke

cardel'lino *sm* goldfinch

car'diaco, -a, -ci, -che *ag* cardiac, heart *cpd*

cardi'nale *ag, sm* cardinal

'cardine *sm* hinge

'cardo *sm* thistle

ca'rente *ag* **~ di** lacking in

cares'tia *sf* famine; (*penuria*) scarcity, dearth

ca'rezza [ka'rettsa] *sf* caress

'carica, -che *sf* (*mansione ufficiale*) office, position; (*Mil, Tecn, Elettr*) charge; **ha una forte ~ di simpatia** he's very likeable; *vedi anche* **carico**

caricabatte'ria *sm inv* battery charger

cari'care *vt* (*merce, Inform*) to load; (*orologio*) to wind up; (*batteria, Mil*) to charge

'carico, a, chi, che *ag* (*che porta un peso*): **~ di** loaded o laden with; (*fucile*) loaded; (*orologio*) wound up; (*batteria*) charged; (*colore*) deep; (*caffè, tè*) strong ▷ *sm* (*il caricare*) loading; (*ciò che si carica*) load; (*fig: peso*) burden, weight; **persona a ~** dependent; **essere a ~ di qn** (*spese ecc*) to be charged to sb

'carie *sf* (*dentaria*) decay

ca'rino, -a *ag* (*grazioso*) lovely, pretty, nice; (*riferito a uomo, anche simpatico*) nice

carità *sf* charity; **per ~!** (*escl di rifiuto*) good heavens, no!

carnagi'one [karna'dʒone] *sf* complexion

'carne *sf* flesh; (*bovina, ovina ecc*) meat; **non mangio ~** I don't eat meat; **carne di maiale/manzo/pecora** pork/beef/mutton; **carne in scatola** tinned o canned meat; **carne tritata** o **macinata** mince (BRIT), hamburger meat (US), minced (BRIT) o ground (US) meat

carne'vale *sm* carnival

● **CARNEVALE**
●
● **Carnevale** is the period between
● Epiphany (Jan. 6th) and the
● beginning of Lent. People wear
● fancy dress, and there are parties,
● processions of floats and bonfires.
● It culminates immediately before
● Lent in the festivities of **martedì**
● **grasso** (Shrove Tuesday).

'caro, -a *ag* (*amato*) dear; (*costoso*)

dear, expensive; **è troppo ~** it's too expensive

ca'rogna [ka'roɲɲa] *sf* carrion; (*anche*: **fig**: *fam*) swine

ca'rota *sf* carrot

caro'vana *sf* caravan

car'poni *av* on all fours

car'rabile *ag* suitable for vehicles; **"passo ~"** "keep clear"

carreggi'ata [karred'dʒata] *sf* carriageway (BRIT), (road)way

car'rello *sm* trolley; (*Aer*) undercarriage; (*Cinema*) dolly; (*di macchina da scrivere*) carriage

carri'era *sf* career; **fare ~** to get on; **a gran ~** at full speed

carri'ola *sf* wheelbarrow

'carro *sm* cart, wagon; **carro armato** tank; **carro attrezzi** breakdown van

car'rozza [kar'rɔttsa] *sf* carriage, coach

carrozze'ria [karrottse'ria] *sf* body, coachwork; (BRIT); (*officina*) coachbuilder's workshop (BRIT), body shop

carroz'zina [karrot'tsina] *sf* pram (BRIT), baby carriage (US)

'carta *sf* paper; (*al ristorante*) menu; (*Geo*) map; plan; (*documento*) card; (*costituzione*) charter; **carte** *sfpl* (*documenti*) papers, documents; **alla ~** (*al ristorante*) à la carte; **carta assegni** bank card; **carta assorbente** blotting paper; **carta bollata** *o* **da bollo** official stamped paper; **carta (da gioco)** playing card; **carta di credito** credit card; **carta fedeltà** loyalty card; **carta (geografica)** map; **carta d'identità** identity card; **carta igienica** toilet paper; **carta d'imbarco** (*Aer, Naut*) boarding card; **carta da lettere** writing paper; **carta da pacchi** wrapping paper; **carta da parati** wallpaper; **carta libera** (*Amm*) unstamped paper; **carta stradale** road map; **carta verde** (*Aut*) green card; **carta vetrata** sandpaper; **carta**

da visita visiting card

car'taccia, -ce [kar'tattʃa] *sf* waste paper

carta'pesta *sf* papier-mâché

car'tella *sf* (*scheda*) card; (*Inform, custodia: di cartone*) folder; (: *di uomo d'affari ecc*) briefcase; (: *di scolaro*) schoolbag, satchel; **cartella clinica** (*Med*) case sheet

cartel'lino *sm* (*etichetta*) label; (*su porta*) notice; (*scheda*) card; **timbrare il ~** (*all'entrata*) to clock in; (*all'uscita*) to clock out; **cartellino di presenza** clock card, timecard

car'tello *sm* sign; (*pubblicitario*) poster; (*stradale*) sign, signpost; (*Econ*) cartel; (*in dimostrazioni*) placard; **cartello stradale** sign; **cartel'lone** *sm* (*della tombola*) scoring frame; (*Teatro*) playbill; **tenere il cartellone** (*spettacolo*) to have a long run; **cartellone pubblicitario** advertising poster

car'tina *sf* (*Aut, Geo*) map; **può indicarmelo sulla ~?** can you show it to me on the map?

car'toccio [kar'tɔttʃo] *sm* paper bag

cartole'ria *sf* stationer's (shop)

carto'lina *sf* postcard; **cartolina postale** ready-stamped postcard

car'tone *sm* cardboard; (*Arte*) cartoon; **cartoni animati** (*Cinema*) cartoons

car'tuccia, -ce [kar'tuttʃa] *sf* cartridge

'casa *sf* house; (*in senso astratto*) home; (*Comm*) firm, house; **essere a ~** to be at home; **vado a ~ mia/tua** I'm going home/to your house; **vino della ~** house wine; **casa di cura** nursing home; **casa editrice** publishing house; **Casa delle Libertà** centre-right coalition; **casa di riposo** (old people's) home, care home; **case popolari** ≈ council houses (*o* flats) (BRIT), ≈ public housing units (US); **casa dello studente** student hostel

ca'sacca, -che sf military coat; (di fantino) blouse

casa'linga, -ghe sf housewife

casa'lingo, -a, -ghi, -ghe ag household, domestic; (fatto a casa) home-made; (semplice) homely; (amante della casa) home-loving

cas'care vi to fall; **cas'cata** sf fall; (d'acqua) cascade, waterfall

cascherò ecc [kaske'rɔ] vb vedi **cascare**

'casco, -schi sm helmet; (del parrucchiere) hair-drier; (di banane) bunch; **casco blu** (Mil) blue helmet (UN soldier)

casei'ficio [kazei'fitʃo] sm creamery

ca'sella sf pigeon-hole; **casella di posta elettronica** mailbox; **casella postale** post office box

ca'sello sm (di autostrada) toll-house

ca'serma sf barracks pl

ca'sino (fam) sm brothel; (confusione) row, racket

casinò sm inv casino

'caso sm chance; (fatto, vicenda) event, incident; (possibilità) possibility; (Med, Ling) case; **a ~** at random; **per ~** by chance, by accident; **in ogni ~, in tutti i casi** in any case, at any rate; **al ~** should the opportunity arise; **nel ~ che** in case; **~ mai** if by chance; **caso limite** borderline case

caso'lare sm cottage

'caspita escl (di sorpresa) good heavens!; (di impazienza) for goodness' sake!

'cassa sf case, crate, box; (bara) coffin; (mobile) chest; (involucro: di orologio ecc) case; (macchina) cash register, till; (luogo di pagamento) checkout (counter); (fondo) fund; (istituto bancario) bank; **cassa automatica prelievi** cash dispenser; **cassa continua** night safe; **cassa mutua** o **malattia** health insurance scheme; **cassa integrazione: mettere in cassa integrazione** ≈ to lay off; **cassa**

di risparmio savings bank; **cassa toracica** (Anat) chest

cassa'forte (pl **casse'forti**) sf safe; **lo potrebbe mettere nella ~?** could you put this in the safe, please?

cassa'panca (pl **cassa'panche** o **casse'panche**) sf settle

casseru'ola sf saucepan

cas'setta sf box; (per registratore) cassette; (Cinema, Teatro) box-office takings pl; **film di ~** box-office draw; **cassetta di sicurezza** strongbox; **cassetta delle lettere** letterbox

cas'setto sm drawer

cassi'ere, -a sm/f cashier; (di banca) teller

casso'netto sm wheelie-bin

cas'tagna [kas'taɲɲa] sf chestnut

cas'tagno [kas'taɲɲo] sm chestnut (tree)

cas'tano, -a ag chestnut (brown)

cas'tello sm castle; (Tecn) scaffolding

casti'gare vt to punish; **cas'tigo, -ghi** sm punishment

cas'toro sm beaver

casu'ale ag chance cpd; (Inform) random cpd

catalizza'tore [kataliddza'tore] sm (anche fig) catalyst; (Aut) catalytic converter

ca'talogo, -ghi sm catalogue

catarifran'gente [katarifran'dʒɛnte] sm (Aut) reflector

ca'tarro sm catarrh

ca'tastrofe sf catastrophe, disaster; **catastro'fista, -i, -e** agg, sm/f doom-monger

catego'ria sf category

ca'tena sf chain; **catena di montaggio** assembly line; **catene da neve** (Aut) snow chains; **cate'nina** sf (gioiello) (thin) chain

cate'ratta sf cataract; (chiusa) sluice-gate

ca'tino sm basin

ca'trame sm tar

'cattedra sf teacher's desk; (di

docente) chair

catte'drale *sf* cathedral

catti'veria *sf* malice, spite; naughtiness; *(atto)* spiteful act; *(parole)* malicious o spiteful remark

cat'tivo, -a *ag* bad; *(malvagio)* bad, wicked; *(turbolento: bambino)* bad, naughty; *(: mare)* rough; *(odore, sapore)* nasty, bad

cat'tolico, -a, -ci, -che *ag, sm/f* (Roman) Catholic

cattu'rare *vt* to capture

'causa *sf* cause; *(Dir)* lawsuit, case, action; **a ~ di, per ~ di** because of; **fare** *o* **muovere ~ a qn** to take legal action against sb

cau'sare *vt* to cause

cau'tela *sf* caution, prudence

'cauto, -a *ag* cautious, prudent

cauzi'one [kaut'tsjone] *sf* security; *(Dir)* bail

'cava *sf* quarry

caval'care *vt* *(cavallo)* to ride; *(muro)* to sit astride; *(ponte)* to span; **caval'cata** *sf* ride; *(gruppo di persone)* riding party

cavalca'via *sm inv* flyover

cavalci'oni [kaval'tʃoni]: **a ~ di** *prep* astride

cavali'ere *sm* rider; *(feudale, titolo)* knight; *(soldato)* cavalryman; *(al ballo)* partner

caval'letta *sf* grasshopper

caval'letto *sm* *(Fot)* tripod; *(da pittore)* easel

ca'vallo *sm* horse; *(Scacchi)* knight; *(Aut: anche: ~ vapore)* horsepower; *(dei pantaloni)* crotch; **a ~** on horseback; **a ~ di** astride, straddling; **cavallo di battaglia** *(fig)* hobby-horse; **cavallo da corsa** racehorse; **cavallo a dondolo** rocking horse

ca'vare *vt* *(togliere)* to draw out, extract, take out; *(: giacca, scarpe)* to take off; *(: fame, sete, voglia)* to satisfy; **cavarsela** to manage, get on all right; *(scamparla)* to get away with it

cava'tappi *sm inv* corkscrew

ca'verna *sf* cave

'cavia *sf* guinea pig

cavi'ale *sm* caviar

ca'viglia [ka'viʎʎa] *sf* ankle

'cavo, -a *ag* hollow ▷ *sm* *(Anat)* cavity; *(corda, Elettr, Tel)* cable

cavo'letto *sm*: **~ di Bruxelles** Brussels sprout

cavolfi'ore *sm* cauliflower

'cavolo *sm* cabbage; *(fam)*: **non m'importa un ~** I don't give a damn

'cazzo ['kattso] *sm* *(fam!: pene)* prick (!); **non gliene importa un ~** *(fig fam!)* he doesn't give a damn about it; **fatti i cazzi tuoi** *(fig fam!)* mind your own damn business

C.C.D. *sigla m* (= *Centro Cristiano Democratico*) *Italian political party of the centre*

CD *sm inv* CD; *(lettore)* CD player

CD-Rom [tʃidi'rom] *sm inv* CD-ROM

C.D.U. *sigla m* (= *Cristiano Democratici Uniti*) *Italian centre-right political party*

ce [tʃe] *pron, av vedi* **ci**

Ce'cenia [tʃe'tʃenia] *sf* **la ~** Chechnya

ce'ceno, -a [tʃe'tʃeno] *sm/f, ag* Chechen

'ceco, -a, -chi, -che ['tʃɛko] *ag, sm/f* Czech; **la Repubblica Ceca** the Czech Republic

'cedere ['tʃedere] *vt* *(concedere posto)* to give up; *(Dir)* to transfer, make over ▷ *vi* *(cadere)* to give way, subside; **~ (a)** to surrender (to), yield (to), give in (to)

'cedola ['tʃedola] *sf* *(Comm)* coupon; voucher

'ceffo ['tʃeffo] *(peg)* *sm* ugly mug

cef'fone [tʃef'fone] *sm* slap, smack

cele'brare [tʃele'brare] *vt* to celebrate

'celebre ['tʃelebre] *ag* famous, celebrated

ce'leste [tʃe'lɛste] *ag* celestial; heavenly; *(colore)* sky-blue

'celibe ['tʃɛlibe] *ag* single, unmarried

'cella ['tʃella] *sf* cell; **cella frigorifera** cold store

'cellula ['tʃɛllula] *sf* (*Biol, Elettr, Pol*) cell; **cellu'lare** *sm* cellphone

cellu'lite [tʃellu'lite] *sf* cellulite

cemen'tare [tʃemen'tare] *vt* (*anche fig*) to cement

ce'mento [tʃe'mento] *sm* cement; **cemento armato** reinforced concrete

'cena ['tʃena] *sf* dinner; (*leggera*) supper

ce'nare [tʃe'nare] *vi* to dine, have dinner

'cenere ['tʃenere] *sf* ash

'cenno ['tʃenno] *sm* (*segno*) sign, signal; (*gesto*) gesture; (*col capo*) nod; (*con la mano*) wave; (*allusione*) hint, mention; (*breve esposizione*) short account; **far ~ di sì/no** to nod (one's head)/shake one's head

censi'mento [tʃensi'mento] *sm* census

cen'sura [tʃen'sura] *sf* censorship; censor's office; (*fig*) censure

cente'nario, -a [tʃente'narjo] *ag* (*che ha cento anni*) hundred-year-old; (*che ricorre ogni cento anni*) centennial, centenary *cpd* ▷ *sm/f* centenarian ▷ *sm* centenary

cen'tesimo, -a [tʃen'tezimo] *ag, sm* hundredth; (*di euro, dollaro*) cent

cen'tigrado, -a [tʃen'tigrado] *ag* centigrade; **20 gradi centigradi** 20 degrees centigrade

cen'timetro [tʃen'timetro] *sm* centimetre

centi'naio [tʃenti'najo] (*pl(f)* **-aia**) *sm* **un ~ (di)** a hundred; about a hundred

'cento ['tʃɛnto] *num* a hundred, one hundred

cento'mila [tʃento'mila] *num* a o one hundred thousand; **te l'ho detto ~ volte** (*fig*) I've told you a thousand times

cen'trale [tʃen'trale] *ag* central ▷ *sf*: **centrale telefonica** (telephone) exchange; **centrale elettrica** electric power station; **centrali'nista** *sm/f* operator; **centra'lino** *sm* (telephone) exchange; (*di albergo ecc*) switchboard; **centralizzato, -a** [tʃentralid'dzato] *ag* central

cen'trare [tʃen'trare] *vt* to hit the centre of; (*Tecn*) to centre

cen'trifuga [tʃen'trifuɡa] *sf* spin-drier

'centro ['tʃɛntro] *sm* centre; **centro civico** civic centre; **centro commerciale** shopping centre; (*città*) commercial centre; **centro di permanenza temporanea** reception centre

centro'destra [tʃentro'dɛstra] *sm* (*Pol*) centre right

centrosi'nistra [tʃentrosi'nistra] (*Pol*) centre left

'ceppo ['tʃeppo] *sm* (*di albero*) stump; (*pezzo di legno*) log

'cera ['tʃera] *sf* wax; (*aspetto*) appearance

ce'ramica, -che [tʃe'ramika] *sf* ceramic; (*Arte*) ceramics *sg*

cerbi'atto [tʃer'bjatto] *sm* (*Zool*) fawn

cer'care [tʃer'kare] *vt* to look for, search for ▷ *vi* **~ di fare qc** to try to do sth; **stiamo cercando un albergo/ristorante** we're looking for a hotel/restaurant

cerche'rò *ecc* [tʃerke'rɔ] *vb vedi* **cercare**

'cerchia ['tʃerkja] *sf* circle

cerchi'etto [tʃer'kjetto] *sm* (*per capelli*) hairband

'cerchio ['tʃerkjo] *sm* circle; (*giocattolo, di botte*) hoop

cere'ali [tʃere'ali] *smpl* cereal *sg*

ceri'monia [tʃeri'mɔnja] *sf* ceremony

ce'rino [tʃe'rino] *sm* wax match

'cernia ['tʃernja] *sf* (*Zool*) stone bass

cerni'era [tʃer'njera] *sf* hinge; **cerniera lampo** zip (fastener) (BRIT), zipper (US)

'cero ['tʃero] *sm* (church) candle

ce'rotto [tʃe'rɔtto] *sm* sticking plaster
certa'mente [tʃerta'mente] *av*
certainly
certifi'cato *sm* certificate;
certificato medico medical
certificate; **certificato di nascita/di
morte** birth/death certificate

 PAROLA CHIAVE

'certo, -a ['tʃɛrto] *ag* (*sicuro*): **certo
(di/che)** certain *o* sure (of/that)
▷ *det* **1** (*tale*) certain; **un certo signor
Smith** a (certain) Mr Smith
2 (*qualche: con valore intensivo*)
some; **dopo un certo tempo** after
some time; **un fatto di una certa
importanza** a matter of some
importance; **di una certa età** past
one's prime, not so young
▷ *pron* **certi, e** *pl* some ▷ *av*
(*certamente*) certainly; (*senz'altro*) of
course; **di certo** certainly; **no (di)
certo!, certo che no!** certainly not!;
sì certo yes indeed, certainly

cer'vello, -i [tʃer'vɛllo] (*Anat*) (*pl(f)*
-a) *sm* brain; **cervello elettronico**
computer
'cervo, -a ['tʃɛrvo] *sm/f* stag/doe
▷ *sm* deer; **cervo volante** stag beetle
ces'puglio [tʃes'puʎʎo] *sm* bush
ces'sare [tʃes'sare] *vi, vt* to stop, cease;
~ di fare qc to stop doing sth
ces'tino [tʃes'tino] *sm* basket; (*per
la carta straccia*) wastepaper basket;
cestino da viaggio (*Ferr*) packed
lunch (*o* dinner)
'cesto ['tʃesto] *sm* basket
'ceto ['tʃɛto] *sm* (*social*) class
cetrio'lino [tʃetrio'lino] *sm* gherkin
cetri'olo [tʃetri'olo] *sm* cucumber
Cfr. *abbr* (= *confronta*) cf.
CGIL *sigla f* (= *Confederazione Generale
Italiana del Lavoro*) trades union
organization
chat line [tʃæt'laen] *sf inv* chat room

chattare [tʃat'tare] *vi* (*Inform*) to chat
online; **chat'tata** [tʃat'tata] *sf* chat

 PAROLA CHIAVE

che [ke] *pron* **1** (*relativo: persona:
soggetto*) who; (: *oggetto*) whom,
that; (: *cosa, animale*) which, that; **il
ragazzo che è venuto** the boy who
came; **l'uomo che io vedo** the man
(whom) I see; **il libro che è sul tavolo**
the book which *o* that is on the table; **il
libro che vedi** the book (which *o* that)
you see; **la sera che ti ho visto** the
evening I saw you
2 (*interrogativo, esclamativo*) what; **che
(cosa) fai?** what are you doing?; **a che
(cosa) pensi?** what are you thinking
about?; **non sa che (cosa) fare** he
doesn't know what to do; **ma che
dici!** what are you saying!
3 (*indefinito*): **quell'uomo ha un che
di losco** there's something suspicious
about that man; **un certo non so che**
an indefinable something
▷ *det* **1** (*interrogativo: tra tanti*) what;
(: *tra pochi*) which; **che tipo di film
preferisci?** what sort of film do you
prefer?; **che vestito ti vuoi mettere?**
what (*o* which) dress do you want to
put on?
2 (*esclamativo: seguito da aggettivo*)
how; (: *seguito da sostantivo*) what;
che buono! how delicious!; **che bel
vestito!** what a lovely dress!
▷ *cong* **1** (*con proposizioni subordinate*)
that; **credo che verrà** I think he'll
come; **voglio che tu studi** I want you
to study; **so che tu c'eri** I know (that)
you were there; **non che, non che sia
sbagliato, ma ...** not that it's wrong,
but ...
2 (*finale*) so that; **vieni qua, che ti
veda** come here, so (that) I can see
you
3 (*temporale*): **arrivai che eri già
partito** you had already left when I

arrived; **sono anni che non lo vedo** I haven't seen him for years

4 (*in frasi imperative, concessive*): **che venga pure!** let him come by all means!; **che tu sia benedetto!** may God bless you!

5 (*comparativo: con più, meno*) than; *vedi anche* **più**; **meno**; **così** *ecc*

chemiotera'pia [kemjotera'pia] *sf* chemotherapy

chero'sene [kero'zɛne] *sm* kerosene

 PAROLA CHIAVE

chi [ki] *pron* **1** (*interrogativo: soggetto*) who; (*: oggetto*) who, whom; **chi è?** who is it?; **di chi è questo libro?** whose book is this?, whose is this book?; **con chi parli?** who are you talking to?; **a chi pensi?** who are you thinking about?; **chi di voi?** which of you?; **non so a chi rivolgermi** I don't know who to ask

2 (*relativo*) whoever, anyone who; **dillo a chi vuoi** tell whoever you like

3 (*indefinito*) **chi ... chi ...** some ... others ...; **chi dice una cosa, chi dice un'altra** some say one thing, others say another

chiacchie'rare [kjakkje'rare] *vi* to chat; (*discorrere futilmente*) to chatter; (*far pettegolezzi*) to gossip; **chi'acchiere** *sfpl* **fare due** *o* **quattro chiacchiere** to have a chat

chia'mare [kja'mare] *vt* to call; (*rivolgersi a qn*) to call (in), send for; **chiamarsi** *vpr* to be called; **come ti chiami?** what's your name?; **mi chiamo Paolo** my name is Paolo, I'm called Paolo; **~ alle armi** to call up; **~ in giudizio** (*aver nome*) to summon; **chia'mata** *sf* (*Tel*) call; (*Mil*) call-up

chia'rezza [kja'rettsa] *sf* clearness; clarity

chia'rire [kja'rire] *vt* to make clear;

(*fig: spiegare*) to clear up, explain

chi'aro, -a ['kjaro] *ag* clear; (*luminoso*) clear, bright; (*colore*) pale, light

chi'asso ['kjasso] *sm* uproar, row

chi'ave ['kjave] *sf key* ▷ *ag inv* key *cpd*; **posso avere la mia ~?** can I have my key?; **chiave d'accensione** (*Aut*) ignition key; **chiave di volta** keystone; **chiave inglese** monkey wrench; **chiave USB** (*Inform*) USB key

chi'azza ['kjattsa] *sf* stain; splash

'chicco, -chi ['kikko] *sm* grain; (*di caffè*) bean; **chicco d'uva** grape

chi'edere ['kjɛdere] *vt* (*per sapere*) to ask; (*per avere*) to ask for ▷ *vi* **~ di qn** to ask after sb; (*al telefono*) to ask for *o* want sb; **~ qc a qn** to ask sb sth; to ask sb for sth; **chiedersi** *vpr* **chiedersi (se)** to wonder (whether)

chi'esa ['kjɛza] *sf* church

chi'esi *ecc* ['kjɛzi] *vb vedi* **chiedere**

'chiglia ['kiʎʎa] *sf* keel

'chilo ['kilo] *sm* kilo; **chi'lometro** *sm* kilometre

'chimica ['kimika] *sf* chemistry

'chimico, -a, -ci, -che ['kimiko] *ag* chemical ▷ *sm/f* chemist

chi'nare [ki'nare] *vt* to lower, bend; **chinarsi** *vpr* to stoop, bend

chi'occiola ['kjɔttʃola] *sf* snail; (*di indirizzo e-mail*) at sign, @; **scala a ~** spiral staircase

chi'odo ['kjɔdo] *sm* nail; (*fig*) obsession; **chiodo di garofano** (*Cuc*) clove

chi'osco, -schi ['kjɔsko] *sm* kiosk, stall

chi'ostro ['kjɔstro] *sm* cloister

chiro'mante [kiro'mante] *sm/f* palmist

chirur'gia [kirur'dʒia] *sf* surgery; **chirurgia estetica** cosmetic surgery; **chi'rurgo, -ghi** *o* **gi** *sm* surgeon

chissà [kis'sa] *av* who knows, I wonder

chi'tarra [ki'tarra] *sf* guitar

chitar'rista, -i, e [kitar'rista] *sm/f*

guitarist, guitar player

chi'udere ['kjudere] *vt* to close, shut; (*luce, acqua*) to put off, turn off; (*definitivamente: fabbrica*) to close down, shut down; (*strada*) to close; (*recingere*) to enclose; (*porre termine a*) to end ▷ *vi* to close, shut; (*definitivamente: fabbrica*) to close down, shut down; to end; **chiudersi** *vpr* to shut, close; (*ritirarsi: anche fig*) to shut o.s. away; (*ferita*) to close up; **a che ora chiudete?** what time do you close?

chi'unque [ki'unkwe] *pron* (*relativo*) whoever; (*indefinito*) anyone, anybody; **~ sia** whoever it is

'chiusi *ecc* ['kjusi] *vb vedi* **chiudere**

chi'uso, -a ['kjuso] *pp di* **chiudere** ▷ *sf* (*di corso d'acqua*) sluice, lock; (*recinto*) enclosure; (*di discorso ecc*) conclusion, ending; **chiu'sura** *sf* (*vedi* **chiudere**) closing; shutting; closing o shutting down; enclosing; putting o turning off; ending; (*dispositivo*) catch; fastening; fastener; **chiusura lampo®** zip (fastener) (BRIT), zipper (US)

C.I. *abbr* = **carta d'identità**

PAROLA CHIAVE

ci [tʃi] (*dav lo, la, li, le, ne diventa* **ce**) *pron*
1 (*personale: complemento oggetto*) us; (*: a noi: complemento di termine*) (to) us; (*: riflessivo*) ourselves; (*: reciproco*) each other, one another; (*impersonale*): **ci si veste** we get dressed; **ci ha visti** he's seen us; **non ci ha dato niente** he gave us nothing; **ci vestiamo** we get dressed; **ci amiamo** we love one another o each other
2 (*dimostrativo: di ciò, su ciò, in ciò ecc*) about (o on o of) it; **non so cosa farci** I don't know what to do about it; **che c'entro io?** what have I got to do with it?
▷ *av* (*qui*) here; (*lì*) there; (*moto attraverso luogo*): **ci passa sopra un**

ponte a bridge passes over it; **non ci passa più nessuno** nobody comes this way any more; **esserci** *vedi* **essere**

cia'batta [tʃa'batta] *sf* slipper; (*pane*) ciabatta

ciam'bella [tʃam'bɛlla] *sf* (Cuc) ring-shaped cake; (*salvagente*) rubber ring

ci'ao ['tʃao] *escl* (*all'arrivo*) hello!; (*alla partenza*) cheerio! (BRIT), bye!

cias'cuno, -a [tʃas'kuno] (*det: dav sm:* **ciascun** +C, V, **ciascuno** +s *impura*, *gn, pn, ps, x, z*; *dav sf:* **ciascuna** +C, **ciascun'** +V) *det* every, each; (*ogni*) every ▷ *pron* each (one); (*tutti*) everyone, everybody

ci'barie [tʃi'barje] *sfpl* foodstuffs

cibernauta, -i, -e [tʃiber'nauta] *sm/f* Internet surfer

ciberspazio [tʃiber'spattsjo] *sm* cyberspace

'cibo ['tʃibo] *sm* food

ci'cala [tʃi'kala] *sf* cicada

cica'trice [tʃika'tritʃe] *sf* scar

'cicca ['tʃikka] *sf* cigarette end

'ciccia ['tʃittʃa] (*fam*) *sf* fat

cicci'one, -a [tʃit'tʃone] *sm/f* (*fam*) fatty

cicla'mino [tʃikla'mino] *sm* cyclamen

ci'clismo [tʃi'klizmo] *sm* cycling; **ci'clista, -i, -e** *sm/f* cyclist

'ciclo ['tʃiklo] *sm* cycle; (*di malattia*) course

ciclomo'tore [tʃiklomo'tore] *sm* moped

ci'clone [tʃi'klone] *sm* cyclone

ci'cogna [tʃi'koɲɲa] *sf* stork

ci'eco, -a, -chi, -che ['tʃɛko] *ag* blind ▷ *sm/f* blind man/woman

ci'elo ['tʃɛlo] *sm* sky; (Rel) heaven

'cifra ['tʃifra] *sf* (*numero*) figure; numeral; (*somma di denaro*) sum, figure; (*monogramma*) monogram, initials *pl*; (*codice*) code, cipher

'ciglio, -i ['tʃiʎʎo] (*delle palpebre*) (*pl(f)* **ciglia**) *sm* (*margine*) edge, verge;

(eye)lash; (eye)lid; (*sopracciglio*) eyebrow

'cigno ['tʃiɲɲo] *sm* swan

cigo'lare [tʃigo'lare] *vi* to squeak, creak

'Cile ['tʃile] *sm*: **il ~** Chile

ci'leno, -a [tʃi'lɛno] *ag, sm/f* Chilean

cili'egia, -gie *o* **ge** [tʃi'liɛdʒa] *sf* cherry

ciliegina [tʃilje'dʒina] *sf* glacé cherry

cilin'drata [tʃilin'drata] *sf* (*Aut*) (cubic) capacity; **una macchina di grossa ~** a big-engined car

ci'lindro [tʃi'lindro] *sm* cylinder; (*cappello*) top hat

'cima ['tʃima] *sf* (*sommità*) top; (*di monte*) top, summit; (*estremità*) end; **in ~ a** at the top of; **da ~ a fondo** from top to bottom; (*fig*) from beginning to end

'cimice ['tʃimitʃe] *sf* (*Zool*) bug; (*puntina*) drawing pin (*BRIT*), thumbtack (*US*)

cimini'era [tʃimi'njɛra] *sf* chimney; (*di nave*) funnel

cimi'tero [tʃimi'tɛro] *sm* cemetery

'Cina ['tʃina] *sf*: **la ~** China

cin'cin [tʃin'tʃin] *escl* cheers!

'cinema ['tʃinema] *sm inv* cinema

ci'nese [tʃi'nese] *ag, sm/f, sm* Chinese *inv*

'cinghia ['tʃiŋgja] *sf* strap; (*cintura, Tecn*) belt

cinghi'ale [tʃin'gjale] *sm* wild boar

cinguet'tare [tʃingwet'tare] *vi* to twitter

'cinico, -a, -ci, -che ['tʃiniko] *ag* cynical ▷ *sm/f* cynic

cin'quanta [tʃin'kwanta] *num* fifty; **cinquan'tesimo, -a** *num* fiftieth

cinquan'tina [tʃinkwan'tina] *sf* (*serie*): **una ~ (di)** about fifty; (*età*): **essere sulla ~** to be about fifty

'cinque ['tʃinkwe] *num* five; **avere ~ anni** to be five (years old); **il ~ dicembre 1998** the fifth of December 1998; **alle ~** (*ora*) at five (o'clock)

cinque'cento [tʃinkwe'tʃɛnto] *num* five hundred ▷ *sm* **il C~** the sixteenth century

cin'tura [tʃin'tura] *sf* belt; **cintura di salvataggio** lifebelt (*BRIT*), life preserver (*US*); **cintura di sicurezza** (*Aut, Aer*) safety *o* seat belt

cintu'rino [tʃintu'rino] *sm* strap; **~ dell'orologio** watch strap

ciò [tʃɔ] *pron* this; that; **~ che** what; **~ nonostante** *o* **nondimeno** nevertheless, in spite of that

ci'occa, -che ['tʃɔkka] *sf* (*di capelli*) lock

ciocco'lata [tʃokko'lata] *sf* chocolate; (*bevanda*) (hot) chocolate; **cioccola'tino** *sm* chocolate

cioè [tʃo'ɛ] *av* that is (to say)

ci'otola ['tʃɔtola] *sf* bowl

ci'ottolo ['tʃɔttolo] *sm* pebble; (*di strada*) cobble(stone)

ci'polla [tʃi'polla] *sf* onion; (*di tulipano ecc*) bulb

cipol'lina [tʃipol'lina] *sf* **cipolline sottaceto** pickled onions

ci'presso [tʃi'presso] *sm* cypress (tree)

'cipria ['tʃiprja] *sf* (face) powder

'Cipro ['tʃipro] *sm* Cyprus

'circa ['tʃirka] *av* about, roughly ▷ *prep* about, concerning; **a mezzogiorno ~** about midday

'circo, -chi ['tʃirko] *sm* circus

circo'lare [tʃirko'lare] *vi* to circulate; (*Aut*) to drive (along), move (along) ▷ *ag* circular ▷ *sf* (*Amm*) circular; (*di autobus*) circle (line)

'circolo ['tʃirkolo] *sm* circle

circon'dare [tʃirkon'dare] *vt* to surround; **circondarsi** *vpr* **circondarsi di** to surround o.s. with

circonvallazi'one [tʃirkonvallat'tsjone] *sf* ring road (*BRIT*), beltway (*US*); (*per evitare una città*) by-pass

circos'petto, -a [tʃirkos'pɛtto] *ag* circumspect, cautious

circos'tante [tʃirkos'tante] *ag*

surrounding, neighbouring

circos'tanza [tʃirkos'tantsa] *sf*
circumstance; (*occasione*) occasion

cir'cuito [tʃir'kuito] *sm* circuit

CISL *sigla f* (= *Confederazione Italiana
Sindacati Lavoratori*) trades union
organization

cis'terna [tʃis'tɛrna] *sf* tank, cistern

'cisti ['tʃisti] *sf* cyst

cis'tite [tʃis'tite] *sf* cystitis

ci'tare [tʃi'tare] *vt* (*Dir*) to summon;
(*autore*) to quote; (*a esempio, modello*)
to cite

ci'tofono [tʃi'tɔfono] *sm* entry phone;
(*in uffici*) intercom

città [tʃit'ta] *sf inv* town; (*importante*)
city; **città universitaria** university
campus

cittadi'nanza [tʃittadi'nantsa] *sf*
citizens *pl*; (*Dir*) citizenship

citta'dino, -a [tʃitta'dino] *ag* town
cpd; city *cpd* ▷ *sm/f* (*di uno Stato*)
citizen; (*abitante di città*) townsman,
city dweller

ci'uccio ['tʃuttʃo] *sm* (*fam*) comforter,
dummy (BRIT), pacifier (US)

ci'uffo ['tʃuffo] *sm* tuft

ci'vetta [tʃi'vetta] *sf* (*Zool*) owl; (*fig:
donna*) coquette, flirt ▷ *ag inv* **auto/
nave ~** decoy car/ship

'civico, -a, -ci, -che ['tʃivico] *ag* civic;
(*museo*) municipal, town *cpd*; city *cpd*

ci'vile [tʃi'vile] *ag* civil; (*non militare*)
civilian; (*nazione*) civilized ▷ *sm* civilian

civiltà [tʃivil'ta] *sf* civilization;
(*cortesia*) civility

'clacson *sm inv* (*Aut*) horn

clandes'tino, -a *ag* clandestine; (*Pol*)
underground, clandestine; (*immigrato*)
illegal ▷ *sm/f* stowaway; (*anche:*
immigrato ~) illegal immigrant

'classe *sf* class; **di ~** (*fig*) with class;
of excellent quality; **classe operaia**
working class; **classe turistica** (*Aer*)
economy class

'classico, -a, -ci, -che *ag* classical;
(*tradizionale: moda*) classic(al) ▷ *sm*

classic; classical author

clas'sifica *sf* classification; (*Sport*)
placings *pl*

classifi'care *vt* to classify; (*candidato,
compito*) to grade; **classificarsi** *vpr* to
be placed

'clausola *sf* (*Dir*) clause

clavi'cembalo [klavi'tʃembalo] *sm*
harpsichord

cla'vicola *sf* (*Anat*) collar bone

clic'care *vi* (*Inform*): **~ su** to click on

cli'ente *sm/f* customer, client

'clima, -i *sm* climate; **climatizzatore**
sm air conditioning system

'clinica, -che *sf* (*scienza*) clinical
medicine; (*casa di cura*) clinic, nursing
home; (*settore d'ospedale*) clinic

clo'nare *vt* to clone; **clonazione**
[klona'tsjone] *sf* cloning

'cloro *sm* chlorine

club *sm inv* club

c.m. *abbr* = **corrente mese**

cm *abbr* (= *centimetro*) cm

coalizi'one [koalit'tsjone] *sf*
coalition

'COBAS *sigla mpl* (= *Comitati di base*)
independent trades unions

'coca *sf* (*bibita*) Coke®; (*droga*) cocaine

coca'ina *sf* cocaine

cocci'nella [kottʃi'nɛlla] *sf* ladybird
(BRIT), ladybug (US)

cocci'uto, -a [kot'tʃuto] *ag* stubborn,
pigheaded

'cocco, -chi *sm* (*pianta*) coconut
palm; (*frutto*): **noce di ~** coconut
▷ *sm/f* (*fam*) darling

cocco'drillo *sm* crocodile

cocco'lare *vt* to cuddle, fondle

cocerò *ecc* [kotʃe'rɔ] *vb vedi* **cuocere**

co'comero *sm* watermelon

'coda *sf* tail; (*fila di persone, auto*)
queue (BRIT), line (US); (*di abiti*) train;
con la ~ dell'occhio out of the
corner of one's eye; **mettersi in ~** to
queue (up) (BRIT), line up (US); to join
the queue (BRIT) o line (US); **coda di
cavallo** (*acconciatura*) ponytail

co'dardo, -a ag cowardly ▷ sm/f coward

'**codice** ['kɔditʃe] sm code; **codice di avviamento postale** postcode (BRIT), zip code (US); **codice a barre** bar code; **codice civile** civil code; **codice fiscale** tax code; **codice penale** penal code; **codice segreto** (di tessera magnetica) PIN (number); **codice della strada** highway code

coe'rente ag coherent

coe'taneo, -a ag, sm/f contemporary

'**cofano** sm (Aut) bonnet (BRIT), hood (US); (forziere) chest

'**cogliere** ['kɔʎʎere] vt (fiore: frutto) to pick, gather; (sorprendere) to catch, surprise; (bersaglio) to hit; (fig: momento opportuno ecc) to grasp, seize, take; (: capire) to grasp; **~ qn in flagrante o in fallo** to catch sb red-handed

co'gnato, -a [koɲ'ɲato] sm/f brother-/sister-in-law

co'gnome [koɲ'ɲome] sm surname

coinci'denza [kointʃi'dɛntsa] sf coincidence; (Ferr, Aer, di autobus) connection

coin'cidere [koin'tʃidere] vi to coincide

coin'volgere [koin'vɔldʒere] vt: **~ in** to involve in

cola'pasta sm inv colander

co'lare vt (liquido) to strain; (pasta) to drain; (oro fuso) to pour ▷ vi (sudore) to drip; (botte) to leak; (cera) to melt; **~ a picco** vt, vi (nave) to sink

colazi'one [kolat'tsjone] sf breakfast; **fare ~** to have breakfast; **a che ora è servita la ~?** what time is breakfast?

co'lera sm (Med) cholera

'**colgo** ecc vb vedi **cogliere**

'**colica** sf (Med) colic

co'lino sm strainer

'**colla** sf glue; (di farina) paste

collabo'rare vi to collaborate; **~ a** to collaborate on; (giornale) to contribute to; **collabora'tore, -'trice** sm/f collaborator; contributor; **collaboratore esterno** freelance; **collaboratrice familiare** home help

col'lana sf necklace; (collezione) collection, series

col'lant [kɔ'lā] sm inv tights pl

col'lare sm collar

col'lasso sm (Med) collapse

collau'dare vt to test, try out

col'lega, -ghi, -ghe sm/f colleague

collega'mento sm connection; (Mil) liaison

colle'gare vt to connect, join, link; **collegarsi** vpr (Radio, TV) to link up; **collegarsi con** (Tel) to get through to

col'legio [kol'lɛdʒo] sm college; (convitto) boarding school; **collegio elettorale** (Pol) constituency

'**collera** sf anger

col'lerico, -a, -ci, -che ag quick-tempered, irascible

col'letta sf collection

col'letto sm collar

collezio'nare [kollettsjo'nare] vt to collect

collezi'one [kollet'tsjone] sf collection

col'lina sf hill

col'lirio sm eyewash

'**collo** sm neck; (di abito) neck, collar; (pacco) parcel; **collo del piede** instep

colloca'mento sm (impiego) employment; (disposizione) placing, arrangement

collo'care vt (libri, mobili) to place; (Comm: merce) to find a market for

collocazi'one [kollokat'tsjone] sf placing; (di libro) classification

col'loquio sm conversation, talk; (ufficiale, per un lavoro) interview; (Ins) preliminary oral exam

col'mare vt **~ di** (anche fig) to fill with; (dare in abbondanza) to load o overwhelm with

co'lombo, -a sm/f dove; pigeon

co'lonia sf colony; (per bambini)

holiday camp; **(acqua di) ~** (eau de) cologne

co'lonna *sf* column; **colonna sonora** (*Cinema*) sound track; **colonna vertebrale** spine, spinal column

colon'nello *sm* colonel

colo'rante *sm* colouring

colo'rare *vt* to colour; (*disegno*) to colour in

co'lore *sm* colour; **a colori** in colour, colour *cpd*; **farne di tutti i colori** to get up to all sorts of mischief; **vorrei un ~ diverso** I'd like a different colour

colo'rito, -a *ag* coloured; (*viso*) rosy, pink; (*linguaggio*) colourful ▷ *sm* (*tinta*) colour; (*carnagione*) complexion

'colpa *sf* fault; (*biasimo*) blame; (*colpevolezza*) guilt; (*azione colpevole*) offence; (*peccato*) sin; **di chi è la ~?** whose fault is it?; **è ~ sua** it's his fault; **per ~ di** through, owing to; **col'pevole** *ag* guilty

col'pire *vt* to hit, strike; (*fig*) to strike; **rimanere colpito da qc** to be amazed *o* struck by sth

'colpo *sm* (*urto*) knock; (: *affettivo*) blow, shock; (: *aggressivo*) blow; (*di pistola*) shot; (*Med*) stroke; (*rapina*) raid; **di ~** suddenly; **fare ~** to make a strong impression; **colpo d'aria** chill; **colpo in banca** bank job *o* raid; **colpo basso** (*Pugilato, fig*) punch below the belt; **colpo di fulmine** love at first sight; **colpo di grazia** coup de grâce; **colpo di scena** (*Teatro*) coup de théâtre; (*fig*) dramatic turn of events; **colpo di sole** sunstroke; **colpo di Stato** coup d'état; **colpo di telefono** phone call; **colpo di testa** (sudden) impulse *o* whim; **colpo di vento** gust (of wind); **colpi di sole** (*nei capelli*) highlights

'colsi *ecc vb vedi* **cogliere**

coltel'lata *sf* stab

col'tello *sm* knife; **coltello a serramanico** clasp knife

colti'vare *vt* to cultivate; (*verdura*) to grow, cultivate

'colto, -a *pp di* **cogliere** ▷ *ag* (*istruito*) cultured, educated

'coma *sm inv* coma

comanda'mento *sm* (*Rel*) commandment

coman'dante *sm* (*Mil*) commander, commandant; (*di reggimento*) commanding officer; (*Naut, Aer*) captain

coman'dare *vi* to be in command ▷ *vt* to command; (*imporre*) to order, command; **~ a qn di fare** to order sb to do

combaci'are [komba'tʃare] *vi* to meet; (*fig: coincidere*) to coincide

com'battere *vt, vi* to fight

combi'nare *vt* to combine; (*organizzare*) to arrange; (*fam: fare*) to make, cause; **combinazi'one** *sf* combination; (*caso fortuito*) coincidence; **per combinazione** by chance

combus'tibile *ag* combustible ▷ *sm* fuel

⬤ **PAROLA CHIAVE**

'come *av* **1** (*alla maniera di*) like; **ti comporti come lui** you behave like him *o* like he does; **bianco come la neve** (as) white as snow; **come se** as if, as though

2 (*in qualità di*) as a; **lavora come autista** he works as a driver

3 (*interrogativo*) how?; **come ti chiami?** what's your name?; **come sta?** how are you?; **com'è il tuo amico?** what is your friend like?; **come?** (*prego?*) pardon?, sorry?; **come mai?** how come?; **come mai non ci hai avvertiti?** why on earth didn't you warn us?

4 (*esclamativo*): **come sei bravo!** how clever you are!; **come mi dispiace!** I'm terribly sorry!

▷ *cong* **1** (*in che modo*) how; **mi ha**

spiegato come l'ha conosciuto he told me how he met him
2 (*correlativo*) as; (*con comparativi di maggioranza*) than; **non è bravo come pensavo** he isn't as clever as I thought; **è meglio di come pensassi** it's better than I thought
3 (*appena che, quando*) as soon as; **come arrivò, iniziò a lavorare** as soon as he arrived, he set to work; *vedi* **così**; **tanto**

'**comico, -a, -ci, -che** *ag* (*Teatro*) comic; (*buffo*) comical ▷ *sm* (*attore*) comedian, comic actor
cominci'are [komin'tʃare] *vt, vi* to begin, start; **~ a fare/col fare** to begin to do/by doing; **a che ora comincia il film?** when does the film start?
comi'tato *sm* committee
comi'tiva *sf* party, group
co'mizio [ko'mittsjo] *sm* (*Pol*) meeting, assembly
com'media *sf* comedy; (*opera teatrale*) play; (: *che fa ridere*) comedy; (*fig*) playacting *no pl*
commemo'rare *vt* to commemorate
commen'tare *vt* to comment on; (*testo*) to annotate; (*Radio, TV*) to give a commentary on
commerci'ale [kommer'tʃale] *ag* commercial, trading; (*peg*) commercial
commercia'lista, -i, e [kommertʃa'lista] *sm/f* (*laureato*) graduate in economics and commerce; (*consulente*) business consultant
commerci'ante [kommer'tʃante] *sm/f* trader, dealer; (*negoziante*) shopkeeper
commerci'are [kommer'tʃare] *vt, vi* **~ in** to deal o trade in
com'mercio [kom'mɛrtʃo] *sm* trade, commerce; **essere in ~**

(*prodotto*) to be on the market o on sale; **essere nel ~** (*persona*) to be in business; **commercio al dettaglio/all'ingrosso** retail/wholesale trade; **commercio elettronico** e-commerce
com'messo, -a *pp di* **commettere** ▷ *sm/f* shop assistant (BRIT), sales clerk (US) ▷ *sm* (*impiegato*) clerk; **commesso viaggiatore** commercial traveller
commes'tibile *ag* edible
com'mettere *vt* to commit
com'misi *ecc vb vedi* **commettere**
commissari'ato *sm* (*Amm*) commissionership; (: *sede*) commissioner's office; **commissariato di polizia** police station
commis'sario *sm* commissioner; (*di pubblica sicurezza*) ≈ (police) superintendent (BRIT), ≈ (police) captain (US); (*Sport*) steward; (*membro di commissione*) member of a committee o board
commissi'one *sf* (*incarico*) errand; (*comitato, percentuale*) commission; (*Comm: ordinazione*) order; **commissioni** *sfpl* (*acquisti*) shopping *sg*; **commissioni bancarie** bank charges; **commissione d'esame** examining board
com'mosso, -a *pp di* **commuovere**
commo'vente *ag* moving
commozi'one [kommot'tsjone] *sf* emotion, deep feeling; **commozione cerebrale** (*Med*) concussion
commu'overe *vt* to move, affect; **commuoversi** *vpr* to be moved
como'dino *sm* bedside table
comodità *sf inv* comfort; convenience
'**comodo, -a** *ag* comfortable; (*facile*) easy; (*conveniente*) convenient; (*utile*) useful, handy ▷ *sm* comfort; convenience; **con ~** at one's convenience o leisure; **fare il proprio ~** to do as one pleases; **far ~** to be

useful o handy

compa'gnia [kompaɲ'ɲia] sf
company; (gruppo) gathering

com'pagno, -a [kom'paɲɲo]
sm/f (di classe, gioco) companion; (Pol)
comrade

com'paio ecc vb vedi **comparire**

compa'rare vt to compare

compara'tivo, -a ag, sm
comparative

compa'rire vi to appear

com'parvi ecc vb vedi **comparire**

compassi'one sf compassion, pity;
avere ~ di qn to feel sorry for sb, to
pity sb

com'passo sm (pair of) compasses pl;
callipers pl

compa'tibile ag (scusabile)
excusable; (conciliabile, Inform)
compatible

compa'tire vt (aver compassione di)
to sympathize with, feel sorry for;
(scusare) to make allowances for

com'patto, -a ag compact; (roccia)
solid; (folla) dense; (fig: gruppo, partito)
united

compen'sare vt (equilibrare) to
compensate for, make up for; **~ qn di**
(rimunerare) to pay o remunerate sb
for; (risarcire) to pay compensation to
sb for; (fig: fatiche, dolori) to reward sb
for; **com'penso** sm compensation
payment, remuneration; reward; **in
compenso** (d'altra parte) on the other
hand

compe'rare vt = **comprare**

'compere sfpl: **fare ~** to do the
shopping

compe'tente ag competent;
(mancia) apt, suitable

com'petere vi to compete, vie;
(Dir: spettare): **~ a** to lie within the
competence of; **competizi'one** sf
competition

compi'angere [kom'pjandʒere] vt
to sympathize with, feel sorry for

'compiere vt (concludere) to finish;

complete; (adempiere) to carry out,
fulfil; **compiersi** vpr (avverarsi) to be
fulfilled, come true; **~ gli anni** to have
one's birthday

compi'lare vt (modulo) to fill in;
(dizionario, elenco) to compile

'compito sm (incarico) task, duty;
(dovere) duty; (Ins) exercise; (: a casa)
piece of homework; **fare i compiti** to
do one's homework

comple'anno sm birthday

complessità sf complexity

comples'sivo, -a ag (globale)
comprehensive, overall; (totale: cifra)
total

com'plesso, -a ag complex ▷ sm
(Psic, Edil) complex; (Mus: corale)
ensemble; (: orchestrina) band; (: di
musica pop) group; **in o nel ~** on the
whole; **complesso alberghiero** hotel
complex; **complesso edilizio** building
complex; **complesso vitaminico**
vitamin complex

completa'mente av completely

comple'tare vt to complete

com'pleto, -a ag complete; (teatro,
autobus) full ▷ sm suit; **al ~** full; (tutti
presenti) all present; **completo da sci**
ski suit

compli'care vt to complicate;
complicarsi vpr to become
complicated

'complice ['komplitʃe] sm/f
accomplice

complicità [komplitʃi'ta] sf inv
complicity; **un sorriso/uno sguardo
di ~** a knowing smile/look

complimen'tarsi vpr: **~ con** to
congratulate

compli'mento sm compliment;
complimenti smpl (cortesia eccessiva)
ceremony sg; (ossequi) regards,
compliments; **complimenti!**
congratulations!; **senza
complimenti!** don't stand on
ceremony!; make yourself at home!;
help yourself!

complot'tare *vi* to plot, conspire

com'plotto *sm* plot, conspiracy

com'pone *ecc vb vedi* **comporre**

compo'nente *sm/f* member ▷ *sm* component

com'pongo *ecc vb vedi* **comporre**

componi'mento *sm* (*Dir*) settlement; (*Ins*) composition; (*poetico, teatrale*) work

com'porre *vt* (*musica, testo*) to compose; (*mettere in ordine*) to arrange; (*Dir: lite*) to settle; (*Tip*) to set; (*Tel*) to dial; **comporsi** *vpr* **comporsi di** to consist of, be composed of

comporta'mento *sm* behaviour

compor'tare *vt* (*implicare*) to involve; **comportarsi** *vpr* to behave

com'posi *ecc vb vedi* **comporre**

composi'tore, -'trice *sm/f* composer; (*Tip*) compositor, typesetter

com'posto, -a *pp di* **comporre** ▷ *ag* (*persona*) composed, self-possessed; (*: decoroso*) dignified; (*formato da più elementi*) compound *cpd* ▷ *sm* compound

com'prare *vt* to buy; **dove posso ~ delle cartoline?** where can I buy some postcards?

com'prendere *vt* (*contenere*) to comprise, consist of; (*capire*) to understand

compren'sibile *ag* understandable

comprensi'one *sf* understanding

compren'sivo, -a *ag* (*prezzo*): **~ di** inclusive of; (*indulgente*) understanding

> Attenzione! In inglese esiste la parola *comprehensive*, che però in genere significa *completo*.

com'preso, -a *pp di* **comprendere** ▷ *ag* (*incluso*) included; **il servizio è ~?** is service included?

com'pressa *sf* (*Med: garza*) compress; (*: pastiglia*) tablet; *vedi anche* **compresso**

com'primere *vt* (*premere*) to press;

(*Fisica*) to compress; (*fig*) to repress

compro'messo, -a *pp di* **compromettere** ▷ *sm* compromise

compro'mettere *vt* to compromise; **compromettersi** *vpr* to compromise o.s.

com'puter *sm inv* computer

comu'nale *ag* municipal, town *cpd*, ≈ borough *cpd*

co'mune *ag* common; (*consueto*) common, everyday; (*di livello medio*) average; (*ordinario*) ordinary ▷ *sm* (*Amm*) town council; (*: sede*) town hall ▷ *sf* (*di persone*) commune; **fuori del ~** out of the ordinary; **avere in ~** to have in common, share; **mettere in ~** to share

comuni'care *vt* (*notizia*) to pass on, convey; (*malattia*) to pass on; (*ansia ecc*) to communicate; (*trasmettere: calore ecc*) to transmit, communicate; (*Rel*) to administer communion to ▷ *vi* to communicate

comuni'cato *sm* communiqué; **comunicato stampa** press release

comunicazi'one [komunikat'tsjone] *sf* communication; (*annuncio*) announcement; (*Tel*): **dare la ~ a qn** to put sb through; **ottenere la ~** to get through; **comunicazione (telefonica)** (telephone) call

comuni'one *sf* communion; **comunione di beni** (*Dir*) joint ownership of property

comu'nismo *sm* communism

comunità *sf inv* community; **Comunità Europea** European Community

co'munque *cong* however, no matter how ▷ *av* (*in ogni modo*) in any case; (*tuttavia*) however, nevertheless

con *prep* with; **partire col treno** to leave by train; **~ mio grande stupore** to my great astonishment; **~ tutto ciò** for all that

con'cedere [kon'tʃɛdere] *vt*

(*accordare*) to grant; (*ammettere*) to admit, concede; **concedersi qc** to treat o.s. to sth, to allow o.s. sth
concentrarsi *vpr* to concentrate
concentrazi'one *sf* concentration
conce'pire [kontʃe'pire] *vt* (*bambino*) to conceive; (*progetto, idea*) to conceive (of); (*metodo, piano*) to devise
con'certo [kon'tʃɛrto] *sm* (*Mus*) concert; (: *componimento*) concerto
con'cessi *ecc* [kon'tʃɛssi] *vb vedi* **concedere**
con'cetto [kon'tʃetto] *sm* (*pensiero, idea*) concept; (*opinione*) opinion
concezi'one [kontʃet'tsjone] *sf* conception
con'chiglia [kon'kiʎʎa] *sf* shell
conci'are [kon'tʃare] *vt* (*pelli*) to tan; (*tabacco*) to cure; (*fig: ridurre in cattivo stato*) to beat up; **conciarsi** *vpr* (*sporcarsi*) to get in a mess; (*vestirsi male*) to dress badly
concili'are [kontʃi'ljare] *vt* to reconcile; (*contravvenzione*) to pay on the spot; (*sonno*) to be conducive to, induce; **conciliarsi qc** to gain o win sth (for o.s.); **conciliarsi qn** to win sb over; **conciliarsi con** to be reconciled with
con'cime [kon'tʃime] *sm* manure; (*chimico*) fertilizer
con'ciso, -a [kon'tʃizo] *ag* concise, succinct
concitta'dino, -a [kontʃitta'dino] *sm/f* fellow citizen
con'cludere *vt* to conclude; (*portare a compimento*) to conclude, finish, bring to an end; (*operare positivamente*) to achieve ▷ *vi* (*essere convincente*) to be conclusive; **concludersi** *vpr* to come to an end, close
concor'dare *vt* (*tregua, prezzo*) to agree on; (*Ling*) to make agree ▷ *vi* to agree
con'corde *ag* (*d'accordo*) in agreement; (*simultaneo*) simultaneous
concor'rente *sm/f* competitor;

(*Ins*) candidate; **concor'renza** *sf* competition
concorrenzi'ale [konkorren'tsjale] *ag* competitive
con'correre *vi*: ~ **(in)** (*Mat*) to converge o meet (in); ~ **(a)** (*competere*) to compete (for); (: *Ins: a una cattedra*) to apply (for); (*partecipare: a un'impresa*) to take part (in), contribute (to); **con'corso, -a** *pp di* **concorrere** ▷ *sm* competition; (*Ins*) competitive examination; **concorso di colpa** (*Dir*) contributory negligence
con'creto, -a *ag* concrete
con'danna *sf* sentence; conviction; condemnation
condan'nare *vt* (*Dir*): ~ **a** to sentence to; ~ **per** to convict of; (*disapprovare*) to condemn
conden'sare *vt* to condense
condi'mento *sm* seasoning; dressing
con'dire *vt* to season; (*insalata*) to dress
condi'videre *vt* to share
condizio'nale [kondittsjo'nale] *ag* conditional ▷ *sm* (*Ling*) conditional ▷ *sf* (*Dir*) suspended sentence
condizio'nare [kondittsjo'nare] *vt* to condition; **ad aria condizionata** air-conditioned; **condiziona'tore** *sm* air conditioner
condizi'one [kondit'tsjone] *sf* condition
condogli'anze [kondoʎ'ʎantse] *sfpl* condolences
condo'minio *sm* joint ownership; (*edificio*) jointly-owned building
con'dotta *sf* (*modo di comportarsi*) conduct, behaviour; (*di un affare ecc*) handling; (*di acqua*) piping; (*incarico sanitario*) country medical practice controlled by a local authority
condu'cente [kondu'tʃɛnte] *sm* driver
con'duco *ecc vb vedi* **condurre**
con'durre *vt* to conduct; (*azienda*) to manage; (*accompagnare: bambino*) to

take; (*automobile*) to drive; (*trasportare*: *acqua, gas*) to convey, conduct; (*fig*) to lead ▷ *vi* to lead

con'dussi *ecc vb vedi* **condurre**

confe'renza [konfe'rɛntsa] *sf* (*discorso*) lecture; (*riunione*) conference; **conferenza stampa** press conference

con'ferma *sf* confirmation

confer'mare *vt* to confirm

confes'sare *vt* to confess; **confessarsi** *vpr* to confess; **andare a confessarsi** (*Rel*) to go to confession

con'fetto *sm* sugared almond; (*Med*) pill

> Attenzione! In inglese esiste la parola *confetti*, che però significa *coriandoli*.

confet'tura *sf* (*gen*) jam; (*di arance*) marmalade

confezio'nare [konfettsjo'nare] *vt* (*vestito*) to make (up); (*merci, pacchi*) to package

confezi'one [konfet'tsjone] *sf* (*di abiti*: *da uomo*) tailoring; (: *da donna*) dressmaking; (*imballaggio*) packaging; **confezioni per signora** ladies' wear; **confezioni da uomo** menswear; **confezione regalo** gift pack

confic'care *vt* ~ **qc in** to hammer *o* drive sth into; **conficcarsi** *vpr* to stick

confi'dare *vi*: ~ **in** to confide in, rely on ▷ *vt* to confide; **confidarsi con qn** to confide in sb

configu'rare *vt* (*Inform*) to set

configurazi'one [konfigurat'tsjone] *sf* configuration; (*Inform*) setting

confi'nare *vi* ~ **con** to border on ▷ *vt* (*Pol*) to intern; (*fig*) to confine

Confin'dustria *sigla f* (= *Confederazione Generale dell'Industria Italiana*) employers' association, ≈ CBI (BRIT)

con'fine *sm* boundary; (*di paese*) border, frontier

confis'care *vt* to confiscate

con'flitto *sm* conflict; **conflitto**

d'interessi conflict of interests

conflu'enza [konflu'ɛntsa] *sf* (*di fiumi*) confluence; (*di strade*) junction

con'fondere *vt* to mix up, confuse; (*imbarazzare*) to embarrass; **confondersi** *vpr* (*mescolarsi*) to mingle; (*turbarsi*) to be confused; (*sbagliare*) to get mixed up

confor'tare *vt* to comfort, console

confron'tare *vt* to compare

con'fronto *sm* comparison; **in** *o* **a** ~ **di** in comparison with, compared to; **nei miei** (*o* **tuoi** *ecc*) **confronti** towards me (*o* you *ecc*)

con'fusi *ecc vb vedi* **confondere**

confusi'one *sf* confusion; (*chiasso*) racket, noise; (*imbarazzo*) embarrassment

con'fuso, -a *pp di* **confondere** ▷ *ag* (*vedi confondere*) confused; embarrassed

conge'dare [kondʒe'dare] *vt* to dismiss; (*Mil*) to demobilize; **congedarsi** *vpr* to take one's leave

con'gegno *sm* device, mechanism

conge'lare [kondʒe'lare] *vt* to freeze; **congelarsi** *vpr* to freeze; **congela'tore** *sm* freezer

congesti'one [kondʒes'tjone] *sf* congestion

conget'tura [kondʒet'tura] *sf* conjecture

con'giungere [kon'dʒundʒere] *vt* to join (together); **congiungersi** *vpr* to join (together)

congiunti'vite [kondʒunti'vite] *sf* conjunctivitis

congiun'tivo [kondʒun'tivo] *sm* (*Ling*) subjunctive

congi'unto, -a [kon'dʒunto] *pp di* **congiungere** ▷ *ag* (*unito*) joined ▷ *sm/f* relative

congiunzi'one [kondʒun'tsjone] *sf* (*Ling*) conjunction

congi'ura [kon'dʒura] *sf* conspiracy

congratu'larsi *vpr*: ~ **con qn per qc** to congratulate sb on sth

congratulazi'oni
[kongratulat'tsjoni] *sfpl*
congratulations

con'gresso *sm* congress

C.O.N.I. *sigla m* (= *Comitato Olimpico Nazionale Italiano*) Italian Olympic Games Committee

coni'are *vt* to mint, coin; (*fig*) to coin

co'niglio [ko'niʎʎo] *sm* rabbit

coniu'gare *vt* (*Ling*) to conjugate; **coniugarsi** *vpr* to get married

'coniuge ['kɔnjudʒe] *sm/f* spouse

connazio'nale [konnattsjo'nale] *sm/f* fellow-countryman/woman

connessi'one *sf* connection

con'nettere *vt* to connect, join ▷ *vi* (*fig*) to think straight

'cono *sm* cone; **cono gelato** ice-cream cone

co'nobbi *ecc vb vedi* **conoscere**

cono'scente [konoʃʃente] *sm/f* acquaintance

cono'scenza [konoʃʃentsa] *sf* (*il sapere*) knowledge *no pl*; (*persona*) acquaintance; (*facoltà sensoriale*) consciousness *no pl*; **perdere ~** to lose consciousness

co'noscere [ko'noʃʃere] *vt* to know; **ci siamo conosciuti a Firenze** we (first) met in Florence; **conoscersi** *vpr* to know o.s.; (*reciproco*) to know each other; (*incontrarsi*) to meet; **~ qn di vista** to know sb by sight; **farsi ~** (*fig*) to make a name for o.s.; **conosci'uto, -a** *pp di* **conoscere** ▷ *ag* well-known

con'quista *sf* conquest

conquis'tare *vt* to conquer; (*fig*) to gain, win

consa'pevole *ag*: **~ di** aware *o* conscious of

'conscio, -a, -sci, -sce ['kɔnʃo] *ag*: **~ di** aware *o* conscious of

consecu'tivo, -a *ag* consecutive; (*successivo: giorno*) following, next

con'segna [kon'seɲɲa] *sf* delivery; (*merce consegnata*) consignment; (*custodia*) care, custody; (*Mil: ordine*) orders *pl*; (: *punizione*) confinement to barracks; **pagamento alla ~** cash on delivery; **dare qc in ~ a qn** to entrust sth to sb

conse'gnare [konseɲ'ɲare] *vt* to deliver; (*affidare*) to entrust, hand over; (*Mil*) to confine to barracks

consegu'enza [konse'gwɛntsa] *sf* consequence; **per o di ~** consequently

con'senso *sm* approval, consent; **consenso informato** informed consent

consen'tire *vi*: **~ a** to consent *o* agree to ▷ *vt* to allow, permit

con'serva *sf* (*Cuc*) preserve; **conserva di frutta** jam; **conserva di pomodoro** tomato purée

conser'vante *sm* (*per alimenti*) preservative

conser'vare *vt* (*Cuc*) to preserve; (*custodire*) to keep; (: *dalla distruzione ecc*) to preserve, conserve

conserva'tore, -'trice *sm/f* (*Pol*) conservative

conserva'torio *sm* (*di musica*) conservatory

conservazi'one [konservat'tsjone] *sf* preservation; conservation

conside'rare *vt* to consider; (*reputare*) to consider, regard; **considerarsi** *vpr* to consider o.s.

consigli'are [konsiʎ'ʎare] *vt* (*persona*) to advise; (*metodo, azione*) to recommend, advise, suggest; **mi può ~ un buon ristorante?** can you recommend a good restaurant?; **con'siglio** *sm* (*suggerimento*) advice *no pl*, piece of advice; (*assemblea*) council; **consiglio d'amministrazione** board; **Consiglio d'Europa** Council of Europe; **Consiglio dei Ministri** (*Pol*): **il Consiglio dei Ministri** ≈ the Cabinet

consis'tente *ag* thick; solid; (*fig*) sound, valid

con'sistere *vi*: **~ in** to consist of

conso'lare *ag* consular ▷ *vt* (*confortare*) to console, comfort;

(*rallegrare*) to cheer up; **consolarsi** *vpr*
to be comforted; to cheer up
conso'lato *sm* consulate
consolazi'one [konsolat'tsjone] *sf*
consolation, comfort
'console *sm* consul
conso'nante *sf* consonant
'consono, -a *ag* ~ **a** consistent with,
consonant with
con'sorte *sm/f* consort
consta'tare *vt* to establish, verify
consu'eto, -a *ag* habitual, usual
consu'lente *sm/f* consultant
consul'tare *vt* to consult;
consultarsi *vpr* **consultarsi con qn**
to seek the advice of sb
consul'torio *sm*: ~ **familiare** family
planning clinic
consu'mare *vt* (*logorare: abiti, scarpe*)
to wear out; (*usare*) to consume, use
up; (*mangiare, bere*) to consume; (*Dir*)
to consummate; **consumarsi** *vpr* to
wear out; to be used up; (*anche fig*)
to be consumed; (*combustibile*) to
burn out
con'tabile *ag* accounts *cpd*,
accounting ▷ *sm/f* accountant
contachi'lometri [kontaki'lɔmetri]
sm inv ≈ mileometer
conta'dino, -a *sm/f* countryman/
woman, farm worker; (*peg*) peasant
contagi'are [konta'dʒare] *vt* to
infect
contagi'oso, -a *ag* infectious;
contagious
conta'gocce [konta'gottʃe] *sm inv*
(*Med*) dropper
contami'nare *vt* to contaminate
con'tante *sm* cash; **pagare in**
contanti to pay cash; **non ho**
contanti I haven't got any cash
con'tare *vt* to count; (*considerare*)
to consider ▷ *vi* to count, be of
importance; ~ **su qn** to count *o* rely
on sb; ~ **di fare qc** to intend to do sth;
conta'tore *sm* meter
contat'tare *vt* to contact

con'tatto *sm* contact
'conte *sm* count
conteggi'are [konted'dʒare] *vt* to
charge, put on the bill
con'tegno [kon'teɲɲo] *sm*
(*comportamento*) behaviour;
(*atteggiamento*) attitude; **darsi un** ~ to
act nonchalant; to pull o.s. together
contemporanea'mente *av*
simultaneously; at the same time
contempo'raneo, -a *ag, sm/f*
contemporary
conten'dente *sm/f* opponent,
adversary
conte'nere *vt* to contain;
conteni'tore *sm* container
conten'tezza [konten'tettsa] *sf*
contentment
con'tento, -a *ag* pleased, glad; ~ **di**
pleased with
conte'nuto *sm* contents *pl*;
(*argomento*) content
con'tessa *sf* countess
contes'tare *vt* (*Dir*) to notify; (*fig*) to
dispute
con'testo *sm* context
continen'tale *ag, sm/f* continental
conti'nente *ag* continent ▷ *sm* (*Geo*)
continent; (: *terra ferma*) mainland
contin'gente [kontin'dʒɛnte] *ag*
contingent ▷ *sm* (*Comm*) quota; (*Mil*)
contingent
continua'mente *av* (*senza*
interruzione) continuously, nonstop;
(*ripetutamente*) continually
continu'are *vt* to continue (with),
go on with ▷ *vi* to continue, go on; ~
a fare qc to go on *o* continue doing sth
continuità *sf* continuity
con'tinuo, -a *ag* (*numerazione*)
continuous; (*pioggia*) continual,
constant; (*Elettr*): **corrente continua**
direct current; **di** ~ continually
'conto *sm* (*calcolo*) calculation;
(*Comm, Econ*) account; (*di ristorante,*
albergo) bill; (*fig: stima*) consideration,
esteem; **il** ~**, per favore** can I have the

bill, please?; **lo metta sul mio ~** put it on my bill; **fare i conti con qn** to settle one's account with sb; **fare ~ su qn/qc** to count o rely on sb; **rendere ~ a qn di qc** to be accountable to sb for sth; **tener ~ di qn/qc** to take sb/sth into account; **per ~ di** on behalf of; **per ~ mio** as far as I'm concerned; **a conti fatti, in fin dei conti** all things considered; **conto corrente** current account; **conto alla rovescia** countdown

con'torno sm (*linea*) outline, contour; (*ornamento*) border; (*Cuc*) vegetables pl

con'torto, -a pp di **contorcere**

contrabbandi'ere, -a sm/f smuggler

contrab'bando sm smuggling, contraband; **merce di ~** contraband, smuggled goods pl

contrab'basso sm (*Mus*) (double) bass

contraccambi'are vt (*favore ecc*) to return

contraccet'tivo, -a [kontrattʃet'tivo] ag, sm contraceptive

contrac'colpo sm rebound; (*di arma da fuoco*) recoil; (*fig*) repercussion

contrad'dire vt to contradict; **contraddirsi** vpr to contradict o.s.; (*uso reciproco: persone*) to contradict each other o one another; (*: testimonianze ecc*) to be contradictory

contraf'fare vt (*persona*) to mimic; (*alterare: voce*) to disguise; (*firma*) to forge, counterfeit

contraria'mente av: **~ a** contrary to

contrari'are vt (*contrastare*) to thwart, oppose; (*irritare*) to annoy, bother

con'trario, -a ag opposite; (*sfavorevole*) unfavourable ▷ sm opposite; **essere ~ a qc** (*persona*) to be against sth; **in caso ~** otherwise; **avere qc in ~** to have some objection;

al ~ on the contrary

contrasse'gnare [kontrasseɲ'ɲare] vt to mark

contras'tare vt (*avversare*) to oppose; (*impedire*) to bar; (*negare: diritto*) to contest, dispute ▷ vi **~ (con)** (*essere in disaccordo*) to contrast (with); (*lottare*) to struggle (with)

contrat'tacco sm counterattack

contrat'tare vt, vi to negotiate

contrat'tempo sm hitch

con'tratto, -a pp di **contrarre** ▷ sm contract

contravvenzi'one [kontravven'tsjone] sf contravention; (*ammenda*) fine

contrazi'one [kontrat'tsjone] sf contraction; (*di prezzi ecc*) reduction

contribu'ente sm/f taxpayer; ratepayer (*BRIT*), property tax payer (*US*)

contribu'ire vi to contribute

'contro prep against; **~ di me/lui** against me/him; **pastiglie ~ la tosse** throat lozenges; **~ pagamento** (*Comm*) on payment ▷ prefisso: **controfi'gura** sf (*Cinema*) double

control'lare vt (*accertare*) to check; (*sorvegliare*) to watch, control; (*tenere nel proprio potere, fig: dominare*) to control; **controllarsi** vpr to control o.s.; **con'trollo** sm check; watch; control; **controllo delle nascite** birth control; **control'lore** sm (*Ferr, Autobus*) (ticket) inspector

contro'luce [kontro'lutʃe] sf inv (*Fot*) backlit shot ▷ av **(in) ~** against the light; (*fotografare*) into the light

contro'mano av: **guidare ~** to drive on the wrong side of the road; (*in un senso unico*) to drive the wrong way up a one-way street

controprodu'cente [kontroprodu'tʃente] ag counterproductive

contro'senso sm (*contraddizione*) contradiction in terms; (*assurdità*) nonsense

controspio'naggio
[kontrospio'naddʒo] *sm*
counterespionage

contro'versia *sf* controversy; (*Dir*)
dispute

contro'verso, -a *ag* controversial

contro'voglia [kontro'vɔʎʎa] *av*
unwillingly

contusi'one *sf* (*Med*) bruise

convale'scente [konvaleʃʃente] *ag*,
sm/f convalescent

convali'dare *vt* (*Amm*) to validate;
(*fig: sospetto, dubbio*) to confirm

con'vegno [kon'veɲɲo] *sm* (*incontro*)
meeting; (*congresso*) convention,
congress; (*luogo*) meeting place

conve'nevoli *smpl* civilities

conveni'ente *ag* suitable;
(*vantaggioso*) profitable; (*: prezzo*)
cheap

> Attenzione! In inglese esiste
> la parola *convenient*, che però
> significa *comodo*.

conve'nire *vi* (*riunirsi*) to gather,
assemble; (*concordare*) to agree,
(*tornare utile*) to be worthwhile ▷ *vb
impers* **conviene fare questo** it
is advisable to do this; **conviene
andarsene** we should go; **ne
convengo** I agree

con'vento *sm* (*di frati*) monastery; (*di
suore*) convent

convenzio'nale [konventsjo'nale]
ag conventional

convenzi'one [konven'tsjone]
sf (*Dir*) agreement; (*nella società*)
convention

conver'sare *vi* to have a
conversation, converse

conversazi'one [konversat'tsjone]
sf conversation; **fare ~** to chat, have
a chat

conversi'one *sf* conversion;
conversione ad U (*Aut*) U-turn

conver'tire *vt* (*trasformare*) to
change; (*Pol, Rel*) to convert;

convertirsi *vpr* **convertirsi (a)** to be
converted (to)

con'vesso, -a *ag* convex

convin'cente [konvin'tʃente] *ag*
convincing

con'vincere [kon'vintʃere] *vt* to
convince; **~ qn di qc** to convince sb of
sth; **~ qn a fare qc** to persuade sb to
do sth; **convincersi** *vpr* **convincersi
(di qc)** to convince o.s. (of sth); **~ qn di
qc** to convince sb of sth; **~ qn a fare qc**
to convince sb to do sth

convi'vente *sm/f* common-law
husband/wife

con'vivere *vi* to live together

convo'care *vt* to call, convene; (*Dir*)
to summon

convulsi'one *sf* convulsion

coope'rare *vi* **~ (a)** to cooperate (in);
coopera'tiva *sf* cooperative

coordi'nare *vt* to coordinate

co'perchio [ko'perkjo] *sm* cover; (*di
pentola*) lid

co'perta *sf* cover; (*di lana*) blanket; (*da
viaggio*) rug; (*Naut*) deck

coper'tina *sf* (*Stampa*) cover, jacket

co'perto, -a *pp di* **coprire** ▷ *ag*
covered; (*cielo*) overcast ▷ *sm* place
setting; (*posto a tavola*) place; (*al
ristorante*) cover charge; **~ di** covered
in o with

coper'tone *sm* (*Aut*) rubber tyre

coper'tura *sf* (*anche Econ, Mil*) cover;
(*di edificio*) roofing

'copia *sf* copy; **brutta/bella ~** rough/
final copy

copi'are *vt* to copy

copi'one *sm* (*Cinema, Teatro*) script

'coppa *sf* (*bicchiere*) goblet; (*per frutta,
gelato*) dish; (*trofeo*) cup, trophy;
coppa dell'olio oil sump (*BRIT*) o pan
(*US*)

'coppia *sf* (*di persone*) couple; (*di
animali, Sport*) pair

coprifu'oco, -chi *sm* curfew

copri'letto *sm* bedspread

copripiu'mino *sm* duvet cover

co'prire vt to cover; (occupare: carica, posto) to hold; **coprirsi** vpr (cielo) to cloud over; (vestirsi) to wrap up, cover up; (Econ) to cover o.s.; **coprirsi di** (macchie, muffa) to become covered in

coque [kɔk] sf: **uovo alla ~** boiled egg

co'raggio [ko'raddʒo] sm courage, bravery; **~!** (forza!) come on!; (animo!) cheer up!

co'rallo sm coral

Co'rano sm (Rel) Koran

co'razza [ko'rattsa] sf armour; (di animali) carapace, shell; (Mil) armour(-plating)

'corda sf cord; (fune) rope; (spago, Mus) string; **dare ~ a qn** to let sb have his (o her) way; **tenere sulla ~ qn** to keep sb on tenterhooks; **tagliare la ~** to slip away, sneak off; **corda vocale** vocal cords

cordi'ale ag cordial, warm ▷ sm (bevanda) cordial

'cordless ['kɔ:dlɪs] sm inv cordless phone

cor'done sm cord, string; (linea: di polizia) cordon; **cordone ombelicale** umbilical cord

Co'rea sf **la ~** Korea

coreogra'fia sf choreography

cori'andolo sm (Bot) coriander; **coriandoli** smpl confetti sg

cor'nacchia [kor'nakkja] sf crow

corna'musa sf bagpipes pl

cor'netta sf (Mus) cornet; (Tel) receiver

cor'netto sm (Cuc) croissant; (gelato) cone

cor'nice [kor'nitʃe] sf frame; (fig) setting, background

cornici'one [korni'tʃone] sm (di edificio) ledge; (Archit) cornice

'corno (pl(f) **-a**) sm (Zool) horn; (pl(m) **-i**: Mus) horn; **fare le corna a qn** to be unfaithful to sb

Corno'vaglia [korno'vaʎʎa] sf: **la ~** Cornwall

cor'nuto, -a ag (con corna) horned; (fam!: marito) cuckolded ▷ sm (fam!) cuckold; (: insulto) bastard (!)

'coro sm chorus; (Rel) choir

co'rona sf crown; (di fiori) wreath

'corpo sm body; (militare, diplomatico) corps inv; **prendere ~** to take shape; **a ~ a ~** hand-to-hand; **corpo di ballo** corps de ballet; **corpo insegnante** teaching staff

corpora'tura sf build, physique

cor'reggere [kor'rɛddʒere] vt to correct; (compiti) to correct, mark

cor'rente ag (acqua: di fiume) flowing; (: di rubinetto) running; (moneta, prezzo) current; (comune) everyday ▷ sm **essere al ~ (di)** to be well-informed (about); **mettere al ~ (di)** to inform (of) ▷ sf (d'acqua) current, stream; (spiffero) draught; (Elettr, Meteor) current; (fig) trend, tendency; **la vostra lettera del 5 ~ mese** (Comm) your letter of the 5th of this month; **corrente alternata/continua** alternate/direct current; **corrente'mente** av commonly; **parlare una lingua correntemente** to speak a language fluently

'correre vi to run; (precipitarsi) to rush; (partecipare a una gara) to race, run; (fig: diffondersi) to go round ▷ vt (Sport: gara) to compete in; (rischio) to run; (pericolo) to face; **~ dietro a qn** to run after sb; **corre voce che ...** it is rumoured that ...

cor'ressi ecc vb vedi **correggere**

correzi'one [korret'tsjone] sf correction; marking; **correzione di bozze** proofreading

corri'doio sm corridor; (in aereo, al cinema) aisle; **vorrei un posto sul ~** I'd like an aisle seat

corri'dore sm (Sport) runner; (: su veicolo) racer

corri'era sf coach (BRIT), bus

corri'ere sm (diplomatico, di guerra, postale) courier; (Comm) carrier

corri'mano sm handrail

corrispon'dente *ag* corresponding ▷ *sm/f* correspondent

corrispon'denza [korrispon'dɛntsa] *sf* correspondence

corris'pondere *vi (equivalere)*: **~ (a)** to correspond (to) ▷ *vt (stipendio)* to pay; *(fig: amore)* to return

cor'rodere *vt* to corrode

cor'rompere *vt* to corrupt; *(comprare)* to bribe

cor'roso, -a *pp di* **corrodere**

cor'rotto, -a *pp di* **corrompere** ▷ *ag* corrupt

corru'gare *vt* to wrinkle; **~ la fronte** to knit one's brows

cor'ruppi *ecc vb vedi* **corrompere**

corruzi'one [korrut'tsjone] *sf* corruption; bribery

'corsa *sf* running *no pl*; *(gara)* race; *(di autobus, taxi)* journey, trip; **fare una ~** to run, dash; *(Sport)* to run a race; **corsa campestre** cross-country race

'corsi *ecc vb vedi* **correre**

cor'sia *sf (Aut, Sport)* lane; *(di ospedale)* ward

'Corsica *sf* **la ~** Corsica

cor'sivo *sm* cursive (writing); *(Tip)* italics *pl*

'corso, -a *pp di* **correre** ▷ *sm* course; *(strada cittadina)* main street; *(di unità monetaria)* circulation; *(di titoli, valori)* rate, price; **in ~** in progress, under way; *(annata)* current; **corso d'acqua** river, stream; *(artificiale)* waterway; **corso d'aggiornamento** refresher course; **corso serale** evening class

'corte *sf (court)yard; (Dir, regale)* court; **fare la ~ a qn** to court sb; **corte marziale** court-martial

cor'teccia, -ce [kor'tettʃa] *sf* bark

corteggi'are [korted'dʒare] *vt* to court

cor'teo *sm* procession

cor'tese *ag* courteous; **corte'sia** *sf* courtesy; **per cortesia ...** excuse me, please ...

cor'tile *sm* (court)yard

cor'tina *sf* curtain; *(anche fig)* screen

'corto, -a *ag* short; **essere a ~ di qc** to be short of sth; **corto circuito** short-circuit

'corvo *sm* raven

'cosa *sf* thing; *(faccenda)* affair, matter, business *no pl*; **(che) ~?** what?; **(che) cos'è?** what is it?; **a ~ pensi?** what are you thinking about?

'coscia, -sce ['kɔʃʃa] *sf* thigh; **coscia di pollo** *(Cuc)* chicken leg

cosci'ente [koʃʃɛnte] *ag* conscious; **~ di** conscious *o* aware of

 PAROLA CHIAVE

così *av* **1** *(in questo modo)* like this, (in) this way; *(in tal modo)* so; **le cose stanno così** this is the way things stand; **non ho detto così!** I didn't say that!; **come stai? — (e) così così** how are you? — so-so; **e così via** and so on; **per così dire** so to speak

2 *(tanto)* so; **così lontano** so far away; **un ragazzo così intelligente** such an intelligent boy

▷ *ag inv (tale)*: **non ho mai visto un film così** I've never seen such a film ▷ *cong* **1** *(perciò)* so, therefore

2: **così ... come** as ... as; **non è così bravo come te** he's not as good as you; **così ... che** so ... that

cosid'detto, -a *ag* so-called

cos'metico, -a, -ci, -che *ag, sm* cosmetic

cos'pargere [kos'pardʒere] *vt* **~ di** to sprinkle with

cos'picuo, -a *ag* considerable, large

cospi'rare *vi* to conspire

'cossi *ecc vb vedi* **cuocere**

'costa *sf (tra terra e mare)* coast(line); *(litorale)* shore; *(Anat)* rib; **la C~ Azzurra** the French Riviera

cos'tante *ag* constant; *(persona)* steadfast ▷ *sf* constant

cos'tare *vi, vt* to cost; **quanto costa?**

how much does it cost?; **~ caro** to be expensive, cost a lot

cos'tata *sf* (*Cuc*) large chop

costeggi'are [kosted'dʒare] *vt* to be close to; to run alongside

costi'ero, -a *ag* coastal, coast *cpd*

costitu'ire *vt* (*comitato, gruppo*) to set up, form; (*elementi, parti: comporre*) to make up, constitute; (*rappresentare*) to constitute; (*Dir*) to appoint; **costituirsi** *vpr* **costituirsi alla polizia** to give o.s. up to the police

costituzi'one [kostitut'tsjone] *sf* setting up; building up; constitution

'costo *sm* cost; **a ogni** *o* **qualunque ~, a tutti i costi** at all costs

'costola *sf* (*Anat*) rib

cos'toso, -a *ag* expensive, costly

cos'tringere [kos'trindʒere] *vt* **~ qn a fare qc** to force sb to do sth

costru'ire *vt* to construct, build; **costruzi'one** *sf* construction, building

cos'tume *sm* (*uso*) custom; (*foggia di vestire, indumento*) costume; **costume da bagno** bathing *o* swimming costume (*BRIT*), swimsuit; (*da uomo*) bathing *o* swimming trunks *pl*

co'tenna *sf* bacon rind

coto'letta *sf* (*di maiale, montone*) chop; (*di vitello, agnello*) cutlet

co'tone *sm* cotton; **cotone idrofilo** cotton wool (*BRIT*), absorbent cotton (*US*)

'cotta *sf* (*fam: innamoramento*) crush

'cottimo *sm*: **lavorare a ~** to do piecework

'cotto, -a *pp di* **cuocere** ▷ *ag* cooked; (*fam: innamorato*) head-over-heels in love; **ben ~** (*carne*) well done

cot'tura *sf* cooking; (*in forno*) baking; (*in umido*) stewing

co'vare *vt* to hatch; (*fig: malattia*) to be sickening for; (: *odio, rancore*) to nurse ▷ *vi* (*fuoco, fig*) to smoulder

'covo *sm* den

co'vone *sm* sheaf

'cozza ['kɔttsa] *sf* mussel

coz'zare [kot'tsare] *vi*: **~ contro** to bang into, collide with

CPT *sigla m inv* = **Centro di Permanenza Temporanea**

crac'care *vt* (*Inform*) to crack

'crampo *sm* cramp; **ho un ~ alla gamba** I've got cramp in my leg

'cranio *sm* skull

cra'tere *sm* crater

cra'vatta *sf* tie

cre'are *vt* to create

'crebbi *ecc vb vedi* **crescere**

cre'dente *sm/f* (*Rel*) believer

cre'denza [kre'dɛntsa] *sf* belief; (*armadio*) sideboard

'credere *vt* to believe ▷ *vi*: **~ in, ~ a** to believe in; **~ qn onesto** to believe sb (to be) honest; **~ che** to believe *o* think that; **credersi furbo** to think one is clever

'credito *sm* (*anche Comm*) credit; (*reputazione*) esteem, repute; **comprare a ~** to buy on credit

'crema *sf* cream; (*con uova, zucchero ecc*) custard; **crema pasticciera** confectioner's custard; **crema solare** sun cream

cre'mare *vt* to cremate

'crepa *sf* crack

cre'paccio [kre'pattʃo] *sm* large crack, fissure; (*di ghiacciaio*) crevasse

crepacu'ore *sm* broken heart

cre'pare *vi* (*fam: morire*) to snuff it, kick the bucket; **~ dalle risa** to split one's sides laughing

crêpe [krɛp] *sf inv* pancake

cre'puscolo *sm* twilight, dusk

'crescere ['krɛʃʃere] *vi* to grow ▷ *vt* (*figli*) to raise

'cresima *sf* (*Rel*) confirmation

'crespo, -a *ag* (*capelli*) frizzy; (*tessuto*) puckered ▷ *sm* crêpe

'cresta *sf* crest; (*di polli, uccelli*) crest, comb

'creta *sf* chalk; clay

creti'nata *sf* (*fam*): **dire/fare una ~**

to say/do a stupid thing
cre'tino, -a *ag* stupid ▷ *sm/f* idiot, fool
CRI *sigla f* = **Croce Rossa Italiana**
cric *sm inv* (*Tecn*) jack
cri'ceto [kri'tʃeto] *sm* hamster
crimi'nale *ag, sm/f* criminal
criminalità *sf* crime, ci imiiialità organizzata organized crime
'crimine *sm* (*Dir*) crime
crip'tare *vt* (*TV: programma*) to encrypt
crisan'temo *sm* chrysanthemum
'crisi *sf inv* crisis; (*Med*) attack, fit; **crisi di nervi** attack o fit of nerves
cris'tallo *sm* crystal; **cristalli liquidi** liquid crystals
cristia'nesimo *sm* Christianity
cristi'ano, -a *ag, sm/f* Christian
'Cristo *sm* Christ
cri'terio *sm* criterion; (*buon senso*) (common) sense
'critica, -che *sf* criticism; **la ~** (*attività*) criticism; (*persone*) the critics *pl*; *vedi anche* **critico**
criti'care *vt* to criticize
'critico, -a, -ci, -che *ag* critical ▷ *sm* critic
cro'ato, -a *ag, sm/f* Croatian, Croat
Croa'zia [kroa'ttsja] *sf* Croatia
croc'cante *ag* crisp, crunchy
'croce ['krotʃe] *sf* cross; **in ~** (*di traverso*) crosswise; (*fig*) on tenterhooks; **Croce Rossa** Red Cross
croci'ata [kro'tʃata] *sf* crusade
croci'era [kro'tʃɛra] *sf* (*viaggio*) cruise; (*Archit*) transept
croci'fisso, -a *pp di* **crocifiggere**
crol'lare *vi* to collapse; **'crollo** *sm* collapse; (*di prezzi*) slump, sudden fall; **crollo in Borsa** *slump in prices on the Stock Exchange*
cro'mato, -a *ag* chromium-plated
'cromo *sm* chrome, chromium
'cronaca, -che *sf* (*Stampa*) news *sg*; (*: rubrica*) column; (*TV, Radio*) commentary; **fatto** o **episodio di ~**

news item; **cronaca nera** crime news *sg*; crime column
'cronico, -a, -ci, -che *ag* chronic
cro'nista, -i *sm* (*Stampa*) reporter
cro'nometro *sm* chronometer; (*a scatto*) stopwatch
'crosta *sf* crust
cros'tacei [kros'tatʃei] *smpl* shellfish
cros'tata *sf* (*Cuc*) tart
cros'tino *sm* (*Cuc*) crouton; (*: da antipasto*) canapé
cruci'ale [kru'tʃale] *ag* crucial
cruci'verba *sm inv* crossword (puzzle)
cru'dele *ag* cruel
'crudo, -a *ag* (*non cotto*) raw; (*aspro*) harsh, severe
cru'miro (*peg*) *sm* blackleg (*BRIT*), scab
'crusca *sf* bran
crus'cotto *sm* (*Aut*) dashboard
CSI *sigla f inv* (= *Comunità Stati Indipendenti*) CIS
CSM [tʃiɛsse'ɛmme] *sigla m* (= *consiglio superiore della magistratura*) Magistrates' Board of Supervisors
'Cuba *sf* Cuba
cu'bano, -a *ag, sm/f* Cuban
cu'betto *sm*; **cubetto di ghiaccio** ice cube
'cubico, -a, -ci, -che *ag* cubic
cu'bista, -i, -e *ag* (*Arte*) Cubist ▷ *sf* (*in discoteca*) podium dancer
'cubo, -a *ag* cubic ▷ *sm* cube; **elevare al ~** (*Mat*) to cube
cuc'cagna [kuk'kaɲɲa] *sf* **paese della ~** land of plenty; **albero della ~** greasy pole (*fig*)
cuc'cetta [kut'tʃetta] *sf* (*Ferr*) couchette; (*Naut*) berth
cucchiai'ata [kukja'jata] *sf* spoonful
cucchia'ino [kukkja'ino] *sm* teaspoon; coffee spoon
cucchi'aio [kuk'kjajo] *sm* spoon
'cuccia, -ce ['kuttʃa] *sf* dog's bed; **a ~!** down!
'cucciolo ['kuttʃolo] *sm* cub; (*di cane*) puppy

cu'cina [ku'tʃina] sf (locale) kitchen; (arte culinaria) cooking, cookery; (le vivande) food, cooking; (apparecchio) cooker; **cucina componibile** fitted kitchen; **cuci'nare** vt to cook

cu'cire [ku'tʃire] vt to sew, stitch; **cuci'trice** sf stapler

cucù sm inv cuckoo

'cuffia sf bonnet, cap; (da infermiera) cap; (da bagno) (bathing) cap; (per ascoltare) headphones pl, headset

cu'gino, -a [ku'dʒino] sm/f cousin

 PAROLA CHIAVE

'cui pron **1** (nei complementi indiretti: persona) whom; (: oggetto, animale) which; **la persona/le persone a cui accennavi** the person/people you were referring to o to whom you were referring; **i libri di cui parlavo** the books I was talking about o about which I was talking; **il quartiere in cui abito** the district where I live; **la ragione per cui** the reason why **2** (inserito tra articolo e sostantivo) whose; **la donna i cui figli sono scomparsi** the woman whose children have disappeared; **il signore, dal cui figlio ho avuto il libro** the man from whose son I got the book

culi'naria sf cookery

'culla sf cradle

cul'lare vt to rock

'culmine sm top, summit

'culo (fam!) sm arse (BRIT!), ass (US!); (fig: fortuna): **aver ~** to have the luck of the devil

'culto sm (religione) religion; (adorazione) worship, adoration; (venerazione: anche fig) cult

cul'tura sf culture; education, learning; **cultu'rale** ag cultural

cultu'rismo sm body-building

cumula'tivo, -a ag cumulative; (prezzo) inclusive; (biglietto) group cpd

'cumulo sm (mucchio) pile, heap; (Meteor) cumulus

cu'netta sf (avvallamento) dip; (di scolo) gutter

cu'ocere ['kwɔtʃere] vt (alimenti) to cook; (mattoni ecc) to fire ▷ vi to cook; **~ al forno** (pane) to bake; (arrosto) to roast; **cu'oco, -a, -chi, -che** sm/f cook; (di ristorante) chef

cu'oio sm leather; **cuoio capelluto** scalp

cu'ore sm heart; **cuori** smpl (Carte) hearts; **avere buon ~** to be kind-hearted; **stare a ~ a qn** to be important to sb

'cupo, -a ag dark; (suono) dull; (fig) gloomy, dismal

'cupola sf dome; cupola

'cura sf care; (Med: trattamento) (course of) treatment; **aver ~ di** (occuparsi di) to look after; **a ~ di** (libro) edited by; **cura dimagrante** diet

cu'rare vt (malato, malattia) to treat; (: guarire) to cure; (aver cura di) to take care of; (testo) to edit; **curarsi** vpr to take care of o.s.; (Med) to follow a course of treatment; **curarsi di** to pay attention to

curio'sare vi to look round, wander round; (tra libri) to browse; **~ nei negozi** to look o wander round the shops

curiosità sf inv curiosity; (cosa rara) curio, curiosity

curi'oso, -a ag curious; **essere ~ di** to be curious about

cur'sore sm (Inform) cursor

'curva sf curve; (stradale) bend, curve

cur'vare vt to bend ▷ vi (veicolo) to take a bend; (strada) to bend, curve; **curvarsi** vpr to bend; (legno) to warp

'curvo, -a ag curved; (piegato) bent

cusci'netto [kuʃʃi'netto] sm pad; (Tecn) bearing ▷ ag inv **stato ~** buffer state; **cuscinetto a sfere** ball bearing

cu'scino [kuʃʃino] sm cushion; (guanciale) pillow

cus'tode *sm/f* keeper, custodian
cus'todia *sf* care; (*Dir*) custody;
(*astuccio*) case, holder
custo'dire *vt* (*conservare*) to keep;
(*assistere*) to look after, take care of;
(*fare la guardia*) to guard
CV *abbr* (= *cavallo vapore*) h p
cybercaffè [tʃiberka'te] *sm inv*
cybercafé
cybernauta, -i, -e *sm/f* Internet
surfer
cyberspazio *sm* cyberspace

 PAROLA CHIAVE

da (*da+il* = **dal**, *da+lo* = **dallo**, *da+l'* =
dall', *da+la* = **dalla**, *da+i* = **dai**, *da+gli*
= **dagli, da+le = dalle**) *prep* **1** (*agente*)
by; **dipinto da un grande artista**
painted by a great artist
2 (*causa*) with; **tremare dalla paura**
to tremble with fear
3 (*stato in luogo*) at; **abito da lui** I'm
living at his house *o* with him; **sono
dal giornalaio/da Francesco** I'm at
the newsagent's/Francesco's (house)
4 (*moto a luogo*) to; (*moto per luogo*)
through; **vado da Pietro/dal
giornalaio** I'm going to Pietro's
(house)/to the newsagent's; **sono
passati dalla finestra** they came in
through the window
5 (*provenienza, allontanamento*) from;
arrivare/partire da Milano to
arrive/depart from Milan; **scendere
dal treno/dalla macchina** to get off
the train/out of the car; **si trova a 5**

km da qui it's 5 km from here
6 (*tempo: durata*) for; (: *a partire da: nel passato*) since; (: *nel futuro*) from; **vivo qui da un anno** I've been living here for a year; **è dalle 3 che ti aspetto** I've been waiting for you since 3 (o'clock); **da oggi in poi** from today onwards; **da bambino** as a child, when I (*o he ecc*) was a child
7 (*modo, maniera*) like; **comportarsi da uomo** to behave like a man; **l'ho fatto da me** I did it (by) myself
8 (*descrittivo*): **una macchina da corsa** a racing car; **una ragazza dai capelli biondi** a girl with blonde hair; **un vestito da 60 euro** a 60 euros dress

dà *vb vedi* **dare**

dac'capo *av* (*di nuovo*) (once) again; (*dal principio*) all over again, from the beginning

'dado *sm* (*da gioco*) dice *o* die; (*Cuc*) stock (BRIT) *o* bouillon (US) cube; (*Tecn*) (screw)nut; **dadi** *smpl* (game of) dice; **giocare a dadi** to play dice

'daino *sm* (*fallow*) deer *inv*; (*pelle*) buckskin

dal'tonico, -a, -ci, -che *ag* colour-blind

'dama *sf* lady; (*nei balli*) partner; (*gioco*) draughts *sg* (BRIT), checkers *sg* (US)

damigi'ana [dami'dʒana] *sf* demijohn

da'nese *ag* Danish ▷ *sm/f* Dane ▷ *sm* (*Ling*) Danish

Dani'marca *sf* **la ~** Denmark

dannazi'one *sf* damnation

danneggi'are [danned'dʒare] *vt* to damage; (*rovinare*) to spoil; (*nuocere*) to harm

'danno *sm* damage; (*a persona*) harm, injury; **danni** *smpl* (*Dir*) damages; **dan'noso, -a** *ag* **dannoso (a, per)** harmful (to), bad (for)

Da'nubio *sm* **il ~** the Danube

'danza ['dantsa] *sf* **la ~** dancing; **una ~** a dance

dan'zare [dan'tsare] *vt*, *vi* to dance

dapper'tutto *av* everywhere

dap'prima *av* at first

'dare *sm* (*Comm*) debit ▷ *vt* to give; (*produrre: frutti, suono*) to produce ▷ *vi* (*guardare*): **~ su** to look (out) onto; **darsi** *vpr* **darsi a** to dedicate o.s. to; **darsi al commercio** to go into business; **darsi al bere** to take to drink; **~ da mangiare a qn** to give sb sth to eat; **~ per certo qc** to consider sth certain; **~ per morto qn** to give sb up for dead; **darsi per vinto** to give in

'data *sf* date; **~ limite d'utilizzo** *or* **di consumo** best-before date; **data di nascita** date of birth; **data di scadenza** expiry date

'dato, -a *ag* (*stabilito*) given ▷ *sm* datum; **dati** *smpl* data *pl*; **~ che** given that; **un ~ di fatto** a fact; **dati sensibili** personal information

da'tore, -'trice *sm/f*; **datore di lavoro** employer

'dattero *sm* date

dattilogra'fia *sf* typing

datti'lografo, -a *sm/f* typist

da'vanti *av* in front; (*dirimpetto*) opposite ▷ *ag inv* front ▷ *sm* front; **~ a** in front of; facing, opposite; (*in presenza di*) before, in front of

davan'zale [davan'tsale] *sm* windowsill

dav'vero *av* really, indeed

d.C. *adv abbr* (= *dopo Cristo*) A.D.

'dea *sf* goddess

'debbo *ecc vb vedi* **dovere**

'debito, -a *ag* due, proper ▷ *sm* debt; (*Comm: dare*) debit; **a tempo ~** at the right time

'debole *ag* weak, feeble; (*suono*) faint; (*luce*) dim ▷ *sm* weakness; **debo'lezza** *sf* weakness

debut'tare *vi* to make one's debut

deca'denza [deka'dɛntsa] *sf* decline; (*Dir*) loss, forfeiture

decaffei'nato, -a *ag* decaffeinated

decapi'tare *vt* to decapitate, behead

decappot'tabile *ag, sf* convertible

de'cennio [de'tʃennjo] *sm* decade

de'cente [de'tʃɛnte] *ag* decent, respectable, proper; *(accettabile)* satisfactory, decent

de'cesso [de'tʃɛsso] *sm* death

de'cidere [de'tʃidere] *vt*: ~ **qc** to decide on sth; *(questione, lite)* to settle sth; ~ **di fare/che** to decide to do/that; ~ **di qc** *(cosa)* to determine sth; **decidersi (a fare)** to decide (to do), make up one's mind (to do)

deci'frare [detʃi'frare] *vt* to decode; *(fig)* to decipher, make out

deci'male [detʃi'male] *ag* decimal

'decimo, -a ['dɛtʃimo] *num* tenth

de'cina [de'tʃina] *sf* ten; *(circa dieci)*: **una ~ (di)** about ten

de'cisi *ecc* [de'tʃizi] *vb vedi* **decidere**

decisi'one [detʃi'zjone] *sf* decision; **prendere una ~** to make a decision

deci'sivo, -a [detʃi'zivo] *ag* *(gen)* decisive; *(fattore)* deciding

de'ciso, -a [de'tʃizo] *pp di* **decidere**

decli'nare *vi* *(pendio)* to slope down; *(fig: diminuire)* to decline ▷ *vt* to decline

declinazi'one *sf* *(Ling)* declension

de'clino *sm* decline

decodifica'tore *sm* *(Tel)* decoder

decol'lare *vi* *(Aer)* to take off; **de'collo** *sm* take-off

deco'rare *vt* to decorate; **decorazi'one** *sf* decoration

de'creto *sm* decree; **decreto legge** *decree with the force of law*

'dedica, -che *sf* dedication

dedi'care *vt* to dedicate; **dedicarsi** *vpr* **dedicarsi a** to devote o.s. to

dedicherò *ecc* [dedike'rɔ] *vb vedi* **dedicare**

'dedito, -a *ag*: ~ **a** *(studio ecc)* dedicated o devoted to; *(vizio)* addicted to

de'duco *ecc vb vedi* **dedurre**

de'durre *vt* *(concludere)* to deduce; *(defalcare)* to deduct

de'dussi *ecc vb vedi* **dedurre**

defici'ente [defi'tʃɛnte] *ag* *(mancante)*: ~ **di** deficient in; *(insufficiente)* insufficient ▷ *sm/f* mental defective; *(peg: cretino)* idiot

'deficit ['dɛfitʃit] *sm inv* *(Econ)* deficit

defi'nire *vt* to define; *(risolvere)* to settle; **defini'tiva** *sf* **in ~** *(dopotutto)* in the end; *(dunque)* hence; **defini'tivo, -a** *ag* definitive, final; **definizi'one** *sf* definition; settlement

defor'mare *vt* *(alterare)* to put out of shape; *(corpo)* to deform; *(pensiero, fatto)* to distort; **deformarsi** *vpr* to lose its shape

de'forme *ag* deformed; disfigured

de'funto, -a *ag* late *cpd* ▷ *sm/f* deceased

degene'rare [dedʒene'rare] *vi* to degenerate

de'gente [de'dʒɛnte] *sm/f* *(in ospedale)* in-patient

deglu'tire *vt* to swallow

de'gnare [deɲ'ɲare] *vt*: ~ **qn della propria presenza** to honour sb with one's presence; **degnarsi** *vpr* **degnarsi di fare qc** to deign o condescend to do sth

'degno, -a ['deɲɲo] *ag* dignified; ~ **di** worthy of; ~ **di lode** praiseworthy

de'grado *sm*; **degrado urbano** urban decline

'delega, -ghe *sf* *(procura)* proxy

dele'terio, -a *ag* damaging; *(per salute ecc)* harmful

del'fino *sm* *(Zool)* dolphin; *(Storia)* dauphin; *(fig)* probable successor

deli'cato, -a *ag* delicate; *(salute)* delicate, frail; *(fig: gentile)* thoughtful, considerate; (: *che dimostra tatto)* tactful

delin'quente *sm/f* criminal, delinquent; **delinquente abituale** regular offender, habitual offender;

delin'quenza sf criminality, delinquency; **delinquenza minorile** juvenile delinquency

deli'rare vi to be delirious, rave; (fig) to rave

de'lirio sm delirium; (ragionamento insensato) raving; (fig): **andare/ mandare in ~** to go/send into a frenzy

de'litto sm crime

delizi'oso, -a ag delightful; (cibi) delicious

delta'plano sm hang-glider; **volo col ~** hang-gliding

delu'dente ag disappointing

de'ludere vt to disappoint; **delusi'one** sf disappointment; **de'luso, -a** pp di **deludere**

'demmo vb vedi **dare**

demo'cratico, -a, -ci, -che ag democratic

democra'zia [demokrat'tsia] sf democracy

demo'lire vt to demolish

de'monio sm demon, devil; **il D~** the Devil

de'naro sm money

densità sf inv density

'denso, -a ag thick, dense

den'tale ag dental

'dente sm tooth; (di forchetta) prong; **al ~** (Cuc: pasta) al dente; **denti del giudizio** wisdom teeth; **denti da latte** milk teeth; **denti'era** sf (set of) false teeth pl

denti'fricio [denti'fritʃo] sm toothpaste

den'tista, -i, -e sm/f dentist

'dentro av inside; (in casa) indoors; (fig: nell'intimo) inwardly ▷ prep **~ (a)** in; **piegato in ~** folded over; **qui/là ~** in here/there; **~ di sé** (pensare, brontolare) to oneself

de'nuncia, -ce o **cie** [de'nuntʃa] sf denunciation; declaration; **denuncia dei redditi** (income) tax return

denunci'are [denun'tʃare] vt to denounce; (dichiarare) to declare; (persona, smarrimento ecc) report; **vorrei ~ un furto** I'd like to report a theft

denu'trito, -a ag undernourished

denutrizi'one [denutrit'tsjone] sf malnutrition

deodo'rante sm deodorant

depe'rire vi to waste away

depi'larsi vpr: **~ (le gambe)** (con rasoio) to shave (one's legs); (con ceretta) to wax (one's legs)

depila'torio, -a ag hair-removing cpd, depilatory

dépli'ant [depli'ã] sm inv leaflet; (opuscolo) brochure

deplo'revole ag deplorable

de'pone, de'pongo ecc vb vedi **deporre**

de'porre vt (depositare) to put down; (rimuovere: da una carica) to remove; (: re) to depose; (Dir) to testify

depor'tare vt to deport

de'posi ecc vb vedi **deporre**

deposi'tare vt (gen, Geo, Econ) to deposit; (lasciare) to leave; (merci) to store; **depositarsi** vpr (sabbia, polvere) to settle

de'posito sm deposit; (luogo) warehouse; depot; (: Mil) depot; **deposito bagagli** left-luggage office

deposizi'one [depozit'tsjone] sf deposition; (da una carica) removal

depra'vato, -a ag depraved ▷ sm/f degenerate

depre'dare vt to rob, plunder

depressi'one sf depression

de'presso, -a pp di **deprimere** ▷ ag depressed

deprez'zare [depret'tsare] vt (Econ) to depreciate

depri'mente ag depressing

de'primere vt to depress

depu'rare vt to purify

depu'tato sm (Pol) deputy, ≈ Member of Parliament (BRIT), ≈ Member of Congress (US)

deragli'are [deraʎ'ʎare] vi to be

derailed; **far ~** to derail

de'ridere vt to mock, deride

de'risi ecc vb vedi **deridere**

de'riva sf (Naut, Aer) drift; **andare alla ~** (anche fig) to drift

deri'vare vi **~ da** to derive from ▷ vt to derive; (corso d'acqua) to divert

derma'tologo, -a, -gi, -ghe sm/f dermatologist

deru'bare vt to rob

des'crivere vt to describe; **descrizi'one** sf description

de'serto, -a ag deserted ▷ sm (Geo) desert; **isola deserta** desert island

deside'rare vt to want, wish for; (sessualmente) to desire; **~ fare/che qn faccia** to want o wish to do/sb to do; **desidera fare una passeggiata?** would you like to go for a walk?

desi'derio sm wish; (più intenso, carnale) desire

deside'roso, -a ag **~ di** longing o eager for

desi'nenza [dezi'nɛntsa] sf (Ling) ending, inflexion

de'sistere vi **~ da** to give up, desist from

deso'lato, -a ag (paesaggio) desolate; (persona: spiacente) sorry

'dessi ecc vb vedi **dare**

'deste ecc vb vedi **dare**

desti'nare vt to destine; (assegnare) to appoint, assign; (indirizzare) to address; **~ qc a qn** to intend to give sth to sb, intend sb to have sth; **destina'tario, -a** sm/f (di lettera) addressee

destinazi'one [destinat'tsjone] sf destination; (uso) purpose

des'tino sm destiny, fate

destitu'ire vt to dismiss, remove

'destra sf (mano) right hand; (parte) right (side); (Pol): **la ~** the Right; **a ~** (essere) on the right; (andare) to the right

destreggi'arsi [destred'dʒarsi] vpr to manoeuvre (BRIT), maneuver (US)

des'trezza [des'trettsa] sf skill, dexterity

'destro, -a ag right, right-hand

dete'nuto, -a sm/f prisoner

deter'gente [deter'dʒɛnte] ag (crema, latte) cleansing ▷ sm cleanser

Attenzione! In inglese esiste la parola detergent che però significa detersivo.

determi'nare vt to determine

determina'tivo, -a ag determining; **articolo ~** (Ling) definite article

determi'nato, -a ag (gen) certain; (particolare) specific; (risoluto) determined, resolute

deter'sivo sm detergent

detes'tare vt to detest, hate

de'trae, de'traggo ecc vb vedi **detrarre**

de'trarre vt: **~ (da)** to deduct (from), take away (from)

de'trassi ecc vb vedi **detrarre**

'detta sf **a ~ di** according to

det'taglio [det'taʎʎo] sm detail; (Comm): **il ~** retail; **al ~** (Comm) retail; separately

det'tare vt to dictate; **~ legge** (fig) to lay down the law; **det'tato** sm dictation

'detto, -a pp di **dire** ▷ ag (soprannominato) called, known as; (già nominato) above-mentioned ▷ sm saying; **~ fatto** no sooner said than done

devas'tare vt to devastate; (fig) to ravage

devi'are vi **~ (da)** to turn off (from) ▷ vt to divert; **deviazi'one** sf (anche Aut) diversion

'devo ecc vb vedi **dovere**

devoluzi'one [devolut'tsjone] sf (Dir) devolution, transfer

de'volvere vt (Dir) to transfer, devolve

de'voto, -a ag (Rel) devout, pious; (affezionato) devoted

devozi'one [devot'tsjone] sf

devoutness; (*anche Rel*) devotion

 PAROLA CHIAVE

di (*di+il* = **del**, *di+lo* = **dello**, *di+l'* = **dell'**, *di+la* = **della**, *di+i* = **dei**, *di+gli* = **degli**, *di+le* = **delle**) *prep* **1** (*possesso, specificazione*) of; (*composto da, scritto da*) by; **la macchina di Paolo/mio fratello** Paolo's/my brother's car; **un amico di mio fratello** a friend of my brother's, one of my brother's friends; **un quadro di Botticelli** a painting by Botticelli

2 (*caratterizzazione, misura*) of; **una casa di mattoni** a brick house, a house made of bricks; **un orologio d'oro** a gold watch; **un bimbo di 3 anni** a child of 3, a 3-year-old child

3 (*causa, mezzo, modo*) with; **tremare di paura** to tremble with fear; **morire di cancro** to die of cancer; **spalmare di burro** to spread with butter

4 (*argomento*) about, of; **discutere di sport** to talk about sport

5 (*luogo: provenienza*) from; out of; **essere di Roma** to be from Rome; **uscire di casa** to come out of *o* leave the house

6 (*tempo*) in; **d'estate/d'inverno** in (the) summer/winter; **di notte** by night, at night; **di mattina/sera** in the morning/evening; **di lunedì** on Mondays

▷ *det* (*una certa quantità di*) some; (: *negativo*) any; (*interrogativo*) any; some; **del pane** (some) bread; **delle caramelle** (some) sweets; **degli amici miei** some friends of mine; **vuoi del vino?** do you want some *o* any wine?

dia'bete *sm* diabetes *sg*
dia'betico, -a, ci, che *ag, sm/f* diabetic
dia'framma, -i *sm* (*divisione*) screen; (*Anat, Fot, contraccettivo*) diaphragm

di'agnosi [di'aɲɲozi] *sf* diagnosis *sg*
diago'nale *ag, sf* diagonal
dia'gramma, -i *sm* diagram
dia'letto *sm* dialect
di'alisi *sf* dialysis *sg*
di'alogo, -ghi *sm* dialogue
dia'mante *sm* diamond
di'ametro *sm* diameter
diaposi'tiva *sf* transparency, slide
di'ario *sm* diary
diar'rea *sf* diarrhoea
di'avolo *sm* devil
di'battito *sm* debate, discussion
'dice ['ditʃe] *vb vedi* **dire**
di'cembre [di'tʃɛmbre] *sm* December
dice'ria [ditʃe'ria] *sf* rumour, piece of gossip
dichia'rare [dikja'rare] *vt* to declare; **dichiararsi** *vpr* to declare o.s.; (*innamorato*) to declare one's love; **dichiararsi vinto** to acknowledge defeat; **dichiarazi'one** *sf* declaration; **dichiarazione dei redditi** statement of income; (*modulo*) tax return
dician'nove [ditʃan'nɔve] *num* nineteen
dicias'sette [ditʃas'sɛtte] *num* seventeen
dici'otto [di'tʃɔtto] *num* eighteen
dici'tura [ditʃi'tura] *sf* words *pl*, wording
'dico *ecc vb vedi* **dire**
didasca'lia *sf* (*di illustrazione*) caption; (*Cine*) subtitle; (*Teatro*) stage directions *pl*
di'eci ['djɛtʃi] *num* ten
di'edi *ecc vb vedi* **dare**
'diesel ['dizəl] *sm inv* diesel engine
dies'sino, -a *sm/f* member of the DS political party
di'eta *sf* diet; **essere a ~** to be on a diet
di'etro *av* behind; (*in fondo*) at the back ▷ *prep* behind; (*tempo: dopo*) after ▷ *sm* back, rear ▷ *ag inv* back *cpd*; **le zampe di ~** the hind legs; **~ richiesta** on demand; (*scritta*) on application

di'fendere vt to defend; **difendersi** vpr (cavarsela) to get by; **difendersi da/contro** to defend o.s. from/against; **difendersi dal freddo** to protect o.s. from the cold; **difen'sore, -a** sm/f defender; **avvocato difensore** counsel for the defence; **di'fesa** sf defence

di'fesi ecc vb vedi **difendere**

di'fetto sm (mancanza): **~ di** lack of; shortage of; (di fabbricazione) fault, flaw, defect; (morale) fault, failing, defect; (fisico) defect; **far ~** to be lacking; **in ~** at fault; in the wrong; **difet'toso, -a** ag defective, faulty

diffe'rente ag different

diffe'renza [diffe'rentsa] sf difference; **a ~ di** unlike

diffe'rire vt to postpone, defer ▷ vi to be different

diffe'rita sf: **in ~** (trasmettere) prerecorded

dif'ficile [dif'fitʃile] ag difficult; (persona) hard to please, difficult (to please); (poco probabile): **è ~ che sia libero** it is unlikely that he'll be free ▷ sm difficult part; difficulty; **difficoltà** sf inv difficulty

diffi'dente ag suspicious, distrustful

diffi'denza sf suspicion, distrust

dif'fondere vt (luce, calore) to diffuse; (notizie) to spread, circulate; **diffondersi** vpr to spread

dif'fusi ecc vb vedi **diffondere**

dif'fuso, -a pp di **diffondere** ▷ ag (malattia, fenomeno) widespread

'diga, -ghe sf dam; (portuale) breakwater

dige'rente [didʒe'rɛnte] ag (apparato) digestive

dige'rire [didʒe'rire] vt to digest; **digesti'one** sf digestion; **diges'tivo, -a** ag digestive ▷ sm (after-dinner) liqueur

digi'tale [didʒi'tale] ag digital; (delle dita) finger cpd, digital ▷ sf (Bot) foxglove

digi'tare [didʒi'tare] vt, vi (Inform) to key (in)

digiu'nare [didʒu'nare] vi to starve o.s.; (Rel) to fast; **digi'uno, -a** ag **essere digiuno** not to have eaten ▷ sm fast; **a digiuno** on an empty stomach

dignità [diɲɲi'ta] sf inv dignity

'DIGOS [uiɣɔs] sigla f (= Divisione Investigazioni Generali e Operazioni Speciali) police department dealing with political security

digri'gnare [digriɲ'ɲare] vt: **~ i denti** to grind one's teeth

dilapi'dare vt to squander, waste

dila'tare vt to dilate; (gas) to cause to expand; (passaggio, cavità) to open (up); **dilatarsi** vpr to dilate; (Fisica) to expand

dilazio'nare [dilattsjo'nare] vt to delay, defer

di'lemma, -i sm dilemma

dilet'tante sm/f dilettante; (anche Sport) amateur

dili'gente [dili'dʒɛnte] ag (scrupoloso) diligent; (accurato) careful, accurate

dilu'ire vt to dilute

dilun'garsi vpr (fig): **~ su** to talk at length on o about

diluvi'are vb impers to pour (down)

di'luvio sm downpour; (inondazione, fig) flood

dima'grante ag slimming cpd

dima'grire vi to get thinner, lose weight

dime'nare vt to wave, shake; **dimenarsi** vpr to toss and turn; (fig) to struggle; **~ la coda** (cane) to wag its tail

dimensi'one sf dimension; (grandezza) size

dimenti'canza [dimenti'kantsa] sf forgetfulness; (errore) oversight, slip; **per ~** inadvertently

dimenti'care vt to forget; **ho dimenticato la chiave/il passaporto** I forgot the key/my

passport; **dimenticarsi** vpr
dimenticarsi di qc to forget sth

dimesti'chezza [dimesti'kettsa] sf
familiarity

di'mettere vt: ~ **qn da** to dismiss
sb from; (dall'ospedale) to discharge
sb from; **dimettersi** vpr **dimettersi
(da)** to resign (from)

dimez'zare [dimed'dzare] vt to halve

diminu'ire vt to reduce, diminish;
(prezzi) to bring down, reduce ▷ vi to
decrease, diminish; (rumore) to die
down, die away; (prezzi) to fall, go
down

diminu'tivo, -a ag, sm diminutive

diminuzi'one sf decreasing,
diminishing

di'misi ecc vb vedi **dimettere**

dimissi'oni sfpl resignation sg; **dare**
o **presentare le ~** to resign, hand in
one's resignation

dimos'trare vt to demonstrate,
show; (provare) to prove,
demonstrate; **dimostrarsi** vpr
dimostrarsi molto abile to show o.s.
o prove to be very clever; **dimostra
30 anni** he looks about 30 (years old);
dimostrazi'one sf demonstration;
proof

di'namica sf dynamics sg

di'namico, -a, -ci, -che ag dynamic

dina'mite sf dynamite

'dinamo sf inv dynamo

dino'sauro sm dinosaur

din'torni smpl outskirts; **nei ~ di** in the
vicinity o neighbourhood of

'dio (pl **'dei**) sm god; **D~** God; **gli dei**
the gods; **D~ mio!** my goodness!,
my God!

diparti'mento sm department

dipen'dente ag dependent ▷ sm/f
employee; **dipendente statale** state
employee

di'pendere vi: ~ **da** to depend on;
(finanziariamente) to be dependent on;
(derivare) to come from, be due to

di'pesi ecc vb vedi **dipendere**

di'pingere [di'pindʒere] vt to paint

di'pinsi ecc vb vedi **dipingere**

di'pinto, -a pp di **dipingere** ▷ sm
painting

di'ploma, -i sm diploma

diplo'matico, -a, -ci, -che ag
diplomatic ▷ sm diplomat

diploma'zia [diplomat'tsia] sf
diplomacy

di'porto: **imbarcazione da ~** sf
pleasure craft

dira'dare vt to thin (out); (visite) to
reduce, make less frequent; **diradarsi**
vpr to disperse; (nebbia) to clear (up)

'dire vt to say; (segreto, fatto) to tell; ~
qc a qn to tell sb sth; ~ **a qn di fare qc**
to tell sb to do sth; ~ **di si/no** to say
yes/no; **si dice che ...** they say that
...; **si ~bbe che ...** it looks (o sounds)
as though ...; **dica, signora?** (in un
negozio) yes, Madam, can I help you?;
come si dice in inglese...? what's the
English (word) for ...?

di'ressi ecc vb vedi **dirigere**

di'retta sf vedi **diretto**

di'retto, -a pp di **dirigere** ▷ ag direct
▷ sm (Ferr) through train

diret'tore, -'trice sm/f (di azienda)
director: manager/ess; (di scuola
elementare) head (teacher) (BRIT),
principal (US); **direttore d'orchestra**
conductor; **direttore vendite** sales
director o manager

direzi'one [diret'tsjone] sf board
of directors; management; (senso di
movimento) direction; **in ~ di** in the
direction of, towards

diri'gente [diri'dʒɛnte] sm/f
executive; (Pol) leader ▷ ag **classe ~**
ruling class

di'rigere [di'ridʒere] vt to direct;
(impresa) to run, manage; (Mus) to
conduct; **dirigersi** vpr **dirigersi
verso** o **a** to make o head for

dirim'petto av opposite; ~ **a**
opposite, facing

di'ritto, -a ag straight; (onesto)

straight, upright ▷ *av* straight, directly; **andare ~** to go straight on ▷ *sm* right side; (*Tennis*) forehand; (*Maglia*) plain stitch; (*prerogativa*) right; (*leggi, scienza*): **il ~** law; **diritti** *smpl* (*tasse*) duty *sg*; **stare ~** to stand up straight; **aver ~ a qc** to be entitled to sth; **diritti d'autore** royalties

dirotta'mento *sm*; **dirottamento (aereo)** hijack

dirot'tare *vt* (*nave, aereo*) to change the course of; (*aereo sotto minaccia*) to hijack; (*traffico*) to divert ▷ *vi* (*nave, aereo*) to change course; **dirotta'tore, -'trice** *sm/f* hijacker

di'rotto, -a *ag* (*pioggia*) torrential; (*pianto*) unrestrained; **piovere a ~** to pour; **piangere a ~** to cry one's heart out

di'rupo *sm* crag, precipice

di'sabile *sm/f* disabled person ▷ *ag* disabled; **i disabili** the disabled

disabi'tato, -a *ag* uninhabited

disabitu'arsi *vpr*: **~ a** to get out of the habit of

disac'cordo *sm* disagreement

disadat'tato, -a *ag* (*Psic*) maladjusted

disa'dorno, -a *ag* plain, unadorned

disagi'ato, -a [diza'dʒato] *ag* poor, needy; (*vita*) hard

di'sagio [di'zadʒo] *sm* discomfort; (*disturbo*) inconvenience; (*fig: imbarazzo*) embarrassment; **essere a ~** to be ill at ease

disappro'vare *vt* to disapprove of; **disapprovazi'one** *sf* disapproval

disap'punto *sm* disappointment

disar'mare *vt, vi* to disarm; **di'sarmo** *sm* (*Mil*) disarmament

di'sastro *sm* disaster

disas'troso, -a *ag* disastrous

disat'tento, -a *ag* inattentive; **disattenzi'one** *sf* carelessness, lack of attention

disavven'tura *sf* misadventure, mishap

dis'capito *sm*: **a ~ di** to the detriment of

dis'carica, -che *sf* (*di rifiuti*) rubbish tip *o* dump

di'scendere [diʃʃendere] *vt* to go (*o* come) down ▷ *vi* to go (*o* come) down; (*strada*) to go down; (*smontare*) to get off; **~ da** (*famiglia*) to be descended from; **~ dalla macchina/dal treno** to get out of the car/out of *o* off the train; **~ da cavallo** to dismount, get off one's horse

di'scesa [diʃʃesa] *sf* descent; (*pendio*) slope; **in ~** (*strada*) downhill *cpd*, sloping; **discesa libera** (*Sci*) downhill (race)

disci'plina [diʃʃi'plina] *sf* discipline

'disco, -schi *sm* disc; (*Sport*) discus; (*fonografico*) record, (*Inform*) disk; **disco orario** (*Aut*) parking disc; **disco rigido** (*Inform*) hard disk; **disco volante** flying saucer

disco'grafico, -a, ci, che *ag* record *cpd*, recording *cpd* ▷ *sm* record producer; **casa discografica** record(ing) company

dis'correre *vi*: **~ (di)** to talk (about)

dis'corso, -a *pp di* **discorrere** ▷ *sm* speech; (*conversazione*) conversation, talk

disco'teca, -che *sf* (*raccolta*) record library; (*locale*) disco

discount [dis'kaunt] *sm inv* (*supermercato*) cut-price supermarket

discre'panza [diskre'pantsa] *sf* disagreement

dis'creto, -a *ag* discreet; (*abbastanza buono*) reasonable, fair

discriminazi'one [diskriminat'tsjone] *sf* discrimination

dis'cussi *ecc vb vedi* **discutere**

discussi'one *sf* discussion; (*litigio*) argument; **fuori ~** out of the question

dis'cutere *vt* to discuss, debate; (*contestare*) to question ▷ *vi* (*conversare*): **~ (di)** to discuss; (*litigare*) to argue

dis'detta *sf* (*di prenotazione ecc*) cancellation; (*sfortuna*) bad luck

dis'dire *vt* (*prenotazione*) to cancel; (*Dir*): **~ un contratto d'affitto** to give notice (to quit); **vorrei ~ la mia prenotazione** I want to cancel my booking

dise'gnare [disɛɲ'ɲare] *vt* to draw; (*progettare*) to design; (*fig*) to outline

disegna'tore, -'trice *sm/f* designer

di'segno [di'seɲɲo] *sm* drawing; design; outline; **disegno di legge** (*Dir*) bill

diser'bante *sm* weed-killer

diser'tare *vt, vi* to desert

dis'fare *vt* to undo; (*valigie*) to unpack; (*meccanismo*) to take to pieces; (*neve*) to melt; **disfarsi** *vpr* to come undone; (*neve*) to melt; **~ il letto** to strip the bed; **disfarsi di qn** (*liberarsi*) to get rid of sb; **dis'fatto, -a** *pp di* **disfare**

dis'gelo [diz'dʒɛlo] *sm* thaw

dis'grazia [diz'grattsja] *sf* (*sventura*) misfortune; (*incidente*) accident, mishap

disgu'ido *sm* hitch; **disguido postale** error in postal delivery

disgus'tare *vt* to disgust

dis'gusto *sm* disgust; **disgus'toso, -a** *ag* disgusting

disidra'tare *vt* to dehydrate

disimpa'rare *vt* to forget

disinfet'tante *ag, sm* disinfectant

disinfet'tare *vt* to disinfect

disini'bito, -a *ag* uninhibited

disinstal'lare *vt* (*software*) to uninstall

disinte'grare *vt, vi* to disintegrate; **disintegrarsi** *vpr* to disintegrate

disinteres'sarsi *vpr* **~ di** to take no interest in

disinte'resse *sm* indifference; (*generosità*) unselfishness

disintossicarsi *vpr* to clear out one's system; (*alcolizzato, drogato*)

to be treated for alcoholism (*o drug addiction*)

disin'volto, -a *ag* casual, free and easy

dismi'sura *sf* excess; **a ~** to excess, excessively

disoccu'pato, -a *ag* unemployed ▷ *sm/f* unemployed person; **disoccupazi'one** *sf* unemployment

diso'nesto, -a *ag* dishonest

disordi'nato, -a *ag* untidy; (*privo di misura*) irregular, wild

di'sordine *sm* (*confusione*) disorder, confusion; (*sregolatezza*) debauchery; **disordini** *smpl* (*Pol ecc*) disorder *sg*; (*tumulti*) riots

disorien'tare *vt* to disorientate

disorien'tato, -a *ag* disorientated

'dispari *ag inv* odd, uneven

dis'parte: **in ~** *av* (*da lato*) aside, apart; **tenersi** *o* **starsene in ~** to keep to o.s., hold o.s. aloof

dispendi'oso, -a *ag* expensive

dis'pensa *sf* pantry, larder; (*mobile*) sideboard; (*Dir*) exemption; (*Rel*) dispensation; (*fascicolo*) number, issue

dispe'rato, -a *ag* (*persona*) in despair; (*caso, tentativo*) desperate

disperazi'one *sf* despair

dis'perdere *vt* (*disseminare*) to disperse; (*Mil*) to scatter, rout; (*fig: consumare*) to waste, squander; **disperdersi** *vpr* to disperse; to scatter; **dis'perso, -a** *pp di* **disperdere** ▷ *sm/f* missing person

dis'petto *sm* spite *no pl*, spitefulness *no pl*; **fare un ~ a qn** to play a (nasty) trick on sb; **a ~ di** in spite of; **dispet'toso, -a** *ag* spiteful

dispia'cere [dispja'tʃere] *sm* (*rammarico*) regret, sorrow; (*dolore*) grief; **dispiaceri** *smpl* (*preoccupazioni*) troubles, worries *vi* **~ a** to displease *vb impers* **mi dispiace (che)** I am sorry (that); **le dispiace se...?** do you mind if ...?

dis'pone, dis'pongo *ecc vb vedi*

disporre

dispo'nibile *ag* available

dis'porre *vt* (*sistemare*) to arrange; (*preparare*) to prepare; (*Dir*) to order; (*persuadere*): **~ qn a** to incline o dispose sb towards ▷ *vi* (*decidere*) to decide; (*usufruire*): **~ di** to use, have at one's disposal; (*essere dotato*): **~ di** to have

dis'posi *vb vedi* **disporre**

disposi'tivo *sm* (*meccanismo*) device

disposizi'one [dispozit'tsjone] *sf* arrangement, layout; (*stato d'animo*) mood; (*tendenza*) bent, inclination; (*comando*) order; (*Dir*) provision, regulation; **a ~ di qn** at sb's disposal

dis'posto, -a *pp di* **disporre**

disprez'zare [dispret'tsare] *vt* to despise

dis'prezzo [dis'prɛttso] *sm* contempt

'disputa *sf* dispute, quarrel

dispu'tare *vt* (*contendere*) to dispute, contest; (*gara*) to take part in ▷ *vi* to quarrel; **~ di** to discuss; **disputarsi qc** to fight for sth

'disse *vb vedi* **dire**

dissente'ria *sf* dysentery

dissen'tire *vi*: **~ (da)** to disagree (with)

disse'tante *ag* refreshing

'dissi *vb vedi* **dire**

dissimu'lare *vt* (*fingere*) to dissemble; (*nascondere*) to conceal

dissi'pare *vt* to dissipate; (*scialacquare*) to squander, waste

dissu'adere *vt*: **~ qn da** to dissuade sb from

dissua'sore *sm*: **~ di velocità** (*Auto*) speed bump

distac'care *vt* to detach, separate; (*Sport*) to leave behind; **distaccarsi** *vpr* to be detached; (*fig*) to stand out; **distaccarsi da** (*fig: allontanarsi*) to grow away from

dis'tacco, -chi *sm* (*separazione*) separation; (*fig: indifferenza*) detachment; (*Sport*): **vincere con un ~ di ...** to win by a distance of ...

dis'tante *av* far away ▷ *ag*: **~ (da)** distant (from), far away (from)

dis'tanza [dis'tantsa] *sf* distance

distanzi'are [distan'tsjare] *vt* to space out, place at intervals; (*Sport*) to outdistance; (*fig: superare*) to outstrip, surpass

dis'tare *vi*: **distiamo pochi chilometri da Roma** we are only a few kilometres (away) from Rome; **quanto dista il centro da qui?** how far is the town centre?

dis'tendere *vt* (*coperta*) to spread out; (*gambe*) to stretch (out); (*mettere a giacere*) to lay; (*rilassare: muscoli, nervi*) to relax; **distendersi** *vpr* (*rilassarsi*) to relax; (*sdraiarsi*) to lie down

dis'tesa *sf* expanse, stretch

dis'teso, -a *pp di* **distendere**

distil'lare *vt* to distil

distille'ria *sf* distillery

dis'tinguere *vt* to distinguish; **distinguersi** *vpr* (*essere riconoscibile*) to be distinguished; (*emergere*) to stand out, be conspicuous, distinguish o.s.

dis'tinta *sf* (*nota*) note; (*elenco*) list; **distinta di versamento** pay-in slip

distin'tivo, -a *ag* distinctive; distinguishing ▷ *sm* badge

dis'tinto, -a *pp di* **distinguere** ▷ *ag* (*dignitoso ed elegante*) distinguished; **"distinti saluti"** (*in lettera*) yours faithfully

distinzi'one [distin'tsjone] *sf* distinction

dis'togliere [dis'tɔʎʎere] *vt*: **~ da** to take away from; (*fig*) to dissuade from

distorsi'one *sf* (*Med*) sprain; (*Fisica, Ottica*) distortion

dis'trarre *vt* to distract; (*divertire*) to entertain, amuse; **distrarsi** *vpr* (*non fare attenzione*) to be distracted, let one's mind wander; (*svagarsi*) to amuse o enjoy o.s.; **dis'tratto, -a** *pp di* **distrarre** ▷ *ag* absent-minded; (*disattento*) inattentive; **distrazi'one**

sf absent-mindedness; inattention; (*svago*) distraction, entertainment

dis'tretto *sm* district

distribu'ire *vt* to distribute; (*Carte*) to deal (out); (*posta*) to deliver; (*lavoro*) to allocate, assign; (*ripartire*) to share out; **distribu'tore** *sm* (*di benzina*) petrol (BRIT) *o* gas (US) pump; (*Aut, Elettr*) distributor; **distributore automatico** vending machine

distri'care *vt* to disentangle, unravel; **districarsi** *vpr* (*tirarsi fuori*): **districarsi da** to get out of, disentangle o.s. from

dis'truggere [dis'truddʒere] *vt* to destroy; **distruzi'one** *sf* destruction

distur'bare *vt* to disturb, trouble; (*sonno, lezioni*) to disturb, interrupt; **disturbarsi** *vpr* to put o.s. out

dis'turbo *sm* trouble, bother, inconvenience; (*indisposizione*) (slight) disorder, ailment; **scusi il ~** I'm sorry to trouble you

disubbidi'ente *ag* disobedient

disubbi'dire *vi*: **~ (a qn)** to disobey (sb)

disu'mano, -a *ag* inhuman

di'tale *sm* thimble

'dito (*pl(f)* **'dita**) *sm* finger; (*misura*) finger, finger's breadth; **dito (del piede)** toe

'ditta *sf* firm, business

ditta'tore *sm* dictator

ditta'tura *sf* dictatorship

dit'tongo, -ghi *sm* diphthong

di'urno, -a *ag* day *cpd*, daytime *cpd*

'diva *sf vedi* **divo**

di'vano *sm* sofa; divan; **divano letto** bed settee, sofa bed

divari'care *vt* to open wide

di'vario *sm* difference

diven'tare *vi* to become; **~ famoso/ professore** to become famous/a teacher

diversifi'care *vt* to diversify, vary; to differentiate; **diversificarsi** *vpr* **diversificarsi (per)** to differ (in)

diversità *sf inv* difference, diversity; (*varietà*) variety

diver'sivo *sm* diversion, distraction

di'verso, -a *ag* (*differente*): **~ (da)** different (from); **diversi, -e** *det pl* several, various; (*Comm*) sundry *pron pl* several (people), many (people)

diver'tente *ag* amusing

diverti'mento *sm* amusement, pleasure; (*passatempo*) pastime, recreation

diver'tire *vt* to amuse, entertain; **divertirsi** *vpr* to amuse *o* enjoy o.s.

di'videre *vt* (*anche Mat*) to divide; (*distribuire, ripartire*) to divide (up), split (up); **dividersi** *vpr* (*separarsi*) to separate; (*strade*) to fork

divi'eto *sm* prohibition; **"~ di sosta"** (*Aut*) "no parking"

divinco'larsi *vpr* to wriggle, writhe

di'vino, -a *ag* divine

di'visa *sf* (*Mil ecc*) uniform; (*Comm*) foreign currency

di'visi *ecc vb vedi* **dividere**

divisi'one *sf* division

'divo, -a *sm/f* star

divo'rare *vt* to devour

divorzi'are [divor'tsjare] *vi*: **~ (da qn)** to divorce (sb)

di'vorzio [di'vɔrtsjo] *sm* divorce

divul'gare *vt* to divulge, disclose; (*rendere comprensibile*) to popularize

dizio'nario [ditsjo'narjo] *sm* dictionary

DJ [di'dʒei] *sigla m/f* (= *Disc Jockey*) DJ

do *sm* (*Mus*) C; (: *solfeggiando*) do(h)

dobbi'amo *vb vedi* **dovere**

D.O.C. [dɔk] *abbr* (= *denominazione di origine controllata*) label guaranteeing the quality of wine

'doccia, -ce ['dɔttʃa] *sf* (*bagno*) shower; **fare la ~** to have a shower

docciaschi'uma [dottʃas'kjuma] *sm inv* shower gel

do'cente [do'tʃɛnte] *ag* teaching ▷ *sm/f* teacher; (*di università*) lecturer

'docile ['dɔtʃile] *ag* docile

documen'tario *sm* documentary
documentarsi *vpr*: ~ **(su)** to gather information *o* material (about)
docu'mento *sm* document; **documenti** *smpl* (*d'identità ecc*) papers
dodi'cesimo, -a [dodi'tʃɛzimo] *num* twelfth
'dodici ['doditʃi] *num* twelve
do'gana *sf* (*ufficio*) customs *pl*; (*tassa*) (customs) duty; **passare la ~** to go through customs; **dogani'ere** *sm* customs officer
'doglie ['dɔʎʎe] *sfpl* (*Med*) labour *sg*, labour pains
'dolce ['doltʃe] *ag* sweet; (*carattere, persona*) gentle, mild; (*fig: mite: clima*) mild; (*non ripido: pendio*) gentle ▷ *sm* (*sapore dolce*) sweetness, sweet taste; (*Cuc: portata*) sweet, dessert; (: *torta*) cake; **dolcifi'cante** *sm* sweetener
'dollaro *sm* dollar
Dolo'miti *sfpl*: **le ~** the Dolomites
do'lore *sm* (*fisico*) pain; (*morale*) sorrow, grief; **dolo'roso, -a** *ag* painful; sorrowful, sad
do'manda *sf* (*interrogazione*) question; (*richiesta*) demand; (: *cortese*) request; (*Dir: richiesta scritta*) application; (*Econ*): **la ~** demand; **fare una ~ a qn** to ask sb a question; **fare ~ (per un lavoro)** to apply (for a job)
doman'dare *vt* (*per avere*) to ask for; (*per sapere*) to ask; (*esigere*) to demand; **domandarsi** *vpr* to wonder; to ask o.s.; ~ **qc a qn** to ask sb for sth; to ask sb sth
do'mani *av* tomorrow ▷ *sm*: **il ~** (*il futuro*) the future; (*il giorno successivo*) the next day; ~ **l'altro** the day after tomorrow
do'mare *vt* to tame
doma'tore, -'trice *sm/f* (*gen*) tamer; **domatore di cavalli** horsebreaker; **domatore di leoni** lion tamer
domat'tina *av* tomorrow morning
do'menica, -che *sf* Sunday; **di** *o* **la ~** on Sundays
do'mestico, -a, -ci, -che *ag* domestic ▷ *sm/f* servant, domestic
domi'cilio [domi'tʃiljo] *sm* (*Dir*) domicile, place of residence
domi'nare *vt* to dominate; (*fig: sentimenti*) to control, master ▷ *vi* to be in the dominant position
do'nare *vt* to give, present; (*per beneficenza ecc*) to donate ▷ *vi* (*fig*): ~ **a** to suit, become; ~ **sangue** to give blood; **dona'tore, -'trice** *sm/f* donor; **donatore di sangue/di organi** blood/organ donor
dondo'lare *vt* (*cullare*) to rock; **dondolarsi** *vpr* to swing, sway; **'dondolo** *sm* **sedia/cavallo a dondolo** rocking chair/horse
'donna *sf* woman; **donna di casa** housewife; home-loving woman; **donna di servizio** maid
donnai'olo *sm* ladykiller
'donnola *sf* weasel
'dono *sm* gift
doping ['dɔpiŋ] *sm* doping
'dopo *av* (*tempo*) afterwards; (*più tardi*) later; (*luogo*) after, next ▷ *prep* after ▷ *cong* (*temporale*): ~ **aver studiato** after having studied; ~ **mangiato va a dormire** after having eaten *o* after a meal he goes for a sleep ▷ *ag inv* **il giorno ~** the following day; **un anno ~** a year later; ~ **di me/lui** after me/him; ~, **a ~!** see you later!
dopo'barba *sm inv* after-shave
dopodo'mani *av* the day after tomorrow
doposcì [dopoʃʃi] *sm inv* après-ski outfit
dopo'sole *sm inv* aftersun (lotion)
dopo'tutto *av* (*tutto considerato*) after all
doppi'aggio [dop'pjaddʒo] *sm* (*Cinema*) dubbing
doppi'are *vt* (*Naut*) to round; (*Sport*) to lap; (*Cinema*) to dub
'doppio, -a *ag* double; (*fig: falso*)

double-dealing, deceitful ▷ *sm* (*quantità*): **il ~ (di)** twice as much (*o* many), double the amount (*o* number) of; (*Sport*) doubles *pl* ▷ *av* double

doppi'one *sm* duplicate (copy)

doppio'petto *sm* double-breasted jacket

dormicchi'are [dormik'kjare] *vi* to doze

dormigli'one, -a [dormiʎ'ʎone] *sm/f* sleepyhead

dor'mire *vt*, *vi* to sleep; **andare a ~** to go to bed; **dor'mita** *sf* **farsi una dormita** to have a good sleep

dormi'torio *sm* dormitory

dormi'veglia [dormi'veʎʎa] *sm* drowsiness

'dorso *sm* back; (*di montagna*) ridge, crest; (*di libro*) spine; **a ~ di cavallo** on horseback

do'sare *vt* to measure out; (*Med*) to dose

'dose *sf* quantity, amount; (*Med*) dose

do'tato, -a *ag* **~ di** (*attrezzature*) equipped with; (*bellezza, intelligenza*) endowed with; **un uomo ~** a gifted man

'dote *sf* (*di sposa*) dowry; (*assegnata a un ente*) endowment; (*fig*) gift, talent

Dott. *abbr* (= *dottore*) Dr.

dotto'rato *sm* degree; **dottorato di ricerca** doctorate, doctor's degree

dot'tore, -essa *sm/f* doctor; **chiamate un ~** call a doctor

● **DOTTORE**

● In Italy, anyone who has a degree
● in any subject can use the title
● **dottore**. Thus a person who
● is addressed as **dottore** is not
● necessarily a doctor of medicine.

dot'trina *sf* doctrine

Dott.ssa *abbr* (= *dottoressa*) Dr.

'dove *av* (*gen*) where; (*in cui*) where, in which; (*dovunque*) wherever ▷ *cong* (*mentre, laddove*) whereas; **~ sei?/vai?** where are you?/are you going?; **dimmi dov'è** tell me where it is; **di ~ sei?** where are you from?; **per ~ si passa?** which way should we go?; **la città ~ abito** the town where *o* in which I live; **siediti ~ vuoi** sit wherever you like

do'vere *sm* (*obbligo*) duty ▷ *vt* (*essere debitore*): **~ qc (a qn)** to owe (sb) sth ▷ *vi* (*seguito dall'infinito: obbligo*) to have to; **rivolgersi a chi di ~** to apply to the appropriate authority *o* person; **lui deve farlo** he has to do it, he must do it; **quanto le devo?** how much do I owe you?; **è dovuto partire** he had to leave; **ha dovuto pagare** he had to pay; (: *intenzione*): **devo partire domani** I'm (due) to leave tomorrow; (: *probabilità*): **dev'essere tardi** it must be late; **come si deve** (*lavorare, comportarsi*) properly; **una persona come si deve** a respectable person

dove'roso, -a *ag* (right and) proper

dovrò *ecc vb vedi* **dovere**

do'vunque *av* (*in qualunque luogo*) wherever; (*dappertutto*) everywhere; **~ io vada** wherever I go

do'vuto, -a *ag* (*causato*): **~ a** due to

doz'zina [dod'dzina] *sf* dozen; **una ~ di uova** a dozen eggs

dozzi'nale [doddzi'nale] *ag* cheap, second-rate

'drago, -ghi *sm* dragon

'dramma, -i *sm* drama; **dram'matico, -a, -ci, -che** *ag* dramatic

'drastico, -a, -ci, -che *ag* drastic

'dritto, -a *ag*, *av* = **diritto**

'droga, -ghe *sf* (*sostanza aromatica*) spice; (*stupefacente*) drug; **droghe leggere/pesanti** soft/hard drugs

drogarsi *vpr* to take drugs

dro'gato, -a *sm/f* drug addict

droghe'ria [droge'ria] *sf* grocer's shop (BRIT), grocery (store) (US)

drome'dario *sm* dromedary

DS [di'ɛsse] *sigla mpl* (= *Democratici di Sinistra*) Italian left-wing party

'dubbio, -a *ag* (*incerto*) doubtful, dubious; (*ambiguo*) dubious ▷ *sm* (*incertezza*) doubt; **avere il ~ che** to be afraid that, suspect that; **mettere in ~ qc** to question sth

dubi'tare *vi* **~ di** to doubt; (*risultato*) to be doubtful of

Dub'lino *sf* Dublin

'duca, -chi *sm* duke

du'chessa [du'kessa] *sf* duchess

'due *num* two

due'cento [due'tʃɛnto] *num* two hundred ▷ *sm* **il D~** the thirteenth century

due'pezzi [due'pɛttsi] *sm* (*costume da bagno*) two-piece swimsuit; (*abito femminile*) two-piece suit

'dunque *cong* (*perciò*) so, therefore; (*riprendendo il discorso*) well (then) ▷ *sm inv* **venire al ~** to come to the point

du'omo *sm* cathedral

> Attenzione! In inglese esiste la parola *dome*, che però significa *cupola*.

dupli'cato *sm* duplicate

'duplice ['duplitʃe] *ag* double, twofold; **in ~ copia** in duplicate

du'rante *prep* during

du'rare *vi* to last; **~ fatica a** to have difficulty in

du'rezza [du'rettsa] *sf* hardness; stubbornness; harshness; toughness

'duro, -a *ag* (*pietra, lavoro, materasso, problema*) hard; (*persona: ostinato*) stubborn, obstinate; (*severo*) harsh, hard; (*voce*) harsh; (*carne*) tough ▷ *sm* hardness; (*difficoltà*) hard part; (*persona*) tough guy; **tener ~** to stand firm, hold out; **~ d'orecchi** hard of hearing

DVD [divu'di] *sigla m* (= *digital versatile* (*or*) *video disc*) DVD; (*lettore*) DVD player

e (*davV spesso* **ed**) *cong* and; **e lui?** what about him?; **e compralo!** well buy it then!

E *abbr* (= *est*) E

è *vb vedi* **essere**

eb'bene *cong* well (then)

'ebbi *ecc vb vedi* **avere**

e'braico, -a, -ci, -che *ag* Hebrew, Hebraic ▷ *sm* (*Ling*) Hebrew

e'breo, -a *ag* Jewish ▷ *sm/f* Jew/ess

EC *abbr* (= *Eurocity*) fast train connecting Western European cities

ecc. *av abbr* (= *eccetera*) etc

eccel'lente [ettʃel'lɛnte] *ag* excellent

ec'centrico, -a, -ci, -che [et'tʃɛntriko] *ag* eccentric

ecces'sivo, -a [ettʃes'sivo] *ag* excessive

ec'cesso [et'tʃɛsso] *sm* excess; **all'~** (*gentile, generoso*) to excess, excessively; **eccesso di velocità** (*Aut*) speeding

ec'cetera [et'tʃetera] *av* et cetera, and so on

ec'cetto [et'tʃɛtto] prep except, with the exception of; ~ che except, other than; ~ che (non) unless

eccezio'nale [ettʃetsjo'nale] ag exceptional

eccezi'one [ettʃet'sjone] sf exception; (Dir) objection; a ~ di with the exception of, except for; d'~ exceptional

ecci'tare [ettʃi'tare] vt (curiosità, interesse) to excite, arouse; (folla) to incite; eccitarsi vpr to get excited; (sessualmente) to become aroused

'ecco av (per dimostrare): ~ il treno! here's o here comes the train!; (dav pron): ~mi! here I am!; ~ne uno! here's one (of them)!; (dav pp): ~ fatto! there, that's it done!

ec'come av rather; ti piace? — ~! do you like it? — I'll say! o and how! o rather! (BRIT)

e'clisse sf eclipse

'eco (pl(m) 'echi) sm o f echo

ecogra'fia sf (Med) scan

ecolo'gia [ekolo'dʒia] sf ecology

eco'logico, -a, ci, che [eko'lɔdʒiko] ag ecological

econo'mia sf economy; (scienza) economics sg; (risparmio: azione) saving; fare ~ to economize, make economies; eco'nomico, -a, -ci, -che ag economic; (poco costoso) economical

ecstasy ['ɛkstazi] sf Ecstasy

'edera sf ivy

e'dicola sf newspaper kiosk o stand (US)

edi'ficio [edi'fitʃo] sm building

e'dile ag building cpd

Edim'burgo sf Edinburgh

edi'tore, -'trice ag publishing cpd ▷ sm/f publisher

Attenzione! In inglese esiste la parola editor, che però significa redattore.

edizi'one [edit'tsjone] sf edition; (tiratura) printing; edizione

straordinaria special edition

edu'care vt to educate; (gusto, mente) to train; ~ qn a fare to train sb to do; edu'cato, -a ag polite, well-mannered; educazi'one sf education; (familiare) upbringing; (comportamento) (good) manners pl; educazione fisica (Ins) physical training o education

Attenzione! In inglese esiste la parola educated, che però significa istruito.

educherò ecc [eduke'rɔ] vb vedi educare

effemi'nato, -a ag effeminate

efferve'scente [efferveʃ'ʃɛnte] ag effervescent

effet'tivo, -a ag (reale) real, actual; (impiegato, professore) permanent; (Mil) regular ▷ sm (Mil) strength; (di patrimonio ecc) sum total

ef'fetto sm effect; (Comm: cambiale) bill; (fig: impressione) impression; in effetti in fact, actually; effetto serra greenhouse effect; effetti personali personal effects, personal belongings

effi'cace [effi'katʃe] ag effective

effici'ente [effi'tʃɛnte] ag efficient

E'geo [e'dʒɛo] sm l'~, il mare ~ the Aegean (Sea)

E'gitto [e'dʒitto] sm l'~ Egypt

egizi'ano, -a [edʒit'tsjano] ag, sm/f Egyptian

'egli ['eʎʎi] pron he; ~ stesso he himself

ego'ismo sm selfishness, egoism; ego'ista, -i, -e ag selfish, egoistic ▷ sm/f egoist

Egr. abbr = egregio

e'gregio, -a, -gi, -gie [e'grɛdʒo] ag (nelle lettere): E~ Signore Dear Sir

E.I. abbr = Esercito Italiano

elabo'rare vt (progetto) to work out, elaborate; (dati) to process

elasticiz'zato, -a [elastitʃid'dzato] ag stretch cpd

e'lastico, -a, -ci, -che ag elastic; (fig:

andatura) springy; (: *decisione, vedute*)
flexible ▷ *sm* (*di gomma*) rubber band;
(*per il cucito*) elastic *no pl*
ele'fante *sm* elephant
ele'gante *ag* elegant
e'leggere [e'lɛddʒere] *vt* to elect
elemen'tare *ag* elementary; **le
(scuole) elementari** *sfpl* primary
(BRIT) o grade (US) school
ele'mento *sm* element; (*parte
componente*) element, component,
part; **elementi** *smpl* (*della scienza ecc*)
elements, rudiments
ele'mosina *sf* charity, alms *pl*;
chiedere l'~ to beg
elen'care *vt* to list
elencherò *ecc* [elenke'rɔ] *vb vedi*
elencare
e'lenco, -chi *sm* list; **elenco
telefonico** telephone directory
e'lessi *ecc vb vedi* **eleggere**
eletto'rale *ag* electoral, election *cpd*
elet'tore, -'trice *sm/f* voter, elector
elet'trauto *sm inv* workshop for
car electrical repairs; (*tecnico*) car
electrician
elettri'cista, -i [elettri'tʃista] *sm*
electrician
elettricità [elettritʃi'ta] *sf* electricity
e'lettrico, -a, -ci, -che *ag*
electric(al)
elettriz'zante [elettrid'dzante] *ag*
(*fig*) electrifying, thrilling
elettriz'zare [elettrid'dzare] *vt* to
electrify; **elettrizzarsi** *vpr* to become
charged with electricity
e'lettro... *prefisso*;
elettrodo'mestico, -a, -ci, -che
ag **apparecchi elettrodomestici**
domestic (electrical) appliances;
elet'tronico, -a, -ci, -che *ag*
electronic
elezi'one [elet'tsjone] *sf* election;
elezioni *sfpl* (*Pol*) election(s)
'elica, -che *sf* propeller
eli'cottero *sm* helicopter
elimi'nare *vt* to eliminate

elisoc'corso *sm* helicopter
ambulance
el'metto *sm* helmet
elogi'are [elo'dʒare] *vt* to praise
elo'quente *ag* eloquent
e'ludere *vt* to evade
e'lusi *ecc vb vedi* **eludere**
e-mail [i'mɛil] *sf inv* (*messaggio,
sistema*) e-mail ▷ *ag inv* (*indirizzo*)
e-mail
emargi'nato, -a [emardʒi'nato]
sm/f outcast; **emarginazione**
[emardʒinat'tsjone] *sf*
marginalization
embri'one *sm* embryo
emenda'mento *sm* amendment
emer'genza [emer'dʒɛntsa] *sf*
emergency; **in caso di ~** in an
emergency
e'mergere [e'mɛrdʒere] *vi* to
emerge; (*sommergibile*) to surface; (*fig:
distinguersi*) to stand out
e'mersi *ecc vb vedi* **emergere**
e'mettere *vt* (*suono, luce*) to give out,
emit; (*onde radio*) to send out; (*assegno,
francobollo, ordine*) to issue
emi'crania *sf* migraine
emi'grare *vi* to emigrate
emis'fero *sm* hemisphere; **emisfero
australe** southern hemisphere;
emisfero boreale northern
hemisphere
e'misi *ecc vb vedi* **emettere**
emit'tente *ag* (*banca*) issuing; (*Radio*)
broadcasting, transmitting ▷ *sf*
(*Radio*) transmitter
emorra'gia, -'gie [emorra'dʒia] *sf*
haemorrhage
emor'roidi *sfpl* haemorrhoids *pl*
(BRIT), hemorrhoids *pl* (US)
emo'tivo, -a *ag* emotional
emozio'nante [emottsjo'nante] *ag*
exciting, thrilling
emozio'nare [emottsjo'nare] *vt*
(*commuovere*) to move; (*agitare*) to
make nervous; (*elettrizzare*) to excite;
emozionarsi *vpr* to be moved; to be

nervous; to be excited; **emozionato, -a** [emottsjo'nato] *ag* (*commosso*) moved; (*agitato*) nervous; (*elettrizzato*) excited

emozi'one [emot'tsjone] *sf* emotion; (*agitazione*) excitement

enciclope'dia [entʃiklope'dia] *sf* encyclopaedia

endove'noso, -a *ag* (*Med*) intravenous

'E.N.E.L. ['enel] *sigla m* (= *Ente Nazionale per l'Energia Elettrica*) national electricity company

ener'getico, -a, ci, che [ener'dʒetiko] *ag* (*risorse, crisi*) energy *cpd*; (*sostanza, alimento*) energy-giving

ener'gia, -'gie [ener'dʒia] *sf* (*Fisica*) energy; (*fig*) energy, strength, vigour; **energia eolica** wind power; **energia solare** solar energy, solar power; **e'nergico, -a, -ci, -che** *ag* energetic, vigorous

'enfasi *sf* emphasis; (*peg*) bombast, pomposity

en'nesimo, -a *ag* (*Mat, fig*) nth; **per l'ennesima volta** for the umpteenth time

e'norme *ag* enormous, huge

'ente *sm* (*istituzione*) body, board, corporation; (*Filosofia*) being; **enti pubblici** public bodies; **ente di ricerca** research organization

en'trambi, -e *pron pl* both (of them) ▷ *ag pl* **~ i ragazzi** both boys, both of the boys

en'trare *vi* to go (*o come*) in; **~ in** (*luogo*) to enter, go (*o come*) into; (*trovar posto, poter stare*) to fit into; (*essere ammesso a: club ecc*) to join, become a member of; **~ in automobile** to get into the car; **far ~ qn** (*visitatore ecc*) to show sb in; **questo non c'entra** (*fig*) that's got nothing to do with it; **en'trata** *sf* entrance, entry; **dov'è l'entrata?** where's the entrance?; **entrate** *sfpl* (*Comm*) receipts, takings; (*Econ*)

income *sg*

'entro *prep* (*temporale*) within

entusias'mare *vt* to excite, fill with enthusiasm; **entusiasmarsi** *vpr* **entusiasmarsi (per qc/qn)** to become enthusiastic (about sth/sb); **entusi'asmo** *sm* enthusiasm; **entusi'asta, -i, -e** *ag* enthusiastic ▷ *sm/f* enthusiast

epa'tite *sf* hepatitis

epide'mia *sf* epidemic

epiles'sia *sf* epilepsy

epi'lettico, -a, ci, che *ag, sm/f* epileptic

epi'sodio *sm* episode

'epoca, -che *sf* (*periodo storico*) age, era; (*tempo*) time; (*Geo*) age

ep'pure *cong* and yet, nevertheless

EPT *sigla m* (= *Ente Provinciale per il Turismo*) district tourist bureau

equa'tore *sm* equator

equazi'one [ekwat'tsjone] *sf* (*Mat*) equation

e'questre *ag* equestrian

equi'librio *sm* balance, equilibrium; **perdere l'equilibrare** to lose one's balance

e'quino, -a *ag* horse *cpd*, equine

equipaggia'mento [ekwipaddʒa'mento] *sm* (*operazione: di nave*) equipping, fitting out; (*: di spedizione, esercito*) equipping, kitting out; (*attrezzatura*) equipment

equipaggi'are [ekwipad'dʒare] *vt* (*di persone*) to man; (*di mezzi*) to equip; **equipaggiarsi** *vpr* to equip o.s; **equi'paggio** *sm* crew

equitazi'one [ekwitat'tsjone] *sf* (horse-)riding

equiva'lente *ag, sm* equivalent

e'quivoco, -a, -ci, -che *ag* equivocal, ambiguous; (*sospetto*) dubious ▷ *sm* misunderstanding; **a scanso di equivoci** to avoid any misunderstanding; **giocare sull'~** to equivocate

'equo, -a *ag* fair, just

'era *sf* era

'era *ecc vb vedi* **essere**

'erba *sf* grass; **in ~** (*fig*) budding; **erbe aromatiche** herbs; **erba medica** lucerne; **er'baccia, -ce** *sf* weed

erboriste'ria *sf* (*scienza*) study of medicinal herbs; (*negozio*) herbalist's (shop)

e'rede *sm/f* heir; **eredità** *sf* (*Dir*) inheritance; (*Biol*) heredity; **lasciare qc in eredità a qn** to leave *o* bequeath sth to sb; **eredi'tare** *vt* to inherit; **eredi'tario, -a** *ag* hereditary

ere'mita, -i *sm* hermit

er'gastolo *sm* (*Dir: pena*) life imprisonment

'erica *sf* heather

er'metico, -a, -ci, -che *ag* hermetic

'ernia *sf* (*Med*) hernia

'ero *vb vedi* **essere**

e'roe *sm* hero

ero'gare *vt* (*somme*) to distribute; (*gas, servizi*) to supply

e'roico, -a, -ci, -che *ag* heroic

ero'ina *sf* heroine; (*droga*) heroin

erosi'one *sf* erosion

e'rotico, -a, -ci, -che *ag* erotic

er'rato, -a *ag* wrong

er'rore *sm* error, mistake; (*morale*) error; **per ~** by mistake; **ci dev'essere un ~** there must be some mistake; **errore giudiziario** miscarriage of justice

eruzi'one [erut'tsjone] *sf* eruption

esacer'bare [ezatʃer'bare] *vt* to exacerbate

esage'rare [ezadʒe'rare] *vt* to exaggerate ▷ *vi* to exaggerate; (*eccedere*) to go too far

esal'tare *vt* to exalt; (*entusiasmare*) to excite, stir

e'same *sm* examination; (*Ins*) exam, examination; **fare** *o* **dare un ~** to sit *o* take an exam; **esame di guida** driving test; **esame del sangue** blood test

esami'nare *vt* to examine

esaspe'rare *vt* to exasperate; to exacerbate

esatta'mente *av* exactly; accurately, precisely

esat'tezza [ezat'tettsa] *sf* exactitude, accuracy, precision

e'satto, -a *pp di* **esigere** ▷ *ag* (*calcolo, ora*) correct, right, exact; (*preciso*) accurate, precise; (*puntuale*) punctual

esau'dire *vt* to grant, fulfil

esauri'ente *ag* exhaustive

esauri'mento *sm* exhaustion; **esaurimento nervoso** nervous breakdown

esau'rire *vt* (*stancare*) to exhaust, wear out; (*provviste, miniera*) to exhaust; **esaurirsi** *vpr* to exhaust o.s., wear o.s. out; (*provviste*) to run out; **esau'rito, -a** *ag* exhausted; (*merci*) sold out; **registrare il tutto esaurito** (*Teatro*) to have a full house; **e'sausto, -a** *ag* exhausted

'esca (*pl* **'esche**) *sf* bait

'esce ['εʃʃe] *vb vedi* **uscire**

eschi'mese [eski'mese] *ag, sm/f* Eskimo

'esci ['εʃʃi] *vb vedi* **uscire**

escla'mare *vi* to exclaim, cry out

esclama'tivo, -a *ag:* **punto ~** exclamation mark

esclamazi'one *sf* exclamation

es'cludere *vt* to exclude

es'clusi *ecc vb vedi* **escludere**

esclusi'one *sf* exclusion; **a ~ di, fatta ~ per** except (for), apart from; **senza ~ (alcuna)** without exception; **procedere per ~** to follow a process of elimination; **senza ~ di colpi** (*fig*) with no holds barred; **esclusione sociale** social exclusion

esclu'siva *sf* (*Dir, Comm*) exclusive *o* sole rights *pl*

esclusiva'mente *av* exclusively, solely

esclu'sivo, -a *ag* exclusive

es'cluso, -a *pp di* **escludere**

'esco *vb vedi* **uscire**

escogi'tare [eskodʒi'tare] *vt* to

devise, think up

'escono vb vedi **uscire**

escursi'one sf (gita) excursion, trip; (: a piedi) hike, walk; (Meteor) range; **escursione termica** temperature range

esecuzi'one [ezekut'tsjone] sf execution, carrying out; (Mus) performance; **esecuzione capitale** execution

esegu'ire vt to carry out, execute; (Mus) to perform, execute

e'sempio sm example; **per ~** for example, for instance; **fare un ~** to give an example; **esem'plare** ag exemplary ▷ sm example; (copia) copy

eserci'tare [ezertʃi'tare] vt (professione) to practise (BRIT), practice (US); (allenare: corpo, mente) to exercise, train; (diritto) to exercise; (influenza, pressione) to exert; **esercitarsi** vpr to practise; **esercitarsi alla lotta** to practise fighting

e'sercito [e'zertʃito] sm army

eser'cizio [ezer'tʃittsjo] sm practice; exercising; (fisico: di matematica) exercise; (Econ) financial year; (azienda) business, concern; **in ~** (medico ecc) practising; **esercizio pubblico** (Comm) commercial concern

esi'bire vt to exhibit, display; (documenti) to produce, present; **esibirsi** vpr (attore) to perform; (fig) to show off; **esibizi'one** sf exhibition; (di documento) presentation; (spettacolo) show, performance

esi'gente [ezi'dʒɛnte] ag demanding

e'sigere [e'zidʒere] vt (pretendere) to demand; (richiedere) to demand, require; (imposte) to collect

'esile ag (persona) slender, slim; (stelo) thin; (voce) faint

esili'are vt to exile; **e'silio** sm exile

esis'tenza [ezis'tɛntsa] sf existence

e'sistere vi to exist

esi'tare vi to hesitate

'esito sm result, outcome

'esodo sm exodus

esone'rare vt to exempt

e'sordio sm debut

esor'tare vt: **~ qn a fare** to urge sb to do

e'sotico, -a, -ci, -che ag exotic

es'pandere vt to expand; (confini) to extend; (influenza) to extend, spread; **espandersi** vpr to expand; **espansi'one** sf expansion; **espansione di memoria** (Inform) memory upgrade; **espan'sivo, -a** ag expansive, communicative

espatri'are vi to leave one's country

espedi'ente sm expedient

es'pellere vt to expel

esperi'enza [espe'rjɛntsa] sf experience

esperi'mento sm experiment

es'perto, -a ag, sm expert

espi'rare vt, vi to breathe out

es'plicito, -a [es'plitʃito] ag explicit

es'plodere vi (anche fig) to explode ▷ vt to fire

esplo'rare vt to explore

esplosi'one sf explosion

es'pone ecc vb vedi **esporre**

es'pongo, es'poni ecc vb vedi **esporre**

es'porre vt (merci) to display; (quadro) to exhibit, show; (fatti, idee) to explain, set out; (porre in pericolo, Fot) to expose; **esporsi** vpr **esporsi a** (sole, pericolo) to expose o.s. to; (critiche) to lay o.s. open to

espor'tare vt to export

es'pose ecc vb vedi **esporre**

esposizi'one [espozit'tsjone] sf displaying; exhibiting; setting out; (anche Fot) exposure; (mostra) exhibition; (narrazione) explanation, exposition

es'posto, -a pp di **esporre** ▷ ag **~ a nord** facing north ▷ sm (Amm) statement, account; (: petizione) petition

espressi'one sf expression

espres'sivo, -a *ag* expressive
es'presso, -a *pp di* **esprimere** ▷ *ag* express ▷ *sm* (*lettera*) express letter; (*anche:* **treno ~**) express train; (*anche:* **caffè ~**) espresso
es'primere *vt* to express; **esprimersi** *vpr* to express o.s.
es'pulsi *ecc vb vedi* **espellere**
espulsi'one *sf* expulsion
es'senza [es'sɛntsa] *sf* essence; **essenzi'ale** *ag* essential; **l'essenziale** the main o most important thing

🔵 **PAROLA CHIAVE**

'essere *sm* being; **essere umano** human being
▷ *vb copulativo* **1** (*con attributo, sostantivo*) to be; **sei giovane/ simpatico** you are o you're young/ nice; **è medico** he is o he's a doctor
2 (*+ di: appartenere*) to be; **di chi è la penna?** whose pen is it?; **è di Carla** it is o it's Carla's, it belongs to Carla
3 (*+ di: provenire*) to be; **è di Venezia** he is o he's from Venice
4 (*data, ora*): **è il 15 agosto/lunedì** it is o it's the 15th of August/Monday; **che ora è?, che ore sono?** what time is it?; **è l'una** it is o it's one o'clock; **sono le due** it is o it's two o'clock
5 (*costare*): **quant'è?** how much is it?; **sono 10 euro** it's 10 euros
▷ *vb aus* **1** (*attivo*): **essere arrivato/ venuto** to have arrived/come; **è gia partita** she has already left
2 (*passivo*) to be; **essere fatto da** to be made by; **è stata uccisa** she has been killed
3 (*riflessivo*): **si sono lavati** they washed, they got washed
4 (*+ da + infinito*): **è da farsi subito** it must be o is to be done immediately
▷ *vi* **1** (*esistere, trovarsi*) to be; **sono a casa** I'm at home; **essere in piedi/ seduto** to be standing/sitting
2: **esserci**: **c'è** there is; **ci sono** there

are; **che c'è?** what's the matter?, what is it?; **ci sono!** (*fig: ho capito*) I get it!; *vedi anche* **ci**
▷ *vb impers* **è tardi/Pasqua** it's late/ Easter; **è possibile che venga** he may come; **è così** that's the way it is

'essi *pron mpl vedi* **esso**
'esso, -a *pron* it; (*riferito a persona: soggetto*) he/she; (*: complemento*) him/her
est *sm* east
es'tate *sf* summer
esteri'ore *ag* outward, external
es'terno, -a *ag* (*porta, muro*) outer, outside; (*scala*) outside; (*alunno, impressione*) external ▷ *sm* outside, exterior ▷ *sm/f* (*allievo*) day pupil; **all'~** outside; **per uso ~** for external use only; **esterni** *smpl* (*Cinema*) location shots
'estero, -a *ag* foreign ▷ *sm* **all'~** abroad
es'teso, -a *pp di* **estendere** ▷ *ag* extensive, large; **scrivere per ~** to write in full
es'tetico, -a, -ci, -che *ag* aesthetic ▷ *sf* (*disciplina*) aesthetics *sg*; (*bellezza*) attractiveness; **este'tista, -i, -e** *sm/f* beautician
es'tinguere *vt* to extinguish, put out; (*debito*) to pay off; **estinguersi** *vpr* to go out; (*specie*) to become extinct
es'tinsi *ecc vb vedi* **estinguere**
estin'tore *sm* (*fire*) extinguisher
estinzi'one *sf* putting out; (*di specie*) extinction
estir'pare *vt* (*pianta*) to uproot, pull up; (*fig: vizio*) to eradicate
es'tivo, -a *ag* summer *cpd*
es'torcere [es'tɔrtʃere] *vt*: **~ qc (a qn)** to extort sth (from sb)
estradizi'one [estradit'tsjone] *sf* extradition
es'trae, es'traggo *ecc vb vedi* **estrarre**
es'traneo, -a *ag* foreign ▷ *sm/f*

stranger; **rimanere ~ a qc** to take no part in sth

es'trarre vt to extract; (minerali) to mine; (sorteggiare) to draw

es'trassi ecc vb vedi **estrarre**

estrema'mente av extremely

estre'mista, -i, e sm/f extremist

estremità sf inv extremity, end ▷ sfpl (Anat) extremities

es'tremo, -a ag extreme; (ultimo: ora, tentativo) final, last ▷ sm extreme; (di pazienza, forze) limit, end; **estremi** smpl (Amm: dati essenziali) details, particulars; **l'~ Oriente** the Far East

estro'verso, -a ag, sm extrovert

età sf inv age; **all'~ di 8 anni** at the age of 8, at 8 years of age; **ha la mia ~** he (o she) is the same age as me o as I am; **raggiungere la maggiore ~** to come of age; **essere in ~ minore** to be under age

'etere sm ether

eternità sf eternity

e'terno, -a ag eternal

etero'geneo, -a [etero'dʒɛneo] ag heterogeneous

eterosessu'ale ag, sm/f heterosexual

'etica sf ethics sg; vedi anche **etico**

eti'chetta [eti'ketta] sf label; (cerimoniale): **l'~** etiquette

'etico, -a, -ci, -che ag ethical

eti'lometro sm Breathalyzer®

etimolo'gia, -'gie [etimolo'dʒia] sf etymology

Eti'opia sf l'~ Ethiopia

'etnico, -a, -ci, -che ag ethnic

e'trusco, -a, -schi, -sche ag, sm/f Etruscan

'ettaro sm hectare (= 10,000 m²)

'etto sm abbr (= ettogrammo) 100 grams

'euro sm inv (divisa) euro

Eu'ropa sf l'~ Europe

europarlamen'tare sm/f Member of the European Parliament, MEP

euro'peo, -a ag, sm/f European

eutana'sia sf euthanasia

evacu'are vt to evacuate

e'vadere vi (fuggire): **~ da** to escape from ▷ vt (sbrigare) to deal with, dispatch; (tasse) to evade

evapo'rare vi to evaporate

e'vasi ecc vb vedi **evadere**

evasi'one sf (vedi evadere) escape; dispatch; **evasione fiscale** tax evasion

eva'sivo, -a ag evasive

e'vaso, -a pp di **evadere** ▷ sm escapee

e'vento sm event

eventu'ale ag possible

| Attenzione! In inglese esiste la parola eventual, che però significa finale.

eventual'mente av if necessary

| Attenzione! In inglese esiste la parola eventually, che però significa alla fine.

evi'dente ag evident, obvious

evidente'mente av evidently; (palesemente) obviously, evidently

evi'tare vt to avoid; **~ di fare** to avoid doing; **~ qc a qn** to spare sb sth

evoluzi'one [evolut'tsjone] sf evolution

e'volversi vpr to evolve

ev'viva escl hurrah!; **~ il re!** long live the king!, hurrah for the king!

ex prefisso ex, former

'extra ag inv first-rate; top-quality ▷ sm inv extra; **extracomuni'tario, -a** ag from outside the EC ▷ sm/f non-EC citizen

extrater'restre ag, sm/f extraterrestrial

fa *vb vedi* **fare** ▷ *sm inv* (*Mus*) F; (: *solfeggiando la scala*) fa ▷ *av* **10 anni fa** 10 years ago

'fabbrica *sf* factory; **fabbri'care** *vt* to build; (*produrre*) to manufacture, make; (*fig*) to fabricate, invent
Attenzione! In inglese esiste la parola fabric, *che però significa* stoffa.

fac'cenda [fat'tʃɛnda] *sf* matter, affair; (*cosa da fare*) task, chore

fac'chino [fak'kino] *sm* porter

'faccia, -ce ['fattʃa] *sf* face; (*di moneta, medaglia*) side; **faccia a faccia** face to face

facci'ata [fat'tʃata] *sf* façade; (*di pagina*) side

'faccio ['fattʃo] *vb vedi* **fare**

fa'cessi *ecc* [fa'tʃessi] *vb vedi* **fare**

fa'cevo *ecc* [fa'tʃevo] *vb vedi* **fare**

'facile ['fatʃile] *ag* easy; (*disposto*): **~ a** inclined to, prone to; (*probabile*): **è ~ che piova** it's likely to rain

facoltà *sf inv* faculty; (*autorità*) power

facolta'tivo, -a *ag* optional; (*fermata d'autobus*) request *cpd*

'faggio ['faddʒo] *sm* beech

fagi'ano [fa'dʒano] *sm* pheasant

fagio'lino [fadʒo'lino] *sm* French (*BRIT*) o string bean

fagi'olo [fa'dʒolo] *sm* bean

'fai *vb vedi* **fare**

'fai-da-'te *sm inv* DIY, do-it-yourself

'falce ['faltʃe] *sf* scythe; **falci'are** *vt* to cut; (*fig*) to mow down

falcia'trice [faltʃa'tritʃe] *sf* (*per fieno*) reaping machine; (*per erba*) mowing machine

'falco, -chi *sm* hawk

'falda *sf* layer, stratum; (*di cappello*) brim; (*di cappotto*) tails *pl*; (*di monte*) lower slope; (*di tetto*) pitch

fale'gname [faleɲ'ɲame] *sm* joiner

falli'mento *sm* failure; bankruptcy

fal'lire *vi* (*non riuscire*): **~ (in)** to fail (in); (*Dir*) to go bankrupt ▷ *vt* (*colpo, bersaglio*) to miss

'fallo *sm* error, mistake; (*imperfezione*) defect, flaw; (*Sport*) foul; fault; **senza ~** without fail

falò *sm inv* bonfire

falsifi'care *vt* to forge; (*monete*) to forge, counterfeit

'falso, -a *ag* false; (*errato*) wrong; (*falsificato*) forged; fake; (: *oro, gioielli*) imitation *cpd* ▷ *sm* forgery; **giurare il ~** to commit perjury

'fama *sf* fame; (*reputazione*) reputation, name

'fame *sf* hunger; **aver ~** to be hungry

fa'miglia [fa'miʎʎa] *sf* family

famili'are *ag* (*della famiglia*) family *cpd*; (*ben noto*) familiar; (*rapporti, atmosfera*) friendly; (*Ling*) informal, colloquial ▷ *sm/f* relative, relation

fa'moso, -a *ag* famous, well-known

fa'nale *sm* (*Aut*) light, lamp (*BRIT*); (*luce stradale, Naut*) light; (*di faro*) beacon

fa'natico, -a, -ci, -che *ag* fanatical; (*del teatro, calcio ecc*): **~ di** o **per** mad o crazy about ▷ *sm/f* fanatic; (*tifoso*) fan

'fango, -ghi *sm* mud

'fanno *vb vedi* **fare**

fannul'lone, -a *sm/f* idler, loafer

fantasci'enza [fantaʃʃɛntsa] *sf*
science fiction

fanta'sia *sf* fantasy, imagination;
(*capriccio*) whim, caprice ▷ *ag inv*
vestito ~ patterned dress

fan'tasma, -i *sm* ghost, phantom

fan'tastico, -a, -ci, -che *ag*
fantastic; (*potenza, ingegno*)
imaginative

fan'tino *sm* jockey

fara'butto *sm* crook

fard *sm inv* blusher

 PAROLA CHIAVE

'fare *sm* **1** (*modo di fare*): **con fare
distratto** absent-mindedly; **ha un
fare simpatico** he has a pleasant
manner
2: **sul far del giorno/della notte** at
daybreak/nightfall
▷ *vt* **1** (*fabbricare, creare*) to make;
(: *casa*) to build; (: *assegno*) to make
out; **fare un pasto/una promessa/
un film** to make a meal/a promise/a
film; **fare rumore** to make a noise
2 (*effettuare: lavoro, attività, studi*) to
do; (: *sport*) to play; **cosa fa?** (*adesso*)
what are you doing?; (*di professione*)
what do you do?; **fare psicologia/
italiano** (*Ins*) to do psychology/
Italian; **fare un viaggio** to go on a trip
o journey; **fare una passeggiata** to
go for a walk; **fare la spesa** to do the
shopping
3 (*funzione*) to be; (*Teatro*) to play, be;
fare il medico to be a doctor; **fare il
malato** (*fingere*) to act the invalid
4 (*suscitare: sentimenti*): **fare paura
a qn** to frighten sb; **(non) fa niente**
(*non importa*) it doesn't matter
5 (*ammontare*): **3 più 3 fa 6** 3 and 3 are
o make 6; **fanno 3 euro** that's 3 euros;

Roma fa 2.000.000 di abitanti
Rome has 2,000,000 inhabitants;
che ora fai? what time do you make
it?
6 (+ *infinito*): **far fare qc a qn**
(*obbligare*) to make sb do sth;
(*permettere*) to let sb do sth; **fammi
vedere** let me see; **far partire il
motore** to start (up) the engine; **far
riparare la macchina/costruire una
casa** to get *o* have the car repaired/a
house built
7: **farsi: farsi una gonna** to make
o.s. a skirt; **farsi un nome** to make a
name for o.s.; **farsi la permanente**
to get a perm; **farsi tagliare i capelli**
to get one's hair cut; **farsi operare** to
have an operation
8 (*fraseologia*): **farcela** to succeed,
manage; **non ce la faccio più** I can't
go on; **ce la faremo** we'll make it;
me l'hanno fatta! (*imbrogliare*) I've
been done!; **lo facevo più giovane** I
thought he was younger; **fare sì/no
con la testa** to nod/shake one's head
▷ *vi* **1** (*agire*) to act, do; **fate come
volete** do as you like; **fare presto** to
be quick; **fare da** to act as; **non c'è
niente da fare** it's no use; **saperci
fare con qn/qc** to know how to deal
with sb/sth; **faccia pure!** go ahead!
2 (*dire*) to say; **"davvero?" fece**
"really?" he said
3: **fare per** (*essere adatto*) to be suitable
for; **fare per fare qc** to be about to do
sth; **fece per andarsene** he made as
if to leave
4: **farsi: si fa così** you do it like this,
this is the way it's done; **non si fa così!**
(*rimprovero*) that's no way to behave!;
la festa non si fa the party is off
5: **fare a gara con qn** to compete *o*
vie with sb; **fare a pugni** to come to
blows; **fare in tempo a fare** to be in
time to do
▷ *vb impers* **fa bel tempo** the weather
is fine; **fa caldo/freddo** it's hot/cold;

fa notte it's getting dark ▷ *vpr* **farsi**
1 (*diventare*) to become; **farsi prete**
to become a priest; **farsi grande/
vecchio** to grow tall/old
2 (*spostarsi*): **farsi avanti/indietro** to
move forward/back
3 (*fam: drogarsi*) to be a junkie

far'falla *sf* butterfly
fa'rina *sf* flour
farma'cia, -'cie [farma'tʃia] *sf*
pharmacy; (*negozio*) chemist's (shop)
(BRIT), pharmacy; **farma'cista, -i, -e**
sm/f chemist (BRIT), pharmacist
'farmaco, -ci *o* **chi** *sm* drug, medicine
'faro *sm* (*Naut*) lighthouse; (*Aer*)
beacon; (*Aut*) headlight
'fascia, -sce ['faʃʃa] *sf* band, strip;
(*Med*) bandage; (*di sindaco, ufficiale*)
sash; (*parte di territorio*) strip, belt; (*di
contribuenti ecc*) group, band; **essere
in fasce** (*anche fig*) to be in one's
infancy; **fascia oraria** time band
fasci'are [faʃʃare] *vt* to bind; (*Med*) to
bandage
fa'scicolo [faʃʃikolo] *sm* (*di
documenti*) file, dossier; (*di rivista*)
issue, number; (*opuscolo*) booklet,
pamphlet
'fascino ['faʃʃino] *sm* charm,
fascination
fa'scismo [faʃʃizmo] *sm* fascism
'fase *sf* phase; (*Tecn*) stroke; **fuori ~**
(*motore*) rough
fas'tidio *sm* bother, trouble; **dare ~ a
qn** to bother *o* annoy sb; **sento ~ allo
stomaco** my stomach's upset; **avere
fastidi con la polizia** to have trouble
o bother with the police; **fastidi'oso,
-a** *ag* annoying, tiresome

> Attenzione! In inglese esiste
> la parola *fastidious*, che però
> significa *pignolo*.

'fata *sf* fairy
fa'tale *ag* fatal; (*inevitabile*) inevitable;
(*fig*) irresistible
fa'tica, -che *sf* hard work, toil;

(*sforzo*) effort; (*di metalli*) fatigue; **a
~** with difficulty; **fare ~ a fare qc** to
have a job doing sth; **fati'coso, -a** *ag*
tiring, exhausting; (*lavoro*) laborious
'fatto, -a *pp di* **fare** ▷ *ag*: **un uomo
~** a grown man; **~ a mano/in casa**
hand-/home-made ▷ *sm* fact;
(*azione*) deed; (*avvenimento*) event,
occurrence; (*di romanzo, film*) action,
story; **cogliere qn sul ~** to catch sb
red-handed; **il ~ sta** *o* **è che** the fact
remains *o* is that; **in ~ di** as for, as far
as … is concerned; **coppia/unione di
~** long-standing relationship
fat'tore *sm* (*Agr*) farm manager; (*Mat,
elemento costitutivo*) factor; **fattore di
protezione** (*di lozione solare*) factor;
**vorrei una crema solare con ~
di protezione 15** I'd like a factor 15
suntan cream
fatto'ria *sf* farm; farmhouse

> Attenzione! In inglese esiste la
> parola *factory*, che però significa
> *fabbrica*.

fatto'rino *sm* errand-boy; (*di ufficio*)
office-boy; (*d'albergo*) porter
fat'tura *sf* (*Comm*) invoice; (*di abito*)
tailoring; (*malia*) spell
fattu'rato *sm* (*Comm*) turnover
'fauna *sf* fauna
'fava *sf* broad bean
'favola *sf* (*fiaba*) fairy tale; (*d'intento
morale*) fable; (*fandonia*) yarn;
favo'loso, -a *ag* fabulous; (*incredibile*)
incredible
fa'vore *sm* favour; **per ~** please; **fare
un ~ a qn** to do sb a favour
favo'rire *vt* to favour; (*il commercio,
l'industria, le arti*) to promote,
encourage; **vuole ~?** won't you help
yourself?; **favorisca in salotto** please
come into the sitting room
fax *sm inv* fax; **mandare qc via ~** to
fax sth
fazzo'letto [fattso'letto] *sm*
handkerchief; (*per la testa*) (head)scarf;
fazzoletto di carta tissue

feb'braio *sm* February

'febbre *sf* fever; **aver la ~** to have a high temperature; **febbre da fieno** hay fever

'feci *ecc* ['fɛtʃi] *vb vedi* **fare**

fecondazi'one [fekondat'tsjone] *sf* fertilization; **fecondazione artificiale** artificial insemination

fe'condo, -a *ag* fertile

'fede *sf* (*credenza*) belief, faith; (*Rel*) faith; (*fiducia*) faith, trust; (*fedeltà*) loyalty; (*anello*) wedding ring; (*attestato*) certificate; **aver ~ in qn** to have faith in sb; **in buona/cattiva ~** in good/bad faith; **"in ~"** (*Dir*) "in witness whereof"; **fe'dele** *ag* **fedele (a)** faithful (to) ▷ *sm/f* follower; **i fedeli** (*Rel*) the faithful

'federa *sf* pillowslip, pillowcase

fede'rale *ag* federal

'fegato *sm* liver; (*fig*) guts *pl*, nerve

'felce ['feltʃe] *sf* fern

fe'lice [fe'litʃe] *ag* happy; (*fortunato*) lucky; **felicità** *sf* happiness

felici'tarsi [felitʃi'tarsi] *vpr* (*congratularsi*): **~ con qn per qc** to congratulate sb on sth

fe'lino, -a *ag*, *sm* feline

'felpa *sf* sweatshirt

'femmina *sf* (*Zool, Tecn*) female; (*figlia*) girl, daughter; (*spesso peg*) woman; **femmi'nile** *ag* feminine; (*sesso*) female; (*lavoro, giornale, moda*) woman's ▷ *sm* (*Ling*) feminine

'femore *sm* thighbone, femur

fe'nomeno *sm* phenomenon

feri'ale *ag*: **giorno ~** weekday

'ferie *sfpl* holidays (*BRIT*), vacation *sg* (*US*); **andare in ~** to go on holiday *o* vacation

fe'rire *vt* to injure; (*deliberatamente: Mil ecc*) to wound; (*colpire*) to hurt; **ferirsi** *vpr* to hurt o.s., injure o.s; **fe'rita** *sf* injury, wound; **fe'rito, -a** *sm/f* wounded *o* injured man/woman

fer'maglio [fer'maʎʎo] *sm* clasp; (*per documenti*) clip

fer'mare *vt* to stop, halt; (*Polizia*) to detain, hold ▷ *vi* to stop; **fermarsi** *vpr* to stop, halt; **fermarsi a fare qc** to stop to do sth; **può fermarsi qui/all'angolo?** could you stop here/at the corner?

fer'mata *sf* stop; **fermata dell'autobus** bus stop

fer'menti *smpl*: **~ lattici** probiotic bacteria

fer'mezza [fer'mettsa] *sf* (*fig*) firmness, steadfastness

'fermo, -a *ag* still, motionless; (*veicolo*) stationary; (*orologio*) not working; (*saldo: anche fig*) firm; (*voce, mano*) steady ▷ *escl* stop!; keep still! ▷ *sm* (*chiusura*) catch, lock; (*Dir*): **fermo di polizia** police detention

fe'roce [fe'rotʃe] *ag* (*animale*) fierce, ferocious; (*persona*) cruel, fierce; (*fame, dolore*) raging; **le bestie feroci** wild animals

ferra'gosto *sm* (*festa*) feast of the Assumption; (*periodo*) August holidays *pl*

● **FERRAGOSTO**
●
● **Ferragosto**, August 15th, is a
● national holiday. Marking the Feast
● of the Assumption, its origins are
● religious but in recent years it has
● simply become the most important
● public holiday of the summer
● season. Most people take some
● extra time off work and head out of
● town to the holiday resorts.

ferra'menta *sfpl*: **negozio di ~** ironmonger's (*BRIT*), hardware shop *o* store (*US*)

'ferro *sm* iron; **una bistecca ai ferri** a grilled steak; **ferro battuto** wrought iron; **ferro da calza** knitting needle; **ferro di cavallo** horseshoe; **ferro da stiro** iron

ferro'via *sf* railway (*BRIT*), railroad

(US); **ferrovi'ario, -a** ag railway cpd
(BRIT), railroad cpd (US); **ferrovi'ere**
sm railwayman (BRIT), railroad man
(US)

fertile ag fertile

'fesso, -a pp di **fendere** ▷ ag (fam:
sciocco) crazy, cracked

fes'sura sf crack, split; (per gettone,
moneta) slot

'festa sf (religiosa) feast; (pubblica)
holiday; (compleanno) birthday;
(onomastico) name day; (ricevimento)
celebration, party; **far ~** to have a
holiday; to live it up; **far ~ a qn** to give
sb a warm welcome

festeggi'are [fested'dʒare] vt
to celebrate; (persona) to have a
celebration for

fes'tivo, -a ag (atmosfera) festive;
giorno ~ holiday

'feto sm foetus (BRIT), fetus (US)

'fetta sf slice

fettuc'cine [fettut'tʃine] sfpl (Cuc)
ribbon-shaped pasta

FF.SS. abbr = **Ferrovie dello Stato**

FI sigla = **Firenze** ▷ abbr (= Forza Italia)
Italian centre-right political party

fi'aba sf fairy tale

fi'acca sf weariness; (svogliatezza)
listlessness

fi'acco, -a, -chi, -che ag (stanco)
tired, weary; (svogliato) listless;
(debole) weak; (mercato) slack

fi'accola sf torch

fi'ala sf phial

fi'amma sf flame

fiam'mante ag (colore) flaming;
nuovo ~ brand new

fiam'mifero sm match

fiam'mingo, -a, -ghi, -ghe ag
Flemish ▷ sm/f Fleming ▷ sm (Ling)
Flemish; **i Fiamminghi** the Flemish

fi'anco, -chi sm side; (Mil) flank; **di ~**
sideways, from the side; **a ~ a ~** side
by side

fi'asco, -schi sm flask; (fig) fiasco;
fare ~ to fail

fia'tare vi (fig: parlare): **senza ~**
without saying a word

fi'ato sm breath; (resistenza) stamina;
avere il ~ grosso to be out of breath;
prendere ~ to catch one's breath

'fibbia sf buckle

'fibra sf fibre; (fig) constitution

fic'care vt to push, thrust, drive;
ficcarsi vpr (andare a finire) to get to

ficcherò ecc [fikke'rɔ] vb vedi **ficcare**

'fico, -chi sm (pianta) fig tree; (frutto)
fig; **fico d'India** prickly pear; **fico
secco** dried fig

fiction ['fikʃon] sf inv TV drama

> Attenzione! In inglese esiste la
> parola *fiction* che però significa
> narrativa oppure *finzione*.

fidanza'mento [fidantsa'mento] sm
engagement

fidan'zarsi [fidan'tsarsi] vpr to
get engaged; **fidan'zato, -a** sm/f
fiancé/fiancée

fi'darsi vpr **~ di** to trust; **fi'dato, -a** ag
reliable, trustworthy

fi'ducia [fi'dutʃa] sf confidence,
trust; **incarico di ~** position of trust,
responsible position; **persona di ~**
reliable person

fie'nile sm barn; hayloft

fi'eno sm hay

fi'era sf fair

fi'ero, -a ag proud; (audace) bold

'fifa (fam) sf **aver ~** to have the jitters

fig. abbr (= figura) fig.

'figlia ['fiʎʎa] sf daughter

figli'astro, -a [fiʎ'ʎastro] sm/f
stepson/daughter

'figlio ['fiʎʎo] sm son; (senza distinzione
di sesso) child; **figlio di papà** spoilt,
wealthy young man; **figlio unico**
only child

fi'gura sf figure; (forma, aspetto
esterno) form, shape; (illustrazione)
picture, illustration; **far ~** to look
smart; **fare una brutta ~** to make a
bad impression

figu'rina sf figurine; (cartoncino)

picture card

'fila *sf* row, line; (*coda*) queue; (*serie*)
series, string; **di ~** in succession; **fare
la ~** to queue; **in ~ indiana** in single
file

fi'lare *vt* to spin ▷ *vi* (*baco, ragno*) to
spin; (*formaggio fuso*) to go stringy;
(*discorso*) to hang together; (*fam:
amoreggiare*) to go steady; (*muoversi
a forte velocità*) to go at full speed; **~
diritto** (*fig*) to toe the line; **~ via** to
dash off

filas'trocca, -che *sf* nursery rhyme

filate'lia *sf* philately, stamp collecting

fi'letto *sm* (*di vite*) thread; (*di carne*)
fillet

fili'ale *ag* filial ▷ *sf* (*di impresa*) branch

film *sm inv* film

'filo *sm* (*anche fig*) thread; (*filato*) yarn;
(*metallico*) wire; (*di lama, rasoio*) edge;
per ~ e per segno in detail; **con un ~
di voce** in a whisper; **filo d'erba** blade
of grass; **filo interdentale** dental
floss; **filo di perle** string of pearls; **filo
spinato** barbed wire

fi'lone *sm* (*di minerali*) seam, vein;
(*pane*) ≈ Vienna loaf; (*fig*) trend

filoso'fia *sf* philosophy; **fi'losofo, -a**
sm/f philosopher

fil'trare *vt, vi* to filter

'filtro *sm* filter; **filtro dell'olio** (*Aut*)
oil filter

fi'nale *ag* final ▷ *sm* (*di opera*) end,
ending; (: *Mus*) finale ▷ *sf* (*Sport*) final;
final'mente *av* finally, at last

fi'nanza [fi'nantsa] *sf* finance;
finanze *sfpl* (*di individuo, Stato*)
finances

finché [fin'ke] *cong* (*per tutto il tempo
che*) as long as; (*fino al momento in
cui*) until; **aspetta ~ io (non) sia
ritornato** wait until I get back

'fine *ag* (*lamina, carta*) thin; (*capelli,
polvere*) fine; (*vista, udito*) keen,
sharp; (*persona: raffinata*) refined,
distinguished; (*osservazione*) subtle
▷ *sf* end ▷ *sm* aim, purpose; (*esito*)

result, outcome; **secondo ~** ulterior
motive; **in** *o* **alla ~** in the end, finally

fi'nestra *sf* window; **fines'trino** *sm*
window; **vorrei un posto vicino al
finestrino** I'd like a window seat

'fingere ['findʒere] *vt* to feign;
(*supporre*) to imagine, suppose;
fingersi *vpr* **fingersi ubriaco/pazzo**
to pretend to be drunk/mad; **~ di fare**
to pretend to do

fi'nire *vt* to finish ▷ *vi* to finish, end;
quando finisce lo spettacolo?
when does the show finish?; **~ di fare**
(*compiere*) to finish doing; (*smettere*)
to stop doing; **~ in galera** to end up *o*
finish up in prison

finlan'dese *ag, sm* (*Ling*) Finnish
▷ *sm/f* Finn

Fin'landia *sf* **la ~** Finland

'fino, -a *ag* (*capelli, seta*) fine; (*oro*)
pure; (*fig: acuto*) shrewd ▷ *av* (*spesso
troncato in* **fin**: *pure, anche*) even
▷ *prep* (*spesso troncato in* **fin**: *tempo*):
fin quando? till when?; (: *luogo*): **fin
qui** as far as here; **~ a** (*tempo*) until,
till; (*luogo*) as far as, (up) to; **fin da
domani** from tomorrow onwards;
fin da ieri since yesterday; **fin dalla
nascita** from *o* since birth

fi'nocchio [fi'nɔkkjo] *sm* fennel; (*fam:
peg: omosessuale*) queer

fi'nora *av* up till now

'finsi *ecc vb vedi* **fingere**

'finta *sf* pretence, sham; (*Sport*) feint;
far ~ (di fare) to pretend (to do)

'finto, -a *pp di* **fingere** ▷ *ag* false;
artificial

finzi'one [fin'tsjone] *sf* pretence,
sham

fi'occo, -chi *sm* (*di nastro*) bow;
(*di stoffa, lana*) flock; (*di neve*) flake;
(*Naut*) jib; **coi fiocchi** (*fig*) first-rate;
fiocchi di avena oatflakes; **fiocchi di
granturco** cornflakes

fi'ocina ['fjɔtʃina] *sf* harpoon

fi'oco, -a, -chi, -che *ag* faint, dim

fi'onda *sf* catapult

fio'raio, -a *sm/f* florist

fi'ore *sm* flower; **fiori** *smpl* (*Carte*) clubs; **a fior d'acqua** on the surface of the water; **avere i nervi a fior di pelle** to be on edge; **fior di latte** cream; **fiori di campo** wild flowers

fioren'tino, -a *ag* Florentine

fio'retto *sm* (*Scherma*) foil

fio'rire *vi* (*rosa*) to flower; (*albero*) to blossom; (*fig*) to flourish

Fi'renze [fi'rɛntse] *sf* Florence

'firma *sf* signature

> ▌ Attenzione! In inglese esiste la parola *firm*, che però significa *ditta*.

fir'mare *vt* to sign; **un abito firmato** a designer suit; **dove devo ~?** where do I sign?

fisar'monica, -che *sf* accordion

fis'cale *ag* fiscal, tax *cpd*; **medico ~** *doctor employed by Social Security to verify cases of sick leave*

fischi'are [fis'kjare] *vi* to whistle ▷ *vt* to whistle; (*attore*) to boo, hiss

fischi'etto [fis'kjetto] *sm* (*strumento*) whistle

'fischio ['fiskjo] *sm* whistle

'fisco *sm* tax authorities *pl*, ≈ Inland Revenue (*BRIT*), ≈ Internal Revenue Service (*US*)

'fisica *sf* physics *sg*

'fisico, -a, -ci, -che *ag* physical ▷ *sm/f* physicist ▷ *sm* physique

fisiotera'pia *sf* physiotherapy

fisiotera'pista *sm/f* physiotherapist

fis'sare *vt* to fix, fasten; (*guardare intensamente*) to stare at; (*data, condizioni*) to fix, establish, set; (*prenotare*) to book; **fissarsi** *vpr* **fissarsi su** (*sguardo, attenzione*) to focus on; (*fig: idea*) to become obsessed with

'fisso, -a *ag* fixed; (*stipendio, impiego*) regular ▷ *av* **guardare ~ qc/qn** to stare at sth/sb; **telefono ~** landline

'fitta *sf* sharp pain; *vedi anche* **fitto**

fit'tizio, -a *ag* fictitious, imaginary

'fitto, -a *ag* thick, dense; (*pioggia*) heavy ▷ *sm* depths *pl*, middle; (*affitto, pigione*) rent

fi'ume *sm* river

fiu'tare *vt* to smell, sniff; (*animale*) to scent; (*fig: inganno*) to get wind of, smell; **~ tabacco/cocaina** to take snuff/cocaine

fla'grante *ag*: **cogliere qn in ~** to catch sb red-handed

fla'nella *sf* flannel

flash [flaʃ] *sm inv* (*Fot*) flash; (*giornalistico*) newsflash

'flauto *sm* flute

fles'sibile *ag* pliable; (*fig: che si adatta*) flexible

flessibili'tà *sf* (*anche fig*) flexibility

flessi'one *sf* (*gen*) bending; (*Ginnastica: a terra*) sit-up; (*: in piedi*) forward bend; (*: sulle gambe*) knee-bend; (*diminuzione*) slight drop, slight fall; (*Ling*) inflection; **fare una ~** to bend; **una ~ economica** a downward trend in the economy

'flettere *vt* to bend

'flipper *sm inv* pinball machine

F.lli *abbr* (= *fratelli*) Bros

'flora *sf* flora

'florido, -a *ag* flourishing; (*fig*) glowing with health

'floscio, -a, -sci, -sce ['flɔʃʃo] *ag* (*cappello*) floppy, soft; (*muscoli*) flabby

'flotta *sf* fleet

'fluido, -a *ag, sm* fluid

flu'oro *sm* fluorine

'flusso *sm* flow; (*Fisica, Med*) flux; **~ e ri~** ebb and flow

fluvi'ale *ag* river *cpd*, fluvial

FMI *sigla m* (= *Fondo Monetario Internazionale*) IMF

'foca, -che *sf* (*Zool*) seal

fo'caccia, -ce [fo'kattʃa] *sf* kind of pizza; (*dolce*) bun

'foce ['fotʃe] *sf* (*Geo*) mouth

foco'laio *sm* (*Med*) centre of infection; (*fig*) hotbed

foco'lare *sm* hearth, fireside; (*Tecn*)

furnace

'fodera sf (di vestito) lining; (di libro, poltrona) cover

'fodero sm (di spada) scabbard; (di pugnale) sheath; (di pistola) holster

'foga sf enthusiasm, ardour

'foglia ['fɔʎʎa] sf leaf; **foglia d'argento/d'oro** silver/gold leaf

'foglio ['fɔʎʎo] sm (di carta) sheet (of paper); (di metallo) sheet; **foglio di calcolo** (Inform) spreadsheet; **foglio rosa** (Aut) provisional licence; **foglio di via** (Dir) expulsion order; **foglio volante** pamphlet

'fogna ['foɲɲa] sf drain, sewer

föhn [føːn] sm inv hair dryer

'folla sf crowd, throng

'folle ag mad, insane; (Tecn) idle; **in ~** (Aut) in neutral

fol'lia sf folly, foolishness; foolish act; (pazzia) madness, lunacy

'folto, -a ag thick

fon sm inv hair dryer

fondamen'tale ag fundamental, basic

fonda'mento sm foundation; **fondamenta** sfpl (Edil) foundations

fon'dare vt to found; (fig: dar base): **~ qc su** to base sth on

fon'dente ag: **cioccolato ~** plain o dark chocolate

'fondere vt (neve) to melt; (metallo) to fuse, melt; (fig: colori) to merge, blend; (: imprese, gruppi) to merge ▷ vi to melt; **fondersi** vpr to melt; (fig: partiti, correnti) to unite, merge

'fondo, -a ag deep ▷ sm (di recipiente, pozzo) bottom; (di stanza) back; (quantità di liquido che resta, deposito) dregs pl; (sfondo) background; (unità immobiliare) property, estate; (somma di denaro) fund; (Sport) long-distance race; **fondi** smpl (denaro) funds; **a notte fonda** at dead of night; **in ~ a** at the bottom of; at the back of; (strada) at the end of; **andare a ~** (nave) to sink; **conoscere a ~** to know inside

out; **dar ~ a** (fig: provviste, soldi) to use up; **in ~** (fig) after all, all things considered; **andare fino in ~ a** (fig) to examine thoroughly; **a ~ perduto** (Comm) without security; **fondi di magazzino** old o unsold stock sg; **fondi di caffè** coffee grounds; **fondo comune di investimento** investment trust

fondo'tinta sm inv (cosmetico) foundation

fo'netica sf phonetics sg

fon'tana sf fountain

'fonte sf spring, source; (fig) source ▷ sm: **fonte battesimale** (Rel) font; **fonte energetica** source of energy

fo'raggio [fo'raddʒo] sm fodder, forage

fo'rare vt to pierce, make a hole in; (pallone) to burst; (biglietto) to punch; **~ una gomma** to burst a tyre (BRIT) o tire (US)

'forbici ['fɔrbitʃi] sfpl scissors

'forca, -che sf (Agr) fork, pitchfork; (patibolo) gallows sg

for'chetta [for'ketta] sf fork

for'cina [for'tʃina] sf hairpin

fo'resta sf forest

foresti'ero, -a ag foreign ▷ sm/f foreigner

'forfora sf dandruff

'forma sf form; (aspetto esteriore) form, shape; (Dir: procedura) procedure; (per calzature) last; (stampo da cucina) mould

formag'gino [formad'dʒino] sm processed cheese

for'maggio [for'maddʒo] sm cheese

for'male ag formal

for'mare vt to form, shape, make; (numero di telefono) to dial; (fig: carattere) to form, mould; **formarsi** vpr to form, take shape; **for'mato** sm format, size; **formazi'one** sf formation; (fig: educazione) training; **formazione continua** continuing education; **formazione permanente**

lifelong learning; **formazione professionale** vocational training

for'mica¹, -che *sf* ant

formica® ['fɔrmika] *sf* (*materiale*) Formica®

formi'dabile *ag* powerful, formidable; (*straordinario*) remarkable

'formula *sf* formula; **formula di cortesia** courtesy form

formu'lare *vt* to formulate; to express

for'naio *sm* baker

for'nello *sm* (*elettrico, a gas*) ring; (*di pipa*) bowl

for'nire *vt*: ~ **qn di qc, ~ qc a qn** to provide o supply sb with sth, supply sth to sb

'forno *sm* (*di cucina*) oven; (*panetteria*) bakery; (*Tecn: per calce ecc*) kiln; (: *per metalli*) furnace; **forno a microonde** microwave oven

'foro *sm* (*buco*) hole; (*Storia*) forum; (*tribunale*) (law) court

'forse *av* perhaps, maybe; (*circa*) about; **essere in ~** to be in doubt

'forte *ag* strong; (*suono*) loud; (*spesa*) considerable, great; (*passione, dolore*) great, deep ▷ *av* strongly; (*velocemente*) fast; (*a voce alta*) loud(ly); (*violentemente*) hard ▷ *sm* (*edificio*) fort; (*specialità*) forte, strong point; **essere ~ in qc** to be good at sth

for'tezza [for'tettsa] *sf* (*morale*) strength; (*luogo fortificato*) fortress

for'tuito, -a *ag* fortuitous, chance

for'tuna *sf* (*destino*) fortune, luck; (*buona sorte*) success, fortune; (*eredità, averi*) fortune; **per ~** luckily, fortunately; **di ~** makeshift, improvised; **atterraggio di ~** emergency landing; **fortu'nato, -a** *ag* lucky, fortunate; (*coronato da successo*) successful

'forza ['fɔrtsa] *sf* strength; (*potere*) power; (*Fisica*) force; **forze** *sfpl* (*fisiche*) strength *sg*; (*Mil*) forces *escl* come on!; **per ~** against one's will;

(*naturalmente*) of course; **a viva ~** by force; **a ~ di** by dint of; **~ maggiore** circumstances beyond one's control; **la ~ pubblica** the police *pl*; **forze armate** armed forces; **forze dell'ordine** the forces of law and order; **Forza Italia** *Italian centre-right political party*; **forza di pace** peacekeeping force

for'zare [for'tsare] *vt* to force; **~ qn a fare** to force sb to do

for'zista, -i, e [for'tsista] *ag* of Forza Italia ▷ *sm/f* member (o supporter) of Forza Italia

fos'chia [fos'kia] *sf* mist, haze

'fosco, -a, -schi, -sche *ag* dark, gloomy

'fosforo *sm* phosphorous

'fossa *sf* pit; (*di cimitero*) grave; **fossa biologica** septic tank

fos'sato *sm* ditch; (*di fortezza*) moat

fos'setta *sf* dimple

'fossi *ecc vb vedi* **essere**

'fossile *ag, sm* fossil

'fosso *sm* ditch; (*Mil*) trench

'foste *ecc vb vedi* **essere**

'foto *sf* photo; **può farci una ~, per favore?** would you take a picture of us, please? ▷ *prefisso*: **foto ricordo** souvenir photo; **foto tessera** passport(-type) photo; **foto'camera** *sf* **fotocamera digitale** digital camera; **foto'copia** *sf* photocopy; **fotocopi'are** *vt* to photocopy; **fotocopia'trice** [fotokopja'tritʃe] *sf* photocopier; **fotofo'nino** *sm* camera phone; **fotogra'fare** *vt* to photograph; **fotogra'fia** *sf* (*procedimento*) photography; (*immagine*) photograph; **fare una fotografia** to take a photograph; **una fotografia a colori/in bianco e nero** a colour/black and white photograph; **foto'grafico, -a, ci, che** *ag* photographic; **macchina fotografica** camera; **fo'tografo, -a** *sm/f* photographer; **fotoro'manzo** sm romantic picture story

fou'lard [fu'lar] sm inv scarf

fra prep = **tra**

'fradicio, -a, -ci, -ce ['fraditʃo] ag (molto bagnato) soaking (wet); **ubriaco ~** blind drunk

'fragile ['fradʒile] ag fragile; (fig: salute) delicate

'fragola sf strawberry

fra'grante ag fragrant

frain'tendere vt to misunderstand

fram'mento sm fragment

'frana sf landslide; (fig: persona): **essere una ~** to be useless

fran'cese [fran'tʃeze] ag French ▷ sm/f Frenchman/woman ▷ sm (Ling) French; **i Francesi** the French

'Francia ['frantʃa] sf: **la ~** France

'franco, -a, -chi, -che ag (Comm) free; (sincero) frank, open, sincere ▷ sm (moneta) franc; **farla franca** (fig) to get off scot-free; **prezzo ~ fabbrica** ex-works price; **franco di dogana** duty-free

franco'bollo sm (postage) stamp

'frangia, -ge ['frandʒa] sf fringe

frap'pé sm milk shake

'frase sf (Ling) sentence; (locuzione, espressione, Mus) phrase; **frase fatta** set phrase

'frassino sm ash (tree)

frastagli'ato, -a [frastaʎ'ʎato] ag (costa) indented, jagged

frastor'nare vt to daze; to befuddle

frastu'ono sm hubbub, din

'frate sm friar, monk

fratel'lastro sm stepbrother; (con genitore in comune) half-brother

fra'tello sm brother; **fratelli** smpl brothers; (nel senso di fratelli e sorelle) brothers and sisters

fra'terno, -a ag fraternal, brotherly

frat'tempo sm **nel ~** in the meantime, meanwhile

frat'tura sf fracture; (fig) split, break

frazi'one [frat'tsjone] sf fraction; (di comune) small town

'freccia, -ce ['frettʃa] sf arrow; **freccia di direzione** (Aut) indicator

fred'dezza [fred'dettsa] sf coldness

'freddo, -a ag, sm cold; **fa ~** it's cold; **aver ~** to be cold; **a ~** (fig) deliberately; **freddo'loso, -a** ag sensitive to the cold

fre'gare vt to rub; (fam: truffare) to take in, cheat; (: rubare) to swipe, pinch; **fregarsene** (fam!): **chi se ne frega?** who gives a damn (about it)?

fregherò ecc [frege'rɔ] vb vedi **fregare**

fre'nare vt (veicolo) to slow down; (cavallo) to rein in; (lacrime) to restrain, hold back ▷ vi to brake; **frenarsi** vpr (fig) to restrain o.s., control o.s.

'freno sm brake; (morso) bit; **tenere a ~** to restrain; **freno a disco** disc brake; **freno a mano** handbrake

frequen'tare vt (scuola, corso) to attend; (locale, bar) to go to, frequent; (persone) to see (often)

frequen'tato, -a ag (locale) busy

fre'quente ag frequent; **di ~** frequently

fres'chezza [fres'kettsa] sf freshness

'fresco, -a, -schi, -sche ag fresh; (temperatura) cool; (notizia) recent, fresh ▷ sm **godere il ~** to enjoy the cool air; **stare ~** (fig) to be in for it; **mettere al ~** to put in a cool place

'fretta sf hurry, haste; **in ~** in a hurry; **in ~ e furia** in a mad rush; **aver ~** to be in a hurry

'friggere ['friddʒere] vt to fry ▷ vi (olio ecc) to sizzle

'frigido, -a ['fridʒido] ag (Med) frigid

'frigo sm fridge

frigo'bar sm inv minibar

frigo'rifero, -a ag refrigerating ▷ sm refrigerator

fringu'ello sm chaffinch

'frissi ecc vb vedi **friggere**

frit'tata sf omelette; **fare una ~** (fig) to make a mess of things

frit'tella sf (Cuc) fritter

'fritto, -a pp di **friggere** ▷ ag fried

▷ *sm* fried food; **fritto misto** mixed fry

frit'tura *sf* (*Cuc*): **frittura di pesce** mixed fried fish

'frivolo, -a *ag* frivolous

frizi'one [frit'tsjone] *sf* friction; (*sulla pelle*) rub, rub-down; (*Aut*) clutch

friz'zante [frid'dzante] *ag* (*anche fig*) sparkling

fro'dare *vt* to defraud, cheat

'frode *sf* fraud, **frode fiscale** tax evasion

'fronda *sf* (leafy) branch; (*di partito politico*) internal opposition; **fronde** *sfpl* (*di albero*) foliage *sg*

fron'tale *ag* frontal; (*scontro*) head-on

'fronte *sf* (*Anat*) forehead; (*di edificio*) front, façade ▷ *sm* (*Mil, Pol, Meteor*) front; **a ~, di ~** facing, opposite; **di ~ a** (*posizione*) opposite, facing, in front of; (*a paragone di*) compared with

fronti'era *sf* border, frontier

'frottola *sf* fib

fru'gare *vi* to rummage ▷ *vt* to search

frugherò *ecc* [fruge'rɔ] *vb vedi* **frugare**

frul'lare *vt* (*Cuc*) to whisk ▷ *vi* (*uccelli*) to flutter; **frul'lato** *sm* milk shake, fruit drink; **frulla'tore** *sm* electric mixer

fru'mento *sm* wheat

fru'scio [fruʃʃio] *sm* rustle; rustling; (*di acque*) murmur

'frusta *sf* whip; (*Cuc*) whisk

frus'tare *vt* to whip

frus'trato, -a *ag* frustrated

'frutta *sf* fruit; (*portata*) dessert; **frutta candita** candied fruit; **frutta secca** dried fruit

frut'tare *vi* to bear dividends, give a return

frut'teto *sm* orchard

frutti'vendolo, -a *sm/f* greengrocer (*BRIT*), produce dealer (*US*)

'frutto *sm* fruit; (*fig: risultato*) result(s); (*Econ: interesse*) interest; (: *reddito*) income; **frutti di bosco** berries; **frutti di mare** seafood *sg*

FS *abbr* = **Ferrovie dello Stato**

fu *vb vedi* **essere** ▷ *ag inv* **il fu Paolo Bianchi** the late Paolo Bianchi

fuci'lare [futʃi'lare] *vt* to shoot

fu'cile [fu'tʃile] *sm* rifle, gun; (*da caccia*) shotgun, gun

'fucsia *sf* fuchsia

'fuga *sf* escape, flight; (*di gas, liquidi*) leak; (*Mus*) fugue; **fuga di cervelli** brain drain

fug'gire [fud'dʒire] *vi* to flee, run away; (*fig: passar veloce*) to fly ▷ *vt* to avoid

'fui *vb vedi* **essere**

fu'liggine [fu'liddʒine] *sf* soot

'fulmine *sm* thunderbolt; lightning *no pl*

fu'mare *vi* to smoke; (*emettere vapore*) to steam ▷ *vt* to smoke; **le dà fastidio se fumo?** do you mind if I smoke?; **fuma'tore, -'trice** *sm/f* smoker

fu'metto *sm* comic strip; **giornale** *sm*, **a fumetti** comic

'fummo *vb vedi* **essere**

'fumo *sm* smoke; (*vapore*) steam; (*il fumare tabacco*) smoking; **fumi** *smpl* (*industriali ecc*) fumes; **i fumi dell'alcool** the after-effects of drink; **vendere ~** to deceive, cheat; **fumo passivo** passive smoking

'fune *sf* rope, cord; (*più grossa*) cable

'funebre *ag* (*rito*) funeral; (*aspetto*) gloomy, funereal

fune'rale *sm* funeral

'fungere ['fundʒere] *vi* **~ da** to act as

'fungo, -ghi *sm* fungus; (*commestibile*) mushroom; **fungo velenoso** toadstool

funico'lare *sf* funicular railway

funi'via *sf* cable railway

'funsi *ecc vb vedi* **fungere**

funzio'nare [funtsjo'nare] *vi* to work, function; (*fungere*): **~ da** to act as; **come funziona?** how does this work?; **la TV non funziona** the TV isn't working

funzio'nario [funtsjo'narjo] *sm*

official; **funzionario statale** civil servant

funzi'one [fun'tsjone] *sf* function; (*carica*) post, position; (*Rel*) service; **in ~** (*meccanismo*) in operation; **in ~ di** (*come*) as; **fare la ~ di qn** (*farne le veci*) to take sb's place

fu'oco, -chi *sm* fire; (*fornello*) ring; (*Fot, Fisica*) focus; **dare ~ a qc** to set fire to sth; **far ~** (*sparare*) to fire; **al ~!** fire!; **fuoco d'artificio** firework

fuorché [fwor'ke] *cong, prep* except

fu'ori *av* outside; (*all'aperto*) outdoors, outside; (*fuori di casa, Sport*) out; (*esclamativo*) get out! ▷ *prep* **~ (di)** out of, outside ▷ *sm* outside; **lasciar ~ qc/qn** to leave sth/sb out; **far ~ qn** (*fam*) to kill sb, do sb in; **essere ~ di sé** to be beside o.s.; **~ luogo** (*inopportuno*) out of place, uncalled for; **~ mano** out of the way, remote; **~ pericolo** out of danger; **~ uso** old-fashioned; obsolete; **fuorigi'oco** *sm* offside; **fuori'strada** *sm* (*Aut*) cross-country vehicle

'furbo, -a *ag* clever, smart; (*peg*) cunning

fu'rente *ag* **~ (contro)** furious (with)

fur'fante *sm* rascal, scoundrel

fur'gone *sm* van

'furia *sf* (*ira*) fury, rage; (*fig: impeto*) fury, violence; (*fretta*) rush; **a ~ di** by dint of; **andare su tutte le furie** to get into a towering rage; **furi'bondo, -a** *ag* furious

furi'oso, -a *ag* furious

'furono *vb vedi* **essere**

fur'tivo, -a *ag* furtive

'furto *sm* theft; **vorrei denunciare un ~** I'd like to report a theft; **furto con scasso** burglary

'fusa *sfpl* **fare le ~** to purr

fu'seaux [fy'zo] *smpl inv* leggings

'fusi *ecc vb vedi* **fondere**

fu'sibile *sm* (*Elettr*) fuse

fusi'one *sf* (*di metalli*) fusion, melting; (*colata*) casting; (*Comm*) merger; (*fig*) merging

'fuso, -a *pp di* **fondere** ▷ *sm* (*Filatura*) spindle; **fuso orario** time zone

fus'tino *sm* (*di detersivo*) tub

'fusto *sm* stem; (*Anat, di albero*) trunk; (*recipiente*) drum, can

fu'turo, -a *ag, sm* future

g

'gabbia sf cage; (da imballaggio) crate; **gabbia dell'ascensore** lift (BRIT) o elevator (US) shaft; **gabbia toracica** (Anat) rib cage

gabbi'ano sm (sea)gull

gabi'netto sm (Med ecc) consulting room; (Pol) ministry; (WC) toilet, lavatory; (Ins: di fisica ecc) laboratory

'gaffe [gaf] sf inv blunder

ga'lante ag gallant, courteous; (avventura) amorous

ga'lassia sf galaxy

ga'lera sf (Naut) galley; (prigione) prison

'galla sf **a ~** afloat; **venire a ~** to surface, come to the surface; (fig: verità) to come out

galleggi'are [galled'dʒare] vi to float

galle'ria sf (traforo) tunnel; (Archit, d'arte) gallery; (Teatro) circle; (strada coperta con negozi) arcade

'Galles sm **il ~** Wales

gal'lina sf hen

'gallo sm cock

galop'pare vi to gallop

ga'loppo sm gallop; **al** o **di ~** at a gallop

'gamba sf leg; (asta: di lettera) stem; **in ~** (in buona salute) well; (bravo, sveglio) bright, smart; **prendere qc sotto ~** (fig) to treat sth too lightly

gambe'retto sm shrimp

'gambero sm (di acqua dolce) crayfish; (di mare) prawn

'gambo sm stem; (di frutta) stalk

'gamma sf (Mus) scale; (di colori, fig) range

'gancio ['gantʃo] sm hook

'gara sf competition; (Sport) competition; contest; match; (: corsa) race; **fare a ~** to compete, vie

ga'rage [ga'raʒ] sm inv garage

garan'tire vt to guarantee; (debito) to stand surety for; (dare per certo) to assure

garan'zia [garan'tsia] sf guarantee; (pegno) security

gar'bato, -a ag courteous, polite

gareggi'are [gared'dʒare] vi to compete

garga'rismo sm gargle; **fare i gargarismi** to gargle

ga'rofano sm carnation; **chiodo di ~** clove

'garza ['gardza] sf (per bende) gauze

gar'zone [gar'dzone] sm (di negozio) boy

gas sm inv gas; **sento odore di ~** I can smell gas; **a tutto ~** at full speed; **dare ~** (Aut) to accelerate

ga'solio sm diesel (oil)

gas'sato, -a ag fizzy

gas'trite sf gastritis

gastrono'mia sf gastronomy

gat'tino sm kitten

'gatto, -a sm/f cat, tomcat/she-cat; **gatto delle nevi** (Aut, Sci) snowcat; **gatto selvatico** wildcat

'gazza ['gaddza] sf magpie

gel [dʒɛl] sm inv gel

ge'lare [dʒe'lare] vt, vi, vb impers to

freeze

gelate'ria [dʒelate'ria] *sf* ice-cream shop

gela'tina [dʒela'tina] *sf* gelatine; **gelatina esplosiva** dynamite; **gelatina di frutta** fruit jelly

ge'lato, -a [dʒe'lato] *ag* frozen ▷ *sm* ice cream

'gelido, -a [dʒɛlido] *ag* icy, ice-cold

'gelo [dʒɛlo] *sm* (*temperatura*) intense cold; (*brina*) frost; (*fig*) chill

gelo'sia [dʒelo'sia] *sf* jealousy

ge'loso, -a [dʒe'loso] *ag* jealous

'gelso [dʒɛlso] *sm* mulberry (tree)

gelso'mino [dʒelso'mino] *sm* jasmine

ge'mello, -a [dʒe'mɛllo] *ag, sm/f* twin; **gemelli** *smpl* (*di camicia*) cufflinks; (*dello zodiaco*): **Gemelli** Gemini *sg*

'gemere [dʒɛmere] *vi* to moan, groan; (*cigolare*) to creak

'gemma [dʒɛmma] *sf* (*Bot*) bud; (*pietra preziosa*) gem

gene'rale [dʒene'rale] *ag, sm* general; **in ~** (*per sommi capi*) in general terms; (*di solito*) usually, in general

gene'rare [dʒene'rare] *vt* (*dar vita*) to give birth to; (*produrre*) to produce; (*causare*) to arouse; (*Tecn*) to produce, generate; **generazi'one** *sf* generation

'genere [dʒɛnere] *sm* kind, type, sort; (*Biol*) genus; (*merce*) article, product; (*Ling*) gender; (*Arte, Letteratura*) genre; **in ~** generally, as a rule; **genere umano** mankind; **generi alimentari** foodstuffs

ge'nerico, -a, -ci, -che [dʒe'nɛriko] *ag* generic; (*vago*) vague, imprecise

'genero [dʒɛnero] *sm* son-in-law

gene'roso, -a [dʒene'roso] *ag* generous

ge'netica [dʒe'nɛtika] *sf* genetics *sg*

ge'netico, -a, -ci, -che [dʒe'nɛtiko] *ag* genetic

gen'giva [dʒen'dʒiva] *sf* (*Anat*) gum

geni'ale [dʒen'jale] *ag* (*persona*) of genius; (*idea*) ingenious, brilliant

'genio [dʒɛnjo] *sm* genius; **andare a ~ a qn** to be to sb's liking, appeal to sb

geni'tore [dʒeni'tore] *sm* parent, father o mother; **i miei genitori** my parents, my father and mother

gen'naio [dʒen'najo] *sm* January

'Genova [dʒɛnova] *sf* Genoa

'gente [dʒɛnte] *sf* people *pl*

gen'tile [dʒen'tile] *ag* (*persona, atto*) kind; (: *garbato*) courteous, polite; (*nelle lettere*): **G~ Signore** Dear Sir; (: *sulla busta*): **G~ Signor Fernando Villa** Mr Fernando Villa

genu'ino, -a [dʒenu'ino] *ag* (*prodotto*) natural; (*persona, sentimento*) genuine, sincere

geogra'fia [dʒeogra'fia] *sf* geography

geolo'gia [dʒeolo'dʒia] *sf* geology

ge'ometra, -i, -e [dʒe'ometra] *sm/f* (*professionista*) surveyor

geome'tria [dʒeome'tria] *sf* geometry

ge'ranio [dʒe'ranjo] *sm* geranium

gerar'chia [dʒerar'kia] *sf* hierarchy

'gergo, -ghi [dʒɛrgo] *sm* jargon; slang

geria'tria [dʒerja'tria] *sf* geriatrics *sg*

Ger'mania [dʒer'manja] *sf*: **la ~** Germany; **la ~ occidentale/orientale** West/East Germany

'germe [dʒɛrme] *sm* germ; (*fig*) seed

germogli'are [dʒermoʎ'ʎare] *vi* to sprout; to germinate

gero'glifico, -ci [dʒero'glifiko] *sm* hieroglyphic

ge'rundio [dʒe'rundjo] *sm* gerund

'gesso [dʒɛsso] *sm* chalk; (*Scultura, Med, Edil*) plaster; (*statua*) plaster figure; (*minerale*) gypsum

gesti'one [dʒes'tjone] *sf* management

ges'tire [dʒes'tire] *vt* to run, manage

'gesto [dʒɛsto] *sm* gesture

Gesù [dʒe'zu] *sm* Jesus

gesu'ita, -i [dʒezu'ita] *sm* Jesuit

get'tare [dʒet'tare] vt to throw;
(anche: **~ via**) to throw away o out;
(Scultura) to cast; (Edil) to lay; (acqua)
to spout; (grido) to utter; **gettarsi** vpr
gettarsi in (fiume) to flow into; **~ uno
sguardo su** to take a quick look at

'getto ['dʒɛtto] sm (di gas, liquido, Aer)
jet; **a ~ continuo** uninterruptedly; **di
~** (fig) straight off, in one go

get'tone [dʒet'tone] sm token; (per
giochi) counter; (: roulette ecc) chip;
gettone telefonico telephone token

ghiacci'aio [gjat'tʃajo] sm glacier

ghiacci'ato, -a ag frozen; (bevanda)
ice-cold

ghi'accio ['gjattʃo] sm ice

ghiacci'olo [gjat'tʃɔlo] sm icicle; (tipo
di gelato) ice lolly (BRIT), Popsicle® (US)

ghi'aia ['gjaja] sf gravel

ghi'anda ['gjanda] sf (Bot) acorn

ghi'andola ['gjandola] sf gland

ghi'otto, -a ['gjotto] ag greedy; (cibo)
delicious, appetizing

ghir'landa [gir'landa] sf garland,
wreath

'ghiro ['giro] sm dormouse

'ghisa ['giza] sf cast iron

già [dʒa] av already; (ex, in precedenza)
formerly ▷ escl of course!, yes indeed!

gi'acca, -che ['dʒakka] sf jacket;
giacca a vento windcheater (BRIT),
windbreaker (US)

giacché [dʒak'ke] cong since, as

giac'cone [dʒak'kone] sm heavy
jacket

gi'ada ['dʒada] sf jade

giagu'aro [dʒa'gwaro] sm jaguar

gi'allo ['dʒallo] ag yellow; (carnagione)
sallow ▷ sm yellow; (anche: **romanzo
~**) detective novel; (anche: **film ~**)
detective film; **giallo dell'uovo** yolk

Giamaica [dʒa'maika] sf **la ~** Jamaica

Giap'pone [dʒap'pone] sm Japan;
giappo'nese ag, sm/f, sm Japanese inv

giardi'naggio [dʒardi'naddʒo] sm
gardening

giardini'ere, -a [dʒardi'njɛre] sm/f
gardener

giar'dino [dʒar'dino] sm garden;
giardino d'infanzia nursery school;
giardino pubblico public gardens pl,
(public) park; **giardino zoologico** zoo

giavel'lotto [dʒavel'lɔtto] sm javelin

gigabyte [dʒiga'bait] sm inv gigabyte

gi'gante, -'essa [dʒi'gante] sm/f
giant ▷ ag giant, gigantic; (Comm)
giant-size

'giglio ['dʒiʎʎo] sm lily

gilè [dʒi'lɛ] sm inv waistcoat

gin [dʒin] sm inv gin

gine'cologo, -a, -gi, -ghe
[dʒine'kɔlogo] sm/f gynaecologist

gi'nepro [dʒi'nepro] sm juniper

gi'nestra [dʒi'nɛstra] sf (Bot) broom

Gi'nevra [dʒi'nevra] sf Geneva

gin'nastica sf gymnastics sg;
(esercizio fisico) keep-fit exercises; (Ins)
physical education

gi'nocchio [dʒi'nɔkkjo] (pl(m)
gi'nocchi, o pl(f) **gi'nocchia**) sm
knee; **stare in ~** to kneel, be on one's
knees; **mettersi in ~** to kneel (down)

gio'care [dʒo'kare] vt to play;
(scommettere) to stake, wager, bet;
(ingannare) to take in ▷ vi to play; (a
roulette ecc) to gamble; (fig) to play a
part, be important; **~ a** (gioco, sport)
to play; (cavalli) to bet on; **giocarsi
la carriera** to put one's career at
risk; **gioca'tore, -'trice** sm/f player;
gambler

gio'cattolo [dʒo'kattolo] sm toy

giocherò ecc [dʒoke'rɔ] vb vedi
giocare

gi'oco, -chi ['dʒɔko] sm game;
(divertimento, Tecn) play; (al casinò)
gambling; (Carte) hand; (insieme di
pezzi ecc necessari per un gioco) set; **per
~** for fun; **fare il doppio ~ con qn** to
double-cross sb; **i Giochi Olimpici**
the Olympic Games; **gioco d'azzardo**
game of chance; **gioco degli scacchi**
chess set

giocoli'ere [dʒoko'ljɛre] sm juggler

gi'oia ['dʒɔja] *sf* joy, delight; (*pietra preziosa*) jewel, precious stone

gioielle'ria [dʒojelle'ria] *sf* jeweller's craft; jeweller's (shop)

gioiel'liere, -a [dʒojeʎ'ljɛre] *sm/f* jeweller

gioi'ello [dʒo'jɛllo] *sm* jewel, piece of jewellery; **i miei gioielli** my jewels *o* jewellery; **gioielli** *smpl* (*anelli, collane ecc*) jewellery; **i gioielli della Corona** the crown jewels

Gior'dania [dʒor'danja] *sf*: **la ~** Jordan

giorna'laio, -a [dʒorna'lajo] *sm/f* newsagent (BRIT), newsdealer (US)

gior'nale [dʒor'nale] *sm* (*news*) paper; (*diario*) journal, diary; (*Comm*) journal; **giornale di bordo** log; **giornale radio** radio news *sg*

giornali'ero, -a [dʒorna'ljɛro] *ag* daily; (*che varia: umore*) changeable ▷ *sm* day labourer

giorna'lismo [dʒorna'lizmo] *sm* journalism

giorna'lista, -i, -e [dʒorna'lista] *sm/f* journalist

gior'nata [dʒor'nata] *sf* day; **giornata lavorativa** working day

gi'orno ['dʒorno] *sm* day; (*opposto alla notte*) day, daytime; (*anche*: **luce del ~**) daylight; **al ~** per day; **di ~** by day; **al ~ d'oggi** nowadays

gi'ostra ['dʒɔstra] *sf* (*per bimbi*) merry-go-round; (*torneo storico*) joust

gi'ovane ['dʒovane] *ag* young; (*aspetto*) youthful ▷ *sm/f* youth/girl, young man/woman; **i giovani** young people

gio'vare [dʒo'vare] *vi*: **~ a** (*essere utile*) to be useful to; (*far bene*) to be good for ▷ *vb impers* (*essere bene, utile*) to be useful; **giovarsi di qc** to make use of sth

giovedì [dʒove'di] *sm inv* Thursday; **di** *o* **il ~** on Thursdays

gioventù [dʒoven'tu] *sf* (*periodo*) youth; (*i giovani*) young people *pl*, youth

G.I.P. [dʒip] *sigla m inv* (= *Giudice per le Indagini Preliminari*) judge for preliminary enquiries

gira'dischi [dʒira'diski] *sm inv* record player

gi'raffa [dʒi'raffa] *sf* giraffe

gi'rare [dʒi'rare] *vt* (*far ruotare*) to turn; (*percorrere, visitare*) to go round; (*Cinema*) to shoot; to make; (*Comm*) to endorse ▷ *vi* to turn; (*più veloce*) to spin; (*andare in giro*) to wander, go around; **girarsi** *vpr* to turn; **~ attorno a** to go round; to revolve round; **al prossimo incrocio giri a destra/sinistra** turn right/left at the next junction; **far ~ la testa a qn** to make sb dizzy; (*fig*) to turn sb's head

girar'rosto [dʒirar'rɔsto] *sm* (*Cuc*) spit

gira'sole [dʒira'sole] *sm* sunflower

gi'revole [dʒi'revole] *ag* revolving, turning

gi'rino [dʒi'rino] *sm* tadpole

'giro ['dʒiro] *sm* (*circuito, cerchio*) circle; (*di chiave, manovella*) turn; (*viaggio*) tour, excursion; (*passeggiata*) stroll, walk; (*in macchina*) drive; (*in bicicletta*) ride; (*Sport: della pista*) lap; (*di denaro*) circulation; (*Carte*) hand; (*Tecn*) revolution; **prendere in ~ qn** (*fig*) to pull sb's leg; **fare un ~** to go for a walk (*o* a drive *o* a ride); **andare in ~** to go about, walk around; **a stretto ~ di posta** by return of post; **nel ~ di un mese** in a month's time; **essere nel ~** (*fig*) to belong to a circle (of friends); **giro d'affari** (*Comm*) turnover; **giro di parole** circumlocution; **giro di prova** (*Aut*) test drive; **giro turistico** sightseeing tour; **giro'collo** *sm* **a girocollo** crew-neck *cpd*

gironzo'lare [dʒirondzo'lare] *vi* to stroll about

'gita ['dʒita] *sf* excursion, trip; **fare una ~** to go for a trip, go on an outing

gi'tano, -a [dʒi'tano] *sm/f* gipsy

giù [dʒu] *av* down; (*dabbasso*)

downstairs; **in ~** downwards, down; **~ di lì** (*pressappoco*) thereabouts; **bambini dai 6 anni in ~** children aged 6 and under; **~ per: cadere ~ per le scale** to fall down the stairs; **essere ~** (*fig: di salute*) to be run down; (: *di spirito*) to be depressed

giub'botto [dʒub'bɔtto] *sm* jerkin; **giubbotto antiproiettile** bulletproof vest; **giubbotto salvagente** life jacket

giudi'care [dʒudi'kare] *vt* to judge, (*accusato*) to try; (*lite*) to arbitrate in; **~ qn/qc bello** to consider sb/sth (to be) beautiful

gi'udice ['dʒuditʃe] *sm* judge; **giudice conciliatore** justice of the peace; **giudice istruttore** examining (*BRIT*) o committing (*US*) magistrate; **giudice popolare** member of a jury

giu'dizio [dʒu'dittsjo] *sm* judgment; (*opinione*) opinion; (*Dir*) judgment, sentence; (: *processo*) trial; (: *verdetto*) verdict; **aver ~** to be wise o prudent; **citare in ~** to summons

gi'ugno ['dʒuɲɲo] *sm* June

gi'ungere ['dʒundʒere] *vi* to arrive ▷ *vt* (*mani ecc*) to join; **~ a** to arrive at, reach

gi'ungla ['dʒungla] *sf* jungle

gi'unsi *ecc* ['dʒunsi] *vb vedi* **giungere**

giura'mento [dʒura'mento] *sm* oath; **giuramento falso** perjury

giu'rare [dʒu'rare] *vt* to swear ▷ *vi* to swear, take an oath

giu'ria [dʒu'ria] *sf* jury

giu'ridico, -a, -ci, -che [dʒu'ridiko] *ag* legal

giustifi'care [dʒustifi'kare] *vt* to justify; **giustificazi'one** *sf* justification; (*Ins*) (note of) excuse

gius'tizia [dʒus'tittsja] *sf* justice; **giustizi'are** *vt* to execute, put to death

gi'usto, -a ['dʒusto] *ag* (*equo*) fair, just; (*vero*) true, correct; (*adatto*) right, suitable; (*preciso*) exact, correct ▷ *av*

(*esattamente*) exactly, precisely; (*per l'appunto, appena*) just; **arrivare ~** to arrive just in time; **ho ~ bisogno di te** you're just the person I need

glaci'ale [gla'tʃale] *ag* glacial

gli [ʎi] (*davV, s impura, gn, pn, ps, x, z*) *det mpl* the ▷ *pron* (*a lui*) to him; (*a esso*) to it; (*in coppia con lo, la, li, le, ne: a lui, a lei, a loro ecc*): **gliele do** I'm giving them to him (o her o them); *vedi anche* **il**

glo'bale *ag* overall

'globo *sm* globe

'globulo *sm* (*Anat*): **globulo rosso/ bianco** red/white corpuscle

'gloria *sf* glory

'gnocchi ['ɲɔkki] *smpl* (*Cuc*) small dumplings made of semolina pasta or potato

'gobba *sf* (*Anat*) hump; (*protuberanza*) bump

'gobbo, -a *ag* hunchbacked; (*ricurvo*) round-shouldered ▷ *sm/f* hunchback

'goccia, -ce ['gottʃa] *sf* drop; **goccio'lare** *vi, vt* to drip

go'dere *vi* (*compiacersi*): **~ (di)** to be delighted (at), rejoice (at); (*trarre vantaggio*): **~ di** benefit from ▷ *vt* to enjoy; **godersi la vita** to enjoy life; **godersela** to have a good time, enjoy o.s.

godrò *ecc vb vedi* **godere**

'goffo, -a *ag* clumsy, awkward

'gola *sf* (*Anat*) throat; (*golosità*) gluttony, greed; (*di camino*) flue; (*di monte*) gorge; **fare ~** (*anche fig*) to tempt

golf *sm inv* (*Sport*) golf; (*maglia*) cardigan

'golfo *sm* gulf

go'loso, -a *ag* greedy

gomi'tata *sf*: **dare una ~ a qn** to elbow sb; **farsi avanti a (forza o furia di) gomitate** to elbow one's way through; **fare a gomitate per qc** to fight to get sth

'gomito *sm* elbow; (*di strada ecc*) sharp bend

go'mitolo sm ball

'gomma sf rubber; (per cancellare) rubber, eraser; (di veicolo) tyre (BRIT), tire (US); **gomma americana** o **da masticare** chewing gum; **gomma a terra** flat tyre (BRIT) o tire (US); **ho una ~ a terra** I've got a flat tyre; **gom'mone** sm rubber dinghy

gonfi'are vt (pallone) to blow up, inflate; (dilatare, ingrossare) to swell; (fig: notizia) to exaggerate; **gonfiarsi** vpr to swell; (fiume) to rise; **'gonfio, -a** ag swollen; (stomaco) bloated; (vela) full; **gonfi'ore** sm swelling

'gonna sf skirt; **gonna pantalone** culottes pl

'gorgo, -ghi sm whirlpool

gorgogli'are [gorgoʎ'ʎare] vi to gurgle

go'rilla sm inv gorilla; (guardia del corpo) bodyguard

'gotico, -a, ci, che ag, sm Gothic

'gotta sf gout

gover'nare vt (stato) to govern, rule; (pilotare, guidare) to steer; (bestiame) to tend, look after

go'verno sm government

GPL sigla m (= Gas di Petrolio Liquefatto) LPG

GPS sigla m (= Global Positioning System) GPS

graci'dare [gratʃi'dare] vi to croak

'gracile ['gratʃile] ag frail, delicate

gradazi'one [gradat'tsjone] sf (sfumatura) gradation; **gradazione alcolica** alcoholic content, strength

gra'devole ag pleasant, agreeable

gradi'nata sf flight of steps; (in teatro, stadio) tiers pl

gra'dino sm step; (Alpinismo) foothold

gra'dire vt (accettare con piacere) to accept; (desiderare) to wish, like; **gradisce una tazza di tè?** would you like a cup of tea?

'grado sm (Mat, Fisica ecc) degree; (stadio) degree, level; (Mil, sociale) rank; **essere in ~ di fare** to be in a position to do

gradu'ale ag gradual

graf'fetta sf paper clip

graffi'are vt to scratch; **graffiarsi** vpr to get scratched; (con unghie) to scratch o.s.

'graffio sm scratch

gra'fia sf spelling; (scrittura) handwriting

'grafico, -a, -ci, -che ag graphic ▷ sm graph; (persona) graphic designer

gram'matica, -che sf grammar

'grammo sm gram(me)

'grana sf (granello, di minerali, corpi spezzati) grain; (fam: seccatura) trouble; (: soldi) cash ▷ sm inv Parmesan (cheese)

gra'naio sm granary, barn

gra'nata sf (proiettile) grenade

Gran Bre'tagna [-bre'taɲɲa] sf: **la ~** Great Britain

'granchio ['grankjo] sm crab; (fig) blunder; **prendere un ~** (fig) to blunder

'grande (qualche volta **gran** + C, **grand'** + V) ag (grosso, largo, vasto) big, large; (alto) tall; (lungo) long; (in sensi astratti) great ▷ sm/f (persona adulta) adult, grown-up; (chi ha ingegno e potenza) great man/woman; **fare le cose in ~** to do things in style; **una gran bella donna** a very beautiful woman; **non è una gran cosa** o **un gran che** it's nothing special; **non ne so gran che** I don't know very much about it

gran'dezza [gran'dettsa] sf (dimensione) size; magnitude; (fig) greatness; **in ~ naturale** life-size(d)

grandi'nare vb impers to hail

'grandine sf hail

gra'nello sm (di cereali, uva) seed; (di frutta) pip; (di sabbia, sale ecc) grain

gra'nito sm granite

'grano sm (in quasi tutti i sensi) grain; (frumento) wheat; (di rosario, collana) bead; **grano di pepe** peppercorn

gran'turco sm maize

'grappa sf rough, strong brandy
'grappolo sm bunch, cluster
gras'setto sm (Tip) bold (type)
'grasso, -a ag fat; (cibo) fatty; (pelle) greasy; (terreno) rich; (fig: guadagno, annata) plentiful ▷ sm (di persona, animale) fat; (sostanza che unge) grease
'grata sf grating
gra'ticola sf grill
'gratis av free, for nothing
grati'tudine sf gratitude
'grato, -a ag grateful; (gradito) pleasant, agreeable
gratta'capo sm worry, headache
grattaci'elo [gratta'tʃɛlo] sm skyscraper
gratta e 'sosta sm inv scratch card used to pay for parking
gratta e vinci ['gratta e 'vintʃi] sm inv (biglietto) scratchcard; (lotteria) scratchcard lottery
grat'tare vt (pelle) to scratch; (raschiare) to scrape; (pane, formaggio, carote) to grate; (fam: rubare) to pinch ▷ vi (stridere) to grate; (Aut) to grind; **grattarsi** vpr to scratch o.s.; **grattarsi la pancia** (fig) to twiddle one's thumbs
grat'tugia, -gie [grat'tudʒa] sf grater; **grattugi'are** vt to grate; **pane grattugiato** breadcrumbs pl
gra'tuito, -a ag free; (fig) gratuitous
'grave ag (danno, pericolo, peccato ecc) grave, serious; (responsabilità) heavy, grave; (contegno) grave, solemn; (voce, suono) deep, low-pitched; (Ling): **accento ~** grave accent; **un malato ~** a person who is seriously ill
grave'mente av (ammalato, ferito) seriously
gravi'danza [gravi'dantsa] sf pregnancy
gravità sf seriousness; (anche Fisica) gravity
gra'voso, -a ag heavy, onerous
'grazia ['grattsja] sf grace; (favore) favour; (Dir) pardon

'grazie ['grattsje] escl thank you!; **~ mille!** o **tante!** o **infinite!** thank you very much!; **~ a** thanks to
grazi'oso, -a [grat'tsjoso] ag charming, delightful; (gentile) gracious
'Grecia ['grɛtʃa] sf **la ~** Greece; **'greco, -a, -ci, -che** ag, sm/f, sm Greek
'gregge ['greddʒe] (pl(f) **-i**) sm flock
grembi'ule sm apron; (sopravveste) overall
'grembo sm lap; (ventre della madre) womb
'grezzo, -a ['greddzo] ag raw, unrefined; (diamante) rough, uncut; (tessuto) unbleached
gri'dare vi (per chiamare) to shout, cry (out); (strillare) to scream, yell ▷ vt to shout (out), yell (out); **~ aiuto** to cry o shout for help
'grido (pl(m) **-i**, o pl(f) **-a**) sm shout, cry; scream, yell; (di animale) cry; **di ~** famous
'grigio, -a, -gi, -gie ['gridʒo] ag, sm grey
'griglia ['griʎʎa] sf (per arrostire) grill; (Elettr) grid; (inferriata) grating; **alla ~** (Cuc) grilled
gril'letto sm trigger
'grillo sm (Zool) cricket; (fig) whim
'grinta sf grim expression; (Sport) fighting spirit
gris'sino sm bread-stick
Groen'landia sf **la ~** Greenland
gron'daia sf gutter
gron'dare vi to pour; (essere bagnato): **~ di** to be dripping with ▷ vt to drip with
'groppa sf (di animale) back, rump; (fam: dell'uomo) back, shoulders pl
gros'sezza [gros'settsa] sf size; thickness
gros'sista, -i, -e sm/f (Comm) wholesaler
'grosso, -a ag big, large; (di spessore) thick; (grossolano: anche fig) coarse; (grave, insopportabile) serious, great;

(*tempo, mare*) rough ▷ *sm*: **il ~ di**
the bulk of; **un pezzo ~** (*fig*) a VIP, a
bigwig; **farla grossa** to do something
very stupid; **dirle grosse** to tell
tall stories; **sbagliarsi di ~** to be
completely wrong

'grotta *sf* cave; grotto

grot'tesco, -a, -schi, -sche *ag*
grotesque

gro'viglio [groˈviʎʎo] *sm* tangle; (*fig*)
muddle

gru *sf inv* crane

'gruccia, -ce [ˈgruttʃa] *sf* (*per
camminare*) crutch; (*per abiti*) coat-
hanger

'grumo *sm* (*di sangue*) clot; (*di farina
ecc*) lump

'gruppo *sm* group; **gruppo
sanguigno** blood group

GSM *sigla m* (= *Global System for Mobile
Communication*) GSM

guada'gnare [gwadaɲˈɲare] *vt*
(*ottenere*) to gain; (*soldi, stipendio*) to
earn; (*vincere*) to win; (*raggiungere*)
to reach

gua'dagno [gwaˈdaɲɲo] *sm* earnings
pl; (*Comm*) profit; (*vantaggio, utile*)
advantage, gain; **guadagno lordo/
netto** gross/net earnings *pl*

gu'ado *sm* ford; **passare a ~** to ford

gu'ai *escl* **~ a te** (*o lui ecc*)**!** woe betide
you (*o him ecc*)!

gu'aio *sm* trouble, mishap;
(*inconveniente*) trouble, snag

gua'ire *vi* to whine, yelp

gu'ancia, -ce [ˈgwantʃa] *sf* cheek

guanci'ale [gwanˈtʃale] *sm* pillow

gu'anto *sm* glove

guarda'linee *sm inv* (*Sport*) linesman

guar'dare *vt* (*con lo sguardo: osservare*)
to look at; (*film, televisione*) to watch;
(*custodire*) to look after, take care
of ▷ *vi* to look; (*badare*): **~ a** to pay
attention to; (*luoghi: esser orientato*):
~ a to face; **guardarsi** *vpr* to look at
o.s.; **guardarsi da** (*astenersi*) to refrain
from; (*stare in guardia*) to beware of;

guardarsi dal fare to take care not
to do; **guarda di non sbagliare** try
not to make a mistake; **~ a vista qn** to
keep a close watch on sb

guarda'roba *sm inv* wardrobe;
(*locale*) cloakroom

gu'ardia *sf* (*individuo, corpo*) guard;
(*sorveglianza*) watch; **fare la ~ a qc/qn**
to guard sth/sb; **stare in ~** (*fig*) to be
on one's guard; **di ~** (*medico*) on call;
guardia carceraria (*prison*) warder;
guardia del corpo bodyguard;
Guardia di finanza (*corpo*) customs
pl; (*persona*) customs officer; **guardia
medica** emergency doctor service

● **GUARDIA DI FINANZA**
●
● The **Guardia di Finanza** is
● a military body which deals
● with infringements of the laws
● governing income tax and
● monopolies. It reports to the
● Ministers of Finance, Justice or
● Agriculture, depending on the
● function it is performing.

guardi'ano, -a *sm/f* (*di carcere*)
warder; (*di villa ecc*) caretaker; (*di
museo*) custodian; (*di zoo*) keeper;
guardiano notturno night
watchman

guarigi'one [gwariˈdʒone] *sf*
recovery

gua'rire *vt* (*persona, malattia*) to cure;
(*ferita*) to heal ▷ *vi* to recover, be
cured; to heal (up)

guar'nire *vt* (*ornare: abiti*) to trim;
(*Cuc*) to garnish

guasta'feste *sm/f inv* spoilsport

guas'tarsi *vpr* (*cibo*) to go bad;
(*meccanismo*) to break down; (*tempo*)
to change for the worse

gu'asto, -a *ag* (*non funzionante*)
broken; (: *telefono ecc*) out of order;
(*andato a male*) bad, rotten; (: *dente*)
decayed, bad; (*fig: corrotto*) depraved

▷ *sm* breakdown; (*avaria*) failure;
guasto al motore engine failure
gu'erra *sf* war; (*tecnica: atomica,
chimica ecc*) warfare; **fare la ~ (a)**
to wage war (against); **guerra
mondiale** world war; **guerra
preventiva** preventive war
'gufo *sm* owl
gu'ida *sf* (*libro*) guidebook; (*persona*)
guide; (*comando, direzione*) guidance,
direction; (*Aut*) driving; (*tappeto: di
tenda, cassetto*) runner; **avete una ~ in
italiano?** do you have a guidebook in
Italian?; **c'è una ~ che parla italiano?**
is there an Italian-speaking guide?;
guida a destra/a sinistra (*Aut*)
right-/left-hand drive; **guida
telefonica** telephone directory;
guida turistica tourist guide
gui'dare *vt* to guide; (*squadra,
rivolta*) to lead; (*auto*) to drive; (*aereo,
nave*) to pilot; **sai ~?** can you drive?;
guida'tore, -trice *sm/f* (*conducente*)
driver
guin'zaglio [gwin'tsaʎʎo] *sm* leash,
lead
'guscio ['guʃʃo] *sm* shell
gus'tare *vt* (*cibi*) to taste; (: *assaporare
con piacere*) to enjoy, savour; (*fig*) to
enjoy, appreciate ▷ *vi* ~ **a** to please;
non mi gusta affatto I don't like it
at all
'gusto *sm* taste; (*sapore*) flavour;
(*godimento*) enjoyment; **che gusti
avete?** which flavours do you
have?; **al ~ di fragola** strawberry-
flavoured; **mangiare di ~** to eat
heartily; **prenderci ~: ci ha preso ~**
he's acquired a taste for it, he's got
to like it; **gus'toso, -a** *ag* tasty; (*fig*)
agreeable

H, h ['akka] *sf o m inv* (*lettera*) H, h
▷ *abbr* (= *ora*) hr; (= *etto, altezza*) h; **H
come hotel** ≈ H for Harry (*BRIT*), H for
How (*US*)
ha, 'hai [a, ai] *vb vedi* **avere**
ha'cker ['hakər] *sm inv* hacker
hall [hɔl] *sf inv* hall, foyer
hamburger [am'burger] *sm inv*
(*carne*) hamburger; (*panino*) burger
'handicap ['handikap] *sm inv*
handicap; **handicap'pato, -a** *ag*
handicapped ▷ *sm/f* handicapped
person, disabled person
'hanno ['anno] *vb vedi* **avere**
hard discount [ardis'kaunt] *sm inv*
discount supermarket
hard disk [ar'disk] *sm inv* hard disk
hardware ['ardwer] *sm inv* hardware
hascisch [aʃ'ʃiʃ] *sm* hashish
Hawaii [a'vai] *sfpl* **le ~** Hawaii *sg*
help [ɛlp] *sm inv* (*Inform*) help
'herpes ['ɛrpes] *sm* (*Med*) herpes *sg*;
herpes zoster shingles *sg*
'hi-fi ['haifai] *sm inv, ag inv* hi-fi

ho [ɔ] *vb vedi* **avere**
'hobby ['hɔbi] *sm inv* hobby
'hockey ['hɔki] *sm* hockey; **hockey su ghiaccio** ice hockey
home page ['houm'pɛidʒ] *sf inv* home page
Hong Kong ['ɔŋ'kɔŋg] *sf* Hong Kong
'hostess ['houstis] *sf inv* air hostess (*BRIT*) *o* stewardess
hot dog ['hɔtdɔg] *sm inv* hot dog
ho'tel *sm inv* hotel
humour ['jumor] *sm inv* (sense of) humour
'humus *sm* humus
husky ['aski] *sm inv* (*cane*) husky *m inv*

i *det mpl* the
IC *abbr* (= *Intercity*) Intercity
ICI ['itʃi] *sigla f* (= *Imposta Comunale sugli Immobili*) ≈ Council Tax
i'cona *sf* (*Rel, Inform, fig*) icon
i'dea *sf* idea; (*opinione*) opinion, view; (*ideale*) ideal; **dare l'~ di** to seem, look like; **neanche** *o* **neppure per ~!** certainly not!; **idea fissa** obsession
ide'ale *ag, sm* ideal
ide'are *vt* (*immaginare*) to think up, conceive; (*progettare*) to plan
i'dentico, -a, -ci, -che *ag* identical
identifi'care *vt* to identify; **identificarsi** *vpr* **identificarsi (con)** to identify o.s. (with)
identità *sf inv* identity
ideolo'gia, -'gie [ideolo'dʒia] *sf* ideology
idio'matico, -a, -ci, -che *ag* idiomatic; **frase idiomatica** idiom
idi'ota, -i, -e *ag* idiotic ▷ *sm/f* idiot
'idolo *sm* idol
idoneità *sf* suitability

i'doneo, -a ag: ~ a suitable for, fit for; (Mil) fit for; (qualificato) qualified for

i'drante sm hydrant

idra'tante ag moisturizing ▷ sm moisturizer

i'draulico, -a, -ci, -che ag hydraulic ▷ sm plumber

idroe'lettrico, -a, -ci, -che ag hydroelectric

i'drofilo, -a ag vedi cotone

i'drogeno [i'drɔdʒeno] sm hydrogen

idrovo'lante sm seaplane

i'ena sf hyena

i'eri av, sm yesterday; il giornale di ~ yesterday's paper; ~ l'altro the day before yesterday; ~ sera yesterday evening

igi'ene [i'dʒɛne] sf hygiene; igiene pubblica public health; igi'enico, -a, -ci, -he ag hygienic; (salubre) healthy

i'gnaro, -a [iɲ'naro] ag ~ di unaware of, ignorant of

i'gnobile [iɲ'nɔbile] ag despicable, vile

igno'rante [iɲɲo'rante] ag ignorant

igno'rare [iɲɲo'rare] vt (non sapere, conoscere) to be ignorant o unaware of, not to know; (fingere di non vedere, sentire) to ignore

i'gnoto, -a [iɲ'nɔto] ag unknown

 PAROLA CHIAVE

il (pl(m) i; diventa lo (pl gli) davanti a s impura, gn, pn, ps, x, z; f la (pl le)) det m

1 the; il libro/lo studente/l'acqua the book/the student/the water; gli scolari the pupils

2 (astrazione): il coraggio/l'amore/la giovinezza courage/love/youth

3 (tempo): il mattino/la sera in the morning/evening; il venerdì ecc (abitualmente) on Fridays ecc; (quel giorno) on (the) Friday ecc; la settimana prossima next week

4 (distributivo) a, an; 2 euro il chilo/paio 2 euros a o per kilo/pair

5 (partitivo) some, any; hai messo lo zucchero? have you added sugar?; hai comprato il latte? did you buy (some o any) milk?

6 (possesso): aprire gli occhi to open one's eyes; rompersi la gamba to break one's leg; avere i capelli neri/il naso rosso to have dark hair/a red nose

7 (con nomi propri): il Petrarca Petrarch; il Presidente Bush President Bush; dov'è la Francesca? where's Francesca?

8 (con nomi geografici): il Tevere the Tiber; l'Italia Italy; il Regno Unito the United Kingdom; l'Everest Everest

ille'gale ag illegal

illeg'gibile [illed'dʒibile] ag illegible

ille'gittimo, -a [ille'dʒittimo] ag illegitimate

il'leso, -a ag unhurt, unharmed

illimi'tato, -a ag boundless; unlimited

ill.mo abbr = illustrissimo

il'ludere vt to deceive, delude; illudersi vpr to deceive o.s., delude o.s.

illumi'nare vt to light up, illuminate; (fig) to enlighten; illuminarsi vpr to light up; ~ a giorno to floodlight; illuminazi'one sf lighting; illumination; floodlighting; (fig) flash of inspiration

il'lusi ecc vb vedi illudere

illusi'one sf illusion; farsi delle illusioni to delude o.s.; illusione ottica optical illusion

il'luso, -a pp di illudere

illus'trare vt to illustrate; illustrazi'one sf illustration

il'lustre ag eminent, renowned; illus'trissimo, -a ag (negli indirizzi) very revered

imbal'laggio [imbal'laddʒo] sm packing no pl

imbal'lare vt to pack; (Aut) to race

imbalsa'mare vt to embalm

imbambo'lato, -a ag (sguardo) vacant, blank

imbaraz'zante [imbarat'tsante] ag embarrassing, awkward

imbaraz'zare [imbarat'tsare] vt (mettere a disagio) to embarrass; (ostacolare movimenti) to hamper

imbaraz'zato, -a [imbarat'tsato] ag embarrassed; **avere lo stomaco ~** to have an upset stomach

imba'razzo [imba'rattso] sm (disagio) embarrassment; (perplessità) puzzlement, bewilderment; **imbarazzo di stomaco** indigestion

imbar'care vt (passeggeri) to embark; (merci) to load; **imbarcarsi** vpr **imbarcarsi su** to board; **imbarcarsi per l'America** to sail for America; **imbarcarsi in** (fig: affare ecc) to embark on

imbarcazi'one [imbarkat'tsjone] sf (small) boat, (small) craft inv; **imbarcazione di salvataggio** lifeboat

im'barco, -chi sm embarkation; loading; boarding; (banchina) landing stage

imbas'tire vt (cucire) to tack; (fig: abbozzare) to sketch, outline

im'battersi vpr: **~ in** (incontrare) to bump o run into

imbat'tibile ag unbeatable, invincible

imbavagli'are [imbavaʎ'ʎare] vt to gag

imbe'cille [imbe'tʃille] ag idiotic ▷ sm/f idiot; (Med) imbecile

imbian'care vt to whiten; (muro) to whitewash ▷ vi to become o turn white

imbian'chino [imbjan'kino] sm (house) painter, painter and decorator

imboc'care vt (bambino) to feed; (entrare: strada) to enter, turn into

imbocca'tura sf mouth; (di strada, porto) entrance; (Mus, del morso) mouthpiece

imbos'cata sf ambush

imbottigli'are [imbottiʎ'ʎare] vt to bottle; (Naut) to blockade; (Mil) to hem in; **imbottigliarsi** vpr to be stuck in a traffic jam

imbot'tire vt to stuff; (giacca) to pad; **imbottirsi** vpr **imbottirsi di** (rimpinzarsi) to stuff o.s. with; **imbot'tito, -a** ag stuffed; (giacca) padded; **panino imbottito** filled roll

imbra'nato, -a ag clumsy, awkward ▷ sm/f clumsy person

imbrogli'are [imbroʎ'ʎare] vt to mix up; (fig: raggirare) to deceive, cheat; (: confondere) to confuse, mix up; **imbrogli'one, -a** sm/f cheat, swindler

imbronci'ato, -a ag sulky

imbu'care vt to post; **dove posso ~ queste cartoline?** where can I post these cards?

imbur'rare vt to butter

im'buto sm funnel

imi'tare vt to imitate; (riprodurre) to copy; (assomigliare) to look like

immagazzi'nare [immagaddzi'nare] vt to store

immagi'nare [immadʒi'nare] vt to imagine; (supporre) to suppose; (inventare) to invent; **s'immagini!** don't mention it!, not at all!; **immaginazi'one** sf imagination; (cosa immaginata) fancy

im'magine [im'madʒine] sf image; (rappresentazione grafica, mentale) picture

imman'cabile ag certain; unfailing

im'mane ag (smisurato) enormous; (spaventoso) terrible

immangi'abile [imman'dʒabile] ag inedible

immatrico'lare vt to register; **immatricolarsi** vpr (Ins) to matriculate, enrol

imma'turo, -a ag (frutto) unripe; (persona) immature; (prematuro) premature

immedesi'marsi vpr: **~ in** to identify with

immediata'mente av immediately, at once

immedi'ato, -a ag immediate

im'menso, -a ag immense

im'mergere [im'mɛrdʒere] vt to immerse, plunge; **immergersi** vpr to plunge; (sommergibile) to dive, submerge; (dedicarsi a): **immergersi in** to immerse o.s. in

immeri'tato, -a ag undeserved

immersi'one sf immersion; (di sommergibile) submersion, dive; (di palombaro) dive

im'mettere vt: **~ (in)** to introduce (into); **~ dati in un computer** to enter data on a computer

immi'grato, -a sm/f immigrant

immi'nente ag imminent

immischiarsi vpr: **~ in** to interfere o meddle in

im'mobile ag motionless, still; **immobili'are** ag (Dir) property cpd

immon'dizia [immon'dittsja] sf dirt, filth; (spesso al pl: spazzatura, rifiuti) rubbish no pl, refuse no pl

immo'rale ag immoral

immor'tale ag immortal

im'mune ag (esente) exempt; (Med, Dir) immune

immu'tabile ag immutable; unchanging

impacchet'tare [impakket'tare] vt to pack up

impacci'ato, -a ag awkward, clumsy; (imbarazzato) embarrassed

im'pacco, -chi sm (Med) compress

impadro'nirsi vpr: **~ di** to seize, take possession of; (fig: apprendere a fondo) to master

impa'gabile ag priceless

impa'lato, -a ag (fig) stiff as a board

impalca'tura sf scaffolding

impalli'dire vi to turn pale; (fig) to fade

impa'nato, -a ag (Cuc) coated in breadcrumbs

impanta'narsi vpr to sink (in the mud); (fig) to get bogged down

impappi'narsi vpr to stammer, falter

impa'rare vt to learn

impar'tire vt to bestow, give

imparzi'ale [impar'tsjale] ag impartial, unbiased

impas'sibile ag impassive

impas'tare vt (pasta) to knead

impastic'carsi vpr to pop pills

im'pasto sm (l'impastare: di pane) kneading; (: di cemento) mixing; (pasta) dough; (anche fig) mixture

im'patto sm impact

impau'rire vt to scare, frighten ▷ vi (anche: **impaurirsi**) to become scared o frightened

impazi'ente [impat'tsjɛnte] ag impatient

impaz'zata [impat'tsata] sf: **all'~** (precipitosamente) at breakneck speed

impaz'zire [impat'tsire] vi to go mad; **~ per qn/qc** to be crazy about sb/sth

impec'cabile ag impeccable

impedi'mento sm obstacle, hindrance

impe'dire vt (vietare): **~ a qn di fare** to prevent sb from doing; (ostruire) to obstruct; (impacciare) to hamper, hinder

impegnarsi vpr (vincolarsi): **~ a fare** to undertake to do; (mettersi risolutamente): **~ in qc** to devote o.s. to sth; **~ con qn** (accordarsi) to come to an agreement with sb

impegna'tivo, -a ag binding; (lavoro) demanding, exacting

impe'gnato, -a ag (occupato) busy; (fig: romanzo, autore) committed, engagé

im'pegno [im'peɲɲo] sm (obbligo) obligation; (promessa) promise, pledge; (zelo) diligence, zeal; (compito, d'autore) commitment

impel'lente ag pressing, urgent
impen'narsi vpr (cavallo) to rear up; (Aer) to nose up; (fig) to bridle
impensie'rire vt to worry; **impensierirsi** vpr to worry
impera'tivo, -a ag, sm imperative
impera'tore, -'trice sm/f emperor/empress
imperdo'nabile ag unforgivable, unpardonable
imper'fetto, -a ag imperfect ▷ sm (Ling) imperfect (tense)
imperi'ale ag imperial
imperi'oso, -a ag (persona) imperious; (motivo, esigenza) urgent, pressing
imperme'abile ag waterproof ▷ sm raincoat
im'pero sm empire; (forza, autorità) rule, control
imperso'nale ag impersonal
imperso'nare vt to personify; (Teatro) to play, act (the part of)
imperter'rito, -a ag fearless, undaunted; impassive
imperti'nente ag impertinent
'impeto sm (moto, forza) force, impetus; (assalto) onslaught; (fig: impulso) impulse; (: slancio) transport; **con ~** energetically; vehemently
impet'tito, -a ag stiff, erect
impetu'oso, -a ag (vento) strong, raging; (persona) impetuous
impi'anto sm (installazione) installation; (apparecchiature) plant; (sistema) system; **impianto elettrico** wiring; **impianto di risalita** (Sci) ski lift; **impianto di riscaldamento** heating system; **impianto sportivo** sports complex
impic'care vt to hang; **impiccarsi** vpr to hang o.s.
impicciarsi [impit'tʃarsi] vpr (immischiarsi): **~ (in)** to meddle (in); **impicciati degli affari tuoi!** mind your own business!
impicci'one, -a [impit'tʃone] sm/f busybody

impie'gare vt (usare) to use, employ; (spendere: denaro, tempo) to spend; (investire) to invest; **impie'gato, -a** sm/f employee
impi'ego, -ghi sm (uso) use; (occupazione) employment; (posto di lavoro) (regular) job, post; (Econ) investment
impieto'sire vt to move to pity; **impietosirsi** vpr to be moved to pity
impigli'arsi vpr to get caught up o entangled
impi'grirsi vpr to grow lazy
impli'care vt to imply; (coinvolgere) to involve
im'plicito, -a [im'plitʃito] ag implicit
implo'rare vt to implore; (pietà ecc) to beg for
impolve'rarsi vpr to get dusty
im'pone ecc vb vedi **imporre**
impo'nente ag imposing, impressive
im'pongo ecc vb vedi **imporre**
impo'nibile ag taxable ▷ sm taxable income
impopo'lare ag unpopular
im'porre vt to impose; (costringere) to force, make; (far valere) to impose, enforce; **imporsi** vpr (persona) to assert o.s.; (cosa: rendersi necessario) to become necessary; (aver successo: moda, attore) to become popular; **~ a qn di fare** to force sb to do, make sb do
impor'tante ag important; **impor'tanza** sf importance; **dare importanza a qc** to attach importance to sth; **darsi importanza** to give o.s. airs
impor'tare vt (introdurre dall'estero) to import ▷ vi to matter, be important ▷ vb impers (essere necessario) to be necessary; (interessare) to matter; **non importa!** it doesn't matter!; **non me ne importa!** I don't care!
im'porto sm (total) amount
importu'nare vt to bother

im'posi ecc vb vedi **imporre**

imposizi'one [impozit'tsjone] sf imposition; order, command; (onere, imposta) tax

imposses'sarsi vpr: **~ di** to seize, take possession of

impos'sibile ag impossible; **fare l'~** to do one's utmost, do all one can

im'posta sf (di finestra) shutter; (tassa) tax; **imposta sul reddito** income tax; **imposta sul valore aggiunto** value added tax (BRIT), sales tax (US)

impos'tare vt (imbucare) to post; (preparare) to plan, set out; (avviare) to begin, start off; (voce) to pitch

impostazi'one [impostat'tsjone] sf (di lettera) posting (BRIT), mailing (US); (di problema, questione) formulation, statement; (di lavoro) organization, planning; (di attività) setting up; (Mus: di voce) pitch; **impostazioni** sfpl (di computer) settings

impo'tente ag weak, powerless; (anche Med) impotent

imprati'cabile ag (strada) impassable; (campo da gioco) unplayable

impre'care vi to curse, swear; **~ contro** to hurl abuse at

imprecazi'one [imprekat'tsjone] sf abuse, curse

impre'gnare [impren'nare] vt: **~ (di)** (imbevere) to soak o impregnate (with); (riempire) to fill (with)

imprendi'tore sm (industriale) entrepreneur; (appaltatore) contractor; **piccolo ~** small businessman

im'presa sf (iniziativa) enterprise; (azione) exploit; (azienda) firm, concern

impressio'nante ag impressive; upsetting

impressio'nare vt to impress; (turbare) to upset; (Fot) to expose; **impressionarsi** vpr to be easily upset

impressi'one sf impression; (fig: sensazione) sensation, feeling; (stampa) printing; **fare ~** (colpire) to impress; (turbare) to frighten, upset; **fare buona/cattiva ~ a** to make a good/bad impression on

impreve'dibile ag unforeseeable; (persona) unpredictable

impre'visto, -a ag unexpected, unforeseen ▷ sm unforeseen event; **salvo imprevisti** unless anything unexpected happens

imprigio'nare [impridʒo'nare] vt to imprison

impro'babile ag improbable, unlikely

im'pronta sf imprint, impression, sign; (di piede, mano) print; (fig) mark, stamp; **impronta digitale** fingerprint

improvvisa'mente av suddenly; unexpectedly

improvvi'sare vt to improvise

improv'viso, -a ag (imprevisto) unexpected; (subitaneo) sudden; **all'~** unexpectedly; suddenly

impru'dente ag unwise, rash

impu'gnare [impun'nare] vt to grasp, grip; (Dir) to contest

impul'sivo, -a ag impulsive

im'pulso sm impulse

impun'tarsi vpr to stop dead, refuse to budge; (fig) to be obstinate

impu'tato, -a sm/f (Dir) accused, defendant

 PAROLA CHIAVE

in (in + il = **nel**, in + lo = **nello**, in + l' = **nell'**, in + la = **nella**, in + i = **nei**, in + gli = **negli**, in + le = **nelle**) prep **1** (stato in luogo) in; **vivere in Italia/città** to live in Italy/town; **essere in casa/ufficio** to be at home/the office; **se fossi in te** if I were you

2 (moto a luogo) to; (: dentro) into; **andare in Germania/città** to go to Germany/town; **andare in ufficio** to go to the office; **entrare in macchina/casa** to get into the

car/go into the house
3 (*tempo*) in; **nel 1989** in 1989; **in giugno/estate** in June/summer
4 (*modo, maniera*) in; **in silenzio** in silence; **in abito da sera** in evening dress; **in guerra** at war; **in vacanza** on holiday; **Maria Bianchi in Rossi** Maria Rossi née Bianchi
5 (*mezzo*) by; **viaggiare in autobus/ treno** to travel by bus/train
6 (*materia*) made of; **in marmo** made of marble, marble *cpd*; **una collana in oro** a gold necklace
7 (*misura*) in; **siamo in quattro** there are four of us; **in tutto** in all
8 (*fine*): **dare in dono** to give as a gift; **spende tutto in alcool** he spends all his money on drink; **in onore di** in honour of

inabi'tabile *ag* uninhabitable
inacces'sibile [inattʃes'sibile] *ag* (*luogo*) inaccessible; (*persona*) unapproachable
inaccet'tabile [inattʃet'tabile] *ag* unacceptable
ina'datto, -a *ag*: **~ (a)** unsuitable *o* unfit (for)
inadegu'ato, -a *ag* inadequate
inaffi'dabile *ag* unreliable
inami'dato, -a *ag* starched
inar'care *vt* (*schiena*) to arch; (*sopracciglia*) to raise
inaspet'tato, -a *ag* unexpected
inas'prire *vt* (*disciplina*) to tighten up, make harsher; (*carattere*) to embitter; **inasprirsi** *vpr* to become harsher; to become bitter; to become worse
inattac'cabile *ag* (*anche fig*) unassailable; (*alibi*) cast-iron
inatten'dibile *ag* unreliable
inat'teso, -a *ag* unexpected
inattu'abile *ag* impracticable
inau'dito, -a *ag* unheard of
inaugu'rare *vt* to inaugurate, open; (*monumento*) to unveil
inaugurazi'one [inaugurat'tsjone]

sf inauguration; unveiling
incal'lito, -a *ag* calloused; (*fig*) hardened, inveterate; (: *insensibile*) hard
incande'scente [inkandeʃʃɛnte] *ag* incandescent, white-hot
incan'tare *vt* to enchant, bewitch; **incantarsi** *vpr* (*rimanere intontito*) to be spellbound; to be in a daze; (*meccanismo: bloccarsi*) to jam; **incan'tevole** *ag* charming, enchanting
in'canto *sm* spell, charm, enchantment; (*asta*) auction; **come per ~** as if by magic; **mettere all'~** to put up for auction
inca'pace [inka'patʃe] *ag* incapable
incarce'rare [inkartʃe'rare] *vt* to imprison
incari'care *vt*: **~ qn di fare** to give sb the responsibility of doing; **incaricarsi di** to take care *o* charge of
in'carico, -chi *sm* task, job
incarta'mento *sm* dossier, file
incar'tare *vt* to wrap (in paper)
incas'sare *vt* (*merce*) to pack (in cases); (*gemma: incastonare*) to set; (*Econ: riscuotere*) to collect; (*Pugilato: colpi*) to take, stand up to; **in'casso** *sm* cashing, encashment; (*introito*) takings *pl*
incas'trare *vt* to fit in, insert; (*fig: intrappolare*) to catch; **incastrarsi** *vpr* (*combaciare*) to fit together; (*restare bloccato*) to become stuck
incate'nare *vt* to chain up
in'cauto, -a *ag* imprudent, rash
inca'vato, -a *ag* hollow; (*occhi*) sunken
incendi'are [intʃen'djare] *vt* to set fire to; **incendiarsi** *vpr* to catch fire, burst into flames
in'cendio [in'tʃɛndjo] *sm* fire
inceneri'tore [intʃeneri'tore] *sm* incinerator
in'censo [in'tʃɛnso] *sm* incense
incensu'rato, -a [intʃensu'rato] *ag*

(*Dir*): **essere ~** to have a clean record
incenti'vare [intʃenti'vare] *vt*
(*produzione, vendite*) to boost; (*persona*)
to motivate
incen'tivo [intʃen'tivo] *sm* incentive
incepparsi *vpr* to jam
incer'tezza [intʃer'tettsa] *sf*
uncertainty
in'certo, -a [in'tʃɛrto] *ag* uncertain;
(*irresoluto*) undecided, hesitating ▷ *sm*
uncertainty
in'cetta [in'tʃetta] *sf* buying up, **fare
~ di qc** to buy up sth
inchi'esta [in'kjɛsta] *sf*
investigation, inquiry
inchinarsi *vpr* to bend down; (*per
riverenza*) to bow; (: *donna*) to curtsy
inchio'dare [inkjo'dare] *vt* to nail
(down); **~ la macchina** (*Aut*) to jam on
the brakes
inchi'ostro [in'kjɔstro] *sm* ink;
inchiostro simpatico invisible ink
inciam'pare [intʃam'pare] *vi* to trip,
stumble
inci'dente [intʃi'dɛnte] *sm* accident;
ho avuto un ~ I've had an accident;
incidente automobilistico o d'auto
car accident; **incidente diplomatico**
diplomatic incident
in'cidere [in'tʃidere] *vi:* **~ su** to bear
upon, affect ▷ *vt* (*tagliare incavando*)
to cut into; (*Arte*) to engrave; to etch;
(*canzone*) to record
in'cinta [in'tʃinta] *ag f* pregnant
incipri'are [intʃi'prjare] *vt* to
powder; **incipriarsi** ▷ *vpr* to powder
one's face
in'circa [in'tʃirka] *av:* **all'~** more or
less, very nearly
in'cisi *ecc* [in'tʃizi] *vb vedi* **incidere**
incisi'one [intʃi'zjone] *sf* cut;
(*disegno*) engraving; etching;
(*registrazione*) recording; (*Med*)
incision
in'ciso, -a [in'tʃizo] *pp di* **incidere**
▷ *sm* **per ~** incidentally, by the way
inci'tare [intʃi'tare] *vt* to incite

inci'vile [intʃi'vile] *ag* uncivilized;
(*villano*) impolite
incl. *abbr* (= *incluso*) encl.
incli'nare *vt* to tilt; **inclinarsi** *vpr*
(*barca*) to list; (*aereo*) to bank
in'cludere *vt* to include; (*accludere*) to
enclose; **in'cluso, -a** *pp di* **includere**
▷ *ag* included; enclosed
incoe'rente *ag* incoherent;
(*contraddittorio*) inconsistent
in'cognita [in'kɔɲita] *sf* (*Mat, fig*)
unknown quantity
in'cognito, -a [in'kɔɲito] *ag*
unknown ▷ *sm* **in ~** incognito
incol'lare *vt* to glue, gum; (*unire con
colla*) to stick together
inco'lore *ag* colourless
incol'pare *vt:* **~ qn di** to charge sb
with
in'colto, -a *ag* (*terreno*) uncultivated;
(*trascurato: capelli*) neglected; (*persona*)
uneducated
in'columne *ag* safe and sound, unhurt
incom'benza [inkom'bɛntsa] *sf*
duty, task
in'combere *vi* (*sovrastare
minacciando*): **~ su** to threaten, hang
over
incominci'are [inkomin'tʃare] *vi, vt*
to begin, start
incompe'tente *ag* incompetent
incompi'uto, -a *ag* unfinished,
incomplete
incom'pleto, -a *ag* incomplete
incompren'sibile *ag*
incomprehensible
inconce'pibile [inkontʃe'pibile] *ag*
inconceivable
inconcili'abile [inkontʃi'ljabile] *ag*
irreconcilable
inconclu'dente *ag* inconclusive;
(*persona*) ineffectual
incondizio'nato, -a
[inkondittsjo'nato] *ag*
unconditional
inconfon'dibile *ag* unmistakable
inconsa'pevole *ag:* **~ di** unaware of,

ignorant of

in'conscio, -a, -sci, -sce [in'kɔnʃo]
ag unconscious ▷ *sm* (*Psic*): **l'~** the
unconscious

inconsis'tente *ag* insubstantial;
unfounded

inconsu'eto, -a *ag* unusual

incon'trare *vt* to meet; (*difficoltà*) to
meet with; **incontrarsi** *vpr* to meet

in'contro *av* **~ a** (*verso*) towards ▷ *sm*
meeting; (*Sport*) match; meeting;
incontro di calcio football match

inconveni'ente *sm* drawback, snag

incoraggia'mento
[inkoraddʒa'mento] *sm*
encouragement

incoraggi'are [inkorad'dʒare] *vt* to
encourage

incornici'are [inkorni'tʃare] *vt* to
frame

incoro'nare *vt* to crown

in'correre *vi*: **~ in** to meet with, run
into

incosci'ente [inkoʃʃente]
ag (*inconscio*) unconscious;
(*irresponsabile*) reckless, thoughtless

incre'dibile *ag* incredible,
unbelievable

in'credulo, -a *ag* incredulous,
disbelieving

incremen'tare *vt* to increase; (*dar
sviluppo a*) to promote

incre'mento *sm* (*sviluppo*)
development; (*aumento numerico*)
increase, growth

incresci'oso, -a [inkreʃʃoso] *ag*
(*incidente ecc*) regrettable

incrimi'nare *vt* (*Dir*) to charge

incri'nare *vt* to crack; (*fig: rapporti,
amicizia*) to cause to deteriorate;
incrinarsi *vpr* to crack; to deteriorate

incroci'are [inkro'tʃare] *vt* to cross;
(*incontrare*) to meet ▷ *vi* (*Naut, Aer*)
to cruise; **incrociarsi** *vpr* (*strade*)
to cross, intersect; (*persone, veicoli*)
to pass each other; **~ le braccia/le
gambe** to fold one's arms/cross one's

legs

in'crocio [in'krotʃo] *sm* (*anche Ferr*)
crossing; (*di strade*) crossroads

incuba'trice [inkuba'tritʃe] *sf*
incubator

'incubo *sm* nightmare

incu'rabile *ag* incurable

incu'rante *ag*: **~ (di)** heedless (of),
careless (of)

incurio'sire *vt* to make curious;
incuriosirsi *vpr* to become curious

incursi'one *sf* raid

incur'vare *vt* to bend, curve;
incurvarsi *vpr* to bend, curve

incusto'dito, -a *ag* unguarded,
unattended

in'cutere *vt*: **~ timore/rispetto a qn**
to strike fear into sb/command sb's
respect

'indaco *sm* indigo

indaffa'rato, -a *ag* busy

inda'gare *vt* to investigate

in'dagine [in'dadʒine] *sf*
investigation, inquiry; (*ricerca*)
research, study; **indagine di mercato**
market survey

indebi'tarsi *vpr* to run o get into debt

indebo'lire *vt, vi* (*anche*: **indebolirsi**)
to weaken

inde'cente [inde'tʃente] *ag* indecent

inde'ciso, -a [inde'tʃizo] *ag*
indecisive; (*irresoluto*) undecided

indefi'nito, -a *ag* (*anche Ling*)
indefinite; (*impreciso, non determinato*)
undefined

in'degno, -a [in'deɲɲo] *ag* (*atto*)
shameful; (*persona*) unworthy

indemoni'ato, -a *ag* possessed (by
the devil)

in'denne *ag* unhurt, uninjured

indenniz'zare [indennid'dzare] *vt*
to compensate

indetermina'tivo, -a *ag* (*Ling*)
indefinite

'India *sf* **l'~** India; **indi'ano, -a**
ag Indian ▷ *sm/f* (*d'India*) Indian;
(*d'America*) Native American,

(American) Indian

indi'care vt (mostrare) to show, indicate; (: col dito) to point to, point out; (consigliare) to suggest, recommend; **indica'tivo, -a** ag indicative ▷ sm (Ling) indicative (mood); **indicazi'one** sf indication; (informazione) piece of information

'**indice** ['inditʃe] sm index; (fig) sign; (dito) index finger, forefinger; **indice di gradimento** (Radio, TV) popularity rating

indicherò ecc [indike'rɔ] vb vedi **indicare**

indi'cibile [indi'tʃibile] ag inexpressible

indietreggi'are [indietred'dʒare] vi to draw back, retreat

indi'etro av back; (guardare) behind, back; (andare, cadere: anche: **all'~**) backwards; **rimanere ~** to be left behind; **essere ~** (col lavoro) to be behind; (orologio) to be slow; **rimandare qc ~** to send sth back

indi'feso, -a ag (città ecc) undefended; (persona) defenceless

indiffe'rente ag indifferent

in'digeno, -a [in'didʒeno] ag indigenous, native ▷ sm/f native

indigesti'one [indidʒes'tjone] sf indigestion

indi'gesto, -a [indi'dʒɛsto] ag indigestible

indi'gnare [indiɲ'ɲare] vt to fill with indignation; **indignarsi** vpr to get indignant

indimenti'cabile ag unforgettable

indipen'dente ag independent

in'dire vt (concorso) to announce; (elezioni) to call

indi'retto, -a ag indirect

indiriz'zare [indirit'tsare] vt (dirigere) to direct; (mandare) to send; (lettera) to address

indi'rizzo [indi'rittso] sm address; (direzione) direction; (avvio) trend, course; **il mio ~ è...** my address is ...

indis'creto, -a ag indiscreet

indis'cusso, -a ag unquestioned

indispen'sabile ag indispensable, essential

indispet'tire vt to irritate, annoy ▷ vi (anche: **indispettirsi**) to get irritated o annoyed

individu'ale ag individual

individu'are vt (dar forma distinta a) to characterize; (determinare) to locate; (riconoscere) to single out

indi'viduo sm individual

indizi'ato, -a ag suspected ▷ sm/f suspect

in'dizio [in'dittsjo] sm (segno) sign, indication; (Polizia) clue; (Dir) piece of evidence

'**indole** sf nature, character

indolen'zito, -a [indolen'tsito] ag stiff, aching; (intorpidito) numb

indo'lore ag painless

indo'mani sm **l'~** the next day, the following day

Indo'nesia sf **l'~** Indonesia

indos'sare vt (mettere indosso) to put on; (avere indosso) to have on; **indossa'tore, -'trice** sm/f model

indottri'nare vt to indoctrinate

indovi'nare vt (scoprire) to guess; (immaginare) to imagine, guess; (il futuro) to foretell; **indovi'nello** sm riddle

indubbia'mente av undoubtedly

in'dubbio, -a ag certain, undoubted

in'duco ecc vb vedi **indurre**

indugi'are [indu'dʒare] vi to take one's time, delay

in'dugio [in'dudʒo] sm (ritardo) delay; **senza ~** without delay

indul'gente [indul'dʒɛnte] ag indulgent; (giudice) lenient

indu'mento sm article of clothing, garment

indu'rire vt to harden ▷ vi (anche: **indurirsi**) to harden, become hard

in'durre vt **~ qn a fare qc** to induce o persuade sb to do sth; **~ qn in errore**

to mislead sb

in'dussi *ecc vb vedi* **indurre**

in'dustria *sf* industry; **industri'ale** *ag* industrial ▷ *sm* industrialist

inecce'pibile [inettʃe'pibile] *ag* unexceptionable

i'nedito, -a *ag* unpublished

ine'rente *ag* ~ **a** concerning, regarding

i'nerme *ag* unarmed; defenceless

inerpi'carsi *vpr* ~ **(su)** to clamber (up)

i'nerte *ag* inert; (*inattivo*) indolent, sluggish

ine'satto, -a *ag* (*impreciso*) inexact; (*erroneo*) incorrect; (*Amm: non riscosso*) uncollected

inesis'tente *ag* non-existent

inesperi'enza [inespe'rjɛntsa] *sf* inexperience

ines'perto, -a *ag* inexperienced

inevi'tabile *ag* inevitable

i'nezia [i'nɛttsja] *sf* trifle, thing of no importance

infagot'tare *vt* to bundle up, wrap up; **infagottarsi** *vpr* to wrap up

infal'libile *ag* infallible

infa'mante *ag* defamatory

in'fame *ag* infamous; (*fig: cosa, compito*) awful, dreadful

infan'gare *vt* to cover with mud; (*fig: reputazione*) to sully; **infangarsi** *vpr* to get covered in mud; to be sullied

infan'tile *ag* child *cpd*; childlike; (*adulto, azione*) childish; **letteratura ~** children's books *pl*

in'fanzia [in'fantsja] *sf* childhood; (*bambini*) children *pl*; **prima ~** babyhood, infancy

infari'nare *vt* to cover with (*o sprinkle with o dip in*) flour; **infarina'tura** *sf* (*fig*) smattering

in'farto *sm* (*Med*) heart attack

infasti'dire *vt* to annoy, irritate; **infastidirsi** *vpr* to get annoyed *o* irritated

infati'cabile *ag* tireless, untiring

in'fatti *cong* actually, as a matter of fact

Attenzione! In inglese esiste l'espressione *in fact* che però vuol dire *in effetti*.

infatu'arsi *vpr*: ~ **di** to become infatuated with, fall for

infe'dele *ag* unfaithful

infe'lice [infe'litʃe] *ag* unhappy; (*sfortunato*) unlucky, unfortunate; (*inopportuno*) inopportune, ill-timed; (*mal riuscito: lavoro*) bad, poor

inferi'ore *ag* lower; (*per intelligenza, qualità*) inferior ▷ *sm/f* inferior; ~ **a** (*numero, quantità*) less o smaller than; (*meno buono*) inferior to; ~ **alla media** below average; **inferiorità** *sf* inferiority

inferme'ria *sf* infirmary; (*di scuola, nave*) sick bay

infermi'ere, -a *sm/f* nurse

infermità *sf inv* illness; infirmity; **infermità mentale** mental illness; (*Dir*) insanity

in'fermo, -a *ag* (*ammalato*) ill; (*debole*) infirm

infer'nale *ag* infernal; (*proposito, complotto*) diabolical

in'ferno *sm* hell

inferri'ata *sf* grating

infes'tare *vt* to infest

infet'tare *vt* to infect; **infettarsi** *vpr* to become infected; **infezi'one** *sf* infection

infiam'mabile *ag* inflammable

infiam'mare *vt* to set alight; (*fig, Med*) to inflame; **infiammarsi** *vpr* to catch fire; (*Med*) to become inflamed; **infiammazi'one** *sf* (*Med*) inflammation

infie'rire *vi*: ~ **su** (*fisicamente*) to attack furiously; (*verbalmente*) to rage at

infi'lare *vt* (*ago*) to thread; (*mettere: chiave*) to insert; (: *anello, vestito*) to slip o put on; (*strada*) to turn into, take; **infilarsi** *vpr* **infilarsi in** to slip into; (*indossare*) to slip on; ~ **l'uscio** to slip

in; to slip out
infil'trarsi *vpr* to penetrate, seep through; (*Mil*) to infiltrate
infil'zare [infil'tsare] *vt* (*infilare*) to string together; (*trafiggere*) to pierce
'infimo, -a *ag* lowest
in'fine *av* finally; (*insomma*) in short
infinità *sf* infinity; (*in quantità*): **un'~ di** an infinite number of
infi'nito, -a *ag* infinite; (*Ling*) infinitive ▷ *sm* infinity; (*Ling*) infinitive; (*senza fine*) endlessly
infinocchi'are [infinok'kjare] (*fam*) *vt* to hoodwink
infischi'arsi [infis'kjarsi] *vpr*: **~ di** not to care about
in'fisso, -a *pp di* **infiggere** ▷ *sm* fixture; (*di porta, finestra*) frame
inflazi'one [inflat'tsjone] *sf* inflation
in'fliggere [in'fliddʒere] *vt* to inflict
in'flissi *ecc vb vedi* **infliggere**
influ'ente *ag* influential; **influ'enza** *sf* influence; (*Med*) influenza, flu
influen'zare [influen'tsare] *vt* to influence, have an influence on
influ'ire *vi*: **~ su** to influence
in'flusso *sm* influence
infon'dato, -a *ag* unfounded, groundless
in'fondere *vt*: **~ qc in qn** to instill sth in sb
infor'mare *vt* to inform, tell; **informarsi** *vpr* **informarsi (di o su)** to inquire (about)
infor'matica *sf* computer science
informa'tivo, -a *ag* informative
infor'mato, -a *ag* informed; **tenersi ~ to keep o.s. (well-)informed
informa'tore *sm* informer
informazi'one [informat'tsjone] *sf* piece of information; **prendere informazioni sul conto di qn** to get information about sb; **chiedere un'~ to ask for (some) information
in'forme *ag* shapeless
informico'larsi *vpr* to have pins and needles

infortu'nato, -a *ag* injured, hurt ▷ *sm/f* injured person
infor'tunio *sm* accident; **infortunio sul lavoro** industrial accident, accident at work
infra'dito *sm inv* (*calzatura*) flip flop (BRIT), thong (US)
infrazi'one [infrat'tsjone] *sf*: **~ a** breaking of, violation of
infredda'tura *sf* slight cold
infreddo'lito, -a *ag* cold, chilled
infu'ori *av* out; **all'~** outwards; **all'~ di** (*eccetto*) except, with the exception of
infuri'arsi *vpr* to fly into a rage
infusi'one *sf* infusion
in'fuso, -a *pp di* **infondere** ▷ *sm* infusion
Ing. *abbr* = **ingegnere**
ingaggi'are [ingad'dʒare] *vt* (*assumere con compenso*) to take on, hire; (*Sport*) to sign on; (*Mil*) to engage
ingan'nare *vt* to deceive; (*fisco*) to cheat; (*eludere*) to dodge, elude; (*fig: tempo*) to while away ▷ *vi* (*apparenza*) to be deceptive; **ingannarsi** *vpr* to be mistaken, be wrong
in'ganno *sm* deceit, deception; (*azione*) trick; (*menzogna, frode*) cheat, swindle; (*illusione*) illusion
inge'gnarsi [indʒeɲ'narsi] *vpr* to do one's best, try hard; **~ per vivere** to live by one's wits
inge'gnere [indʒeɲ'ɲere] *sm* engineer; **~ civile/navale** civil/naval engineer; **ingegne'ria** *sf* engineering; **ingegnere genetica** genetic engineering
in'gegno [in'dʒeɲɲo] *sm* (*intelligenza*) intelligence, brains *pl*; (*capacità creativa*) ingenuity; (*disposizione*) talent; **inge'gnoso, -a** *ag* ingenious, clever
ingelo'sire [indʒelo'zire] *vt* to make jealous ▷ *vi* (*anche*: **ingelosirsi**) to become jealous
in'gente [in'dʒɛnte] *ag* huge,

enormous

ingenuità [indʒenui'ta] *sf* ingenuousness

in'genuo, -a [in'dʒɛnuo] *ag* naïve
Attenzione! In inglese esiste la parola *ingenious*, che però significa *ingegnoso*.

inge'rire [indʒe'rire] *vt* to ingest

inges'sare [indʒes'sare] *vt* (*Med*) to put in plaster; **ingessa'tura** *sf* plaster

Inghil'terra [ingil'tɛrra] *sf*: **l'~** England

inghiot'tire [ingjot'tire] *vt* to swallow

ingial'lire [indʒal'lire] *vi* to go yellow

inginocchi'arsi [indʒinok'kjarsi] *vpr* to kneel (down)

ingiù [in'dʒu] *av* down, downwards

ingi'uria [in'dʒurja] *sf* insult; (*fig: danno*) damage

ingius'tizia [indʒus'tittsja] *sf* injustice

ingi'usto, -a [in'dʒusto] *ag* unjust, unfair

in'glese *ag* English ▷ *sm/f* Englishman/woman ▷ *sm* (*Ling*) English; **gli inglesi** the English; **andarsene** *o* **filare all'~** to take French leave

ingoi'are *vt* to gulp (down); (*fig*) to swallow (up)

ingol'farsi *vpr* to flood

ingom'brante *ag* cumbersome

ingom'brare *vt* (*strada*) to block; (*stanza*) to clutter up

in'gordo, -a *ag*: **~ di** greedy for; (*fig*) greedy *o* avid for

in'gorgo, -ghi *sm* blockage, obstruction; (*anche*: **~ stradale**) traffic jam

ingoz'zarsi *vpr*: **~ (di)** to stuff o.s. (with)

ingra'naggio [ingra'naddʒo] *sm* (*Tecn*) gear; (*di orologio*) mechanism; **gli ingranaggi della burocrazia** the bureaucratic machinery

ingra'nare *vi* to mesh, engage ▷ *vt* to engage; **~ la marcia** to get into gear

ingrandi'mento *sm* enlargement; extension

ingran'dire *vt* (*anche Fot*) to enlarge; (*estendere*) to extend; (*Ottica, fig*) to magnify ▷ *vi* (*anche*: **ingrandirsi**) to become larger *o* bigger; (*aumentare*) to grow, increase; (*espandersi*) to expand

ingras'sare *vt* to make fat; (*animali*) to fatten; (*lubrificare*) to oil, lubricate ▷ *vi* (*anche*: **ingrassarsi**) to get fat, put on weight

in'grato, -a *ag* ungrateful; (*lavoro*) thankless, unrewarding

ingredi'ente *sm* ingredient

in'gresso *sm* (*porta*) entrance; (*atrio*) hall; (*l'entrare*) entrance, entry; (*facoltà di entrare*) admission; **ingresso libero** admission free

ingros'sare *vt* to increase; (*folla, livello*) to swell ▷ *vi* (*anche*: **ingrossarsi**) to increase; to swell

in'grosso *av*: **all'~** (*Comm*) wholesale; (*all'incirca*) roughly, about

ingua'ribile *ag* incurable

'inguine *sm* (*Anat*) groin

ini'bire *vt* to forbid, prohibit; (*Psic*) to inhibit; **inibirsi** *vpr* to restrain o.s.

ini'bito, -a *ag* inhibited ▷ *sm/f* inhibited person

iniet'tare *vt* to inject; **iniezi'one** *sf* injection

ininterrotta'mente *av* non-stop, continuously

ininter'rotto, -a *ag* unbroken; uninterrupted

inizi'ale [init'tsjale] *ag, sf* initial

inizi'are [init'tsjare] *vi, vt* to begin, start; **a che ora inizia il film?** when does the film start?; **~ qn a** to initiate sb into; (*pittura ecc*) to introduce sb to; **~ a fare qc** to start doing sth

inizia'tiva [inittsja'tiva] *sf* initiative; **iniziativa privata** private enterprise

i'nizio [i'nittsjo] *sm* beginning; **all'~** at the beginning, at the start; **dare ~ a qc** to start sth, get sth going

innaffi'are *ecc* = **annaffiare** *ecc*

innamo'rarsi *vpr*: **~ (di qn)** to fall in love (with sb); **innamo'rato, -a** *ag* (*che nutre amore*): **innamorato (di)** in love (with); (*appassionato*): **innamorato di** very fond of ▷ *sm/f* lover; sweetheart

innanzi'tutto *av* first of all

in'nato, -a *ag* innate

innatu'rale *ag* unnatural

inne'gabile *ag* undeniable

innervo'sire *vt*: **~ qn** to get on sb's nerves; **innervosirsi** *vpr* to get irritated *o* upset

innes'care *vt* to prime

'inno *sm* hymn; **inno nazionale** national anthem

inno'cente [inno'tʃɛnte] *ag* innocent

in'nocuo, -a *ag* innocuous, harmless

innova'tivo, -a *ag* innovative

innume'revole *ag* innumerable

inol'trare *vt* (*Amm*) to pass on, forward

i'noltre *av* besides, moreover

inon'dare *vt* to flood

inoppor'tuno, -a *ag* untimely, ill-timed; inappropriate; (*momento*) inopportune

inorri'dire *vt* to horrify ▷ *vi* to be horrified

inosser'vato, -a *ag* (*non notato*) unobserved; (*non rispettato*) not observed, not kept

inossi'dabile *ag* stainless

INPS *sigla m* (= *Istituto Nazionale Previdenza Sociale*) social security service

inqua'drare *vt* (*foto, immagine*) to frame; (*fig*) to situate, set

inqui'eto, -a *ag* restless; (*preoccupato*) worried, anxious

inqui'lino, -a *sm/f* tenant

inquina'mento *sm* pollution

inqui'nare *vt* to pollute

insabbi'are *vt* (*fig*: *pratica*) to shelve; **insabbiarsi** *vpr* (*arenarsi*: *barca*) to run aground; (*fig*: *pratica*) to be shelved

insac'cati *smpl* (*Cuc*) sausages

insa'lata *sf* salad; **insalata mista** mixed salad; **insalata russa** (*Cuc*) Russian salad (*comprised of cold diced cooked vegetables in mayonnaise*); **insalati'era** *sf* salad bowl

insa'nabile *ag* (*piaga*) which cannot be healed; (*situazione*) irremediable; (*odio*) implacable

insa'puta *sf*: **all'~ di qn** without sb knowing

inse'diarsi *vpr* to take up office; (*popolo, colonia*) to settle

in'segna [in'seɲɲa] *sf* sign; (*emblema*) sign, emblem; (*bandiera*) flag, banner

insegna'mento [inseɲɲa'mento] *sm* teaching

inse'gnante [inseɲ'ɲante] *ag* teaching ▷ *sm/f* teacher

inse'gnare [inseɲ'ɲare] *vt, vi* to teach; **~ a qn qc** to teach sb sth; **~ a qn a fare qc** to teach sb (how) to do sth

insegui'mento *sm* pursuit, chase

insegu'ire *vt* to pursue, chase

insena'tura *sf* inlet, creek

insen'sato, -a *ag* senseless, stupid

insen'sibile *ag* (*nervo*) insensible; (*persona*) indifferent

inse'rire *vt* to insert; (*Elettr*) to connect; (*allegare*) to enclose; (*annuncio*) to put in, place; **inserirsi** *vpr* (*fig*): **inserirsi in** to become part of

inservi'ente *sm/f* attendant

inserzi'one [inser'tsjone] *sf* insertion; (*avviso*) advertisement; **fare un'~ sul giornale** to put an advertisement in the paper

insetti'cida, -i [insetti'tʃida] *sm* insecticide

in'setto *sm* insect

insi'curo, -a *ag* insecure

insi'eme *av* together ▷ *prep* **~ a** *o* **con** together with ▷ *sm* whole; (*Mat, servizio, assortimento*) set; (*Moda*) ensemble, outfit; **tutti ~** all together; **tutto ~** all together; (*in una volta*) at one go; **nell'~** on the whole; **d'~** (*veduta ecc*) overall

in'signe [in'siɲɲe] *ag* (*persona*) famous, distinguished; (*città, monumento*) notable

insignifi'cante [insiɲɲifi'kante] *ag* insignificant

insinu'are *vt* (*introdurre*): **~ qc in** to slip *o* slide sth into; (*fig*) to insinuate, imply; **insinuarsi** *vpr* **insinuarsi in** to seep into; (*fig*) to creep into; to worm one's way into

in'sipido, -a *ag* insipid

insis'tente *ag* insistent; persistent

in'sistere *vi*: **~ su qc** to insist on sth; **~ in qc/a fare** (*perseverare*) to persist in sth/in doing

insoddis'fatto, -a *ag* dissatisfied

insoffe'rente *ag* intolerant

insolazi'one [insolat'tsjone] *sf* (*Med*) sunstroke

inso'lente *ag* insolent

in'solito, -a *ag* unusual, out of the ordinary

inso'luto, -a *ag* (*non risolto*) unsolved

in'somma *av* (*in conclusione*) in short; (*dunque*) well ▷ *escl* for heaven's sake!

in'sonne *ag* sleepless; **in'sonnia** *sf* insomnia, sleeplessness

insonno'lito, -a *ag* sleepy, drowsy

insoppor'tabile *ag* unbearable

in'sorgere [in'sordʒere] *vi* (*ribellarsi*) to rise up, rebel; (*apparire*) to come up, arise

in'sorsi *ecc vb vedi* **insorgere**

insospet'tire *vt* to make suspicious ▷ *vi* (*anche*: **insospettirsi**) to become suspicious

inspi'rare *vt* to breathe in, inhale

in'stabile *ag* (*carico, indole*) unstable; (*tempo*) unsettled; (*equilibrio*) unsteady

instal'lare *vt* to install

instan'cabile *ag* untiring, indefatigable

instau'rare *vt* to introduce, institute

insuc'cesso [insut'tʃesso] *sm* failure, flop

insuffici'ente [insuffi'tʃɛnte]

ag insufficient; (*compito, allievo*) inadequate; **insuffici'enza** *sf* insufficiency; inadequacy; (*Ins*) fail; **insufficienza di prove** (*Dir*) lack of evidence; **insufficienza renale** renal insufficiency

insu'lina *sf* insulin

in'sulso, -a *ag* (*sciocco*) inane, silly; (*persona*) dull, insipid

insul'tare *vt* to insult, affront

in'sulto *sm* insult, affront

intac'care *vt* (*fare tacche*) to cut into; (*corrodere*) to corrode; (*fig: cominciare ad usare: risparmi*) to break into; (: *ledere*) to damage

intagli'are [intaʎ'ʎare] *vt* to carve

in'tanto *av* (*nel frattempo*) meanwhile, in the meantime; (*per cominciare*) just to begin with; **~ che** while

inta'sare *vt* to choke (up), block (up); (*Aut*) to obstruct, block; **intasarsi** *vpr* to become choked *o* blocked

intas'care *vt* to pocket

in'tatto, -a *ag* intact; (*puro*) unsullied

intavo'lare *vt* to start, enter into

inte'grale *ag* complete; (*pane, farina*) wholemeal (*BRIT*), whole-wheat (*US*); (*Mat*): **calcolo ~** integral calculus

inte'grante *ag*: **parte ~** integral part

inte'grare *vt* to complete; (*Mat*) to integrate; **integrarsi** *vpr* (*persona*) to become integrated

integra'tore *sm*: **integratori alimentari** nutritional supplements

integrità *sf* integrity

'integro, -a *ag* (*intatto, intero*) complete, whole; (*retto*) upright

intelaia'tura *sf* frame; (*fig*) structure, framework

intel'letto *sm* intellect; **intellettu'ale** *ag, sm/f* intellectual

intelli'gente [intelli'dʒɛnte] *ag* intelligent

intem'perie *sfpl* bad weather *sg*

in'tendere *vt* (*avere intenzione*): **~ fare qc** to intend *o* mean to do sth; (*comprendere*) to understand; (*udire*) to hear; (*significare*) to mean; **intendersi** *vpr* (*conoscere*): **intendersi di** to know a lot about, be a connoisseur of; (*accordarsi*) to get on (well); **intendersela con qn** (*avere una relazione amorosa*) to have an affair with sb; **intendi'tore, -'trice** *sm/f* connoisseur, expert

inten'sivo, -a *ag* intensive

in'tenso, -a *ag* intense

in'tento, -a *ag* (*teso, assorto*): **~ (a)** Intent (on), absorbed (in) ▷ *sm* aim, purpose

intenzio'nale [intentsjo'nale] *ag* intentional

intenzi'one [inten'tsjone] *sf* intention; (*Dir*) intent; **avere ~ di fare qc** to intend to do sth, have the intention of doing sth

interat'tivo, -a *ag* interactive

intercet'tare [intertʃet'tare] *vt* to intercept

intercity [inter'siti] *sm inv* (*Ferr*) ≈ intercity (train)

inter'detto, -a *pp di* **interdire** ▷ *ag* forbidden, prohibited; (*sconcertato*) dumbfounded ▷ *sm* (*Rel*) interdict

interes'sante *ag* interesting; **essere in stato ~** to be expecting (a baby)

interes'sare *vt* to interest; (*concernere*) to concern, be of interest to; (*far intervenire*): **~ qn a** to draw sb's attention to ▷ *vi*: **~ a** to interest, matter to; **interessarsi** *vpr* (*mostrare interesse*): **interessarsi a** to take an interest in, be interested in; (*occuparsi*): **interessarsi di** to take care of

inte'resse *sm* (*anche Comm*) interest

inter'faccia, -ce [inter'fattʃa] *sf* (*Inform*) interface

interfe'renza [interfe'rɛntsa] *sf* interference

interfe'rire *vi* to interfere

interiezi'one [interjet'tsjone] *sf* exclamation, interjection

interi'nale *agg*: **lavoro ~** temporary

work (*gained through an agency*)

interi'ora *sfpl* entrails

interi'ore *ag* interior, inner, inside, internal; (*fig*) inner

inter'medio, -a *ag* intermediate

inter'nare *vt* (*arrestare*) to intern; (*Med*) to commit (to a mental institution)

inter'nauta *sm/f* Internet user

internazio'nale [internattsjo'nale] *ag* international

'Internet ['internet] *sf* Internet; **in ~** on the Internet

in'terno, -a *ag* (*di dentro*) internal, interior, inner; (: *mare*) inland; (*nazionale*) domestic; (*allievo*) boarding ▷ *sm* inside, interior; (*di paese*) interior; (*fodera*) lining; (*di appartamento*) flat (number); (*Tel*) extension ▷ *sm/f* (*Ins*) boarder; **interni** *smpl* (*Cinema*) interior shots; **all'~** inside; **Ministero degli Interni** Ministry of the Interior, ≈ Home Office (BRIT), Department of the Interior (US)

in'tero, -a *ag* (*integro, intatto*) whole, entire; (*completo, totale*) complete; (*numero*) whole; (*non ridotto: biglietto*) full; (*latte*) full-cream

interpel'lare *vt* to consult

interpre'tare *vt* to interpret; **in'terprete** *sm/f* interpreter; (*Teatro*) actor/actress, performer; (*Mus*) performer; **ci potrebbe fare da interprete?** could you act as an interpreter for us?

interregio'nale [interredʒo'nale] *sm train that travels between two or more regions of Italy, stopping frequently*

interro'gare *vt* to question; (*Ins*) to test; **interrogazi'one** *sf* questioning *no pl*; (*Ins*) oral test

inter'rompere *vt* to interrupt; (*studi, trattative*) to break off, interrupt; **interrompersi** *vpr* to break off, stop

interrut'tore *sm* switch

interruzi'one [interrut'tsjone] *sf* interruption; break

interur'bana *sf* trunk *o* long-distance call

inter'vallo *sm* interval; (*spazio*) space, gap

interve'nire *vi* (*partecipare*): **~ a** to take part in; (*intromettersi: anche Pol*) to intervene; (*Med: operare*) to operate; **inter'vento** *sm* participation; (*intromissione*) intervention; (*Med*) operation; **fare un intervento nel corso di** (*dibattito, programma*) to take part in

inter'vista *sf* interview; **intervis'tare** *vt* to interview

intes'tare *vt* (*lettera*) to address; (*proprietà*): **~ a** to register in the name of; **~ un assegno a qn** to make out a cheque to sb

intes'tato, -a *ag* (*proprietà, casa, conto*) in the name of; (*assegno*) made out to; **carta intestata** headed paper

intes'tino *sm* (*Anat*) intestine

intimidazi'one [intimidat'tsjone] *sf* intimidation

intimi'dire *vt* to intimidate ▷ *vi* (*intimidirsi*) to grow shy

intimità *sf* intimacy; privacy; (*familiarità*) familiarity

'intimo, -a *ag* intimate; (*affetti, vita*) private; (*fig: profondo*) inmost ▷ *sm* (*persona*) intimate *o* close friend; (*dell'animo*) bottom, depths *pl*; **parti intime** (*Anat*) private parts

in'tingolo *sm* sauce; (*pietanza*) stew

intito'lare *vt* to give a title to; (*dedicare*) to dedicate; **intitolarsi** *vpr* (*libro, film*) to be called

intolle'rabile *ag* intolerable

intolle'rante *ag* intolerant

in'tonaco, -ci *o* **chi** *sm* plaster

into'nare *vt* (*canto*) to start to sing; (*armonizzare*) to match; **intonarsi** *vpr* (*colori*) to go together; **intonarsi a** (*carnagione*) to suit; (*abito*) to go with, match

inton'tito, -a *ag* stunned, dazed; **~ dal sonno** stupid with sleep

in'toppo *sm* stumbling block, obstacle

in'torno *av* around; **~ a** (*attorno a*) around; (*riguardo, circa*) about

intossi'care *vt* to poison; **intossicazi'one** *sf* poisoning

intralci'are [intral'tʃare] *vt* to hamper, hold up

intransi'tivo, -a *ag, sm* intransitive

intrapren'dente *ag* enterprising, go-ahead

intra'prendere *vt* to undertake

intrat'tabile *ag* intractable

intratte'nere *vt* to entertain; to engage in conversation; **intrattenersi** *vpr* to linger; **intrattenersi su qc** to dwell on sth

intrave'dere *vt* to catch a glimpse of; (*fig*) to foresee

intrecci'are [intret'tʃare] *vt* (*capelli*) to plait, braid; (*intessere: anche fig*) to weave, interweave, intertwine

intri'gante *ag* scheming ▷ *sm/f* schemer, intriguer

in'trinseco, -a, -ci, -che *ag* intrinsic

in'triso, -a *ag*: **~ (di)** soaked (in)

intro'durre *vt* to introduce; (*chiave ecc*): **~ qc in** to insert sth into; (*persone: far entrare*) to show in; **introdursi** *vpr* (*moda, tecniche*) to be introduced; **introdursi in** (*persona: penetrare*) to enter; (*: entrare furtivamente*) to steal *o* slip into; **introduzi'one** *sf* introduction

in'troito *sm* income, revenue

intro'mettersi *vpr* to interfere, meddle; (*interporsi*) to intervene

in'truglio [in'truʎʎo] *sm* concoction

intrusi'one *sf* intrusion; interference

in'truso, -a *sm/f* intruder

intu'ire *vt* to perceive by intuition; (*rendersi conto*) to realize; **in'tuito** *sm* intuition; (*perspicacia*) perspicacity

inu'mano, -a *ag* inhuman

inumi'dire *vt* to dampen, moisten; **inumidirsi** *vpr* to become damp *o* wet

i'nutile *ag* useless; (*superfluo*)

pointless, unnecessary

inutil'mente av unnecessarily; (senza risultato) in vain

inva'dente ag (fig) interfering, nosey

in'vadere vt to invade; (affollare) to swarm into, overrun; (acque) to flood

inva'ghirsi [inva'girsi] vpr: ~ **di** to take a fancy to

invalidità sf infirmity; disability; (Dir) invalidity

in'valido, -a ag (infermo) infirm, invalid; (al lavoro) disabled; (Dir: nullo) invalid ▷ sm/f invalid; disabled person

in'vano av in vain

invasi'one sf invasion

inva'sore, invadi'trice [invadi'tritʃe] ag invading ▷ sm invader

invecchi'are [invek'kjare] vi (persona) to grow old; (vino, popolazione) to age; (moda) to become dated ▷ vt to age; (far apparire più vecchio) to make look older

in'vece [in'vetʃe] av instead; (al contrario) on the contrary; ~ **di** instead of

inve'ire vi ~ **contro** to rail against

inven'tare vt to invent; (pericoli, pettegolezzi) to make up, invent

inven'tario sm inventory; (Comm) stocktaking no pl

inven'tore sm inventor

invenzi'one [inven'tsjone] sf invention; (bugia) lie, story

inver'nale ag winter cpd; (simile all'inverno) wintry

in'verno sm winter

invero'simile ag unlikely

inversi'one sf inversion; reversal; **"divieto d'~"** (Aut) "no U-turns"

in'verso, -a ag opposite; (Mat) inverse ▷ sm contrary, opposite; **in senso ~** in the opposite direction; **in ordine ~** in reverse order

inver'tire vt to invert, reverse; ~ **la marcia** (Aut) to do a U-turn

investi'gare vt, vi to investigate;

investiga'tore, -'trice sm/f investigator, detective; **investigatore privato** private investigator

investi'mento sm (Econ) investment

inves'tire vt (denaro) to invest; (veicolo: pedone) to knock down; (: altro veicolo) to crash into; (apostrofare) to assail; (incaricare): ~ **qn di** to invest sb with

invi'are vt to send; **invi'ato, -a** sm/f envoy; (Stampa) correspondent; **inviato speciale** (Pol) special envoy; (di giornale) special correspondent

in'vidia sf envy; **invidi'are** vt **invidiare qn (per qc)** to envy sb for sth; **invidiare qc a qn** to envy sb sth; **invidi'oso, -a** ag envious

in'vio, -'vii sm sending; (insieme di merci) consignment; (tasto) return (key), enter (key)

invipe'rito, -a ag furious

invi'sibile ag invisible

invi'tare vt to invite; ~ **qn a fare** to invite sb to do; **invi'tato, -a** sm/f guest; **in'vito** sm invitation

invo'care vt (chiedere: aiuto, pace) to cry out for; (appellarsi: la legge, Dio) to appeal to, invoke

invogli'are [invoʎ'ʎare] vt: ~ **qn a fare** to tempt sb to do, induce sb to do

involon'tario, -a ag (errore) unintentional; (gesto) involuntary

invol'tino sm (Cuc) roulade

in'volto sm (pacco) parcel; (fagotto) bundle

in'volucro sm cover, wrapping

inzup'pare [intsup'pare] vt to soak; **inzupparsi** vpr to get soaked

'io pron I ▷ sm inv I'~ the ego, the self; ~ **stesso(a)** I myself

i'odio sm iodine

l'onio sm: **lo ~, il mar ~** the Ionian (Sea)

ipermer'cato sm hypermarket

ipertensi'one sf high blood pressure, hypertension

iper'testo sm hypertext;

ipertestu'ale agg (Inform) hypertext cpd

ip'nosi sf hypnosis; **ipnotiz'zare** vt to hypnotize

ipocri'sia sf hypocrisy

i'pocrita, -i, -e ag hypocritical ▷ sm/f hypocrite

ipo'teca, -che sf mortgage

i'potesi sf inv hypothesis

'ippica sf horseracing

'ippico, -a, -ci, -che ag horse cpd

ippocas'tano sm horse chestnut

ip'podromo sm racecourse

ippo'potamo sm hippopotamus

'ipsilon sf o m inv (lettera) Y, y; (: dell'alfabeto greco) epsilon

IR abbr (= Interregionale) long distance train which stops frequently

ira'cheno, -a [ira'kɛno] ag, sm/f Iraqi

I'ran sm **l'~** Iran

irani'ano, -a ag, sm/f Iranian

I'raq sm **l'~** Iraq

'iride sf (arcobaleno) rainbow; (Anat, Bot) iris

'iris sm inv iris

Ir'landa sf: **l'~** Ireland; **l'~ del Nord** Northern Ireland, Ulster; **la Repubblica d'~** Eire, the Republic of Ireland; **irlan'dese** ag Irish ▷ sm/f Irishman/woman; **gli Irlandesi** the Irish

iro'nia sf irony; **i'ronico, -a, -ci, -che** ag ironic(al)

irragio'nevole [irradʒo'nevole] ag irrational; unreasonable

irrazio'nale [irrattsjo'nale] ag irrational

irre'ale ag unreal

irrego'lare ag irregular; (terreno) uneven

irremo'vibile ag (fig) unshakeable, unyielding

irrequi'eto, -a ag restless

irresis'tibile ag irresistible

irrespon'sabile ag irresponsible

irri'gare vt (annaffiare) to irrigate; (fiume ecc) to flow through

irrigi'dire [irridʒi'dire] vt to stiffen; **irrigidirsi** vpr to stiffen

irri'sorio, -a ag derisory

irri'tare vt (mettere di malumore) to irritate, annoy; (Med) to irritate; **irritarsi** vpr (stizzirsi) to become irritated o annoyed; (Med) to become irritated

ir'rompere vi: **~ in** to burst into

irru'ente ag (fig) impetuous, violent

ir'ruppi ecc vb vedi **irrompere**

irruzi'one [irrut'tsjone] sf **fare ~ in** to burst into; (polizia) to raid

is'crissi ecc vb vedi **iscrivere**

is'critto, -a pp di **iscrivere** ▷ sm/f member; **per o in** ~ in writing

is'crivere vt to register, enter; (persona): **~ (a)** to register (in), enrol (in); **iscriversi** vpr **iscriversi (a)** (club, partito) to join; (università) to register o enrol (at); (esame, concorso) to register o enter (for); **iscrizi'one** sf (epigrafe ecc) inscription; (a scuola, società) enrolment, registration; (registrazione) registration

Is'lam sm: **l'~** Islam

Is'landa sf: **l'~** Iceland

islan'dese ag Icelandic ▷ sm/f Icelander ▷ sm (Ling) Icelandic

'isola sf island; **isola pedonale** (Aut) pedestrian precinct

isola'mento sm isolation; (Tecn) insulation

iso'lante ag insulating ▷ sm insulator

iso'lare vt to isolate; (Tecn) to insulate; (: acusticamente) to soundproof; **isolarsi** vpr to isolate o.s.; **iso'lato, -a** ag isolated; insulated ▷ sm (gruppo di edifici) block

ispet'tore sm inspector

ispezio'nare [ispettsjo'nare] vt to inspect

'ispido, -a ag bristly, shaggy

ispi'rare vt to inspire

Isra'ele sm **l'~** Israel; **israeli'ano, -a** ag, sm/f Israeli

is'sare vt to hoist

istan'taneo, -a *ag* instantaneous
▷ *sf* (*Fot*) snapshot

is'tante *sm* instant, moment; **all'~, sull'~** instantly, immediately

is'terico, -a, -ci, -che *ag* hysterical

isti'gare *vt* to incite

is'tinto *sm* instinct

istitu'ire *vt* (*fondare*) to institute, found; (*porre: confronto*) to establish; (*intraprendere: inchiesta*) to set up

isti'tuto *sm* institute; (*di università*) department; (*ente, Dir*) institution; **istituto di bellezza** beauty salon; **istituto di credito** bank, banking institution; **istituto di ricerca** research institute

istituzi'one [istitut'tsjone] *sf* institution

'istmo *sm* (*Geo*) isthmus

'istrice ['istritʃe] *sm* porcupine

istru'ito, -a *ag* educated

istrut'tore, -'trice *sm/f* instructor ▷ *ag* **giudice ~** *vedi* **giudice**

istruzi'one *sf* education; training; (*direttiva*) instruction; **istruzioni** *sfpl* (*norme*) instructions; **istruzioni per l'uso** instructions for use; **~ obbligatoria** (*Scol*) compulsory education

l'talia *sf*: **l'~** Italy

itali'ano, -a *ag* Italian ▷ *sm/f* Italian ▷ *sm* (*Ling*) Italian; **gli Italiani** the Italians

itine'rario *sm* itinerary

'ittico, -a, -ci, -che *ag* fish *cpd*; fishing *cpd*

Iugos'lavia = **Jugoslavia**

IVA ['iva] *sigla f* (= *imposta sul valore aggiunto*) VAT

j

jazz [dʒaz] *sm* jazz

jeans [dʒinz] *smpl* jeans

jeep® [dʒip] *sm inv* jeep

'jogging ['dʒɔgin] *sm* jogging; **fare ~** to go jogging

'jolly ['dʒɔli] *sm inv* joker

joystick [dʒɔis'tik] *sm inv* joystick

ju'do [dʒu'dɔ] *sm* judo

Jugos'lavia [jugoz'lavja] *sf* (*Storia*): **la ~** Yugoslavia; **la ex-~** former Yugoslavia; **jugos'lavo, -a** *ag, sm/f* (*Storia*) Yugoslav(ian)

k l

k *abbr* (= kilo-, chilo-) k; *(Inform)* K

kamikaze [kami'kaddze] *sm inv* kamikaze

karaoke [ka'raokɛ] *sm inv* karaoke

karatè *sm* karate

ka'yak [ka'jak] *sm inv* kayak

Kenia ['kenja] *sm*: **il ~** Kenya

kg *abbr* (= chilogrammo) kg

'killer *sm inv* gunman, hired gun

kitsch [kitʃ] *sm* kitsch

'kiwi ['kiwi] *sm inv* kiwi fruit

km *abbr* (= chilometro) km

K.O. [kappa'o] *sm inv* knockout

ko'ala [ko'ala] *sm inv* koala (bear)

koso'varo, -a [koso'varo] *ag, sm/f* Kosovan

Ko'sovo *sm* Kosovo

'krapfen *sm inv* (*Cuc*) doughnut

Kuwait [ku'vait] *sm*: **il ~** Kuwait

l' *det vedi* **la**; **lo**; **il**

la (*dav V* **l'**) *det f* the ▷ *pron (oggetto: persona)* her; (: *cosa*) it; (: *forma di cortesia*) you; *vedi anche* **il**

là *av* there; **di là** (*da quel luogo*) from there; (*in quel luogo*) in there; (*dall'altra parte*) over there; **di là di** beyond; **per di là** that way; **più in là** further on; (*tempo*) later on; **fatti in là** move up; **là dentro/sopra/sotto** in/up (*o* on)/under there; *vedi anche* **quello**

'labbro (*pl(f)* **labbra**) (*solo nel senso Anat*) *sm* lip

labi'rinto *sm* labyrinth, maze

labora'torio *sm* (*di ricerca*) laboratory; (*di arti, mestieri*) workshop; **laboratorio linguistico** language laboratory

labori'oso, -a *ag* (*faticoso*) laborious; (*attivo*) hard-working

'lacca, -che *sf* lacquer

'laccio ['lattʃo] *sm* noose; (*legaccio, tirante*) lasso; (*di scarpa*) lace; **laccio emostatico** tourniquet

lace'rare [latʃe'rare] *vt* to tear to shreds, lacerate; **lacerarsi** *vpr* to tear

'lacrima *sf* tear; **in lacrime** in tears; **lacri'mogeno, -a** *ag* **gas lacrimogeno** tear gas

la'cuna *sf* (*fig*) gap

'ladro *sm* thief

laggiù [lad'dʒu] *av* down there; (*di là*) over there

la'gnarsi [laɲ'ɲarsi] *vpr*: **~ (di)** to complain (about)

'lago, -ghi *sm* lake

la'guna *sf* lagoon

'laico, -a, -ci, -che *ag* (*apostolato*) lay; (*vita*) secular; (*scuola*) non-denominational ▷ *sm/f* layman/woman

'lama *sm inv* (*Zool*) llama; (*Rel*) lama ▷ *sf* blade

lamentarsi *vpr* (*emettere lamenti*) to moan, groan; (*rammaricarsi*): **~ (di)** to complain (about)

lamen'tela *sf* complaining *no pl*

la'metta *sf* razor blade

'lamina *sf* (*lastra sottile*) thin sheet (*o* layer *o* plate); **lamina d'oro** gold leaf, gold foil

'lampada *sf* lamp; **lampada a gas** gas lamp; **lampada da tavolo** table lamp

lampa'dario *sm* chandelier

lampa'dina *sf* light bulb; **lampadina tascabile** pocket torch (*BRIT*) *o* flashlight (*US*)

lam'pante *ag* (*fig: evidente*) crystal clear, evident

lampeggi'are [lamped'dʒare] *vi* (*luce, fari*) to flash ▷ *vb impers* **lampeggia** there's lightning; **lampeggia'tore** *sm* (*Aut*) indicator

lampi'one *sm* street light *o* lamp (*BRIT*)

'lampo *sm* (*Meteor*) flash of lightning; (*di luce: fig*) flash

lam'pone *sm* raspberry

'lana *sf* wool; **pura ~ vergine** pure new wool; **lana d'acciaio** steel wool;

lana di vetro glass wool

lan'cetta [lan'tʃetta] *sf* (*indice*) pointer, needle; (*di orologio*) hand

'lancia ['lantʃa] *sf* (*arma*) lance; (: *picca*) spear; (*di pompa antincendio*) nozzle; (*imbarcazione*) launch; **lancia di salvataggio** lifeboat

lanciafi'amme [lantʃa'fjamme] *sm inv* flamethrower

lanci'are [lan'tʃare] *vt* to throw, hurl, fling; (*Sport*) to throw; (*far partire: automobile*) to get up to full speed; (*bombe*) to drop; (*razzo, prodotto, moda*) to launch; **lanciarsi** *vpr* **lanciarsi contro/su** to throw *o* hurl *o* fling o.s. against/on; **lanciarsi in** (*fig*) to embark on

lanci'nante [lantʃi'nante] *ag* (*dolore*) shooting, throbbing; (*grido*) piercing

'lancio ['lantʃo] *sm* throwing *no pl*; throw; dropping *no pl*; drop; launching *no pl*; launch; **lancio del disco** (*Sport*) throwing the discus; **lancio del peso** putting the shot

'languido, -a *ag* (*fiacco*) languid, weak; (*tenero, malinconico*) languishing

lan'terna *sf* lantern; (*faro*) lighthouse

'lapide *sf* (*di sepolcro*) tombstone; (*commemorativa*) plaque

'lapsus *sm inv* slip

'lardo *sm* bacon fat, lard

lar'ghezza [lar'gettsa] *sf* width; breadth; looseness; generosity; **larghezza di vedute** broad-mindedness

'largo, -a, -ghi, -ghe *ag* wide; broad; (*maniche*) wide; (*abito: troppo ampio*) loose; (*fig*) generous ▷ *sm* width; breadth; (*mare aperto*): **il ~** the open sea ▷ *sf* **stare** *o* **tenersi alla larga (da qn/qc)** to keep one's distance (from sb/sth), keep away (from sb/sth); **~ due metri** two metres wide; **~ di spalle** broad-shouldered; **di larghe**

vedute broad-minded; **su larga scala** on a large scale; **di manica larga** generous, open-handed; **al ~ di Genova** off (the coast of) Genoa; **farsi ~ tra la folla** to push one's way through the crowd

'larice ['laritʃe] *sm* (*Bot*) larch

larin'gite [larin'dʒite] *sf* laryngitis

'larva *sf* larva; (*fig*) shadow

la'sagne [la'zaɲɲe] *sfpl* lasagna *sg*

lasci'are [laʃʃare] *vt* to leave; (*abbandonare*) to leave, abandon, give up; (*cessare di tenere*) to let go of ▷ *vb aus* **~ fare qn** to let sb do; **~ andare** *o* **correre** *o* **perdere** to let things go their own way; **~ stare qc/qn** to leave sth/sb alone; **lasciarsi** *vpr* (*persone*) to part; (*coppia*) to split up; **lasciarsi andare** to let o.s. go

'laser ['lazer] *ag, sm inv:* **(raggio) ~** laser (beam)

lassa'tivo, -a *ag, sm* laxative

'lasso *sm;* **lasso di tempo** interval, lapse of time

lassù *av* up there

'lastra *sf* (*di pietra*) slab; (*di metallo, Fot*) plate; (*di ghiaccio, vetro*) sheet; (*radiografica*) X-ray (plate)

lastri'cato *sm* paving

late'rale *ag* lateral, side *cpd;* (*uscita, ingresso ecc*) side *cpd* ▷ *sm* (*Calcio*) half-back

la'tino, -a *ag, sm* Latin

lati'tante *sm/f* fugitive (from justice)

lati'tudine *sf* latitude

'lato, -a *ag* (*fig*) wide, broad ▷ *sm* side; (*fig*) aspect, point of view; **in senso ~** broadly speaking

'latta *sf* tin (plate); (*recipiente*) tin, can

lat'tante *ag* unweaned

'latte *sm* milk; **latte detergente** cleansing milk *o* lotion; **latte intero** full-cream milk; **latte a lunga conservazione** UHT milk, long-life milk; **latte magro** *o* **scremato** skimmed milk; **latte in polvere** dried

o powdered milk; **latte solare** suntan lotion; **latti'cini** *smpl* dairy products

lat'tina *sf* (*di birra ecc*) can

lat'tuga, -ghe *sf* lettuce

'laurea *sf* degree; **laurea in ingegneria** engineering degree; **laurea in lettere** ≈ arts degree

● **LAUREA**
●
● The **laurea** is awarded to students
● who successfully complete their
● degree courses. Traditionally,
● this takes between four and six
● years; a major element of the final
● examinations is the presentation
● and discussion of a dissertation.
● A shorter, more vocational course
● of study, taking from two to three
● years, is also available; at the end
● of this time students receive a
● diploma called the **laurea breve**.

laure'arsi *vpr* to graduate

laure'ato, -a *ag, sm/f* graduate

'lauro *sm* laurel

'lauto, -a *ag* (*pranzo, mancia*) lavish

'lava *sf* lava

la'vabo *sm* washbasin

la'vaggio [la'vaddʒo] *sm* washing *no pl;* **lavaggio del cervello** brainwashing *no pl;* **lavaggio a secco** dry-cleaning

la'vagna [la'vaɲɲa] *sf* (*Geo*) slate; (*di scuola*) blackboard

la'vanda *sf* (*anche Med*) wash; (*Bot*) lavender; **lavande'ria** *sf* laundry; **lavanderia automatica** launderette; **lavanderia a secco** dry-cleaner's; **lavan'dino** *sm* sink

lavapi'atti *sm/f* dishwasher

la'vare *vt* to wash; **lavarsi** *vpr* to wash, have a wash; **~ a secco** to dry-clean; **lavarsi le mani/i denti** to wash one's hands/clean one's teeth

lava'secco *sm o f inv* dry cleaner's

lavasto'viglie [lavasto'viʎʎe] *sm o f inv* (*macchina*) dishwasher

lava'trice [lava'tritʃe] *sf* washing machine

lavo'rare *vi* to work; (*fig: bar, studio ecc*) to do good business ▷ *vt* to work; **lavorarsi qn** (*persuaderlo*) to work on sb; **~ a** to work on; **~ a maglia** to knit; **lavora'tivo, -a** *ag* working; **lavora'tore, -'trice** *sm/f* worker ▷ *ag* working

la'voro *sm* work; (*occupazione*) job, work *no pl*; (*opera*) piece of work, job; (*Econ*) labour; **che ~ fa?** what do you do?; **lavori forzati** hard labour *sg*; **lavoro interinale** *o* **in affitto** temporary work

le *det fpl* the ▷ *pron* (*oggetto*) them; (: *a lei, a essa*) (to) her; (: *forma di cortesia*) (to) you; *vedi anche* **il**

le'ale *ag* loyal; (*sincero*) sincere; (*onesto*) fair

'lecca 'lecca *sm inv* lollipop

leccapi'edi (*peg*) *sm/f inv* toady, bootlicker

lec'care *vt* to lick; (*gatto: latte ecc*) to lick *o* lap up; (*fig*) to flatter; **leccarsi i baffi** to lick one's lips

leccherò *ecc* [lekke'rɔ] *vb vedi* **leccare**

'leccio ['lettʃo] *sm* holm oak, ilex

leccor'nia *sf* titbit, delicacy

'lecito, -a ['lɛtʃito] *ag* permitted, allowed

'lega, -ghe *sf* league; (*di metalli*) alloy

le'gaccio [le'gattʃo] *sm* string, lace

le'gale *ag* legal ▷ *sm* lawyer; **legaliz'zare** *vt* to authenticate; (*regolarizzare*) to legalize

le'game *sm* (*corda, fig: affettivo*) tie, bond; (*nesso logico*) link, connection

le'gare *vt* (*prigioniero, capelli, cane*) to tie (up); (*libro*) to bind; (*Chim*) to alloy; (*fig: collegare*) to bind, join ▷ *vi* (*far lega*) to unite; (*fig*) to get on well

le'genda [le'dʒɛnda] *sf* (*di carta geografica ecc*) = **leggenda**

'legge ['lɛddʒe] *sf* law

leg'genda [led'dʒɛnda] *sf* (*narrazione*) legend; (*di carta geografica ecc*) key, legend

'leggere ['lɛddʒere] *vt, vi* to read

legge'rezza [leddʒe'rettsa] *sf* lightness; thoughtlessness; fickleness

leg'gero, -a [led'dʒero] *ag* light; (*agile, snello*) nimble, agile, light; (*tè, caffè*) weak; (*fig: non grave, piccolo*) slight; (: *spensierato*) thoughtless; (: *incostante*) fickle; free and easy; **alla leggera** thoughtlessly

leg'gio, -'gii [led'dʒio] *sm* lectern; (*Mus*) music stand

legherò *ecc* [lege'rɔ] *vb vedi* **legare**

legisla'tivo, -a [ledʒizla'tivo] *ag* legislative

legisla'tura [ledʒizla'tura] *sf* legislature

le'gittimo, -a [le'dʒittimo] *ag* legitimate; (*fig: giustificato, lecito*) justified, legitimate; **legittima difesa** (*Dir*) self-defence

'legna ['leɲɲa] *sf* firewood

'legno ['leɲɲo] *sm* wood; (*pezzo di legno*) piece of wood; **di ~** wooden; **legno compensato** plywood

'lei *pron* (*soggetto*) she; (*oggetto: per dare rilievo, con preposizione*) her; (*forma di cortesia: anche:* **L~**) you ▷ *sm* **dare del ~ a qn** to address sb as "lei"; **~ stessa** she herself; you yourself

---

● **LEI**
●
●
● **lei** is the third person singular
● pronoun. It is used in Italian to
● address an adult whom you do not
● know or with whom you are on
● formal terms.

lenta'mente *av* slowly

'lente *sf* (*Ottica*) lens *sg*; **lenti a contatto** *o* **corneali** contact lenses; **·lenti (a contatto) morbide/rigide**

soft/hard contact lenses; **lente d'ingrandimento** magnifying glass; **lenti** *sfpl* (*occhiali*) lenses
len'tezza [len'tettsa] *sf* slowness
len'ticchia [len'tikkja] *sf* (*Bot*) lentil
len'tiggine [len'tidd3ine] *sf* freckle
'lento, -a *ag* slow; (*molle: fune*) slack; (*non stretto: vite, abito*) loose ▷ *sm* (*ballo*) slow dance
'lenza ['lɛntsa] *sf* fishing-line
lenzu'olo [len'tswɔlo] *sm* sheet
le'one *sm* lion; (*dello zodiaco*): **L~** Leo
lepo'rino, -a *ag* **labbro ~** harelip
'lepre *sf* hare
'lercio, -a, -ci, -cie ['lɛrtʃo] *ag* filthy
lesi'one *sf* (*Med*) lesion; (*Dir*) injury, damage; (*Edil*) crack
les'sare *vt* (*Cuc*) to boil
'lessi *ecc vb vedi* **leggere**
'lessico, -ci *sm* vocabulary; lexicon
'lesso, -a *ag* boiled ▷ *sm* boiled meat
le'tale *ag* lethal; fatal
leta'maio *sm* dunghill
le'tame *sm* manure, dung
le'targo, -ghi *sm* lethargy; (*Zool*) hibernation
'lettera *sf* letter; **lettere** *sfpl* (*letteratura*) literature *sg*; (*studi umanistici*) arts (subjects); **alla ~** literally; **in lettere** in words, in full
letteral'mente *av* literally
lette'rario, -a *ag* literary
lette'rato, -a *ag* well-read, scholarly
lettera'tura *sf* literature
let'tiga, -ghe *sf* (*barella*) stretcher
let'tino *sm* cot (*BRIT*), crib (*US*); **lettino solare** sunbed
'letto, -a *pp di* **leggere** ▷ *sm* bed; **andare a ~** to go to bed; **letto a castello** bunk beds *pl*; **letto a una piazza** single; **letto a due piazze** *o* **matrimoniale** double bed
let'tore, -'trice *sm/f* reader; (*Ins*) (foreign language) assistant (*BRIT*), (foreign) teaching assistant (*US*) ▷ *sm* (*Tecn*): **~ ottico** optical character

reader; **lettore CD** CD player; **lettore DVD** DVD player
let'tura *sf* reading
▎ Attenzione! In inglese esiste la parola *lecture*, che però significa *lezione* oppure *conferenza*.
leuce'mia [leutʃe'mia] *sf* leukaemia
'leva *sf* lever; (*Mil*) conscription; **far ~ su qn** to work on sb; **leva del cambio** (*Aut*) gear lever
le'vante *sm* east; (*vento*) East wind; **il L~** the Levant
le'vare *vt* (*occhi, braccio*) to raise; (*sollevare, togliere: tassa, divieto*) to lift; (*indumenti*) to take off, remove; (*rimuovere*) to take away; (: *dal di sopra*) to take off; (: *dal di dentro*) to take out
leva'toio, -a *ag*: **ponte ~** drawbridge
lezi'one [let'tsjone] *sf* lesson; (*Univ*) lecture; **fare ~** to teach; to lecture; **dare una ~ a qn** to teach sb a lesson; **lezioni private** private lessons
li *pron pl* (*oggetto*) them
lì *av* there; **di** *o* **da lì** from there; **per di lì** that way; **di lì a pochi giorni** a few days later; **lì per lì** there and then; at first; **essere lì (lì) per fare** to be on the point of doing, be about to do; **lì dentro** in there; **lì sotto** under there; **lì sopra** on there; up there; *vedi anche* **quello**
liba'nese *ag, sm/f* Lebanese *inv*
Li'bano *sm*: **il ~** the Lebanon
'libbra *sf* (*peso*) pound
li'beccio [li'bettʃo] *sm* south-west wind
li'bellula *sf* dragonfly
libe'rale *ag, sm/f* liberal
liberaliz'zare [liberalid'dzare] *vt* to liberalize
libe'rare *vt* (*rendere libero: prigioniero*) to release; (: *popolo*) to free, liberate; (*sgombrare: passaggio*) to clear; (: *stanza*) to vacate; (*produrre: energia*) to release; **liberarsi** *vpr* **liberarsi di qc/qn** to get rid of sth/sb;

liberazi'one sf liberation, freeing; release; rescuing

● **LIBERAZIONE**
●
● The **Liberazione** is a national
● holiday which falls on April 25th.
● It commemorates the liberation
● of Italy at the end of the Second
● World War.

'**libero, -a** ag free; (strada) clear; (non occupato: posto ecc) vacant; free; not taken; empty; not engaged; **~ di fare qc** free to do sth; **~ da** free from; **è ~ questo posto?** is this seat free?; **~ arbitrio** free will; **~ professionista** self-employed professional person; **~ scambio** free trade; **libertà** sf inv freedom; (tempo disponibile) free time ▷ sfpl (licenza) liberties; **in libertà provvisoria/vigilata** released without bail/on probation

'**Libia** sf **la ~** Libya; '**libico, -a, -ci, -che** ag, sm/f Libyan

li'bidine sf lust

li'braio sm bookseller

li'brarsi vpr to hover

libre'ria sf (bottega) bookshop; (mobile) bookcase

▌ Attenzione! In inglese esiste la parola library, che però significa biblioteca.

li'bretto sm booklet; (taccuino) notebook; (Mus) libretto; **libretto degli assegni** cheque book; **libretto di circolazione** (Aut) logbook; **libretto di risparmio** (savings) bank-book, passbook; **libretto universitario** student's report book

'**libro** sm book; **libro di cassa** cash book; **libro mastro** ledger; **libro paga** payroll; **libro di testo** textbook

li'cenza [li'tʃɛntsa] sf (permesso) permission, leave; (di pesca, caccia, circolazione) permit, licence; (Mil) leave; (Ins) school leaving

certificate; (libertà) liberty; licence; licentiousness; **andare in ~** (Mil) to go on leave

licenzia'mento [litʃentsja'mento] sm dismissal

licenzi'are [litʃen'tsjare] vt (impiegato) to dismiss; (Comm: per eccesso di personale) to make redundant; (Ins) to award a certificate to; **licenziarsi** vpr (impiegato) to resign, hand in one's notice; (Ins) to obtain one's school-leaving certificate

li'ceo [li'tʃɛo] sm (Ins) secondary (BRIT) o high (US) school (for 14- to 19-year-olds)

'**lido** sm beach, shore

Liechtenstein ['liktənstain] sm: **il ~** Liechtenstein

li'eto, -a ag happy, glad; "**molto ~**" (nelle presentazioni) "pleased to meet you"

li'eve ag light; (di poco conto) slight; (sommesso: voce) faint, soft

lievi'tare vi (anche fig) to rise ▷ vt to leaven

li'evito sm yeast; **lievito di birra** brewer's yeast

'**ligio, -a, -gi, -gie** ['lidʒo] ag faithful, loyal

'**lilla** sm inv lilac

'**lillà** sm inv lilac

'**lima** sf file; **lima da unghie** nail file

limacci'oso, -a [limat'tʃoso] ag slimy; muddy

li'mare vt to file (down); (fig) to polish

limi'tare vt to limit, restrict; (circoscrivere) to bound, surround; **limitarsi** vpr **limitarsi nel mangiare** to limit one's eating; **limitarsi a qc/a fare qc** to limit o.s. to sth/to doing sth

'**limite** sm limit; (confine) border, boundary; **limite di velocità** speed limit

limo'nata sf lemonade (BRIT), (lemon) soda (US); lemon squash (BRIT), lemonade (US)

li'mone sm (pianta) lemon tree; (frutto) lemon

'limpido, -a *ag* clear; (*acqua*) limpid, clear

'lince ['lintʃe] *sf* lynx

linci'are *vt* to lynch

'linea *sf* line; (*di mezzi pubblici di trasporto: itinerario*) route; (: *servizio*) service; **a grandi linee** in outline; **mantenere la ~** to look after one's figure; **aereo di ~** airliner; **nave di ~** liner; **volo di ~** scheduled flight; **linea aerea** airline; **linea di partenza/ d'arrivo** (*Sport*) starting/finishing line; **linea di tiro** line of fire

linea'menti *smpl* features; (*fig*) outlines

line'are *ag* linear; (*fig*) coherent, logical

line'etta *sf* (*trattino*) dash; (*d'unione*) hyphen

lin'gotto *sm* ingot, bar

'lingua *sf* (*Anat, Cuc*) tongue; (*idioma*) language; **mostrare la ~** to stick out one's tongue; **di ~ italiana** Italian-speaking; **che lingue parla?** what languages do you speak?; **una ~ di terra** a spit of land; **lingua madre** mother tongue

lingu'aggio [lin'gwaddʒo] *sm* language

lingu'etta *sf* (*di strumento*) reed; (*di scarpa, Tecn*) tongue; (*di busta*) flap

'lino *sm* (*pianta*) flax; (*tessuto*) linen

li'noleum *sm inv* linoleum, lino

liposuzi'one [liposut'tsjone] *sf* liposuction

lique'fatto, -a *pp di* **liquefare**

liqui'dare *vt* (*società, beni: persona: uccidere*) to liquidate; (*persona: sbarazzarsene*) to get rid of; (*conto, problema*) to settle; (*Comm: merce*) to sell off, clear; **liquidazi'one** *sf* liquidation; settlement; clearance sale

liquidità *sf* liquidity

'liquido, -a *ag, sm* liquid; **liquido per freni** brake fluid

liqui'rizia [likwi'rittsja] *sf* liquorice

li'quore *sm* liqueur

'lira *sf* (*Storia: unità monetaria*) lira; (*Mus*) lyre; **lira sterlina** pound sterling

'lirico, -a, -ci, -che *ag* lyric(al); (*Mus*) lyric; **cantante/teatro ~** opera singer/house

Lis'bona *sf* Lisbon

'lisca, -sche *sf* (*di pesce*) fishbone

lisci'are [liʃʃare] *vt* to smooth; (*fig*) to flatter

'liscio, -a, -sci, -sce ['liʃʃo] *ag* smooth; (*capelli*) straight; (*mobile*) plain; (*bevanda alcolica*) neat; (*fig*) straightforward, simple ▷ *av* **andare ~** to go smoothly; **passarla liscia** to get away with it

'liso, -a *ag* worn out, threadbare

'lista *sf* (*elenco*) list; **lista elettorale** electoral roll; **lista delle spese** shopping list; **lista dei vini** wine list; **lista delle vivande** menu

lis'tino *sm* list; **listino dei cambi** (foreign) exchange rate; **listino dei prezzi** price list

'lite *sf* quarrel, argument; (*Dir*) lawsuit

liti'gare *vi* to quarrel; (*Dir*) to litigate

li'tigio [li'tidʒo] *sm* quarrel

lito'rale *ag* coastal, coast *cpd* ▷ *sm* coast

'litro *sm* litre

livel'lare *vt* to level, make level

li'vello *sm* level; (*fig*) level, standard; **ad alto ~** (*fig*) high-level; **livello del mare** sea level

'livido, -a *ag* livid; (*per percosse*) bruised, black and blue; (*cielo*) leaden ▷ *sm* bruise

Li'vorno *sf* Livorno, Leghorn

'lizza ['littsa] *sf* lists *pl*; **scendere in ~** to enter the lists

lo (*dav s impura, gn, pn, ps, x, z; dav∨* **l'**) *det m* the ▷ *pron* (*oggetto: persona*) him; (: *cosa*) it; **lo sapevo** I knew it; **lo so** I know; **sii buono, anche se lui non lo è** be good, even if he isn't; *vedi anche* **il**

lo'cale *ag* local ▷ *sm* room; (*luogo*

pubblico) premises *pl*; **locale notturno** nightclub; **località** *sf inv* locality

lo'canda *sf* inn

locomo'tiva *sf* locomotive

locuzi'one [lokut'tsjone] *sf* phrase, expression

lo'dare *vt* to praise

'lode *sf* praise; (*Ins*): **laurearsi con 110 e ~** ≈ to graduate with a first-class honours degree (*BRIT*), graduate summa cum laude (*US*)

'loden *sm inv* (*stoffa*) loden; (*cappotto*) loden overcoat

lo'devole *ag* praiseworthy

loga'ritmo *sm* logarithm

'loggia, -ge ['lɔddʒa] *sf* (*Archit*) loggia; (*circolo massonico*) lodge; **loggi'one** *sm* (*di teatro*): **il loggione** the Gods *sg*

'logico, -a, -ci, -che ['lɔdʒiko] *ag* logical

logo'rare *vt* to wear out; (*sciupare*) to waste; **logorarsi** *vpr* to wear out; (*fig*) to wear o.s. out

'logoro, -a *ag* (*stoffa*) worn out, threadbare; (*persona*) worn out

Lombar'dia *sf* **la ~** Lombardy

lom'bata *sf* (*taglio di carne*) loin

lom'brico, -chi *sm* earthworm

londi'nese *ag* London *cpd* ▷ *sm/f* Londoner

'Londra *sf* London

lon'gevo, -a [lon'dʒevo] *ag* long-lived

longi'tudine [londʒi'tudine] *sf* longitude

lonta'nanza [lonta'nantsa] *sf* distance; absence

lon'tano, -a *ag* (*distante*) distant, faraway; (*assente*) absent; (*vago: sospetto*) slight, remote; (*tempo: remoto*) far-off, distant; (*parente*) distant, remote ▷ *av* far; **è lontana la casa?** is it far to the house?, is the house far from here?; **è ~ un chilometro** it's a kilometre away *o* a kilometre from here; **più ~** farther; **da** *o* **di ~** from a distance; **~ da** a long way

from; **è molto ~ da qui?** is it far from here?; **alla lontana** slightly, vaguely

lo'quace [lo'kwatʃe] *ag* talkative, loquacious; (*fig: gesto ecc*) eloquent

'lordo, -a *ag* dirty, filthy; (*peso, stipendio*) gross

'loro *pron pl* (*oggetto, con preposizione*) them; (*complemento di termine*) to them; (*soggetto*) they; (*forma di cortesia: anche: L~*) you; to you; **il (la) ~, i (le) ~** *det* their; (*forma di cortesia: anche: L~*) your ▷ *pron* theirs; (*forma di cortesia: anche: L~*) yours; **~ stessi(e)** they themselves; you yourselves

'losco, -a, -schi, -sche *ag* (*fig*) shady, suspicious

'lotta *sf* struggle, fight; (*Sport*) wrestling; **lotta libera** all-in wrestling; **lot'tare** *vi* to fight, struggle; to wrestle

lotte'ria *sf* lottery; (*di gara ippica*) sweepstake

'lotto *sm* (*gioco*) (state) lottery; (*parte*) lot; (*Edil*) site

● **LOTTO**
●
● The **Lotto** is an official lottery run
● by the Italian Finance Ministry.
● It consists of a weekly draw of
● numbers and is very popular.

lozi'one [lot'tsjone] *sf* lotion

lubrifi'cante *sm* lubricant

lubrifi'care *vt* to lubricate

luc'chetto [luk'ketto] *sm* padlock

lucci'care [luttʃi'kare] *vi* to sparkle, glitter, twinkle

'luccio ['luttʃo] *sm* (*Zool*) pike

'lucciola ['luttʃola] *sf* (*Zool*) firefly; glowworm

'luce ['lutʃe] *sf* light; (*finestra*) window; **alla ~ di** by the light of; **fare ~ su qc** (*fig*) to shed *o* throw light on sth; **~ del sole/della luna** sun/moonlight

lucer'nario [lutʃer'narjo] *sm* skylight

lu'certola [lu'tʃertola] *sf* lizard

luci'dare [lutʃi'dare] *vt* to polish

lucida'trice [lutʃida'tritʃe] *sf* floor polisher

'lucido, -a ['lutʃido] *ag* shining, bright; (*lucidato*) polished; (*fig*) lucid ▷ *sm* shine, lustre; (*disegno*) tracing; **lucido per scarpe** shoe polish

'lucro *sm* profit, gain

'luglio ['luʎʎo] *sm* July

'lugubre *ag* gloomy

'lui *pron* (*soggetto*) he; (*oggetto: per dare rilievo, con preposizione*) him; **~ stesso** he himself

lu'maca, -che *sf* slug; (*chiocciola*) snail

lumi'noso, -a *ag* (*che emette luce*) luminous; (*cielo, colore, stanza*) bright; (*sorgente*) of light, light *cpd*; (*fig: sorriso*) bright, radiant

'luna *sf* moon; **luna nuova/piena** new/full moon; **luna di miele** honeymoon; **siamo in ~ di miele** we're on honeymoon

'luna park *sm inv* amusement park, funfair

lu'nare *ag* lunar, moon *cpd*

lu'nario *sm* almanac; **sbarcare il ~** to make ends meet

lu'natico, -a, -ci, -che *ag* whimsical, temperamental

lunedì *sm inv* Monday; **di** *o* **il ~** on Mondays

lun'ghezza [lun'gettsa] *sf* length; **lunghezza d'onda** (*Fisica*) wavelength

'lungo, -a, -ghi, -ghe *ag* long; (*lento: persona*) slow; (*diluito: caffè, brodo*) weak, watery, thin ▷ *sm* length ▷ *prep* along; **~ 3 metri** 3 metres long; **a ~** for a long time; **a ~ andare** in the long run; **di gran lunga** (*molto*) by far; **andare in ~** *o* **per le lunghe** to drag on; **saperla lunga** to know what's what; **in ~ e in largo** far and wide, all over; **~ il corso dei secoli** throughout the centuries

lungo'mare *sm* promenade

lu'notto *sm* (*Aut*) rear *o* back window; **lunotto termico** heated rear window

lu'ogo, -ghi *sm* place; (*posto: di incidente ecc*) scene, site; (*punto, passo di libro*) passage; **in ~ di** instead of; **in primo ~** in the first place; **aver ~** to take place; **dar ~ a** to give rise to; **luogo di nascita** birthplace; (*Amm*) place of birth; **luogo di provenienza** place of origin; **luogo comune** commonplace

'lupo, -a *sm/f* wolf

'luppolo *sm* (*Bot*) hop

'lurido, -a *ag* filthy

lusin'gare *vt* to flatter

Lussem'burgo *sm* (*stato*): **il ~** Luxembourg ▷ *sf* (*città*) Luxembourg

'lusso *sm* luxury; **di ~** luxury *cpd*; **lussu'oso, -a** *ag* luxurious

lus'suria *sf* lust

lus'trino *sm* sequin

'lutto *sm* mourning; **essere in/ portare il ~** to be in/wear mourning

m

m. *abbr* = **mese**; **metro**; **miglia**; **monte**

ma *cong* but; **ma insomma!** for goodness sake!; **ma no!** of course not!

'macabro, -a *ag* gruesome, macabre

macché [mak'ke] *escl* not at all!, certainly not!

macche'roni [makke'roni] *smpl* macaroni *sg*

'macchia ['makkja] *sf* stain, spot; *(chiazza di diverso colore)* spot, splash, patch; *(tipo di boscaglia)* scrub; **alla ~** *(fig)* in hiding; **macchi'are** *vt* *(sporcare)* to stain, mark; **macchiarsi** *vpr* *(persona)* to get o.s. dirty; *(stoffa)* to stain; *(fig)* to get stained *o* marked

macchi'ato, -a [mak'kjato] *ag* *(pelle, pelo)* spotted; **~ di** stained with; **caffè ~** coffee with a dash of milk

'macchina ['makkina] *sf* machine; *(motore, locomotiva)* engine; *(automobile)* car; *(fig: meccanismo)* machinery; **andare in ~** *(Aut)* to go by car; *(Stampa)* to go to press; **macchina da cucire** sewing machine; **macchina fotografica** camera; **macchina da presa** *cine o* movie camera; **macchina da scrivere** typewriter; **macchina a vapore** steam engine

macchi'nario [makki'narjo] *sm* machinery

macchi'nista, -i [makki'nista] *sm* *(di treno)* engine-driver; *(di nave)* engineer

Macedonia [matʃe'dɔnja] *sf*: **la ~** Macedonia

mace'donia [matʃe'dɔnja] *sf* fruit salad

macel'laio [matʃel'lajo] *sm* butcher

macelle'ria *sf* butcher's (shop)

ma'cerie [ma'tʃɛrje] *sfpl* rubble *sg*, debris *sg*

ma'cigno [ma'tʃinno] *sm* *(masso)* rock, boulder

maci'nare [matʃi'nare] *vt* to grind; *(carne)* to mince (BRIT), grind (US)

macrobi'otico, -a *ag* macrobiotic ▷ *sf* macrobiotics *sg*

Ma'donna *sf* *(Rel)* Our Lady

mador'nale *ag* enormous, huge

'madre *sf* mother; *(matrice di bolletta)* counterfoil ▷ *ag inv* mother *cpd*; **ragazza ~** unmarried mother; **scena ~** *(Teatro)* principal scene; *(fig)* terrible scene

madre'lingua *sf* mother tongue, native language

madre'perla *sf* mother-of-pearl

ma'drina *sf* godmother

maestà *sf inv* majesty

ma'estra *sf vedi* **maestro**

maes'trale *sm* north-west wind, mistral

ma'estro, -a *sm/f* *(Ins: anche: ~ di scuola o elementare)* primary (BRIT) *o* grade school (US) teacher; *(esperto)* expert ▷ *sm* *(artigiano, fig: guida)* master; *(Mus)* maestro ▷ *ag* *(principale)* main; *(di grande abilità)* masterly, skilful; **maestra d'asilo**

nursery teacher; **~ di cerimonie** master of ceremonies

'mafia sf Mafia

'maga sf sorceress

ma'gari escl (esprime desiderio): **~ fosse vero!** if only it were true!; **ti piacerebbe andare in Scozia? — ~!** would you like to go to Scotland? — and how! ▷ av (anche) even; (forse) perhaps

magaz'zino [magad'dzino] sm warehouse; **grande ~** department store

> Attenzione! In inglese esiste la parola magazine che però significa rivista.

'maggio ['maddʒo] sm May

maggio'rana [maddʒo'rana] sf (Bot) (sweet) marjoram

maggio'ranza [maddʒo'rantsa] sf majority

maggior'domo [maddʒor'dɔmo] sm butler

maggi'ore [mad'dʒore] ag (comparativo: più grande) bigger, larger; taller; greater; (: più vecchio: sorella, fratello) older, elder; (: di grado superiore) senior; (: più importante: Mil, Mus) major; (superlativo) biggest, largest; tallest; greatest; oldest, eldest ▷ sm/f (di grado) superior; (di età) elder; (Mil) major; (: Aer) squadron leader; **la maggior parte** the majority; **andare per la ~** (cantante ecc) to be very popular; **maggio'renne** ag of age ▷ sm/f person who has come of age

ma'gia [ma'dʒia] sf magic; **'magico, -a, -ci, -che** ag magic; (fig) fascinating, charming, magical

magis'trato [madʒis'trato] sm magistrate

'maglia ['maʎʎa] sf stitch; (lavoro ai ferri) knitting no pl; (tessuto) jersey; (maglione) jersey, sweater; (di catena) link; (di rete) mesh; **maglia diritta/rovescia** plain/purl;

magli'etta sf (canottiera) vest; (tipo camicia) T-shirt

magli'one sm sweater, jumper

ma'gnetico, -a, -ci, -che ag magnetic

ma'gnifico, -a, -ci, -che [maɲ'ɲifiko] ag magnificent, splendid; (ospite) generous

ma'gnolia [maɲ'ɲɔlja] sf magnolia

'mago, -ghi sm (stregone) magician, wizard; (illusionista) magician

ma'grezza [ma'grettsa] sf thinness

'magro, -a ag (very) thin, skinny; (carne) lean; (formaggio) low-fat; (fig: scarso, misero) meagre, poor; (: meschino: scusa) poor, lame; **mangiare di ~** not to eat meat

'mai av (nessuna volta) never; (talvolta) ever; **non ... ~** never; **~ più** never again; **non sono ~ stato in Spagna** I've never been to Spain; **come ~?** why (o how) on earth?; **chi/dove/quando ~?** whoever/wherever/whenever?

mai'ale sm (Zool) pig; (carne) pork

maio'nese sf mayonnaise

'mais sm inv maize

mai'uscolo, -a ag (lettera) capital; (fig) enormous, huge

mala'fede sf bad faith

malan'dato, -a ag (persona: di salute) in poor health; (: di condizioni finanziarie) badly off; (trascurato) shabby

ma'lanno sm (disgrazia) misfortune; (malattia) ailment

mala'pena sf: **a ~** hardly, scarcely

ma'laria sf (Med) malaria

ma'lato, -a ag ill, sick; (gamba) bad; (pianta) diseased ▷ sm/f sick person; (in ospedale) patient; **malat'tia** sf (infettiva ecc) illness, disease; (cattiva salute) illness, sickness; (di pianta) disease

mala'vita sf underworld

mala'voglia [mala'vɔʎʎa] sf: **di ~** unwillingly, reluctantly

Ma'laysia sf Malaysia

mal'concio, -a, -ci, -ce [mal'kontʃo] *ag* in a sorry state

malcon'tento *sm* discontent

malcos'tume *sm* immorality

mal'destro, -a *ag* (*inabile*) inexpert, inexperienced; (*goffo*) awkward

'male *av* badly ▷ *sm* (*ciò che è ingiusto, disonesto*) evil; (*danno, svantaggio*) harm; (*sventura*) misfortune; (*dolore fisico, morale*) pain, ache; **di ~ in peggio** from bad to worse; **sentirsi ~** to feel ill; **far ~** (*dolere*) to hurt; **far ~ alla salute** to be bad for one's health; **far del ~ a qn** to hurt o harm sb; **restare** *o* **rimanere ~** to be sorry; to be disappointed; to be hurt; **andare a ~** to go bad; **come va? — non c'è ~** how are you? — not bad; **avere mal di gola/testa** to have a sore throat/a headache; **aver ~ ai piedi** to have sore feet; **mal d'auto** carsickness; **mal di cuore** heart trouble; **male di dente** toothache; **mal di mare** seasickness

male'detto, -a *pp di* **maledire** ▷ *ag* cursed, damned; (*fig: fam*) damned, blasted

male'dire *vt* to curse; **maledizi'one** *sf* curse; **maledizione!** damn it!

maledu'cato, -a *ag* rude, ill-mannered

maleducazi'one [maledukat'tsjone] *sf* rudeness

ma'lefico, -a, -ci, -che *ag* (*influsso, azione*) evil

ma'lessere *sm* indisposition, slight illness; (*fig*) uneasiness

malfa'mato, -a *ag* notorious

malfat'tore, -'trice *sm/f* wrongdoer

mal'fermo, -a *ag* unsteady, shaky; (*salute*) poor, delicate

mal'grado *prep* in spite of, despite ▷ *cong* although; **mio** (*o* **tuo** *ecc*) **~** against my (*o* your *ecc*) will

ma'ligno, -a [ma'liɲɲo] *ag* (*malvagio*) malicious, malignant; (*Med*) malignant

malinco'nia *sf* melancholy, gloom;

malin'conico, -a, -ci, -che *ag* melancholy

malincu'ore: a ~ *av* reluctantly, unwillingly

malin'teso, -a *ag* misunderstood; (*riguardo, senso del dovere*) mistaken, wrong ▷ *sm* misunderstanding; **c'è stato un ~** there's been a misunderstanding

ma'lizia [ma'littsja] *sf* (*malignità*) malice; (*furbizia*) cunning; (*espediente*) trick; **malizi'oso, -a** *ag* malicious; cunning; (*vivace, birichino*) mischievous

malme'nare *vt* to beat up

ma'locchio [ma'lɔkkjo] *sm* evil eye

ma'lora *sf*: **andare in ~** to go to the dogs

ma'lore *sm* (*sudden*) illness

mal'sano, -a *ag* unhealthy

'malta *sf* (*Edil*) mortar

mal'tempo *sm* bad weather

'malto *sm* malt

maltrat'tare *vt* to ill-treat

malu'more *sm* bad mood; (*irritabilità*) bad temper; (*discordia*) ill feeling; **di ~** in a bad mood

'malva *sf* (*Bot*) mallow ▷ *ag, sm inv* mauve

mal'vagio, -a, -gi, -gie [mal'vadʒo] *ag* wicked, evil

malvi'vente *sm* criminal

malvolenti'eri *av* unwillingly, reluctantly

'mamma *sf* mummy, mum; **~ mia!** my goodness!

mam'mella *sf* (*Anat*) breast; (*di vacca, capra ecc*) udder

mam'mifero *sm* mammal

ma'nata *sf* (*colpo*) slap; (*quantità*) handful

man'canza [man'kantsa] *sf* lack; (*carenza*) shortage, scarcity; (*fallo*) fault; (*imperfezione*) failing, shortcoming; **per ~ di tempo** through lack of time; **in ~ di meglio** for lack of anything better

man'care vi (essere insufficiente) to be lacking; (venir meno) to fail; (sbagliare) to be wrong, make a mistake; (non esserci) to be missing, not to be there; (essere lontano): **~ (da)** to be away (from) ▷ vt to miss; **~ di** to lack; **~ a** (promessa) to fail to keep; **tu mi manchi** I miss you; **mancò poco che morisse** he very nearly died; **mancano ancora 10 sterline** we're still £10 short; **manca un quarto alle 6** it's a quarter to 6

mancherò ecc [manke'rɔ] vb vedi **mancare**

'mancia, -ce ['mantʃa] sf tip; **quanto devo lasciare di ~?** how much should I tip?; **~ competente** reward

manci'ata [man'tʃata] sf handful

man'cino, -a [man'tʃino] ag (braccio) left; (persona) left-handed; (fig) underhand

manda'rancio [manda'rantʃo] sm clementine

man'dare vt to send; (far funzionare: macchina) to drive; (emettere) to send out; (: grido) to give, utter, let out; **~ a chiamare qn** to send for sb; **~ avanti** (fig: famiglia) to provide for; (: fabbrica) to run, look after; **~ giù** to send down; (anche fig) to swallow; **~ via** to send away; (licenziare) to fire

manda'rino sm mandarin (orange); (cinese) mandarin

man'data sf (quantità) lot, batch; (di chiave) turn; **chiudere a doppia ~** to double-lock

man'dato sm (incarico) commission; (Dir: provvedimento) warrant; (di deputato ecc) mandate; (ordine di pagamento) postal o money order; **mandato d'arresto** warrant for arrest

man'dibola sf mandible, jaw

'mandorla sf almond; **'mandorlo** sm almond tree

'mandria sf herd

maneggi'are [maned'dʒare] vt

(creta, cera) to mould, work, fashion; (arnesi, utensili) to handle; (: adoperare) to use; (fig: persone, denaro) to handle, deal with; **ma'neggio** sm moulding; handling; use; (intrigo) plot, scheme; (per cavalli) riding school

ma'nesco, -a, -schi, -sche ag free with one's fists

ma'nette sfpl handcuffs

manga'nello sm club

mangi'are [man'dʒare] vt to eat; (intaccare) to eat into o away; (Carte, Scacchi ecc) to take ▷ vi to eat ▷ sm eating; (cibo) food; (cucina) cooking; **possiamo ~ qualcosa?** can we have something to eat?; **mangiarsi le parole** to mumble; **mangiarsi le unghie** to bite one's nails

man'gime [man'dʒime] sm fodder

'mango, -ghi sm mango

ma'nia sf (Psic) mania; (fig) obsession, craze; **ma'niaco, -a, -ci, -che** ag suffering from a mania; **maniaco (di)** obsessed (by), crazy (about)

'manica sf sleeve; (fig: gruppo) gang, bunch; (Geo): **la M~, il Canale della M~** the (English) Channel; **essere di ~ larga/stretta** to be easy-going/strict; **manica a vento** (Aer) wind sock

mani'chino [mani'kino] sm (di sarto, vetrina) dummy

'manico, -ci sm handle; (Mus) neck

mani'comio sm mental hospital; (fig) madhouse

mani'cure sm o f inv manicure ▷ sf inv manicurist

mani'era sf way, manner; (stile) style, manner; **maniere** sfpl (comportamento) manners; **in ~ che** so that; **in ~ da** so as to; **in tutte le maniere** at all costs

manifes'tare vt to show, display; (esprimere) to express; (rivelare) to reveal, disclose ▷ vi to demonstrate; **manifestazi'one** sf show, display; expression; (sintomo) sign,

symptom; (*dimostrazione pubblica*)
demonstration; (*cerimonia*) event
mani'festo, -a *ag* obvious, evident
▷ *sm* poster, bill; (*scritto ideologico*)
manifesto
ma'niglia [ma'niʎʎa] *sf* handle;
(*sostegno: negli autobus ecc*) strap
manipo'lare *vt* to manipulate;
(*alterare: vino*) to adulterate
man'naro: lupo ~ *sm* werewolf
'mano, -i *sf* hand; (*strato: di vernice ecc*)
coat; **di prima ~** (*notizia*) first-hand; **di
seconda ~** second-hand; **man ~ che** as;
darsi *o* **stringersi la ~** to shake hands;
mettere le mani avanti (*fig*) to
safeguard o.s.; **restare a mani vuote**
to be left empty-handed; **venire alle
mani** to come to blows; **a ~** by hand;
mani in alto! hands up!
mano'dopera *sf* labour
ma'nometro *sm* gauge, manometer
mano'mettere *vt* (*alterare*) to
tamper with; (*aprire indebitamente*) to
break open illegally
ma'nopola *sf* (*dell'armatura*) gauntlet;
(*guanto*) mitt; (*di impugnatura*) hand-
grip; (*pomello*) knob
manos'critto, -a *ag* handwritten
▷ *sm* manuscript
mano'vale *sm* labourer
mano'vella *sf* handle; (*Tecn*) crank
ma'novra *sf* manoeuvre (BRIT),
maneuver (US); (*Ferr*) shunting
man'sarda *sf* attic
mansi'one *sf* task, duty, job
mansu'eto, -a *ag* gentle, docile
man'tello *sm* cloak; (*fig: di neve ecc*)
blanket, mantle; (*Zool*) coat
mante'nere *vt* to maintain;
(*adempiere: promesse*) to keep, abide
by; (*provvedere a*) to support, maintain;
mantenersi *vpr* **mantenersi calmo/
giovane** to stay calm/young
'Mantova *sf* Mantua
manu'ale *ag* manual ▷ *sm* (*testo*)
manual, handbook

ma'nubrio *sm* handle; (*di bicicletta
ecc*) handlebars *pl*; (*Sport*) dumbbell
manutenzi'one [manuten'tsjone]
sf maintenance, upkeep; (*d'impianti*)
maintenance, servicing
'manzo ['mandzo] *sm* (*Zool*) steer;
(*carne*) beef
'mappa *sf* (*Geo*) map; **mappa'mondo**
sm map of the world; (*globo girevole*)
globe
mara'tona *sf* marathon
'marca, -che *sf* (*Comm: di prodotti*)
brand; (*contrassegno, scontrino*) ticket,
check; **prodotto di ~** (*di buona qualità*)
high-class product; **marca da bollo**
official stamp
mar'care *vt* (*munire di contrassegno*)
to mark; (*a fuoco*) to brand; (*Sport:
gol*) to score; (*: avversario*) to mark;
(*accentuare*) to stress; **~ visita** (*Mil*) to
report sick
marcherò *ecc* [marke'rɔ] *vb vedi*
marcare
mar'chese, -a [mar'keze] *sm/f*
marquis *o* marquess/marchioness
marchi'are [mar'kjare] *vt* to brand
'marcia, -ce ['martʃa] *sf* (*anche Mus,
Mil*) march; (*funzionamento*) running;
(*il camminare*) walking; (*Aut*) gear;
mettere in ~ to start; **mettersi in ~**
to get moving; **far ~ indietro** (*Aut*) to
reverse; (*fig*) to back-pedal
marciapi'ede [martʃa'pjɛde] *sm* (*di
strada*) pavement (BRIT), sidewalk
(US); (*Ferr*) platform
marci'are [mar'tʃare] *vi* to march;
(*andare: treno, macchina*) to go;
(*funzionare*) to run, work
'marcio, -a, -ci, -ce ['martʃo] *ag*
(*frutta, legno*) rotten, bad; (*Med*)
festering; (*fig*) corrupt, rotten
mar'cire [mar'tʃire] *vi* (*andare a male*)
to go bad, rot; (*suppurare*) to fester;
(*fig*) to rot, waste away
'marco, -chi *sm* (*unità monetaria*)
mark
'mare *sm* sea; **in ~** at sea; **andare al ~**

(*in vacanza ecc*) to go to the seaside; **il M~ del Nord** the North Sea

ma'rea *sf* tide; **alta/bassa ~** high/low tide

mareggi'ata [mared'dʒata] *sf* heavy sea

mare'moto *sm* seaquake

maresci'allo [mareʃʃallo] *sm* (*Mil*) marshal; (: *sottufficiale*) warrant officer

marga'rina *sf* margarine

marghe'rita [marge'rita] *sf* (ox-eye) daisy, marguerite; (*di stampante*) daisy wheel

'margine ['mardʒine] *sm* margin; (*di bosco, via*) edge, border

mariju'ana [mæri'wa:nə] *sf* marijuana

ma'rina *sf* navy; (*costa*) coast; (*quadro*) seascape; **marina mercantile/militare** navy/merchant navy (BRIT) o marine (US)

mari'naio *sm* sailor

mari'nare *vt* (*Cuc*) to marinate; **~ la scuola** to play truant

ma'rino, -a *ag* sea *cpd*, marine

mario'netta *sf* puppet

ma'rito *sm* husband

ma'rittimo, -a *ag* maritime, sea *cpd*

marmel'lata *sf* jam; (*di agrumi*) marmalade

mar'mitta *sf* (*recipiente*) pot; (*Aut*) silencer; **marmitta catalitica** catalytic converter

'marmo *sm* marble

mar'motta *sf* (*Zool*) marmot

maroc'chino, -a [marok'kino] *ag, sm/f* Moroccan

Ma'rocco *sm* **il ~** Morocco

mar'rone *ag inv* brown ▷ *sm* (*Bot*) chestnut

> Attenzione! In inglese esiste la parola *maroon*, che però indica un altro colore, il rosso bordeaux.

mar'supio *sm* pouch; (*per denaro*) bum bag; (*per neonato*) sling

martedì *sm inv* Tuesday; **di** o **il ~** on Tuesdays; **martedì grasso** Shrove Tuesday

martel'lare *vt* to hammer ▷ *vi* (*pulsare*) to throb; (: *cuore*) to thump

mar'tello *sm* hammer; (: *di uscio*) knocker; **martello pneumatico** pneumatic drill

'martire *sm/f* martyr

mar'xista, -i, -e *ag, sm/f* Marxist

marza'pane [martsa'pane] *sm* marzipan

'marzo ['martso] *sm* March

mascal'zone [maskal'tsone] *sm* rascal, scoundrel

mas'cara *sm inv* mascara

ma'scella [maʃʃɛlla] *sf* (*Anat*) jaw

'maschera ['maskera] *sf* mask; (*travestimento*) disguise; (: *per un ballo ecc*) fancy dress; (*Teatro, Cinema*) usher/usherette; (*personaggio del teatro*) stock character; **masche'rare** *vt* to mask; (*travestire*) to disguise; to dress up; (*fig: celare*) to hide, conceal; (*Mil*) to camouflage; **mascherarsi da** to disguise o.s. as; to dress up as; (*fig*) to masquerade as

mas'chile [mas'kile] *ag* masculine; (*sesso, popolazione*) male; (*abiti*) men's; (*per ragazzi: scuola*) boys'

mas'chilista, -i, -e *ag, sm/f* (*uomo*) (male) chauvinist, sexist; (*donna*) sexist

'maschio, -a ['maskjo] *ag* (*Biol*) male; (*virile*) manly ▷ *sm* (*anche Zool, Tecn*) male; (*uomo*) man; (*ragazzo*) boy; (*figlio*) son

masco'lino, -a *ag* masculine

'massa *sf* mass; (*di errori ecc*): **una ~ di** heaps of, masses of; (*di gente*) mass, multitude; (*Elettr*) earth; **in ~** (*Comm*) in bulk; (*tutti insieme*) en masse; **adunata in ~** mass meeting; **di ~** (*cultura, manifestazione*) mass *cpd*

mas'sacro *sm* massacre, slaughter; (*fig*) mess, disaster

massaggi'are [massad'dʒare] *vt* to massage

mas'saggio [mas'saddʒo] sm massage; **massaggio cardiaco** cardiac massage

mas'saia sf housewife

masse'rizie [masse'rittsje] sfpl (household) furnishings

mas'siccio, -a, -ci, -ce [mas'sittʃo] ag (oro, legno) solid; (palazzo) massive; (corporatura) stout ▷ sm (Geo) massif

'massima sf (sentenza, regola) maxim; (Meteor) maximum temperature; **in linea di ~** generally speaking; vedi **massimo**

massi'male sm maximum

'massimo, -a ag, sm maximum; **al ~** at (the) most

'masso sm rock, boulder

masteriz'zare [masterid'dzare] vt (CD, DVD) to burn

masterizza'tore [masteriddza'tore] sm CD burner o recorder

masti'care vt to chew

'mastice ['mastitʃe] sm mastic; (per vetri) putty

mas'tino sm mastiff

ma'tassa sf skein

mate'matica sf mathematics sg

mate'matico, -a, -ci, -che ag mathematical ▷ sm/f mathematician

materas'sino sm mat; **materassino gonfiabile** air bed

mate'rasso sm mattress; **materasso a molle** spring o interior-sprung mattress

ma'teria sf (Fisica) matter; (Tecn, Comm) material, matter no pl; (disciplina) subject; (argomento) subject matter, material; **in ~ di** (per quanto concerne) on the subject of; **materie prime** raw materials

materi'ale ag material; (fig: grossolano) rough, rude ▷ sm material; (insieme di strumenti ecc) equipment no pl, materials pl

mater'nità sf motherhood, maternity; (reparto) maternity ward

ma'terno, -a ag (amore, cura ecc) maternal, motherly; (nonno) maternal; (lingua, terra) mother cpd

ma'tita sf pencil; **matite colorate** coloured pencils; **matita per gli occhi** eyeliner (pencil)

ma'tricola sf (registro) register; (numero) registration number; (nell'università) freshman, fresher

ma'trigna [ma'trinna] sf stepmother

matrimoni'ale ag matrimonial, marriage cpd

matri'monio sm marriage, matrimony; (durata) marriage, married life; (cerimonia) wedding

mat'tina sf morning

'matto, -a ag mad, crazy; (fig: falso) false, imitation ▷ sm/f madman/woman; **avere una voglia matta di qc** to be dying for sth

mat'tone sm brick; (fig): **questo libro/film è un ~** this book/film is heavy going

matto'nella sf tile

matu'rare vi (anche: maturarsi: frutta, grano) to ripen; (ascesso) to come to a head; (fig: persona, idea, Econ) to mature ▷ vt to ripen, to (make) mature

maturità sf maturity; (di frutta) ripeness, maturity; (Ins) school-leaving examination, ≈ GCE A-levels (BRIT)

ma'turo, -a ag mature; (frutto) ripe, mature

max. abbr (= massimo) max

maxischermo [maxis'kermo] sm giant screen

'mazza ['mattsa] sf (bastone) club; (martello) sledge-hammer; (Sport: da golf) club; (: da baseball, cricket) bat

maz'zata [mat'tsata] sf (anche fig) heavy blow

'mazzo ['mattso] sm (di fiori, chiavi ecc) bunch; (di carte da gioco) pack

me pron me; **me stesso(-a)** myself; **sei bravo quanto me** you are as clever as

I (am) *o* as me

mec'canico, -a, -ci, -che *ag*
mechanical ▷ *sm* mechanic; **può
mandare un ~?** can you send a
mechanic?

mecca'nismo *sm* mechanism

me'daglia [me'daʎʎa] *sf* medal

me'desimo, -a *ag* same; (*in persona*):
io ~ I myself

'media *sf* average; (*Mat*) mean; (*Ins:
voto*) end-of-term average; **le medie**
sfpl = **scuola media**; **in ~** on average;
vedi anche medio

medi'ante *prep* by means of

media'tore, -'trice *sm/f* mediator;
(*Comm*) middle man, agent

medi'care *vt* to treat; (*ferita*) to dress

medi'cina [medi'tʃina] *sf* medicine;
medicina legale forensic medicine

'medico, -a, -ci, -che *ag* medical
▷ *sm* doctor; **chiamate un ~** call a
doctor; **medico generico** general
practitioner, GP

medie'vale *ag* medieval

'medio, -a *ag* average; (*punto, ceto*)
middle; (*altezza, statura*) medium ▷ *sm*
(*dito*) middle finger; **licenza media**
*leaving certificate awarded at the end of
3 years of secondary education*; **scuola
media** *first 3 years of secondary school*

medi'ocre *ag* mediocre, poor

medi'tare *vt* to ponder over,
meditate on; (*progettare*) to plan, think
out ▷ *vi* to meditate

mediter'raneo, -a *ag*
Mediterranean; **il (mare) M~** the
Mediterranean (Sea)

me'dusa *sf* (*Zool*) jellyfish

mega'byte *sm inv* (*Comput*)
megabyte

me'gafono *sm* megaphone

'meglio ['mɛʎʎo] *av, ag inv* better; (*con
senso superlativo*) best ▷ *sm* (*la cosa
migliore*): **il ~** the best (thing); **faresti
~ ad andartene** you had better leave;
alla ~ as best one can; **andar di bene
in ~** to get better and better; **fare del**

proprio ~ to do one's best; **per il ~** for
the best; **aver la ~ su qn** to get the
better of sb

'mela *sf* apple; **mela cotogna** quince

mela'grana *sf* pomegranate

melan'zana [melan'dzana] *sf*
aubergine (*BRIT*), eggplant (*US*)

melato'nina *sf* melatonin

'melma *sf* mud, mire

'melo *sm* apple tree

melo'dia *sf* melody

me'lone *sm* (musk)melon

'membro *sm* member; (*pl(f)*
membra) (*arto*) limb

memo'randum *sm inv*
memorandum

me'moria *sf* memory; **memorie** *sfpl*
(*opera autobiografica*) memoirs; **a ~**
(*imparare, sapere*) by heart; **a ~ d'uomo**
within living memory

mendi'cante *sm/f* beggar

 PAROLA CHIAVE

'meno *av* **1** (*in minore misura*) less;
dovresti mangiare meno you should
eat less, you shouldn't eat so much
2 (*comparativo*): **meno ... di** not as ...
as, less ... than; **sono meno alto di te**
I'm not as tall as you (are), I'm less tall
than you (are); **meno ... che** not as ...
as, less ... than; **meno che mai** less
than ever; **è meno intelligente che
ricco** he's more rich than intelligent;
meno fumo più mangio the less I
smoke the more I eat
3 (*superlativo*) least; **il meno dotato
degli studenti** the least gifted of
the students; **è quello che compro
meno spesso** it's the one I buy least
often
4 (*Mat*) minus; **8 meno 5** 8 minus 5,
8 take away 5; **sono le 8 meno un
quarto** it's a quarter to 8; **meno 5
gradi** 5 degrees below zero, minus 5
degrees; **1 euro in meno** 1 euro less
5 (*fraseologia*): **quanto meno poteva**

telefonare he could at least have phoned; **non so se accettare o meno** I don't know whether to accept or not; **fare a meno di qc/qn** to do without sth/sb; **non potevo fare a meno di ridere** I couldn't help laughing; **meno male!** thank goodness!; **meno male che sei arrivato** it's a good job that you've come
▷ *ag inv (tempo, denaro)* less; *(errori, persone)* fewer; **ha fatto meno errori di tutti** he made fewer mistakes than anyone, he made the fewest mistakes of all
▷ *sm inv* **1**: **il meno** *(il minimo)* the least; **parlare del più e del meno** to talk about this and that
2 *(Mat)* minus
▷ *prep (eccetto)* except (for), apart from; **a meno che, a meno di** unless; **a meno che non piova** unless it rains; **non posso, a meno di prendere ferie** I can't, unless I take some leave

meno'pausa *sf* menopause
'**mensa** *sf (locale)* canteen; (: *Mil*) mess; (: *nelle università*) refectory
men'sile *ag* monthly ▷ *sm (periodico)* monthly (magazine); *(stipendio)* monthly salary
'**mensola** *sf* bracket; *(ripiano)* shelf; *(Archit)* corbel
'**menta** *sf* mint; *(anche:* **~ piperita**) peppermint; *(bibita)* peppermint cordial; *(caramella)* mint, peppermint
men'tale *ag* mental; **mentalità** *sf inv* mentality
'**mente** *sf* mind; **imparare/sapere qc a ~** to learn/know sth by heart; **avere in ~ qc** to have sth in mind; **passare di ~ a qn** to slip sb's mind
men'tire *vi* to lie
'**mento** *sm* chin
'**mentre** *cong (temporale)* while; *(avversativo)* whereas
menù *sm inv* menu; **ci può portare il ~?** could we see the menu?; **menù**

turistico set menu
menzio'nare [mentsjo'nare] *vt* to mention
men'zogna [men'tsɔɲɲa] *sf* lie
mera'viglia [mera'viʎʎa] *sf* amazement, wonder; *(persona, cosa)* marvel, wonder; **a ~** perfectly, wonderfully; **meravigli'are** *vt* to amaze, astonish; **meravigliarsi (di)** to marvel (at); *(stupirsi)* to be amazed (at), be astonished (at); **meravigli'oso, -a** *ag* wonderful, marvellous
mer'cante *sm* merchant; **mercante d'arte** art dealer
merca'tino *sm (rionale)* local street market; *(Econ)* unofficial stock market
mer'cato *sm* market; **mercato dei cambi** exchange market; **mercato nero** black market
'**merce** ['mɛrtʃe] *sf* goods *pl*, merchandise
mercé [mer'tʃe] *sf* mercy
merce'ria [mertʃe'ria] *sf (articoli)* haberdashery (BRIT), notions *pl* (US); *(bottega)* haberdasher's shop (BRIT), notions store (US)
mercoledì *sm inv* Wednesday; **di** *o* **il ~** on Wednesdays; **mercoledì delle Ceneri** Ash Wednesday
mer'curio *sm* mercury
'**merda** *sf (fam!)* shit (!)
me'renda *sf* afternoon snack
meren'dina *sf* snack
meridi'ana *sf (orologio)* sundial
meridi'ano, -a *ag* meridian; midday *cpd*, noonday ▷ *sm* meridian
meridio'nale *ag* southern ▷ *sm/f* southerner
meridi'one *sm* south
me'ringa, -ghe *sf (Cuc)* meringue
meri'tare *vt* to deserve, merit ▷ *vb impers* **merita andare** it's worth going
meri'tevole *ag* worthy
'**merito** *sm* merit; *(valore)* worth; **in ~ a** as regards, with regard to; **dare ~ a qn di** to give sb credit for; **finire**

a pari ~ to finish joint first (o second ecc); to tie

mer'letto sm lace

'merlo sm (Zool) blackbird; (Archit) battlement

mer'luzzo [mer'luttso] sm (Zool) cod

mes'chino, -a [mes'kino] ag wretched; (scarso) scanty, poor; (persona: gretta) mean; (: limitata) narrow-minded, petty

mesco'lare vt to mix; (vini, colori) to blend; (mettere in disordine) to mix up, muddle up; (carte) to shuffle

'mese sm month

'messa sf (Rel) mass; (il mettere): **messa in moto** starting; **messa in piega** set; **messa a punto** (Tecn) adjustment; (Aut) tuning; (fig) clarification; **messa in scena** = **messinscena**

messag'gero [messad'dʒɛro] sm messenger

messaggi'arsi [messad'dʒarsi] vip: **messaggiamoci** let's text each other

messaggino [messad'dʒino] sm (di telefonino) text (message)

mes'saggio [mes'saddʒo] sm message; **posso lasciare un ~?** can I leave a message?; **ci sono messaggi per me?** are there any messages for me?; **messaggio di posta elettronica** e-mail message

messag'gistica [messad'dʒistica] sf **~ immediata** (Inform) instant messaging; **programma di ~ immediata** instant messenger

mes'sale sm (Rel) missal

messi'cano, -a ag, sm/f Mexican

'Messico sm **il ~** Mexico

messin'scena [messin'ʃena] sf (Teatro) production

'messo, -a pp di **mettere** ▷ sm messenger

mesti'ere sm (professione) job; (: manuale) trade; (: artigianale) craft; (fig: abilità nel lavoro) skill, technique; **essere del ~** to know the tricks of the trade

'mestolo sm (Cuc) ladle

mestruazi'one [mestruat'tsjone] sf menstruation

'meta sf destination; (fig) aim, goal

metà sf inv half; (punto di mezzo) middle; **dividere qc a o per ~** to divide sth in half, halve sth; **fare a ~ (di qc con qn)** to go halves (with sb in sth); **a ~ prezzo** at half price; **a ~ strada** halfway

meta'done sm methadone

me'tafora sf metaphor

me'tallico, -a, -ci, -che ag (di metallo) metal cpd; (splendore, rumore ecc) metallic

me'tallo sm metal

metalmec'canico, -a, -ci, -che ag engineering cpd ▷ sm engineering worker

me'tano sm methane

me'ticcio, -a, -ci, -ce [me'tittʃo] sm/f half-caste, half-breed

me'todico, -a, -ci, -che ag methodical

'metodo sm method

'metro sm metre; (nastro) tape measure; (asta) (metre) rule

metropoli'tana sf underground, subway

metrosessu'ale agg metrosexual

'mettere vt to put; (abito) to put on; (: portare) to wear; (installare: telefono) to put in; (fig: provocare): **~ fame/allegria a qn** to make sb hungry/happy; (supporre): **mettiamo che ...** let's suppose o say that ...; **mettersi** vpr (persona) to put o.s.; (oggetto) to go; (disporsi: faccenda) to turn out; **mettersi a sedere** to sit down; **mettersi a letto** to get into bed; (per malattia) to take to one's bed; **mettersi il cappello** to put on one's hat; **mettersi a** (cominciare) to begin to, start to; **mettersi al lavoro** to set to work; **mettersi con qn** (in società) to team up with sb; (in coppia) to start going out with sb; **metterci: metterci molta cura/molto tempo** to take a lot of care/a lot of time; **ci ho messo 3 ore per venire** it's taken me 3 hours to get here; **mettercela tutta** to do one's best; **~ a tacere qn/qc** to keep sb/sth quiet; **~ su casa** to set up house; **~ su un negozio** to start a shop; **~ via** to put away

mezza'notte [meddza'nɔtte] *sf* midnight

'mezzo, -a ['mɛddzo] *ag* half; **un ~ litro/panino** half a litre/roll ▷ *av* half-; **~ morto** half-dead ▷ *sm (metà)* half; *(parte centrale: di strada ecc)* middle; *(per raggiungere un fine)* means *sg*; *(veicolo)* vehicle; *(nell'indicare l'ora)*: **le nove e ~** half past nine; **~giorno e ~** half past twelve; **mezzi** *smpl (possibilità economiche)* means; **di mezza età** middle-aged; **un soprabito di mezza stagione** a spring (*o* autumn) coat; **di ~** middle, in the middle; **andarci di ~** *(patir danno)* to suffer; **levarsi** *o* **togliersi di ~** to get out of the way; **in ~ a** in the middle of; **per** *o* **a ~ di** by means of; **mezzi di comunicazione di massa** mass media *pl*; **mezzi pubblici** public transport *sg*; **mezzi di trasporto** means of transport

mezzogi'orno [meddzo'dʒorno] *sm* midday, noon; **a ~** at 12 (o'clock) *o* midday *o* noon; **il ~ d'Italia** southern Italy

mi *(dav lo, la, li, le, ne diventa* **me)** *pron (oggetto)* me; *(complemento di termine)* to me; *(riflessivo)* myself ▷ *sm (Mus)* E; *(: solfeggiando la scala)* mi

miago'lare *vi* to miaow, mew

'mica *av (fam)*: **non ... ~** not ... at all; **non sono ~ stanco** I'm not a bit tired; **non sarà ~ partito?** he wouldn't have left, would he?; **~ male** not bad

'miccia, -ce ['mittʃa] *sf* fuse

micidi'ale [mitʃi'djale] *ag* fatal; *(dannosissimo)* deadly

micro'fibra *sf* microfibre

mi'crofono *sm* microphone

micros'copio *sm* microscope

mi'dollo *(pl(f)* **midolla)** *sm (Anat)* marrow; **midollo osseo** bone marrow

mi'ele *sm* honey

'miglia ['miʎʎa] *sfpl di* **miglio**

migli'aio [miʎ'ʎajo] *((pl)f* **migliaia)** *sm* thousand; **un ~ (di)** about a thousand; **a migliaia** by the thousand, in thousands

'miglio ['miʎʎo] *sm (Bot)* millet; *(pl(f)* **miglia)** *(unità di misura)* mile; **~ marino** *o* **nautico** nautical mile

migliora'mento [miʎʎora'mento] *sm* improvement

miglio'rare [miʎʎo'rare] *vt, vi* to improve

migli'ore [miʎ'ʎore] *ag (comparativo)* better; *(superlativo)* best ▷ *sm* **il ~** the best (thing) ▷ *sm/f* **il(la) ~** the best (person); **il miglior vino di questa regione** the best wine in this area

'mignolo ['miɲɲolo] *sm (Anat)* little finger, pinkie; *(: dito del piede)* little toe

Mi'lano *sf* Milan

miliar'dario, -a *sm/f* millionaire

mili'ardo *sm* thousand million, billion *(us)*

mili'one *sm* million

mili'tante *ag, sm/f* militant

mili'tare *vi (Mil)* to be a soldier, serve; *(fig: in un partito)* to be a militant ▷ *ag* military ▷ *sm* serviceman; **fare il ~** to do one's military service

'mille *(pl* **mila)** *num* *a o* one thousand; **dieci mila** ten thousand; **mille euro** one thousand euros

mil'lennio *sm* millennium

millepi'edi *sm inv* centipede

mil'lesimo, -a *ag, sm* thousandth

milli'grammo *sm* milligram(me)

mil'limetro *sm* millimetre

'milza ['miltsa] *sf (Anat)* spleen

mimetiz'zare [mimetid'dzare] *vt* to camouflage; **mimetizzarsi** *vpr* to camouflage o.s.

'**mimo** *sm* (*attore, componimento*)
mime

mi'mosa *sf* mimosa

min. *abbr* (= *minuto, minimo*) min.

'**mina** *sf* (*esplosiva*) mine; (*di matita*)
lead

mi'naccia, -ce [mi'nattʃa] *sf*
threat; **minacci'are** *vt* to threaten;
minacciare qn di morte to threaten
to kill sb; **minacciare di fare qc** to
threaten to do sth

mi'nare *vt* (*Mil*) to mine; (*fig*) to
undermine

mina'tore *sm* miner

mine'rale *ag, sm* mineral

mine'rario, -a *ag* (*delle miniere*)
mining; (*dei minerali*) ore *cpd*

mi'nestra *sf* soup; **minestra in
brodo** noodle soup; **minestra di
verdure** vegetable soup

minia'tura *sf* miniature

mini'bar *sm inv* minibar

mini'era *sf* mine

mini'gonna *sf* miniskirt

'**minimo, -a** *ag* minimum, least,
slightest; (*piccolissimo*) very small,
slight; (*il più basso*) lowest, minimum
▷ *sm* minimum; **al ~** at least; **girare al
~** (*Aut*) to idle

minis'tero *sm* (*Pol, Rel*) ministry;
(*governo*) government; **M~ delle
Finanze** Ministry of Finance,
≈ Treasury

mi'nistro *sm* (*Pol, Rel*) minister

mino'ranza [mino'rantsa] *sf*
minority

mi'nore *ag* (*comparativo*) less; (*più
piccolo*) smaller; (*numero*) lower;
(*inferiore*) lower, inferior; (*meno
importante*) minor; (*più giovane*)
younger; (*superlativo*) least;
smallest; lowest; youngest ▷ *sm/f*
= **minorenne**

mino'renne *ag* under age ▷ *sm/f*
minor, person under age

mi'nuscolo, -a *ag* (*scrittura, carattere*)
small; (*piccolissimo*) tiny ▷ *sf* small

letter

mi'nuto, -a *ag* tiny, minute; (*pioggia*)
fine; (*corporatura*) delicate, fine ▷ *sm*
(*unità di misura*) minute; **al ~** (*Comm*)
retail

'**mio** (*f* '**mia**, *pl* **mi'ei** *or* '**mie**) *det* **il ~,
la mia** *ecc* my ▷ *pron* **il ~, la mia** *ecc*
mine; **i miei** my family; **un ~ amico** a
friend of mine

'**miope** *ag* short-sighted

'**mira** *sf* (*anche fig*) aim; **prendere la ~**
to take aim; **prendere di ~ qn** (*fig*) to
pick on sb

mi'racolo *sm* miracle

mi'raggio [mi'raddʒo] *sm* mirage

mi'rare *vi* **~ a** to aim at; **mi'rato, -a**
agg (*targetted*)

mi'rino *sm* (*Tecn*) sight; (*Fot*) viewer,
viewfinder

mir'tillo *sm* bilberry (*BRIT*), blueberry
(*US*), whortleberry

mi'scela [miʃ'ʃela] *sf* mixture; (*di
caffè*) blend

'**mischia** ['miskja] *sf* scuffle; (*Rugby*)
scrum, scrummage

mis'cuglio [mis'kuʎʎo] *sm* mixture,
hotchpotch, jumble

'**mise** *vb vedi* **mettere**

mise'rabile *ag* (*infelice*) miserable,
wretched; (*povero*) poverty-stricken;
(*di scarso valore*) miserable

mi'seria *sf* extreme poverty;
(*infelicità*) misery

miseri'cordia *sf* mercy, pity

'**misero, -a** *ag* miserable,
wretched; (*povero*) poverty-stricken;
(*insufficiente*) miserable

'**misi** *vb vedi* **mettere**

mi'sogino [mi'zɔdʒino] *sm*
misogynist

'**missile** *sm* missile

missio'nario, -a *ag, sm/f* missionary

missi'one *sf* mission

misteri'oso, -a *ag* mysterious

mis'tero *sm* mystery

'**misto, -a** *ag* mixed; (*scuola*) mixed,
coeducational ▷ *sm* mixture

mis'tura *sf* mixture

mi'sura *sf* measure; (*misurazione, dimensione*) measurement; (*taglia*) size; (*provvedimento*) measure, step; (*moderazione*) moderation; (*Mus*) time; (: *divisione*) bar; (*fig: limite*) bounds *pl*, limit; **nella ~ in cui** inasmuch as, insofar as; **(fatto) su ~** made to measure

misu'rare *vt* (*ambiente, stoffa*) to measure; (*terreno*) to survey; (*abito*) to try on; (*pesare*) to weigh; (*fig: parole ecc*) to weigh up; (: *spese, cibo*) to limit ▷ *vi* to measure; **misurarsi** *vpr* **misurarsi con qn** to have a confrontation with sb; to compete with sb

'mite *ag* mild

'mitico, -a, ci, che *ag* mythical

'mito *sm* myth; **mitolo'gia, -'gie** *sf* mythology

'mitra *sf* (*Rel*) mitre ▷ *sm inv* (*arma*) sub-machine gun

mit'tente *sm/f* sender

mm *abbr* (= *millimetro*) mm

'mobile *ag* mobile; (*parte di macchina*) moving; (*Dir: bene*) movable, personal ▷ *sm* (*arredamento*) piece of furniture; **mobili** *smpl* (*mobilia*) furniture *sg*

mocas'sino *sm* moccasin

'moda *sf* fashion; **alla ~, di ~** fashionable, in fashion

modalità *sf inv* formality

mo'della *sf* model

mo'dello *sm* model; (*stampo*) mould ▷ *ag inv* model *cpd*

'modem *sm inv* modem

modera'tore, -'trice *sm/f* moderator

mo'derno, -a *ag* modern

mo'desto, -a *ag* modest

'modico, -a, -ci, -che *ag* reasonable, moderate

mo'difica, -che *sf* modification

modifi'care *vt* to modify, alter

'modo *sm* way, manner; (*mezzo*) means, way; (*occasione*) opportunity; (*Ling*) mood; (*Mus*) mode; **modi** *smpl*

(*comportamento*) manners; **a suo ~, a ~ suo** in his own way; **ad o in ogni ~** anyway; **di o in ~ che** so that; **in ~ da** so as to; **in tutti i modi** at all costs; (*comunque sia*) anyway; (*in ogni caso*) in any case; **in qualche ~** somehow or other; **per ~ di dire** so to speak; **modo di dire** turn of phrase

'modulo *sm* (*modello*) form; (*Archit, lunare, di comando*) module

'mogano *sm* mahogany

'mogio, -a, -gi, -gie ['mɔdʒo] *ag* down in the dumps, dejected

'moglie ['moʎʎe] *sf* wife

mo'ine *sfpl* cajolery *sg*; (*leziosità*) affectation *sg*

mo'lare *sm* (*dente*) molar

'mole *sf* mass; (*dimensioni*) size; (*edificio grandioso*) massive structure

moles'tare *vt* to bother, annoy; **mo'lestia** *sf* annoyance, bother; **recar molestia a qn** to bother sb; **molestie sessuali** sexual harassment *sg*

'molla *sf* spring; **molle** *sfpl* (*per camino*) tongs

mol'lare *vt* to release, let go; (*Naut*) to ease; (*fig: ceffone*) to give ▷ *vi* (*cedere*) to give in

'molle *ag* soft; (*muscoli*) flabby

mol'letta *sf* (*per capelli*) hairgrip; (*per panni stesi*) clothes peg

'mollica, -che *sf* crumb, soft part

mol'lusco, -schi *sm* mollusc

'molo *sm* mole, breakwater, jetty

moltipli'care *vt* to multiply; **moltiplicarsi** *vpr* to multiply; to increase in number; **moltiplicazi'one** *sf* multiplication

 PAROLA CHIAVE

'molto, -a *det* (*quantità*) a lot of, much; (*numero*) a lot of, many; **molto pane/ carbone** a lot of bread/coal; **molta gente** a lot of people, many people; **molti libri** a lot of books, many books;

non ho molto tempo I haven't got much time; **per molto (tempo)** for a long time
▷ *av* **1** a lot, (very) much; **viaggia molto** he travels a lot; **non viaggia molto** he doesn't travel much *o* a lot **2** (*intensivo: con aggettivi, avverbi*) very; (: *con participio passato*) (very) much; **molto buono** very good; **molto migliore, molto meglio** much *o* a lot better
▷ *pron* much, a lot

momentanea'mente *av* at the moment, at present

momen'taneo, -a *ag* momentary, fleeting

mo'mento *sm* moment; **da un ~ all'altro** at any moment; (*all'improvviso*) suddenly; **al ~ di fare** just as I was (*o* you were *o* he was *ecc*) doing; **per il ~** for the time being; **dal ~ che** ever since; (*dato che*) since; **a momenti** (*da un momento all'altro*) any time *o* moment now; (*quasi*) nearly

'monaca, -che *sf* nun

'Monaco *sf* Monaco; **Monaco (di Baviera)** Munich

'monaco, -ci *sm* monk

monar'chia *sf* monarchy

monas'tero *sm* (*di monaci*) monastery; (*di monache*) convent

mon'dano, -a *ag* (*anche fig*) worldly; (*anche: **dell'alta società***) society *cpd*; fashionable

mondi'ale *ag* (*campionato, popolazione*) world *cpd*; (*influenza*) world-wide

'mondo *sm* world; (*grande quantità*): **un ~ di** lots of, a host of; **il bel ~** high society

mo'nello, -a *sm/f* street urchin; (*ragazzo vivace*) scamp, imp

mo'neta *sf* (*pezzo*) coin; (*Econ: valuta*) currency; (*denaro spicciolo*) (small) change; **moneta estera** foreign currency; **moneta legale** legal tender

mongol'fiera *sf* hot-air balloon

'monitor *sm inv* (*Tecn, TV*) monitor

monolo'cale *sm* studio flat

mono'polio *sm* monopoly

mo'notono, -a *ag* monotonous

monovo'lume *ag inv, sf inv* **(automobile) ~** people carrier, MPV

mon'sone *sm* monsoon

monta'carichi [monta'kariki] *sm inv* hoist, goods lift

mon'taggio [mon'taddʒo] *sm* (*Tecn*) assembly; (*Cinema*) editing

mon'tagna [mon'taɲɲa] *sf* mountain; (*zona montuosa*): **la ~** the mountains *pl*; **andare in ~** to go to the mountains; **montagne russe** roller coaster *sg*, big dipper *sg* (*BRIT*)

monta'naro, -a *ag* mountain *cpd*
▷ *sm/f* mountain dweller

mon'tano, -a *ag* mountain *cpd*; alpine

mon'tare *vt* to go (*o* come) up; (*cavallo*) to ride; (*apparecchiatura*) to set up, assemble; (*Cuc*) to whip; (*Zool*) to cover; (*incastonare*) to mount, set; (*Cinema*) to edit; (*Fot*) to mount ▷ *vi* to go (*o* come) up; (*a cavallo*): **~ bene/male** to ride well/badly; (*aumentare di livello, volume*) to rise

monta'tura *sf* assembling *no pl*; (*di occhiali*) frames *pl*; (*di gioiello*) mounting, setting; (*fig*): **montatura pubblicitaria** publicity stunt

'monte *sm* mountain; **a ~** upstream; **mandare a ~ qc** to upset sth, cause sth to fail; **il M~ Bianco** Mont Blanc; **monte di pietà** pawnshop; **monte premi** prize

mon'tone *sm* (*Zool*) ram; **carne di ~** mutton

montu'oso, -a *ag* mountainous

monu'mento *sm* monument

mo'quette [mɔ'kɛt] *sf inv* fitted carpet

'mora *sf* (*del rovo*) blackberry; (*del gelso*) mulberry; (*Dir*) delay; (: *somma*) arrears *pl*

mo'rale *ag* moral ▷ *sf* (*scienza*) ethics *sg*, moral philosophy; (*complesso di norme*) moral standards *pl*, morality; (*condotta*) morals *pl*; (*insegnamento morale*) moral ▷ *sm* morale; **essere giù di ~** to be feeling down

'morbido, -a *ag* soft; (*pelle*) soft, smooth

> Attenzione! In inglese esiste la parola *morbid*, che però significa *morboso*.

mor'billo *sm* (*Med*) measles *sg*

'morbo *sm* disease

mor'boso, -a *ag* (*fig*) morbid

'mordere *vt* to bite; (*addentare*) to bite into

mori'bondo, -a *ag* dying, moribund

mo'rire *vi* to die; (*abitudine, civiltà*) to die out; **~ di fame** to die of hunger; (*fig*) to be starving; **~ di noia/paura** to be bored/scared to death; **fa un caldo da ~** it's terribly hot

mormo'rare *vi* to murmur; (*brontolare*) to grumble

'moro, -a *ag* dark(-haired), dark(-complexioned)

'morsa *sf* (*Tecn*) vice; (*fig: stretta*) grip

morsi'care *vt* to nibble (at), gnaw (at); (*insetto*) to bite

'morso, -a *pp di* **mordere** ▷ *sm* bite; (*di insetto*) sting; (*parte della briglia*) bit; **morsi della fame** pangs of hunger

morta'della *sf* (*Cuc*) mortadella (*type of salted pork meat*)

mor'taio *sm* mortar

mor'tale *ag, sm* mortal

'morte *sf* death

'morto, -a *pp di* **morire** ▷ *ag* dead ▷ *sm* dead; **i morti** the dead; **fare il ~** (*nell'acqua*) to float on one's back; **il Mar M~** the Dead Sea

mo'saico, -ci *sm* mosaic

'Mosca *sf* Moscow

'mosca, -sche *sf* fly; **mosca cieca** blind-man's-buff

mosce'rino [moʃʃe'rino] *sm* midge, gnat

mos'chea [mos'kɛa] *sf* mosque

'moscio, -a, -sci, -sce ['mɔʃʃo] *ag* (*fig*) lifeless

mos'cone *sm* (*Zool*) bluebottle; (*barca*) pedalo; (: *a remi: a*) kind of pedalo with oars

'mossa *sf* movement; (*nel gioco*) move

'mossi *ecc vb vedi* **muovere**

'mosso, -a *pp di* **muovere** ▷ *ag* (*mare*) rough; (*capelli*) wavy; (*Fot*) blurred

mos'tarda *sf* mustard; **mostarda di Cremona** pickled fruit with mustard

'mostra *sf* exhibition, show; (*ostentazione*) show; **in ~** on show; **far ~ di** (*fingere*) to pretend; **far ~ di sé** to show off

mos'trare *vt* to show; **può mostrarmi dov'è, per favore?** can you show me where it is, please?

'mostro *sm* monster; **mostru'oso, -a** *ag* monstrous

mo'tel *sm inv* motel

moti'vare *vt* (*causare*) to cause; (*giustificare*) to justify, account for

mo'tivo *sm* (*causa*) reason, cause; (*movente*) motive; (*letterario*) (central) theme; (*disegno*) motif, design, pattern; (*Mus*) motif; **per quale ~?** why?, for what reason?

'moto *sm* (*anche Fisica*) motion; (*movimento, gesto*) movement; (*esercizio fisico*) exercise; (*sommossa*) rising, revolt; (*commozione*) feeling, impulse ▷ *sf inv* (*motocicletta*) motorbike; **mettere in ~** to set in motion; (*Aut*) to start up

motoci'clista, -i, -e *sm/f* motorcyclist

mo'tore, -'trice *ag* motor; (*Tecn*) driving ▷ *sm* engine, motor; **a ~** motor *cpd*, power-driven; **~ a combustione interna/a reazione** internal combustion/jet engine; **motore di ricerca** (*Inform*) search engine; **moto'rino** *sm* moped; **motorino di avviamento** (*Aut*) starter

motos'cafo *sm* motorboat

'motto sm (battuta scherzosa) witty remark; (frase emblematica) motto, maxim

'mouse ['maus] sm inv (Inform) mouse

mo'vente sm motive

movi'mento sm movement; (fig) activity, hustle and bustle; (Mus) tempo, movement

mozi'one [mot'tsjone] sf (Pol) motion

mozza'rella [mottsa'rella] sf mozzarella, a moist Neapolitan curd cheese

mozzi'cone [mottsi'kone] sm stub, butt, end; (anche: ~ di sigaretta) cigarette end

'mucca, -che sf cow; **mucca pazza** mad cow disease

'mucchio ['mukkjo] sm pile, heap; (fig) **un ~ di** lots of, heaps of

'muco, -chi sm mucus

'muffa sf mould, mildew

mug'gire [mud'dʒire] vi (vacca) to low, moo; (toro) to bellow; (fig) to roar

mu'ghetto [mu'getto] sm lily of the valley

mu'lino sm mill; **mulino a vento** windmill

'mulo sm mule

'multa sf fine

multi'etnico, -a, -ci, -che ag multiethnic

multirazziale [multirat'tsjale] ag multiracial

multi'sala ag inv multiscreen

multivitami'nico, -a, -ci, -che ag **complesso ~** multivitamin

'mummia sf mummy

'mungere ['mundʒere] vt (anche fig) to milk

munici'pale [munitʃi'pale] ag municipal; town cpd

muni'cipio [muni'tʃipjo] sm town council, corporation; (edificio) town hall

munizi'oni [munit'tsjoni] sfpl (Mil) ammunition sg

'munsi ecc vb vedi **mungere**

mu'oio ecc vb vedi **morire**

mu'overe vt to move; (ruota, macchina) to drive; (sollevare: questione, obiezione) to raise, bring up; (: accusa) to make, bring forward; **muoversi** vpr to move; **muoviti!** hurry up!, get a move on!

'mura sfpl vedi **muro**

mu'rale ag wall cpd; mural

mura'tore sm mason; bricklayer

'muro sm wall

'muschio ['muskjo] sm (Zool) musk; (Bot) moss

musco'lare ag muscular, muscle cpd

'muscolo sm (Anat) muscle

mu'seo sm museum

museru'ola sf muzzle

'musica sf music; **musica da ballo/ camera** dance/chamber music; **musi'cale** ag musical; **musi'cista, -i, -e** sm/f musician

'müsli ['mysli] sm muesli

'muso sm muzzle; (di auto, aereo) nose; **tenere il ~** to sulk

mussul'mano, -a ag, sm/f Muslim, Moslem

'muta sf (di animali) moulting; (di serpenti) sloughing; (per immersioni subacquee) diving suit; (gruppo di cani) pack

mu'tande sfpl (da uomo) (under)pants

'muto, -a ag (Med) dumb; (emozione, dolore, Cinema) silent; (Ling) silent, mute; (carta geografica) blank; **~ per lo stupore** ecc speechless with amazement ecc

'mutuo, -a ag (reciproco) mutual ▷ sm (Econ) (long-term) loan

n

N *abbr* (= *nord*) N

n. *abbr* (= *numero*) no.

'nafta *sf* naphtha; (*per motori diesel*) diesel oil

nafta'lina *sf* (*Chim*) naphthalene; (*tarmicida*) mothballs *pl*

'naia *sf* (*Mil*) *slang term for national service*

na'ïf [na'if] *ag inv* naïve

'nanna *sf* (*linguaggio infantile*): **andare a ~** to go to beddy-byes

'nano, -a *ag, sm/f* dwarf

napole'tano, -a *ag, sm/f* Neapolitan

'Napoli *sf* Naples

nar'ciso [nar'tʃizo] *sm* narcissus

nar'cotico, -ci *sm* narcotic

na'rice [na'ritʃe] *sf* nostril

nar'rare *vt* to tell the story of, recount; **narra'tiva** *sf* (*branca letteraria*) fiction

na'sale *ag* nasal

'nascere ['naʃʃere] *vi* (*bambino*) to be born; (*pianta*) to come o spring up; (*fiume*) to rise, have its source; (*sole*) to rise; (*dente*) to come through; (*fig: derivare, conseguire*): **~ da** to arise from, be born out of; **è nata nel 1952** she was born in 1952; **'nascita** *sf* birth

nas'condere *vt* to hide, conceal; **nascondersi** *vpr* to hide; **nascon'diglio** *sm* hiding place; **nascon'dino** *sm* (*gioco*) hide-and-seek; **nas'cosi** *ecc vb vedi* **nascondere**; **nas'costo, -a** *pp di* **nascondere** ▷ *ag* hidden; **di nascosto** secretly

na'sello *sm* (*Zool*) hake

'naso *sm* nose

'nastro *sm* ribbon; (*magnetico, isolante, Sport*) tape; **nastro adesivo** adhesive tape; **nastro trasportatore** conveyor belt

nas'turzio [nas'turtsjo] *sm* nasturtium

na'tale *ag* of one's birth ▷ *sm* (*Rel*): **N~** Christmas; (*giorno della nascita*) birthday; **nata'lizio, -a** *ag* (*del Natale*) Christmas *cpd*

'natica, -che *sf* (*Anat*) buttock

'nato, -a *pp di* **nascere** ▷ *ag* **un attore ~** a born actor, **nata Pieri** née Pieri

na'tura *sf* nature; **pagare in ~** to pay in kind; **natura morta** still life

natu'rale *ag* natural

natural'mente *av* naturally; (*certamente, sì*) of course

natu'rista, -i, e *ag, sm/f* naturist, nudist

naufra'gare *vi* (*nave*) to be wrecked; (*persona*) to be shipwrecked; (*fig*) to fall through; **'naufrago, -ghi** *sm* castaway, shipwreck victim

'nausea *sf* nausea; **nause'ante** *ag* (*odore*) nauseating; (*sapore*) disgusting; (*fig*) sickening

'nautico, -a, -ci, -che *ag* nautical

na'vale *ag* naval

na'vata *sf* (*anche: ~ centrale*) nave; (*anche: ~ laterale*) aisle

'nave *sf* ship, vessel; **nave cisterna**

tanker; **nave da guerra** warship;
nave passeggeri passenger ship
na'vetta *sf* shuttle; (*servizio di
collegamento*) shuttle (service)
navi'cella [navi'tʃɛlla] *sf* (*di aerostato*)
gondola; **navicella spaziale**
spaceship
navi'gare *vi* to sail; **~ in Internet**
to surf the Net; **navigazi'one** *sf*
navigation
nazio'nale [nattsjo'nale] *ag*
national ▷ *sf* (*Sport*) national team;
nazionalità *sf inv* nationality
nazi'one [nat'tsjone] *sf* nation
naziskin ['na:tsiskin] *sm inv* Nazi
skinhead
NB *abbr* (= *nota bene*) NB

 PAROLA CHIAVE

ne *pron* **1** (*di lui, lei, loro*) of him/her/
them; about him/her/them; **ne
riconosco la voce** I recognize his (*o
her*) voice
2 (*di questa, quella cosa*) of it; about it;
ne voglio ancora I want some more
(*of it o them*); **non parliamone più!**
let's not talk about it any more!
3 (*con valore partitivo*): **hai dei libri?
— sì, ne ho** have you any books?
— yes, I have (some); **hai del pane?
— no, non ne ho** have you any bread?
— no, I haven't any; **quanti anni hai?
— ne ho 17** how old are you? — I'm 17
▷ *av* (*moto a luogo: da lì*) from there;
ne vengo ora I've just come from
there

né *cong*: **né ... né** neither ... nor; **né
l'uno né l'altro lo vuole** neither
of them wants it; **non parla né
l'italiano né il tedesco** he speaks
neither Italian nor German, he doesn't
speak either Italian or German; **non
piove né nevica** it isn't raining or
snowing
ne'anche [ne'anke] *av, cong* not even;

non ... ~ not even; **~ se volesse
potrebbe venire** he couldn't come
even if he wanted to; **non l'ho visto
— io** I didn't see him — neither did I *o*
I didn't either; **~ per idea *o* sogno!** not
on your life!
'nebbia *sf* fog; (*foschia*) mist
necessaria'mente
[netʃessarjamente] *av* necessarily
neces'sario, -a [netʃes'sarjo] *ag*
necessary
necessità [netʃessi'ta] *sf inv*
necessity; (*povertà*) need, poverty
necro'logio [nekro'lɔdʒo] *sm*
obituary notice
ne'gare *vt* to deny; (*rifiutare*) to deny,
refuse; **~ di aver fatto/che** to deny
having done/that; **nega'tivo, -a** *ag*,
sf, sm negative
negherò ecc [nege'rɔ] *vb vedi* **negare**
negli'gente [negli'dʒɛnte] *ag*
negligent, careless
negozi'ante [negot'tsjante] *sm/f*
trader, dealer; (*bottegaio*) shopkeeper
(*BRIT*), storekeeper (*US*)
negozi'are [negot'tsjare] *vt* to
negotiate ▷ *vi*: **~ in** to trade *o* deal in;
negozi'ato *sm* negotiation
ne'gozio [ne'gɔttsjo] *sm* (*locale*) shop
(*BRIT*), store (*US*)
'negro, -a *ag, sm/f* Negro
ne'mico, -a, -ci, -che *ag* hostile;
(*Mil*) enemy *cpd* ▷ *sm/f* enemy; **essere
~ di** to be strongly averse *o* opposed to
nem'meno *av, cong* = **neanche**
'neo *sm* mole; (*fig*) (slight) flaw
'neon *sm* (*Chim*) neon
neo'nato, -a *ag* newborn ▷ *sm/f*
newborn baby
neozelan'dese [neoddzelan'dese]
ag New Zealand *cpd* ▷ *sm/f* New
Zealander
'Nepal *sm* **il ~** Nepal
nep'pure *av, cong* = **neanche**
'nero, -a *ag* black; (*scuro*) dark ▷ *sm*
black; **il Mar N~** the Black Sea
'nervo *sm* (*Anat*) nerve; (*Bot*) vein;

avere i nervi to be on edge; **dare sui nervi a qn** to get on sb's nerves; **ner'voso, -a** ag nervous; (irritabile) irritable ▷ sm (fam): **far venire il nervoso a qn** to get on sb's nerves

'**nespola** sf (Bot) medlar; (fig) blow, punch

'**nesso** sm connection, link

PAROLA CHIAVE

nes'suno, -a (det: dav sm **nessun** +C, V, **nessuno** +s impura, gn, pn, ps, x, z; dav sf **nessuna** +C, **nessun'** +V) det 1 (non uno) no; (, espressione negativa +) any; **non c'è nessun libro** there isn't any book, there is no book; **nessun altro** no one else, nobody else; **nessun'altra cosa** nothing else; **in nessun luogo** nowhere
2 (qualche) any; **hai nessuna obiezione?** do you have any objections?
▷ pron 1 (non uno) no one, nobody, espressione negativa + any(one); (: cosa) none, espressione negativa + any; **nessuno è venuto, non è venuto nessuno** nobody came
2 (qualcuno) anyone, anybody; **ha telefonato nessuno?** did anyone phone?

net'tare vt to clean
net'tezza [net'tettsa] sf cleanness, cleanliness; **nettezza urbana** cleansing department
'**netto, -a** ag (pulito) clean; (chiaro) clear, clear-cut; (deciso) definite; (Econ) net
nettur'bino sm dustman (BRIT), garbage collector (US)
neu'trale ag neutral
'**neutro, -a** ag neutral; (Ling) neuter ▷ sm (Ling) neuter
'**neve** sf snow; **nevi'care** vb impers to snow; **nevi'cata** sf snowfall
ne'vischio [ne'viskjo] sm sleet

ne'voso, -a ag snowy; snow-covered
nevral'gia [nevral'dʒia] sf neuralgia
nevras'tenico, -a, -ci, -che ag (Med) neurasthenic; (fig) hot-tempered
ne'vrosi sf neurosis
ne'vrotico, -a, ci, che ag, sm/f (anche fig) neurotic
'**nicchia** ['nikkja] sf niche; (naturale) cavity, hollow; **nicchia di mercato** (Comm) niche market
nicchi'are [nik'kjare] vi to shilly-shally, hesitate
'**nichel** ['nikel] sm nickel
nico'tina sf nicotine
'**nido** sm nest; **a ~ d'ape** (tessuto ecc) honeycomb cpd

PAROLA CHIAVE

ni'ente pron 1 (nessuna cosa) nothing; **niente può fermarlo** nothing can stop him; **niente di niente** absolutely nothing; **nient'altro** nothing else; **nient'altro che** nothing but, just, only; **niente affatto** not at all, not in the least; **come se niente fosse** as if nothing had happened; **cose da niente** trivial matters; **per niente** (gratis, invano) for nothing
2 (qualcosa): **hai bisogno di niente?** do you need anything?
3: **non ... niente** nothing; (espressione negativa +) anything; **non ho visto niente** I saw nothing, I didn't see anything; **non ho niente da dire** I have nothing o haven't anything to say
▷ sm nothing; **un bel niente** absolutely nothing; **basta un niente per farla piangere** the slightest thing is enough to make her cry
▷ av (in nessuna misura): **non ... niente** not ... at all; **non è (per) niente buono** it isn't good at all

Ni'geria [ni'dʒɛrja] sf **la ~** Nigeria
'**ninfa** sf nymph

nin'fea *sf* water lily

ninna-'nanna *sf* lullaby

'ninnolo *sm* (*gingillo*) knick-knack

ni'pote *sm/f* (*di zii*) nephew/niece; (*di nonni*) grandson/daughter, grandchild

'nitido, -a *ag* clear; (*specchio*) bright

ni'trire *vi* to neigh

ni'trito *sm* (*di cavallo*) neighing *no pl*; neigh; (*Chim*) nitrite

nitroglice'rina [nitroglitʃe'rina] *sf* nitroglycerine

no *av* (*risposta*) no; **vieni o no?** are you coming or not?; **perché no?** why not?; **lo conosciamo? — tu no ma io sì** do we know him? — you don't but I do; **verrai, no?** you'll come, won't you?

'nobile *ag* noble ▷ *sm/f* noble, nobleman/woman

'nocca, -che *sf* (*Anat*) knuckle

'noccio *ecc* ['nɔttʃo] *vb vedi* **nuocere**

nocci'ola [not'tʃɔla] *ag inv* (*colore*) hazel, light brown ▷ *sf* hazelnut

noccio'lina [nottʃo'lina] *sf*: **nocciolina americana** peanut

'nocciolo ['nɔttʃolo] *sm* (*di frutto*) stone; (*fig*) heart, core

'noce ['nɔtʃe] *sm* (*albero*) walnut tree ▷ *sf* (*frutto*) walnut; **noce di cocco** coconut; **noce moscata** nutmeg

no'cevo *ecc* [no'tʃevo] *vb vedi* **nuocere**

no'civo, -a [no'tʃivo] *ag* harmful, noxious

'nocqui *ecc vb vedi* **nuocere**

'nodo *sm* (*di cravatta, legname, Naut*) knot; (*Aut, Ferr*) junction; (*Med, Astr, Bot*) node; (*fig: legame*) bond, tie; (: *punto centrale*) heart, crux; **avere un ~ alla gola** to have a lump in one's throat

no-'global *sm/f* anti-globalization protester ▷ *ag* (*movimento, manifestante*) anti-globalization

'noi *pron* (*soggetto*) we; (*oggetto: per dare rilievo, con preposizione*) us; **~ stessi(e)** we ourselves; (*oggetto*) ourselves

'noia *sf* boredom; (*disturbo, impaccio*)

bother *no pl*, trouble *no pl*; **avere qn/qc a ~** not to like sb/sth; **mi è venuto a ~** I'm tired of it; **dare ~ a** to annoy; **avere delle noie con qn** to have trouble with sb

noi'oso, -a *ag* boring; (*fastidioso*) annoying, troublesome

> Attenzione! In inglese esiste la parola *noisy*, che però significa *rumoroso*.

noleggi'are [noled'dʒare] *vt* (*prendere a noleggio*) to hire (BRIT), rent; (*dare a noleggio*) to hire out (BRIT), rent (out); (*aereo, nave*) to charter; **vorrei ~ una macchina** I'd like to hire a car; **no'leggio** *sm* hire (BRIT), rental; charter

'nomade *ag* nomadic ▷ *sm/f* nomad

'nome *sm* name; (*Ling*) noun; **in/a ~ di** in the name of; **di o per ~** (*chiamato*) called, named; **conoscere qn di ~** to know sb by name; **nome d'arte** stage name; **nome di battesimo** Christian name; **nome di famiglia** surname

no'mignolo [no'miɲɲolo] *sm* nickname

'nomina *sf* appointment

nomi'nale *ag* nominal; (*Ling*) noun *cpd*

nomi'nare *vt* to name; (*eleggere*) to appoint; (*citare*) to mention

nomina'tivo, -a *ag* (*Ling*) nominative; (*Econ*) registered ▷ *sm* (*Ling: anche:* **caso ~**) nominative (case); (*Amm*) name

non *av* not ▷ *prefisso* non-; *vedi* **affatto**; **appena** *ecc*

nonché [non'ke] *cong* (*tanto più, tanto meno*) let alone; (*e inoltre*) as well as

noncu'rante *ag*: **~ (di)** careless (of), indifferent (to)

'nonno, -a *sm/f* grandfather/mother; (*in senso più familiare*) grandma/grandpa; **i nonni** *smpl* the grandparents

non'nulla *sm inv*: **un ~** nothing, a trifle

'nono, -a *ag, sm* ninth

nonos'tante prep in spite of, notwithstanding ▷ cong although, even though

nontiscordardimé sm inv (Bot) forget-me-not

nord sm North ▷ ag inv north; northern; **il Mare del N~** the North Sea; **nor'dest** sm north-east; **nor'dovest** sm north-west

'norma sf (principio) norm; (regola) regulation, rule; (consuetudine) custom, rule; **a ~ di legge** according to law, as laid down by law; **norme per l'uso** instructions for use; **norme di sicurezza** safety regulations

nor'male ag normal; standard cpd

normal'mente av normally

norve'gese [norve'dʒese] ag, sm/f, sm Norwegian

Nor'vegia [nor'vedʒa] sf: **la ~** Norway

nostal'gia [nostal'dʒia] sf (di casa, paese) homesickness; (del passato) nostalgia

nos'trano, -a ag local; national; home-produced

'nostro, -a det **il (la) ~(-a)** ecc our ▷ pron **il (la) ~(-a)** ecc ours ▷ sm **il ~** our money; our belongings; **i nostri** our family; our own people; **è dei nostri** he's one of us

'nota sf (segno) mark; (comunicazione scritta, Mus) note; (fattura) bill; (elenco) list; **degno di ~** noteworthy, worthy of note

no'taio sm notary

no'tare vt (segnare: errori) to mark; (registrare) to note (down), write down; (rilevare, osservare) to note, notice; **farsi ~** to get o.s. noticed

no'tevole ag (talento) notable, remarkable; (peso) considerable

no'tifica, -che sf notification

no'tizia [no'tittsja] sf (piece of) news sg; (informazione) piece of information; **notizi'ario** sm (Radio, TV, Stampa) news sg

'noto, -a ag (well-)known

notorietà sf fame; notoriety

no'torio, -a ag well-known; (peg) notorious

not'tambulo, -a sm/f night-bird; (fig)

not'tata sf night

'notte sf night; **di ~** at night; (durante la notte) in the night, during the night; **notte bianca** sleepless night

not'turno, -a ag nocturnal; (servizio, guardiano) night cpd

no'vanta num ninety; **novan'tesimo, -a** num ninetieth

'nove num nine

nove'cento [nove't∫ɛnto] num nine hundred ▷ sm: **il N~** the twentieth century

no'vella sf (Letteratura) short story

no'vello, -a ag (piante, patate) new; (insalata, verdura) early; (sposo) newly-married

no'vembre sm November

novità sf inv novelty; (innovazione) innovation; (cosa originale, insolita) something new; (notizia) (piece of) news sg; **le ~ della moda** the latest fashions

nozi'one [not'tsjone] sf notion, idea

'nozze ['nɔttse] sfpl wedding sg, marriage sg; **nozze d'argento/d'oro** silver/golden wedding

'nubile ag (donna) unmarried, single

'nuca sf nape of the neck

nucle'are ag nuclear

'nucleo sm nucleus; (gruppo) team, unit, group; (Mil, Polizia) squad; **nucleo familiare** family unit

nu'dista, -i, -e sm/f nudist

'nudo, -a ag (persona) bare, naked, nude; (membra) bare, naked; (montagna) bare ▷ sm (Arte) nude

'nulla pron, av = **niente** ▷ sm **il nulla** nothing

nullità sf inv nullity; (persona) nonentity

'nullo, -a ag useless, worthless; (Dir) null (and void); (Sport): **incontro ~**

draw
nume'rale *ag, sm* numeral
nume'rare *vt* to number
nu'merico, -a, -ci, -che *ag*
numerical
'numero *sm* number; (*romano,
arabo*) numeral; (*di spettacolo*) act,
turn; **numero civico** house number;
numero di scarpe shoe size; **numero
di telefono** telephone number;
nume'roso, -a *ag* numerous, many;
(*con sostantivo sg*) large
nu'occio *ecc* ['nwɔttʃo] *vb vedi*
nuocere
nu'ocere ['nwɔtʃere] *vi*: **~ a** to harm,
damage
nu'ora *sf* daughter-in-law
nuo'tare *vi* to swim; (*galleggiare:
oggetti*) to float; **nuota'tore, -'trice**
sm/f swimmer; **nu'oto** *sm* swimming
nu'ova *sf* (*notizia*) (piece of) news *sg*;
vedi anche **nuovo**
nuova'mente *av* again
Nu'ova Ze'landa [-dze'landa] *sf*: **la
~** New Zealand
nu'ovo, -a *ag* new; **di ~** again; **~
fiammante** *o* **di zecca** brand-new
nutri'ente *ag* nutritious, nourishing
nutri'mento *sm* food, nourishment
nu'trire *vt* to feed; (*fig: sentimenti*) to
harbour, nurse; **nutrirsi** *vpr* **nutrirsi
di** to feed on, to eat
'nuvola *sf* cloud; **nuvo'loso, -a** *ag*
cloudy
nuzi'ale [nut'tsjale] *ag* nuptial;
wedding *cpd*
'nylon ['nailən] *sm* nylon

o (*dav V spesso* **od**) *cong* or; **o ... o**
either ... or; **o l'uno o l'altro** either
(of them)
O *abbr* (= *ovest*) W
'oasi *sf inv* oasis
obbedi'ente *ecc* = **ubbidiente** *ecc*
obbli'gare *vt* (*costringere*): **~ qn a fare**
to force *o* oblige sb to do; (*Dir*) to bind;
obbliga'torio, -a *ag* compulsory,
obligatory; **'obbligo, -ghi** *sm*
obligation; (*dovere*) duty; **avere
l'obbligo di fare** to be obliged to do;
essere d'obbligo (*discorso, applauso*)
to be called for
o'beso, -a *ag* obese
obiet'tare *vt* **~ che** to object that; **~
su qc** to object to sth, raise objections
concerning sth
obiet'tivo, -a *ag* objective ▷ *sm*
(*Ottica, Fot*) lens *sg*, objective; (*Mil, fig*)
objective
obiet'tore *sm* objector; **obiettore di
coscienza** conscientious objector
obiezi'one [objet'tsjone] *sf* objection

obi'torio sm morgue, mortuary

o'bliquo, -a ag oblique; (inclinato) slanting; (fig) devious, underhand

obli'terare vt (biglietto) to stamp; (francobollo) to cancel

oblò sm inv porthole

'oboe sm (Mus) oboe

'oca (pl **'oche**) sf goose

occasi'one sf (caso favorevole) opportunity; (causa, motivo, circostanza) occasion; (Comm) bargain; **d'~** (a buon prezzo) bargain cpd; (usato) secondhand

occhi'aia [ok'kjaja] sf: **avere le occhiaie** to have shadows under one's eyes

occhi'ali [ok'kjali] smpl glasses, spectacles; **occhiali da sole/da vista** sunglasses/(prescription) glasses

occhi'ata [ok'kjata] sf look, glance; **dare un'~ a** to have a look at

occhi'ello [ok'kjɛllo] sm buttonhole; (asola) eyelet

'occhio [ˈɔkkjo] sm eye; **~!** careful!, watch out!; **a ~ nudo** with the naked eye; **a quattr'occhi** privately, tête-à-tête; **dare all'~** o **nell'~ a qn** to catch sb's eye; **fare l'~ a qc** to get used to sth; **tenere d'~ qn** to keep an eye on sb; **vedere di buon/mal ~ qc** to look favourably/unfavourably on sth

occhio'lino [okkjo'lino] sm: **fare l'~ a qn** to wink at sb

occiden'tale [ottʃiden'tale] ag western ▷ sm/f Westerner

occi'dente [ottʃi'dɛnte] sm west; (Pol): **l'O~** the West; **a ~** in the west

occor'rente ag necessary ▷ sm all that is necessary

occor'renza [okkor'rɛntsa] sf necessity, need; **all'~** in case of need

oc'correre vi to be needed, be required ▷ vb impers **occorre farlo** it must be done; **occorre che tu parta** you must leave, you'll have to

leave; **mi occorrono i soldi** I need the money

> Attenzione! In inglese esiste il verbo to occur, che però significa succedere.

oc'culto, -a ag hidden, concealed; (scienze, forze) occult

occu'pare vt to occupy; (manodopera) to employ; (ingombrare) to occupy, take up; **occuparsi** vpr to occupy o.s., keep o.s. busy; (impiegarsi) to get a job; **occuparsi di** (interessarsi) to take an interest in; (prendersi cura di) to look after, take care of; **occu'pato, -a** ag (Mil, Pol) occupied; (persona: affaccendato) busy; (posto, sedia) taken; (toilette, Tel) engaged; **la linea è occupata** the line's engaged; **è occupato questo posto?** is this seat taken?; **occupazi'one** sf occupation; (impiego, lavoro) job; (Econ) employment

o'ceano [o'tʃeano] sm ocean

'ocra sf ochre

'OCSE sigla f (= Organizzazione per la Cooperazione e lo Sviluppo Economico) OECD (Organization for Economic Cooperation and Development)

ocu'lare ag ocular, eye cpd; **testimone ~** eye witness

ocu'lato, -a ag (attento) cautious, prudent; (accorto) shrewd

ocu'lista, -i, -e sm/f eye specialist, oculist

odi'are vt to hate, detest

odi'erno, -a ag today's, of today; (attuale) present

'odio sm hatred; **avere in ~ qc/qn** to hate o detest sth/sb; **odi'oso, -a** ag hateful, odious

odo'rare vt (annusare) to smell; (profumare) to perfume, scent ▷ vi **~ (di)** to smell (of)

o'dore sm smell; **odori** smpl (Cuc) (aromatic) herbs

of'fendere vt to offend; (violare) to break, violate; (insultare) to insult;

(*ferire*) to hurt; **offendersi** *vpr* (*con senso reciproco*) to insult one another; (*risentirsi*): **offendersi (di)** to take offence (at), be offended (by)

offe'rente *sm* (*in aste*): **al maggior ~** to the highest bidder

of'ferta *sf* offer; (*donazione, anche Rel*) offering; (*in gara d'appalto*) tender; (*in aste*) bid; (*Econ*) supply; **fare un'~** to make an offer; to tender; to bid; **"offerte d'impiego"** "situations vacant"; **offerta speciale** special offer

of'fesa *sf* insult, affront; (*Mil*) attack; (*Dir*) offence; *vedi anche* **offeso**

of'feso, -a *pp di* **offendere** ▷ *ag* offended; (*fisicamente*) hurt, injured ▷ *sm/f* offended party; **essere ~ con qn** to be annoyed with sb; **parte offesa** (*Dir*) plaintiff

offi'cina [offi'tʃina] *sf* workshop

of'frire *vt* to offer; **offrirsi** *vpr* (*proporsi*) to offer (o.s.), volunteer; (*occasione*) to present itself; (*esporsi*): **offrirsi a** to expose o.s. to; **ti offro da bere** I'll buy you a drink

offus'care *vt* to obscure, darken; (*fig: intelletto*) to dim, cloud; (: *fama*) to obscure, overshadow; **offuscarsi** *vpr* to grow dark; to cloud, grow dim; to be obscured

ogget'tivo, -a [oddʒet'tivo] *ag* objective

og'getto [od'dʒetto] *sm* object; (*materia, argomento*) subject (matter); **oggetti smarriti** lost property *sg*

'oggi ['ɔddʒi] *av, sm* today; **~ a otto** a week today; **oggigi'orno** *av* nowadays

OGM *sigla m* (= *organismo geneticamente modificato*) GMO

'ogni ['oɲɲi] *det* every, each; (*tutti*) all; (*con valore distributivo*) every; **~ uomo è mortale** all men are mortal; **viene ~ due giorni** he comes every two days; **~ cosa** everything; **ad ~ costo** at all costs, at any price; **in ~ luogo** everywhere; **~ tanto** every so often; **~**

volta che every time that

Ognis'santi [oɲɲis'santi] *sm* All Saints' Day

o'gnuno [oɲ'ɲuno] *pron* everyone, everybody

O'landa *sf* **l'~** Holland; **olan'dese** *ag* Dutch ▷ *sm* (*Ling*) Dutch ▷ *sm/f* Dutchman/woman; **gli Olandesi** the Dutch

ole'andro *sm* oleander

oleo'dotto *sm* oil pipeline

ole'oso, -a *ag* oily; (*che contiene olio*) oil-yielding

ol'fatto *sm* sense of smell

oli'are *vt* to oil

oli'era *sf* oil cruet

Olim'piadi *sfpl* Olympic games; **o'limpico, -a, -ci, -che** *ag* Olympic

'olio *sm* oil; **sott'~** (*Cuc*) in oil; **~ di fegato di merluzzo** cod liver oil; **oli essenziali** essential oils; **olio d'oliva** olive oil; **olio di semi** vegetable oil

o'liva *sf* olive; **o'livo** *sm* olive tree

'olmo *sm* elm

OLP *sigla f* (= *Organizzazione per la Liberazione della Palestina*) PLO

ol'traggio [ol'traddʒo] *sm* outrage; offence, insult; **~ a pubblico ufficiale** (*Dir*) insulting a public official; **oltraggio al pudore** (*Dir*) indecent behaviour

ol'tranza [ol'trantsa] *sf* **a ~** to the last, to the bitter end

'oltre *av* (*più in là*) further; (*di più: aspettare*) longer, more ▷ *prep* (*di là da*) beyond, over, on the other side of; (*più di*) more than, over; (*in aggiunta a*) besides; (*eccetto*): **~ a** except, apart from; **oltrepas'sare** *vt* to go beyond, exceed

o'maggio [o'maddʒo] *sm* (*dono*) gift; (*segno di rispetto*) homage, tribute; **omaggi** *smpl* (*complimenti*) respects; **rendere ~ a** to pay homage o tribute to; **in ~** (*copia, biglietto*) complimentary

ombe'lico, -chi *sm* navel

'ombra sf (zona non assolata, fantasma) shade; (sagoma scura) shadow; **sedere all'~** to sit in the shade; **restare nell'~** (fig) to remain in obscurity

om'brello sm umbrella; **ombrel'lone** sm beach umbrella

om'bretto sm eye shadow

O.M.C. sigla f (= Organizzazione Mondiale del Commercio) WTO

ome'lette [ɔmə'lɛt] sf inv omelet(te)

ome'lia sf (Rel) homily, sermon

omeopa'tia sf homoeopathy

omertà sf conspiracy of silence

o'mettere vt to omit, leave out; **~ di fare** to omit o fail to do

omi'cida, -i, -e [omi'tʃida] ag homicidal, murderous ▷ sm/f murderer/eress

omi'cidio [omi'tʃidjo] sm murder; **omicidio colposo** culpable homicide

o'misi ecc vb vedi **omettere**

omissi'one sf omission; **omissione di soccorso** (Dir) failure to stop and give assistance

omogeneiz'zato [omodʒeneid'dzato] sm baby food

omo'geneo, -a [omo'dʒɛnɛo] ag homogeneous

o'monimo, -a sm/f namesake ▷ sm (Ling) homonym

omosessu'ale ag, sm/f homosexual

O.M.S. sigla f (= Organizzazione Mondiale della Sanità) WHO

On. abbr (Pol) = **onorevole**

'onda sf wave; **mettere** o **mandare in ~** (Radio, TV) to broadcast; **andare in ~** (Radio, TV) to go on the air; **onde corte/lunghe/medie** short/long/medium wave

'onere sm burden; **oneri fiscali** taxes

onestà sf honesty

o'nesto, -a ag (probo, retto) honest; (giusto) fair; (casto) chaste, virtuous

ONG sigla f inv (= Organizzazione Non Governativa) NGO

onnipo'tente ag omnipotent

ono'mastico, -ci sm name-day

ono'rare vt to honour; (far onore a) to do credit to

ono'rario, -a ag honorary ▷ sm fee

o'nore sm honour; **in ~ di** in honour of; **fare gli onori di casa** to play host (o hostess); **fare ~ a** to honour; (pranzo) to do justice to; (famiglia) to be a credit to; **farsi ~** to distinguish o.s.; **ono'revole** ag honourable ▷ sm/f (Pol) ≈ Member of Parliament (BRIT), ≈ Congressman/woman (US)

on'tano sm (Bot) alder

'O.N.U. ['ɔnu] sigla f (= Organizzazione delle Nazioni Unite) UN, UNO

o'paco, -a, -chi, -che ag (vetro) opaque; (metallo) dull, matt

o'pale sm o f opal

'opera sf work; (azione rilevante) action, deed, work; (Mus) work; opus; (: melodramma) opera; (: teatro) opera house; (ente) institution, organization; **opere pubbliche** public works; **opera d'arte** work of art; **opera lirica** (grand) opera

ope'raio, -a ag working-class; workers' ▷ sm/f worker; **classe operaia** working class

ope'rare vt to carry out, make; (Med) to operate on ▷ vi to operate, work; (rimedio) to act, work; (Med) to operate; **operarsi** vpr (Med) to have an operation; **operarsi d'appendicite** to have one's appendix out; **operazi'one** sf operation

ope'retta sf (Mus) operetta, light opera

opini'one sf opinion; **opinione pubblica** public opinion

'oppio sm opium

op'pongo ecc vb vedi **opporre**

op'porre vt to oppose; **opporsi** vpr **opporsi (a qc)** to oppose (sth); to object (to sth); **~ resistenza/un rifiuto** to offer resistance/refuse

opportu'nista, -i, -e sm/f opportunist

opportunità sf inv opportunity;

(*convenienza*) opportuneness, timeliness

oppor'tuno, -a *ag* timely, opportune

op'posi *ecc vb vedi* **opporre**

opposizi'one [oppozit'tsjone] *sf* opposition; (*Dir*) objection

op'posto, -a *pp di* **opporre** ▷ *ag* opposite; (*opinioni*) conflicting ▷ *sm* opposite, contrary; **all'~** on the contrary

oppressi'one *sf* oppression

oppri'mente *ag* (*caldo, noia*) oppressive; (*persona*) tiresome; (*deprimente*) depressing

op'primere *vt* (*premere, gravare*) to weigh down; (*estenuare: caldo*) to suffocate, oppress; (*tiranneggiare: popolo*) to oppress

op'pure *cong* or (else)

op'tare *vi*: **~ per** to opt for

o'puscolo *sm* booklet, pamphlet

opzi'one [op'tsjone] *sf* option

'ora *sf* (*60 minuti*) hour; (*momento*) time; **che ~ è?, che ore sono?** what time is it?; **a che ~ apre il museo/negozio?** what time does the museum/shop open?; **non veder l'~ di fare** to long to do, look forward to doing; **di buon'~** early; **alla buon'~!** at last!; **~ legale** *o* **estiva** summer time (*BRIT*), daylight saving time (*US*); **ora di cena** dinner time; **ora locale** local time; **ora di pranzo** lunchtime; **ora di punta** (*Aut*) rush hour

o'racolo *sm* oracle

o'rale *ag, sm* oral

o'rario, -a *ag* hourly; (*fuso, segnale*) time *cpd*; (*velocità*) per hour ▷ *sm* timetable, schedule; (*di ufficio, visite ecc*) hours *pl*, time(s *pl*); **in ~** on time

o'rata *sf* (*Zool*) sea bream

ora'tore, -'trice *sm/f* speaker; orator

'orbita *sf* (*Astr, Fisica*) orbit; (*Anat*) (eye-)socket

or'chestra [or'kɛstra] *sf* orchestra

orchi'dea [orki'dɛa] *sf* orchid

or'digno [or'diɲɲo] *sm* (*esplosivo*)

explosive device

ordi'nale *ag, sm* ordinal

ordi'nare *vt* (*mettere in ordine*) to arrange, organize; (*Comm*) to order; (*prescrivere: medicina*) to prescribe; (*comandare*): **posso ~ per favore?** can I order now please?; **~ a qn di fare qc** to order *o* command sb to do sth; (*Rel*) to ordain

ordi'nario, -a *ag* (*comune*) ordinary; everyday; standard; (*grossolano*) coarse, common ▷ *sm* ordinary; (*Ins: di università*) full professor

ordi'nato, -a *ag* tidy, orderly

ordinazi'one [ordinat'tsjone] *sf* (*Comm*) order; (*Rel*) ordination; **eseguire qc su ~** to make sth to order

'ordine *sm* order; (*carattere*): **d'~ pratico** of a practical nature; **all'~** (*Comm: assegno*) to order; **di prim'~** first-class; **fino a nuovo ~** until further notice; **essere in ~** (*documenti*) to be in order; (*stanza, persona*) to be tidy; **mettere in ~** to put in order, tidy (up); **l'~ pubblico** law and order; **ordini (sacri)** (*Rel*) holy orders; **ordine del giorno** (*di seduta*) agenda; (*Mil*) order of the day; **ordine di pagamento** (*Comm*) order for payment

orec'chino [orek'kino] *sm* earring

o'recchio [o'rekkjo] (*pl(f)* **o'recchie**) *sm* (*Anat*) ear

orecchi'oni [orek'kjoni] *smpl* (*Med*) mumps *sg*

o'refice [o'rɛfitʃe] *sm* goldsmith; jeweller; **orefice'ria** *sf* (*arte*) goldsmith's art; (*negozio*) jeweller's (shop)

'orfano, -a *ag* orphan(ed) ▷ *sm/f* orphan; **~ di padre/madre** fatherless/motherless

orga'netto *sm* barrel organ; (*fam: armonica a bocca*) mouth organ; (: *fisarmonica*) accordion

or'ganico, -a, -ci, -che *ag* organic ▷ *sm* personnel, staff

organi'gramma, -i sm organization chart

orga'nismo sm (Biol) organism; (corpo umano) body; (Amm) body, organism

organiz'zare [organid'dzare] vt to organize; **organizzarsi** vpr to get organized; **organizzazi'one** sf organization

'organo sm organ; (di congegno) part; (portavoce) spokesman, mouthpiece

'orgia, -ge ['ɔrdʒa] sf orgy

or'goglio [or'gɔʎʎo] sm pride; **orgogli'oso, -a** ag proud

orien'tale ag oriental; eastern; east

orienta'mento sm positioning; orientation; direction; **senso di ~** sense of direction; **perdere l'~** to lose one's bearings; **orientamento professionale** careers guidance

orientarsi vpr to find one's bearings; (fig: tendere) to tend, lean; (: indirizzarsi): **~ verso** to take up, go in for

ori'ente sm east; **l'O~** the East, the Orient; **a ~** in the east

o'rigano sm oregano

origi'nale [oridʒi'nale] ag original; (bizzarro) eccentric ⊳ sm original

origi'nario, -a [oridʒi'narjo] ag original; **essere ~ di** to be a native of; (provenire da) to originate from; to be native to

o'rigine [o'ridʒine] sf origin; **all'~** originally; **d'~ inglese** of English origin; **dare ~ a** to give rise to

origli'are [oriʎ'ʎare] vi **~ (a)** to eavesdrop (on)

o'rina sf urine

ori'nare vi to urinate ⊳ vt to pass

orizzon'tale [oriddzon'tale] ag horizontal

oriz'zonte [orid'dzonte] sm horizon

'orlo sm edge, border; (di recipiente) rim, brim; (di vestito ecc) hem

'orma sf (di persona) footprint; (di animale) track; (impronta, traccia)

mark, trace

or'mai av by now, by this time; (adesso) now; (quasi) almost, nearly

ormeggi'are [ormed'dʒare] vt (Naut) to moor

or'mone sm hormone

ornamen'tale ag ornamental, decorative

or'nare vt to adorn, decorate; **ornarsi** vpr **ornarsi (di)** to deck o.s. (out) (with)

ornitolo'gia [ornitolo'dʒia] sf ornithology

'oro sm gold; **d'~, in ~** gold cpd; **d'~** (colore, occasione) golden; (persona) marvellous

oro'logio [oro'lɔdʒo] sm clock; (da tasca, da polso) watch; **orologio al quarzo** quartz watch; **orologio da polso** wristwatch

o'roscopo sm horoscope

or'rendo, -a ag (spaventoso) horrible, awful; (bruttissimo) hideous

or'ribile ag horrible

or'rore sm horror; **avere in ~ qn/qc** to loathe o detest sb/sth; **mi fanno ~ I** loathe o detest them

orsacchi'otto [orsak'kjɔtto] sm teddy bear

'orso sm bear; **orso bruno/bianco** brown/polar bear

or'taggio [or'taddʒo] sm vegetable

or'tensia sf hydrangea

or'tica, -che sf (stinging) nettle

orti'caria sf nettle rash

'orto sm vegetable garden, kitchen garden; (Agr) market garden (BRIT), truck farm (US); **orto botanico** botanical garden(s) (pl)

orto'dosso, -a ag orthodox

ortogra'fia sf spelling

orto'pedico, -a, -ci, -che ag orthopaedic ⊳ sm orthopaedic specialist

orzai'olo [ordza'jɔlo] sm (Med) stye

'orzo ['ɔrdzo] sm barley

o'sare vt, vi to dare; **~ fare** to dare

(to) do

oscenità [oʃʃeni'ta] *sf inv* obscenity

o'sceno, -a [oʃʃeno] *ag* obscene; (*ripugnante*) ghastly

oscil'lare [oʃʃil'lare] *vi* (*pendolo*) to swing; (*dondolare: al vento ecc*) to rock; (*variare*) to fluctuate; (*Tecn*) to oscillate; (*fig*): **~ fra** to waver o hesitate between

oscu'rare *vt* to darken, obscure; (*fig*) to obscure; **oscurarsi** *vpr* (*cielo*) to darken, cloud over; (*persona*): **si oscurò in volto** his face clouded over

oscurità *sf* (*vedi ag*) darkness; obscurity

os'curo, -a *ag* dark; (*fig*) obscure; humble, lowly ▷ *sm* **all'~** in the dark; **tenere qn all'~ di qc** to keep sb in the dark about sth

ospe'dale *sm* hospital; **dov'è l'~ più vicino?** where's the nearest hospital?

ospi'tale *ag* hospitable

ospi'tare *vt* to give hospitality to; (*albergo*) to accommodate

'ospite *sm/f* (*persona che ospita*) host/hostess; (*persona ospitata*) guest

os'pizio [os'pittsjo] *sm* (*per vecchi ecc*) home

osser'vare *vt* to observe, watch; (*esaminare*) to examine; (*notare, rilevare*) to notice, observe; (*Dir: la legge*) to observe, respect; (*mantenere: silenzio*) to keep, observe; **far ~ qc a qn** to point sth out to sb; **osservazi'one** *sf* observation; (*di legge ecc*) observance; (*considerazione critica*) observation, remark; (*rimprovero*) reproof; **in osservazione** under observation

ossessio'nare *vt* to obsess, haunt; (*tormentare*) to torment, harass

ossessi'one *sf* obsession

os'sia *cong* that is, to be precise

'ossido *sm* oxide; **ossido di carbonio** carbon monoxide

ossige'nare [ossidʒe'nare] *vt* to oxygenate; (*decolorare*) to bleach;

acqua ossigenata hydrogen peroxide

os'sigeno *sm* oxygen

'osso (*pl(f)* **ossa**) *sm* bone; **d'~** (*bottone ecc*) of bone, bone *cpd*; **osso di seppia** cuttlebone

ostaco'lare *vt* to block, obstruct

os'tacolo *sm* obstacle; (*Equitazione*) hurdle, jump

os'taggio [os'taddʒo] *sm* hostage

os'tello *sm*: **~ della gioventù** youth hostel

osten'tare *vt* to make a show of, flaunt

oste'ria *sf* inn

os'tetrico, -a, -ci, -che *ag* obstetric ▷ *sm* obstetrician

'ostia *sf* (*Rel*) host; (*per medicinali*) wafer

'ostico, -a, -ci, -che *ag* (*fig*) harsh; hard, difficult; unpleasant

os'tile *ag* hostile

osti'narsi *vpr* to insist, dig one's heels in; **~ a fare** to persist (obstinately) in doing; **osti'nato, -a** *ag* (*caparbio*) obstinate; (*tenace*) persistent, determined

'ostrica, -che *sf* oyster

> Attenzione! In inglese esiste la parola *ostrich*, che però significa *struzzo*.

ostru'ire *vt* to obstruct, block

o'tite *sf* ear infection

ot'tanta *num* eighty

ot'tavo, -a *num* eighth

otte'nere *vt* to obtain, get; (*risultato*) to achieve, obtain

'ottica *sf* (*scienza*) optics *sg*; (*Fot: lenti, prismi ecc*) optics *pl*

'ottico, -a, -ci, -che *ag* (*della vista: nervo*) optic; (*dell'ottica*) optical ▷ *sm* optician

ottima'mente *av* excellently, very well

otti'mismo *sm* optimism; **otti'mista, -i, -e** *sm/f* optimist

'ottimo, -a *ag* excellent, very good

'otto *num* eight

ot'tobre *sm* October

otto'cento [otto't∫εnto] *num* eight hundred ▷ *sm* **l'O~** the nineteenth century

ot'tone *sm* brass; **gli ottoni** (*Mus*) the brass

ottu'rare *vt* to close (up); (*dente*) to fill; **il lavandino è otturato** the sink is blocked; **otturarsi** *vpr* to become *o* get blocked up; **otturazi'one** *sf* closing (up); (*dentaria*) filling

ot'tuso, -a *ag* (*Mat, fig*) obtuse; (*suono*) dull

o'vaia *sf* (*Anat*) ovary

o'vale *ag, sm* oval

o'vatta *sf* cotton wool; (*per imbottire*) padding, wadding

'ovest *sm* west

o'vile *sm* pen, enclosure

ovulazi'one [ovulat'tsjone] *sf* ovulation

'ovulo *sm* (*Fisiol*) ovum

o'vunque *av* = **dovunque**

ovvi'are *vi* **~ a** to obviate

'ovvio, -a *ag* obvious

ozi'are [ot'tsjare] *vi* to laze, idle

'ozio ['ɔttsjo] *sm* idleness; (*tempo libero*) leisure; **ore d'~** leisure time; **stare in ~** to be idle

o'zono [o'dzɔno] *sm* ozone

p

P *abbr* (= *parcheggio*) P; (*Aut*: = *principiante*) L

p. *abbr* (= *pagina*) p.

pac'chetto [pak'ketto] *sm* packet; **pacchetto azionario** (*Comm*) shareholding

'pacco, -chi *sm* parcel; (*involto*) bundle; **pacco postale** parcel

'pace ['pat∫e] *sf* peace; **darsi ~** to resign o.s.; **fare la ~ con** to make it up with

pa'cifico, -a, -ci, -che [pa't∫i:fiko] *ag* (*persona*) peaceable; (*vita*) peaceful; (*fig: indiscusso*) indisputable; (: *ovvio*) obvious, clear ▷ *sm* **il P~, l'Oceano P~** the Pacific (Ocean)

paci'fista, -i, -e [pat∫i'fista] *sm/f* pacifist

PACS *sigla mpl* civil partnership

pa'della *sf* frying pan; (*per infermi*) bedpan

padigli'one [padiʎ'ʎone] *sm* pavilion

'Padova *sf* Padua

'padre *sm* father

pa'drino sm godfather

padro'nanza [padro'nantsa] sf command, mastery

pa'drone, -a sm/f master/mistress; (proprietario) owner; (datore di lavoro) employer; **essere ~ di sé** to be in control of o.s.; **padrone(a) di casa** master/mistress of the house; (per gli inquilini) landlord/lady

pae'saggio [pae'zaddʒo] sm landscape

pa'ese sm (nazione) country, nation; (terra) country, land; (villaggio) village, (small) town; **i Paesi Bassi** the Netherlands; **paese di provenienza** country of origin

'paga, -ghe sf pay, wages pl

paga'mento sm payment

pa'gare vt to pay; (acquisto, fig: colpa) to pay for; (contraccambiare) to repay, pay back ▷ vi to pay; **quanto l'hai pagato?** how much did you pay for it?; **posso ~ con la carta di credito?** can I pay by credit card?; **~ in contanti** to pay cash

pa'gella [pa'dʒɛlla] sf (Ins) report card

pagherò [page'rɔ] sm inv acknowledgement of a debt, IOU

'pagina ['padʒina] sf page; **pagine bianche** phone book, telephone directory; **pagine gialle** Yellow Pages

'paglia ['paʎʎa] sf straw

pagli'accio [paʎ'ʎattʃo] sm clown

pagli'etta [paʎ'ʎetta] sf (cappello per uomo) (straw) boater; (per tegami ecc) steel wool

pa'gnotta [paɲ'ɲɔtta] sf round loaf

'paio (pl(f) **'paia**) sm pair; **un ~ di** (alcuni) a couple of

'Pakistan sm **il ~** Pakistan

'pala sf shovel; (di remo, ventilatore, elica) blade; (di ruota) paddle

pa'lato sm palate

pa'lazzo [pa'lattso] sm (reggia) palace; (edificio) building; **palazzo di giustizia** courthouse; **palazzo dello sport** sports stadium

'palco, -chi sm (Teatro) box; (tavolato) platform, stand; (ripiano) layer

palco'scenico, -ci [palkoʃ'ʃeniko] sm (Teatro) stage

pa'lese ag clear, evident

Pales'tina sf **la ~** Palestine

palesti'nese ag, sm/f Palestinian

pa'lestra sf gymnasium; (esercizio atletico) exercise, training; (fig) training ground, school

pa'letta sf spade; (per il focolare) shovel; (del capostazione) signalling disc

pa'letto sm stake, peg; (spranga) bolt

'palio sm (gara): **il P~** horse race run at Siena; **mettere qc in ~** to offer sth as a prize

● **PALIO**
●
●
● The **palio** is a horse race which
● takes place in a number of Italian
● towns, the most famous being
● the one in Siena. This is usually
● held twice a year on July 2nd
● and August 16th in the Piazza
● del Campo in Siena. 10 of the 17
● **contrade** or districts take part,
● each represented by a horse and
● rider. The winner is the first horse
● to complete the course, whether it
● has a rider or not.

'palla sf ball; (pallottola) bullet; **palla di neve** snowball; **palla ovale** rugby ball; **pallaca'nestro** sf basketball; **palla'mano** sf handball; **pallanu'oto** sf water polo; **palla'volo** sf volleyball

palleggi'are [palled'dʒare] vi (Calcio) to practise with the ball; (Tennis) to knock up

pallia'tivo sm palliative; (fig) stopgap measure

'pallido, -a ag pale

pal'lina sf (bilia) marble

pallon'cino [pallon'tʃino] sm

balloon; (*lampioncino*) Chinese lantern

pal'lone *sm* (*palla*) ball; (*Calcio*) football; (*aerostato*) balloon; **gioco del ~** football

pal'lottola *sf* pellet; (*proiettile*) bullet

'**palma** *sf* (*Anat*) = **palmo**; (*Bot, simbolo*) palm; **palma da datteri** date palm

'**palmo** *sm* (*Anat*) palm; **restare con un ~ di naso** to be badly disappointed

'**palo** *sm* (*legno appuntito*) stake; (*sostegno*) pole; **fare da *o* il ~** (*fig*) to act as look-out

palom'baro *sm* diver

pal'pare *vt* to feel, finger

'**palpebra** *sf* eyelid

pa'lude *sf* marsh, swamp

pan'cetta [pan'tʃetta] *sf* (*Cuc*) bacon

pan'china [pan'kina] *sf* garden seat; (*di giardino pubblico*) (park) bench

'**pancia, -ce** ['pantʃa] *sf* belly, stomach; **mettere *o* fare ~** to be getting a paunch; **avere mal di ~** to have stomachache *o* a sore stomach

panci'otto [pan'tʃɔtto] *sm* waistcoat

'**pancreas** *sm inv* pancreas

'**panda** *sm inv* panda

pande'mia *sf* pandemic

'**pane** *sm* bread; (*pagnotta*) loaf (of bread); (*forma*) **un ~ di burro** a pat of butter; **guadagnarsi il ~** to earn one's living; **pane a cassetta** sliced bread; **pane di Spagna** sponge cake; **pane integrale** wholemeal bread; **pane tostato** toast

panette'ria *sf* (*forno*) bakery; (*negozio*) baker's (shop), bakery

panetti'ere, -a *sm/f* baker

panet'tone *sm a kind of spiced brioche with sultanas, eaten at Christmas*

pangrat'tato *sm* breadcrumbs *pl*

'**panico, -a, -ci, -che** *ag, sm* panic

pani'ere *sm* basket

pani'ficio [pani'fitʃo] *sm* (*forno*) bakery; (*negozio*) baker's (shop), bakery

pa'nino *sm* roll; **panino caldo** toasted sandwich; **panino imbottito** filled roll; sandwich

'**panna** *sf* (*Cuc*) cream; (*Tecn*) = **panne**; **panna da cucina** cooking cream; **panna montata** whipped cream

'**panne** *sf inv*: **essere in ~** (*Aut*) to have broken down

pan'nello *sm* panel; **pannello solare** solar panel

'**panno** *sm* cloth; **panni** *smpl* (*abiti*) clothes; **mettiti nei miei panni** (*fig*) put yourself in my shoes

pan'nocchia [pan'nɔkkja] *sf* (*di mais ecc*) ear

panno'lino *sm* (*per bambini*) nappy (*BRIT*), diaper (*US*)

panno'lone *sm* incontinence pad

pano'rama, -i *sm* panorama

panta'loni *smpl* trousers (*BRIT*), pants (*US*), pair *sg*, of trousers *o* pants

pan'tano *sm* bog

pan'tera *sf* panther

pan'tofola *sf* slipper

'**Papa, -i** *sm* pope

papà *sm inv* dad(dy)

pa'pavero *sm* poppy

'**pappa** *sf* baby cereal; **pappa reale** royal jelly

pappa'gallo *sm* parrot; (*fig: uomo*) Romeo, wolf

pa'rabola *sf* (*Mat*) parabola; (*Rel*) parable

para'bolico, -a, ci, che *ag* (*Mat*) parabolic; *vedi anche* **antenna**

para'brezza [para'breddza] *sm inv* (*Aut*) windscreen (*BRIT*), windshield (*US*)

paraca'dute *sm inv* parachute

para'diso *sm* paradise

parados'sale *ag* paradoxical

para'fulmine *sm* lightning conductor

pa'raggi [pa'raddʒi] *smpl*: **nei ~** in the vicinity, in the neighbourhood

parago'nare *vt*: **~ con/a** to compare

with/to

para'gone sm comparison; (esempio analogo) analogy, parallel; **reggere al ~** to stand comparison

pa'ragrafo sm paragraph

pa'ralisi sf paralysis

paral'lelo, -a ag parallel ▷ sm (Geo) parallel; (comparazione): **fare un ~ tra** to draw a parallel between

para'lume sm lampshade

pa'rametro sm parameter

para'noia paranoia; **para'noico, -a, -ci, -che** ag, sm/f paranoid

para'occhi [para'ɔkki] smpl blinkers

paraolim'piadi sfpl paralympics

para'petto sm balustrade

pa'rare vt (addobbare) to adorn, deck; (proteggere) to shield, protect; (scansare: colpo) to parry; (Calcio) to save ▷ vi **dove vuole andare a ~?** what are you driving at?

pa'rata sf (Sport) save; (Mil) review, parade

para'urti sm inv (Aut) bumper

para'vento sm folding screen; **fare da ~ a qn** (fig) to shield sb

par'cella [par'tʃɛlla] sf account, fee (of lawyer etc)

parcheggi'are [parked'dʒare] vt to park; **posso ~ qui?** can I park here?; **parcheggiatore, -trice** [parkedd3a'tore] sm/f (Aut) parking attendant

par'cheggio sm parking no pl; (luogo) car park; (singolo posto) parking space

par'chimetro [par'kimetro] sm parking meter

'parco, -chi sm park; (spazio per deposito) depot; (complesso di veicoli) fleet

par'cometro sm (pay-and-display) ticket machine

pa'recchio, -a [pa'rekkjo] det quite a lot of; (tempo) quite a lot of, a long

pareggi'are [pared'dʒare] vt to make equal; (terreno) to level, make

level; (bilancio, conti) to balance ▷ vi (Sport) to draw; **pa'reggio** sm (Econ) balance; (Sport) draw

pa'rente sm/f relative, relation

⚠️ Attenzione! In inglese esiste la parola parent, che però significa genitore.

paren'tela sf (vincolo di sangue, fig) relationship

pa'rentesi sf (segno grafico) bracket, parenthesis; (frase incisa) parenthesis; (digressione) parenthesis, digression

pa'rere sm (opinione) opinion; (consiglio) advice, opinion; **a mio ~ in** my opinion ▷ vi to seem, appear ▷ vb impers **pare che** it seems o appears that, they say that; **mi pare che** it seems to me that; **mi pare di sì** I think so; **fai come ti pare** do as you like; **che ti pare del mio libro?** what do you think of my book?

pa'rete sf wall

'pari ag inv (uguale) equal, same; (in giochi) equal; drawn, tied; (Mat) even ▷ sm inv (Pol: di Gran Bretagna) peer ▷ sm/f inv peer, equal; **copiato ~ ~** copied word for word; **alla ~** on the same level; **ragazza alla ~** au pair girl; **mettersi alla ~ con** to place o.s. on the same level as; **mettersi in ~ con** to catch up with; **andare di ~ passo con qn** to keep pace with sb

Pa'rigi [pa'ridʒi] sf Paris

pari'gino, -a [pari'dʒino] ag, sm/f Parisian

parità sf parity, equality; (Sport) draw, tie

parlamen'tare ag parliamentary ▷ sm/f ≈ Member of Parliament (BRIT), ≈ Congressman/woman (US) ▷ vi to negotiate, parley

parla'mento sm parliament

⬤ **PARLAMENTO**
⬤
⬤ The Italian **Parlamento** is made
⬤ up of two chambers, the **Camera**

● **dei deputati** and the **Senato**.
● Parliamentary elections are held
● every 5 years.

parlan'tina *(fam)* sf talkativeness;
avere ~ to have the gift of the gab

par'lare vi to speak, talk; *(confidare
cose segrete)* to talk ▷ vt to speak; **~ (a
qn) di** to speak o talk (to sb) about;
posso ~ con...? can I speak to ...?;
parla italiano? do you speak Italian?;
non parlo inglese I don't speak
English

parmigi'ano [parmi'dʒano] sm
(grana) Parmesan (cheese)

pa'rola sf word; *(facoltà)* speech;
parole sfpl *(chiacchiere)* talk sg;
chiedere la ~ to ask permission to
speak; **prendere la ~** to take the floor;
parola d'onore word of honour;
parola d'ordine *(Mil)* password;
parole incrociate crossword (puzzle)
sg; **paro'laccia, -ce** sf bad word,
swearword

parrò ecc vb vedi **parere**

par'rocchia [par'rɔkkja] sf parish;
parish church

par'rucca, -che sf wig

parrucchi'ere, -a [parruk'kjɛre]
sm/f hairdresser ▷ sm barber

'parte sf part; *(lato)* side; *(quota
spettante a ciascuno)* share; *(direzione)*
direction; *(Pol)* party; faction;
(Dir) party; **a ~** ag separate ▷ av
separately; **scherzi a ~** joking aside;
a ~ ciò apart from that; **da ~** *(in
disparte)* to one side, aside; **d'altra ~**
on the other hand; **da ~ di** *(per conto
di)* on behalf of; **da ~ mia** as far as
I'm concerned, as for me; **da ~ a ~**
right through; **da ogni ~** on all sides,
everywhere; *(moto da luogo)* from all
sides; **da nessuna ~** nowhere; **da
questa ~** *(in questa direzione)* this way;
prendere ~ a qc to take part in sth;
mettere da ~ to put aside; **mettere
qn a ~ di** to inform sb of

parteci'pare [partetʃi'pare] vi **~ a** to
take part in, participate in; *(utili ecc)*
to share in; *(spese ecc)* to contribute to;
(dolore, successo di qn) to share (in)

parteggi'are [parted'dʒare] vi: **~ per**
to side with, be on the side of

par'tenza [par'tɛntsa] sf departure;
(Sport) start; **essere in ~** to be about
to leave, be leaving

parti'cipio [parti'tʃipjo] sm participle

partico'lare ag *(specifico)* particular;
(proprio) personal, private; *(speciale)*
special, particular; *(caratteristico)*
distinctive, characteristic; *(fuori
dal comune)* peculiar ▷ sm detail,
particular; **in ~** in particular,
particularly

par'tire vi to go, leave; *(allontanarsi)*
to go (o drive ecc) away o off; *(petardo,
colpo)* to go off; *(fig: avere inizio, Sport)*
to start; **sono partita da Roma alle
7** I left Rome at 7; **a che ora parte il
treno/l'autobus?** what time does
the train/bus leave?; **il volo parte
da Ciampino** the flight leaves from
Ciampino; **a ~ da** from

par'tita sf *(Comm)* lot, consignment;
(Econ: registrazione) entry, item; *(Carte,
Sport: gioco)* game; *(: competizione)*
match, game; **partita di caccia**
hunting party; **partita IVA** VAT
registration number

par'tito sm *(Pol)* party; *(decisione)*
decision, resolution; *(persona da
maritare)* match

'parto sm *(Med)* delivery, (child)birth;
labour

'parvi ecc vb vedi **parere**

parzi'ale [par'tsjale] ag *(limitato)*
partial; *(non obiettivo)* biased, partial

pasco'lare vt, vi to graze

'pascolo sm pasture

'Pasqua sf Easter; **Pas'quetta** sf
Easter Monday

pas'sabile ag fairly good, passable

pas'saggio [pas'saddʒo] sm passing
no pl, passage; *(traversata)* crossing

no pl, passage; (*luogo, prezzo della traversata, brano di libro ecc*) passage; (*su veicolo altrui*) lift (BRIT), ride; (*Sport*) pass; **di ~** (*persona*) passing through; **può darmi un ~ fino alla stazione?** can you give me a lift to the station?; **passaggio a livello** level (BRIT) o grade (US) crossing; **passaggio pedonale** pedestrian crossing

passamon'tagna [passamon'taɲɲa] *sm inv* balaclava

pas'sante *sm/f* passer-by ▷ *sm* loop

passa'porto *sm* passport

pas'sare *vi* (*andare*) to go; (*veicolo, pedone*) to pass (by), go by; (*fare una breve sosta: postino ecc*) to come, call; (*: amico: per fare una visita*) to call o drop in; (*sole, aria, luce*) to get through; (*trascorrere: giorni, tempo*) to pass, go by; (*fig: proposta di legge*) to be passed; (*: dolore*) to pass, go away; (*Carte*) to pass ▷ *vt* (*attraversare*) to cross; (*trasmettere: messaggio*): **~ qc a qn** to pass sth on to sb; (*dare*): **~ qc a qn** to pass sth to sb, give sb sth; (*trascorrere: tempo*) to spend; (*superare: esame*) to pass; (*triturare: verdura*) to strain; (*approvare*) to pass, approve; (*oltrepassare, sorpassare: anche fig*) to go beyond, pass; (*fig: subire*) to go through; **mi passa il sale/l'olio per favore?** could you pass the salt/oil please?; **~ da ... a** to pass from ... to; **~ di padre in figlio** to be handed down o to pass from father to son; **~ per** (*anche fig*) to go through; **~ per stupido/un genio** to be taken for a fool/a genius; **~ sopra** (*anche fig*) to pass over; **~ attraverso** (*anche fig*) to go through; **~ alla storia** to pass into history; **~ a un esame** to go up (to the next class) after an exam; **~ inosservato** to go unnoticed; **~ di moda** to go out of fashion; **le passo il Signor X** (*al telefono*) here is Mr X; I'm putting you through to Mr X; **lasciar ~ qn/qc** to let sb/sth through; **come**

te la passi? how are you getting on o along?

passa'tempo *sm* pastime, hobby

pas'sato, -a *ag* past; (*sfiorito*) faded ▷ *sm* past; (*Ling*) past (tense); **passato prossimo/remoto** (*Ling*) present perfect/past historic; **passato di verdura** (*Cuc*) vegetable purée

passeg'gero, -a [passed'dʒero] *ag* passing ▷ *sm/f* passenger

passeggi'are [passed'dʒare] *vi* to go for a walk; (*in veicolo*) to go for a drive; **passeggi'ata** *sf* walk; drive; (*luogo*) promenade; **fare una passeggiata** to go for a walk (o drive); **passeg'gino** *sm* pushchair (BRIT), stroller (US)

passe'rella *sf* footbridge; (*di nave, aereo*) gangway; (*pedana*) catwalk

'passero *sm* sparrow

passi'one *sf* passion

pas'sivo, -a *ag* passive ▷ *sm* (*Ling*) passive; (*Econ*) debit; (*: complesso dei debiti*) liabilities *pl*

'passo *sm* step; (*andatura*) pace; (*rumore*) (foot)step; (*orma*) footprint; (*passaggio, fig: brano*) passage; (*valico*) pass; **a ~ d'uomo** at walking pace; **~ (a) ~** step by step; **fare due o quattro passi** to go for a walk o a stroll; **di questo ~** at this rate; **"passo carraio"** "vehicle entrance — keep clear"

'pasta *sf* (*Cuc*) dough; (: *impasto per dolce*) pastry; (: *anche: ~ alimentare*) pasta; (*massa molle di materia*) paste; (*fig: indole*) nature; **paste** *sfpl* (*pasticcini*) pastries; **pasta in brodo** noodle soup; **pasta sfoglia** puff pastry o paste (US)

pastasci'utta [pastaʃʃutta] *sf* pasta

pas'tella *sf* batter

pas'tello *sm* pastel

pasticce'ria [pastittʃe'ria] *sf* (*pasticcini*) pastries *pl*, cakes *pl*; (*negozio*) cake shop; (*arte*) confectionery

pasticci'ere, -a [pastit'tʃere] *sm/f* pastrycook; confectioner

pastic'cino [pastit'tʃino] *sm* petit four

pas'ticcio [pas'tittʃo] *sm* (*Cuc*) pie; (*lavoro disordinato, imbroglio*) mess; **trovarsi nei pasticci** to get into trouble

pas'tiglia [pas'tiʎʎa] *sf* pastille, lozenge

pas'tina *sf* small pasta shapes used in soup

'pasto *sm* meal

pas'tore *sm* shepherd; (*Rel*) pastor, minister; (*anche:* **cane ~**) sheepdog; **pastore tedesco** (*Zool*) Alsatian, German shepherd

pa'tata *sf* potato; **patate fritte** chips (*BRIT*), French fries; **pata'tine** *sfpl* (*potato*) crisps; **patatine fritte** chips

pa'tente *sf* licence; **patente di guida** driving licence (*BRIT*), driver's license (*US*); **patente a punti** *driving licence with penalty points*

> Attenzione! In inglese esiste la parola *patent*, che però significa *brevetto*.

paternità *sf* paternity, fatherhood

pa'tetico, -a, -ci, -che *ag* pathetic; (*commovente*) moving, touching

pa'tibolo *sm* gallows *sg*, scaffold

'patina *sf* (*su rame ecc*) patina; (*sulla lingua*) fur, coating

pa'tire *vt, vi* to suffer

pa'tito, -a *sm/f* enthusiast, fan, lover

patolo'gia [patolo'dʒia] *sf* pathology

'patria *sf* homeland

pa'trigno [pa'triɲɲo] *sm* stepfather

patri'monio *sm* estate, property; (*fig*) heritage

pa'trono *sm* (*Rel*) patron saint; (*socio di patronato*) patron; (*Dir*) counsel

patteggi'are [patted'dʒare] *vt, vi* to negotiate; (*Dir*) to plea-bargain

patti'naggio [patti'naddʒo] *sm* skating; **pattinaggio a rotelle/sul ghiaccio** roller-/ice-skating

patti'nare *vi* to skate; **~ sul ghiaccio** to ice-skate; **pattina'tore, -'trice**

sm/f skater; **'pattino** *sm* skate; (*di slitta*) runner; (*Aer*) skid; (*Tecn*) sliding block; **pattini in linea** Rollerblades®; **pattini da ghiaccio/a rotelle** ice/roller skates

'patto *sm* (*accordo*) pact, agreement; (*condizione*) term, condition; **a ~ che** on condition that

pat'tuglia [pat'tuʎʎa] *sf* (*Mil*) patrol

pattu'ire *vt* to reach an agreement on

pattumi'era *sf* (dust)bin (*BRIT*), ashcan (*US*)

pa'ura *sf* fear; **aver ~ di/di fare/che** to be frightened *o* afraid of/of doing/that; **far ~ a** to frighten; **per ~ di/che** for fear of/that; **pau'roso, -a** *ag* (*che fa paura*) frightening; (*che ha paura*) fearful, timorous

'pausa *sf* (*sosta*) break; (*nel parlare, Mus*) pause

pavi'mento *sm* floor

> Attenzione! In inglese esiste la parola *pavement*, che però significa *marciapiede*.

pa'vone *sm* peacock

pazien'tare [pattsjen'tare] *vi* to be patient

pazi'ente [pat'tsjɛnte] *ag, sm/f* patient; **pazi'enza** *sf* patience

paz'zesco, -a, -schi, -sche [pat'tsesko] *ag* mad, crazy

paz'zia [pat'tsia] *sf* (*Med*) madness, insanity; (*azione*) folly; (*di azione, decisione*) madness, folly

'pazzo, -a ['pattso] *ag* (*Med*) mad, insane; (*strano*) wild, mad ▷ *sm/f* madman/woman; **~ di** (*gioia, amore ecc*) mad *o* crazy with; **~ per qc/qn** mad *o* crazy about sth/sb

PC [pit'tʃi] *sigla m inv* (= *personal computer*) PC; **PC portatile** laptop

pec'care *vi* to sin; (*fig*) to err

pec'cato *sm* sin; **è un ~ che** it's a pity that; **che ~!** what a shame *o* pity!

pecche'rò *ecc* [pekke'rɔ] *vb vedi* peccare

'pece ['petʃe] *sf* pitch

Pe'chino [pe'kino] *sf* Beijing
'pecora *sf* sheep; **peco'rino** *sm* sheep's milk cheese
pe'daggio [pe'daddʒo] *sm* toll
pedago'gia [pedago'dʒia] *sf* pedagogy, educational methods *pl*
peda'lare *vi* to pedal; *(andare in bicicletta)* to cycle
pe'dale *sm* pedal
pe'dana *sf* footboard; *(Sport: nel salto)* springboard; *(: nella scherma)* piste
pe'dante *ag* pedantic ▷ *sm/f* pedant
pe'data *sf (impronta)* footprint; *(colpo)* kick; **prendere a pedate qn/qc** to kick sb/sth
pedi'atra, -i, -e *sm/f* paediatrician
pedi'cure *sm/f inv* chiropodist
pe'dina *sf (della dama)* draughtsman (BRIT), draftsman (US); *(fig)* pawn
pedi'nare *vt* to shadow, tail
pe'dofilo, -a *ag, sm/f* paedophile
pedo'nale *ag* pedestrian
pe'done, -a *sm/f* pedestrian ▷ *sm (Scacchi)* pawn
'peggio ['pɛddʒo] *av, ag inv* worse ▷ *sm of:* **il o la ~** the worst; **alla ~** at worst, if the worst comes to the worst; **peggio'rare** *vt* to make worse, worsen ▷ *vi* to grow worse, worsen; **peggi'ore** *ag (comparativo)* worse; *(superlativo)* worst ▷ *sm/f:* **il(la) peggiore** the worst (person)
'pegno ['peɲɲo] *sm (Dir)* security, pledge; *(nei giochi di società)* forfeit; *(fig)* pledge, token; **dare in ~ qc** to pawn sth
pe'lare *vt (spennare)* to pluck; *(spellare)* to skin; *(sbucciare)* to peel; *(fig)* to make pay through the nose
pe'lato, -a *ag:* **pomodori pelati** tinned tomatoes
'pelle *sf* skin; *(di animale)* skin, hide; *(cuoio)* leather; **avere la ~ d'oca** to have goose pimples *o* goose flesh
pellegri'naggio [pellegri'naddʒo] *sm* pilgrimage

pelle'rossa *(pl* **pelli'rosse)** *sm/f* Red Indian
pelli'cano *sm* pelican
pel'liccia, -ce [pel'littʃa] *sf (mantello di animale)* coat, fur; *(indumento)* fur coat; **pelliccia ecologica** fake fur
pel'licola *sf (membrana sottile)* film, layer; *(Fot, Cinema)* film
'pelo *sm* hair; *(pelame)* coat, hair; *(pelliccia)* fur; *(di tappeto)* pile; *(di liquido)* surface; **per un ~: per un ~ non ho perduto il treno** I very nearly missed the train; **c'è mancato un ~ che affogasse** he escaped drowning by the skin of his teeth; **pe'loso, -a** *ag* hairy
'peltro *sm* pewter
pe'luche [pə'lyʃ] *sm* plush; **giocattoli di ~** soft toys
pe'luria *sf* down
'pena *sf (Dir)* sentence; *(punizione)* punishment; *(sofferenza)* sadness *no pl,* sorrow; *(fatica)* trouble *no pl,* effort; *(difficoltà)* difficulty; **far ~** to be pitiful; **mi fai ~** I feel sorry for you; **prendersi o darsi la ~ di fare** to go to the trouble of doing; **pena di morte** death sentence; **pena pecuniaria** fine; **pe'nale** *ag* penal
pen'dente *ag* hanging; leaning ▷ *sm (ciondolo)* pendant; *(orecchino)* drop earring
'pendere *vi (essere appeso):* **~ da** to hang from; *(essere inclinato)* to lean; *(fig: incombere):* **~ su** to hang over
pen'dio, -'dii *sm* slope, slant; *(luogo in pendenza)* slope
'pendola *sf* pendulum clock
pendo'lare *sm/f* commuter
pendo'lino *sm* high-speed train
pene'trante *ag* piercing, penetrating
pene'trare *vi* to come *o* get in ▷ *vt* to penetrate; **~ in** to enter; *(proiettile)* to penetrate; *(: acqua, aria)* to go *o* come into
penicil'lina [penitʃil'lina] *sf*

penicillin

pe'nisola sf peninsula

penitenzi'ario [peniten'tsjarjo] sm
prison

'penna sf (di uccello) feather; (per
scrivere) pen; **penne** sfpl (Cuc) quills
(type of pasta); **penna a sfera**
ballpoint pen; **penna stilografica**
fountain pen

penna'rello sm felt(-tip) pen

pen'nello sm brush; (per dipingere)
(paint)brush; **a ~** (perfettamente) to
perfection, perfectly; **pennello per la
barba** shaving brush

pe'nombra sf half-light, dim light

pen'sare vi to think ▷ vt to think;
(inventare, escogitare) to think out; **~ a**
to think of; (amico, vacanze) to think of
o about; (problema) to think about; **~ di
fare qc** to think of doing sth; **ci penso
io** I'll see to o take care of it

pensi'ero sm thought; (modo di
pensare, dottrina) thinking no pl;
(preoccupazione) worry, care, trouble;
stare in ~ per qn to be worried about
sb; **pensie'roso, -a** ag thoughtful

'pensile ag hanging

pensio'nato, -a sm/f pensioner

pensi'one sf (al prestatore di lavoro)
pension; (vitto e alloggio) board and
lodging; (albergo) boarding house;
andare in ~ to retire; **mezza ~** half
board; **pensione completa** full board

pen'tirsi vpr **~ di** to repent of;
(rammaricarsi) to regret, be sorry for

'pentola sf pot; **pentola a pressione**
pressure cooker

pe'nultimo, -a ag last but one (BRIT),
next to last, penultimate

penzo'lare [pendzo'lare] vi to
dangle, hang loosely

'pepe sm pepper; **pepe in grani/
macinato** whole/ground pepper

peperon'cino [peperon'tʃino] sm
chilli pepper

pepe'rone sm pepper, capsicum;
(piccante) chili

pe'pita sf nugget

 PAROLA CHIAVE

per prep **1** (moto attraverso luogo)
through; **i ladri sono passati per
la finestra** the thieves got in (o out)
through the window; **l'ho cercato
per tutta la casa** I've searched the
whole house o all over the house for it
2 (moto a luogo) for, to; **partire per
la Germania/il mare** to leave for
Germany/the sea; **il treno per Roma**
the Rome train, the train for o to
Rome
3 (stato in luogo): **seduto/sdraiato
per terra** sitting/lying on the ground
4 (tempo) for; **per anni/lungo tempo**
for years/a long time; **per tutta
l'estate** throughout the summer, all
summer long; **lo rividi per Natale** I
saw him again at Christmas; **lo faccio
per lunedì** I'll do it for Monday
5 (mezzo, maniera) by; **per lettera/via
aerea/ferrovia** by letter/airmail/rail;
prendere qn per un braccio to take
sb by the arm
6 (causa, scopo) for; **assente per
malattia** absent because of o through
o owing to illness; **ottimo per il mal
di gola** excellent for sore throats
7 (limitazione) for; **è troppo difficile
per lui** it's too difficult for him; **per
quel che mi riguarda** as far as I'm
concerned; **per poco che sia** however
little it may be; **per questa volta ti
perdono** I'll forgive you this time
8 (prezzo, misura) for; (distributivo) a,
per; **venduto per 3 milioni** sold for 3
million; **1 euro per persona** 1 euro a
o per person; **uno per volta** one at a
time; **uno per uno** one by one; **5 per
cento** 5 per cent; **3 per 4 fa 12** 3 times
4 equals 12; **dividere/moltiplicare 12
per 4** to divide/multiply 12 by 4
9 (in qualità di) as; (al posto di) for;
avere qn per professore to have sb

as a teacher; **ti ho preso per Mario** I mistook you for Mario, I thought you were Mario; **dare per morto qn** to give sb up for dead

10 (seguito da vb: finale): **per fare qc** so as to do sth, in order to do sth; (: causale): **per aver fatto qc** for having done sth; (: consecutivo): **è abbastanza grande per andarci da solo** he's big enough to go on his own

'pera sf pear

per'bene ag inv respectable, decent ▷ av (con cura) properly, well

percentu'ale [pertʃentu'ale] sf percentage

perce'pire [pertʃe'pire] vt (sentire) to perceive; (ricevere) to receive

 PAROLA CHIAVE

perché [per'ke] av why; **perché no?** why not?; **perché non vuoi andarci?** why don't you want to go?; **spiegami perché l'hai fatto** tell me why you did it

▷ cong **1** (causale) because; **non posso uscire perché ho da fare** I can't go out because o as I've a lot to do

2 (finale) in order that, so that; **te lo do perché tu lo legga** I'm giving it to you so (that) you can read it

3 (consecutivo): **è troppo forte perché si possa batterlo** he's too strong to be beaten

▷ sm inv reason; **il perché di** the reason for

perciò [per'tʃɔ] cong so, for this (o that) reason

per'correre vt (luogo) to go all over; (: paese) to travel up and down, go all over; (distanza) to cover

per'corso, -a pp di **percorrere** ▷ sm (tragitto) journey; (tratto) route

percu'otere vt to hit, strike

percussi'one sf percussion;

strumenti a ~ (Mus) percussion instruments

'perdere vt to lose; (lasciarsi sfuggire) to miss; (sprecare: tempo, denaro) to waste ▷ vi to lose; (serbatoio ecc) to leak; **perdersi** vpr (smarrirsi) to get lost; (svanire) to disappear, vanish; **mi sono perso** I'm lost; **ho perso il portafoglio/passaporto** I've lost my wallet/passport; **abbiamo perso il treno** we missed our train; **saper ~** to be a good loser; **lascia ~!** forget it!, never mind!

perdigi'orno [perdi'dʒorno] sm/f idler, waster

'perdita sf loss; (spreco) waste; (fuoriuscita) leak; (Comm): **siamo in ~** we are running at a loss; **a ~ d'occhio** as far as the eye can see

perdo'nare vt to pardon, forgive; (scusare) to excuse, pardon

per'dono sm forgiveness; (Dir) pardon

perduta'mente av desperately, passionately

pe'renne ag eternal, perpetual, perennial; (Bot) perennial

perfetta'mente av perfectly; **sai ~ che ...** you know perfectly well that ...

per'fetto, -a ag perfect ▷ sm (Ling) perfect (tense)

perfeziona'mento [perfettsjona'mento] sm **~ (di)** improvement (in), perfection (of); **corso di ~** proficiency course

perfezio'nare [perfettsjo'nare] vt to improve, perfect; **perfezionarsi** vpr to improve

perfezi'one [perfet'tsjone] sf perfection

per'fino av even

perfo'rare vt to perforate, to punch a hole (o holes) in; (banda, schede) to punch; (trivellare) to drill

perga'mena sf parchment

perico'lante ag precarious

pe'ricolo sm danger; **mettere in ~** to endanger, put in danger;

perico'loso, -a *ag* dangerous

perife'ria *sf* (*di città*) outskirts *pl*

pe'rifrasi *sf* circumlocution

pe'rimetro *sm* perimeter

peri'odico, -a, -ci, -che *ag* periodic(al); (*Mat*) recurring ▷ *sm* periodical

pe'riodo *sm* period

peripe'zie [peripet'tsie] *sfpl* ups and downs, vicissitudes

pe'rito, -a *ag* expert, skilled ▷ *sm/f* expert; (*agronomo, navale*) surveyor; **perito chimico** qualified chemist

peri'zoma, -i [peri'dzoma] *sm* G-string

'perla *sf* pearl; **per'lina** *sf* bead

perlus'trare *vt* to patrol

perma'loso, -a *ag* touchy

perma'nente *ag* permanent ▷ *sf* permanent wave, perm; **perma'nenza** *sf* permanence; (*soggiorno*) stay

perme'are *vt* to permeate

per'messo, -a *pp di* **permettere** ▷ *sm* (*autorizzazione*) permission, leave; (*dato a militare, impiegato*) leave; (*licenza*) licence, permit; (*Mil: foglio*) pass; **~?, è ~?** (*posso entrare?*) may I come in?; (*posso passare?*) excuse me; **permesso di lavoro/pesca** work/fishing permit; **permesso di soggiorno** residence permit

per'mettere *vt* to allow, permit; **~ a qn qc/di fare qc** to allow sb sth/to do sth; **permettersi qc/di fare qc** to allow o.s. sth/to do sth; (*avere la possibilità*) to afford sth/to do sth

per'misi *ecc vb vedi* **permettere**

per'nacchia [per'nakkja] (*fam*) *sf* **fare una ~** to blow a raspberry

per'nice [per'nitʃe] *sf* partridge

'perno *sm* pivot

pernot'tare *vi* to spend the night, stay overnight

'pero *sm* pear tree

però *cong* (*ma*) but; (*tuttavia*) however, nevertheless

perpendico'lare *ag, sf* perpendicular

per'plesso, -a *ag* perplexed; uncertain, undecided

perqui'sire *vt* to search; **perquisizi'one** *sf* (*police*) search

'perse *ecc vb vedi* **perdere**

persecuzi'one [persekut'tsjone] *sf* persecution

persegui'tare *vt* to persecute

perseve'rante *ag* persevering

'persi *ecc vb vedi* **perdere**

persi'ana *sf* shutter; **persiana avvolgibile** roller shutter

per'sino *av* = **perfino**

persis'tente *ag* persistent

'perso, -a *pp di* **perdere**

per'sona *sf* person; (*qualcuno*): **una ~** someone, somebody; (*espressione interrogativa*) anyone *o* anybody

perso'naggio [perso'naddʒo] *sm* (*persona ragguardevole*) personality, figure; (*tipo*) character, individual; (*Letteratura*) character

perso'nale *ag* personal ▷ *sm* staff; personnel; (*figura fisica*) build

personalità *sf inv* personality

perspi'cace [perspi'katʃe] *ag* shrewd, discerning

persu'adere *vt*: **~ qn (di qc/a fare)** to persuade sb (of sth/to do)

per'tanto *cong* (*quindi*) so, therefore

'pertica, -che *sf* pole

perti'nente *ag* **~ (a)** relevant (to), pertinent (to)

per'tosse *sf* whooping cough

perturbazi'one [perturbat'tsjone] *sf* disruption; perturbation; **perturbazione atmosferica** atmospheric disturbance

per'vadere *vt* to pervade

per'verso, -a *ag* depraved; perverse

perver'tito, -a *sm/f* pervert

p.es. *abbr* (= *per esempio*) e.g.

pe'sante *ag* heavy; **è troppo ~** it's too heavy

pe'sare *vt* to weigh ▷ *vi* (*avere un peso*) to weigh; (*essere pesante*) to be heavy; *(fig)* to carry weight; **~ su** *(fig)* to lie heavy on; to influence; to hang over; **pesarsi** *vpr* to weigh o.s.; **~ le parole** to weigh one's words; **~ sulla coscienza** to weigh on sb's conscience; **mi pesa ammetterlo** I don't like admitting it; **tutta la responsabilità pesa su di lui** all the responsibility rests on him; **è una situazione che mi pesa** I find the situation difficult; **il suo parere pesa molto** his opinion counts for a lot

'pesca *(pl* **pesche:** *frutto)* *sf* peach; *(il pescare)* fishing; **andare a ~** to go fishing; **~ con la lenza** angling; **pesca di beneficenza** *(lotteria)* lucky dip

pes'care *vt (pesce)* to fish for; to catch; *(qc nell'acqua)* to fish out; *(fig: trovare)* to get hold of, find; **andare a ~** to go fishing

pesca'tore *sm* fisherman; angler

'pesce ['peʃʃe] *sm* fish *gen inv;* **Pesci** *(dello zodiaco)* Pisces; **pesce d'aprile!** April Fool!; **pesce rosso** goldfish; **pesce spada** swordfish; **pesce'cane** *sm* shark

pesche'reccio [peske'rettʃo] *sm* fishing boat

pesche'ria [peske'ria] *sf* fishmonger's (shop) *(BRIT)*, fish store *(US)*

pescherò *ecc* [peske'rɔ] *vb vedi* **pescare**

'peso *sm* weight; *(Sport)* shot; **rubare sul ~** to give short weight; **essere di ~ a qn** *(fig)* to be a burden to sb; **peso lordo/netto** gross/net weight; **peso massimo/medio** *(Pugilato)* heavy/middleweight

pessi'mismo *sm* pessimism; **pessi'mista, -i, -e** *ag* pessimistic ▷ *sm/f* pessimist

'pessimo, -a *ag* very bad, awful

pes'tare *vt* to tread on, trample on; *(sale, pepe)* to grind; *(uva, aglio)* to crush; *(fig: picchiare)*: **~ qn** to beat sb up

'peste *sf* plague; *(persona)* nuisance, pest

pes'tello *sm* pestle

'petalo *sm (Bot)* petal

pe'tardo *sm* firecracker, banger *(BRIT)*

petizi'one [petit'tsjone] *sf* petition

petroli'era *sf (nave)* oil tanker

pe'trolio *sm* oil, petroleum; *(per lampada, fornello)* paraffin

> Attenzione! In inglese esiste la parola *petrol* che però significa *benzina*.

pettego'lare *vi* to gossip

pettego'lezzo [pettego'leddzo] *sm* gossip *no pl;* **fare pettegolezzi** to gossip

pet'tegolo, -a *ag* gossipy ▷ *sm/f* gossip

petti'nare *vt* to comb (the hair of); **pettinarsi** *vpr* to comb one's hair; **pettina'tura** *sf (acconciatura)* hairstyle

'pettine *sm* comb; *(Zool)* scallop

petti'rosso *sm* robin

'petto *sm* chest; *(seno)* breast, bust; *(Cuc: di carne bovina)* brisket; *(: di pollo ecc)* breast; **a doppio ~** *(abito)* double-breasted

petu'lante *ag* insolent

'pezza ['pɛttsa] *sf* piece of cloth; *(toppa)* patch; *(cencio)* rag, cloth

pez'zente [pet'tsɛnte] *sm/f* beggar

'pezzo ['pɛttso] *sm (gen)* piece; *(brandello, frammento)* piece, bit; *(di macchina, arnese ecc)* part; *(Stampa)* article; *(di tempo)*: **aspettare un ~** to wait quite a while *o* some time; **in** *o* **a pezzi** in pieces; **andare in pezzi** to break into pieces; **un bel ~ d'uomo** a fine figure of a man; **abito a due pezzi** two-piece suit; **pezzo di cronaca** *(Stampa)* report; **pezzo grosso** *(fig)* bigwig; **pezzo di ricambio** spare part

pi'accio *ecc* ['pjattʃo] *vb vedi* **piacere**

pia'cente [pja'tʃɛnte] *ag* attractive

pia'cere [pja'tʃere] *vi* to please; **una ragazza che piace** a likeable girl;

an attractive girl; **~ a: mi piace** I like it; **quei ragazzi non mi piacciono** I don't like those boys; **gli piacerebbe andare al cinema** he would like to go to the cinema ▷ *sm* pleasure; (*favore*) favour; **"~!"** (*nelle presentazioni*) "pleased to meet you!"; **~ (di conoscerla)** nice to meet you; **con ~** certainly, with pleasure; **per ~!** please; **fare un ~ a qn** to do sb a favour; **pia'cevole** *ag* pleasant, agreeable

pi'acqui *ecc vb vedi* **piacere**

pi'aga, -ghe *sf* (*lesione*) sore; (*ferita: anche fig*) wound; (*fig: flagello*) scourge, curse; (: *persona*) pest, nuisance

piagnuco'lare [pjaɲɲuko'lare] *vi* to whimper

pianeggi'ante [pjaned'dʒante] *ag* flat, level

piane'rottolo *sm* landing

pia'neta *sm* (*Astr*) planet

pi'angere ['pjandʒere] *vi* to cry, weep; (*occhi*) to water ▷ *vt* to cry, weep; (*lamentare*) to bewail, lament; **~ la morte di qn** to mourn sb's death

pianifi'care *vt* to plan

pia'nista, -i, -e *sm/f* pianist

pi'ano, -a *ag* (*piatto*) flat, level; (*Mat*) plane; (*chiaro*) clear, plain ▷ *av* (*adagio*) slowly; (*a bassa voce*) softly; (*con cautela*) slowly, carefully ▷ *sm* (*Mat*) plane; (*Geo*) plain; (*livello*) level, plane; (*di edificio*) floor; (*programma*) plan; (*Mus*) piano; **a che ~ si trova?** what floor is it on?; **pian ~** very slowly; (*poco a poco*) little by little; **in primo/secondo ~** in the foreground/background; **di primo ~** (*fig*) prominent, high-ranking

piano'forte *sm* piano, pianoforte

piano'terra *sm inv* ground floor

pi'ansi *ecc vb vedi* **piangere**

pi'anta *sf* (*Bot*) plant; (*Anat: anche: ~ del piede*) sole (of the foot); (*grafico*) plan; (*topografica*) map; **in ~ stabile** on the permanent staff; **pian'tare** *vt* to plant; (*conficcare*) to drive *o* hammer in; (*tenda*) to put up, pitch; (*fig: lasciare*) to leave, desert; **piantarsi** *vpr* **piantarsi davanti a qn** to plant o.s. in front of sb; **piantala!** (*fam*) cut it out!

pianter'reno *sm* = **pianoterra**

pia'nura *sf* plain

pi'astra *sf* plate; (*di pietra*) slab; (*di fornello*) hotplate; **panino alla ~** ≈ toasted sandwich; **piastra di registrazione** tape deck

pias'trella *sf* tile

pias'trina *sf* (*Mil*) identity disc

piatta'forma *sf* (*anche fig*) platform

piat'tino *sm* saucer

pi'atto, -a *ag* flat; (*fig: scialbo*) dull ▷ *sm* (*recipiente, vivanda*) dish; (*portata*) course; (*parte piana*) flat (part); **piatti** *smpl* (*Mus*) cymbals; **piatto fondo** soup dish; **piatto forte** main course; **piatto del giorno** dish of the day, plat du jour; **piatto del giradischi** turntable; **piatto piano** dinner plate

pi'azza ['pjattsa] *sf* square; (*Comm*) market; **far ~ pulita** to make a clean sweep; **piazza d'armi** (*Mil*) parade ground; **piaz'zale** *sm* (large) square

piaz'zola [pjat'tsɔla] *sf* (*Aut*) lay-by; (*di tenda*) pitch

pic'cante *ag* hot, pungent; (*fig*) racy; biting

pic'chetto [pik'ketto] *sm* (*Mil, di scioperanti*) picket; (*di tenda*) peg

picchi'are [pik'kjare] *vt* (*persona: colpire*) to hit, strike; (: *prendere a botte*) to beat (up); (*battere*) to beat; (*sbattere*) to bang ▷ *vi* (*bussare*) to knock; (: *con forza*) to bang; (*colpire*) to hit, strike; (*sole*) to beat down; **picchi'ata** *sf* (*Aer*) dive

'picchio ['pikkjo] *sm* woodpecker

pic'cino, -a [pit'tʃino] *ag* tiny, very small

picci'one [pit'tʃone] *sm* pigeon

'picco, -chi *sm* peak; **a ~** vertically

'piccolo, -a *ag* small; (*oggetto, mano, di età: bambino*) small, little; (*dav* *sostantivo: di breve durata: viaggio)* short; *(fig)* mean, petty ▷ *sm/f* child, little one

pic'cone *sm* pick(-axe)

pic'cozza [pik'kɔttsa] *sf* ice-axe

pic'nic *sm inv* picnic

pi'docchio [pi'dɔkkjo] *sm* louse

pi'ede *sm* foot; *(di mobile)* leg; **in piedi** standing; **a piedi** on foot; **a piedi nudi** barefoot; **su due piedi** *(fig)* at once; **prendere ~** *(fig)* to gain ground, catch on; **sul ~ di guerra** *(Mil)* ready for action; **piede di porco** crowbar

pi'ega, -ghe *sf (piegatura, Geo)* fold; *(di gonna)* pleat; *(di pantaloni)* crease; *(grinza)* wrinkle, crease; **prendere una brutta ~** *(fig)* to take a turn for the worse

pie'gare *vt* to fold; *(braccia, gambe, testa)* to bend ▷ *vi* to bend; **piegarsi** *vpr* to bend; *(fig)*: **piegarsi (a)** to yield (to), submit (to)

piegherò *ecc* [pjege'rɔ] *vb vedi* **piegare**

pie'ghevole *ag* pliable, flexible; *(porta)* folding

Pie'monte *sm*: **il ~** Piedmont

pi'ena *sf (di fiume)* flood, spate

pi'eno, -a *ag* full; *(muro, mattone)* solid ▷ *sm (colmo)* height, peak; *(carico)* full load; **~ di** full of; **in ~ giorno** in broad daylight; **il ~, per favore** *(Aut)* fill it up, please

piercing ['pirsing] *sm* piercing; **farsi il ~ all'ombelico** to have one's navel pierced

pietà *sf* pity; *(Rel)* piety; **senza ~** pitiless, merciless; **avere ~ di** *(compassione)* to pity, feel sorry for; *(misericordia)* to have pity o mercy on

pie'tanza [pje'tantsa] *sf* dish, course

pie'toso, -a *ag (compassionevole)* pitying, compassionate; *(che desta pietà)* pitiful

pi'etra *sf* stone; **pietra preziosa** precious stone, gem

'piffero *sm (Mus)* pipe

pigi'ama, -i [pi'dʒama] *sm* pyjamas *pl*

pigli'are [piʎ'ʎare] *vt* to take, grab; *(afferrare)* to catch

'pigna ['piɲɲa] *sf* pine cone

pi'gnolo, -a [piɲ'ɲɔlo] *ag* pernickety

pi'grizia [pi'grittsja] *sf* laziness

'pigro, -a *ag* lazy

PIL *sigla m* (= *prodotto interno lordo*) GDP

'pila *sf (catasta, di ponte)* pile; *(Elettr)* battery; *(torcia)* torch *(BRIT)*, flashlight

pi'lastro *sm* pillar

'pile ['pail] *sm inv* fleece

'pillola *sf* pill; **prendere la ~** to be on the pill

pi'lone *sm (di ponte)* pier; *(di linea elettrica)* pylon

pi'lota, -i, -e *sm/f* pilot; *(Aut)* driver ▷ *ag inv* pilot *cpd*; **pilota automatico** automatic pilot

pinaco'teca, -che *sf* art gallery

pi'neta *sf* pinewood

ping-'pong [piŋ'pɔn] *sm* table tennis

pingu'ino *sm (Zool)* penguin

'pinna *sf (di pesce)* fin; *(di cetaceo, per nuotare)* flipper

'pino *sm* pine (tree); **pi'nolo** *sm* pine kernel

'pinza ['pintsa] *sf* pliers *pl*; *(Med)* forceps *pl*; *(Zool)* pincer

pinzette [pin'tsette] *sfpl* tweezers

pi'oggia, -ge ['pjɔddʒa] *sf* rain; **pioggia acida** acid rain

pi'olo *sm* peg; *(di scala)* rung

piom'bare *vi* to fall heavily; *(gettarsi con impeto)*: **~ su** to fall upon, assail ▷ *vt (dente)* to fill; **piomba'tura** *sf (di dente)* filling

piom'bino *sm (sigillo)* (lead) seal; *(del filo a piombo)* plummet; *(Pesca)* sinker

pi'ombo *sm (Chim)* lead; **a ~** *(cadere)* straight down; **senza ~** *(benzina)* unleaded

pioni'ere, -a *sm/f* pioneer

pi'oppo *sm* poplar

pi'overe *vb impers* to rain ▷ *vi (fig: scendere dall'alto)* to rain down; *(lettere, regali)* to pour into; **pioviggi'nare**

vb impers to drizzle; **pio'voso, -a** *ag* rainy

pi'ovra *sf* octopus

pi'ovve *ecc vb vedi* **piovere**

'pipa *sf* pipe

pipì (*fam*) *sf*: **fare ~** to have a wee (wee)

pipis'trello *sm* (*Zool*) bat

pi'ramide *sf* pyramid

pi'rata, -i *sm* pirate; **pirata della strada** hit-and-run driver; **pirata informatica** hacker

Pire'nei *smpl* **i ~** the Pyrenees

pi'romane *sm/f* pyromaniac; arsonist

pi'roscafo *sm* steamer, steamship

pisci'are [piʃʃare] (*fam!*) *vi* to piss (!), pee (!)

pi'scina [piʃʃina] *sf* (swimming) pool; (*stabilimento*) (swimming) baths *pl*

pi'sello *sm* pea

piso'lino *sm* nap

'pista *sf* (*traccia*) track, trail; (*di stadio*) track; (*di pattinaggio*) rink; (*da sci*) run; (*Aer*) runway; (*di circo*) ring; **pista da ballo** dance floor

pis'tacchio [pis'takkjo] *sm* pistachio (tree); pistachio (nut)

pis'tola *sf* pistol, gun

pis'tone *sm* piston

pi'tone *sm* python

pit'tore, -'trice *sm/f* painter; **pitto'resco, -a, -schi, -sche** *ag* picturesque

pit'tura *sf* painting; **pittu'rare** *vt* to paint

 PAROLA CHIAVE

più *av* **1** (*in maggiore quantità*) more; **più del solito** more than usual; **in più, di più** more; **ne voglio di più** I want some more; **ci sono 3 persone in** *o* **di più** there are 3 more *o* extra people; **più o meno** more or less; **per di più** (*inoltre*) what's more, moreover

2 (*comparativo*) more; (*se monosillabo, spesso*): + ...er; **più ... di/che** more ... than; **lavoro più di te/Paola** I

work harder than you/Paola; **è più intelligente che ricco** he's more intelligent than rich

3 (*superlativo*) most; (*se monosillabo, spesso*): + ...est; **il più grande/ intelligente** the biggest/most intelligent; **è quello che compro più spesso** that's the one I buy most often; **al più presto** as soon as possible; **al più tardi** at the latest

4 (*negazione*): **non ... più** no more, no longer; **non ho più soldi** I've got no more money, I don't have any more money; **non lavoro più** I'm no longer working, I don't work any more; **a più non posso** (*gridare*) at the top of one's voice; (*correre*) as fast as one can

5 (*Mat*) plus; **4 più 5 fa 9** 4 plus 5 equals 9; **più 5 gradi** 5 degrees above freezing, plus 5

▷ *prep* plus ▷ *ag inv* **1**: **più ... (di)** more ... (than); **più denaro/tempo** more money/time; **più persone di quante ci aspettassimo** more people than we expected

2 (*numerosi, diversi*) several; **l'aspettai per più giorni** I waited for it for several days

▷ *sm* **1** (*la maggior parte*): **il più è fatto** most of it is done

2 (*Mat*) plus (sign)

3: **i più** the majority

pi'uma *sf* feather; **piu'mino** *sm* (eider)down; (*per letto*) eiderdown; (: *tipo danese*) duvet, continental quilt; (*giacca*) quilted jacket (*with goose-feather padding*); (*per cipria*) powder puff; (*per spolverare*) feather duster

piut'tosto *av* rather; **~ che** (*anziché*) rather than

'pizza ['pittsa] *sf* pizza; **pizze'ria** *sf* place where pizzas are made, sold or eaten

pizzi'care [pittsi'kare] *vt* (*stringere*) to nip, pinch; (*pungere*) to sting; to bite; (*Mus*) to pluck ▷ *vi* (*prudere*) to itch, be itchy; (*cibo*) to be hot *o* spicy

'pizzico, -chi ['pittsiko] *sm*
(*pizzicotto*) pinch, nip; (*piccola quantità*)
pinch, dash; (*d'insetto*) sting; bite
pizzi'cotto [pittsi'kɔtto] *sm* pinch,
nip
'pizzo ['pittso] *sm* (*merletto*) lace;
(*barbetta*) goatee beard
plagi'are [pla'dʒare] *vt* (*copiare*) to
plagiarize
plaid [plɛd] *sm inv* (travelling) rug
(BRIT), lap robe (US)
pla'nare *vi* (Aer) to glide
'plasma *sm* plasma
plas'mare *vt* to mould, shape
'plastica, -che *sf* (*arte*) plastic arts
pl; (*Med*) plastic surgery; (*sostanza*)
plastic; **plastica facciale** face lift
'platano *sm* plane tree
pla'tea *sf* (Teatro) stalls *pl*
'platino *sm* platinum
plau'sibile *ag* plausible
pleni'lunio *sm* full moon
'plettro *sm* plectrum
pleu'rite *sf* pleurisy
'plico, -chi *sm* (*pacco*) parcel; **in ~ a
parte** (Comm) under separate cover
plo'tone *sm* (Mil) platoon; **plotone
d'esecuzione** firing squad
plu'rale *ag, sm* plural
PM *abbr* (Pol) = **Pubblico Ministero**;
(= *Polizia Militare*) MP (*Military Police*)
PMI *sigla fpl*: **Piccole e Medie
Imprese** SME (*Small and Medium-sized
Enterprises*)
pneu'matico, -a, -ci, -che *ag*
inflatable; pneumatic ▷ *sm* (Aut) tyre
(BRIT), tire (US)
po' *av, sm vedi* **poco**

PAROLA CHIAVE

'poco, -a, -chi, -che *ag* (*quantità*)
little, not much; (*numero*) few, not
many; **poco pane/denaro/spazio**
little *o* not much bread/money/space;
poche persone/idee few *o* not many
people/ideas; **ci vediamo tra poco**

(*sottinteso: tempo*) see you soon
▷ *av* **1** (*in piccola quantità*) little, not
much; (*numero limitato*) few, not
many; **guadagna poco** he doesn't
earn much, he earns little
2 (*con ag, av*) (a) little, not very; **sta
poco bene** he isn't very well; **è poco
più vecchia di lui** she's a little *o*
slightly older than him
3 (*tempo*): **poco dopo/prima** shortly
afterwards/before; **il film dura poco**
the film doesn't last very long; **ci
vediamo molto poco** we don't see
each other very often, we hardly ever
see each other
4: **un po'** a little, a bit; **è un po' corto**
it's a little *o* a bit short; **arriverà fra un
po'** he'll arrive shortly *o* in a little while
5: **a dir poco** to say the least; **a poco
a poco** little by little; **per poco
non cadevo** I nearly fell; **è una
cosa da poco** it's nothing, it's of no
importance; **una persona da poco** a
worthless person
▷ *pron* (a) little

po'dere *sm* (Agr) farm
'podio *sm* dais, platform; (Mus)
podium
po'dismo *sm* (Sport) track events *pl*
poe'sia *sf* (*arte*) poetry;
(*componimento*) poem
po'eta, -'essa *sm/f* poet/poetess
poggi'are [pod'dʒare] *vt* to lean, rest;
(*posare*) to lay, place; **poggia'testa** *sm
inv* (Aut) headrest
'poggio ['pɔddʒo] *sm* hillock, knoll
'poi *av* then; (*alla fine*) finally, at last;
e ~ (*inoltre*) and besides; **questa ~ (è
bella)!** (*ironico*) that's a good one!
poiché [poi'ke] *cong* since, as
'poker *sm* poker
po'lacco, -a, -chi, -che *ag* Polish
▷ *sm/f* Pole
po'lare *ag* polar
po'lemica, -che *sf* controversy
po'lemico, -a, -ci, -che *ag*

polemic(al), controversial

po'lenta sf (Cuc) sort of thick porridge made with maize flour

'polio(mie'lite) sf polio(myelitis)

'polipo sm polyp

polisti'rolo sm polystyrene

po'litica, -che sf politics sg; (linea di condotta) policy; **politica'mente** av politically; **politicamente corretto** politically correct

po'litico, -a, -ci, -che ag political ▷ sm/f politician

poli'zia [polit'tsia] sf police; **polizia giudiziaria** ≈ Criminal Investigation Department (BRIT), ≈ Federal Bureau of Investigation (US); **polizia stradale** traffic police; **polizi'esco, -a, -schi, -sche** ag police cpd; (film, romanzo) detective cpd; **polizi'otto** sm policeman; **cane poliziotto** police dog; **donna poliziotto** policewoman; **poliziotto di quartiere** local police officer

● **POLIZIA DI STATO**
●
● The function of the **polizia di**
● **stato** is to maintain public order,
● to uphold the law and prevent and
● investigate crime. It is a civil body,
● reporting to the Minister of the
● Interior.

'polizza ['politsa] sf (Comm) bill; **~ di assicurazione** insurance policy; **polizza di carico** bill of lading

pol'laio sm henhouse

'pollice ['pollitfe] sm thumb

'polline sm pollen

'pollo sm chicken

pol'mone sm lung; **polmone d'acciaio** (Med) iron lung; **polmo'nite** sf pneumonia; **polmonite atipica** SARS

'polo sm (Geo, Fisica) pole; (gioco) polo; **polo nord/sud** North/South Pole

Po'lonia sf **la ~** Poland

'polpa sf flesh, pulp; (carne) lean meat

pol'paccio [pol'pattfo] sm (Anat) calf

polpas'trello sm fingertip

pol'petta sf (Cuc) meatball

'polpo sm octopus

pol'sino sm cuff

'polso sm (Anat) wrist; (pulsazione) pulse; (fig: forza) drive, vigour

pol'trire vi to laze about

pol'trona sf armchair; (Teatro: posto) seat in the front stalls (BRIT) o orchestra (US)

'polvere sf dust; (sostanza ridotta minutissima) powder, dust; **latte in ~** dried o powdered milk; **caffè in ~** instant coffee; **sapone in ~** soap powder; **polvere da sparo/pirica** gunpowder

po'mata sf ointment, cream

po'mello sm knob

pome'riggio [pome'riddʒo] sm afternoon

'pomice ['pomitfe] sf pumice

'pomo sm (mela) apple; (ornamentale) knob; (di sella) pommel; **pomo d'Adamo** (Anat) Adam's apple

pomo'doro sm tomato; **pomodori pelati** skinned tomatoes

'pompa sf pump; (sfarzo) pomp (and ceremony); **pompe funebri** funeral parlour sg (BRIT), undertaker's sg; **pompa di benzina** petrol (BRIT) o gas (US) pump; (distributore) filling o gas (US) station; **pom'pare** vt to pump; (trarre) to pump out; (gonfiare d'aria) to pump up

pom'pelmo sm grapefruit

pompi'ere sm fireman

po'nente sm west

pongo, poni ecc vb vedi **porre**

'ponte sm bridge; (di nave) deck; (: anche: **~ di comando**) bridge; (impalcatura) scaffold; **fare il ~** (fig) to take the extra day off (between 2 public holidays); **governo ~** interim government; **ponte aereo** airlift;

ponte levatoio drawbridge; **ponte sospeso** suspension bridge

pon'tefice [pon'tɛfitʃe] sm (Rel) pontiff

'popcorn ['pɔpkɔːn] sm inv popcorn

popo'lare ag popular; (quartiere, clientela) working-class ▷ vt (rendere abitato) to populate; **popolarsi** vpr to fill with people, get crowded; **popolazi'one** sf population

'popolo sm people

'poppa sf (di nave) stern; (seno) breast

porcel'lana [portʃel'lana] sf porcelain, china; piece of china

porcel'lino, -a [portʃel'lino] sm/f piglet; **porcellino d'India** guinea pig

porche'ria [porke'ria] sf filth, muck; (fig: oscenità) obscenity; (: azione disonesta) dirty trick; (: cosa mal fatta) rubbish

por'cile [por'tʃile] sm pigsty

por'cino, -a [por'tʃino] ag of pigs, pork cpd ▷ sm (fungo) type of edible mushroom

'porco, -ci sm pig; (carne) pork

porcos'pino sm porcupine

'porgere ['pɔrdʒere] vt to hand, give; (tendere) to hold out

pornogra'fia sf pornography; **porno'grafico, -a, -ci, -che** ag pornographic

'poro sm pore

'porpora sf purple

'porre vt (mettere) to put; (collocare) to place; (posare) to lay (down), put (down); (fig: supporre): **poniamo (il caso) che ...** let's suppose that ...

'porro sm (Bot) leek; (Med) wart

'porsi ecc vb vedi **porgere**

'porta sf door; (Sport) goal; **portaba'gagli** sm inv (facchino) porter; (Aut, Ferr) luggage rack; **porta-CD** [portatʃi'di] sm inv (mobile) CD rack; (astuccio) CD holder; **porta'cenere** sm inv ashtray; **portachi'avi** sm inv keyring; **porta'erei** sf inv (nave)

aircraft carrier; **portafi'nestra** (pl **portefi'nestre**) sf French window; **porta'foglio** sm wallet; (Pol, Borsa) portfolio; **non trovo il portafoglio** I can't find my wallet; **portafor'tuna** sm inv lucky charm; mascot

por'tale sm (di chiesa, Inform) portal

porta'mento sm carriage, bearing

portamo'nete sm inv purse

por'tante ag (muro ecc) supporting, load-bearing

portan'tina sf sedan chair; (per ammalati) stretcher

portaom'brelli sm inv umbrella stand

porta'pacchi [porta'pakki] sm inv (di moto, bicicletta) luggage rack

por'tare vt (sostenere, sorreggere: peso, bambino, pacco) to carry; (indossare: abito, occhiali) to wear; (: capelli lunghi) to have; (avere: nome, titolo) to have, bear; (recare?): **~ qc a qn** to take (o bring) sth to sb; (fig: sentimenti) to bear

portasiga'rette sm inv cigarette case

por'tata sf (vivanda) course; (Aut) carrying (o loading) capacity; (di arma) range; (volume d'acqua) (rate of) flow; (fig: limite) scope, capability; (: importanza) impact, import; **alla ~ di tutti** (conoscenza) within everybody's capabilities; (prezzo) within everybody's means; **a/fuori ~ (di)** within/out of reach (of); **a ~ di mano** within (arm's) reach

por'tatile ag portable

por'tato, -a ag (incline): **~ a** inclined o apt to

portau'ovo sm inv eggcup

porta'voce [porta'votʃe] sm/f inv spokesman/woman

por'tento sm wonder, marvel

porti'era sf (Aut) door

porti'ere sm (portinaio) concierge, caretaker; (di hotel) porter; (nel calcio) goalkeeper

porti'naio, -a sm/f concierge,

caretaker

portine'ria sf caretaker's lodge

'porto, -a pp di **porgere** ▷ sm (Naut) harbour, port ▷ sm inv port (wine); **porto d'armi** (documento) gun licence

Porto'gallo sm: **il ~** Portugal; **porto'ghese** ag, sm/f, sm Portuguese inv

por'tone sm main entrance, main door

portu'ale ag harbour cpd, port cpd ▷ sm dock worker

porzi'one [por'tsjone] sf portion, share; (di cibo) portion, helping

'posa sf (Fot) exposure; (atteggiamento, di modello) pose

po'sare vt to put (down), lay (down) ▷ vi (ponte, edificio, teoria): **~ su** to rest on; (Fot: atteggiarsi) to pose; **posarsi** vpr (aereo) to land; (uccello) to alight; (sguardo) to settle

po'sata sf piece of cutlery

pos'critto sm postscript

'posi ecc vb vedi **porre**

posi'tivo, -a ag positive

posizi'one [pozit'tsjone] sf position; **prendere ~** (fig) to take a stand; **luci di ~** (Aut) sidelights

pos'porre vt to place after; (differire) to postpone, defer

posse'dere vt to own, possess; (qualità, virtù) to have, possess

posses'sivo, -a ag possessive

pos'sesso sm ownership no pl; possession

posses'sore sm owner

pos'sibile ag possible ▷ sm **fare tutto il ~** to do everything possible; **nei limiti del ~** as far as possible; **al più tardi ~** as late as possible; **possibilità** sf inv possibility ▷ sfpl (mezzi) means; **aver la possibilità di fare** to be in a position to do; to have the opportunity to do

possi'dente sm/f landowner

possi'edo ecc vb vedi **possedere**

'posso ecc vb vedi **potere**

'posta sf (servizio) post, postal service; (corrispondenza) post, mail; (ufficio postale) post office; (nei giochi d'azzardo) stake; **Poste** sfpl (amministrazione) post office; **c'è ~ per me?** are there any letters for me?; **ministro delle Poste e Telecomunicazioni** Postmaster General; **posta aerea** airmail; **posta elettronica** E-mail, e-mail, electronic mail; **posta ordinaria** ≈ second-class mail; **posta prioritaria** ≈ first-class post; **pos'tale** ag postal, post office cpd

posteggi'are [posted'dʒare] vt, vi to park; **pos'teggio** sm car park (BRIT), parking lot (US); (di taxi) rank (BRIT), stand (US)

'poster sm inv poster

posteri'ore ag (dietro) back; (dopo) later ▷ sm (fam: sedere) behind

postici'pare [postitʃi'pare] vt to defer, postpone

pos'tino sm postman (BRIT), mailman (US)

'posto, -a pp di **porre** ▷ sm (sito, posizione) place; (impiego) job; (spazio libero) room, space; (di parcheggio) space; (sedile: al teatro, in treno ecc) seat; (Mil) post; **a ~** (in ordine) in place, tidy; (fig) settled; (: persona) reliable; **vorrei prenotare due posti** I'd like to book two seats; **al ~ di** in place of; **sul ~** on the spot; **mettere a ~** to tidy (up), put in order; (faccende) to straighten out; **posto di blocco** roadblock; **posto di lavoro** job; **posti in piedi** (in teatro, in autobus) standing room; **posto di polizia** police station

po'tabile ag drinkable; **acqua ~** drinking water

po'tare vt to prune

po'tassio sm potassium

po'tente ag (nazione) strong, powerful; (veleno, farmaco) potent, strong; **po'tenza** sf power; (forza) strength

potenzi'ale [poten'tsjale] *ag, sm*
potential

🔘 **PAROLA CHIAVE**

po'tere *sm* power; **al potere** (*partito ecc*) in power; **potere d'acquisto**
purchasing power
▷ *vb aus* **1** (*essere in grado di*) can, be
able to; **non ha potuto ripararlo** he
couldn't *o* he wasn't able to repair it;
non è potuto venire he couldn't *o*
he wasn't able to come; **spiacente
di non poter aiutare** sorry not to be
able to help
2 (*avere il permesso*) can, may, be
allowed to; **posso entrare?** can *o* may
I come in?; **si può sapere dove sei
stato?** where on earth have you been?
3 (*eventualità*) may, might, could;
potrebbe essere vero it might *o*
could be true; **può aver avuto un
incidente** he may *o* might *o* could
have had an accident; **può darsi**
perhaps; **può darsi** *o* **essere che non
venga** he may *o* might not come
4 (*augurio*): **potessi almeno
parlargli!** if only I could speak to him!
5 (*suggerimento*): **potresti almeno
scusarti!** you could at least apologize!
▷ *vt* can, be able to; **può molto
per noi** he can do a lot for us; **non
ne posso più** (*per stanchezza*) I'm
exhausted; (*per rabbia*) I can't take
any more

potrò *ecc vb vedi* **potere**
'povero, -a *ag* poor; (*disadorno*) plain,
bare ▷ *sm/f* poor man/woman;
i poveri the poor; **~ di** lacking in,
having little; **povertà** *sf* poverty
poz'zanghera [pot'tsangera] *sf*
puddle
'pozzo ['pottso] *sm* well; (*cava: di
carbone*) pit; (*di miniera*) shaft; **pozzo
petrolifero** oil well
P.R.A. [pra] *sigla m* (= *Pubblico Registro*

Automobilistico) ≈ DVLA
pran'zare [pran'dzare] *vi* to dine,
have dinner; to lunch, have lunch
'pranzo ['prandzo] *sm* dinner; (*a
mezzogiorno*) lunch
'prassi *sf* usual procedure
'pratica, -che *sf* practice; (*esperienza*)
experience; (*conoscenza*) knowledge,
familiarity; (*tirocinio*) training,
practice; (*Amm: affare*) matter, case;
(: *incartamento*) file, dossier; **in ~**
(*praticamente*) in practice; **mettere in
~** to put into practice
prati'cabile *ag* (*progetto*) practicable,
feasible; (*luogo*) passable, practicable
pratica'mente *av* (*in modo pratico*)
in a practical way, practically; (*quasi*)
practically, almost
prati'care *vt* to practise; (*Sport:
tennis ecc*) to play; (: *nuoto, scherma
ecc*) to go in for; (*eseguire: apertura,
buco*) to make; **~ uno sconto** to give
a discount
'pratico, -a, -ci, -che *ag* practical;
~ di (*esperto*) experienced *o* skilled in;
(*familiare*) familiar with
'prato *sm* meadow; (*di giardino*) lawn
preav'viso *sm* notice; **telefonata
con ~** personal *o* person to person call
pre'cario, -a *ag* precarious; (*Ins*)
temporary
precauzi'one [prekaut'tsjone] *sf*
caution, care; (*misura*) precaution
prece'dente [pretʃe'dɛnte] *ag*
previous ▷ *sm* precedent; **il discorso/
film ~** the previous *o* preceding
speech/film; **senza precedenti**
unprecedented; **precedenti penali**
criminal record *sg*; **precedenza** *sf*
priority, precedence; (*Aut*) right of way
pre'cedere [pre'tʃedere] *vt* to
precede, go (*o* come) before
precipi'tare [pretʃipi'tare] *vi* (*cadere*)
to fall headlong; (*fig: situazione*) to get
out of control ▷ *vt* (*gettare dall'alto
in basso*) to hurl, fling; (*fig: affrettare*)
to rush; **precipitarsi** *vpr* (*gettarsi*)

to hurl *o* fling o.s.; *(affrettarsi)* to
rush; **precipi'toso, -a** *ag (caduta,*
fuga) headlong; *(fig: avventato)* rash,
reckless; (: *affrettato)* hasty, rushed
preci'pizio [pretʃi'pittsjo] *sm*
precipice; **a ~** *(fig: correre)* headlong
precisa'mente [pretʃiza'mente] *av*
(gen) precisely; *(con esattezza)* exactly
preci'sare [pretʃi'zare] *vt* to state,
specify; *(spiegare)* to explain (in detail)
precisi'one [pretʃi'zjone] *sf*
precision; accuracy
pre'ciso, -a [pre'tʃizo] *ag (esatto)*
precise; *(accurato)* accurate, precise;
(deciso: idee) precise, definite; *(uguale)*:
2 vestiti precisi 2 dresses exactly the
same; **sono le 9 precise** it's exactly
9 o'clock
pre'cludere *vt* to block, obstruct
pre'coce [pre'kotʃe] *ag* early;
(bambino) precocious; *(vecchiaia)*
premature
precon'cetto [prekon'tʃetto] *sm*
preconceived idea, prejudice
precur'sore *sm* forerunner, precursor
'preda *sf (bottino)* booty; *(animale, fig)*
prey; **essere ~ di** to fall prey to; **essere**
in ~ a to be prey to
'predica, -che *sf* sermon; *(fig)*
lecture, talking-to
predi'care *vt, vi* to preach
predi'cato *sm (Ling)* predicate
predi'letto, -a *pp di* **prediligere**
▷ *ag, sm/f* favourite
predi'ligere [predi'lidʒere] *vt* to
prefer, have a preference for
pre'dire *vt* to foretell, predict
predis'porre *vt* to get ready, prepare;
~ qn a qc to predispose sb to sth
predizi'one [predit'tsjone] *sf*
prediction
prefazi'one [prefat'tsjone] *sf*
preface, foreword
prefe'renza [prefe'rentsa] *sf*
preference
prefe'rire *vt* to prefer, like better; **~ il**
caffè al tè to prefer coffee to tea, like

coffee better than tea
pre'figgersi [pre'fiddʒersi] *vpr*: **~**
uno scopo to set o.s. a goal
pre'fisso, -a *pp di* **prefiggere** ▷ *sm*
(Ling) prefix; *(Tel)* dialling (BRIT) *o* dial
(US) code; **qual è il ~ telefonico di**
Londra? what is the dialling code for
London?
pre'gare *vi* to pray ▷ *vt (Rel)* to pray
to; *(implorare)* to beg; *(chiedere)*: **~ qn**
di fare to ask sb to do; **farsi ~** to need
coaxing *o* persuading
pre'gevole [pre'dʒevole] *ag* valuable
pregherò *ecc* [prege'rɔ] *vb vedi*
pregare
preghi'era [pre'gjɛra] *sf (Rel)* prayer;
(domanda) request
pregi'ato, -a [pre'dʒato] *ag (di valore)*
valuable; **vino ~** vintage wine
'pregio ['prɛdʒo] *sm (stima)* esteem,
regard; *(qualità)* (good) quality, merit;
(valore) value, worth
pregiudi'care [predʒudi'kare] *vt* to
prejudice, harm, be detrimental to
pregiu'dizio [predʒu'dittsjo] *sm (idea*
errata) prejudice; *(danno)* harm *no pl*
'prego *escl (a chi ringrazia)* don't
mention it!; *(invitando qn ad*
accomodarsi) please sit down!;
(invitando qn ad andare prima) after you!
pregus'tare *vt* to look forward to
prele'vare *vt (denaro)* to withdraw;
(campione) to take; *(polizia)* to take,
capture
preli'evo *sm (di denaro)* withdrawal;
(Med): **fare un ~ (di)** to take a sample
(of); **prelievo di sangue**; **fare un ~ di**
sangue to take a blood sample
prelimi'nare *ag* preliminary
'premere *vt* to press ▷ *vi* **~ su** to press
down on; *(fig)* to put pressure on; **~ a**
(fig: importare) to matter to
pre'mettere *vt* to put before; *(dire*
prima) to start by saying, state first
premi'are *vt* to give a prize to; *(fig:*
merito, onestà) to reward
premiazi'one [premjat'tsjone] *sf*

prize giving

'premio sm prize; (ricompensa) reward; (Comm) premium; (Amm: indennità) bonus

pre'misi ecc vb vedi **premettere**

premu'nirsi vpr: ~ **di** to provide o.s. with; ~ **contro** to protect o.s. from, guard o.s. against

pre'mura sf (fretta) haste, hurry; (riguardo) attention, care; **premure** sfpl (attenzioni, cure) care sg; **aver ~** to be in a hurry; **far ~ a qn** to hurry sb; **usare ogni ~ nei riguardi di qn** to be very attentive to sb; **premu'roso, -a** ag thoughtful, considerate

'prendere vt to take; (andare a prendere) to get, fetch; (ottenere) to get; (guadagnare) to get, earn; (catturare: ladro, pesce) to catch; (collaboratore, dipendente) to take on; (passeggero) to pick up; (chiedere: somma, prezzo) to charge, ask; (trattare: persona) to handle ▷ vi (colla, cemento) to set; (pianta) to take; (fuoco: nel camino) to catch; (voltare): ~ **a destra** to turn (to the) right; **prendersi** vpr (azzuffarsi): **prendersi a pugni** to come to blows; **dove si prende il traghetto per...** where do we get the ferry to ...; **prendi qualcosa?** (da bere, da mangiare) would you like something to eat (o drink)?; **prendo un caffè** I'll have a coffee; ~ **qn/qc per** (scambiare) to take sb/sth for; ~ **fuoco** to catch fire; ~ **parte a** to take part in; **prendersi cura di qn/qc** to look after sb/sth; **prendersela** (adirarsi) to get annoyed; (preoccuparsi) to get upset, worry

preno'tare vt to book, reserve; **vorrei ~ una camera doppia** I'd like to book a double room; **ho prenotato un tavolo al nome di ...** I booked a table in the name of ...; **prenotazi'one** sf booking, reservation; **ho confermato la prenotazione per fax/e-mail** I confirmed my booking by fax/e-mail

preoccu'pare vt to worry; to preoccupy; **preoccuparsi** vpr **preoccuparsi di qn/qc** to worry about sb/sth; **preoccuparsi per qn** to be anxious for sb; **preoccupazi'one** sf worry, anxiety

prepa'rare vt to prepare; (esame, concorso) to prepare for; **prepararsi** vpr (vestirsi) to get ready; **prepararsi a qc/a fare** to get ready o prepare (o.s.) for sth/to do; ~ **da mangiare** to prepare a meal; **prepara'tivi** smpl preparations

preposizi'one [prepozit'tsjone] sf (Ling) preposition

prepo'tente ag (persona) domineering, arrogant; (bisogno, desiderio) overwhelming, pressing ▷ sm/f bully

'presa sf taking no pl; catching no pl; (di città) capture; (indurimento: di cemento) setting; (appiglio, Sport) hold; (di acqua, gas) (supply) point; (piccola quantità: di sale ecc) pinch; (Carte) trick; **far ~** (colla) to set; **far ~ sul pubblico** to catch the public's imagination; **essere alle prese con** (fig) to be struggling with; **presa d'aria** air inlet; **presa (di corrente)** (Elettr) socket; (: al muro) point

pre'sagio [pre'zadʒo] sm omen

'presbite ag long-sighted

pres'crivere vt to prescribe

'prese ecc vb vedi **prendere**

presen'tare vt to present; (far conoscere): ~ **qn (a)** to introduce sb (to); (Amm: inoltrare) to submit; **presentarsi** vpr (recarsi, farsi vedere) to present o.s., appear; (farsi conoscere) to introduce o.s.; (occasione) to arise; **presentarsi come candidato** (Pol) to stand as a candidate; **presentarsi bene/male** to have a good/poor appearance

pre'sente ag present; (questo) this ▷ sm present; **i presenti** those present; **aver ~ qc/qn** to remember sth/sb; **presenti** (*persone*) people present; **aver ~ qc/qn** to remember sth/sb; **tenere ~ qn/qc** to keep sth/sb in mind

presenti'mento *sm* premonition

pre'senza [pre'zɛntsa] *sf* presence; (*aspetto esteriore*) appearance; **presenza di spirito** presence of mind

pre'sepio, pre'sepe *sm* crib

preser'vare *vt* to protect; to save; **preserva'tivo** *sm* sheath, condom

'**presi** *ecc vb vedi* **prendere**

'**preside** *sm/f* (*Ins*) head (teacher) (BRIT), principal (US); (*di facoltà universitaria*) dean; **preside di facoltà** (*Univ*) dean of faculty

presi'dente *sm* (*Pol*) president; (*di assemblea, Comm*) chairman; **presidente del consiglio** prime minister

presi'edere *vt* to preside over ▷ *vi* **~ a** to direct, be in charge of

pressap'poco *av* about, roughly

pres'sare *vt* to press

pressi'one *sf* pressure; **far ~ su qn** to put pressure on sb; **pressione sanguigna** blood pressure; **pressione atmosferica** atmospheric pressure

'**presso** *av* (*vicino*) nearby, close at hand ▷ *prep* (*vicino a*) near; (*accanto a*) beside, next to; (*in casa di*): **~ qn** at sb's home; (*nelle lettere*) care of, c/o; (*alle dipendenze di*): **lavora ~ di noi** he works for 0 with us ▷ *smpl* **nei pressi di** near, in the vicinity of

pres'tante *ag* good-looking

pres'tare *vt*: **~ (qc a qn)** to lend (sb sth 0 sth to sb); **prestarsi** *vpr* (*offrirsi*): **prestarsi a fare** to offer to do; (*essere adatto*): **prestarsi a** to lend itself to, be suitable for; **mi può ~ dei soldi?** can you lend me some money?; **~ aiuto** to lend a hand; **~ attenzione** to pay attention; **~ fede a qc/qn** to give credence to sth/sb; **~ orecchio** to listen; **prestazi'one** *sf* (*Tecn, Sport*)

performance

prestigia'tore, -'trice [prestidʒa'tore] *sm/f* conjurer

pres'tigio [pres'tidʒo] *sm* (*fama*) prestige; (*illusione*): **gioco di ~** conjuring trick

'**prestito** *sm* lending *no pl*; loan; **dar in ~** to lend; **prendere in ~** to borrow

'**presto** *av* (*tra poco*) soon; (*in fretta*) quickly; (*di buon'ora*) early; **a ~** see you soon; **fare ~ a fare qc** to hurry up and do sth; (*non costare fatica*) to have no trouble doing sth; **si fa ~ a criticare** it's easy to criticize

pre'sumere *vt* to presume, assume

pre'sunsi *ecc vb vedi* **presumere**

presuntu'oso, -a *ag* presumptuous

presunzi'one [prezun'tsjone] *sf* presumption

'**prete** *sm* priest

preten'dente *sm/f* pretender ▷ *sm* (*corteggiatore*) suitor

pre'tendere *vt* (*esigere*) to demand, require; (*sostenere*): **~ che** to claim that; **pretende di aver sempre ragione** he thinks he's always right

▍ Attenzione! In inglese esiste il verbo *to pretend*, che però significa *far finta*.

pre'tesa *sf* (*esigenza*) claim, demand; (*presunzione, sfarzo*) pretentiousness; **senza pretese** unpretentious

pre'testo *sm* pretext, excuse

preva'lere *vi* to prevail

preve'dere *vt* (*indovinare*) to foresee; (*presagire*) to foretell; (*considerare*) to make provision for

preve'nire *vt* (*anticipare*) to forestall; to anticipate; (*evitare*) to avoid, prevent

preven'tivo, -a *ag* preventive ▷ *sm* (*Comm*) estimate

prevenzi'one [preven'tsjone] *sf* prevention; (*preconcetto*) prejudice

previ'dente *ag* showing foresight; prudent; **previ'denza** *sf* foresight; **istituto di previdenza** provident institution; **previdenza sociale** social security (BRIT), welfare (US)

pre'vidi ecc vb vedi **prevedere**

previsi'one sf forecast, prediction; **previsioni meteorologiche** weather forecast sg; **previsioni del tempo** weather forecast sg

pre'visto, -a pp di **prevedere** ▷ sm **più/meno del ~** more/less than expected

prezi'oso, -a [pret'tsjoso] ag precious; invaluable ▷ sm jewel; valuable

prez'zemolo [pret'tsemolo] sm parsley

'prezzo ['prɛttso] sm price; **prezzo d'acquisto/di vendita** buying/selling price

prigi'one [pri'dʒone] sf prison; **prigioni'ero, -a** ag captive ▷ sm/f prisoner

'prima sf (Teatro) first night; (Cinema) première; (Aut) first gear; vedi anche **primo** ▷ av before; (in anticipo) in advance, beforehand; (per l'addietro) at one time, formerly; (più presto) sooner, earlier; (in primo luogo) first ▷ cong **~ di fare/che parta** before doing/he leaves; **~ di** before; **~ o poi** sooner or later

pri'mario, -a ag primary; (principale) chief, leading, primary ▷ sm (Med) chief physician

prima'tista, -i, e sm/f (Sport) record holder

pri'mato sm supremacy; (Sport) record

prima'vera sf spring

primi'tivo, -a ag primitive; original

pri'mizie [pri'mittsje] sfpl early produce sg

'primo, -a ag first; (fig) initial; basic; prime ▷ sm/f first (one) ▷ sm (Cuc) first course; (in date): **il ~ luglio** the first of July; **le prime ore del mattino** the early hours of the morning; **ai primi di maggio** at the beginning of

May; **viaggiare in prima** to travel first-class; **in ~ luogo** first of all, in the first place; **di prim'ordine** o **prima qualità** first-class, first-rate; **in un ~ tempo** at first; **prima donna** leading lady; (di opera lirica) prima donna

primordi'ale ag primordial

'primula sf primrose

princi'pale [printʃi'pale] ag main, principal ▷ sm manager, boss

principal'mente [printʃipal'mente] av mainly, principally

'principe ['printʃipe] sm prince; **principe ereditario** crown prince; **princi'pessa** sf princess

principi'ante [printʃi'pjante] sm/f beginner

prin'cipio [prin'tʃipjo] sm (inizio) beginning, start; (origine) origin, cause; (concetto, norma) principle; **al** o **in ~** at first; **per ~** on principle; **principi** smpl (concetti fondamentali) principles; **una questione di ~** a matter of principle

priorità sf priority

priori'tario, -a ag having priority, of utmost importance

pri'vare vt **~ qn di** to deprive sb of; **privarsi di** to go o do without

pri'vato, -a ag private ▷ sm/f private citizen; **in ~** in private

privilegi'are [privile'dʒare] vt to grant a privilege to

privilegi'ato, -a [privile'dʒato] ag (individuo, classe) privileged; (trattamento, Comm: credito) preferential; **azioni ~e** preference shares (BRIT), preferred stock (US)

privi'legio [privi'lɛdʒo] sm privilege

'privo, -a ag **~ di** without, lacking

pro prep for, on behalf of ▷ sm inv (utilità) advantage, benefit; **a che ~?** what's the use?; **il ~ e il contro** the pros and cons

pro'babile ag probable, likely; **probabilità** sf inv probability

probabil'mente av probably

pro'blema, -i sm problem
pro'boscide [pro'bɔʃʃide] sf (di elefante) trunk
pro'cedere [pro'tʃɛdere] vi to proceed; (comportarsi) to behave; (iniziare): **~ a** to start; **~ contro** (Dir) to start legal proceedings against; **proce'dura** sf (Dir) procedure
proces'sare [protʃes'sare] vt (Dir) to try
processi'one [protʃes'sjone] sf procession
pro'cesso [pro'tʃɛsso] sm (Dir) trial; proceedings pl; (metodo) process
pro'cinto [pro'tʃinto] sm: **in ~ di fare** about to do, on the point of doing
procla'mare vt to proclaim
procre'are vt to procreate
procu'rare vt: **~ qc a qn** (fornire) to get o obtain sth for sb; (causare: noie ecc) to bring o give sb sth
pro'digio [pro'didʒo] sm marvel, wonder; (persona) prodigy
pro'dotto, -a pp di **produrre** ▷ sm product; **prodotti agricoli** farm produce sg
pro'duco ecc vb vedi **produrre**
pro'durre vt to produce
pro'dussi ecc vb vedi **produrre**
produzi'one sf production; (rendimento) output
Prof. abbr (= professore) Prof.
profa'nare vt to desecrate
profes'sare vt to profess; (medicina ecc) to practise
professio'nale ag professional
professi'one sf profession; **professio'nista, -i, -e** sm/f professional
profes'sore, -'essa sm/f (Ins) teacher; (: di università) lecturer; (: titolare di cattedra) professor
pro'filo sm profile; (breve descrizione) sketch, outline; **di ~** in profile
pro'fitto sm advantage, profit, benefit; (fig: progresso) progress; (Comm) profit

profondità sf inv depth
pro'fondo, -a ag deep; (rancore, meditazione) profound ▷ sm depth(s pl), bottom; **quanto è profonda l'acqua?** how deep is the water?; **~ 8 metri** 8 metres deep
'profugo, -a, -ghi, -ghe sm/f refugee
profu'mare vt to perfume ▷ vi to be fragrant; **profumarsi** vpr to put on perfume o scent
profu'mato, -a ag (fiore, aria) fragrant; (fazzoletto, saponetta) scented; (pelle) sweet-smelling; (persona) with perfume on
profume'ria sf perfumery; (negozio) perfume shop
pro'fumo sm (prodotto) perfume, scent; (fragranza) scent, fragrance
proget'tare [prodʒet'tare] vt to plan; (edificio) to plan, design; **pro'getto** sm plan, project; (idea) plan, project; **progetto di legge** bill
pro'gramma, -i sm programme; (TV, Radio) programmes pl; (Ins) syllabus, curriculum; (Inform) program; **program'mare** vt (TV, Radio) to put on; (Inform) to program; (Econ) to plan; **programma'tore, -'trice** sm/f (Inform) computer programmer
progre'dire vi to progress, make progress
pro'gresso sm progress no pl; **fare progressi** to make progress
proi'bire vt to forbid, prohibit
proiet'tare vt (gen, Geom, Cinema) to project; (: presentare) to show, screen; (luce, ombra) to throw, cast, project; **proi'ettile** sm projectile, bullet (o shell ecc); **proiet'tore** sm (Cinema) projector; (Aut) headlamp; (Mil) searchlight; **proiezi'one** sf (Cinema) projection; showing
prolife'rare vi (fig) to proliferate
pro'lunga, -ghe sf (di cavo ecc) extension
prolun'gare vt (discorso, attesa) to

prolong; (*linea, termine*) to extend
prome'moria *sm inv* memorandum
pro'messa *sf* promise
pro'mettere *vt* to promise ▷ *vi* to
be *o* look promising; **~ a qn di fare** to
promise sb that one will do
promi'nente *ag* prominent
pro'misi *ecc vb vedi* **promettere**
promon'torio *sm* promontory,
headland
promozi'one [promot'tsjone] *sf*
promotion
promu'overe *vt* to promote
proni'pote *sm/f* (*di nonni*) great-
grandchild, great-grandson/
granddaughter; (*di zii*) great-nephew/
niece
pro'nome *sm* (*Ling*) pronoun
pron'tezza [pron'tettsa] *sf*
readiness; quickness, promptness
'pronto, -a *ag* ready; (*rapido*) fast,
quick, prompt; **quando saranno
pronte le mie foto?** when will my
photos be ready?; **~!** (*Tel*) hello!; **~
all'ira** quick-tempered; **pronto
soccorso** (*cure*) first aid; (*reparto*) A&E
(*BRIT*), ER (*US*)
prontu'ario *sm* manual, handbook
pro'nuncia [pro'nuntʃa] *sf*
pronunciation
pronunci'are [pronun'tʃare] *vt*
(*parola, sentenza*) to pronounce; (*dire*)
to utter; (*discorso*) to deliver; **come si
pronuncia?** how do you pronounce it?
propa'ganda *sf* propaganda
pro'pendere *vi* **~ per** to favour, lean
towards
propi'nare *vt* to administer
pro'porre *vt* (*suggerire*): **~ qc (a qn)** to
suggest sth (to sb); (*candidato*) to put
forward; (*legge, brindisi*) to propose;
~ di fare to suggest *o* propose doing;
proporsi di fare to propose *o* intend
to do; **proporsi una meta** to set o.s.
a goal
proporzio'nale [proportsjo'nale] *ag*
proportional

proporzi'one [propor'tsjone] *sf*
proportion; **in ~ a** in proportion
to; **proporzioni** *sfpl* (*dimensioni*)
proportions; **di vaste proporzioni**
huge
pro'posito *sm* (*intenzione*) intention,
aim; (*argomento*) subject, matter; **a
~ di** regarding, with regard to; **di ~**
(*apposta*) deliberately, on purpose;
a ~ by the way; **capitare a ~** (*cosa,
persona*) to turn up at the right time
proposizi'one [propozit'tsjone] *sf*
(*Ling*) clause; (*: periodo*) sentence
pro'posta *sf* proposal; (*suggerimento*)
suggestion; **proposta di legge** bill
proprietà *sf inv* (*ciò che si possiede*)
property *gen no pl*, estate;
(*caratteristica*) property; (*correttezza*)
correctness; **proprietà privata**
private property; **proprie'tario, -a**
sm/f owner; (*di albergo ecc*) proprietor,
owner; (*per l'inquilino*) landlord/lady
'proprio, -a *ag* (*possessivo*) own;
(*: impersonale*) one's; (*esatto*) exact,
correct, proper; (*senso, significato*)
literal; (*Ling: nome*) proper;
(*particolare*): **~ di** characteristic of,
peculiar to ▷ *av* (*precisamente*) just,
exactly; (*davvero*) really; (*affatto*):
non ... ~ not ... at all; **l'ha visto con i
(suoi) propri occhi** he saw it with his
own eyes
proro'gare *vt* to extend; (*differire*) to
postpone, defer
'prosa *sf* prose
pro'sciogliere [proʃʃɔʎʎere] *vt* to
release; (*Dir*) to acquit
prosciu'gare [proʃʃu'gare] *vt* (*terreni*)
to drain, reclaim; **prosciugarsi** *vpr*
to dry up
prosci'utto [proʃʃutto] *sm* ham;
prosciutto cotto/crudo cooked/
cured ham
prosegui'mento *sm* continuation;
buon ~! all the best!; (*a chi viaggia*)
enjoy the rest of your journey!
prosegu'ire *vt* to carry on with,

continue ▷ *vi* to carry on, go on
prospe'rare *vi* to thrive
prospet'tare *vt* (*esporre*) to point out, show; **prospettarsi** *vpr* to look, appear
prospet'tiva *sf* (*Arte*) perspective; (*veduta*) view; (*fig: previsione, possibilità*) prospect
pros'petto *sm* (*Disegno*) elevation; (*veduta*) view, prospect; (*facciata*) façade, front; (*tabella*) table; (*sommario*) summary; **prospetto informativo** prospectus
prossimità *sf* nearness, proximity; **in ~ di** near (to), close to
'prossimo, -a *ag* (*vicino*): **~ a** near (to), close to; (*che viene subito dopo*) next; (*parente*) close ▷ *sm* neighbour, fellow man
prostitu'irsi *vpr* to prostitute o.s.
prosti'tuta *sf* prostitute
protago'nista, -i, -e *sm/f* protagonist
pro'teggere [pro'tɛddʒere] *vt* to protect
prote'ina *sf* protein
pro'tendere *vt* to stretch out
pro'testa *sf* protest
protes'tante *ag, sm/f* Protestant
protes'tare *vt, vi* to protest
pro'tetto, -a *pp di* **proteggere**
protezi'one [protet'tsjone] *sf* protection; (*patrocinio*) patronage
pro'totipo *sm* prototype
pro'trarre *vt* (*prolungare*) to prolong; **protrarsi** *vpr* to go on, continue
protube'ranza [protube'rantsa] *sf* protuberance, bulge
'prova *sf* (*esperimento, cimento*) test, trial; (*tentativo*) attempt, try; (*Mat, testimonianza, documento ecc*) proof; (*Dir*) evidence *no pl*, proof; (*Ins*) exam, test; (*Teatro*) rehearsal; (*di abito*) fitting; **a ~ di** (*in testimonianza di*) as proof of; **a ~ di fuoco** fireproof; **fino a ~ contraria** until it is proved otherwise; **mettere alla ~** to put

to the test; **giro di ~** test *o* trial run; **prova generale** (*Teatro*) dress rehearsal
pro'vare *vt* (*sperimentare*) to test; (*tentare*) to try, attempt; (*assaggiare*) to try, taste; (*sperimentare in sé*) to experience; (*sentire*) to feel; (*cimentare*) to put to the test; (*dimostrare*) to prove; (*abito*) to try on; **~ a fare** to try *o* attempt to do
proveni'enza [prove'njentsa] *sf* origin, source
prove'nire *vi* **~ da** to come from
pro'venti *smpl* revenue *sg*
pro'verbio *sm* proverb
pro'vetta *sf* test tube; **bambino in ~** test-tube baby
pro'vider [pro'vaider] *sm inv* (*Inform*) service provider
pro'vincia, -ce *o* **cie** [pro'vintʃa] *sf* province
pro'vino *sm* (*Cinema*) screen test; (*campione*) specimen
provo'cante *ag* (*attraente*) provocative
provo'care *vt* (*causare*) to cause, bring about; (*eccitare: riso, pietà*) to arouse; (*irritare, sfidare*) to provoke; **provocazi'one** *sf* provocation
provve'dere *vi* (*disporre*): **~ (a)** to provide (for); (*prendere un provvedimento*) to take steps, act; **provvedi'mento** *sm* measure; (*di previdenza*) precaution
provvi'denza [provvi'dentsa] *sf*: **la ~** providence
provvigi'one [provvi'dʒone] *sf* (*Comm*) commission
provvi'sorio, -a *ag* temporary
prov'viste *sfpl* supplies
'prua *sf* (*Naut*) bow(s) (*pl*), prow
pru'dente *ag* cautious, prudent; (*assennato*) sensible, wise; **pru'denza** *sf* prudence, caution; wisdom
'prudere *vi* to itch, be itchy
'prugna ['pruɲɲa] *sf* plum; **prugna secca** prune

pru'rito *sm* itchiness *no pl*; itch
P.S. *abbr* (= *postscriptum*) P.S.; (*Polizia*) = **Pubblica Sicurezza**
pseu'donimo *sm* pseudonym
psica'nalisi *sf* psychoanalysis
psicana'lista, -i, -e *sm/f* psychoanalyst
'psiche ['psike] *sf* (*Psic*) psyche
psichi'atra, -i, -e [psi'kjatra] *sm/f* psychiatrist; **psichi'atrico, -a, -ci, -che** *ag* psychiatric
psicolo'gia [psikolo'dʒia] *sf* psychology; **psico'logico, -a, -ci, -che** *ag* psychological; **psi'cologo, -a, -gi, -ghe** *sm/f* psychologist
psico'patico, -a, -ci, -che *ag* psychopathic ▷ *sm/f* psychopath
pubbli'care *vt* to publish
pubblicazi'one [pubblikat'tsjone] *sf* publication
pubblicità [pubblitʃi'ta] *sf* (*diffusione*) publicity; (*attività*) advertising; (*annunci nei giornali*) advertisements *pl*
'pubblico, -a, -ci, -che *ag* public; (*statale: scuola ecc*) state *cpd* ▷ *sm* public; (*spettatori*) audience; **in ~** in public; **P~ Ministero** Public Prosecutor's Office; **la Pubblica Sicurezza** the police; **pubblico funzionario** civil servant
'pube *sm* (*Anat*) pubis
pubertà *sf* puberty
'pudico, -a, -ci, -che *ag* modest
pu'dore *sm* modesty
pue'rile *ag* childish
pugi'lato [pudʒi'lato] *sm* boxing
'pugile ['pudʒile] *sm* boxer
pugna'lare [puɲɲa'lare] *vt* to stab
pu'gnale [puɲ'ɲale] *sm* dagger
'pugno ['puɲɲo] *sm* fist; (*colpo*) punch; (*quantità*) fistful
'pulce ['pultʃe] *sf* flea
pul'cino [pul'tʃino] *sm* chick
pu'lire *vt* to clean; (*lucidare*) to polish; **pu'lito, -a** *ag* (*anche fig*) clean; (*ordinato*) neat, tidy; **puli'tura** *sf* cleaning; **pulitura a secco** dry

cleaning; **puli'zia** *sf* cleaning; cleanness; **fare le pulizie** to do the cleaning *o* the housework; **pulizia etnica** ethnic cleansing
'pullman *sm inv* coach
pul'lover *sm inv* pullover, jumper
pullu'lare *vi* to swarm, teem
pul'mino *sm* minibus
'pulpito *sm* pulpit
pul'sante *sm* (push-)button
pul'sare *vi* to pulsate, beat
pul'viscolo *sm* fine dust; **pulviscolo atmosferico** specks *pl* of dust
'puma *sm inv* puma
pun'gente [pun'dʒɛnte] *ag* prickly; stinging; (*anche fig*) biting
'pungere ['pundʒere] *vt* to prick; (*insetto, ortica*) to sting; (*freddo*) to bite
pungigli'one [pundʒiʎ'ʎone] *sm* sting
pu'nire *vt* to punish; **punizi'one** *sf* punishment; (*Sport*) penalty
'punsi *ecc vb vedi* **pungere**
'punta *sf* point; (*parte terminale*) tip, end; (*di monte*) peak; (*di costa*) promontory; (*minima parte*) touch, trace; **in ~ di piedi** on tip-toe; **ore di ~** peak hours; **uomo di ~** front-rank *o* leading man
pun'tare *vt* (*piedi a terra, gomiti sul tavolo*) to plant; (*dirigere: pistola*) to point; (*scommettere*) to bet ▷ *vi* (*mirare*): **~ a** to aim at; **~ su** (*dirigersi*) to head *o* make for; (*fig: contare*) to count *o* rely on
pun'tata *sf* (*gita*) short trip; (*scommessa*) bet; (*parte di opera*) instalment; **romanzo a puntate** serial
punteggia'tura [punteddʒa'tura] *sf* (*Ling*) punctuation
pun'teggio [pun'teddʒo] *sm* score
puntel'lare *vt* to support
pun'tello *sm* prop, support
pun'tina *sf*: **puntina da disegno** drawing pin

pun'tino *sm* dot; **fare qc a ~** to do sth properly

'punto, -a *pp di* **pungere** ▷ *sm* (*segno, macchiolina*) dot; (*Ling*) full stop; (*di indirizzo e-mail*) dot; (*Mat, momento, di punteggio: fig: argomento*) point; (*posto*) spot; (*a scuola*) mark; (*nel cucire, nella maglia, Med*) stitch ▷ *av* **non ... ~** not at all; **punto cardinale** point of the compass, cardinal point; **punto debole** weak point; **punto esclamativo** exclamation mark; **punto interrogativo** question mark; **punto nero** (*comedone*) blackhead; **punto di partenza** (*anche fig*) starting point; **punto di riferimento** landmark; (*fig*) point of reference; **punto (di) vendita** retail outlet; **punto e virgola** semicolon; **punto di vista** (*fig*) point of view

puntu'ale *ag* punctual

pun'tura *sf* (*di ago*) prick; (*Med*) puncture; (*: iniezione*) injection; (*dolore*) sharp pain; **puntura d'insetto** sting, bite

> Attenzione! In inglese esiste la parola *puncture*, che si usa per indicare la foratura di una gomma.

punzecchi'are [puntsek'kjare] *vt* to prick; (*fig*) to tease

può *ecc*, **-pu'oi** *vb vedi* **potere**

pu'pazzo [pu'pattso] *sm* puppet

pu'pilla *sf* (*Anat*) pupil

purché [pur'ke] *cong* provided that, on condition that

'pure *cong* (*tuttavia*) and yet, nevertheless; (*anche se*) even if ▷ *av* (*anche*) too, also; **pur di** (*al fine di*) just to; **faccia ~!** go ahead!, please do!

purè *sm* (*Cuc*) purée; (*: di patate*) mashed potatoes

pu'rezza [pu'rettsa] *sf* purity

pur'gante *sm* (*Med*) purgative, purge

purga'torio *sm* purgatory

purifi'care *vt* to purify; (*metallo*) to refine

'puro, -a *ag* pure; (*acqua*) clear, limpid; (*vino*) undiluted; **puro'sangue** *sm/f inv* thoroughbred

pur'troppo *av* unfortunately

pus *sm* pus

'pustola *sf* pimple

puti'ferio *sm* rumpus, row

putre'fatto, -a *pp di* **putrefare**

put'tana (*fam!*) *sf* whore (!)

puz'zare [put'tsare] *vi* to stink

'puzzo ['puttso] *sm* stink, foul smell

'puzzola ['puttsola] *sf* polecat

puzzo'lente [puttso'lente] *ag* stinking

pvc [pivi'tʃi] *sigla m* (= *polyvinyl chloride*) PVC

q

q *abbr* (= quintale) q.

qua *av* here; **in ~** (*verso questa parte*) this way; **da un anno in ~** for a year now; **da ~ndo in ~?** since when?; **per di ~** (*passare*) this way; **al di ~ di** (*fiume, strada*) on this side of; **~ dentro/fuori** *ecc* in/out here *ecc*; *vedi anche* **questo**

qua'derno *sm* notebook; (*per scuola*) exercise book

qua'drante *sm* quadrant; (*di orologio*) face

qua'drare *vi* (*bilancio*) to balance, tally; (*descrizione*) to correspond ▷ *vt* (*Mat*) to square; **non mi quadra** I don't like it; **qua'drato, -a** *ag* square; (*fig: equilibrato*) level-headed, sensible; (*: peg*) square ▷ *sm* (*Mat*) square; (*Pugilato*) ring; **5 al quadrato** 5 squared

quadri'foglio [kwadri'fɔʎʎo] *sm* four-leaf clover

quadri'mestre *sm* (*periodo*) four-month period; (*Ins*) term

'quadro *sm* (*pittura*) painting, picture; (*quadrato*) square; (*tabella*) table, chart; (*Tecn*) board, panel; (*Teatro: scena, spettacolo*) scene; (*fig: scena, spettacolo*) sight; (*: descrizione*) outline, description; **quadri** *smpl* (*Pol*) party organizers; (*Mil*) cadres; (*Comm*) managerial staff; (*Carte*) diamonds

'quadruplo, -a *ag, sm* quadruple

quaggiù [kwad'dʒu] *av* down here

'quaglia ['kwaʎʎa] *sf* quail

PAROLA CHIAVE

'qualche ['kwalke] *det* **1** some, a few; (*in interrogative*) any; **ho comprato qualche libro** I've bought some *o* a few books; **qualche volta** sometimes; **hai qualche sigaretta?** have you any cigarettes?
2 (*uno*): **c'è qualche medico?** is there a doctor?; **in qualche modo** somehow
3 (*un certo, parecchio*) some; **un personaggio di qualche rilievo** a figure of some importance
4: **qualche cosa = qualcosa**

qual'cosa *pron* something; (*in espressioni interrogative*) anything; **qualcos'altro** something else; anything else; **~ di nuovo** something new; anything new; **~ da mangiare** something to eat; anything to eat; **c'è ~ che non va?** is there something *o* anything wrong?

qual'cuno *pron* (*persona*) someone, somebody; (*: in espressioni interrogative*) anyone, anybody; (*alcuni*) some; **~ è favorevole a noi** some are on our side; **qualcun altro** someone *o* somebody else; anyone *o* anybody else

PAROLA CHIAVE

'quale (*spesso troncato in qual*) *det* **1** (*interrogativo*) what; (*: scegliendo tra* *due o più cose o persone*) which; **quale uomo/denaro?** what man/money?, which man/money?; **quali sono i tuoi programmi?** what are your plans?; **quale stanza preferisci?** which room do you prefer?

2 (*relativo: come*): **il risultato fu quale ci si aspettava** the result was as expected

3 (*esclamativo*) what; **quale disgrazia!** what bad luck!

▷ *pron* **1** (*interrogativo*) which; **quale dei due scegli?** which of the two do you want?

2 (*relativo*): **il (la) quale** (*persona: soggetto*) who; (: *oggetto, con preposizione*) whom; (*cosa*) which; (*possessivo*) whose; **suo padre, il quale è avvocato, ...** his father, who is a lawyer, ...; **il signore con il quale parlavo** the gentleman to whom I was speaking; **l'albergo al quale ci siamo fermati** the hotel where we stayed o which we stayed at; **la signora della quale ammiriamo la bellezza** the lady whose beauty we admire

3 (*relativo: in elenchi*) such as, like; **piante quali l'edera** plants like o such as ivy; **quale sindaco di questa città** as mayor of this town

qua'lifica, -che *sf* qualification; (*titolo*) title

qualifi'cato, -a *ag* (*dotato di qualifica*) qualified; (*esperto, abile*) skilled; **non mi ritengo ~ per questo lavoro** I don't think I'm qualified for this job; **è un medico molto ~** he is a very distinguished doctor

qualificazi'one *sf*: **gara di ~** (*Sport*) qualifying event

qualità *sf inv* quality; **in ~ di** in one's capacity as

qua'lora *cong* in case, if

qual'siasi *det inv* = **qualunque**

qua'lunque *det inv* any; (*quale che sia*) whatever; (*discriminativo*) whichever; (*posposto: mediocre*) poor, indifferent; ordinary; **mettiti un vestito ~** put on any old dress; **~ cosa** anything; **~ cosa accada** whatever happens; **a ~ costo** at any cost, whatever the cost; **l'uomo ~** the man in the street; **~ persona** anyone, anybody

'quando *cong, av* when; **~ sarò ricco** when I'm rich; **da ~** (*dacché*) since; (*interrogativo*): **da ~ sei qui?** how long have you been here?; **quand'anche** even if

quantità *sf inv* quantity; (*gran numero*): **una ~ di** a great deal of; a lot of; **in grande ~** in large quantities

 PAROLA CHIAVE

'quanto, -a *det* **1** (*interrogativo: quantità*) how much; (: *numero*) how many; **quanto pane/denaro?** how much bread/money?; **quanti libri/ragazzi?** how many books/boys?; **quanto tempo?** how long?; **quanti anni hai?** how old are you?

2 (*esclamativo*): **quante storie!** what a lot of nonsense!; **quanto tempo sprecato!** what a waste of time!

3 (*relativo: quantità*) as much ... as; (: *numero*) as many ... as; **ho quanto denaro mi occorre** I have as much money as I need; **prendi quanti libri vuoi** take as many books as you like

▷ *pron* **1** (*interrogativo: quantità*) how much; (: *numero*) how many; (: *tempo*) how long; **quanto mi dai?** how much will you give me?; **quanti me ne hai portati?** how many did you bring me?; **da quanto sei qui?** how long have you been here?; **quanti ne abbiamo oggi?** what's the date today?

2 (*relativo: quantità*) as much as; (: *numero*) as many as; **farò quanto posso** I'll do as much as I can; **possono venire quanti sono stati**

invitati all those who have been invited can come
▷ *av* **1** (*interrogativo: con ag, av*) how; (: *con vb*) how much; **quanto stanco ti sembrava?** how tired did he seem to you?; **quanto corre la tua moto?** how fast can your motorbike go?; **quanto costa?** how much does it cost?; **quant'è?** how much is it?
2 (*esclamativo: con ag, av*) how; (: *con vb*) how much; **quanto sono felice!** how happy I am!; **sapessi quanto abbiamo camminato!** if you knew how far we've walked!; **studierò quanto posso** I'll study as much as *o* all I can; **quanto prima** as soon as possible
3: **in quanto** (*in qualità di*) as; (*perché, per il fatto che*) as, since; **(in) quanto a** (*per ciò che riguarda*) as for, as regards
4: **per quanto** (*nonostante, anche se*) however; **per quanto si sforzi, non ce la farà** try as he may, he won't manage it; **per quanto sia brava, fa degli errori** however good she may be, she makes mistakes; **per quanto io sappia** as far as I know

qua'ranta *num* forty
quaran'tena *sf* quarantine
quaran'tesimo, -a *num* fortieth
quaran'tina *sf* **una ~ (di)** about forty
'quarta *sf* (*Aut*) fourth (gear); *vedi anche* **quarto**
quar'tetto *sm* quartet(te)
quarti'ere *sm* district, area; (*Mil*) quarters *pl*; **quartier generale** headquarters *pl*
'quarto, -a *ag* fourth ▷ *sm* fourth; (*quarta parte*) quarter; **le 6 e un ~ a** quarter past six; **quarti di finale** quarter final; **quarto d'ora** quarter of an hour
'quarzo ['kwartso] *sm* quartz
'quasi *av* almost, nearly ▷ *cong*

(*anche*: **~ che**) as if; **(non) … ~ mai** hardly ever; **~ ~ me ne andrei** I've half a mind to leave
quassù *av* up here
quat'tordici [kwat'torditʃi] *num* fourteen
quat'trini *smpl* money *sg*, cash *sg*
'quattro *num* four; **in ~ e quattr'otto** in less than no time; **quattro'cento** *num* four hundred
▷ *sm* **il Quattrocento** the fifteenth century

⬤ **PAROLA CHIAVE**

'quello, -a (*dav sm* **quel** + C, **quell'** + V, **quello** + *s impura, gn, pn, ps, x, z; pl* **quei** + C, **quegli** + V *o s impura, gn, pn, ps, x, z; dav sf* **quella** + C, **quell'** + V; *pl* **quelle**) *det* that; those *pl*; **quella casa** that house; **quegli uomini** those men; **voglio quella camicia** (**lì** *o* **là**) I want that shirt
▷ *pron* **1** (*dimostrativo*) that (one), those (ones) *pl*; (*ciò*) that; **conosci quella?** do you know that woman?; **prendo quello bianco** I'll take the white one; **chi è quello?** who's that?; **prendi quello** (**lì** *o* **là**) take that one (there)
2 (*relativo*): **quello(a) che** (*persona*) the one (who); (*cosa*) the one (which), the one (that); **quelli(e) che** (*persone*) those who; (*cose*) those which; **è lui quello che non voleva venire** he's the one who didn't want to come; **ho fatto quello che potevo** I did what I could

'quercia, -ce ['kwɛrtʃa] *sf* oak (tree); (*legno*) oak
que'rela *sf* (*Dir*) (legal) action
que'sito *sm* question, query; problem
questio'nario *sm* questionnaire
questi'one *sf* problem, question; (*controversia*) issue; (*litigio*) quarrel;

in ~ in question; **è ~ di tempo** it's a
matter o question of time

PAROLA CHIAVE

'**questo, -a** det 1 (dimostrativo) this;
these pl; **questo libro (qui** o **qua)** this
book; **io prendo questo cappotto,
tu quello** I'll take this coat, you take
that one; **quest'oggi** today; **questa
sera** this evening
2 (enfatico): **non fatemi più prendere
di queste paure** don't frighten me
like that again
▷ pron (dimostrativo) this (one); these
(ones) pl; (ciò) this; **prendo questo
(qui** o **qua)** I'll take this one; **preferisci
questi o quelli?** do you prefer these
(ones) or those (ones)?; **questo
intendevo io** this is what I meant;
**vengono Paolo e Luca: questo da
Roma, quello da Palermo** Paolo and
Luca are coming: the former from
Palermo, the latter from Rome

ques'**tura** sf police headquarters
qui av here; **da** o **di ~** from here; **di ~ in
avanti** from now on; **di ~ a poco/una
settimana** in a little while/a week's
time; **~ dentro/sopra/vicino** in/up/
near here; vedi anche **questo**
quie'**tanza** [kwje'tantsa] sf receipt
qui'**ete** sf quiet, quietness; calmness;
stillness; peace
qui'**eto, -a** ag quiet; (notte) calm, still;
(mare) calm
'**quindi** av then ▷ cong therefore, so
'**quindici** ['kwinditʃi] num fifteen; **~
giorni** a fortnight (BRIT), two weeks
quindi'**cina** [kwindi'tʃina] sf (serie):
una ~ (di) about fifteen; **fra una ~ di
giorni** in a fortnight
'**quinta** sf vedi **quinto**
quin'**tale** sm quintal (100 kg)
'**quinto, -a** num fifth
'**quiz** [kwidz] sm inv (domanda)
question; (anche): **gioco a ~** quiz game

'**quota** sf (parte) quota, share;
(Aer) height, altitude; (Ippica) odds
pl; **prendere/perdere ~** (Aer) to
gain/lose height o altitude; **quota
d'iscrizione** enrolment fee; (a club)
membership fee
quotidi'**ano, -a** ag daily; (banale)
everyday ▷ sm (giornale) daily (paper)
quozi'**ente** [kwot'tsjɛnte] sm (Mat)
quotient; **quoziente d'intelligenza**
intelligence quotient, IQ

r

R, r ['ɛrre] *sf o m* (*lettera*) R, r; **R come Roma** ≈ R for Robert (*BRIT*), R for Roger (*US*)

'rabbia *sf* (*ira*) anger, rage; (*accanimento, furia*) fury; (*Med: idrofobia*) rabies *sg*

rab'bino *sm* rabbi

rabbi'oso, -a *ag* angry, furious; (*facile all'ira*) quick-tempered; (*forze, acqua ecc*) furious, raging; (*Med*) rabid, mad

rabbo'nire *vt* to calm down

rabbrivi'dire *vi* to shudder, shiver

raccapez'zarsi [rakkapet'tsarsi] *vpr* **non ~** to be at a loss

raccapricci'ante [rakkaprit'tʃante] *ag* horrifying

raccatta'palle *sm inv* (*Sport*) ballboy

raccat'tare *vt* to pick up

rac'chetta [rak'ketta] *sf* (*per tennis*) racket; (*per ping-pong*) bat; **racchetta da neve** snowshoe; **racchetta da sci** ski stick

racchi'udere [rak'kjudere] *vt* to contain

rac'cogliere [rak'kɔʎʎere] *vt* to collect; (*raccattare*) to pick up; (*frutti, fiori*) to pick, pluck; (*Agr*) to harvest; (*approvazione, voti*) to win

rac'colta *sf* collecting *no pl*; collection; (*Agr*) harvesting *no pl*, gathering *no pl*; harvest, crop; (*adunata*) gathering; **raccolta differenziata** (*dei rifiuti*) separate collection of different kinds of household waste

rac'colto, -a *pp di* **raccogliere** ▷ *ag* (*persona: pensoso*) thoughtful; (*luogo: appartato*) secluded, quiet ▷ *sm* (*Agr*) crop, harvest

raccoman'dabile *ag* (highly) commendable; **è un tipo poco ~** he is not to be trusted

raccoman'dare *vt* to recommend; (*affidare*) to entrust; (*esortare*): **~ a qn di non fare** to tell *o* warn sb not to do; **raccoman'data** *sf* (*anche:* **lettera raccomandata**) recorded-delivery letter

raccon'tare *vt* **~ (a qn)** (*dire*) to tell (sb); (*narrare*) to relate (to sb), tell (sb) about; **rac'conto** *sm* telling *no pl*, relating *no pl*; (*fatto raccontato*) story, tale; **racconti per bambini** children's stories

rac'cordo *sm* (*Tecn: giunto*) connection, joint; (*Aut*): **raccordo anulare** (*Aut*) ring road (*BRIT*), beltway (*US*); **raccordo autostradale** slip road (*BRIT*), entrance (*o exit*) ramp (*US*); **raccordo ferroviario** siding; **raccordo stradale** link road

racimo'lare [ratʃimo'lare] *vt* (*fig*) to scrape together, glean

'rada *sf* (natural) harbour

'radar *sm* radar

raddoppi'are *vt, vi* to double

raddriz'zare [raddrit'tsare] *vt* to straighten; (*fig: correggere*) to put straight, correct

'radere *vt* (*barba*) to shave off; (*mento*) to shave; (*fig: rasentare*) to graze; to

skim; **radersi** *vpr* to shave (o.s.); **~ al suolo** to raze to the ground
radi'are *vt* to strike off
radia'tore *sm* radiator
radiazi'one [radjat'tsjone] *sf* (*Fisica*) radiation; (*cancellazione*) striking off
radi'cale *ag* radical ▷ *sm* (*Ling*) root; **radicali liberi** free radicals
ra'dicchio [ra'dikkjo] *sm* chicory
ra'dice [ra'ditʃe] *sf* root
'radio *sf inv* radio ▷ *sm* (*Chim*) radium; **radioat'tivo, -a** *ag* radioactive; **radio'cronaca, -che** *sf* radio commentary; **radiogra'fia** *sf* radiography; (*foto*) X-ray photograph
radi'oso, -a *ag* radiant
radios'veglia [radjoz'veʎʎa] *sf* radio alarm
'rado, -a *ag* (*capelli*) sparse, thin; (*visite*) infrequent; **di ~** rarely
radu'nare *vt* to gather, assemble; **radunarsi** *vpr* to gather, assemble
ra'dura *sf* clearing
raf'fermo, -a *ag* stale
'raffica, -che *sf* (*Meteor*) gust (of wind); (*di colpi: scarica*) burst of gunfire
raffigu'rare *vt* to represent
raffi'nato, -a *ag* refined
raffor'zare [raffor'tsare] *vt* to reinforce
raffredda'mento *sm* cooling
raffred'dare *vt* to cool; (*fig*) to dampen, have a cooling effect on; **raffreddarsi** *vpr* to grow cool *o* cold; (*prendere un raffreddore*) to catch a cold; (*fig*) to cool (off)
raffred'dato, -a *ag* (*Med*): **essere ~** to have a cold
raffred'dore *sm* (*Med*) cold
raf'fronto *sm* comparison
'rafia *sf* (*fibra*) raffia
rafting ['rafting] *sm* white-water rafting
ra'gazza [ra'gattsa] *sf* girl; (*fam: fidanzato*) girlfriend; **nome da ~** maiden name; **ragazza madre** unmarried mother

ra'gazzo [ra'gattso] *sm* boy; (*fam: fidanzato*) boyfriend; **ragazzi** *smpl* (*figli*) kids; **ciao ragazzi!** (*gruppo*) hi guys!
raggi'ante [rad'dʒante] *ag* radiant, shining
'raggio ['raddʒo] *sm* (*di sole ecc*) ray; (*Mat, distanza*) radius; (*di ruota ecc*) spoke; **raggio d'azione** range; **raggi X** X-rays
raggi'rare [raddʒi'rare] *vt* to take in, trick
raggi'ungere [rad'dʒundʒere] *vt* to reach; (*persona: riprendere*) to catch up (with); (*bersaglio*) to hit; (*fig: meta*) to achieve
raggomito'larsi *vpr* to curl up
raggranel'lare *vt* to scrape together
raggrup'pare *vt* to group (together)
ragiona'mento [radʒona'mento] *sm* reasoning *no pl*; arguing *no pl*; argument
ragio'nare [radʒo'nare] *vi* to reason; **~ di** (*discorrere*) to talk about
ragi'one [ra'dʒone] *sf* reason; (*dimostrazione, prova*) argument, reason; (*diritto*) right; **aver ~** to be right; **aver ~ di qn** to get the better of sb; **dare ~ a qn** to agree with sb; to prove sb right; **perdere la ~** to become insane; (*fig*) to take leave of one's senses; **in ~ di** at the rate of; to the amount of; according to; **a** *o* **con ~** rightly, justly; **a ragion veduta** after due consideration; **ragione sociale** (*Comm*) corporate name
ragione'ria [radʒone'ria] *sf* accountancy; accounts department
ragio'nevole [radʒo'nevole] *ag* reasonable
ragioni'ere, -a [radʒo'njɛre] *sm/f* accountant
ragli'are [raʎ'ʎare] *vi* to bray
ragna'tela [raɲɲa'tela] *sf* cobweb, spider's web
'ragno ['raɲɲo] *sm* spider
ragù *sm inv* (*Cuc*) meat sauce; stew

RAI-TV [raiti'vu] *sigla f* = **Radio televisione italiana**

ralle'grare *vt* to cheer up; **rallegrarsi** *vpr* to cheer up; (*provare allegrezza*) to rejoice; **rallegrarsi con qn** to congratulate sb

rallen'tare *vt* to slow down; (*fig*) to lessen, slacken ▷ *vi* to slow down

rallenta'tore *sm* (*Cinema*) slow-motion camera; **al ~** (*anche fig*) in slow motion

raman'zina [raman'dzina] *sf* lecture, telling-off

'rame *sm* (*Chim*) copper

rammari'carsi *vpr*: **~ (di)** (*rincrescersi*) to be sorry (about), regret; (*lamentarsi*) to complain (about)

rammen'dare *vt* to mend; (*calza*) to darn

'ramo *sm* branch

ramo'scello [ramoʃʃello] *sm* twig

'rampa *sf* flight (of stairs); **rampa di lancio** launching pad

rampi'cante *ag* (*Bot*) climbing

'rana *sf* frog

'rancido, -a ['rantʃido] *ag* rancid.

ran'core *sm* rancour, resentment

ran'dagio, -a, -gi, -gie *o* **ge** [ran'dadʒo] *ag* (*gatto, cane*) stray

ran'dello *sm* club, cudgel

'rango, -ghi *sm* (*condizione sociale, Mil, riga*) rank

rannicchi'arsi [rannik'kjarsi] *vpr* to crouch, huddle

rannuvo'larsi *vpr* to cloud over, become overcast

'rapa *sf* (*Bot*) turnip

ra'pace [ra'patʃe] *ag* (*animale*) predatory; (*fig*) rapacious, grasping ▷ *sm* bird of prey

ra'pare *vt* (*capelli*) to crop, cut very short

rapida'mente *av* quickly, rapidly

rapidità *sf* speed

'rapido, -a *ag* fast; (*esame, occhiata*) quick, rapid ▷ *sm* (*Ferr*) express (train)

rapi'mento *sm* kidnapping; (*fig*)

rapture

ra'pina *sf* robbery; **rapina in banca** bank robbery; **rapina a mano armata** armed robbery; **rapi'nare** *vt* to rob; **rapina'tore, -'trice** *sm/f* robber

ra'pire *vt* (*cose*) to steal; (*persone*) to kidnap; (*fig*) to enrapture, delight; **rapi'tore, -'trice** *sm/f* kidnapper

rap'porto *sm* (*resoconto*) report; (*legame*) relationship; (*Mat, Tecn*) ratio; **rapporti sessuali** sexual intercourse *sg*

rappre'saglia [rappre'saʎʎa] *sf* reprisal, retaliation

rappresen'tante *sm/f* representative

rappresen'tare *vt* to represent; (*Teatro*) to perform; **rappresentazi'one** *sf* representation; performing *no pl*; (*spettacolo*) performance

rara'mente *av* seldom, rarely

rare'fatto, -a *ag* rarefied

'raro, -a *ag* rare

ra'sare *vt* (*barba ecc*) to shave off; (*siepi, erba*) to trim, cut; **rasarsi** *vpr* to shave (o.s.)

raschi'are [ras'kjare] *vt* to scrape; (*macchia, fango*) to scrape off ▷ *vi* to clear one's throat

ra'sente *prep*: **~ (a)** close to, very near

'raso, -a *pp di* **radere** ▷ *ag* (*barba*) shaved; (*capelli*) cropped; (*con misure di capacità*) level; (*pieno: bicchiere*) full to the brim ▷ *sm* (*tessuto*) satin; **un cucchiaio ~** a level spoonful; **raso terra** close to the ground

ra'soio *sm* razor; **rasoio elettrico** electric shaver *o* razor

ras'segna [ras'seɲɲa] *sf* (*Mil*) inspection, review; (*esame*) inspection; (*resoconto*) review, survey; (*pubblicazione letteraria ecc*) review; (*mostra*) exhibition, show; **passare in ~** (*Mil, fig*) to review

rassegnarsi *vpr* (*accettare*): **~ (a qc/a**

fare) to resign o.s. (to sth/to doing)

rassicu'rare vt to reassure

rasso'dare vt to harden, stiffen; **rassodarsi** vpr to harden, to strengthen

rassomigli'anza [rassomiʎ'ʎantsa] sf resemblance

rassomigli'are [rassomiʎ'ʎare] vi: ~ **a** to resemble, look like

rastrel'lare vt to rake; (fig: perlustrare) to comb

ras'trello sm rake

'**rata** sf (quota) instalment; **pagare a rate** to pay by instalments o on hire purchase (BRIT)

ratifi'care vt (Dir) to ratify

'**ratto** sm (Dir) abduction; (Zool) rat

rattop'pare vt to patch

rattris'tare vt to sadden; **rattristarsi** vpr to become sad

'**rauco, -a, -chi, -che** ag hoarse

rava'nello sm radish

ravi'oli smpl ravioli sg

ravvi'vare vt to revive; (fig) to brighten up, enliven

razio'nale [rattsjo'nale] ag rational

razio'nare [rattsjo'nare] vt to ration

razi'one [rat'tsjone] sf ration; (porzione) portion, share

'**razza** ['rattsa] sf race; (Zool) breed; (discendenza, stirpe) stock, race; (sorta) sort, kind

razzi'ale [rat'tsjale] ag racial

raz'zismo [rat'tsizmo] sm racism, racialism

raz'zista, -i, -e [rat'tsista] ag, sm/f racist, racialist

'**razzo** ['raddzo] sm rocket

R.C. sigla m (= partito della Rifondazione Comunista) left-wing Italian political party

re sm inv king; (Mus) D; (: solfeggiando) re

rea'gire [rea'dʒire] vi to react

re'ale ag real; (di, da re) royal ▷ sm il ~ reality

reality [ri'aliti] sm inv reality show

realiz'zare [realid'dzare] vt (progetto ecc) to realize, carry out; (sogno, desiderio) to realize, fulfil; (scopo) to achieve; (Comm: titoli ecc) to realize; (Calcio ecc) to score; **realizzarsi** vpr to be realized

real'mente av really, actually

realtà sf inv reality

re'ato sm offence

reat'tore sm (Fisica) reactor; (Aer: aereo) jet; (: motore) jet engine

reazio'nario, -a [reattsjo'narjo] ag (Pol) reactionary

reazi'one [reat'tsjone] sf reaction

'**rebus** sm inv rebus; (fig) puzzle; enigma

recapi'tare vt to deliver

re'capito sm (indirizzo) address; (consegna) delivery; **recapito a domicilio** home delivery (service); **recapito telefonico** phone number

re'cedere [re'tʃedere] vi to withdraw

recensi'one [retʃen'sjone] sf review

re'cente [re'tʃɛnte] ag recent; **di ~** recently; **recente'mente** av recently

re'cidere [re'tʃidere] vt to cut off, chop off

recin'tare [retʃin'tare] vt to enclose, fence off

re'cinto [re'tʃinto] sm enclosure; (ciò che recinge) fence; surrounding wall

recipi'ente [retʃi'pjɛnte] sm container

re'ciproco, -a, -ci, -che [re'tʃiproko] ag reciprocal

'**recita** ['rɛtʃita] sf performance

reci'tare [retʃi'tare] vt (poesia, lezione) to recite; (dramma) to perform; (ruolo) to play o act (the part of)

recla'mare vi to complain ▷ vt (richiedere) to demand

re'clamo sm complaint

recli'nabile ag (sedile) reclining

reclusi'one sf (Dir) imprisonment

'**recluta** sf recruit

re'condito, -a ag secluded; (fig) secret, hidden

'record *ag inv* record *cpd* ▷ *sm inv*
record; **in tempo ~, a tempo di ~** in
record time; **detenere il ~ di** to hold
the record for; **record mondiale**
world record

recriminazi'one
[rekriminat'tsjone] *sf* recrimination

recupe'rare *vt* (*rientrare in possesso di*)
to recover, get back; (*tempo perduto*)
to make up for; (*Naut*) to salvage;
(: *naufraghi*) to rescue; (*delinquente*) to
rehabilitate; **~ lo svantaggio** (*Sport*)
to close the gap

redargu'ire *vt* to rebuke

re'dassi *ecc vb vedi* **redigere**

reddi'tizio, -a [reddi'tittsjo] *ag*
profitable

'reddito *sm* income; (*dello Stato*)
revenue; (*di un capitale*) yield

re'digere [re'didʒere] *vt* to write;
(*contratto*) to draw up

'redini *sfpl* reins

'reduce ['rɛdutʃe] *ag*: **~ da** returning
from, back from ▷ *sm/f* survivor

refe'rendum *sm inv* referendum

referenze [refe'rɛntse] *sfpl*
references

re'ferto *sm* medical report

rega'lare *vt* to give (as a present),
make a present of

re'galo *sm* gift, present

re'gata *sf* regatta

'reggere ['rɛddʒere] *vt* (*tenere*) to
hold; (*sostenere*) to support, bear, hold
up; (*portare*) to carry, bear; (*resistere*)
to withstand; (*dirigere: impresa*) to
manage, run; (*governare*) to rule,
govern; (*Ling*) to take, be followed
by ▷ *vi* (*resistere*): **~ a** to stand up to,
hold out against; (*sopportare*): **~ a** to
stand; (*durare*) to last; (*fig: teoria ecc*) to
hold water; **reggersi** *vpr* (*stare ritto*)
to stand

'reggia, -ge ['rɛddʒa] *sf* royal palace

reggi'calze [reddʒi'kaltse] *sm inv*
suspender belt

reggi'mento [reddʒi'mento] *sm* (*Mil*)
regiment

reggi'seno [reddʒi'seno] *sm* bra

re'gia, -'gie [re'dʒia] *sf* (*TV, Cinema
ecc*) direction

re'gime [re'dʒime] *sm* (*Pol*) regime;
(*Dir: aureo, patrimoniale ecc*) system;
(*Med*) diet; (*Tecn*) (engine) speed

re'gina [re'dʒina] *sf* queen

regio'nale [redʒo'nale] *ag* regional
▷ *sm* local train (*stopping frequently*)

regi'one [re'dʒone] *sf* region;
(*territorio*) region, district, area

re'gista, -i, -e [re'dʒista] *sm/f* (*TV,
Cinema ecc*) director

regis'trare [redʒis'trare] *vt* (*Amm*)
to register; (*Comm*) to enter; (*notare*)
to note, take note of; (*canzone,
conversazione: strumento di misura*)
to record; (*mettere a punto*) to
adjust, regulate; (*bagagli*) to check
in; **registra'tore** *sm* (*strumento*)
recorder, register; (*magnetofono*) tape
recorder; **registratore di cassa** cash
register; **registratore a cassette**
cassette recorder

re'gistro [re'dʒistro] *sm* (*libro, Mus,
Tech*) register; ledger; logbook; (*Dir*)
registry

re'gnare [ren'nare] *vi* to reign, rule

'regno ['renno] *sm* kingdom; (*periodo*)
reign; (*fig*) realm; **il R~ Unito** the
United Kingdom; **regno animale/
vegetale** animal/vegetable kingdom

'regola *sf* rule; **a ~ d'arte** duly;
perfectly; **in ~** in order

rego'labile *ag* adjustable

regola'mento *sm* (*complesso di
norme*) regulations *pl*; (*di debito*)
settlement; **regolamento di conti**
(*fig*) settling of scores

rego'lare *ag* regular; (*in regola:
domanda*) in order, lawful ▷ *vt* to
regulate, control; (*apparecchio*) to
adjust, regulate; (*questione, conto,
debito*) to settle; **regolarsi** *vpr*
(*moderarsi*): **regolarsi nel bere/nello
spendere** to control one's drinking/

spending; (*comportarsi*) to behave, act

rela'tivo, -a *ag* relative

relazi'one [relat'tsjone] *sf* (*fra cose, persone*) relation(ship); (*resoconto*) report, account

rele'gare *vt* to banish; (*fig*) to relegate

religi'one [reli'dʒone] *sf* religion

re'liquia *sf* relic

re'litto *sm* wreck; (*fig*) down-and-out

re'mare *vi* to row

remini'scenze [reminiʃʃentse] *sfpl* reminiscences

remis'sivo, -a *ag* submissive, compliant

'remo *sm* oar

re'moto, -a *ag* remote

'rendere *vt* (*ridare*) to return, give back; (: *saluto ecc*) to return; (*produrre*) to yield, bring in; (*esprimere, tradurre*) to render; **~ qc possibile** to make sth possible; **rendersi** *vpr* **rendersi utile** to make o.s. useful; **rendersi conto di qc** to realize sth; **~ qc possibile** to make sth possible; **~ grazie a qn** give thanks to sb; **~ omaggio a qn** to pay homage to sb; **~ un servizio a qn** to do sb a service; **~ una testimonianza** to give evidence; **non so se rendo l'idea** I don't know if I'm making myself clear

rendi'mento *sm* (*reddito*) yield; (*di manodopera, Tecn*) efficiency; (*capacità di produrre*) output; (*di studenti*) performance

'rendita *sf* (*di individuo*) private o unearned income; (*Comm*) revenue; **rendita annua** annuity

'rene *sm* kidney

'renna *sf* reindeer *inv*

re'parto *sm* department, section; (*Mil*) detachment

repel'lente *ag* repulsive

repen'taglio [repen'taʎʎo] *sm* **mettere a ~** to jeopardize, risk

repen'tino, -a *ag* sudden, unexpected

reper'torio *sm* (*Teatro*) repertory;

(*elenco*) index, (alphabetical) list

'replica, -che *sf* repetition; reply, answer; (*obiezione*) objection; (*Teatro, Cinema*) repeat performance; (*copia*) replica

repli'care *vt* (*ripetere*) to repeat; (*rispondere*) to answer, reply

repressi'one *sf* repression

re'presso, -a *pp di* **reprimere**

re'primere *vt* to suppress, repress

re'pubblica, -che *sf* republic

reputazi'one [reputat'tsjone] *sf* reputation

requi'sire *vt* to requisition

requi'sito *sm* requirement

'resa *sf* (*l'arrendersi*) surrender; (*restituzione, rendimento*) return; **resa dei conti** rendering of accounts; (*fig*) day of reckoning

'resi *ecc vb vedi* **rendere**

resi'dente *ag* resident; **residenzi'ale** *ag* residential

re'siduo, -a *ag* residual, remaining ▷ *sm* remainder; (*Chim*) residue

'resina *sf* resin

resis'tente *ag* (*che resiste*): **~ a** resistant to; (*forte*) strong; (*duraturo*) long-lasting, durable; **~ al caldo** heat-resistant; **resis'tenza** *sf* resistance; (*di persona: fisica*) stamina, endurance; (: *mentale*) endurance, resistance

● **RESISTENZA**
●
● The **Resistenza** in Italy fought
● against the Nazis and the Fascists
● during the Second World War.
● Members of the **Resistenza**
● spanned a wide political spectrum
● and played a vital role in the
● Liberation and in the formation of
● the new democratic government at
● the end of the war.

re'sistere *vi* to resist; **~ a** (*assalto, tentazioni*) to resist; (*dolore*) to withstand; (*non patir danno*) to be resistant to

reso'conto *sm* report, account

res'pingere [res'pindʒere] *vt* to drive back, repel; (*rifiutare*) to reject; (*Ins: bocciare*) to fail

respi'rare *vi* to breathe; (*fig*) to get one's breath; to breathe again ▷ *vt* to breathe (in), inhale; **respirazi'one** *sf* breathing; **respirazione artificiale** artificial respiration; **res'piro** *sm* breathing *no pl*; (*singolo atto*) breath; (*fig*) respite, rest; **mandare un respiro di sollievo** to give a sigh of relief

respon'sabile *ag* responsible ▷ *sm/f* person responsible; (*capo*) person in charge; **~ di** responsible for; (*Dir*) liable for; **responsabilità** *sf inv* responsibility; (*legale*) liability

res'ponso *sm* answer

'ressa *sf* crowd, throng

'ressi *ecc vb vedi* **reggere**

res'tare *vi* (*rimanere*) to remain, stay; (*avanzare*) to be left, remain; **~ orfano/cieco** to become *o* be left an orphan/become blind; **~ d'accordo** to agree; **non resta più niente** there's nothing left; **restano pochi giorni** there are only a few days left

restau'rare *vt* to restore

res'tio, -a, -'tii, -'tie *ag*: **~ a** reluctant to

restitu'ire *vt* to return, give back; (*energie, forze*) to restore

'resto *sm* remainder, rest; (*denaro*) change; (*Mat*) remainder; **resti** *smpl* (*di cibo*) leftovers; (*di città*) remains; **del ~** moreover, besides; **tenga pure il ~** keep the change; **resti mortali** (mortal) remains

res'tringere [res'trindʒere] *vt* to reduce; (*vestito*) to take in; (*stoffa*) to shrink; (*fig*) to restrict, limit; **restringersi** *vpr* (*strada*) to narrow; (*stoffa*) to shrink

'rete *sf* net; (*fig*) trap, snare; (*di recinzione*) wire netting; (*Aut, Ferr,* *di spionaggio ecc*) network; **segnare una ~** (*Calcio*) to score a goal; **la R~** the Web; **rete ferroviaria** railway network; **rete del letto** (sprung) bed base; **rete stradale** road network; **rete (televisiva)** (*sistema*) network; (*canale*) channel

reti'cente [reti'tʃɛnte] *ag* reticent

retico'lato *sm* grid; (*rete*) wire netting; (*di filo spinato*) barbed wire (fence)

'retina *sf* (*Anat*) retina

re'torico, -a, -ci, -che *ag* rhetorical

retribu'ire *vt* to pay

'retro *sm inv* back ▷ *av* (*dietro*): **vedi ~** see over(leaf)

retro'cedere [retro'tʃɛdere] *vi* to withdraw ▷ *vt* (*Calcio*) to relegate; (*Mil*) to degrade

re'trogrado, -a *ag* (*fig*) reactionary, backward-looking

retro'marcia [retro'martʃa] *sf* (*Aut*) reverse; (*: dispositivo*) reverse gear

retro'scena [retro'ʃɛna] *sm inv* (*Teatro*) backstage; **i ~** (*fig*) the behind-the-scenes activities

retrovi'sore *sm* (*Aut*) (rear-view) mirror

'retta *sf* (*Mat*) straight line; (*di convitto*) charge for bed and board; (*fig: ascolto*): **dar ~ a** to listen to, pay attention to

rettango'lare *ag* rectangular

ret'tangolo, -a *ag* right-angled ▷ *sm* rectangle

ret'tifica, -che *sf* rectification, correction

'rettile *sm* reptile

retti'lineo, -a *ag* rectilinear

'retto, -a *pp di* **reggere** ▷ *ag* straight; (*Mat*): **angolo ~** right angle; (*onesto*) honest, upright; (*giusto, esatto*) correct, proper, right

ret'tore *sm* (*Rel*) rector; (*di università*) ≈ chancellor

reuma'tismo *sm* rheumatism

revisi'one *sf* auditing *no pl*; audit;

servicing *no pl*; overhaul; review; revision; **revisione di bozze** proofreading

revi'sore *sm*; **revisore di bozze** proofreader; **revisore di conti** auditor

revival [ri'vaivəl] *sm inv* revival

'revoca *sf* revocation

revo'care *vt* to revoke

re'volver *sm inv* revolver

ri'abbia *ecc vb vedi* **riavere**

riabili'tare *vt* to rehabilitate

rianimazi'one [rianimat'tsjone] *sf (Med)* resuscitation; **centro di ~** intensive care unit

ria'prire *vt* to reopen, open again; **riaprirsi** *vpr* to reopen, open again

ri'armo *sm (Mil)* rearmament

rias'sumere *vt (riprendere)* to resume; *(impiegare di nuovo)* to re-employ; *(sintetizzare)* to summarize; **rias'sunto, -a** *pp di* **riassumere** ▷ *sm* summary

riattac'care *vt (attaccare di nuovo)*: **~ (a)** *(manifesto, francobollo)* to stick back (on); *(bottone)* to sew back (on); *(quadro, chiavi)* to hang back up (on); **~ (il telefono** *o* **il ricevitore)** to hang up (the receiver)

ria'vere *vt* to have again; *(avere indietro)* to get back; *(riacquistare)* to recover; **riaversi** *vpr* to recover

riba'dire *vt (fig)* to confirm

ri'balta *sf* flap; *(Teatro: proscenio)* front of the stage; *(fig)* limelight; **luci della ~** footlights *pl*

ribal'tabile *ag (sedile)* tip-up

ribal'tare *vt, vi (anche:* **ribaltarsi***)* to turn over, tip over

ribas'sare *vt* to lower, bring down ▷ *vi* to come down, fall

ri'battere *vt* to return, hit back; *(confutare)* to refute; **~ che** to retort that

ribel'larsi *vpr*: **~ (a)** to rebel (against); **ri'belle** *ag (soldati)* rebel; *(ragazzo)* rebellious ▷ *sm/f* rebel

'ribes *sm inv* currant; **ribes nero** blackcurrant; **ribes rosso** redcurrant

ri'brezzo [ri'breddzo] *sm* disgust, loathing; **far ~ a** to disgust

ribut'tante *ag* disgusting, revolting

rica'dere *vi* to fall again; *(scendere a terra: fig: nel peccato ecc)* to fall back; *(vestiti, capelli ecc)* to hang (down); *(riversarsi: fatiche, colpe)*: **~ su** to fall on; **rica'duta** *sf (Med)* relapse

rica'mare *vt* to embroider

ricambi'are *vt* to change again; *(contraccambiare)* to repay, return; **ri'cambio** *sm* exchange, return; *(Fisiol)* metabolism

ri'camo *sm* embroidery

ricapito'lare *vt* to recapitulate, sum up

ricari'care *vt (arma, macchina fotografica)* to reload; *(pipa)* to refill; *(orologio)* to rewind; *(batteria)* to recharge

ricat'tare *vt* to blackmail; **ri'catto** *sm* blackmail

rica'vare *vt (estrarre)* to draw out, extract; *(ottenere)* to obtain, gain

ric'chezza [rik'kettsa] *sf* wealth; *(fig)* richness

'riccio, -a ['rittʃo] *ag* curly ▷ *sm (Zool)* hedgehog; **riccio di mare** sea urchin; **'ricciolo** *sm* curl

'ricco, -a, -chi, -che *ag* rich; *(persona, paese)* rich, wealthy ▷ *sm/f* rich man/woman; **i ricchi** the rich; **~ di** full of; rich in

ri'cerca, -che [ri'tʃerka] *sf* search; *(indagine)* investigation, inquiry; *(studio)*: **la ~** research; **una ~** piece of research; **ricerca di mercato** market research

ricer'care [ritʃer'kare] *vt (motivi, cause)* to look for, try to determine; *(successo, piacere)* to pursue; *(onore, gloria)* to seek; **ricer'cato, -a** *ag (apprezzato)* much sought-after; *(affettato)* studied, affected ▷ *sm/f (Polizia)* wanted man/woman

ricerca'tore, -'trice [ritʃerka'tore]
sm/f (*Ins*) researcher

ri'cetta [ri'tʃetta] *sf* (*Med*)
prescription; (*Cuc*) recipe; **mi può fare
una ~ medica?** could you write me a
prescription?

ricettazi'one [ritʃettat'tsjone] *sf*
(*Dir*) receiving (stolen goods)

ri'cevere [ri'tʃevere] *vt* to receive;
(*stipendio, lettera*) to get, receive;
(*accogliere: ospite*) to welcome;
(*vedere: cliente, rappresentante ecc*) to
see; **ricevi'mento** *sm* receiving *no
pl*; (*festa*) reception; **ricevi'tore** *sm*
(*Tecn*) receiver; **rice'vuta** *sf* receipt;
**posso avere una ricevuta, per
favore?** can I have a receipt, please?;
ricevuta fiscale receipt for tax
purposes; **ricevuta di ritorno** (*Posta*)
advice of receipt

richia'mare [rikja'mare] *vt* (*chiamare
indietro, ritelefonare*) to call back;
(*ambasciatore, truppe*) to recall;
(*rimproverare*) to reprimand; (*attirare*)
to attract, draw; **può ~ più tardi?** can
you call back later?; **richiamarsi a**
(*riferirsi a*) to refer to

richi'edere [ri'kjɛdere] *vt* to ask
again for; (*chiedere indietro*): **~ qc** to
ask for sth back; (*chiedere: per sapere*)
to ask; (*: per avere*) to ask for; (*Amm:
documenti*) to apply for; (*esigere*) to
need, require; **richi'esta** *sf* (*domanda*)
request; (*Amm*) application, request;
(*esigenza*) demand, request; **a
richiesta** on request

rici'clare [ritʃi'klare] *vt* to recycle

'ricino ['ritʃino] *sm*: **olio di ~** castor oil

ricogni'zi'one [rikoɲɲit'tsjone]
sf (*Mil*) reconnaissance; (*Dir*)
recognition, acknowledgement

ricominci'are [rikomin'tʃare] *vt, vi* to
start again, begin again

ricom'pensa *sf* reward

ricompen'sare *vt* to reward

riconciliarsi *vpr* to be reconciled

ricono'scente [rikonoʃʃente] *ag*
grateful

rico'noscere [riko'noʃʃere] *vt* to
recognize; (*Dir: figlio, debito*) to
acknowledge; (*ammettere: errore*) to
admit, acknowledge

rico'perto, -a *pp di* **ricoprire**

ricopi'are *vt* to copy

rico'prire *vt* (*coprire*) to cover;
(*occupare: carica*) to hold

ricor'dare *vt* to remember, recall;
(*richiamare alla memoria*): **~ qc a
qn** to remind sb of sth; **ricordarsi**
vpr **ricordarsi (di)** to remember;
ricordarsi di qc/di aver fatto to
remember sth/having done

ri'cordo *sm* memory; (*regalo*)
keepsake, souvenir; (*di viaggio*)
souvenir

ricor'rente *ag* recurrent, recurring;
ricor'renza *sf* recurrence; (*festività*)
anniversary

ri'correre *vi* (*ripetersi*) to recur; **~ a**
(*rivolgersi*) to turn to; (*: Dir*) to appeal
to; (*servirsi di*) to have recourse to

ricostitu'ente *ag* (*Med*): **cura ~** tonic

ricostru'ire *vt* (*casa*) to rebuild; (*fatti*)
to reconstruct

ri'cotta *sf* soft white unsalted cheese
made from sheep's milk

ricove'rare *vt* to give shelter to; **~ qn
in ospedale** to admit sb to hospital

ri'covero *sm* shelter, refuge; (*Mil*)
shelter; (*Med*) admission (to hospital)

ricreazi'one [rikreat'tsjone] *sf*
recreation, entertainment; (*Ins*) break

ri'credersi *vpr* to change one's mind

ridacchi'are [ridak'kjare] *vi* to
snigger

ri'dare *vt* to return, give back

'ridere *vi* to laugh; (*deridere, beffare*): **~
di** to laugh at, make fun of

ri'dicolo, -a *ag* ridiculous, absurd

ridimensio'nare *vt* to reorganize;
(*fig*) to see in the right perspective

ri'dire *vt* to repeat; (*criticare*) to find
fault with; to object to; **trova sempre
qualcosa da ~** he always manages to

find fault

ridon'dante *ag* redundant

ri'dotto, -a *pp di* **ridurre** ▷ *ag* (*biglietto*) reduced; (*formato*) small

ri'duco *ecc vb vedi* **ridurre**

ri'durre *vt* (*anche Chim, Mat*) to reduce; (*prezzo, spese*) to cut, reduce; (*accorciare: opera letteraria*) to abridge; (: *Radio, TV*) to adapt; **ridursi** *vpr* (*diminuirsi*) to be reduced, shrink; **ridursi a** to be reduced to; **ridursi pelle e ossa** to be reduced to skin and bone; **ri'dussi** *ecc vb vedi* **ridurre**; **ridut'tore** *sm* (*Elec*) adaptor; **riduzi'one** *sf* reduction; abridgement; adaptation; **ci sono riduzioni per i bambini/gli studenti?** is there a reduction for children/students?

ri'ebbi *ecc vb vedi* **riavere**

riem'pire *vt* to fill (up); (*modulo*) to fill in *o* out; **riempirsi** *vpr* to fill (up); **~ qc di** to fill sth (up) with

rien'tranza [rien'trantsa] *sf* recess; indentation

rien'trare *vi* (*entrare di nuovo*) to go (*o* come) back in; (*tornare*) to return; (*fare una rientranza*) to go in, curve inwards; to be indented; (*riguardare*): **~ in** to be included among, form part of

riepilo'gare *vt* to summarize ▷ *vi* to recapitulate

ri'esco *ecc vb vedi* **riuscire**

ri'fare *vt* to do again; (*ricostruire*) to make again; (*nodo*) to tie again, do up again; (*imitare*) to imitate, copy; **rifarsi** *vpr* (*risarcirsi*): **rifarsi di** to make up for; (*vendicarsi*): **rifarsi di qc su qn** to get one's own back on sb for sth; (*riferirsi*): **rifarsi a** to go back to; to follow; **~ il letto** to make the bed; **rifarsi una vita** to make a new life for o.s.

riferi'mento *sm* reference; **in** *o* **con ~ a** with reference to

rife'rire *vt* (*riportare*) to report ▷ *vi* to do a report; **riferirsi** *vpr* **riferirsi a** to refer to

rifi'nire *vt* to finish off, put the finishing touches to

rifiu'tare *vt* to refuse; **~ di fare** to refuse to do; **rifi'uto** *sm* refusal; **rifiuti** *smpl* (*spazzatura*) rubbish *sg*, refuse *sg*

riflessi'one *sf* (*Fisica, meditazione*) reflection; (*il pensare*) thought, reflection; (*osservazione*) remark

rifles'sivo, -a *ag* (*persona*) thoughtful, reflective; (*Ling*) reflexive

ri'flesso, -a *pp di* **riflettere** ▷ *sm* (*di luce, allo specchio*) reflection; (*Fisiol*) reflex; **di** *o* **per ~** indirectly

riflessologia [riflessolo'dʒia] *sf* reflexology

ri'flettere *vt* to reflect ▷ *vi* to think; **riflettersi** *vpr* to be reflected; **~ su** to think over

riflet'tore *sm* reflector; (*proiettore*) floodlight; searchlight

ri'flusso *sm* flowing back; (*della marea*) ebb; **un'epoca di ~** an era of nostalgia

ri'forma *sf* reform; **la R~** (*Rel*) the Reformation

riforma'torio *sm* (*Dir*) community home (*BRIT*), reformatory (*US*)

riforni'mento *sm* supplying, providing; restocking; **rifornimenti** *smpl* (*provviste*) supplies, provisions

rifor'nire *vt* (*provvedere*): **~ di** to supply *o* provide with; (*fornire di nuovo: casa ecc*) to restock; **rifornirsi** *vpr* **rifornirsi di qc** to stock up on sth

rifugi'arsi [rifu'dʒarsi] *vpr* to take refuge; **rifugi'ato, -a** *sm/f* refugee

ri'fugio [ri'fudʒo] *sm* refuge, shelter; (*in montagna*) shelter; **rifugio antiaereo** air-raid shelter

'riga, -ghe *sf* line; (*striscia*) stripe; (*di persone, cose*) line, row; (*regolo*) ruler; (*scriminatura*) parting; **mettersi in ~** to line up; **a righe** (*foglio*) lined; (*vestito*) striped

ri'gare *vt* (*foglio*) to rule ▷ *vi* **~ diritto**

(fig) to toe the line

rigatti'ere sm junk dealer

righerò ecc [riɡeˈrɔ] vb vedi **rigare**

'rigido, -a [ˈridʒido] ag rigid, stiff; *(membra ecc: indurite)* stiff; *(Meteor)* harsh, severe; *(fig)* strict

rigogli'oso, -a [riɡoʎˈʎoso] ag *(pianta)* luxuriant; *(fig: commercio, sviluppo)* thriving

ri'gore sm *(Meteor)* harshness, rigours pl; *(fig)* severity, strictness; *(anche:* **calcio di ~)** penalty; **di ~** compulsory; **a rigor di termini** strictly speaking

riguar'dare vt to look at again; *(considerare)* to regard, consider; *(concernere)* to regard, concern; **riguardarsi** vpr *(aver cura di sé)* to look after o.s.

rigu'ardo sm *(attenzione)* care; *(considerazione)* regard, respect; **~ a** concerning, with regard to; **non aver riguardi nell'agire/nel parlare** to act/speak freely

rilasci'are [rilaʃˈʃare] vt *(rimettere in libertà)* to release; *(Amm: documenti)* to issue

rilassarsi vpr to relax; *(fig: disciplina)* to become slack

rile'gare vt *(libro)* to bind

ri'leggere [riˈlɛddʒere] vt to reread, read again; *(rivedere)* to read over

ri'lento: **a ~** av slowly

rile'vante ag considerable; important

rile'vare vt *(ricavare)* to find; *(notare)* to notice; *(mettere in evidenza)* to point out; *(venire a conoscere: notizia)* to learn; *(raccogliere: dati)* to gather, collect; *(Topografia)* to survey; *(Mil)* to relieve; *(Comm)* to take over

rili'evo sm *(Arte, Geo)* relief; *(fig: rilevanza)* importance; *(Topografia)* survey; **dar ~ a** o **mettere in ~ qc** *(fig)* to bring sth out, highlight sth

rilut'tante ag reluctant

'rima sf rhyme; *(verso)* verse

riman'dare vt to send again; *(restituire, rinviare)* to send back, return; *(differire)*: **~ qc (a)** to postpone sth o put sth off (till); *(fare riferimento)*: **~ qn a** to refer sb to; **essere rimandato** *(Ins)* to have to repeat one's exams

ri'mando sm *(rinvio)* return; *(dilazione)* postponement; *(riferimento)* cross-reference

rima'nente ag remaining ▷ sm rest, remainder; **i rimanenti** *(persone)* the rest of them, the others

rima'nere vi *(restare)* to remain, stay; *(avanzare)* to be left, remain; *(restare stupito)* to be amazed; *(restare, mancare)*: **rimangono poche settimane a Pasqua** there are only a few weeks left till Easter; **rimane da vedere se** it remains to be seen whether; *(diventare)*: **~ vedovo** to be left a widower; *(trovarsi)*: **~ sorpreso** to be surprised

rimangi'are [rimanˈdʒare] vt to eat again; **~rsi la parola/una promessa** *(fig)* to go back on one's word/one's promise

ri'mango ecc vb vedi **rimanere**

rimargi'narsi vpr to heal

rimbal'zare [rimbalˈtsare] vi to bounce back, rebound; *(proiettile)* to ricochet

rimbam'bito, -a ag senile, in one's dotage

rimboc'care vt *(coperta)* to tuck in; *(maniche, pantaloni)* to turn o roll up

rimbom'bare vi to resound

rimbor'sare vt to pay back, repay

rimedi'are vi **~ a** to remedy ▷ vt *(fam: procurarsi)* to get o scrape together

ri'medio sm *(medicina)* medicine; *(cura, fig)* remedy, cure

ri'mettere vt *(mettere di nuovo)* to put back; *(indossare di nuovo)*: **~ qc** to put sth back on, put sth on again; *(affidare)* to entrust; *(: decisione)* to refer; *(condonare)* to remit; *(Comm: merci)* to deliver; *(: denaro)* to remit; *(vomitare)* to bring up; (*perdere: anche*: **rimetterci**) to lose; **rimettersi al bello** (*tempo*) to clear up; **rimettersi in salute** to get better, recover one's health

ri'misi *ecc vb vedi* **rimettere**

'rimmel® *sm inv* mascara

rimoder'nare *vt* to modernize

rimorchi'are [rimor'kjare] *vt* to tow; (*fig: ragazza*) to pick up

ri'morchio [ri'mɔrkjo] *sm* tow; (*veicolo*) trailer

ri'morso *sm* remorse

rimozi'one [rimot'tsjone] *sf* removal; (*da un impiego*) dismissal; (*Psic*) repression

rimpatri'are *vi* to return home ▷ *vt* to repatriate

rimpi'angere [rim'pjandʒere] *vt* to regret; (*persona*) to miss; **rimpi'anto, -a** *pp di* **rimpiangere** ▷ *sm* regret

rimpiaz'zare [rimpjat'tsare] *vt* to replace

rimpiccio'lire [rimpittʃo'lire] *vt* to make smaller ▷ *vi* (*anche*: **rimpicciolirsi**) to become smaller

rimpinzarsi [rimpin'tsarsi] *vpr* **~ (di qc)** to stuff o.s. (with sth)

rimprove'rare *vt* to rebuke, reprimand

rimu'overe *vt* to remove; (*destituire*) to dismiss

Rinasci'mento [rinaʃʃi'mento] *sm* **il ~** the Renaissance

ri'nascita [ri'naʃʃita] *sf* rebirth, revival

rinca'rare *vt* to increase the price of ▷ *vi* to go up, become more expensive

rinca'sare *vi* to go home

rinchi'udere [rin'kjudere] *vt* to shut (*o lock*) up; **rinchiudersi** *vpr* **rinchiudersi in** to shut o.s. up in; **rinchiudersi in se stesso** to withdraw into o.s.

rin'correre *vt* to chase, run after; **rin'corsa** *sf* short run

rin'crescere [rin'kreʃʃere] *vb impers* **mi rincresce che/di non poter**

fare I'm sorry that/I can't do, I regret that/being unable to do

rinfacci'are [rinfat'tʃare] *vt* (*fig*): **~ qc a qn** to throw sth in sb's face

rinfor'zare [rinfor'tsare] *vt* to reinforce, strengthen ▷ *vi* (*anche*: **rinforzarsi**) to grow stronger

rinfres'care *vt* (*atmosfera, temperatura*) to cool (down); (*abito, pareti*) to freshen up ▷ *vi* (*tempo*) to grow cooler; **rinfrescarsi** *vpr* (*ristorarsi*) to refresh o.s.; (*lavarsi*) to freshen up; **rin'fresco, -schi** *sm* (*festa*) party; **rinfreschi** *smpl* refreshments

rin'fusa *sf* **alla ~** in confusion, higgledy-piggledy

ringhi'are [rin'gjare] *vi* to growl, snarl

ringhi'era [rin'gjɛra] *sf* railing; (*delle scale*) banister(s) (*pl*)

ringiova'nire [rindʒova'nire] *vt* (*vestito, acconciatura ecc*): **~ qn** to make sb look younger; (*: vacanze ecc*) to rejuvenate ▷ *vi* (*anche*: **ringiovanirsi**) to become (*o look*) younger

ringrazia'mento [ringrattsja'mento] *sm* thanks *pl*

ringrazi'are [ringrat'tsjare] *vt* to thank; **~ qn di qc** to thank sb for sth

rinne'gare *vt* (*fede*) to renounce; (*figlio*) to disown, repudiate

rinnova'mento *sm* renewal; (*economico*) revival

rinno'vare *vt* to renew; (*ripetere*) to repeat, renew

rinoce'ronte [rinotʃe'ronte] *sm* rhinoceros

rino'mato, -a *ag* renowned, celebrated

rintracci'are [rintrat'tʃare] *vt* to track down

rintro'nare *vi* to boom, roar ▷ *vt* (*assordare*) to deafen; (*stordire*) to stun

rinunci'are [rinun'tʃare] *vi* **~ a** to give up, renounce; **~ a fare qc** to give up doing sth

rinvi'are vt (*rimandare indietro*) to send back, return; (*differire*): ~ **qc (a)** to postpone sth o put sth off (till); to adjourn sth (till); (*fare un rimando*): ~ **qn a** to refer sb to

rin'vio, -'vii sm (*rimando*) return; (*differimento*) postponement; (: *di seduta*) adjournment; (*in un testo*) cross-reference; **rinvio a giudizio** (*Dir*) indictment

riò ecc vb vedi **riavere**

ri'one sm district, quarter

riordi'nare vt (*rimettere in ordine*) to tidy; (*riorganizzare*) to reorganize

riorganiz'zare [riorganid'dzare] vt to reorganize

ripa'gare vt to repay

ripa'rare vt (*proteggere*) to protect, defend; (*correggere: male, torto*) to make up for; (: *errore*) to put right; (*aggiustare*) to repair ▷ vi (*mettere rimedio*): ~ **a** to make up for; **ripararsi** vpr (*rifugiarsi*) to take refuge o shelter; **dove lo posso far ~?** where can I get this repaired?; **riparazi'one** sf (*di un torto*) reparation; (*di guasto, scarpe*) repairing no pl; repair; (*risarcimento*) compensation

ri'paro sm (*protezione*) shelter, protection; (*rimedio*) remedy

ripar'tire vt (*dividere*) to divide up; (*distribuire*) to share out ▷ vi to set off again; to leave again

ripas'sare vi to come (o go) back ▷ vt (*scritto, lezione*) to go over (again)

ripen'sare vi to think; (*cambiare pensiero*) to change one's mind; (*tornare col pensiero*): ~ **a** to recall

ripercu'otersi vpr ~ **su** (*fig*) to have repercussions on

ripercussi'one sf (*fig*): **avere una ~ o delle ripercussioni su** to have repercussions on

ripes'care vt (*pesce*) to catch again; (*persona, cosa*) to fish out; (*fig: ritrovare*) to dig out

ri'petere vt to repeat; (*ripassare*) to go over; **può ~ per favore?** can you repeat that please?; **ripetizi'one** sf repetition; (*di lezione*) revision; **ripetizioni** sfpl (*Ins*) private tutoring o coaching sg

ripi'ano sm (*di mobile*) shelf

ri'picca sf **per ~** out of spite

'ripido, -a ag steep

ripie'gare vt to refold; (*piegare più volte*) to fold (up) ▷ vi (*Mil*) to retreat, fall back; (*fig: accontentarsi*): ~ **su** to make do with

ripi'eno, -a ag full; (*Cuc*) stuffed; (: *panino*) filled ▷ sm (*Cuc*) stuffing

ri'pone, ri'pongo ecc vb vedi **riporre**

ri'porre vt (*porre al suo posto*) to put back, replace; (*mettere via*) to put away; (*fiducia, speranza*): ~ **qc in qn** to place o put sth in sb

ripor'tare vt (*portare indietro*) to bring (o take) back; (*riferire*) to report; (*citare*) to quote; (*vittoria*) to gain; (*successo*) to have; (*Mat*) to carry; **riportarsi a** (*anche fig*) to go back to; (*riferirsi a*) to refer to; ~ **danni** to suffer damage

ripo'sare vt, vi to rest; **riposarsi** vpr to rest

ri'posi ecc vb vedi **riporre**

ri'poso sm rest; (*Mil*): ~! at ease!; **a ~** (*in pensione*) retired; **giorno di ~** day off

ripos'tiglio [ripos'tiʎʎo] sm lumber-room

ri'prendere vt (*prigioniero, fortezza*) to recapture; (*prendere indietro*) to take back; (*ricominciare: lavoro*) to resume; (*andare a prendere*) to fetch, come back for; (*riassumere: impiegati*) to take on again, re-employ; (*rimproverare*) to tell off; (*restringere: abito*) to take in; (*Cinema*) to shoot; **riprendersi** vpr to recover; (*correggersi*) to correct o.s.; **ri'presa** sf recapture; resumption; (*economica, da malattia, emozione*) recovery; (*Aut*) acceleration no pl; (*Teatro, Cinema*) rerun; (*Cinema: presa*) shooting no pl; shot; (*Sport*) second

half; (: Pugilato) round; **a più riprese**
on several occasions, several times;
ripresa cinematografica shot

ripristi'nare vt to restore

ripro'durre vt to reproduce;
riprodursi vpr (Biol) to reproduce;
(riformarsi) to form again

ripro'vare vt (provare di nuovo: gen)
to try again; (vestito) to try on again;
(: sensazione) to experience again ▷ vi
(tentare): **~ (a fare qc)** to try (to do
sth) again; **riproverò più tardi** I'll try
again later

ripudi'are vt to repudiate, disown

ripu'gnante [ripuɲ'ɲante] ag
disgusting, repulsive

ri'quadro sm square; (Archit) panel

ri'saia sf paddy field

risa'lire vi (ritornare in su) to go back
up; **~ a** (ritornare con la mente) to go
back to; (datare da) to date back to,
go back to

risal'tare vi (fig: distinguersi) to stand
out; (Archit) to project, jut out

risa'puto, -a ag **è ~ che ...** everyone
knows that ..., it is common
knowledge that ...

risarci'mento [risartʃi'mento]
sm **~ (di)** compensation (for);
risarcimento danni damages

risar'cire [risar'tʃire] vt (cose) to pay
compensation for; (persona): **~ qn di
qc** to compensate sb for sth

ri'sata sf laugh

riscalda'mento sm heating;
riscaldamento centrale central
heating

riscal'dare vt (scaldare) to heat;
(: mani, persona) to warm; (minestra) to
reheat; **riscaldarsi** vpr to warm up

ris'catto sm ransom; redemption

rischia'rare [riskja'rare] vt
(illuminare) to light up; (colore) to make
lighter; **rischiararsi** vpr (tempo) to
clear up; (cielo) to clear; (fig: volto) to
brighten up; **rischiararsi la voce** to
clear one's throat

rischi'are [ris'kjare] vt to risk ▷ vi
~ di fare qc to risk o run the risk of
doing sth

'rischio ['riskjo] sm risk; **rischi'oso, -a**
ag risky, dangerous

riscia'cquare [riʃʃa'kware] vt to rinse

riscon'trare vt (rilevare) to find

ris'cuotere vt (ritirare: somma) to
collect; (: stipendio) to draw, collect;
(assegno) to cash; (fig: successo ecc) to
win, earn

'rise ecc vb vedi **ridere**

risenti'mento sm resentment

risen'tire vt to hear again; (provare)
to feel ▷ vi **~ di** to feel (o show) the
effects of; **risentirsi** vpr **risentirsi
di** o **per** to take offence at, resent;
risen'tito, -a ag resentful

ri'serbo sm reserve

ri'serva sf reserve; (di caccia, pesca)
preserve; (restrizione, di indigeni)
reservation; **di ~** (provviste ecc) in
reserve

riser'vare vt (tenere in serbo) to
keep, put aside; (prenotare) to book,
reserve; **ho riservato un tavolo a
nome...** I booked a table in the name
of ...; **riser'vato, -a** ag (prenotato:
fig: persona) reserved; (confidenziale)
confidential

'risi ecc vb vedi **ridere**

risi'edere vi **~ a o in** to reside in

'risma sf (di carta) ream; (fig) kind, sort

'riso (pl(f) **risa**) (: il ridere) sm **il ~**
laughter; (pianta) rice ▷ pp di **ridere**

riso'lino sm snigger

ri'solsi ecc vb vedi **risolvere**

ri'solto, -a pp di **risolvere**

riso'luto, -a ag determined, resolute

risoluzi'one [risolut'tsjone] sf
solving no pl; (Mat) solution; (decisione,
di schermo, immagine) resolution

ri'solvere vt (difficoltà, controversia) to
resolve; (problema) to solve; (decidere):
~ di fare to resolve to do; **risolversi**
vpr (decidersi): **risolversi a fare** to
make up one's mind to do; (andare a

finire): **risolversi in** to end up, turn out; **risolversi in nulla** to come to nothing

riso'nanza [riso'nantsa] *sf* resonance; **aver vasta ~** (*fig: fatto ecc*) to be known far and wide

ri'sorgere [ri'sordʒere] *vi* to rise again; **risorgi'mento** *sm* revival; **il Risorgimento** (*Storia*) the Risorgimento

● **RISORGIMENTO**
●
● The **Risorgimento** was the
● political movement which led to
● the proclamation of the Kingdom
● of Italy in 1861, and eventually to
● unification in 1871.

ri'sorsa *sf* expedient, resort; **risorse umane** human resources

ri'sorsi *ecc vb vedi* **risorgere**

ri'sotto *sm* (*Cuc*) risotto

risparmi'are *vt* to save; (*non uccidere*) to spare ▷ *vi* to save; **~ qc a qn** to spare sb sth

ris'parmio *sm* saving *no pl*; (*denaro*) savings *pl*; **risparmi** *smpl* (*denaro*) savings

rispec'chiare [rispek'kjare] *vt* to reflect

rispet'tabile *ag* respectable

rispet'tare *vt* to respect; **farsi ~ to** command respect

rispet'tivo, -a *ag* respective

ris'petto *sm* respect; **rispetti** *smpl* (*saluti*) respects, regards; **~ a** (*in paragone a*) compared to; (*in relazione a*) as regards, as for

ris'pondere *vi* to answer, reply; (*freni*) to respond; **~ a** (*domanda*) to answer, reply to; (*persona*) to answer; (*invito*) to reply to; (*provocazione: veicolo, apparecchio*) to respond to; (*corrispondere a*) to correspond to; (*: speranze, bisogno*) to answer; **~ di** to answer for; **ris'posta** *sf* answer,

reply; **in risposta a** in reply to

'rissa *sf* brawl

ris'tampa *sf* reprinting *no pl*; reprint

risto'rante *sm* restaurant; **mi può consigliare un buon ~?** can you recommend a good restaurant?

ris'tretto, -a *pp di* **restringere** ▷ *ag* (*racchiuso*) enclosed, hemmed in; (*angusto*) narrow; (*limitato*): **~ (a)** restricted o limited (to); (*Cuc: brodo*) thick; (*: caffè*) extra strong

ristruttu'rare *vt* (*azienda*) to reorganize; (*edificio*) to restore; (*appartamento*) to alter; (*crema, balsamo*) to repair

risucchi'are [risuk'kjare] *vt* to suck in

risul'tare *vi* (*dimostrarsi*) to prove (to be), turn out (to be); (*riuscire*): **~ vincitore** to emerge as the winner; **~ da** (*provenire*) to result from, be the result of; **mi risulta che ...** I understand that ...; **non mi risulta** not as far as I know; **risul'tato** *sm* result

risuo'nare *vi* (*rimbombare*) to resound

risurrezi'one [risurret'tsjone] *sf* (*Rel*) resurrection

risusci'tare [risuʃʃi'tare] *vt* to resuscitate, restore to life; (*fig*) to revive, bring back ▷ *vi* to rise (from the dead)

ris'veglio [riz'veʎʎo] *sm* waking up; (*fig*) revival

ris'volto *sm* (*di giacca*) lapel; (*di pantaloni*) turn-up; (*di manica*) cuff; (*di tasca*) flap; (*di libro*) inside flap; (*fig*) implication

ritagli'are [ritaʎ'ʎare] *vt* (*tagliar via*) to cut out

ritar'dare *vi* (*persona, treno*) to be late; (*orologio*) to be slow ▷ *vt* (*rallentare*) to slow down; (*impedire*) to delay, hold up; (*differire*) to postpone, delay

ri'tardo *sm* delay; (*di persona aspettata*) lateness *no pl*; (*fig: mentale*) backwardness; **in ~** late; **il volo ha**

due ore di ~ the flight is two hours late; **scusi il ~** sorry I'm late

ri'tegno [ri'teɲɲo] *sm* restraint

rite'nere *vt* (*trattenere*) to hold back; (: *somma*) to deduct; (*giudicare*) to consider, believe

ri'tengo, ri'tenni *ecc vb vedi* **ritenere**

riterrò, ritiene *ecc vb vedi* **ritenere**

riti'rare *vt* to withdraw; (*Pol: richiamare*) to recall; (*andare a prendere: pacco ecc*) to collect, pick up; **ritirarsi** *vpr* to withdraw; (*da un'attività*) to retire; (*stoffa*) to shrink; (*marea*) to recede

'ritmo *sm* rhythm; (*fig*) rate; (: *della vita*) pace, tempo

'rito *sm* rite; **di ~** usual, customary

ritoc'care *vt* (*disegno, fotografia*) to touch up; (*testo*) to alter

ritor'nare *vi* to return, go (*o* come) back, to get back; (*ripresentarsi*) to recur; (*ridiventare*): **~ ricco** to become rich again ▷ *vt* (*restituire*) to return, give back; **quando ritorniamo?** when do we get back?

ritor'nello *sm* refrain

ri'torno *sm* return; **essere di ~** to be back; **avere un ~ di fiamma** (*Aut*) to backfire; (*fig: persona*) to be back in love again

ri'trarre *vt* (*trarre indietro, via*) to withdraw; (*distogliere: sguardo*) to turn away; (*rappresentare*) to portray, depict; (*ricavare*) to get, obtain

ritrat'tare *vt* (*disdire*) to retract, take back; (*trattare nuovamente*) to deal with again

ri'tratto, -a *pp di* **ritrarre** ▷ *sm* portrait

ritro'vare *vt* to find; (*salute*) to regain; (*persona*) to find; to meet again; **ritrovarsi** *vpr* (*essere, capitare*) to find o.s.; (*raccapezzarsi*) to find one's way; (*con senso reciproco*) to meet (again)

'ritto, -a *ag* (*in piedi*) standing, on one's feet; (*levato in alto*) erect, raised;

(: *capelli*) standing on end; (*posto verticalmente*) upright

ritu'ale *ag, sm* ritual

riuni'one *sf* (*adunanza*) meeting; (*riconciliazione*) reunion

riu'nire *vt* (*ricongiungere*) to join (together); (*riconciliare*) to reunite, bring together (again); **riunirsi** *vpr* (*adunarsi*) to meet; (*tornare insieme*) to be reunited

riu'scire [riuʃʃire] *vi* (*uscire di nuovo*) to go out again, go back out; (*aver esito: fatti, azioni*) to go, turn out; (*aver successo*) to succeed, be successful; (*essere, apparire*) to be, prove; (*raggiungere il fine*) to manage, succeed; **~ a fare qc** to manage to do *o* succeed in doing *o* be able to do sth

'riva *sf* (*di fiume*) bank; (*di lago, mare*) shore

ri'vale *sm/f* rival; **rivalità** *sf* rivalry

rivalu'tare *vt* (*Econ*) to revalue

rive'dere *vt* to see again; (*ripassare*) to revise; (*verificare*) to check

rivedrò *ecc vb vedi* **rivedere**

rive'lare *vt* to reveal; (*divulgare*) to reveal, disclose; (*dare indizio*) to reveal, show; **rivelarsi** *vpr* (*manifestarsi*) to be revealed; **rivelarsi onesto** *ecc* to prove to be honest *ecc*; **rivelazi'one** *sf* revelation

rivendi'care *vt* to claim, demand

rivendi'tore, -'trice *sm/f* retailer; **rivenditore autorizzato** (*Comm*) authorized dealer

ri'verbero *sm* (*di luce, calore*) reflection; (*di suono*) reverberation

rivesti'mento *sm* covering; coating

rives'tire *vt* to dress again; (*ricoprire*) to cover; to coat; (*fig: carica*) to hold

ri'vidi *ecc vb vedi* **rivedere**

ri'vincita [ri'vintʃita] *sf* (*Sport*) return match; (*fig*) revenge

ri'vista *sf* review; (*periodico*) magazine, review; (*Teatro*) revue; variety show

ri'volgere [ri'vɔldʒere] *vt* (*attenzione*,

sguardo) to turn, direct; (*parole*) to address; **rivolgersi** *vpr* to turn round; (*fig: dirigersi per informazioni*): **rivolgersi a** to go and see, go and speak to; (: *ufficio*) to enquire at

ri'volsi *ecc vb vedi* **rivolgere**

ri'volta *sf* revolt, rebellion

rivol'tella *sf* revolver

rivoluzio'nare [rivoluttsjo'nare] *vt* to revolutionize

rivoluzio'nario, -a [rivoluttsjo'narjo] *ag, sm/f* revolutionary

rivoluzi'one [rivolut'tsjone] *sf* revolution

riz'zare [rit'tsare] *vt* to raise, erect; **rizzarsi** *vpr* to stand up; (*capelli*) to stand on end

'roba *sf* stuff, things *pl*; (*possessi, beni*) belongings *pl*, things *pl*, possessions *pl*; ~ **da mangiare** things *pl* to eat, food; ~ **da matti** sheer madness *o* lunacy

'robot *sm inv* robot

ro'busto, -a *ag* robust, sturdy; (*solido: catena*) strong

roc'chetto [rok'ketto] *sm* reel, spool

'roccia, -ce ['rɔttʃa] *sf* rock; **fare ~** (*Sport*) to go rock climbing

'roco, -a, chi, che *ag* hoarse

ro'daggio [ro'daddʒo] *sm* running (BRIT) *o* breaking (US) in; **in ~** running (BRIT) *o* breaking (US) in

rodi'tore *sm* (*Zool*) rodent

rodo'dendro *sm* rhododendron

ro'gnone [roɲ'ɲone] *sm* (*Cuc*) kidney

'rogo, -ghi *sm* (*per cadaveri*) (funeral) pyre; (*supplizio*): **il ~** the stake

rol'lio *sm* roll(ing)

'Roma *sf* Rome

Roma'nia *sf:* **la ~** Romania

ro'manico, -a, -ci, -che *ag* Romanesque

ro'mano, -a *ag, sm/f* Roman

ro'mantico, -a, -ci, -che *ag* romantic

romanzi'ere [roman'dzjɛre] *sm* novelist

ro'manzo, -a [ro'mandzo] *ag* (*Ling*) romance *cpd* ▷ *sm* novel; **romanzo d'appendice** serial (story); **romanzo giallo/poliziesco** detective story; **romanzo rosa** romantic novel

'rombo *sm* rumble, thunder, roar; (*Mat*) rhombus; (*Zool*) turbot; brill

'rompere *vt* to break; (*fidanzamento*) to break off ▷ *vi* to break; **rompersi** *vpr* to break; **mi rompe le scatole** (*fam*) he (*o* she) is a pain in the neck; **rompersi un braccio** to break an arm; **mi si è rotta la macchina** my car has broken down; **rompis'catole** (*fam*) *sm/f inv* pest, pain in the neck

'rondine *sf* (*Zool*) swallow

ron'zare [ron'dzare] *vi* to buzz, hum

ron'zio [ron'dzio] *sm* buzzing

'rosa *sf* rose ▷ *ag inv, sm* pink; **ro'sato, -a** *ag* pink, rosy ▷ *sm* (*vino*) rosé (wine)

rosicchi'are [rosik'kjare] *vt* to gnaw (at); (*mangiucchiare*) to nibble (at)

rosma'rino *sm* rosemary

roso'lare *vt* (*Cuc*) to brown

roso'lia *sf* (*Med*) German measles *sg*, rubella

ro'sone *sm* rosette; (*vetrata*) rose window

'rospo *sm* (*Zool*) toad

ros'setto *sm* (*per labbra*) lipstick

'rosso, -a *ag, sm, sm/f* red; **il mar R~** the Red Sea; **rosso d'uovo** egg yolk

rosticce'ria [rostittʃe'ria] *sf* shop selling roast meat and other cooked food

ro'taia *sf* rut, track; (*Ferr*) rail

ro'tella *sf* small wheel; (*di mobile*) castor

roto'lare *vt, vi* to roll; **rotolarsi** *vpr* to roll (about)

'rotolo *sm* roll; **andare a rotoli** (*fig*) to go to rack and ruin

ro'tondo, -a *ag* round

'rotta *sf* (*Aer, Naut*) course, route; (*Mil*) rout; **a ~ di collo** at breakneck speed; **essere in ~ con qn** to be on bad terms with sb

rotta'mare vt to scrap

rottamazione [rottama'tsjone] sf (come incentivo) the scrapping of old vehicles in return for incentives

rot'tame sm fragment, scrap, broken bit; **rottami** smpl (di nave, aereo ecc) wreckage sg

'rotto, -a pp di **rompere** ▷ ag broken; (calzoni) torn, split; **per il ~ della cuffia** by the skin of one's teeth

rot'tura sf breaking no pl; break; breaking off; (Med) fracture, break

rou'lotte [ru'lɔt] sf caravan

ro'vente ag red-hot

'rovere sm oak

ro'vescia [ro'veʃʃa] sf **alla ~** upside-down; inside-out; **oggi mi va tutto alla ~** everything is going wrong (for me) today

rovesci'are [roveʃʃare] vt (versare in giù) to pour; (: accidentalmente) to spill; (capovolgere) to turn upside down; (gettare a terra) to knock down; (: fig: governo) to overthrow; (piegare all'indietro: testa) to throw back; **rovesciarsi** vpr (sedia, macchina) to overturn; (barca) to capsize; (liquido) to spill; (fig: situazione) to be reversed

ro'vescio, -sci [ro'veʃʃo] sm other side, wrong side; (della mano) back; (di moneta) reverse; (pioggia) sudden downpour; (fig) setback; (Maglia: anche: **punto ~**) purl (stitch); (Tennis) backhand (stroke); **a ~** upside-down; inside-out; **capire qc a ~** to misunderstand sth

ro'vina sf ruin; **andare in ~** (andare a pezzi) to collapse; (fig) to go to rack and ruin; **rovine** sfpl (ruderi) ruins; **mandare in ~** to ruin

rovi'nare vi to collapse, fall down ▷ vt (danneggiare: fig) to ruin; **rovinarsi** vpr (persona) to ruin o.s.; (oggetto, vestito) to be ruined

rovis'tare vt (casa) to ransack; (tasche) to rummage in (o through)

'rovo sm (Bot) blackberry bush, bramble bush

'rozzo, -a ['roddzo] ag rough, coarse

ru'bare vt to steal; **~ qc a qn** to steal sth from sb; **mi hanno rubato il portafoglio** my wallet has been stolen

rubi'netto sm tap, faucet (US)

ru'bino sm ruby

ru'brica, -che sf (Stampa) column; (quadernetto) index book; address book; **rubrica d'indirizzi** address book; **rubrica telefonica** list of telephone numbers

'rudere sm (rovina) ruins pl

rudimen'tale ag rudimentary, basic

rudi'menti smpl rudiments; basic principles; basic knowledge sg

ruffi'ano sm pimp

'ruga, -ghe sf wrinkle

'ruggine ['ruddʒine] sf rust

rug'gire [rud'dʒire] vi to roar

rugi'ada [ru'dʒada] sf dew

ru'goso, -a ag wrinkled

rul'lino sm (Fot) spool; (: pellicola) film; **vorrei un ~ da 36 pose** I'd like a 36-exposure film

'rullo sm (di tamburi) roll; (arnese cilindrico, Tip) roller; **rullo compressore** steam roller; **rullo di pellicola** roll of film

rum sm rum

ru'meno, -a ag, sm/f, sm Romanian

rumi'nare vt (Zool) to ruminate

ru'more sm **un ~** a noise, a sound; **il ~** noise; **non riesco a dormire a causa del ~** I can't sleep for the noise; **rumo'roso, -a** ag noisy

> Attenzione! In inglese esiste la parola *rumour*, che però significa *voce* nel senso *diceria*.

ru'olo sm (Teatro: fig) role, part; (elenco) roll, register, list; **di ~** permanent, on the permanent staff

ru'ota sf wheel; **ruota anteriore/ posteriore** front/back wheel; **ruota di scorta** spare wheel

ruo'tare *vt, vi* to rotate
'rupe *sf* cliff
'ruppi *ecc vb vedi* **rompere**
ru'rale *ag* rural, country *cpd*
ru'scello [ruʃʃɛllo] *sm* stream
'ruspa *sf* excavator
rus'sare *vi* to snore
'Russia *sf* **la ~** Russia; **'russo, -a** *ag, sm/f, sm* Russian
'rustico, -a, -ci, -che *ag* rustic; (*fig*) rough, unrefined
rut'tare *vi* to belch; **'rutto** *sm* belch
'ruvido, -a *ag* rough, coarse

S

S. *abbr* (= *sud*) S; (= *santo*) St
sa *vb vedi* **sapere**
'sabato *sm* Saturday; **di** *o* **il ~** on Saturdays
'sabbia *sf* sand; **sabbie mobili** quicksand(s); **sabbi'oso, -a** *ag* sandy
'sacca, -che *sf* bag; (*bisaccia*) haversack; **sacca da viaggio** travelling bag
sacca'rina *sf* saccharin(e)
sacheggi'are [sakkedˈdʒare] *vt* to sack, plunder
sac'chetto [sakˈketto] *sm* (small) bag, (small) sack; **sacchetto di carta/di plastica** paper/plastic bag
'sacco, -chi *sm* bag; (*per carbone ecc*) sack; (*Anat, Biol*) sac; (*tela*) sacking; (*saccheggio*) sack(ing); (*fig: grande quantità*): **un ~ di** lots of, heaps of; **sacco a pelo** sleeping bag; **sacco per i rifiuti** bin bag
sacer'dote [satʃerˈdɔte] *sm* priest
sacrifi'care *vt* to sacrifice; **sacrificarsi** *vpr* to sacrifice o.s.;

(*privarsi di qc*) to make sacrifices
sacri'ficio [sakri'fitʃo] *sm* sacrifice
'sacro, -a *ag* sacred
'sadico, -a, -ci, -che *ag* sadistic
▷ *sm/f* sadist
sa'etta *sf* arrow; (*fulmine*)
thunderbolt; flash of lightning
sa'fari *sm inv* safari
sag'gezza [sad'dʒettsa] *sf* wisdom
'saggio, -a, -gi, -ge ['saddʒo] *ag*
wise ▷ *sm* (*persona*) sage; (*esperimento*)
test; (*fig: prova*) proof; (*campione*)
sample; (*scritto*) essay
Sagit'tario [sadʒit'tarjo] *sm*
Sagittarius
'sagoma *sf* (*profilo*) outline, profile;
(*forma*) form, shape; (*Tecn*) template;
(*bersaglio*) target; (*fig: persona*)
character
'sagra *sf* festival
sagres'tano *sm* sacristan; sexton
sagres'tia *sf* sacristy
Sa'hara [sa'ara] *sm*: **il (deserto del) ~**
the Sahara (Desert)
'sai *vb vedi* **sapere**
'sala *sf* hall; (*stanza*) room; (*Cinema:
di proiezione*) cinema; **sala d'aspetto**
waiting room; **sala da ballo**
ballroom; **sala giochi** amusement
arcade; **sala operatoria** operating
theatre; **sala da pranzo** dining room;
sala per concerti concert hall
sa'lame *sm* salami *no pl*, salami
sausage
sala'moia *sf* (*Cuc*) brine
sa'lato, -a *ag* (*sapore*) salty; (*Cuc*)
salted, salt *cpd*; (*fig: prezzo*) steep, stiff
sal'dare *vt* (*congiungere*) to join,
bind; (*parti metalliche*) to solder; (*: con
saldatura autogena*) to weld; (*conto*) to
settle, pay
'saldo, -a *ag* (*resistente, forte*) strong,
firm; (*fermo*) firm, steady, stable; (*fig*)
firm, steadfast ▷ *sm* (*svendita*) sale;
(*di conto*) settlement; (*Econ*) balance;
saldi *smpl* (*Comm*) sales; **essere ~
nella propria fede** (*fig*) to stick to

one's guns
'sale *sm* salt; (*fig*): **ha poco ~ in zucca**
he doesn't have much sense; **sale fino**
table salt; **sale grosso** cooking salt
'salgo *ecc vb vedi* **salire**
'salice ['salitʃe] *sm* willow; **salice
piangente** weeping willow
sali'ente *ag* (*fig*) salient, main
sali'era *sf* salt cellar
sa'lire *vi* to go (*o* come) up; (*aereo ecc*)
to climb, go up; (*passeggero*) to get
on; (*sentiero, prezzi, livello*) to go up,
rise ▷ *vt* (*scale, gradini*) to go (*o* come)
up; **~ su** to climb (up); **~ sul treno/
sull'autobus** to board the train/the
bus; **~ in macchina** to get into the
car; **sa'lita** *sf* climb, ascent; (*erta*) hill,
slope; **in salita** *ag, av* uphill
sa'liva *sf* saliva
'salma *sf* corpse
'salmo *sm* psalm
sal'mone *sm* salmon
sa'lone *sm* (*stanza*) sitting room,
lounge; (*in albergo*) lounge; (*su nave*)
lounge, saloon; (*mostra*) show,
exhibition; **salone di bellezza** beauty
salon
sa'lotto *sm* lounge, sitting room;
(*mobilio*) lounge suite
sal'pare *vi* (*Naut*) to set sail; (*anche: ~
l'ancora*) to weigh anchor
'salsa *sf* (*Cuc*) sauce; **salsa di
pomodoro** tomato sauce
sal'siccia, -ce [sal'sittʃa] *sf* pork
sausage
sal'tare *vi* to jump, leap; (*esplodere*)
to blow up, explode; (*: valvola*) to
blow; (*venir via*) to pop off; (*non aver
luogo: corso ecc*) to be cancelled ▷ *vt* to
jump (over), leap (over); (*fig: pranzo,
capitolo*) to skip, miss (out); (*Cuc*) to
sauté; **far ~** to blow up; to burst open;
~ fuori (*fig: apparire all'improvviso*) to
turn up
saltel'lare *vi* to skip; to hop
'salto *sm* jump; (*Sport*) jumping; **fare
un ~** to jump, leap; **fare un ~ da qn** to

pop over to sb's (place); **salto in alto/ lungo** high/long jump; **salto con l'asta** pole vaulting; **salto mortale** somersault

saltu'ario, -a *ag* occasional, irregular

sa'lubre *ag* healthy, salubrious

salume'ria *sf* delicatessen

sa'lumi *smpl* salted pork meats

salu'tare *ag* healthy; (*fig*) salutary, beneficial ▷ *vt* (*incontrandosi*) to greet; (*congedandosi*) to say goodbye to; (*Mil*) to salute

sa'lute *sf* health; **~!** (*a chi starnutisce*) bless you!; (*nei brindisi*) cheers!; **bere alla ~ di qn** to drink (to) sb's health

sa'luto *sm* (*gesto*) wave; (*parola*) greeting; (*Mil*) salute

salvada'naio *sm* money box, piggy bank

salva'gente [salva'dʒɛnte] *sm* (*Naut*) lifebuoy; (*ciambella*) life belt; (*giubbotto*) life jacket; (*stradale*) traffic island

salvaguar'dare *vt* to safeguard

sal'vare *vt* to save; (*trarre da un pericolo*) to rescue; (*proteggere*) to protect; **salvarsi** *vpr* to save o.s.; to escape; **salvaschermo** [salvas'kermo] *sm* (*Inform*) screen saver; **salvaslip** [salva'zlip] *sm inv* panty liner; **salva'taggio** *sm* rescue

'salve (*fam*) *escl* hi!

'salvia *sf* (*Bot*) sage

salvi'etta *sf* napkin; **salvietta umidificata** baby wipe

'salvo, -a *ag* safe, unhurt, unharmed; (*fuori pericolo*) safe, out of danger ▷ *sm* **in ~** safe ▷ *prep* (*eccetto*) except; **mettere qc in ~** to put sth in a safe place; **~ che** (*a meno che*) unless; (*eccetto che*) except (that); **~ imprevisti** barring accidents

sam'buco *sm* elder (tree)

'sandalo *sm* (*Bot*) sandalwood; (*calzatura*) sandal

'sangue *sm* blood; **farsi cattivo ~** to fret, get in a state; **sangue freddo**

(*fig*) sang-froid, calm; **a ~ freddo** in cold blood; **sangui'nare** *vi* to bleed

sanità *sf* health; (*salubrità*) healthiness; **Ministero della S~** Department of Health; **sanità mentale** sanity

sani'tario, -a *ag* health *cpd*; (*condizioni*) sanitary ▷ *sm* (*Amm*) doctor; **sanitari** *smpl* (*impianti*) bathroom *o* sanitary fittings

'sanno *vb vedi* **sapere**

'sano, -a *ag* healthy; (*denti, costituzione*) healthy, sound; (*integro*) whole, unbroken; (*fig: politica, consigli*) sound; **~ di mente** sane; **di sana pianta** completely, entirely; **~ e salvo** safe and sound

'santo, -a *ag* holy; (*fig*) saintly; (*seguito da nome proprio*) saint ▷ *sm/f* saint; **la Santa Sede** the Holy See

santu'ario *sm* sanctuary

sanzi'one [san'tsjone] *sf* sanction; (*penale, civile*) sanction, penalty

sa'pere *vt* to know; (*essere capace di*): **so nuotare** I know how to swim, I can swim ▷ *vi* **~ di** (*aver sapore*) to taste of; (*aver odore*) to smell of ▷ *sm* knowledge; **far ~ qc a qn** to inform sb about sth, let sb know sth; **mi sa che non sia vero** I don't think that's true; **non lo so** I don't know; **non so l'inglese** I don't speak English; **sa dove posso...?** do you know where I can ...?

sa'pone *sm* soap; **sapone da bucato** washing soap

sa'pore *sm* taste, flavour; **sapo'rito, -a** *ag* tasty

sappi'amo *vb vedi* **sapere**

saprò *ecc vb vedi* **sapere**

sarà *ecc vb vedi* **essere**

saraci'nesca [saratʃi'neska] *sf* (*serranda*) rolling shutter

sar'castico, -a, ci, che *ag* sarcastic

Sar'degna [sar'deɲɲa] *sf*: **la ~** Sardinia

sar'dina *sf* sardine

sa'rei ecc vb vedi **essere**

SARS sigla f (Med: = severe acute respiratory syndrome) SARS

'**sarta** sf vedi **sarto**

'**sarto, -a** sm/f tailor/dressmaker

'**sasso** sm stone; (ciottolo) pebble; (masso) rock

sas'sofono sm saxophone

sas'soso, -a ag stony; pebbly

'**Satana** sm Satan

satelli'tare agg satellite cpd

sa'tellite sm, ag satellite

'**satira** sf satire

'**sauna** sf sauna

sazi'are [sat'tsjare] vt to satisfy, satiate; **saziarsi** vpr **saziarsi (di)** to eat one's fill (of); (fig) **saziarsi di** to grow tired o weary of

'**sazio, -a** ['sattsjo] ag: ~ **(di)** sated (with), full (of); (fig: stufo) fed up (with), sick (of); **sono ~** I'm full (up)

sba'dato, -a ag careless, inattentive

sbadigli'are [zbadiʎ'ʎare] vi to yawn; **sba'diglio** sm yawn

sbagli'are [zbaʎ'ʎare] vt to make a mistake in, get wrong ▷ vi to make a mistake, be mistaken, be wrong; (operare in modo non giusto) to err; **sbagliarsi** vpr to make a mistake, be mistaken, be wrong; ~ **strada/la mira** to take the wrong road/miss one's aim

sbagli'ato, -a [zbaʎ'ʎato] ag (gen) wrong; (compito) full of mistakes; (conclusione) erroneous

'**sbaglio** sm mistake, error; (morale) error; **fare uno ~** to make a mistake

sbalor'dire vt to stun, amaze ▷ vi to be stunned, be amazed

sbal'zare [zbal'tsare] vt to throw, hurl ▷ vi (balzare) to bounce; (saltare) to leap, bound

sban'dare vi (Naut) to list; (Aer) to bank; (Aut) to skid

sba'raglio [zba'raʎʎo] sm rout; defeat; **gettarsi allo ~** to risk everything

sbaraz'zarsi [zbarat'tsarsi] vpr: ~ **di** to get rid of, rid o.s. of

sbar'care vt (passeggeri) to disembark; (merci) to unload ▷ vi to disembark

'**sbarra** sf bar; (di passaggio a livello) barrier; (Dir): **presentarsi alla ~** to appear before the court

sbar'rare vt (strada ecc) to block, bar; (assegno) to cross; ~ **il passo** to bar the way; ~ **gli occhi** to open one's eyes wide

'**sbattere** vt (porta) to slam, bang; (tappeti, ali, Cuc) to beat; (urtare) to knock, hit ▷ vi (porta, finestra) to bang; (agitarsi: ali, vele ecc) to flap; **me ne sbatto!** (fam) I don't give a damn!

sba'vare vi to dribble; (colore) to smear, smudge

'**sberla** sf slap

sbia'dire vi, vt to fade; **sbia'dito, -a** ag faded; (fig) colourless, dull

sbian'care vt to whiten; (tessuto) to bleach ▷ vi (impallidire) to grow pale o white

sbirci'ata [zbir'tʃata] sf: **dare una ~ a qc** to glance at sth, have a look at sth

sbloc'care vt to unblock, free; (freno) to release; (prezzi, affitti) to decontrol; **sbloccarsi** vpr (gen) to become unblocked; (passaggio, strada) to clear, become unblocked

sboc'care vi: ~ **in** (fiume) to flow into; (strada) to lead into; (persona) to come (out) into; (fig: concludersi) to end (up) in

sboc'cato, -a ag (persona) foul-mouthed; (linguaggio) foul

sbocci'are [zbot'tʃare] vi (fiore) to bloom, open (out)

sbol'lire vi (fig) to cool down, calm down

'**sbornia** (fam) sf: **prendersi una ~** to get plastered

sbor'sare vt (denaro) to pay out

sbot'tare vi: ~ **in una risata/per la collera** to burst out laughing/explode with anger

sbotto'nare *vt* to unbutton, undo

sbrai'tare *vi* to yell, bawl

sbra'nare *vt* to tear to pieces

sbricio'lare [zbritʃo'lare] *vt* to crumble; **sbriciolarsi** *vpr* to crumble

sbri'gare *vt* to deal with; **sbrigarsi** *vpr* to hurry (up)

'sbronza ['zbrontsa] (*fam*) *sf* (*ubriaco*): **prendersi una ~** to get plastered

sbron'zarsi [zbron'tsarsi] *vpr* (*fam*) to get sozzled

'sbronzo, -a ['zbrontso] (*fam*) *ag* plastered

sbruf'fone, -a *sm/f* boaster

sbu'care *vi* to come out, emerge; (*improvvisamente*) to pop out (o up)

sbucci'are [zbut'tʃare] *vt* (*arancia, patata*) to peel; (*piselli*) to shell; **sbucciarsi un ginocchio** to graze one's knee

sbucherò *ecc* [zbuke'rɔ] *vb vedi* **sbucare**

sbuf'fare *vi* (*persona, cavallo*) to snort; (*ansimare*) to puff, pant; (*treno*) to puff

sca'broso, -a *ag* (*fig: difficile*) difficult, thorny; (: *imbarazzante*) embarrassing; (: *sconcio*) indecent

scacchi *smpl* (*gioco*) chess *sg*; **a ~** (*tessuto*) check(ed)

scacchi'era [skak'kjɛra] *sf* chessboard

scacci'are [skat'tʃare] *vt* to chase away o out, drive away o out

'scaddi *ecc vb vedi* **scadere**

sca'dente *ag* shoddy, of poor quality

sca'denza [ska'dɛntsa] *sf* (*di cambiale, contratto*) maturity; (*di passaporto*) expiry date; **a breve/lunga ~** short-/long-term; **data di ~** expiry date

sca'dere *vi* (*contratto ecc*) to expire; (*debito*) to fall due; (*valore, forze, peso*) to decline, go down

sca'fandro *sm* (*di palombaro*) diving suit; (*di astronauta*) space-suit

scaf'fale *sm* shelf; (*mobile*) set of shelves

'scafo *sm* (*Naut, Aer*) hull

scagio'nare [skadʒo'nare] *vt* to exonerate, free from blame

'scaglia ['skaʎʎa] *sf* (*Zool*) scale; (*scheggia*) chip, flake

scagli'are [skaʎ'ʎare] *vt* (*lanciare: anche fig*) to hurl, fling; **scagliarsi** (*anche*: **vr**): **scagliarsi su** *o* **contro** to hurl *o* fling o.s. at; (*fig*) to rail at

'scala *sf* (*a gradini ecc*) staircase, stairs *pl*; (*a pioli, di corda*) ladder; (*Mus, Geo, di colori, valori, fig*) scale; **scale** *sfpl* (*scalinata*) stairs; **su vasta ~/~ ridotta** on a large/small scale; **~ mobile (dei salari)** index-linked pay scale; **scala a libretto** stepladder; **scala mobile** escalator; (*Econ*) sliding scale

● **SCALA**
●
● Milan's world-famous **la Scala**
● theatre first opened its doors in
● 1778 with a performance of Salieri's
● opera, "L'Europa riconosciuta". It
● suffered serious damage in the
● bombing of Milan in 1943 and
● reopened in 1946 with a concert
● conducted by Toscanini. It also has
● a famous classical dance school.

sca'lare *vt* (*Alpinismo, muro*) to climb, scale; (*debito*) to scale down, reduce

scalda'bagno [skalda'baɲɲo] *sm* water-heater

scal'dare *vt* to heat; **scaldarsi** *vpr* to warm up, heat up; (*al fuoco, al sole*) to warm o.s.; (*fig*) to get excited

scal'fire *vt* to scratch

scali'nata *sf* staircase

sca'lino *sm* (*anche fig*) step; (*di scala a pioli*) rung

'scalo *sm* (*Naut*) slipway; (: *porto d'approdo*) port of call; (*Aer*) stopover; **fare ~ (a)** (*Naut*) to call (at), put in (at); (*Aer*) to land (at), make a stop (at); **scalo merci** (*Ferr*) goods (BRIT) o freight yard

scalop'pina sf (Cuc) escalope

scal'pello sm chisel

scal'pore sm noise, row; **far ~** (notizia) to cause a sensation o a stir

'scaltro, -a ag cunning, shrewd

'scalzo, -a ['skaltso] ag barefoot

scambi'are vt to exchange; (confondere): **~ qn/qc per** to take o mistake sb/sth for; **mi hanno scambiato il cappello** they've given me the wrong hat; **scambiarsi** vpr (auguri, confidenze, visite) to exchange; **~ qn/qc per** (confondere) to mistake sth/sb for

'scambio sm exchange; (Ferr) points pl; **fare (uno) ~** to make a swap

scampa'gnata [skampaɲ'ɲata] sf trip to the country

scam'pare vt (salvare) to rescue, save; (evitare: morte, prigione) to escape ▷ vi **~ (a qc)** to survive (sth), escape (sth); **scamparla bella** to have a narrow escape

'scampo sm (salvezza) escape; (Zool) prawn; **cercare ~ nella fuga** to seek safety in flight

'scampolo sm remnant

scanala'tura sf (incavo) channel, groove

scandagli'are [skandaʎ'ʎare] vt (Naut) to sound; (fig) to sound out; to probe

scandaliz'zare [skandalid'dzare] vt to shock, scandalize; **scandalizzarsi** vpr to be shocked

'scandalo sm scandal

Scandi'navia sf: **la ~** Scandinavia; **scandi'navo, -a** ag, sm/f Scandinavian

scanner ['skanner] sm inv (Inform) scanner

scansafa'tiche [skansafa'tike] sm/f inv idler, loafer

scan'sare vt (rimuovere) to move (aside), shift; (schivare: schiaffo) to dodge; (sfuggire) to avoid; **scansarsi**

vpr to move aside

scan'sia sf shelves pl; (per libri) bookcase

'scanso sm: **a ~ di** in order to avoid, as a precaution against

scanti'nato sm basement

scapacci'one [skapat'tʃone] sm clout

scapes'trato, -a ag dissolute

'scapola sf shoulder blade

'scapolo sm bachelor

scappa'mento sm (Aut) exhaust

scap'pare vi (fuggire) to escape; (andare via in fretta) to rush off; **lasciarsi ~ un'occasione** to let an opportunity go by; **~ di prigione** to escape from prison; **~ di mano** (oggetto) to slip out of one's hands; **~ di mente a qn** to slip sb's mind; **mi scappò detto** I let it slip; **scappa'toia** sf way out

scara'beo sm beetle

scarabocchi'are [skarabok'kjare] vt to scribble, scrawl; **scara'bocchio** sm scribble, scrawl

scara'faggio [skara'faddʒo] sm cockroach

scaraman'zia [skaraman'tsia] sf **per ~** for luck

scaraven'tare vt to fling, hurl; **scaraventarsi** vpr to fling o.s.

scarce'rare [skartʃe'rare] vt to release (from prison)

scardi'nare vt: **~ una porta** to take a door off its hinges

scari'care vt (merci, camion ecc) to unload; (passeggeri) to set down, put off; (arma) to unload; (: sparare, Elettr) to discharge; (corso d'acqua) to empty, pour; (fig: liberare da un peso) to unburden, relieve; (da Internet) to download; **scaricarsi** vpr (orologio) to run o wind down; (batteria, accumulatore) to go flat o dead; (fig: rilassarsi) to unwind; (: sfogarsi) to let off steam

'scarico, -a, -chi, -che ag unloaded;

(*orologio*) run down; (*accumulatore*) dead, flat ▷ *sm* (*di merci, materiali*) unloading; (*di immondizie*) dumping, tipping (BRIT); (*Tecn: deflusso*) draining; (: *dispositivo*) drain; (*Aut*) exhaust

scarlat'tina *sf* scarlet fever

scar'latto, -a *ag* scarlet

'scarpa *sf* shoe; **scarpe da ginnastica/tennis** gym/tennis shoes

scar'pata *sf* escarpment

scarpi'era *sf* shoe rack

scar'pone *sm* boot; **scarponi da montagna** climbing boots; **scarponi da sci** ski-boots

scarseggi'are [skarsed'dʒare] *vi* to be scarce; **~ di** to be short of, lack

'scarso, -a *ag* (*insufficiente*) insufficient, meagre; (*povero: annata*) poor, lean; (*Ins: voto*) poor; **~ di** lacking in; **3 chili scarsi** just under 3 kilos, barely 3 kilos

scar'tare *vt* (*pacco*) to unwrap; (*idea*) to reject; (*Mil*) to declare unfit for military service; (*carte da gioco*) to discard; (*Calcio*) to dodge (past) ▷ *vi* to swerve

'scarto *sm* (*cosa scartata: anche Comm*) reject; (*di veicolo*) swerve; (*differenza*) gap, difference

scassi'nare *vt* to break, force

scate'nare *vt* (*fig*) to incite, stir up; **scatenarsi** *vpr* (*temporale*) to break; (*rivolta*) to break out; (*persona: infuriarsi*) to rage

'scatola *sf* box; (*di latta*) tin (BRIT), can; **cibi in ~** tinned (BRIT) *o* canned foods; **scatola cranica** cranium; **scato'lone** *sm* (big) box

scat'tare *vt* (*fotografia*) to take ▷ *vi* (*congegno, molla ecc*) to be released; (*balzare*) to spring up; (*Sport*) to put on a spurt; (*fig: per l'ira*) to fly into a rage; **~ in piedi** to spring to one's feet

'scatto *sm* (*dispositivo*) release; (: *di arma da fuoco*) trigger mechanism; (*rumore*) click; (*balzo*) jump, start; (*Sport*) spurt; (*fig: di ira ecc*) fit; (: *di*

stipendio) increment; **di ~** suddenly

scaval'care *vt* (*ostacolo*) to pass (*o* climb) over; (*fig*) to get ahead of, overtake

sca'vare *vt* (*terreno*) to dig; (*legno*) to hollow out; (*pozzo, galleria*) to bore; (*città sepolta ecc*) to excavate

'scavo *sm* excavating *no pl*; excavation

'scegliere ['ʃeʎʎere] *vt* to choose, select

sce'icco, -chi [ʃe'ikko] *sm* sheik

'scelgo *ecc* ['ʃelgo] *vb vedi* **scegliere**

scel'lino [ʃel'lino] *sm* shilling

'scelta ['ʃelta] *sf* choice; selection; **di prima ~** top grade *o* quality; **frutta o formaggi a ~** choice of fruit or cheese

'scelto, -a ['ʃelto] *pp di* **scegliere** ▷ *ag* (*gruppo*) carefully selected; (*frutta, verdura*) choice, top quality; (*Mil: specializzato*) crack *cpd*, highly skilled

'scemo, -a ['ʃemo] *ag* stupid, silly

'scena ['ʃena] *sf* (*gen*) scene; (*palcoscenico*) stage; **le scene** (*fig: teatro*) the stage; **fare una ~** to make a scene; **andare in ~** to be staged *o* put on *o* performed; **mettere in ~** to stage

sce'nario [ʃe'narjo] *sm* scenery; (*di film*) scenario

sce'nata [ʃe'nata] *sf* row, scene

'scendere ['ʃendere] *vi* to go (*o* come) down; (*strada, sole*) to go down; (*notte*) to fall; (*passeggero: fermarsi*) to get out, alight; (*fig: temperatura, prezzi*) to go *o* come down, fall, drop ▷ *vt* (*scale, pendio*) to go (*o* come) down; **~ dalle scale** to go (*o* come) down the stairs; **~ dal treno** to get off *o* out of the train; **dove devo ~?** where do I get off?; **~ dalla macchina** to get out of the car; **~ da cavallo** to dismount, get off one's horse

sceneggi'ato [ʃened'dʒato] *sm* television drama

'scettico, -a, -ci, -che ['ʃettiko] *ag* sceptical

'scettro ['ʃettro] *sm* sceptre

'**scheda** ['skɛda] *sf* (index) card; **scheda elettorale** ballot paper; **scheda ricaricabile** (Tel) top-up card; **scheda telefonica** phone card; **sche'dario** *sm* file; (mobile) filing cabinet

sche'dina [ske'dina] *sf* ≈ pools coupon (BRIT)

'**scheggia, -ge** ['skeddʒa] *sf* splinter, sliver

'**scheletro** ['skɛletro] *sm* skeleton

'**schema, -i** ['skɛma] *sm* (diagramma) diagram, sketch; (progetto, abbozzo) outline, plan

'**scherma** ['skerma] *sf* fencing

scher'maglia [sker'maʎʎa] *sf* (fig) skirmish

'**schermo** ['skermo] *sm* shield, screen; (Cinema, TV) screen; **a ~ panoramico** (TV) widescreen

scher'nire [sker'nire] *vt* to mock, sneer at

scher'zare [sker'tsare] *vi* to joke

'**scherzo** ['skertso] *sm* joke; (tiro) trick; (Mus) scherzo; **è uno ~!** (una cosa facile) it's child's play!, it's easy!; **per ~** in jest; for a joke o a laugh; **fare un brutto ~ a qn** to play a nasty trick on sb

schiaccia'noci [skjattʃa'notʃi] *sm inv* nutcracker

schiacci'are [skjat'tʃare] *vt* (dito) to crush; (noci) to crack; **~ un pisolino** (appiattirsi) to have a nap; **schiacciarsi** *vpr* (appiattirsi) to get squashed; (frantumarsi) to get crushed

schiaffeggi'are [skjaffed'dʒare] *vt* to slap

schi'affo ['skjaffo] *sm* slap

schiantarsi *vpr* to break (up), shatter

schia'rire [skja'rire] *vt* to lighten, make lighter; **schiarirsi** *vpr* to grow lighter; (tornar sereno) to clear, brighten up; **schiarirsi la voce** to clear one's throat

schiavitù [skjavi'tu] *sf* slavery

schi'avo, -a ['skjavo] *sm/f* slave

schi'ena ['skjɛna] *sf* (Anat) back;

schie'nale *sm* (di sedia) back

schi'era ['skjera] *sf* (Mil) rank; (gruppo) group, band

schiera'mento [skjera'mento] *sm* (Mil, Sport) formation; (fig) alliance

schie'rare [skje'rare] *vt* (esercito) to line up, draw up, marshal; **schierarsi** *vpr* to line up; (fig): **schierarsi con o dalla parte di/contro qn** to side with/oppose sb

'**schifo** ['skifo] *sm* disgust; **fare ~** (essere fatto male, dare pessimi risultati) to be awful; **mi fa ~** it makes me sick, it's disgusting; **quel libro è uno ~** that book's rotten; **schi'foso, -a** *ag* disgusting, revolting; (molto scadente) rotten, lousy

schioc'care [skjok'kare] *vt* (frusta) to crack; (dita) to snap; (lingua) to click; **~ le labbra** to smack one's lips

schiudersi *vpr* to open

schi'uma ['skjuma] *sf* foam; (di sapone) lather; (di latte) froth; (fig: feccia) scum

schi'vare [ski'vare] *vt* to dodge, avoid

'**schivo, -a** ['skivo] *ag* (ritroso) stand-offish, reserved; (timido) shy

schiz'zare [skit'tsare] *vt* (spruzzare) to spurt, squirt; (sporcare) to splash, spatter; (fig: abbozzare) to sketch ▷ *vi* to spurt, squirt; (saltar fuori) to dart up (o off ecc)

schizzi'noso, -a [skittsi'noso] *ag* fussy, finicky

'**schizzo** ['skittso] *sm* (di liquido) spurt; splash, spatter; (abbozzo) sketch

sci [ʃi] *sm* (attrezzo) ski; (attività) skiing; **sci d'acqua** water-skiing; **sci di fondo** cross-country skiing, ski touring (us); **sci nautico** water-skiing

'**scia** ['ʃia] (pl **scie**) *sf* (di imbarcazione) wake; (di profumo) trail

scià [ʃa] *sm inv* shah

sci'abola ['ʃabola] *sf* sabre

scia'callo [ʃa'kallo] *sm* jackal

sciac'quare [ʃak'kware] *vt* to rinse

scia'gura [ʃaˈgura] *sf* disaster, calamity; misfortune

scialac'quare [ʃalakˈkware] *vt* to squander

sci'albo, -a [ˈʃalbo] *ag* pale, dull; (*fig*) dull, colourless

sci'alle [ˈʃalle] *sm* shawl

scia'luppa [ʃaˈluppa] *sf*; **scialuppa di salvataggio** lifeboat

sci'ame [ˈʃame] *sm* swarm

sci'are [ʃiˈare] *vi* to ski

sci'arpa [ˈʃarpa] *sf* scarf; (*fascia*) sash

scia'tore, -'trice [ʃiaˈtore] *sm/f* skier

sci'atto, -a [ˈʃatto] *ag* (*persona*) slovenly, unkempt

scien'tifico, -a, -ci, -che [ʃenˈtifiko] *ag* scientific

sci'enza [ˈʃɛntsa] *sf* science; (*sapere*) knowledge; **scienze** *sfpl* (*Ins*) science *sg*; **scienze naturali** natural sciences; **scienzi'ato, -a** *sm/f* scientist

'scimmia [ˈʃimmja] *sf* monkey

scimpanzé [ʃimpanˈtse] *sm inv* chimpanzee

scin'tilla [ʃinˈtilla] *sf* spark; **scintil'lare** *vi* to spark; (*acqua, occhi*) to sparkle

scioc'chezza [ʃokˈkettsa] *sf* stupidity *no pl*; stupid *o* foolish thing; **dire sciocchezze** to talk nonsense

sci'occo, -a, -chi, -che [ˈʃɔkko] *ag* stupid, foolish

sci'ogliere [ˈʃɔʎʎere] *vt* (*nodo*) to untie; (*capelli*) to loosen; (*persona, animale*) to untie, release; (*fig: persona*): **~ da** to release from; (*neve*) to melt; (*nell'acqua: zucchero ecc*) to dissolve; (*fig: mistero*) to solve; (*porre fine a: contratto*) to cancel; (: *società, matrimonio*) to dissolve; (: *riunione*) to bring to an end; **sciogliersi** *vpr* to loosen, come untied; to melt; to dissolve; (*assemblea ecc*) to break up; **~ i muscoli** to limber up; **scioglilingua** [ʃoʎʎiˈlingwa] *sm inv* tongue-twister

sci'olgo *ecc* [ˈʃɔlgo] *vb vedi* **sciogliere**

sci'olto, -a [ˈʃɔlto] *pp di* **sciogliere**

▷ *ag* loose; (*agile*) agile, nimble; supple; (*disinvolto*) free and easy; **versi sciolti** (*Poesia*) blank verse

sciope'rare [ʃopeˈrare] *vi* to strike, go on strike

sci'opero [ˈʃɔpero] *sm* strike; **fare ~** to strike; **sciopero bianco** work-to-rule (*BRIT*), slowdown (*US*); **sciopero selvaggio** wildcat strike; **sciopero a singhiozzo** on-off strike

scio'via [ʃioˈvia] *sf* ski lift

scip'pare [ʃipˈpare] *vt*: **~ qn** to snatch sb's bag; **mi hanno scippato** they snatched my bag

sci'rocco [ʃiˈrɔkko] *sm* sirocco

sci'roppo [ʃiˈrɔppo] *sm* syrup

'scisma, -i [ˈʃizma] *sm* (*Rel*) schism

scissi'one [ʃisˈsjone] *sf* (*anche fig*) split, division; (*Fisica*) fission

sciu'pare [ʃuˈpare] *vt* (*abito, libro, appetito*) to spoil, ruin; (*tempo, denaro*) to waste

scivo'lare [ʃivoˈlare] *vi* to slide *o* glide along; (*involontariamente*) to slip, slide; **'scivolo** *sm* slide; (*Tecn*) chute; **scivo'loso, -a** *ag* slippery

scle'rosi *sf* sclerosis

scoc'care *vt* (*freccia*) to shoot ▷ *vi* (*guizzare*) to shoot up; (*battere: ora*) to strike

scoccherò *ecc* [skokkeˈrɔ] *vb vedi* **scoccare**

scocci'are [skotˈtʃare] (*fam*) *vt* to bother, annoy; **scocciarsi** *vpr* to be bothered *o* annoyed

sco'della *sf* bowl

scodinzo'lare [skodintsoˈlare] *vi* to wag its tail

scogli'era [skoʎˈʎɛra] *sf* reef; cliff

'scoglio [ˈskɔʎʎo] *sm* (*al mare*) rock

scoi'attolo *sm* squirrel

scola'pasta *sm inv* colander

scolapi'atti *sm inv* drainer (*for plates*)

sco'lare *ag* **età scolare** school age ▷ *vt* to drain ▷ *vi* to drip

scola'resca *sf* schoolchildren *pl*, pupils *pl*

sco'laro, -a *sm/f* pupil, schoolboy/
girl

> Attenzione! In inglese esiste la
> parola *scholar*, che però significa
> *studioso*.

sco'lastico, -a, -ci, -che *ag* school
cpd; scholastic

scol'lato, -a *ag* (*vestito*) low-cut, low-
necked; (*donna*) wearing a low-cut
dress (*o blouse ecc*)

scolla'tura *sf* neckline

scolle'gare *vt* (*fili, apparecchi*) to
disconnect

'scolo *sm* drainage

scolo'rire *vt* to fade; to discolour;
scolorirsi *vpr* to fade; to become
discoloured; (*impallidire*) to turn pale

scol'pire *vt* to carve, sculpt

scombusso'lare *vt* to upset

scom'messa *sf* bet, wager

scom'mettere *vt, vi* to bet

scomo'dare *vt* to trouble, bother; to
disturb; **scomodarsi** *vpr* to put o.s.
out; **scomodarsi a fare** to go to the
bother *o* trouble of doing

'scomodo, -a *ag* uncomfortable;
(*sistemazione, posto*) awkward,
inconvenient

scompa'rire *vi* (*sparire*) to disappear,
vanish; (*fig*) to be insignificant

scomparti'mento *sm*
compartment; **uno ~ per
non-fumatori** a non-smoking
compartment

scompigli'are [skompiʎ'ʎare]
vt (*cassetto, capelli*) to mess up,
disarrange; (*fig: piani*) to upset

scomuni'care *vt* to excommunicate

'sconcio, -a, -ci, -ce ['skontʃo] *ag*
(*osceno*) indecent, obscene ▷ *sm*
disgrace

scon'figgere [skon'fiddʒere] *vt* to
defeat, overcome

sconfi'nare *vi* to cross the border; (*in
proprietà privata*) to trespass; (*fig*): **~ da**
to stray *o* digress from

scon'fitta *sf* defeat

scon'forto *sm* despondency

sconge'lare [skondʒe'lare] *vt* to
defrost

scongiu'rare [skondʒu'rare] *vt*
(*implorare*) to entreat, beseech,
implore; (*eludere: pericolo*) to ward
off, avert; **scongi'uro** *sm* entreaty;
(*esorcismo*) exorcism; **fare gli
scongiuri** to touch wood (BRIT),
knock on wood (US)

scon'nesso, -a *ag* incoherent

sconosci'uto, -a [skonoʃ'ʃuto]
ag unknown; new, strange ▷ *sm/f*
stranger; unknown person

sconsigli'are [skonsiʎ'ʎare] *vt*: **~ qc
a qn** to advise sb against sth; **~ qn dal
fare qc** to advise sb not to do *o* against
doing sth

sconso'lato, -a *ag* inconsolable;
desolate

scon'tare *vt* (*Comm: detrarre*) to
deduct; (: *debito*) to pay off; (: *cambiale*)
to discount; (*pena*) to serve; (*colpa,
errori*) to pay for, suffer for

scon'tato, -a *ag* (*previsto*) foreseen,
taken for granted; **dare per ~ che** to
take it for granted that

scon'tento, -a *ag*: **~ (di)** dissatisfied
(with) ▷ *sm* dissatisfaction

'sconto *sm* discount; **fare uno ~** to
give a discount; **ci sono sconti per
studenti?** are there discounts for
students?

scon'trarsi *vpr* (*treni ecc*) to crash,
collide; (*venire ad uno scontro, fig*) to
clash; **~ con** to crash into, collide with

scon'trino *sm* ticket; (*di cassa*)
receipt; **potrei avere lo ~ per favore?**
can I have a receipt, please?

'scontro *sm* clash, encounter; crash,
collision

scon'troso, -a *ag* sullen, surly;
(*permaloso*) touchy

sconveni'ente *ag* unseemly,
improper

scon'volgere [skon'vɔldʒere] *vt* to
throw into confusion, upset; (*turbare*)

to shake, disturb, upset; **scon'volto, -a** *pp di* **sconvolgere**

scooter ['skuter] *sm inv* scooter

'**scopa** *sf* broom; (*Carte*) *Italian card game*; **sco'pare** *vt* to sweep

sco'perta *sf* discovery

sco'perto, -a *pp di* **scoprire** ▷ *ag* uncovered; (*capo*) uncovered, bare; (*macchina*) open; (*Mil*) exposed, without cover; (*conto*) overdrawn

'**scopo** *sm* aim, purpose; **a che ~?** what for?

scoppi'are *vi* (*spaccarsi*) to burst; (*esplodere*) to explode; (*fig*) to break out; **~ in pianto** *o* **a piangere** to burst out crying; **~ dalle risa** *o* **dal ridere** to split one's sides laughing

scoppiet'tare *vi* to crackle

'**scoppio** *sm* explosion; (*di tuono, arma ecc*) crash, bang; (*fig: di risa, ira*) fit, outburst; (: *di guerra*) outbreak; **a ~ ritardato** delayed-action

sco'prire *vt* to discover; (*liberare da ciò che copre*) to uncover; (: *monumento*) to unveil; **scoprirsi** *vpr* to put on lighter clothes; (*fig*) to give o.s. away

scoraggi'are [skorad'dʒare] *vt* to discourage; **scoraggiarsi** *vpr* to become discouraged, lose heart

scorcia'toia [skortʃa'toja] *sf* short cut

'**scorcio** ['skortʃo] *sm* (*Arte*) foreshortening; (*di secolo, periodo*) end, close; **scorcio panoramico** vista

scor'dare *vt* to forget; **scordarsi** *vpr* **scordarsi di qc/di fare** to forget sth/to do

'**scorgere** ['skordʒere] *vt* to make out, distinguish, see

scorpacci'ata [skorpat'tʃata] *sf*: **fare una ~ (di)** to stuff o.s. (with), eat one's fill (of)

scorpi'one *sm* scorpion; (*dello zodiaco*): **S~** Scorpio

'**scorrere** *vt* (*giornale, lettera*) to run *o* skim through ▷ *vi* (*liquido, fiume*) to run, flow; (*fune*) to run; (*cassetto, porta*)

to slide easily; (*tempo*) to pass (by)

scor'retto, -a *ag* incorrect; (*sgarbato*) impolite; (*sconveniente*) improper

scor'revole *ag* (*porta*) sliding; (*fig: stile*) fluent, flowing

'**scorsi** *ecc vb vedi* **scorgere**

'**scorso, -a** *pp di* **scorrere** ▷ *ag* last

scor'soio, -a *ag*: **nodo ~** noose

'**scorta** *sf* (*di personalità, convoglio*) escort; (*provvista*) supply, stock

scor'tese *ag* discourteous, rude

'**scorza** ['skordza] *sf* (*di albero*) bark; (*di agrumi*) peel, skin

sco'sceso, -a [skoʃ'ʃeso] *ag* steep

'**scossa** *sf* jerk, jolt, shake; (*Elettr: fig*) shock; **scossa di terremoto** earth tremor

'**scosso, -a** *pp di* **scuotere** ▷ *ag* (*turbato*) shaken, upset

scos'tante *ag* (*fig*) off-putting (*BRIT*), unpleasant

scotch [skotʃ] *sm inv* (*whisky*) Scotch; (*nastro adesivo*) Scotch tape®, Sellotape®

scot'tare *vt* (*ustionare*) to burn; (: *con liquido bollente*) to scald ▷ *vi* to burn; (*caffè*) to be too hot; **scottarsi** *vpr* to burn/scald o.s.; (*fig*) to have one's fingers burnt; **scotta'tura** *sf* burn; scald

'**scotto, -a** *ag* overcooked ▷ *sm* (*fig*): **pagare lo ~ (di)** to pay the penalty (for)

sco'vare *vt* to drive out, flush out; (*fig*) to discover

'**Scozia** ['skottsia] *sf*: **la ~** Scotland; **scoz'zese** *ag* Scottish ▷ *sm/f* Scot

scredi'tare *vt* to discredit

screen saver ['skriin'seivər] *sm inv* (*Inform*) screen saver

scre'mato, -a *ag* skimmed; **parzialmente ~** semi-skimmed

screpo'lato, -a *ag* (*labbra*) chapped; (*muro*) cracked

'**screzio** ['skrettsjo] *sm* disagreement

scricchio'lare [skrikkjo'lare] *vi* to creak, squeak

'scrigno ['skriɲɲo] *sm* casket

scrimina'tura *sf* parting

'scrissi *ecc vb vedi* **scrivere**

'scritta *sf* inscription

'scritto, -a *pp di* **scrivere** ▷ *ag* written ▷ *sm* writing; (*lettera*) letter, note

scrit'toio *sm* writing desk

scrit'tore, -'trice *sm/f* writer

scrit'tura *sf* writing; (*Comm*) entry; (*contratto*) contract; (*Rel*): **la Sacra S~** the Scriptures *pl*

scrittu'rare *vt* (*Teatro, Cinema*) to sign up, engage; (*Comm*) to enter

scriva'nia *sf* desk

'scrivere *vt* to write; **come si scrive?** how is it spelt?, how do you write it?

scroc'cone, -a *sm/f* scrounger

'scrofa *sf* (*Zool*) sow

scrol'lare *vt* to shake; **scrollarsi** *vpr* (*anche fig*) to give o.s. a shake; (*anche*: **~ le spalle/il capo**) to shrug one's shoulders/shake one's head

'scrupolo *sm* scruple; (*meticolosità*) care, conscientiousness

scrupo'loso, -a *ag* scrupulous; conscientious

scru'tare *vt* to scrutinize; (*intenzioni, causa*) to examine, scrutinize

scu'cire [sku'tʃire] *vt* (*orlo ecc*) to unpick, undo; **scucirsi** *vpr* to come unstitched

scude'ria *sf* stable

scu'detto *sm* (*Sport*) (championship) shield; (*distintivo*) badge

'scudo *sm* shield

sculacci'are [skulat'tʃare] *vt* to spank

scul'tore, -'trice *sm/f* sculptor

scul'tura *sf* sculpture

scu'ola *sf* school; **scuola elementare/materna** primary (*BRIT*) *o* grade (*US*) /nursery school; **scuola guida** driving school; **scuola media** secondary (*BRIT*) *o* high (*US*) school; **scuola dell'obbligo** compulsory education; **scuola tecnica** technical college; **scuole serali** evening classes, night school *sg*

scu'otere *vt* to shake

'scure *sf* axe

'scuro, -a *ag* dark; (*fig: espressione*) grim ▷ *sm* darkness; dark colour; (*imposta*) (window) shutter; **verde/rosso** *ecc* **~** dark green/red *ecc*

'scusa *sf* apology; (*pretesto*) excuse; **chiedere ~ a qn (per)** to apologize to sb (for); **chiedo ~** I'm sorry; (*disturbando ecc*) excuse me

scu'sare *vt* to excuse; **scusarsi** *vpr* **scusarsi (di)** to apologize (for); **(mi) scusi** I'm sorry; (*per richiamare l'attenzione*) excuse me

sde'gnato, -a [zdeɲ'ɲato] *ag* indignant, angry

'sdegno ['zdeɲɲo] *sm* scorn, disdain

sdolci'nato, -a [zdoltʃi'nato] *ag* mawkish, oversentimental

sdrai'arsi *vpr* to stretch out, lie down

'sdraio *sm* **sedia a ~** deck chair

sdruccio'levole [zdruttʃo'levole] *ag* slippery

⬤ **PAROLA CHIAVE**

se *pron vedi* **si**
▷ *cong* **1** (*condizionale, ipotetica*) if; **se nevica non vengo** I won't come if it snows; **sarei rimasto se me l'avessero chiesto** I would have stayed if they'd asked me; **non puoi fare altro se non telefonare** all you can do is phone; **se mai** if, if ever; **siamo noi se mai che le siamo grati** it is we who should be grateful to you; **se no** (*altrimenti*) or (else), otherwise **2** (*in frasi dubitative, interrogative indirette*) if, whether; **non so se scrivere o telefonare** I don't know whether *o* if I should write or phone

sé *pron* (*gen*) oneself; (*esso, essa, lui, lei, loro*) itself; himself; herself; themselves; **sé stesso(a)** *pron* oneself; itself; himself; herself

seb'bene *cong* although, though

sec. *abbr* (= *secolo*) c.

'secca *sf* (*del mare*) shallows *pl*; *vedi anche* **secco**

sec'care *vt* to dry; (*prosciugare*) to dry up; (*fig*: *importunare*) to annoy, bother ▷ *vi* to dry; to dry up; **seccarsi** *vpr* to dry; to dry up; (*fig*) to grow annoyed

sec'cato, -a *ag* (*fig*: *infastidito*) bothered, annoyed; (: *stufo*) fed up

secca'tura *sf* (*fig*) bother *no pl*, trouble *no pl*

seccherò *ecc* [sekke'rɔ] *vb vedi* **seccare**

secchi'ello *sm* bucket; **secchiello del ghiaccio** ice bucket

'secchio ['sekkjo] *sm* bucket, pail

'secco, -a, -chi, -che *ag* dry; (*fichi, pesce*) dried; (*foglie, ramo*) withered; (*magro*: *persona*) thin, skinny; (*fig*: *risposta, modo di fare*) curt, abrupt; (: *colpo*) clean, sharp ▷ *sm* (*siccità*) drought; **restarci ~** (*fig*: *morire sul colpo*) to drop dead; **mettere in ~** (*barca*) to beach; **rimanere a ~** (*fig*) to be left in the lurch

seco'lare *ag* age-old, centuries-old; (*laico, mondano*) secular

'secolo *sm* century; (*epoca*) age

se'conda *sf* (*Aut*) second (gear); **viaggiare in ~** to travel second-class; *vedi anche* **secondo**; **seconda colazione** lunch

secon'dario, -a *ag* secondary

se'condo, -a *ag* second ▷ *sm* second; (*di pranzo*) main course ▷ *prep* according to; (*nel modo prescritto*) in accordance with; **~ me** in my opinion, to my mind; **di seconda mano** second-hand; **a seconda di** according to; in accordance with; **seconda classe** second-class

'sedano *sm* celery

seda'tivo, -a *ag, sm* sedative

'sede *sf* seat; (*di ditta*) head office; (*di organizzazione*) headquarters *pl*; **sede centrale** head office; **sede sociale** registered office

seden'tario, -a *ag* sedentary

se'dere *vi* to sit, be seated

'sedia *sf* chair; **sedia elettrica** electric chair; **sedia a rotelle** wheelchair

'sedici ['seditʃi] *num* sixteen

se'dile *sm* seat; (*panchina*) bench

sedu'cente [sedu'tʃɛnte] *ag* seductive; (*proposta*) very attractive

se'durre *vt* to seduce

se'duta *sf* session, sitting; (*riunione*) meeting; **seduta spiritica** séance; **seduta stante** (*fig*) immediately

seduzi'one [sedut'tsjone] *sf* seduction; (*fascino*) charm, appeal

SEeO *abbr* (= *salvo errori e omissioni*) E and OE

'sega, -ghe *sf* saw

'segale *sf* rye

se'gare *vt* to saw; (*recidere*) to saw off

'seggio ['sɛddʒo] *sm* seat; **seggio elettorale** polling station

seggi'ola ['sɛddʒola] *sf* chair; **seggio'lone** *sm* (*per bambini*) highchair

seggio'via [sɛddʒo'via] *sf* chairlift

segherò *ecc* [sege'rɔ] *vb vedi* **segare**

segna'lare [seɲɲa'lare] *vt* (*manovra ecc*) to signal; to indicate; (*annunciare*) to announce; to report; (*fig*: *far conoscere*) to point out; (: *persona*) to single out

se'gnale [seɲ'ɲale] *sm* signal; (*cartello*) sign; **segnale acustico** acoustic o sound signal; **segnale d'allarme** alarm; (*Ferr*) communication cord; **segnale orario** (*Radio*) time signal; **segnale stradale** road sign

segna'libro [seɲɲa'libro] *sm* (*anche Inform*) bookmark

se'gnare [seɲ'ɲare] *vt* to mark; (*prendere nota*) to note; (*indicare*) to indicate, mark; (*Sport*: *goal*) to score

'segno ['seɲɲo] *sm* sign; (*impronta,*

contrassegno) mark; (limite) limit, bounds pl; (bersaglio) target; **fare ~ di sì/no** to nod (one's head)/shake one's head; **fare ~ a qn di fermarsi** to motion (to) sb to stop; **cogliere o colpire nel ~** (fig) to hit the mark; **segno zodiacale** star sign

segre'tario, -a sm/f secretary; **segretario comunale** town clerk; **Segretario di Stato** Secretary of State

segrete'ria sf (di ditta, scuola) (secretary's) office; (d'organizzazione internazionale) secretariat; (Pol ecc: carica) office of Secretary; **segreteria telefonica** answering service

se'greto, -a ag secret ▷ sm secret; secrecy no pl; **in ~** in secret, secretly

segu'ace [se'gwatʃe] sm/f follower, disciple

segu'ente ag following, next

segu'ire vt to follow; (frequentare: corso) to attend ▷ vi to follow; (continuare: testo) to continue

segui'tare vt to continue, carry on with ▷ vi to continue, carry on

'seguito sm (scorta) suite, retinue; (discepoli) followers pl; (favore) following; (continuazione) continuation; (conseguenza) result; **di ~** at a stretch, on end; **in ~** later on; **in ~ a, a ~ di** following; (a causa di) as a result of, owing to

'sei vb vedi **essere** ▷ num six

sei'cento [sei'tʃɛnto] num six hundred ▷ sm **il S~** the seventeenth century

selci'ato [sel'tʃato] sm cobbled surface

selezio'nare [selettsjo'nare] vt to select

selezi'one [selet'tsjone] sf selection

'sella sf saddle

sel'lino sm saddle

selvag'gina [selvad'dʒina] sf (animali) game

sel'vaggio, -a, -gi, -ge [sel'vaddʒo]

ag wild; (tribù) savage, uncivilized; (fig) savage, brutal ▷ sm/f savage

sel'vatico, -a, -ci, -che ag wild

se'maforo sm (Aut) traffic lights pl

sem'brare vi to seem ▷ vb impers **sembra che** it seems that; **mi sembra che** it seems to me that, I think (that); **~ di essere** to seem to be

'seme sm seed; (sperma) semen; (Carte) suit

se'mestre sm half-year, six-month period

semifi'nale sf semifinal

semi'freddo sm ice-cream cake

semi'nare vt to sow

semi'nario sm seminar; (Rel) seminary

seminter'rato sm basement; (appartamento) basement flat

'semola sf; **semola di grano duro** durum wheat

semo'lino sm semolina

'semplice ['semplitʃe] ag simple; (di un solo elemento) single

'sempre av always; (ancora) still; **posso ~ tentare** I can always o still try; **da ~** always; **per ~** forever; **una volta per ~** once and for all; **~ che** provided (that); **~ più** more and more; **~ meno** less and less

sempre'verde ag, sm o f (Bot) evergreen

'senape sf (Cuc) mustard

se'nato sm senate; **sena'tore, -'trice** sm/f senator

'senno sm judgment, (common) sense; **col ~ di poi** with hindsight

'seno sm (Anat: petto, mammella) breast; (: grembo, fig) womb; (: cavità) sinus

sen'sato, -a ag sensible

sensazio'nale [sensattsjo'nale] ag sensational

sensazi'one [sensat'tsjone] sf feeling, sensation; **avere la ~ che** to have a feeling that; **fare ~** to cause a sensation, create a stir

sen'sibile *ag* sensitive; (*ai sensi*) perceptible; (*rilevante, notevole*) appreciable, noticeable; **~ a** sensitive to

> Attenzione! In inglese esiste la parola *sensible*, che però significa *ragionevole*.

'senso *sm* (*Fisiol, istinto*) sense; (*impressione, sensazione*) feeling, sensation; (*significato*) meaning, sense; (*direzione*) direction; **sensi** *smpl* (*coscienza*) consciousness *sg*; (*sensualità*) senses; **ciò non ha ~** that doesn't make sense; **fare ~ a** (*ripugnare*) to disgust, repel; **in ~ orario/antiorario** clockwise/anticlockwise; **senso di colpa** sense of guilt; **senso comune** common sense; **senso unico** (*strada*) one-way; **senso vietato** (*Aut*) no entry

sensu'ale *ag* sensual; sensuous

sen'tenza [sen'tentsa] *sf* (*Dir*) sentence; (*massima*) maxim

senti'ero *sm* path

sentimen'tale *ag* sentimental; (*vita, avventura*) love *cpd*

senti'mento *sm* feeling

senti'nella *sf* sentry

sen'tire *vt* (*percepire al tatto, fig*) to feel; (*udire*) to hear; (*ascoltare*) to listen to; (*odore*) to smell; (*avvertire con il gusto, assaggiare*) to taste ▷ *vi* **~ di** (*avere sapore*) to taste of; (*avere odore*) to smell of; **sentirsi** *vpr* (*uso reciproco*) to be in touch; **sentirsi bene/male** to feel well/unwell *o* ill; **non mi sento bene** I don't feel well; **sentirsi di fare qc** (*essere disposto*) to feel like doing sth

sen'tito, -a *ag* (*sincero*) sincere, warm; **per ~ dire** by hearsay

'senza ['sentsa] *prep, cong* without; **~ dir nulla** without saying a word; **fare ~ qc** to do without sth; **~ di me** without me; **~ che io lo sapessi** without me *o* my knowing; **senz'altro** of course, certainly; **~ dubbio** no doubt; **~ scrupoli** unscrupulous; **~**

amici friendless

sepa'rare *vt* to separate; (*dividere*) to divide; (*tenere distinto*) to distinguish; **separarsi** *vpr* (*coniugi*) to separate, part; (*amici*) to part, leave each other; **separarsi da** (*coniuge*) to separate *o* part from; (*amico, socio*) to part company with; (*oggetto*) to part with; **sepa'rato, -a** *ag* (*letti, conto ecc*) separate; (*coniugi*) separated

seppel'lire *vt* to bury

'seppi *ecc vb vedi* **sapere**

'seppia *sf* cuttlefish ▷ *ag inv* sepia

se'quenza [se'kwentsa] *sf* sequence

seques'trare *vt* (*Dir*) to impound; (*rapire*) to kidnap; **se'questro** *sm* (*Dir*) impoundment; **sequestro di persona** kidnapping

'sera *sf* evening; **di ~** in the evening; **domani ~** tomorrow evening, tomorrow night; **se'rale** *ag* evening *cpd*; **se'rata** *sf* evening; (*ricevimento*) party

ser'bare *vt* to keep; (*mettere da parte*) to put aside; **~ rancore/odio verso qn** to bear sb a grudge/hate sb

serba'toio *sm* tank; (*cisterna*) cistern

'Serbia *sf* **la ~** Serbia

'serbo *ag* Serbian ▷ *sm/f* Serbian, Serb ▷ *sm* (*Ling*) Serbian; (*il serbare*): **mettere/tenere** *o* **avere in ~ qc** to put/keep sth aside

se'reno, -a *ag* (*tempo, cielo*) clear; (*fig*) serene, calm

ser'gente [ser'dʒɛnte] *sm* (*Mil*) sergeant

'serie *sf inv* (*successione*) series *inv*; (*gruppo, collezione*) set; (*Sport*) division; league; (*Comm*): **modello di ~/fuori ~** standard/custom-built model; **in ~** in quick succession; (*Comm*) mass *cpd*

serietà *sf* seriousness; reliability

'serio, -a *ag* serious; (*impiegato*) responsible, reliable; (*ditta, cliente*) reliable, dependable; **sul ~** (*davvero*) really, truly; (*seriamente*) seriously, in earnest

ser'pente sm snake; **serpente a sonagli** rattlesnake
'serra sf greenhouse; hothouse
ser'randa sf roller shutter
serra'tura sf lock
server ['sɛrvər] sm inv (Inform) server
ser'vire vt to serve; (clienti: al ristorante) to wait on; (: al negozio) to serve, attend to; (fig: giovare) to aid, help; (Carte) to deal ▷ vi (Tennis) to serve; (essere utile): **~ a qn** to be of use to sb; **~ a qc/a fare** (utensile ecc) to be used for sth/for doing; **~ (a qn) da** to serve as (for sb); **servirsi** vpr (usare): **servirsi di** to use; (prendere: cibo): **servirsi (di)** to help o.s. (to); **serviti pure!** help yourself!; (essere cliente abituale): **servirsi da** to be a regular customer at, go to
servizi'evole [servit'tsjevole] ag obliging, willing to help
ser'vizio [ser'vittsjo] sm service; (al ristorante: sul conto) service (charge); (Stampa, TV, Radio) report; (da tè, caffè ecc) set, service; **servizi** smpl (di casa) kitchen and bathroom; (Econ) services; **essere di ~** to be on duty; **fuori ~** (telefono ecc) out of order; **~ compreso** service included; **servizio militare** military service; **servizio di posate** set of cutlery; **servizi segreti** secret service sg; **servizio da tè** tea set
ses'santa num sixty; **sessan'tesimo, -a** num sixtieth
sessi'one sf session
'sesso sm sex; **sessu'ale** ag sexual, sex cpd
ses'tante sm sextant
'sesto, -a ag, sm sixth
'seta sf silk
'sete sf thirst; **avere ~** to be thirsty
'setola sf bristle
'setta sf sect
set'tanta num seventy; **settan'tesimo, -a** num seventieth
set'tare vt (Inform) to set up

'sette num seven
sette'cento [sette'tʃɛnto] num seven hundred ▷ sm **il S~** the eighteenth century
set'tembre sm September
settentrio'nale ag northern
settentri'one sm north
setti'mana sf week; **settima'nale** ag, sm weekly

● **SETTIMANA BIANCA**
●
● **Settimana bianca** is the name
● given to a week-long winter-sports
● holiday taken by many Italians
● some time in the skiing season.

'settimo, -a ag, sm seventh
set'tore sm sector
severità sf severity
se'vero, -a ag severe
sevizi'are [sevit'tsjare] vt to torture
sezio'nare [settsjo'nare] vt to divide into sections; (Med) to dissect
sezi'one [set'tsjone] sf section
sfacchi'nata [sfakki'nata] sf (fam) chore, drudgery no pl
sfacci'ato, -a [sfat'tʃato] ag (maleducato) cheeky, impudent; (vistoso) gaudy
sfa'mare vt to feed; (cibo) to fill; **sfamarsi** vpr to satisfy one's hunger, fill o.s. up
sfasci'are [sfaʃʃare] vt (ferita) to unbandage; (distruggere) to smash, shatter; **sfasciarsi** vpr (rompersi) to smash, shatter
sfavo'revole ag unfavourable
'sfera sf sphere
sfer'rare vt (fig: colpo) to land, deal; (: attacco) to launch
'sfida sf challenge
sfi'dare vt to challenge; (fig) to defy, brave
sfi'ducia [sfi'dutʃa] sf distrust, mistrust
sfi'gato, -a (fam) ag (sfortunato)

unlucky

sfigu'rare vt (persona) to disfigure; (quadro, statua) to deface ▷ vi (far cattiva figura) to make a bad impression

sfi'lare vt (ago) to unthread; (abito, scarpe) to slip off ▷ vi (truppe) to march past; (atleti) to parade; **sfilarsi** vpr (perle ecc) to come unstrung; (orlo, tessuto) to fray; (calza) to run, ladder; **sfi'lata** sf march past; parade; **sfilata di moda** fashion show

'sfinge ['sfindʒe] sf sphinx

sfi'nito, -a ag exhausted

sfio'rare vt to brush (against); (argomento) to touch upon

sfio'rire vi to wither, fade

sfo'cato, -a ag (Fot) out of focus

sfoci'are [sfo'tʃare] vi: ~ **in** to flow into; (fig: malcontento) to develop into

sfode'rato, -a ag (vestito) unlined

sfogarsi vpr (sfogare la propria rabbia) to give vent to one's anger; (confidarsi): ~ **(con)** to confide one's feelings (to); **non sfogarti su di me!** don't take your bad temper out on me!

sfoggi'are [sfod'dʒare] vt, vi to show off

'sfoglia ['sfoʎʎa] sf sheet of pasta dough; **pasta ~** (Cuc) puff pastry

sfogli'are [sfoʎ'ʎare] vt (libro) to leaf through

'sfogo, -ghi sm (eruzione cutanea) rash; (fig) outburst; **dare ~ a** (fig) to give vent to

sfon'dare vt (porta) to break down; (scarpe) to wear a hole in; (cesto, scatola) to burst, knock the bottom out of; (Mil) to break through ▷ vi (riuscire) to make a name for o.s.

'sfondo sm background

sfor'mato sm (Cuc) type of soufflé

sfor'tuna sf misfortune, ill luck no pl; **avere ~** to be unlucky; **sfortu'nato, -a** ag unlucky; (impresa, film) unsuccessful

sforzarsi vpr: ~ **di** o **a** o **per fare** to try

hard to do

'sforzo ['sfɔrtso] sm effort; (tensione eccessiva, Tecn) strain; **fare uno ~** to make an effort

sfrat'tare vt to evict; **'sfratto** sm eviction

sfrecci'are [sfret'tʃare] vi to shoot o flash past

sfre'gare vt (strofinare) to rub; (graffiare) to scratch; **sfregarsi le mani** to rub one's hands; ~ **un fiammifero** to strike a match

sfregi'are [sfre'dʒare] vt to slash, gash; (persona) to disfigure; (quadro) to deface

sfre'nato, -a ag (fig) unrestrained, unbridled

sfron'tato, -a ag shameless

sfrutta'mento sm exploitation

sfrut'tare vt (terreno) to overwork, exhaust; (miniera) to exploit, work; (fig: operai, occasione, potere) to exploit

sfug'gire [sfud'dʒire] vi to escape; ~ **a** (custode) to escape (from); (morte) to escape; ~ **a qn** (dettaglio, nome) to escape sb; ~ **di mano a qn** to slip out of sb's hand (o hands)

sfu'mare vt (colori, contorni) to soften, shade off ▷ vi to shade (off), fade; (fig: svanire) to vanish, disappear; (: speranze) to come to nothing

sfuma'tura sf shading off no pl; (tonalità) shade, tone; (fig) touch, hint

sfuri'ata sf (scatto di collera) fit of anger; (rimprovero) sharp rebuke

sga'bello sm stool

sgabuz'zino [sgabud'dzino] sm lumber room

sgambet'tare vi to kick one's legs about

sgam'betto sm **far lo ~ a qn** to trip sb up; (fig) to oust sb

sganci'are [zgan'tʃare] vt to unhook; (Ferr) to uncouple; (bombe: da aereo) to release, drop; (fig: fam: soldi) to fork out; **sganciarsi** vpr (fig): **sganciarsi (da)** to get away (from)

sganghe'rato, -a [zgange'rato] *ag* (*porta*) off its hinges; (*auto*) ramshackle; (*risata*) wild, boisterous

sgar'bato, -a *ag* rude, impolite

'sgarbo *sm* **fare uno ~ a qn** to be rude to sb

sgargi'ante [zgar'dʒante] *ag* gaudy, showy

sgattaio'lare *vi* to sneak away *o* off

sge'lare [zdʒe'lare] *vi, vt* to thaw

sghignaz'zare [zgiɲɲat'tsare] *vi* to laugh scornfully

sgob'bare (*fam*) *vi* (*scolaro*) to swot; (*operaio*) to slog

sgombe'rare *vt* (*tavolo, stanza*) to clear; (*piazza, città*) to evacuate ▷ *vi* to move

'sgombro, -a *ag*: **~ (di)** clear (of), free (from) ▷ *sm* (*Zool*) mackerel; (*anche:* **sgombero**) clearing; vacating; evacuation; (*: trasloco*) removal

sgonfi'are *vt* to let down, deflate; **sgonfiarsi** *vpr* to go down

'sgonfio, -a *ag* (*pneumatico, pallone*) flat

'sgorbio *sm* blot; scribble

sgra'devole *ag* unpleasant, disagreeable

sgra'dito, -a *ag* unpleasant, unwelcome

sgra'nare *vt* (*piselli*) to shell; **~ gli occhi** to open one's eyes wide

sgranchire [zgran'kire] *vt* (*anche:* **sgranchirsi**) to stretch; **~ le gambe** to stretch one's legs

sgranocchi'are [zgranok'kjare] *vt* to munch

'sgravio *sm* **~ fiscale** tax relief

sgrazi'ato, -a [zgrat'tsjato] *ag* clumsy, ungainly

sgri'dare *vt* to scold

sgual'cire [zgwal'tʃire] *vt* to crumple (up), crease

sgual'drina (*peg*) *sf* slut

sgu'ardo *sm* (*occhiata*) look, glance; (*espressione*) look (in one's eye)

sguaz'zare [zgwat'tsare] *vi*

(*nell'acqua*) to splash about; (*nella melma*) to wallow; **~ nell'oro** to be rolling in money

sguinzagli'are [zgwintsaʎ'ʎare] *vt* to let off the leash; (*fig: persona*): **~ qn dietro a qn** to set sb on sb

sgusci'are [zguʃ'ʃare] *vt* to shell ▷ *vi* (*sfuggire di mano*) to slip; **~ via** to slip *o* slink away

'shampoo ['ʃampo] *sm inv* shampoo

shiatzu [ʃi'atstsu] *sm inv* shiatsu

shock [ʃɔk] *sm inv* shock

PAROLA CHIAVE

si (*dav lo, la, li, le, ne diventa* **se**) *pron*
1 (*riflessivo: maschile*) himself; (*: femminile*) herself; (*: neutro*) itself; (*: impersonale*) oneself; (*: pl*) themselves; **lavarsi** to wash (oneself); **si è tagliato** he has cut himself; **si credono importanti** they think a lot of themselves
2 (*riflessivo: con complemento oggetto*): **lavarsi le mani** to wash one's hands; **si sta lavando i capelli** he (*o* she) is washing his (*o* her) hair
3 (*reciproco*) one another, each other; **si amano** they love one another *o* each other
4 (*passivo*): **si ripara facilmente** it is easily repaired
5 (*impersonale*): **si dice che ...** they *o* people say that ...; **si vede che è vecchio** one *o* you can see that it's old
6 (*noi*) we; **tra poco si parte** we're leaving soon

sì *av* yes; **un giorno sì e uno no** every other day

'sia *cong* **~ ... ~** (*o ... o*): **~ che lavori, ~ che non lavori** whether he works or not; (*tanto ... quanto*): **verranno ~ Luigi ~ suo fratello** both Luigi and his brother will be coming

si'amo *vb vedi* **essere**

si'cario *sm* hired killer

sicché [sik'ke] *cong (perciò)* so (that), therefore; *(e quindi) (and)* so
siccità [sittʃi'ta] *sf* drought
sic'come *cong* since, as
Si'cilia [si'tʃilja] *sf* **la ~** Sicily
si'cura *sf* safety catch; *(Aut)* safety lock
sicu'rezza [siku'rettsa] *sf* safety; security; *(fiducia)* confidence; *(certezza)* certainty; **di ~** safety *cpd*; **la ~ stradale** road safety
si'curo, -a *ag* safe; *(ben difeso)* secure; *(fiducioso)* confident; *(certo)* sure, certain; *(notizia, amico)* reliable; *(esperto)* skilled ▷ *av (anche:* **di ~)** certainly; **essere/mettere al ~** to be safe/put in a safe place; **~ di sé** self-confident, sure of o.s.; **sentirsi ~** to feel safe o secure
si'edo *ecc vb vedi* **sedere**
si'epe *sf* hedge
si'ero *sm (Med)* serum; **sieronega'tivo, -a** *ag* HIV-negative; **sieroposi'tivo, -a** *ag* HIV-positive
si'ete *vb vedi* **essere**
si'filide *sf* syphilis
Sig. *abbr (= signore)* Mr
siga'retta *sf* cigarette
'sigaro *sm* cigar
Sigg. *abbr (= signori)* Messrs
sigil'lare [sidʒil'lare] *vt* to seal
si'gillo [si'dʒillo] *sm* seal
'sigla *sf* initials *pl*; acronym, abbreviation; **sigla automobilistica** *abbreviation of province on vehicle number plate*; **sigla musicale** signature tune
Sig.na *abbr (= signorina)* Miss
signifi'care [siɲɲifi'kare] *vt* to mean; **signifi'cato** *sm* meaning
si'gnora [siɲ'ɲora] *sf* lady; **la ~ X** Mrs X; **buon giorno S~/Signore/ Signorina** good morning; *(deferente)* good morning Madam/Sir/Madam; *(quando si conosce il nome)* good morning Mrs/Mr/Miss X; **Gentile S~/Signore/Signorina** *(in una*

lettera) Dear Madam/Sir/Madam; **il signor Rossi e ~** Mr Rossi and his wife; **signore e signori** ladies and gentlemen
si'gnore [siɲ'ɲore] *sm* gentleman; *(padrone)* lord, master; *(Rel):* **il S~** the Lord; **il signor X** Mr X; **i signori Bianchi** *(coniugi)* Mr and Mrs Bianchi; *vedi anche* **signora**
signo'rile [siɲɲo'rile] *ag* refined
signo'rina [siɲɲo'rina] *sf* young lady; **la ~ X** Miss X; *vedi anche* **signora**
Sig.ra *abbr (= signora)* Mrs
silenzia'tore [silentsja'tore] *sm* silencer
si'lenzio [si'lɛntsjo] *sm* silence; **fare ~** to be quiet, stop talking; **silenzi'oso, -a** *ag* silent, quiet
si'licio [si'litʃo] *sm* silicon
sili'cone *sm* silicone
'sillaba *sf* syllable
si'luro *sm* torpedo
simboleggi'are [simboled'dʒare] *vt* to symbolize
'simbolo *sm* symbol
'simile *ag (analogo)* similar; *(di questo tipo):* **un uomo ~** such a man, a man like this; **libri simili** such books; **~ a** similar to; **i suoi simili** one's fellow men; one's peers
simme'tria *sf* symmetry
simpa'tia *sf (qualità)* pleasantness; *(inclinazione)* liking; **avere ~ per qn** to like sb, have a liking for sb; **sim'patico, -a, -ci, -che** *ag (persona)* nice, pleasant, likeable; *(casa, albergo ecc)* nice, pleasant

> Attenzione! In inglese esiste la parola *sympathetic*, che però significa *comprensivo*.

simpatiz'zare [simpatid'dzare] *vi* **~ con** to take a liking to
simu'lare *vt* to sham, simulate; *(Tecn)* to simulate
simul'taneo, -a *ag* simultaneous
sina'goga, -ghe *sf* synagogue
sincerità [sintʃeri'ta] *sf* sincerity

sin'cero, -a [sin'tʃero] *ag* sincere; genuine; heartfelt

sinda'cale *ag* (trade-)union *cpd*

sinda'cato *sm* (*di lavoratori*) (trade) union; (*Amm, Econ, Dir*) syndicate, trust, pool

'sindaco, -ci *sm* mayor

sinfo'nia *sf* (*Mus*) symphony

singhioz'zare [singjot'tsare] *vi* to sob; to hiccup

singhi'ozzo [sin'gjottso] *sm* sob; (*Med*) hiccup; **avere il ~** to have the hiccups; **a ~** (*fig*) by fits and starts

single ['singol] *ag inv, sm/f inv* single

singo'lare *ag* (*insolito*) remarkable, singular; (*Ling*) singular ▷ *sm* (*Ling*) singular; (*Tennis*): **~ maschile/femminile** men's/women's singles

'singolo, -a *ag* single, individual ▷ *sm* (*persona*) individual; (*Tennis*) **= singolare**

si'nistra *sf* (*Pol*) left (wing); **a ~** on the left; (*direzione*) to the left

si'nistro, -a *ag* left, left-hand; (*fig*) sinister ▷ *sm* (*incidente*) accident

si'nonimo *sm* synonym; **~ di** synonymous with

sin'tassi *sf* syntax

'sintesi *sf* synthesis; (*riassunto*) summary, résumé

sin'tetico, -a, -ci, -che *ag* synthetic

sintetiz'zare [sintetid'dzare] *vt* to synthesize; (*riassumere*) to summarize

sinto'matico, -a, -ci, -che *ag* symptomatic

'sintomo *sm* symptom

sintonizzarsi *vpr* **~ su** to tune in to

si'pario *sm* (*Teatro*) curtain

si'rena *sf* (*apparecchio*) siren; (*nella mitologia, fig*) siren, mermaid

'Siria *sf* **la ~** Syria

si'ringa, -ghe *sf* syringe

'sismico, -a, -ci, -che *ag* seismic

sis'tema, -i *sm* system; method, way; **sistema nervoso** nervous system; **sistema operativo** (*Inform*) operating system; **sistema solare** solar system

siste'mare *vt* (*mettere a posto*) to tidy, put in order; (*risolvere: questione*) to sort out, settle; (*procurare un lavoro a*) to find a job for; (*dare un alloggio a*) to settle, find accommodation for; **sistemarsi** *vpr* (*problema*) to be settled; (*persona: trovare alloggio*) to find accommodation (*BRIT*) o accommodations (*US*); (: *trovarsi un lavoro*) to get fixed up with a job; **ti sistemo io!** I'll soon sort you out!

siste'matico, -a, -ci, -che *ag* systematic

sistemazi'one [sistemat'tsjone] *sf* arrangement, order; settlement; employment; accommodation (*BRIT*), accommodations (*US*)

'sito *sm* **~ Internet** website

situazi'one [situat'tsjone] *sf* situation

ski-lift ['ski:lift] *sm inv* ski tow

slacci'are [zlat'tʃare] *vt* to undo, unfasten

slanci'ato, -a [zlan'tʃato] *ag* slender

'slancio *sm* dash, leap; (*fig*) surge; **di ~** impetuously

'slavo, -a *ag* Slav(onic), Slavic

sle'ale *ag* disloyal; (*concorrenza ecc*) unfair

sle'gare *vt* to untie

slip [zlip] *sm inv* briefs *pl*

'slitta *sf* sledge; (*trainata*) sleigh

slit'tare *vi* to slip, slide; (*Aut*) to skid

s.l.m. *abbr* (= *sul livello del mare*) a.s.l.

slo'gare *vt* (*Med*) to dislocate

sloggi'are [zlod'dʒare] *vt* (*inquilino*) to turn out ▷ *vi* to move out

Slo'vacchia [zlo'vakkja] *sf* Slovakia

slo'vacco, -a, -chi, -che *ag, sm/f* Slovak

Slovenia [zlo'vɛnja] *sf* Slovenia

slo'veno, -a *ag, sm/f* Slovene, Slovenian ▷ *sm* (*Ling*) Slovene

smacchi'are [zmak'kjare] *vt* to remove stains from; **smacchia'tore** *sm* stain remover

'smacco, -chi sm humiliating defeat

smagli'ante [zmaʎ'ʎante] ag brilliant, dazzling

smaglia'tura [zmaʎʎa'tura] sf (su maglia, calza) ladder; (della pelle) stretch mark

smalizi'ato, -a [smalit'tsjato] ag shrewd, cunning

smalti'mento sm (di rifiuti) disposal

smal'tire vt (merce) to sell off; (rifiuti) to dispose of; (cibo) to digest; (peso) to lose; (rabbia) to get over; **~ la sbornia** to sober up

'smalto sm (anche: **di denti**) enamel; (per ceramica) glaze; **smalto per unghie** nail varnish

smantel'lare vt to dismantle

smarri'mento sm loss; (fig) bewilderment; dismay

smar'rire vt to lose; (non riuscire a trovare) to mislay; **smarrirsi** vpr (perdersi) to lose one's way, get lost; (: oggetto) to go astray

smasche'rare [zmaske'rare] vt to unmask

SME sigla m (= Sistema Monetario Europeo) EMS (European Monetary System)

smen'tire vt (negare) to deny; (testimonianza) to refute; **smentirsi** vpr to be inconsistent

sme'raldo sm emerald

'smesso, -a pp di **smettere**

'smettere vt to stop; (vestiti) to stop wearing ▷ vi to stop, cease; **~ di fare** to stop doing

'smilzo, -a ['zmiltso] ag thin, lean

sminu'ire vt to diminish, lessen; (fig) to belittle

sminuz'zare [zminut'tsare] vt to break into small pieces; to crumble

'smisi ecc vb vedi **smettere**

smis'tare vt (pacchi ecc) to sort; (Ferr) to shunt

smisu'rato, -a ag boundless, immeasurable; (grandissimo) immense, enormous

smoking ['sməukɪŋ] sm inv dinner jacket

smon'tare vt (mobile, macchina ecc) to take to pieces, dismantle; (fig: scoraggiare) to dishearten ▷ vi (scendere: da cavallo) to dismount; (: da treno) to get off; (terminare il lavoro) to stop (work); **smontarsi** vpr to lose heart; to lose one's enthusiasm

'smorfia sf grimace; (atteggiamento lezioso) simpering; **fare smorfie** to make faces; to simper

'smorto, -a ag (viso) pale, wan; (colore) dull

smor'zare [zmor'tsare] vt (suoni) to deaden; (colori) to tone down; (luce) to dim; (sete) to quench; (entusiasmo) to dampen; **smorzarsi** vpr (suono, luce) to fade; (entusiasmo) to dampen

SMS sigla m inv (= short message service) text (message)

smu'overe vt to move, shift; (fig: commuovere) to move; (: dall'inerzia) to rouse, stir

snatu'rato, -a ag inhuman, heartless

'snello, -a ag (agile) agile; (svelto) slender, slim

sner'vante ag (attesa, lavoro) exasperating

snob'bare vt to snub

sno'dare vt (rendere agile, mobile) to loosen; **snodarsi** vpr to come loose; (articolarsi) to bend; (strada, fiume) to wind

sno'dato, -a ag (articolazione, persona) flexible; (fune ecc) undone

so vb vedi **sapere**

sobbar'carsi vpr: **~ a** to take on, undertake

'sobrio, -a ag sober

socchi'udere [sok'kjudere] vt (porta) to leave ajar; (occhi) to half-close; **socchi'uso, -a** pp di **socchiudere**

soc'correre vt to help, assist

soccorri'tore, -'trice sm/f rescuer

soc'corso, -a pp di **soccorrere**
▷ sm help, aid, assistance; **soccorso**
stradale breakdown service

soci'ale [so'tʃale] ag social; (di
associazione) club cpd, association cpd

socia'lismo [sotʃa'lizmo] sm
socialism; **socia'lista, -i, -e** ag, sm/f
socialist

società [sotʃe'ta] sf inv society;
(sportiva) club; (Comm) company; ~
a responsabilità limitata type of
limited liability company; **società per**
azioni limited (BRIT) o incorporated
(US) company

soci'evole [so'tʃevole] ag sociable

'socio ['sɔtʃo] sm (Dir, Comm) partner;
(membro di associazione) member

'soda sf (Chim) soda; (bibita) soda
(water)

soddisfa'cente [soddisfa'tʃɛnte] ag
satisfactory

soddis'fare vt, vi: ~ **a** to satisfy;
(impegno) to fulfil; (debito) to pay off;
(richiesta) to meet, comply with;
soddis'fatto, -a pp di **soddisfare**
▷ ag satisfied; **soddisfatto di** happy
o satisfied with; pleased with;
soddisfazi'one sf satisfaction

'sodo, -a ag firm, hard; (uovo) hard-
boiled ▷ av (picchiare, lavorare) hard;
(dormire) soundly

sofà sm inv sofa

soffe'renza [soffe'rɛntsa] sf
suffering

sof'ferto, -a pp di **soffrire**

soffi'are vt to blow; (notizia, segreto)
to whisper ▷ vi to blow; (sbuffare) to
puff (and blow); **soffiarsi il naso** to
blow one's nose; ~ **qc/qn a qn** (fig) to
pinch o steal sth/sb from sb; ~ **via qc**
to blow sth away

soffi'ata sf (fam) tip-off; **fare una ~**
alla polizia to tip off the police

'soffice ['sɔffitʃe] ag soft

'soffio sm (di vento) breath; **soffio al**
cuore heart murmur

sof'fitta sf attic

sof'fitto sm ceiling

soffo'cante ag suffocating, stifling

soffo'care vi (anche: **soffocarsi**) to
suffocate, choke ▷ vt to suffocate,
choke; (fig) to stifle, suppress

sof'frire vt to suffer, endure;
(sopportare) to bear, stand ▷ vi to
suffer; to be in pain; ~ **(di) qc** (Med) to
suffer from sth

sof'fritto, -a pp di **soffriggere** ▷ sm
(Cuc) fried mixture of herbs, bacon and
onions

sofisti'cato, -a ag sophisticated;
(vino) adulterated

'software ['sɔftwɛə] sm ~
applicativo applications package

sogget'tivo, -a [soddʒet'tivo] ag
subjective

sog'getto, -a [sod'dʒɛtto] ag: ~ **a**
(sottomesso) subject to; (esposto: a
variazioni, danni ecc) subject o liable to
▷ sm subject

soggezi'one [soddʒet'tsjone] sf
subjection; (timidezza) awe; **avere ~**
di qn to stand in awe of sb; to be ill at
ease in sb's presence

soggi'orno sm (invernale, marino)
stay; (stanza) living room

'soglia ['sɔʎʎa] sf doorstep; (anche fig)
threshold

'sogliola ['sɔʎʎola] sf (Zool) sole

so'gnare [son'ɲare] vt, vi to dream; ~
a occhi aperti to daydream

'sogno ['sonɲo] sm dream

'soia sf (Bot) soya

sol sm (Mus) G; (: solfeggiando) so(h)

so'laio sm (soffitta) attic

sola'mente av only, just

so'lare ag solar, sun cpd

'solco, -chi sm (scavo, fig: ruga)
furrow; (incavo) rut, track; (di disco)
groove

sol'dato sm soldier; **soldato**
semplice private

soldi smpl (denaro) money sg; **non ho ~**
I haven't got any money

'sole sm sun; (luce) sun(light); (tempo

assolato) sun(shine); **prendere il ~** to sunbathe

soleggi'ato, -a [soled'dʒato] *ag* sunny

so'lenne *ag* solemn

soli'dale *ag:* **essere ~ (con)** to be in agreement (with)

solidarietà *sf* solidarity

'solido, -a *ag* solid; *(forte, robusto)* sturdy, solid; *(fig: ditta)* sound, solid ▷ *sm* (Mat) solid

so'lista, -i, -e *ag* solo ▷ *sm/f* soloist

solita'mente *av* usually, as a rule

soli'tario, -a *ag (senza compagnia)* solitary, lonely; *(solo, isolato)* solitary, lone; *(deserto)* lonely ▷ *sm (gioiello, gioco)* solitaire

'solito, -a *ag* usual; **essere ~ fare** to be in the habit of doing; **di ~** usually; **più tardi del ~** later than usual; **come al ~** as usual

soli'tudine *sf* solitude

sol'letico *sm* tickling; **soffrire il ~** to be ticklish

solleva'mento *sm* raising; lifting; revolt; **sollevamento pesi** *(Sport)* weight-lifting

solle'vare *vt* to lift, raise; *(fig: persona: alleggerire):* **~ (da)** to relieve (of); *(: dar conforto)* to comfort, relieve; *(: questione)* to raise; *(: far insorgere)* to stir (to revolt); **sollevarsi** *vpr* to rise; *(fig: riprendersi)* to recover; *(: ribellarsi)* to rise up

solli'evo *sm* relief; *(conforto)* comfort

'solo, -a *ag* alone; *(in senso spirituale: isolato)* lonely; *(unico):* **un ~ libro** only one book, a single book; *(con ag numerale):* **veniamo noi tre soli** just o only the three of us are coming ▷ *av (soltanto)* only, just; **non ~ ... ma anche** not only ... but also; **fare qc da ~** to do sth (all) by oneself

sol'tanto *av* only

so'lubile *ag (sostanza)* soluble

soluzi'one [solut'tsjone] *sf* solution

sol'vente *ag, sm* solvent

so'maro *sm* ass, donkey

somigli'anza [somiʎ'ʎantsa] *sf* resemblance

somigli'are [somiʎ'ʎare] *vi:* **~ a** to be like, resemble; *(nell'aspetto fisico)* to look like; **somigliarsi** *vpr* to be (o look) alike

'somma *sf* (Mat) sum; *(di denaro)* sum (of money)

som'mare *vt* to add up; *(aggiungere)* to add; **tutto sommato** all things considered

som'mario, -a *ag (racconto, indagine)* brief; *(giustizia)* summary ▷ *sm* summary

sommer'gibile [sommer'dʒibile] *sm* submarine

som'merso, -a *pp di* **sommergere**

sommità *sf inv* summit, top; *(fig)* height

som'mossa *sf* uprising

'sonda *sf* (Med, Meteor, Aer) probe; *(Mineralogia)* drill ▷ *ag inv* **pallone** *m* **~** weather balloon

son'daggio [son'daddʒo] *sm* sounding; probe; boring, drilling; *(indagine)* survey; **sondaggio d'opinioni** opinion poll

son'dare *vt* (Naut) to sound; *(atmosfera, piaga)* to probe; *(Mineralogia)* to bore, drill; *(fig: opinione ecc)* to survey, poll

so'netto *sm* sonnet

son'nambulo, -a *sm/f* sleepwalker

sonnel'lino *sm* nap

son'nifero *sm* sleeping drug *(o pill)*

'sonno *sm* sleep; **prendere ~** to fall asleep; **aver ~** to be sleepy

'sono *vb vedi* **essere**

so'noro, -a *ag (ambiente)* resonant; *(voce)* sonorous, ringing; *(onde, film)* sound *cpd*

sontu'oso, -a *ag* sumptuous; lavish

sop'palco, -chi *sm* mezzanine

soppor'tare *vt (subire: perdita, spese)* to bear, sustain; *(soffrire: dolore)* to bear, endure; *(cosa: freddo)* to withstand; (*persona: freddo, vino*) to take; (*tollerare*) to put up with, tolerate

> ▌ Attenzione! In inglese esiste il verbo *to support*, che però non significa *sopportare*.

sop'primere *vt* (*carica, privilegi, testimone*) to do away with; (*pubblicazione*) to suppress; (*parola, frase*) to delete

'**sopra** *prep* (*gen*) on; (*al di sopra di, più in alto di*) above; over; (*riguardo a*) on, about ▷ *av* on top; (*attaccato, scritto*) on it; (*al di sopra*) above; (*al piano superiore*) upstairs; **donne ~ i 30 anni** women over 30 (years of age); **abito di ~** I live upstairs; **dormirci ~** (*fig*) to sleep on it

so'prabito *sm* overcoat

soprac'ciglio [soprat'tʃiʎʎo] (*pl(f)* **soprac'ciglia**) *sm* eyebrow

sopraf'fare *vt* to overcome, overwhelm

sopral'luogo, -ghi *sm* (*di esperti*) inspection; (*di polizia*) on-the-spot investigation

sopram'mobile *sm* ornament

soprannatu'rale *ag* supernatural

sopran'nome *sm* nickname

so'prano, -a *sm/f* (*persona*) soprano ▷ *sm* (*voce*) soprano

soprappensi'ero *av* lost in thought

sopras'salto *sm*: **di ~** with a start; suddenly

soprasse'dere *vi*: **~ a** to delay, put off

soprat'tutto *av* (*anzitutto*) above all; (*specialmente*) especially

sopravvalu'tare *vt* to overestimate

soprav'vento *sm* **avere/prendere il ~ su** to have/get the upper hand over

sopravvis'suto, -a *pp di* **sopravvivere**

soprav'vivere *vi* to survive; (*continuare a vivere*): **~ (in)** to live on (in); **~ a** (*incidente ecc*) to survive; (*persona*) to outlive

so'pruso *sm* abuse of power; **subire un ~** to be abused

soq'quadro *sm*: **mettere a ~** to turn upside-down

sor'betto *sm* sorbet, water ice

sor'dina *sf* **in ~** softly; (*fig*) on the sly

'**sordo, -a** *ag* deaf; (*rumore*) muffled; (*dolore*) dull; (*odio, rancore*) veiled ▷ *sm/f* deaf person; **sordo'muto, -a** *ag* deaf-and-dumb ▷ *sm/f* deaf-mute

so'rella *sf* sister; **sorel'lastra** *sf* stepsister; (*con genitore in comune*) half-sister

sor'gente [sor'dʒɛnte] *sf* (*d'acqua*) spring; (*di fiume, Fisica, fig*) source

'**sorgere** ['sordʒere] *vi* to rise; (*scaturire*) to spring, rise; (*fig: difficoltà*) to arise

sorni'one, -a *ag* sly

sorpas'sare *vt* (*Aut*) to overtake; (*fig*) to surpass; (: *eccedere*) to exceed, go beyond; **~ in altezza** to be higher than; (*persona*) to be taller than

sorpren'dente *ag* surprising

sor'prendere *vt* (*cogliere: in flagrante ecc*) to catch; (*stupire*) to surprise; **sorprendersi** *vpr*: **sorprendersi (di)** to be surprised (at); **sor'presa** *sf* surprise; **fare una sorpresa a qn** to give sb a surprise; **sor'preso, -a** *pp di* **sorprendere**

sor'reggere [sor'rɛddʒere] *vt* to support, hold up; (*fig*) to sustain; **sorreggersi** *vpr* (*tenersi ritto*) to stay upright

sor'ridere *vi* to smile; **sor'riso, -a** *pp di* **sorridere** ▷ *sm* smile

'**sorsi** *ecc vb vedi* **sorgere**

'**sorso** *sm* sip

'**sorta** *sf* sort, kind; **di ~** whatever, of any kind, at all

'**sorte** *sf* (*fato*) fate, destiny; (*evento fortuito*) chance; **tirare a ~** to draw lots

sor'teggio [sor'teddʒo] *sm* draw

sorvegli'ante [sorveʎ'ʎante] *sm/f* (*di carcere*) guard, warder (BRIT); (*di fabbrica ecc*) supervisor

sorvegli'anza [sorveʎ'ʎantsa] *sf*

watch; supervision; (*Polizia, Mil*) surveillance

sorvegli'are [sorveʎ'ʎare] *vt* (*bambino, bagagli, prigioniero*) to watch, keep an eye on; (*malato*) to watch over; (*territorio, casa*) to watch o keep watch over; (*lavori*) to supervise

sorvo'lare *vt* (*territorio*) to fly over ▷ *vi* ~ **su** (*fig*) to skim over

S.O.S. *sigla m* mayday, SOS

'sosia *sm inv* double

sos'pendere *vt* (*appendere*) to hang (up); (*interrompere, privare di una carica*) to suspend; (*rimandare*) to defer; (*appendere*) to hang

sospet'tare *vt* to suspect ▷ *vi*: ~ **di** to suspect; (*diffidare*) to be suspicious of

sos'petto, -a *ag* suspicious ▷ *sm* suspicion; **sospet'toso, -a** *ag* suspicious

sospi'rare *vi* to sigh ▷ *vt* to long for, yearn for; **sos'piro** *sm* sigh

'sosta *sf* (*fermata*) stop, halt; (*pausa*) pause, break; **senza ~** non-stop, without a break

sostan'tivo *sm* noun, substantive

sos'tanza [sos'tantsa] *sf* substance; **sostanze** *sfpl* (*ricchezze*) wealth *sg*, possessions; **in ~** in short, to sum up

sos'tare *vi* (*fermarsi*) to stop (for a while), stay; (*fare una pausa*) to take a break

sos'tegno [sos'teɲɲo] *sm* support

soste'nere *vt* to support; (*prendere su di sé*) to take on, bear; (*resistere*) to withstand, stand up to; (*affermare*): ~ **che** to maintain that; **sostenersi** *vpr* to hold o.s. up, support o.s.; (*fig*) to keep up one's strength; ~ **gli esami** to sit exams

sostena'mento *sm* maintenance, support

sostitu'ire *vt* (*mettere al posto di*): ~ **qn/qc a** to substitute sb/sth for; (*prendere il posto di: persona*) to substitute for; (*: cosa*) to take the place of

sosti'tuto, -a *sm/f* substitute

sostituzi'one [sostitut'tsjone] *sf* substitution; **in ~ di** as a substitute for, in place of

sotta'ceti [sotta'tʃeti] *smpl* pickles

sot'tana *sf* (*sottoveste*) underskirt; (*gonna*) skirt; (*Rel*) soutane, cassock

sotter'fugio [sotter'fudʒo] *sm* subterfuge

sotter'raneo, -a *ag* underground ▷ *sm* cellar

sotter'rare *vt* to bury

sot'tile *ag* thin; (*figura, caviglia*) thin, slim, slender; (*fine: polvere, capelli*) fine; (*fig: leggero*) light; (*: vista*) sharp, keen; (*: olfatto*) fine, discriminating; (*: mente*) subtle; shrewd ▷ *sm* **non andare per il ~** not to mince matters

sottin'teso, -a *pp di* **sottintendere** ▷ *sm* allusion; **parlare senza sottintesi** to speak plainly

'sotto *prep* (*gen*) under; (*più in basso di*) below ▷ *av* underneath, beneath; below; (**al piano) di ~** downstairs; ~ **forma di** in the form of; ~ **il monte** at the foot of the mountain; **siamo** ~ **Natale** it's nearly Christmas; ~ **la pioggia/il sole** in the rain/sun(shine); ~ **terra** underground; **chiuso ~ vuoto** vacuum-packed

sotto'fondo *sm* background; **sottofondo musicale** background music

sottoline'are *vt* to underline; (*fig*) to emphasize, stress

sottoma'rino, -a *ag* (*flora*) submarine; (*cavo, navigazione*) underwater ▷ *sm* (*Naut*) submarine

sottopas'saggio [sottopas'saddʒo] *sm* (*Aut*) underpass; (*pedonale*) subway, underpass

sotto'porre *vt* (*costringere*) to subject; (*fig: presentare*) to submit; **sottoporsi** *vpr* to submit; **sottoporsi a** (*subire*) to undergo

sottos'critto, -a *pp di* **sottoscrivere**

sotto'sopra *av* upside-down

sotto'terra av underground
sotto'titolo sm subtitle
sottovalu'tare vt to underestimate
sotto've ste sf underskirt
sotto'voce [sotto'votʃe] av in a low voice
sottovu'oto av: **confezionare ~** to vacuum-pack ▷ ag **confezione** f **~** vacuum packed
sot'trarre vt (Mat) to subtract, take away; **~ qn/qc a** (togliere) to remove sb/sth from; (salvare) to save o rescue sb/sth from; **~ qc a qn** (rubare) to steal sth from sb; **sottrarsi** vpr **sottrarsi a** (sfuggire) to escape; (evitare) to avoid; **sottrazi'one** sf subtraction; removal
souve'nir [suv(ə)'nir] sm inv souvenir
sovi'etico, -a, -ci, -che ag Soviet ▷ sm/f Soviet citizen
sovrac'carico, -a, -chi, che ag: **~ (di)** overloaded (with) ▷ sm excess load; **~ di lavoro** extra work
sovraffol'lato, -a ag overcrowded
sovrannatu'rale ag = **soprannatu'rale**
so'vrano, -a ag sovereign; (fig: sommo) supreme ▷ sm/f sovereign, monarch
sovrap'porre vt to place on top of, put on top of
sovvenzi'one [sovven'tsjone] sf subsidy, grant
'sozzo, -a ['sottso] ag filthy, dirty
S.P.A. abbr = **società per azioni**
spac'care vt to split, break; (legna) to chop; **spaccarsi** vpr to split, break; **spacca'tura** sf split
spaccherò ecc [spakke'rɔ] vb vedi **spaccare**
spacci'are [spat'tʃare] vt (vendere) to sell (off); (mettere in circolazione) to circulate; (droga) to peddle, push; **spacciarsi** vpr **spacciarsi per** (farsi credere) to pass o.s. off as, pretend to be; **spaccia'tore, -'trice** sm/f (di droga) pusher; (di denaro falso) dealer; **'spaccio** sm (di merce rubata, droga):

spaccio (di) trafficking (in); **spaccio (di)** passing (of); (vendita) sale; (bottega) shop
'spacco, -chi sm (fenditura) split, crack; (strappo) tear; (di gonna) slit
spac'cone sm/f boaster, braggart
'spada sf sword
spae'sato, -a ag disorientated, lost
spa'ghetti [spa'getti] smpl (Cuc) spaghetti sg
'Spagna ['spaɲɲa] sf: **la ~** Spain; **spa'gnolo, -a** ag Spanish ▷ sm/f Spaniard ▷ sm (Ling) Spanish; **gli Spagnoli** the Spanish
'spago, -ghi sm string, twine
spai'ato, -a ag (calza, guanto) odd
spalan'care vt to open wide; **spalancarsi** vpr to open wide
spa'lare vt to shovel
'spalla sf shoulder; (fig: Teatro) stooge; **spalle** sfpl (dorso) back
spalli'era sf (di sedia ecc) back; (di letto: da capo) head(board); (: da piedi) foot(board); (Ginnastica) wall bars pl
spal'lina sf (bretella) strap; (imbottitura) shoulder pad
spal'mare vt to spread
'spalti smpl (di stadio) terracing
spandere vt to spread; (versare) to pour (out)
spa'rare vt to fire ▷ vi (far fuoco) to fire; (tirare) to shoot; **spara'toria** sf exchange of shots
sparecchi'are [sparek'kjare] vt: **~ (la tavola)** to clear the table
spa'reggio [spa'reddʒo] sm (Sport) play-off
'spargere ['spardʒere] vt (sparpagliare) to scatter; (versare: vino) to spill; (: lacrime, sangue) to shed; (diffondere) to spread; (emanare) to give off (o out); **spargersi** vpr to spread
spa'rire vi to disappear, vanish
spar'lare vi **~ di** to run down, speak ill of
'sparo sm shot
spar'tire vt (eredità, bottino) to share

out; (*avversari*) to separate
spar'tito *sm* (*Mus*) score
sparti'traffico *sm inv* (*Aut*) central
reservation (*BRIT*), median (strip) (*US*)
sparvi'ero *sm* (*Zool*) sparrowhawk
spasi'mante *sm* suitor
spassio'nato, -a *ag* dispassionate,
impartial
'spasso *sm* (*divertimento*)
amusement, enjoyment; **andare a ~**
to go out for a walk; **essere a ~** (*fig*) to
be out of work; **mandare qn a ~** (*fig*)
to give sb the sack
'spatola *sf* spatula; (*di muratore*)
trowel
spa'valdo, -a *ag* arrogant, bold
spaventa'passeri *sm inv* scarecrow
spaven'tare *vt* to frighten, scare;
spaventarsi *vpr* to be frightened,
be scared; to get a fright; **spa'vento**
sm fear, fright; **far spavento a qn**
to give sb a fright; **spaven'toso,**
-a *ag* frightening, terrible; (*fig: fam*)
tremendous, fantastic
spazientirsi [spattsjen'tirsi] *vpr* to
lose one's patience
'spazio ['spattsjo] *sm* space; **spazio**
aereo airspace; **spazi'oso, -a** *ag*
spacious
spazzaca'mino [spattsaka'mino]
sm chimney sweep
spazza'neve [spattsa'neve] *sm inv*
snowplough
spaz'zare [spat'tsare] *vt* to sweep;
(*foglie ecc*) to sweep up; (*cacciare*)
to sweep away; **spazza'tura** *sf*
sweepings *pl*; (*immondizia*) rubbish;
spaz'zino *sm* street sweeper
'spazzola ['spattsola] *sf* brush;
spazzola da capelli hairbrush;
spazzola per abiti clothesbrush;
spazzo'lare *vt* to brush; **spazzo'lino**
sm (small) brush; **spazzolino da**
denti toothbrush
specchi'arsi [spek'kjarsi] *vpr* to look
at o.s. in a mirror; (*riflettersi*) to be
mirrored, be reflected

specchi'etto [spek'kjetto] *sm*
(*tabella*) table, chart; **specchietto da**
borsetta pocket mirror; **specchietto**
retrovisore (*Aut*) rear-view mirror
'specchio ['spɛkkjo] *sm* mirror
speci'ale [spe'tʃale] *ag* special;
specia'lista, -i, -e *sm/f* specialist;
specialità *sf inv* speciality; (*branca di*
studio) special field, speciality; **vorrei**
assaggiare una specialità del
posto I'd like to try a local speciality;
special'mente *av* especially,
particularly
'specie ['spɛtʃe] *sf inv* (*Biol, Bot, Zool*)
species *inv*; (*tipo*) kind, sort ▷ *av*
especially, particularly; **una ~ di** a
kind of; **fare ~ a qn** to surprise sb; **la ~**
umana mankind
specifi'care [spetʃifi'kare] *vt* to
specify, state
spe'cifico, -a, -ci, -che [spe'tʃifiko]
ag specific
specu'lare *vi*: **~ su** (*Comm*) to
speculate in; (*sfruttare*) to exploit;
(*meditare*) to speculate on;
speculazi'one *sf* speculation
spe'dire *vt* to send
'spegnere ['spɛɲɲere] *vt* (*fuoco,*
sigaretta) to put out, extinguish;
(*apparecchio elettrico*) to turn o
switch off; (*gas*) to turn off; (*fig:*
suoni, passioni) to stifle; (*debito*)
to extinguish; **spegnersi** *vpr* to
go out; to go off; (*morire*) to pass
away; **puoi ~ la luce?** could you
switch off the light?; **non riesco a**
~ il riscaldamento I can't turn the
heating off
spellarsi *vpr* to peel
'spendere *vt* to spend
'spengo *ecc vb vedi* **spegnere**
'spensi *ecc vb vedi* **spegnere**
spensie'rato, -a *ag* carefree
'spento, -a *pp di* **spegnere** ▷ *ag*
(*suono*) muffled; (*colore*) dull; (*sigaretta*)
out; (*civiltà, vulcano*) extinct
spe'ranza [spe'rantsa] *sf* hope

spe'rare vt to hope for ▷ vi ~ **in** to trust in; ~ **che/di fare** to hope that/to do; **lo spero, spero di sì** I hope so

sper'duto, -a ag (isolato) out-of-the-way; (persona: smarrita, a disagio) lost

sperimen'tale ag experimental

sperimen'tare vt to experiment with, test; (fig) to test, put to the test

'sperma, -i sm sperm

spe'rone sm spur

sperpe'rare vt to squander

'spesa sf (somma di denaro) expense; (costo) cost; (acquisto) purchase; (fam: acquisto del cibo quotidiano) shopping; **spese postali** postage sg; **spese di viaggio** travelling expenses

'spesso, -a ag (fitto) thick; (frequente) frequent ▷ av often; **spesse volte** frequently, often

spes'sore sm thickness

Spett. abbr vedi **spettabile**

spet'tabile (abbr: **Spett.**: in lettere) ag ~ **Ditta X** Messrs X and Co.

spet'tacolo sm (rappresentazione) performance, show; (vista, scena) sight; **dare ~ di sé** to make an exhibition o a spectacle of o.s.

spet'tare vi: ~ **a** (decisione) to be up to; (stipendio) to be due to; **spetta a te decidere** it's up to you to decide

spetta'tore, -'trice sm/f (Cinema, Teatro) member of the audience; (di avvenimento) onlooker, witness

spettego'lare vi to gossip

spetti'nato, -a ag dishevelled

'spettro sm (fantasma) spectre; (Fisica) spectrum

'spezie ['spɛttsje] sfpl (Cuc) spices

spez'zare [spet'tsare] vt (rompere) to break; (fig: interrompere) to break up; **spezzarsi** vpr to break

spezza'tino [spettsa'tino] sm (Cuc) stew

spezzet'tare [spettset'tare] vt to break up (o chop) into small pieces

'spia sf spy; (confidente della polizia) informer; (Elettr) indicating light;

warning light; (fessura) peep-hole; (fig: sintomo) sign, indication

spia'cente [spja'tʃɛnte] ag sorry; **essere ~ di qc/di fare qc** to be sorry about sth/for doing sth

spia'cevole [spja'tʃevole] ag unpleasant

spi'aggia, -ge ['spjaddʒa] sf beach; **spiaggia libera** public beach

spia'nare vt (terreno) to level, make level; (edificio) to raze to the ground; (pasta) to roll out; (rendere liscio) to smooth (out)

spi'are vt to spy on

spi'azzo ['spjattso] sm open space; (radura) clearing

'spicchio ['spikkjo] sm (di agrumi) segment; (di aglio) clove; (parte) piece, slice

spicciarsi vpr to hurry up

spiccioli smpl (small) change; **mi dispiace, non ho ~** sorry, I don't have any change

'spicco, -chi sm: **di ~** outstanding; (tema) main, principal; **fare ~** to stand out

spie'dino sm (utensile) skewer; (pietanza) kebab

spi'edo sm (Cuc) spit

spie'gare vt (far capire) to explain; (tovaglia) to unfold; (vele) to unfurl; **spiegarsi** vpr to explain o.s., make o.s. clear; ~ **qc a qn** to explain sth to sb; **spiegazi'one** sf explanation

spiegherò ecc [spjege'rɔ] vb vedi **spiegare**

spie'tato, -a ag ruthless, pitiless

spiffe'rare (fam) vt to blurt out, blab

'spiffero sm draught (BRIT), draft (US)

'spiga, -ghe sf (Bot) ear

spigli'ato, -a [spiʎ'ʎato] ag self-possessed, self-confident

'spigolo sm corner; (Mat) edge

'spilla sf brooch; (da cravatta, cappello) pin; ~ **di sicurezza** o **da balia** safety pin

'spillo sm pin; **spillo da balia** o **di**

sicurezza safety pin

spi'lorcio, -a, -ci, -ce [spi'lortʃo] *ag*
mean, stingy

'spina *sf* (*Bot*) thorn; (*Zool*) spine,
prickle; (*di pesce*) bone; (*Elettr*) plug; (*di
botte*) bunghole; **birra alla ~** draught
beer; **spina dorsale** (*Anat*) backbone

spinaci [spi'natʃi] *smpl* spinach *sg*

spi'nello *sm* (*Droga: gergo*) joint

'spingere ['spindʒere] *vt* to
push; (*condurre: anche fig*) to drive;
(*stimolare*): **~ qn a fare** to urge o press
sb to do

spi'noso, -a *ag* thorny, prickly

'spinsi *ecc vb vedi* **spingere**

'spinta *sf* (*urto*) push; (*Fisica*)
thrust; (*fig: stimolo*) incentive, spur;
(: *appoggio*) string-pulling *no pl*; **dare
una ~ a qn** (*fig*) to pull strings for sb

'spinto, -a *pp di* **spingere**

spio'naggio [spio'naddʒo] *sm*
espionage, spying

spion'cino [spion'tʃino] *sm* peephole

spi'raglio [spi'raʎʎo] *sm* (*fessura*)
chink, narrow opening; (*raggio di luce,
fig*) glimmer, gleam

spi'rale *sf* spiral; (*contraccettivo*) coil; **a
~** spiral(-shaped)

spiri'tato, -a *ag* possessed; (*fig:
persona, espressione*) wild

spiri'tismo *sm* spiritualism

'spirito *sm* (*Rel, Chim, disposizione
d'animo, di legge ecc, fantasma*) spirit;
(*pensieri, intelletto*) mind; (*arguzia*) wit;
(*umorismo*) humour, wit; **lo S~ Santo**
the Holy Spirit o Ghost

spirito'saggine [spirito'saddʒine] *sf*
witticism; (*peg*) wisecrack

spiri'toso, -a *ag* witty

spiritu'ale *ag* spiritual

'splendere *sm* to shine

'splendido, -a *ag* splendid;
(*splendente*) shining; (*sfarzoso*)
magnificent, splendid

splen'dore *sm* splendour; (*luce
intensa*) brilliance, brightness

spogli'are [spoʎ'ʎare] *vt* (*svestire*)

to undress; (*privare, fig: depredare*): **~
qn di qc** to deprive sb of sth; (*togliere
ornamenti: anche fig*): **~ qn/qc di** to
strip sb/sth of; **spogliarsi** *vpr* to
undress, strip; **spogliarsi di** (*ricchezze
ecc*) to deprive o.s. of, give up;
(*pregiudizi*) to rid o.s. of; **spoglia'rello**
[spoʎʎa'rello] *sm* striptease;
spoglia'toio *sm* dressing room;
(*di scuola ecc*) cloakroom; (*Sport*)
changing room

'spola *sf* (*bobina di filo*) spool; **fare
la ~ (fra)** to go to and fro o shuttle
(between)

spolve'rare *vt* (*anche Cuc*) to dust;
(*con spazzola*) to brush; (*con battipanni*)
to beat; (*fig*) to polish off ▷ *vi* to dust

spon'taneo, -a *ag* spontaneous;
(*persona*) unaffected, natural

spor'care *vt* to dirty, make dirty; (*fig*)
to sully, soil; **sporcarsi** *vpr* to get dirty

spor'cizia [spor'tʃittsja] *sf* (*stato*)
dirtiness; (*sudiciume*) dirt, filth; (*cosa
sporca*) dirt *no pl*, something dirty

'sporco, -a, -chi, -che *ag* dirty, filthy

spor'genza [spor'dʒentsa] *sf*
projection

'sporgere ['spordʒere] *vt* to put out,
stretch out ▷ *vi* (*venire in fuori*) to stick
out; **sporgersi** *vpr* to lean out; **~
querela contro qn** (*Dir*) to take legal
action against sb

'sporsi *ecc vb vedi* **sporgere**

sport *sm inv* sport

spor'tello *sm* (*di treno, auto ecc*) door;
(*di banca, ufficio*) window, counter;
sportello automatico (*Banca*) cash
dispenser, automated telling machine

spor'tivo, -a *ag* (*gara, giornale,
centro*) sports *cpd*; (*persona*) sporty;
(*abito*) casual; (*spirito, atteggiamento*)
sporting

'sposa *sf* bride; (*moglie*) wife

sposa'lizio [spoza'littsjo] *sm*
wedding

spo'sare *vt* to marry; (*fig: idea, fede*) to
espouse; **sposarsi** *vpr* to get married,

marry; **sposarsi con qn** to marry sb,
get married to sb; **spo'sato, -a** ag
married

'**sposo** sm (bride)groom; (marito)
husband

spos'sato, -a ag exhausted, weary

spos'care vt to waste

spos'tare vt to move, shift; (cambiare:
orario) to change; **spostarsi** vpr to
move; **può ~ la macchina, per
favore?** can you move your car please?

'**spranga, -ghe** sf (sbarra) bar

spre'care vt to waste

spre'gevole [spre'dʒevole] ag
contemptible, despicable

'**spremere** vt to squeeze

spremia'grumi sm inv lemon
squeezer

spre'muta sf fresh juice; **spremuta
d'arancia** fresh orange juice

sprez'zante [spret'tsante] ag
scornful, contemptuous

sprofon'dare vi to sink; (casa) to
collapse; (suolo) to give way, subside

spro'nare vt to spur (on)

sproporzio'nato, -a
[sproportsjo'nato] ag
disproportionate, out of all
proportion

sproporzi'one [spropor'tsjone] sf
disproportion

spro'posito sm blunder; **a ~** at the
wrong time; (rispondere, parlare)
irrelevantly

sprovve'duto, -a ag inexperienced,
naïve

sprov'visto, -a ag (mancante): **~ di**
lacking in, without; **alla sprovvista**
unawares

spruz'zare [sprut'tsare] vt (a
nebulizzazione) to spray; (aspergere) to
sprinkle; (inzaccherare) to splash

'**spugna** ['spuɲɲa] sf (Zool) sponge;
(tessuto) towelling

'**spuma** sf (schiuma) foam; (bibita)
fizzy drink

spu'mante sm sparkling wine

spun'tare vt (coltello) to break the

point of; (capelli) to trim ▷ vi (uscire:
germogli) to sprout; (: capelli) to begin
to grow; (: denti) to come through;
(apparire) to appear (suddenly)

spun'tino sm snack

'**spunto** sm (Teatro, Mus) cue; (fig)
starting point; **dare lo ~ a** (fig) to give
rise to

spu'tare vt to spit out; (fig) to belch
(out) ▷ vi to spit

'**squadra** sf (strumento) (set) square;
(gruppo) team, squad; (di operai)
gang, squad; (Mil) squad; (: Aer, Naut)
squadron; (Sport) team; **lavoro a
squadre** teamwork

squagli'arsi [skwaʎ'ʎarsi] vpr to
melt; (fig) to sneak off

squa'lifica sf disqualification

squalifi'care vt to disqualify

'**squallido, -a** ag wretched, bleak

'**squalo** sm shark

'**squama** sf scale

squarcia'gola [skwartʃa'gola]: **a ~** av
at the top of one's voice

squattri'nato, -a ag penniless

squili'brato, -a ag (Psic) unbalanced

squil'lante ag shrill, sharp

squil'lare vi (campanello, telefono) to
ring (out); (tromba) to blare; '**squillo**
sm ring, ringing no pl; blare; **ragazza** f
squillo inv call girl

squi'sito, -a ag exquisite; (cibo)
delicious; (persona) delightful

squit'tire vi (uccello) to squawk; (topo)
to squeak

sradi'care vt to uproot; (fig) to
eradicate

srego'lato, -a ag (senza ordine: vita)
disorderly; (smodato) immoderate;
(dissoluto) dissolute

S.r.l. abbr = **società a responsabilità
limitata**

sroto'lare vt, sroto'larsi ▷ vpr to
unroll

SS sigla = **strada statale**

S.S.N. abbr (= Servizio Sanitario
Nazionale) ≈ NHS

sta *ecc vb vedi* **stare**

'stabile *ag* stable, steady; (*tempo: non variabile*) settled; (*Teatro: compagnia*) resident ▷ *sm* (*edificio*) building

stabili'mento *sm* (*edificio*) establishment; (*fabbrica*) plant, factory

stabi'lire *vt* to establish; (*fissare: prezzi, data*) to fix; (*decidere*) to decide; **stabilirsi** *vpr* (*prendere dimora*) to settle

stac'care *vt* (*levare*) to detach, remove; (*separare: anche fig*) to separate, divide; (*strappare*) to tear off (*o* out); (*scandire: parole*) to pronounce clearly; (*Sport*) to leave behind; **staccarsi** *vpr* (*bottone ecc*) to come off; (*scostarsi*): **staccarsi (da)** to move away (from); (*fig: separarsi*): **staccarsi da** to leave; **non ~ gli occhi da qn** not to take one's eyes off sb

'stadio *sm* (*Sport*) stadium; (*periodo, fase*) phase, stage

'staffa *sf* (*di sella, Tecn*) stirrup; **perdere le staffe** (*fig*) to fly off the handle

staf'fetta *sf* (*messo*) dispatch rider; (*Sport*) relay race

stagio'nale [stadʒo'nale] *ag* seasonal

stagio'nato, -a [stadʒo'nato] *ag* (*vedi vb*) seasoned; matured; (*scherzoso: attempato*) getting on in years

stagi'one [sta'dʒone] *sf* season; **alta/bassa ~** high/low season

stagista, -i, -e [sta'd[gh]ista] *sm/f* trainee, intern (*US*)

'stagno, -a ['staɲɲo] *ag* watertight; (*a tenuta d'aria*) airtight ▷ *sm* (*acquitrino*) pond; (*Chim*) tin

sta'gnola [staɲ'ɲola] *sf* tinfoil

'stalla *sf* (*per bovini*) cowshed; (*per cavalli*) stable

stal'lone *sm* stallion

stamat'tina *av* this morning

stam'becco, -chi *sm* ibex

stami'nale *agg*: **cellula ~** stem cell

'stampa *sf* (*Tip, Fot: tecnica*) printing; (*impressione, copia fotografica*) print; (*insieme di quotidiani, giornalisti ecc*) press

stam'pante *sf* (*Inform*) printer

stam'pare *vt* to print; (*pubblicare*) to publish; (*coniare*) to strike, coin; (*imprimere: anche fig*) to impress

stampa'tello *sm* block letters *pl*

stam'pella *sf* crutch

'stampo *sm* mould; (*fig: indole*) type, kind, sort

sta'nare *vt* to drive out

stan'care *vt* to tire, make tired; (*annoiare*) to bore; (*infastidire*) to annoy; **stancarsi** *vpr* to get tired, tire o.s. out; **stancarsi (di)** to grow weary (of), grow tired (of)

stan'chezza [stan'kettsa] *sf* tiredness, fatigue

'stanco, -a, -chi, -che *ag* tired; **~ di** tired of, fed up with

stan'ghetta [stan'getta] *sf* (*di occhiali*) leg; (*Mus, di scrittura*) bar

'stanno *vb vedi* **stare**

sta'notte *av* tonight; (*notte passata*) last night

'stante *prep* **a sé ~** (*appartamento, casa*) independent, separate

stan'tio, -a, -'tii, -'tie *ag* stale; (*burro*) rancid; (*fig*) old

stan'tuffo *sm* piston

'stanza ['stantsa] *sf* room; (*Poesia*) stanza; **stanza da bagno** bathroom; **stanza da letto** bedroom

stap'pare *vt* to uncork; to uncap

'stare *vi* (*restare in un luogo*) to stay, remain; (*abitare*) to stay, live; (*essere situato*) to be, be situated; (*anche*: **~ in piedi**) to be, stand; (*essere, trovarsi*) to be; (*dipendere*): **se stesse in me** if it were up to me, if it depended on me; (*seguito da gerundio*): **sta studiando** he's studying; **starci** (*esserci spazio*): **nel baule non ci sta più niente** there's no more room in the boot;

(*accettare*) to accept; **ci stai?** is that okay with you?; **~ a** (*attenersi a*) to follow, stick to; (*seguito dall'infinito*): **stiamo a discutere** we're talking; (*toccare a*): **sta a te giocare** it's your turn to play; **~ per fare qc** to be about to do sth; **come sta?** how are you?; **io sto bene/male** I'm very well/not very well; **~ a qn** (*abiti ecc*) to fit sb; **queste scarpe mi stanno strette** these shoes are tight on me; **il rosso ti sta bene** red suits you

starnu'tire *vi* to sneeze; **star'nuto** *sm* sneeze

sta'sera *av* this evening, tonight

sta'tale *ag* state *cpd*; government *cpd* ▷ *sm/f* state employee, local authority employee; (*nell'amministrazione*) ≈ civil servant; **strada statale** ≈ trunk (*Brit*) *o* main road

sta'tista, -i *sm* statesman

sta'tistica *sf* statistics *sg*

'stato, -a *pp di* **essere; stare** ▷ *sm* (*condizione*) state, condition; (*Pol*) state; (*Dir*) status; **essere in ~ d'accusa** (*Dir*) to be committed for trial; **~ d'assedio/d'emergenza** state of siege/emergency; **~ civile** (*Amm*) marital status; **gli Stati Uniti (d'America)** the United States (of America); **stato d'animo** mood; **stato maggiore** (*Mil*) staff

'statua *sf* statue

statuni'tense *ag* United States *cpd*, of the United States

sta'tura *sf* (*Anat*) height, stature; (*fig*) stature

sta'tuto *sm* (*Dir*) statute; constitution

sta'volta *av* this time

stazio'nario, -a [stattsjo'narjo] *ag* stationary; (*fig*) unchanged

stazi'one [stat'tsjone] *sf* station; (*balneare, termale*) resort; **stazione degli autobus** bus station; **stazione balneare** seaside resort; **stazione ferroviaria** railway (*BRIT*) *o* railroad (*US*) station; **stazione invernale** winter sports resort; **stazione di polizia** police station (*in small town*); **stazione di servizio** service *o* petrol (*BRIT*) *o* filling station

'stecca, -che *sf* stick; (*di ombrello*) rib; (*di sigarette*) carton; (*Med*) splint; (*stonatura*): **fare una ~** to sing (*o play*) a wrong note

stec'cato *sm* fence

'stella *sf* star; **stella alpina** (*Bot*) edelweiss; **stella cadente** shooting star; **stella di mare** (*Zool*) starfish

'stelo *sm* stem; (*asta*) rod; **lampada a ~** standard lamp

'stemma, -i *sm* coat of arms

'stemmo *vb vedi* **stare**

stempi'ato, -a *ag* with a receding hairline

'stendere *vt* (*braccia, gambe*) to stretch (out); (*tovaglia*) to spread (out); (*bucato*) to hang out; (*mettere a giacere*) to lay (down); (*spalmare: colore*) to spread; (*mettere per iscritto*) to draw up; **stendersi** *vpr* (*coricarsi*) to stretch out, lie down; (*estendersi*) to extend, stretch

stenogra'fia *sf* shorthand

sten'tare *vi* **~ a fare** to find it hard to do, have difficulty doing

'stento *sm* (*fatica*) difficulty; **stenti** *smpl* (*privazioni*) hardship *sg*, privation *sg*; **a ~** with difficulty, barely

'sterco *sm* dung

stereo ['stɛrɛo] *ag inv* stereo ▷ *sm inv* (*impianto*) stereo

'sterile *ag* sterile; (*terra*) barren; (*fig*) futile, fruitless

steriliz'zare [sterilid'dzare] *vt* to sterilize

ster'lina *sf* pound (sterling)

stermi'nare *vt* to exterminate, wipe out

stermi'nato, -a *ag* immense; endless

ster'minio *sm* extermination, destruction

'sterno sm (Anat) breastbone

ste'roide sm steroid

ster'zare [ster'tsare] vt, vi (Aut) to steer; **'sterzo** sm steering; (volante) steering wheel

'stessi ecc vb vedi **stare**

'stesso, -a ag same; (rafforzativo: in persona, proprio): **il re ~** the king himself o in person ▷ pron **lo(la) ~(a)** the same (one); **i suoi stessi avversari lo ammirano** even his enemies admire him; **fa lo ~** it doesn't matter; **per me è lo ~** it's all the same to me, it doesn't matter to me; vedi **io**; **tu** ecc

ste'sura sf drafting no pl, drawing up no pl; draft

'stetti ecc vb vedi **stare**

'stia ecc vb vedi **stare**

sti'lare vt to draw up, draft

'stile sm style; **stile libero** freestyle; **sti'lista, -i** sm designer

stilo'grafica, -che sf (anche: **penna ~**) fountain pen

'stima sf esteem; valuation; assessment, estimate

sti'mare vt (persona) to esteem, hold in high regard; (terreno, casa ecc) to value; (stabilire in misura approssimativa) to estimate, assess; (ritenere): **~ che** to consider that; **stimarsi fortunato** to consider o.s. (to be) lucky

stimo'lare vt to stimulate; (incitare): **~ qn (a fare)** to spur sb on (to do)

'stimolo sm (anche fig) stimulus

'stingere ['stindʒere] vt, vi (anche: **stingersi**) to fade; **'stinto, -a** pp di **stingere**

sti'pare vt to cram, pack; **stiparsi** vpr (accalcarsi) to crowd, throng

sti'pendio sm salary

'stipite sm (di porta, finestra) jamb

stipu'lare vt (redigere) to draw up

sti'rare vt (abito) to iron; (distendere) to stretch; (strappare: muscolo) to strain; **stirarsi** vpr to stretch (o.s.)

stiti'chezza [stiti'kettsa] sf constipation

'stitico, -a, -ci, -che ag constipated

'stiva sf (di nave) hold

sti'vale sm boot

'stizza ['stittsa] sf anger, vexation

'stoffa sf material, fabric; (fig): **aver la ~ di** to have the makings of

'stomaco, -chi sm stomach; **dare di ~** to vomit, be sick

sto'nato, -a ag (persona) off-key; (strumento) off-key, out of tune

stop sm inv (Tel) stop; (Aut: cartello) stop sign; (: fanalino d'arresto) brake-light

'storcere ['stɔrtʃere] vt to twist; **storcersi** vpr to writhe, twist; **~ il naso** (fig) to turn up one's nose; **storcersi la caviglia** to twist one's ankle

stor'dire vt (intontire) to stun, daze; **stor'dito, -a** ag stunned

'storia sf (scienza, avvenimenti) history; (racconto, bugia) story; (faccenda, questione) business no pl; (pretesto) excuse, pretext; **storie** sfpl (smancerie) fuss sg; **'storico, -a, -ci, -che** ag historic(al) ▷ sm historian

stori'one sm (Zool) sturgeon

'stormo sm (di uccelli) flock

'storpio, -a ag crippled, maimed

'storsi ecc vb vedi **storcere**

'storta sf (distorsione) sprain, twist

'storto, -a pp di **storcere** ▷ ag (chiodo) twisted, bent; (gamba, quadro) crooked

sto'viglie [sto'viʎʎe] sfpl dishes, crockery sg

'strabico, -a, -ci, -che ag squint-eyed; (occhi) squint

strac'chino [strak'kino] sm type of soft cheese

stracci'are [strat'tʃare] vt to tear; **stracciarsi** vpr to tear

'straccio, -a, -ci, -ce ['strattʃo] ag **carta straccia** waste paper ▷ sm rag; (per pulire) cloth, duster; **stracci** smpl (*peg: indumenti*) rags; **si è ridotto a uno ~** he's worn himself out; **non ha uno ~ di lavoro** he's not got a job of any sort

'**strada** *sf* road; (*di città*) street; (*cammino, via, fig*) way; **che ~ devo prendere per andare a …?** which road do I take for …?; **farsi ~** (*fig*) to do well for o.s.; **essere fuori ~** (*fig*) to be on the wrong track; **~ facendo** on the way; **strada senza uscita** dead end; **stra'dale** *ag* road *cpd*

strafalci'one [strafal'tʃone] *sm* blunder, howler

stra'fare *vi* to overdo it

strafot'tente *ag*: **è ~** he doesn't give a damn, he couldn't care less

'**strage** ['stradʒe] *sf* massacre, slaughter

stralu'nato, -a *ag* (*occhi*) rolling; (*persona*) beside o.s., very upset

'**strambo, -a** *ag* strange, queer

strampa'lato, -a *ag* odd, eccentric

stra'nezza [stra'nettsa] *sf* strangeness

strango'lare *vt* to strangle

strani'ero, -a *ag* foreign ▷ *sm/f* foreigner

> Attenzione! In inglese esiste la parola *stranger*, che però significa *sconosciuto* oppure *estraneo*.

'**strano, -a** *ag* strange, odd

straordi'nario, -a *ag* extraordinary; (*treno ecc*) special ▷ *sm* (*lavoro*) overtime

strapi'ombo *sm* overhanging rock; **a ~** overhanging

strap'pare *vt* (*gen*) to tear, rip; (*pagina ecc*) to tear off, tear out; (*sradicare*) to pull up; (*togliere*): **~ qc a qn** to snatch sth from sb; (*fig*) to wrest sth from sb; **strapparsi** *vpr* (*lacerarsi*) to rip, tear; (*rompersi*) to break; **strapparsi un muscolo** to tear a muscle;

'**strappo** *sm* pull, tug; tear, rip; **fare uno strappo alla regola** to make

an exception to the rule; **strappo muscolare** torn muscle

strari'pare *vi* to overflow

'**strascico, -chi** ['straʃʃiko] *sm* (*di abito*) train; (*conseguenza*) after-effect

strata'gemma, -i [strata'dʒɛmma] *sm* stratagem

strate'gia, -'gie [strate'dʒia] *sf* strategy; **stra'tegico, -a, -ci, -che** *ag* strategic

'**strato** *sm* layer; (*rivestimento*) coat, coating; (*Geo, fig*) stratum; (*Meteor*) stratus; **strato d'ozono** ozone layer

strat'tone *sm* tug, jerk; **dare uno ~ a qc** to tug o jerk sth, give sth a tug o jerk

strava'gante *ag* odd, eccentric

stra'volto, -a *pp di* **stravolgere**

'**strazio** *sm* torture; (*fig: cosa fatta male*): **essere uno ~** to be appalling

'**strega, -ghe** *sf* witch

stre'gare *vt* to bewitch

stre'gone *sm* (*mago*) wizard; (*di tribù*) witch doctor

strepi'toso, -a *ag* clamorous, deafening; (*fig: successo*) resounding

stres'sante *ag* stressful

stres'sato, -a *ag* under stress

stretch [stretʃ] *ag inv* stretch

'**stretta** *sf* (*di mano*) grasp; (*finanziaria*) squeeze; (*fig: dolore, turbamento*) pang; **una ~ di mano** a handshake; **essere alle strette** to have one's back to the wall; *vedi anche* **stretto**

stretta'mente *av* tightly; (*rigorosamente*) strictly

'**stretto, -a** *pp di* **stringere** ▷ *ag* (*corridoio, limiti*) narrow; (*gonna, scarpe, nodo, curva*) tight; (*intimo: parente, amico*) close; (*rigoroso: osservanza*) strict; (*preciso: significato*) precise, exact ▷ *sm* (*braccio di mare*) strait; **a denti stretti** with clenched teeth; **lo ~ necessario** the bare minimum; **stret'toia** *sf* bottleneck; (*fig*) tricky situation

stri'ato, -a *ag* streaked

'**stridulo, -a** *ag* shrill

stril'lare vt, vi to scream, shriek; **'strillo** sm scream, shriek

strimin'zito, -a [strimin'tsito] ag (misero) shabby; (molto magro) skinny

strimpel'lare vt (Mus) to strum

'stringa, -ghe sf lace

strin'gato, -a ag (fig) concise

'stringere ['strindʒere] vt (avvicinare due cose) to press (together), squeeze (together); (tenere stretto) to hold tight, clasp, clutch; (pugno, mascella, denti) to clench; (labbra) to compress; (avvitare) to tighten; (abito) to take in; (scarpe) to pinch, be tight for; (fig: concludere: patto) to make; (: accelerare: passo, tempo) to quicken ▷ vi (essere stretto) to be tight; (tempo: incalzare) to be pressing

'strinsi ecc vb vedi **stringere**

'striscia, -sce ['striʃʃa] sf (di carta, tessuto ecc) strip; (riga) stripe; **strisce (pedonali)** zebra crossing sg

strisci'are [striʃʃare] vt (piedi) to drag; (muro, macchina) to graze ▷ vi to crawl, creep

'striscio ['striʃʃo] sm graze; (Med) smear; **colpire di ~** to graze

strisci'one [striʃʃone] sm banner

strito'lare vt to grind

striz'zare [strit'tsare] vt (panni) to wring (out); **~ l'occhio** to wink

'strofa sf strophe

strofi'naccio [strofi'nattʃo] sm duster, cloth; (per piatti) dishcloth; (per pavimenti) floorcloth

strofi'nare vt to rub

stron'care vt to break off; (fig: ribellione) to suppress, put down; (: film, libro) to tear to pieces

'stronzo ['strontso] sm (sterco) turd; (fig fam!: persona) shit (!)

stroz'zare [strot'tsare] vt (soffocare) to choke, strangle

struccarsi vpr to remove one's make-up

strumen'tale ag (Mus) instrumental

strumentaliz'zare [strumentalid'dzare] vt to exploit, use to one's own ends

stru'mento sm (arnese, fig) instrument, tool; (Mus) instrument; **~ a corda** o **ad arco/a fiato** stringed/ wind instrument

'strutto sm lard

strut'tura sf structure

'struzzo ['struttso] sm ostrich

stuc'care vt (muro) to plaster; (vetro) to putty; (decorare con stucchi) to stucco

'stucco, -chi sm plaster; (da vetri) putty; (ornamentale) stucco; **rimanere di ~** (fig) to be dumbfounded

stu'dente, -'essa sm/f student; (scolaro) pupil, schoolboy/girl

studi'are vt to study

'studio sm studying; (ricerca, saggio, stanza) study; (di professionista) office; (di artista, Cinema, TV, Radio) studio; **studi** smpl (Ins) studies; **studio medico** doctor's surgery (BRIT) o office (US)

studi'oso, -a ag studious, hardworking ▷ sm/f scholar

'stufa sf stove; **stufa elettrica** electric fire o heater

stu'fare vt (Cuc) to stew; (fig: fam) to bore; **stufarsi** vpr (fam): **stufarsi (di)** (fig) to get fed up (with); **'stufo, -a** (fam) ag **essere stufo di** to be fed up with, be sick and tired of

stu'oia sf mat

stupefa'cente [stupefa'tʃente] ag stunning, astounding ▷ sm drug, narcotic

stupe'fatto, -a pp di **stupefare**

stu'pendo, -a ag marvellous, wonderful

stupi'daggine [stupi'daddʒine] sf stupid thing (to do o say)

stupidità sf stupidity

'stupido, -a ag stupid

stu'pire vt to amaze, stun ▷ vi **stupirsi; ~ (di)** to be amazed (at), be stunned (by)

stu'pore sm amazement, astonishment

stu'prare vt to rape

'stupro sm rape

stu'rare vt (lavandino) to clear

stuzzica'denti [stuttsika'dɛnti] sm toothpick

stuzzi'care [stuttsi'kare] vt (ferita ecc) to poke (at), prod (at); (fig) to tease; (: appetito) to whet; (: curiosità) to stimulate; **~ i denti** to pick one's teeth

 PAROLA CHIAVE

su (su +il = **sul**, su +lo = **sullo**, su +l' = **sull'**, su +la = **sulla**, su +i = **sui**, su +gli = **sugli**, su +le = **sulle**) prep 1 (gen) on; (moto) on(to); (in cima a) on (top of); **mettilo sul tavolo** put it on the table; **un paesino sul mare** a village by the sea

2 (argomento) about, on; **un libro su Cesare** a book on o about Caesar

3 (circa) about; **costerà sui 3 milioni** it will cost about 3 million; **una ragazza sui 17 anni** a girl of about 17 (years of age)

4: **su misura** made to measure; **su richiesta** on request; **3 casi su dieci** 3 cases out of 10

▷ av 1 (in alto, verso l'alto) up; **vieni su** come on up; **guarda su** look up; **su le mani!** hands up!; **in su** (verso l'alto) up(wards); (in poi) onwards; **dai 20 anni in su** from the age of 20 onwards

2 (addosso) on; **cos'hai su?** what have you got on?

▷ escl come on!; **su coraggio!** come on, cheer up!

su'bacqueo, -a ag underwater ▷ sm skin-diver

sub'buglio [sub'buʎʎo] sm confusion, turmoil

'subdolo, -a ag underhand, sneaky

suben'trare vi: **~ a qn in qc** to take over sth from sb

su'bire vt to suffer, endure

'subito av immediately, at once, straight away

subodo'rare vt (insidia ecc) to smell, suspect

subordi'nato, -a ag subordinate; (dipendente): **~ a** dependent on, subject to

suc'cedere [sut'tʃedere] vi (prendere il posto di qn): **~ a** to succeed; (venire dopo): **~ a** to follow; (accadere) to happen; **cos'è successo?** what happened?; **succes'sivo, -a** ag successive; **suc'cesso, -a** pp di **succedere** ▷ sm (esito) outcome; (buona riuscita) success; **di successo** (libro, personaggio) successful

succhi'are [suk'kjare] vt to suck (up)

succhi'otto [suk'kjɔtto] sm dummy (BRIT), pacifier (US), comforter (US)

suc'cinto, -a [sut'tʃinto] ag (discorso) succinct; (abito) brief

'succo, -chi sm juice; (fig) essence, gist; **succo di frutta/pomodoro** fruit/tomato juice

succur'sale sf branch (office)

sud sm south ▷ ag inv south; (lato) south, southern

Su'dafrica sm **il ~** South Africa; **sudafri'cano, -a** ag, sm/f South African

Suda'merica sm: **il ~** South America

su'dare vi to perspire, sweat; **~ freddo** to come out in a cold sweat

su'dato, -a ag (persona, mani) sweaty; (fig: denaro) hard-earned ▷ sf (anche fig) sweat; **una vittoria sudata** a hard-won victory; **ho fatto una bella sudata per finirlo in tempo** it was a real sweat to get it finished in time

suddi'videre vt to subdivide

su'dest sm south-east

'sudicio, -a, -ci, -ce ['suditʃo] ag dirty, filthy

sudoku sm inv sudoku

su'dore sm perspiration, sweat
su'dovest sm south-west
suffici'ente [suffi'tʃɛnte] ag enough, sufficient; (borioso) self-important; (Ins) satisfactory; **suffici'enza** sf self-importance; pass mark; **a sufficienza** enough; **ne ho avuto a sufficienza!** I've had enough of this!
suf'fisso sm (Ling) suffix
suggeri'mento [suddʒeri'mento] sm suggestion; (consiglio) piece of advice, advice no pl
sugge'rire [suddʒe'rire] vt (risposta) to tell; (consigliare) to advise; (proporre) to suggest; (Teatro) to prompt
suggestio'nare [suddʒestjo'nare] vt to influence
sugges'tivo, -a [suddʒes'tivo] ag (paesaggio) evocative; (teoria) interesting, attractive
'sughero ['sugero] sm cork
'sugo, -ghi sm (succo) juice; (di carne) gravy; (condimento) sauce; (fig) gist, essence
sui'cida, -i, -e [sui'tʃida] ag suicidal ▷ sm/f suicide
suici'darsi [suitʃi'darsi] vpr to commit suicide
sui'cidio [sui'tʃidjo] sm suicide
su'ino, -a ag: **carne suina** pork ▷ sm pig
sul'tano, -a sm/f sultan/sultana
'suo (f 'sua, pl 'sue, su'oi) det **il ~, la sua** ecc (di lui) his; (di lei) her; (di esso) its; (con valore indefinito) one's, his/her; (anche: **S~**: forma di cortesia) your ▷ pron **il ~, la sua** ecc his; hers; yours; **i ~i** his (o her o one's o your) family
su'ocero, -a ['swɔtʃero] sm/f father/mother-in-law
su'ola sf (di scarpa) sole
su'olo sm (terreno) ground; (terra) soil
suo'nare vt (Mus) to play; (campana) to ring; (ore) to strike; (clacson, allarme) to sound ▷ vi to play; (telefono, campana) to ring; (ore) to strike; (clacson, fig: parole) to sound

suone'ria sf alarm
su'ono sm sound
su'ora sf (Rel) sister
'super sf (anche: **benzina ~**) ≈ four-star (petrol) (BRIT), premium (US)
supe'rare vt (oltrepassare: limite) to exceed, surpass; (percorrere) to cover; (attraversare: fiume) to cross; (sorpassare: veicolo) to overtake; (fig: essere più bravo di) to surpass, outdo; (: difficoltà) to overcome; (: esame) to get through; **~ qn in altezza/peso** to be taller/heavier than sb; **ha superato la cinquantina** he's over fifty (years of age)
su'perbia sf pride; **su'perbo, -a** ag proud; (fig) magnificent, superb
superfici'ale [superfi'tʃale] ag superficial
super'ficie, -ci [super'fitʃe] sf surface
su'perfluo, -a ag superfluous
superi'ore ag (piano, arto, classi) upper; (più elevato: temperatura, livello): **~ (a)** higher (than); (migliore): **~ (a)** superior (to)
superla'tivo, -a ag, sm superlative
supermer'cato sm supermarket
su'perstite ag surviving ▷ sm/f survivor
superstizi'one [superstit'tsjone] sf superstition; **superstizi'oso, -a** ag superstitious
super'strada sf ≈ (toll-free) motorway
su'pino, -a ag supine
supplemen'tare ag extra; (treno) relief cpd; (entrate) additional
supple'mento sm supplement
sup'plente sm/f temporary member of staff, supply (o substitute) teacher
'supplica, -che sf (preghiera) plea; (domanda scritta) petition, request
suppli'care vt to implore, beseech
sup'plizio [sup'plittsjo] sm torture
sup'pongo, sup'poni ecc vb vedi

suppore
sup'porre vt to suppose
sup'porto sm (sostegno) support
sup'posta sf (Med) suppository
su'premo, -a ag supreme
surge'lare [surdʒe'lare] vt to (deep-) freeze
surge'lato, -a [surdʒe'lato] ag (deep-)frozen ▷ smpl **i surgelati** frozen food sg
sur'plus sm inv (Econ) surplus
surriscal'dare vt to overheat
suscet'tibile [suʃʃet'tibile] ag (sensibile) touchy, sensitive
susci'tare [suʃʃi'tare] vt to provoke, arouse
su'sina sf plum
susseguirsi vpr to follow one another
sus'sidio sm subsidy; **sussidi didattici** teaching aids
sussul'tare vi to shudder
sussur'rare vt, vi to whisper, murmur; **sus'surro** sm whisper, murmur
svagarsi vpr to amuse o.s.; to enjoy o.s.
'svago, -ghi sm (riposo) relaxation; (ricreazione) amusement; (passatempo) pastime
svaligi'are [zvali'dʒare] vt to rob, burgle (BRIT), burglarize (US)
svalutarsi vpr (Econ) to be devalued
svalutazi'one sf devaluation
sva'nire vi to disappear, vanish
svantaggi'ato, -a [zvantad'dʒato] ag at a disadvantage
svan'taggio [zvan'taddʒo] sm disadvantage; (inconveniente) drawback, disadvantage
svari'ato, -a ag varied; various
'svastica sf swastika
sve'dese ag Swedish ▷ sm/f Swede ▷ sm (Ling) Swedish
'sveglia ['zveʎʎa] sf waking up; (orologio) alarm (clock); **sveglia telefonica** alarm call
svegli'are [zveʎ'ʎare] vt to wake up; (fig) to awaken, arouse; **svegliarsi**

vpr to wake up; (fig) to be revived, reawaken; **vorrei essere svegliato alle 7, per favore** could I have an alarm call at 7 am, please?
'sveglio, -a ['zveʎʎo] ag awake; (fig) quick-witted
sve'lare vt to reveal
'svelto, -a ag (passo) quick; (mente) quick, alert; **alla svelta** quickly
'svendere vt to sell off, clear
'svendita sf (Comm) (clearance) sale
'svengo ecc vb vedi **svenire**
sveni'mento sm fainting fit, faint
sve'nire vi to faint
sven'tare vt to foil, thwart
sven'tato, -a ag (distratto) scatterbrained; (imprudente) rash
svento'lare vt, vi to wave, flutter
sven'tura sf misfortune
sverrò ecc vb vedi **svenire**
sves'tire vt to undress; **svestirsi** vpr to get undressed
'Svezia ['zvɛttsja] sf: **la ~** Sweden
svi'are vt to divert; (fig) to lead astray
svi'gnarsela [zviɲ'ɲarsela] vpr to slip away, sneak off
svilup'pare vt to develop; **svilupparsi** vpr to develop; **può ~ questo rullino?** can you develop this film?
svi'luppo sm development
'svincolo sm (stradale) motorway (BRIT) o expressway (US) intersection
'svista sf oversight
svi'tare vt to unscrew
'Svizzera ['zvittsera] sf: **la ~** Switzerland
'svizzero, -a ['zvittsero] ag, sm/f Swiss
svogli'ato, -a [zvoʎ'ʎato] ag listless; (pigro) lazy
'svolgere ['zvɔldʒere] vt to unwind; (srotolare) to unroll; (fig: argomento) to develop; (: piano, programma) to carry out; **svolgersi** vpr to unwind; to unroll; (fig: aver luogo) to take place; (: procedere) to go on

'svolsi *ecc vb vedi* **svolgere**
'svolta *sf (atto)* turning *no pl; (curva)* turn, bend; *(fig)* turning-point
svol'tare *vi* to turn
svuo'tare *vt* to empty (out)

T, t [ti] *sf o m inv (lettera)* T, t; **T come Taranto** ≈ T for Tommy
t *abbr* = **tonnellata**
tabacche'ria [tabakke'ria] *sf* tobacconist's (shop)

- **TABACCHERIA**
-
- **Tabaccherie** sell cigarettes and
- tobacco and can easily be identified
- by their sign, a large white "T" on
- a black background. You can buy
- postage stamps and bus tickets at
- a **tabaccheria** and some also sell
- newspapers.

ta'bacco, -chi *sm* tobacco
ta'bella *sf (tavola)* table; *(elenco)* list
tabel'lone *sm (pubblicitario)* billboard; *(con orario)* timetable board
tabu'lato *sm (Inform)* printout
TAC *sigla f (Med: = Tomografia Assiale Computerizzata)* CAT

tac'chino [tak'kino] *sm* turkey

'tacco, -chi *sm* heel; **tacchi a spillo** stiletto heels

taccu'ino *sm* notebook

ta'cere [ta'tʃere] *vi* to be silent *o* quiet; (*smettere di parlare*) to fall silent ▷ *vt* to keep to oneself, say nothing about; **far ~ qn** to make sb be quiet; (*fig*) to silence sb

ta'chimetro [ta'kimetro] *sm* speedometer

'tacqui *ecc vb vedi* **tacere**

ta'fano *sm* horsefly

'taglia ['taʎʎa] *sf* (*statura*) height; (*misura*) size; (*riscatto*) ransom; (*ricompensa*) reward; **taglia forte** (*di abito*) large size

taglia'carte [taʎʎa'karte] *sm inv* paperknife

tagli'ando [taʎ'ʎando] *sm* coupon

tagli'are [taʎ'ʎare] *vt* to cut; (*recidere, interrompere*) to cut off; (*intersecare*) to cut across, intersect; (*carne*) to carve; (*vini*) to blend ▷ *vi* to cut; (*prendere una scorciatoia*) to take a short-cut; **tagliarsi** *vpr* to cut o.s.; **mi sono tagliato** I've cut myself; **~ corto** (*fig*) to cut short; **~ la corda** (*fig*) to sneak off; **~ i ponti (con)** (*fig*) to break off relations (with); **~ la strada a qn** to cut across sb

taglia'telle [taʎʎa'tɛlle] *sfpl* tagliatelle *pl*

taglia'unghie [taʎʎa'ungje] *sm inv* nail clippers *pl*

tagli'ente [taʎ'ʎɛnte] *ag* sharp

'taglio ['taʎʎo] *sm* cutting *no pl*; cut; (*parte tagliente*) cutting edge; (*di abito*) cut, style; (*di stoffa: lunghezza*) length; (*di vini*) blending; **di ~** on edge, edgeways; **banconote di piccolo/grosso ~** notes of small/large denomination; **taglio cesareo** Caesarean section

tailan'dese *ag, sm/f, sm* Thai

Tai'landia *sf*: **la ~** Thailand

'talco *sm* talcum powder

 PAROLA CHIAVE

'tale *det* **1** (*simile, così grande*) such; **un(a) tale ...** such (a) ...; **non accetto tali discorsi** I won't allow such talk; **è di una tale arroganza** he is so arrogant; **fa una tale confusione!** he makes such a mess!
2 (*persona o cosa indeterminata*) such-and-such; **il giorno tale all'ora tale** on such-and-such a day at such-and-such a time; **la tal persona** that person; **ha telefonato una tale Giovanna** somebody called Giovanna phoned
3 (*nelle similitudini*): **tale ... tale** like ... like; **tale padre tale figlio** like father, like son; **hai il vestito tale quale il mio** your dress is just *o* exactly like mine
▷ *pron* (*indefinito: persona*): **un(a) tale** someone; **quel** (*o* **quella**) **tale** that person, that man (*o* woman); **il tal dei tali** what's-his-name

tale'bano *sm* Taliban

ta'lento *sm* talent

talis'mano *sm* talisman

tallon'cino [tallon'tʃino] *sm* counterfoil

tal'lone *sm* heel

tal'mente *av* so

'talpa *sf* (*Zool*) mole

tal'volta *av* sometimes, at times

tambu'rello *sm* tambourine

tam'buro *sm* drum

Ta'migi [ta'midʒi] *sm* **il ~** the Thames

tampo'nare *vt* (*otturare*) to plug; (*urtare: macchina*) to crash *o* ram into

tam'pone *sm* (*Med*) wad, pad; (*per timbri*) ink-pad; (*respingente*) buffer; **tampone assorbente** tampon

'tana *sf* lair, den

'tanga *sm inv* G-string

tan'gente [tan'dʒɛnte] *ag* (*Mat*): **~**

a tangential to ▷ *sf* tangent; (*quota*) share

tangenzi'ale [tandʒen'tsjale] *sf* (*Aut*) bypass

'tanica *sf* (*contenitore*) jerry can

 PAROLA CHIAVE

'tanto, -a *det* **1** (*molto: quantità*) a lot of, much; (: *numero*) a lot of, many; (*così tanto: quantità*) so much, such a lot of; (: *numero*) so many, such a lot of; **tante volte** so many times, so often; **tanti auguri!** all the best!; **tante grazie** many thanks; **tanto tempo** so long, such a long time; **ogni tanti chilometri** every so many kilometres **2**: **tanto ... quanto** (*quantità*) as much ... as; (*numero*) as many ... as; **ho tanta pazienza quanta ne hai tu** I have as much patience as you have *o* as you; **ha tanti amici quanti nemici** he has as many friends as he has enemies **3** (*rafforzativo*) such; **ho aspettato per tanto tempo** I waited so long *o* for such a long time

▷ *pron* **1** (*molto*) much, a lot; (*così tanto*) so much, such a lot; **tanti, e** many, a lot; so many, such a lot; **credevo ce ne fosse tanto** I thought there was (such) a lot, I thought there was plenty **2**: **tanto quanto** (*denaro*) as much as; (*cioccolatini*) as many as; **ne ho tanto quanto basta** I have as much as I need; **due volte tanto** twice as much **3** (*indeterminato*) so much; **tanto per l'affitto, tanto per il gas** so much for the rent, so much for the gas; **costa un tanto al metro** it costs so much per metre; **di tanto in tanto, ogni tanto** every so often; **tanto vale che ...** I (*o* we ecc) may as well ...; **tanto meglio!** so much the better!; **tanto peggio per lui!** so much the worse for him!

▷ *av* **1** (*molto*) very; **vengo tanto volentieri** I'd be very glad to come; **non ci vuole tanto a capirlo** it doesn't take much to understand it **2** (*così tanto: con ag, av*) so; (: *con vb*) so much, such a lot; **è tanto bella!** she's so beautiful!; **non urlare tanto** don't shout so much; **sto tanto meglio adesso** I'm so much better now; **tanto ... che** so ... (that); **tanto ... da** so ... as **3**: **tanto ... quanto** as ... as; **conosco tanto Carlo quanto suo padre** I know both Carlo and his father; **non è poi tanto complicato quanto sembri** it's not as difficult as it seems; **tanto più insisti, tanto più non mollerà** the more you insist, the more stubborn he'll be; **quanto più ... tanto meno** the more ... the less **4** (*solamente*) just; **tanto per cambiare/scherzare** just for a change/a joke; **una volta tanto** for once **5** (*a lungo*) (for) long ▷ *cong* after all

'tappa *sf* (*luogo di sosta, fermata*) stop, halt; (*parte di un percorso*) stage, leg; (*Sport*) lap; **a tappe** in stages

tap'pare *vt* to plug, stop up; (*bottiglia*) to cork; **tapparsi** *vpr* **tapparsi in casa** to shut o.s. up at home; **tapparsi la bocca** to shut up; **tapparsi le orecchie** to turn a deaf ear

tappa'rella *sf* rolling shutter

tappe'tino *sm* (*per auto*) car mat; **tappetino antiscivolo** (*da bagno*) non-slip mat

tap'peto *sm* carpet; (*anche:* **tappetino**) rug; (*Sport*): **andare al ~** to go down for the count; **mettere sul ~** (*fig*) to bring up for discussion

tappez'zare [tappet'tsare] *vt* (*con carta*) to paper; (*rivestire*): **~ qc (di)** to cover sth (with); **tappezze'ria** *sf* (*tessuto*) tapestry; (*carta da parati*) wallpaper; (*arte*) upholstery; **far da tappezzeria** (*fig*) to be a wallflower

'tappo *sm* stopper; (*in sughero*) cork

tar'dare *vi* to be late ▷ *vt* to delay; **~ a fare** to delay doing

'tardi *av* late; **più ~** later (on); **al più ~** at the latest; **sul ~** (*verso sera*) late in the day; **far ~** to be late; (*restare alzato*) to stay up late; **è troppo ~** it's too late

'targa, -ghe *sf* plate; (*Aut*) number (*BRIT*) o license (*US*) plate; **tar'ghetta** *sf* (*su bagaglio*) name tag; (*su porta*) nameplate

ta'riffa *sf* (*gen*) rate, tariff; (*di trasporti*) fare; (*elenco*) price list; tariff

'tarlo *sm* woodworm

'tarma *sf* moth

tarocchi *smpl* (*gioco*) tarot *sg*

tarta'ruga, -ghe *sf* tortoise; (*di mare*) turtle; (*materiale*) tortoiseshell

tar'tina *sf* canapé

tar'tufo *sm* (*Bot*) truffle

'tasca, -sche *sf* pocket; **tas'cabile** *ag* (*libro*) pocket *cpd*

'tassa *sf* (*imposta*) tax; (*doganale*) duty; (*per iscrizione: a scuola ecc*) fee; **tassa di circolazione** road tax; **tassa di soggiorno** tourist tax

tas'sare *vt* to tax; to levy a duty on

tas'sello *sm* plug; wedge

tassì *sm inv* = **taxi**; **tas'sista, -i, -e** *sm/f* taxi driver

'tasso *sm* (*di natalità, d'interesse ecc*) rate; (*Bot*) yew; (*Zool*) badger; **tasso di cambio/d'interesse** rate of exchange/interest

tas'tare *vt* to feel; **~ il terreno** (*fig*) to see how the land lies

tasti'era *sf* keyboard

'tasto *sm* key; (*tatto*) touch, feel

tas'toni *av*: **procedere (a) ~** to grope one's way forward

'tatto *sm* (*senso*) touch; (*fig*) tact; **duro al ~** hard to the touch; **aver ~** to be tactful, have tact

tatu'aggio [tatu'addʒo] *sm* tattooing; (*disegno*) tattoo

tatu'are *vt* to tattoo

TAV *sigla fsg* = **Treni Alta Velocità**; (*treno*) high-speed train; (*sistema*) high-speed rail system

'tavola *sf* table; (*asse*) plank, board; (*lastra*) tablet; (*quadro*) panel (painting); (*illustrazione*) plate; **tavola calda** snack bar; **tavola rotonda** (*fig*) round table; **tavola a vela** windsurfer

tavo'letta *sf* tablet, bar; **a ~** (*Aut*) flat out

tavo'lino *sm* small table; (*scrivania*) desk

'tavolo *sm* table; **un ~ per 4 per favore** a table for 4, please

'taxi *sm inv* taxi; **può chiamarmi un ~ per favore?** can you call me a taxi, please?

'tazza ['tattsa] *sf* cup; **una ~ di caffè/tè** a cup of coffee/tea; **tazza da tè/caffè** tea/coffee cup

TBC *abbr f* (= *tubercolosi*) TB

te *pron* (*soggetto: in forme comparative, oggetto*) you

tè *sm inv* tea; (*trattenimento*) tea party

tea'trale *ag* theatrical

te'atro *sm* theatre

techno ['tɛkno] *ag inv* (*musica*) techno

'tecnica, -che *sf* technique; (*tecnologia*) technology

'tecnico, -a, -ci, -che *ag* technical ▷ *sm/f* technician

tecnolo'gia [teknolo'dʒia] *sf* technology

te'desco, -a, -schi, -sche *ag, sm/f, sm* German

te'game *sm* (*Cuc*) pan

'tegola *sf* tile

tei'era *sf* teapot

tel. *abbr* (= *telefono*) tel.

'tela *sf* (*tessuto*) cloth; (*per vele, quadri*) canvas; (*dipinto*) canvas, painting; **di ~** (*calzoni*) (heavy) cotton *cpd*; (*scarpe, borsa*) canvas *cpd*; **tela cerata** oilcloth

te'laio *sm* (*apparecchio*) loom; (*struttura*) frame

tele'camera *sf* television camera

teleco'mando *sm* remote control

tele'cronaca *sf* television report

telefo'nare *vi* to telephone, ring; to make a phone call ▷ *vt* to telephone; **~ a** to phone up, ring up, call up

telefo'nata *sf* (telephone) call; **~ a carico del destinatario** reverse charge (*BRIT*) o collect (*US*) call

tele'fonico, -a, -ci, -che *ag* (tele)phone *cpd*

telefon'ino *sm* mobile phone

te'lefono *sm* telephone; **telefono a gettoni** ≈ pay phone

telegior'nale [teledʒor'nale] *sm* television news (programme)

tele'gramma, -i *sm* telegram

tela'voro *sm* teleworking

Tele'pass® *sm inv automatic payment card for use on Italian motorways*

telepa'tia *sf* telepathy

teles'copio *sm* telescope

teleselezi'one [teleselet'tsjone] *sf* direct dialling

telespetta'tore, -'trice *sm/f* (television) viewer

tele'vendita *sf* teleshopping

televisi'one *sf* television

televi'sore *sm* television set

'tema, -i *sm* theme, (*Ins*) essay, composition

te'mere *vt* to fear, be afraid of; (*essere sensibile a: freddo, calore*) to be sensitive to ▷ *vi* to be afraid; (*essere preoccupato*): **~ per** to worry about, fear for; **~ di/che** to be afraid of/that

temperama'tite *sm inv* pencil sharpener

tempera'mento *sm* temperament

tempera'tura *sf* temperature

tempe'rino *sm* penknife

tem'pesta *sf* storm; **tempesta di sabbia/neve** sand/snowstorm

'tempia *sf* (*Anat*) temple

'tempio *sm* (*edificio*) temple

'tempo *sm* (*Meteor*) weather; (*cronologico*) time; (*epoca*) time, times *pl*; (*di film, gioco: parte*) part; (*Mus*) time; (: *battuta*) beat; (*Ling*) tense; **che ~ fa?** what's the weather like?; **un ~** once; **~ fa** some time ago; **al ~ stesso** o **a un ~** at the same time; **per ~** early; **ha fatto il suo ~** it has had its day; **primo/secondo ~** (*Teatro*) first/second part; (*Sport*) first/second half; **in ~ utile** in due time o course; **a ~ pieno** full-time; **tempo libero** free time

tempo'rale *ag* temporal ▷ *sm* (*Meteor*) (thunder)storm

tempo'raneo, -a *ag* temporary

te'nace [te'natʃe] *ag* strong, tough; (*fig*) tenacious

te'naglie [te'naʎʎe] *sfpl* pincers *pl*

'tenda *sf* (*riparo*) awning; (*di finestra*) curtain; (*per campeggio ecc*) tent

ten'denza [ten'dɛntsa] *sf* tendency; (*orientamento*) trend; **avere ~ a** o **per qc** to have a bent for sth

'tendere *vt* (*allungare al massimo*) to stretch, draw tight; (*porgere: mano*) to hold out; (*fig: trappola*) to lay, set ▷ *vi* **~ a qc/a fare** to tend towards sth/to do; **~ l'orecchio** to prick up one's ears; **il tempo tende al caldo** the weather is getting hot; **un blu che tende al verde** a greenish blue

'tendine *sm* tendon, sinew

ten'done *sm* (*da circo*) tent

'tenebre *sfpl* darkness *sg*

te'nente *sm* lieutenant

te'nere *vt* to hold; (*conservare, mantenere*) to keep; (*ritenere, considerare*) to consider; (*spazio: occupare*) to take up, occupy; (*seguire: strada*) to keep to ▷ *vi* to hold; (*colori*) to be fast; (*dare importanza*): **~ a** to care about; **~ a fare** to want to do, be keen to do; **tenersi** *vpr* (*stare in una determinata posizione*) to stand; (*stimarsi*) to consider o.s.; (*aggrapparsi*): **tenersi a** to hold on to; (*attenersi*): **tenersi a** to stick to; **~ una conferenza** to give a lecture; **~ conto di qc** to take sth into consideration; **~**

presente qc to bear sth in mind
'tenero, -a ag tender; (pietra, cera, colore) soft; (fig) tender, loving
'tengo ecc vb vedi **tenere**
'tenni ecc vb vedi **tenere**
'tennis sm tennis
ten'nista, -i, e sm/f tennis player
te'nore sm (tono) tone; (Mus) tenor; **tenore di vita** (livello) standard of living
tensi'one sf tension
ten'tare vt (indurre) to tempt; (provare): **~ qc/di fare** to attempt o try sth/to do; **tenta'tivo** sm attempt; **tentazi'one** sf temptation
tenten'nare vi to shake, be unsteady; (fig) to hesitate, waver
ten'toni av **andare a ~** (anche fig) to grope one's way
'tenue ag (sottile) fine; (colore) soft; (fig) slender, slight
te'nuta sf (capacità) capacity; (divisa) uniform; (abito) dress; (Agr) estate; **a ~ d'aria** airtight; **tenuta di strada** roadholding power
teolo'gia [teolo'dʒia] sf theology
teo'ria sf theory
te'pore sm warmth
tep'pista, -i sm hooligan
tera'pia sf therapy; **terapia intensiva** intensive care
tergicris'tallo [terdʒikris'tallo] sm windscreen (BRIT) o windshield (US) wiper
tergiver'sare [terdʒiver'sare] vi to shilly-shally
ter'male ag thermal; **stazione** sf **~** spa
'terme sfpl thermal baths
termi'nale ag, sm terminal
termi'nare vt to end; (lavoro) to finish ▷ vi to end
'termine sm term; (fine, estremità) end; (di territorio) boundary, limit; **contratto a ~** (Comm) forward contract; **a breve/lungo ~** short-/long-term; **parlare senza mezzi**

termini to talk frankly, not to mince one's words
ter'mometro sm thermometer
'termos sm inv = **thermos**®
termosi'fone sm radiator
ter'mostato sm thermostat
'terra sf (gen, Elettr) earth; (sostanza) soil, earth; (opposto al mare) land no pl; (regione, paese) land; (argilla) clay; **terre** sfpl (possedimento) lands, land sg; **a o per ~** (stato) on the ground (o floor); (moto) to the ground, down; **mettere a ~** (Elettr) to earth
terra'cotta sf terracotta; **vasellame** sm **di ~** earthenware
terra'ferma sf dry land, terra firma; (continente) mainland
ter'razza [ter'rattsa] sf terrace
ter'razzo [ter'rattso] sm = **terrazza**
terre'moto sm earthquake
ter'reno, -a ag (vita, beni) earthly ▷ sm (suolo, fig) ground; (Comm) land no pl, plot (of land); site; (Sport, Mil) field
ter'restre ag (superficie) of the earth, earth's; (di terra: battaglia, animale) land cpd; (Rel) earthly, worldly
ter'ribile ag terrible, dreadful
terrifi'cante ag terrifying
ter'rina sf tureen
territori'ale ag territorial
terri'torio sm territory
ter'rore sm terror; **terro'rismo** sm terrorism; **terro'rista, -i, -e** sm/f terrorist
terroriz'zare [terrorid'dzare] vt to terrorize
terza ['tɛrtsa] sf (Scol: elementare) third year at primary school; (: media) third year at secondary school; (: superiore) sixth year at secondary school; (Aut) third gear
ter'zino [ter'tsino] sm (Calcio) fullback, back
'terzo, -a ['tɛrtso] ag third ▷ sm (frazione) third; (Dir) third party; **terza pagina** (Stampa) Arts page; **terzi** smpl

(*altri*) others, other people

teschio ['teskjo] *sm* skull

tesi[1] *sf* thesis; **tesi di laurea** degree thesis

tesi *ecc*[2] *vb vedi* **tendere**

teso, -a *pp di* **tendere** ▷ *ag* (*tirato*) taut, tight; (*fig*) tense

te'soro *sm* treasure; **il Ministero del T~** the Treasury

tessera *sf* (*documento*) card

tes'suto *sm* fabric, material; (*Biol*) tissue

test ['test] *sm inv* test

testa *sf* head; (*di cose: estremità, parte anteriore*) head, front; **di ~** (*vettura ecc*) front; **tenere ~ a qn** (*nemico ecc*) to stand up to sb; **fare di ~ propria** to go one's own way; **in ~** (*Sport*) in the lead; **~ o croce?** heads or tails?; **avere la ~ dura** to be stubborn; **testa d'aglio** bulb of garlic; **testa di serie** (*Tennis*) seed, seeded player

testa'mento *sm* (*atto*) will; **l'Antico/il Nuovo T~** (*Rel*) the Old/New Testament

tes'tardo, -a *ag* stubborn, pigheaded

tes'tata *sf* (*parte anteriore*) head; (*intestazione*) heading

tes'ticolo *sm* testicle

testi'mone *sm/f* (*Dir*) witness; **testimone oculare** eye witness

testimoni'are *vt* to testify; (*fig*) to bear witness to, testify to ▷ *vi* to give evidence, testify

testo *sm* text; **fare ~** (*opera, autore*) to be authoritative; **questo libro non fa ~** this book is not essential reading

tes'tuggine [tes'tuddʒine] *sf* tortoise; (*di mare*) turtle

tetano *sm* (*Med*) tetanus

tetto *sm* roof; **tet'toia** *sf* roofing; canopy

tettuccio [tet'tuttʃo] *sm* **~ apribile** (*Aut*) sunroof

Tevere *sm* **il ~** the Tiber

TG, Tg *abbr* = **telegiornale**

thermos® ['tɛrmos] *sm inv* vacuum o Thermos® flask

ti *pron* (*dav lo, la, li, le, ne diventa* **te**) ▷ *pron* (*oggetto*) you; (*complemento di termine*) (to) you; (*riflessivo*) yourself

Tibet *sm*: **il ~** Tibet

tibia *sf* tibia, shinbone

tic *sm inv* tic, (*nervous*) twitch; (*fig*) mannerism

ticchet'tio [tikket'tio] *sm* (*di macchina da scrivere*) clatter; (*di orologio*) ticking; (*della pioggia*) patter

ticket *sm inv* (*su farmaci*) prescription charge

ti'ene *ecc vb vedi* **tenere**

ti'epido, -a *ag* lukewarm, tepid

tifo *sm* (*Med*) typhus; (*fig*): **fare il ~ per** to be a fan of

ti'fone *sm* typhoon

ti'foso, -a *sm/f* (*Sport ecc*) fan

tigì [ti'dʒi] *sm inv* TV news

tiglio ['tiʎʎo] *sm* lime (tree), linden (tree)

tigre *sf* tiger

tim'brare *vt* to stamp; (*annullare: francobolli*) to postmark; **~ il cartellino** to clock in

timbro *sm* stamp; (*Mus*) timbre, tone

timido, -a *ag* shy; timid

timo *sm* thyme

ti'mone *sm* (*Naut*) rudder

ti'more *sm* (*paura*) fear; (*rispetto*) awe

timpano *sm* (*Anat*) eardrum

tingere ['tindʒere] *vt* to dye

tinsi *ecc vb vedi* **tingere**

tinta *sf* (*materia colorante*) dye; (*colore*) colour, shade

tintin'nare *vi* to tinkle

tinto'ria *sf* (*lavasecco*) dry cleaner's (shop)

tin'tura *sf* (*operazione*) dyeing; (*colorante*) dye; **tintura di iodio** tincture of iodine

tipico, -a, -ci, -che *ag* typical

tipo *sm* type; (*genere*) kind, type; (*fam*) chap, fellow; **che ~ di...?** what kind of ...?

tipogra'fia *sf* typography; (*procedimento*) letterpress (printing); (*officina*) printing house

TIR *sigla m* (= *Transports Internationaux Routiers*) International Heavy Goods Vehicle

ti'rare *vt* (*gen*) to pull; (*estrarre*): **~ qc da** to take *o* pull sth out of; to get sth out of; to extract sth from; (*chiudere: tenda ecc*) to draw, pull; (*tracciare, disegnare*) to draw, trace; (*lanciare: sasso, palla*) to throw; (*stampare*) to print; (*pistola, freccia*) to fire ▷ *vi* (*pipa, camino*) to draw; (*vento*) to blow; (*abito*) to be tight; (*fare fuoco*) to fire; (*fare del tiro, Calcio*) to shoot; **~ avanti** *vi* to struggle on ▷ *vt* to keep going; **~ fuori** (*estrarre*) to take out, pull out; **~ giù** (*abbassare*) to bring down, to lower; (*da scaffale ecc.*) to take down; **~ su** to pull up; (*capelli*) to put up; (*fig: bambino*) to bring up; **tirarsi** *vpr* **tirarsi indietro** to draw back; (*fig*) to back out; **~ a indovinare** to take a guess; **~ sul prezzo** to bargain; **tirar dritto** to keep right on going; **tirati su!** (*fig*) cheer up!; **~ via** (*togliere*) to take off

tira'tura *sf* (*azione*) printing; (*di libro*) (print) run; (*di giornale*) circulation

'tirchio, -a ['tirkjo] *ag* mean, stingy

'tiro *sm* shooting *no pl*, firing *no pl*; (*colpo, sparo*) shot; (*di palla: lancio*) throwing *no pl*; throw; (*fig*) trick; **cavallo da ~** draught (*BRIT*) *o* draft (*US*) horse; **tiro a segno** target shooting; (*luogo*) shooting range; **tiro con l'arco** archery

tiro'cinio [tiro'tʃinjo] *sm* apprenticeship; (*professionale*) training

ti'roide *sf* thyroid (gland)

Tir'reno *sm*: **il (mar) ~** the Tyrrhenian Sea

ti'sana *sf* herb tea

tito'lare *sm/f* incumbent; (*proprietario*) owner; (*Calcio*) regular player

'titolo *sm* title; (*di giornale*) headline; (*diploma*) qualification; (*Comm*) security; (: *azione*) share; **a che ~?** for what reason?; **a ~ di amicizia** out of friendship; **a ~ di premio** as a prize; **titolo di credito** share; **titoli di stato** government securities; **titoli di testa** (*Cinema*) credits

titu'bante *ag* hesitant, irresolute

toast [toust] *sm inv* toasted sandwich (*generally with ham and cheese*)

toc'cante *ag* touching

toc'care *vt* to touch; (*tastare*) to feel; (*fig: riguardare*) to concern; (: *commuovere*) to touch, move; (: *pungere*) to hurt, wound; (: *far cenno a: argomento*) to touch on, mention ▷ *vi* **~ a** (*accadere*) to happen to; (*spettare*) to be up to; **~ (il fondo)** (*in acqua*) to touch the bottom; **tocca a te difenderci** it's up to you to defend us; **a chi tocca?** whose turn is it?; **mi toccò pagare** I had to pay

tocche'rò *ecc* [tokke'rɔ] *vb vedi* **toccare**

'togliere ['tɔʎʎere] *vt* (*rimuovere*) to take away (*o* off), remove; (*riprendere, non concedere più*) to take away, remove; (*Mat*) to take away, subtract; **~ qc a qn** to take sth (away) from sb; **ciò non toglie che** nevertheless, be that as it may; **togliersi il cappello** to take off one's hat

toi'lette [twa'lɛt] *sf inv* toilet; (*mobile*) dressing table; **dov'è la ~?** where's the toilet?

'Tokyo *sf* Tokyo

'tolgo *ecc vb vedi* **togliere**

tolle'rare *vt* to tolerate

'tolsi *ecc vb vedi* **togliere**

'tomba *sf* tomb

tom'bino *sm* manhole cover

'tombola *sf* (*gioco*) tombola; (*ruzzolone*) tumble

'tondo, -a *ag* round

'tonfo *sm* splash; (*rumore sordo*) thud; (*caduta*): **fare un ~** to take a tumble

tonifi'care vt (muscoli, pelle) to tone up; (irrobustire) to invigorate, brace
tonnel'lata sf ton
'**tonno** sm (gen) tone; (Mus: di pezzo) key; (di colore) shade, tone
ton'silla sf tonsil
'**tonto, -a** ag dull, stupid
to'pazio [to'pattsjo] sm topaz
'**topo** sm mouse
'**toppa** sf (serratura) keyhole; (pezza) patch
to'race [to'ratʃe] sm chest
'**torba** sf peat
'**torcere** ['tɔrtʃere] vt to twist; **torcersi** vpr to twist, writhe
'**torcia, -ce** ['tɔrtʃa] sf torch; **torcia elettrica** torch (BRIT), flashlight (US)
torci'collo [tortʃi'kɔllo] sm stiff neck
'**tordo** sm thrush
To'rino sf Turin
tor'menta sf snowstorm
tormen'tare vt to torment; **tormentarsi** vpr to fret, worry o.s.
tor'nado sm tornado
tor'nante sm hairpin bend
tor'nare vi to return, go (o come) back; (ridiventare: anche fig) to become (again); (riuscire giusto, esatto: conto) to work out; (risultare) to turn out (to be), prove (to be); **~ utile** to prove o turn out (to be) useful; **~ a casa** to go (o come) home; **torno a casa martedì** I'm going home on Tuesday
tor'neo sm tournament
'**tornio** sm lathe
'**toro** sm bull; (dello zodiaco): **T~** Taurus
'**torre** sf tower; (Scacchi) rook, castle; **torre di controllo** (Aer) control tower
tor'rente sm torrent
torri'one sm keep
tor'rone sm nougat
'**torsi** ecc vb vedi **torcere**
torsi'one sf twisting; torsion
'**torso** sm torso, trunk; (Arte) torso
'**torsolo** sm (di cavolo ecc) stump; (di frutta) core

'**torta** sf cake
tortel'lini smpl (Cuc) tortellini
'**torto, -a** pp di **torcere** ▷ ag (ritorto) twisted; (storto) twisted, crooked ▷ sm (ingiustizia) wrong; (colpa) fault; **a ~** wrongly; **aver ~** to be wrong
'**tortora** sf turtle dove
tor'tura sf torture; **tortu'rare** vt to torture
to'sare vt (pecora) to shear; (siepe) to clip
Tos'cana sf: **la ~** Tuscany
'**tosse** sf cough; **ho la ~** I've got a cough
'**tossico, -a, -ci, -che** ag toxic
tossicodipen'dente sm/f drug addict
tos'sire vi to cough
tosta'pane sm inv toaster
to'tale ag, sm total
toto'calcio [toto'kaltʃo] sm gambling pool betting on football results, ≈ (football) pools pl (BRIT)
to'vaglia [to'vaʎʎa] sf tablecloth; **tovagli'olo** sm napkin
tra prep (di due persone, cose) between; (di più persone, cose) among(st); (tempo: entro) within, in; **~ 5 giorni** in 5 days' time; **sia detto ~ noi ...** between you and me ...; **litigano ~ (di) loro** they're fighting amongst themselves; **~ breve** soon; **~ sé e sé** (parlare ecc) to oneself
traboc'care vi to overflow
traboc'chetto [trabok'ketto] sm (fig) trap
'**traccia, -ce** ['trattʃa] sf (segno, striscia) trail, track; (orma) tracks pl; (residuo, testimonianza) trace, sign; (abbozzo) outline
tracci'are [trat'tʃare] vt to trace, mark (out); (disegnare) to draw; (fig: abbozzare) to outline
tra'chea [tra'kɛa] sf windpipe, trachea
tra'colla sf shoulder strap; **borsa a ~** shoulder bag

tradi'mento sm betrayal; (Dir, Mil) treason

tra'dire vt to betray; (coniuge) to be unfaithful to; (doveri: mancare) to fail in; (rivelare) to give away, reveal; **tradirsi** vpr to give o.s. away

tradizio'nale [tradittsjo'nale] ag traditional

tradizi'one [tradit'tsjone] sf tradition

tra'durre vt to translate; (spiegare) to render, convey; **me lo può ~?** can you translate this for me?; **traduzi'one** sf translation

'trae vb vedi **trarre**

traffi'cante sm/f dealer; (peg) trafficker

traffi'care vi (commerciare): **~ (in)** to trade (in), deal (in); (affaccendarsi) to busy o.s. ▷ vt (peg) to traffic in

'traffico, -ci sm traffic; (commercio) trade, traffic; **traffico di armi/droga** arms/drug trafficking

tra'gedia [tra'dʒɛdja] sf tragedy

'traggo ecc vb vedi **trarre**

tra'ghetto [tra'getto] sm ferry(boat)

'tragico, -a, -ci, -che ['tradʒiko] ag tragic

tra'gitto [tra'dʒitto] sm (passaggio) crossing; (viaggio) journey

tragu'ardo sm (Sport) finishing line; (fig) goal, aim

'trai ecc vb vedi **trarre**

traiet'toria sf trajectory

trai'nare vt to drag, haul; (rimorchiare) to tow

tralasci'are [tralaʃ'ʃare] vt (studi) to neglect; (dettagli) to leave out, omit

tra'liccio [tra'littʃo] sm (Elettr) pylon

tram sm inv tram

'trama sf (filo) weft, woof; (fig: argomento, maneggio) plot

traman'dare vt to pass on, hand down

tram'busto sm turmoil

tramez'zino [tramed'dzino] sm sandwich

'tramite prep through

tramon'tare vi to set, go down; **tra'monto** sm setting; (del sole) sunset

trampo'lino sm (per tuffi) springboard, diving board; (per lo sci) ski-jump

tra'nello sm trap

'tranne prep except (for), but (for); **~ che** unless

tranquil'lante sm (Med) tranquillizer

tranquillità sf calm, stillness; quietness; peace of mind

tranquilliz'zare [trankwillid'dzare] vt to reassure

> Attenzione! In inglese esiste il verbo to tranquillize, che però significa "calmare con un tranquillante".

tran'quillo, -a ag calm, quiet; (bambino, scolaro) quiet; (sereno) with one's mind at rest; **sta' ~** don't worry

transazi'one [transat'tsjone] sf compromise; (Dir) settlement; (Comm) transaction, deal

tran'senna sf barrier

transgenico, -a, -ci, -che [trans'dʒɛniko] ag genetically modified

tran'sigere [tran'sidʒere] vi (venire a patti) to compromise, come to an agreement

transi'tabile ag passable

transi'tare vi to pass

transi'tivo, -a ag transitive

'transito sm transit; **di ~** (merci) in transit; (stazione) transit cpd; **"divieto di ~"** "no entry"

'trapano sm (utensile) drill; (Med) trepan

trape'lare vi to leak, drip; (fig) to leak out

tra'pezio [tra'pɛtsjo] sm (Mat) trapezium; (attrezzo ginnico) trapeze

trapian'tare vt to transplant; **trapi'anto** sm transplanting; (Med) transplant; **trapianto cardiaco** heart

transplant
'trappola sf trap
tra'punta sf quilt
'trarre vt to draw, pull; (*portare*) to take; (*prendere, tirare fuori*) to take (out), draw; (*derivare*) to obtain; **~ origine da qc** to have its origins o originate in sth
trasa'lire vi to start, jump
trasan'dato, -a ag shabby
trasci'nare [traʃʃiˈnare] vt to drag; **trascinarsi** vpr to drag o.s. along; (*fig*) to drag on
tras'correre vt (*tempo*) to spend, pass ▷ vi to pass
tras'crivere vt to transcribe
trascu'rare vt to neglect; (*non considerare*) to disregard
trasferi'mento sm transfer; (*trasloco*) removal, move; **trasferimento di chiamata** (*Tel*) call forwarding
trasfe'rire vt to transfer; **trasferirsi** vpr to move; **tras'ferta** sf transfer; (*indennità*) travelling expenses pl; (*Sport*) away game
trasfor'mare vt to transform, change; **trasformarsi** vpr to be transformed; **trasformarsi in qc** to turn into sth; **trasforma'tore** sm (*Elec*) transformer
trasfusi'one sf (*Med*) transfusion
trasgre'dire vt to disobey, contravene
traslo'care vt to move, transfer; **tras'loco, -chi** sm removal
tras'mettere vt (*passare*): **~ qc a qn** to pass sth on to sb; (*mandare*) to send; (*Tecn, Tel, Med*) to transmit; (*TV, Radio*) to broadcast; **trasmissi'one** sf (*gen, Fisica, Tecn*) transmission; (*passaggio*) transmission, passing on; (*TV, Radio*) broadcast
traspa'rente ag transparent
traspor'tare vt to carry, move; (*merce*) to transport, convey; **lasciarsi ~ (da qc)** (*fig*) to let o.s. be

carried away (by sth); **tras'porto** sm transport
'trassi ecc vb vedi **trarre**
trasver'sale ag transverse, cross(-); running at right angles
'tratta sf (*Econ*) draft; (*di persone*): **la ~ delle bianche** the white slave trade
tratta'mento sm treatment; (*servizio*) service
trat'tare vt (*gen*) to treat; (*commerciare*) to deal in; (*svolgere: argomento*) to discuss, deal with; (*negoziare*) to negotiate ▷ vi **~ di** to deal with; **~ con** (*persona*) to deal with; **si tratta di ...** it's about ...
tratte'nere vt (*far rimanere: persona*) to detain; (*intrattenere: ospiti*) to entertain; (*tenere, frenare, reprimere*) to hold back, keep back; (*astenersi dal consegnare*) to hold, keep; (*detrarre: somma*) to deduct; **trattenersi** vpr (*astenersi*) to restrain o.s., stop o.s.; (*soffermarsi*) to stay, remain
trat'tino sm dash; (*in parole composte*) hyphen
'tratto, -a pp di **trarre** ▷ sm (*di penna, matita*) stroke; (*parte*) part, piece; (*di strada*) stretch; (*di mare, cielo*) expanse; (*di tempo*) period (of time)
trat'tore sm tractor
tratto'ria sf restaurant
'trauma, -i sm trauma
tra'vaglio [traˈvaʎʎo] sm (*angoscia*) pain, suffering; (*Med*) pains pl
trava'sare vt to decant
tra'versa sf (*trave*) crosspiece; (*via*) side street; (*Ferr*) sleeper (*BRIT*), (*railroad*) tie (*US*); (*Calcio*) crossbar
traver'sata sf crossing; (*Aer*) flight, trip; **quanto dura la ~?** how long does the crossing take?
traver'sie sfpl mishaps, misfortunes
tra'verso, -a ag oblique; **di ~** ag askew ▷ av sideways; **andare di ~** (*cibo*) to go down the wrong way; **guardare di ~** to look askance at
travesti'mento sm disguise

travestirsi *vpr* to disguise o.s.

tra'volgere [tra'vɔldʒere] *vt* to sweep away, carry away; (*fig*) to overwhelm

tre *num* three

'treccia, -ce ['trettʃa] *sf* plait, braid

tre'cento [tre'tʃɛnto] *num* three hundred ▷ *sm*: **il T~** the fourteenth century

'tredici ['treditʃi] *num* thirteen

'tregua *sf* truce; (*fig*) respite

tre'mare *vi*: ~ **di** (*freddo ecc*) to shiver o tremble with; (*paura, rabbia*) to shake o tremble with

tre'mendo, -a *ag* terrible, awful

> Attenzione! In inglese esiste la parola *tremendous*, che però significa *enorme* oppure *fantastico, strepitoso*.

'tremito *sm* trembling *no pl*; shaking *no pl*; shivering *no pl*

'treno *sm* train; **è questo il ~ per...?** is this the train for ...?; **treno di gomme** set of tyres (*BRIT*) o tires (*US*); **treno merci** goods (*BRIT*) o freight train; **treno viaggiatori** passenger train

⬤ **TRENI**

⬤ There are various types of train in
⬤ Italy. For short journeys there are
⬤ the "Regionali" (R), which generally
⬤ operate within a particular region,
⬤ and the "Interregionali" (IR),
⬤ which operate beyond regional
⬤ boundaries. Medium- and long-
⬤ distance passenger journeys are
⬤ carried out by "Intercity" (I) and
⬤ "Eurocity" (EC) trains. The "Eurostar"
⬤ service (ES) offers fast connections
⬤ between the major Italian cities.
⬤ Night services are operated by
⬤ "Intercity Notte" (ICN), "Euronight"
⬤ (EN) and "Espressi" (EXP).

'trenta *num* thirty; **tren'tesimo, -a** *num* thirtieth; **tren'tina** *sf* **una**

trentina (di) thirty or so, about thirty

'trepidante *ag* anxious

tri'angolo *sm* triangle

tribù *sf inv* tribe

tri'buna *sf* (*podio*) platform; (*in aule ecc*) gallery; (*di stadio*) stand

tribu'nale *sm* court

tri'ciclo [tri'tʃiklo] *sm* tricycle

tri'foglio [tri'fɔʎʎo] *sm* clover

'triglia ['triʎʎa] *sf* red mullet

tri'mestre *sm* period of three months; (*Ins*) term, quarter (*US*); (*Comm*) quarter

trin'cea [trin'tʃea] *sf* trench

trion'fare *vi* to triumph, win; ~ **su** to triumph over, overcome; **tri'onfo** *sm* triumph

tripli'care *vt* to triple

'triplo, -a *ag* triple; treble ▷ *sm*: **il ~ (di)** three times as much (as); **la spesa è tripla** it costs three times as much

'trippa *sf* (*Cuc*) tripe

'triste *ag* sad; (*luogo*) dreary, gloomy

tri'tare *vt* to mince, grind (*US*)

trivi'ale *ag* vulgar, low

tro'feo *sm* trophy

'tromba *sf* (*Mus*) trumpet; (*Aut*) horn; **tromba d'aria** whirlwind; **tromba delle scale** stairwell

trom'bone *sm* trombone

trom'bosi *sf* thrombosis

tron'care *vt* to cut off; (*spezzare*) to break off

'tronco, -a, -chi, -che *ag* cut off; broken off; (*Ling*) truncated; (*fig*) cut short ▷ *sm* (*Bot, Anat*) trunk; (*fig: tratto*) section; **licenziare qn in ~** to fire sb on the spot

'trono *sm* throne

tropi'cale *ag* tropical

 PAROLA CHIAVE

'troppo, -a *det* (*in eccesso: quantità*) too much; (: *numero*) too many; **c'era troppa gente** there were too many people; **fa troppo caldo** it's too hot

▷ pron (in eccesso: quantità) too much; (: numero) too many; **ne hai messo troppo** you've put in too much; **meglio troppi che pochi** better too many than too few ▷ av (eccessivamente: con ag, av) too; (: con vb) too much; **troppo amaro/tardi** too bitter/late; **lavora troppo** he works too much; **costa troppo** it costs too much; **di troppo** too much; too many; **qualche tazza di troppo** a few cups too many; **2 euro di troppo** 2 euros too many; **essere di troppo** to be in the way

'**trota** sf trout

'**trottola** sf spinning top

tro'**vare** vt to find; (giudicare): **trovo che** I find o think that; **trovarsi** vpr (reciproco: incontrarsi) to meet; (essere, stare) to be; (arrivare, capitare) to find o.s.; **non trovo più il portafoglio** I can't find my wallet; **andare a ~ qn** to go and see sb; **~ qn colpevole** to find sb guilty; **trovarsi bene** (in un luogo, con qn) to get on well

truc'**care** vt (falsare) to fake; (attore ecc) to make up; (travestire) to disguise; (Sport) to fix; (Aut) to soup up; **truccarsi** vpr to make up (one's face)

'**trucco, -chi** sm trick; (cosmesi) make-up

'**truffa** sf fraud, swindle; **truf'fare** vt to swindle, cheat

truffa'**tore, -'trice** sm/f swindler, cheat

'**truppa** sf troop

tu pron you; **tu stesso(a)** you yourself; **dare del tu a qn** to address sb as "tu"

'**tubo** sm tube; pipe; **tubo digerente** (Anat) alimentary canal, digestive tract; **tubo di scappamento** (Aut) exhaust pipe

tuf'**farsi** vpr to plunge, dive

'**tuffo** sm dive; (breve bagno) dip

tuli'**pano** sm tulip

tu'**more** sm (Med) tumour

Tuni'**sia** sf: **la ~** Tunisia

'**tuo** (f'**tua**, pl **tu'oi**,'**tue**) det **il ~**, **la tua** ecc your ▷ pron **il ~**, **la tua** ecc yours

tuo'**nare** vi to thunder; **tuona** it is thundering, there's some thunder

tu'**ono** sm thunder

tu'**orlo** sm yolk

tur'**bante** sm turban

tur'**bare** vt to disturb, trouble

tur'**bato, -a** ag upset; (preoccupato, ansioso) anxious

turbo'**lenza** [turbo'lɛntsa] sf turbulence

tur'**chese** [tur'kese] sf turquoise

Tur'**chia** [tur'kia] sf: **la ~** Turkey

'**turco, -a, -chi, -che** ag Turkish ▷ sm/f Turk/Turkish woman ▷ sm (Ling) Turkish; **parlare ~** (fig) to talk double-dutch

tu'**rismo** sm tourism; tourist industry; **tu'rista, -i, -e** sm/f tourist; **turismo sessuale** sex tourism; **tu'ristico, -a, -ci, -che** ag tourist cpd

'**turno** sm turn; (di lavoro) shift; **di ~** (soldato, medico, custode) on duty; **a ~** (rispondere) in turn; (lavorare) in shifts; **fare a ~ a fare qc** to take turns to do sth; **è il suo ~** it's your (o his ecc turn)

'**turpe** ag filthy, vile

'**tuta** sf overalls pl; (Sport) tracksuit

tu'**tela** sf (Dir: di minore) guardianship; (: protezione) protection; (difesa) defence

tutta'**via** cong nevertheless, yet

 PAROLA CHIAVE

'**tutto, -a** det **1** (intero) all; **tutto il latte** all the milk; **tutta la notte** all night, the whole night; **tutto il libro** the whole book; **tutta una bottiglia** a whole bottle

2 (pl, collettivo) all; every; **tutti i libri** all the books; **tutte le notti** every night; **tutti i venerdì** every

Friday; **tutti gli uomini** all the men; (*collettivo*) all men; **tutto l'anno** all year long; **tutti e due** both *o* each of us (*o* them *o* you); **tutti e cinque** all five of us (*o* them *o* you)
3 (*completamente*): **era tutta sporca** she was all dirty; **tremava tutto** he was trembling all over; **è tutta sua madre** she's just *o* exactly like her mother
4: **a tutt'oggi** so far, up till now; **a tutta velocità** at full *o* top speed
▷ *pron* 1 (*ogni cosa*) everything, all; (*qualsiasi cosa*) anything; **ha mangiato tutto** he's eaten everything; **tutto considerato** all things considered; **in tutto: 5 euro in tutto** 5 euros in all; **in tutto eravamo 50** there were 50 of us in all
2: **tutti, e** (*ognuno*) all, everybody; **vengono tutti** they are all coming, everybody's coming; **tutti quanti** all and sundry
▷ *av* (*completamente*) entirely, quite; **è tutto il contrario** it's quite *o* exactly the opposite; **tutt'al più: saranno stati tutt'al più una cinquantina** there were about fifty of them at (the very) most; **tutt'al più possiamo prendere un treno** if the worst comes to the worst we can take a train; **tutt'altro** on the contrary; **è tutt'altro che felice** he's anything but happy; **tutt'a un tratto** suddenly
▷ *sm* **il tutto** the whole lot, all of it

tut'tora *av* still
TV [ti'vu] *sf inv* (= *televisione*) TV ▷ *sigla* = **Treviso**

ubbidi'ente *ag* obedient
ubbi'dire *vi* to obey; **~ a** to obey; (*veicolo, macchina*) to respond to
ubria'care *vt* **~ qn** to get sb drunk; (*alcool*) to make sb drunk; (*fig*) to make sb's head spin *o* reel; **ubriacarsi** *vpr* to get drunk; **ubriacarsi di** (*fig*) to become intoxicated with
ubri'aco, -a, -chi, -che *ag, sm/f* drunk
uc'cello [ut'tʃello] *sm* bird
uc'cidere [ut'tʃidere] *vt* to kill; **uccidersi** *vpr* (*suicidarsi*) to kill o.s.; (*perdere la vita*) to be killed
u'dito *sm* (sense of) hearing
UE *sigla f* (= *Unione Europea*) EU
UEM *sigla f* (= *Unione economica e monetaria*) EMU
'uffa *escl* tut!
uffici'ale [uffi'tʃale] *ag* official ▷ *sm* (*Amm*) official, officer; (*Mil*) officer; **~ di stato civile** registrar
uf'ficio [uf'fitʃo] *sm* (*gen*) office; (*dovere*) duty; (*mansione*) task,

function, job; (*agenzia*) agency,
bureau; (*Rel*) service; **d'~** *ag* office
cpd; official ▷ *av* officially; **ufficio di
collocamento** employment office;
ufficio informazioni information
bureau; **ufficio oggetti smarriti**
lost property office (*BRIT*), lost and
found (*US*); **ufficio (del) personale**
personnel department; **ufficio
postale** post office

uffici'oso, -a [uffi'tʃoso] *ag* unofficial

uguagli'anza [ugwaʎ'ʎantsa] *sf*
equality

uguagli'are [ugwaʎ'ʎare] *vt* to make
equal; (*essere uguale*) to equal, be equal
to; (*livellare*) to level; **uguagliarsi a
o con qn** (*paragonarsi*) to compare
o.s. to sb

ugu'ale *ag* equal; (*identico*) identical,
the same; (*uniforme*) level, even ▷ *av*
costano ~ they cost the same; **sono
bravi ~** they're equally good

UIL *sigla f* (= Unione Italiana del Lavoro)
trade union federation

'ulcera ['ultʃera] *sf* ulcer

U'livo *sm*: **l'~** *centre-left Italian political
grouping*

u'livo = **olivo**

ulteri'ore *ag* further

ultima'mente *av* lately, of late

ulti'mare *vt* to finish, complete

'ultimo, -a *ag* (*finale*) last;
(*estremo*) farthest, utmost; (*recente:
notizia, moda*) latest; (*fig: sommo,
fondamentale*) ultimate ▷ *sm/f* last
(one); **fino all'~** to the last, until the
end; **da ~, in ~** in the end; **abitare
all'~ piano** to live on the top floor; **per
~** (*entrare, arrivare*) last

ulu'lare *vi* to howl

umanità *sf* humanity

u'mano, -a *ag* human; (*comprensivo*)
humane

umidità *sf* dampness; humidity

'umido, -a *ag* damp; (*mano, occhi*)
moist; (*clima*) humid ▷ *sm* dampness,
damp; **carne in ~** stew

'umile *ag* humble

umili'are *vt* to humiliate; **umiliarsi**
vpr to humble o.s.

u'more *sm* (*disposizione d'animo*)
mood; (*carattere*) temper; **di buon/
cattivo ~** in a good/bad mood

umo'rismo *sm* humour; **avere
il senso dell'~** to have a sense of
humour; **umo'ristico, -a, -ci, -che** *ag*
humorous, funny

u'nanime *ag* unanimous

unci'netto [untʃi'netto] *sm* crochet
hook

un'cino [un'tʃino] *sm* hook

undi'cenne [undi'tʃenne] *ag, sm/f*
eleven-year-old

undi'cesimo, -a [undi'tʃezimo] *num*
eleventh

'undici ['unditʃi] *num* eleven

'ungere ['undʒere] *vt* to grease, oil;
(*Rel*) to anoint; (*fig*) to flatter, butter
up

unghe'rese [unge'rese] *ag, sm/f, sm*
Hungarian

Unghe'ria [unge'ria] *sf* **l'~** Hungary

'unghia ['ungja] *sf* (*Anat*) nail; (*di
animale*) claw; (*di rapace*) talon; (*di
cavallo*) hoof

ungu'ento *sm* ointment

'unico, -a, -ci, -che *ag* (*solo*) only;
(*ineguagliabile*) unique; (*singolo:
binario*) single; **figlio(a) ~(a)** only
son/daughter, only child

unifi'care *vt* to unite, unify; (*sistemi*)
to standardize; **unificazi'one** *sf*
uniting; unification; standardization

uni'forme *ag* uniform; (*superficie*)
even ▷ *sf* (*divisa*) uniform

uni'one *sf* union; (*fig: concordia*) unity,
harmony; **Unione europea** European
Union; **ex Unione Sovietica** former
Soviet Union

u'nire *vt* to unite; (*congiungere*) to
join, connect; (: *ingredienti, colori*) to
combine; (*in matrimonio*) to unite,
join together; **unirsi** *vpr* to unite; (*in
matrimonio*) to be joined together; **~ qc**

a to unite sth with; to join o connect sth with; to combine sth with; **unirsi a** (*gruppo, società*) to join

unità *sf inv* (*unione, concordia*) unity; (*Mat, Mil, Comm, di misura*) unit; **unità di misura** unit of measurement

u'nito, -a *ag* (*paese*) united; (*amici, famiglia*) close; **in tinta unita** plain, self-coloured

univer'sale *ag* universal; general

università *sf inv* university

uni'verso *sm* universe

○ **PAROLA CHIAVE**

'uno, -a (*dav sm* **un** + *C, V,* **uno** + *s impura, gn, pn, ps, x, z; dav sf* **un'** +*V,* **una** + *C*) *art indef* **1** a; (*dav vocale*) an; **un bambino** a child; **una strada** a street; **uno zingaro** a gypsy
2 (*intensivo*): **ho avuto una paura!** I got such a fright!
▷ *pron* **1** one; **prendine uno** take one (of them); **l'uno o l'altro** either (of them); **l'uno e l'altro** both (of them); **aiutarsi l'un l'altro** to help one another o each other; **sono entrati l'uno dopo l'altro** they came in one after the other
2 (*un tale*) someone, somebody
3 (*con valore impersonale*) one, you; **se uno vuole** if one wants, if you want
▷ *num* one; **una mela e due pere** an apple and two pears; **uno più uno fa due** one plus one equals two, one and one are two ▷ *sf* **è l'una** it's one (o'clock)

'unsi *ecc vb vedi* ungere

'unto, -a *pp di* ungere ▷ *ag* greasy, oily ▷ *sm* grease

u'omo (*pl* **u'omini**) *sm* man; **da ~** (*abito, scarpe*) men's, for men; **uomo d'affari** businessman; **uomo di paglia** stooge; **uomo politico** politician; **uomo rana** frogman

u'ovo (*pl(f)* **u'ova**) *sm* egg; **uovo affogato/alla coque** poached/boiled egg; **uovo bazzotto/sodo** soft-/hard-boiled egg; **uovo di Pasqua** Easter egg; **uovo in camicia** poached egg; **uova strapazzate/al tegame** scrambled/fried eggs

ura'gano *sm* hurricane

urba'nistica *sf* town planning

ur'bano, -a *ag* urban, city *cpd*, town *cpd*; (*Tel: chiamata*) local; (*fig*) urbane

ur'gente [ur'dʒɛnte] *ag* urgent; **ur'genza** *sf* urgency; **in caso d'urgenza** in (case of) an emergency; **d'urgenza** *ag* emergency ▷ *av* urgently, as a matter of urgency

ur'lare *vi* (*persona*) to scream, yell; (*animale, vento*) to howl ▷ *vt* to scream, yell

'urlo (*pl(m)* **'urli**, *pl(f)* **'uria**) *sm* scream, yell; howl

URP *sigla m* (= *Ufficio Relazioni con il Pubblico*) PR Office

urrà *escl* hurrah!

U.R.S.S. *abbr f* **l'U.R.S.S.** the USSR

ur'tare *vt* to bump into, knock against; (*fig: irritare*) to annoy ▷ *vi* **~ contro** o **in** to bump into, knock against, crash into; (*fig: imbattersi*) to come up against; **urtarsi** *vpr* (*reciproco: scontrarsi*) to collide; (: *fig*) to clash; (*irritarsi*) to get annoyed

'U.S.A. ['uza] *smpl* **gli U.S.A.** the USA

u'sanza [u'zantsa] *sf* custom; (*moda*) fashion

u'sare *vt* to use, employ ▷ *vi* (*servirsi*): **~ di** to use; (: *diritto*) to exercise; (*essere di moda*) to be fashionable; (*essere solito*): **~ fare** to be in the habit of doing, be accustomed to doing ▷ *vb impers* **qui usa così** it's the custom round here; **u'sato, -a** *ag* used; (*consumato*) worn; (*di seconda mano*) used, second-hand ▷ *sm* second-hand goods *pl*

u'scire [uʃʃire] *vi* (*gen*) to come out; (*partire, andare a passeggio, a uno spettacolo ecc*) to go out; (*essere*

sorteggiato: numero) to come up;
~ da (*gen*) to leave; (*posto*) to go (*o*
come) out of, leave; (*solco, vasca ecc*)
to come out of; (*muro*) to stick out
of; (*competenza ecc*) to be outside;
(*infanzia, adolescenza*) to leave behind;
(*famiglia nobile ecc*) to come from; **~**
da *o* **di casa** to go out; (*fig*) to leave
home; **~ in automobile** to go out in
the car, go for a drive; **~ di strada** (*Aut*)
to go off *o* leave the road

u'scita [uʃʃita] *sf* (*passaggio, varco*)
exit, way out; (*per divertimento*) outing;
(*Econ: somma*) expenditure; (*Teatro*)
entrance; (*fig: battuta*) witty remark;
dov'è l'~? where's the exit?; **uscita di**
sicurezza emergency exit

usi'gnolo [uziɲ'ɲɔlo] *sm* nightingale

'uso *sm* (*utilizzazione*) use; (*esercizio*)
practice; (*abitudine*) custom; **a ~ di**
for (the use of); **d'~** (*corrente*) in use;
fuori ~ out of use; **uso esterno**; **per ~**
esterno for external use only

usti'one *sf* burn

usu'ale *ag* common, everyday

u'sura *sf* usury; (*logoramento*) wear
(and tear)

uten'sile *sm* tool, implement;
utensili da cucina kitchen utensils

u'tente *sm/f* user

'utero *sm* uterus

'utile *ag* useful ▷ *sm* (*vantaggio*)
advantage, benefit; (*Econ: profitto*)
profit

utiliz'zare [utilid'dzare] *vt* to use,
make use of, utilize

'uva *sf* grapes *pl*; **uva passa** raisins *pl*;
uva spina gooseberry

UVA *abbr* (= *ultravioletto prossimo*) UVA

UVB *abbr* (= *ultravioletto remoto*) UVB

v. *abbr* (= *vedi*) v

va, va' *vb vedi* **andare**

va'cante *ag* vacant

va'canza [va'kantsa] *sf* (*riposo, ferie*)
holiday(s) *pl* (BRIT), vacation (US);
(*giorno di permesso*) day off, holiday;
vacanze *sfpl* (*periodo di ferie*) holidays
(BRIT), vacation *sg* (US); **essere/**
andare in ~ to be/go on holiday *o*
vacation; **sono qui in ~** I'm on holiday
here; **vacanze estive** summer
holiday(s) *o* vacation; **vacanze**
natalizie Christmas holidays *o*
vacation

> Attenzione! In inglese esiste la
> parola *vacancy* che però indica
> un posto vacante o una camera
> disponibile.

'vacca, -che *sf* cow

vacci'nare [vattʃi'nare] *vt* to
vaccinate

vac'cino [vat'tʃino] *sm* (*Med*) vaccine

vacil'lare [vatʃil'lare] *vi* to sway,
wobble; (*luce*) to flicker; (*fig: memoria,*

coraggio) to be failing, falter

'vacuo, -a *ag* (*fig*) empty, vacuous

'vado *ecc vb vedi* **andare**

vaga'bondo, -a *sm/f* tramp, vagrant

va'gare *vi* to wander

vagherò *ecc* [vaɡe'rɔ] *vb vedi* **vagare**

va'gina [va'dʒina] *sf* vagina

'vaglia ['vaʎʎa] *sm inv* money order; **vaglia postale** postal order

vagli'are [vaʎ'ʎare] *vt* to sift; (*fig*) to weigh up

'vago, -a, -ghi, -ghe *ag* vague

va'gone *sm* (*Ferr: per passeggeri*) coach; (*: per merci*) truck, wagon; **vagone letto** sleeper, sleeping car; **vagone ristorante** dining o restaurant car

'vai *vb vedi* **andare**

vai'olo *sm* smallpox

va'langa, -ghe *sf* avalanche

va'lere *vi* (*avere forza, potenza*) to have influence; (*essere valido*) to be valid; (*avere vigore, autorità*) to hold, apply; (*essere capace: poeta, studente*) to be good, be able ▷ *vt* (*prezzo, sforzo*) to be worth; (*corrispondere*) to correspond to; (*procurare*): **~ qc a qn** to earn sb sth; **valersi di** to make use of, take advantage of; **far ~** (*autorità ecc*) to assert; **vale a dire** that is to say; **~ la pena** to be worth the effort o worth it

'valgo *ecc vb vedi* **valere**

vali'care *vt* to cross

'valico, -chi *sm* (*passo*) pass

'valido, -a *ag* valid; (*rimedio*) effective; (*aiuto*) real; (*persona*) worthwhile

vali'getta [vali'dʒetta] *sf* briefcase; **valigetta ventiquattrore** overnight bag o case

va'ligia, -gie o **ge** [va'lidʒa] *sf* (*suit*)case; **fare le valigie** to pack (up)

'valle *sf* valley; **a ~** (*di fiume*) downstream; **scendere a ~** to go downhill

va'lore *sm* (*gen*) value; (*merito*) merit, worth; (*coraggio*) valour, courage; (*Comm: titolo*) security; **valori** *smpl*

(*oggetti preziosi*) valuables

valoriz'zare [valorid'dzare] *vt* (*terreno*) to develop; (*fig*) to make the most of

va'luta *sf* currency, money; (*Banca*): **~ 15 gennaio** interest to run from January 15th

valu'tare *vt* (*casa, gioiello, fig*) to value; (*stabilire: peso, entrate, fig*) to estimate

'valvola *sf* (*Tecn, Anat*) valve; (*Elettr*) fuse

'valzer ['valtser] *sm inv* waltz

vam'pata *sf* (*di fiamma*) blaze; (*di calore*) blast; (*: al viso*) flush

vam'piro *sm* vampire

vanda'lismo *sm* vandalism

'vandalo *sm* vandal

vaneggi'are [vaned'dʒare] *vi* to rave

'vanga, -ghe *sf* spade

van'gelo [van'dʒɛlo] *sm* gospel

va'niglia [va'niʎʎa] *sf* vanilla

vanità *sf* vanity; (*di promessa*) emptiness; (*di sforzo*) futility; **vani'toso, -a** *ag* vain, conceited

'vanno *vb vedi* **andare**

'vano, -a *ag* vain ▷ *sm* (*spazio*) space; (*apertura*) opening; (*stanza*) room

van'taggio [van'taddʒo] *sm* advantage; **essere/portarsi in ~** (*Sport*) to be in/take the lead; **vantaggi'oso, -a** *ag* advantageous; favourable

vantarsi *vpr*: **~ (di/di aver fatto)** to boast o brag (about/about having done)

'vanvera *sf* **a ~** haphazardly; **parlare a ~** to talk nonsense

va'pore *sm* vapour; (*anche*: **~ acqueo**) steam; (*nave*) steamer; **~** (*turbina ecc*) steam *cpd*; **al ~** (*Cuc*) steamed

va'rare *vt* (*Naut, fig*) to launch; (*Dir*) to pass

var'care *vt* to cross

'varco, -chi *sm* passage; **aprirsi un ~ tra la folla** to push one's way through the crowd

vare'china [vare'kina] *sf* bleach
vari'abile *ag* variable; (*tempo, umore*) changeable, variable ▷ *sf* (*Mat*) variable
vari'cella [vari'tʃɛlla] *sf* chickenpox
vari'coso, -a *ag* varicose
varietà *sf inv* variety ▷ *sm inv* variety show
'vario, -a *ag* varied; (*parecchi: col sostantivo al pl*) various; (*mutevole: umore*) changeable
'varo *sm* (*Naut: fig*) launch; (*di leggi*) passing
varrò *ecc vb vedi* **valere**
Var'savia *sf* Warsaw
va'saio *sm* potter
'vasca, -sche *sf* basin; **vasca da bagno** bathtub, bath
vas'chetta [vas'ketta] *sf* (*per gelato*) tub; (*per sviluppare fotografie*) dish
vase'lina *sf* Vaseline®
'vaso *sm* (*recipiente*) pot; (: *barattolo*) jar; (: *decorativo*) vase; (*Anat*) vessel; **vaso da fiori** vase; (*per piante*) flowerpot
vas'soio *sm* tray
'vasto, -a *ag* vast, immense
Vati'cano *sm*: **il ~** the Vatican
ve *pron, av vedi* **vi**
vecchi'aia [vek'kjaja] *sf* old age
'vecchio, -a ['vɛkkjo] *ag* old ▷ *sm/f* old man/woman; **i vecchii** the old
ve'dere *vt, vi* to see; **vedersi** *vpr* to meet, see one another; **avere a che ~ con** to have something to do with; **far ~ qc a qn** to show sb sth; **farsi ~** to show o.s.; (*farsi vivo*) to show one's face; **vedi di non farlo** make sure o see you don't do it; **non (ci) si vede** (*è buio ecc*) you can't see a thing; **non lo posso ~** (*fig*) I can't stand him
ve'detta *sf* (*sentinella, posto*) look-out; (*Naut*) patrol boat
'vedovo, -a *sm/f* widower/widow
vedrò *ecc vb vedi* **vedere**
ve'duta *sf* view; **vedute** *sfpl* (*fig: opinioni*) views; **di larghe** o **ampie**

vedute broad-minded; **di vedute limitate** narrow-minded
vege'tale [vedʒe'tale] *ag, sm* vegetable
vegetari'ano, -a [vedʒeta'rjano] *ag, sm/f* vegetarian; **avete piatti vegetariani?** do you have any vegetarian dishes?
vegetazi'one [vedʒetat'tsjone] *sf* vegetation
'vegeto, -a ['vɛdʒeto] *ag* (*pianta*) thriving; (*persona*) strong, vigorous
'veglia ['veʎʎa] *sf* wakefulness; (*sorveglianza*) watch; (*trattenimento*) evening gathering; **fare la ~ a un malato** to watch over a sick person
vegli'one [veʎ'ʎone] *sm* ball, dance; **veglione di Capodanno** New Year's Eve party
ve'icolo *sm* vehicle
'vela *sf* (*Naut: tela*) sail; (*Sport*) sailing
ve'leno *sm* poison; **vele'noso, -a** *ag* poisonous
veli'ero *sm* sailing ship
vel'luto *sm* velvet; **velluto a coste** cord
'velo *sm* veil; (*tessuto*) voile
ve'loce [ve'lotʃe] *ag* fast, quick ▷ *av* fast, quickly; **velocità** *sf* speed; **a forte velocità** at high speed; **velocità di crociera** cruising speed
'vena *sf* (*gen*) vein; (*filone*) vein, seam; (*fig: ispirazione*) inspiration; (: *umore*) mood; **essere in ~ di qc** to be in the mood for sth
ve'nale *ag* (*prezzo, valore*) market *cpd*; (*fig*) venal; mercenary
ven'demmia *sf* (*raccolta*) grape harvest; (*quantità d'uva*) grape crop, grapes *pl*; (*vino ottenuto*) vintage
'vendere *vt* to sell; **"vendesi"** "for sale"
ven'detta *sf* revenge
vendicarsi *vpr*: **~ (di)** to avenge o.s. (for); (*per rancore*) to take one's revenge (for); **~ su qn** to revenge o.s. on sb

'vendita sf sale; **la ~** (attività) selling; (smercio) sales pl; **in ~** on sale; **vendita all'asta** sale by auction; **vendita per telefono** telesales sg

vene'rare vt to venerate

venerdì sm inv Friday; **di** o **il ~** on Fridays; **V~ Santo** Good Friday

ve'nereo, -a ag venereal

Ve'nezia [ve'nɛttsja] sf Venice

'vengo ecc vb vedi **venire**

veni'ale ag venial

ve'nire vi to come; (riuscire: dolce, fotografia) to turn out; (come ausiliare: essere): **viene ammirato da tutti** he is admired by everyone; **~ da** to come from; **quanto viene?** how much does it cost?; **far ~** (mandare a chiamare) to send for; **~ giù** to come down; **~ meno** (svenire) to faint; **~ meno a qc** not to fulfil sth; **~ su** to come up; **~ a trovare qn** to come and see sb; **~ via** to come away

'venni ecc vb vedi **venire**

ven'taglio [ven'taλλo] sm fan

ven'tata sf gust (of wind)

ven'tenne ag: **una ragazza ~** a twenty-year-old girl, a girl of twenty

ven'tesimo, -a num twentieth

'venti num twenty

venti'lare vt (stanza) to air, ventilate; (fig: idea, proposta) to air; **ventila'tore** sm ventilator, fan

ven'tina sf: **una ~ (di)** around twenty, twenty or so

'vento sm wind

ven'tola sf (Aut, Tecn) fan

ven'tosa sf (Zool) sucker; (di gomma) suction pad

ven'toso, -a ag windy

'ventre sm stomach

'vera sf wedding ring

vera'mente av really

ve'randa sf veranda(h)

ver'bale ag verbal ▷ sm (di riunione) minutes pl

'verbo sm (Ling) verb; (parola) word; (Rel): **il V~** the Word

'verde ag, sm green; **essere al ~** to be broke; **verde bottiglia/oliva** bottle/olive green

ver'detto sm verdict

ver'dura sf vegetables pl

'vergine ['vɛrdʒine] sf virgin; (dello zodiaco): **V~** Virgo ▷ ag virgin; (ragazza): **essere ~** to be a virgin

ver'gogna [ver'ɡoɲɲa] sf shame; (timidezza) shyness, embarrassment; **vergo'gnarsi** vpr **vergognarsi (di)** to be o feel ashamed (of); to be shy (about), be embarrassed (about); **vergo'gnoso, -a** ag ashamed; (timido) shy, embarrassed; (causa di vergogna: azione) shameful

ve'rifica, -che sf checking no pl, check

verifi'care vt (controllare) to check; (confermare) to confirm, bear out

verità sf inv truth

'verme sm worm

ver'miglio [ver'miλλo] sm vermilion, scarlet

ver'nice [ver'nitʃe] sf (colorazione) paint; (trasparente) varnish; (pelle) patent leather; **"~ fresca"** "wet paint"; **vernici'are** vt to paint; to varnish

'vero, -a ag (veridico: fatti, testimonianza) true; (autentico) real ▷ sm (verità) truth; (realtà) (real) life; **un ~ e proprio delinquente** a real criminal, an out-and-out criminal

vero'simile ag likely, probable

verrò ecc vb vedi **venire**

ver'ruca, -che sf wart

versa'mento sm (pagamento) payment; (deposito di denaro) deposit

ver'sante sm slopes pl, side

ver'sare vt (fare uscire: vino, farina) to pour (out); (spargere: lacrime, sangue) to shed; (rovesciare) to spill; (Econ) to pay; (: depositare) to deposit, pay in

versa'tile ag versatile

versi'one sf version; (traduzione) translation

'verso sm (di poesia) verse, line; (di animale, uccello) cry; (direzione) direction; (*modo*) way; (*di foglio di carta*) verso; (*di moneta*) reverse; **versi** *smpl* (*poesia*) verse *sg*; **non c'è ~ di persuaderlo** there's no way of persuading him, he can't be persuaded *prep* (*in direzione di*) toward(s); (*nei pressi di*) near, around (about); (*in senso temporale*) about, around; (*nei confronti di*) for; **~ di me** towards me; **~ sera** towards evening

'**vertebra** *sf* vertebra

verte'brale *ag* vertebral; **colonna ~** spinal column, spine

verti'cale *ag*, *sf* vertical

'**vertice** ['vertitʃe] *sm* summit, top; (*Mat*) vertex; **conferenza al ~** (*Pol*) summit conference

ver'tigine [ver'tidʒine] *sf* dizziness *no pl*; dizzy spell; (*Med*) vertigo; **avere le vertigini** to feel dizzy

ve'scica, -che [veʃʃika] *sf* (*Anat*) bladder; (*Med*) blister

'**vescovo** *sm* bishop

'**vespa** *sf* wasp

ves'taglia [ves'taʎʎa] *sf* dressing gown

ves'tire *vt* (*bambino, malato*) to dress; (*avere indosso*) to have on, wear; **vestirsi** *vpr* to dress, get dressed; **ves'tito, -a** *ag* dressed ▷ *sm* garment; (*da donna*) dress; (*da uomo*) suit; **vestiti** *smpl* (*indumenti*) clothes; **vestito di bianco** dressed in white

veteri'nario, -a *ag* veterinary ▷ *sm* veterinary surgeon (*BRIT*), veterinarian (*US*), vet

'**veto** *sm inv* veto

ve'traio *sm* glassmaker; glazier

ve'trata *sf* glass door (*o window*); (*di chiesa*) stained glass window

ve'trato, -a *ag* (*porta, finestra*) glazed; (*che contiene vetro*) glass *cpd* ▷ *sf* glass door (*o window*); (*di chiesa*) stained glass window; **carta vetrata** sandpaper

ve'trina *sf* (*di negozio*) (shop) window; (*armadio*) display cabinet; **vetri'nista,**

-i, -e *sm/f* window dresser

'**vetro** *sm* glass; (*per finestra, porta*) pane (of glass)

'**vetta** *sf* peak, summit, top

vet'tura *sf* (*carrozza*) carriage; (*Ferr*) carriage (*BRIT*), car (*US*); (*auto*) car (*BRIT*), automobile (*US*)

vezzeggia'tivo [vettseddʒa'tivo] *sm* (*Ling*) term of endearment

vi (*dav lo, la, li, le, ne diventa* **ve**) *pron* (*oggetto*) you; (*complemento di termine*) (to) you; (*riflessivo*) yourselves; (*reciproco*) each other ▷ *av* (*lì*) there; (*qui*) here; (*per questo/quel luogo*) through here/there; **vi è/sono** there is/are

'**via** *sf* (*gen*) way; (*strada*) street; (*sentiero, pista*) path, track; (*Amm: procedimento*) channels *pl* ▷ *prep* (*passando per*) via, by way of ▷ *av* away ▷ *escl* go away!; (*suvvia*) come on!; (*Sport*) go! ▷ *sm* (*Sport*) starting signal; **in ~ di guarigione** on the road to recovery; **per ~ di** (*a causa di*) because of, on account of; **in o per ~** on the way; **per ~ aerea** by air; (*lettere*) by airmail; **andare/essere ~** to go/be away; **~ ~ che** (*a mano a mano*) as; **dare il ~** (*Sport*) to give the starting signal; **dare il ~ a** (*fig*) to start; **in ~ provvisoria** provisionally; **Via lattea** (*Astr*) Milky Way; **via di mezzo** middle course; **via d'uscita** (*fig*) way out

via'dotto *sm* viaduct

viaggi'are [viad'dʒare] *vi* to travel; **viaggia'tore, -'trice** *ag* travelling ▷ *sm* traveller; (*passeggero*) passenger

vi'aggio ['vjaddʒo] *sm* travel(ling); (*tragitto*) journey, trip; **buon ~!** have a good trip!; **com'è andato il ~?** how was your journey?; **il ~ dura due ore** the journey takes two hours; **viaggio di nozze** honeymoon; **siamo in ~ di nozze** we're on honeymoon

vi'ale *sm* avenue

via'vai sm coming and going, bustle

vi'brare vi to vibrate

'vice ['vitʃe] sm/f deputy

vi'cenda [vi'tʃɛnda] sf event; **a ~** in turn

vice'versa [vitʃe'vɛrsa] av vice versa; **da Roma a Pisa e ~** from Rome to Pisa and back

vici'nanza [vitʃi'nantsa] sf nearness, closeness

vi'cino, -a [vi'tʃino] ag (gen) near; (nello spazio) near, nearby; (accanto) next; (nel tempo) near, close at hand ▷ sm/f neighbour ▷ av near, close; **da ~** (guardare) close up; (esaminare, seguire) closely; (conoscere) well, intimately; **~ a** near (to), close to; (accanto a) beside; **c'è una banca qui ~?** is there a bank nearby?; **~ di casa** neighbour

'vicolo sm alley; **vicolo cieco** blind alley

'video sm inv (TV: schermo) screen; **video'camera** sf camcorder; **videocas'setta** sf videocassette; **videochia'mare** [videokja'mare] vt to video call; **video'clip** [video'klip] sm inv videoclip; **videogi'oco, -chi** [video'dʒɔko] sm video game; **videoregistra'tore** sm video (recorder); **videote'lefono** sm videophone

'vidi ecc vb vedi **vedere**

vie'tare vt to forbid; (Amm) to prohibit; **~ a qn di fare** to forbid sb to do; to prohibit sb from doing

vie'tato, -a ag (vedi vb) forbidden; prohibited; banned; **"~ fumare/ l'ingresso"** "no smoking/ admittance"; **~ ai minori di 14/18 anni** prohibited to children under 14/18; **"senso ~"** (Aut) "no entry"; **"sosta vietata"** (Aut) "no parking"

Viet'nam sm: **il ~** Vietnam; **vietna'mita, -i, -e** ag, sm/f, sm Vietnamese inv

vi'gente [vi'dʒɛnte] ag in force

'vigile ['vidʒile] ag watchful ▷ sm (anche: **~ urbano**) policeman (in towns); **vigile del fuoco** fireman

vi'gilia [vi'dʒilja] sf (giorno antecedente) eve; **la ~ di Natale** Christmas Eve

vigli'acco, -a, -chi, -che [viʎ'ʎakko] ag cowardly ▷ sm/f coward

vi'gneto [viɲ'ɲeto] sm vineyard

vi'gnetta [viɲ'ɲetta] sf cartoon

vi'gore sm vigour; (Dir): **essere/ entrare in ~** to be in/come into force

'vile ag (spregevole) low, mean, base, (codardo) cowardly

'villa sf villa

vil'laggio [vil'laddʒo] sm village; **villaggio turistico** holiday village

vil'lano, -a ag rude, ill-mannered

villeggia'tura [villeddʒa'tura] sf holiday(s) pl (BRIT), vacation (US)

vil'letta sf, **vil'lino** ▷ sm small house (with a garden), cottage

'vimini smpl: **di ~** wicker

'vincere ['vintʃere] vt (in guerra, al gioco, a una gara) to defeat, beat; (premio, guerra, partita) to win; (fig) to overcome, conquer ▷ vi to win; **~ qn in bellezza** to be better-looking than sb; **vinci'tore** sm winner; (Mil) victor

vi'nicolo, -a ag wine cpd

'vino sm wine; **vino bianco/rosato/ rosso** white/rosé/red wine; **vino da pasto** table wine

'vinsi ecc vb vedi **vincere**

vi'ola sf (Bot) violet; (Mus) viola ▷ ag, sm inv (colore) purple

vio'lare vt (chiesa) to desecrate, violate; (giuramento, legge) to violate

violen'tare vt to use violence on; (donna) to rape

vio'lento, -a ag violent; **vio'lenza** sf violence; **violenza carnale** rape

vio'letta sf (Bot) violet

vio'letto, -a ag sm (colore) violet

violi'nista, -i, -e sm/f violinist

vio'lino sm violin

violon'cello [violon'tʃɛllo] sm cello

vi'ottolo *sm* path, track

vip [vip] *sigla m* (= *very important person*) VIP

'vipera *sf* viper, adder

vi'rare *vi* (*Naut, Aer*) to turn; (*Fot*) to tone; **~ di bordo** (*Naut*) to tack

'virgola *sf* (*Ling*) comma; (*Mat*) point; **virgo'lette** *sfpl* inverted commas, quotation marks

vi'rile *ag* (*proprio dell'uomo*) masculine; (*non puerile, da uomo*) manly, virile

virtù *sf inv* virtue; **in** *o* **per ~ di** by virtue of, by

virtu'ale *ag* virtual

'virus *sm inv* (*anche Inform*) virus

'viscere ['viʃʃere] *sfpl* (*di animale*) entrails *pl*; (*fig*) bowels *pl*

'vischio ['viskjo] *sm* (*Bot*) mistletoe; (*pania*) birdlime

'viscido, -a ['viʃʃido] *ag* slimy

vi'sibile *ag* visible

visibilità *sf* visibility

visi'era *sf* (*di elmo*) visor; (*di berretto*) peak

visi'one *sf* vision; **prendere ~ di qc** to examine sth, look sth over; **prima/ seconda ~** (*Cinema*) first/second showing

'visita *sf* visit; (*Med*) visit, call; (: *esame*) examination; **visita guidata** guided tour; **a che ora comincia la ~ guidata?** what time does the guided tour start?; **visita medica** medical examination; **visi'tare** *vt* to visit; (*Med*) to visit, call on; (: *esaminare*) to examine; **visita'tore, -'trice** *sm/f* visitor

vi'sivo, -a *ag* visual

'viso *sm* face

vi'sone *sm* mink

'vispo, -a *ag* quick, lively

'vissi *ecc vb vedi* **vivere**

'vista *sf* (*facoltà*) (eye)sight; (*fatto di vedere*): **la ~ di** the sight of; (*veduta*) view; **sparare a ~** to shoot on sight; **in ~** in sight; **perdere qn di ~** to lose sight of sb; (*fig*) to lose touch with sb;

a ~ d'occhio as far as the eye can see; (*fig*) before one's very eyes; **far ~ di fare** to pretend to do

'visto, -a *pp di* **vedere** ▷ *sm* visa; **~ che** seeing (that)

vis'toso, -a *ag* gaudy, garish; (*ingente*) considerable

visu'ale *ag* visual

'vita *sf* life; (*Anat*) waist; **a ~** for life

vi'tale *ag* vital

vita'mina *sf* vitamin

'vite *sf* (*Bot*) vine; (*Tecn*) screw

vi'tello *sm* (*Zool*) calf; (*carne*) veal; (*pelle*) calfskin

'vittima *sf* victim

'vitto *sm* food; (*in un albergo ecc*) board; **vitto e alloggio** board and lodging

vit'toria *sf* victory

'viva *escl*: **~ il re!** long live the king!

vi'vace [vi'vatʃe] *ag* (*vivo, animato*) lively; (: *mente*) lively, sharp; (*colore*) bright

vi'vaio *sm* (*di pesci*) hatchery; (*Agr*) nursery

vivavoce [viva'votʃe] *sm inv* (*dispositivo*) loudspeaker; **mettere il ~** to switch on the loudspeaker

vi'vente *ag* living, alive; **i viventi** the living

'vivere *vi* to live ▷ *vt* to live; (*passare: brutto momento*) to live through, go through; (*sentire: gioie, pene di qn*) to share ▷ *sm* life; (*anche*: **modo di ~**) way of life; **viveri** *smpl* (*cibo*) food *sg*, provisions; **~ di** to live on

'vivido, -a *ag* (*colore*) vivid, bright

vivisezi'one [viviset'tsjone] *sf* vivisection

'vivo, -a *ag* (*vivente*) alive, living; (: *animale*) live; (*fig*) lively; (: *colore*) bright, brilliant; **i vivi** the living; **~ e vegeto** hale and hearty; **farsi ~** to show one's face; to be heard from; **ritrarre dal ~** to paint from life; **pungere qn nel ~** (*fig*) to cut sb to the quick

vivrò *ecc vb vedi* **vivere**

vizi'are [vit'tsjare] *vt* (*bambino*) to spoil; (*corrompere moralmente*) to corrupt; **vizi'ato, -a** *ag* spoilt; (*aria, acqua*) polluted

'vizio ['vittsjo] *sm* (*morale*) vice; (*cattiva abitudine*) bad habit; (*imperfezione*) flaw, defect; (*errore*) fault, mistake

V.le *abbr* = **viale**

vocabo'lario *sm* (*dizionario*) dictionary; (*lessico*) vocabulary

vo'cabolo *sm* word

vo'cale *ag* vocal ▷ *sf* vowel

vocazi'one [vokat'tsjone] *sf* vocation; (*fig*) natural bent

'voce ['votʃe] *sf* voice; (*diceria*) rumour; (*di un elenco, in bilancio*) item; **aver ~ in capitolo** (*fig*) to have a say in the matter

'voga *sf* (*Naut*) rowing; (*usanza*): **essere in ~** to be in fashion *o* in vogue

vo'gare *vi* to row

vogherò [voge'rɔ] *vb vedi* **vogare**

'voglia ['vɔʎʎa] *sf* desire, wish; (*macchia*) birthmark; **aver ~ di qc/di fare** to feel like sth/like doing; (*più forte*) to want sth/to do

'voglio *ecc* ['vɔʎʎo] *vb vedi* **volere**

'voi *pron* you; **voi'altri** *pron* you

vo'lante *ag* flying ▷ *sm* (steering) wheel

volan'tino *sm* leaflet

vo'lare *vi* (*uccello, aereo, fig*) to fly; (*cappello*) to blow away *o* off, fly away *o* off; **~ via** to fly away *o* off

vo'latile *ag* (*Chim*) volatile ▷ *sm* (*Zool*) bird

volente'roso, -a *ag* willing

volenti'eri *av* willingly; **"~"** "with pleasure", "I'd be glad to"

PAROLA CHIAVE

vo'lere *sm* will, wish(es); **contro il volere di** against the wishes of; **per volere di qn** in obedience to sb's will

o wishes

▷ *vt* **1** (*esigere, desiderare*) to want; **voler fare/che qn faccia** to want to do/sb to do; **volete del caffè?** would you like *o* do you want some coffee?; **vorrei questo/fare** I would *o* I'd like this/to do; **come vuoi** as you like; **senza volere** (*inavvertitamente*) without meaning to, unintentionally

2 (*consentire*): **vogliate attendere, per piacere** please wait; **vogliamo andare?** shall we go?; **vuole essere così gentile da ...?** would you be so kind as to ...?; **non ha voluto ricevermi** he wouldn't see me

3: **volerci** (*essere necessario: materiale, attenzione*) to need; (: *tempo*) to take; **quanta farina ci vuole per questa torta?** how much flour do you need for this cake?; **ci vuole un'ora per arrivare a Venezia** it takes an hour to get to Venice

4: **voler bene a qn** (*amore*) to love sb; (*affetto*) to be fond of sb, like sb very much; **voler male a qn** to dislike sb; **volerne a qn** to bear sb a grudge; **voler dire** to mean

vol'gare *ag* vulgar

voli'era *sf* aviary

voli'tivo, -a *ag* strong-willed

'volli *ecc vb vedi* **volere**

'volo *sm* flight; **al ~: colpire qc al ~** to hit sth as it flies past; **capire al ~** to understand straight away; **volo charter** charter flight; **volo di linea** scheduled flight

volontà *sf* will; **a ~** (*mangiare, bere*) as much as one likes; **buona/cattiva ~** goodwill/lack of goodwill

volon'tario, -a *ag* voluntary ▷ *sm* (*Mil*) volunteer

'volpe *sf* fox

'volta *sf* (*momento, circostanza*) time; (*turno, giro*) turn; (*curva*) turn, bend; (*Archit*) vault; (*direzione*): **partire alla ~ di** to set off for; **a mia (*o* tua *ecc*) ~**

in turn; **una ~** once; **una ~ sola** only once; **due volte** twice; **una cosa per ~** one thing at a time; **una ~ per tutte** once and for all; **a volte** at times, sometimes; **una ~ che** (*temporale*) once; (*causale*) since; **3 volte 4** 3 times 4

volta'faccia [volta'fattʃa] *sm inv* (*fig*) volte-face

vol'taggio [vol'taddʒo] *sm* (*Elettr*) voltage

vol'tare *vt* to turn; (*girare: moneta*) to turn over; (*rigirare*) to turn round ▷ *vi* to turn; **voltarsi** *vpr* to turn; to turn over; to turn round

voltas'tomaco *sm* nausea; (*fig*) disgust

'volto, -a *pp di* **volgere** ▷ *sm* face

vo'lubile *ag* changeable, fickle

vo'lume *sm* volume

vomi'tare *vt, vi* to vomit; **'vomito** *sm* vomiting *no pl*; vomit

'vongola *sf* clam

vo'race [vo'ratʃe] *ag* voracious, greedy

vo'ragine [vo'radʒine] *sf* abyss, chasm

vorrò *ecc vb vedi* **volere**

'vortice ['vɔrtitʃe] *sm* whirlwind; whirlpool; (*fig*) whirl

'vostro, -a *det*: **il(la) ~(a)** *ecc* your ▷ *pron* **il(la) ~(a)** *ecc* yours

vo'tante *sm/f* voter

vo'tare *vi* to vote ▷ *vt* (*sottoporre a votazione*) to take a vote on; (*approvare*) to vote for; (*Rel*): **~ qc a** to dedicate sth to

'voto *sm* (*Pol*) vote; (*Ins*) mark; (*Rel*) vow; (*: offerta*) votive offering; **aver voti belli/brutti** (*Ins*) to get good/ bad marks

vs. *abbr* (*Comm*) = **vostro**

vul'cano *sm* volcano

vulne'rabile *ag* vulnerable

vu'oi, vu'ole *vb vedi* **volere**

vuo'tare *vt* to empty; **vuotarsi** *vpr* to empty

vu'oto, -a *ag* empty; (*fig: privo*): **~ di** (*senso ecc*) devoid of ▷ *sm* empty space, gap; (*spazio in bianco*) blank; (*Fisica*) vacuum; (*fig: mancanza*) gap, void; **a mani vuote** empty-handed; **vuoto d'aria** air pocket; **vuoto a rendere** returnable bottle

W   X

'wafer ['vafer] *sm inv (Cuc, Elettr)*
   wafer
'water ['wɔːtər] *sm inv* toilet
watt [vat] *sm inv* watt
W.C. *sm inv* WC
web [ueb] *sm:* **il ~** the Web; **cercare**
   nel ~ to search the Web ▷ *ag inv*
   pagina ~ web page
'weekend ['wiːkɛnd] *sm inv* weekend
'western ['wɛstern] *ag (Cinema)*
   cowboy *cpd* ▷ *sm inv* western, cowboy
   film; **western all'italiana** spaghetti
   western
'whisky ['wiski] *sm inv* whisky
'windsurf ['windsəːf] *sm inv (tavola)*
   windsurfer; *(sport)* windsurfing
'würstel ['vyrstəl] *sm inv* frankfurter

xe'nofobo, -a [kse'nɔfobo] *ag*
   xenophobic ▷ *sm/f* xenophobe
xi'lofono [ksi'lɔfono] *sm* xylophone

y z

yacht [jɔt] *sm inv* yacht
'yoga ['jɔga] *ag inv, sm* yoga (*cpd*)
yogurt ['jɔgurt] *sm inv* yog(h)urt

zabai'one [dzaba'jone] *sm dessert made of egg yolks, sugar and marsala*
zaf'fata [tsaf'fata] *sf (tanfo)* stench
zaffe'rano [dzaffe'rano] *sm* saffron
zaf'firo [dzaf'firo] *sm* sapphire
'zaino ['dzaino] *sm* rucksack
'zampa ['tsampa] *sf (di animale: gamba)* leg; (: *piede*) paw; **a quattro zampe** on all fours
zampil'lare [tsampil'lare] *vi* to gush, spurt
zan'zara [dzan'dzara] *sf* mosquito; **zanzari'era** *sf* mosquito net
'zappa ['tsappa] *sf* hoe
'zapping ['tsapiŋ] *sm (TV)* channel-hopping
zar, za'rina [tsar, tsa'rina] *sm/f* tsar/tsarina
'zattera ['dzattera] *sf* raft
'zebra ['dzɛbra] *sf* zebra; **zebre** *sfpl (Aut)* zebra crossing *sg (BRIT)*, crosswalk *sg (US)*
'zecca, -che ['tsekka] *sf (Zool)* tick; (*officina di monete*) mint

'zelo ['dzɛlo] *sm* zeal

'zenzero ['dzendzero] *sm* ginger

'zeppa ['tseppa] *sf* wedge

'zeppo, -a ['tseppo] *ag*: **~ di** crammed o packed with

zer'bino [dzer'bino] *sm* doormat

'zero ['dzɛro] *sm* zero, nought; **vincere per tre a ~** (*Sport*) to win three-nil

'zia ['tsia] *sf* aunt

zibel'lino [dzibel'lino] *sm* sable

'zigomo ['dzigomo] *sm* cheekbone

zig'zag [dzig'dzag] *sm inv* zigzag; **andare a ~** to zigzag

Zimbabwe [tsim'babwe] *sm*: **lo ~** Zimbabwe

'zinco ['dzinko] *sm* zinc

'zingaro, -a ['dzingaro] *sm/f* gipsy

'zio ['tsio] (*pl* **'zii**) *sm* uncle

zip'pare *vt* (*Inform: file*) to zip

zi'tella [dzi'tɛlla] *sf* spinster; (*peg*) old maid

'zitto, -a ['tsitto] *ag* quiet, silent; **sta' ~!** be quiet!

'zoccolo ['tsɔkkolo] *sm* (*calzatura*) clog; (*di cavallo ecc*) hoof; (*basamento*) base; plinth

zodia'cale [dzodia'kale] *ag* zodiac *cpd*; **segno ~** sign of the zodiac

zo'diaco [dzo'diako] *sm* zodiac

'zolfo ['tsolfo] *sm* sulphur

'zolla ['dzɔlla] *sf* clod (of earth)

zol'letta [dzol'letta] *sf* sugar lump

'zona ['dzɔna] *sf* zone, area; **zona di depressione** (*Meteor*) trough of low pressure; **zona disco** (*Aut*) ≈ meter zone; **zona industriale** industrial estate; **zona pedonale** pedestrian precinct; **zona verde** (*di abitato*) green area

'zonzo ['dzondzo]: **a ~** *av*, **andare a ~** to wander about, stroll about

zoo ['dzɔo] *sm inv* zoo

zoolo'gia [dzoolo'dʒia] *sf* zoology

zoppi'care [tsoppi'kare] *vi* to limp; to be shaky, rickety

'zoppo, -a ['tsɔppo] *ag* lame; (*fig:*

mobile) shaky, rickety

Z.T.L. *sigla f* (= *Zona a Traffico Limitato*) controlled traffic zone

'zucca, -che ['tsukka] *sf* (*Bot*) marrow; pumpkin

zucche'rare [tsukke'rare] *vt* to put sugar in; **zucche'rato, -a** *ag* sweet, sweetened

zuccheri'era [tsukke'rjɛra] *sf* sugar bowl

'zucchero ['tsukkero] *sm* sugar; **zucchero di canna** cane sugar; **zucchero filato** candy floss, cotton candy (*US*)

zuc'china [tsuk'kina] *sf* courgette (*BRIT*), zucchini (*US*)

'zuffa ['tsuffa] *sf* brawl

'zuppa ['tsuppa] *sf* soup; (*fig*) mixture, muddle; **zuppa inglese** (*Cuc*) dessert made with sponge cake, custard and chocolate, ≈ trifle (*BRIT*)

'zuppo, -a ['tsuppo] *ag*: **~ (di)** drenched (with), soaked (with)

Italian in focus

Introduction

Italian in focus gives you an introduction to various aspects of Italy and the Italian language. The following pages help you get to know the country where the language is spoken and the people who speak it.

Practical language tips and helpful notes on common translation difficulties will enable you to become a more confident Italian speaker. A useful correspondence section gives you all the information you need to be able to communicate effectively.

We've also included a number of links to useful websites, which will give you the opportunity to read more about Italy and the Italian language.

We hope you will enjoy using your *Italian in focus* supplement. We are sure it will help you find out more about Italy and Italians and become more confident in writing and speaking Italian.

Cominciamo!

Italy and its regions

©Collins Bartholomew Ltd 2006

Italy's neighbours
Italian is an official language in two Swiss cantons – Ticino and Grigioni, in the republic of San Marino and in Vatican City. Italian is also spoken in Malta, part of Croatia, and part of Slovenia.

3

Italy and its regions

The six biggest Italian cities

City	Name of inhabitants	Population
Roma	i romani	2,542,003
Milano	i milanesi	1,272,898
Napoli	i napoletani	1,000,449
Torino	i torinesi	867,857
Palermo	i palermitani	679,430
Genova	i genovesi	601,338

Italy consists of the mainland and two large islands, Sardegna and Sicilia, together with smaller islands such as Elba and Capri.

There are 20 administrative regions, five of which are *regioni autonome*, which have more decision-making powers than the others. Three of the 'autonomous regions' are in the north – Valle d'Aosta, Friuli-Venezia Giulia and Trentino-Alto Adige. The other two are the islands of Sardegna and Sicilia. Central government retains jurisdiction for matters such as defence, foreign affairs and the legal system, which affect the country as a whole.

Italy has only been a unified country since 1870. Before then parts of the peninsula were under the control of various countries, such as Spain, Austria and France. There was, and still is, a strong regional identity, with many people speaking one of the diverse local dialects. Nowadays everyone learns standard Italian at school; however many people speak *dialetto* with neighbours, friends and family.

As is often the case in areas bordering other countries, there are some bilingual communities. For example, in the Trentino-Alto Adige area in the far north of Italy, the majority language is German.

A snapshot of Italy

- In area, Italy (301, 323 km²) is somewhat bigger than the UK (244,110 km²).

- The Po (652 km) is Italy's longest river. It rises in the Alps and flows into the Adriatic near Venice.

- The population of Italy is about 58.4 million, which is slightly less than that of the UK. The birth rate is very low (1.2 children per woman). Deaths outnumber births.

- The Italian economy is the fourth biggest in the EU and seventh biggest in the world.

- Italy is the world's biggest wine-producing country.

- Gran Paradiso (4061) is Italy's highest peak.

- About 37 million tourists visit Italy every year, making it the 5th most popular tourist destination in the world.

- Italy has four active volcanoes: Etna, Vesuvius, Stromboli and Vulcano. Etna erupts frequently and is Europe's most active volcano.

Some useful links are:
www. governo.it
Website of the Italian government.
www.istat.it
The Italian statistics office.
www.enit.it
Italian state tourist board.

The Italian-speaking world

COUNTRIES OR REGIONS WHERE ITALIAN IS THE MOTHER TONGUE OR AN OFFICIAL LANGUAGE

Countries with large numbers of Italian speakers

Artico

Belgio
Germania
GRIGIONI
Slovenia
Croazia
SAN MARINO
ITALIA
Albania
MALTA

Somalia

Oceano
Pacifico

Oceano
Indiano

Australia

©Collins Bartholomew Ltd 2006

Many Italians went to the Americas – particularly to the US and Argentina – and to Australia. There are 1 ½ million Italian speakers in Argentina and nearly a milion in the US. Italian has had a major influence on the way Spanish is spoken in Argentina

The Italian State

- Italy has dozens of political parties. The two main political groupings are the centre-right and the centre-left. The government tends to be formed by a coalition consisting of several parties.

- Italy has two houses of parliament: the Senate (*il Senato*) and the Chamber of Deputies (*la Camera dei Deputati*). The President of the Republic (*il Presidente della Repubblica*), who is the head of state, has a tenure of seven years.

- The Prime Minister (*il Presidente del Consiglio*) is the head of government.

- Inside Italy there are two tiny independent states: San Marino and Vatican City.

- San Marino is the smallest republic in Europe.

- Vatican City is the spiritual and administrative centre of the Roman Catholic Church. It has two official languages, Italian and Latin.

Italian words that have travelled the world

An important part of the language Italians took to foreign countries was to do with food – many immigrants opened cafés and restaurants. These days people all over the world drink cappuccinos and espressos, and eat ciabatta, spaghetti, minestrone and pizza.

While everyone is familiar with these food items, they may not realize that the Italian words themselves have interesting, highly descriptive meanings. Here are just a few:

• cappuccino
  This comes from the word capuchin. Capuchins are friars whose habits are brown – the colour of cappuccino coffee.

• ciabatta
  This means 'slipper'. The bread has this name because of its shape.

• macchiato
  macchiato means 'stained' and describes the look of a dark coffee with a little spot of milk on it .

• spaghetti
  spago means 'string' – so *spaghetti* are 'little strings'. There's another pasta called *orecchiette*. If you bear in mind that *un orecchio* is an ear, you can probably guess what this pasta looks like.

• tiramisù
  This word doesn't describe the appearance of the dessert, but the effect it has, as it means 'pick-me-up' (a reference to the stimulating effect of the coffee it contains).

• vermicelli
  This kind of pasta is very, very thin, and its name means 'little worms'.

Italian words used in English

Apart from lots of words to do with food, there are other Italian words that are very often used in English. Here are a few interesting examples:

- solo
  This means 'alone' in Italian and was originally borrowed as a musical term – but it's now used in all kinds of contexts.

- fiasco
  English has borrowed only one of this word's two senses: the other one is 'wine bottle'!

- piano
  This is the Italian for 'soft'. When the pianoforte was invented it was so called because it could be played either soft (*piano*), or loud (*forte*), unlike its predecessor, the harpsichord.

- prima donna
  This word for leading lady means 'first woman'. This is another musical term which has come to be used more generally.

- bimbo
  Unlike in English, in Italian this is not a derogatory word for a woman – it just means 'little boy'. *Una bimba* is a little girl.

- al fresco
  In Italian this doesn't mean 'outside' but 'in the cool', and in a figurative sense, 'in jail'.

English words used in Italian

Italians have as great an appetite for English words as other people have for Italian food. Words from every conceivable field are borrowed; daily life, popular culture, science, computing, sport, business and so on.

• Countless words are borrowed in their original form:

lo stress	la privacy
lo shopping	il gay
il fast food	il blues
il jazz	lo show
il talk show	il computer
il mouse	il golf
lo sport	il supporter,
il record	il training
il manager	il target.

In the plural, these words get a plural article (i, gli or le) but no final 's':

Singular	Plural
il talk show	i talk show
lo sport	gli sport
la star	le star

• Other words are Italianized, but still recognizably English:

chattare	to chat
craccare	to crack
dribblare	to dribble
sprintare	to sprint
scrollare	to scroll
standardizzare	to standardize
interfaccia	interface
reality	reality show

• Some words look English, but have taken on a different meaning:

un box	a garage
un golf	a cardigan (it also means the sport)
un ticket	a prescription charge
uno smoking	a dinner jacket
uno spot	a tv or radio advert

Improving your pronunciation

Italian sounds

Vowels

Each English vowel can be pronounced in several quite different ways – think of the sound the letter **i** has, for example, in the words m**i**lk, k**i**nd and c**i**rcus. Italian vowels vary much less in their pronunciation:

a – is like the *a* in father
e – is like the *e* in set
i – is like the *ee* in sheep OR is
    pronounced like *y* in yard
o – is like the *o* in orange
u – is like the *oo* in soon

Avoid saying Italian words like their English lookalikes: the *i* in *Milano* and in *aprile*, for example is the long *ee* sound, not the short i used in Milan and April.

Unlike English, Italian is pronounced exactly as it is written, so *interessante*, for example, has five syllables, with a clearly pronounced vowel in each one: *in-te-res-san-te*.

• Italian vowels never disappear as they do in English words like interesting (int-res-ting) and camera (cam-ra). Always pronounce them fully.

• Italian vowels never have the indistinct 'uh' sound to be heard at the end of many English words, for example, hos<u>tel</u>, hospi<u>tal</u> and cir<u>cus</u>. Always pronounce Italian vowels clearly.

• When *i* is pronounced **y**, make sure that it's **y** as in yard, not **y** as in very:

andiamo	an-dya-mo
	(not an-dy-a-mo)
ravioli	rav-yo-lee
	(not ra-vee-o-lee)
stazione	sta-zyo-ne
	(not sta-zee-o-ne)

Improving your pronunciation

Consonants

- The presence of a double consonant in Italian makes the consonant sound longer: *cat-ti-vo*, *inte-res-san-te*, *An-na*.

- *c* followed by *e* or *i*, is pronounced *tch* as in *centro* and *facile*.

- *ch* is pronounced *k*, as in *fuochi* and *chiuso*.

- *g* followed by *e* and *i* is pronounced *j* as in *leggero* and *giardino*.

- *gh* is pronounced like *g* in get, as in *lunghi* and *spaghetti*.

- *gl* followed by *e* and *i* is normally pronounced like the *lli* in million, for example *luglio*, *bagagli*.

- *gn* is pronounced *ny*, for example *gnocchi*, *giugno*.

- *sc* followed by *e* and *i* is pronounced *sh*, as in *lasciare* and *sciare*.

Stress

- Italian words are usually stressed on the next to the last syllable, for example *cucina*, *studente*, *straniero*, *diciassette*, *parlare*, *avere*.

- If a word is spelled with an accent on the last vowel, for example, *fedeltà*, *università*, *però*, *così*, *caffè*, put the stress on this vowel.

- Some words are stressed on other syllables; the 'they' form of verbs, for example, usually stresses the second to last syllable: *capiscono* (= they understand); *parlano* (= they speak).

- Other words, such as *subito*, *macchina*, *vendere* and *camera* stress the first syllable. Be aware that words aren't always stressed as you'd expect and when in doubt look in the dictionary: you'll see that in each headword there's a mark that looks like an apostrophe. The syllable immediately following this apostrophe is the one you stress.

A useful link is:
www.accademiadellacrusca.it
National language academy of Italy.

Improving your fluency

Conversational words and phrases

In English we insert lots of words and phrases, such as *so, then, by the way*, into our conversation, to give our thoughts a structure and often to show our attitude. The Italian words below do the same thing. If you use them you'll sound more fluent and natural.

- *allora*
  Allora, che facciamo stasera? (= so)

- *va bene*
  Va bene, ho capito. (= okay)

- *ecco*
  Ecco perché non sono venuti.
  (= that's)
  Ecco Mario! (= here's)
  Eccolo! (= there … is)

- *forse*
  Sì, ma **forse** hanno ragione.
  (= maybe)

- *certo*
  Certo che puoi. (= of course)

- *dunque*
  Dunque, come dicevo … (= well)
  Dunque ha ragione lui. (= so)

- *può darsi*
  Sì, lo so, ma **può darsi** che …
  (= perhaps)

- *purtroppo*
  Sì, **purtroppo**. (= unfortunately)

- *sinceramente*
  Sinceramente, non m'importa niente.
  (= really)

- *comunque*
  Comunque, non è sempre così.
  (= however)

- *senz'altro*
  Mi scriverai? – **Senz'altro!**
  (= of course)
  È **senz'altro** meglio lui. (= definitely)

- *davvero*
  Ha pagato lui. – **Davvero**? (= really)

Improving your fluency

Varying the words you use to get your message across will also make you sound more fluent in Italian. For example, instead of *Mi piace molto il calcio*, you could say *Il calcio è la mia passione*. Here are some other suggestions.

Saying what you like or dislike

Adoro le ciliege.	I love ...
Mi è piaciuto molto il tuo regalo.	I (really) liked ...
Non mi piace il tennis.	I don't like ...
Il suo ultimo film *non mi piace per niente*.	I don't like ... (at all).
Detesto mentire.	I hate ...

Expressing your opinion

Credo che sia giusto.	I think ...
Penso che costino di più.	I think ...
Sono sicuro/sicura che ti piacerà.	I'm sure ...
Secondo me è stato un errore.	In my opinion ...
A mio parere vincerà lui.	In my opinion ...
A me sembra che qualche volta ...	It seems to me ...

Agreeing or disagreeing

Ha ragione.	You're right.
Giusto!	Quite right!
(Non) sono d'accordo.	I (don't) agree.
Non direi.	I wouldn't say so.
Certo!	Of course!

Correspondence

The following section on correspondence has been designed to help you communicate confidently in written as well as spoken Italian. Sample letters, e-mails and sections on text messaging and making telephone calls will ensure that you have all the vocabulary you need to correspond successfully.

Text messaging

un sms *(esse emme esse)*   = text message
mandare un sms a qualcuno = to text somebody

Abbreviation	Italian	English
+ tardi	più tardi	later
+o-	più o meno	more or less
ba	bacio	kiss
bn	bene	well
C6?	ci sei?	are you there?
cs	cosa	what
c ved	ci vediamo	see you soon
dv	dove	where
k6?	chi sei?	who are you?
ke cs?	che cosa?	what?
tu6	tu sei	you are
k	che	that, what
qd	quando	when
nn	non	not
k fai?	che fai?	what are you doing?
qnd	quando	when
TVB	ti voglio bene	I love you
TVTB	ti voglio tanto bene	I love you so much
x	per	for
xke	perché	because
xke?	perché?	why?
TAT	ti amo tanto	love you loads

Writing an e-mail

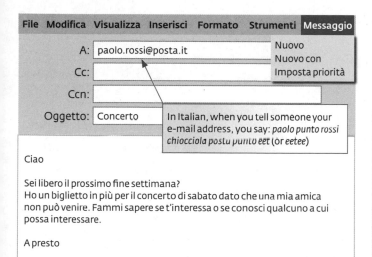

File Modifica Visualizza Inserisci Formato Strumenti **Messaggio**

Nuovo
Nuovo con
Imposta priorità

A: paolo.rossi@posta.it

Cc:

Ccn:

Oggetto: Concerto

In Italian, when you tell someone your e-mail address, you say: *paolo punto rossi chiocciola posta punto eet* (or *eetee*)

Ciao

Sei libero il prossimo fine settimana?
Ho un biglietto in più per il concerto di sabato dato che una mia amica non può venire. Fammi sapere se t'interessa o se conosci qualcuno a cui possa interessare.

A presto

file	file	*rispondi al mittente*	reply to sender
modifica	edit	*rispondi a tutti*	reply to all
visualizza	view	*inoltrare*	to forward
formato	format	*allega*	attachment
inserisci	insert	*A*	to
?	help	*Cc (copia carbone)*	cc (carbon copy)
strumenti	tools	*Ccn (copia carbone nascosta)*	bcc (blind carbon copy)
scrivere	to compose	*oggetto*	subject
help	help	*da*	from
invia	send	*dat*	sent
crea messaggio	new message		

Here is some additional useful Internet vocabulary:

ADSL	broadband	*Internet*	the Internet
avanti	forward	*la Rete*	the (World-Wide) Web
cartella	folder	*motore di recerca*	search engine
cercare	to search	*navigare in Internet*	to surf the Net
cliccare	to click	*pagina iniziale*	home page
collegamenti	links	*pagina web*	web page
collegarsi	to log on	*prefereti*	favorites
copiare	to copy	*programma*	program
cronologia	history	*provider*	Internet Service Provider
domande frequenti	FAQs	*salvare*	to save
fare doppio click	to double-click	*scaricare*	to download
finestra	window	*scollegarsi*	to log off
foglio di calcolo	spreadsheet	*sito Internet*	website
icona	icon	*stampare*	print
impostazioni	settings	*tagliare*	to cut
incollare	to paste	*tartiera*	keyboard
indietro	back	*visualizzare*	to view

Writing a personal letter

Town/city you are writing from, and the date → *Siena, 5 giugno 2006*

Cara Maria,

No capital for start of letter

ti ringrazio moltissimo del biglietto che mi hai mandato per il mio compleanno, che è arrivato proprio il giorno della mia festa!

Mi dispiace che tu non sia potuta venire a Milano per il mio compleanno e spero che ti sia ripresa dopo l'influenza. Mi piacerebbe poterti incontrare presto perché ho molte novità da raccontarti. Forse tra due settimane verrò a Torino con degli amici. Pensi di essere libera il giorno 12? Ti telefono la prossima settimana, così ci mettiamo d'accordo.

Baci,

Anna

Writing a personal letter

Other ways of starting a personal letter	Other ways of ending a personal letter
Carissima Maria *Mia cara Maria* *Cari Luigi e Silvia*	*Un abbraccio* *Bacioni* *Con affetto* *A presto*

Some useful phrases

Ti ringrazio per la tua lettera.	Thank you for your letter.
Mi ha fatto piacere ricevere tue notizie.	It was lovely to hear from you.
Scusami se non ti ho scritto prima.	I'm sorry I didn't reply sooner.
Salutami tanto Lucia.	Give my love to Lucia.
Tanti saluti anche da Paolo.	Paolo sends his best wishes.
Scrivi presto!	Write soon!

Writing a formal letter

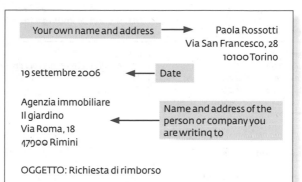

Your own name and address ➡️ Paola Rossotti
Via San Francesco, 28
10100 Torino

19 settembre 2006 ⬅️ Date

Agenzia immobiliare
Il giardino ⬅️ Name and address of the
Via Roma, 18 person or company you
17000 Rimini are writing to

OGGETTO: Richiesta di rimborso

Egr. signori,
vi scrivo per presentare reclamo in merito all'appartamento
che ho affittato nel condominio Le Torri per il periodo 5-12
agosto. Avevo espressamente richiesto un appartamento
con due camere e invece mi è stato assegnato un
appartamento con una camera sola; mancava inoltre
il condizionatore d'aria di cui il contratto di locazione fa
specifica menzione.
Chiedo quindi un rimborso di 1000 euro comprensivo
della differenza tra la tariffa che ho pagato per un
appartamento con due camere e aria condizionata e quella
per un appartamento con una camera sola senza aria
condizionata, e di un risarcimento per i disagi subiti.

Allego fotocopia del contratto di locazione.

Distinti saluti

Paola Rossotti

Writing a formal letter

Other ways of starting a formal letter	Other ways of ending a formal letter
Egregio signore, *Gentile signora,* *Egregio Signor Paolozzo,* *Gentile Signora Paolozzo,* *Spett. Ditta,* (when writing to a firm)	*Distinti saluti* *La prego di accettare i miei più distinti saluti* *Cordiali saluti*

Some useful phrases

La ringrazio della sua lettera del …	Thank you for your letter of …
In riferimento a …	With reference to …
Vi prego di inviarmi …	Please send me …
In attesa di una sua risposta la ringrazio per l'attenzione.	I look forward to hearing from you.
La ringrazio in anticipo per …	Thank you in advance for …

Agenzia immobiliare
Il giardino
Via Roma, 18
47900 Rimini

The house number comes after the street name, and the postcode comes before the name of the town.

Making a call

Asking for information

Qual è il prefisso di Livorno?	What's the code for Livorno?
Cosa devo fare per ottenere la linea esterna?	How do I get an outside line?
Può darmi il numero dell'interno della Signora Busi?	Could you give me Ms Busi's extension number?

When your number answers

Buongiorno, c'è Andrea?	Hello! Is Andrea there?
Potrei parlare con Lucia, per favore?	Could I speak to Lucia, please?
Parla la signora de Maggio?	Is that Mrs de Maggio?
Può chiedergli/chiederle di richiamarmi?	Could you ask him/her to call me back?
Richiamo fra mezz'ora.	I'll call back in half an hour.
Posso lasciare un messaggio, per favore?	Could I leave a message, please?

When you answer the telephone

Pronto!	Hello!
Chi parla?	Who's speaking?
Sono Marco.	It's Marco speaking.
Sì, sono io.	Speaking.
Vuole lasciare un messaggio?	Would you like to leave a message?

What you may hear

Chi devo dire?	Who shall I say is calling?
Le passo la comunicazione.	I'm putting you through now.
Attenda in linea.	Please hold.
Non risponde nessuno.	There's no reply.
La linea è occupata.	The line is engaged (Brit)/busy (US).
Vuole lasciare un messaggio?	Would you like to leave a message?

If you have a problem

Scusi, ho sbagliato numero.	Sorry, I dialled the wrong number.
La linea è molto disturbata.	This is a very bad line.
Qui non c'è campo.	There's no signal here.
Ho la batteria quasi scarica.	My battery's low.
Non ti sento.	I can't hear you.

Italian phrases and sayings

In Italian, as in many languages, people use vivid expressions based on images from their experience of real life. We've grouped the common expressions below according to the type of image they use. For fun, we have given you the word-for-word translation as well as the English equivalent.

Food and drink

dire pane al pane e vino al vino
word for word:
→ to call a spade a spade
to call bread bread and wine wine

Se non è zuppa è pan bagnato.
word for word:
→ It's much of a muchness.
if it's not soup it's wet bread

rendere pan per focaccia
word for word:
→ to give as good as you get
to give bread for focaccia

avere le mani in pasta
word for word:
→ to have a finger in the pie
to have your hands in the dough

lavorare per la pagnotta
word for word:
→ to earn your living
to work for your loaf

Ormai la frittata è fatta.
word for word:
→ The damage is done.
the omelette is made now

Weather

fare il bello e il cattivo tempo
word for word:
→ to do as one pleases
to make the good and bad weather

una tempesta in un bicchier d'acqua
word for word:
→ a storm in a teacup
a storm in a glass of water

sposa bagnata sposa fortunata
word for word:
→ rain on your wedding day is lucky
wet bride, lucky bride

Italian phrases and sayings

Animals

prendere due piccioni con una fava
word for word:
→ to kill two birds with one stone
to get two pigeons with one broad bean

Quando il gatto non c'è i topi ballano.
word for word:
→ When the cat's away the mice will play.
when the cat's not there the mice dance

Chi dorme non piglia pesci.
word for word:
→ The early bird catches the worm.
if you're asleep you don't catch any fish

In bocca al lupo!
word for word:
→ Break a leg!
into the wolf's mouth!

Meglio un uovo oggi che una gallina domani.
word for word:
→ A bird in the hand is worth two in the bush.
better an egg today than a hen tomorrow

L'ospite è come il pesce, dopo tre giorni puzza.
word for word:
→ It's nice when they come and it's nice when they go.
guests are like fish – after three days they start to smell

Parts of the body

essere un pugno in un occhio
word for word:
→ to be an eyesore
to be a punch in the eye

Chi non ha testa ha gambe.
word for word:
→ Use your head to save your legs.
people who have no head have legs

rimanere a bocca aperta
word for word:
→ to be amazed
to be left open-mouthed

avere le mani bucate
word for word:
→ to spend money like water
to have holes in your hands

Italian phrases and sayings

nascere con la camicia → to be born with a silver spoon in your
mouth

word for word: *to be born with with a shirt on*

sudare sette camicie → to work like a dog
word for word: *to sweat seven shirts*

tirare qualcuno per la giacca → to twist someone's arm
word for word: *to pull someone by the coat*

Se sono rose fioriranno. → The proof of the pudding is in the
eating.

word for word: *if they're roses they'll bloom*

fare di ogni erba un fascio → to lump everything together
word for word: *to put all the grasses into one bundle*

Non sono tutte rose e fiori. → It's not all a bed of roses.
word for word: *it's not all roses and flowers*

Rosso di sera, bel tempo si spera. → Red sky at night, shepherd's delight.
word for word: *(if the sky's) red at night you can hope
for good weather*

vedere tutto nero → to look on the black side
word for word: *to see everything as black*

Al buio tutti i gatti sono neri. → At night all cats are grey.
word for word: *in the dark all cats are black*

Some common translation difficulties

On the following pages we have shown some of the translation difficulties you are most likely to come across. We hope that the tips we have given will help you to avoid these common pitfalls when writing or speaking Italian.

How to say 'you' in Italian

There are three ways of saying *you* in Italian: **tu** and **lei** are used to speak to one person, and **voi** is used to speak to more than one person.

• Use **tu** when you are speaking to a person you know well, or to a child. If you are a student you can call another student **tu**.

> And how old are you, Roberto? → E **tu**, Roberto, quanti anni hai?

• Use **lei** when speaking to strangers, or anyone you're not on familiar terms with. As you get to know someone better they may suggest that you call each other **tu** instead of **lei**. In shops, hotels and restaurants customers are always addressed as **lei**.

> Would you like a coffee too, madam? → Vuole un caffè anche **lei**, signora?

It may seem potentially confusing that **lei** also means 'she', but in practice it's quite obvious that if someone speaks directly to you using **lei**, the meaning is *you*.

• Use **voi** when you are speaking to more than one person.

> Where are you boys from? → **Voi** ragazzi, di dove siete?

'You' has to go with the verb in English, but in Italian you often use the verb alone:

> How old are you? → Quanti anni hai?
> You speak good Italian, madam. → Parla bene l'italiano, signora.
> You're young. → Siete giovani.

Some common translation difficulties

You use the words **tu**, **lei** and **voi** to attract someone's attention, or for the sake of emphasis.

<u>Tu</u> cosa pensi? → What do <u>you</u> think?
<u>Lei</u> quale preferisce? → Which one do <u>you</u> prefer?

Showing possession

In English -'s is a common way of showing who or what something belongs to. In Italian you have to use **di**:

my brother**'s** car → la macchina **di** mio fratello
Maria**'s** house → la casa **di** Maria

Translating 'to like'

There are two ways of saying you like something, depending whether it is singular or plural:

I like Italy. → **Mi piace** l'Italia.
word-for-word meaning of Italian: *to me is pleasing Italy*

I like dogs. → **Mi piacciono** i cani.
word-for-word meaning of Italian: *to me are pleasing dogs*

If you bear in mind the word-for-word meaning of the Italian you'll have no trouble deciding whether to use **piace** or **piacciono**.

To say 'we like', change **mi** to **ci**.

We like the sea. → **Ci piace** il mare.
We like his films. → **Ci piacciono** i suoi film.

Some common translation difficulties

If you want to ask someone if they like something:

• Use *ti* when asking someone you know well.

> Do you like my shoes?   →   ***Ti piacciono** le mie scarpe?*

• Use *le* when speaking politely

> Do you like Italian food, madam? →   ***Le piace** la cucina italiana, signora?*

• Use *vi* when talking to more than one person.

> Do you like football, boys?   →   ***Vi piace** il calcio, ragazzi?*

Translating *-ing*

The English *-ing* form is used to talk about something you are doing or were doing. This can be translated into Italian by using the Italian present continuous tense (the verb form that ends *-ando* or *-endo*).

> They were gett**ing** bored.   →   *Si stavano annoi**ando**.*
> He's read**ing** the paper.   →   *Sta legg**endo** il giornale.*
> She's talk**ing** to Mum.   →   *Sta parl**ando** con la mamma.*

It is, however, just as common to translate the *-ing* form in English with the present simple tense in Italian.

> He's read**ing** the paper.   →   ***Legge** il giornale.*
> She's talk**ing** to Mum.   →   ***Parla** con la mamma.*

In other cases the Italian infinitive (the verb form that ends in *-are*, *-ere*, or *-ire*) is often used where the *-ing* form is used in English.

• Use the infinitive when talking about activities:

> I love **reading**.   →   *Mi piace moltissimo **leggere**.*
> We don't like **walking**.   →   *Non ci piace **camminare**.*
> **Smoking** is bad for you.   →   ***Fumare** fa male.*

Some common translation difficulties

Use the infinitive to translate prepositions such as without + -ing (**senza** + infinitive), before + -ing (**prima di** + infinitive), after + -ing (**dopo aver** + past participle).

He went away **without saying** anything. → *È andato via **senza dire** niente.*

Before opening the packet, read the instructions. → ***Prima di aprire** il pacchetto, leggi le istruzioni.*

After making a phone call she went out. → ***Dopo aver** telefonato è uscita.*

More on prepositions

Sentences that have no preposition in English may contain a preposition in Italian. The dictionary can help you with these. For example:

They started **laughing**. → *Hanno cominciato **a ridere**.*

Have you finished **eating**? → *Hai finito **di mangiare**?*

When did you stop **smoking**? → *Quando hai smesso **di fumare**?*

Saying Sorry

• To apologize about something, use **scusi** to someone you're on formal terms with, and **scusa** to a friend. Use **scusate** to more than one person.

Sorry. → *Scusi.*

Sorry I'm late. → *Scusi il ritardo.*

Sorry, Paola, I've got to go. → *Scusa, Paola, devo andare.*

Sorry to disturb you. → *Scusate il disturbo.*

• **Scusi** is also used to mean *'excuse me'* when you stop somebody to ask something.

Excuse me, where is the station? → *Scusi, dov'è la stazione?*

Some common translation difficulties

When you haven't heard what someone said, say **come, scusi**?

• To express regret use **mi dispiace**:

My grandfather has died. –
Oh, **I'm sorry**. → È morto mio nonno. –
Oh, **mi dispiace**.
I haven't got time, **sorry**. → Non ho tempo, **mi dispiace**.
I'm sorry but I can't come. → **Mi dispiace** ma non posso venire.
I'm sorry for them. → **Mi dispiace** per loro.

Translating 'to be'

'To be' usually corresponds to **essere**, but remember:

• In phrases describing how you feel, use **avere**:

I **am** hot/cold → **ho** caldo/freddo
they **are** hungry/thirsty → **hanno** fame/sete
he **is** scared → **ha** paura

• To describe the weather, use **fare**:

It**'s** nice weather today. → **Fa** bel tempo oggi.

• To say your age, use **avere**:

I**'m** fifteen. → **Ho** guindici anni.

• To talk about your health, use **stare**:

I**'m** fine, thanks. → **Sto** bene, grazie

Some common translation difficulties

'Have' or 'have got' usually correspond to *avere*:

I've **got** two brothers.	→ *Ho due fratelli.*
Have you **got** a bike?	→ *Hai una bici?*
I**'ve** spent a lot of money.	→ *Ho speso molti soldi.*
What **have** you done?	→ *Cos' hai fatto?*

Remember, though that 'have' and 'has' are translated by *essere*.

• In the perfect tense of some common verbs such as to go (*andare*), to come (*venire*) and to arrive (*arrivare*):

Where **have** they gone?	→ *Dove sono andati?*
She **has** come too.	→ *È venuta anche lei.*
We**'ve** arrived.	→ *Siamo arrivati.*

• In the perfect tense of all reflexive verbs:

I**'ve** hurt myself.	→ *Mi sono fatto male.*
Has she had a good time?	→ *Si è divertita?*

A [eɪ] *n* (*Mus*) la *m*

A2 *n abbr* (*BRIT: Scol*) seconda parte del diploma di studi superiori chiamato "A level"

KEYWORD

a [ə] (*before vowel or silent h* **an**) *indef art* **1** un (uno + *s impure, gn, pn, ps, x, z*), una *f* (un' + *vowel*); **a book** un libro; **a mirror** uno specchio; **an apple** una mela; **she's a doctor** è medico
2 (*instead of the number "one"*) un(o), *f* una; **a year ago** un anno fa; **a hundred/thousand** *etc* **pounds** cento/mille *etc* sterline
3 (*in expressing ratios, prices etc*) a, per; **3 a day/week** 3 al giorno/alla settimana; **10 km an hour** 10 km all'ora; **£5 a person** 5 sterline a persona *or* per persona

A.A. *n abbr* (= *Alcoholics Anonymous*) AA; (*BRIT:* = *Automobile Association*)

≈ A.C.I. *m*
A.A.A. (*US*) *n abbr* (= *American Automobile Association*) ≈ A.C.I. *m*
aback [ə'bæk] *adv* **to be taken ~** essere sbalordito(-a)
abandon [ə'bændən] *vt* abbandonare ▷ *n* **with ~** sfrenatamente, spensieratamente
abattoir ['æbətwɑː^r] (*BRIT*) *n* mattatoio
abbey ['æbɪ] *n* abbazia, badia
abbreviation [əbriː'veɪʃən] *n* abbreviazione *f*
abdomen ['æbdəmən] *n* addome *m*
abduct [æb'dʌkt] *vt* rapire
abide [ə'baɪd] *vt* **I can't ~ it/him** non lo posso soffrire *or* sopportare; **abide by** *vt fus* conformarsi a
ability [ə'bɪlɪtɪ] *n* abilità *f inv*
able ['eɪbl] *adj* capace; **to be ~ to do sth** essere capace di fare qc, poter fare qc
abnormal [æb'nɔːməl] *adj* anormale
aboard [ə'bɔːd] *adv* a bordo ▷ *prep* a bordo di
abolish [ə'bɔlɪʃ] *vt* abolire
abolition [æbəu'lɪʃən] *n* abolizione *f*
abort [ə'bɔːt] *vt* abortire; **abortion** [ə'bɔːʃən] *n* aborto; **to have an abortion** abortire

KEYWORD

about [ə'baut] *adv* **1** (*approximately*) circa, quasi; **about a hundred/thousand** *etc* un centinaio/migliaio *etc*, circa cento/mille *etc*; **it takes about 10 hours** ci vogliono circa 10 ore; **at about 2 o'clock** verso le 2; **I've just about finished** ho quasi finito
2 (*referring to place*) qua e là, in giro; **to leave things lying about** lasciare delle cose in giro; **to run about** correre qua e là; **to walk about** camminare
3: **to be about to do sth** stare per fare qc

▷ *prep* **1** (*relating to*) su, di; **a book about London** un libro su Londra; **what is it about?** di che si tratta?; (*book, film etc*) di cosa tratta?; **we talked about it** ne abbiamo parlato; **what** or **how about doing this?** che ne dici di fare questo?
2 (*referring to place*): **to walk about the town** camminare per la città; **her clothes were scattered about the room** i suoi vestiti erano sparsi or in giro per tutta la stanza

above [əˈbʌv] *adv, prep* sopra; **mentioned ~** suddetto; **~ all** soprattutto

abroad [əˈbrɔːd] *adv* all'estero

abrupt [əˈbrʌpt] *adj* (*sudden*) improvviso(-a); (*gruff, blunt*) brusco(-a)

abscess [ˈæbsɪs] *n* ascesso

absence [ˈæbsəns] *n* assenza

absent [ˈæbsənt] *adj* assente; **absent-minded** *adj* distratto(-a)

absolute [ˈæbsəluːt] *adj* assoluto(-a); **absolutely** [-ˈluːtlɪ] *adv* assolutamente

absorb [əbˈzɔːb] *vt* assorbire; **to be ~ed in a book** essere immerso in un libro; **absorbent cotton** [əbˈzɔːbənt-] (*us*) *n* cotone *m* idrofilo; **absorbing** *adj* avvincente, molto interessante

abstain [əbˈsteɪn] *vi* **to ~ (from)** astenersi (da)

abstract [ˈæbstrækt] *adj* astratto(-a)

absurd [əbˈsɜːd] *adj* assurdo(-a)

abundance [əˈbʌndəns] *n* abbondanza

abundant [əˈbʌndənt] *adj* abbondante

abuse [*n* əˈbjuːs, *vb* əˈbjuːz] *n* abuso; (*insults*) ingiurie *fpl* ▷ *vt* abusare di; **abusive** *adj* ingiurioso(-a)

abysmal [əˈbɪzməl] *adj* spaventoso(-a)

academic [ækəˈdɛmɪk] *adj* accademico(-a); (*pej: issue*) puramente formale ▷ *n* universitario(-a);

academic year *n* anno accademico

academy [əˈkædəmɪ] *n* (*learned body*) accademia; (*school*) scuola privata; **academy of music** *n* conservatorio

accelerate [ækˈsɛləreɪt] *vt, vi* accelerare; **acceleration** *n* accelerazione *f*; **accelerator** *n* acceleratore *m*

accent [ˈæksɛnt] *n* accento

accept [əkˈsɛpt] *vt* accettare; **acceptable** *adj* accettabile; **acceptance** *n* accettazione *f*

access [ˈæksɛs] *n* accesso; **accessible** [ækˈsɛsəbl] *adj* accessibile

accessory [ækˈsɛsərɪ] *n* accessorio; (*Law*): **~ to** complice *m/f* di

accident [ˈæksɪdənt] *n* incidente *m*; (*chance*) caso; **I've had an ~** ho avuto un incidente; **by ~** per caso; **accidental** [-ˈdɛntl] *adj* accidentale; **accidentally** [-ˈdɛntəlɪ] *adv* per caso; **Accident and Emergency Department** *n* (*BRIT*) pronto soccorso; **accident insurance** *n* assicurazione *f* contro gli infortuni

acclaim [əˈkleɪm] *n* acclamazione *f*

accommodate [əˈkɔmədeɪt] *vt* alloggiare; (*oblige, help*) favorire

accommodation [əkɔməˈdeɪʃən] (*us* **accommodations**) *n* alloggio

accompaniment [əˈkʌmpənɪmənt] *n* accompagnamento

accompany [əˈkʌmpənɪ] *vt* accompagnare

accomplice [əˈkʌmplɪs] *n* complice *m/f*

accomplish [əˈkʌmplɪʃ] *vt* compiere; (*goal*) raggiungere; **accomplishment** *n* compimento; realizzazione *f*

accord [əˈkɔːd] *n* accordo ▷ *vt* accordare; **of his own ~** di propria iniziativa; **accordance** *n* **in accordance with** in conformità con; **according: according to** *prep* secondo; **accordingly** *adv* in conformità

account [əˈkaunt] *n* (*Comm*) conto;

(*report*) descrizione *f*; **accounts** *npl* (*Comm*) conti *mpl*; **of no ~** di nessuna importanza; **on ~** in acconto; **on no ~** per nessun motivo; **on ~ of** a causa di; **to take into ~, take ~ of** tener conto di; **account for** *vt fus* spiegare; giustificare; **accountable** *adj* **accountable (to)** responsabile (verso); **accountant** [ə'kauntənt] *n* ragioniere(-a); **account number** *n* numero di conto

accumulate [ə'kju:mjuleɪt] *vt* accumulare ▷ *vi* accumularsi

accuracy ['ækjurəsɪ] *n* precisione *f*

accurate ['ækjurɪt] *adj* preciso(-a); **accurately** *adv* precisamente

accusation [ækju'zeɪʃən] *n* accusa

accuse [ə'kju:z] *vt* accusare; **accused** *n* accusato(-a)

accustomed [ə'kʌstəmd] *adj* **~ to** abituato(-a) a

ace [eɪs] *n* asso

ache [eɪk] *n* male *m*, dolore *m* ▷ *vi* (*be sore*) far male, dolere; **my head ~s** mi fa male la testa

achieve [ə'tʃi:v] *vt* (*aim*) raggiungere; (*victory, success*) ottenere; **achievement** *n* compimento; successo

acid ['æsɪd] *adj* acido(-a) ▷ *n* acido

acknowledge [ək'nɔlɪdʒ] *vt* (*letter: also:* **~ receipt of**) confermare la ricevuta di; (*fact*) riconoscere; **acknowledgement** *n* conferma; riconoscimento

acne ['æknɪ] *n* acne *f*

acorn ['eɪkɔ:n] *n* ghianda

acoustic [ə'ku:stɪk] *adj* acustico(-a)

acquaintance [ə'kweɪntəns] *n* conoscenza; (*person*) conoscente *m/f*

acquire [ə'kwaɪəʳ] *vt* acquistare; **acquisition** [ækwɪ'zɪʃən] *n* acquisto

acquit [ə'kwɪt] *vt* assolvere; **to ~ o.s. well** comportarsi bene

acre ['eɪkəʳ] *n* acro, ≈ 4047 m²

acronym ['ækrənɪm] *n* acronimo

across [ə'krɔs] *prep* (*on the other side*) dall'altra parte di; (*crosswise*) attraverso ▷ *adv* dall'altra parte; in larghezza; **to run/swim ~** attraversare di corsa/a nuoto; **~ from** di fronte a

acrylic [ə'krɪlɪk] *adj* acrilico(-a)

act [ækt] *n* atto; (*in music-hall etc*) numero; (*Law*) decreto ▷ *vi* agire; (*Theatre*) recitare; (*pretend*) fingere ▷ *vt* (*part*) recitare; **to ~ as** agire da; **act up** (*inf*) *vi* (*person*) comportarsi male; (*knee, back, injury*) fare male; (*machine*) non funzionare; **acting** *adj* che fa le funzioni di ▷ *n* (*of actor*) recitazione *f*; (*activity*): **to do some acting** fare del teatro (*or* del cinema)

action ['ækʃən] *n* azione *f*; (*Mil*) combattimento; (*Law*) processo; **out of ~** fuori combattimento; fuori servizio; **to take ~** agire; **action replay** *n* (*TV*) replay *m inv*

activate ['æktɪveɪt] *vt* (*mechanism*) attivare

active ['æktɪv] *adj* attivo(-a); **actively** *adv* (*participate*) attivamente; (*discourage, dislike*) vivamente

activist ['æktɪvɪst] *n* attivista *m/f*

activity [æk'tɪvɪtɪ] *n* attività *f inv*; **activity holiday** *n* vacanza organizzata con attività ricreative per ragazzi

actor ['æktəʳ] *n* attore *m*

actress ['æktrɪs] *n* attrice *f*

actual ['æktjuəl] *adj* reale, effettivo(-a)

> Be careful not to translate *actual* by the Italian word *attuale*.

actually ['æktjuəlɪ] *adv* veramente; (*even*) addirittura

> Be careful not to translate *actually* by the Italian word *attualmente*.

acupuncture ['ækjupʌŋktʃəʳ] *n* agopuntura

acute [ə'kju:t] *adj* acuto(-a); (*mind, person*) perspicace

ad [æd] *n abbr* = **advertisement**

A.D. *adv abbr* (= *Anno Domini*) d.C.

adamant ['ædəmənt] *adj* irremovibile

adapt [ə'dæpt] *vt* adattare ▷ *vi* **to ~ (to)** adattarsi (a); **adapter, adaptor** *n* (*Elec*) adattatore *m*

add [æd] *vt* aggiungere ▷ *vi* **to ~ to** (*increase*) aumentare; **add up** *vt* (*figures*) addizionare ▷ *vi* (*fig*): **it doesn't add up** non ha senso; **add up to** *vt fus* (*Math*) ammontare a; (*fig*: *mean*) significare; **it doesn't add up to much** non è un granché

addict ['ædɪkt] *n* tossicomane *m/f*; (*fig*) fanatico(-a); **addicted** [ə'dɪktɪd] *adj* **to be addicted to** (*drink etc*) essere dedito(-a) a; (*fig*: *football etc*) essere tifoso(-a) di; **addiction** [ə'dɪkʃən] *n* (*Med*) tossicodipendenza; **addictive** [ə'dɪktɪv] *adj* che dà assuefazione

addition [ə'dɪʃən] *n* addizione *f*; (*thing added*) aggiunta; **in ~** inoltre; **in ~ to** oltre; **additional** *adj* supplementare

additive ['ædɪtɪv] *n* additivo

address [ə'drɛs] *n* indirizzo; (*talk*) discorso ▷ *vt* indirizzare; (*speak to*) fare un discorso a; (*issue*) affrontare; **my ~ is ...** il mio indirizzo è...; **address book** *n* rubrica

adequate ['ædɪkwɪt] *adj* adeguato(-a), sufficiente

adhere [əd'hɪər] *vi* **to ~ to** aderire a; (*fig*: *rule, decision*) seguire

adhesive [əd'hi:zɪv] *n* adesivo; **adhesive tape** *n* (BRIT: *for parcels etc*) nastro adesivo; (US *Med*) cerotto adesivo

adjacent [ə'dʒeɪsənt] *adj* adiacente; **~ to** accanto a

adjective ['ædʒɛktɪv] *n* aggettivo

adjoining [ə'dʒɔɪnɪŋ] *adj* accanto *inv*, adiacente

adjourn [ə'dʒəːn] *vt* rimandare ▷ *vi* essere aggiornato(-a)

adjust [ə'dʒʌst] *vt* aggiustare; (*change*) rettificare ▷ *vi* **to ~ (to)** adattarsi (a); **adjustable** *adj* regolabile; **adjustment** *n* (*Psych*) adattamento; (*of machine*) regolazione *f*; (*of prices, wages*) modifica

administer [əd'mɪnɪstər] *vt* amministrare; (*justice, drug*) somministrare; **administration** [ədmɪnɪs'treɪʃən] *n* amministrazione *f*; **administrative** [əd'mɪnɪstrətɪv] *adj* amministrativo(-a)

administrator [əd'mɪnɪstreɪtər] *n* amministratore(-trice)

admiral ['ædmərəl] *n* ammiraglio

admiration [ædmə'reɪʃən] *n* ammirazione *f*

admire [əd'maɪər] *vt* ammirare; **admirer** *n* ammiratore(-trice)

admission [əd'mɪʃən] *n* ammissione *f*; (*to exhibition, nightclub etc*) ingresso; (*confession*) confessione *f*

admit [əd'mɪt] *vt* ammettere; far entrare; (*agree*) riconoscere; **admit to** *vt fus* riconoscere; **admittance** *n* ingresso; **admittedly** *adv* bisogna pur riconoscere (che)

adolescent [ædəu'lɛsnt] *adj*, *n* adolescente *m/f*

adopt [ə'dɔpt] *vt* adottare; **adopted** *adj* adottivo(-a); **adoption** [ə'dɔpʃən] *n* adozione *f*

adore [ə'dɔːr] *vt* adorare

adorn [ə'dɔːn] *vt* ornare

Adriatic [eɪdrɪ'ætɪk] *n*: **the ~ (Sea)** il mare Adriatico, l'Adriatico

adrift [ə'drɪft] *adv* alla deriva

adult ['ædʌlt] *adj* adulto(-a); (*work, education*) per adulti ▷ *n* adulto(-a); **adult education** *n* scuola per adulti

adultery [ə'dʌltərɪ] *n* adulterio

advance [əd'vɑːns] *n* avanzamento; (*money*) anticipo ▷ *adj* (*booking etc*) in anticipo ▷ *vt* (*money*) anticipare ▷ *vi* avanzare; **in ~** in anticipo; **do I need to book in ~?** occorre che prenoti in anticipo?; **advanced** *adj* avanzato(-a); (*Scol*: *studies*) superiore

advantage [əd'vɑːntɪdʒ] *n* (*also Tennis*) vantaggio; **to take ~ of**

approfittarsi di

advent ['ædvənt] n avvento; (Rel): **A~** Avvento

adventure [əd'ventʃər] n avventura; **adventurous** [əd'ventʃərəs] adj avventuroso(-a)

adverb ['ædvə:b] n avverbio

adversary ['ædvəsərɪ] n avversario(-a)

adverse ['ædvə:s] adj avverso(-a)

advert ['ædvə:t] (BRIT) n abbr = **advertisement**

advertise ['ædvətaɪz] vi, vt fare pubblicità or réclame (a); fare un'inserzione (per vendere); **to ~ for** (staff) mettere un annuncio sul giornale per trovare; **advertisement** [əd'və:tɪsmənt] n (Comm) réclame f inv, pubblicità f inv; (in classified ads) inserzione f; **advertiser** n azienda che reclamizza un prodotto; (in newspaper) inserzionista m/f; **advertising** ['ædvətaɪzɪŋ] n pubblicità

advice [əd'vaɪs] n consigli mpl; **piece of ~** consiglio; **to take legal ~** consultare un avvocato

advisable [əd'vaɪzəbl] adj consigliabile

advise [əd'vaɪz] vt consigliare; **to ~ sb of sth** informare qn di qc; **to ~ sb against sth/doing sth** sconsigliare qc a qn/a qn di fare qc; **adviser** n consigliere(-a); (in business) consulente m/f, consigliere(-a); **advisory** [-ərɪ] adj consultivo(-a)

advocate [n 'ædvəkɪt, vb 'ædvəkeɪt] n (upholder) sostenitore(-trice); (Law) avvocato (difensore) ▷ vt propugnare

Aegean [ɪ'dʒi:ən] n: **the ~ (Sea)** il mar Egeo, l'Egeo

aerial ['ɛərɪəl] n antenna ▷ adj aereo(-a)

aerobics [ɛə'rəubɪks] n aerobica

aeroplane ['ɛərəpleɪn] (BRIT) n aeroplano

aerosol ['ɛərəsɔl] (BRIT) n aerosol

affair [ə'fɛər] n affare m; (also: **love ~**) relazione f amorosa; **~s** (business) affari

affect [ə'fɛkt] vt toccare; (influence) influire su, incidere su; (feign) fingere; **affected** adj affettato(-a); **affection** [ə'fɛkʃən] n affezione f; **affectionate** adj affettuoso(-a)

afflict [ə'flɪkt] vt affliggere

affluent ['æfluənt] adj ricco(-a); **the ~ society** la società del benessere

afford [ə'fɔ:d] vt permettersi; (provide) fornire; **affordable** adj (che ha un prezzo) abbordabile

Afghanistan [æf'gænɪstɑ:n] n Afganistan m

afraid [ə'freɪd] adj impaurito(-a); **to be ~ of or to/that** aver paura di/che; **I am ~ so/not** ho paura di sì/no

Africa ['æfrɪkə] n Africa; **African** adj, n africano(-a); **African-American** adj, n afroamericano(-a)

after ['ɑ:ftər] prep, adv dopo ▷ conj dopo che; **what/who are you ~?** che/chi cerca?; **~ he left/having done** dopo che se ne fu andato/dopo aver fatto; **to name sb ~ sb** dare a qn il nome di qn; **it's twenty ~ eight** (US) sono le otto e venti; **to ask ~ sb** chiedere di qn; **~ all** dopo tutto; **~ you!** dopo di lei!; **after-effects** npl conseguenze fpl; (of illness) postumi mpl; **aftermath** n conseguenze fpl; **in the aftermath of** nel periodo dopo; **afternoon** n pomeriggio; **after-shave (lotion)** ['ɑ:ftəʃeɪv-] n dopobarba m inv; **aftersun (lotion/cream)** n doposole m inv; **afterwards** (US **afterward**) adv dopo

again [ə'gɛn] adv di nuovo; **to begin/see ~** ricominciare/rivedere; **not ... ~** non ... più; **~ and ~** ripetutamente

against [ə'gɛnst] prep contro

age [eɪdʒ] n età f inv ▷ vt, vi invecchiare; **it's been ~s since** sono secoli che; **he is 20 years of ~** ha

20 anni; **to come of ~** diventare maggiorenne; **~d 10** di 10 anni; **the ~d** ['eɪdʒɪd] gli anziani; **age group** n generazione f; **age limit** n limite m d'età

agency ['eɪdʒənsɪ] n agenzia

agenda [ə'dʒɛndə] n ordine m del giorno

agent ['eɪdʒənt] n agente m

aggravate ['æɡrəveɪt] vt aggravare; (person) irritare

aggression [ə'ɡrɛʃən] n aggressione f

aggressive [ə'ɡrɛsɪv] adj aggressivo(-a)

agile ['ædʒaɪl] adj agile

agitated ['ædʒɪteɪtɪd] adj agitato(-a), turbato(-a)

AGM n abbr = **annual general meeting**

ago [ə'ɡəʊ] adv **2 days ~** 2 giorni fa; **not long ~** poco tempo fa; **how long ~?** quanto tempo fa?

agony ['æɡənɪ] n dolore m atroce; **to be in ~** avere dolori atroci

agree [ə'ɡriː] vt (price) pattuire ▷ vi **to ~ (with)** essere d'accordo (con); (Ling) concordare (con); **to ~ to sth/to do sth** accettare qc/di fare qc; **to ~ that** (admit) ammettere che; **to ~ on sth** accordarsi su qc; **garlic doesn't ~ with me** l'aglio non mi va; **agreeable** adj gradevole; (willing) disposto(-a); **agreed** adj (time, place) stabilito(-a); **agreement** n accordo; **in agreement** d'accordo

agricultural [æɡrɪ'kʌltʃərəl] adj agricolo(-a)

agriculture ['æɡrɪkʌltʃəʳ] n agricoltura

ahead [ə'hɛd] adv avanti; davanti; **~ of** davanti a; (fig: schedule etc) in anticipo su; **~ of time** in anticipo; **go right** or **straight ~** tiri diritto

aid [eɪd] n aiuto ▷ vt aiutare; **in ~ of** a favore di

aide [eɪd] n (person) aiutante m/f

AIDS [eɪdz] n abbr (= acquired immune deficiency syndrome) AIDS f

ailing ['eɪlɪŋ] adj sofferente; (fig: economy, industry etc) in difficoltà

ailment ['eɪlmənt] n indisposizione f

aim [eɪm] vt **to ~ sth at** (such as gun) mirare qc a, puntare qc a; (camera) rivolgere qc a; (missile) lanciare qc contro ▷ vi (also: **to take ~**) prendere la mira ▷ n mira; **to ~ at** mirare; **to ~ to do** aver l'intenzione di fare

ain't [eɪnt] (inf) = **am not**; **aren't**; **isn't**

air [ɛəʳ] n aria ▷ vt (room) arieggiare; (clothes) far prendere aria a; (grievances, ideas) esprimere pubblicamente ▷ cpd (currents) d'aria; (attack) aereo(-a); **to throw sth into the ~** lanciare qc in aria; **by ~** (travel) in aereo; **on the ~** (Radio, TV) in onda; **airbag** n airbag m inv; **airbed** (BRIT) n materassino; **airborne** ['ɛəbɔːn] adj (plane) in volo; (troops) aerotrasportato(-a); **as soon as the plane was airborne** appena l'aereo ebbe decollato; **air-conditioned** adj con or ad aria condizionata; **air conditioning** n condizionamento d'aria; **aircraft** n inv apparecchio; **airfield** n campo d'aviazione; **Air Force** n aviazione f militare; **air hostess** (BRIT) n hostess f inv; **airing cupboard** ['ɛərɪŋ-] n armadio riscaldato per asciugare panni.; **airlift** n ponte m aereo; **airline** n linea aerea; **airliner** n aereo di linea; **airmail** n **by airmail** per via aerea; **airplane** (US) n aeroplano; **airport** n aeroporto; **air raid** n incursione f aerea; **airsick** adj **to be airsick** soffrire di mal d'aria; **airspace** n spazio aereo; **airstrip** n pista d'atterraggio; **air terminal** n air-terminal m inv; **airtight** adj ermetico(-a); **air-traffic controller** n controllore m del traffico aereo; **airy** adj arioso(-a); (manners) noncurante

aisle [aɪl] n (of church) navata laterale; navata centrale; (of plane) corridoio; **aisle seat** n (on plane) posto sul corridoio

ajar [ə'dʒɑːʳ] *adj* socchiuso(-a)

à la carte [ɑːlɑːˈkɑːt] *adv* alla carta

alarm [ə'lɑːm] *n* allarme *m* ▷ *vt* allarmare; **alarm call** *n* (*in hotel etc*) sveglia; **could I have an alarm call at 7 am, please?** vorrei essere svegliato alle 7, per favore; **alarm clock** *n* sveglia; **alarmed** *adj* (*person*) allarmato(-a); (*house, car etc*) dotato(-a) di allarme; **alarming** *adj* allarmante, preoccupante

Albania [æl'beɪnɪə] *n* Albania

albeit [ɔːl'biːɪt] *conj* sebbene + *sub*, benché + *sub*

album ['ælbəm] *n* album *m inv*

alcohol ['ælkəhɔl] *n* alcool *m*; **alcohol-free** *adj* analcolico(-a); **alcoholic** [-'hɔlɪk] *adj* alcolico(-a) ▷ *n* alcolizzato(-a)

alcove ['ælkəʊv] *n* alcova

ale [eɪl] *n* birra

alert [ə'ləːt] *adj* vigile ▷ *n* allarme *m* ▷ *vt* avvertire; mettere in guardia; **on the ~** all'erta

algebra ['ældʒɪbrə] *n* algebra

Algeria [æl'dʒɪərɪə] *n* Algeria

alias ['eɪlɪəs] *adv* alias ▷ *n* pseudonimo, falso nome *m*

alibi ['ælɪbaɪ] *n* alibi *m inv*

alien ['eɪlɪən] *n* straniero(-a); (*extraterrestrial*) alieno(-a) ▷ *adj* **~ (to)** estraneo(-a) (a); **alienate** *vt* alienare

alight [ə'laɪt] *adj* acceso(-a) ▷ *vi* scendere; (*bird*) posarsi

align [ə'laɪn] *vt* allineare

alike [ə'laɪk] *adj* simile ▷ *adv* sia … sia; **to look ~** assomigliarsi

alive [ə'laɪv] *adj* vivo(-a); (*lively*) vivace

KEYWORD

all [ɔːl] *adj* tutto(-a); **all day** tutto il giorno; **all night** tutta la notte; **all men** tutti gli uomini; **all five came** sono venuti tutti e cinque; **all the books** tutti i libri; **all the food** tutto

il cibo; **all the time** sempre; tutto il tempo; **all his life** tutta la vita

▷ *pron* **1** tutto(-a); **I ate it all, I ate all of it** l'ho mangiato tutto; **all of us went** tutti noi siamo andati; **all of the boys went** tutti i ragazzi sono andati

2 (*in phrases*): **above all** soprattutto; **after all** dopotutto; **at all: not at all** (*in answer to question*) niente affatto; (*in answer to thanks*) prego!, di niente!, s'immagini!; **I'm not at all tired** non sono affatto stanco(-a); **anything at all will do** andrà bene qualsiasi cosa; **all in all** tutto sommato

▷ *adv* **all alone** tutto(-a) solo(-a); **it's not as hard as all that** non è poi così difficile; **all the more/the better** tanto più/meglio; **all but** quasi; **the score is two all** il punteggio è di due a due

Allah ['ælə] *n* Allah *m*

allegation [ælɪ'geɪʃən] *n* asserzione *f*

alleged [ə'lɛdʒd] *adj* presunto(-a); **allegedly** [ə'lɛdʒɪdlɪ] *adv* secondo quanto si asserisce

allegiance [ə'liːdʒəns] *n* fedeltà

allergic [ə'ləːdʒɪk] *adj* **~ to** allergico(-a) a; **I'm ~ to penicillin** sono allergico alla penicillina

allergy ['ælədʒɪ] *n* allergia

alleviate [ə'liːvɪeɪt] *vt* sollevare

alley ['ælɪ] *n* vicolo

alliance [ə'laɪəns] *n* alleanza

allied ['ælaɪd] *adj* alleato(-a)

alligator ['ælɪgeɪtəʳ] *n* alligatore *m*

all-in ['ɔːlɪn] *adj* (BRIT: *also adv: charge*) tutto compreso

allocate ['æləkeɪt] *vt* assegnare

allot [ə'lɔt] *vt* assegnare

all-out ['ɔːlaut] *adj* (*effort etc*) totale ▷ *adv* **to go all out for** mettercela tutta per

allow [ə'lau] *vt* (*practice, behaviour*) permettere; (*sum to spend etc*) accordare; (*sum, time estimated*) dare; (*concede*): **to ~ that** ammettere che;

to ~ **sb to do** permettere a qn di fare; **he is ~ed to** lo può fare; **allow for** vt fus tener conto di; **allowance** n (money received) assegno; indennità f inv; (Tax) detrazione f di imposta; **to make allowances for** tener conto di

all right adv (feel, work) bene; (as answer) va bene

ally ['ælaɪ] n alleato

almighty [ɔːl'maɪtɪ] adj onnipotente; (row etc) colossale

almond ['ɑːmənd] n mandorla

almost ['ɔːlməʊst] adv quasi

alone [ə'ləʊn] adj, adv solo(-a); **to leave sb ~** lasciare qn in pace; **to leave sth ~** lasciare stare qc; **let ~ ...** figuriamoci poi ..., tanto meno ...

along [ə'lɒŋ] prep lungo ▷ adv **is he coming ~?** viene con noi?; **he was limping ~** veniva zoppicando; **~ with** insieme con; **all ~** (all the time) sempre, fin dall'inizio; **alongside** prep accanto a; lungo ▷ adv accanto

aloof [ə'luːf] adj distaccato(-a) ▷ adv **to stand ~** tenersi a distanza or in disparte

aloud [ə'laʊd] adv ad alta voce

alphabet ['ælfəbɛt] n alfabeto

Alps [ælps] npl: **the ~** le Alpi

already [ɔːl'rɛdɪ] adv già

alright ['ɔːl'raɪt] (BRIT) adv = **all right**

also ['ɔːlsəʊ] adv anche

altar ['ɒltər] n altare m

alter ['ɒltər] vt, vi alterare; **alteration** [ɒltə'reɪʃən] n modificazione f, alterazione f; **alterations** (Sewing, Archit) modifiche fpl; **timetable subject to alteration** orario soggetto a variazioni

alternate [adj ɒl'tɜːnɪt, vb 'ɒltə:neɪt] adj alterno(-a); (US: plan etc) alternativo(-a) ▷ vi **to ~ (with)** alternarsi (a); **on ~ days** ogni due giorni

alternative [ɒl'tɜːnətɪv] adj alternativo(-a) ▷ n (choice) alternativa; **alternatively** adv

alternatively one could ... come alternativa si potrebbe ...

although [ɔːl'ðəʊ] conj benché + sub, sebbene + sub

altitude ['æltɪtjuːd] n altitudine f

altogether [ɔːltə'gɛðər] adv del tutto, completamente; (on the whole) tutto considerato; (in all) in tutto

aluminium [ælju'mɪnɪəm] (BRIT), **aluminum** [ə'luːmɪnəm] (US) n alluminio

always ['ɔːlweɪz] adv sempre

Alzheimer's (disease) ['æltshaɪməz-] n (malattia di) Alzheimer

am [æm] vb see **be**

amalgamate [ə'mælgəmeɪt] vt amalgamare ▷ vi amalgamarsi

amass [ə'mæs] vt ammassare

amateur ['æmətər] n dilettante m/f ▷ adj (Sport) dilettante

amaze [ə'meɪz] vt stupire; **amazed** adj sbalordito(-a); **to be amazed (at)** essere sbalordito (da); **amazement** n stupore m; **amazing** adj sorprendente, sbalorditivo(-a)

Amazon ['æməzən] n (Mythology) Amazzone f; (river): **the ~** il Rio delle Amazzoni ▷ cpd (basin, jungle) amazzonico(-a)

ambassador [æm'bæsədər] n ambasciatore(-trice)

amber ['æmbər] n ambra; **at ~** (BRIT Aut) giallo

ambiguous [æm'bɪgjuəs] adj ambiguo(-a)

ambition [æm'bɪʃən] n ambizione f; **ambitious** [æm'bɪʃəs] adj ambizioso(-a)

ambulance ['æmbjuləns] n ambulanza; **call an ~!** chiamate un'ambulanza!

ambush ['æmbuʃ] n imboscata

amen ['ɑː'mɛn] excl così sia, amen

amend [ə'mɛnd] vt (law) emendare; (text) correggere; **to make ~s** fare ammenda; **amendment** n emendamento; correzione f

amenities [ə'mi:nɪtɪz] npl
attrezzature fpl ricreative e culturali

America [ə'mɛrɪkə] n America;
American adj, n americano(-a);
American football n (BRIT) football
m americano

amicable ['æmɪkəbl] adj amichevole

amid(st) [ə'mɪd(st)] prep in mezzo a

ammunition [æmju'nɪʃən] n
munizioni fpl

amnesty ['æmnɪstɪ] n amnistia; **to
grant an ~ to** concedere l'amnistia a,
amnistiare

among(st) [ə'mʌŋ(st)] prep fra, tra,
in mezzo a

amount [ə'maunt] n somma;
ammontare m; quantità f inv ▷ vi **to
~ to** (total) ammontare a; (be same as)
essere come

amp(ère) ['æmp(ɛəʳ)] n ampère m inv

ample ['æmpl] adj ampio(-a);
spazioso(-a); (enough): **this is ~** questo
è più che sufficiente

amplifier ['æmplɪfaɪəʳ] n
amplificatore m

amputate ['æmpjuteɪt] vt amputare

Amtrak ['æmtræk] (US) n società
ferroviaria americana

amuse [ə'mju:z] vt divertire;
amusement n divertimento;
amusement arcade n sala giochi;
amusement park n luna park m inv

amusing [ə'mju:zɪŋ] adj divertente

an [æn] indef art see **a**

anaemia [ə'ni:mɪə] (US **anemia**) n
anemia

anaemic [ə'ni:mɪk] (US **anemic**) adj
anemico(-a)

anaesthetic [æmɪs'θɛtɪk] (US
anesthetic) adj anestetico(-a) ▷ n
anestetico

analog(ue) ['ænəlɔg] adj (watch,
computer) analogico(-a)

analogy [ə'nælədʒɪ] n analogia; **to
draw an ~ between** fare un'analogia
tra

analyse ['ænəlaɪz] (US **analyze**) vt
analizzare; **analysis** [ə'næləsɪs] (pl
analyses) n analisi f inv; **analyst**
['ænəlɪst] n (Pol etc) analista m/f; (US)
(psic)analista m/f

analyze ['ænəlaɪz] (US) vt = **analyse**

anarchy ['ænəkɪ] n anarchia

anatomy [ə'nætəmɪ] n anatomia

ancestor ['ænsɪstəʳ] n antenato(-a)

anchor ['æŋkəʳ] n ancora ▷ vi (also:
to drop ~) gettare l'ancora ▷ vt
ancorare; **to weigh ~** salpare or levare
l'ancora

anchovy ['æntʃəvɪ] n acciuga

ancient ['eɪnʃənt] adj antico(-a);
(person, car) vecchissimo(-a)

and [ænd] conj e; (often ed before vowel):
~ so on e così via; **try ~ come** cerca
di venire; **he talked ~ talked** non
la finiva di parlare; **better ~ better**
sempre meglio

Andes ['ændi:z] npl **the ~** le Ande

anemia etc [ə'ni:mɪə] (US) = **anaemia**
etc

anesthetic [æmɪs'θɛtɪk] (US) adj, n
= **anaesthetic**

angel ['eɪndʒəl] n angelo

anger ['æŋgəʳ] n rabbia

angina [æn'dʒaɪnə] n angina pectoris

angle ['æŋgl] n angolo; **from their ~**
dal loro punto di vista

angler ['æŋgləʳ] n pescatore m con
la lenza

Anglican ['æŋglɪkən] adj, n
anglicano(-a)

angling ['æŋglɪŋ] n pesca con la
lenza

angrily ['æŋgrɪlɪ] adv con rabbia

angry ['æŋgrɪ] adj arrabbiato(-a),
furioso(-a); (wound) infiammato(-a);
to be ~ with sb/at sth essere in
collera con qn/per qc; **to get ~**
arrabbiarsi; **to make sb ~** fare
arrabbiare qn

anguish ['æŋgwɪʃ] n angoscia

animal ['ænɪməl] adj animale ▷ n
animale m

animated ['ænɪmeɪtɪd] *adj*
animato(-a)

animation [ænɪ'meɪʃən] *n*
animazione *f*

aniseed ['ænɪsi:d] *n* semi *mpl* di anice

ankle ['æŋkl] *n* caviglia

annex [*n* 'æneks, *vb* ə'neks] *n* (BRIT:
also: **~e**) (edificio) annesso ▷ *vt*
annettere

anniversary [ænɪ'və:sərɪ] *n*
anniversario

announce [ə'naʊns] *vt* annunciare;
announcement *n* annuncio; (*letter,
card*) partecipazione *f*; **announcer**
n (*Radio, TV: between programmes*)
annunciatore(-trice); (: *in a programme*)
presentatore(-trice)

annoy [ə'nɔɪ] *vt* dare fastidio a; **don't
get ~ed!** non irritarti!; **annoying** *adj*
noioso(-a)

annual ['ænjʊəl] *adj* annuale ▷ *n*
(*Bot*) pianta annua; (*book*) annuario;
annually *adv* annualmente

annum ['ænəm] *n see* **per**

anonymous [ə'nɒnɪməs] *adj*
anonimo(-a)

anorak ['ænəræk] *n* giacca a vento

anorexia [ænə'reksɪə] *n* (*Med: also:* **~
nervosa**) anoressia

anorexic [ænə'reksɪk] *adj, n*
anoressico(-a)

another [ə'nʌðəʳ] *adj* **~ book** (*one
more*) un altro libro, ancora un libro;
(*a different one*) un altro libro ▷ *pron*
un altro(un'altra), ancora uno(-a); *see
also* **one**

answer ['ɑ:nsəʳ] *n* risposta; soluzione
f ▷ *vi* rispondere ▷ *vt* (*reply to*)
rispondere a; (*problem*) risolvere;
(*prayer*) esaudire; **in ~ to your letter**
in risposta alla sua lettera; **to ~ the
phone** rispondere (al telefono); **to ~
the bell** rispondere al campanello; **to
~ the door** aprire la porta; **answer
back** *vi* ribattere; **answerphone** *n*
(*esp* BRIT) segreteria telefonica

ant [ænt] *n* formica

Antarctic [ænt'ɑ:ktɪk] *n* **the ~**
l'Antartide *f*

antelope ['æntɪləʊp] *n* antilope *f*

antenatal ['æntɪ'neɪtl] *adj* prenatale

antenna [æn'tenə, -ni:] (*pl*
antennae) *n* antenna

anthem ['ænθəm] *n* **national ~** inno
nazionale

anthology [æn'θɒlədʒɪ] *n* antologia

anthrax ['ænθræks] *n* antrace *m*

anthropology [ænθrə'pɒlədʒɪ] *n*
antropologia

anti [æntɪ] *prefix* anti; **antibiotic**
['æntɪbaɪ'ɒtɪk] *n* antibiotico;
antibody ['æntɪbɒdɪ] *n* anticorpo

anticipate [æn'tɪsɪpeɪt] *vt*
prevedere; pregustare; (*wishes,
request*) prevenire; **anticipation**
[æntɪsɪ'peɪʃən] *n* anticipazione *f*;
(*expectation*) aspettative *fpl*

anticlimax ['æntɪ'klaɪmæks] *n* **it
was an ~** fu una completa delusione

anticlockwise ['æntɪ'klɒkwaɪz] *adj,
adv* in senso antiorario

antics ['æntɪks] *npl* buffonerie *fpl*

anti: **antidote** ['æntɪdəʊt] *n*
antidoto; **antifreeze** ['æntɪ'fri:z]
n anticongelante *m*; **anti-
globalization** [æntɪgləʊbəlaɪ'zeɪʃən]
n antiglobalizzazione *f*;
antihistamine [æntɪ'hɪstəmɪn]
n antistaminico; **antiperspirant**
['æntɪ'pə:spərənt] *adj*
antitraspirante

antique [æn'ti:k] *n* antichità *f inv*
▷ *adj* antico(-a); **antique shop** *n*
negozio d'antichità

antiseptic [æntɪ'septɪk] *n*
antisettico

antisocial ['æntɪ'səʊʃəl] *adj* asociale

antivirus [æntɪ'vaɪərəs] *adj* antivirus
inv; **~ program** antivirus *m inv*

antlers ['æntləz] *npl* palchi *mpl*

anxiety [æŋ'zaɪətɪ] *n* ansia;
(*keenness*) smania di fare

anxious ['æŋkʃəs] *adj* ansioso(-a),
inquieto(-a); (*worrying*) angosciante;

(keen): **~ to do/that** impaziente di fare/che + *sub*

O **KEYWORD**

any [ˈɛnɪ] *adj* **1** (*in questions etc*): **have you any butter?** hai del burro?, hai un po' di burro?; **have you any children?** hai bambini?; **if there are any tickets left** se ci sono ancora (dei) biglietti, se c'è ancora qualche biglietto
2 (*with negative*): **I haven't any money/books** non ho soldi/libri
3 (*no matter which*) qualsiasi, qualunque; **choose any book you like** scegli un libro qualsiasi
4 (*in phrases*): **in any case** in ogni caso; **any day now** da un giorno all'altro; **at any moment** in qualsiasi momento, da un momento all'altro; **at any rate** ad ogni modo
▷ *pron* **1** (*in questions, with negative*): **have you got any?** ne hai?; **can any of you sing?** qualcuno di voi sa cantare?; **I haven't any (of them)** non ne ho
2 (*no matter which one(s)*): **take any of those books (you like)** prendi uno qualsiasi di quei libri
▷ *adv* **1** (*in questions etc*): **do you want any more soup/sandwiches?** vuoi ancora un po' di minestra/degli altri panini?; **are you feeling any better?** ti senti meglio?
2 (*with negative*): **I can't hear him any more** non lo sento più; **don't wait any longer** non aspettare più

any: **anybody** [ˈɛnɪbɔdɪ] *pron* (*in questions etc*) qualcuno, nessuno; (*with negative*) nessuno; (*no matter who*) chiunque; **can you see anybody?** vedi qualcuno *or* nessuno?; **if anybody should phone ...** se telefona qualcuno ...; **I can't see anybody** non vedo nessuno; **anybody could do it** chiunque

potrebbe farlo; **anyhow** [ˈɛnɪhau] *adv* (*at any rate*) ad ogni modo, comunque; (*haphazard*): **do it anyhow you like** fallo come ti pare; **I shall go anyhow** ci andrò lo stesso *or* comunque; **she leaves things just anyhow** lascia tutto come capita; **anyone** [ˈɛnɪwʌn] *pron* = **anybody**; **anything** [ˈɛnɪθɪŋ] *pron* (*in question etc*) qualcosa, niente; (*with negative*) niente; (*no matter what*): **you can say anything you like** puoi dire quello che ti pare; **can you see anything?** vedi niente *or* qualcosa?; **if anything happens to me ...** se mi dovesse succedere qualcosa ...; **I can't see anything** non vedo niente; **anything will do** va bene qualsiasi cosa *or* tutto; **anytime** *adv* in qualunque momento; quando vuole; **anyway** [ˈɛnɪweɪ] *adv* (*at any rate*) ad ogni modo, comunque; (*besides*) ad ogni modo; **anywhere** [ˈɛnɪwɛəʳ] *adv* (*in questions etc*) da qualche parte; (*with negative*) da nessuna parte; (*no matter where*) da qualsiasi *or* qualunque parte, dovunque; **can you see him anywhere?** lo vedi da qualche parte?; **I can't see him anywhere** non lo vedo da nessuna parte; **anywhere in the world** dovunque nel mondo

apart [əˈpɑːt] *adv* (*to one side*) a parte; (*separately*) separatamente; **with one's legs ~** con le gambe divaricate; **10 miles ~** a 10 miglia di distanza (l'uno dall'altro); **to take ~** smontare; **~ from** a parte, eccetto

apartment [əˈpɑːtmənt] (*US*) *n* appartamento; (*room*) locale *m*; **apartment building** (*US*) *n* stabile *m*, caseggiato

apathy [ˈæpəθɪ] *n* apatia

ape [eɪp] *n* scimmia ▷ *vt* scimmiottare

aperitif [əˈpɛrɪtiːf] *n* aperitivo

aperture [ˈæpətʃuəʳ] *n* apertura

APEX *n abbr* (= *advance purchase*

excursion) APEX *m inv*

apologize [əˈpɒlədʒaɪz] *vi* **to ~ (for sth to sb)** scusarsi (di qc a qn), chiedere scusa (a qn per qc)

apology [əˈpɒlədʒɪ] *n* scuse *fpl*

apostrophe [əˈpɒstrəfɪ] *n (sign)* apostrofo

appal [əˈpɔːl] *(US* **appall**) *vt* scioccare; **appalling** *adj* spaventoso(-a)

apparatus [æpəˈreɪtəs] *n* apparato; *(in gymnasium)* attrezzatura

apparent [əˈpærənt] *adj* evidente; **apparently** *adv* evidentemente

appeal [əˈpiːl] *vi (Law)* appellarsi alla legge ▷ *n (Law)* appello; *(request)* richiesta; *(charm)* attrattiva; **to ~ for** chiedere (con insistenza); **to ~ to** *(person)* appellarsi a; *(thing)* piacere a; **it doesn't ~ to me** mi dice poco; **appealing** *adj (nice)* attraente

appear [əˈpɪəʳ] *vi* apparire; *(Law)* comparire; *(publication)* essere pubblicato(-a); *(seem)* sembrare; **it would ~ that** sembra che; **appearance** *n* apparizione *f*; apparenza; *(look, aspect)* aspetto

appendicitis [əpɛndɪˈsaɪtɪs] *n* appendicite *f*

appendix [əˈpɛndɪks] *(pl* **appendices**) *n* appendice *f*

appetite [ˈæpɪtaɪt] *n* appetito

appetizer [ˈæpɪtaɪzəʳ] *n* stuzzichino

applaud [əˈplɔːd] *vt, vi* applaudire

applause [əˈplɔːz] *n* applauso

apple [ˈæpl] *n* mela; **apple pie** *n* torta di mele

appliance [əˈplaɪəns] *n* apparecchio

applicable [əˈplɪkəbl] *adj* applicabile; **to be ~ to** essere valido per; **the law is ~ from January** la legge entrerà in vigore in gennaio

applicant [ˈæplɪkənt] *n* candidato(-a)

application [æplɪˈkeɪʃən] *n* applicazione *f*; *(for a job, a grant etc)* domanda; **application form** *n* modulo per la domanda

apply [əˈplaɪ] *vt* **to ~ (to)** *(paint, ointment)* dare (a); *(theory, technique)* applicare (a) ▷ *vi* **to ~ to** *(ask)* rivolgersi a; *(be suitable for, relevant to)* riguardare, riferirsi a; **to ~ (for)** *(permit, grant, job)* fare domanda (per); **to ~ o.s. to** dedicarsi a

appoint [əˈpɔɪnt] *vt* nominare; **appointment** *n* nomina; *(arrangement to meet)* appuntamento; **I have an appointment (with) ...** ho un appuntamento (con) ...; **I'd like to make an appointment (with)** vorrei prendere un appuntamento (con)

appraisal [əˈpreɪzl] *n* valutazione *f*

appreciate [əˈpriːʃɪeɪt] *vt (like)* apprezzare; *(be grateful for)* essere riconoscente di; *(be aware of)* rendersi conto di ▷ *vi (Finance)* aumentare; **I'd ~ your help** ti sono grato per l'aiuto; **appreciation** [əpriːʃɪˈeɪʃən] *n* apprezzamento; *(Finance)* aumento del valore

apprehension [æprɪˈhɛnʃən] *n (fear)* inquietudine *f*

apprehensive [æprɪˈhɛnsɪv] *adj* apprensivo(-a)

apprentice [əˈprɛntɪs] *n* apprendista *m/f*

approach [əˈprəʊtʃ] *vi* avvicinarsi ▷ *vt (come near)* avvicinarsi a; *(ask, apply to)* rivolgersi a; *(subject, passer-by)* avvicinare ▷ *n* approccio; accesso; *(to problem)* modo di affrontare

appropriate [*adj* əˈprəʊprɪɪt, *vb* əˈprəʊprɪeɪt] *adj* appropriato(-a), adatto(-a) ▷ *vt (take)* appropriarsi

approval [əˈpruːvəl] *n* approvazione *f*; **on ~** *(Comm)* in prova, in esame

approve [əˈpruːv] *vt, vi* approvare; **approve of** *vt fus* approvare

approximate [əˈprɒksɪmɪt] *adj* approssimativo(-a); **approximately** *adv* circa

Apr. *abbr (= April)* apr.

apricot [ˈeɪprɪkɒt] *n* albicocca

April [ˈeɪprəl] *n* aprile *m*; **~ fool!** pesce

d'aprile!; **April Fools' Day** n vedi nota nel riquadro

● **APRIL FOOLS' DAY**

● **April Fool's Day** è il primo aprile,
● il giorno degli scherzi e delle burle.
● Il nome deriva dal fatto che, se
● una persona cade nella trappola
● che gli è stata tesa, fa la figura
● del "fool", cioè dello sciocco.
● Tradizionalmente, gli scherzi
● vengono fatti entro mezzogiorno.

apron ['eɪprən] n grembiule m
apt [æpt] adj (suitable) adatto(-a); (able) capace; (likely): **to be ~ to do** avere tendenza a fare
aquarium [ə'kwɛərɪəm] n acquario
Aquarius [ə'kwɛərɪəs] n Acquario
Arab ['ærəb] adj, n arabo(-a)
Arabia [ə'reɪbɪə] n Arabia; **Arabian** [ə'reɪbɪən] adj arabo(-a); **Arabic** ['ærəbɪk] adj arabico(-a), arabo(-a) ▷ n arabo; **Arabic numerals** n numeri mpl arabi, numerazione f araba
arbitrary ['ɑːbɪtrərɪ] adj arbitrario(-a)
arbitration [ɑːbɪ'treɪʃən] n (Law) arbitrato; (Industry) arbitraggio
arc [ɑːk] n arco
arcade [ɑː'keɪd] n portico; (passage with shops) galleria
arch [ɑːtʃ] n arco; (of foot) arco plantare ▷ vt inarcare
archaeology [ɑːkɪ'ɔlədʒɪ] (US **archeology**) n archeologia
archbishop [ɑːtʃ'bɪʃəp] n arcivescovo
archeology etc [ɑːkɪ'ɔlədʒɪ] (US) = **archaeology** etc
architect ['ɑːkɪtɛkt] n architetto; **architectural** [ɑːkɪ'tɛktʃərəl] adj architettonico(-a); **architecture** ['ɑːkɪtɛktʃər] n architettura
archive ['ɑːkaɪv] n (often pl: also Comput) archivio
Arctic ['ɑːktɪk] adj artico(-a) ▷ n: **the**

~ l'Artico
are [ɑːr] vb see **be**
area ['ɛərɪə] n (Geom) area; (zone) zona; (: smaller) settore m; **area code** (US) n (Tel) prefisso
arena [ə'riːnə] n arena
aren't [ɑːnt] = **are not**
Argentina [ɑːdʒən'tiːnə] n Argentina; **Argentinian** [-'tɪnɪən] adj, n argentino(-a)
arguably ['ɑːgjuəblɪ] adv **it is ~ ...** si può sostenere che sia ...
argue ['ɑːgjuː] vi (quarrel) litigare; (reason) ragionare; **to ~ that** sostenere che
argument ['ɑːgjumənt] n (reasons) argomento; (quarrel) lite f
Aries ['ɛərɪz] n Ariete m
arise [ə'raɪz] (pt **arose**, pp **arisen**) vi (opportunity, problem) presentarsi
arithmetic [ə'rɪθmətɪk] n aritmetica
arm [ɑːm] n braccio ▷ vt armare; **arms** npl (weapons) armi fpl; **~ in ~** a braccetto; **armchair** n poltrona
armed [ɑːmd] adj armato(-a); **armed robbery** n rapina a mano armata
armour ['ɑːmər] (US **armor**) n armatura; (Mil: tanks) mezzi mpl blindati
armpit ['ɑːmpɪt] n ascella
armrest ['ɑːmrɛst] n bracciolo
army ['ɑːmɪ] n esercito
A road n strada statale
aroma [ə'rəumə] n aroma; **aromatherapy** n aromaterapia
arose [ə'rəuz] pt of **arise**
around [ə'raund] adv attorno, intorno ▷ prep intorno a; (fig: about): **~ £5/3 o'clock** circa 5 sterline/le 3; **is he ~?** è in giro?
arouse [ə'rauz] vt (sleeper) svegliare; (curiosity, passions) suscitare
arrange [ə'reɪndʒ] vt sistemare; (programme) preparare; **to ~ to do sth** mettersi d'accordo per fare qc; **arrangement** n sistemazione f; (agreement) accordo; **arrangements**

npl (plans) progetti mpl, piani mpl
array [əˈreɪ] n ~ **of** fila di
arrears [əˈrɪəz] npl arretrati mpl; **to
be in ~ with one's rent** essere in
arretrato con l'affitto
arrest [əˈrɛst] vt arrestare; (sb's
attention) attirare ▷ n arresto; **under
~** in arresto
arrival [əˈraɪvəl] n arrivo; (person)
arrivato(-a); **a new ~** un nuovo
venuto; (baby) un neonato
arrive [əˈraɪv] vi arrivare; **what time
does the train from Rome ~?** a che
ora arriva il treno da Roma?; **arrive at**
vt fus arrivare a
arrogance [ˈærəgəns] n arroganza
arrogant [ˈærəgənt] adj arrogante
arrow [ˈærəʊ] n freccia
arse [ɑːs] (inf!) n culo (!)
arson [ˈɑːsn] n incendio doloso
art [ɑːt] n arte f; (craft) mestiere m; **art
college** n scuola di belle arti
artery [ˈɑːtərɪ] n arteria
art gallery n galleria d'arte
arthritis [ɑːˈθraɪtɪs] n artrite f
artichoke [ˈɑːtɪtʃəʊk] n carciofo;
Jerusalem ~ topinambur m inv
article [ˈɑːtɪkl] n articolo
articulate [adj ɑːˈtɪkjʊlɪt, vb
ɑːˈtɪkjʊleɪt] adj (person) che si esprime
forbitamente; (speech) articolato(-a)
▷ vi articolare
artificial [ɑːtɪˈfɪʃəl] adj artificiale
artist [ˈɑːtɪst] n artista m/f; **artistic**
[ɑːˈtɪstɪk] adj artistico(-a)
art school n scuola d'arte

◯ **KEYWORD**

as [æz] conj **1** (referring to time) mentre;
as the years went by col passare
degli anni; **he came in as I was
leaving** arrivò mentre stavo uscendo;
as from tomorrow da domani
2 (in comparisons): **as big as** grande
come; **twice as big as** due volte più
grande di; **as much/many as** tanto

quanto/tanti quanti; **as soon as
possible** prima possibile
3 (since, because) dal momento che,
siccome
4 (referring to manner, way) come; **do as
you wish** fa' come vuoi; **as she said**
come ha detto lei
5 (concerning): **as for** or **to that** per
quanto riguarda or quanto a quello
6: **as if** or **as though** come se; **he
looked as if he was ill** sembrava
stare male; see also **long**; **such**; **well**
▷ prep **he works as a driver** fa
l'autista; **as chairman of the
company he ...** come presidente
della compagnia lui ...; **he gave me it
as a present** me lo ha regalato

a.s.a.p. abbr = **as soon as possible**
asbestos [æzˈbɛstəs] n asbesto,
amianto
ASBO n abbr (BRIT: = Antisocial
Behaviour Order) provvedimento
restrittivo per comportamento
antisociale
ascent [əˈsɛnt] n salita
ash [æʃ] n (dust) cenere f; (wood, tree)
frassino
ashamed [əˈʃeɪmd] adj
vergognoso(-a); **to be ~ of**
vergognarsi di
ashore [əˈʃɔːʳ] adv a terra
ashtray [ˈæʃtreɪ] n portacenere m
Ash Wednesday n mercoledì m inv
delle Ceneri
Asia [ˈeɪʃə] n Asia; **Asian** adj, n
asiatico(-a)
aside [əˈsaɪd] adv da parte ▷ n a
parte m
ask [ɑːsk] vt (question) domandare;
(invite) invitare; **to ~ sb sth/sb to do
sth** chiedere qc a qn/a qn di fare qc; **to
~ sb about sth** chiedere a qn di qc; **to
~ (sb) a question** fare una domanda
(a qn); **to ~ sb out to dinner** invitare
qn a mangiare fuori; **ask for** vt fus
chiedere; (trouble etc) cercare

asleep [ə'sli:p] *adj* addormentato(-a);
to be ~ dormire; **to fall ~**
addormentarsi

AS level *n abbr* (= *Advanced Subsidiary level*) *prima parte del diploma di studi superiori chiamato "A level"*

asparagus [əs'pærəgəs] *n* asparagi *mpl*

aspect ['æspɛkt] *n* aspetto

aspirations [æspə'reɪʃənz] *npl*
aspirazioni *fpl*

aspire [əs'paɪə'] *vi*: **to ~ to** aspirare a

aspirin ['æsprɪn] *n* aspirina

ass [æs] *n* asino; (*inf*) scemo(-a); (*us: inf!*) culo (*!*)

assassin [ə'sæsɪn] *n* assassino;
assassinate [ə'sæsɪneɪt] *vt*
assassinare

assault [ə'sɔ:lt] *n* (*Mil*) assalto; (*gen: attack*) aggressione *f* ▷ *vt* assaltare;
aggredire; (*sexually*) violentare

assemble [ə'sɛmbl] *vt* riunire; (*Tech*)
montare ▷ *vi* riunirsi

assembly [ə'sɛmblɪ] *n* (*meeting*)
assemblea; (*construction*) montaggio

assert [ə'sə:t] *vt* asserire; (*insist on*)
far valere; **assertion** [ə'sə:ʃən] *n*
asserzione *f*

assess [ə'sɛs] *vt* valutare;
assessment *n* valutazione *f*

asset ['æsɛt] *n* vantaggio; **assets** *npl*
(*Finance: of individual*) beni *mpl*; (: *of company*) attivo

assign [ə'saɪn] *vt*: **to ~ (to)** (*task*)
assegnare (a); (*resources*) riservare
(a); (*cause, meaning*) attribuire (a); **to
~ a date to sth** fissare la data di qc;
assignment *n* compito

assist [ə'sɪst] *vt* assistere, aiutare;
assistance *n* assistenza, aiuto;
assistant *n* assistente *m/f*; (*BRIT: also*: **shop assistant**) commesso(-a)

associate [*adj, n* ə'səuʃɪɪt, *vb*
ə'səuʃɪeɪt] *adj* associato(-a);
(*member*) aggiunto(-a) ▷ *n* collega
m/f ▷ *vt* associare ▷ *vi* **to ~ with sb**
frequentare qn

association [əsəusɪ'eɪʃən] *n*
associazione *f*

assorted [ə'sɔ:tɪd] *adj* assortito(-a)

assortment [ə'sɔ:tmənt] *n*
assortimento

assume [ə'sju:m] *vt* supporre;
(*responsibilities etc*) assumere;
(*attitude, name*) prendere

assumption [ə'sʌmpʃən] *n*
supposizione *f*, ipotesi *f inv*; (*of power*)
assunzione *f*

assurance [ə'ʃuərəns] *n*
assicurazione *f*; (*self-confidence*) fiducia
in se stesso

assure [ə'ʃuə'] *vt* assicurare

asterisk ['æstərɪsk] *n* asterisco

asthma ['æsmə] *n* asma

astonish [ə'stɔnɪʃ] *vt* stupire;
astonished *adj* stupito(-a),
sorpreso(-a); **to be astonished (at)**
essere stupito(-a) (da); **astonishing**
adj sorprendente, stupefacente; **I find
it astonishing that …** mi stupisce
che …; **astonishment** *n* stupore *m*

astound [ə'staund] *vt* sbalordire

astray [ə'streɪ] *adv* **to go ~** smarrirsi;
to lead ~ portare sulla cattiva strada

astrology [əs'trɔlədʒɪ] *n* astrologia

astronaut ['æstrənɔ:t] *n* astronauta
m/f

astronomer [əs'trɔnəmə'] *n*
astronomo(-a)

astronomical [æstrə'nɔmɪkl] *adj*
astronomico(-a)

astronomy [əs'trɔnəmɪ] *n*
astronomia

astute [əs'tju:t] *adj* astuto(-a)

asylum [ə'saɪləm] *n* (*politico*) asilo;
(*per malati*) manicomio

 KEYWORD

at [æt] *prep* **1** (*referring to position,
direction*) a; **at the top** in cima; **at
the desk** al banco, alla scrivania; **at
home/school** a casa/scuola; **at the
baker's** dal panettiere; **to look at**

sth guardare qc; **to throw sth at sb**
lanciare qc a qn
2 (*referring to time*) a; **at 4 o'clock** alle
4; **at night** di notte; **at Christmas** a
Natale; **at times** a volte
3 (*referring to rates, speed etc*) a; **at £1 a
kilo** a 1 sterlina al chilo; **two at a time**
due alla volta, due per volta; **at 50
km/h** a 50 km/h
4 (*referring to manner*): **at a stroke** d'un
solo colpo; **at peace** in pace
5 (*referring to activity*): **to be at work**
essere al lavoro; **to play at cowboys**
giocare ai cowboy; **to be good at
sth/doing sth** essere bravo in qc/fare
qc
6 (*referring to cause*): **shocked/
surprised/annoyed at sth** colpito
da/sorpreso da/arrabbiato per qc;
I went at his suggestion ci sono
andato dietro suo consiglio
7 (*Comput: symbol*) chiocciola
ate [eɪt] *pt of* **eat**
atheist ['eɪθɪɪst] *n* ateo(-a)
Athens ['æθɪnz] *n* Atene *f*
athlete ['æθliːt] *n* atleta *m/f*
athletic [æθ'letɪk] *adj* atletico(-a);
athletics *n* atletica
Atlantic [ət'læntɪk] *adj* atlantico(-a)
▷ *n*: **the ~ (Ocean)** l'Atlantico,
l'Oceano Atlantico
atlas ['ætləs] *n* atlante *m*
A.T.M. *n abbr* (= *automated telling
machine*) cassa automatica prelievi,
sportello automatico
atmosphere ['ætməsfɪə^r] *n*
atmosfera
atom ['ætəm] *n* atomo; **atomic**
[ə'tɒmɪk] *adj* atomico(-a); **atom(ic)
bomb** *n* bomba atomica
A to Z® *n* (*map*) stradario
atrocity [ə'trɒsɪtɪ] *n* atrocità *f inv*
attach [ə'tætʃ] *vt* attaccare;
(*document, letter*) allegare; (*importance
etc*) attribuire; **to be ~ed to sb/sth** (*to
like*) essere affezionato(-a) a qn/qc;

attachment [ə'tætʃmənt] *n* (*tool*)
accessorio; (*love*): **attachment (to)**
affetto (per)
attack [ə'tæk] *vt* attaccare; (*person*)
aggredire; (*task etc*) iniziare; (*problem*)
affrontare ▷ *n* attacco; **heart ~**
infarto; **attacker** *n* aggressore *m*
attain [ə'teɪn] *vt* (*also:* **to ~ to**)
arrivare a, raggiungere
attempt [ə'tɛmpt] *n* tentativo ▷ *vt*
tentare; **to make an ~ on sb's life**
attentare alla vita di qn
attend [ə'tɛnd] *vt* frequentare;
(*meeting, talk*) andare a; (*patient*)
assistere; **attend to** *vt fus* (*needs,
affairs etc*) prendersi cura di; (*customer*)
occuparsi di; **attendance** *n* (*being
present*) presenza; (*people present*)
gente *f* presente; **attendant** *n*
custode *m/f*; persona di servizio ▷ *adj*
concomitante

> Be careful not to translate
> *attend* by the Italian word
> *attendere*.

attention [ə'tɛnʃən] *n* attenzione
f ▷ *excl* (*Mil*) attenti!; **for the ~ of**
(*Admin*) per l'attenzione di
attic ['ætɪk] *n* soffitta
attitude ['ætɪtjuːd] *n* atteggiamento;
posa
attorney [ə'təːnɪ] *n* (*lawyer*) avvocato;
(*having proxy*) mandatario; **Attorney
General** *n* (BRIT) Procuratore *m*
Generale; (US) Ministro della Giustizia
attract [ə'trækt] *vt* attirare;
attraction [ə'trækʃən] *n* (*gen pl:
pleasant things*) attrattiva; (*Physics, fig:
towards sth*) attrazione *f*; **attractive**
adj attraente
attribute [*n* 'ætrɪbjuːt, *vb* ə'trɪbjuːt]
n attributo ▷ *vt* **to ~ sth to** attribuire
qc a
aubergine ['əubəʒiːn] *n* melanzana
auburn ['ɔːbən] *adj* tizianesco(-a)
auction ['ɔːkʃən] *n* (*also:* **sale by ~**)
asta ▷ *vt* (*also:* **to sell by ~**) vendere
all'asta; (*also:* **to put up for ~**) mettere

all'asta

audible ['ɔ:dɪbl] *adj* udibile

audience ['ɔ:dɪəns] *n* (*people*) pubblico; spettatori *mpl*; ascoltatori *mpl*; (*interview*) udienza

audit ['ɔ:dɪt] *vt* rivedere, verificare

audition [ɔ:'dɪʃən] *n* audizione *f*

auditor ['ɔ:dɪtəʳ] *n* revisore *m*

auditorium [ɔ:dɪ'tɔ:rɪəm] *n* sala, auditorio

Aug. *abbr* (= *August*) ago., ag.

August ['ɔ:gəst] *n* agosto

aunt [ɑ:nt] *n* zia; **auntie** *n* zietta; **aunty** *n* zietta

au pair ['əu'pɛəʳ] *n* (*also*: **~ girl**) (*ragazza f*) alla pari *inv*

aura ['ɔ:rə] *n* aura

austerity [ɔs'tɛrɪtɪ] *n* austerità *f inv*

Australia [ɔs'treɪlɪə] *n* Australia; **Australian** *adj, n* australiano(-a)

Austria ['ɔstrɪə] *n* Austria; **Austrian** *adj, n* austriaco(-a)

authentic [ɔ:'θɛntɪk] *adj* autentico(-a)

author ['ɔ:θəʳ] *n* autore(-trice)

authority [ɔ:'θɔrɪtɪ] *n* autorità *f inv*; (*permission*) autorizzazione *f*; **the authorities** *npl* (*government etc*) le autorità

authorize ['ɔ:θəraɪz] *vt* autorizzare

auto ['ɔ:təu] (*US*) *n* auto *f inv*; **autobiography** [ɔ:təbaɪ'ɔgrəfɪ] *n* autobiografia; **autograph** ['ɔ:təgrɑ:f] *n* autografo ▷ *vt* firmare; **automatic** [ɔ:tə'mætɪk] *adj* automatico(-a) ▷ *n* (*gun*) arma automatica; (*washing machine*) lavatrice *f* automatica; (*car*) automobile *f* con cambio automatico; **automatically** *adv* automaticamente; **automobile** ['ɔ:təməbi:l] (*US*) *n* automobile *f*; **autonomous** [ɔ:'tɔnəməs] *adj* autonomo(-a); **autonomy** [ɔ:'tɔnəmɪ] *n* autonomia

autumn ['ɔ:təm] *n* autunno

auxiliary [ɔ:g'zɪlɪərɪ] *adj* ausiliario(-a) ▷ *n* ausiliare *m/f*

avail [ə'veɪl] *vt* **to ~ o.s. of** servirsi di; approfittarsi di ▷ *n* **to no ~** inutilmente

availability [əveɪlə'bɪlɪtɪ] *n* disponibilità

available [ə'veɪləbl] *adj* disponibile

avalanche ['ævəlɑ:nʃ] *n* valanga

Ave. *abbr* = **avenue**

avenue ['ævənju:] *n* viale *m*; (*fig*) strada, via

average ['ævərɪdʒ] *n* media ▷ *adj* medio(-a) ▷ *vt* (*a certain figure*) fare di or in media; **on ~** in media

avert [ə'və:t] *vt* evitare, prevenire; (*one's eyes*) distogliere

avid ['ævɪd] *adj* (*supporter etc*) accanito(-a)

avocado [ævə'kɑ:dəu] *n* (*BRIT: also*: **~ pear**) avocado *m inv*

avoid [ə'vɔɪd] *vt* evitare

await [ə'weɪt] *vt* aspettare

awake [ə'weɪk] (*pt* **awoke**, *pp* **awoken, awaked**) *adj* sveglio(-a) ▷ *vt* svegliare ▷ *vi* svegliarsi

award [ə'wɔ:d] *n* premio; (*Law*) risarcimento ▷ *vt* assegnare; (*Law: damages*) accordare

aware [ə'wɛəʳ] *adj* **~ of** (*conscious*) conscio(-a) di; (*informed*) informato(-a) di; **to become ~ of** accorgersi di; **awareness** *n* consapevolezza

away [ə'weɪ] *adj, adv* via; lontano(-a); **two kilometres ~** a due chilometri di distanza; **two hours ~ by car** a due ore di distanza in macchina; **the holiday was two weeks ~** mancavano due settimane alle vacanze; **he's ~ for a week** è andato via per una settimana; **to take ~** togliere; **he was working/pedalling** *etc* **~** (*la particella indica la continuità e l'energia dell'azione*) lavorava/pedalava *etc* più che poteva; **to fade/wither** *etc* **~** (*la particella rinforza l'idea della diminuzione*)

awe [ɔ:] *n* timore *m*; **awesome** *adj* imponente

awful ['ɔːfəl] *adj* terribile; **an ~ lot of** un mucchio di; **awfully** *adv* (*very*) terribilmente

awkward ['ɔːkwəd] *adj* (*clumsy*) goffo(-a); (*inconvenient*) scomodo(-a); (*embarrassing*) imbarazzante

awoke [ə'wəuk] *pt of* **awake**

awoken [ə'wəukn] *pp of* **awake**

axe [æks] (*us* **ax**) *n* scure *f* ▷ *vt* (*project etc*) abolire; (*jobs*) sopprimere

axle ['æksl] *n* (*also:* **~-tree**) asse *m*

ay(e) [aɪ] *excl* (*yes*) sì

azalea [ə'zeɪlɪə] *n* azalea

B [biː] *n* (*Mus*) si *m*

B.A. *n abbr* = **Bachelor of Arts**

baby ['beɪbɪ] *n* bambino(-a); **baby carriage** (*us*) *n* carrozzina; **baby-sit** *vi* fare il (*or* la) baby-sitter; **baby-sitter** *n* baby-sitter *m/f inv*; **baby wipe** *n* salvietta umidificata

bachelor ['bætʃələr] *n* scapolo; **B~ of Arts/Science** ≈ laureato(-a) in lettere/scienze

back [bæk] *n* (*of person, horse*) dorso, schiena; (*as opposed to front*) dietro; (*of hand*) dorso; (*of train*) coda; (*of chair*) schienale *m*; (*of page*) rovescio; (*of book*) retro; (*Football*) difensore *m* ▷ *vt* (*candidate*) appoggiare; (*horse: at races*) puntare su; (*car*) guidare a marcia indietro ▷ *vi* indietreggiare; (*car etc*) fare marcia indietro ▷ *cpd* posteriore, di dietro; (*Aut: seat, wheels*) posteriore ▷ *adv* (*not forward*) indietro; (*returned*): **he's ~** è tornato; **he ran ~** tornò indietro di corsa; (*restitution*): **throw the ball ~** ritira la palla; **can I**

have it ~? posso riaverlo?; (*again*): **he called ~** ha richiamato; **back down** *vi* fare marcia indietro; **back out** *vi* (*of promise*) tirarsi indietro; **back up** *vt* (*support*) appoggiare, sostenere; (*Comput*) fare una copia di riserva di; **backache** *n* mal *m* di schiena; **backbencher** (BRIT) *n* membro del Parlamento senza potere amministrativo; **backbone** *n* spina dorsale; **back door** *n* porta sul retro; **backfire** *vi* (*Aut*) dar ritorni di fiamma; (*plans*) fallire; **backgammon** *n* tavola reale; **background** *n* sfondo; (*of events*) background *m inv*; (*basic knowledge*) base *f*; (*experience*) esperienza; **family background** ambiente *m* familiare; **backing** *n* (*fig*) appoggio; **backlog** *n* **backlog of work** lavoro arretrato; **backpack** *n* zaino; **backpacker** *n* chi viaggia con zaino e sacco a pelo; **backslash** *n* backslash *m inv*, barra obliqua inversa; **backstage** *adv* nel retroscena; **backstroke** *n* nuoto sul dorso; **backup** *adj* (*train, plane*) supplementare; (*Comput*) di riserva ▷ *n* (*support*) appoggio, sostegno; (*also*: **backup file**) file *m inv* di riserva; **backward** *adj* (*movement*) indietro *inv*; (*person*) tardivo(-a); (*country*) arretrato(-a); **backwards** *adv* indietro; (*fall, walk*) all'indietro; **backyard** *n* cortile *m* dietro la casa

bacon ['beɪkən] *n* pancetta

bacteria [bæk'tɪərɪə] *npl* batteri *mpl*

bad [bæd] *adj* cattivo(-a); (*accident, injury*) brutto(-a); (*meat, food*) andato(-a) a male; **his ~ leg** la sua gamba malata; **to go ~** andare a male

badge [bædʒ] *n* insegna; (*of policeman*) stemma *m*

badger ['bædʒər] *n* tasso

badly ['bædlɪ] *adv* (*work, dress etc*) male; **~ wounded** gravemente ferito; **he needs it ~** ne ha un gran bisogno

bad-mannered [bæd'mænəd] *adj* maleducato(-a), sgarbato(-a)

badminton ['bædmɪntən] *n* badminton *m*

bad-tempered ['bæd'tɛmpəd] *adj* irritabile; di malumore

bag [bæg] *n* sacco; (*handbag etc*) borsa; **~s of** (*inf: lots of*) un sacco di; **baggage** *n* bagagli *mpl*; **baggage allowance** *n* franchigia *f* bagaglio *inv*; **baggage reclaim** *n* ritiro *m* bagaglio *inv*; **baggy** *adj* largo(-a), sformato(-a); **bagpipes** *npl* cornamusa

bail [beɪl] *n* cauzione *f* ▷ *vt* (*prisoner: also*: **grant - to**) concedere la libertà provvisoria su cauzione a; (*boat: also*: **~ out**) aggottare; **on ~** in libertà provvisoria su cauzione

bait [beɪt] *n* esca ▷ *vt* (*hook*) innescare; (*trap*) munire di esca; (*fig*) tormentare

bake [beɪk] *vt* cuocere al forno ▷ *vi* cuocersi al forno; **baked beans** [-biːnz] *npl* fagioli *mpl* in salsa di pomodoro; **baked potato** *n* patata cotta al forno con la buccia; **baker** *n* fornaio(-a), panettiere(-a); **bakery** *n* panetteria; **baking** *n* cottura (al forno); **baking powder** *n* lievito in polvere

balance ['bæləns] *n* equilibrio; (*Comm: sum*) bilancio; (*remainder*) resto; (*scales*) bilancia ▷ *vt* tenere in equilibrio; (*budget*) far quadrare; (*account*) pareggiare; (*compensate*) contrappesare; **~ of trade/ payments** bilancia commerciale/dei pagamenti; **balanced** *adj* (*personality, diet*) equilibrato(-a); **balance sheet** *n* bilancio

balcony ['bælkənɪ] *n* balcone *m*; (*in theatre*) balconata; **do you have a room with a ~?** avete una camera con balcone?

bald [bɔːld] *adj* calvo(-a); (*tyre*) liscio(-a)

Balearics [bælɪ'ærɪks] *npl*: **the ~** le Baleari *fpl*

ball [bɔːl] *n* palla; (*football*) pallone *m*; (*for golf*) pallina; (*of wool, string*) gomitolo; (*dance*) ballo; **to play ~** (*fig*)

stare al gioco
ballerina [bæləˈriːnə] n ballerina
ballet [ˈbæleɪ] n balletto; **ballet
dancer** n ballerino(-a) classico(-a)
balloon [bəˈluːn] n pallone m
ballot [ˈbælət] n scrutinio
ballpoint (pen) [ˈbɔːlpɔɪnt(-)] n
penna a sfera
ballroom [ˈbɔːlrum] n sala da ballo
Baltic [ˈbɔːltɪk] adj, **the ~ Sea** il
(mar) Baltico
bamboo [bæmˈbuː] n bambù m
ban [bæn] n interdizione f ▷ vt
interdire
banana [bəˈnɑːnə] n banana
band [bænd] n banda; (at a dance)
orchestra; (Mil) fanfara
bandage [ˈbændɪdʒ] n benda, fascia
Band-Aid® [ˈbændeɪd] (US) n cerotto
B. & B. n abbr = **bed and breakfast**
bandit [ˈbændɪt] n bandito
bang [bæŋ] n (of door) lo sbattere;
(of gun, blow) colpo ▷ vt battere
(violentemente); (door) sbattere ▷ vi
scoppiare; sbattere
Bangladesh [bɑːŋɡləˈdɛʃ] n
Bangladesh m
bangle [ˈbæŋɡl] n braccialetto
bangs [bæŋz] (US) npl (fringe) frangia,
frangetta
banish [ˈbænɪʃ] vt bandire
banister(s) [ˈbænɪstə(z)] n(pl)
ringhiera
banjo [ˈbændʒəu] (pl **banjoes** or
banjos) n banjo m inv
bank [bæŋk] n banca, banco; (of river,
lake) riva, sponda; (of earth) banco
▷ vi (Aviat) inclinarsi in virata; **bank
on** vt fus contare su; **bank account**
n conto in banca; **bank balance** n
saldo; **a healthy bank balance** un
solido conto in banca; **bank card** n
carta f assegni inv; **bank charges** npl
(BRIT) spese fpl bancarie; **banker** n
banchiere m; **bank holiday** (BRIT) n
giorno di festa; vedi nota nel riquadro;
banking n attività bancaria;

professione f di banchiere; **bank
manager** n direttore m di banca;
banknote n banconota

● **BANK HOLIDAY**
●
● Una **bank holiday**, in Gran
● Bretagna, è una giornata in cui
● banche e molti negozi sono chiusi.
● Generalmente le **bank holidays**
● cadono di lunedì e molti ne
● approfittano per fare una breve
● vacanza fuori città.

bankrupt [ˈbæŋkrʌpt] adj fallito(-a);
to go ~ fallire; **bankruptcy** n
fallimento
bank statement n estratto conto
banner [ˈbænəʳ] n striscione m
bannister(s) [ˈbænɪstə(z)] n(pl) see
banister(s)
banquet [ˈbæŋkwɪt] n banchetto
baptism [ˈbæptɪzəm] n battesimo
baptize [bæpˈtaɪz] vt battezzare
bar [bɑːʳ] n (place) bar m inv; (counter)
banco; (rod) barra; (of window etc)
sbarra; (of chocolate) tavoletta; (fig)
ostacolo; restrizione f; (Mus) battuta
▷ vt (road, window) sbarrare; (person)
escludere; (activity) interdire; **~ of
soap** saponetta; **the B~** (Law) l'Ordine
m degli avvocati; **behind ~s** (prisoner)
dietro le sbarre; **~ none** senza
eccezione
barbaric [bɑːˈbærɪk] adj barbarico(-a)
barbecue [ˈbɑːbɪkjuː] n barbecue
m inv
barbed wire [ˈbɑːbd-] n filo spinato
barber [ˈbɑːbəʳ] n barbiere m;
barber's (shop) (US **barber (shop)**)
n barbiere m
bar code n (on goods) codice m a barre
bare [bɛəʳ] adj nudo(-a) ▷ vt scoprire,
denudare; (teeth) mostrare; **the ~
necessities** lo stretto necessario;
barefoot adj, adv scalzo(-a); **barely**
adv appena

bargain ['bɑːgɪn] n (transaction) contratto; (good buy) affare m ▷ vi trattare; **into the ~** per giunta; **bargain for** vt fus **he got more than he bargained for** gli è andata peggio di quel che si aspettasse

barge [bɑːdʒ] n chiatta; **barge in** vi (walk in) piombare dentro; (interrupt talk) intromettersi a sproposito

bark [bɑːk] n (of tree) corteccia; (of dog) abbaio ▷ vi abbaiare

barley ['bɑːlɪ] n orzo

barmaid ['bɑːmeɪd] n cameriera al banco

barman ['bɑːmən] (irreg) n barista m

barn [bɑːn] n granaio

barometer [bə'rɒmɪtə'] n barometro

baron ['bærən] n barone m; **baroness** n baronessa

barracks ['bærəks] npl caserma

barrage ['bærɑːʒ] n (Mil, dam) sbarramento; (fig) fiume m

barrel ['bærəl] n barile m; (of gun) canna

barren ['bærən] adj sterile; (soil) arido(-a)

barrette [bə'rɛt] (US) n fermaglio per capelli

barricade [bærɪ'keɪd] n barricata

barrier ['bærɪə'] n barriera

barring ['bɑːrɪŋ] prep salvo

barrister ['bærɪstə'] (BRIT) n avvocato(-essa) (con diritto di parlare davanti a tutte le corti)

barrow ['bærəu] n (cart) carriola

bartender ['bɑːtɛndə'] (US) n barista m

base [beɪs] n base f ▷ vt **to ~ sth on** basare qc su ▷ adj vile

baseball ['beɪsbɔːl] n baseball m; **baseball cap** n berretto da baseball

basement ['beɪsmənt] n seminterrato; (of shop) interrato

bases¹ ['beɪsiːz] npl of **basis**

bases² ['beɪsɪz] npl of **base**

bash [bæʃ] (inf) vt picchiare

basic ['beɪsɪk] adj rudimentale; essenziale; **basically** [-lɪ]

adv fondamentalmente; sostanzialmente; **basics** npl **the basics** l'essenziale m

basil ['bæzl] n basilico

basin ['beɪsn] n (vessel: also Geo) bacino; (also: **wash~**) lavabo

basis ['beɪsɪs] (pl **bases**) n base f; **on a part-time ~** part-time; **on a trial ~** in prova

basket ['bɑːskɪt] n cesta; (smaller) cestino; (with handle) paniere m; **basketball** n pallacanestro f

bass [beɪs] n (Mus) basso

bastard ['bɑːstəd] n bastardo(-a); (infl) stronzo (!)

bat [bæt] n pipistrello; (for baseball etc) mazza; (BRIT: for table tennis) racchetta ▷ vt **he didn't ~ an eyelid** non battè ciglio

batch [bætʃ] n (of bread) infornata; (of papers) cumulo

bath [bɑːθ] n bagno; (bathtub) vasca da bagno ▷ vt far fare il bagno a; **to have a ~** fare un bagno; see also **baths**

bathe [beɪð] vi fare il bagno ▷ vt (wound) lavare

bathing ['beɪðɪŋ] n bagni mpl; **bathing costume** (US **bathing suit**) n costume m da bagno

bath: bathrobe ['bɑːθrəub] n accappatoio; **bathroom** ['bɑːθrum] n stanza da bagno; **baths** [bɑːðz] npl bagni mpl pubblici; **bath towel** n asciugamano da bagno; **bathtub** n (vasca da) bagno

baton ['bætən] n (Mus) bacchetta; (Athletics) testimone m; (club) manganello

batter ['bætə'] vt battere ▷ n pastetta; **battered** adj (hat) sformato(-a); (pan) ammaccato(-a)

battery ['bætərɪ] n batteria; (of torch) pila; **battery farming** n allevamento in batteria

battle ['bætl] n battaglia ▷ vi battagliare, lottare; **battlefield** n campo di battaglia

bay [beɪ] n (*of sea*) baia; **to hold sb at ~** tenere qn a bada

bazaar [bəˈzɑːʳ] n bazar m inv; vendita di beneficenza

BBC n abbr (= *British Broadcasting Corporation*) rete nazionale di radiotelevisione in Gran Bretagna

- **BBC**
-
- La **BBC** è l'azienda statale che
- fornisce il servizio radiofonico
- e televisivo in Gran Bretagna.
- Ha due reti televisive terrestri
- (BBC1 e BBC2), e cinque stazioni
- radiofoniche nazionali. Oggi la BBC
- ha anche diverse stazioni digitali
- radiofoniche e televisive. Da molti
- anni fornisce inoltre un servizio di
- intrattenimento e informazione
- internazionale, il "BBC World
- Service", trasmesso in tutto il
- mondo.

B.C. adv abbr (= *before Christ*) a.C.

○ **KEYWORD**

be [biː] (pt **was, were**, pp **been**) aux vb **1** (*with present participle: forming continuous tenses*): **what are you doing?** che fa?, che sta facendo?; **they're coming tomorrow** vengono domani; **I've been waiting for her for hours** sono ore che l'aspetto
2 (*with pp: forming passives*) essere; **to be killed** essere or venire ucciso(-a); **the box had been opened** la scatola era stata aperta; **the thief was nowhere to be seen** il ladro non si trovava da nessuna parte
3 (*in tag questions*): **it was fun, wasn't it?** è stato divertente, no?; **he's good-looking, isn't he?** è un bell'uomo, vero?; **she's back, is she?** così è tornata, eh?
4 (+ *to* + *infinitive*): **the house is to be sold** abbiamo or hanno etc intenzione di vendere casa; **you're to be congratulated for all your work** dovremo farvi i complimenti per tutto il vostro lavoro; **he's not to open it** non deve aprirlo
▷ vb + complement **1** (*gen*) essere; **I'm English** sono inglese; **I'm tired** sono stanco(-a); **I'm hot/cold** ho caldo/freddo; **he's a doctor** è medico; **2 and 2 are 4** 2 più 2 fa 4; **be careful!** sta attento(-a)!; **be good** sii buono(-a)
2 (*of health*) stare; **how are you?** come sta?; **he's very ill** sta molto male
3 (*of age*): **how old are you?** quanti anni hai?; **I'm sixteen (years old)** ho sedici anni
4 (*cost*) costare; **how much was the meal?** quant'era or quanto costava il pranzo?; **that'll be £5, please** (fa) 5 sterline, per favore
▷ vi **1** (*exist, occur etc*) essere, esistere; **the best singer that ever was** il migliore cantante mai esistito or di tutti tempi; **be that as it may** comunque sia, sia come sia; **so be it** sia pure, e sia
2 (*referring to place*) essere, trovarsi; **I won't be here tomorrow** non ci sarò domani; **Edinburgh is in Scotland** Edimburgo si trova in Scozia
3 (*referring to movement*): **where have you been?** dov'è stato?; **I've been to China** sono stato in Cina
▷ impers vb **1** (*referring to time, distance*) essere; **it's 5 o'clock** sono le 5; **it's the 28th of April** è il 28 aprile; **it's 10 km to the village** di qui al paese sono 10 km
2 (*referring to the weather*) fare; **it's too hot/cold** fa troppo caldo/freddo; **it's windy** c'è vento
3 (*emphatic*): **it's me** sono io; **it was Maria who paid the bill** è stata Maria che ha pagato il conto

beach [biːtʃ] n spiaggia ▷ vt tirare

in secco

beacon ['biːkən] n (lighthouse) faro; (marker) segnale m

bead [biːd] n perlina; **beads** npl (necklace) collana

beak [biːk] n becco

beam [biːm] n trave f; (of light) raggio ▷ vi brillare

bean [biːn] n fagiolo; (of coffee) chicco; **runner ~** fagiolino; **beansprouts** npl germogli mpl di soia

bear [bɛəʳ] (pt **bore**, pp **borne**) n orso ▷ vt portare; (endure) sopportare; (produce) generare ▷ vi **to ~ right/left** piegare a destra/sinistra

beard [bɪəd] n barba

bearer ['bɛərəʳ] n portatore m

bearing ['bɛərɪŋ] n portamento; (connection) rapporto

beast [biːst] n bestia

beat [biːt] (pt **beat**, pp **beaten**) n colpo; (of heart) battito; (Mus) tempo; battuta; (of policeman) giro ▷ vt battere; (eggs, cream) sbattere ▷ vi battere; **off the ~ en track** fuori mano; **~ it!** (inf) fila!, fuori dai piedi!; **beat up** vt (person) picchiare; (eggs) sbattere; **beating** n bastonata

beautiful ['bjuːtɪful] adj bello(-a); **beautifully** adv splendidamente

beauty ['bjuːtɪ] n bellezza; **beauty parlour** [-'pɑːləʳ] (us **beauty parlor**) n salone m di bellezza; **beauty salon** n istituto di bellezza; **beauty spot** (BRIT) n (Tourism) luogo pittoresco

beaver ['biːvəʳ] n castoro

became [bɪ'keɪm] pt of **become**

because [bɪ'kɔz] conj perché; **~ of** a causa di

beckon ['bɛkən] vt (also: **~ to**) chiamare con un cenno

become [bɪ'kʌm] (irreg: like **come**) vt diventare; **to ~ fat/thin** ingrassarsi/dimagrire

bed [bɛd] n letto; (of flowers) aiuola; (of coal, clay) strato; **single/double ~** letto a una piazza/a due piazze or matrimoniale; **bed and breakfast** n (place) ≈ pensione f familiare; (terms) camera con colazione; vedi nota nel riquadro; **bedclothes** ['bɛdkləuðz] npl biancheria e coperte fpl da letto; **bedding** n coperte e lenzuola fpl; **bed linen** n biancheria da letto; **bedroom** n camera da letto; **bedside** n **at sb's bedside** al capezzale di qn; **bedside lamp** n lampada da comodino; **bedside table** n comodino; **bedsit(ter)** (BRIT) n monolocale m; **bedspread** n copriletto; **bedtime** n **it's bedtime** è ora di andare a letto

● **BED AND BREAKFAST**
●
● I **bed and breakfasts**, anche
● **B & Bs**, sono piccole pensioni
● a conduzione familiare, più
● economiche rispetto agli alberghi,
● dove al mattino viene servita la
● tradizionale colazione all'inglese.

bee [biː] n ape f

beech [biːtʃ] n faggio

beef [biːf] n manzo; **roast ~** arrosto di manzo; **beefburger** n hamburger m inv; **Beefeater** n guardia della Torre di Londra

been [biːn] pp of **be**

beer [bɪəʳ] n birra; **beer garden** n (BRIT) giardino (di pub)

beet [biːt] (us) n (also: **red ~**) barbabietola rossa

beetle ['biːtl] n scarafaggio; coleottero

beetroot ['biːtruːt] (BRIT) n barbabietola

before [bɪ'fɔːʳ] prep (in time) prima di; (in space) davanti a ▷ conj prima che + sub; prima di ▷ adv prima; **~ going** prima di andare; **~ she goes** prima che vada; **the week ~** la settimana prima; **I've seen it ~** l'ho già visto; **I've never seen it ~** è la prima volta che lo vedo; **beforehand** adv in anticipo

beg [bɛg] vi chiedere l'elemosina ▷ vt (also: ~ **for**) chiedere in elemosina; (favour) chiedere; **to ~ sb to do** pregare qn di fare

began [bɪ'gæn] pt of **begin**

beggar ['bɛgəʳ] n mendicante m/f

begin [bɪ'gɪn] (pt **began**, pp **begun**) vt, vi cominciare; **to ~ doing** or **to do sth** incominciare or iniziare a fare qc; **beginner** n principiante m/f; **beginning** n inizio, principio

begun [bɪ'gʌn] pp of **begin**

behalf [bɪ'hɑːf] n **on ~ of** per conto di; a nome di

behave [bɪ'heɪv] vi comportarsi; (well: also: ~ **o.s.**) comportarsi bene; **behaviour** [bɪ'heɪvjəʳ] (us **behavior**) n comportamento, condotta

behind [bɪ'haɪnd] prep dietro; (followed by pronoun) dietro di; (time) in ritardo con ▷ adv dietro; (leave, stay) indietro ▷ n didietro; **to be ~ (schedule)** essere in ritardo rispetto al programma; **~ the scenes** (fig) dietro le quinte

beige [beɪʒ] adj beige inv

Beijing ['beɪ'dʒɪŋ] n Pechino f

being ['biːɪŋ] n essere m

belated [bɪ'leɪtɪd] adj tardo(-a)

belch [bɛltʃ] vi ruttare ▷ vt (gen: belch out: smoke etc) eruttare

Belgian ['bɛldʒən] adj, n belga m/f

Belgium ['bɛldʒəm] n Belgio m

belief [bɪ'liːf] n (opinion) opinione f, convinzione f; (trust, faith) fede f

believe [bɪ'liːv] vt, vi credere; **to ~ in** (God) credere in; (ghosts) credere a; (method) avere fiducia in; **believer** n (Rel) credente m/f; (in idea, activity): **to be a believer in** credere in

bell [bɛl] n campana; (small, on door, electric) campanello

bellboy ['bɛlbɔɪ], (us) **bellhop** ['bɛlhɔp] n ragazzo d'albergo, fattorino d'albergo

bellow ['bɛləu] vi muggire

bell pepper (esp us) n peperone m

belly ['bɛlɪ] n pancia; **belly button** n ombelico

belong [bɪ'lɔŋ] vi **to ~ to** appartenere a; (club etc) essere socio di; **this book ~s here** questo libro va qui; **belongings** npl cose fpl, roba

beloved [bɪ'lʌvɪd] adj adorato(-a)

below [bɪ'ləu] prep sotto, al di sotto di ▷ adv sotto, di sotto; giù; **see ~** vedi sotto or oltre

belt [bɛlt] n cintura; (Tech) cinghia ▷ vt (thrash) picchiare ▷ vi (inf) filarsela; **beltway** (us) n (Aut: ring road) circonvallazione f; (: motorway) autostrada

bemused [bɪ'mjuːzd] adj perplesso(-a), stupito(-a)

bench [bɛntʃ] n panca; (in workshop, Pol) banco; **the B~** (Law) la Corte

bend [bɛnd] (pt, pp **bent**) vt curvare; (leg, arm) piegare ▷ vi curvarsi; piegarsi ▷ n (BRIT: in road) curva; (in pipe, river) gomito; **bend down** vi chinarsi; **bend over** vi piegarsi

beneath [bɪ'niːθ] prep sotto, al di sotto di; (unworthy of) indegno(-a) di ▷ adv sotto, di sotto

beneficial [bɛnɪ'fɪʃəl] adj che fa bene; vantaggioso(-a)

benefit ['bɛnɪfɪt] n beneficio, vantaggio; (allowance of money) indennità f inv ▷ vt far bene a ▷ vi **he'll ~ from it** ne trarrà beneficio or profitto

benign [bɪ'naɪn] adj (person, smile) benevolo(-a); (Med) benigno(-a)

bent [bɛnt] pt, pp of **bend** ▷ n inclinazione f ▷ adj (inf: dishonest) losco(-a); **to be ~ on** essere deciso(-a) a

bereaved [bɪ'riːvd] n **the ~** i familiari in lutto

beret ['bɛreɪ] n berretto

Berlin [bəː'lɪn] n Berlino f

Bermuda [bəː'mjuːdə] n **le** Bermude

berry ['bɛrɪ] n bacca

berth [bəːθ] n (bed) cuccetta; (for ship) ormeggio ▷ vi (in harbour) entrare in

porto; (at anchor) gettare l'ancora
beside [bɪ'saɪd] prep accanto a; **to be
~ o.s. (with anger)** essere fuori di sé
(dalla rabbia); **that's ~ the point** non
c'entra; **besides** [bɪ'saɪdz] adv inoltre,
per di più ▷ prep oltre a; a parte
best [bɛst] adj migliore ▷ adv meglio;
the ~ part of (quantity) la maggior
parte di; **at ~** tutt'al più; **to make
the ~ of sth** cavare il meglio possibile
da qc; **to do one's ~** fare del proprio
meglio; **to the ~ of my knowledge**
per quel che ne so; **to the ~ of my
ability** al massimo delle mie capacità;
best-before date n scadenza; **best
man** (irreg) n testimone m dello
sposo; **bestseller** n bestseller m inv
bet [bɛt] (pt, pp **bet** or **betted**) n
scommessa ▷ vt, vi scommettere; **to
~ sb sth** scommettere qc con qn
betray [bɪ'treɪ] vt tradire
better ['bɛtə'] adj migliore ▷ adv
meglio ▷ vt migliorare ▷ n **to get the
~ of** avere la meglio su; **you had ~ do
it** è meglio che lo faccia; **he thought ~
of it** cambiò idea; **to get ~** migliorare
betting ['bɛtɪŋ] n scommesse
fpl; **betting shop** (BRIT) n ufficio
dell'allibratore
between [bɪ'twiːn] prep tra ▷ adv in
mezzo, nel mezzo
beverage ['bɛvərɪdʒ] n bevanda
beware [bɪ'wɛə'] vt, vi **to ~ (of)**
stare attento(-a) (a); **"~ of the dog"**
"attenti al cane"
bewildered [bɪ'wɪldəd] adj
sconcertato(-a), confuso(-a)
beyond [bɪ'jɔnd] prep (in space) oltre;
(exceeding) al di sopra di ▷ adv di
là; **~ doubt** senza dubbio; **~ repair**
irreparabile
bias ['baɪəs] n (prejudice) pregiudizio;
(preference) preferenza; **bias(s)ed** adj
parziale
bib [bɪb] n bavaglino
Bible ['baɪbl] n Bibbia
bicarbonate of soda [baɪ'kɑːbənɪt-]

n bicarbonato (di sodio)
biceps ['baɪsɛps] n bicipite m
bicycle ['baɪsɪkl] n bicicletta; **bicycle
pump** n pompa della bicicletta
bid [bɪd] (pt **bade** or **bid**, pp **bidden** or
bid) n offerta; (attempt) tentativo ▷ vi
fare un'offerta ▷ vt fare un'offerta di;
to ~ sb good day dire buon giorno a
qn; **bidder** n **the highest bidder** il
maggior offerente
bidet ['biːdeɪ] n bidè m inv
big [bɪg] adj grande; grosso(-a);
Big Apple n vedi nota nel riquadro;
bigheaded ['bɪg'hɛdɪd] adj
presuntuoso(-a); **big toe** n alluce m

● **BIG APPLE**

● Tutti sanno che **The Big Apple**, la
● Grande Mela, è New York ("apple"
● in gergo significa grande città),
● ma sicuramente i soprannomi
● di altre città americane non
● sono così conosciuti. Chicago è
● soprannominata "the Windy City"
● perché è ventosa, New Orleans si
● chiama "the Big Easy" per il modo
● di vivere tranquillo e rilassato
● dei suoi abitanti, e l'industria
● automobilistica ha fatto sì che
● Detroit fosse soprannominata
● "Motown".

bike [baɪk] n bici f inv; **bike lane** n
pista ciclabile
bikini [bɪ'kiːnɪ] n bikini m inv
bilateral [baɪ'lætərl] adj bilaterale
bilingual [baɪ'lɪŋgwəl] adj bilingue
bill [bɪl] n conto; (Pol) atto; (US:
banknote) banconota; (of bird) becco;
(of show) locandina; **can I have the ~,
please** il conto, per favore; **put it on
my ~** lo metta sul mio conto; **"post
no ~s"** "divieto di affissione"; **to fit or
fill the ~** (fig) fare al caso; **billboard** n
tabellone m; **billfold** ['bɪlfəuld] (US) n
portafoglio

billiards ['bɪljədz] n biliardo
billion ['bɪljən] num (BRIT) bilione m;
(US) miliardo
bin [bɪn] n (for coal, rubbish) bidone
m; (for bread) cassetta; (dustbin)
pattumiera; (litter bin) cestino
bind [baɪnd] (pt, pp **bound**) vt legare;
(oblige) obbligare ▷ n (inf) scocciatura
binge [bɪndʒ] (inf) n **to go on a ~** fare
baldoria; **binge drinker** n persona che
di norma beve troppo
bingo ['bɪŋgəu] n gioco simile alla
tombola
binoculars [bɪ'nɔkjuləz] npl binocolo
bio... [baɪə'...] prefix; **biochemistry**
n biochimica; **biodegradable**
adj biodegradabile; **biography**
[baɪ'ɔgrəfɪ] n biografia; **biological**
adj biologico(-a); **biology** [baɪ'ɔlədʒɪ]
n biologia; **biometric** [baɪə'mɛtrɪk]
adj biometrico(-a)
birch [bəːtʃ] n betulla
bird [bəːd] n uccello; (BRIT: inf: girl)
bambola; **bird flu** n influenza aviaria;
bird of prey n (uccello) rapace m;
birdwatching n birdwatching m
Biro® ['baɪrəu] n biro® f inv
birth [bəːθ] n nascita; **to give ~
to** partorire; **birth certificate**
n certificato di nascita; **birth
control** n controllo delle nascite;
contraccezione f; **birthday** n
compleanno ▷ cpd di compleanno;
birthmark n voglia; **birthplace** n
luogo di nascita
biscuit ['bɪskɪt] (BRIT) n biscotto
bishop ['bɪʃəp] n vescovo
bistro ['biːstrəu] n bistrò m inv
bit [bɪt] pt of **bite** ▷ n pezzo; (Comput)
bit m inv; (of horse) morso; **a ~ of** un
po' di; **a ~ mad** un po' matto; **~ by ~** a
poco a poco
bitch [bɪtʃ] n (dog) cagna; (inf!) vacca
bite [baɪt] (pt, pp **bit, bitten**) vt, vi
mordere; (insect) pungere ▷ n morso;
(insect bite) puntura; (mouthful)
boccone m; **let's have a ~ to eat**

mangiamo un boccone; **to ~ one's
nails** mangiarsi le unghie
bitten ['bɪtn] pp of **bite**
bitter ['bɪtər] adj amaro(-a); (wind,
criticism) pungente ▷ n (BRIT: beer)
birra amara
bizarre [bɪ'zɑːr] adj bizzarro(-a)
black [blæk] adj nero(-a) ▷ n nero;
(person): **B~** negro(-a) ▷ vt (BRIT
Industry) boicottare; **to give sb a ~
eye** fare un occhio nero a qn; **in the ~**
(bank account) in attivo; **black out** vi
(faint) svenire; **blackberry** n mora;
blackbird n merlo; **blackboard** n
lavagna; **black coffee** n caffè m inv
nero; **blackcurrant** n ribes m inv;
black ice n strato trasparente di
ghiaccio; **blackmail** n ricatto ▷ vt
ricattare; **black market** n mercato
nero; **blackout** n oscuramento;
(TV, Radio) interruzione f delle
trasmissioni; (fainting) svenimento;
black pepper n pepe m nero; **black
pudding** n sanguinaccio; **Black Sea**
n **the Black Sea** il Mar Nero
bladder ['blædər] n vescica
blade [bleɪd] n lama; (of oar) pala; **~ of
grass** filo d'erba
blame [bleɪm] n colpa ▷ vt **to ~ sb/
sth for sth** dare la colpa di qc a qn/qc;
who's to ~? chi è colpevole?
bland [blænd] adj mite; (taste)
blando(-a)
blank [blæŋk] adj bianco(-a); (look)
distratto(-a) ▷ n spazio vuoto;
(cartridge) cartuccia a salve
blanket ['blæŋkɪt] n coperta
blast [blɑːst] n (of wind) raffica; (of
bomb etc) esplosione f ▷ vt far saltare
blatant ['bleɪtənt] adj flagrante
blaze [bleɪz] n (fire) incendio; (fig)
vampata; splendore m ▷ vi (fire)
ardere, fiammeggiare; (guns) sparare
senza sosta; (fig: eyes) ardere ▷ vt **to ~
a trail** (fig) tracciare una via nuova; **in
a ~ of publicity** circondato da grande
pubblicità

blazer ['bleɪzə'] n blazer m inv
bleach [bli:tʃ] n (also: **household ~**) varechina ▷ vt (material) candeggiare; **bleachers** (US) npl (Sport) posti mpl di gradinata
bleak [bli:k] adj tetro(-a)
bled [blɛd] pt, pp of **bleed**
bleed [bli:d] (pt, pp **bled**) vi sanguinare; **my nose is ~ing** mi viene fuori sangue dal naso
blemish ['blɛmɪʃ] n macchia
blend [blɛnd] n miscela ▷ vt mescolare ▷ vi (colours etc: also: **~ in**) armonizzare; **blender** n (Culin) frullatore m
bless [blɛs] (pt, pp **blessed** or **blest**) vt benedire; **~ you!** (after sneeze) salute!; **blessing** n benedizione f; fortuna
blew [blu:] pt of **blow**
blight [blaɪt] vt (hopes etc) deludere; (life) rovinare
blind [blaɪnd] adj cieco(-a) ▷ n (for window) avvolgibile m; (Venetian blind) veneziana ▷ vt accecare; **the blind** npl i ciechi; **blind alley** n vicolo cieco; **blindfold** n benda ▷ adj, adv bendato(-a) ▷ vt bendare gli occhi a
blink [blɪŋk] vi battere gli occhi; (light) lampeggiare
bliss [blɪs] n estasi f
blister ['blɪstə'] n (on skin) vescica; (on paintwork) bolla ▷ vi (paint) coprirsi di bolle
blizzard ['blɪzəd] n bufera di neve
bloated ['bləʊtɪd] adj gonfio(-a)
blob [blɔb] n (drop) goccia; (stain, spot) macchia
block [blɔk] n blocco; (in pipes) ingombro; (toy) cubo; (of buildings) isolato ▷ vt bloccare; **the sink is ~ed** il lavandino è otturato; **block up** vt bloccare; (pipe) ingorgare, intasare; **blockade** [-'keɪd] n blocco; **blockage** n ostacolo; **blockbuster** n (film, book) grande successo; **block capitals** npl stampatello; **block letters** npl stampatello

blog [blɔg] n blog m inv ▷ vi scrivere un blog
bloke [bləʊk] (BRIT: inf) n tizio
blond(e) [blɔnd] adj, n biondo(-a)
blood [blʌd] n sangue m; **blood donor** n donatore(-trice) di sangue; **blood group** n gruppo sanguigno; **blood poisoning** n setticemia; **blood pressure** n pressione f sanguigna; **bloodshed** n spargimento di sangue; **bloodshot** adj **bloodshot eyes** occhi iniettati di sangue; **bloodstream** n flusso del sangue; **blood test** n analisi f inv del sangue; **blood transfusion** n trasfusione f di sangue; **blood type** n gruppo sanguigno; **blood vessel** n vaso sanguigno; **bloody** adj (fight) sanguinoso(-a); (nose) sanguinante; (BRIT: inf!): **this bloody ...** questo maledetto ...; **bloody awful/good** (inf!) veramente terribile/forte
bloom [blu:m] n fiore m ▷ vi (tree) essere in fiore; (flower) aprirsi
blossom ['blɔsəm] n fiore m; (with pl sense) fiori mpl ▷ vi essere in fiore
blot [blɔt] n macchia ▷ vt macchiare
blouse [blauz] n (feminine garment) camicetta
blow [bləʊ] (pt **blew**, pp **blown**) n colpo ▷ vi soffiare ▷ vt (fuse) far saltare; (wind) spingere; (instrument) suonare; **to ~ one's nose** soffiarsi il naso; **to ~ a whistle** fischiare; **blow away** vt portare via; **blow out** vi scoppiare; **blow up** vi saltare in aria ▷ vt far saltare in aria; (tyre) gonfiare; (Phot) ingrandire; **blow-dry** n messa in piega a föhn
blown [bləʊn] pp of **blow**
blue [blu:] adj azzurro(-a); (depressed) giù inv; **~ film/joke** film/barzelletta pornografico(-a); **out of the ~** (fig) all'improvviso; **bluebell** n giacinto dei boschi; **blueberry** n mirtillo; **blue cheese** n formaggio tipo gorgonzola; **blues** npl **the blues** (Mus) il blues; **to**

have the blues (*inf*: *feeling*) essere a terra; **bluetit** *n* cinciarella
bluff [blʌf] *vi* bluffare ▷ *n* bluff *m inv* ▷ *adj* (*person*) brusco(-a); **to call sb's ~** mettere alla prova il bluff di qn
blunder ['blʌndə'] *n* abbaglio ▷ *vi* prendere un abbaglio
blunt [blʌnt] *adj* smussato(-a); spuntato(-a); (*person*) brusco(-a)
blur [blə:'] *n* forma indistinta ▷ *vt* offuscare; **blurred** *adj* (*photo*) mosso(-a); (*TV*) sfuocato(-a)
blush [blʌʃ] *vi* arrossire ▷ *n* rossore *m*; **blusher** *n* fard *m inv*
board [bɔ:d] *n* tavola; (*on wall*) tabellone *m*; (*committee*) consiglio, comitato; (*in firm*) consiglio d'amministrazione; (*Naut, Aviat*): **on ~** a bordo ▷ *vt* (*ship*) salire a bordo di; (*train*) salire su; **full ~** (*BRIT*) pensione completa; **half ~** (*BRIT*) mezza pensione; **~ and lodging** vitto e alloggio; **which goes by the ~** (*fig*) che viene abbandonato; **board game** *n* gioco da tavolo; **boarding card** *n* = **boarding pass**; **boarding pass** *n* (*Aviat, Naut*) carta d'imbarco; **boarding school** *n* collegio; **board room** *n* sala del consiglio
boast [bəust] *vi*: **to ~ (about** *or* **of)** vantarsi (di)
boat [bəut] *n* nave *f*; (*small*) barca
bob [bɔb] *vi* (*boat, cork on water: also:* **~ up and down**) andare su e giù
bobby pin ['bɔbɪ-] (*US*) *n* fermaglio per capelli
body ['bɔdɪ] *n* corpo; (*of car*) carrozzeria; (*of plane*) fusoliera; (*fig: group*) gruppo; (: *organization*) organizzazione *f*; (: *quantity*) quantità *f inv*; **body-building** *n* culturismo; **bodyguard** *n* guardia del corpo; **bodywork** *n* carrozzeria
bog [bɔg] *n* palude *f* ▷ *vt* **to get ~ged down** (*fig*) impantanarsi
bogus ['bəugəs] *adj* falso(-a); finto(-a)
boil [bɔɪl] *vt, vi* bollire ▷ *n* (*Med*)

foruncolo; **to come to the** (*BRIT*) *or* **a** (*US*) **~** raggiungere l'ebollizione; **boil over** *vi* traboccare (bollendo); **boiled egg** *n* uovo alla coque; **boiled potatoes** *npl* patate *fpl* bollite *or* lesse; **boiler** *n* caldaia; **boiling** *adj* bollente; **I'm boiling (hot)** (*inf*) sto morendo di caldo; **boiling point** *n* punto di ebollizione
bold [bəuld] *adj* audace; (*child*) impudente; (*colour*) deciso(-a)
Bolivia [bə'lɪvɪə] *n* Bolivia
Bolivian [bə'lɪvɪən] *adj, n* boliviano(-a)
bollard ['bɔləd] (*BRIT*) *n* (*Aut*) colonnina luminosa
bolt [bəult] *n* chiavistello; (*with nut*) bullone *m* ▷ *adv* **~ upright** diritto(-a) come un fuso ▷ *vt* serrare; (*also:* **~ together**) imbullonare; (*food*) mangiare in fretta ▷ *vi* scappare via
bomb [bɔm] *n* bomba ▷ *vt* bombardare; **bombard** [bɔm'bɑ:d] *vt* bombardare; **bomber** *n* (*Aviat*) bombardiere *m*; **bomb scare** *n* stato di allarme (*per sospetta presenza di una bomba*)
bond [bɔnd] *n* legame *m*; (*binding promise, Finance*) obbligazione *f*; (*Comm*): **in ~** in attesa di sdoganamento
bone [bəun] *n* osso; (*of fish*) spina, lisca ▷ *vt* disossare; togliere le spine di ...
bonfire ['bɔnfaɪə'] *n* falò *m inv*
bonnet ['bɔnɪt] *n* cuffia; (*BRIT: of car*) cofano
bonus ['bəunəs] *n* premio; (*fig*) sovrappiù *m inv*
boo [bu:] *excl* ba! ▷ *vt* fischiare
book [buk] *n* libro; (*of stamps etc*) blocchetto ▷ *vt* (*ticket, seat, room*) prenotare; (*driver*) multare; (*football player*) ammonire; **books** *npl* (*Comm*) conti *mpl*; **I'd like to ~ a double room** vorrei prenotare una camera doppia; **I ~ed a table in the name of ...** ho prenotato un tavolo al nome di...; **book in** *vi* (*BRIT: at hotel*) prendere

una camera; **book up** vt riservare, prenotare; **the hotel is booked up** l'albergo è al completo; **all seats are booked up** è tutto esaurito; **bookcase** n scaffale m; **booking** n (BRIT) prenotazione f; **I confirmed my booking by fax/e-mail** ho confermato la mia prenotazione tramite fax/e-mail; **booking office** (BRIT) n (Rail) biglietteria; (Theatre) botteghino; **book-keeping** n contabilità; **booklet** n libricino; **bookmaker** n allibratore m; **bookmark** (also Comput) n segnalibro ▷ vt (Comput) mettere un segnalibro a; (Internet Explorer) aggiungere a "Preferiti"; **bookseller** n libraio; **bookshelf** n mensola (per libri); **bookshop, bookstore** n libreria

boom [bu:m] n (noise) rimbombo; (in prices etc) boom m inv ▷ vi rimbombare; andare a gonfie vele

boost [bu:st] n spinta ▷ vt spingere

boot [bu:t] n stivale m; (for hiking) scarpone m da montagna; (for football etc) scarpa; (BRIT: of car) portabagagli m inv ▷ vt (Comput) inizializzare, to ~ (in addition) per giunta, in più

booth [bu:ð] n cabina; (at fair) baraccone m

booze [bu:z] (inf) n alcool m

border ['bɔ:də'] n orlo; margine m; (of a country) frontiera; (for flowers) aiuola (laterale) ▷ vt (road) costeggiare; (another country: also: ~ **on**) confinare con; **the B~s** la zona di confine tra l'Inghilterra e la Scozia; **borderline** n (fig): **on the borderline** incerto(-a)

bore [bɔ:'] pt of **bear** ▷ vt (hole etc) scavare; (person) annoiare ▷ n (person) seccatore(-trice); (of gun) calibro; **bored** adj annoiato(-a); **to be bored** annoiarsi; **he's bored to tears** or **to death** or **stiff** è annoiato a morte; **boredom** n noia

boring ['bɔ:rɪŋ] adj noioso(-a)

born [bɔ:n] adj **to be ~** nascere; **I was**

~ in 1960 sono nato nel 1960

borne [bɔ:n] pp of **bear**

borough ['bʌrə] n comune m

borrow ['bɔrəu] vt **to ~ sth (from sb)** prendere in prestito qc (da qn)

Bosnia(-Herzegovina) ['bɔznɪə(hɛrzə'gəuvi:nə)] n Bosnia-Erzegovina; **Bosnian** ['bɔznɪən] n, adj bosniaco(-a) m/f

bosom ['buzəm] n petto; (fig) seno

boss [bɔs] n capo ▷ vt comandare; **bossy** adj prepotente

both [bəuθ] adj entrambi(-e), tutt'e due ▷ pron ~ **of them** entrambi(-e); ~ **of us went, we ~ went** ci siamo andati tutt'e due ▷ adv **they sell ~ meat and poultry** vendono insieme la carne ed il pollame

bother ['bɔðə'] vt (worry) preoccupare; (annoy) infastidire ▷ vi (also: ~ **o.s.**) preoccuparsi ▷ n **it is a ~ to have to do** è una seccatura dover fare; **it was no ~** non c'era problema; **to ~ doing sth** darsi la pena di fare qc

bottle ['bɔtl] n bottiglia; (baby's) biberon m inv ▷ vt imbottigliare; **bottle bank** n contenitore m per la raccolta del vetro; **bottle-opener** n apribottiglie m inv

bottom ['bɔtəm] n fondo; (buttocks) sedere m ▷ adj più basso(-a); ultimo(-a); **at the ~ of** in fondo a

bought [bɔ:t] pt, pp of **buy**

boulder ['bəuldə'] n masso (tondeggiante)

bounce [bauns] vi (ball) rimbalzare; (cheque) essere restituito(-a) ▷ vt far rimbalzare ▷ n (rebound) rimbalzo; **bouncer** (inf) n buttafuori m inv

bound [baund] pt, pp of **bind** ▷ n (gen pl) limite m; (leap) salto ▷ vi saltare ▷ vt (limit) delimitare ▷ adj ~ **by law** obbligato(-a) per legge; **to be ~ to do sth** (obliged) essere costretto(-a) a fare qc; **he's ~ to fail** (likely) fallirà di certo; ~ **for** diretto(-a) a; **out of ~s** il cui accesso è vietato

boundary ['baʊndrɪ] n confine m
bouquet ['bʊkeɪ] n bouquet m inv
bourbon ['bʊəbən] (US) n (also: ~
whiskey) bourbon m inv
bout [baʊt] n periodo; (of malaria etc)
attacco; (Boxing etc) incontro
boutique [buː'tiːk] n boutique f inv
bow¹ [bəʊ] n nodo; (weapon) arco;
(Mus) archetto
bow² [baʊ] n (with body) inchino; (Naut:
also: ~s) prua ▷ vi inchinarsi; (yield): **to**
~ **to** or **before** sottomettersi a
bowels ['baʊəlz] npl intestini mpl; (fig)
viscere fpl
bowl [bəʊl] n (for eating) scodella;
(for washing) bacino; (ball) boccia ▷ vi
(Cricket) servire (la palla); **bowler**
['bəʊlə'] n (Cricket, Baseball) lanciatore
m; (BRIT: also: **bowler hat**) bombetta;
bowling ['bəʊlɪŋ] n (game) gioco
delle bocce; **bowling alley** n pista da
bowling; **bowling green** n campo
di bocce; **bowls** [bəʊlz] n gioco delle
bocce
bow tie n cravatta a farfalla
box [bɒks] n scatola; (also: **cardboard**
~) cartone m; (Theatre) palco ▷ vt
inscatolare ▷ vi fare del pugilato;
boxer n (person) pugile m; **boxer**
shorts ['bɒksəʃɔːts] pl n boxer; **a pair**
of boxer shorts un paio di boxer;
boxing n (Sport) pugilato; **Boxing**
Day (BRIT) n ≈ Santo Stefano; vedi
nota nel riquadro; **boxing gloves** npl
guantoni mpl da pugile; **boxing ring** n
ring m inv; **box office** n biglietteria

> ● **BOXING DAY**
> ●
> ● Il **Boxing Day** è un giorno di festa
> ● e cade in genere il 26 dicembre.
> ● Prende il nome dalla tradizionale
> ● usanza di donare pacchi regalo
> ● natalizi, chiamati "Christmas
> ● boxes", a fornitori e dipendenti.

boy [bɔɪ] n ragazzo

boycott ['bɔɪkɒt] n boicottaggio ▷ vt
boicottare
boyfriend ['bɔɪfrɛnd] n ragazzo
bra [brɑː] n reggipetto, reggiseno
brace [breɪs] n (on teeth) apparecchio
correttore; (tool) trapano ▷ vt
rinforzare, sostenere; **braces** (BRIT)
npl (Dress) bretelle fpl; **to ~ o.s.** (also
fig) tenersi forte
bracelet ['breɪslɪt] n braccialetto
bracket ['brækɪt] n (Tech) mensola;
(group) gruppo; (Typ) parentesi f inv
▷ vt mettere fra parentesi
brag [bræg] vi vantarsi
braid [breɪd] n (trimming) passamano;
(of hair) treccia
brain [breɪn] n cervello; **brains** npl
(intelligence) cervella fpl; **he's got ~s** è
intelligente
braise [breɪz] vt brasare
brake [breɪk] n (on vehicle) freno ▷ vi
frenare; **brake light** n (fanalino dello)
stop m inv
bran [bræn] n crusca
branch [brɑːntʃ] n ramo; (Comm)
succursale f; **branch off** vi diramarsi;
branch out vi (fig) intraprendere una
nuova attività
brand [brænd] n marca; (fig) tipo
▷ vt (cattle) marcare (a ferro rovente);
brand name n marca; **brand-new**
adj nuovo(-a) di zecca
brandy ['brændɪ] n brandy m inv
brash [bræʃ] adj sfacciato(-a)
brass [brɑːs] n ottone m; **the ~** (Mus)
gli ottoni; **brass band** n fanfara
brat [bræt] (pej) n marmocchio,
monello(-a)
brave [breɪv] adj coraggioso(-a) ▷ vt
affrontare; **bravery** n coraggio
brawl [brɔːl] n rissa
Brazil [brə'zɪl] n Brasile m; **Brazilian**
adj, n brasiliano(-a)
breach [briːtʃ] vt aprire una breccia
in ▷ n (gap) breccia, varco; (breaking):
~ **of contract** rottura di contratto; ~
of the peace violazione f dell'ordine

pubblico

bread [brɛd] *n* pane *m*; **breadbin** *n* cassetta *f* portapane *inv*; **breadbox** (US) *n* cassetta *f* portapane *inv*; **breadcrumbs** *npl* briciole *fpl*; (*Culin*) pangrattato

breadth [brɛtθ] *n* larghezza; (*fig*: *of knowledge etc*) ampiezza

break [breɪk] (*pt* **broke**, *pp* **broken**) *vt* rompere; (*law*) violare; (*record*) battere ▷ *vi* rompersi; (*storm*) scoppiare; (*weather*) cambiare; (*dawn*) spuntare; (*news*) saltare fuori ▷ *n* (*gap*) breccia; (*fracture*) rottura; (*rest*, *also Scol*) intervallo; (*: short*) pausa; (*chance*) possibilità *f* *inv*; **to ~ one's leg** *etc* rompersi la gamba *ecc*; **to ~ the news to sb** comunicare per primo la notizia a qn; **to ~ even** coprire le spese; **to ~ free** *or* **loose** spezzare i legami; **to ~ open** (*door etc*) sfondare; **break down** *vt* (*figures, data*) analizzare ▷ *vi* (*person*) avere un esaurimento (nervoso); (*Aut*) guastarsi; **my car has broken down** mi si è rotta la macchina; **break in** *vt* (*horse etc*) domare ▷ *vi* (*burglar*) fare irruzione; (*interrupt*) interrompere; **break into** *vt fus* (*house*) fare irruzione in; **break off** *vi* (*speaker*) interrompersi; (*branch*) troncarsi; **break out** *vi* evadere; (*war, fight*) scoppiare; **to break out in spots** coprirsi di macchie; **break up** *vi* (*ship*) sfondarsi; (*meeting*) sciogliersi; (*crowd*) disperdersi; (*marriage*) andare a pezzi; (*Scol*) chiudere ▷ *vt* fare a pezzi, spaccare; (*fight etc*) interrompere, far cessare; **the line's** *or* **you're breaking up** la linea è disturbata; **breakdown** *n* (*Aut*) guasto; (*in communications*) interruzione *f*; (*of marriage*) rottura; (*Med: also*: **nervous breakdown**) esaurimento nervoso; (*of statistics*) resoconto; **breakdown truck, breakdown van** *n* carro *m* attrezzi *inv*

breakfast ['brɛkfəst] *n* colazione *f*; **what time is ~?** a che ora è servita la colazione?

break: **break-in** *n* irruzione *f*; **breakthrough** *n* (*fig*) passo avanti

breast [brɛst] *n* (*of woman*) seno; (*chest, Culin*) petto; **breast-feed** (*irreg*: *like* **feed**) *vt*, *vi* allattare (al seno); **breast-stroke** *n* nuoto a rana

breath [brɛθ] *n* respiro; **out of ~** senza fiato

Breathalyser® ['brɛθəlaɪzəʳ] (BRIT) *n* alcoltest *m inv*

breathe [briːð] *vt*, *vi* respirare; **breathe in** *vt* respirare ▷ *vi* inspirare; **breathe out** *vt*, *vi* espirare; **breathing** *n* respiro, respirazione *f*

breath: **breathless** ['brɛθlɪs] *adj* senza fiato; **breathtaking** ['brɛθteɪkɪŋ] *adj* mozzafiato *inv*; **breath test** *n* = prova del palloncino

bred [brɛd] *pt*, *pp of* **breed**

breed [briːd] (*pt*, *pp* **bred**) *vt* allevare ▷ *vi* riprodursi ▷ *n* razza; (*type, class*) varietà *f inv*

breeze [briːz] *n* brezza

breezy ['briːzɪ] *adj* allegro(-a), ventilato(-a)

brew [bruː] *vt* (*tea*) fare un infuso di; (*beer*) fare ▷ *vi* (*storm, fig: trouble etc*) prepararsi; **brewery** *n* fabbrica di birra

bribe [braɪb] *n* bustarella ▷ *vt* comprare; **bribery** *n* corruzione *f*

bric-a-brac ['brɪkəbræk] *n* bric-a-brac *m*

brick [brɪk] *n* mattone *m*; **bricklayer** *n* muratore *m*

bride [braɪd] *n* sposa; **bridegroom** *n* sposo; **bridesmaid** *n* damigella d'onore

bridge [brɪdʒ] *n* ponte *m*; (*Naut*) ponte di comando; (*of nose*) dorso; (*Cards*) bridge *m inv* ▷ *vt* (*fig: gap*) colmare

bridle ['braɪdl] *n* briglia

brief [briːf] *adj* breve ▷ *n* (*Law*) comparsa; (*gen*) istruzioni *fpl* ▷ *vt* mettere al corrente; **briefs** *npl* (*underwear*) mutande *fpl*; **briefcase**

n cartella; **briefing** *n* briefing *m*
inv; **briefly** *adv* (*glance*) di sfuggita;
(*explain, say*) brevemente
brigadier [brɪgə'dɪəʳ] *n* generale *m*
di brigata
bright [braɪt] *adj* luminoso(-a); (*clever*)
sveglio(-a); (*lively*) vivace
brilliant ['brɪljənt] *adj* brillante; (*light,
smile*) radioso(-a); (*inf*) splendido(-a)
brim [brɪm] *n* orlo
brine [braɪn] *n* (*Culin*) salamoia
bring [brɪŋ] (*pt, pp* **brought**) *vt*
portare; **bring about** *vt* causare;
bring back *vt* riportare; **bring
down** *vt* portare giù; abbattere;
bring in *vt* (*person*) fare entrare;
(*object*) portare; (*Pol: bill*) presentare;
(: *legislation*) introdurre; (*Law: verdict*)
emettere; (*produce: income*) rendere;
bring on *vt* (*illness, attack*) causare,
provocare; (*player, substitute*) far
scendere in campo; **bring out** *vt* tirar
fuori; (*meaning*) mettere in evidenza;
(*book, album*) far uscire; **bring up** *vt*
(*carry up*) portare su; (*child*) allevare;
(*question*) introdurre; (*food: vomit*)
rimettere, rigurgitare
brink [brɪŋk] *n* orlo
brisk [brɪsk] *adj* (*manner*) spiccio(-a);
(*trade*) vivace; (*pace*) svelto(-a)
bristle ['brɪsl] *n* setola ▷ *vi* rizzarsi;
bristling with irto(-a) di
Brit [brɪt] *n abbr* (*inf*: = *British person*)
britannico(-a)
Britain ['brɪtən] *n* (*also*: **Great ~**) Gran
Bretagna
British ['brɪtɪʃ] *adj* britannico(-a);
British Isles *npl* Isole Britanniche
Briton ['brɪtən] *n* britannico(-a)
brittle ['brɪtl] *adj* fragile
broad [brɔːd] *adj* largo(-a); (*distinction*)
generale; (*accent*) spiccato(-a); **in ~
daylight** in pieno giorno; **broadband**
adj (*Comput*) a banda larga ▷ *n*
banda larga; **broad bean** *n* fava;
broadcast (*pt, pp* **broadcast**) *n*
trasmissione *f* ▷ *vt* trasmettere per

radio (*or* per televisione) ▷ *vi* fare una
trasmissione; **broaden** *vt* allargare
▷ *vi* allargarsi; **broadly** *adv* (*fig*) in
generale; **broad-minded** *adj* di
mente aperta
broccoli ['brɔkəlɪ] *n* broccoli *mpl*
brochure ['brəʊʃjuəʳ] *n* dépliant *m inv*
broil [brɔɪl] *vt* cuocere a fuoco vivo
broiler ['brɔɪləʳ] (*US*) *n* (*grill*) griglia
broke [brəʊk] *pt of* **break** ▷ *adj* (*inf*)
squattrinato(-a)
broken ['brəʊkn] *pp of* **break** ▷ *adj*
rotto(-a); **a ~ leg** una gamba rotta; **in
~ English** in un inglese stentato
broker ['brəʊkəʳ] *n* agente *m*
bronchitis [brɔŋ'kaɪtɪs] *n* bronchite *f*
bronze [brɔnz] *n* bronzo
brooch [brəʊtʃ] *n* spilla
brood [bruːd] *n* covata ▷ *vi* (*person*)
rimuginare
broom [brum] *n* scopa; (*Bot*) ginestra
Bros. *abbr* (= *Brothers*) F.lli
broth [brɔθ] *n* brodo
brothel ['brɔθl] *n* bordello
brother ['brʌðəʳ] *n* fratello; **brother-
in-law** *n* cognato
brought [brɔːt] *pt, pp of* **bring**
brow [brau] *n* fronte *f*; (*rare, gen:
eyebrow*) sopracciglio; (*of hill*) cima
brown [braun] *adj* bruno(-a),
marrone; (*tanned*) abbronzato(-a) ▷ *n*
(*colour*) color *m* bruno *or* marrone ▷ *vt*
(*Culin*) rosolare; **brown bread** *n* pane
m integrale, pane nero
Brownie ['braunɪ] *n* giovane
esploratrice *f*
brown rice *n* riso greggio
brown sugar *n* zucchero greggio
browse [brauz] *vi* (*among books*)
curiosare fra i libri; **to ~ through a
book** sfogliare un libro; **browser** *n*
(*Comput*) browser *m inv*
bruise [bruːz] *n* (*on person*) livido ▷ *vt*
farsi un livido a
brunette [bruː'nɛt] *n* bruna
brush [brʌʃ] *n* spazzola; (*for
painting, shaving*) pennello; (*quarrel*)

schermaglia ▷ vt spazzolare; (also: ~
against) sfiorare
Brussels ['brʌslz] n Bruxelles f
Brussels sprout [spraut] n cavolo
di Bruxelles
brutal ['bruːtl] adj brutale
B.Sc. n abbr (Univ) = **Bachelor of
Science**
BSE n abbr (= bovine spongiform
encephalopathy) encefalite f bovina
spongiforme
bubble ['bʌbl] n bolla ▷ vi ribollire;
(sparkle: fig) essere effervescente;
bubble bath n bagnoschiuma m inv;
bubble gum n gomma americana
buck [bʌk] n maschio (di camoscio,
caprone, coniglio ecc); (us: inf) dollaro
▷ vi sgroppare; **to pass the ~ to
sb** scaricare (su di qn) la propria
responsabilità
bucket ['bʌkɪt] n secchio
buckle ['bʌkl] n fibbia ▷ vt allacciare
▷ vi (wheel etc) piegarsi
bud [bʌd] n gemma; (of flower)
bocciolo ▷ vi germogliare; (flower)
sbocciare
Buddhism ['budɪzəm] n buddismo
Buddhist ['budɪst] adj, n buddista
(m/f)
buddy ['bʌdɪ] n (us) n compagno
budge [bʌdʒ] vt scostare; (fig)
smuovere ▷ vi spostarsi; smuoversi
budgerigar ['bʌdʒərɪgaːʳ] n
pappagallino
budget ['bʌdʒɪt] n bilancio preventivo
▷ vi **to ~ for sth** fare il bilancio per qc
budgie ['bʌdʒɪ] n = **budgerigar**
buff [bʌf] adj color camoscio ▷ n (inf:
enthusiast) appassionato(-a)
buffalo ['bʌfələu] (pl **buffalo** or
buffaloes) n bufalo; (us) bisonte m
buffer ['bʌfəʳ] n respingente m;
(Comput) memoria tampone, buffer
m inv
buffet¹ ['bʌfɪt] vt sferzare
buffet² ['bufeɪ] n (food, BRIT: bar)
buffet m inv; **buffet car** (BRIT) n (Rail)

≈ servizio ristoro
bug [bʌg] n (esp us: insect) insetto;
(Comput, fig: germ) virus m inv; (spy
device) microfono spia ▷ vt mettere
sotto controllo; (inf: annoy) scocciare
buggy ['bʌgɪ] n (baby buggy)
passeggino
build [bɪld] (pt, pp **built**) n (of person)
corporatura ▷ vt costruire; **build
up** vt accumulare; aumentare;
builder n costruttore m; **building**
n costruzione f; edificio; (industry)
edilizia; **building site** n cantiere m di
costruzione; **building society** (BRIT)
n società f inv immobiliare
built [bɪlt] pt, pp of **build**; **built-
in** adj (cupboard) a muro; (device)
incorporato(-a); **built-up** adj **built-
up area** abitato
bulb [bʌlb] n (Bot) bulbo; (Elec)
lampadina
Bulgaria [bʌl'gɛərɪə] n Bulgaria;
Bulgarian adj bulgaro(-a) ▷ n
bulgaro(-a); (Ling) bulgaro
bulge [bʌldʒ] n rigonfiamento ▷ vi
essere protuberante or rigonfio(-a); **to
be bulging with** essere pieno(-a) or
zeppo(-a) di
bulimia [bə'lɪmɪə] n bulimia
bulimic [bju:'lɪmɪk] adj, n
bulimico(-a)
bulk [bʌlk] n massa, volume m; **in
~** a pacchi or cassette etc; (Comm)
all'ingrosso; **the ~ of** il grosso di;
bulky adj grosso(-a), voluminoso(-a)
bull [bul] n toro; (male elephant, whale)
maschio
bulldozer ['buldəuzəʳ] n bulldozer
m inv
bullet ['bulɪt] n pallottola
bulletin ['bulɪtɪn] n bollettino;
bulletin board n (Comput) bulletin
board m inv
bullfight ['bulfaɪt] n corrida;
bullfighter n torero; **bullfighting** n
tauromachia
bully ['bulɪ] n prepotente m ▷ vt

angariare; (frighten) intimidire

bum [bʌm] (inf) n (backside) culo; (tramp) vagabondo(-a)

bumblebee ['bʌmblbiː] n bombo

bump [bʌmp] n (in car) piccolo tamponamento; (jolt) scossa; (on road etc) protuberanza; (on head) bernoccolo ▷ vt battere; **bump into** vt fus scontrarsi con; (person) imbattersi in; **bumper** n paraurti m inv ▷ adj **bumper harvest** raccolto eccezionale; **bumpy** ['bʌmpɪ] adj (road) dissestato(-a)

bun [bʌn] n focaccia; (of hair) crocchia

bunch [bʌntʃ] n (of flowers, keys) mazzo; (of bananas) casco; (of people) gruppo; **~ of grapes** grappolo d'uva; **bunches** npl (in hair) codine fpl

bundle ['bʌndl] n fascio ▷ vt (also: **~ up**) legare in un fascio; (put): **to ~ sth/sb into** spingere qc/qn in

bungalow ['bʌŋgələu] n bungalow m inv

bungee jumping ['bʌndʒiː'dʒʌmpɪŋ] n salto nel vuoto da ponti, grattacieli etc con un cavo fissato alla caviglia

bunion ['bʌnjən] n callo (al piede)

bunk [bʌŋk] n cuccetta; **bunk beds** npl letti mpl a castello

bunker ['bʌŋkər] n (coal store) ripostiglio per il carbone; (Mil, Golf) bunker m inv

bunny ['bʌnɪ] n (also: **~ rabbit**) coniglietto

buoy [bɔɪ] n boa; **buoyant** adj galleggiante; (fig) vivace

burden ['bəːdn] n carico, fardello ▷ vt **to ~ sb with** caricare qn di

bureau [bjuə'rəu] (pl **bureaux**) n (BRIT: writing desk) scrivania; (US: chest of drawers) cassettone m; (office) ufficio, agenzia

bureaucracy [bjuə'rɔkrəsɪ] n burocrazia

bureaucrat ['bjuərəkræt] n burocrate m/f

bureau de change [-də'ʃɑ̃ʒ] (pl

bureaux de change) n cambiavalute m inv

bureaux [bjuə'rəuz] npl of **bureau**

burger ['bəːgər] n hamburger m inv

burglar ['bəːglər] n scassinatore m; **burglar alarm** n campanello antifurto; **burglary** n furto con scasso

burial ['bɛrɪəl] n sepoltura

burn [bəːn] (pt, pp **burned** or **burnt**) vt, vi bruciare ▷ n bruciatura, scottatura; **burn down** vt distruggere col fuoco; **burn out** vt (writer etc): **to burn o.s. out** esaurirsi; **burning** adj in fiamme; (sand) che scotta; (ambition) bruciante

Burns Night n vedi nota nel riquadro

● **BURNS NIGHT**

●
● **Burns Night** è la festa celebrata
● il 25 gennaio per commemorare
● il poeta scozzese Robert Burns
● (1759-1796). Gli scozzesi festeggiano
● questa data con una cena, la "Burns
● supper", a base di "haggis", piatto
● tradizionale scozzese, e whisky.

burnt [bəːnt] pt, pp of **burn**

burp [bəːp] (inf) n rutto ▷ vi ruttare

burrow ['bʌrəu] n tana ▷ vt scavare

burst [bəːst] (pt, pp **burst**) vt far scoppiare ▷ vi esplodere; (tyre) scoppiare ▷ n scoppio; (also: **~ pipe**) rottura nel tubo, perdita; **a ~ of speed** uno scatto di velocità; **to ~ into flames/tears** scoppiare in fiamme/lacrime; **to ~ out laughing** scoppiare a ridere; **to be ~ing with** scoppiare di; **burst into** vt fus (room etc) irrompere in

bury ['bɛrɪ] vt seppellire

bus [bʌs] (pl **buses**) n autobus m inv; **bus conductor** n autista m/f (dell'autobus)

bush [buʃ] n cespuglio; (scrub land) macchia; **to beat about the ~** menare il cane per l'aia

business ['bɪznɪs] n (matter) affare m;

(*trading*) affari *mpl*; (*firm*) azienda; (*job, duty*) lavoro; **to be away on ~** essere andato via per affari; **it's none of my ~** questo non mi riguarda; **he means ~** non scherza; **business class** *n* (*Aer*) business class *f*; **businesslike** *adj* serio(-a), efficiente; **businessman** (*irreg*) *n* uomo d'affari; **business trip** *n* viaggio d'affari; **businesswoman** (*irreg*) *n* donna d'affari

busker ['bʌskə^r] (*BRIT*) *n* suonatore(-trice) ambulante

bus: **bus pass** *n* tessera dell'autobus; **bus shelter** *n* pensilina (*alla fermata dell'autobus*); **bus station** *n* stazione *f* delle corriere, autostazione *f*; **bus-stop** *n* fermata d'autobus

bust [bʌst] *n* busto; (*Anat*) seno ▷ *adj* (*inf*: *broken*) rotto(-a); **to go ~** fallire

bustling ['bʌslɪŋ] *adj* movimentato(-a)

busy ['bɪzɪ] *adj* occupato(-a); (*shop, street*) molto frequentato(-a) ▷ *vt* **to ~ o.s.** darsi da fare; **busy signal** (*US*) *n* (*Tel*) segnale *m* di occupato

 KEYWORD

but [bʌt] *conj* ma; **I'd love to come, but I'm busy** vorrei tanto venire, ma ho da fare
▷ *prep* (*apart from, except*) eccetto, tranne, meno; **he was nothing but trouble** non dava altro che guai; **no-one but him can do it** nessuno può farlo tranne lui; **but for you/your help** se non fosse per te/per il tuo aiuto; **anything but that** tutto ma non questo
▷ *adv* (*just, only*) solo, soltanto; **she's but a child** è solo una bambina; **had I but known** se solo avessi saputo; **I can but try** tentar non nuoce; **all but finished** quasi finito

butcher ['butʃə^r] *n* macellaio ▷ *vt* macellare; **butcher's (shop)** *n*

macelleria

butler ['bʌtlə^r] *n* maggiordomo

butt [bʌt] *n* (*cask*) grossa botte *f*; (*of gun*) calcio; (*of cigarette*) mozzicone *m*; (*BRIT*: *fig*: *target*) oggetto ▷ *vt* cozzare

butter ['bʌtə^r] *n* burro ▷ *vt* imburrare; **buttercup** *n* ranuncolo

butterfly ['bʌtəflaɪ] *n* farfalla; (*Swimming*: *also*: **~ stroke**) (nuoto a) farfalla

buttocks ['bʌtəks] *npl* natiche *fpl*

button ['bʌtn] *n* bottone *m*; (*US*: *badge*) distintivo ▷ *vt* (*also*: **~ up**) abbottonare ▷ *vi* abbottonarsi

buy [baɪ] (*pt, pp* **bought**) *vt* comprare ▷ *n* acquisto; **where can I ~ some postcards?** dove posso comprare delle cartoline?; **to ~ sb sth/sth from sb** comprare qc per qn/qc da qn; **to ~ sb a drink** offrire da bere a qn; **buy out** *vt* (*business*) rilevare; **buy up** *vt* accaparrare; **buyer** *n* compratore(-trice)

buzz [bʌz] *n* ronzio; (*inf*: *phone call*) colpo di telefono ▷ *vi* ronzare; **buzzer** ['bʌzə^r] *n* cicalino

 KEYWORD

by [baɪ] *prep* **1** (*referring to cause, agent*) da; **killed by lightning** ucciso da un fulmine; **surrounded by a fence** circondato da uno steccato; **a painting by Picasso** un quadro di Picasso
2 (*referring to method, manner, means*): **by bus/car/train** in autobus/ macchina/treno, con l'autobus/la macchina/il treno; **to pay by cheque** pagare con (un) assegno; **by moonlight** al chiaro di luna; **by saving hard, he ...** risparmiando molto, lui ...
3 (*via, through*) per; **we came by Dover** siamo venuti via Dover
4 (*close to, past*) accanto a; **the house by the river** la casa sul fiume; **a**

holiday by the sea una vacanza al mare; **she sat by his bed** si sedette accanto al suo letto; **she rushed by me** mi è passata accanto correndo; **I go by the post office every day** passo davanti all'ufficio postale ogni giorno

5 (*not later than*) per, entro; **by 4 o'clock** per *or* entro le 4; **by this time tomorrow** domani a quest'ora; **by the time I got here it was too late** quando sono arrivato era ormai troppo tardi

6 (*during*): **by day/night** di giorno/ notte

7 (*amount*) a; **by the kilo/metre** a chili/metri; **paid by the hour** pagato all'ora; **one by one** uno per uno; **little by little** a poco a poco

8 (*Math, measure*): **to divide/ multiply by 3** dividere/moltiplicare per 3; **it's broader by a metre** è un metro più largo, è più largo di un metro

9 (*according to*) per; **to play by the rules** attenersi alle regole; **it's all right by me** per me va bene

10: **(all) by oneself** *etc* (tutto(-a)) solo(-a); **he did it (all) by himself** lo ha fatto (tutto) da solo

11: **by the way** a proposito; **this wasn't my idea by the way** tra l'altro l'idea non è stata mia

▷ *adv* 1 *see* **go; pass** *etc*

2: **by and by** (*in past*) poco dopo; (*in future*) fra breve; **by and large** nel complesso

bye(-bye) ['baɪ('baɪ)] *excl* ciao!, arrivederci!

by-election ['baɪɪlɛkʃən] (*BRIT*) *n* elezione *f* straordinaria

bypass ['baɪpɑːs] *n* circonvallazione *f*; (*Med*) by-pass *m inv* ▷ *vt* fare una deviazione intorno a

byte [baɪt] *n* (*Comput*) byte *m inv*, bicarattere *m*

C [siː] *n* (*Mus*) do

cab [kæb] *n* taxi *m inv*; (*of train, truck*) cabina

cabaret ['kæbəreɪ] *n* cabaret *m inv*

cabbage ['kæbɪdʒ] *n* cavolo

cabin ['kæbɪn] *n* capanna; (*on ship*) cabina; **cabin crew** *n* equipaggio

cabinet ['kæbɪnɪt] *n* (*Pol*) consiglio dei ministri; (*furniture*) armadietto; (*also*: **display ~**) vetrinetta; **cabinet minister** *n* ministro (*membro del Consiglio*)

cable ['keɪbl] *n* cavo; fune *f*; (*Tel*) cablogramma *m* ▷ *vt* telegrafare; **cable car** *n* funivia; **cable television** *n* televisione *f* via cavo

cactus ['kæktəs] (*pl* **cacti**) *n* cactus *m inv*

café ['kæfeɪ] *n* caffè *m inv*

cafeteria [kæfɪ'tɪərɪə] *n* self-service *m inv*

caffein(e) ['kæfiːn] *n* caffeina

cage [keɪdʒ] *n* gabbia

cagoule [kə'guːl] *n* K-way® *m inv*

cake [keɪk] *n* (*large*) torta; (*small*) pasticcino; **cake of soap** *n* saponetta

calcium [ˈkælsɪəm] *n* calcio

calculate [ˈkælkjuleɪt] *vt* calcolare; **calculation** [-ˈleɪʃən] *n* calcolo; **calculator** *n* calcolatrice *f*

calendar [ˈkæləndəʳ] *n* calendario

calf [kɑːf] (*pl* **calves**) *n* (*of cow*) vitello; (*of other animals*) piccolo; (*also*: **~skin**) (*pelle f di*) vitello; (*Anat*) polpaccio

calibre [ˈkælɪbəʳ] (*US* **caliber**) *n* calibro

call [kɔːl] *vt* (*gen: also Tel*) chiamare; (*meeting*) indire ▷ *vi* chiamare; (*visit: also*: **~ in, ~ round**) passare ▷ *n* (*shout*) grido, urlo; (*Tel*) telefonata; **to be ~ed** (*person, object*) chiamarsi; **can you ~ back later?** può richiamare più tardi?; **can I make a ~ from here?** posso telefonare da qui?; **to be on ~** essere a disposizione; **call back** *vi* (*return*) ritornare; (*Tel*) ritelefonare, richiamare; **call for** *vt fus* richiedere; (*fetch*) passare a prendere; **call in** *vt* (*doctor, expert, police*) chiamare, far venire; **call off** *vt* disdire; **call on** *vt fus* (*visit*) passare da; (*appeal to*) chiedere a; **call out** *vi* (*in pain*) urlare; (*to person*) chiamare; (*Tel*) telefonare a; **call up** *vt* (*Mil*) richiamare; (*Tel*) telefonare a; **callbox** (*BRIT*) *n* cabina telefonica; **call centre** (*US* **call center**) *n* centro informazioni telefoniche; **caller** *n* persona che chiama, visitatore(-trice)

callous [ˈkæləs] *adj* indurito(-a), insensibile

calm [kɑːm] *adj* calmo(-a) ▷ *n* calma ▷ *vt* calmare; **calm down** *vi* calmarsi ▷ *vt* calmare; **calmly** *adv* con calma

Calor gas® [ˈkæləʳ-] *n* butano

calorie [ˈkælərɪ] *n* caloria

calves [kɑːvz] *npl of* **calf**

camcorder [ˈkæmkɔːdəʳ] *n* camcorder *f inv*

came [keɪm] *pt of* **come**

camel [ˈkæməl] *n* cammello

camera [ˈkæmərə] *n* macchina fotografica; (*Cinema, TV*) cinepresa; **in ~** a porte chiuse; **cameraman** (*irreg*) *n* cameraman *m inv*; **camera phone** *n* telefono cellulare con fotocamera incorporata

camouflage [ˈkæməflɑːʒ] *n* (*Mil, Zool*) mimetizzazione *f* ▷ *vt* mimetizzare

camp [kæmp] *n* campeggio; (*Mil*) campo ▷ *vi* accamparsi ▷ *adj* effeminato(-a)

campaign [kæmˈpeɪn] *n* (*Mil, Pol etc*) campagna ▷ *vi* (*also fig*) fare una campagna; **campaigner** *n* **campaigner for** fautore(-trice) di; **campaigner against** oppositore(-trice) di

camp: campbed *n* (*BRIT*) brandina; **camper** [ˈkæmpəʳ] *n* campeggiatore(-trice); (*vehicle*) camper *m inv*; **campground** (*US*) *n* campeggio; **camping** [ˈkæmpɪŋ] *n* campeggio; **to go camping** andare in campeggio; **campsite** [ˈkæmpsaɪt] *n* campeggio

campus [ˈkæmpəs] *n* campus *m inv*

can¹ [kæn] *n* (*of milk*) scatola; (*of oil*) bidone *m*; (*of water*) tanica; (*tin*) scatola ▷ *vt* mettere in scatola

 KEYWORD

can² [kæn] (*negative* **cannot, can't**, *conditional and pt* **could**) *aux vb* **1** (*be able to*) potere; **I can't go any further** non posso andare oltre; **you can do it if you try** sei in grado di farlo — basta provarci; **I'll help you all I can** ti aiuterò come potrò; **I can't see you** non ti vedo

2 (*know how to*) sapere, essere capace di; **I can swim** so nuotare; **can you speak French?** parla francese?

3 (*may*) potere; **could I have a word with you?** posso parlarle un momento?

4 (*expressing disbelief, puzzlement etc*):

it can't be true! non può essere vero!;
what can he want? cosa può mai
volere?
5 (*expressing possibility, suggestion etc*):
he could be in the library può darsi
che sia in biblioteca; **she could have
been delayed** può aver avuto un
contrattempo

Canada ['kænədə] *n* Canada *m*;
Canadian [kə'neɪdɪən] *adj, n*
canadese *m/f*
canal [kə'næl] *n* canale *m*
canary [kə'nɛərɪ] *n* canarino
Canary Islands, Canaries
[kə'nɛərɪz] *npl* **the ~** le (isole) Canarie
cancel ['kænsəl] *vt* annullare; (*train*)
sopprimere; (*cross out*) cancellare; **I
want to ~ my booking** vorrei disdire
la mia prenotazione; **cancellation**
[-'leɪʃən] *n* annullamento;
soppressione *f*; cancellazione *f*;
(*Tourism*) prenotazione *f* annullata
cancer ['kænsə'] *n* cancro
Cancer ['kænsə'] *n* (*sign*) Cancro
candidate ['kændɪdeɪt] *n*
candidato(-a)
candle ['kændl] *n* candela; (*in church*)
cero; **candlestick** *n* bugia; (*bigger,
ornate*) candeliere *m*
candy ['kændɪ] *n* zucchero candito;
(*US*) caramella; caramelle *fpl*; **candy
bar** (*US*) *n* lungo biscotto, in genere
ricoperto di cioccolata; **candyfloss**
['kændɪflɒs] *n* (*BRIT*) zucchero filato
cane [keɪn] *n* canna; (*for furniture*)
bambù *m*; (*stick*) verga ▷ *vt* (*BRIT Scol*)
punire a colpi di verga
canister ['kænɪstə'] *n* scatola
metallica
cannabis ['kænəbɪs] *n* canapa
indiana
canned ['kænd] *adj* (*food*) in scatola
cannon ['kænən] (*pl* **cannon** or
cannons) *n* (*gun*) cannone *m*
cannot ['kænɒt] = **can not**
canoe [kə'nuː] *n* canoa; **canoeing** *n*

canottaggio
canon ['kænən] *n* (*clergyman*)
canonico; (*standard*) canone *m*
can-opener ['kænəupnə'] *n*
apriscatole *m inv*
can't [kænt] = **can not**
canteen [kæn'tiːn] *n* mensa; (*BRIT: of
cutlery*) portaposate *m inv*

> Be careful not to translate
> *canteen* by the Italian word
> *cantina*.

canter ['kæntə'] *vi* andare al piccolo
galoppo
canvas ['kænvəs] *n* tela
canvass ['kænvəs] *vi* (*Pol*): **to ~
for** raccogliere voti per ▷ *vt* fare un
sondaggio di
canyon ['kænjən] *n* canyon *m inv*
cap [kæp] *n* (*hat*) berretto; (*of pen*)
coperchio; (*of bottle, toy gun*) tappo;
(*contraceptive*) diaframma *m* ▷ *vt*
(*outdo*) superare; (*limit*) fissare un
tetto (a)
capability [keɪpə'bɪlɪtɪ] *n* capacità *f
inv*, abilità *f inv*
capable ['keɪpəbl] *adj* capace
capacity [kə'pæsɪtɪ] *n* capacità *f inv*;
(*of lift etc*) capienza
cape [keɪp] *n* (*garment*) cappa; (*Geo*)
capo
caper ['keɪpə'] *n* (*Culin*) cappero;
(*prank*) scherzetto
capital ['kæpɪtl] *n* (*also:* **~ city**)
capitale *f*; (*money*) capitale *m*;
(*also:* **~ letter**) (lettera) maiuscola;
capitalism *n* capitalismo; **capitalist**
adj, n capitalista *m/f*; **capital
punishment** *n* pena capitale
Capitol ['kæpɪtl] *n* **the ~** il
Campidoglio
Capricorn ['kæprɪkɔːn] *n* Capricorno
capsize [kæp'saɪz] *vt* capovolgere ▷ *vi*
capovolgersi
capsule ['kæpsjuːl] *n* capsula
captain ['kæptɪn] *n* capitano
caption ['kæpʃən] *n* leggenda
captivity [kæp'tɪvɪtɪ] *n* cattività

capture ['kæptʃər] vt catturare; (Comput) registrare ▷ n cattura; (data) registrazione f or rilevazione f di dati

car [kɑːr] n (Aut) macchina, automobile f; (Rail) vagone m

carafe [kəˈræf] n caraffa

caramel ['kærəməl] n caramello

carat ['kærət] n carato; **18 ~ gold** oro a 18 carati

caravan ['kærəvæn] n (BRIT) roulotte f inv; (of camels) carovana; **caravan site** (BRIT) n campeggio per roulotte

carbohydrate [kɑːbəʊˈhaɪdreɪt] n carboidrato

carbon ['kɑːbən] n carbonio; **carbon dioxide** [-daɪˈɔksaɪd] n diossido di carbonio; **carbon monoxide** [-mɔˈnɔksaɪd] n monossido di carbonio

car boot sale n vedi nota nel riquadro

● ● **CAR BOOT SALE**
●
● Il **car boot sale** è un mercatino
● dell'usato molto popolare in Gran
● Bretagna. Normalmente ha luogo
● in un parcheggio o in un grande
● spiazzo, e la merce viene in genere
● esposta nei bagagliai, in inglese
● appunto "boots", aperti delle
● macchine.

carburettor [kɑːbjuˈrɛtər] (US **carburetor**) n carburatore m

card [kɑːd] n carta; (visiting card etc) biglietto; (Christmas card etc) cartolina; **cardboard** n cartone m; **card game** n gioco di carte

cardigan ['kɑːdɪgən] n cardigan m inv

cardinal ['kɑːdɪnl] adj cardinale ▷ n cardinale m

cardphone ['kɑːdfəʊn] n telefono a scheda

care [kɛər] n cura, attenzione f; (worry) preoccupazione f ▷ vi **to ~ about** curarsi di; (thing, idea) interessarsi di; **~ of** presso; **in sb's ~** alle cure di

qn; **to take ~ (to do)** fare attenzione (a fare); **to take ~ of** curarsi di; (bill, problem) occuparsi di; **I don't ~** non me ne importa; **I couldn't ~ less** non m'interessa affatto; **care for** vt fus aver cura di; (like) volere bene a

career [kəˈrɪər] n carriera ▷ vi (also: ~ **along**) andare di (gran) carriera

care: **carefree** ['kɛəfriː] adj sgombro(-a) di preoccupazioni; **careful** ['kɛəful] adj attento(-a), (cautious) cauto(-a); **(be) careful!** attenzione!; **carefully** adv con cura; cautamente; **caregiver** (US) n (professional) badante m/f; (unpaid) persona che si prende cura di un parente malato o anziano; **careless** ['kɛəlɪs] adj negligente; (heedless) spensierato(-a); **carelessness** n negligenza, mancanza di tatto; **carer** ['kɛərər] n assistente m/f (di persone malata o handicappata); **caretaker** ['kɛəteɪkər] n custode m

car-ferry ['kɑːfɛrɪ] n traghetto

cargo ['kɑːgəʊ] (pl **cargoes**) n carico

car hire n autonoleggio

Caribbean [kærɪˈbiːən] adj: **the ~ Sea** il Mar dei Caraibi

caring ['kɛərɪŋ] adj (person) premuroso(-a); (society, organization) umanitario(-a)

carnation [kɑːˈneɪʃən] n garofano

carnival ['kɑːnɪvəl] n (public celebration) carnevale m; (US: funfair) luna park m inv

carol ['kærəl] n: **Christmas ~** canto di Natale

carousel [kærəˈsɛl] (US) n giostra

car park (BRIT) n parcheggio

carpenter ['kɑːpɪntər] n carpentiere m

carpet ['kɑːpɪt] n tappeto ▷ vt coprire con tappeto

car rental (US) n autonoleggio

carriage ['kærɪdʒ] n vettura; (of goods) trasporto; **carriageway** (BRIT) n (part of road) carreggiata

carrier ['kærɪə'] n (of disease) portatore(-trice); (Comm) impresa di trasporti; **carrier bag** (BRIT) n sacchetto

carrot ['kærət] n carota

carry ['kærɪ] vt (person) portare; (: vehicle) trasportare; (involve: responsibilities etc) comportare; (Med) essere portatore(-trice) di ▷ vi (sound) farsi sentire; **to be** or **get carried away** (fig) entusiasmarsi; **carry on** vi **to carry on with sth/doing** continuare qc/a fare ▷ vt mandare avanti; **carry out** vt (orders) eseguire; (investigation) svolgere

cart [kɑːt] n carro ▷ vt (inf) trascinare

carton ['kɑːtən] n (box) scatola di cartone; (of yogurt) cartone m; (of cigarettes) stecca

cartoon [kɑːˈtuːn] n (Press) disegno umoristico; (comic strip) fumetto; (Cinema) disegno animato

cartridge ['kɑːtrɪdʒ] n (for gun, pen) cartuccia; (music tape) cassetta

carve [kɑːv] vt (meat) trinciare; (wood, stone) intagliare; **carving** n (in wood etc) scultura

car wash n lavaggio auto

case [keɪs] n caso; (Law) causa, processo; (box) scatola; (BRIT: also: **suit~**) valigia; **in ~ of** in caso di; **in ~ he** caso mai lui; **in any ~** in ogni caso; **just in ~** in caso di bisogno

cash [kæʃ] n denaro; (coins, notes) denaro liquido ▷ vt incassare; **I haven't got any ~** non ho contanti; **to pay (in) ~** pagare in contanti; **~ on delivery** pagamento alla consegna; **cashback** n (discount) sconto; (at supermarket etc) anticipo di contanti ottenuto presso la cassa di un negozio tramite una carta di debito; **cash card** (BRIT) n tesserino di prelievo; **cash desk** (BRIT) n cassa; **cash dispenser** (BRIT) n sportello automatico

cashew [kæˈʃuː] n (also: **~ nut**) anacardio

cashier [kæˈʃɪə'] n cassiere(-a)

cashmere ['kæʃmɪə'] n cachemire m

cash point n sportello bancario automatico, Bancomat® m inv

cash register n registratore m di cassa

casino [kəˈsiːnəu] n casinò m inv

casket ['kɑːskɪt] n cofanetto; (US: coffin) bara

casserole ['kæsərəul] n casseruola; (food): **chicken ~** pollo in casseruola

cassette [kæˈsɛt] n cassetta; **cassette player** n riproduttore m a cassette

cast [kɑːst] (pt, pp **cast**) vt (throw) gettare; (metal) gettare, fondere; (Theatre): **to ~ sb as Hamlet** scegliere qn per la parte di Amleto ▷ n (Theatre) cast m inv; (also: **plaster ~**) ingessatura; **to ~ one's vote** votare, dare il voto; **cast off** vi (Naut) salpare; (Knitting) calare

castanets [kæstəˈnɛts] npl castagnette fpl

caster sugar ['kɑːstə'-] (BRIT) n zucchero semolato

cast-iron ['kɑːstaɪən] adj (lit) di ghisa; (fig: case) di ferro

castle ['kɑːsl] n castello

casual ['kæʒjul] adj (chance) casuale, fortuito(-a); (: work etc) avventizio(-a); (unconcerned) noncurante, indifferente; **~ wear** casual m

casualty ['kæʒjultɪ] n ferito(-a); (dead) morto(-a), vittima; (Med: department) pronto soccorso

cat [kæt] n gatto

catalogue ['kætəlɔg] (US **catalog**) n catalogo ▷ vt catalogare

catalytic converter [kætəlɪtɪk-] n marmitta catalitica, catalizzatore m

cataract ['kætərækt] n (also Med) cateratta

catarrh [kəˈtɑː'] n catarro

catastrophe [kəˈtæstrəfɪ] n catastrofe f

catch [kætʃ] (pt, pp **caught**) vt

prendere; (*ball*) afferrare; (*surprise: person*) sorprendere; (*attention*) attirare; (*comment, whisper*) cogliere; (*person*) raggiungere ▷ *vi* (*fire*) prendere ▷ *n* (*fish etc caught*) retata; (*of ball*) presa; (*trick*) inganno; (*Tech*) gancio; (*game*) catch *m inv*; **to ~ fire** prendere fuoco; **to ~ sight of** scorgere; **catch up** *vi* mettersi in pari ▷ *vt* (*also*: **~ up with**) raggiungere; **catching** ['kætʃɪŋ] *adj* (*Med*) contagioso(-a)

category ['kætɪɡərɪ] *n* categoria

cater ['keɪtər] *vi*: **~ for** (*BRIT: needs*) provvedere a; (: *readers, consumers*) incontrare i gusti di; (*Comm: provide food*) provvedere alla ristorazione di

caterpillar ['kætəpɪlər] *n* bruco

cathedral [kə'θiːdrəl] *n* cattedrale *f*, duomo

Catholic ['kæθəlɪk] *adj, n* (*Rel*) cattolico(-a)

Catseye® [kæts'aɪ] (*BRIT*) *n* (*Aut*) catarifrangente *m*

cattle ['kætl] *npl* bestiame *m*, bestie *fpl*

catwalk ['kætwɔːk] *n* passerella

caught [kɔːt] *pt, pp of* **catch**

cauliflower ['kɒlɪflauər] *n* cavolfiore *m*

cause [kɔːz] *n* causa ▷ *vt* causare

caution ['kɔːʃən] *n* prudenza; (*warning*) avvertimento ▷ *vt* avvertire; ammonire; **cautious** ['kɔːʃəs] *adj* cauto(-a), prudente

cave [keɪv] *n* caverna, grotta; **cave in** *vi* (*roof etc*) crollare

caviar(e) ['kævɪɑːr] *n* caviale *m*

cavity ['kævɪtɪ] *n* cavità *f inv*

cc *abbr* = **cubic centimetres**; **carbon copy**

CCTV *n abbr* (= *closed-circuit television*) televisione *f* a circuito chiuso

CD *abbr* (*disc*) CD *m inv*; (*player*) lettore *m* CD *inv*; **CD burner** *n* masterizzatore *m* (di) CD; **CD player** *n* lettore *m* CD; **CD-ROM** [-rɔm] *n abbr* CD-ROM *m inv*

cease [siːs] *vt, vi* cessare; **ceasefire** *n* cessate il fuoco *m inv*

cedar ['siːdər] *n* cedro

ceilidh ['keɪlɪ] *n* festa con musiche e danze popolari scozzesi o irlandesi

ceiling ['siːlɪŋ] *n* soffitto; (*on wages etc*) tetto

celebrate ['sɛlɪbreɪt] *vt, vi* celebrare; **celebration** [-'breɪʃən] *n* celebrazione *f*

celebrity [sɪ'lɛbrɪtɪ] *n* celebrità *f inv*

celery ['sɛlərɪ] *n* sedano

cell [sɛl] *n* cella; (*of revolutionaries, Biol*) cellula; (*Elec*) elemento (di batteria)

cellar ['sɛlər] *n* sottosuolo; cantina

cello ['tʃɛləu] *n* violoncello

Cellophane® ['sɛləfeɪn] *n* cellophane® *m*

cellphone ['sɛlfəun] *n* cellulare *m*

Celsius ['sɛlsɪəs] *adj* Celsius *inv*

Celtic ['kɛltɪk, 'sɛltɪk] *adj* celtico(-a)

cement [sə'mɛnt] *n* cemento

cemetery ['sɛmɪtrɪ] *n* cimitero

censor ['sɛnsər] *n* censore *m* ▷ *vt* censurare; **censorship** *n* censura

census ['sɛnsəs] *n* censimento

cent [sɛnt] *n* (*us: coin*) centesimo (= 1.100 di un dollaro); (*unit of euro*) centesimo; *see also* **per**

centenary [sɛn'tiːnərɪ] *n* centenario

centennial [sɛn'tɛnɪəl] (*us*) *n* centenario

center ['sɛntər] (*us*) *n, vt* = **centre**

centi... [sɛntɪ] *prefix*: **centigrade** ['sɛntɪɡreɪd] *adj* centigrado(-a); **centimetre** ['sɛntɪmiːtər] (*us* **centimeter**) *n* centimetro; **centipede** ['sɛntɪpiːd] *n* centopiedi *m inv*

central ['sɛntrəl] *adj* centrale; **Central America** *n* America centrale; **central heating** *n* riscaldamento centrale; **central reservation** *n* (*BRIT Aut*) banchina *f* spartitraffico *inv*

centre ['sɛntər] (*us* **center**) *n* centro ▷ *vt* centrare; **centre-forward** *n* (*Sport*) centroavanti *m inv*; **centre-half** *n* (*Sport*) centromediano

century ['sɛntjʊrɪ] n secolo;
twentieth ~ ventesimo secolo

CEO n abbr = **chief executive officer**

ceramic [sɪ'ræmɪk] adj ceramico(-a)

cereal ['siːrɪəl] n cereale m

ceremony ['sɛrɪmənɪ] n cerimonia;
to stand on ~ fare complimenti

certain ['səːtən] adj certo(-a);
to make ~ of assicurarsi di; **for ~**
per certo, di sicuro; **certainly** adv
certamente, certo; **certainty** n
certezza

certificate [sə'tɪfɪkɪt] n certificato;
diploma m

certify ['səːtɪfaɪ] vt certificare; (award
diploma to) conferire un diploma a;
(declare insane) dichiarare pazzo(-a)

cf. abbr (= compare) cfr.

CFC n (= chlorofluorocarbon) CFC m inv

chain [tʃeɪn] n catena ▷ vt (also: **~ up**)
incatenare; **chain-smoke** vi fumare
una sigaretta dopo l'altra

chair [tʃɛəʳ] n sedia; (armchair)
poltrona; (of university) cattedra; (of
meeting) presidenza ▷ vt (meeting)
presiedere; **chairlift** n seggiovia;
chairman (irreg) n presidente m;
chairperson n presidente(-essa);
chairwoman (irreg) n presidentessa

chalet ['ʃæleɪ] n chalet m inv

chalk [tʃɔːk] n gesso; **chalkboard** (US)
n lavagna

challenge ['tʃælɪndʒ] n sfida ▷ vt
sfidare; (statement, right) mettere
in dubbio; **to ~ sb to do** sfidare
qn a fare; **challenging** adj (task)
impegnativo(-a); (look) di sfida

chamber ['tʃeɪmbəʳ] n camera;
chambermaid n cameriera

champagne [ʃæm'peɪn] n
champagne m inv

champion ['tʃæmpɪən] n
campione(-essa); **championship** n
campionato

chance [tʃɑːns] n caso; (opportunity)
occasione f; (likelihood) possibilità f
inv ▷ vt **to ~ it** rischiare, provarci ▷ adj

fortuito(-a); **to take a ~** rischiare; **by
~** per caso

chancellor ['tʃɑːnsələʳ] n cancelliere
m; **Chancellor of the Exchequer**
[-ɪks'tʃɛkəʳ] (BRIT) n Cancelliere dello
Scacchiere

chandelier [ʃændə'lɪəʳ] n lampadario

change [tʃeɪndʒ] vt cambiare;
(transform): **to ~ sb into** trasformare
qn in ▷ vi cambiare; (change one's
clothes) cambiarsi; (be transformed):
to ~ into trasformarsi in ▷ n
cambiamento; (of clothes) cambio;
(money returned) resto; (coins) spiccioli;
where can I ~ some money? dove
posso cambiare dei soldi?; **to ~ one's
mind** cambiare idea; **keep the ~!**
tenga pure il resto!; **sorry, I don't
have any ~** mi dispiace, non ho
spiccioli; **for a ~** tanto per cambiare;
change over vi (from sth to sth)
passare; (players etc) scambiarsi
(di posto o di campo) ▷ vt cambiare;
changeable adj (weather) variabile;
change machine n distributore
automatico di monete; **changing
room** n (BRIT: in shop) camerino;
(: Sport) spogliatoio

channel ['tʃænl] n canale m; (of river,
sea) alveo ▷ vt canalizzare; **Channel
Tunnel** n: **the Channel Tunnel** il
tunnel sotto la Manica

chant [tʃɑːnt] n canto; salmodia ▷ vt
cantare; salmodiare

chaos ['keɪɔs] n caos m

chaotic [keɪ'ɔtɪk] adj caotico(-a)

chap [tʃæp] (BRIT: inf) n (man) tipo

chapel ['tʃæpəl] n cappella

chapped [tʃæpt] adj (skin, lips)
screpolato(-a)

chapter ['tʃæptəʳ] n capitolo

character ['kærɪktəʳ] n carattere
m; (in novel, film) personaggio;
characteristic [-'rɪstɪk] adj
caratteristico(-a) ▷ n caratteristica;
characterize ['kærɪktəraɪz]
vt caratterizzare; (describe): **to**

characterize (as) descrivere (come)
charcoal ['tʃɑːkəʊl] n carbone m di
legna
charge [tʃɑːdʒ] n accusa; (cost)
prezzo; (responsibility) responsabilità
▷ vt (gun, battery, Mil: enemy) caricare;
(customer) fare pagare a; (sum) fare
pagare; (Law): **to ~ sb (with)** accusare
qn (di) ▷ vi (gen with: up, along etc)
lanciarsi; **charge card** n carta f
clienti inv; **charger** n (also: **battery
charger**) caricabatterie m inv; (old:
warhorse) destriero
charismatic [kærɪzˈmætɪk] adj
carismatico(-a)
charity ['tʃærɪtɪ] n carità;
(organization) opera pia; **charity shop**
n (BRIT) negozi che vendono articoli di
seconda mano e devolvono il ricavato in
beneficenza
charm [tʃɑːm] n fascino; (on bracelet)
ciondolo ▷ vt affascinare, incantare;
charming adj affascinante
chart [tʃɑːt] n tabella; grafico; (map)
carta nautica ▷ vt fare una carta
nautica di; **charts** npl (Mus) hit
parade f
charter ['tʃɑːtəʳ] vt (plane) noleggiare
▷ n (document) carta; **chartered
accountant** ['tʃɑːtəd-] (BRIT) n
ragioniere(-a) professionista; **charter
flight** n volo m charter inv
chase [tʃeɪs] vt inseguire; (also: ~
away) cacciare ▷ n caccia
chat [tʃæt] vi (also: **have a ~**)
chiacchierare ▷ n chiacchierata; (on
the Internet) chattare; **chat up** vt
(BRIT inf: girl) abbordare; **chat room** n
(Internet) chat room f inv; **chat show**
(BRIT) n talk show m inv
chatter ['tʃætəʳ] vi (person) ciarlare;
(bird) cinguettare; (teeth) battere ▷ n
ciarle fpl; cinguettio
chauffeur ['ʃəʊfəʳ] n autista m
chauvinist ['ʃəʊvɪnɪst] n (male
chauvinist) maschilista m; (nationalist)
sciovinista m/f

cheap [tʃiːp] adj economico(-a);
(joke) grossolano(-a); (poor quality)
di cattiva qualità ▷ adv a buon
mercato; **can you recommend a ~
hotel/restaurant, please?** potrebbe
indicarmi un albergo/ristorante non
troppo caro?; **cheap day return**
n biglietto ridotto di andata e ritorno
valido in giornata; **cheaply** adv a buon
prezzo, a buon mercato
cheat [tʃiːt] vi imbrogliare; (at
school) copiare ▷ vt ingannare ▷ n
imbroglione m; **to ~ sb out of sth**
defraudare qn di qc; **cheat on** vt fus
(husband, wife) tradire
Chechnya [tʃɪtʃˈnjɑː] n Cecenia
check [tʃɛk] vt verificare; (passport,
ticket) controllare; (halt) fermare;
(restrain) contenere ▷ n verifica;
controllo; (curb) freno; (US: bill)
conto; (pattern: gen pl) quadretti mpl;
(US) = **cheque** ▷ adj (pattern, cloth)
a quadretti; **check in** vi (in hotel)
registrare; (at airport) presentarsi
all'accettazione ▷ vt (luggage)
depositare; **check off** vt segnare;
check out vi (in hotel) saldare il conto;
check up vi **to check up (on sth)**
investigare (qc); **to check up on sb**
informarsi sul conto di qn; **checkbook**
(US) n = **chequebook**; **checked** adj
a quadretti; **checkers** (US) n dama;
check-in n (also: **check-in desk**: at
airport) check-in m inv, accettazione
f (bagagli inv); **checking account**
(US) n conto corrente; **checklist**
n lista di controllo; **checkmate**
n scaccomatto; **checkout** n (in
supermarket) cassa; **checkpoint** n
posto di blocco; **checkroom** (US) n
deposito m bagagli inv; **checkup** n
(Med) controllo medico
cheddar ['tʃɛdəʳ] n formaggio duro di
latte di mucca di colore bianco o arancione
cheek [tʃiːk] n guancia; (impudence)
faccia tosta; **cheekbone** n zigomo;
cheeky adj sfacciato(-a)

cheer [tʃɪəʳ] vt applaudire; (*gladden*) rallegrare ▷ vi applaudire ▷ n grido (di incoraggiamento); **cheer up** vi rallegrarsi, farsi animo ▷ vt rallegrare; **cheerful** adj allegro(-a)

cheerio ['tʃɪərɪ'əu] (BRIT) excl ciao!

cheerleader ['tʃɪəli:dəʳ] n cheerleader f inv

cheese [tʃi:z] n formaggio; **cheeseburger** n cheeseburger m inv; **cheesecake** n specie di torta di ricotta, a volte con frutta

chef [ʃɛf] n capocuoco

chemical ['kɛmɪkəl] adj chimico(-a) ▷ n prodotto chimico

chemist ['kɛmɪst] n (BRIT: pharmacist) farmacista m/f; (scientist) chimico(-a); **chemistry** n chimica; **chemist's (shop)** (BRIT) n farmacia

cheque [tʃɛk] (US **check**) n assegno; **chequebook** n libretto degli assegni; **cheque card** n carta f assegni inv

cherry ['tʃɛrɪ] n ciliegia; (also: **~ tree**) ciliegio

chess [tʃɛs] n scacchi mpl

chest [tʃɛst] n petto; (box) cassa

chestnut ['tʃɛsnʌt] n castagna; (also: **~ tree**) castagno

chest of drawers n cassettone m

chew [tʃu:] vt masticare; **chewing gum** n chewing gum m

chic [ʃi:k] adj elegante

chick [tʃɪk] n pulcino; (inf) pollastrella

chicken ['tʃɪkɪn] n pollo; (inf: coward) coniglio; **chicken out** (inf) vi avere fifa; **chickenpox** n varicella

chickpea ['tʃɪkpi:] n cece m

chief [tʃi:f] n capo ▷ adj principale; **chief executive (officer)** n direttore m generale; **chiefly** adv per lo più, soprattutto

child [tʃaɪld] (pl **children**) n bambino(-a); **child abuse** n molestie fpl a minori; **child benefit** n (BRIT) ≈ assegni mpl familiari; **childbirth** n parto; **child-care** n il badare ai bambini; **childhood** n infanzia;

childish adj puerile; **child minder** [-'maɪndəʳ] (BRIT) n bambinaia; **children** ['tʃɪldrən] npl of **child**

Chile ['tʃɪlɪ] n Cile m

Chilean ['tʃɪlɪən] adj, n cileno(-a)

chill [tʃɪl] n freddo; (Med) infreddatura ▷ vt raffreddare; **chill out** (esp US) vi (inf) darsi una calmata

chil(l)i ['tʃɪlɪ] n peperoncino

chilly ['tʃɪlɪ] adj freddo(-a), fresco(-a); **to feel ~** sentirsi infreddolito(-a)

chimney ['tʃɪmnɪ] n camino

chimpanzee [tʃɪmpæn'zi:] n scimpanzé m inv

chin [tʃɪn] n mento

China ['tʃaɪnə] n Cina

china ['tʃaɪnə] n porcellana

Chinese [tʃaɪ'ni:z] adj cinese ▷ n inv cinese m/f; (Ling) cinese m

chip [tʃɪp] n (gen pl: Culin) patatina fritta; (: US: also: **potato ~**) patatina; (of wood, glass, stone) scheggia; (also: **micro~**) chip m inv ▷ vt (cup, plate) scheggiare; **chip and PIN card** n (BRIT) scheda a chip con PIN; **chip shop** n (BRIT) vedi nota nel riquadro

● **CHIP SHOP**
●
● I **chip shops**, anche chiamati "fish
● and chip shops", sono friggitorie che
● vendono principalmente filetti di
● pesce impanati e patatine fritte.

chiropodist [kɪ'rɔpədɪst] (BRIT) n pedicure m/f inv

chisel ['tʃɪzl] n cesello

chives [tʃaɪvz] npl erba cipollina

chlorine ['klɔ:ri:n] n cloro

choc-ice ['tʃɔkaɪs] n (BRIT) gelato ricoperto al cioccolato

chocolate ['tʃɔklɪt] ▷ n (substance) cioccolato, cioccolata; (drink) cioccolata; (a sweet) cioccolatino

choice [tʃɔɪs] n scelta ▷ adj scelto(-a)

choir ['kwaɪəʳ] n coro

choke [tʃəuk] vi soffocare ▷ vt

soffocare; (block): **to be ~d with** essere intasato(-a) di ▷ n (Aut) valvola dell'aria

cholesterol [kə'lɛstərɔl] n colesterolo

choose [tʃuːz] (pt **chose**, pp **chosen**) vt scegliere; **to ~ to do** decidere di fare; preferire fare

chop [tʃɔp] vt (wood) spaccare; (Culin: also: **~ up**) tritare ▷ n (Culin) costoletta; **chop down** vt (tree) abbattere; **chop off** vt tagliare; **chopsticks** ['tʃɔpstɪks] npl bastoncini mpl cinesi

chord [kɔːd] n (Mus) accordo

chore [tʃɔːʳ] n faccenda; **household ~s** faccende fpl domestiche

chorus ['kɔːrəs] n coro; (repeated part of song: also fig) ritornello

chose [tʃəuz] pt of **choose**

chosen ['tʃəuzn] pp of **choose**

Christ [kraɪst] n Cristo

christen ['krɪsn] vt battezzare; **christening** n battesimo

Christian ['krɪstɪən] adj, n cristiano(-a); **Christianity** [-'ænɪtɪ] n cristianesimo; **Christian name** n nome m (di battesimo)

Christmas ['krɪsməs] n Natale m; **Merry ~!** Buon Natale!; **Christmas card** n cartolina di Natale; **Christmas carol** n canto natalizio; **Christmas Day** n il giorno di Natale; **Christmas Eve** n la vigilia di Natale; **Christmas pudding** n (esp BRIT) specie di budino con frutta secca, spezie e brandy; **Christmas tree** n albero di Natale

chrome [krəum] n cromo

chronic ['krɔnɪk] adj cronico(-a)

chrysanthemum [krɪ'sænθəməm] n crisantemo

chubby ['tʃʌbɪ] adj paffuto(-a)

chuck [tʃʌk] (inf) vt buttare, gettare; (BRIT: also: **~ up**) piantare; **chuck out** vt buttar fuori

chuckle ['tʃʌkl] vi ridere

sommessamente

chum [tʃʌm] n compagno(-a)

chunk [tʃʌŋk] n pezzo

church [tʃəːtʃ] n chiesa; **churchyard** n sagrato

churn [tʃəːn] n (for butter) zangola; (for milk) bidone m

chute [ʃuːt] n (also: **rubbish ~**) canale m di scarico; (BRIT: children's slide) scivolo

chutney ['tʃʌtnɪ] n salsa piccante (di frutta, zucchero e spezie)

CIA (US) n abbr (= Central Intelligence Agency) CIA f

CID (BRIT) n abbr (= Criminal Investigation Department) ≈ polizia giudiziaria

cider ['saɪdəʳ] n sidro

cigar [sɪ'gɑːʳ] n sigaro

cigarette [sɪgə'rɛt] n sigaretta; **cigarette lighter** n accendino

cinema ['sɪnəmə] n cinema m inv

cinnamon ['sɪnəmən] n cannella

circle ['səːkl] n cerchio; (of friends etc) circolo; (in cinema) galleria ▷ vi girare in circolo ▷ vt (surround) circondare; (move round) girare intorno a

circuit ['səːkɪt] n circuito

circular ['səːkjuləʳ] adj circolare ▷ n circolare f

circulate ['səːkjuleɪt] vi circolare ▷ vt far circolare; **circulation** [-'leɪʃən] n circolazione f; (of newspaper) tiratura

circumstances ['səːkəmstənsɪz] npl circostanze fpl; (financial condition) condizioni fpl finanziarie

circus ['səːkəs] n circo

cite [saɪt] vt citare

citizen ['sɪtɪzn] n (of country) cittadino(-a); (of town) abitante m/f; **citizenship** n cittadinanza

citrus fruits ['sɪtrəs-] npl agrumi mpl

city ['sɪtɪ] n città f inv; **the C~** la Città di Londra (centro commerciale); **city centre** n centro della città; **city technology college** n (BRIT) istituto tecnico superiore (finanziato *dall'industria)*

civic ['sɪvɪk] *adj* civico(-a)

civil ['sɪvɪl] *adj* civile; **civilian** [sɪ'vɪlɪən] *adj, n* borghese *m/f*

civilization [sɪvɪlaɪ'zeɪʃən] *n* civiltà *f inv*

civilized ['sɪvɪlaɪzd] *adj* civilizzato(-a); *(fig)* cortese

civil: **civil law** *n* codice *m*, civile; *(study)* diritto civile; **civil rights** *npl* diritti *mpl* civili; **civil servant** *n* impiegato(-a) statale; **Civil Service** *n* amministrazione *f* statale; **civil war** *n* guerra civile

CJD *abbr* (= *Creutzfeld Jacob disease*) malattia di Creutzfeldt-Jacob

claim [kleɪm] *vt (assert)*: **to ~ (that)/to be** sostenere (che)/di essere; *(credit, rights etc)* rivendicare; *(damages)* richiedere ▷ *vi (for insurance)* fare una domanda d'indennizzo ▷ *n* pretesa; rivendicazione *f*, richiesta; **claim form** *n (gen)* modulo di richiesta; *(for expenses)* modulo di rimborso spese

clam [klæm] *n* vongola

clamp [klæmp] *n* pinza; morsa ▷ *vt* stringere con una morsa; *(Aut: wheel)* applicare i ceppi bloccaruote a

clan [klæn] *n* clan *m inv*

clap [klæp] *vi* applaudire

claret ['klærət] *n* vino di Bordeaux

clarify ['klærɪfaɪ] *vt* chiarificare, chiarire

clarinet [klærɪ'nɛt] *n* clarinetto

clarity ['klærɪtɪ] *n* clarità

clash [klæʃ] *n* frastuono; *(fig)* scontro ▷ *vi* scontrarsi; cozzare

clasp [klɑːsp] *n (hold)* stretta; *(of necklace, bag)* fermaglio, fibbia ▷ *vt* stringere

class [klɑːs] *n* classe *f* ▷ *vt* classificare

classic ['klæsɪk] *adj* classico(-a) ▷ *n* classico; **classical** *adj* classico(-a)

classification [klæsɪfɪ'keɪʃən] *n* classificazione *f*

classify ['klæsɪfaɪ] *vt* classificare

classmate ['klɑːsmeɪt] *n* compagno(-a) di classe

classroom ['klɑːsrum] *n* aula

classy ['klɑːsɪ] *adj (inf)* chic *inv*, elegante

clatter ['klætər] *n* tintinnio; scalpitio ▷ *vi* tintinnare; scalpitare

clause [klɔːz] *n* clausola; *(Ling)* proposizione *f*

claustrophobic [klɔːstrə'fəubɪk] *adj* claustrofobico(-a)

claw [klɔː] *n (of bird of prey)* artiglio; *(of lobster)* pinza

clay [kleɪ] *n* argilla

clean [kliːn] *adj* pulito(-a); *(clear, smooth)* liscio(-a) ▷ *vt* pulire; **clean up** *vt (also fig)* ripulire; **cleaner** *n (person)* donna delle pulizie; **cleaner's** *n (also:* **dry cleaner's**) tintoria; **cleaning** *n* pulizia

cleanser ['klɛnzər] *n* detergente *m*

clear [klɪər] *adj* chiaro(-a); *(glass etc)* trasparente; *(road, way)* libero(-a); *(conscience)* pulito(-a) ▷ *vt* sgombrare; liberare; *(table)* sparecchiare; *(cheque)* fare la compensazione di; *(Law: suspect)* discolpare; *(obstacle)* superare ▷ *vi (weather)* rasserenarsi; *(fog)* andarsene ▷ *adv* ~ **of** distante da; **clear away** *vt (things, clothes etc)* mettere a posto; **to clear away the dishes** sparecchiare la tavola; **clear up** *vt* mettere in ordine; *(mystery)* risolvere; **clearance** *n (removal)* sgombro; *(permission)* autorizzazione *f*, permesso; **clear-cut** *adj* ben delineato(-a), distinto(-a); **clearing** *n* radura; **clearly** *adv* chiaramente; **clearway** (BRIT) *n* strada con divieto di sosta

clench [klɛntʃ] *vt* stringere

clergy ['klɜːdʒɪ] *n* clero

clerk [klɑːk, *(US)* klɜːrk] *n (BRIT)* impiegato(-a); *(US)* commesso(-a)

clever ['klɛvər] *adj (mentally)* intelligente; *(deft, skilful)* abile; *(device, arrangement)* ingegnoso(-a)

cliché ['kliːʃeɪ] n cliché m inv

click [klɪk] vi scattare ▷ vt (heels etc) battere; (tongue) far schioccare

client ['klaɪənt] n cliente m/f

cliff [klɪf] n scogliera scoscesa, rupe f

climate ['klaɪmɪt] n clima m; **climate change** nsg cambiamenti mpl climatici

climax ['klaɪmæks] n culmine m; (sexual) orgasmo

climb [klaɪm] vi salire; (clamber) arrampicarsi ▷ vt salire; (Climbing) scalare ▷ n salita; arrampicata; scalata; **climb down** vi scendere; (BRIT fig) far marcia indietro; **climber** n rocciatore(-trice); alpinista m/f; **climbing** n alpinismo

clinch [klɪntʃ] vt (deal) concludere

cling [klɪŋ] (pt, pp **clung**) vi **to ~ (to)** aggrapparsi (a); (of clothes) aderire strettamente (a)

Clingfilm® ['klɪŋfɪlm] n pellicola trasparente (per alimenti)

clinic ['klɪnɪk] n clinica

clip [klɪp] n (for hair) forcina; (also: **paper ~**) graffetta; (TV, Cinema) sequenza ▷ vt attaccare insieme, (hair, nails) tagliare; (hedge) tosare; **clipping** n (from newspaper) ritaglio

cloak [kləuk] n mantello ▷ vt avvolgere; **cloakroom** n (for coats etc) guardaroba m inv; (BRIT: W.C.) gabinetti mpl

clock [klɔk] n orologio; **clock in** or **on** vi timbrare il cartellino (all'entrata); **clock off** or **out** vi timbrare il cartellino (all'uscita); **clockwise** adv in senso orario; **clockwork** n movimento or meccanismo a orologeria ▷ adj a molla

clog [klɔg] n zoccolo ▷ vt intasare ▷ vi (also: **~ up**) intasarsi, bloccarsi

clone [kləun] n clone m

close¹ [kləus] adj **~ (to)** vicino(-a) (a); (watch, link, relative) stretto(-a); (examination) attento(-a); (contest) combattuto(-a); (weather) afoso(-a)

▷ adv vicino, dappresso; **~ to** vicino a; **~ by, ~ at hand** a portata di mano; **a ~ friend** un amico intimo; **to have a ~ shave** (fig) scamparla bella

close² [kləuz] vt chiudere ▷ vi (shop etc) chiudere; (lid, door etc) chiudersi; (end) finire ▷ n (end) fine f; **what time do you ~?** a che ora chiudete?; **close down** vi cessare (definitivamente); **closed** adj chiuso(-a)

closely ['kləuslɪ] adv (examine, watch) da vicino; (related) strettamente

closet ['klɔzɪt] n (cupboard) armadio

close-up ['kləusʌp] n primo piano

closing time n orario di chiusura

closure ['kləuʒər] n chiusura

clot [klɔt] n (also: **blood ~**) coagulo; (inf: idiot) scemo(-a) ▷ vi coagularsi

cloth [klɔθ] n (material) tessuto, stoffa; (rag) strofinaccio

clothes [kləuðz] npl abiti mpl, vestiti mpl; **clothes line** n corda (per stendere il bucato); **clothes peg** (US **clothes pin**) n molletta

clothing ['kləuðɪŋ] n = **clothes**

cloud [klaud] n nuvola; **cloud over** vi rannuvolarsi; (fig) offuscarsi; **cloudy** adj nuvoloso(-a); (liquid) torbido(-a)

clove [kləuv] n chiodo di garofano; **clove of garlic** n spicchio d'aglio

clown [klaun] n pagliaccio ▷ vi (also: **~ about, ~ around**) fare il pagliaccio

club [klʌb] n (society) club m inv, circolo; (weapon, Golf) mazza ▷ vt bastonare ▷ vi **to ~ together** associarsi; **clubs** npl (Cards) fiori mpl; **club class** n (Aviat) classe f club inv

clue [kluː] n indizio; (in crosswords) definizione f; **I haven't a ~** non ho la minima idea

clump [klʌmp] n (of flowers, trees) gruppo; (of grass) ciuffo

clumsy ['klʌmzɪ] adj goffo(-a)

clung [klʌŋ] pt, pp of **cling**

cluster ['klʌstər] n gruppo ▷ vi raggrupparsi

clutch [klʌtʃ] n (grip, grasp) presa,

stretta; (*Aut*) frizione *f* ▷ *vt* afferrare, stringere forte

cm *abbr* (= *centimetre*) cm

Co. *abbr* = **county**; **company**

c/o *abbr* (= *care of*) presso

coach [kəutʃ] *n* (*bus*) pullman *m inv*; (*horse-drawn, of train*) carrozza; (*Sport*) allenatore(-trice); (*tutor*) chi dà ripetizioni ▷ *vt* allenare; dare ripetizioni a; **coach station** (*BRIT*) *n* stazione *f* delle corriere; **coach trip** *n* viaggio in pullman

coal [kəul] *n* carbone *m*

coalition [kəuə'lɪʃən] *n* coalizione *f*

coarse [kɔːs] *adj* (*salt, sand etc*) grosso(-a); (*cloth, person*) rozzo(-a)

coast [kəust] *n* costa ▷ *vi* (*with cycle etc*) scendere a ruota libera; **coastal** *adj* costiero(-a); **coastguard** *n* guardia costiera; **coastline** *n* linea costiera

coat [kəut] *n* cappotto; (*of animal*) pelo; (*of paint*) mano *f* ▷ *vt* coprire; **coat hanger** *n* attaccapanni *m inv*; **coating** *n* rivestimento

coax [kəuks] *vt* indurre (con moine)

cob [kɔb] *n see* **corn**

cobbled ['kɔbld] *adj*: ~ **street** strada pavimentata a ciottoli

cobweb ['kɔbwɛb] *n* ragnatela

cocaine [kə'keɪn] *n* cocaina

cock [kɔk] *n* (*rooster*) gallo; (*male bird*) maschio ▷ *vt* (*gun*) armare; **cockerel** *n* galletto

cockney ['kɔknɪ] *n* cockney *m/f inv* (*abitante dei quartieri popolari dell'East End di Londra*)

cockpit ['kɔkpɪt] *n* abitacolo

cockroach ['kɔkrəutʃ] *n* blatta

cocktail ['kɔkteɪl] *n* cocktail *m inv*

cocoa ['kəukəu] *n* cacao

coconut ['kəukənʌt] *n* noce *f* di cocco

cod [kɔd] *n* merluzzo

C.O.D. *abbr* = **cash on delivery**

code [kəud] *n* codice *m*

coeducational ['kəuɛdju'keɪʃənl] *adj* misto(-a)

coffee ['kɔfɪ] *n* caffè *m inv*; **coffee bar** (*BRIT*) *n* caffè *m inv*; **coffee bean** *n* grano *or* chicco di caffè; **coffee break** *n* pausa per il caffè; **coffee maker** *n* bollitore *m* per il caffè; **coffeepot** *n* caffettiera; **coffee shop** *n* ≈ caffè *m inv*; **coffee table** *n* tavolino

coffin ['kɔfɪn] *n* bara

cog [kɔg] *n* dente *m*

cognac ['kɔnjæk] *n* cognac *m inv*

coherent [kəu'hɪərənt] *adj* coerente

coil [kɔɪl] *n* rotolo; (*Elec*) bobina; (*contraceptive*) spirale *f* ▷ *vt* avvolgere

coin [kɔɪn] *n* moneta ▷ *vt* (*word*) coniare

coincide [kəuɪn'saɪd] *vi* coincidere; **coincidence** [kəu'ɪnsɪdəns] *n* combinazione *f*

Coke® [kəuk] *n* coca

coke [kəuk] *n* coke *m*

colander ['kɔləndəʳ] *n* colino

cold [kəuld] *adj* freddo(-a) ▷ *n* freddo; (*Med*) raffreddore *m*; **it's** ~ fa freddo; **to be** ~ (*person*) aver freddo; (*object*) essere freddo(-a); **to catch** ~ prendere freddo; **to catch a** ~ prendere un raffreddore; **in** ~ **blood** a sangue freddo; **cold sore** *n* erpete *m*

coleslaw ['kəulslɔː] *n* insalata di cavolo bianco

colic ['kɔlɪk] *n* colica

collaborate [kə'læbəreɪt] *vi* collaborare

collapse [kə'læps] *vi* crollare ▷ *n* crollo; (*Med*) collasso

collar ['kɔləʳ] *n* (*of coat, shirt*) colletto; (*of dog, cat*) collare *m*; **collarbone** *n* clavicola

colleague ['kɔliːg] *n* collega *m/f*

collect [kə'lɛkt] *vt* (*gen*) raccogliere; (*as a hobby*) fare collezione di; (*BRIT: call and pick up*) prendere; (*money owed, pension*) riscuotere; (*donations, subscriptions*) fare una colletta di ▷ *vi* adunarsi, riunirsi; ammucchiarsi; **to call** ~ (*us Tel*) fare una chiamata a carico del destinatario; **collection**

[kə'lɛkʃən] n raccolta; collezione f; (for money) colletta; **collective** adj collettivo(-a) ▷ n collettivo; **collector** [kə'lɛktə^r] n collezionista m/f

college ['kɔlɪdʒ] n college m inv; (of technology etc) istituto superiore

collide [kə'laɪd] vi: **to ~ with** scontrarsi (con)

collision [kə'lɪʒən] n collisione f, scontro

cologne [kə'ləun] n (also: **eau de ~**) acqua di colonia

Colombia [kə'lɔmbɪə] n Colombia; **Colombian** adj, n colombiano(-a)

colon ['kəulən] n (sign) due punti mpl; (Med) colon m inv

colonel ['kə:nl] n colonnello

colonial [kə'ləunɪəl] adj coloniale

colony ['kɔlənɪ] n colonia

colour etc ['kʌlə^r] (US **color**) n colore m ▷ vt colorare; (tint, dye) tingere; (fig: affect) influenzare ▷ vi (blush) arrossire; **colour in** vt colorare; **colour-blind** adj daltonico(-a); **coloured** adj (photo) a colori; (person) di colore; **colour film** n (for camera) pellicola a colori; **colourful** adj pieno(-a) di colore, a vivaci colori; (personality) colorato(-a); **colouring** n (substance) colorante m; (complexion) colorito; **colour television** n televisione f a colori

column ['kɔləm] n colonna

coma ['kəumə] n coma m inv

comb [kəum] n pettine m ▷ vt (hair) pettinare; (area) battere a tappeto

combat ['kɔmbæt] n combattimento ▷ vt combattere, lottare contro

combination [kɔmbɪ'neɪʃən] n combinazione f

combine [vb kəm'baɪn, n 'kɔmbaɪn] vt **to ~ (with)** combinare (con); (one quality with another) unire (a) ▷ vi unirsi; (Chem) combinarsi ▷ n (Econ) associazione f

come [kʌm] (pt **came**, pp **come**) vi venire; arrivare; **to ~ to** (decision etc)

raggiungere; **I've ~ to like him** ha cominciato a piacermi; **to ~ undone** slacciarsi; **to ~ loose** allentarsi; **come across** vt fus trovare per caso; **come along** vi (pupil, work) fare progressi; **come along!** avanti!, andiamo!, forza!; **come back** vi ritornare; **come down** vi scendere; (prices) calare; (buildings) essere demolito(-a); **come from** vt fus venire da; provenire da; **come in** vi entrare; **come off** vi (button) staccarsi; (stain) andar via; (attempt) riuscire; **come on** vi (pupil, work, project) fare progressi; (lights) accendersi; (electricity) entrare in funzione; **come on!** avanti!, andiamo!, forza!; **come out** vi uscire; (stain) andare via; **come round** vi (after faint, operation) riprendere conoscenza, rinvenire; **come to** vi rinvenire; **come up** vi (sun) salire; (problem) sorgere; (event) essere in arrivo; (in conversation) saltar fuori; **come up with** vt fus **he came up with an idea** venne fuori con un'idea

comeback ['kʌmbæk] n (Theatre etc) ritorno

comedian [kə'mi:dɪən] n comico

comedy ['kɔmɪdɪ] n commedia

comet ['kɔmɪt] n cometa

comfort ['kʌmfət] n comodità f inv, benessere m; (relief) consolazione f, conforto ▷ vt consolare, confortare; **comfortable** adj comodo(-a); (financially) agiato(-a); **comfort station** (US) n gabinetti mpl

comic ['kɔmɪk] adj (also: **~al**) comico(-a) ▷ n (BRIT: magazine) giornaletto; **comic book** (US) n giornalino (a fumetti); **comic strip** n fumetto

comma ['kɔmə] n virgola

command [kə'mɑ:nd] n ordine m, comando; (Mil: authority) comando; (mastery) padronanza ▷ vt comandare; **to ~ sb to do** ordinare a qn di fare; **commander** n capo; (Mil) comandante *m*

commemorate [kə'mɛməreɪt] *vt* commemorare

commence [kə'mɛns] *vt, vi* cominciare; **commencement** (*US*) *n* (*Univ*) cerimonia di consegna dei diplomi

commend [kə'mɛnd] *vt* lodare; raccomandare

comment ['kɔmɛnt] *n* commento ▷ *vi* **to ~ (on)** fare commenti (su); **commentary** ['kɔməntəri] *n* commentario; (*Sport*) radiocronaca; telecronaca; **commentator** ['kɔmənteɪtər] *n* commentatore(-trice); radiocronista *m/f*; telecronista *m/f*

commerce ['kɔməːs] *n* commercio

commercial [kə'məːʃəl] *adj* commerciale ▷ *n* (*TV, Radio: advertisement*) pubblicità *f inv*; **commercial break** *n* intervallo pubblicitario

commission [kə'mɪʃən] *n* commissione *f* ▷ *vt* (*work of art*) commissionare; **out of ~** (*Naut*) in disarmo; **commissioner** *n* (*Police*) questore *m*

commit [kə'mɪt] *vt* (*act*) commettere; (*to sb's care*) affidare; **to ~ o.s. to do** impegnarsi (a fare); **to ~ suicide** suicidarsi; **commitment** *n* impegno; promessa

committee [kə'mɪtɪ] *n* comitato

commodity [kə'mɔdɪtɪ] *n* prodotto, articolo

common ['kɔmən] *adj* comune; (*pej*) volgare; (*usual*) normale ▷ *n* terreno comune; **the C~s** (*BRIT*) ▷ *npl* la Camera dei Comuni; **in ~** in comune; **commonly** *adv* comunemente, usualmente; **commonplace** *adj* banale, ordinario(-a); **Commons** *npl* (*BRIT Pol*): **the (House of) Commons** la Camera dei Comuni; **common sense** *n* buon senso; **Commonwealth** *n* **the**

Commonwealth il Commonwealth

● **COMMONWEALTH**
●
● Il **Commonwealth** è
● un'associazione di stati sovrani
● indipendenti e di alcuni territori
● annessi che facevano parte
● dell'antico Impero Britannico.
● Nel 1931 questi assunsero il nome
● di "Commonwealth of Nations",
● denominazione successivamente
● semplificata in "Commonwealth".
● Attualmente gli stati del
● "Commonwealth" riconoscono
● ancora il proprio capo di stato.

communal ['kɔmjuːnl] *adj* (*for common use*) pubblico(-a)

commune [*n* 'kɔmjuːn, *vb* kə'mjuːn] *n* (*group*) comune *f* ▷ *vi* **to ~ with** mettersi in comunione con

communicate [kə'mjuːnɪkeɪt] *vt* comunicare, trasmettere ▷ *vi* **to ~ with** comunicare (con)

communication [kəmjuːnɪ'keɪʃən] *n* comunicazione *f*

communion [kə'mjuːnɪən] *n* (*also:* **Holy C~**) comunione *f*

communism ['kɔmjunɪzəm] *n* comunismo; **communist** *adj, n* comunista *m/f*

community [kə'mjuːnɪtɪ] *n* comunità *f inv*; **community centre** (*US* **community center**) *n* circolo ricreativo; **community service** *n* (*BRIT*) ≈ lavoro sostitutivo

commute [kə'mjuːt] *vi* fare il pendolare ▷ *vt* (*Law*) commutare; **commuter** *n* pendolare *m/f*

compact [*adj* kəm'pækt, *n* 'kɔmpækt] *adj* compatto(-a) ▷ *n* (*also:* **powder ~**) portacipria *m inv*; **compact disc** *n* compact disc *m inv*; **compact disc player** *n* lettore *m* CD *inv*

companion [kəm'pænɪən] *n* compagno(-a)

company ['kʌmpənɪ] n (also Comm, Mil, Theatre) compagnia; **to keep sb ~** tenere compagnia a qn; **company car** n macchina (di proprietà) della ditta; **company director** n amministratore m, consigliere m di amministrazione

comparable ['kɔmpərəbl] adj simile

comparative [kəm'pærətɪv] adj relativo(-a); (adjective etc) comparativo(-a); **comparatively** adv relativamente

compare [kəm'pɛəʳ] vt **to ~ sth/sb with/to** confrontare qc/qn con/a ▷ vi **to ~ (with)** reggere il confronto (con); **comparison** [-'pærɪsn] n confronto; **in comparison (with)** in confronto (a)

compartment [kəm'pɑːtmənt] n compartimento; (Rail) scompartimento; **a non-smoking ~** uno scompartimento per non-fumatori

compass ['kʌmpəs] n bussola; **compasses** npl (Math) compasso

compassion [kəm'pæʃən] n compassione f

compatible [kəm'pætɪbl] adj compatibile

compel [kəm'pɛl] vt costringere, obbligare; **compelling** adj (fig: argument) irresistibile

compensate ['kɔmpənseɪt] vt risarcire ▷ vi **to ~ for** compensare; **compensation** [-'seɪʃn] n compensazione f; (money) risarcimento

compete [kəm'piːt] vi (take part) concorrere; (vie): **to ~ with** fare concorrenza (a)

competent ['kɔmpɪtənt] adj competente

competition [kɔmpɪ'tɪʃən] n gara; concorso; (Econ) concorrenza

competitive [kəm'pɛtɪtɪv] adj (Econ) concorrenziale; (sport) agonistico(-a); (person) che ha spirito di competizione; che ha spirito agonistico

competitor [kəm'pɛtɪtəʳ] n concorrente m/f

complacent [kəm'pleɪsnt] adj compiaciuto(-a) di sé

complain [kəm'pleɪn] vi lagnarsi, lamentarsi; **complaint** n lamento; (in shop etc) reclamo; (Med) malattia

complement [n 'kɔmplɪmənt, vb 'kɔmplɪment] n complemento; (especially of ship's crew etc) effettivo ▷ vt (enhance) accompagnarsi bene a; **complementary** [kɔmplɪ'mentərɪ] adj complementare

complete [kəm'pliːt] adj completo(-a) ▷ vt completare; (a form) riempire; **completely** adv completamente; **completion** n completamento

complex ['kɔmplɛks] adj complesso(-a) ▷ n (Psych, of buildings etc) complesso

complexion [kəm'plɛkʃən] n (of face) carnagione f

compliance [kəm'plaɪəns] n acquiescenza; **in ~ with** (orders, wishes etc) in conformità con

complicate ['kɔmplɪkeɪt] vt complicare; **complicated** adj complicato(-a); **complication** [-'keɪʃən] n complicazione f

compliment [n 'kɔmplɪmənt, vb 'kɔmplɪment] n complimento ▷ vt fare un complimento a; **complimentary** [-'mentərɪ] adj complimentoso(-a), elogiativo(-a); (free) in omaggio

comply [kəm'plaɪ] vi **to ~ with** assentire a; conformarsi a

component [kəm'pəunənt] adj componente ▷ n componente m

compose [kəm'pəuz] vt (form): **to be ~d of** essere composto di; (music, poem etc) comporre; **to ~ o.s.** ricomporsi; **composer** n (Mus) compositore(-trice); **composition** [kɔmpə'zɪʃən] n composizione f

composure [kəm'pəʊʒəʳ] n calma
compound ['kɒmpaʊnd] n (Chem, Ling) composto; (enclosure) recinto ▷ adj composto(-a)
comprehension [kɒmprɪ'hɛnʃən] n comprensione f
comprehensive [kɒmprɪ'hɛnsɪv] adj completo(-a); **comprehensive (school)** (BRIT) n scuola secondaria aperta a tutti

> Be careful not to translate **comprehensive** by the Italian word **comprensivo**.

compress [vb kəm'prɛs, n n'kɒmprɛs] vt comprimere ▷ n (Med) compressa
comprise [kəm'praɪz] vt (also: **be ~d**) comprendere
compromise ['kɒmprəmaɪz] n compromesso ▷ vt compromettere ▷ vi venire a un compromesso
compulsive [kəm'pʌlsɪv] adj (liar, gambler) che non riesce a controllarsi; (viewing, reading) cui non si può fare a meno
compulsory [kəm'pʌlsərɪ] adj obbligatorio(-a)
computer [kəm'pju:təʳ] n computer m inv, elaboratore m elettronico; **computer game** n gioco per computer; **computer-generated** adj realizzato(-a) al computer; **computerize** vt computerizzare; **computer programmer** n programmatore(-trice); **computer programming** n programmazione f di computer; **computer science** n informatica; **computer studies** npl informatica; **computing** n informatica
con [kɒn] (inf) vt truffare ▷ n truffa
conceal [kən'si:l] vt nascondere
concede [kən'si:d] vt ammettere
conceited [kən'si:tɪd] adj presuntuoso(-a), vanitoso(-a)
conceive [kən'si:v] vt concepire ▷ vi concepire un bambino
concentrate ['kɒnsəntreɪt] vi concentrarsi ▷ vt concentrare
concentration [kɒnsən'treɪʃən] n concentrazione f
concept ['kɒnsɛpt] n concetto
concern [kən'sə:n] n affare m; (Comm) azienda, ditta; (anxiety) preoccupazione f ▷ vt riguardare; **to be ~ed (about)** preoccuparsi (di); **concerning** prep riguardo a, circa
concert ['kɒnsə:t] n concerto; **concert hall** n sala da concerti
concerto [kən'tʃə:təʊ] n concerto
concession [kən'sɛʃən] n concessione f
concise [kən'saɪs] adj conciso(-a)
conclude [kən'klu:d] vt concludere; **conclusion** [-'klu:ʒən] n conclusione f
concrete ['kɒnkri:t] n calcestruzzo ▷ adj concreto(-a), di calcestruzzo
concussion [kən'kʌʃən] n commozione f cerebrale
condemn [kən'dɛm] vt condannare; (building) dichiarare pericoloso(-a)
condensation [kɒndɛn'seɪʃən] n condensazione f
condense [kən'dɛns] vi condensarsi ▷ vt condensare
condition [kən'dɪʃən] n condizione f; (Med) malattia ▷ vt condizionare; **on ~ that** a condizione che + sub, a condizione di; **conditional** adj condizionale; **to be conditional upon** dipendere da; **conditioner** n (for hair) balsamo; (for fabrics) ammorbidente m
condo ['kɒndəʊ] (US) n abbr (inf) = **condominium**
condom ['kɒndəm] n preservativo
condominium [kɒndə'mɪnɪəm] (US) n condominio
condone [kən'dəʊn] vt condonare
conduct [n 'kɒndʌkt, vb kən'dʌkt] n condotta ▷ vt condurre; (manage) dirigere; amministrare; (Mus) dirigere; **to ~ o.s.** comportarsi; **conducted tour** [kən'dʌktɪd-] n

gita accompagnata; **conductor** n (of orchestra) direttore m d'orchestra; (on bus) bigliettaio; (us: on train) controllore m; (Elec) conduttore m

cone [kəun] n cono; (Bot) pigna; (traffic cone) birillo

confectionery [kən'fɛkʃənrɪ] n dolciumi mpl

confer [kən'fəːʳ] vt **to ~ sth on** conferire qc a ▷ vi conferire

conference ['kɔnfərns] n congresso

confess [kən'fɛs] vt confessare, ammettere ▷ vi confessare; **confession** [kən'fɛʃən] n confessione f

confide [kən'faɪd] vi **to ~ in** confidarsi con

confidence ['kɔnfɪdns] n confidenza; (trust) fiducia; (self-assurance) sicurezza di sé; **in ~** (speak, write) in confidenza, confidenzialmente; **confident** adj sicuro(-a), sicuro(-a) di sé; **confidential** [kɔnfɪ'dɛnʃəl] adj riservato(-a), confidenziale

confine [kən'faɪn] vt limitare; (shut up) rinchiudere; **confined** adj (space) ristretto(-a)

confirm [kən'fəːm] vt confermare; **confirmation** [kɔnfə'meɪʃən] n conferma; (Rel) cresima

confiscate ['kɔnfɪskeɪt] vt confiscare

conflict [n 'kɔnflɪkt, vb kən'flɪkt] n conflitto ▷ vi essere in conflitto

conform [kən'fɔːm] vi **to ~ to** conformarsi (a)

confront [kən'frʌnt] vt (enemy, danger) affrontare; **confrontation** [kɔnfrən'teɪʃən] n scontro

confuse [kən'fjuːz] vt (one thing with another) confondere; **confused** adj confuso(-a); **confusing** adj che fa confondere; **confusion** [-'fjuːʒən] n confusione f

congestion [kən'dʒɛstʃən] n congestione f

congratulate [kən'grætjuleɪt] vt **to ~ sb (on)** congratularsi con qn (per or

di); **congratulations** [-'leɪʃənz] npl auguri mpl; (on success) complimenti mpl, congratulazioni fpl

congregation [kɔŋgrɪ'geɪʃən] n congregazione f

congress ['kɔŋgrɛs] n congresso; **congressman** (irreg: us) n membro del Congresso; **congresswoman** (irreg: us) n (donna) membro del Congresso

conifer ['kɔnɪfəʳ] n conifero

conjugate ['kɔndʒugeɪt] vt coniugare

conjugation [kɔndʒə'geɪʃən] n coniugazione f

conjunction [kən'dʒʌŋkʃən] n congiunzione f

conjure ['kʌndʒəʳ] vi fare giochi di prestigio

connect [kə'nɛkt] vt connettere, collegare; (Elec, Tel) collegare; (fig) associare ▷ vi (train): **to ~ with** essere in coincidenza con; **to be ~ed with** (associated) aver rapporti con; **connecting flight** n volo in coincidenza; **connection** [-ʃən] ▷ n relazione f, rapporto; (Elec) connessione f; (train, plane) coincidenza; (Tel) collegamento

conquer ['kɔŋkəʳ] vt conquistare; (feelings) vincere

conquest ['kɔŋkwɛst] n conquista

cons [kɔnz] npl see **convenience; pro**

conscience ['kɔnʃəns] n coscienza

conscientious [kɔnʃɪ'ɛnʃəs] adj coscienzioso(-a)

conscious ['kɔnʃəs] adj consapevole; (Med) cosciente; **consciousness** n consapevolezza; coscienza

consecutive [kən'sɛkjutɪv] adj consecutivo(-a); **on 3 ~ occasions** 3 volte di fila

consensus [kən'sɛnsəs] n consenso; **the ~ of opinion** l'opinione f unanime or comune

consent [kən'sɛnt] n consenso ▷ vi **to ~ (to)** acconsentire (a)

consequence ['kɔnsɪkwəns] n
consequenza, risultato; importanza

consequently ['kɔnsɪkwəntlɪ] adv di
conseguenza, dunque

conservation [kɔnsə'veɪʃən] n
conservazione f

conservative [kən'sə:vətɪv] adj
conservatore(-trice); (cautious)
cauto(-a); **Conservative** (BRIT) adj, n
(Pol) conservatore(-trice)

conservatory [kən'sə:vətrɪ]
n (greenhouse) serra; (Mus)
conservatorio

consider [kən'sɪdəʳ] vt considerare;
(take into account) tener conto di; **to ~
doing sth** considerare la possibilità di
fare qc; **considerable** [kən'sɪdərəbl]
adj considerevole, notevole;
considerably adv notevolmente,
decisamente; **considerate**
[kən'sɪdərɪt] adj premuroso(-a);
consideration [kənsɪdə'reɪʃən]
n considerazione f; **considering**
[kən'sɪdərɪŋ] prep in considerazione
di

consignment [kən'saɪnmənt] n (of
goods) consegna; spedizione f

consist [kən'sɪst] vi **to ~ of** constare
di, essere composto(-a) di

consistency [kən'sɪstənsɪ] n
consistenza; (fig) coerenza

consistent [kən'sɪstənt] adj coerente

consolation [kɔnsə'leɪʃən] n
consolazione f

console¹ [kən'səul] vt consolare

console² ['kɔnsəul] n quadro di
comando

consonant ['kɔnsənənt] n
consonante f

conspicuous [kən'spɪkjuəs] adj
cospicuo(-a)

conspiracy [kən'spɪrəsɪ] n congiura,
cospirazione f

constable ['kʌnstəbl] (BRIT) n
≈ poliziotto, agente m di polizia; **chief
~** ≈ questore m

constant ['kɔnstənt] adj costante,

continuo(-a); **constantly** adv
costantemente; continuamente

constipated ['kɔnstɪpeɪtɪd]
adj stitico(-a); **constipation**
[kɔnstɪ'peɪʃən] n stitichezza

constituency [kən'stɪtjuənsɪ] n
collegio elettorale

constitute ['kɔnstɪtjuːt] vt
costituire

constitution [kɔnstɪ'tjuːʃən] n
costituzione f

constraint [kən'streɪnt] n
costrizione f

construct [kən'strʌkt] vt costruire;
construction [-ʃən] n costruzione f;
constructive adj costruttivo(-a)

consul ['kɔnsl] n console m;
consulate ['kɔnsjulɪt] n consolato

consult [kən'sʌlt] vt consultare;
consultant n (Med) consulente m
medico; (other specialist) consulente;
consultation [-'teɪʃən] n (Med)
consulto; (discussion) consultazione f;
consulting room [kən'sʌltɪŋ-] (BRIT)
n ambulatorio

consume [kən'sjuːm] vt consumare;
consumer n consumatore(-trice)

consumption [kən'sʌmpʃən] n
consumo

cont. abbr = **continued**

contact ['kɔntækt] n contatto;
(person) conoscenza ▷ vt mettersi in
contatto con; **contact lenses** npl
lenti fpl a contatto

contagious [kən'teɪdʒəs] adj (also fig)
contagioso(-a)

contain [kən'teɪn] vt contenere;
to ~ o.s. contenersi; **container**
n recipiente m; (for shipping etc)
container m inv

contaminate [kən'tæmɪneɪt] vt
contaminare

cont'd abbr = **continued**

contemplate ['kɔntəmpleɪt] vt
contemplare; (consider) pensare a
(or di)

contemporary [kən'tɛmpərərɪ] adj,

n contemporaneo(-a)

contempt [kən'tɛmpt] *n* disprezzo; **~ of court** (*Law*) oltraggio alla Corte

contend [kən'tɛnd] *vt* **to ~ that** sostenere che ▷ *vi* **to ~ with** lottare contro

content¹ ['kɔntɛnt] *n* contenuto; **contents** *npl* (*of box, case etc*) contenuto; **(table of) ~s** indice *m*

content² [kən'tɛnt] *adj* contento(-a), soddisfatto(-a) ▷ *vt* contentare, soddisfare; **contented** *adj* contento(-a), soddisfatto(-a)

contest [*n* 'kɔntɛst, *vb* kən'tɛst] *n* lotta; (*competition*) gara, concorso ▷ *vt* contestare; impugnare; (*compete for*) essere in lizza per; **contestant** [kən'tɛstənt] *n* concorrente *m/f*; (*in fight*) avversario(-a)

context ['kɔntɛkst] *n* contesto

continent ['kɔntɪnənt] *n* continente *m*; **the C~** (*BRIT*) l'Europa continentale; **continental** [-'nɛntl] *adj* continentale; **continental breakfast** *n* colazione f all'europea (*senza piatti caldi*); **continental quilt** (*BRIT*) *n* piumino

continual [kən'tɪnjuəl] *adj* continuo(-a); **continually** *adv* di continuo

continue [kən'tɪnjuː] *vi* continuare ▷ *vt* continuare; (*start again*) riprendere

continuity [kɔntɪ'njuːɪtɪ] *n* continuità; (*TV, Cinema*) (ordine *m* della) sceneggiatura

continuous [kən'tɪnjuəs] *adj* continuo(-a), ininterrotto(-a); **continuous assessment** *n* (*BRIT*) valutazione f continua; **continuously** *adv* (*repeatedly*) continuamente; (*uninterruptedly*) ininterrottamente

contour ['kɔntuəʳ] *n* contorno, profilo; (*also*: **~ line**) curva di livello

contraception [kɔntrə'sɛpʃən] *n* contraccezione f

contraceptive [kɔntrə'sɛptɪv] *adj*

contraccettivo(-a) ▷ *n* contraccettivo

contract [*n* 'kɔntrækt, *vb* kən'trækt] *n* contratto ▷ *vi* (*become smaller*) contrarsi; (*Comm*) **to ~ to do sth** fare un contratto per fare qc ▷ *vt* (*illness*) contrarre; **contractor** *n* imprenditore *m*

contradict [kɔntrə'dɪkt] *vt* contraddire; **contradiction** [kɔntrə'dɪkʃən] *n* contraddizione f; **to be in contradiction with** discordare con

contrary¹ ['kɔntrərɪ] *adj* contrario(-a); (*unfavourable*) avverso(-a), contrario(-a) ▷ *n* contrario; **on the ~** al contrario; **unless you hear to the ~** salvo contrordine

contrary² [kən'trɛərɪ] *adj* (*perverse*) bisbetico(-a)

contrast [*n* 'kɔntrɑːst, *vb* kən'trɑːst] *n* contrasto ▷ *vt* mettere in contrasto; **in ~ to** contrariamente a

contribute [kən'trɪbjuːt] *vi* contribuire ▷ *vt* **to ~ £10/an article to** dare 10 sterline/un articolo a; **to ~ to** contribuire a; (*newspaper*) scrivere per; **contribution** [kɔntrɪ'bjuːʃən] *n* contributo; **contributor** *n* (*to newspaper*) collaboratore(-trice)

control [kən'trəul] *vt* controllare; (*firm, operation etc*) dirigere ▷ *n* controllo; **controls** *npl* (*of vehicle etc*) comandi *mpl*; (*governmental*) controlli *mpl*; **under ~** sotto controllo; **to be in ~ of** avere il controllo di; **to go out of ~** (*car*) non rispondere ai comandi; (*situation*) sfuggire di mano; **control tower** *n* (*Aviat*) torre f di controllo

controversial [kɔntrə'vəːʃl] *adj* controverso(-a), polemico(-a)

controversy ['kɔntrəvəːsɪ] *n* controversia, polemica

convenience [kən'viːnɪəns] *n* comodità f inv; **at your ~** a suo comodo; **all modern ~s** (*BRIT*), **all mod cons** tutte le comodità moderne

convenient [kən'viːnɪənt] *adj*
comodo(-a)

> Be careful not to translate
> *convenient* by the Italian word
> *conveniente*.

convent ['kɒnvənt] *n* convento
convention [kən'vɛnʃən] *n*
convenzione *f*; (*meeting*) convegno;
conventional *adj* convenzionale
conversation [kɒnvə'seɪʃən] *n*
conversazione *f*
conversely [kɒn'vɜːslɪ] *adv* al
contrario, per contro
conversion [kən'vɜːʃən] *n*
conversione *f*; (BRIT: *of house*)
trasformazione *f*, rimodernamento
convert [*vb* kən'vɜːt, *n* 'kɒnvɜːt]
vt (*Comm, Rel*) convertire; (*alter*)
trasformare ▷ *n* convertito(-a);
convertible *n* macchina
decappottabile
convey [kən'veɪ] *vt* trasportare;
(*thanks*) comunicare; (*idea*) dare;
conveyor belt [kən'veɪəʳ-] *n* nastro
trasportatore
convict [*vb* kən'vɪkt, *n* 'kɒnvɪkt]
vt dichiarare colpevole ▷ *n*
carcerato(-a); **conviction** [-ʃən] *n*
condanna; (*belief*) convinzione *f*
convince [kən'vɪns] *vt* convincere,
persuadere; **convinced** *adj*
convinced of/that convinto(-a)
di/che; **convincing** *adj* convincente
convoy ['kɒnvɔɪ] *n* convoglio
cook [kʊk] *vt* cucinare, cuocere
▷ *vi* cuocere; (*person*) cucinare ▷ *n*
cuoco(-a); **cook book** *n* libro di
cucina; **cooker** *n* fornello, cucina;
cookery *n* cucina; **cookery book**
(BRIT) *n* = **cook book**; **cookie** (US) *n*
biscotto; **cooking** *n* cucina
cool [kuːl] *adj* fresco(-a); (*not afraid,
calm*) calmo(-a); (*unfriendly*) freddo(-a)
▷ *vt* raffreddare; (*room*) rinfrescare ▷ *vi*
(*water*) raffreddarsi; (*air*) rinfrescarsi;
cool down *vi* raffreddarsi; (*fig: person,
situation*) calmarsi; **cool off** *vi* (*become*

calmer) calmarsi; (*lose enthusiasm*)
perdere interesse
cop [kɒp] (*inf*) *n* sbirro
cope [kəup] *vi* **to ~ with** (*problems*)
far fronte a
copper ['kɒpəʳ] *n* rame *m*; (*inf:
policeman*) sbirro
copy ['kɒpɪ] *n* copia ▷ *vt* copiare;
copyright *n* diritto d'autore
coral ['kɒrəl] *n* corallo
cord [kɔːd] *n* corda; (*Elec*) filo; **cords**
npl (*trousers*) calzoni *mpl* (di velluto) a
coste; **cordless** *adj* senza cavo
corduroy ['kɔːdərɔɪ] *n* fustagno
core [kɔːʳ] *n* (*of fruit*) torsolo; (*of
organization etc*) cuore *m* ▷ *vt* estrarre
il torsolo da
coriander [kɒrɪ'ændəʳ] *n* coriandolo
cork [kɔːk] *n* sughero; (*of bottle*) tappo;
corkscrew *n* cavatappi *m inv*
corn [kɔːn] *n* (BRIT: *wheat*) grano; (US:
maize) granturco; (*on foot*) callo; **~ on
the cob** (*Culin*) pannocchia cotta
corned beef ['kɔːnd-] *n* carne *f* di
manzo in scatola
corner ['kɔːnəʳ] *n* angolo; (*Aut*)
curva ▷ *vt* intrappolare; mettere
con le spalle al muro; (*Comm: market*)
accaparrare ▷ *vi* prendere una curva
corner shop (BRIT) *n* piccolo negozio di
generi alimentari
cornflakes ['kɔːnfleɪks] *npl* fiocchi
mpl di granturco
cornflour ['kɔːnflauəʳ] (BRIT) *n* farina
finissima di granturco
cornstarch ['kɔːnstɑːtʃ] (US) *n*
= **cornflour**
Cornwall ['kɔːnwɔːl] *n* Cornovaglia
coronary ['kɒrənərɪ] *n* ~
(thrombosis) trombosi *f* coronaria
coronation [kɒrə'neɪʃən] *n*
incoronazione *f*
coroner ['kɒrənəʳ] *n* magistrato
*incaricato di indagare la causa di morte in
circostanze sospette*
corporal ['kɔːpərəl] *n* caporalmaggiore
m ▷ *adj* **~ punishment** pena

corporale

corporate ['kɔːpərɪt] adj
costituito(-a) (in corporazione),
comune

corporation [kɔːpə'reɪʃən] n (of town)
consiglio comunale; (Comm) ente m

corps [kɔː, pl kɔːz] n inv corpo

corpse [kɔːps] n cadavere m

correct [kə'rɛkt] adj (accurate)
corretto(-a), esatto(-a); (proper)
corretto(-a) ▷ vt correggere;
correction [-ʃən] n correzione f

correspond [kɔrɪs'pɔnd] vi
corrispondere; **correspondence** n
corrispondenza; **correspondent** n
corrispondente m/f; **corresponding**
adj corrispondente

corridor ['kɔrɪdɔːʳ] n corridoio

corrode [kə'rəud] vt corrodere ▷ vi
corrodersi

corrupt [kə'rʌpt] adj corrotto(-a);
(Comput) alterato(-a) ▷ vt
corrompere; **corruption** n
corruzione f

Corsica ['kɔːsɪkə] n Corsica

cosmetic [kɔz'mɛtɪk] n cosmetico
▷ adj (fig: measure etc) superficiale;
cosmetic surgery n chirurgia
plastica

cosmopolitan [kɔzmə'pɔlɪtn] adj
cosmopolita

cost [kɔst] (pt, pp **cost**) n costo ▷ vt
costare; (find out the cost of) stabilire
il prezzo di; **costs** npl (Comm, Law)
spese fpl; **how much does it ~?**
quanto costa?; **at all ~s** a ogni costo

co-star ['kəustɑːʳ] n attore/trice della
stessa importanza del protagonista

Costa Rica ['kɔstə'riːkə] n Costa Rica

costly ['kɔstlɪ] adj costoso(-a),
caro(-a)

cost of living adj **~ allowance**
indennità f inv di contingenza

costume ['kɔstjuːm] n costume m;
(lady's suit) tailleur m inv; (BRIT: also:
swimming ~) costume m da bagno

cosy ['kəuzi] (US **cozy**) adj intimo(-a);

I'm very **~ here** sto proprio bene qui

cot [kɔt] n (BRIT: child's) lettino; (US:
campbed) brandina

cottage ['kɔtɪdʒ] n cottage m inv;
cottage cheese n fiocchi mpl di latte
magro

cotton ['kɔtn] n cotone m; **cotton
on** vi (inf): **to cotton on (to sth)**
afferrare (qc); **cotton bud** n (BRIT)
cotton fioc® m inv; **cotton candy** (US)
n zucchero filato; **cotton wool** (BRIT)
n cotone idrofilo

couch [kautʃ] n sofà m inv

cough [kɔf] vi tossire ▷ n tosse f; **I've
got a ~** ho la tosse; **cough mixture,
cough syrup** n sciroppo per la tosse

could [kud] pt of **can²**

couldn't = **could not**

council ['kaunsl] n consiglio; **city** or
town ~ consiglio comunale; **council
estate** (BRIT) n quartiere m di case
popolari; **council house** (BRIT) n casa
popolare; **councillor** (US **councilor**)
n consigliere(-a); **council tax** n (BRIT)
tassa comunale sulla proprietà

counsel ['kaunsl] n avvocato;
consultazione f ▷ vt consigliare;
counselling (US **counseling**) n
(Psych) assistenza psicologica;
counsellor (US **counselor**) n
consigliere(-a); (US) avvocato

count [kaunt] vt, vi contare ▷ n (of
votes etc) conteggio; (of pollen etc)
livello; (nobleman) conte m; **count in**
(inf) vt includere; **count me in** ci sto
anch'io; **count on** vt fus contare su;
countdown n conto alla rovescia

counter ['kauntəʳ] n banco ▷ vt
opporsi a ▷ adv **~ to** contro; in
opposizione a; **counterclockwise**
[-'klɔkwaɪz] (US) adv in senso
antiorario

counterfeit ['kauntəfɪt] n
contraffazione f, falso ▷ vt
contraffare, falsificare ▷ adj falso(-a)

counterpart ['kauntəpɑːt] n (of
document etc) copia; (of person)

corrispondente *m/f*

counterterrorism
[kauntə'terərızəm] *n* antiterrorismo
countess ['kauntıs] *n* contessa
countless ['kauntlıs] *adj*
innumerevole
country ['kʌntrı] *n* paese *m*; (*native
land*) patria; (*as opposed to town*)
campagna; (*region*) regione *f*; **country
and western (music)** *n* musica
country e western, country *m*;
country house *n* villa in campagna;
countryside *n* campagna
county ['kauntı] *n* contea
coup [ku:] (*pl* **coups**) *n* colpo; (*also:* ~
d'état) colpo di Stato
couple ['kʌpl] *n* coppia; **a ~ of** un
paio di
coupon ['ku:pɔn] *n* buono;
(*detachable form*) coupon *m inv*
courage ['kʌrıdʒ] *n* coraggio;
courageous *adj* coraggioso(-a)
courgette [kuə'ʒet] (*BRIT*) *n* zucchina
courier ['kurıə^r] *n* corriere *m*; (*for
tourists*) guida
course [kɔ:s] *n* corso; (*of ship*) rotta;
(*for golf*) campo; (*part of meal*) piatto;
of ~ senz'altro, naturalmente;
~ of action modo d'agire; **a ~ of
treatment** (*Med*) una cura
court [kɔ:t] *n* corte *f*; (*Tennis*) campo
▷ *vt* (*woman*) fare la corte a; **to take to
~** citare in tribunale
courtesy ['kə:təsı] *n* cortesia; **(by)
~ of** per gentile concessione di;
courtesy bus, courtesy coach
n autobus *m inv* gratuito (*di hotel,
aeroporto*)
court: court-house (*US*) *n* palazzo di
giustizia; **courtroom** *n* tribunale *m*;
courtyard *n* cortile *m*
cousin ['kʌzn] *n* cugino(-a); **first ~**
cugino di primo grado
cover ['kʌvə^r] *vt* coprire; (*book, table*)
rivestire; (*include*) comprendere;
(*Press*) fare un servizio su ▷ *n* (*of pan*)
coperchio; (*over furniture*) fodera; (*of

bed*) copriletto; (*of book*) copertina;
(*shelter*) riparo; (*Comm, Insurance, of
spy*) copertura; **covers** *npl* (*on bed*)
lenzuola *fpl* e coperte *fpl*; **to take ~**
(*shelter*) ripararsi; **under ~** al riparo;
under ~ of darkness protetto
dall'oscurità; **under separate ~**
(*Comm*) a parte, in plico separato;
cover up *vi* **to cover up for sb**
coprire qn; **coverage** *n* (*Press, Radio,
TV*): **to give full coverage to sth** fare
un ampio servizio su qc; **cover charge**
n coperto; **cover-up** *n* occultamento
(di informazioni)
cow [kau] *n* vacca ▷ *vt* (*person*)
intimidire
coward ['kauəd] *n* vigliacco(-a);
cowardly *adj* vigliacco(-a)
cowboy ['kaubɔı] *n* cow-boy *m inv*
cozy ['kauzı] (*US*) *adj* = **cosy**
crab [kræb] *n* granchio
crack [kræk] *n* fessura, crepa;
incrinatura; (*noise*) schiocco; (: *of
gun*) scoppio; (*drug*) crack *m inv* ▷ *vt*
spaccare; incrinare; (*whip*) schioccare;
(*nut*) schiacciare; (*problem*) risolvere;
(*code*) decifrare ▷ *adj* (*troops*) fuori
classe; **to ~ a joke** fare una battuta;
crack down on *vt fus* porre freno a;
cracked *adj* (*inf*) matto(-a); **cracker**
n cracker *m inv*; petardo
crackle ['krækl] *vi* crepitare
cradle ['kreıdl] *n* culla
craft [krɑ:ft] *n* mestiere *m*; (*cunning*)
astuzia; (*boat*) naviglio; **craftsman**
(*irreg*) *n* artigiano; **craftsmanship**
n abilità
cram [kræm] *vt* (*fill*): **to ~ sth with**
riempire qc di; (*put*): **to ~ sth into**
stipare qc in ▷ *vi* (*for exams*) prepararsi
(in gran fretta)
cramp [kræmp] *n* crampo; **I've got ~
in my leg** ho un crampo alla gamba;
cramped *adj* ristretto(-a)
cranberry ['krænbərı] *n* mirtillo
crane [kreın] *n* gru *f inv*
crap [kræp] *n* (*inf!*) fesserie *fpl*; **to

have a ~ cacare (!)
crash [kræʃ] n fragore m; (of car) incidente m; (of plane) caduta; (of business etc) crollo ▷ vt fracassare ▷ vi (plane) fracassarsi; (car) avere un incidente; (two cars) scontrarsi; (business etc) fallire, andare in rovina; **crash course** n corso intensivo; **crash helmet** n casco
crate [kreɪt] n cassa
crave [kreɪv] vt, vi **to ~ (for)** desiderare ardentemente
crawl [krɔːl] vi strisciare carponi; (vehicle) avanzare lentamente ▷ n (Swimming) crawl m
crayfish ['kreɪfɪʃ] n inv (freshwater) gambero (d'acqua dolce); (saltwater) gambero
crayon ['kreɪən] n matita colorata
craze [kreɪz] n mania
crazy ['kreɪzɪ] adj matto(-a); (inf: keen): **~ about sb** pazzo(-a) di qn; **~ about sth** matto(-a) per qc
creak [kriːk] vi cigolare, scricchiolare
cream [kriːm] n crema; (fresh) panna ▷ adj (colour) color crema inv; **cream cheese** n formaggio fresco; **creamy** adj cremoso(-a)
crease [kriːs] n grinza; (deliberate) piega ▷ vt sgualcire ▷ vi sgualcirsi
create [kriː'eɪt] vt creare; **creation** [-ʃən] n creazione f; **creative** adj creativo(-a); **creator** n creatore(-trice)
creature ['kriːtʃə^r] n creatura
crèche [krɛʃ] n asilo infantile
credentials [krɪ'dɛnʃlz] npl credenziali fpl
credibility [krɛdɪ'bɪlɪtɪ] n credibilità
credible ['krɛdɪbl] adj credibile; (witness, source) attendibile
credit ['krɛdɪt] n credito; onore m ▷ vt (Comm) accreditare; (believe: also: **give ~ to**) credere, prestar fede a; **credits** npl (Cinema) titoli mpl; **to ~ sb with** (fig) attribuire a qn; **to be in ~** (person) essere creditore(-trice); (bank account)

essere coperto(-a); **credit card** n carta di credito; **do you take credit cards?** accettate carte di credito?
creek [kriːk] n insenatura; (US) piccolo fiume m
creep [kriːp] (pt, pp **crept**) vi avanzare furtivamente (or pian piano)
cremate [krɪ'meɪt] vt cremare
crematorium [krɛmə'tɔːrɪəm] (pl **crematoria**) n forno crematorio
crept [krɛpt] pt, pp of **creep**
crescent ['krɛsnt] n (shape) mezzaluna; (street) strada semicircolare
cress [krɛs] n crescione m
crest [krɛst] n cresta; (of coat of arms) cimiero
crew [kruː] n equipaggio; **crew-neck** n girocollo
crib [krɪb] n culla ▷ vt (inf) copiare
cricket ['krɪkɪt] n (insect) grillo; (game) cricket m; **cricketer** n giocatore m di cricket
crime [kraɪm] n crimine m; **criminal** ['krɪmɪnl] adj, n criminale m/f
crimson ['krɪmzn] adj color cremisi inv
cringe [krɪndʒ] vi acquattarsi; (in embarrassment) sentirsi sprofondare
cripple ['krɪpl] n zoppo(-a) ▷ vt azzoppare
crisis ['kraɪsɪs] (pl **crises**) n crisi f inv
crisp [krɪsp] adj croccante; (fig) frizzante; vivace; deciso(-a); **crispy** adj croccante
criterion [kraɪ'tɪərɪən] (pl **criteria**) n criterio
critic ['krɪtɪk] n critico; **critical** adj critico(-a); **criticism** ['krɪtɪsɪzm] n critica; **criticize** ['krɪtɪsaɪz] vt criticare
Croat ['krəuæt] adj, n = **Croatian**
Croatia [krəu'eɪʃə] n Croazia; **Croatian** adj croato(-a) ▷ n croato(-a); (Ling) croato
crockery ['krɔkərɪ] n vasellame m
crocodile ['krɔkədaɪl] n coccodrillo

crocus ['krəukəs] n croco

croissant ['krwas] n brioche f inv, croissant m inv

crook [kruk] n truffatore m; (of shepherd) bastone m; **crooked** ['krukɪd] adj curvo(-a), storto(-a); (action) disonesto(-a)

crop [krɔp] n (produce) coltivazione f; (amount produced) raccolto; (riding crop) frustino ▷ vt (hair) rapare; **crop up** vi presentarsi

cross [krɔs] n croce f; (Biol) incrocio ▷ vt (street etc) attraversare; (arms, legs, Biol) incrociare; (cheque) sbarrare ▷ adj di cattivo umore; **cross off** vt cancellare (tirando una riga con la penna); **cross out** vt cancellare; **cross over** vi attraversare; **cross-Channel ferry** ['krɔs'tʃænl-] n traghetto che attraversa la Manica; **crosscountry (race)** n cross-country m inv; **crossing** n incrocio; (sea passage) traversata; (also: **pedestrian crossing**) passaggio pedonale; **how long does the crossing take?** quanto dura la traversata?; **crossing guard** (US) n dipendente comunale che aiuta i bambini ad attraversare la strada; **crossroads** n incrocio; **crosswalk** (US) n strisce fpl pedonali, passaggio pedonale; **crossword** n cruciverba m inv

crotch [krɔtʃ] n (Anat) inforcatura; (of garment) pattina

crouch [krautʃ] vi acquattarsi; rannicchiarsi

crouton ['kru:tɔn] n crostino

crow [krəu] n (bird) cornacchia; (of cock) canto del gallo ▷ vi (cock) cantare

crowd [kraud] n folla ▷ vt affollare, stipare ▷ vi **to ~ round/in** affollarsi intorno a/in; **crowded** adj affollato(-a); **crowded with** stipato(-a) di

crown [kraun] n corona; (of head) calotta cranica; (of hat) cocuzzolo; (of hill) cima ▷ vt incoronare; (fig: career) coronare; **crown jewels** npl gioielli mpl della Corona

crucial ['kru:ʃl] adj cruciale, decisivo(-a)

crucifix ['kru:sɪfɪks] n crocifisso

crude [kru:d] adj (materials) greggio(-a), non raffinato(-a); (fig: basic) crudo(-a), primitivo(-a); (: vulgar) rozzo(-a), grossolano(-a); **crude (oil)** n (petrolio) greggio

cruel ['kruəl] adj crudele; **cruelty** n crudeltà f inv

cruise [kru:z] n crociera ▷ vi andare a velocità di crociera; (taxi) circolare

crumb [krʌm] n briciola

crumble ['krʌmbl] vt sbriciolare ▷ vi sbriciolarsi; (plaster etc) sgretolarsi; (land, earth) franare; (building, fig) crollare

crumpet ['krʌmpɪt] n specie di frittella

crumple ['krʌmpl] vt raggrinzare, spiegazzare

crunch [krʌntʃ] vt sgranocchiare; (underfoot) scricchiolare ▷ n (fig) punto or momento cruciale; **crunchy** adj croccante

crush [krʌʃ] n folla; (love): **to have a ~ on sb** avere una cotta per qn; (drink): **lemon ~** spremuta di limone ▷ vt schiacciare; (crumple) sgualcire

crust [krʌst] n crosta; **crusty** adj (bread) croccante; (person) brontolone(-a); (remark) brusco(-a)

crutch [krʌtʃ] n gruccia

cry [kraɪ] vi piangere; (shout) urlare ▷ n urlo, grido; **cry out** vi, vt gridare

crystal ['krɪstl] n cristallo

cub [kʌb] n cucciolo; (also: **~ scout**) lupetto

Cuba ['kju:bə] n Cuba

Cuban ['kju:bən] adj, n cubano(-a)

cube [kju:b] n cubo ▷ vt (Math) elevare al cubo; **cubic** adj cubico(-a); (metre, foot) cubo(-a)

cubicle ['kju:bɪkl] n scompartimento separato; cabina

cuckoo ['kuku:] n cucù m inv

cucumber ['kju:kʌmbə^r] n cetriolo
cuddle ['kʌdl] vt abbracciare, coccolare ▷ vi abbracciarsi
cue [kju:] n (snooker cue) stecca; (Theatre etc) segnale m
cuff [kʌf] n (BRIT: of shirt, coat etc) polsino; (US: of trousers) risvolto; **off the** ~ improvvisando; **cufflinks** npl gemelli mpl
cuisine [kwɪ'zi:n] n cucina
cul-de-sac ['kʌldəsæk] n vicolo cieco
cull [kʌl] vt (ideas etc) scegliere ▷ n (of animals) abbattimento selettivo
culminate ['kʌlmɪneɪt] vi **to** ~ **in** culminare con
culprit ['kʌlprɪt] n colpevole m/f
cult [kʌlt] n culto
cultivate ['kʌltɪveɪt] vt (also fig) coltivare
cultural ['kʌltʃərəl] adj culturale
culture ['kʌltʃə^r] n (also fig) cultura
cumin ['kʌmɪn] n (spice) cumino
cunning ['kʌnɪŋ] n astuzia, furberia ▷ adj astuto(-a), furbo(-a)
cup [kʌp] n tazza; (prize, of bra) coppa
cupboard ['kʌbəd] n armadio
cup final n (BRIT Football) finale f di coppa
curator [kjuə'reɪtə^r] n direttore m (di museo ecc)
curb [kə:b] vt tenere a freno ▷ n freno; (US) bordo del marciapiede
curdle ['kə:dl] vi cagliare
cure [kjuə^r] vt guarire; (Culin) trattare; affumicare; essiccare ▷ n rimedio
curfew ['kə:fju:] n coprifuoco
curiosity [kjuərɪ'ɔsɪtɪ] n curiosità
curious ['kjuərɪəs] adj curioso(-a)
curl [kə:l] n riccio ▷ vt ondulare; (tightly) arricciare ▷ vi arricciarsi; **curl up** vi rannicchiarsi; **curler** n bigodino; **curly** ['kə:lɪ] adj ricciuto(-a)
currant ['kʌrnt] n (dried) sultanina; (bush, fruit) ribes m inv
currency ['kʌrnsɪ] n moneta; **to gain** ~ (fig) acquistare larga diffusione
current ['kʌrnt] adj corrente ▷ n corrente f; **current account** (BRIT) n conto corrente; **current affairs** npl attualità fpl; **currently** adv attualmente
curriculum [kə'rɪkjuləm] (pl **curriculums** or **curricula**) n curriculum m inv; **curriculum vitae** [-'vi:taɪ] n curriculum vitae m inv
curry ['kʌrɪ] n curry m inv ▷ vt **to** ~ **favour with** cercare di attirarsi i favori di; **curry powder** n curry m
curse [kə:s] vt maledire ▷ vi bestemmiare ▷ n maledizione f; bestemmia
cursor ['kə:sə^r] n (Comput) cursore m
curt [kə:t] adj secco(-a)
curtain ['kə:tn] n tenda; (Theatre) sipario
curve [kə:v] n curva ▷ vi curvarsi; **curved** adj curvo(-a)
cushion ['kuʃən] n cuscino ▷ vt (shock) fare da cuscinetto a
custard ['kʌstəd] n (for pouring) crema
custody ['kʌstədɪ] n (of child) tutela; **to take into** ~ (suspect) mettere in detenzione preventiva
custom ['kʌstəm] n costume m, consuetudine f; (Comm) clientela
customer ['kʌstəmə^r] n cliente m/f
customized ['kʌstəmaɪzd] adj (car etc) fuoriserie inv
customs ['kʌstəmz] npl dogana; **customs officer** n doganiere m
cut [kʌt] (pt, pp **cut**) vt tagliare; (shape, make) intagliare; (reduce) ridurre ▷ vi tagliare ▷ n taglio; (in salary etc) riduzione f; **I've** ~ **myself** mi sono tagliato; **to** ~ **a tooth** mettere un dente; **cut back** vt (plants) tagliare; (production, expenditure) ridurre; **cut down** vt (tree etc) abbattere ▷ vt fus (also: ~ **down on**) ridurre; **cut off** vt tagliare; (fig) isolare; **cut out** vt tagliare fuori; eliminare; ritagliare; **cut up** vt tagliare a pezzi; **cutback** n riduzione f
cute [kju:t] adj (sweet) carino(-a)

cutlery ['kʌtlərɪ] *n* posate *fpl*
cutlet ['kʌtlɪt] *n* costoletta; (*nut etc cutlet*) cotoletta vegetariana
cut: **cut-price** (BRIT) *adj* a prezzo ridotto; **cut-rate** (US) *adj* = **cut-price**; **cutting** ['kʌtɪŋ] *adj* tagliente ▷ *n* (*from newspaper*) ritaglio (di giornale); (*from plant*) talea
CV *n abbr* = **curriculum vitae**
cwt *abbr* = **hundredweight(s)**
cybercafé ['saɪbəkaefeɪ] *n* cybercaffè *m inv*
cybercrime [saɪbəkraɪm] *n* delinquenza informatica
cyberspace ['saɪbəspeɪs] *n* ciberspazio
cycle ['saɪkl] *n* ciclo; (*bicycle*) bicicletta ▷ *vi* andare in bicicletta; **cycle hire** *n* noleggio *m* biciclette *inv*; **cycle lane** *n* pista ciclabile; **cycle path** *n* pista ciclabile; **cycling** ['saɪklɪŋ] *n* ciclismo; **cyclist** ['saɪklɪst] *n* ciclista *m/f*
cyclone ['saɪkləun] *n* ciclone *m*
cylinder ['sɪlɪndər] *n* cilindro
cymbal ['sɪmbl] *n* piatto
cynical ['sɪnɪkl] *adj* cinico(-a)
Cypriot ['sɪprɪət] *adj, n* cipriota (*m/f*)
Cyprus ['saɪprəs] *n* Cipro
cyst [sɪst] *n* cisti *f inv*; **cystitis** [sɪs'taɪtɪs] *n* cistite *f*
czar [zɑːr] *n* zar *m inv*
Czech [tʃɛk] *adj* ceco(-a) ▷ *n* ceco(-a); (*Ling*) ceco; **Czech Republic** *n*: **the Czech Republic** la Repubblica Ceca

d

D [diː] *n* (*Mus*) re *m*
dab [dæb] *vt* (*eyes, wound*) tamponare; (*paint, cream*) applicare (con leggeri colpetti)
dad, daddy [dæd, 'dædɪ] *n* babbo, papà *m inv*
daffodil ['dæfədɪl] *n* trombone *m*, giunchiglia
daft [dɑːft] *adj* sciocco(-a)
dagger ['dægər] *n* pugnale *m*
daily ['deɪlɪ] *adj* quotidiano(-a), giornaliero(-a) ▷ *n* quotidiano ▷ *adv* tutti i giorni
dairy ['dɛərɪ] *n* (*BRIT: shop*) latteria; (*on farm*) caseificio ▷ *adj* caseario(-a); **dairy produce** *npl* latticini *mpl*
daisy ['deɪzɪ] *n* margherita
dam [dæm] *n* diga ▷ *vt* sbarrare; costruire dighe su
damage ['dæmɪdʒ] *n* danno, danni *mpl*; (*fig*) danno ▷ *vt* danneggiare; **damages** *npl* (*Law*) danni
damn [dæm] *vt* condannare; (*curse*) maledire ▷ *n* (*inf*): **I don't give a ~**

non me ne frega niente ▷ *adj* (*inf*: *also*: **~ed**): **this ~ ...** questo maledetto ...; **~ it !** accidenti!

damp [dæmp] *adj* umido(-a) ▷ *n* umidità, umido ▷ *vt* (*also*: **~en**: *cloth*, *rag*) inumidire, bagnare; (: *enthusiasm etc*) spegnere

dance [dɑːns] *n* danza, ballo; (*ball*) ballo ▷ *vi* ballare; **dance floor** *n* pista da ballo; **dancer** *n* danzatore(-trice); (*professional*) ballerino(-a); **dancing** ['dɑːnsɪŋ] *n* danza, ballo

dandelion ['dændɪlaɪən] *n* dente *m* di leone

dandruff ['dændrəf] *n* forfora

Dane [deɪn] *n* danese *m/f*

danger ['deɪndʒər] *n* pericolo; **there is a ~ of fire** c'è pericolo di incendio; **in ~** in pericolo; **he was in ~ of falling** rischiava di cadere; **dangerous** *adj* pericoloso(-a)

dangle ['dæŋgl] *vt* dondolare; (*fig*) far balenare ▷ *vi* pendolare

Danish ['deɪnɪʃ] *adj* danese ▷ *n* (*Ling*) danese *m*

dare [dɛər] *vt* **to ~ sb to do** sfidare qn a fare ▷ *vi* **to ~ to do sth** osare fare qc; **I ~ say** (*I suppose*) immagino (che); **daring** *adj* audace, ardito(-a) ▷ *n* audacia

dark [dɑːk] *adj* (*night*, *room*) buio(-a), scuro(-a); (*colour*, *complexion*) scuro(-a); (*fig*) cupo(-a), tetro(-a), nero(-a) ▷ *n* **in the ~** al buio; **in the ~ about** (*fig*) all'oscuro di; **after ~** a notte fatta; **darken** *vt* (*colour*) scurire ▷ *vi* (*sky*, *room*) oscurarsi; **darkness** *n* oscurità, buio; **darkroom** *n* camera oscura

darling ['dɑːlɪŋ] *adj* caro(-a) ▷ *n* tesoro

dart [dɑːt] *n* freccetta; (*Sewing*) pince *f inv* ▷ *vi* **to ~ towards** precipitarsi verso; **to ~ away/along** sfrecciare via/lungo; **dartboard** *n* bersaglio (per freccette); **darts** *n* tiro al bersaglio (con freccette)

dash [dæʃ] *n* (*sign*) lineetta; (*small quantity*) punta ▷ *vt* (*missile*) gettare; (*hopes*) infrangere ▷ *vi* **to ~ towards** precipitarsi verso

dashboard ['dæʃbɔːd] *n* (*Aut*) cruscotto

data ['deɪtə] *npl* dati *mpl*; **database** *n* base *f* di dati, data base *m inv*; **data processing** *n* elaborazione *f* (elettronica) dei dati

date [deɪt] *n* data; appuntamento; (*fruit*) dattero ▷ *vt* datare; (*person*) uscire con; **what's the ~ today?** quanti ne abbiamo oggi?; **~ of birth** data di nascita; **to ~** (*until now*) fino a oggi; **dated** *adj* passato(-a) di moda

daughter ['dɔːtər] *n* figlia; **daughter-in-law** *n* nuora

daunting ['dɔːntɪŋ] *adj* non invidiabile

dawn [dɔːn] *n* alba ▷ *vi* (*day*) spuntare; (*fig*): **it ~ed on him that ...** gli è venuto in mente che ...

day [deɪ] *n* giorno; (*as duration*) giornata; (*period of time, age*) tempo, epoca; **the ~ before** il giorno avanti *or* prima, **the ~ after, the following ~** il giorno dopo *or* seguente; **the ~ after tomorrow** dopodomani; **the ~ before yester~** l'altroieri; **by ~** di giorno; **day-care centre** *n* scuola materna; **daydream** *vi* sognare a occhi aperti; **daylight** *n* luce *f* del giorno; **day return** (*BRIT*) *n* biglietto giornaliero di andata e ritorno; **daytime** *n* giorno; **day-to-day** *adj* (*life, organization*) quotidiano(-a); **day trip** *n* gita (di un giorno)

dazed [deɪzd] *adj* stordito(-a)

dazzle ['dæzl] *vt* abbagliare; **dazzling** *adj* (*light*) abbagliante; (*colour*) violento(-a); (*smile*) smagliante

DC *abbr* (= *direct current*) c.c.

dead [dɛd] *adj* morto(-a); (*numb*) intirizzito(-a); (*telephone*) muto(-a); (*battery*) scarico(-a) ▷ *adv* assolutamente, perfettamente ▷ *npl*

the ~ i morti; **he was shot ~** fu colpito a morte; **~ tired** stanco(-a) morto(-a); **to stop ~** fermarsi di colpo; **dead end** n vicolo cieco; **deadline** n scadenza; **deadly** adj mortale; (weapon, poison) micidiale; **Dead Sea** n: **the Dead Sea** il mar Morto

deaf [dɛf] adj sordo(-a); **deafen** vt assordare; **deafening** adj fragoroso(-a), assordante

deal [diːl] (pt, pp **dealt**) n accordo; (business deal) affare m ▷ vt (blow, cards) dare; **a great ~ (of)** molto(-a); **deal with** vt fus (Comm) fare affari con, trattare con; (handle) occuparsi di; (be about: book etc) trattare di; **dealer** n commerciante m/f; **dealings** npl (Comm) relazioni fpl; (relations) rapporti mpl

dealt [dɛlt] pt, pp of **deal**

dean [diːn] n (Rel) decano; (Scol) preside m di facoltà (or di collegio)

dear [dɪəʳ] adj caro(-a) ▷ n **my ~** caro mio/cara mia ▷ excl **~ me!** Dio mio!; **D~ Sir/Madam** (in letter) Egregio Signore/Egregia Signora; **D~ Mr/Mrs X** Gentile Signor/Signora X; **dearly** adv (love) moltissimo; (pay) a caro prezzo

death [dɛθ] n morte f; (Admin) decesso; **death penalty** n pena di morte; **death sentence** n condanna a morte

debate [dɪˈbeɪt] n dibattito ▷ vt dibattere; discutere

debit [ˈdɛbɪt] n debito ▷ vt **to ~ a sum to sb** or **to sb's account** addebitare una somma a qn; **debit card** n carta di debito

debris [ˈdɛbriː] n detriti mpl

debt [dɛt] n debito; **to be in ~** essere indebitato(-a)

debut [ˈdeɪbjuː] n debutto

Dec. abbr (= December) dic.

decade [ˈdɛkeɪd] n decennio

decaffeinated [dɪˈkæfɪneɪtɪd] adj decaffeinato(-a)

decay [dɪˈkeɪ] n decadimento; (also: **tooth ~**) carie f ▷ vi (rot) imputridire

deceased [dɪˈsiːst] n defunto(-a)

deceit [dɪˈsiːt] n inganno; **deceive** [dɪˈsiːv] vt ingannare

December [dɪˈsɛmbəʳ] n dicembre m

decency [ˈdiːsənsɪ] n decenza

decent [ˈdiːsənt] adj decente; (respectable) per bene; (kind) gentile

deception [dɪˈsɛpʃən] n inganno

deceptive [dɪˈsɛptɪv] adj ingannevole

decide [dɪˈsaɪd] vt (person) far prendere una decisione a; (question, argument) risolvere, decidere ▷ vi decidere, decidersi; **to ~ to do/that** decidere di fare/che; **to ~ on** decidere per

decimal [ˈdɛsɪməl] adj decimale ▷ n decimale m

decision [dɪˈsɪʒən] n decisione f

decisive [dɪˈsaɪsɪv] adj decisivo(-a); (person) deciso(-a)

deck [dɛk] n (Naut) ponte m; (of bus): **top ~** imperiale m; (record deck) piatto; (of cards) mazzo; **deckchair** n sedia a sdraio

declaration [dɛkləˈreɪʃən] n dichiarazione f

declare [dɪˈklɛəʳ] vt dichiarare

decline [dɪˈklaɪn] n (decay) declino; (lessening) ribasso ▷ vt declinare; rifiutare ▷ vi declinare; diminuire

decorate [ˈdɛkəreɪt] vt (adorn, give a medal to) decorare; (paint and paper) tinteggiare e tappezzare; **decoration** [-ˈreɪʃən] n (medal etc, adornment) decorazione f; **decorator** n decoratore m

decrease [n ˈdiːkriːs, vb diːˈkriːs] n diminuzione f ▷ vt, vi diminuire

decree [dɪˈkriː] n decreto

dedicate [ˈdɛdɪkeɪt] vt consacrare; (book etc) dedicare; **dedicated** adj coscienzioso(-a); (Comput) specializzato(-a); dedicato(-a); **dedication** [dɛdɪˈkeɪʃən] n (devotion) dedizione f; (in book etc) dedica

deduce [dɪ'dju:s] vt dedurre
deduct [dɪ'dʌkt] vt **to ~ sth from** dedurre qc (da); **deduction** [dɪ'dʌkʃən] n deduzione f
deed [di:d] n azione f, atto; (Law) atto
deem [di:m] vt (formal) giudicare, ritenere; **to ~ it wise to do** ritenere prudente fare
deep [di:p] adj profondo(-a); **4 metres ~** profondo(-a) 4 metri ▷ adv **spectators stood 20 ~** c'erano 20 file di spettatori; **how ~ is the water?** quanto è profonda l'acqua?; **deep-fry** vt friggere in olio abbondante; **deeply** adv profondamente
deer [dɪə^r] n inv **the ~** i cervidi; **(red) ~** cervo; **(fallow) ~** daino; **roe ~** capriolo
default [dɪ'fɔ:lt] n (Comput: also: **~ value**) default m inv; **by ~** (Sport) per abbandono
defeat [dɪ'fi:t] n sconfitta ▷ vt (team, opponents) sconfiggere
defect [n 'di:fɛkt, vb dɪ'fɛkt] n difetto ▷ vi: **to ~ to the enemy** passare al nemico; **defective** [dɪ'fɛktɪv] adj difettoso(-a)
defence [dɪ'fɛns] (us **defense**) n difesa
defend [dɪ'fɛnd] vt difendere; **defendant** n imputato(-a); **defender** n difensore(-a)
defense [dɪ'fɛns] (us) n = **defence**
defensive [dɪ'fɛnsɪv] adj difensivo(-a) ▷ n **on the ~** sulla difensiva
defer [dɪ'fə:^r] vt (postpone) differire, rinviare
defiance [dɪ'faɪəns] n sfida; **in ~ of** a dispetto di; **defiant** [dɪ'faɪənt] adj (attitude) di sfida; (person) ribelle
deficiency [dɪ'fɪʃənsɪ] n deficienza; carenza; **deficient** adj deficiente; insufficiente; **to be deficient in** mancare di
deficit ['dɛfɪsɪt] n deficit m inv
define [dɪ'faɪn] vt definire
definite ['dɛfɪnɪt] adj (fixed) definito(-a), preciso(-a); (clear, obvious) ben definito(-a), esatto(-a); (Ling) determinativo(-a); **he was ~ about it** ne era sicuro; **definitely** adv indubbiamente
definition [dɛfɪ'nɪʃən] n definizione f
deflate [di:'fleɪt] vt sgonfiare
deflect [dɪ'flɛkt] vt deflettere, deviare
defraud [dɪ'frɔ:d] vt defraudare
defrost [di:'frɔst] vt (fridge) disgelare
defuse [di:'fju:z] vt disinnescare; (fig) distendere
defy [dɪ'faɪ] vt sfidare; (efforts etc) resistere a; **it defies description** supera ogni descrizione
degree [dɪ'gri:] n grado; (Scol) laurea (universitaria); **a first ~ in maths** una laurea in matematica; **by ~s** (gradually) gradualmente, a poco a poco; **to some ~** fino a un certo punto, in certa misura
dehydrated [di:haɪ'dreɪtɪd] adj disidratato(-a); (milk, eggs) in polvere
de-icer ['di:aɪsə^r] n sbrinatore m
delay [dɪ'leɪ] vt ritardare ▷ vi **to ~ (in doing sth)** ritardare (a fare qc) ▷ n ritardo; **to be ~ed** subire un ritardo; (person) essere trattenuto(-a)
delegate [n 'dɛlɪgɪt, vb 'dɛlɪgeɪt] n delegato(-a) ▷ vt delegare
delete [dɪ'li:t] vt cancellare
deli ['dɛlɪ] n = **delicatessen**
deliberate [adj dɪ'lɪbərɪt, vb dɪ'lɪbəreɪt] adj (intentional) intenzionale; (slow) misurato(-a) ▷ vi deliberare, riflettere; **deliberately** adv (on purpose) deliberatamente
delicacy ['dɛlɪkəsɪ] n delicatezza
delicate ['dɛlɪkɪt] adj delicato(-a)
delicatessen [dɛlɪkə'tɛsn] n ≈ salumeria
delicious [dɪ'lɪʃəs] adj delizioso(-a), squisito(-a)
delight [dɪ'laɪt] n delizia, gran piacere m ▷ vt dilettare; **to take (a) ~ in** dilettarsi in; **delighted** adj **delighted (at or with)** contentissimo(-a) (di), felice (di); **delighted to do** felice di

fare; **delightful** adj delizioso(-a), incantevole

delinquent [dɪ'lɪŋkwənt] adj, n delinquente m/f

deliver [dɪ'lɪvəʳ] vt (mail) distribuire; (goods) consegnare; (speech) pronunciare; (Med) far partorire; **delivery** n distribuzione f; consegna; (of speaker) dizione f; (Med) parto

delusion [dɪ'luːʒən] n illusione f

de luxe [də'lʌks] adj di lusso

delve [dɛlv] vi **to ~ into** frugare in; (subject) far ricerche in

demand [dɪ'mɑːnd] vt richiedere; (rights) rivendicare ▷ n domanda; (claim) rivendicazione f; **in ~** ricercato(-a), richiesto(-a); **on ~** a richiesta; **demanding** adj (boss) esigente; (work) impegnativo(-a)

demise [dɪ'maɪz] n decesso

demo ['dɛməu] (inf) n abbr (= demonstration) manifestazione f

democracy [dɪ'mɔkrəsɪ] n democrazia; **democrat** ['dɛməkræt] n democratico(-a); **democratic** [dɛmə'krætɪk] adj democratico(-a)

demolish [dɪ'mɔlɪʃ] vt demolire

demolition [dɛmə'lɪʃən] n demolizione f

demon ['diːmən] n (also fig) demonio ▷ cpd **a ~ squash player** un mago dello squash; **a ~ driver** un guidatore folle

demonstrate ['dɛmənstreɪt] vt dimostrare, provare ▷ vi dimostrare, manifestare; **demonstration** [-'streɪʃən] n dimostrazione f; (Pol) dimostrazione, manifestazione f; **demonstrator** n (Pol) dimostrante m/f; (Comm) dimostratore(-trice)

demote [dɪ'məut] vt far retrocedere

den [dɛn] n tana, covo; (room) buco

denial [dɪ'naɪəl] n diniego; rifiuto

denim ['dɛnɪm] n tessuto di cotone ritorto; **denims** npl (jeans) blue jeans mpl

Denmark ['dɛnmɑːk] n Danimarca

denomination [dɪnɔmɪ'neɪʃən] n (money) valore m; (Rel) confessione f

denounce [dɪ'nauns] vt denunciare

dense [dɛns] adj fitto(-a); (smoke) denso(-a); (inf: person) ottuso(-a), duro(-a)

density ['dɛnsɪtɪ] n densità f inv

dent [dɛnt] n ammaccatura ▷ vt (also: **make a ~ in**) ammaccare

dental ['dɛntl] adj dentale; **dental floss** [-flɔs] n filo interdentale; **dental surgery** n ambulatorio del dentista

dentist ['dɛntɪst] n dentista m/f

dentures ['dɛntʃəz] npl dentiera

deny [dɪ'naɪ] vt negare; (refuse) rifiutare

deodorant [diː'əudərənt] n deodorante m

depart [dɪ'pɑːt] vi partire; **to ~ from** (fig) deviare da

department [dɪ'pɑːtmənt] n (Comm) reparto; (Scol) sezione f, dipartimento; (Pol) ministero; **department store** n grande magazzino

departure [dɪ'pɑːtʃəʳ] n partenza; (fig): **~ from** deviazione f da; **a new ~** una svolta (decisiva); **departure lounge** n (at airport) sala d'attesa

depend [dɪ'pɛnd] vi **to ~ on** dipendere da; (rely on) contare su; **it ~s** dipende; **~ing on the result ...** a seconda del risultato ...; **dependant** n persona a carico; **dependent** adj **to be dependent on** dipendere da; (child, relative) essere a carico di ▷ n = **dependant**

depict [dɪ'pɪkt] vt (in picture) dipingere; (in words) descrivere

deport [dɪ'pɔːt] vt deportare; espellere

deposit [dɪ'pɔzɪt] n (Comm, Geo) deposito; (of ore, oil) giacimento; (Chem) sedimento; (part payment) acconto; (for hired goods etc) cauzione f ▷ vt depositare; dare in acconto; mettere or lasciare in deposito;

deposit account n conto vincolato

depot ['dɛpəʊ] n deposito; (US) stazione f ferroviaria

depreciate [dɪ'priːʃɪeɪt] vi svalutarsi

depress [dɪ'prɛs] vt deprimere; (price, wages) abbassare; (press down) premere; **depressed** adj (person) depresso(-a), abbattuto(-a); (price) in ribasso; (industry) in crisi; **depressing** adj deprimente; **depression** [dɪ'prɛʃən] n depressione f

deprive [dɪ'praɪv] vt: **to ~ sb of** privare qn di; **deprived** adj disgraziato(-a)

dept. abbr = **department**

depth [dɛpθ] n profondità f inv; **in the ~s of** nel profondo di; nel cuore di; **out of one's ~** (in water) dove non si tocca; (fig) a disagio

deputy ['dɛpjʊtɪ] adj **~ head** (BRIT: Scol) vicepreside m/f ▷ n (assistant) vice m/f inv; (US: also: **~ sheriff**) vicesceriffo

derail [dɪ'reɪl] vt: **to be ~ed** deragliare

derelict ['dɛrɪlɪkt] adj abbandonato(-a)

derive [dɪ'raɪv] vt: **to ~ sth from** derivare qc da, trarre qc da ▷ vi **to ~ from** derivare da

descend [dɪ'sɛnd] vt, vi discendere, scendere; **to ~ from** discendere da; **to ~ to** (lying, begging) abbassarsi a; **descendant** n discendente m/f; **descent** [dɪ'sɛnt] n discesa; (origin) discendenza, famiglia

describe [dɪs'kraɪb] vt descrivere; **description** [-'krɪpʃən] n descrizione f; (sort) genere m, specie f

desert [n 'dɛzət, vb dɪ'zəːt] n deserto ▷ vt lasciare, abbandonare ▷ vi (Mil) disertare; **deserted** [dɪ'zəːtɪd] adj deserto(-a)

deserve [dɪ'zəːv] vt meritare

design [dɪ'zaɪn] n (art, sketch) disegno; (layout, shape) linea; (pattern) fantasia; (intention) intenzione f ▷ vt disegnare; progettare; **design and technology** n (BRIT: Scol)

progettazione f sg e tecnologie f pl

designate vt [vb 'dɛzɪgneɪt, adj 'dɛzɪgnɪt] designare ▷ adj designato(-a)

designer [dɪ'zaɪnə'] n (Art, Tech) disegnatore(-trice); (of fashion) modellista m/f

desirable [dɪ'zaɪərəbl] adj desiderabile; **it is ~ that** è opportuno che + sub

desire [dɪ'zaɪə'] n desiderio, voglia ▷ vt desiderare, volere

desk [dɛsk] n (in office) scrivania; (for pupil) banco; (BRIT: in shop, restaurant) cassa; (in hotel) ricevimento; (at airport) accettazione f; **desk-top publishing** n desktop publishing m

despair [dɪs'pɛə'] n disperazione f ▷ vi **to ~ of** disperare di

despatch [dɪs'pætʃ] n, vt = **dispatch**

desperate ['dɛspərɪt] adj disperato(-a); (fugitive) capace di tutto; **to be ~ for sth/to do** volere disperatamente qc/fare; **desperately** adv disperatamente; (very) terribilmente, estremamente; **desperation** [dɛspə'reɪʃən] n disperazione f

despise [dɪs'paɪz] vt disprezzare, sdegnare

despite [dɪs'paɪt] prep malgrado, a dispetto di, nonostante

dessert [dɪ'zəːt] n dolce m; frutta; **dessertspoon** n cucchiaio da dolci

destination [dɛstɪ'neɪʃən] n destinazione f

destined ['dɛstɪnd] adj: **to be ~ to do/for** essere destinato(-a) a fare/per

destiny ['dɛstɪnɪ] n destino

destroy [dɪs'trɔɪ] vt distruggere

destruction [dɪs'trʌkʃən] n distruzione f

destructive [dɪs'trʌktɪv] adj distruttivo(-a)

detach [dɪ'tætʃ] vt staccare, distaccare; **detached** adj (attitude) distante; **detached house** n villa

detail ['di:teɪl] n particolare
m, dettaglio ▷ vt dettagliare,
particolareggiare; **in ~** nei particolari;
detailed adj particolareggiato(-a)

detain [dɪ'teɪn] vt trattenere; (in
captivity) detenere

detect [dɪ'tɛkt] vt scoprire, scorgere;
(Med, Police, Radar etc) individuare;
detection [dɪ'tɛkʃən] n scoperta;
individuazione f; **detective** n
investigatore(-trice); **detective story**
n giallo

detention [dɪ'tɛnʃən] n detenzione f;
(Scol) permanenza forzata per punizione

deter [dɪ'tə:ʳ] vt dissuadere

detergent [dɪ'tə:dʒənt] n detersivo

deteriorate [dɪ'tɪərɪəreɪt] vi
deteriorarsi

determination [dɪtə:mɪ'neɪʃən] n
determinazione f

determine [dɪ'tə:mɪn] vt
determinare; **determined** adj
(person) risoluto(-a), deciso(-a);
determined to do deciso(-a) a fare

deterrent [dɪ'tɛrənt] n deterrente m;
to act as a ~ fungere da deterrente

detest [dɪ'tɛst] vt detestare

detour ['di:tuəʳ] n deviazione f

detract [dɪ'trækt] vi **to ~ from**
detrarre da

detrimental [dɛtrɪ'mɛntl] adj **~ to**
dannoso(-a) a, nocivo(-a) a

devastating ['dɛvəsteɪtɪŋ] adj
devastatore(-trice), sconvolgente

develop [dɪ'vɛləp] vt sviluppare;
(habit) prendere (gradualmente) ▷ vi
svilupparsi; (facts, symptoms: appear)
manifestarsi, rivelarsi; **can you ~ this
film?** può sviluppare questo rullino?;
developing country n paese m in via
di sviluppo; **development** n sviluppo

device [dɪ'vaɪs] n (apparatus)
congegno

devil ['dɛvl] n diavolo; demonio

devious ['di:vɪəs] adj (person)
subdolo(-a)

devise [dɪ'vaɪz] vt escogitare,

concepire

devote [dɪ'vəut] vt **to ~ sth
to** dedicare qc a; **devoted** adj
devoto(-a); **to be devoted to sb**
essere molto affezionato(-a) a qn;
devotion [dɪ'vəuʃən] n devozione f,
attaccamento; (Rel) atto di devozione,
preghiera

devour [dɪ'vauəʳ] vt divorare

devout [dɪ'vaut] adj pio(-a),
devoto(-a)

dew [dju:] n rugiada

diabetes [daɪə'bi:ti:z] n diabete m

diabetic [daɪə'bɛtɪk] adj, n
diabetico(-a)

diagnose [daɪəg'nəuz] vt
diagnosticare

diagnosis [daɪəg'nəusɪs] (pl
diagnoses) n diagnosi f inv

diagonal [daɪ'ægənl] adj diagonale
▷ n diagonale f

diagram ['daɪəgræm] n diagramma m

dial ['daɪəl] n quadrante m; (on
radio) lancetta; (on telephone) disco
combinatore ▷ vt (number) fare

dialect ['daɪəlɛkt] n dialetto

dialling code (us **area code**) n
prefisso; **what's the ~ for Paris?** qual
è il prefisso telefonico di Parigi?

dialling tone ['daɪəlɪŋ-] (us **dial
tone**) n segnale m di linea libera

dialogue ['daɪəlɔg] (us **dialog**) n
dialogo

diameter [daɪ'æmɪtəʳ] n diametro

diamond ['daɪəmənd] n diamante m;
(shape) rombo; **diamonds** npl (Cards)
quadri mpl

diaper ['daɪəpəʳ] (us) n pannolino

diarrhoea [daɪə'ri:ə] (us **diarrhea**)
n diarrea

diary ['daɪərɪ] n (daily account) diario;
(book) agenda

dice [daɪs] n inv dado ▷ vt (Culin)
tagliare a dadini

dictate [dɪk'teɪt] vt dettare;
dictation [dɪk'teɪʃən] n dettatura;
(Scol) dettato

dictator [dɪk'teɪtə'] n dittatore m
dictionary ['dɪkʃənrɪ] n dizionario
did [dɪd] pt of **do**
didn't ['dɪdnt] = **did not**
die [daɪ] vi morire; **to be dying for
sth/to do sth** morire dalla voglia di
qc/di fare qc; **die down** vi abbassarsi;
die out vi estinguersi
diesel ['di:zəl] n (vehicle) diesel m inv
diet ['daɪət] n alimentazione f;
(restricted food) dieta ▷ vi (also: **be on a
~**) stare a dieta
differ ['dɪfə'] vi **to ~ from sth** differire
da qc, essere diverso(-a) da qc; **to ~
from sb over sth** essere in disaccordo
con qn su qc; **difference** n differenza;
(disagreement) screzio; **different** adj
diverso(-a); **differentiate** [-'rɛnʃɪeɪt]
vi **to differentiate between**
discriminare or fare differenza fra;
differently adv diversamente
difficult ['dɪfɪkəlt] adj difficile;
difficulty n difficoltà f inv
dig [dɪg] (pt, pp **dug**) vt (hole) scavare;
(garden) vangare ▷ n (prod) gomitata;
(archaeological) scavo; (fig) frecciata;
dig up vt (tree etc) sradicare;
(information) scavare fuori
digest [vb daɪ'dʒɛst, n 'daɪdʒɛst] vt
digerire ▷ n compendio; **digestion**
[dɪ'dʒɛstʃən] n digestione f
digit ['dɪdʒɪt] n cifra; (finger) dito;
digital adj digitale; **digital camera** n
macchina fotografica digitale; **digital
TV** n televisione f digitale
dignified ['dɪgnɪfaɪd] adj
dignitoso(-a)
dignity ['dɪgnɪtɪ] n dignità
digs [dɪgz] (BRIT: inf) npl camera
ammobiliata
dilemma [daɪ'lɛmə] n dilemma m
dill [dɪl] n aneto
dilute [daɪ'lu:t] vt diluire; (with water)
annacquare
dim [dɪm] adj (light) debole; (shape etc)
vago(-a); (room) in penombra; (inf:
person) tonto(-a) ▷ vt (light) abbassare

dime [daɪm] (US) n = 10 cents
dimension [daɪ'mɛnʃən] n
dimensione f
diminish [dɪ'mɪnɪʃ] vt, vi diminuire
din [dɪn] n chiasso, fracasso
dine [daɪn] vi pranzare; **diner** n
(person) cliente m/f; (US: place) tavola
calda
dinghy ['dɪŋgɪ] n battello
pneumatico; (also: **rubber ~**)
gommone m
dingy ['dɪndʒɪ] adj grigio(-a)
dining car ['daɪnɪŋ-] (BRIT) n vagone
m ristorante
dining room n sala da pranzo
dining table n tavolo da pranzo
dinner ['dɪnə'] n (lunch) pranzo;
(evening meal) cena; (public)
banchetto; **dinner jacket** n smoking
m inv; **dinner party** n cena; **dinner
time** n ora di pranzo (or cena)
dinosaur ['daɪnəsɔ:'] n dinosauro
dip [dɪp] n discesa; (in sea) bagno;
(Culin) salsetta ▷ vt immergere;
bagnare; (BRIT Aut: lights) abbassare
▷ vi abbassarsi
diploma [dɪ'pləumə] n diploma m
diplomacy [dɪ'pləuməsɪ] n
diplomazia
diplomat ['dɪpləmæt] n diplomatico;
diplomatic [dɪplə'mætɪk] adj
diplomatico(-a)
dipstick ['dɪpstɪk] n (Aut) indicatore m
di livello dell'olio
dire [daɪə'] adj terribile; estremo(-a)
direct [daɪ'rɛkt] adj diretto(-a) ▷ vt
dirigere; (order): **to ~ sb to do sth**
dare direttive a qn di fare qc ▷ adv
direttamente; **can you ~ me to ...?** mi
può indicare la strada per ...?; **direct
debit** n (Banking) addebito effettuato
per ordine di un cliente di banca
direction [dɪ'rɛkʃən] n direzione
f; **directions** npl (advice)
chiarimenti mpl; **sense of ~** senso
dell'orientamento; **~s for use**
istruzioni f pl

directly [dɪˈrɛktlɪ] adv (in straight line) direttamente; (at once) subito

director [dɪˈrɛktəˈ] n direttore(-trice), amministratore(-trice); (Theatre, Cinema) regista m/f

directory [dɪˈrɛktərɪ] n elenco; **directory enquiries** (us **directory assistance**) n informazioni fpl elenco abbonati inv

dirt [dəːt] n sporcizia; immondizia; (earth) terra; **dirty** adj sporco(-a) ▷ vt sporcare

disability [dɪsəˈbɪlɪtɪ] n invalidità f inv; (Law) incapacità f inv

disabled [dɪsˈeɪbld] adj invalido(-a); (mentally) ritardato(-a) ▷ npl: **the ~** gli invalidi

disadvantage [dɪsədˈvɑːntɪdʒ] n svantaggio

disagree [dɪsəˈɡriː] vi (differ) discordare; (be against, think otherwise): **to ~ (with)** essere in disaccordo (con), dissentire (da); **disagreeable** adj sgradevole; (person) antipatico(-a); **disagreement** n disaccordo; (argument) dissapore m

disappear [dɪsəˈpɪəˈ] vi scomparire; **disappearance** n scomparsa

disappoint [dɪsəˈpɔɪnt] vt deludere; **disappointed** adj deluso(-a); **disappointing** adj deludente; **disappointment** n delusione f

disapproval [dɪsəˈpruːvəl] n disapprovazione f

disapprove [dɪsəˈpruːv] vi: **to ~ of** disapprovare

disarm [dɪsˈɑːm] vt disarmare; **disarmament** n disarmo

disaster [dɪˈzɑːstəˈ] n disastro; **disastrous** [dɪˈzɑːstrəs] adj disastroso(-a)

disbelief [ˈdɪsbəˈliːf] n incredulità

disc [dɪsk] n disco; (Comput) = **disk**

discard [dɪsˈkɑːd] vt (old things) scartare; (fig) abbandonare

discharge [vb dɪsˈtʃɑːdʒ, n ˈdɪstʃɑːdʒ] vt (duties) compiere; (Elec, waste etc) scaricare; (Med) emettere; (patient) dimettere; (employee) licenziare; (soldier) congedare; (defendant) liberare ▷ n (Elec) scarica; (Med) emissione f; (dismissal) licenziamento; congedo; liberazione f

discipline [ˈdɪsɪplɪn] n disciplina ▷ vt disciplinare; (punish) punire

disc jockey n disc jockey m inv

disclose [dɪsˈkləuz] vt rivelare, svelare

disco [ˈdɪskəu] n abbr discoteca

discoloured [dɪsˈkʌləd] (us **discolored**) adj scolorito(-a), ingiallito(-a)

discomfort [dɪsˈkʌmfət] n disagio; (lack of comfort) scomodità f inv

disconnect [dɪskəˈnɛkt] vt sconnettere, staccare; (Elec, Radio) staccare; (gas, water) chiudere

discontent [dɪskənˈtɛnt] n scontentezza

discontinue [dɪskənˈtɪnjuː] vt smettere, cessare; **"~d"** (Comm) "fuori produzione"

discount [n ˈdɪskaunt, vb dɪsˈkaunt] n sconto ▷ vt scontare; (idea) non badare a; **are there ~s for students?** ci sono sconti per studenti?

discourage [dɪsˈkʌrɪdʒ] vt scoraggiare

discover [dɪsˈkʌvəˈ] vt scoprire; **discovery** n scoperta

discredit [dɪsˈkrɛdɪt] vt screditare; mettere in dubbio

discreet [dɪˈskriːt] adj discreto(-a)

discrepancy [dɪˈskrɛpənsɪ] n discrepanza

discretion [dɪˈskrɛʃən] n discrezione f; **use your own ~** giudichi lei

discriminate [dɪˈskrɪmɪneɪt] vi: **to ~ between** distinguere tra; **to ~ against** discriminare contro; **discrimination** [-ˈneɪʃən] n discriminazione f; (judgment) discernimento

discuss [dɪˈskʌs] vt discutere; (debate)

dibattere; **discussion** [dɪˈskʌʃən] n
discussione f; **discussion forum** n (on
the Internet) forum m inv di discussione
disease [dɪˈziːz] n malattia
disembark [dɪsɪmˈbɑːk] vt, vi sbarcare
disgrace [dɪsˈɡreɪs] n vergogna;
(disfavour) disgrazia ▷ vt disonorare,
far cadere in disgrazia; **disgraceful**
adj scandaloso(-a), vergognoso(-a)
disgruntled [dɪsˈɡrʌntld] adj
scontento(-a), di cattivo umore
disguise [dɪsˈɡaɪz] n travestimento
▷ vt **to ~ (as)** travestire (da); **in ~**
travestito(-a)
disgust [dɪsˈɡʌst] n disgusto,
nausea ▷ vt disgustare, far schifo
a; **disgusted** [dɪsˈɡʌstɪd] adj
indignato(-a); **disgusting** [dɪsˈɡʌstɪŋ]
adj disgustoso(-a), ripugnante
dish [dɪʃ] n piatto; **to do** or **wash
the ~es** fare i piatti; **dishcloth** n
strofinaccio
dishonest [dɪsˈɒnɪst] adj
disonesto(-a)
dishtowel [ˈdɪʃtauəl] (us) n
strofinaccio dei piatti
dishwasher [ˈdɪʃwɔʃəʳ] n
lavastoviglie f inv
disillusion [dɪsɪˈluːʒən] vt disilludere,
disingannare
disinfectant [dɪsɪnˈfɛktənt] n
disinfettante m
disintegrate [dɪsˈɪntɪɡreɪt] vi
disintegrarsi
disk [dɪsk] n (Comput) disco; **single-
/double-sided ~** disco a facciata
singola/doppia; **disk drive** n lettore
m; **diskette** (us) n = **disk**
dislike [dɪsˈlaɪk] n antipatia,
avversione f; (gen pl) cosa che non
piace ▷ vt **he ~s it** non gli piace
dislocate [ˈdɪsləkeɪt] vt slogare
disloyal [dɪsˈlɔɪəl] adj sleale
dismal [ˈdɪzml] adj triste, cupo(-a)
dismantle [dɪsˈmæntl] vt (machine)
smontare
dismay [dɪsˈmeɪ] n costernazione f

▷ vt sgomentare
dismiss [dɪsˈmɪs] vt congedare;
(employee) licenziare; (idea) scacciare;
(Law) respingere; **dismissal** n
congedo; licenziamento
disobedient [dɪsəˈbiːdɪənt] adj
disubbidiente
disobey [dɪsəˈbeɪ] vt disubbidire a
disorder [dɪsˈɔːdəʳ] n disordine m;
(rioting) tumulto; (Med) disturbo
disorganized [dɪsˈɔːɡənaɪzd] adj
(person, life) disorganizzato(-a);
(system, meeting) male organizzato(-a)
disown [dɪsˈəun] vt rinnegare
dispatch [dɪsˈpætʃ] vt spedire, inviare
▷ n spedizione f, invio; (Mil, Press)
dispaccio
dispel [dɪsˈpɛl] vt dissipare, scacciare
dispense [dɪsˈpɛns] vt distribuire,
amministrare; **dispense with** vt
fus fare a meno di; **dispenser** n
(container) distributore m
disperse [dɪsˈpəːs] vt disperdere;
(knowledge) disseminare ▷ vi
disperdersi
display [dɪsˈpleɪ] n esposizione f; (of
feeling etc) manifestazione f; (screen)
schermo ▷ vt mostrare; (goods)
esporre; (pej) ostentare
displease [dɪsˈpliːz] vt dispiacere a,
scontentare; **~d with** scontento di
disposable [dɪsˈpəuzəbl] adj (pack
etc) a perdere; (income) disponibile
disposal [dɪsˈpəuzl] n eliminazione f;
(of property) cessione f; **at one's ~** alla
sua disposizione
dispose [dɪsˈpəuz] vi **~ of** sbarazzarsi
di; **disposition** [-ˈzɪʃən] n disposizione
f; (temperament) carattere m
disproportionate [dɪsprəˈpɔːʃənət]
adj sproporzionato(-a)
dispute [dɪsˈpjuːt] n in disputa; (also:
industrial ~) controversia (sindacale)
▷ vt contestare; (matter) discutere;
(victory) disputare
disqualify [dɪsˈkwɔlɪfaɪ] vt (Sport)
squalificare; **to ~ sb from sth/from**

doing rendere qn incapace a qc/a fare; squalificare qn da qc/da fare; **to ~ sb from driving** ritirare la patente a qn

disregard [dısrı'gɑːd] vt non far caso a, non badare a

disrupt [dıs'rʌpt] vt disturbare; creare scompiglio in; **disruption** [dıs'rʌpʃən] n disordine m; interruzione f

dissatisfaction [dıssætıs'fækʃən] n scontentezza, insoddisfazione f

dissatisfied [dıs'sætısfaıd] adj: ~ **(with)** scontento(a) or insoddisfatto(a) (di)

dissect [dı'sɛkt] vt sezionare

dissent [dı'sɛnt] n dissenso

dissertation [dısə'teıʃən] n tesi f inv, dissertazione f

dissolve [dı'zɔlv] vt dissolvere, sciogliere; (Pol, marriage etc) sciogliere ▷ vi dissolversi, sciogliersi

distance [dıstns] n distanza; **in the ~** in lontananza

distant [dıstnt] adj lontano(-a), distante; (manner) riservato(-a), freddo(-a)

distil [dıs'tıl] (US **distill**) vt distillare; **distillery** n distilleria

distinct [dıs'tıŋkt] adj distinto(-a); **as ~ from** a differenza di; **distinction** [dıs'tıŋkʃən] n distinzione f; (in exam) lode f; **distinctive** adj distintivo(-a)

distinguish [dıs'tıŋgwıʃ] vt distinguere; discernere; **distinguished** adj (eminent) eminente

distort [dıs'tɔːt] vt distorcere; (Tech) deformare

distract [dıs'trækt] vt distrarre; **distracted** adj distratto(-a); **distraction** [dıs'trækʃən] n distrazione f

distraught [dıs'trɔːt] adj stravolto(-a)

distress [dıs'trɛs] n angoscia ▷ vt affliggere; **distressing** adj doloroso(-a)

distribute [dıs'trıbjuːt] vt distribuire; **distribution** [-'bjuːʃən] n distribuzione f; **distributor** n distributore m

district ['dıstrıkt] n (of country) regione f; (of town) quartiere m; (Admin) distretto; **district attorney** (US) n ≈ sostituto procuratore m della Repubblica

distrust [dıs'trʌst] n diffidenza, sfiducia ▷ vt non aver fiducia in

disturb [dıs'təːb] vt disturbare; **disturbance** n disturbo; (political etc) disordini mpl; **disturbed** adj (worried, upset) turbato(-a); **emotionally disturbed** con turbe emotive; **disturbing** adj sconvolgente

ditch [dıtʃ] n fossa ▷ vt (inf) piantare in asso

ditto ['dıtəu] adv idem

dive [daıv] n tuffo; (of submarine) immersione f ▷ vi tuffarsi; immergersi; **diver** n tuffatore(-trice), palombaro

diverse [daı'vəːs] adj vario(-a)

diversion [daı'vəːʃən] n (Brit Aut) deviazione f; (distraction) divertimento

diversity [daı'vəːsıtı] n diversità f inv, varietà f inv

divert [daı'vəːt] vt deviare

divide [dı'vaıd] vt dividere; (separate) separare ▷ vi dividersi; **divided highway** (US) n strada a doppia carreggiata

divine [dı'vaın] adj divino(-a)

diving ['daıvıŋ] n tuffo; **diving board** n trampolino

division [dı'vıʒən] n divisione f; separazione f; (esp Football) serie f

divorce [dı'vɔːs] n divorzio ▷ vt divorziare da; (dissociate) separare; **divorced** adj divorziato(-a); **divorcee** [-'siː] n divorziato(-a)

D.I.Y. (Brit) n abbr = **do-it-yourself**

dizzy ['dızı] adj **to feel ~** avere il capogiro

DJ n abbr = **disc jockey**

DNA n abbr (= deoxyribonucleic acid)
DNA m; **DNA test** n test m inv del DNA

○ KEYWORD

do [duː] (pt **did**, pp **done**) n (inf: party
etc) festa; **it was rather a grand
do** è stato un ricevimento piuttosto
importante
▷ vb **1** (in negative constructions: non
tradotto): **I don't understand** non
capisco
2 (to form questions: non tradotto):
didn't you know? non lo sapevi?;
why didn't you come? perché non
sei venuto?
3 (for emphasis, in polite expressions):
she does seem rather late sembra
essere piuttosto in ritardo; **do sit
down** ti accomodi la prego, prego si
sieda; **do take care!** mi raccomando,
sta attento!
4 (used to avoid repeating vb): **she
swims better than I do** lei nuota
meglio di me; **do you agree? — yes, I
do/no, I don't** sei d'accordo? — sì/no;
she lives in Glasgow — so do I lei
vive a Glasgow — anch'io; **he asked
me to help him and I did** mi ha
chiesto di aiutarlo ed io l'ho fatto
5 (in question tags): **you like him,
don't you?** ti piace, vero?; **I don't
know him, do I?** non lo conosco, vero?
▷ vt (gen, carry out, perform etc) fare;
what are you doing tonight? che fa
stasera?; **to do the cooking** cucinare;
to do the washing-up fare i piatti;
to do one's teeth lavarsi i denti; **to
do one's hair/nails** farsi i capelli/le
unghie; **the car was doing 100** la
macchina faceva i 100 all'ora
▷ vi **1** (act, behave) fare; **do as I do**
faccia come me, faccia come faccio io
2 (get on, fare) andare; **he's doing
well/badly at school** va bene/male a
scuola; **how do you do?** piacere!
3 (suit) andare bene; **this room will**
do questa stanza va bene
4 (be sufficient) bastare; **will £10 do?**
basteranno 10 sterline?; **that'll do**
basta così; **that'll do!** (in annoyance)
ora basta!; **to make do (with)**
arrangiarsi (con)
do away with vt fus (kill) far fuori;
(abolish) abolire
do up vt (laces) allacciare; (dress,
buttons) abbottonare; (renovate: room,
house) rimettere a nuovo, rifare
do with vt fus (need) aver bisogno di;
(be connected): **what has it got to do
with you?** e tu che c'entri?; **I won't
have anything to do with it** non
voglio avere niente a che farci; **it has
to do with money** si tratta di soldi
do without vi fare senza ▷ vt fus fare
a meno di

dock [dɔk] n (Naut) bacino; (Law)
banco degli imputati ▷ vi entrare in
bacino; (Space) agganciarsi; **docks** npl
(Naut) dock m inv
doctor ['dɔktə'] n medico(-a); (Ph.
D. etc) dottore(-essa) ▷ vt (drink etc)
adulterare; **call a ~!** chiamate un
dottore!; **Doctor of Philosophy** n
dottorato di ricerca; (person) titolare
m/f di un dottorato di ricerca
document ['dɔkjumənt] n
documento; **documentary**
[-'mɛntərɪ] adj (evidence)
documentato(-a) ▷ n documentario;
documentation [dɔkjumən'teɪʃən]
n documentazione f
dodge [dɔdʒ] n trucco; schivata ▷ vt
schivare, eludere
dodgy ['dɔdʒɪ] adj (inf: uncertain)
rischioso(-a); (untrustworthy)
sospetto(-a)
does [dʌz] vb see **do**
doesn't ['dʌznt] = **does not**
dog [dɔg] n cane m ▷ vt (follow
closely) pedinare; (fig: memory etc)
perseguitare; **doggy bag** n sacchetto
per gli avanzi (da portare a casa)

do-it-yourself ['duːɪtjɔːˈsɛlf] *n* il far da sé

dole [dəul] (*BRIT*) *n* sussidio di disoccupazione; **to be on the ~** vivere del sussidio

doll [dɔl] *n* bambola

dollar ['dɔlər] *n* dollaro

dolphin ['dɔlfɪn] *n* delfino

dome [dəum] *n* cupola

domestic [dəˈmɛstɪk] *adj* (*duty, happiness, animal*) domestico(-a); (*policy, affairs, flights*) nazionale; **domestic appliance** *n* elettrodomestico

dominant ['dɔmɪnənt] *adj* dominante

dominate ['dɔmɪneɪt] *vt* dominare

domino ['dɔmɪnəu] (*pl* **dominoes**) *n* domino; **dominoes** *n* (*game*) gioco del domino

donate [dəˈneɪt] *vt* donare; **donation** [dəˈneɪʃən] *n* donazione *f*

done [dʌn] *pp of* **do**

donkey ['dɔŋkɪ] *n* asino

donor ['dəunər] *n* donatore(-trice); **donor card** *n* tessera di donatore di organi

don't [dəunt] = **do not**

donut ['dəunʌt] (*US*) *n* = **doughnut**

doodle ['duːdl] *vi* scarabocchiare

doom [duːm] *n* destino; rovina ▷ *vt*: **to be ~ed (to failure)** essere predestinato(-a) (a fallire)

door [dɔːʳ] *n* porta; **doorbell** *n* campanello; **door handle** *n* maniglia; **doorknob** ['dɔːnɔb] *n* pomello, maniglia; **doorstep** *n* gradino della porta; **doorway** *n* porta

dope [dəup] *n* (*inf: drugs*) roba ▷ *vt* (*horse etc*) drogare

dormitory ['dɔːmɪtrɪ] *n* dormitorio; (*US*) casa dello studente

DOS [dɔs] *n abbr* (= *disk operating system*) DOS *m*

dosage ['dəusɪdʒ] *n* posologia

dose [dəus] *n* dose *f*; (*bout*) attacco

dot [dɔt] *n* punto; macchiolina ▷ *vt*

~ted with punteggiato(-a) di; **on the ~** in punto; **dotcom** [dɔtˈkɔm] *n* azienda che opera in Internet; **dotted line** ['dɔtɪd-] *n* linea punteggiata

double ['dʌbl] *adj* doppio(-a) ▷ *adv* (*twice*): **to cost ~ sth** costare il doppio (di qc) ▷ *n* sosia *m inv* ▷ *vt* raddoppiare; (*fold*) piegare doppio *or* in due ▷ *vi* raddoppiarsi; **at the ~** (*BRIT*), **on the ~** a passo di corsa; **double back** *vi* (*person*) tornare sui propri passi; **double bass** *n* contrabbasso; **double bed** *n* letto matrimoniale; **double-check** *vt, vi* ricontrollare; **double-click** *vi* (*Comput*) fare doppio click; **double-cross** *vt* fare il doppio gioco con; **doubledecker** *n* autobus *m inv* a due piani; **double glazing** (*BRIT*) *n* doppi vetri *mpl*; **double room** *n* camera matrimoniale; **doubles** *n* (*Tennis*) doppio; **double yellow lines** *npl* (*BRIT: Aut*) linea gialla doppia continua che segnala il divieto di sosta

doubt [daut] *n* dubbio ▷ *vt* dubitare di; **to ~ that** dubitare che + *sub*; **doubtful** *adj* dubbioso(-a), incerto(-a); (*person*) equivoco(-a); **doubtless** *adv* indubbiamente

dough [dəu] *n* pasta, impasto; **doughnut** (*US* **donut**) *n* bombolone *m*

dove [dʌv] *n* colombo(-a)

down [daun] *n* piume *fpl* ▷ *adv* giù, di sotto ▷ *prep* giù per ▷ *vt* (*inf: drink*) scolarsi; **~ with X!** abbasso X!; **down-and-out** *n* barbone *m*; **downfall** *n* caduta; rovina; **downhill** *adv*: **to go downhill** andare in discesa; (*fig*) lasciarsi andare; andare a rotoli

Downing Street ['daunɪŋ-] *n* lo **~** *residenza del primo ministro inglese*

● **DOWNING STREET**
●
● Al numero 10 di **Downing Street**,
● nel quartiere di Westminster a
● Londra, si trova la residenza del

● primo ministro inglese, al numero
● 11 quella del **Chancellor of the**
● **Exchequer**.

down: **download** vt (Comput)
scaricare; **downright** adj franco(-a);
(refusal) assoluto(-a)

Down's syndrome n sindrome f di
Down

down: **downstairs** adv di sotto; al
piano inferiore; **down-to-earth** adj
pratico(-a); **downtown** adv in città;
down under (Australia etc) agli
antipodi; **downward** ['daʊnwəd] adj,
adv in giù, in discesa; **downwards**
['daʊnwədz] adv = **downward**

doz. abbr = **dozen**

doze [dəʊz] vi sonnecchiare

dozen ['dʌzn] n dozzina; **a ~ books**
una dozzina di libri; **~s of** decine fpl di

Dr. abbr (= doctor) dott.; (in street
names) = **drive**

drab [dræb] adj tetro(-a), grigio(-a)

draft [drɑːft] n abbozzo; (Pol) bozza;
(Comm) tratta; (us: call-up) leva ▷ vt
abbozzare; see also **draught**

drag [dræg] vt trascinare; (river)
dragare ▷ vi trascinarsi ▷ n (inf)
noioso(-a); noia, fatica; (women's
clothing): **in ~** travestito (da donna)

dragon ['drægən] n drago

dragonfly ['drægənflaɪ] n libellula

drain [dreɪn] n (for sewage) fogna; (on
resources) salasso ▷ vt (land, marshes)
prosciugare; (vegetables) scolare
▷ vi (water) defluire (via); **drainage**
n prosciugamento; fognatura;
drainpipe n tubo di scarico

drama ['drɑːmə] n (art) dramma
m, teatro; (play) commedia; (event)
dramma; **dramatic** [drə'mætɪk] adj
drammatico(-a)

drank [dræŋk] pt of **drink**

drape [dreɪp] vt drappeggiare; **drapes**
(us) npl (curtains) tende fpl

drastic ['dræstɪk] adj drastico(-a)

draught [drɑːft] (us **draft**) n corrente

f d'aria; (Naut) pescaggio; **on ~** (beer)
alla spina; **draught beer** n birra alla
spina; **draughts** (BRIT) n (gioco della)
dama

draw [drɔː] (pt **drew**, pp **drawn**) vt
tirare; (take out) estrarre; (attract)
attirare; (picture) disegnare; (line,
circle) tracciare; (money) ritirare ▷ vi
(Sport) pareggiare ▷ n pareggio;
(in lottery) estrazione f; **to ~ near**
avvicinarsi; **draw out** vi (lengthen)
allungarsi ▷ vt (money) ritirare; **draw
up** vi (stop) arrestarsi, fermarsi
▷ vt (chair) avvicinare; (document)
compilare; **drawback** n svantaggio,
inconveniente m

drawer [drɔːʳ] n cassetto

drawing ['drɔːɪŋ] n disegno; **drawing
pin** (BRIT) n puntina da disegno;
drawing room n salotto

drawn [drɔːn] pp of **draw**

dread [dred] n terrore m ▷ vt tremare
all'idea di; **dreadful** adj terribile

dream [driːm] (pt, pp **dreamed** or
dreamt) n sogno ▷ vt, vi sognare;
dreamer n sognatore(-trice)

dreamt [dremt] pt, pp of **dream**

dreary ['drɪərɪ] adj tetro(-a);
monotono(-a)

drench [drentʃ] vt inzuppare

dress [dres] n vestito; (no pl: clothing)
abbigliamento ▷ vt vestire; (wound)
fasciare ▷ vi vestirsi; **to get ~ed**
vestirsi; **dress up** vi vestirsi a festa;
(in fancy dress) vestirsi in costume;
dress circle (BRIT) n prima galleria;
dresser n (BRIT: cupboard) credenza;
(us) cassettone m; **dressing** n (Med)
benda; (Culin) condimento; **dressing
gown** (BRIT) n vestaglia; **dressing
room** n (Theatre) camerino; (Sport)
spogliatoio; **dressing table** n toilette
f inv; **dressmaker** n sarta

drew [druː] pt of **draw**

dribble ['drɪbl] vi (baby) sbavare ▷ vt
(ball) dribblare

dried [draɪd] adj (fruit, beans)

secco(-a); (*eggs, milk*) in polvere

drier ['draɪə^r] *n* = **dryer**

drift [drɪft] *n* (*of current etc*) direzione *f*; forza; (*of snow*) cumulo; turbine *m*; (*general meaning*) senso ▷ *vi* (*boat*) essere trasportato(-a) dalla corrente; (*sand, snow*) ammucchiarsi

drill [drɪl] *n* trapano; (*Mil*) esercitazione *f* ▷ *vt* trapanare; (*troops*) addestrare ▷ *vi* (*for oil*) fare trivellazioni

drink [drɪŋk] (*pt* **drank**, *pp* **drunk**) *n* bevanda, bibita; (*alcoholic drink*) bicchierino; (*sip*) sorso ▷ *vt*, *vi* bere; **to have a ~** bere qualcosa; **would you like a ~?** vuoi qualcosa da bere?; **a ~ of water** un po' d'acqua; **drink-driving** *n* guida in stato di ebbrezza; **drinker** *n* bevitore(-trice); **drinking water** *n* acqua potabile

drip [drɪp] *n* goccia; gocciolamento; (*Med*) fleboclisi *f inv* ▷ *vi* gocciolare; (*tap*) sgocciolare

drive [draɪv] (*pt* **drove**, *pp* **driven**) *n* passeggiata *or* giro in macchina; (*also:* **~way**) viale *m* d'accesso; (*energy*) energia; (*campaign*) campagna; (*also:* **disk ~**) lettore *m* ▷ *vt* guidare; (*nail*) piantare; (*push*) cacciare, spingere; (*Tech: motor*) azionare; far funzionare ▷ *vi* (*Aut: at controls*) guidare; (: *travel*) andare in macchina; **left-/right-hand ~** guida a sinistra/destra; **to ~ sb mad** far impazzire qn; **drive out** *vt* (*force out*) cacciare, mandare via; **drive-in** (*esp US*) *adj*, *n* drive-in (*m inv*)

driven ['drɪvn] *pp of* **drive**

driver ['draɪvə^r] *n* conducente *m/f*; (*of taxi*) tassista *m*; (*chauffeur: of bus*) autista *m/f*; **driver's license** (*US*) *n* patente *f* di guida

driveway ['draɪvweɪ] *n* viale *m* d'accesso

driving ['draɪvɪŋ] *n* guida; **driving instructor** *n* istruttore(-trice) di scuola guida; **driving lesson** *n* lezione *f* di guida; **driving licence**

(*BRIT*) *n* patente *f* di guida; **driving test** *n* esame *m* di guida

drizzle ['drɪzl] *n* pioggerella

droop [druːp] *vi* (*flower*) appassire; (*head, shoulders*) chinarsi

drop [drɔp] *n* (*of water*) goccia; (*lessening*) diminuzione *f*; (*fall*) caduta ▷ *vt* lasciare cadere; (*voice, eyes, price*) abbassare; (*set down from car*) far scendere; (*name from list*) lasciare fuori ▷ *vi* cascare; (*wind*) abbassarsi; **drop in** *vi* (*inf: visit*): **to drop in (on)** fare un salto (da), passare (da); **drop off** *vi* (*sleep*) addormentarsi ▷ *vt* (*passenger*) far scendere; **drop out** *vi* (*withdraw*) ritirarsi; (*student etc*) smettere di studiare

drought [draut] *n* siccità *f inv*

drove [drəuv] *pt of* **drive**

drown [draun] *vt* affogare; (*fig: noise*) soffocare ▷ *vi* affogare

drowsy ['drauzɪ] *adj* sonnolento(-a), assonnato(-a)

drug [drʌg] *n* farmaco; (*narcotic*) droga ▷ *vt* drogare; **to be on ~s** drogarsi; (*Med*) prendere medicinali; **hard/soft ~s** droghe pesanti/leggere; **drug addict** *n* tossicomane *m/f*; **drug dealer** *n* trafficante *m/f* di droga; **druggist** (*US*) *n* persona che gestisce un *drugstore*; **drugstore** (*US*) *n* drugstore *m inv*

drum [drʌm] *n* tamburo; (*for oil, petrol*) fusto ▷ *vi* tamburellare; **drums** *npl* (*set of drums*) batteria; **drummer** *n* batterista *m/f*

drunk [drʌŋk] *pp of* **drink** ▷ *adj* ubriaco(-a), ebbro(-a) ▷ *n* (*also:* **~ard**) ubriacone(-a); **drunken** *adj* ubriaco(-a); da ubriaco

dry [draɪ] *adj* secco(-a); (*day, clothes*) asciutto(-a) ▷ *vt* seccare; (*clothes, hair, hands*) asciugare ▷ *vi* asciugarsi; **dry off** *vi* asciugarsi ▷ *vt* asciugare; **dry up** *vi* seccarsi; **dry-cleaner's** *n* lavasecco *m inv*; **dry-cleaning** *n* pulitura a secco; **dryer** *n* (*for hair*) föhn *m inv*, asciugacapelli *m inv*; *(for clothes)* asciugabiancheria; *(US: spin-dryer)* centrifuga

DSS *n abbr* (= Department of Social Security) ministero della Previdenza sociale

DTP *n abbr* (= desk-top publishing) desktop publishing *m inv*

dual ['dju:əl] *adj* doppio(-a); **dual carriageway** (BRIT) *n* strada a doppia carreggiata

dubious ['dju:bɪəs] *adj* dubbio(-a)

Dublin ['dʌblɪn] *n* Dublino *f*

duck [dʌk] *n* anatra ▷ *vi* abbassare la testa

due [dju:] *adj* dovuto(-a); *(expected)* atteso(-a); *(fitting)* giusto(-a) ▷ *n* dovuto ▷ *adv* **~ north** diritto verso nord

duel ['dju:əl] *n* duello

duet [dju:'ɛt] *n* duetto

dug [dʌg] *pt, pp of* **dig**

duke [dju:k] *n* duca *m*

dull [dʌl] *adj* (light) debole; (boring) noioso(-a); (slow-witted) ottuso(-a); (sound, pain) sordo(-a); (weather, day) fosco(-a), scuro(-a) ▷ *vt* (pain, grief) attutire; (mind, senses) intorpidire

dumb [dʌm] *adj* muto(-a); (pej) stupido(-a)

dummy ['dʌmɪ] *n* (tailor's model) manichino; (Tech, Comm) riproduzione *f*; (BRIT: for baby) tettarella ▷ *adj* falso(-a), finto(-a)

dump [dʌmp] *n* (also: **rubbish ~**) discarica di rifiuti; (inf: place) buco ▷ *vt* (put down) scaricare; mettere giù; (get rid of) buttar via

dumpling ['dʌmplɪŋ] *n* specie di gnocco

dune [dju:n] *n* duna

dungarees [dʌŋgə'ri:z] *npl* tuta

dungeon ['dʌndʒən] *n* prigione *f* sotterranea

duplex ['dju:plɛks] (US) *n* (house) casa con muro divisorio in comune con un'altra; (apartment) appartamento su due piani

duplicate [*n* 'dju:plɪkət, *vb* 'dju:plɪkeɪt] *n* doppio ▷ *vt* duplicare; **in ~** in doppia copia

durable ['djuərəbl] *adj* durevole; (clothes, metal) resistente

duration [djuə'reɪʃən] *n* durata

during ['djuərɪŋ] *prep* durante, nel corso di

dusk [dʌsk] *n* crepuscolo

dust [dʌst] *n* polvere *f* ▷ *vt* (furniture) spolverare; (cake etc) cospargere con; **dustbin** (BRIT) *n* pattumiera; **duster** *n* straccio per la polvere; **dustman** (irreg: BRIT) *n* netturbino; **dustpan** *n* pattumiera; **dusty** *adj* polveroso(-a)

Dutch [dʌtʃ] *adj* olandese ▷ *n* (Ling) olandese *m*; **the Dutch** *npl* gli Olandesi; **to go ~** (inf) fare alla romana; **Dutchman, Dutchwoman** (irreg) *n* olandese *m/f*

duty ['dju:tɪ] *n* dovere *m*; (tax) dazio, tassa; **on ~** di servizio; **off ~** libero(-a), fuori servizio; **duty-free** *adj* esente da dazio

duvet ['du:veɪ] (BRIT) *n* piumino, piumone *m*

DVD *n abbr* (= digital versatile or video disk) DVD *m inv*; **DVD burner, DVD writer** *n* masterizzatore *m* di DVD; **DVD player** *n* lettore *m* DVD

dwarf [dwɔ:f] *n* nano(-a) ▷ *vt* far apparire piccolo

dwell [dwɛl] (pt, pp **dwelt**) *vi* dimorare; **dwell on** *vt fus* indugiare su

dwelt [dwɛlt] *pt, pp of* **dwell**

dwindle ['dwɪndl] *vi* diminuire

dye [daɪ] *n* tinta ▷ *vt* tingere

dying ['daɪɪŋ] *adj* morente, moribondo(-a)

dynamic [daɪ'næmɪk] *adj* dinamico(-a)

dynamite ['daɪnəmaɪt] *n* dinamite *f*

dyslexia [dɪs'lɛksɪə] *n* dislessia

dyslexic [dɪs'lɛksɪk] *adj, n* dislessico(-a)

E [iː] n (Mus) mi m

E111 n abbr (also: **form ~**) E111 (modulo CEE per rimborso spese mediche)

each [iːtʃ] adj ogni, ciascuno(-a) ▷ pron ciascuno(-a), ognuno(-a); **~ one** ognuno(-a); **~ other** si or ci etc; **they hate ~ other** si odiano (l'un l'altro); **you are jealous of ~ other** siete gelosi l'uno dell'altro; **they have 2 books ~** hanno 2 libri ciascuno

eager [ˈiːgəʳ] adj impaziente, desideroso(-a); ardente; **to be ~ for** essere desideroso di, aver gran voglia di

eagle [ˈiːgl] n aquila

ear [ɪəʳ] n orecchio; (of corn) pannocchia; **earache** n mal m d'orecchi; **eardrum** n timpano

earl [əːl] (BRIT) n conte m

earlier [ˈəːlɪəʳ] adj precedente ▷ adv prima

early [ˈəːlɪ] adv presto, di buon'ora; (ahead of time) in anticipo ▷ adj (near the beginning) primo(-a); (sooner than expected) prematuro(-a); (quick: reply) veloce; **at an ~ hour** di buon'ora; **to have an ~ night** andare a letto presto; **in the ~** or **~ in the spring/19th century** all'inizio della primavera/dell'Ottocento; **early retirement** n ritiro anticipato

earmark [ˈɪəmɑːk] vt: **to ~ sth for** destinare qc a

earn [əːn] vt guadagnare; (rest, reward) meritare

earnest [ˈəːnɪst] adj serio(-a); **in ~** sul serio

earnings [ˈəːnɪŋz] npl guadagni mpl; (salary) stipendio

ear: **earphones** [ˈɪəfəʊnz] npl cuffia; **earplugs** npl tappi mpl per le orecchie; **earring** [ˈɪərɪŋ] n orecchino

earth [əːθ] n terra ▷ vt (BRIT Elec) mettere a terra; **earthquake** n terremoto

ease [iːz] n agio, comodo ▷ vt (soothe) calmare; (loosen) allentare; **to ~ sth out/in** tirare fuori/infilare qc con delicatezza; facilitare l'uscita/l'entrata di qc; **at ~** a proprio agio; (Mil) a riposo

easily [ˈiːzɪlɪ] adv facilmente

east [iːst] n est m ▷ adj dell'est ▷ adv a oriente; **the E~** l'Oriente m; (Pol) l'Est; **eastbound** [ˈiːstbaʊnd] adj (traffic) diretto(-a) a est; (carriageway) che porta a est

Easter [ˈiːstəʳ] n Pasqua; **Easter egg** n uovo di Pasqua

eastern [ˈiːstən] adj orientale, d'oriente; dell'est

Easter Sunday n domenica di Pasqua

easy [ˈiːzɪ] adj facile; (manner) disinvolto(-a) ▷ adv **to take it** or **things ~** prendersela con calma; **easy-going** adj accomodante

eat [iːt] (pt **ate**, pp **eaten**) vt, vi mangiare; **can we have something to ~?** possiamo mangiare qualcosa?; **eat out** vi mangiare fuori

eavesdrop ['iːvzdrɔp] *vi* **to ~ (on a conversation)** origliare (una conversazione)

e-book ['iːbuk] *n* libro elettronico

e-business ['iːbɪznɪs] *n* (*company*) azienda che opera in Internet; (*commerce*) commercio elettronico

EC *n abbr* (= *European Community*) CE *f*

eccentric [ɪk'sɛntrɪk] *adj, n* eccentrico(-a)

echo ['ɛkəʊ] (*pl* **echoes**) *n* eco *m or f* ▷ *vt* ripetere; fare eco a ▷ *vi* echeggiare; dare un eco

eclipse [ɪ'klɪps] *n* eclissi *f inv*

eco-friendly [iːkəʊ'frɛndlɪ] *adj* ecologico(-a)

ecological [iːkə'lɔdʒɪkəl] *adj* ecologico(-a)

ecology [ɪ'kɔlədʒɪ] *n* ecologia

e-commerce [iːkɔmə:s] *n* commercio elettronico

economic [iːkə'nɔmɪk] *adj* economico(-a); **economical** *adj* economico(-a); (*person*) economo(-a); **economics** *n* economia ▷ *npl* lato finanziario

economist [ɪ'kɔnəmɪst] *n* economista *m/f*

economize [ɪ'kɔnəmaɪz] *vi* risparmiare, fare economia

economy [ɪ'kɔnəmɪ] *n* economia; **economy class** *n* (*Aviat*) classe *f* turistica; **economy class syndrome** *n* sindrome *f* della classe economica

ecstasy ['ɛkstəsɪ] *n* estasi *f inv*; **ecstatic** [ɛks'tætɪk] *adj* estatico(-a), in estasi

eczema ['ɛksɪmə] *n* eczema *m*

edge [ɛdʒ] *n* margine *m*; (*of table, plate, cup*) orlo; (*of knife etc*) taglio ▷ *vt* bordare; **on ~** (*fig*) **= edgy**; **to edge away from** sgattaiolare da

edgy ['ɛdʒɪ] *adj* nervoso(-a)

edible ['ɛdɪbl] *adj* commestibile; (*meal*) mangiabile

Edinburgh ['ɛdɪnbərə] *n* Edimburgo *f*

edit ['ɛdɪt] *vt* curare; **edition** [ɪ'dɪʃən]

n edizione *f*; **editor** *n* (*in newspaper*) redattore(-trice), redattore(-trice) capo; (*of sb's work*) curatore(-trice); **editorial** [-'tɔːrɪəl] *adj* redazionale, editoriale ▷ *n* editoriale *m*

> Be careful not to translate *editor* by the Italian word *editore*.

educate ['ɛdjukeɪt] *vt* istruire; educare; **educated** *adj* istruito(-a)

education [ɛdju'keɪʃən] *n* educazione *f*; (*schooling*) istruzione *f*; **educational** *adj* pedagogico(-a); scolastico(-a); istruttivo(-a)

eel [iːl] *n* anguilla

eerie ['ɪərɪ] *adj* che fa accapponare la pelle

effect [ɪ'fɛkt] *n* effetto ▷ *vt* effettuare; **to take ~** (*law*) entrare in vigore; (*drug*) fare effetto; **in ~** effettivamente; **effects** *npl* (*Theat*) effetti *mpl* scenici; (*property*) effetti *mpl*; **effective** *adj* efficace; (*actual*) effettivo(-a); **effectively** *adv* efficacemente; effettivamente

efficiency [ɪ'fɪʃənsɪ] *n* efficienza; rendimento effettivo

efficient [ɪ'fɪʃənt] *adj* efficiente; **efficiently** *adv* efficientemente; efficacemente

effort ['ɛfət] *n* sforzo; **effortless** *adj* senza sforzo, facile

e.g. *adv abbr* (= *exempli gratia*) per esempio, p.es.

egg [ɛg] *n* uovo; **hard-boiled/soft-boiled ~** uovo sodo/alla coque; **eggcup** *n* portauovo *m inv*; **eggplant** (*esp us*) *n* melanzana; **eggshell** *n* guscio d'uovo; **egg white** *n* albume *m*, bianco d'uovo; **egg yolk** *n* tuorlo, rosso (d'uovo)

ego ['iːgəʊ] *n* ego *m inv*

Egypt ['iːdʒɪpt] *n* Egitto; **Egyptian** [ɪ'dʒɪpʃən] *adj, n* egiziano(-a)

eight [eɪt] *num* otto; **eighteen** *num* diciotto; **eighteenth** *num* diciottesimo(-a); **eighth** [eɪtθ] *num* ottavo(-a); **eightieth** ['eɪtɪɪθ] *num* ottantesimo(-a); **eighty** num ottanta

Eire ['εərə] n Repubblica d'Irlanda

either ['aɪðəʳ] adj l'uno(-a) o l'altro(-a); (both, each) ciascuno(-a) ▷ pron **~ (of them)** (o) l'uno(-a) o l'altro(-a) ▷ adv neanche ▷ conj **~ good or bad** o buono o cattivo; **on ~ side** su ciascun lato; **I don't like ~** non mi piace né l'uno né l'altro; **no, I don't ~** no, neanch'io

eject [ɪ'dʒεkt] vt espellere; lanciare

elaborate [adj ɪ'læbərɪt, vb ɪ'læbəreɪt] adj elaborato(-a), minuzioso(-a) ▷ vt elaborare ▷ vi fornire i particolari

elastic [ɪ'læstɪk] adj elastico(-a) ▷ n elastico; **elastic band** (BRIT) n elastico

elbow ['εlbəu] n gomito

elder ['εldəʳ] adj maggiore, più vecchio(-a) ▷ n (tree) sambuco; **one's ~s** i più anziani; **elderly** adj anziano(-a) ▷ npl **the elderly** gli anziani

eldest ['εldɪst] adj, n **the ~ (child)** il(la) maggiore (dei bambini)

elect [ɪ'lεkt] vt eleggere ▷ adj **the president ~** il presidente designato; **to ~ to do** decidere di fare; **election** [ɪ'lεkʃən] n elezione f; **electoral** [ɪ'lεktərəl] adj elettorale; **electorate** n elettorato

electric [ɪ'lεktrɪk] adj elettrico(-a); **electrical** adj elettrico(-a); **electric blanket** n coperta elettrica; **electric fire** n stufa elettrica; **electrician** [ɪlεk'trɪʃən] n elettricista m; **electricity** [ɪlεk'trɪsɪtɪ] n elettricità; **electric shock** n scossa (elettrica); **electrify** [ɪ'lεktrɪfaɪ] vt (Rail) elettrificare; (audience) elettrizzare

electronic [ɪlεk'trɔnɪk] adj elettronico(-a); **electronic mail** n posta elettronica; **electronics** n elettronica

elegance ['εlɪgəns] n eleganza

elegant ['εlɪgənt] adj elegante

element ['εlɪmənt] n elemento; (of heater, kettle etc) resistenza

elementary [εlɪ'mεntərɪ] adj elementare; **elementary school** (US) n scuola elementare

elephant ['εlɪfənt] n elefante(-essa)

elevate ['εlɪveɪt] vt elevare

elevator ['εlɪveɪtəʳ] n elevatore m; (US: lift) ascensore m

eleven [ɪ'lεvn] num undici; **eleventh** adj undicesimo(-a)

eligible ['εlɪdʒəbl] adj eleggibile; (for membership) che ha i requisiti

eliminate [ɪ'lɪmɪneɪt] vt eliminare

elm [εlm] n olmo

eloquent ['εləkwənt] adj eloquente

else [εls] adv altro; **something ~** qualcos'altro; **somewhere ~** altrove; **everywhere ~** in qualsiasi altro luogo; **nobody ~** nessun altro; **where ~?** in quale altro luogo?; **little ~** poco altro; **elsewhere** adv altrove

elusive [ɪ'lu:sɪv] adj elusivo(-a)

e-mail ['i:meɪl] n abbr (= electronic mail) posta elettronica ▷ vt mandare un messaggio di posta elettronica a; **e-mail address** n indirizzo di posta elettronica

embankment [ɪm'bæŋkmənt] n (of road, railway) terrapieno

embargo [ɪm'bɑ:gəu] n (pl **embargoes**) (Comm, Naut) embargo ▷ vt mettere l'embargo su; **to put an ~ on sth** mettere l'embargo su qc

embark [ɪm'bɑ:k] vi **to ~ (on)** imbarcarsi (su) ▷ vt imbarcare; **to ~ on** (fig) imbarcarsi in

embarrass [ɪm'bærəs] vt imbarazzare; **embarrassed** adj imbarazzato(-a); **embarrassing** adj imbarazzante; **embarrassment** n imbarazzo

embassy ['εmbəsɪ] n ambasciata

embrace [ɪm'breɪs] vt abbracciare ▷ vi abbracciarsi ▷ n abbraccio

embroider [ɪm'brɔɪdəʳ] vt ricamare; **embroidery** n ricamo

embryo ['εmbrɪəu] n embrione m

emerald ['ɛmərəld] n smeraldo
emerge [ɪ'məːdʒ] vi emergere
emergency [ɪ'məːdʒənsɪ] n
emergenza; **in an ~** in caso di
emergenza; **emergency brake** (US)
n freno a mano; **emergency exit**
n uscita di sicurezza; **emergency
landing** n atterraggio forzato;
emergency room (US: Med) n pronto
soccorso; **emergency services** npl
(fire, police, ambulance) servizi mpl di
pronto intervento
emigrate ['ɛmɪgreɪt] vi emigrare;
emigration [ɛmɪ'greɪʃən] n
emigrazione f
eminent ['ɛmɪnənt] adj eminente
emissions [ɪ'mɪʃənz] npl emissioni fpl
emit [ɪ'mɪt] vt emettere
emotion [ɪ'məuʃən] n emozione f;
emotional adj (person) emotivo(-a);
(scene) commovente; (tone, speech)
carico(-a) d'emozione
emperor ['ɛmpərər] n imperatore m
emphasis ['ɛmfəsɪs] (pl **-ases**) n
enfasi f inv; importanza
emphasize ['ɛmfəsaɪz] vt (word,
point) sottolineare; (feature) mettere
in evidenza
empire ['ɛmpaɪər] n impero
employ [ɪm'plɔɪ] vt impiegare;
employee [-'iː] n impiegato(-a);
employer n principale m/f, datore m
di lavoro; **employment** n impiego;
employment agency n agenzia di
collocamento
empower [ɪm'pauər] vt **to ~ sb to do**
concedere autorità a qn di fare
empress ['ɛmprɪs] n imperatrice f
emptiness ['ɛmptɪnɪs] n vuoto
empty ['ɛmptɪ] adj vuoto(-a); (threat,
promise) vano(-a) ▷ vt vuotare ▷ vi
vuotarsi; (liquid) scaricarsi; **empty-
handed** adj a mani vuote
EMU n abbr (= economic and monetary
union) unione f economica e
monetaria
emulsion [ɪ'mʌlʃən] n emulsione f

enable [ɪ'neɪbl] vt **to ~ sb to do**
permettere a qn di fare
enamel [ɪ'næməl] n smalto; (also: ~
paint) vernice f a smalto
enchanting [ɪn'tʃɑːntɪŋ] adj
incantevole, affascinante
encl. abbr (= enclosed) all.
enclose [ɪn'kləuz] vt (land)
circondare, recingere; (letter etc): **to ~
(with)** allegare (con); **please find ~d**
trovi qui accluso
enclosure [ɪn'kləuʒər] n recinto
encore [ɔŋ'kɔːr] excl bis ▷ n bis m inv
encounter [ɪn'kauntər] n incontro
▷ vt incontrare
encourage [ɪn'kʌrɪdʒ] vt
incoraggiare; **encouragement** n
incoraggiamento
encouraging [ɪn'kʌrɪdʒɪŋ] adj
incoraggiante
encyclop(a)edia [ɛnsaɪkləu'piːdɪə]
n enciclopedia
end [ɛnd] n fine f; (aim) fine m; (of table)
bordo estremo; (of pointed object)
punta ▷ vt finire; (also: **bring to an ~,
put an ~ to**) mettere fine a ▷ vi finire;
in the ~ alla fine; **on ~** (object) ritto(-a);
to stand on ~ (hair) rizzarsi; **for hours
on ~** per ore ed ore; **end up** vi **to end
up in** finire in
endanger [ɪn'deɪndʒər] vt mettere
in pericolo
endearing [ɪn'dɪərɪŋ] adj
accattivante
endeavour [ɪn'dɛvər] (US **endeavor**)
n sforzo, tentativo ▷ vi **to ~ to do**
cercare or sforzarsi di fare
ending ['ɛndɪŋ] n fine f, conclusione f;
(Ling) desinenza
endless ['ɛndlɪs] adj senza fine
endorse [ɪn'dɔːs] vt (cheque) girare;
(approve) approvare, appoggiare;
endorsement n approvazione f;
(on driving licence) contravvenzione
registrata sulla patente
endurance [ɪn'djuərəns] n
resistenza; pazienza

endure [ɪn'djuəʳ] vt sopportare, resistere a ▷ vi durare

enemy ['ɛnəmɪ] adj, n nemico(-a)

energetic [ɛnə'dʒɛtɪk] adj energico(-a), attivo(-a)

energy ['ɛnədʒɪ] n energia

enforce [ɪn'fɔːs] vt (Law) applicare, far osservare

engaged [ɪn'geɪdʒd] adj (BRIT: busy, in use) occupato(-a); (betrothed) fidanzato(-a); **the line's ~** la linea è occupata; **to get ~** fidanzarsi; **engaged tone** (BRIT) n (Tel) segnale m di occupato

engagement [ɪn'geɪdʒmənt] n impegno, obbligo; appuntamento; (to marry) fidanzamento; **engagement ring** n anello di fidanzamento

engaging [ɪn'geɪdʒɪŋ] adj attraente

engine ['ɛndʒɪn] n (Aut) motore m; (Rail) locomotiva

engineer [ɛndʒɪ'nɪəʳ] n ingegnere m; (BRIT: for repairs) tecnico; (on ship: US: Rail) macchinista m; **engineering** n ingegneria

England ['ɪŋglənd] n Inghilterra

English ['ɪŋglɪʃ] adj inglese ▷ n (Ling) inglese m; **the English** npl gli Inglesi; **English Channel** n: **the English Channel** la Manica; **Englishman** (irreg) n inglese m; **Englishwoman** (irreg) n inglese f

engrave [ɪn'greɪv] vt incidere

engraving [ɪn'greɪvɪŋ] n incisione f

enhance [ɪn'hɑːns] vt accrescere

enjoy [ɪn'dʒɔɪ] vt godere; (have: success, fortune) avere; **to ~ o.s.** godersela, divertirsi; **enjoyable** adj piacevole; **enjoyment** n piacere m, godimento

enlarge [ɪn'lɑːdʒ] vt ingrandire ▷ vi **to ~ on** (subject) dilungarsi su; **enlargement** n (Phot) ingrandimento

enlist [ɪn'lɪst] vt arruolare; (support) procurare ▷ vi arruolarsi

enormous [ɪ'nɔːməs] adj enorme

enough [ɪ'nʌf] adj, n **~ time/books** assai tempo/libri; **have you got ~?** ne ha abbastanza or a sufficienza? ▷ adv **big ~** abbastanza grande; **he has not worked ~** non ha lavorato abbastanza; **~!** basta!; **that's ~, thanks** basta così, grazie; **I've had ~ of him** ne ho abbastanza di lui; **... which, funnily** or **oddly ~** ... che, strano a dirsi

enquire [ɪn'kwaɪəʳ] vt, vi (esp BRIT) = **inquire**

enquiry [ɪn'kwaɪərɪ] n (esp BRIT) = **inquiry**

enrage [ɪn'reɪdʒ] vt fare arrabbiare

enrich [ɪn'rɪtʃ] vt arricchire

enrol [ɪn'rəul] (US **enroll**) vt iscrivere ▷ vi iscriversi; **enrolment** (US **enrollment**) n iscrizione f

en route [ɔn'ruːt] adv **~ for/from/to** in viaggio per/da/a

en suite [ɔn'swiːt] adj **room with ~ bathroom** camera con bagno

ensure [ɪn'ʃuəʳ] vt assicurare; garantire

entail [ɪn'teɪl] vt comportare

enter ['ɛntəʳ] vt entrare in; (army) arruolarsi in; (competition) partecipare a; (sb for a competition) iscrivere; (write down) registrare; (Comput) inserire ▷ vi entrare

enterprise ['ɛntəpraɪz] n (undertaking, company) impresa; (spirit) iniziativa; **free ~** liberalismo economico; **private ~** iniziativa privata; **enterprising** ['ɛntəpraɪzɪŋ] adj intraprendente

entertain [ɛntə'teɪn] vt divertire; (invite) ricevere; (idea, plan) nutrire; **entertainer** n comico(-a); **entertaining** adj divertente; **entertainment** n (amusement) divertimento; (show) spettacolo

enthusiasm [ɪn'θuːzɪæzəm] n entusiasmo

enthusiast [ɪn'θuːzɪæst] n entusiasta m/f; **enthusiastic** ['-'æstɪk] *adj* entusiasta, entusiastico(-a); **to be enthusiastic about sth/sb** essere appassionato(-a) di qc/entusiasta di qn

entire [ɪn'taɪə^r] *adj* intero(-a); **entirely** *adv* completamente, interamente

entitle [ɪn'taɪtl] *vt* (*give right*): **to ~ sb to sth/to do** dare diritto a qn a qc/a fare; **entitled** *adj* (*book*) che si intitola; **to be entitled to do** avere il diritto di fare

entrance [*n* 'ɛntrns, *vb* ɪn'trɑːns] *n* entrata, ingresso; (*of person*) entrata ▷ *vt* incantare, rapire; **where's the ~?** dov'è l'entrata?; **to gain ~ to** (*university etc*) essere ammesso a; **entrance examination** *n* esame *m* di ammissione; **entrance fee** *n* tassa d'iscrizione; (*to museum etc*) prezzo d'ingresso; **entrance ramp** (*US*) *n* (*Aut*) rampa di accesso; **entrant** ['ɛntrnt] *n* partecipante *m/f*; concorrente *m/f*

entrepreneur [ɔntrəprə'nə:^r] *n* imprenditore *m*

entrust [ɪn'trʌst] *vt* **to ~ sth to** affidare qc a

entry ['ɛntrɪ] *n* entrata; (*way in*) entrata, ingresso; (*item: on list*) iscrizione *f*; (*in dictionary*) voce *f*; **no ~** vietato l'ingresso; (*Aut*) divieto di accesso; **entry phone** *n* citofono

envelope ['ɛnvələup] *n* busta

envious ['ɛnvɪəs] *adj* invidioso(-a)

environment [ɪn'vaɪərnmənt] *n* ambiente *m*; **environmental** [-'mɛntl] *adj* ecologico(-a); ambientale; **environmentally** [ɪnvaɪərən'mɛntəlɪ] *adv* **environmentally sound/friendly** che rispetta l'ambiente

envisage [ɪn'vɪzɪdʒ] *vt* immaginare; prevedere

envoy ['ɛnvɔɪ] *n* inviato(-a)

envy ['ɛnvɪ] *n* invidia ▷ *vt* invidiare; **to ~ sb sth** invidiare qn per qc

epic ['ɛpɪk] *n* poema *m* epico ▷ *adj* epico(-a)

epidemic [ɛpɪ'dɛmɪk] *n* epidemia

epilepsy ['ɛpɪlɛpsɪ] *n* epilessia

epileptic [ɛpɪ'lɛptɪk] *adj, n* epilettico(-a); **epileptic fit** *n* attacco epilettico

episode ['ɛpɪsəud] *n* episodio

equal ['iːkwl] *adj* uguale ▷ *n* pari *m/f* inv ▷ *vt* uguagliare; **~ to** (*task*) all'altezza di; **equality** [iː'kwɔlɪtɪ] *n* uguaglianza; **equalize** *vi* pareggiare; **equally** *adv* ugualmente

equation [ɪ'kweɪʃən] *n* (*Math*) equazione *f*

equator [ɪ'kweɪtə^r] *n* equatore *m*

equip [ɪ'kwɪp] *vt* equipaggiare, attrezzare; **to ~ sb/sth with** fornire qn/qc di; **to be well ~ped** (*office etc*) essere ben attrezzato(-a); **he is well ~ped for the job** ha i requisiti necessari per quel lavoro; **equipment** *n* attrezzatura; (*electrical etc*) apparecchiatura

equivalent [ɪ'kwɪvəlnt] *adj* equivalente ▷ *n* equivalente *m*; **to be ~ to** equivalere a

ER *abbr* (*BRIT*) = **Elizabeth Regina** (*US: Med*) = **emergency room**

era ['ɪərə] *n* era, età *f inv*

erase [ɪ'reɪz] *vt* cancellare; **eraser** *n* gomma

erect [ɪ'rɛkt] *adj* eretto(-a) ▷ *vt* costruire; (*assemble*) montare; **erection** [ɪ'rɛkʃən] *n* costruzione *f*; montaggio; (*Physiol*) erezione *f*

ERM *n* (= *Exchange Rate Mechanism*) ERM *m*

erode [ɪ'rəud] *vt* erodere; (*metal*) corrodere

erosion [ɪ'rəuʒən] *n* erosione *f*

erotic [ɪ'rɔtɪk] *adj* erotico(-a)

errand ['ɛrnd] *n* commissione *f*

erratic [ɪ'rætɪk] *adj* imprevedibile; (*person, mood*) incostante

error ['ɛrə^r] *n* errore *m*

erupt [ɪ'rʌpt] *vi* (*volcano*) mettersi

(or essere) in eruzione; (war, crisis) scoppiare; **eruption** [ɪ'rʌpʃən] n eruzione f; scoppio

escalate ['ɛskəleɪt] vi intensificarsi

escalator ['ɛskəleɪtə'] n scala mobile

escape [ɪ'skeɪp] n evasione f; fuga; (of gas etc) fuga, fuoriuscita ▷ vi fuggire; (from jail) evadere, scappare; (leak) uscire ▷ vt sfuggire a; **to ~ from** (place) fuggire da; (person) sfuggire a

escort [n 'ɛskɔːt, vb ɪ'skɔːt] n scorta; (male companion) cavaliere m ▷ vt scortare; accompagnare

especially [ɪ'spɛʃlɪ] adv specialmente; soprattutto; espressamente

espionage ['ɛspɪənɑːʒ] n spionaggio

essay ['ɛseɪ] n (Scol) composizione f; (Literature) saggio

essence ['ɛsns] n essenza

essential [ɪ'sɛnʃl] adj essenziale ▷ n elemento essenziale; **essentially** adv essenzialmente; **essentials** npl **the essentials** l'essenziale msg

establish [ɪ'stæblɪʃ] vt stabilire; (business) mettere su; (one's power etc) affermare; **establishment** n stabilimento; **the Establishment** la classe dirigente, l'establishment m

estate [ɪ'steɪt] n proprietà f inv; beni mpl, patrimonio; (BRIT: also: **housing ~**) complesso edilizio; **estate agent** (BRIT) n agente m immobiliare; **estate car** (BRIT) n giardiniera

estimate [n 'ɛstɪmət, vb 'ɛstɪmeɪt] n stima; (Comm) preventivo ▷ vt stimare, valutare

etc abbr (= et cetera) etc., ecc.

eternal [ɪ'təːnl] adj eterno(-a)

eternity [ɪ'təːnɪtɪ] n eternità

ethical ['ɛθɪkl] adj etico(-a), morale; **ethics** ['ɛθɪks] n etica ▷ npl morale f

Ethiopia [iːθɪ'əupɪə] n Etiopia

ethnic ['ɛθnɪk] adj etnico(-a); **ethnic minority** n minoranza etnica

e-ticket ['iːtɪkɪt] n biglietto elettronico

etiquette ['ɛtɪkɛt] n etichetta

EU n abbr (= European Union) UE f

euro ['juərəu] n (currency) euro m inv

Europe ['juərəp] n Europa; **European** [-'piːən] adj, n europeo(-a); **European Community** n Comunità Europea; **European Union** n Unione f europea

Eurostar® ['juərəustɑː'] n Eurostar® m inv

evacuate [ɪ'vækjueɪt] vt evacuare

evade [ɪ'veɪd] vt (tax) evadere; (duties etc) sottrarsi a; (person) schivare

evaluate [ɪ'væljueɪt] vt valutare

evaporate [ɪ'væpəreɪt] vi evaporare

eve [iːv] n: **on the ~ of** alla vigilia di

even ['iːvn] adj regolare; (number) pari inv ▷ adv anche, perfino; **~ if, ~ though** anche se; **~ more** ancora di più; **~ so** ciò nonostante; **not ~** nemmeno; **to get ~ with sb** dare la pari a qn

evening ['iːvnɪŋ] n sera; (as duration, event) serata; **in the ~** la sera; **evening class** n corso serale; **evening dress** n (woman's) abito da sera; **in evening dress** (man) in abito scuro; (woman) in abito lungo

event [ɪ'vɛnt] n avvenimento; (Sport) gara; **in the ~ of** in caso di; **eventful** adj denso(-a) di eventi

eventual [ɪ'vɛntʃuəl] adj finale

> Be careful not to translate *eventual* by the Italian word *eventuale*.

eventually [ɪ'vɛntʃuəlɪ] adv alla fine

> Be careful not to translate *eventually* by the Italian word *eventualmente*.

ever ['ɛvə'] adv mai; (at all times) sempre; **the best ~** il migliore che ci sia mai stato; **have you ~ seen it?** l'ha mai visto?; **~ since** adv da allora ▷ conj sin da quando; **~ so pretty** così bello(-a); **evergreen** n sempreverde m

every ['ɛvrɪ] adj ogni; **~ day** tutti i giorni, ogni giorno; **~ other/third day** ogni due/tre giorni; **~ other car** una

macchina su due; **~ now and then**
ogni tanto, di quando in quando;
everybody pron = **everyone**;
everyday adj quotidiano(-a); di ogni
giorno; **everyone** pron ognuno, tutti
pl; **everything** pron tutto, ogni cosa;
everywhere adv (gen) dappertutto;
(wherever) ovunque

evict [ɪ'vɪkt] vt sfrattare

evidence ['ɛvɪdns] n (proof) prova;
(of witness) testimonianza; (sign): **to
show ~ of** dare segni di; **to give ~**
deporre

evident ['ɛvɪdnt] adj evidente;
evidently adv evidentemente

evil ['iːvl] adj cattivo(-a), maligno(-a)
▷ n male m

evoke [ɪ'vəuk] vt evocare

evolution [iːvə'luːʃən] n evoluzione f

evolve [ɪ'vɔlv] vt elaborare ▷ vi
svilupparsi, evolversi

ewe [juː] n pecora

ex (inf) [ɛks] n: **my ex** il (la) mio(-a) ex

ex- [ɛks] prefix ex

exact [ɪg'zækt] adj esatto(-a) ▷ vt: **to
~ sth (from)** estorcere qc (da); esigere
qc (da); **exactly** adv esattamente

exaggerate [ɪg'zædʒəreɪt] vt, vi
esagerare; **exaggeration** [-'reɪʃən] n
esagerazione f

exam [ɪg'zæm] n abbr (Scol)
= **examination**

examination [ɪgzæmɪ'neɪʃən] n
(Scol) esame m; (Med) controllo

examine [ɪg'zæmɪn] vt esaminare;
examiner n esaminatore(-trice)

example [ɪg'zɑːmpl] n esempio; **for ~**
ad or per esempio

exasperated [ɪg'zɑːspəreɪtɪd] adj
esasperato(-a)

excavate ['ɛkskəveɪt] vt scavare

exceed [ɪk'siːd] vt superare; (one's
powers, time limit) oltrepassare;
exceedingly adv eccessivamente

excel [ɪk'sɛl] vi eccellere ▷ vt
sorpassare; **to ~ o.s** (BRIT) superare
se stesso

excellence ['ɛksələns] n eccellenza

excellent ['ɛksələnt] adj eccellente

except [ɪk'sɛpt] prep (also: **~ for,
~ing**) salvo, all'infuori di, eccetto
▷ vt escludere; **~ if/when** salvo
se/quando; **~ that** salvo che;
exception [ɪk'sɛpʃən] n eccezione
f; **to take exception to** trovare a
ridire su; **exceptional** [ɪk'sɛpʃənl]
adj eccezionale; **exceptionally**
[ɪk'sɛpʃənəlɪ] adv eccezionalmente

excerpt ['ɛksəːpt] n estratto

excess [ɪk'sɛs] n eccesso; **excess
baggage** n bagaglio in eccedenza;
excessive adj eccessivo(-a)

exchange [ɪks'tʃeɪndʒ] n scambio;
(also: **telephone ~**) centralino ▷ vt: **to
~ (for)** scambiare (con); **could I ~ this,
please?** posso cambiarlo, per favore?;
exchange rate n tasso di cambio

excite [ɪk'saɪt] vt eccitare; **to get ~d**
eccitarsi; **excited** adj: **to get excited**
essere elettrizzato(-a); **excitement**
n eccitazione f; agitazione f; **exciting**
adj avventuroso(-a); (film, book)
appassionante

exclaim [ɪk'skleɪm] vi esclamare;
exclamation [ɛkskləˈmeɪʃən] n
esclamazione f; **exclamation mark**
(US **exclamation point**) n punto
esclamativo

exclude [ɪk'skluːd] vt escludere

excluding [ɪk'skluːdɪŋ] prep **~ VAT**
IVA esclusa

exclusion [ɪk'skluːʒən] n esclusione
f; **to the ~ of** escludendo

exclusive [ɪk'skluːsɪv] adj
esclusivo(-a); **~ of VAT** I.V.A. esclusa;
exclusively adv esclusivamente

excruciating [ɪk'skruːʃɪeɪtɪŋ] adj
straziante, atroce

excursion [ɪk'skəːʃən] n escursione
f, gita

excuse [n ɪk'skjuːs, vb ɪk'skjuːz] n
scusa ▷ vt scusare; **to ~ sb from**
(activity) dispensare qn da; **~ me!** mi
scusi!; **now, if you will ~ me ...** ora,

mi scusi ma …

ex-directory ['ɛksdɪ'rɛktərɪ] (BRIT)
adj (Tel): **to be ~** non essere sull'elenco
execute ['ɛksɪkjuːt] vt (prisoner)
giustiziare; (plan etc) eseguire;
execution [ɛksɪ'kjuːʃən] n
esecuzione f
executive [ɪg'zɛkjutɪv] n (Comm)
dirigente m; (Pol) esecutivo ▷ adj
esecutivo(-a)
exempt [ɪg'zɛmpt] adj esentato(-a)
▷ vt **to ~ sb from** esentare qn da
exercise ['ɛksəsaɪz] n (keep fit) moto;
(Scol, Mil etc) esercizio ▷ vt esercitare;
(patience) usare; (dog) portar fuori ▷ vi
(also: **take ~**) fare del moto; **exercise
book** n quaderno
exert [ɪg'zəːt] vt esercitare; **to ~ o.s.**
sforzarsi; **exertion** [-ʃən] n sforzo
exhale [ɛks'heɪl] vt, vi espirare
exhaust [ɪg'zɔːst] n (also: **~ fumes**)
scappamento; (also: **~ pipe**) tubo
di scappamento ▷ vt esaurire;
exhausted adj esaurito(-a);
exhaustion [ɪg'zɔːstʃən] n
esaurimento; **nervous exhaustion**
sovraffaticamento mentale
exhibit [ɪg'zɪbɪt] n (Art) oggetto
esposto; (Law) documento or oggetto
esibito ▷ vt esporre; (courage, skill)
dimostrare; **exhibition** [ɛksɪ'bɪʃən] n
mostra, esposizione f
exhilarating [ɪg'zɪləreɪtɪŋ] adj
esilarante; stimolante
exile ['ɛksaɪl] n esilio; (person)
esiliato(-a) ▷ vt esiliare
exist [ɪg'zɪst] vi esistere; **existence** n
esistenza; **existing** adj esistente
exit ['ɛksɪt] n uscita ▷ vi (Theatre,
Comput) uscire; **where's the ~?** dov'è
l'uscita?; **exit ramp** (US) n (Aut)
rampa di uscita
exotic [ɪg'zɔtɪk] adj esotico(-a)
expand [ɪk'spænd] vt espandere;
estendere; allargare ▷ vi (business,
gas) espandersi; (metal) dilatarsi
expansion [ɪk'spænʃən] n (gen)

espansione f; (of town, economy)
sviluppo; (of metal) dilatazione f
expect [ɪk'spɛkt] vt (anticipate)
prevedere, aspettarsi, prevedere
or aspettarsi che + sub; (require)
richiedere, esigere; (suppose) supporre;
(await, also baby) aspettare ▷ vi **to be
~ing** essere in stato interessante; **to
~ sb to do** aspettarsi che qn faccia;
expectation [ɛkspɛk'teɪʃən] n
aspettativa; speranza
expedition [ɛkspə'dɪʃən] n
spedizione f
expel [ɪk'spɛl] vt espellere
expenditure [ɪk'spɛndɪtʃəʳ] n spesa
expense [ɪk'spɛns] n spesa; (high
cost) costo; **expenses** npl (Comm)
spese fpl, indennità fpl; **at the ~ of** a
spese di; **expense account** n conto
m spese inv
expensive [ɪk'spɛnsɪv] adj caro(-a),
costoso(-a); **it's too ~** è troppo caro
experience [ɪk'spɪərɪəns] n
esperienza ▷ vt (pleasure) provare;
(hardship) soffrire; **experienced** adj
esperto(-a)
experiment [n ɪk'spɛrɪmənt, vb
ɪk'spɛrɪmɛnt] n esperimento,
esperienza ▷ vi **to ~ (with/on)** fare
esperimenti (con/su); **experimental**
[ɪkspɛrɪ'mɛntl] adj sperimentale;
at the experimental stage in via di
sperimentazione
expert ['ɛkspəːt] adj, n esperto(-a);
expertise [-'tiːz] n competenza
expire [ɪk'spaɪəʳ] vi (period of time,
licence) scadere; **expiry** n scadenza;
expiry date n (of medicine, food item)
data di scadenza
explain [ɪk'spleɪn] vt spiegare;
explanation [ɛksplə'neɪʃən] n
spiegazione f
explicit [ɪk'splɪsɪt] adj esplicito(-a)
explode [ɪk'spləud] vi esplodere
exploit [n 'ɛksplɔɪt, vb ɪk'splɔɪt] n
impresa ▷ vt sfruttare; **exploitation**
[-'teɪʃən] n sfruttamento

explore [ɪk'splɔːʳ] vt esplorare; (*possibilities*) esaminare; **explorer** n esploratore(-trice)

explosion [ɪk'spləuʒən] n esplosione f; **explosive** [ɪk'spləusɪv] adj esplosivo(-a) ▷ n esplosivo

export [vb ɛk'spɔːt, n 'ɛkspɔːt] vt esportare ▷ n esportazione f; articolo di esportazione ▷ cpd d'esportazione; **exporter** n esportatore m

expose [ɪk'spəuz] vt esporre; (*unmask*) smascherare; **exposed** adj (*position*) esposto(-a); **exposure** [ɪk'spəuʒəʳ] n esposizione f; (*Phot*) posa; (*Med*) assideramento

express [ɪk'sprɛs] adj (*definite*) chiaro(-a), espresso(-a); (*BRIT*: *letter etc*) espresso inv ▷ n (*train*) espresso ▷ vt esprimere; **expression** [ɪk'sprɛʃən] n espressione f; **expressway** (*US*) n (*urban motorway*) autostrada che attraversa la città

exquisite [ɛk'skwɪzɪt] adj squisito(-a)

extend [ɪk'stɛnd] vt (*visit*) protrarre; (*road, deadline*) prolungare; (*building*) ampliare; (*offer*) offrire, porgere ▷ vi (*land, period*) estendersi; **extension** [ɪk'stɛnʃən] n (*of road, term*) prolungamento; (*of contract, deadline*) proroga; (*building*) annesso; (*to wire, table*) prolunga; (*telephone*) interno; (: *in private house*) apparecchio supplementare; **extension lead** n prolunga

extensive [ɪk'stɛnsɪv] adj esteso(-a), ampio(-a); (*damage*) su larga scala; (*coverage, discussion*) esauriente; (*use*) grande

extent [ɪk'stɛnt] n estensione f; **to some ~** fino a un certo punto; **to such an ~ that ...** a un tal punto che ...; **to what ~?** fino a che punto?; **to the ~ of ...** fino al punto di ...

exterior [ɛk'stɪərɪəʳ] adj esteriore, esterno(-a) ▷ n esteriore m, esterno; aspetto (esteriore)

external [ɛk'stəːnl] adj esterno(-a),

esteriore

extinct [ɪk'stɪŋkt] adj estinto(-a); **extinction** [ɪk'stɪŋkʃən] n estinzione f

extinguish [ɪk'stɪŋgwɪʃ] vt estinguere

extra ['ɛkstrə] adj extra inv, supplementare ▷ adv (*in addition*) di più ▷ n extra m inv; (*surcharge*) supplemento; (*Cinema, Theatre*) comparsa

extract [vb ɪk'strækt, n 'ɛkstrækt] vt estrarre; (*money, promise*) strappare ▷ n estratto; (*passage*) brano

extradite ['ɛkstrədaɪt] vt estradare

extraordinary [ɪk'strɔːdnrɪ] adj straordinario(-a)

extravagance [ɪk'strævəgəns] n sperpero; stravaganza

extravagant [ɪk'strævəgənt] adj (*lavish*) prodigo(-a); (*wasteful*) dispendioso(-a)

> Be careful not to translate **extravagant** by the Italian word **stravagante**.

extreme [ɪk'striːm] adj estremo(-a) ▷ n estremo; **extremely** adv estremamente

extremist [ɪk'striːmɪst] adj, n estremista (m/f)

extrovert ['ɛkstrəvəːt] n estroverso(-a)

eye [aɪ] n occhio; (*of needle*) cruna ▷ vt osservare; **to keep an ~ on** tenere d'occhio; **eyeball** n globo dell'occhio; **eyebrow** n sopracciglio; **eyedrops** npl gocce fpl oculari, collirio; **eyelash** n ciglio; **eyelid** n palpebra; **eyeliner** n eye-liner m inv; **eyeshadow** n ombretto; **eyesight** n vista; **eye witness** n testimone m/f oculare

f

F [ɛf] n (Mus) fa m

fabric ['fæbrɪk] n stoffa, tessuto

fabulous ['fæbjuləs] adj favoloso(-a); (super) favoloso(-a), fantastico(-a)

face [feɪs] n faccia, viso, volto; (expression) faccia; (of clock) quadrante m; (of building) facciata ▷ vt essere di fronte a; (facts, situation) affrontare; **~ down** faccia in giù; **to make** or **pull a ~** fare una smorfia; **in the ~ of** (difficulties etc) di fronte a; **on the ~ of it** a prima vista; **~ to ~** faccia a faccia; **face up to** vt fus affrontare, far fronte a; **face cloth** n (BRIT) guanto di spugna; **face pack** n (BRIT) maschera di bellezza

facial ['feɪʃəl] adj del viso

facilitate [fə'sɪlɪteɪt] vt facilitare

facilities [fə'sɪlɪtɪz] npl attrezzature fpl; **credit ~** facilitazioni fpl di credito

fact [fækt] n fatto; **in ~** in effetti

faction ['fækʃən] n fazione f

factor ['fæktər] n fattore m; **I'd like a ~ 15 suntan lotion** vorrei una crema solare con fattore di protezione 15

factory ['fæktərɪ] n fabbrica, stabilimento

> Be careful not to translate *factory* by the Italian word *fattoria*.

factual ['fæktjuəl] adj che si attiene ai fatti

faculty ['fækəltɪ] n facoltà f inv; (US) corpo insegnante

fad [fæd] n mania; capriccio

fade [feɪd] vi sbiadire, sbiadirsi; (light, sound, hope) attenuarsi, affievolirsi; (flower) appassire; **fade away** vi (sound) affievolirsi

fag [fæg] (BRIT: inf) n (cigarette) cicca

Fahrenheit ['fɑːrənhaɪt] n Fahrenheit m inv

fail [feɪl] vt (exam) non superare; (candidate) bocciare; (courage, memory) mancare a ▷ vi fallire; (student) essere respinto(-a); (eyesight, health, light) venire a mancare; **to ~ to do sth** (neglect) mancare di fare qc; (be unable) non riuscire a fare qc; **without ~** senza fallo; certamente; **failing** n difetto ▷ prep in mancanza di; **failure** ['feɪljər] n fallimento; (person) fallito(-a); (mechanical etc) guasto

faint [feɪnt] adj debole; (recollection) vago(-a); (mark) indistinto(-a) ▷ n (Med) svenimento ▷ vi svenire; **to feel ~** sentirsi svenire; **faintest** adj: **I haven't the faintest idea** non ho la più pallida idea; **faintly** adv debolmente; vagamente

fair [feər] adj (person, decision) giusto(-a), equo(-a); (quite large, quite good) discreto(-a); (hair etc) biondo(-a); (skin, complexion) chiaro(-a); (weather) bello(-a), clemente ▷ adv (play) lealmente ▷ n fiera; (BRIT: funfair) luna park m inv; **fairground** n luna park m inv; **fair-haired** [feə'hɛəd] adj (person) biondo(-a); **fairly** adv equamente; (quite) abbastanza; **fair trade** n commercio equo e solidale; **fairway** n

(*Golf*) fairway m *inv*

fairy ['fɛərɪ] n fata; **fairy tale** n fiaba

faith [feɪθ] n fede f; (*trust*) fiducia; (*sect*) religione f, fede f; **faithful** *adj* fedele; **faithfully** *adv* fedelmente; **yours faithfully** (BRIT: *in letters*) distinti saluti

fake [feɪk] n imitazione f; (*picture*) falso; (*person*) impostore(-a) ▷ *adj* falso(-a) ▷ *vt* (*accounts*) falsificare; (*illness*) fingere; (*painting*) contraffare

falcon ['fɔːlkən] n falco, falcone m

fall [fɔːl] (*pt* **fell**, *pp* **fallen**) n caduta; (*in temperature*) abbassamento; (*in price*) ribasso; (*us: autumn*) autunno ▷ *vi* cadere; (*temperature, price, night*) scendere; **falls** *npl* (*waterfall*) cascate *fpl*; **to ~ flat** (*on one's face*) cadere bocconi; (*joke*) fare cilecca; (*plan*) fallire; **fall apart** *vi* cadere a pezzi; **fall down** *vi* (*person*) cadere; (*building*) crollare; **fall for** *vt fus* (*person*) prendere una cotta per; **to fall for a trick** (*or a story etc*) cascarci; **fall off** *vi* cadere; (*diminish*) diminuire, abbassarsi; **fall out** *vi* (*hair, teeth*) cadere; (*friends etc*) litigare; **fall over** *vi* cadere; **fall through** *vi* (*plan, project*) fallire

fallen ['fɔːlən] *pp of* **fall**

fallout ['fɔːlaut] n fall-out m

false [fɔːls] *adj* falso(-a); **under ~ pretences** con l'inganno; **false alarm** n falso allarme m; **false teeth** (BRIT) *npl* denti *mpl* finti

fame [feɪm] n fama, celebrità

familiar [fə'mɪlɪər] *adj* familiare; (*close*) intimo(-a); **to be ~ with** (*subject*) conoscere; **familiarize** [fə'mɪlɪəraɪz] *vt* **to familiarize o.s. with** familiarizzare con

family ['fæmɪlɪ] n famiglia; **family doctor** n medico di famiglia; **family planning** n pianificazione f familiare

famine ['fæmɪn] n carestia

famous ['feɪməs] *adj* famoso(-a)

fan [fæn] n (*folding*) ventaglio;

(*Elec*) ventilatore m; (*person*) ammiratore(-trice), tifoso(-a) ▷ *vt* far vento a; (*fire, quarrel*) alimentare

fanatic [fə'nætɪk] n fanatico(-a)

fan belt n cinghia del ventilatore

fan club n fan club m *inv*

fancy ['fænsɪ] n immaginazione f, fantasia; (*whim*) capriccio ▷ *adj* (*hat*) stravagante; (*hotel, food*) speciale ▷ *vt* (*feel like, want*) aver voglia di; (*imagine, think*) immaginare; **to take a ~ to** incapricciarsi di; **he fancies her** (*inf*) gli piace; **fancy dress** n costume m (per maschera)

fan heater n (BRIT) stufa ad aria calda

fantasize ['fæntəsaɪz] *vi* fantasticare, sognare

fantastic [fæn'tæstɪk] *adj* fantastico(-a)

fantasy ['fæntəsɪ] n fantasia, immaginazione f; fantasticheria; chimera

fanzine ['fænziːn] n rivista specialistica (per appassionati)

FAQs *abbr* (= *frequently asked questions*) FAQ *fpl*

far [fɑːʳ] *adj* lontano(-a) ▷ *adv* lontano; (*much, greatly*) molto; **is it ~ from here?** è molto lontano da qui?; **how ~?** quanto lontano?; (*referring to activity etc*) fino a dove?; **how ~ is the town centre?** quanto dista il centro da qui?; **~ away, ~ off** lontano, distante; **~ better** assai migliore; **~ from** lontano da; **by ~** di gran lunga; **go as ~ as the farm** vada fino alla fattoria; **as ~ as I know** per quel che so

farce [fɑːs] n farsa

fare [fɛəʳ] n (*on trains, buses*) tariffa; (*in taxi*) prezzo della corsa; (*food*) vitto, cibo; **half ~** metà tariffa; **full ~** tariffa intera

Far East n: **the ~** l'Estremo Oriente m

farewell [fɛə'wɛl] *excl*, n addio

farm [fɑːm] n fattoria, podere m ▷ *vt* coltivare; **farmer** n coltivatore(-trice), agricoltore(-trice);

farmhouse n fattoria; **farming** n (gen) agricoltura; (of crops) coltivazione f; (of animals) allevamento; **farmyard** n aia

far-reaching [fɑːˈriːtʃɪŋ] adj di vasta portata

fart [fɑːt] (infl) vi scoreggiare (!)

farther [ˈfɑːðəʳ] adv più lontano ▷ adj più lontano(-a)

farthest [ˈfɑːðɪst] superl of **far**

fascinate [ˈfæsɪneɪt] vt affascinare; **fascinated** adj affascinato(-a); **fascinating** adj affascinante; **fascination** [-ˈneɪʃən] n fascino

fascist [ˈfæʃɪst] adj, n fascista (m/f)

fashion [ˈfæʃən] n moda; (manner) maniera, modo ▷ vt foggiare, formare; **in ~** alla moda; **out of ~** passato(-a) di moda; **fashionable** adj alla moda, di moda; **fashion show** n sfilata di moda

fast [fɑːst] adj rapido(-a), svelto(-a), veloce; (clock): **to be ~** andare avanti; (dye, colour) solido(-a) ▷ adv rapidamente; (stuck, held) saldamente ▷ n digiuno ▷ vi digiunare; **~ asleep** profondamente addormentato

fasten [ˈfɑːsn] vt chiudere, fissare; (coat) abbottonare, allacciare ▷ vi chiudersi, fissarsi; abbottonarsi, allacciarsi

fast food n fast food m

fat [fæt] adj grasso(-a); (book, profit etc) grosso(-a) ▷ n grasso m

fatal [ˈfeɪtl] adj fatale; mortale; disastroso(-a); **fatality** [fəˈtælɪtɪ] n (road death etc) morto(-a), vittima; **fatally** adv a morte

fate [feɪt] n destino; (of person) sorte f

father [ˈfɑːðəʳ] n padre m; **Father Christmas** n Babbo Natale; **father-in-law** n suocero

fatigue [fəˈtiːg] n stanchezza

fattening [ˈfætnɪŋ] adj (food) che fa ingrassare

fatty [ˈfætɪ] adj (food) grasso(-a) ▷ n (inf) ciccione(-a)

faucet [ˈfɔːsɪt] (US) n rubinetto

fault [fɔːlt] n colpa; (Tennis) fallo; (defect) difetto; (Geo) faglia ▷ vt criticare; **it's my ~** è colpa mia; **to find ~ with** trovare da ridire su; **at ~** in fallo; **faulty** adj difettoso(-a)

fauna [ˈfɔːnə] n fauna

favour etc [ˈfeɪvəʳ] (US **favor**) n favore m ▷ vt (proposition) favorire, essere favorevole a; (pupil etc) favorire; (team, horse) dare per vincente; **to do sb a ~** fare un favore or una cortesia a qn; **to find ~ with** (person) entrare nelle buone grazie di; (: suggestion) avere l'approvazione di; **in ~ of** in favore di; **favourable** adj favorevole; **favourite** [-rɪt] adj, n favorito(-a)

fawn [fɔːn] n daino ▷ adj (also: **~-coloured**) marrone chiaro inv ▷ vi: **to ~ (up)on** adulare servilmente

fax [fæks] n (document) facsimile m inv, telecopia; (machine) telecopiatrice f ▷ vt telecopiare, trasmettere in facsimile

FBI (US) n abbr (= Federal Bureau of Investigation) F.B.I. f

fear [fɪəʳ] n paura, timore m ▷ vt aver paura di, temere; **for ~ of** per paura di; **fearful** adj pauroso(-a); (sight, noise) terribile, spaventoso(-a); **fearless** adj intrepido(-a), senza paura

feasible [ˈfiːzəbl] adj possibile, realizzabile

feast [fiːst] n festa, banchetto; (Rel: also: **~ day**) festa ▷ vi banchettare

feat [fiːt] n impresa, fatto insigne

feather [ˈfɛðəʳ] n penna

feature [ˈfiːtʃəʳ] n caratteristica; (Press, TV) articolo ▷ vt (film) avere come protagonista ▷ vi figurare; **features** npl (of face) fisionomia; **feature film** n film m inv principale

Feb. [fɛb] abbr (= February) feb

February [ˈfɛbruərɪ] n febbraio

fed [fɛd] pt, pp of **feed**

federal [ˈfɛdərəl] adj federale

federation [fɛdəˈreɪʃən] n

federazione f

fed up adj **to be ~** essere stufo(-a)

fee [fi:] n pagamento; (of doctor, lawyer) onorario; (for examination) tassa d'esame; **school ~s** tasse fpl scolastiche

feeble ['fi:bl] adj debole

feed [fi:d] (pt, pp **fed**) n (of baby) pappa; (of animal) mangime m; (on printer) meccanismo di alimentazione ▷ vt nutrire; (baby) allattare; (horse etc) dare da mangiare a; (fire, machine) alimentare; (data, information): **to ~ into** inserire in; **feedback** n feedback m

feel [fi:l] (pt, pp **felt**) n consistenza; (sense of touch) tatto ▷ vt toccare; palpare; tastare; (cold, pain, anger) sentire; (think, believe): **to ~ (that)** pensare che; **to ~ hungry/cold** aver fame/freddo; **to ~ lonely/better** sentirsi solo/meglio; **I don't ~ well** non mi sento bene; **it ~s soft** è morbido al tatto; **to ~ like** (want) aver voglia di; **to ~ about** or **around for** cercare a tastoni; **feeling** n sensazione f; (emotion) sentimento

feet [fi:t] npl of **foot**

fell [fɛl] pt of **fall** ▷ vt (tree) abbattere

fellow ['fɛləu] n individuo, tipo; compagno; (of learned society) membro cpd; **fellow citizen** n concittadino(-a); **fellow countryman** (irreg) n compatriota m; **fellow men** npl simili mpl; **fellowship** n associazione f; compagnia; specie di borsa di studio universitaria

felony ['fɛlənɪ] n reato, crimine m

felt [fɛlt] pt, pp of **feel** ▷ n feltro

female ['fi:meɪl] n (Zool) femmina; (pej: woman) donna, femmina ▷ adj (Biol, Elec) femmina inv; (sex, character) femminile; (vote etc) di donne

feminine ['fɛmɪnɪn] adj femminile

feminist ['fɛmɪnɪst] n femminista m/f

fence [fɛns] n recinto ▷ vt (also: ~ in) recingere ▷ vi (Sport) tirare di scherma; **fencing** n (Sport) scherma

fend [fɛnd] vi **to ~ for o.s.** arrangiarsi; **fend off** vt (attack, questions) respingere, difendersi da

fender ['fɛndə^r] n parafuoco; (on boat) parabordo; (us) parafango; paraurti m inv

fennel ['fɛnl] n finocchio

ferment [vb fə'mɛnt, n 'fə:mɛnt] vi fermentare ▷ n (fig) agitazione f, eccitazione f

fern [fə:n] n felce f

ferocious [fə'rəuʃəs] adj feroce

ferret ['fɛrɪt] n furetto

ferry ['fɛrɪ] n (small) traghetto; (large: also: ~ **boat**) nave f traghetto inv ▷ vt traghettare

fertile ['fə:taɪl] adj fertile; (Biol) fecondo(-a); **fertilize** ['fə:tɪlaɪz] vt fertilizzare; fecondare; **fertilizer** ['fə:tɪlaɪzə] n fertilizzante m

festival ['fɛstɪvəl] n (Rel) festa; (Art, Mus) festival m inv

festive ['fɛstɪv] adj di festa; **the ~ season** (BRIT: Christmas) il periodo delle feste

fetch [fɛtʃ] vt andare a prendere; (sell for) essere venduto(-a) per

fête [feɪt] n festa

fetus ['fi:təs] (us) n = **foetus**

feud [fju:d] n contesa, lotta

fever ['fi:və^r] n febbre f; **feverish** adj febbrile

few [fju:] adj pochi(-e); **a ~** adj qualche inv ▷ pron alcuni(-e); **fewer** adj meno inv, meno numerosi(-e); **fewest** adj il minor numero di

fiancé [fɪ'ɑ̃:ŋseɪ] n fidanzato; **fiancée** n fidanzata

fiasco [fɪ'æskəu] n fiasco

fib [fɪb] n piccola bugia

fibre ['faɪbə^r] (us **fiber**) n fibra; **Fibreglass®** ['faɪbəglɑ:s] (us **fiberglass**) n fibra di vetro

fickle ['fɪkl] adj incostante, capriccioso(-a)

fiction ['fɪkʃən] n narrativa, romanzi

mpl; (*sth made up*) finzione *f*; **fictional** *adj* immaginario(-a)

fiddle ['fɪdl] *n* (*Mus*) violino; (*cheating*) imbroglio; truffa ▷ *vt* (*BRIT: accounts*) falsificare, falsare; **fiddle with** *vt fus* gingillarsi con

fidelity [fɪ'dɛlɪtɪ] *n* fedeltà; (*accuracy*) esattezza

field [fiːld] *n* campo; **field marshal** *n* feldmaresciallo

fierce [fɪəs] *adj* (*animal, person, fighting*) feroce; (*loyalty*) assoluto(-a); (*wind*) furioso(-a); (*heat*) intenso(-a)

fifteen [fɪf'tiːn] *num* quindici; **fifteenth** *num* quindicesimo(-a)

fifth [fɪfθ] *num* quinto(-a)

fiftieth ['fɪftɪɪθ] *num* cinquantesimo(-a)

fifty ['fɪftɪ] *num* cinquanta; **fifty-fifty** *adj*: **a fifty-fifty chance** una possibilità su due ▷ *adv* fifty-fifty, metà per ciascuno

fig [fɪg] *n* fico

fight [faɪt] (*pt, pp* **fought**) *n* zuffa, rissa; (*Mil*) battaglia, combattimento; (*against cancer etc*) lotta ▷ *vt* (*person*) azzuffarsi con; (*enemy: also Mil*) combattere; (*cancer, alcoholism, emotion*) lottare contro, combattere; (*election*) partecipare a ▷ *vi* combattere; **fight back** *vi* difendersi; (*Sport, after illness*) riprendersi ▷ *vt* (*tears*) ricacciare; **fight off** *vt* (*attack, attacker*) respingere; (*disease, sleep, urge*) lottare contro; **fighting** *n* combattimento

figure ['fɪgəʳ] *n* figura; (*number, cipher*) cifra ▷ *vt* (*think: esp US*) pensare ▷ *vi* (*appear*) figurare; **figure out** *vt* riuscire a capire; calcolare

file [faɪl] *n* (*tool*) lima; (*dossier*) incartamento; (*folder*) cartellina; (*Comput*) archivio; (*row*) fila ▷ *vt* (*nails, wood*) limare; (*papers*) archiviare; (*Law: claim*) presentare; passare agli atti; **filing cabinet** ['faɪlɪŋ-] *n* casellario

Filipino [fɪlɪ'piːnəu] *n* filippino(-a);

(*Ling*) tagal *m*

fill [fɪl] *vt* riempire; (*job*) coprire ▷ *n* **to eat one's** ~ mangiare a sazietà; **fill in** *vt* (*hole*) riempire; (*form*) compilare; **fill out** *vt* (*form, receipt*) riempire; **fill up** *vt* riempire; **fill it up, please** (*Aut*) il pieno, per favore

fillet ['fɪlɪt] *n* filetto; **fillet steak** *n* bistecca di filetto

filling ['fɪlɪŋ] *n* (*Culin*) impasto, ripieno; (*for tooth*) otturazione *f*; **filling station** *n* stazione *f* di rifornimento

film [fɪlm] *n* (*Cinema*) film *m inv*; (*Phot*) pellicola, rullino; (*of powder, liquid*) sottile strato ▷ *vt, vi* girare; **I'd like a 36-exposure** ~ vorrei un rullino da 36 pose; **film star** *n* divo(-a) dello schermo

filter ['fɪltəʳ] *n* filtro ▷ *vt* filtrare; **filter lane** (*BRIT*) *n* (*Aut*) corsia di svincolo

filth [fɪlθ] *n* sporcizia; **filthy** *adj* lordo(-a), sozzo(-a); (*language*) osceno(-a)

fin [fɪn] *n* (*of fish*) pinna

final ['faɪnl] *adj* finale, ultimo(-a); definitivo(-a) ▷ *n* (*Sport*) finale *f*; **finals** *npl* (*Scol*) esami *mpl* finali; **finale** [fɪ'nɑːlɪ] *n* finale *m*; **finalist** ['faɪnəlɪst] *n* (*Sport*) finalista *m/f*; **finalize** ['faɪnəlaɪz] *vt* mettere a punto; **finally** ['faɪnəlɪ] *adv* (*lastly*) alla fine; (*eventually*) finalmente

finance [faɪ'næns] *n* finanza; (*capital*) capitale *m* ▷ *vt* finanziare; **finances** *npl* (*funds*) finanze *fpl*; **financial** [faɪ'nænʃəl] *adj* finanziario(-a); **financial year** *n* anno finanziario, esercizio finanziario

find [faɪnd] (*pt, pp* **found**) *vt* trovare; (*lost object*) ritrovare ▷ *n* trovata, scoperta; **to** ~ **sb guilty** (*Law*) giudicare qn colpevole; **find out** *vt* (*truth, secret*) scoprire; (*person*) cogliere in fallo; **to find out about** informarsi su; (*by chance*) scoprire; **findings** *npl* (*Law*) sentenza, conclusioni *fpl*; (*of report*) conclusioni

fine [faɪn] adj bello(-a); ottimo(-a); (thin, subtle) fine ▷ adv (well) molto bene ▷ n (Law) multa ▷ vt (Law) multare; **to be ~** (person) stare bene; (weather) far bello; **fine arts** npl belle arti fpl

finger ['fɪŋgəʳ] n dito ▷ vt toccare, tastare; **little~ index ~** mignolo/(dito) indice m; **fingernail** n unghia; **fingerprint** n impronta digitale; **fingertip** n punta del dito

finish ['fɪnɪʃ] n fine f; (polish etc) finitura ▷ vt, vi finire; **when does the show ~?** quando finisce lo spettacolo?; **to ~ doing sth** finire di fare qc; **to ~ third** arrivare terzo(-a); **finish off** vt compiere; (kill) uccidere; **finish up** vi, vt finire

Finland ['fɪnlənd] n Finlandia; **Finn** [fɪn] n finlandese m/f; **Finnish** adj finlandese ▷ n (Ling) finlandese m

fir [fəːʳ] n abete m

fire [faɪəʳ] n fuoco; (destructive) incendio; (gas fire, electric fire) stufa ▷ vt (gun) far fuoco con; (arrow) sparare; (fig) infiammare; (inf: dismiss) licenziare ▷ vi sparare, far fuoco; **~!** al fuoco!; **on ~** in fiamme; **fire alarm** n allarme m d'incendio; **firearm** n arma da fuoco; **fire brigade** [-brɪ'geɪd] (US **fire department**) n (corpo dei) pompieri mpl; **fire engine** n autopompa; **fire escape** n scala di sicurezza; **fire exit** n uscita di sicurezza; **fire extinguisher** [-ɪk'stɪŋgwɪʃəʳ] n estintore m; **fireman** (irreg) n pompiere m; **fireplace** n focolare m; **fire station** n caserma dei pompieri; **firetruck** (US) n = **fire engine**; **firewall** n (Internet) firewall m inv; **firewood** n legna; **fireworks** npl fuochi mpl d'artificio

firm [fəːm] adj fermo(-a) ▷ n ditta, azienda; **firmly** adv fermamente

first [fəːst] adj primo(-a) ▷ adv (before others) il primo, la prima; (before other things) per primo; (when listing reasons etc) per prima cosa ▷ n (person: in race) primo(-a); (BRIT: Scol) laurea con lode; (Aut) prima; **at ~** dapprima, all'inizio; **~ of all** prima di tutto; **first aid** n pronto soccorso; **first-aid kit** n cassetta pronto soccorso; **first-class** adj di prima classe; **first-hand** adj di prima mano; **first lady** (US) n moglie f del presidente; **firstly** adv in primo luogo; **first name** n prenome m; **first-rate** adj di prima qualità, ottimo(-a)

fiscal ['fɪskəl] adj fiscale; **fiscal year** n anno fiscale

fish [fɪʃ] n inv pesce m ▷ vt (river, area) pescare in ▷ vi pescare; **to go ~ing** andare a pesca; **fish and chip shop** n see **chip shop**; **fisherman** (irreg) n pescatore m; **fish fingers** (BRIT) npl bastoncini mpl di pesce (surgelati); **fishing** n pesca; **fishing boat** n barca da pesca; **fishing line** n lenza; **fishmonger** n pescivendolo; **fishmonger's (shop)** n pescheria; **fish sticks** (US) npl = **fish fingers**; **fishy** (inf) adj (tale, story) sospetto(-a)

fist [fɪst] n pugno

fit [fɪt] adj (Med, Sport) in forma; (proper) adatto(-a), appropriato(-a); conveniente ▷ vt (clothes) stare bene a; (put in, attach) mettere; installare; (equip) fornire, equipaggiare ▷ vi (clothes) stare bene; (parts) andare bene, adattarsi; (in space, gap) entrare ▷ n (Med) accesso, attacco; **~ to** in grado di; **~ for** adatto(-a) a, degno(-a) di; **a ~ of anger** un accesso d'ira; **this dress is a good ~** questo vestito sta bene; **by ~s and starts** a sbalzi; **fit in** vi accordarsi; adattarsi; **fitness** n (Med) forma fisica; **fitted** adj: **fitted cupboards** armadi mpl a muro; **fitted carpet** moquette f inv; **fitted kitchen** (BRIT) cucina componibile; **fitting** adj appropriato(-a) ▷ n (of dress) prova; (of piece of equipment) montaggio, aggiustaggio; **fitting room** n camerino; **fittings** npl (in building) impianti mpl

five [faɪv] num cinque; **fiver** (inf) n (BRIT) biglietto da cinque sterline; (US) biglietto da cinque dollari

fix [fɪks] vt fissare; (mend) riparare; (meal, drink) preparare ▷ n **to be in a ~** essere nei guai; **fix up** vt (meeting) fissare; **to fix sb up with sth** procurare qc a qn; **fixed** [fɪkst] adj (prices etc) fisso(-a); **fixture** ['fɪkstʃəʳ] n impianto (fisso); (Sport) incontro (del calendario sportivo)

fizzy ['fɪzɪ] adj frizzante; gassato(-a)

flag [flæg] n bandiera; (also: **~stone**) pietra da lastricare ▷ vi stancarsi; affievolirsi; **flagpole** ['flægpəul] n albero

flair [flɛəʳ] n (for business etc) fiuto; (for languages etc) facilità; (style) stile m

flak [flæk] n (Mil) fuoco d'artiglieria; (inf: criticism) critiche fpl

flake [fleɪk] n (of rust, paint) scaglia; (of snow, soap powder) fiocco ▷ vi (also: **~ off**) sfaldarsi

flamboyant [flæm'bɔɪənt] adj sgargiante

flame [fleɪm] n fiamma

flamingo [flə'mɪŋgəu] n fenicottero, fiammingo

flammable ['flæməbl] adj infiammabile

flan [flæn] (BRIT) n flan m inv

flank [flæŋk] n fianco ▷ vt fiancheggiare

flannel ['flænl] n (BRIT: also: **face ~**) guanto di spugna; (fabric) flanella

flap [flæp] n (of pocket) patta; (of envelope) lembo ▷ vt (wings) battere ▷ vi (sail, flag) sbattere; (inf: also: **be in a ~**) essere in agitazione

flare [flɛəʳ] n razzo; (in skirt etc) svasatura; **flares** (trousers) pantaloni mpl a zampa d'elefante; **flare up** vi andare in fiamme; (fig: person) infiammarsi di rabbia; (: revolt) scoppiare

flash [flæʃ] n vampata; (also: **news ~**) notizia flampo inv; (Phot) flash m inv ▷ vt accendere e spegnere; (send: message) trasmettere; (: look, smile) lanciare ▷ vi brillare; (light on ambulance, eyes etc) lampeggiare; **in a ~** in un lampo; **to ~ one's headlights** lampeggiare; **he ~ed by** or **past** ci passò davanti come un lampo; **flashback** n flashback m inv; **flashbulb** n cubo m flash inv; **flashlight** n lampadina tascabile

flask [flɑːsk] n fiasco; (also: **vacuum ~**) Thermos® m inv

flat [flæt] adj piatto(-a); (tyre) sgonfio(-a), a terra; (battery) scarico(-a); (beer) svampito(-a); (denial) netto(-a); (Mus) bemolle inv; (: voice) stonato(-a); (rate, fee) unico(-a) ▷ n (BRIT: rooms) appartamento; (Aut) pneumatico sgonfio; (Mus) bemolle m; **to work ~ out** lavorare a più non posso; **flatten** vt (also: **flatten out**) appiattire; (building, city) spianare

flatter ['flætəʳ] vt lusingare; **flattering** adj lusinghiero(-a); (dress) che dona

flaunt [flɔːnt] vt fare mostra di

flavour etc ['fleɪvəʳ] (US **flavor**) n gusto ▷ vt insaporire, aggiungere sapore a; **what ~s do you have?** che gusti avete?; **strawberry-~ed** al gusto di fragola; **flavouring** n essenza (artificiale)

flaw [flɔː] n difetto; **flawless** adj senza difetti

flea [fliː] n pulce f; **flea market** n mercato delle pulci

flee [fliː] (pt, pp **fled**) vt fuggire da ▷ vi fuggire, scappare

fleece [fliːs] n vello ▷ vt (inf) pelare

fleet [fliːt] n flotta; (of lorries etc) convoglio; parco

fleeting ['fliːtɪŋ] adj fugace, fuggitivo(-a); (visit) volante

Flemish ['flɛmɪʃ] adj fiammingo(-a)

flesh [flɛʃ] n carne f; (of fruit) polpa

flew [fluː] pt of **fly**

flex [flɛks] n filo (flessibile) ▷ vt flettere; (*muscles*) contrarre; **flexibility** n flessibilità; **flexible** adj flessibile; **flexitime** ['flɛksɪtaɪm] n orario flessibile

flick [flɪk] n colpetto; scarto ▷ vt dare un colpetto a; **flick through** vt fus sfogliare

flicker ['flɪkə^r] vi tremolare

flies [flaɪz] npl of **fly**

flight [flaɪt] n volo; (*escape*) fuga; (*also:* ~ **of steps**) scalinata; **flight attendant** (US) n steward m inv, hostess f inv

flimsy ['flɪmzɪ] adj (*shoes, clothes*) leggero(-a); (*building*) poco solido(-a); (*excuse*) che non regge

flinch [flɪntʃ] vi ritirarsi; **to ~ from** tirarsi indietro di fronte a

fling [flɪŋ] (pt, pp **flung**) vt lanciare, gettare

flint [flɪnt] n selce f; (*in lighter*) pietrina

flip [flɪp] vt (*switch*) far scattare; (*coin*) lanciare in aria

flip-flops ['flɪpflɔps] npl (*esp* BRIT: *sandals*) infradito mpl

flipper ['flɪpə^r] n pinna

flirt [fləːt] vi flirtare ▷ n civetta

float [fləʊt] n galleggiante m; (*in procession*) carro; (*money*) somma ▷ vi galleggiare

flock [flɔk] n (*of sheep, Rel*) gregge m; (*of birds*) stormo ▷ vi: **to ~ to** accorrere in massa a

flood [flʌd] n alluvione m; (*of letters etc*) marea ▷ vt allagare; (*people*) invadere ▷ vi (*place*) allagarsi; (*people*): **to ~ into** riversarsi in; **flooding** n inondazione f; **floodlight** n riflettore m ▷ vt illuminare a giorno

floor [flɔː^r] n pavimento; (*storey*) piano; (*of sea, valley*) fondo ▷ vt (*blow*) atterrare; (*: question*) ridurre al silenzio; **which ~ is it on?** a che piano si trova?; **ground ~** (BRIT), **first ~** (US) pianterreno; **first ~** (BRIT), **second**

~ (US) primo piano; **floorboard** n tavellone m di legno; **flooring** n (*floor*) pavimento; (*material*) materiale m per pavimentazioni; **floor show** n spettacolo di varietà

flop [flɔp] n fiasco ▷ vi far fiasco; (*fall*) lasciarsi cadere; **floppy** ['flɔpɪ] adj floscio(-a), molle

floral ['flɔːrl] adj floreale

Florence ['flɔrəns] n Firenze f

Florentine ['flɔrəntaɪn] adj fiorentino(-a)

florist ['flɔrɪst] n fioraio(-a); **florist's (shop)** n fioraio(-a)

flotation [fləʊ'teɪʃən] n (*Comm*) lancio

flour ['flaʊə^r] n farina

flourish ['flʌrɪʃ] vi fiorire ▷ n (*bold gesture*): **with a ~** con ostentazione

flow [fləʊ] n flusso; circolazione f ▷ vi fluire; (*traffic, blood in veins*) circolare; (*hair*) scendere

flower ['flaʊə^r] n fiore m ▷ vi fiorire; **flower bed** n aiuola; **flowerpot** n vaso da fiori

flown [fləʊn] pp of **fly**

fl. oz. abbr = **fluid ounce**

flu [fluː] n influenza

fluctuate ['flʌktjueɪt] vi fluttuare, oscillare

fluent ['fluːənt] adj (*speech*) facile, sciolto(-a); corrente; **he speaks ~ Italian, he's ~ in Italian** parla l'italiano correntemente

fluff [flʌf] n lanugine f; **fluffy** adj lanuginoso(-a); (*toy*) di peluche

fluid ['fluːɪd] adj fluido(-a) ▷ n fluido; **fluid ounce** n (BRIT) = 0.028 l; 0.05 pints

fluke [fluːk] (*inf*) n colpo di fortuna

flung [flʌŋ] pt, pp of **fling**

fluorescent [fluə'rɛsnt] adj fluorescente

fluoride ['fluəraɪd] n fluoruro

flurry ['flʌrɪ] n (*of snow*) tempesta; **a ~ of activity** uno scoppio di attività

flush [flʌʃ] n rossore m; (*fig: of youth,*

beauty etc) rigoglio, pieno vigore ▷ *vt* ripulire con un getto d'acqua ▷ *vi* arrossire ▷ *adj* **~ with** a livello di, pari a; **to ~ the toilet** tirare l'acqua

flute [flu:t] *n* flauto

flutter ['flʌtə^r] *n* agitazione *f*; (*of wings*) battito ▷ *vi* (*bird*) battere le ali

fly [flaɪ] (*pt* **flew**, *pp* **flown**) *n* (*insect*) mosca; (*on trousers: also:* **flies**) chiusura ▷ *vt* pilotare; (*passengers, cargo*) trasportare (in aereo); (*distances*) percorrere ▷ *vi* volare; (*passengers*) andare in aereo; (*escape*) fuggire; (*flag*) sventolare; **fly away** *vi* volar via; **fly-drive** *n*: **fly-drive holiday** fly and drive *m inv*; **flying** *n* (*activity*) aviazione *f*; (*action*) volo ▷ *adj* **flying visit** visita volante; **with flying colours** con risultati brillanti; **flying saucer** *n* disco volante; **flyover** (BRIT) *n* (*bridge*) cavalcavia *m inv*

FM *abbr* (= *frequency modulation*) FM

foal [fəul] *n* puledro

foam [fəum] *n* schiuma; (*also:* **~ rubber**) gommapiuma® ▷ *vi* schiumare; (*soapy water*) fare la schiuma

focus ['fəukəs] (*pl* **focuses**) *n* fuoco; (*of interest*) centro ▷ *vt* (*field glasses etc*) mettere a fuoco ▷ *vi* **to ~ on** (*with camera*) mettere a fuoco; (*person*) fissare lo sguardo su; **in ~** a fuoco; **out of ~** sfocato(-a)

foetus ['fi:təs] (US **fetus**) *n* feto

fog [fɔg] *n* nebbia; **foggy** *adj* **it's foggy** c'è nebbia; **fog lamp** (US **fog light**) *n* (Aut) faro *m* antinebbia *inv*

foil [fɔɪl] *vt* confondere, frustrare ▷ *n* lamina di metallo; (*kitchen foil*) foglio di alluminio; (*Fencing*) fioretto; **to act as a ~ to** (*fig*) far risaltare

fold [fəuld] *n* (*bend, crease*) piega; (Agr) ovile *m*; (*fig*) gregge *m* ▷ *vt* piegare; (*arms*) incrociare; **fold up** *vi* (*map, bed, table*) piegarsi; (*business*) crollare ▷ *vt* (*map etc*) piegare, ripiegare; **folder** *n* (*for papers*) cartella, cartellina; **folding**

adj (*chair, bed*) pieghevole

foliage ['fəulɪɪdʒ] *n* fogliame *m*

folk [fəuk] *npl* gente *f* ▷ *adj* popolare; **folks** *npl* (*family*) famiglia; **folklore** ['fəuklɔ:^r] *n* folclore *m*; **folk music** *n* musica folk *inv*; **folk song** *n* canto popolare

follow ['fɔləu] *vt* seguire ▷ *vi* seguire; (*result*) conseguire, risultare; **to ~ suit** fare lo stesso; **follow up** *vt* (*letter, offer*) fare seguito a; (*case*) seguire; **follower** *n* seguace *m/f*, discepolo(-a); **following** *adj* seguente ▷ *n* seguito, discepoli *mpl*; **follow-up** *n* seguito

fond [fɔnd] *adj* (*memory, look*) tenero(-a), affettuoso(-a); **to be ~ of sb** volere bene a qn; **he's ~ of walking** gli piace fare camminate

food [fu:d] *n* cibo; **food mixer** *n* frullatore *m*; **food poisoning** *n* intossicazione *f*; **food processor** [-'prəusesə] *n* tritatutto *m inv* elettrico; **food stamp** (US) *n* buono alimentare dato agli indigenti

fool [fu:l] *n* sciocco(-a); (Culin) frullato ▷ *vt* ingannare ▷ *vi* (*gen: fool around*) fare lo sciocco; **fool about**, **fool around** *vi* (*waste time*) perdere tempo; **foolish** *adj* scemo(-a), stupido(-a); imprudente; **foolproof** *adj* (*plan etc*) sicurissimo(-a)

foot [fut] (*pl* **feet**) *n* piede *m*; (*measure*) piede (= 304 mm; 12 inches); (*of animal*) zampa ▷ *vt* (*bill*) pagare; **on ~** a piedi; **footage** *n* (Cinema: length) ≈ metraggio; (: material) sequenza; **foot-and-mouth (disease)** [futənd'mauθ-] *n* afta epizootica; **football** *n* pallone *m*; (sport: BRIT) calcio; (: US) football *m* americano; **footballer** *n* (BRIT) = **football player**; **football match** *n* (BRIT) partita di calcio; **football player** *n* (BRIT: *also:* **footballer**) calciatore *m*; (US) giocatore *m* di football americano; **footbridge** *n* passerella; **foothills**

npl contrafforti *fpl*; **foothold** *n* punto d'appoggio; **footing** *n* (*fig*) posizione *f*; **to lose one's footing** mettere un piede in fallo; **footnote** *n* nota (a piè di pagina); **footpath** *n* sentiero; (*in street*) marciapiede *m*; **footprint** *n* orma, impronta; **footstep** *n* passo; (*footprint*) orma, impronta; **footwear** *n* calzatura

 KEYWORD

for [fɔːʳ] *prep* **1** (*indicating destination, intention, purpose*) per; **the train for London** il treno per Londra; **he went for the paper** è andato a prendere il giornale; **it's time for lunch** è ora di pranzo; **what's it for?** a che serve?; **what for?** (*why*) perché?
2 (*on behalf of, representing*) per; **to work for sb/sth** lavorare per qn/qc; **I'll ask him for you** glielo chiederò a nome tuo; **G for George** G come George
3 (*because of*) per, a causa di; **for this reason** per questo motivo
4 (*with regard to*) per; **it's cold for July** è freddo per luglio; **for everyone who voted yes, 50 voted no** per ogni voto a favore ce n'erano 50 contro
5 (*in exchange for*) per; **I sold it for £5** l'ho venduto per 5 sterline
6 (*in favour of*) per, a favore di; **are you for or against us?** è con noi o contro di noi?; **I'm all for it** sono completamente a favore
7 (*referring to distance, time*) per; **there are roadworks for 5 km** ci sono lavori in corso per 5 km; **he was away for 2 years** è stato via per 2 anni; **she will be away for a month** starà via un mese; **it hasn't rained for 3 weeks** non piove da 3 settimane; **can you do it for tomorrow?** può farlo per domani?
8 (*with infinitive clauses*): **it is not for me to decide** non sta a me decidere;

it would be best for you to leave sarebbe meglio che lei se ne andasse; **there is still time for you to do it** ha ancora tempo per farlo; **for this to be possible …** perché ciò sia possibile …
9 (*in spite of*) nonostante; **for all his complaints, he's very fond of her** nonostante tutte le sue lamentele, le vuole molto bene
▷ *conj* (*since, as: rather formal*) dal momento che, poiché

forbid [fəˈbɪd] (*pt* **forbad(e)**, *pp* **forbidden**) *vt* vietare, interdire; **to ~ sb to do sth** proibire a qn di fare qc; **forbidden** *pt of* **forbid** ▷ *adj* (*food*) proibito(-a); (*area, territory*) vietato(-a); (*word, subject*) tabù *inv*
force [fɔːs] *n* forza ▷ *vt* forzare; **forced** *adj* forzato(-a); **forceful** *adj* forte, vigoroso(-a)
ford [fɔːd] *n* guado
fore [fɔːʳ] *n* **to come to the ~** mettersi in evidenza; **forearm** [ˈfɔːrɑːm] *n* avambraccio; **forecast** [ˈfɔːkɑːst] (*irreg: like* **cast**) *n* previsione *f* ▷ *vt* prevedere; **forecourt** [ˈfɔːkɔːt] *n* (*of garage*) corte *f* esterna; **forefinger** [ˈfɔːfɪŋgəʳ] *n* (*dito*) indice *m*; **forefront** [ˈfɔːfrʌnt] *n* **in the forefront of** all'avanguardia in; **foreground** [ˈfɔːgraʊnd] *n* primo piano; **forehead** [ˈfɔrɪd] *n* fronte *f*
foreign [ˈfɔrɪn] *adj* straniero(-a); (*trade*) estero(-a); (*object, matter*) estraneo(-a); **foreign currency** *n* valuta estera; **foreigner** *n* straniero(-a); **foreign exchange** *n* cambio con l'estero; (*currency*) valuta estera; **Foreign Office** (BRIT) *n* Ministero degli Esteri; **Foreign Secretary** (BRIT) *n* ministro degli Affari esteri
fore: **foreman** [ˈfɔːmən] (*irreg*) *n* caposquadra *m*; **foremost** [ˈfɔːməust] *adj* principale; più in vista ▷ *adv*: **first and foremost**

innanzitutto; **forename** n nome m di battesimo

forensic [fə'rɛnsɪk] adj **~ medicine** medicina legale

foresee [fɔː'siː] (irreg: like **see**) vt prevedere; **foreseeable** adj prevedibile

forest ['fɒrɪst] n foresta; **forestry** ['fɒrɪstrɪ] n silvicoltura

forever [fə'rɛvəʳ] adv per sempre; (endlessly) sempre, di continuo

foreword ['fɔːwəːd] n prefazione f

forfeit ['fɔːfɪt] vt perdere; (one's happiness, health) giocarsi

forgave [fə'geɪv] pt of **forgive**

forge [fɔːdʒ] n fucina ▷ vt (signature, money) contraffare, falsificare; (wrought iron) fucinare, foggiare; **forger** n contraffattore m; **forgery** n falso; (activity) contraffazione f

forget [fə'gɛt] (pt **forgot**, pp **forgotten**) vt, vi dimenticare; **I've forgotten my key/passport** ho dimenticato la chiave/il passaporto; **forgetful** adj di corta memoria; **forgetful of** dimentico(-a) di

forgive [fə'gɪv] (pt **forgave**, pp **forgiven**) vt perdonare; **to ~ sb for sth** perdonare qc a qn

forgot [fə'gɒt] pt of **forget**

forgotten [fə'gɒtn] pp of **forget**

fork [fɔːk] n (for eating) forchetta; (for gardening) forca; (of roads, rivers, railways) biforcazione f ▷ vi (road etc) biforcarsi

forlorn [fə'lɔːn] adj (person) sconsolato(-a); (place) abbandonato(-a); (attempt) disperato(-a); (hope) vano(-a)

form [fɔːm] n forma; (Scol) classe f; (questionnaire) scheda ▷ vt formare; **in top ~** in gran forma

formal ['fɔːməl] adj formale; (gardens) simmetrico(-a), regolare; **formality** [fɔː'mælɪtɪ] n formalità f inv

format ['fɔːmæt] n formato ▷ vt (Comput) formattare

formation [fɔː'meɪʃən] n formazione f

former ['fɔːməʳ] adj vecchio(-a); (before n) ex inv (before n); **the ~ ... the latter** quello ... questo; **formerly** adv in passato

formidable ['fɔːmɪdəbl] adj formidabile

formula ['fɔːmjulə] n formula

fort [fɔːt] n forte m

forthcoming [fɔːθ'kʌmɪŋ] adj (event) prossimo(-a); (help) disponibile; (character) aperto(-a), comunicativo(-a)

fortieth ['fɔːtɪɪθ] num quarantesimo(-a)

fortify ['fɔːtɪfaɪ] vt (city) fortificare; (person) armare

fortnight ['fɔːtnaɪt] (BRIT) n quindici giorni mpl, due settimane fpl; **fortnightly** adj bimensile ▷ adv ogni quindici giorni

fortress ['fɔːtrɪs] n fortezza, rocca

fortunate ['fɔːtʃənɪt] adj fortunato(-a); **it is ~ that** è una fortuna che; **fortunately** adv fortunatamente

fortune ['fɔːtʃən] n fortuna; **fortune-teller** n indovino(-a)

forty ['fɔːtɪ] num quaranta

forum ['fɔːrəm] n foro

forward ['fɔːwəd] adj (ahead of schedule) in anticipo; (movement, position) in avanti; (not shy) aperto(-a), diretto(-a) ▷ n (Sport) avanti m inv ▷ vt (letter) inoltrare; (parcel, goods) spedire; (career, plans) promuovere, appoggiare; **to move ~** avanzare; **forwarding address** n nuovo recapito cui spedire la posta; **forward(s)** adv avanti; **forward slash** n barra obliqua

fossil ['fɒsl] adj fossile ▷ n fossile m

foster ['fɒstəʳ] vt incoraggiare, nutrire; (child) avere in affidamento; **foster child** n bambino(-a) preso(-a) in affidamento; **foster mother** n madre f affidataria

fought [fɔːt] pt, pp of **fight**

foul [faul] adj (smell, food, temper etc) cattivo(-a); (weather) brutto(-a); (language) osceno(-a) ▷ n (Sport) fallo ▷ vt sporcare; **foul play** n (Law): **the police suspect foul play** la polizia sospetta un atto criminale

found [faund] pt, pp of **find** ▷ vt (establish) fondare; **foundation** [-'deɪʃən] n (act) fondazione f; (base) base f; (also: **foundation cream**) fondo tinta; **foundations** npl (of building) fondamenta fpl

founder ['faundə'] n fondatore(-trice) ▷ vi affondare

fountain ['fauntɪn] n fontana; **fountain pen** n penna stilografica

four [fɔː'] num quattro; **on all ~s** a carponi; **four-letter word** ['fɔːletə-'] n parolaccia; **four-poster** n (also: **four-poster bed**) letto a quattro colonne; **fourteen** num quattordici; **fourteenth** num quattordicesimo(-a); **fourth** num quarto(-a); **four-wheel drive** ['fɔːwiːl-] n (Aut): **with four-wheel drive** con quattro ruote motrici

fowl [faul] n pollame m; volatile m

fox [fɔks] n volpe f ▷ vt confondere

foyer ['fɔɪeɪ] n atrio; (Theatre) ridotto

fraction ['frækʃən] n frazione f

fracture ['fræktʃə'] n frattura

fragile ['frædʒaɪl] adj fragile

fragment ['frægmənt] n frammento

fragrance ['freɪgrəns] n fragranza, profumo

frail [freɪl] adj debole, delicato(-a)

frame [freɪm] n (of building) armatura; (of human, animal) ossatura, corpo; (of picture) cornice f; (of door, window) telaio; (of spectacles: also: **~s**) montatura ▷ vt (picture) incorniciare; **framework** n struttura

France [frɑːns] n Francia

franchise ['fræntʃaɪz] n (Pol) diritto di voto; (Comm) concessione f

frank [fræŋk] adj franco(-a), aperto(-a) ▷ vt (letter) affrancare; **frankly** adv francamente, sinceramente

frantic ['fræntɪk] adj frenetico(-a)

fraud [frɔːd] n truffa; (Law) frode f; (person) impostore(-a)

fraught [frɔːt] adj: **~ with** pieno(-a) di, intriso(-a) da

fray [freɪ] vt logorare ▷ vi logorarsi

freak [friːk] n fenomeno, mostro

freckle ['frekl] n lentiggine f

free [friː] adj libero(-a); (gratis) gratuito(-a) ▷ vt (prisoner, jammed person) liberare; (jammed object) districare; **is this seat ~?** è libero questo posto?; **~ of charge, for ~** gratuitamente; **freedom** ['friːdəm] n libertà; **Freefone®** n numero verde; **free gift** n regalo, omaggio; **free kick** n calcio libero; **freelance** adj indipendente; **freely** adv liberamente; (liberally) liberalmente; **Freepost®** n affrancatura a carico del destinatario; **free-range** adj (hen) ruspante; (eggs) di gallina ruspante; **freeway** (us) n superstrada; **free will** n libero arbitrio; **of one's own free will** di spontanea volontà

freeze [friːz] (pt **froze**, pp **frozen**) vi gelare ▷ vt gelare; (food) congelare; (prices, salaries) bloccare ▷ n gelo; blocco; **freezer** n congelatore m; **freezing** ['friːzɪŋ] adj (wind, weather) gelido(-a); **freezing point** n punto di congelamento; **3 degrees below freezing point** 3 gradi sotto zero

freight [freɪt] n (goods) merce f, merci fpl; (money charged) spese fpl di trasporto; **freight train** (us) n treno m merci inv

French [frentʃ] adj francese ▷ n (Ling) francese m; **the French** npl i Francesi; **French bean** n fagiolino; **French bread** n baguette f inv; **French**

dressing n (Culin) condimento per insalata; **French fried potatoes** (US **French fries**) npl patate fpl fritte; **Frenchman** (irreg) n francese m; **French stick** n baguette f inv; **French window** n portafinestra; **Frenchwoman** (irreg) n francese f

frenzy ['frɛnzɪ] n frenesia

frequency ['friːkwənsɪ] n frequenza

frequent [adj 'friːkwənt, vb frɪ'kwɛnt] adj frequente ▷ vt frequentare; **frequently** adv frequentemente, spesso

fresh [frɛʃ] adj fresco(-a); (new) nuovo(-a); (cheeky) sfacciato(-a); **freshen** vi (wind, air) rinfrescare; **freshen up** vi rinfrescarsi; **fresher** (BRIT: inf) n (Scol) matricola; **freshly** adv di recente, di fresco; **freshman** (irreg: US) n = **fresher**; **freshwater** adj (fish) d'acqua dolce

fret [frɛt] vi agitarsi, affliggersi

Fri. abbr (= Friday) ven.

friction ['frɪkʃən] n frizione f, attrito

Friday ['fraɪdɪ] n venerdì m inv

fridge [frɪdʒ] (BRIT) n frigo, frigorifero

fried [fraɪd] pt, pp of **fry** ▷ adj fritto(-a)

friend [frɛnd] n amico(-a); **friendly** adj amichevole; **friendship** n amicizia

fries [fraɪz] (esp US) npl patate fpl fritte

frigate ['frɪgɪt] n (Naut: modern) fregata

fright [fraɪt] n paura, spavento; **to take ~** spaventarsi; **frighten** vt spaventare, far paura a; **frightened** adj spaventato(-a); **frightening** adj spaventoso(-a), pauroso(-a); **frightful** adj orribile

frill [frɪl] n balza

fringe [frɪndʒ] n (decoration: BRIT: of hair) frangia; (edge: of forest etc) margine m

Frisbee® ['frɪzbɪ] n frisbee® m inv

fritter ['frɪtər] n frittella

frivolous ['frɪvələs] adj frivolo(-a)

fro [frəu] see **to**

frock [frɔk] n vestito

frog [frɔg] n rana; **frogman** (irreg) n uomo m rana inv

 KEYWORD

from [frɔm] prep **1** (indicating starting place, origin etc) da; **where do you come from?, where are you from?** da dove viene?, di dov'è?; **from London to Glasgow** da Londra a Glasgow; **a letter from my sister** una lettera da mia sorella; **tell him from me that ...** gli dica da parte mia che ...
2 (indicating time) da; **from one o'clock to** or **until** or **till two** dall'una alle due; **from January (on)** da gennaio, a partire da gennaio
3 (indicating distance) da; **the hotel is 1 km from the beach** l'albergo è a 1 km dalla spiaggia
4 (indicating price, number etc) da; **prices range from £10 to £50** i prezzi vanno dalle 10 alle 50 sterline
5 (indicating difference) da; **he can't tell red from green** non sa distinguere il rosso dal verde
6 (because of, on the basis of): **from what he says** da quanto dice lui; **weak from hunger** debole per la fame

front [frʌnt] n (of house, dress) davanti m inv; (of train) testa; (of book) copertina; (promenade: also: **sea ~**) lungomare m; (Mil, Pol, Meteor) fronte m; (fig: appearances) fronte f ▷ adj primo(-a); anteriore, davanti inv; **in ~ of** davanti a; **front door** n porta d'entrata; (of car) sportello anteriore; **frontier** ['frʌntɪər] n frontiera; **front page** n prima pagina; **front-wheel drive** ['frʌntwiːl-] n trasmissione f anteriore

frost [frɔst] n gelo; (also: **hoar~**) brina; **frostbite** n congelamento; **frosting**

(US) n (on cake) glassa; **frosty** adj (weather, look) gelido(-a)

froth ['frɔθ] n spuma; schiuma

frown [fraun] vi accigliarsi

froze [frəuz] pt of **freeze**

frozen ['frəuzn] pp of **freeze**

fruit [fru:t] n inv (also fig) frutto; (collectively) frutta; **fruit juice** n succo di frutta; **fruit machine** (BRIT) n macchina f mangiasoldi inv; **fruit salad** n macedonia

frustrate [frʌs'treɪt] vt frustrare; **frustrated** adj frustrato(-a)

fry [fraɪ] (pt, pp **fried**) vt friggere; see also **small**; **frying pan** n padella

ft. abbr = **foot**; **feet**

fudge [fʌdʒ] n (Culin) specie di caramella a base di latte, burro e zucchero

fuel [fjuəl] n (for heating) combustibile m; (for propelling) carburante m; **fuel tank** n deposito m nafta inv; (on vehicle) serbatoio (della benzina)

fulfil [ful'fɪl] vt (function) compiere; (order) eseguire; (wish, desire) soddisfare, appagare

full [ful] adj pieno(-a); (details, skirt) ampio(-a) ▷ adv **to know ~ well that** sapere benissimo che; **I'm ~ (up)** sono sazio; **a ~ two hours** due ore intere; **at ~ speed** a tutta velocità; **in ~** per intero; **full-length** adj a lungometraggio; (coat, novel) lungo(-a); (portrait) in piedi; **full moon** n luna piena; **full-scale** adj (attack, war) su larga scala; (model) in grandezza naturale; **full stop** n punto; **full-time** adj, adv (work) a tempo pieno; **fully** adv interamente, pienamente, completamente; (at least) almeno

fumble ['fʌmbl] vi **to ~ with sth** armeggiare con qc

fume [fju:m] vi essere furioso(-a); **fumes** npl esalazioni fpl, vapori mpl

fun [fʌn] n divertimento, spasso; **to have ~** divertirsi; **for ~** per scherzo; **to make ~ of** prendersi gioco di

function ['fʌŋkʃən] n funzione f; cerimonia, ricevimento ▷ vi funzionare

fund [fʌnd] n fondo, cassa; (source) fondo; (store) riserva; **funds** npl (money) fondi mpl

fundamental [fʌndə'mɛntl] adj fondamentale

funeral ['fju:nərəl] n funerale m; **funeral director** n impresario di pompe funebri; **funeral parlour** [-'pɑ:lər] n impresa di pompe funebri

funfair ['fʌnfɛər] n luna park m inv

fungus ['fʌŋgəs] (pl **fungi**) n fungo; (mould) muffa

funnel ['fʌnl] n imbuto; (of ship) ciminiera

funny ['fʌnɪ] adj divertente, buffo(-a); (strange) strano(-a), bizzarro(-a)

fur [fə:r] n pelo; pelliccia; (BRIT: in kettle etc) deposito calcare; **fur coat** n pelliccia

furious ['fjuərɪəs] adj furioso(-a); (effort) accanito(-a)

furnish ['fə:nɪʃ] vt ammobiliare; (supply) fornire; **furnishings** npl mobili mpl, mobilia

furniture ['fə:nɪtʃər] n mobili mpl; **piece of ~** mobile m

furry ['fə:rɪ] adj (animal) peloso(-a)

further ['fə:ðər] adj supplementare, altro(-a); nuovo(-a); più lontano(-a) ▷ adv più lontano; (more) di più; (moreover) inoltre ▷ vt favorire, promuovere; **further education** n ≈ corsi mpl di formazione; **college of further education** istituto statale con corsi specializzati (di formazione professionale, aggiornamento professionale ecc); **furthermore** [fə:ðə'mɔ:r] adv inoltre, per di più

furthest ['fə:ðɪst] superl of **far**

fury ['fjuərɪ] n furore m

fuse [fju:z] (US **fuze**) n fusibile m; (for bomb etc) miccia, spoletta ▷ vt fondere ▷ vi fondersi; **to ~ the lights** (BRIT: Elec) far saltare i fusibili; **fuse**

box n cassetta dei fusibili
fusion ['fjuːʒən] n fusione f
fuss [fʌs] n agitazione f; (complaining)
storie fpl; **to make a ~** fare delle storie;
fussy adj (person) puntiglioso(-a),
esigente; che fa le storie; (dress)
carico(-a) di fronzoli; (style)
elaborato(-a)
future ['fjuːtʃəʳ] adj futuro(-a) ▷ n
futuro, avvenire m; (Ling) futuro;
in ~ in futuro; **futures** npl (Comm)
operazioni fpl a termine
fuze [fjuːz] (US) = **fuse**
fuzzy ['fʌzɪ] adj (Phot) indistinto(-a),
sfocato(-a); (hair) crespo(-a)

G [dʒiː] n (Mus) sol m
g. abbr (= gram, gravity) g.
gadget ['gædʒɪt] n aggeggio
Gaelic ['geɪlɪk] adj gaelico(-a) ▷ n
(Ling) gaelico
gag [gæg] n bavaglio; (joke) facezia,
scherzo ▷ vt imbavagliare
gain [geɪn] n guadagno, profitto ▷ vt
guadagnare ▷ vi (clock, watch) andare
avanti; (benefit): **to ~ (from)** trarre
beneficio (da); **to ~ 3lbs (in weight)**
aumentare di 3 libbre; **to ~ on sb** (in
race etc) guadagnare su qn
gal. abbr = **gallon**
gala ['gɑːlə] n gala; **swimming ~**
manifestazione f di nuoto
galaxy ['gæləksɪ] n galassia
gale [geɪl] n vento forte; burrasca
gall bladder ['gɔːl-] n cistifellea
gallery ['gælərɪ] n galleria
gallon ['gælən] n gallone m (= 8 pints;
BRIT = 4.543l; US = 3.785l)
gallop ['gæləp] n galoppo ▷ vi
galoppare

gallstone ['gɔːlstəun] n calcolo biliare
gamble ['gæmbl] n azzardo, rischio calcolato ▷ vt, vi giocare; **to ~ on** (fig) giocare su; **gambler** n giocatore(-trice) d'azzardo; **gambling** n gioco d'azzardo
game [geɪm] n gioco; (event) partita; (Tennis) game m inv; (Culin, Hunting) selvaggina ▷ adj (ready): **to be ~ (for sth/to do)** essere pronto(-a) (a qc/a fare); **big ~** selvaggina grossa; **games** npl (Scol) attività fpl sportive; **big ~** selvaggina grossa; **games console** [geɪmz-] n console f inv dei videogame; **game show** ['geɪmʃəu] n gioco a premi
gammon ['gæmən] n (bacon) quarto di maiale; (ham) prosciutto affumicato
gang [gæŋ] n banda, squadra ▷ vi **to ~ up on sb** far combutta contro qn
gangster ['gæŋstər] n gangster m inv
gap [gæp] n (space) buco; (in time) intervallo; (difference): **~ (between)** divario (tra)
gape [geɪp] vi (person) restare a bocca aperta; (shirt, hole) essere spalancato(-a)
gap year n (Scol) anno di pausa durante il quale gli studenti viaggiano o lavorano
garage ['gærɑːʒ] n garage m inv; **garage sale** n vendita di oggetti usati nel garage di un privato
garbage ['gɑːbɪdʒ] (US) n immondizie fpl, rifiuti mpl; (inf) sciocchezze fpl; **garbage can** (US) n bidone m della spazzatura; **garbage collector** (US) n spazzino(-a)
garden ['gɑːdn] n giardino; **gardens** npl (public park) giardini pubblici; **garden centre** n vivaio; **gardener** n giardiniere(-a); **gardening** n giardinaggio
garlic ['gɑːlɪk] n aglio
garment ['gɑːmənt] n indumento
garnish ['gɑːnɪʃ] vt (food) guarnire
garrison ['gærɪsn] n guarnigione f
gas [gæs] n gas m inv; (US: gasoline)

benzina ▷ vt asfissiare con il gas; **I can smell ~** sento odore di gas; **gas cooker** (BRIT) n cucina a gas; **gas cylinder** n bombola del gas; **gas fire** (BRIT) n radiatore m a gas
gasket ['gæskɪt] n (Aut) guarnizione f
gasoline ['gæsəliːn] (US) n benzina
gasp [gɑːsp] n respiro affannoso, ansito ▷ vi ansare, ansimare; (in surprise) restare senza fiato
gas: **gas pedal** (esp US) n pedale m dell'acceleratore; **gas station** (US) n distributore m di benzina; **gas tank** (US) n (Aut) serbatoio (di benzina)
gate [geɪt] n cancello; (at airport) uscita
gateau ['gætəu] (pl **gateaux**) n torta
gatecrash ['geɪtkræʃ] (BRIT) vt partecipare senza invito a
gateway ['geɪtweɪ] n porta
gather ['gæðər] vt (flowers, fruit) cogliere; (pick up) raccogliere; (assemble) radunare; raccogliere; (understand) capire; (Sewing) increspare ▷ vi (assemble) radunarsi; **to ~ speed** acquistare velocità; **gathering** n adunanza
gauge [geɪdʒ] n (instrument) indicatore m ▷ vt misurare; (fig) valutare
gave [geɪv] pt of **give**
gay [geɪ] adj (homosexual) omosessuale; (cheerful) gaio(-a), allegro(-a); (colour) vivace, vivo(-a)
gaze [geɪz] n sguardo fisso ▷ vi **to ~ at** guardare fisso
GB abbr = **Great Britain**
GCSE (BRIT) n abbr General Certificate of Secondary Education
gear [gɪər] n attrezzi mpl, equipaggiamento; (Tech) ingranaggio; (Aut) marcia ▷ vt (fig: adapt): **to ~ sth to** adattare qc a; **in top** or (US) **high/low ~** in quarta (or quinta)/seconda; **in ~** in marcia; **gear up** vi **to gear up (to do)** prepararsi (a fare); **gear box**

n scatola del cambio; **gear lever** *n*
leva del cambio; **gear shift** (*US*), **gear
stick** (*BRIT*) *n* = **gear lever**
geese [giːs] *npl of* **goose**
gel [dʒel] *n* gel *m inv*
gem [dʒem] *n* gemma
Gemini [ˈdʒemɪnaɪ] *n* Gemelli *mpl*
gender [ˈdʒendəʳ] *n* genere *m*
gene [dʒiːn] *n* (*Biol*) gene *m*
general [ˈdʒenərl] *n* generale
m ▷ *adj* generale; **in ~** in genere;
general anaesthetic (*US* **general
anesthetic**) *n* anestesia totale;
general election *n* elezioni *fpl*
generali; **generalize** *vi* generalizzare;
generally *adv* generalmente;
general practitioner *n* medico
generico; **general store** *n* emporio
generate [ˈdʒenəreɪt] *vt* generare
generation [dʒenəˈreɪʃən] *n*
generazione *f*
generator [ˈdʒenəreɪtəʳ] *n*
generatore *m*
generosity [dʒenəˈrɔsɪtɪ] *n*
generosità
generous [ˈdʒenərəs] *adj*
generoso(-a); (*copious*) abbondante
genetic [dʒɪˈnetɪk] *adj* genetico(-a);
~ engineering ingegneria
genetica; **genetically modified**
adj geneticamente modificato(-a),
transgenico(-a); **genetics** *n* genetica
Geneva [dʒɪˈniːvə] *n* Ginevra
genitals [ˈdʒenɪtlz] *npl* genitali *mpl*
genius [ˈdʒiːnɪəs] *n* genio
Genoa [ˈdʒenəuə] *n* Genova
gent [dʒent] *n abbr* = **gentleman**
gentle [ˈdʒentl] *adj* delicato(-a);
(*person*) dolce

▌ Be careful not to translate *gentle*
by the Italian word *gentile*.

gentleman [ˈdʒentlmən] (*irreg*) *n*
signore *m*; (*well-bred man*) gentiluomo
gently [ˈdʒentlɪ] *adv* delicatamente
gents [dʒents] *n* W.C. *m* (per signori)
genuine [ˈdʒenjuɪn] *adj*
autentico(-a); sincero(-a); **genuinely**

adv genuinamente
geographic(al) [dʒɪəˈɡræfɪk(l)] *adj*
geografico(-a)
geography [dʒɪˈɔɡrəfɪ] *n* geografia
geology [dʒɪˈɔlədʒɪ] *n* geologia
geometry [dʒɪˈɔmətrɪ] *n* geometria
geranium [dʒɪˈreɪnjəm] *n* geranio
geriatric [dʒerɪˈætrɪk] *adj*
geriatrico(-a)
germ [dʒəːm] *n* (*Med*) microbo; (*Biol*,
fig) germe *m*
German [ˈdʒəːmən] *adj* tedesco(-a)
▷ *n* tedesco(-a); (*Ling*) tedesco;
German measles (*BRIT*) *n* rosolia
Germany [ˈdʒəːmənɪ] *n* Germania
gesture [ˈdʒestjəʳ] *n* gesto

◯ **KEYWORD**

get [ɡet] (*pt, pp* **got**, (*US*) *pp* **gotten**) *vi* **1**
(*become, be*) diventare, farsi; **to get old**
invecchiare; **to get tired** stancarsi;
to get drunk ubriacarsi; **to get killed**
venire *or* rimanere ucciso(-a); **when
do I get paid?** quando mi pagate?; **it's
getting late** si sta facendo tardi
2 (*go*): **to get to/from** andare a/da;
to get home arrivare *or* tornare a
casa; **how did you get here?** come
sei venuto?
3 (*begin*) mettersi a, cominciare a;
to get to know sb incominciare
a conoscere qn; **let's get going** *or*
started muoviamoci
4 (*modal aux vb*): **you've got to do it**
devi farlo
▷ *vt* **1**: **to get sth done** (*do*) fare qc;
(*have done*) far fare qc; **to get one's
hair cut** farsi tagliare i capelli; **to get
sb to do sth** far fare qc a qn
2 (*obtain: money, permission, results*)
ottenere; (*find: job, flat*) trovare; (*fetch:
person, doctor*) chiamare; (: *object*)
prendere; **to get sth for sb** prendere
or procurare qc a qn; **get me Mr
Jones, please** (*Tel*) mi passi il signor
Jones, per favore; **can I get you a**

drink? le posso offrire da bere?
3 (*receive: present, letter, prize*) ricevere;
(*acquire: reputation*) farsi; **how much
did you get for the painting?** quanto
le hanno dato per il quadro?
4 (*catch*) prendere; (*hit: target etc*)
colpire; **to get sb by the arm/throat**
afferrare qn per un braccio/alla gola;
get him! prendetelo!
5 (*take, move*) portare; **to get sth to
sb** far avere qc a qn; **do you think
we'll get it through the door?** pensi
che riusciremo a farlo passare per la
porta?
6 (*catch, take: plane, bus etc*) prendere;
where do we get the ferry to …?
dove si prende il traghetto per …?
7 (*understand*) afferrare; (*hear*) sentire;
I've got it! ci sono arrivato!, ci sono!;
I'm sorry, I didn't get your name
scusi, non ho capito (*or* sentito) il suo
nome
8 (*have, possess*): **to have got** avere;
how many have you got? quanti
ne ha?
get along *vi* (*agree*) andare d'accordo;
(*depart*) andarsene; (*manage*) = **get by**
get at *vt fus* (*attack*) prendersela con;
(*reach*) raggiungere, arrivare a
get away *vi* partire, andarsene;
(*escape*) scappare
get away with *vt fus* cavarsela; farla
franca
get back *vi* (*return*) ritornare, tornare
▷ *vt* riottenere, riavere; **when do we
get back?** quando ritorniamo?
get by *vi* (*pass*) passare; (*manage*)
farcela
get down *vi, vt fus* scendere ▷ *vt* far
scendere; (*depress*) buttare giù
get down to *vt fus* (*work*) mettersi
a (fare)
get in *vi* entrare; (*train*) arrivare;
(*arrive home*) ritornare, tornare
get into *vt fus* entrare in; **to get into
a rage** incavolarsi
get off *vi* (*from train etc*) scendere;

(*depart: person, car*) andare via; (*escape*)
cavarsela ▷ *vt* (*remove: clothes, stain*)
levare ▷ *vt fus* (*train, bus*) scendere
da; **where do I get off?** dove devo
scendere?
get on *vi* (*at exam etc*) andare; (*agree*):
to get on (with) andare d'accordo
(con) ▷ *vt fus* montare in; (*horse*)
montare su
get out *vi* uscire; (*of vehicle*) scendere
▷ *vt* tirar fuori, far uscire
get out of *vt fus* uscire da; (*duty etc*)
evitare
get over *vt fus* (*illness*) riaversi da
get round *vt fus* aggirare; (*fig: person*)
rigirare
get through *vi* (*Tel*) avere la linea
get through to *vt fus* (*Tel*) parlare a
get together *vi* riunirsi ▷ *vt*
raccogliere; (*people*) adunare
get up *vi* (*rise*) alzarsi ▷ *vt fus* salire
su per
get up to *vt fus* (*reach*) raggiungere;
(*prank etc*) fare

getaway ['gɛtəweɪ] *n* fuga
Ghana ['gɑːnə] *n* Ghana *m*
ghastly ['gɑːstlɪ] *adj* orribile,
orrendo(-a); (*pale*) spettrale
ghetto ['gɛtəu] *n* ghetto
ghost [gəust] *n* fantasma *m*, spettro
giant ['dʒaɪənt] *n* gigante *m* ▷ *adj*
gigantesco(-a), enorme
gift [gɪft] *n* regalo; (*donation, ability*)
dono; **gifted** *adj* dotato(-a); **gift
shop** (*us* **gift store**) *n* negozio di
souvenir
gift token, gift voucher *n* buono *m*
omaggio *inv*
gig [gɪg] *n* (*inf: of musician*) serata
gigabyte [gɪ:gəbaɪt] *n* gigabyte *m inv*
gigantic [dʒaɪˈgæntɪk] *adj*
gigantesco(-a)
giggle ['gɪgl] *vi* ridere scioccamente
gills [gɪlz] *npl* (*of fish*) branchie *fpl*
gilt [gɪlt] *n* doratura ▷ *adj* dorato(-a)
gimmick ['gɪmɪk] *n* trucco

gin [dʒɪn] n (liquor) gin m inv
ginger ['dʒɪndʒər] n zenzero
gipsy ['dʒɪpsɪ] n zingaro(-a)
giraffe [dʒɪ'rɑːf] n giraffa
girl [gəːl] n ragazza; (young unmarried woman) signorina; (daughter) figlia, figliola; **girlfriend** n (of girl) amica; (of boy) ragazza; **Girl Scout** (US) n Giovane Esploratrice f
gist [dʒɪst] n succo
give [gɪv] (pt **gave**, pp **given**) vt dare ▷ vi cedere; **to ~ sb sth, ~ sth to sb** dare qc a qn; **I'll ~ you £5 for it** te lo pago 5 sterline; **to ~ a cry/sigh** emettere un grido/sospiro; **to ~ a speech** fare un discorso; **give away** vt (give free) rivelare; (disclose) rivelare; (bride) condurre all'altare; **give back** vt rendere; **give in** vi cedere ▷ vt consegnare; **give out** vt distribuire; annunciare; **give up** vi rinunciare ▷ vt rinunciare a; **to give up smoking** smettere di fumare; **to give o.s. up** arrendersi
given ['gɪvn] pp of **give** ▷ adj (fixed: time, amount) dato(-a), determinato(-a) ▷ conj **~ (that) ...** dato che ...; **~ the circumstances ...** date le circostanze ...
glacier ['glæsɪər] n ghiacciaio
glad [glæd] adj lieto(-a), contento(-a); **gladly** ['glædlɪ] adv volentieri
glamorous ['glæmərəs] adj affascinante, seducente
glamour ['glæmər] (US **glamor**) n fascino
glance [glɑːns] n occhiata, sguardo ▷ vi **to ~ at** dare un'occhiata a; **to ~ off** (bullet) rimbalzare su
gland [glænd] n ghiandola
glare [glɛər] n (of anger) sguardo furioso; (of light) riverbero, luce f abbagliante; (of publicity) chiasso ▷ vi abbagliare; **to ~ at** guardare male; **glaring** adj (mistake) madornale
glass [glɑːs] n (substance) vetro; (tumbler) bicchiere m; **glasses** npl

(spectacles) occhiali mpl
glaze [gleɪz] vt (door) fornire di vetri; (pottery) smaltare ▷ n smalto
gleam [gliːm] vi luccicare
glen [glɛn] n valletta
glide [glaɪd] vi scivolare; (Aviat, birds) planare; **glider** n (Aviat) aliante m
glimmer ['glɪmər] n barlume m
glimpse [glɪmps] n impressione f fugace ▷ vt vedere al volo
glint [glɪnt] vi luccicare
glisten ['glɪsn] vi luccicare
glitter ['glɪtər] vi scintillare
global ['gləʊbl] adj globale; **globalization** [ˌgləʊbəlaɪ'zeɪʃən] n globalizzazione f; **global warming** n effetto m serra inv
globe [gləʊb] n globo, sfera
gloom [gluːm] n oscurità, buio; (sadness) tristezza, malinconia; **gloomy** adj scuro(-a), fosco(-a), triste
glorious ['glɔːrɪəs] adj glorioso(-a), magnifico(-a)
glory ['glɔːrɪ] n gloria; splendore m
gloss [glɔs] n (shine) lucentezza; (also: **~ paint**) vernice f a olio
glossary ['glɔsərɪ] n glossario
glossy ['glɔsɪ] adj lucente
glove [glʌv] n guanto; **glove compartment** n (Aut) vano portaoggetti
glow [gləʊ] vi ardere; (face) essere luminoso(-a)
glucose ['gluːkəʊs] n glucosio
glue [gluː] n colla ▷ vt incollare
GM adj abbr (= genetically modified) geneticamente modificato(-a)
gm abbr = **gram**
GM-free [dʒiːem'friː] adj privo(-a) di OGM
GMO n abbr (= genetically modified organism) OGM m inv
GMT abbr (= Greenwich Mean Time) T.M.G.
gnaw [nɔː] vt rodere
go [gəʊ] (pt **went**, pp **gone**) (pl **goes**) vi andare; (depart) partire, andarsene;

(*work*) funzionare; (*time*) passare; (*break etc*) rompersi; (*be sold*): **to go for £10** essere venduto per 10 sterline; (*fit, suit*): **to go with** andare bene con; (*become*): **to go pale** diventare pallido(-a); **to go mouldy** ammuffire ▷ *n* **to have a go (at)** provare; **to be on the go** essere in moto; **whose go is it?** a chi tocca?; **he's going to do** sta per fare; **to go for a walk** andare a fare una passeggiata; **to go dancing/shopping** andare a ballare/fare la spesa; **just then the bell went** proprio allora suonò il campanello; **how did it go?** com'è andato?; **to go round the back/by the shop** passare da dietro/davanti al negozio; **go ahead** *vi* andare avanti; **go away** *vi* partire, andarsene; **go back** *vi* tornare, ritornare; **go by** *vi* (*years, time*) scorrere ▷ *vt fus* attenersi a, seguire (alla lettera); prestar fede a; **go down** *vi* scendere; (*ship*) affondare; (*sun*) tramontare ▷ *vt fus* scendere; **go for** *vt fus* (*fetch*) andare a prendere; (*like*) andar matto(-a) per; (*attack*) attaccare; saltare addosso a; **go in** *vi* entrare; **go into** *vt fus* entrare in; (*investigate*) indagare, esaminare; (*embark on*) lanciarsi in; **go off** *vi* partire, andar via; (*food*) guastarsi; (*explode*) esplodere, scoppiare; (*event*) passare ▷ *vt fus* **I've gone off chocolate** la cioccolata non mi piace più; **the gun went off** il fucile si scaricò; **go on** *vi* continuare; (*happen*) succedere; **to go on doing** continuare a fare; **go out** *vi* uscire; (*couple*): **they went out for 3 years** sono stati insieme per 3 anni; (*fire, light*) spegnersi; **go over** *vi* (*ship*) ribaltarsi ▷ *vt fus* (*check*) esaminare; **go past** *vi* passare ▷ *vt fus* passare davanti a; **go round** *vi* (*circulate: news, rumour*) circolare; (*revolve*) girare; (*visit*): **to go round (to sb's)** passare (da qn); (*make a detour*): **to**

~ round (by) passare (per); (*suffice*) bastare (per tutti); **go through** *vt fus* (*town etc*) attraversare; (*files, papers*) passare in rassegna; (*examine: list etc*) leggere da cima a fondo; **go up** *vi* salire; **go with** *vt fus* (*accompany*) accompagnare; **go without** *vt fus* fare a meno di

go-ahead ['gəʊəhɛd] *adj* intraprendente ▷ *n* via *m*

goal [gəʊl] *n* (*Sport*) gol *m*, rete *f*; (: *place*) porta; (*fig: aim*) fine *m*, scopo; **goalkeeper** *n* portiere *m*; **goal-post** *n* palo (della porta)

goat [gəʊt] *n* capra

gobble ['gɔbl] *vt* (*also: ~ down, ~ up*) ingoiare

god [gɔd] *n* dio; **G~** Dio; **godchild** *n* figlioccio(-a); **goddaughter** *n* figlioccia; **goddess** *n* dea; **godfather** *n* padrino; **godmother** *n* madrina; **godson** *n* figlioccio

goggles ['gɔglz] *npl* occhiali *mpl* (di protezione)

going ['gəʊɪŋ] *n* (*conditions*) andare *m*; stato del terreno ▷ *adj* **the ~ rate** la tariffa in vigore

gold [gəʊld] *n* oro ▷ *adj* d'oro; **golden** *adj* (*made of gold*) d'oro; (*gold in colour*) dorato(-a); **goldfish** *n* pesce *m* dorato *or* rosso; **goldmine** *n* (*also fig*) miniera d'oro; **gold-plated** *adj* placcato(-a) oro *inv*

golf [gɔlf] *n* golf *m*; **golf ball** *n* (*for game*) pallina da golf; (*on typewriter*) pallina; **golf club** *n* circolo di golf; (*stick*) bastone *m or* mazza da golf; **golf course** *n* campo di golf; **golfer** *n* giocatore(-trice) di golf

gone [gɔn] *pp of* **go** ▷ *adj* partito(-a)

gong [gɔŋ] *n* gong *m inv*

good [gʊd] *adj* buono(-a); (*kind*) buono(-a), gentile; (*child*) bravo(-a) ▷ *n* bene *m*; **goods** *npl* (*Comm etc*) beni *mpl*; merci *fpl*; **~!** bene!, ottimo!; **to be ~ at** essere bravo(-a) in; **to be ~ for** andare bene per; **it's ~ for you**

fa bene; **would you be ~ enough
to ...?** avrebbe la gentilezza di ...?;
a ~ deal (of) molto(-a), una buona
quantità (di); **a ~ many** molti(-e); **to
make ~** (*loss, damage*) compensare;
it's no ~ complaining brontolare
non serve a niente; **for ~** per sempre,
definitivamente; **~ morning!** buon
giorno!; **~ afternoon/evening!**
buona sera!; **~ night!** buona notte!;
goodbye *excl* arrivederci!; **Good
Friday** *n* Venerdì Santo; **good-
looking** *adj* bello(-a); **good-natured**
adj affabile; **goodness** *n* (*of person*)
bontà; **for goodness sake!** per amor
di Dio!; **goodness gracious!** santo
cielo!, mamma mia!; **goods train**
(BRIT) *n* treno *m* merci *inv*; **goodwill** *n*
amicizia, benevolenza

Google® ['gu:gl] *n* Google® *m* ▷ *vt*
fare ricerche in Internet su

goose [gu:s] (*pl* **geese**) *n* oca

gooseberry ['guzbərı] *n* uva spina; **to
play ~** (BRIT) tenere la candela

goose bumps, goose pimples *npl*
pelle *f* d'oca

gorge [gɔ:dʒ] *n* gola ▷ *vt* **to ~ o.s. (on)**
ingozzarsi (di)

gorgeous ['gɔ:dʒəs] *adj* magnifico(-a)

gorilla [gəˈrɪlə] *n* gorilla *m inv*

gosh (*inf*) [gɔʃ] *excl* perdinci!

gospel ['gɔspl] *n* vangelo

gossip ['gɔsɪp] *n* chiacchiere
fpl; pettegolezzi *mpl*; (*person*)
pettegolo(-a) ▷ *vi* chiacchierare;
gossip column *n* cronaca mondana

got [gɔt] *pt, pp of* **get**

gotten ['gɔtn] (US) *pp of* **get**

gourmet ['guəmeɪ] *n*
buongustaio(-a)

govern ['gʌvn] *vt* governare;
government ['gʌvnmənt] *n*
governo; **governor** ['gʌvənər] *n* (*of
state, bank*) governatore *m*; (*of school,
hospital*) amministratore *m*; (BRIT: *of
prison*) direttore(-trice)

gown [gaun] *n* vestito lungo; (*of*

teacher, BRIT: *of judge*) toga

G.P. *n abbr* = **general practitioner**

GPS *n abbr* (= *global positioning system*)
GPS *m*

grab [græb] *vt* afferrare, arraffare;
(*property, power*) impadronirsi di ▷ *vi*
to ~ at cercare di afferrare

grace [greɪs] *n* grazia ▷ *vt* onorare; **5
days' ~** dilazione *f* di 5 giorni; **graceful**
adj elegante, aggraziato(-a);
gracious ['greɪʃəs] *adj* grazioso(-a),
misericordioso(-a)

grade [greɪd] *n* (*Comm*) qualità *f inv*;
classe *f*; categoria; (*in hierarchy*) grado;
(*Scol: mark*) voto; (US: *school class*)
classe ▷ *vt* classificare; ordinare;
graduare; **grade crossing** (US) *n*
passaggio a livello; **grade school** (US)
n scuola elementare

gradient ['greɪdɪənt] *n* pendenza,
inclinazione *f*

gradual ['grædjuəl] *adj* graduale;
gradually *adv* man mano, a poco
a poco

graduate [*n* 'grædjuːt, *vb* 'grædjueɪt]
n (*of university*) laureato(-a); (US:
of high school) diplomato(-a) ▷ *vi*
laurearsi; diplomarsi; **graduation**
[-'eɪʃən] *n* (*ceremony*) consegna delle
lauree (*or dei diplomi*)

graffiti [grəˈfiːtɪ] *npl* graffiti *mpl*

graft [grɑ:ft] *n* (*Agr, Med*) innesto;
(*bribery*) corruzione *f*; (BRIT: *hard
work*): **it's hard ~** è un lavoraccio ▷ *vt*
innestare

grain [greɪn] *n* grano; (*of sand*)
granello; (*of wood*) venatura

gram [græm] *n* grammo

grammar ['græmər] *n* grammatica;
grammar school (BRIT) *n* ≈ liceo

gramme [græm] *n* = **gram**

gran (*inf*) [græn] *n* (BRIT) nonna

grand [grænd] *adj* grande,
magnifico(-a); grandioso(-a);
grandad (*inf*) *n* = **granddad**;
grandchild (*pl* **-children**) *n* nipote
m; **granddad** (*inf*) *n* nonno;

granddaughter n nipote f;
grandfather n nonno; **grandma**
(inf) n nonna; **grandmother** n
nonna; **grandpa** (inf) n = **granddad**;
grandparents npl nonni mpl; **grand
piano** n pianoforte m a coda; **Grand
Prix** ['grɑ̃:'pri:] n (Aut) Gran Premio,
Grand Prix m inv; **grandson** n nipote m
granite ['grænɪt] n granito
granny ['grænɪ] (inf) n nonna
grant [grɑ:nt] vt accordare; (a request)
accogliere; (admit) ammettere,
concedere ▷ n (Scol) borsa; (Admin)
sussidio, sovvenzione f; **to take sth
for ~ed** dare qc per scontato; **to
take sb for ~ed** dare per scontata la
presenza di qn
grape [greɪp] n chicco d'uva, acino
grapefruit ['greɪpfru:t] n pompelmo
graph [grɑ:f] n grafico; **graphic** adj
grafico(-a); (vivid) vivido(-a), **graphics**
n grafica ▷ npl illustrazioni fpl
grasp [grɑ:sp] vt afferrare ▷ n (grip)
presa; (fig) potere m; comprensione f
grass [grɑ:s] n erba; **grasshopper** n
cavalletta
grate [greɪt] n graticola (del focolare)
▷ vi cigolare, stridere ▷ vt (Culin)
grattugiare
grateful ['greɪtful] adj grato(-a),
riconoscente
grater ['greɪtəʳ] n grattugia
gratitude ['grætɪtjuːd] n gratitudine f
grave [greɪv] n tomba ▷ adj grave,
serio(-a)
gravel ['grævl] n ghiaia
gravestone ['greɪvstəun] n pietra
tombale
graveyard ['greɪvjɑːd] n cimitero
gravity ['grævɪtɪ] n (Physics) gravità;
pesantezza; (seriousness) gravità,
serietà
gravy ['greɪvɪ] n intingolo della carne;
salsa
gray [greɪ] (US) adj = **grey**
graze [greɪz] vi pascolare, pascere
▷ vt (touch lightly) sfiorare; (scrape)

escoriare ▷ n (Med) escoriazione f
grease [griːs] n (fat) grasso; (lubricant)
lubrificante m ▷ vt ingrassare;
lubrificare; **greasy** adj grasso(-a),
untuoso(-a)
great [greɪt] adj grande; (inf)
magnifico(-a), meraviglioso(-a);
Great Britain n Gran Bretagna;
great-grandfather n bisnonno;
great-grandmother n bisnonna;
greatly adv molto
Greece [griːs] n Grecia
greed [griːd] n (also: **~iness**) avarizia;
(for food) golosità, ghiottoneria;
greedy adj avido(-a); goloso(-a),
ghiotto(-a)
Greek [griːk] adj greco(-a) ▷ n
greco(-a); (Ling) greco
green [griːn] adj verde; (inexperienced)
inesperto(-a), ingenuo(-a) ▷ n
verde m; (stretch of grass) prato; (on
golf course) green m inv; **greens** npl
(vegetables) verdura; **green card** n
(BRIT: Aut) carta verde; (US: Admin)
permesso di soggiorno e di lavoro;
greengage ['griːngeɪdʒ] n susina
Regina Claudia; **greengrocer** (BRIT)
n fruttivendolo(-a), erbivendolo(-a);
greenhouse n serra; **greenhouse
effect** n effetto serra
Greenland ['griːnlənd] n
Groenlandia
green salad n insalata verde
greet [griːt] vt salutare; **greeting** n
saluto; **greeting(s) card** n cartolina
d'auguri
grew [gruː] pt of **grow**
grey [greɪ] (US **gray**) adj grigio(-a);
grey-haired adj dai capelli grigi;
greyhound n levriere m
grid [grɪd] n grata; (Elec) rete f;
gridlock ['grɪdlɔk] n (traffic jam)
paralisi f inv del traffico; **gridlocked**
adj paralizzato(-a) dal traffico; (talks
etc) in fase di stallo
grief [griːf] n dolore m
grievance ['griːvəns] n lagnanza

grieve [griːv] vi addolorarsi; rattristarsi ▷ vt addolorare; **to ~ for sb** (dead person) piangere qn

grill [grɪl] n (on cooker) griglia; (also: **mixed ~**) grigliata mista ▷ vt (BRIT) cuocere ai ferri; (inf: question) interrogare senza sosta

grille [grɪl] n grata; (Aut) griglia

grim [grɪm] adj sinistro(-a), brutto(-a)

grime [graɪm] n sudiciume m

grin [grɪn] n sorriso smagliante ▷ vi fare un gran sorriso

grind [graɪnd] (pt, pp **ground**) vt macinare; (make sharp) arrotare ▷ n (work) sgobbata

grip [grɪp] n impugnatura; presa; (holdall) borsa da viaggio ▷ vt (object) afferrare; (attention) catturare; **to come to ~s with** affrontare; cercare di risolvere; **gripping** ['grɪpɪŋ] adj avvincente

grit [grɪt] n ghiaia; (courage) fegato ▷ vt (road) coprire di sabbia; **to ~ one's teeth** stringere i denti

grits [grɪts] (US) npl macinato grosso (di avena etc)

groan [grəʊn] n gemito ▷ vi gemere

grocer ['grəʊsər] n negoziante m di generi alimentari; **groceries** npl provviste fpl; **grocer's (shop)** n negozio di (generi) alimentari

grocery ['grəʊsərɪ] n (shop) (negozio di) alimentari

groin [grɔɪn] n inguine m

groom [gruːm] n palafreniere m; (also: **bride~**) sposo ▷ vt (horse) strigliare; (fig): **to ~ sb for** avviare qn a; **well-~ed** (person) curato(-a)

groove [gruːv] n scanalatura, solco

grope [grəʊp] vi **to ~ for** cercare a tastoni

gross [grəʊs] adj grossolano(-a); (Comm) lordo(-a); **grossly** adv (greatly) molto

grotesque [grəʊ'tɛsk] adj grottesco(-a)

ground [graʊnd] pt, pp of **grind** ▷ n suolo, terra; (land) terreno; (Sport) campo; (reason: gen pl) ragione f; (US: also: **~ wire**) terra ▷ vt (plane) tenere a terra; (US Elec) mettere la presa a terra a; **grounds** npl (of coffee etc) fondi mpl; (gardens etc) terreno, giardini mpl; **on/ to the ~** per/a terra; **to gain/lose ~** guadagnare/perdere terreno; **ground floor** n pianterreno; **groundsheet** (BRIT) n telone m impermeabile; **groundwork** n preparazione f

group [gruːp] n gruppo ▷ vt (also: **~ together**) raggruppare ▷ vi (also: **~ together**) raggrupparsi

grouse [graʊs] n inv (bird) tetraone m ▷ vi (complain) brontolare

grovel ['grɒvl] vi (fig): **to ~ (before)** strisciare (di fronte a)

grow [grəʊ] (pt **grew**, pp **grown**) vi crescere; (increase) aumentare; (develop) svilupparsi; (become): **to ~ rich/weak** arricchirsi/indebolirsi ▷ vt coltivare, far crescere; **grow on** vt fus **that painting is growing on me** quel quadro più lo guardo più mi piace; **grow up** vi farsi grande, crescere

growl [graʊl] vi ringhiare

grown [grəʊn] pp of **grow**; **grown-up** n adulto(-a), grande m/f

growth [grəʊθ] n crescita, sviluppo; (what has grown) crescita; (Med) escrescenza, tumore m

grub [grʌb] n larva; (inf: food) roba (da mangiare)

grubby ['grʌbɪ] adj sporco(-a)

grudge [grʌdʒ] n rancore m ▷ vt **to ~ sb sth** dare qc a qn di malavoglia; invidiare qc a qn; **to bear sb a ~ (for)** serbar rancore a qn (per)

gruelling ['grʊəlɪŋ] (US **grueling**) adj estenuante

gruesome ['gruːsəm] adj orribile

grumble ['grʌmbl] vi brontolare, lagnarsi

grumpy ['grʌmpɪ] adj scorbutico(-a)

grunt [grʌnt] vi grugnire

guarantee [gærən'tiː] n garanzia

▷ *vt* garantire

guard [gɑːd] *n* guardia; (*one man*) guardia, sentinella; (*BRIT Rail*) capotreno; (*on machine*) schermo protettivo; (*also:* **fire~**) parafuoco ▷ *vt* fare la guardia a; (*protect*): **to ~ (against)** proteggere (da); **to be on one's ~** stare in guardia; **guardian** *n* custode *m*; (*of minor*) tutore(-trice)

guerrilla [gə'rɪlə] *n* guerrigliero

guess [gɛs] *vi* indovinare ▷ *vt* indovinare; (*US*) credere, pensare ▷ *n* **to take** *or* **have a ~** provare a indovinare

guest [gɛst] *n* ospite *m/f*; (*in hotel*) cliente *m/f*; **guest house** *n* pensione *f*; **guest room** *n* camera degli ospiti

guidance ['gaɪdəns] *n* guida, direzione *f*

guide [gaɪd] *n* (*person, book etc*) guida; (*BRIT: also:* **girl ~**) giovane esploratrice *f* ▷ *vt* guidare; **is there an English-speaking ~?** c'è una guida che parla inglese?; **guidebook** *n* guida; **do you have a guidebook in English?** avete una guida in inglese?; **guide dog** *n* cane *m* guida *inv*; **guided tour** *n* visita guidata; **what time does the guided tour start?** a che ora comincia la visita guidata?; **guidelines** *npl* (*fig*) indicazioni *fpl*, linee *fpl* direttive

guild [gɪld] *n* arte *f*, corporazione *f*; associazione *f*

guilt [gɪlt] *n* colpevolezza; **guilty** *adj* colpevole

guinea pig ['gɪnɪ-] *n* cavia

guitar [gɪ'tɑːʳ] *n* chitarra; **guitarist** *n* chitarrista *m/f*

gulf [gʌlf] *n* golfo; (*abyss*) abisso

gull [gʌl] *n* gabbiano

gulp [gʌlp] *vi* deglutire; (*from emotion*) avere il nodo in gola ▷ *vt* (*also:* **~ down**) tracannare, inghiottire

gum [gʌm] *n* (*Anat*) gengiva; (*glue*) colla; (*also:* **~drop**) caramella gommosa; (*also:* **chewing ~**) chewing-gum *m inv* ▷ *vt* **to ~**

(together) incollare

gun [gʌn] *n* fucile *m*; (*small*) pistola, rivoltella; (*rifle*) carabina; (*shotgun*) fucile da caccia; (*cannon*) cannone *m*; **gunfire** *n* spari *mpl*; **gunman** (*irreg*) *n* bandito armato; **gunpoint** *n*: **at gunpoint** sotto minaccia di fucile; **gunpowder** *n* polvere *f* da sparo; **gunshot** *n* sparo

gush [gʌʃ] *vi* sgorgare; (*fig*) abbandonarsi ad effusioni

gust [gʌst] *n* (*of wind*) raffica; (*of smoke*) buffata

gut [gʌt] *n* intestino, budello; **guts** *npl* (*Anat*) interiora *fpl*; (*courage*) fegato

gutter ['gʌtəʳ] *n* (*of roof*) grondaia; (*in street*) cunetta

guy [gaɪ] *n* (*inf: man*) tipo, elemento; (*also:* **~rope**) cavo *or* corda di fissaggio; (*figure*) effigie di Guy Fawkes

Guy Fawkes Night [-'fɔːks-] *n* (*BRIT*) vedi nota nel riquadro

● **GUY FAWKES NIGHT**
●
● La sera del 5 novembre, in
● occasione della **Guy Fawkes**
● **Night**, altrimenti chiamata **Bonfire**
● **Night**, viene commemorato con
● falò e fuochi d'artificio il fallimento
● della Congiura delle Polveri contro
● Giacomo I nel 1605. La festa prende
● il nome dal principale congiurato
● della cospirazione, Guy Fawkes, la
● cui effigie viene bruciata durante i
● festeggiamenti.

gym [dʒɪm] *n* (*also:* **~nasium**) palestra; (*also:* **~nastics**) ginnastica; **gymnasium** [dʒɪm'neɪzɪəm] *n* palestra; **gymnast** ['dʒɪmnæst] *n* ginnasta *m/f*; **gymnastics** [-'næstɪks] *n, npl* ginnastica; **gym shoes** *npl* scarpe *fpl* da ginnastica

gynaecologist [gaɪnɪ'kɔlədʒɪst] (*US* **gynecologist**) *n* ginecologo(-a)

gypsy ['dʒɪpsɪ] *n* = **gipsy**

h

haberdashery [ˈhæbəˈdæʃərɪ] (BRIT) n merceria

habit [ˈhæbɪt] n abitudine f; (costume) abito; (Rel) tonaca

habitat [ˈhæbɪtæt] n habitat m inv

hack [hæk] vt tagliare, fare a pezzi ▷ n (pej: writer) scribacchino(-a); **hacker** [ˈhækəʳ] n (Comput) pirata m informatico

had [hæd] pt, pp of **have**

haddock [ˈhædək] (pl **haddock** or **haddocks**) n eglefino

hadn't [ˈhædnt] = **had not**

haemorrhage [ˈhɛmərɪdʒ] (US **hemorrhage**) n emorragia

haemorrhoids [ˈhɛmərɔɪdz] (US **hemorrhoids**) npl emorroidi fpl

haggle [ˈhægl] vi mercanteggiare

Hague [heɪg] n: **The ~** L'Aia

hail [heɪl] n grandine f; (of criticism etc) pioggia ▷ vt (call) chiamare; (flag down: taxi) fermare; (greet) salutare ▷ vi grandinare; **hailstone** n chicco di grandine

hair [hɛəʳ] n capelli mpl; (single hair: on head) capello; (: on body) pelo; **to do one's ~** pettinarsi; **hairband** [ˈhɛəbænd] n (elastic) fascia per i capelli; (rigid) cerchietto; **hairbrush** n spazzola per capelli; **haircut** n taglio di capelli; **hairdo** [ˈhɛəduː] n acconciatura, pettinatura; **hairdresser** n parrucchiere(-a); **hairdresser's** n parrucchiere(-a); **hair dryer** n asciugacapelli m inv; **hair gel** n gel m inv per capelli; **hairpin** n forcina; **hairpin bend** (US **hairpin curve**) n tornante m; **hairraising** adj orripilante; **hair spray** n lacca per capelli; **hairstyle** n pettinatura, acconciatura; **hairy** adj irsuto(-a), peloso(-a); (inf: frightening) spaventoso(-a)

hake [heɪk] (pl **hake** or **hakes**) n nasello

half [hɑːf] (pl **halves**) n mezzo, metà f inv ▷ adj mezzo(-a) ▷ adv a mezzo, a metà; **~ an hour** mezz'ora; **~ a dozen** mezza dozzina; **~ a pound** mezza libbra; **two and a ~** due e mezzo; **a week and a ~** una settimana e mezza; **~ (of it)** la metà; **~ (of)** la metà di; **to cut sth in ~** tagliare qc in due; **~ asleep** mezzo(-a) addormentato(-a); **half board** (BRIT) n mezza pensione; **half-brother** n fratellastro; **half day** n mezza giornata; **half fare** n tariffa a metà prezzo; **half-hearted** adj tiepido(-a); **half-hour** n mezz'ora; **half-price** adj, adv a metà prezzo; **half term** (BRIT) n (Scol) vacanza a or di metà trimestre; **half-time** n (Sport) intervallo; **halfway** adv a metà strada

hall [hɔːl] n sala, salone m; (entrance way) entrata

hallmark [ˈhɔːlmɑːk] n marchio di garanzia; (fig) caratteristica

hallo [həˈləu] excl = **hello**

hall of residence (BRIT) n casa dello studente

Halloween [hæləʊ'i:n] n vigilia
d'Ognissanti

● **HALLOWEEN**
●
● Negli Stati Uniti e in Gran
● Bretagna il 31 ottobre si festeggia
● **Halloween**, la notte delle streghe
● e dei fantasmi. I bambini, travestiti
● da fantasmi, streghe o mostri,
● bussano alle porte e ricevono dolci e
● piccoli doni.

hallucination [həluːsɪ'neɪʃən] n
allucinazione f
hallway ['hɔ:lweɪ] n corridoio;
(entrance) ingresso
halo ['heɪləʊ] n (of saint etc) aureola
halt [hɔ:lt] n fermata ▷ vt fermare ▷ vi
fermarsi
halve [hɑ:v] vt (apple etc) dividere a
metà; (expense) ridurre di metà
halves [hɑ:vz] npl of **half**
ham [hæm] n prosciutto
hamburger ['hæmbə:gəʳ] n
hamburger m inv
hamlet ['hæmlɪt] n paesetto
hammer ['hæməʳ] n martello ▷ vt
martellare ▷ vi **to ~ on** or **at the door**
picchiare alla porta
hammock ['hæmək] n amaca
hamper ['hæmpəʳ] vt impedire ▷ n
cesta
hamster ['hæmstəʳ] n criceto
hamstring ['hæmstrɪŋ] n (Anat)
tendine m del ginocchio
hand [hænd] n mano f; (of clock)
lancetta; (handwriting) scrittura; (at
cards) mano; (: game) partita; (worker)
operaio(-a) ▷ vt dare, passare; **to
give sb a ~** dare una mano a qn; **at ~** a
portata di mano; **in ~** a disposizione;
(work) in corso; **on ~** (person)
disponibile; (services) pronto(-a) a
intervenire; (information etc)
a portata di mano; **on the one ~
..., on the other ~** da un lato ...,

dall'altro; **hand down** vt passare giù;
(tradition, heirloom) tramandare; (us:
sentence, verdict) emettere; **hand in** vt
consegnare; **hand out** vt distribuire;
hand over vt passare; cedere;
handbag n borsetta; **hand baggage**
n bagaglio a mano; **handbook** n
manuale m; **handbrake** n freno a
mano; **handcuffs** npl manette fpl;
handful n manciata, pugno
handicap ['hændɪkæp] n
handicap m inv ▷ vt handicappare;
to be physically ~ped essere
handicappato(-a); **to be mentally
~ped** essere un(a) handicappato(-a)
mentale
handkerchief ['hæŋkətʃɪf] n
fazzoletto
handle ['hændl] n (of door etc)
maniglia; (of cup etc) ansa; (of knife etc)
impugnatura; (of saucepan) manico;
(for winding) manovella ▷ vt toccare,
maneggiare; (deal with) occuparsi
di; (treat: people) trattare; **"~ with
care"** "fragile"; **to fly off the ~** (fig)
perdere le staffe, uscire dai gangheri;
handlebar(s) n(pl) manubrio
hand: **hand luggage** n bagagli mpl
a mano; **handmade** adj fatto(-a)
a mano; **handout** n (money, food)
elemosina; (leaflet) volantino;
(at lecture) prospetto; **hands-
free** n (telephone) con auricolare;
(microphone) vivavoce inv
handsome ['hænsəm] adj bello(-a);
(profit, fortune) considerevole
handwriting ['hændraɪtɪŋ] n
scrittura
handy ['hændɪ] adj (person) bravo(-a);
(close at hand) a portata di mano;
(convenient) comodo(-a)
hang [hæŋ] (pt, pp hung) vt
appendere; (criminal: pt, pp hanged)
impiccare ▷ vi (painting) essere
appeso(-a); (hair) scendere; (drapery)
cadere; **to get the ~ of sth** (inf) capire
come qc funziona; **hang about** or

around vi bighellonare, ciondolare;
hang down vi ricadere; **hang on**
vi (wait) aspettare; **hang out** vt
(washing) stendere (fuori); (inf: live)
stare ▷ vi penzolare, pendere; **hang
round** vi = **hang around**; **hang up** vi
(Tel) riattaccare ▷ vt appendere
hanger ['hæŋə'] n gruccia
hang-gliding ['-glaɪdɪŋ] n volo col
deltaplano
hangover ['hæŋəʊvə'] n (after
drinking) postumi mpl di sbornia
hankie ['hæŋkɪ] n abbr
= **handkerchief**
happen ['hæpən] vi accadere,
succedere; (chance): **to ~ to do sth**
fare qc per caso; **what ~ed?** cos'è
successo?; **as it ~s** guarda caso
happily ['hæpɪlɪ] adv felicemente;
fortunatamente
happiness ['hæpɪnɪs] n felicità,
contentezza
happy ['hæpɪ] adj felice,
contento(-a); **~ with** (arrangements
etc) soddisfatto(-a) di; **to be ~ to do**
(willing) fare volentieri; **~ birthday!**
buon compleanno!
harass ['hærəs] vt molestare;
harassment n molestia
harbour ['hɑːbə'] (us **harbor**) n porto
▷ vt (hope, fear) nutrire; (criminal) dare
rifugio a
hard [hɑːd] adj duro(-a) ▷ adv (work)
sodo; (think, try) bene; **to look ~ at**
guardare fissamente; esaminare
attentamente; **no ~ feelings!** senza
rancore!; **to be ~ of hearing** essere
duro(-a) d'orecchio; **to be ~ done by**
essere trattato(-a) ingiustamente;
hardback n libro rilegato; **hardboard**
n legno precompresso; **hard disk** n
(Comput) disco rigido; **harden** vt, vi
indurire
hardly ['hɑːdlɪ] adv (scarcely) appena;
it's ~ the case non è proprio il caso; **~
anyone/anywhere** quasi nessuno/
da nessuna parte; **~ ever** quasi mai

hard: **hardship** ['hɑːdʃɪp] n avversità
f inv; privazioni fpl; **hard shoulder**
(BRIT) n (Aut) corsia d'emergenza;
hard-up (inf) adj al verde; **hardware**
['hɑːdwɛə'] n ferramenta fpl;
(Comput) hardware m; (Mil)
armamenti mpl; **hardware shop**
(US **hardware store**) n (negozio di)
ferramenta fpl; **hard-working**
[-'wə:kɪŋ] adj lavoratore(-trice)
hardy ['hɑːdɪ] adj robusto(-a); (plant)
resistente al gelo
hare [hɛə'] n lepre f
harm [hɑːm] n male m; (wrong)
danno ▷ vt (person) fare male a; (thing)
danneggiare; **out of ~'s way** al sicuro;
harmful adj dannoso(-a); **harmless**
adj innocuo(-a), inoffensivo(-a)
harmony ['hɑːmənɪ] n armonia
harness ['hɑːnɪs] n (for horse)
bardatura, finimenti mpl; (for child)
briglie fpl; (safety harness) imbracatura
▷ vt (horse) bardare; (resources)
sfruttare
harp [hɑːp] n arpa ▷ vi **to ~ on about**
insistere tediosamente su
harsh [hɑːʃ] adj (life, winter) duro(-a);
(judge, criticism) severo(-a); (sound)
rauco(-a); (light) violento(-a)
harvest ['hɑːvɪst] n raccolto; (of
grapes) vendemmia ▷ vt fare il
raccolto di, raccogliere; vendemmiare
has [hæz] vb see **have**
hasn't ['hæznt] = **has not**
hassle ['hæsl] (inf) n sacco di problemi
haste [heɪst] n fretta; precipitazione
f; **hasten** ['heɪsn] vt affrettare ▷ vi
to hasten (to) affrettarsi (a); **hastily**
adv in fretta; precipitosamente; **hasty**
adj affrettato(-a), precipitoso(-a)
hat [hæt] n cappello
hatch [hætʃ] n (Naut: also: ~way)
boccaporto; (also: **service ~**) portello
di servizio ▷ vi (bird) uscire dal guscio;
(egg) schiudersi
hatchback ['hætʃbæk] n (Aut) tre (or
cinque) porte f inv

hate [heɪt] vt odiare, detestare ▷ n odio; **hatred** ['heɪtrɪd] n odio

haul [hɔːl] vt trascinare, tirare ▷ n (of fish) pescata; (of stolen goods etc) bottino

haunt [hɔːnt] vt (fear) pervadere; (person) frequentare ▷ n rifugio; **this house is ~ed** questa casa è abitata da un fantasma; **haunted** adj (castle etc) abitato(-a) dai fantasmi or dagli spiriti; (look) ossessionato(-a), tormentato(-a)

🔵 **KEYWORD**

have [hæv] (pt, pp **had**) aux vb 1 (gen) avere; essere; **to have arrived/gone** essere arrivato(-a)/andato(-a); **to have eaten/slept** avere mangiato/dormito; **he has been kind/promoted** è stato gentile/promosso; **having finished** or **when he had finished, he left** dopo aver finito, se n'è andato

2 (in tag questions): **you've done it, haven't you?** l'ha fatto, (non è) vero?; **he hasn't done it, has he?** non l'ha fatto, vero?

3 (in short answers and questions): **you've made a mistake — no I haven't/so I have** ha fatto un errore — ma no, niente affatto/sì, è vero; **we haven't paid — yes we have!** non abbiamo pagato — ma sì che abbiamo pagato!; **I've been there before, have you?** ci sono già stato, e lei? ▷ modal aux vb (be obliged): **to have (got) to do sth** dover fare qc; **I haven't got** or **I don't have to wear glasses** non ho bisogno di portare gli occhiali ▷ vt 1 (possess, obtain) avere; **he has (got) blue eyes/dark hair** ha gli occhi azzurri/i capelli scuri; **do you have** or **have you got a car/phone?** ha la macchina/il telefono?; **may I have your address?** potrebbe darmi

il suo indirizzo?; **you can have it for £5** te lo lascio per 5 sterline

2 (+ noun: take, hold etc): **to have breakfast/a swim/a bath** fare colazione/una nuotata/un bagno; **to have lunch** pranzare; **to have dinner** cenare; **to have a drink** bere qualcosa; **to have a cigarette** fumare una sigaretta

3: **to have sth done** far fare qc; **to have one's hair cut** farsi tagliare i capelli; **to have sb do sth** far fare qc a qn

4 (experience, suffer) avere; **to have a cold/flu** avere il raffreddore/l'influenza; **she had her bag stolen** le hanno rubato la borsa

5 (inf: dupe): **you've been had!** ci sei cascato!

have out vt: **to have it out with sb** (settle a problem etc) mettere le cose in chiaro con qn

haven ['heɪvn] n porto; (fig) rifugio

haven't ['hævnt] = **have not**

havoc ['hævək] n caos m

Hawaii [həˈwaɪ] n le Hawaii

hawk [hɔːk] n falco

hawthorn ['hɔːθɔːn] n biancospino

hay [heɪ] n fieno; **hay fever** n febbre f da fieno; **haystack** n pagliaio

hazard ['hæzəd] n azzardo, ventura; pericolo, rischio ▷ vt (guess etc) azzardare; **hazardous** adj pericoloso(-a); **hazard warning lights** npl (Aut) luci fpl di emergenza

haze [heɪz] n foschia

hazel ['heɪzl] n (tree) nocciolo ▷ adj (eyes) (color) nocciola inv; **hazelnut** ['heɪzlnʌt] n nocciola

hazy ['heɪzɪ] adj fosco(-a); (idea) vago(-a)

he [hiː] pron lui, egli; **it is he who ...** è lui che ...

head [hɛd] n testa; (leader) capo; (of school) preside m/f ▷ vt (list) essere in testa a; (group) essere a capo di;

~s or tails testa (o croce), pari (o dispari); **~ first** a capofitto, di testa; **~ over heels in love** pazzamente innamorato(-a); **to ~ the ball** colpire una palla di testa; **head for** *vt fus* dirigersi verso; **head off** *vt* (*threat, danger*) sventare; **headache** *n* mal *m* di testa; **heading** *n* titolo; intestazione *f*; **headlamp** (BRIT) *n* = **headlight**; **headlight** *n* fanale *m*; **headline** *n* titolo; **head office** *n* sede *f* (centrale); **headphones** *npl* cuffia; **headquarters** *npl* ufficio centrale; (*Mil*) quartiere *m* generale; **headroom** *n* (*in car*) altezza dell'abitacolo; (*under bridge*) altezza limite; **headscarf** *n* foulard *m inv*; **headset** *n* = **headphones**; **headteacher** *n* (*of primary school*) direttore(-trice); (*of secondary school*) preside; **head waiter** *n* capocameriere *m*

heal [hi:l] *vt, vi* guarire

health [hɛlθ] *n* salute *f*; **health care** *n* assistenza sanitaria; **health centre** (BRIT) *n* poliambulatorio; **health food** *n* cibo macrobiotico; **Health Service** (BRIT) *n*: **the Health Service** ≈ il Servizio Sanitario Statale; **healthy** *adj* (*person*) sano(-a), in buona salute; (*climate*) salubre; (*appetite, economy etc*) sano(-a)

heap [hi:p] *n* mucchio ▷ *vt* (*stones, sand*) to ~ **(up)** ammucchiare; (*plate, sink*): **to ~ sth with** riempire qc di; **~s of** (*inf*) un mucchio di

hear [hɪəʳ] (*pt, pp* **heard**) *vt* sentire; (*news*) ascoltare ▷ *vi* sentire; **to ~ about** avere notizie di; sentire parlare di; **to ~ from sb** ricevere notizie da qn

hearing [ˈhɪərɪŋ] *n* (*sense*) udito; (*of witnesses*) audizione *f*; (*of a case*) udienza; **hearing aid** *n* apparecchio acustico

hearse [hə:s] *n* carro funebre

heart [hɑ:t] *n* cuore *m*; **hearts** *npl* (*Cards*) cuori *mpl*; **to lose ~** scoraggiarsi; **to take ~** farsi coraggio;

at ~ in fondo; **by ~** (*learn, know*) a memoria; **heart attack** *n* attacco di cuore; **heartbeat** *n* battito del cuore; **heartbroken** *adj*: **to be heartbroken** avere il cuore spezzato; **heartburn** *n* bruciore *m* di stomaco; **heart disease** *n* malattia di cuore

hearth [hɑ:θ] *n* focolare *m*

heartless [ˈhɑ:tlɪs] *adj* senza cuore

hearty [ˈhɑ:tɪ] *adj* caloroso(-a); robusto(-a), sano(-a); vigoroso(-a)

heat [hi:t] *n* calore *m*; (*fig*) ardore *m*; fuoco; (*Sport: also*: **qualifying ~**) prova eliminatoria ▷ *vt* scaldare; **heat up** *vi* (*liquids*) scaldarsi; (*room*) riscaldarsi ▷ *vt* riscaldare; **heated** *adj* riscaldato(-a); (*argument*) acceso(-a); **heater** *n* radiatore *m*; (*stove*) stufa

heather [ˈhɛðəʳ] *n* erica

heating [ˈhi:tɪŋ] *n* riscaldamento

heatwave [ˈhi:tweɪv] *n* ondata di caldo

heaven [ˈhɛvn] *n* paradiso, cielo; **heavenly** *adj* divino(-a), celeste

heavily [ˈhɛvɪlɪ] *adv* pesantemente; (*drink, smoke*) molto

heavy [ˈhɛvɪ] *adj* pesante; (*sea*) grosso(-a); (*rain, blow*) forte; (*weather*) afoso(-a); (*drinker, smoker*) gran (*before noun*); **it's too ~** è troppo pesante

Hebrew [ˈhi:bru:] *adj* ebreo(-a) ▷ *n* (*Ling*) ebraico

hectare [ˈhɛktɑ:ʳ] *n* (BRIT) ettaro

hectic [ˈhɛktɪk] *adj* movimentato(-a)

he'd [hi:d] = **he would**; **he had**

hedge [hɛdʒ] *n* siepe *f* ▷ *vi* essere elusivo(-a); **to ~ one's bets** (*fig*) coprirsi dai rischi

hedgehog [ˈhɛdʒhɔg] *n* riccio

heed [hi:d] *vt* (*also*: **take ~ of**) badare a, far conto di

heel [hi:l] *n* (*Anat*) calcagno; (*of shoe*) tacco ▷ *vt* (*shoe*) rifare i tacchi a

hefty [ˈhɛftɪ] *adj* (*person*) robusto(-a); (*parcel*) pesante; (*profit*) grosso(-a)

height [haɪt] *n* altezza; (*high ground*) altura; (*fig: of glory*) apice *m*; (: of *stupidity*) colmo; **heighten** vt (fig) accrescere

heir [ɛəʳ] n erede m; **heiress** n erede f

held [hɛld] pt, pp of **hold**

helicopter ['hɛlɪkɔptəʳ] n elicottero

hell [hɛl] n inferno; **~!** (inf) porca miseria!, accidenti!

he'll [hi:l] = **he will; he shall**

hello [hə'ləʊ] excl buon giorno!; ciao! (to sb one addresses as "tu"); (surprise) ma guarda!

helmet ['hɛlmɪt] n casco

help [hɛlp] n aiuto; (charwoman) donna di servizio ▷ vt aiutare; **~!** aiuto!; **can you ~ me?** può aiutarmi?; **~ yourself (to bread)** si serva (del pane); **he can't ~ it** non ci può far niente; **help out** vi aiutare ▷ vt **to help sb out** aiutare qn; **helper** n aiutante m/f, assistente m/f; **helpful** adj di grande aiuto; (useful) utile; **helping** n porzione f; **helpless** adj impotente; debole; **helpline** n ≈ telefono amico; (Comm) servizio m informazioni inv (a pagamento)

hem [hɛm] n orlo ▷ vt fare l'orlo a

hemisphere ['hɛmɪsfɪəʳ] n emisfero

hemorrhage ['hɛmərɪdʒ] (US) n = **haemorrhage**

hemorrhoids ['hɛmərɔɪdz] (US) npl = **haemorrhoids**

hen [hɛn] n gallina; (female bird) femmina

hence [hɛns] adv (therefore) dunque; **2 years ~** di qui a 2 anni

hen night n (inf) addio al nubilato

hepatitis [hɛpə'taɪtɪs] n epatite f

her [həːʳ] pron (direct) la, l' + vowel; (indirect) le; (stressed, after prep) lei ▷ adj il (la) suo(-a), i (le) suoi (sue); see also **me; my**

herb [həːb] n erba; **herbal** adj di erbe; **herbal tea** n tisana

herd [həːd] n mandria

here [hɪəʳ] adv qui, qua ▷ excl ehi!; **~!** (at roll call) presente!; **~ is/are** ecco; **~ he/she is** eccolo/eccola

hereditary [hɪ'rɛdɪtrɪ] adj ereditario(-a)

heritage ['hɛrɪtɪdʒ] n eredità; (fig) retaggio

hernia ['həːnɪə] n ernia

hero ['hɪərəʊ] (pl **heroes**) n eroe m; **heroic** [hɪ'rəʊɪk] adj eroico(-a)

heroin ['hɛrəʊɪn] n eroina

heroine ['hɛrəʊɪn] n eroina

heron ['hɛrən] n airone m

herring ['hɛrɪŋ] n aringa

hers [həːz] pron il (la) suo(-a), i (le) suoi (sue); see also **mine¹**

herself [həː'sɛlf] pron (reflexive) si; (emphatic) lei stessa; (after prep) se stessa, sé; see also **oneself**

he's [hi:z] = **he is; he has**

hesitant ['hɛzɪtənt] adj esitante, indeciso(-a)

hesitate ['hɛzɪteɪt] vi **to ~ (about/to do)** esitare (su/a fare); **hesitation** [-'teɪʃən] n esitazione f

heterosexual ['hɛtərəʊ'sɛksjuəl] adj, n eterosessuale m/f

hexagon ['hɛksəgən] n esagono

hey [heɪ] excl ehi!

heyday ['heɪdeɪ] n: **the ~ of** i bei giorni di, l'età d'oro di

HGV n abbr = **heavy goods vehicle**

hi [haɪ] excl ciao!

hibernate ['haɪbəneɪt] vi ibernare

hiccough ['hɪkʌp] vi singhiozzare

hiccup ['hɪkʌp] = **hiccough**

hid [hɪd] pt of **hide**

hidden ['hɪdn] pp of **hide**

hide [haɪd] (pt **hid**, pp **hidden**) n (skin) pelle f ▷ vt **to ~ sth (from sb)** nascondere qc (a qn) ▷ vi **to ~ (from sb)** nascondersi (da qn)

hideous ['hɪdɪəs] adj laido(-a); orribile

hiding ['haɪdɪŋ] n (beating) bastonata; **to be in ~** (concealed) tenersi nascosto(-a)

hi-fi ['haɪfaɪ] n stereo ▷ adj ad alta fedeltà, hi-fi inv

high [haɪ] adj alto(-a); (speed, respect, number) grande; (wind) forte; (voice) acuto(-a) ▷ *adv* alto, in alto; **20m ~** alto(-a) 20m; **highchair** *n* seggiolone *m*; **high-class** *adj* (*neighbourhood*) elegante; (*hotel*) di prim'ordine; (*person*) di gran classe; (*food*) raffinato(-a); **higher education** *n* studi *mpl* superiori; **high heels** *npl* (*heels*) tacchi *mpl* alti; (*shoes*) scarpe *fpl* con i tacchi alti; **high jump** *n* (*Sport*) salto in alto; **highlands** *npl* zona montuosa; **the Highlands** le Highlands scozzesi; **highlight** *n* (*fig: of event*) momento culminante; (*in hair*) colpo di sole ▷ *vt* mettere in evidenza; **highlights** *npl* (*in hair*) colpi *mpl* di sole; **highlighter** *n* (*pen*) evidenziatore *m*; **highly** *adv* molto; **to speak highly of** parlare molto bene di; **highness** *n*: **Her Highness** Sua Altezza; **high-rise** *n* (*also*: **high-rise block**, **high-rise building**) palazzone *m*; **high school** *n* scuola secondaria; (*US*) istituto superiore d'istruzione; **high season** (*BRIT*) *n* alta stagione; **high street** (*BRIT*) *n* strada principale; **high-tech** (*inf*) *adj* high-tech *inv*; **highway** ['haɪweɪ] *n* strada maestra; **Highway Code** (*BRIT*) *n* codice *m* della strada

hijack ['haɪdʒæk] *vt* dirottare; **hijacker** *n* dirottatore(-trice)

hike [haɪk] *vi* fare un'escursione a piedi ▷ *n* escursione *f* a piedi; **hiker** *n* escursionista *m/f*; **hiking** *n* escursioni *fpl* a piedi

hilarious [hɪ'lɛərɪəs] *adj* (*behaviour*, *event*) spassosissimo(-a)

hill [hɪl] *n* collina, colle *m*; (*fairly high*) montagna; (*on road*) salita; **hillside** *n* fianco della collina; **hill walking** *n* escursioni *fpl* in collina; **hilly** *adj* collinoso(-a); montagnoso(-a)

him [hɪm] *pron* (*direct*) lo, l' + *vowel*; (*indirect*) gli; (*stressed, after prep*) lui; *see also* **me**; **himself** *pron* (*reflexive*) si; (*emphatic*) lui stesso; (*after prep*) se stesso, sé; *see also* **oneself**

hind [haɪnd] *adj* posteriore ▷ *n* cerva

hinder ['hɪndər] *vt* ostacolare

hindsight ['haɪndsaɪt] *n* **with ~** con il senno di poi

Hindu ['hɪnduː] *n* indù *m/f inv*; **Hinduism** *n* (*Rel*) induismo

hinge [hɪndʒ] *n* cardine *m* ▷ *vi* (*fig*): **to ~ on** dipendere da

hint [hɪnt] *n* (*suggestion*) allusione *f*; (*advice*) consiglio; (*sign*) accenno ▷ *vt* **to ~ that** lasciar capire che ▷ *vi* **to ~ at** alludere a

hip [hɪp] *n* anca, fianco

hippie ['hɪpɪ] *n* hippy *m/f inv*

hippo ['hɪpəu] (*pl* **hippos**) *n* ippopotamo

hippopotamus [hɪpə'pɒtəməs] (*pl* **hippopotamuses** *or* **hippopotami**) *n* ippopotamo

hippy ['hɪpɪ] *n* = **hippie**

hire ['haɪər] *vt* (*BRIT: car, equipment*) noleggiare; (*worker*) assumere, dare lavoro a ▷ *n* nolo, noleggio; **for ~** da nolo; (*taxi*) libero(-a); **I'd like to ~ a car** vorrei noleggiare una macchina; **hire(d) car** (*BRIT*) *n* macchina a nolo; **hire purchase** (*BRIT*) *n* acquisto (*or* vendita) rateale

his [hɪz] *adj*, *pron* il (la) suo (sua), i suoi (sue); *see also* **my**; **mine¹**

Hispanic [hɪs'pænɪk] *adj* ispanico(-a)

hiss [hɪs] *vi* fischiare; (*cat, snake*) sibilare

historian [hɪ'stɔːrɪən] *n* storico(-a)

historic(al) [hɪ'stɔrɪk(l)] *adj* storico(-a)

history ['hɪstərɪ] *n* storia

hit [hɪt] (*pt, pp* **hit**) *vt* colpire, picchiare; (*knock against*) battere; (*reach: target*) raggiungere; (*collide with: car*) urtare contro; (*fig: affect*) colpire; (*find: problem etc*) incontrare ▷ *n* colpo; (*success, song*) successo; **to ~ it off with sb** andare molto d'accordo con qn; **hit back** *vi* **to hit back at sb** restituire il colpo a qn

hitch [hɪtʃ] *vt* (*fasten*) attaccare;

(also: **~ up**) tirare su ▷ n (difficulty) intoppo, difficoltà f inv; **to ~ a lift** fare l'autostop; **hitch-hike** vi fare l'autostop; **hitch-hiker** n autostoppista m/f; **hitch-hiking** n autostop m

hi-tech ['haɪ'tɛk] adj high-tech inv

hitman (irreg) n (inf) sicario

HIV abbr: **~-negative/-positive** adj sieronegativo(-a)/sieropositivo(-a)

hive [haɪv] n alveare m

hoard [hɔːd] n (of food) provviste fpl; (of money) gruzzolo ▷ vt ammassare

hoarse [hɔːs] adj rauco(-a)

hoax [həʊks] n scherzo; falso allarme

hob [hɔb] n piastra (con fornelli)

hobble ['hɔbl] vi zoppicare

hobby ['hɔbɪ] n hobby m inv, passatempo

hobo ['həʊbəʊ] (US) n vagabondo

hockey ['hɔkɪ] n hockey m; **hockey stick** n bastone m da hockey

hog [hɔg] n maiale m ▷ vt (fig) arraffare; **to go the whole ~** farlo fino in fondo

Hogmanay [hɔgmə'neɪ] n (Scottish) ≈ San Silvestro

hoist [hɔɪst] n paranco ▷ vt issare

hold [həʊld] (pt, pp **held**) vt tenere; (contain) contenere; (keep back) trattenere; (believe) mantenere; considerare; (possess) avere, possedere; detenere ▷ vi (withstand pressure) tenere; (be valid) essere valido(-a) ▷ n presa; (control): **to have a ~ over** avere controllo su; (Naut) stiva; **~ the line!** (Tel) resti in linea!; **to ~ one's own** (fig) difendersi bene; **to catch** or **get (a) ~ of** afferrare; **hold back** vt trattenere; (secret) tenere celato(-a); **hold on** vi tener fermo; (wait) aspettare; **hold on!** (Tel) resti in linea!; **hold out** vt offrire ▷ vi (resist) resistere; **hold up** vt (raise) alzare; (support) sostenere; (delay) ritardare; (rob) assaltare; **holdall** (BRIT) n borsone m; **holder**

n (container) contenitore m; (of ticket, title) possessore/posseditrice; (of office etc) incaricato(-a); (of record) detentore(-trice)

hole [həʊl] n buco, buca

holiday ['hɔlədɪ] n vacanza; (day off) giorno di vacanza; (public) giorno festivo; **on ~** in vacanza; **I'm on ~ here** sono qui in vacanza; **holiday camp** (BRIT) n (also: **holiday centre**) ≈ villaggio (di vacanze); **holiday job** n (BRIT) ≈ lavoro estivo; **holiday-maker** (BRIT) n villeggiante m/f; **holiday resort** n luogo di villeggiatura

Holland ['hɔlənd] n Olanda

hollow ['hɔləʊ] adj cavo(-a); (container, claim) vuoto(-a); (laugh, sound) cupo(-a) ▷ n cavità f inv; (in land) valletta, depressione f ▷ vt **to ~ out** scavare

holly ['hɔlɪ] n agrifoglio

Hollywood ['hɔlɪwʊd] n Hollywood f

holocaust ['hɔləkɔːst] n olocausto

holy ['həʊlɪ] adj santo(-a); (bread, ground) benedetto(-a), consacrato(-a)

home [həʊm] n casa; (country) patria; (institution) casa, ricovero ▷ cpd familiare; (cooking etc) casalingo(-a); (Econ, Pol) nazionale, interno(-a); (Sport) di casa ▷ adv a casa; in patria; (right in: nail etc) fino in fondo; **at ~** a casa; (in situation) a proprio agio; **to go** or **come ~** tornare a casa (or in patria); **make yourself at ~** si metta a suo agio; **home address** n indirizzo di casa; **homeland** n patria; **homeless** adj senza tetto; spiatriato(-a); **homely** adj semplice, alla buona; accogliente; **home-made** adj casalingo(-a); **home match** n partita in casa; **Home Office** (BRIT) n ministero degli Interni; **home owner** n proprietario(-a) di casa; **home page** n (Comput) home page f inv; **Home Secretary** (BRIT) n ministro degli Interni; **homesick** adj: **to be homesick** avere la nostalgia; **home town** n città f inv natale;

homework n compiti mpl (per casa)
homicide ['hɒmɪsaɪd] (us) n omicidio
homoeopathic [həumɪə'pæθɪk] (us **homeopathic**) adj omeopatico(-a)
homoeopathy [həumɪ'ɒpəθɪ] (us **homeopathy**) n omeopatia
homosexual [hɒməu'sɛksjuəl] adj, n omosessuale m/f
honest ['ɒnɪst] adj onesto(-a); sincero(-a); **honestly** adv onestamente; sinceramente; **honesty** n onestà
honey ['hʌnɪ] n miele m; **honeymoon** n luna di miele, viaggio di nozze; **we're on honeymoon** siamo in luna di miele; **honeysuckle** n (Bot) caprifoglio
Hong Kong ['hɒŋ'kɒŋ] n Hong Kong f
honorary ['ɒnərərɪ] adj onorario(-a); (duty, title) onorifico(-a)
honour ['ɒnəʳ] (us **honor**) vt onorare ▷ n onore m; **honourable** (us **honorable**) adj onorevole; **honours degree** n (Scol) laurea specializzata
hood [hud] n cappuccio; (on cooker) cappa; (Brit: Aut) capote f; (us: Aut) cofano
hoof [huːf] (pl **hooves**) n zoccolo
hook [huk] n gancio; (for fishing) amo ▷ vt uncinare; (dress) agganciare
hooligan ['huːlɪɡən] n giovinastro, teppista m
hoop [huːp] n cerchio
hooray [huː'reɪ] excl = **hurray**
hoot [huːt] vi (Aut) suonare il clacson; (siren) ululare; (owl) gufare
Hoover® ['huːvəʳ] (Brit) n aspirapolvere m inv ▷ vt **hoover** pulire con l'aspirapolvere
hooves [huːvz] npl of **hoof**
hop [hɒp] vi saltellare, saltare; (on one foot) saltare su una gamba
hope [həup] vt **to ~ that/to do** sperare che/di fare ▷ vi sperare ▷ n speranza; **I ~ so/not** spero di sì/no; **hopeful** adj (person) pieno(-a) di speranza; (situation) promettente;

hopefully adv con speranza; **hopefully he will recover** speriamo che si riprenda; **hopeless** adj senza speranza, disperato(-a); (useless) inutile
hops [hɒps] npl luppoli mpl
horizon [hə'raɪzn] n orizzonte m; **horizontal** [hɒrɪ'zɒntl] adj orizzontale
hormone ['hɔːməun] n ormone m
horn [hɔːn] n (Zool, Mus) corno; (Aut) clacson m inv
horoscope ['hɒrəskəup] n oroscopo
horrendous [hə'rɛndəs] adj orrendo(-a)
horrible ['hɒrɪbl] adj orribile, tremendo(-a)
horrid ['hɒrɪd] adj orrido(-a); (person) odioso(-a)
horrific [hɒ'rɪfɪk] adj (accident) spaventoso(-a); (film) orripilante
horrifying ['hɒrɪfaɪɪŋ] adj terrificante
horror ['hɒrəʳ] n orrore m; **horror film** n film m inv dell'orrore
hors d'œuvre [ɔː'dəːvrə] n antipasto
horse [hɔːs] n cavallo; **horseback: on horseback** adj, adv a cavallo; **horse chestnut** n ippocastano; **horsepower** n cavallo (vapore); **horse-racing** n ippica; **horseradish** n rafano; **horse riding** n (Brit) equitazione f
hose [həuz] n (also: **~pipe**) tubo; (also: **garden ~**) tubo per annaffiare
hospital ['hɒspɪtl] n ospedale m; **where's the nearest ~?** dov'è l'ospedale più vicino?
hospitality [hɒspɪ'tælɪtɪ] n ospitalità
host [həust] n ospite m; (Rel) ostia; (large number): **a ~ of** una schiera di
hostage ['hɒstɪdʒ] n ostaggio(-a)
hostel ['hɒstl] n ostello; (also: **youth ~**) ostello della gioventù
hostess ['həustɪs] n ospite f; (Brit: air hostess) hostess f inv
hostile ['hɒstaɪl] adj ostile
hostility [hɒ'stɪlɪtɪ] n ostilità f inv

hot [hɔt] *adj* caldo(-a); (*as opposed to only very warm*) molto caldo(-a); (*spicy*) piccante; (*fig*) accanito(-a); ardente; violento(-a), focoso(-a); **to be ~** (*person*) aver caldo; (*object*) essere caldo(-a); (*weather*) far caldo; **hot dog** *n* hot dog *m inv*

hotel [həu'tɛl] *n* albergo

hot spot *n* (*fig*) zona calda

hot-water bottle [hɔt'wɔːtə-] *n* borsa dell'acqua calda

hound [haund] *vt* perseguitare ▷ *n* segugio

hour ['auəʳ] *n* ora; **hourly** *adj* all'ora

house [*n* haus, *pl* 'hauzɪz, *vb* hauz] *n* (*also:* **firm**) casa; (*Pol*) camera; (*Theatre*) sala; pubblico; spettacolo; (*dynasty*) casata ▷ *vt* (*person*) ospitare, alloggiare; **on the ~** (*fig*) offerto(-a) dalla casa; **household** *n* famiglia; casa; **householder** *n* padrone(-a) di casa; (*head of house*) capofamiglia *m/f*; **housekeeper** *n* governante *f*; **housekeeping** *n* (*work*) governo della casa; (*money*) soldi *mpl* per le spese di casa; **housewife** (*irreg*) *n* massaia, casalinga; **house wine** *n* vino della casa; **housework** *n* faccende *fpl* domestiche

housing ['hauzɪŋ] *n* alloggio; **housing development** (BRIT), **housing estate** *n* zona residenziale con case popolari e/o private

hover ['hɔvəʳ] *vi* (*bird*) librarsi; **hovercraft** *n* hovercraft *m inv*

how [hau] *adv* come; **~ are you?** come sta?; **~ do you do?** piacere!; **~ far is it to the river?** quanto è lontano il fiume?; **~ long have you been here?** da quando è qui?; **~ lovely!/ awful!** che bello!/orrore!; **~ many?** quanti(-e)?; **~ much?** quanto(-a)?; **~ much milk?** quanto latte?; **~ many people?** quante persone?; **~ old are you?** quanti anni ha?

however [hau'ɛvəʳ] *adv* in qualsiasi modo or maniera che; (+ *adjective*) per quanto + *sub*; (*in questions*) come ▷ *conj* comunque, però

howl [haul] *vi* ululare; (*baby, person*) urlare

H.P. *abbr* = **hire purchase**; **horsepower**

h.p. *n abbr* = **H.P.**

HQ *n, abbr* = **headquarters**

hr(s) *abbr* (= *hour(s)*) h

HTML *abbr* (= *hypertext markup language*) HTML *m inv*

hubcap ['hʌbkæp] *n* coprimozzo

huddle ['hʌdl] *vi* **to ~ together** rannicchiarsi l'uno contro l'altro

huff [hʌf] *n*: **in a ~** stizzito(-a)

hug [hʌg] *vt* abbracciare; (*shore, kerb*) stringere

huge [hjuːdʒ] *adj* enorme, immenso(-a)

hull [hʌl] *n* (*of ship*) scafo

hum [hʌm] *vt* (*tune*) canticchiare ▷ *vi* canticchiare; (*insect, plane, tool*) ronzare

human ['hjuːmən] (*irreg*) *adj* umano(-a) ▷ *n* essere *m* umano

humane [hjuː'meɪn] *adj* umanitario(-a)

humanitarian [hjuːmænɪ'tɛərɪən] *adj* umanitario(-a)

humanity [hjuː'mænɪtɪ] *n* umanità

human rights *npl* diritti *mpl* dell'uomo

humble ['hʌmbl] *adj* umile, modesto(-a) ▷ *vt* umiliare

humid ['hjuːmɪd] *adj* umido(-a); **humidity** [hjuː'mɪdɪtɪ] *n* umidità

humiliate [hjuː'mɪlɪeɪt] *vt* umiliare; **humiliating** *adj* umiliante; **humiliation** [-'eɪʃən] *n* umiliazione *f*

hummus ['huməs] *n* purè di ceci

humorous ['hjuːmərəs] *adj* umoristico(-a); (*person*) buffo(-a)

humour ['hjuːməʳ] (*US* **humor**) *n* umore *m* ▷ *vt* accontentare

hump [hʌmp] *n* gobba

hunch [hʌntʃ] *n* (*premonition*) intuizione *f*

hundred ['hʌndrəd] *num* cento; **~s of**
centinaia *fpl* di; **hundredth** [-ɪdθ] *num*
centesimo(-a)
hung [hʌŋ] *pt, pp of* **hang**
Hungarian [hʌŋ'gɛərɪən] *adj*
ungherese ▷ *n* ungherese *m/f*; (*Ling*)
ungherese *m*
Hungary ['hʌŋgərɪ] *n* Ungheria
hunger ['hʌŋgəʳ] *n* fame *f* ▷ *vi* **to ~ for**
desiderare ardentemente
hungry ['hʌŋgrɪ] *adj* affamato(-a); **to
be ~** aver fame
hunt [hʌnt] *vt* (*seek*) cercare; (*Sport*)
cacciare ▷ *vi* **to ~ (for)** andare a caccia
(di) ▷ *n* caccia; **hunter** *n* cacciatore
m; **hunting** *n* caccia
hurdle ['hə:dl] *n* (*Sport, fig*) ostacolo
hurl [hə:l] *vt* lanciare con violenza
hurrah [hu'rɑ:] *excl* = **hurray**
hurray [hu'reɪ] *excl* urra!, evviva!
hurricane ['hʌrɪkən] *n* uragano
hurry ['hʌrɪ] *n* fretta ▷ *vi* (*also:* **~ up**)
affrettarsi ▷ *vt* (*also:* **~ up**: *person*)
affrettare; (*work*) far in fretta; **to be in
a ~** aver fretta; **hurry up** *vi* sbrigarsi
hurt [hə:t] (*pt, pp* **hurt**) *vt* (*cause pain
to*) far male a; (*injure, fig*) ferire ▷ *vi*
far male
husband ['hʌzbənd] *n* marito
hush [hʌʃ] *n* silenzio, calma ▷ *vt* zittire
husky ['hʌskɪ] *adj* roco(-a) ▷ *n* cane *m*
eschimese
hut [hʌt] *n* rifugio; (*shed*) ripostiglio
hyacinth ['haɪəsɪnθ] *n* giacinto
hydrangea [haɪ'dreɪnʒə] *n* ortensia
hydrofoil ['haɪdrəufɔɪl] *n* aliscafo
hydrogen ['haɪdrədʒən] *n* idrogeno
hygiene ['haɪdʒi:n] *n* igiene *f*;
hygienic [haɪ'dʒi:nɪk] *adj* igienico(-a)
hymn [hɪm] *n* inno; cantica
hype [haɪp] (*inf*) *n* campagna
pubblicitaria
hyphen ['haɪfn] *n* trattino
hypnotize ['hɪpnətaɪz] *vt* ipnotizzare
hypocrite ['hɪpəkrɪt] *n* ipocrita *m/f*
hypocritical [hɪpə'krɪtɪkl] *adj*
ipocrita

hypothesis [haɪ'pɔθɪsɪs] (*pl*
hypotheses) *n* ipotesi *f inv*
hysterical [hɪ'stɛrɪkl] *adj* isterico(-a)
hysterics [hɪ'stɛrɪks] *npl* accesso di
isteria; (*laughter*) attacco di riso

I [aɪ] *pron* io

ice [aɪs] *n* ghiaccio; (*on road*) gelo; (*ice cream*) gelato ▷ *vt* (*cake*) glassare ▷ *vi* (*also:* **~ over**) ghiacciare; (*also:* **~ up**) gelare; **iceberg** *n* iceberg *m inv*; **ice cream** *n* gelato; **ice cube** *n* cubetto di ghiaccio; **ice hockey** *n* hockey *m* su ghiaccio

Iceland ['aɪslənd] *n* Islanda; **Icelander** *n* islandese *m/f*; **Icelandic** [aɪs'lændɪk] *adj* islandese ▷ *n* (*Ling*) islandese *m*

ice: **ice lolly** (*BRIT*) *n* ghiacciolo; **ice rink** *n* pista di pattinaggio; **ice skating** *n* pattinaggio sul ghiaccio

icing ['aɪsɪŋ] *n* (*Culin*) glassa; **icing sugar** (*BRIT*) *n* zucchero a velo

icon ['aɪkɔn] *n* icona

icy ['aɪsɪ] *adj* ghiacciato(-a); (*weather, temperature*) gelido(-a)

I'd [aɪd] = **I would**; **I had**

ID card *n* = **identity card**

idea [aɪ'dɪə] *n* idea

ideal [aɪ'dɪəl] *adj* ideale ▷ *n* ideale *m*;

ideally [aɪ'dɪəlɪ] *adv* perfettamente, assolutamente; **ideally the book should have ...** l'ideale sarebbe che il libro avesse ...

identical [aɪ'dɛntɪkl] *adj* identico(-a)

identification [aɪdɛntɪfɪ'keɪʃən] *n* identificazione *f*; **(means of) ~** carta d'identità

identify [aɪ'dɛntɪfaɪ] *vt* identificare

identity [aɪ'dɛntɪtɪ] *n* identità *f inv*; **identity card** *n* carta d'identità; **identity theft** *n* furto d'identità

ideology [aɪdɪ'ɔlədʒɪ] *n* ideologia

idiom ['ɪdɪəm] *n* idioma *m*; (*phrase*) espressione *f* idiomatica

idiot ['ɪdɪət] *n* idiota *m/f*

idle ['aɪdl] *adj* inattivo(-a); (*lazy*) pigro(-a), ozioso(-a); (*unemployed*) disoccupato(-a); (*question, pleasures*) ozioso(-a) ▷ *vi* (*engine*) girare al minimo

idol ['aɪdl] *n* idolo

idyllic [ɪ'dɪlɪk] *adj* idillico(-a)

i.e. *adv abbr* (= *that is*) cioè

if [ɪf] *conj* se; **if I were you ...** se fossi in te ..., io al tuo posto ...; **if so** se è così; **if not** se no; **if only** se solo *or* soltanto

ignite [ɪg'naɪt] *vt* accendere ▷ *vi* accendersi

ignition [ɪg'nɪʃən] *n* (*Aut*) accensione *f*; **to switch on/off the ~** accendere/ spegnere il motore

ignorance ['ɪgnərəns] *n* ignoranza; **to keep sb in ~ of sth** tenere qn all'oscuro di qc

ignorant ['ɪgnərənt] *adj* ignorante; **to be ~ of** (*subject*) essere ignorante in; (*events*) essere ignaro(-a) di

ignore [ɪg'nɔːʳ] *vt* non tener conto di; (*person, fact*) ignorare

I'll [aɪl] = **I will**; **I shall**

ill [ɪl] *adj* (*sick*) malato(-a); (*bad*) cattivo(-a) ▷ *n* male *m* ▷ *adv* **to speak** *etc* **~ of sb** parlare *etc* male di qn; **to take** *or* **be taken ~** ammalarsi

illegal [ɪ'liːgl] *adj* illegale

illegible [ɪ'lɛdʒɪbl] *adj* illeggibile

illegitimate [ɪlɪ'dʒɪtɪmət] *adj* illegittimo(-a)

ill health *n* problemi *mpl* di salute

illiterate [ɪ'lɪtərət] *adj* analfabeta, illetterato(-a); (*letter*) scorretto(-a)

illness ['ɪlnɪs] *n* malattia

illuminate [ɪ'luːmɪneɪt] *vt* illuminare

illusion [ɪ'luːʒən] *n* illusione *f*

illustrate ['ɪləstreɪt] *vt* illustrare

illustration [ɪlə'streɪʃən] *n* illustrazione *f*

I'm [aɪm] = **I am**

image ['ɪmɪdʒ] *n* immagine *f*; (*public face*) immagine (pubblica)

imaginary [ɪ'mædʒɪnərɪ] *adj* immaginario(-a)

imagination [ɪmædʒɪ'neɪʃən] *n* immaginazione *f*, fantasia

imaginative [ɪ'mædʒɪnətɪv] *adj* immaginoso(-a)

imagine [ɪ'mædʒɪn] *vt* immaginare

imbalance [ɪm'bæləns] *n* squilibrio

imitate ['ɪmɪteɪt] *vt* imitare; **imitation** [-'teɪʃən] *n* imitazione *f*

immaculate [ɪ'mækjulət] *adj* immacolato(-a); (*dress, appearance*) impeccabile

immature [ɪmə'tjuər] *adj* immaturo(-a)

immediate [ɪ'miːdɪət] *adj* immediato(-a); **immediately** *adv* (*at once*) subito, immediatamente; **immediately next to** proprio accanto a

immense [ɪ'mɛns] *adj* immenso(-a); enorme; **immensely** *adv* immensamente

immerse [ɪ'məːs] *vt* immergere

immigrant ['ɪmɪgrənt] *n* immigrante *m/f*; immigrato(-a); **immigration** [ɪmɪ'greɪʃən] *n* immigrazione *f*

imminent ['ɪmɪnənt] *adj* imminente

immoral [ɪ'mɔrl] *adj* immorale

immortal [ɪ'mɔːtl] *adj*, *n* immortale *m/f*

immune [ɪ'mjuːn] *adj*: **~ (to)** immune (da); **immune system** *n* sistema *m* immunitario

immunize ['ɪmjunaɪz] *vt* immunizzare

impact ['ɪmpækt] *n* impatto

impair [ɪm'pɛər] *vt* danneggiare

impartial [ɪm'pɑːʃl] *adj* imparziale

impatience [ɪm'peɪʃəns] *n* impazienza

impatient [ɪm'peɪʃənt] *adj* impaziente; **to get** *or* **grow ~** perdere la pazienza

impeccable [ɪm'pɛkəbl] *adj* impeccabile

impending [ɪm'pɛndɪŋ] *adj* imminente

imperative [ɪm'pɛrətɪv] *adj* imperativo(-a); necessario(-a), urgente; (*voice*) imperioso(-a)

imperfect [ɪm'pəːfɪkt] *adj* imperfetto(-a); (*goods etc*) difettoso(-a) ▷ *n* (*Ling: also*: **~ tense**) imperfetto

imperial [ɪm'pɪərɪəl] *adj* imperiale; (*measure*) legale

impersonal [ɪm'pəːsənl] *adj* impersonale

impersonate [ɪm'pəːsəneɪt] *vt* impersonare; (*Theatre*) fare la mimica di

impetus ['ɪmpətəs] *n* impeto

implant [ɪm'plɑːnt] *vt* (*Med*) innestare; (*fig: idea, principle*) inculcare

implement [*n* 'ɪmplɪmənt, *vb* 'ɪmplɪmɛnt] *n* attrezzo; (*for cooking*) utensile *m* ▷ *vt* effettuare

implicate ['ɪmplɪkeɪt] *vt* implicare

implication [ɪmplɪ'keɪʃən] *n* implicazione *f*; **by ~** implicitamente

implicit [ɪm'plɪsɪt] *adj* implicito(-a); (*complete*) completo(-a)

imply [ɪm'plaɪ] *vt* insinuare; suggerire

impolite [ɪmpə'laɪt] *adj* scortese

import [*vb* ɪm'pɔːt, *n* 'ɪmpɔːt] *vt* importare ▷ *n* (*Comm*) importazione *f*

importance [ɪm'pɔːtns] *n* importanza

important [ɪm'pɔːtnt] *adj*

importante; **it's not ~** non ha importanza

importer [ɪmˈpɔːtəʳ] n importatore(-trice)

impose [ɪmˈpəuz] vt imporre ▷ vi **to ~ on sb** sfruttare la bontà di qn; **imposing** [ɪmˈpəuzɪŋ] adj imponente

impossible [ɪmˈpɔsɪbl] adj impossibile

impotent [ˈɪmpətnt] adj impotente

impoverished [ɪmˈpɔvərɪʃt] adj impoverito(-a)

impractical [ɪmˈpræktɪkl] adj non pratico(-a)

impress [ɪmˈprɛs] vt impressionare; (mark) imprimere, stampare; **to ~ sth on sb** far capire qc a qn

impression [ɪmˈprɛʃən] n impressione f; **to be under the ~ that** avere l'impressione che

impressive [ɪmˈprɛsɪv] adj notevole

imprison [ɪmˈprɪzn] vt imprigionare; **imprisonment** n imprigionamento

improbable [ɪmˈprɔbəbl] adj improbabile; (excuse) inverosimile

improper [ɪmˈprɔpəʳ] adj scorretto(-a); (unsuitable) inadatto(-a), improprio(-a); sconveniente, indecente

improve [ɪmˈpruːv] vt migliorare ▷ vi migliorare; (pupil etc) fare progressi; **improvement** n miglioramento; progresso

improvise [ˈɪmprəvaɪz] vt, vi improvvisare

impulse [ˈɪmpʌls] n impulso; **on ~** d'impulso, impulsivamente; **impulsive** [ɪmˈpʌlsɪv] adj impulsivo(-a)

⊙ **KEYWORD**

in [ɪn] prep **1** (indicating place, position) in; **in the house/garden** in casa/giardino; **in the box** nella scatola; **in the fridge** nel frigorifero; **I have it in my hand** ce l'ho in mano; **in town/**

the country in città/campagna; **in school** a scuola; **in here/there** qui/lì dentro

2 (with place names: of town, region, country): **in London** a Londra; **in England** in Inghilterra; **in the United States** negli Stati Uniti; **in Yorkshire** nello Yorkshire

3 (indicating time: during, in the space of) in; **in spring/summer** in primavera/estate; **in 1988** nel 1988; **in May** in o a maggio; **I'll see you in July** ci vediamo a luglio; **in the afternoon** nel pomeriggio; **at 4 o'clock in the afternoon** alle 4 del pomeriggio; **I did it in 3 hours/days** l'ho fatto in 3 ore/giorni; **I'll see you in 2 weeks** or **in 2 weeks' time** ci vediamo tra 2 settimane

4 (indicating manner etc) a; **in a loud/soft voice** a voce alta/bassa; **in pencil** a matita; **in English/French** in inglese/francese; **the boy in the blue shirt** il ragazzo con la camicia blu

5 (indicating circumstances): **in the sun** al sole; **in the shade** all'ombra; **in the rain** sotto la pioggia; **a rise in prices** un aumento dei prezzi

6 (indicating mood, state): **in tears** in lacrime; **in anger** per la rabbia; **in despair** disperato(-a); **in good condition** in buono stato, in buone condizioni; **to live in luxury** vivere nel lusso

7 (with ratios, numbers): **1 in 10** 1 su 10; **20 pence in the pound** 20 pence per sterlina; **they lined up in twos** si misero in fila a due a due

8 (referring to people, works) in; **the disease is common in children** la malattia è comune nei bambini; **in (the works of) Dickens** in Dickens

9 (indicating profession etc) in; **to be in teaching** fare l'insegnante, insegnare; **to be in publishing** essere nell'editoria

10 (after superlative) di; **the best in the**

class il migliore della classe
11 (with present participle): **in saying
this** dicendo questo, nel dire questo
▷ adv **to be in** (person: at home, work)
esserci; (train, ship, plane) essere
arrivato(-a); (in fashion) essere di
moda; **to ask sb in** invitare qn ad
entrare; **to run/limp** etc **in** entrare di
corsa/zoppicando etc
▷ n **the ins and outs of the problem**
tutti i particolari del problema

inability [ɪnə'bɪlɪtɪ] n ~ **(to do)**
incapacità (di fare)
inaccurate [ɪn'ækjurət] adj
inesatto(-a), impreciso(-a)
inadequate [ɪn'ædɪkwət] adj
insufficiente
inadvertently [ɪnəd'və:tntlɪ] adv
senza volerlo
inappropriate [ɪnə'prəuprɪət] adj
non adatto(-a); (word, expression)
improprio(-a)
inaugurate [ɪ'nɔ:gjureɪt] vt
inaugurare; (president, official)
insediare
Inc. (US) abbr (= incorporated) S.A.
incapable [ɪn'keɪpəbl] adj incapace
incense [n 'ɪnsɛns, vb ɪn'sɛns] n
incenso ▷ vt (anger) infuriare
incentive [ɪn'sɛntɪv] n incentivo
inch [ɪntʃ] n pollice m (25 mm, 12 in a
foot); **within an ~ of** a un pelo da; **he
didn't give an ~** non ha ceduto di un
millimetro
incidence ['ɪnsɪdns] n (of crime,
disease) incidenza
incident ['ɪnsɪdnt] n incidente m; (in
book) episodio
incidentally [ɪnsɪ'dɛntəlɪ] adv (by the
way) a proposito
inclination [ɪnklɪ'neɪʃən] n
inclinazione f
incline [n 'ɪnklaɪn, vb ɪn'klaɪn] n
pendenza, pendio ▷ vt inclinare
▷ vi (surface) essere inclinato(-a); **to
be ~d to do** tendere a fare; essere

propenso(-a) a fare
include [ɪn'klu:d] vt includere,
comprendere; **is service ~d?** il
servizio è compreso?; **including**
prep compreso(-a), incluso(-a);
inclusion [ɪn'klu:ʒən] n inclusione f;
inclusive [ɪn'klu:sɪv] adj incluso(-a),
compreso(-a); **inclusive of tax** etc
tasse etc comprese
income ['ɪnkʌm] n reddito; **income
support** n (BRIT) sussidio di indigenza
or povertà; **income tax** n imposta
sul reddito
incoming ['ɪnkʌmɪŋ] adj (flight, mail)
in arrivo; (government) subentrante;
(tide) montante
incompatible [ɪnkəm'pætɪbl] adj
incompatibile
incompetence [ɪn'kɔmpɪtns] n
incompetenza, incapacità
incompetent [ɪn'kɔmpɪtnt] adj
incompetente, incapace
incomplete [ɪnkəm'pli:t] adj
incompleto(-a)
inconsistent [ɪnkən'sɪstənt] adj
incoerente; ~ **with** non coerente con
inconvenience [ɪnkən'vi:njəns] n
inconveniente m; (trouble) disturbo
▷ vt disturbare
inconvenient [ɪnkən'vi:njənt] adj
scomodo(-a)
incorporate [ɪn'kɔ:pəreɪt] vt
incorporare; (contain) contenere
incorrect [ɪnkə'rɛkt] adj
scorretto(-a); (statement) inesatto(-a)
increase [n 'ɪnkri:s, vb ɪn'kri:s]
n aumento ▷ vi, vt aumentare;
increasingly adv sempre più
incredible [ɪn'krɛdɪbl] adj incredibile;
incredibly adv incredibilmente
incur [ɪn'kə:ʳ] vt (expenses) incorrere;
(anger, risk) esporsi a; (debt) contrarre;
(loss) subire
indecent [ɪn'di:snt] adj indecente
indeed [ɪn'di:d] adv infatti;
veramente; **yes ~!** certamente!
indefinitely [ɪn'dɛfɪnɪtlɪ] adv (wait)

Negli Stati Uniti il 4 luglio si

indefinitamente
independence [ɪndɪˈpɛndns] n
indipendenza; **Independence Day**
(US) n vedi nota nel riquadro

🔵 **INDEPENDENCE DAY**
🔵
🔵 Negli Stati Uniti il 4 luglio si
🔵 festeggia **l'Independence Day**,
🔵 giorno in cui, nel 1776, 13 colonie
🔵 britanniche proclamarono la
🔵 propria indipendenza dalla
🔵 Gran Bretagna ed entrarono
🔵 ufficialmente a far parte degli Stati
🔵 Uniti d'America.

independent [ɪndɪˈpɛndnt] adj
indipendente; **independent school** n
(BRIT) istituto scolastico indipendente che
si autofinanzia
index [ˈɪndɛks] (pl **indexes**) n (in book)
indice m; (: in library etc) catalogo; (pl
indices: ratio, sign) indice m
India [ˈɪndɪə] n India; **Indian** adj, n
indiano(-a)
indicate [ˈɪndɪkeɪt] vt indicare;
indication [-ˈkeɪʃən] n indicazione
f, segno; **indicative** [ɪnˈdɪkətɪv]
adj: **indicative of** indicativo(-a) di;
indicator [ˈɪndɪkeɪtər] n indicatore
m; (Aut) freccia
indices [ˈɪndɪsiːz] npl of **index**
indict [ɪnˈdaɪt] vt accusare;
indictment [ɪnˈdaɪtmənt] n accusa
indifference [ɪnˈdɪfrəns] n
indifferenza
indifferent [ɪnˈdɪfrənt] adj
indifferente; (poor) mediocre
indigenous [ɪnˈdɪdʒɪnəs] adj
indigeno(-a)
indigestion [ɪndɪˈdʒɛstʃən] n
indigestione f
indignant [ɪnˈdɪgnənt] adj **~ (at
sth/with sb)** indignato(-a) (per
qc/contro qn)
indirect [ɪndɪˈrɛkt] adj indiretto(-a)
indispensable [ɪndɪˈspɛnsəbl] adj

indispensabile
individual [ɪndɪˈvɪdjuəl] n individuo
▷ adj individuale; (characteristic)
particolare, originale; **individually**
adv singolarmente, uno(-a) per
uno(-a)
Indonesia [ɪndəˈniːzɪə] n Indonesia
indoor [ˈɪndɔːr] adj da interno; (plant)
d'appartamento; (swimming pool)
coperto(-a); (sport, games) fatto(-a)
al coperto; **indoors** [ɪnˈdɔːz] adv
all'interno
induce [ɪnˈdjuːs] vt persuadere; (bring
about, Med) provocare
indulge [ɪnˈdʌldʒ] vt (whim)
compiacere, soddisfare; (child)
viziare ▷ vi **to ~ in sth** concedersi qc;
abbandonarsi a qc; **indulgent** adj
indulgente
industrial [ɪnˈdʌstrɪəl] adj
industriale; (injury) sul lavoro;
industrial estate (BRIT) n
zona industriale; **industrialist**
[ɪnˈdʌstrɪəlɪst] n industriale m;
industrial park (US) n = **industrial
estate**
industry [ˈɪndəstrɪ] n industria;
(diligence) operosità
inefficient [ɪnɪˈfɪʃənt] adj inefficiente
inequality [ɪnɪˈkwɔlɪtɪ] n
ineguaglianza
inevitable [ɪnˈɛvɪtəbl] adj inevitabile;
inevitably adv inevitabilmente
inexpensive [ɪnɪkˈspɛnsɪv] adj poco
costoso(-a)
inexperienced [ɪnɪksˈpɪərɪənst] adj
inesperto(-a), senza esperienza
inexplicable [ɪnɪkˈsplɪkəbl] adj
inesplicabile
infamous [ˈɪnfəməs] adj infame
infant [ˈɪnfənt] n bambino(-a)
infantry [ˈɪnfəntrɪ] n fanteria
infant school n (BRIT) scuola
elementare (per bambini dall'età di 5
a 7 anni)
infect [ɪnˈfɛkt] vt infettare; **infection**
[ɪnˈfɛkʃən] n infezione f; **infectious**

[ɪnˈfɛkʃəs] adj (disease) infettivo(-a), contagioso(-a); (person: fig: enthusiasm) contagioso(-a)

infer [ɪnˈfɜː^r] vt inferire, dedurre

inferior [ɪnˈfɪərɪə^r] adj inferiore; (goods) di qualità scadente ▷ n inferiore m/f; (in rank) subalterno(-a)

infertile [ɪnˈfɜːtaɪl] adj sterile

infertility [ɪnfəˈtɪlɪtɪ] n sterilità

infested [ɪnˈfɛstɪd] adj: ~ (with) infestato(-a) (di)

infinite [ˈɪnfɪnɪt] adj infinito(-a); **infinitely** adv infinitamente

infirmary [ɪnˈfɜːmərɪ] n ospedale m; (in school, factory) infermeria

inflamed [ɪnˈfleɪmd] adj infiammato(-a)

inflammation [ɪnfləˈmeɪʃən] n infiammazione f

inflatable [ɪnˈfleɪtəbl] adj gonfiabile

inflate [ɪnˈfleɪt] vt (tyre, balloon) gonfiare; (fig) esagerare; gonfiare; **inflation** [ɪnˈfleɪʃən] n (Econ) inflazione f

inflexible [ɪnˈflɛksɪbl] adj inflessibile, rigido(-a)

inflict [ɪnˈflɪkt] vt **to ~ on** infliggere a

influence [ˈɪnfluəns] n influenza ▷ vt influenzare; **under the ~ of alcohol** sotto l'effetto dell'alcool; **influential** [ɪnfluˈɛnʃl] adj influente

influx [ˈɪnflʌks] n afflusso

info (inf) [ˈɪnfəu] n = **information**

inform [ɪnˈfɔːm] vt **to ~ sb (of)** informare qn (di) ▷ vi **to ~ on sb** denunciare qn

informal [ɪnˈfɔːml] adj informale; (announcement, invitation) non ufficiale

information [ɪnfəˈmeɪʃən] n informazioni fpl; particolari mpl; **a piece of ~** un'informazione; **information office** n ufficio m informazioni inv; **information technology** n informatica

informative [ɪnˈfɔːmətɪv] adj istruttivo(-a)

infra-red [ɪnfrəˈrɛd] adj infrarosso(-a)

infrastructure [ˈɪnfrəstrʌktʃə^r] n infrastruttura

infrequent [ɪnˈfriːkwənt] adj infrequente, raro(-a)

infuriate [ɪnˈfjuərɪeɪt] vt rendere furioso(-a)

infuriating [ɪnˈfjuərɪeɪtɪŋ] adj molto irritante

ingenious [ɪnˈdʒiːnjəs] adj ingegnoso(-a)

ingredient [ɪnˈɡriːdɪənt] n ingrediente m; elemento

inhabit [ɪnˈhæbɪt] vt abitare; **inhabitant** [ɪnˈhæbɪtnt] n abitante m/f

inhale [ɪnˈheɪl] vt inalare ▷ vi (in smoking) aspirare; **inhaler** n inalatore m

inherent [ɪnˈhɪərənt] adj: ~ **(in or to)** inerente (a)

inherit [ɪnˈhɛrɪt] vt ereditare; **inheritance** n eredità

inhibit [ɪnˈhɪbɪt] vt (Psych) inibire; **inhibition** [-ˈbɪʃən] n inibizione f

initial [ɪˈnɪʃl] adj iniziale ▷ n iniziale f ▷ vt siglare; **initials** npl (of name) iniziali fpl; (as signature) sigla; **initially** adv inizialmente, all'inizio

initiate [ɪˈnɪʃɪeɪt] vt (start) avviare; intraprendere; iniziare; (person) iniziare; **to ~ sb into a secret** mettere qn a parte di un segreto; **to ~ proceedings against sb** (Law) intentare causa contro qn

initiative [ɪˈnɪʃətɪv] n iniziativa

inject [ɪnˈdʒɛkt] vt (liquid) iniettare; (patient): **to ~ sb with sth** fare a qn un'iniezione di qc; (funds) immettere; **injection** [ɪnˈdʒɛkʃən] n iniezione f, puntura

injure [ˈɪndʒə^r] vt ferire; (damage: reputation etc) nuocere a; **injured** adj ferito(-a); **injury** [ˈɪndʒərɪ] n ferita

injustice [ɪnˈdʒʌstɪs] n ingiustizia

ink [ɪŋk] n inchiostro; **ink-jet printer** [ˈɪŋkdʒɛt-] n stampante f a getto d'inchiostro

inland [adj 'ɪnlənd, adv ɪn'lænd] adj
interno(-a) ▷ adv all'interno; **Inland
Revenue** (BRIT) n Fisco
in-laws ['ɪnlɔ:z] npl suoceri mpl;
famiglia del marito (or della moglie)
inmate ['ɪnmeɪt] n (in prison)
carcerato(-a); (in asylum)
ricoverato(-a)
inn [ɪn] n locanda
inner ['ɪnəʳ] adj interno(-a), interiore;
inner-city n centro di una zona
urbana
inning ['ɪnɪŋ] n (US: Baseball) ripresa;
~s (Cricket) turno di battuta
innocence ['ɪnəsns] n innocenza
innocent ['ɪnəsnt] adj innocente
innovation [ɪnəʊ'veɪʃən] n
innovazione f
innovative ['ɪnəʊveɪtɪv] adj
innovativo(-a)
in-patient ['ɪnpeɪʃənt] n
ricoverato(-a)
input ['ɪnput] n input m
inquest ['ɪnkwɛst] n inchiesta
inquire [ɪn'kwaɪəʳ] vi informarsi
▷ vt domandare, informarsi su;
inquiry n domanda; (Law) indagine
f, investigazione f; **"inquiries"**
"informazioni"
ins. abbr = **inches**
insane [ɪn'seɪn] adj matto(-a),
pazzo(-a); (Med) alienato(-a)
insanity [ɪn'sænɪtɪ] n follia; (Med)
alienazione f mentale
insect ['ɪnsɛkt] n insetto; **insect
repellent** n insettifugo
insecure [ɪnsɪ'kjuəʳ] adj
malsicuro(-a); (person) insicuro(-a)
insecurity [ɪnsɪ'kjuərɪtɪ] n
mancanza di sicurezza
insensitive [ɪn'sɛnsɪtɪv] adj
insensibile
insert [ɪn'sə:t] vt inserire, introdurre
inside ['ɪn'saɪd] n interno, parte f
interiore ▷ adj interno(-a), interiore
▷ adv dentro, all'interno ▷ prep
dentro, all'interno di; (of time): **~ 10**

minutes entro 10 minuti; **inside lane**
n (Aut) corsia di marcia; **inside out**
adv (turn) a rovescio; (know) a fondo
insight ['ɪnsaɪt] n acume m,
perspicacia; (glimpse, idea) percezione f
insignificant [ɪnsɪg'nɪfɪknt] adj
insignificante
insincere [ɪnsɪn'sɪəʳ] adj insincero(-a)
insist [ɪn'sɪst] vi insistere; **to ~
on doing** insistere per fare; **to ~
that** insistere perché + sub; (claim)
sostenere che; **insistent** adj
insistente
insomnia [ɪn'sɔmnɪə] n insonnia
inspect [ɪn'spɛkt] vt ispezionare;
(BRIT: ticket) controllare; **inspection**
[ɪn'spɛkʃən] n ispezione f; controllo;
inspector n ispettore(-trice); (BRIT:
on buses, trains) controllore m
inspiration [ɪnspə'reɪʃən] n
ispirazione f; **inspire** [ɪn'spaɪəʳ] vt
ispirare; **inspiring** adj stimolante
instability [ɪnstə'bɪlɪtɪ] n instabilità
install [ɪn'stɔ:l] (US **instal**) vt
installare; **installation** [ɪnstə'leɪʃən]
n installazione f
instalment [ɪn'stɔ:lmənt] (US
installment) n rata; (of TV serial etc)
puntata; **in ~s** (pay) a rate; (receive)
una parte per volta; (: publication) a
fascicoli
instance ['ɪnstəns] n esempio, caso;
for ~ per or ad esempio; **in the first ~**
in primo luogo
instant ['ɪnstənt] n istante m,
attimo ▷ adj immediato(-a); urgente;
(coffee, food) in polvere; **instantly**
adv immediatamente, subito;
instant messaging n messaggistica
immediata
instead [ɪn'stɛd] adv invece; **~ of**
invece di
instinct ['ɪnstɪŋkt] n istinto;
instinctive adj istintivo(-a)
institute ['ɪnstɪtjuːt] n istituto ▷ vt
istituire, stabilire; (inquiry) avviare;
(proceedings) iniziare

institution [ɪnstɪˈtjuːʃən] n
istituzione f; (*educational institution,
mental institution*) istituto
instruct [ɪnˈstrʌkt] vt **to ~ sb in
sth** insegnare qc a qn; **to ~ sb to do**
dare ordini a qn di fare; **instruction**
[ɪnˈstrʌkʃən] n istruzione f;
instructions (for use) istruzioni per
l'uso; **instructor** n istruttore(-trice);
(*for skiing*) maestro(-a)
instrument [ˈɪnstrəmənt] n
strumento; **instrumental** [-ˈmɛntl]
adj (*Mus*) strumentale; **to be
instrumental in** essere d'aiuto in
insufficient [ɪnsəˈfɪʃənt] adj
insufficiente
insulate [ˈɪnsjuleɪt] vt isolare;
insulation [-ˈleɪʃən] n isolamento
insulin [ˈɪnsjulɪn] n insulina
insult [n ˈɪnsʌlt, vb ɪnˈsʌlt] n insulto,
affronto ▷ vt insultare; **insulting** adj
offensivo(-a), ingiurioso(-a)
insurance [ɪnˈʃuərəns] n
assicurazione f; **fire/life ~**
assicurazione contro gli incendi/sulla
vita; **insurance company** n società
di assicurazioni; **insurance policy** n
polizza d'assicurazione
insure [ɪnˈʃuəʳ] vt assicurare
intact [ɪnˈtækt] adj intatto(-a)
intake [ˈɪnteɪk] n (*Tech*) immissione f;
(*of food*) consumo; (BRIT: *of pupils etc*)
afflusso
integral [ˈɪntɪɡrəl] adj integrale;
(*part*) integrante
integrate [ˈɪntɪɡreɪt] vt integrare ▷ vi
integrarsi
integrity [ɪnˈtɛɡrɪtɪ] n integrità
intellect [ˈɪntəlɛkt] n intelletto;
intellectual [-ˈlɛktjuəl] adj, n
intellettuale m/f
intelligence [ɪnˈtɛlɪdʒəns] n
intelligenza; (*Mil etc*) informazioni fpl
intelligent [ɪnˈtɛlɪdʒənt] adj
intelligente
intend [ɪnˈtɛnd] vt (*gift etc*): **to ~ sth
for** destinare qc a; **to ~ to do** aver

l'intenzione di fare
intense [ɪnˈtɛns] adj intenso(-a);
(*person*) di forti sentimenti
intensify [ɪnˈtɛnsɪfaɪ] vt intensificare
intensity [ɪnˈtɛnsɪtɪ] n intensità
intensive [ɪnˈtɛnsɪv] adj
intensivo(-a); **intensive care** n
terapia intensiva; **intensive care unit
(ICU)** n reparto terapia intensiva
intent [ɪnˈtɛnt] n intenzione f ▷ adj
~ (on) intento(-a) (a), immerso(-a)
(in); **to all ~s and purposes** a tutti gli
effetti; **to be ~ on doing sth** essere
deciso a fare qc
intention [ɪnˈtɛnʃən] n intenzione
f; **intentional** adj intenzionale,
deliberato(-a)
interact [ɪntərˈækt] vi interagire;
interaction [ɪntərˈækʃən] n azione f
reciproca, interazione f; **interactive**
adj (*Comput*) interattivo(-a)
intercept [ɪntəˈsɛpt] vt intercettare;
(*person*) fermare
interchange [ˈɪntətʃeɪndʒ] n
(*exchange*) scambio; (*on motorway*)
incrocio pluridirezionale
intercourse [ˈɪntəkɔːs] n rapporti mpl
interest [ˈɪntrɪst] n interesse m;
(*Comm: stake, share*) interessi mpl
▷ vt interessare; **interested** adj
interessato(-a); **to be interested
in** interessarsi di; **interesting** adj
interessante; **interest rate** n tasso
di interesse
interface [ˈɪntəfeɪs] n (*Comput*)
interfaccia
interfere [ɪntəˈfɪəʳ] vi **to ~ in** (*quarrel,
other people's business*) immischiarsi
in; **to ~ with** (*object*) toccare; (*plans,
duty*) interferire con; **interference**
[ɪntəˈfɪərəns] n interferenza
interim [ˈɪntərɪm] adj provvisorio(-a)
▷ n **in the ~** nel frattempo
interior [ɪnˈtɪərɪəʳ] n interno; (*of
country*) entroterra ▷ adj interno(-a);
(*minister*) degli Interni; **interior
design** n architettura d'interni

intermediate [ɪntə'miːdɪət] *adj*
intermedio(-a)

intermission [ɪntə'mɪʃən] *n* pausa;
(*Theatre, Cinema*) intermissione *f*,
intervallo

intern [*vb* ɪn'təːn, *n* 'ɪntəːn] *vt*
internare ▷ *n* (*us*) medico interno

internal [ɪn'təːnl] *adj* interno(-a);
Internal Revenue Service (*us*) *n*
Fisco

international [ɪntə'næʃənl] *adj*
internazionale ▷ *n* (*BRIT*: *Sport*)
incontro internazionale

Internet ['ɪntənɛt] *n*: **the ~** Internet
f; **Internet café** *n* cybercaffè *m*
inv; **Internet Service Provider** *n*
Provider *m inv*; **Internet user** *n*
utente *m/f* Internet

interpret [ɪn'təːprɪt] *vt* interpretare
▷ *vi* fare da interprete; **interpretation**
[ɪntəːprɪ'teɪʃən] *n* interpretazione *f*;
interpreter *n* interprete *m/f*; **could
you act as an interpreter for us?** ci
potrebbe fare da interprete?

interrogate [ɪn'tɛrəugeɪt] *vt*
interrogare; **interrogation** [-'geɪʃən]
n interrogazione *f*; (*of suspect etc*)
interrogatorio

interrogative [ɪntə'rɔgətɪv]
adj interrogativo(-a) ▷ *n* (*Ling*)
interrogativo

interrupt [ɪntə'rʌpt] *vt, vi*
interrompere; **interruption** [-'rʌpʃən]
n interruzione *f*

intersection [ɪntə'sɛkʃən] *n*
intersezione *f*; (*of roads*) incrocio

interstate ['ɪntəsteɪt] (*us*) *n* fra stati

interval ['ɪntəvl] *n* intervallo; **at ~s**
a intervalli

intervene [ɪntə'viːn] *vi* (*time*)
intercorrere; (*event, person*) intervenire

interview ['ɪntəvjuː] *n* (*Radio, TV
etc*) intervista; (*for job*) colloquio ▷ *vt*
intervistare; avere un colloquio con;
interviewer *n* intervistatore(-trice)

intimate [*adj* 'ɪntɪmət, *vb* 'ɪntɪmeɪt]
adj intimo(-a); (*knowledge*)

profondo(-a) ▷ *vt* lasciar capire

intimidate [ɪn'tɪmɪdeɪt] *vt*
intimidire, intimorire

intimidating [ɪn'tɪmɪdeɪtɪŋ] *adj*
(*sight*) spaventoso(-a); (*appearance,
figure*) minaccioso(-a)

into ['ɪntu] *prep* dentro, in; **come ~
the house** entra in casa; **he worked
late ~ the night** lavorò fino a tarda
notte; **~ Italian** in italiano

intolerant [ɪn'tɔlərnt] *adj* **~ of**
intollerante di

intranet ['ɪntrənɛt] *n* intranet *f*

intransitive [ɪn'trænsɪtɪv] *adj*
intransitivo(-a)

intricate ['ɪntrɪkət] *adj* intricato(-a),
complicato(-a)

intrigue [ɪn'triːg] *n* intrigo ▷ *vt*
affascinare; **intriguing** *adj*
affascinante

introduce [ɪntrə'djuːs] *vt* introdurre;
to ~ sb (to sb) presentare qn (a qn); **to
~ sb to** (*pastime, technique*) iniziare qn
a; **introduction** [-'dʌkʃən]
n introduzione *f*; (*of person*)
presentazione *f*; (*to new experience*)
iniziazione *f*; **introductory** *adj*
introduttivo(-a)

intrude [ɪn'truːd] *vi* (*person*): **to ~
(on)** intromettersi (in); **intruder** *n*
intruso(-a)

intuition [ɪntjuː'ɪʃən] *n* intuizione *f*

inundate ['ɪnʌndeɪt] *vt* **to ~ with**
inondare di

invade [ɪn'veɪd] *vt* invadere

invalid [*n* 'ɪnvəlɪd, *adj* ɪn'vælɪd]
n malato(-a); (*with disability*)
invalido(-a) ▷ *adj* (*not valid*)
invalido(-a), non valido(-a)

invaluable [ɪn'væljuəbl] *adj*
prezioso(-a); inestimabile

invariably [ɪn'vɛərɪəblɪ] *adv*
invariabilmente; sempre

invasion [ɪn'veɪʒən] *n* invasione *f*

invent [ɪn'vɛnt] *vt* inventare;
invention [ɪn'vɛnʃən] *n* invenzione *f*;
inventor *n* inventore *m*

inventory ['ɪnvəntrɪ] n inventario
inverted commas [ɪn'vəːtɪd-] (BRIT)
npl virgolette fpl
invest [ɪn'vɛst] vt investire ▷ vi **to ~**
(in) investire (in)
investigate [ɪn'vɛstɪgeɪt] vt
investigare, indagare; (crime) fare
indagini su; **investigation** [-'geɪʃən] n
investigazione f; (of crime) indagine f
investigator [ɪn'vɛstɪgeɪtə'] n
investigatore(-trice); **a private ~** un
investigatore privato, un detective
investment [ɪn'vɛstmənt] n
investimento
investor [ɪn'vɛstə'] n
investitore(-trice); azionista m/f
invisible [ɪn'vɪzɪbl] adj invisibile
invitation [ɪnvɪ'teɪʃən] n invito
invite [ɪn'vaɪt] vt invitare; (opinions
etc) sollecitare; **inviting** adj invitante,
attraente
invoice ['ɪnvɔɪs] n fattura ▷ vt
fatturare
involve [ɪn'vɒlv] vt (entail) richiedere,
comportare; (associate): **to ~ sb**
(in) implicare qn (in); coinvolgere
qn (in); **involved** adj involuto(-a),
complesso(-a); **to be involved in**
essere coinvolto(-a) in; **involvement**
n implicazione f; coinvolgimento
inward ['ɪnwəd] adj (movement) verso
l'interno; (thought, feeling) interiore,
intimo(-a); **inward(s)** adv verso
l'interno
iPod® ['aɪpɒd] n iPod® m inv lettore
m MP3
IQ n abbr (= intelligence quotient)
quoziente m d'intelligenza
IRA n abbr (= Irish Republican Army) IRA f
Iran [ɪ'rɑːn] n Iran m; **Iranian**
[ɪ'reɪnɪən] adj, n iraniano(-a)
Iraq [ɪ'rɑːk] n Iraq m; **Iraqi** adj, n
iracheno(-a)
Ireland ['aɪələnd] n Irlanda
iris ['aɪrɪs] (pl **irises**) n iride f; (Bot)
giaggiolo, iride
Irish ['aɪrɪʃ] adj irlandese ▷ npl **the**

~ gli Irlandesi; **Irishman** (irreg) n
irlandese m; **Irish Sea** n Mar m
d'Irlanda; **Irishwoman** (irreg) n
irlandese f
iron ['aɪən] n ferro; (for clothes) ferro da
stiro ▷ adj di or in ferro ▷ vt (clothes)
stirare
ironic(al) [aɪ'rɒnɪk(l)] adj ironico(-a);
ironically adv ironicamente
ironing ['aɪənɪŋ] n (act) stirare m;
(clothes) roba da stirare; **ironing**
board n asse f da stiro
irony ['aɪrənɪ] n ironia
irrational [ɪ'ræʃənl] adj irrazionale
irregular [ɪ'regjulə'] adj irregolare
irrelevant [ɪ'rɛləvənt] adj non
pertinente
irresistible [ɪrɪ'zɪstɪbl] adj irresistibile
irresponsible [ɪrɪ'spɒnsɪbl] adj
irresponsabile
irrigation [ɪrɪ'geɪʃən] n irrigazione f
irritable ['ɪrɪtəbl] adj irritabile
irritate ['ɪrɪteɪt] vt irritare; **irritating**
adj (person, sound etc) irritante;
irritation [-'teɪʃən] n irritazione f
IRS (US) n abbr = **Internal Revenue**
Service
is [ɪz] vb see **be**
ISDN n abbr (= Integrated Services Digital
Network) I.S.D.N. f
Islam ['ɪzlɑːm] n Islam m; **Islamic**
[ɪz'læmɪk] adj islamico(-a)
island ['aɪlənd] n isola; **islander** n
isolano(-a)
isle [aɪl] n isola
isn't ['ɪznt] = **is not**
isolated ['aɪsəleɪtɪd] adj isolato(-a)
isolation [aɪsə'leɪʃən] n isolamento
ISP n abbr (= Internet Service Provider)
provider m inv
Israel ['ɪzreɪl] n Israele m; **Israeli**
[ɪz'reɪlɪ] adj, n israeliano(-a)
issue ['ɪʃjuː] n questione f, problema
m; (of banknotes etc) emissione f; (of
newspaper etc) numero ▷ vt (statement)
rilasciare; (rations, equipment)
distribuire; (book) pubblicare;

(banknotes, cheques, stamps) emettere;
at ~ in gioco, in discussione; **to
take ~ with sb (over sth)** prendere
posizione contro qn (riguardo a qc);
to make an ~ of sth fare un problema
di qc

 KEYWORD

it [ɪt] pron 1 (specific: subject) esso(-a);
(: direct object) lo (la), l'; (: indirect object)
gli (le); **where's my book? — it's
on the table** dov'è il mio libro? — è
sulla tavola; **I can't find it** non lo (or
la) trovo; **give it to me** dammelo (or
dammela); **about/from/of it** ne;
I spoke to him about it gliene ho
parlato; **what did you learn from it?**
quale insegnamento ne hai tratto?;
I'm proud of it ne sono fiero; **did you
go to it?** ci sei andato?; **put the book
in it** mettici il libro
2 (impers): **it's raining** piove; **it's
Friday tomorrow** domani è venerdì;
it's 6 o'clock sono le 6; **who is it?
— it's me** chi è? — sono io

IT n abbr see **information technology**
Italian [ɪˈtæljən] adj italiano(-a) ▷ n
italiano(-a); (Ling) italiano; **the ~s** gli
Italiani; **what's the ~ (word) for ...?**
come si dice in italiano ...?
italics [ɪˈtælɪks] npl corsivo
Italy [ˈɪtəlɪ] n Italia
ITC n (BRIT: = Independent Television
Commission) organo di controllo delle reti
televisive
itch [ɪtʃ] n prurito ▷ vi (person) avere
il prurito; (part of body) prudere; **to ~
to do sth** aver una gran voglia di fare
qc; **itchy** adj che prude; **to be itchy**
= **to itch**
it'd [ˈɪtd] = **it would**; **it had**
item [ˈaɪtəm] n articolo; (on agenda)
punto; (also: **news ~**) notizia
itinerary [aɪˈtɪnərərɪ] n itinerario
it'll [ˈɪtl] = **it will**; **it shall**

its [ɪts] adj il (la) suo(-a), i (le) suoi (sue)
it's [ɪts] = **it is**; **it has**
itself [ɪtˈsɛlf] pron (emphatic) esso(-a)
stesso(-a); (reflexive) si
ITV (BRIT) n abbr (= Independent
Television) rete televisiva in concorrenza
con la BBC
I've [aɪv] = **I have**
ivory [ˈaɪvərɪ] n avorio
ivy [ˈaɪvɪ] n edera

j

jab [dʒæb] vt dare colpetti a ▷ n (Med: inf) puntura; **to ~ sth into** affondare or piantare qc dentro

jack [dʒæk] n (Aut) cricco; (Cards) fante m

jacket ['dʒækɪt] n giacca; (of book) copertura; **jacket potato** n patata cotta al forno con la buccia

jackpot ['dʒækpɔt] n primo premio (in denaro)

Jacuzzi® [dʒə'ku:zɪ] n vasca per idromassaggio Jacuzzi®

jagged ['dʒægɪd] adj seghettato(-a); (cliffs etc) frastagliato(-a)

jail [dʒeɪl] n prigione f ▷ vt mandare in prigione; **jail sentence** n condanna al carcere

jam [dʒæm] n marmellata; (also: **traffic ~**) ingorgo; (inf) pasticcio ▷ vt (passage etc) ingombrare, ostacolare; (mechanism, drawer etc) bloccare; (Radio) disturbare con interferenze ▷ vi incepparsi; **to ~ sth into** forzare qc dentro; infilare qc a forza dentro

Jamaica [dʒə'meɪkə] n Giamaica

jammed [dʒæmd] adj (door) bloccato(-a); (rifle, printer) inceppato(-a)

Jan. abbr (= January) gen., genn.

janitor ['dʒænɪtər] n (caretaker) portiere m; (: Scol) bidello

January ['dʒænjuərɪ] n gennaio

Japan [dʒə'pæn] n Giappone m; **Japanese** [dʒæpə'ni:z] adj giapponese ▷ n inv giapponese m/f; (Ling) giapponese m

jar [dʒɑ:ʳ] n (glass) barattolo, vasetto ▷ vi (sound) stridere; (colours etc) stonare

jargon ['dʒɑ:gən] n gergo

javelin ['dʒævlɪn] n giavellotto

jaw [dʒɔ:] n mascella

jazz [dʒæz] n jazz m

jealous ['dʒɛləs] adj geloso(-a); **jealousy** n gelosia

jeans [dʒi:nz] npl (blue-)jeans mpl

Jello® ['dʒɛləʊ] (us) n gelatina di frutta

jelly ['dʒɛlɪ] n gelatina; **jellyfish** n medusa

jeopardize ['dʒɛpədaɪz] vt mettere in pericolo

jerk [dʒə:k] n sobbalzo, scossa; sussulto; (inf: idiot) tonto(-a) ▷ vt dare una scossa a ▷ vi (vehicles) sobbalzare

Jersey ['dʒə:zɪ] n Jersey m

jersey ['dʒə:zɪ] n maglia; (fabric) jersey m

Jesus ['dʒi:zəs] n Gesù m

jet [dʒɛt] n (of gas, liquid) getto; (Aviat) aviogetto; **jet lag** n (problemi mpl dovuti allo) sbalzo dei fusi orari; **jet-ski** vi acquascooter m inv

jetty ['dʒɛtɪ] n molo

Jew [dʒu:] n ebreo

jewel ['dʒu:əl] n gioiello; **jeweller** (us **jeweler**) n orefice m, gioielliere(-a); **jeweller's (shop)** (us **jewelry store**) n oreficeria, gioielleria; **jewellery** (us **jewelry**) n gioielli mpl

Jewish ['dʒu:ɪʃ] adj ebreo(-a),

ebraico(-a)
jigsaw ['dʒɪgsɔː] n (also: **~ puzzle**)
puzzle m inv
job [dʒɔb] n lavoro; (employment)
impiego, posto; **it's not my ~**
(duty) non è compito mio; **it's a
good ~ that …** meno male che …;
just the ~! proprio quello che ci
vuole; **job centre** (BRIT) n ufficio di
collocamento; **jobless** adj senza
lavoro, disoccupato(-a)
jockey ['dʒɔkɪ] n fantino, jockey m inv
▷ vi **to ~ for position** manovrare per
una posizione di vantaggio
jog [dʒɔg] vt urtare ▷ vi (Sport) fare
footing, fare jogging; **to ~ sb's
memory** rinfrescare la memoria a qn;
to ~ along trottare; (fig) andare avanti
piano piano; **jogging** n footing m,
jogging m
join [dʒɔɪn] vt unire, congiungere;
(become member of) iscriversi a; (meet)
raggiungere; riunirsi a ▷ vi (roads,
rivers) confluire ▷ n giuntura; **join in**
vi partecipare ▷ vt fus unirsi a; **join up**
vi incontrarsi; (Mil) arruolarsi
joiner ['dʒɔɪnəʳ] (BRIT) n falegname m
joint [dʒɔɪnt] n (Tech) giuntura;
giunto; (Anat) articolazione f,
giuntura; (BRIT Culin) arrosto; (inf:
place) locale m; (: of cannabis) spinello
▷ adj comune; **joint account** n (at
bank etc) conto in partecipazione,
conto comune; **jointly** adv in
comune, insieme
joke [dʒəuk] n scherzo; (funny story)
barzelletta; (also: **practical ~**) beffa
▷ vi scherzare; **to play a ~ on sb** fare
uno scherzo a qn; **joker** n (Cards)
matta, jolly m inv
jolly ['dʒɔlɪ] adj allegro(-a), gioioso(-a)
▷ adv (BRIT: inf) veramente, proprio
jolt [dʒəult] n scossa, sobbalzo ▷ vt
urtare
Jordan ['dʒɔːdən] n (country)
Giordania; (river) Giordano
journal ['dʒəːnl] n giornale m; rivista;

diario; **journalism** n giornalismo;
journalist n giornalista m/f
journey ['dʒəːnɪ] n viaggio; (distance
covered) tragitto; **how was your ~?**
com'è andato il viaggio?; **the ~ takes
two hours** il viaggio dura due ore
joy [dʒɔɪ] n gioia; **joyrider** n chi ruba
un'auto per farvi un giro; **joy stick** n
(Aviat) barra di comando; (Comput)
joystick m inv
Jr abbr = **junior**
judge [dʒʌdʒ] n giudice m/f ▷ vt
giudicare
judo ['dʒuːdəu] n judo
jug [dʒʌg] n brocca, bricco
juggle ['dʒʌgl] vi fare giochi di
destrezza; **juggler** n giocoliere(-a)
juice [dʒuːs] n succo; **juicy** ['dʒuːsɪ]
adj succoso(-a)
Jul. abbr (= July) lug., lu.
July [dʒuː'laɪ] n luglio
jumble ['dʒʌmbl] n miscuglio ▷ vt
(also: **~ up**) mischiare; **jumble sale**
(BRIT) n vendita di beneficenza

● **JUMBLE SALE**
●
● Una **jumble sale** è un mercatino
● di oggetti di seconda mano
● organizzato in chiese, scuole o
● in circoli ricreativi, i cui proventi
● vengono devoluti in beneficenza.

jumbo ['dʒʌmbəu] adj ~ **jet** jumbo-jet
m inv; ~ **size** formato gigante
jump [dʒʌmp] vi saltare, balzare;
(start) sobbalzare; (increase) rincarare
▷ vt saltare ▷ n salto, balzo; sobbalzo
jumper ['dʒʌmpəʳ] n (BRIT: pullover)
maglione m, pullover m inv; (US: dress)
scamiciato
jumper cables (US) npl = **jump leads**
jump leads (BRIT) npl cavi mpl per
batteria
Jun. abbr = **junior**
junction ['dʒʌŋkʃən] n (BRIT: of roads)
incrocio; (of rails) nodo ferroviario

June [dʒuːn] *n* giugno

jungle ['dʒʌŋgl] *n* giungla

junior ['dʒuːnɪəʳ] *adj, n* **he's ~ to me by 2 years, he's my ~ by 2 years** è più giovane di me (di 2 anni); **he's ~ to me** (*seniority*) è al di sotto di me, ho più anzianità di lui; **junior high school** (US) *n* scuola media (*da 12 a 15 anni*); **junior school** (BRIT) *n* scuola elementare (*da 8 a 11 anni*)

junk [dʒʌŋk] *n* cianfrusaglie *fpl*; (*cheap goods*) robaccia; **junk food** *n* porcherie *fpl*

junkie ['dʒʌŋkɪ] (*inf*) *n* drogato(-a)

junk mail *n* stampe *fpl* pubblicitarie

Jupiter ['dʒuːpɪtəʳ] *n* (*planet*) Giove *m*

jurisdiction [dʒuərɪs'dɪkʃən] *n* giurisdizione *f*; **it falls** *or* **comes within/outside our ~** è/non è di nostra competenza

jury ['dʒuərɪ] *n* giuria

just [dʒʌst] *adj* giusto(-a) ▷ *adv* **he's ~ done it/left** lo ha appena fatto/è appena partito; **~ right** proprio giusto; **~ 2 o'clock** le 2 precise; **she's ~ as clever as you** è in gamba proprio quanto te; **it's ~ as well that ...** meno male che ...; **~ as I arrived** proprio mentre arrivavo; **it was ~ before/enough/here** era poco prima/appena assai/proprio qui; **it's ~ me** sono solo io; **~ missed/caught** appena perso/preso; **~ listen to this!** senta un po' questo!

justice ['dʒʌstɪs] *n* giustizia

justification [dʒʌstɪfɪ'keɪʃən] *n* giustificazione *f*; (*Typ*) giustezza

justify ['dʒʌstɪfaɪ] *vt* giustificare

jut [dʒʌt] *vi* (*also:* **~ out**) sporgersi

juvenile ['dʒuːvənaɪl] *adj* giovane, giovanile; (*court*) dei minorenni; (*books*) per ragazzi ▷ *n* giovane *m/f*, minorenne *m/f*

K

K *abbr* (= *one thousand*) mille; (= *kilobyte*) K

kangaroo [kæŋgə'ruː] *n* canguro

karaoke [kɑːrə'əukɪ] *n* karaoke *m inv*

karate [kə'rɑːtɪ] *n* karatè *m*

kebab [kə'bæb] *n* spiedino

keel [kiːl] *n* chiglia; **on an even ~** (*fig*) in uno stato normale

keen [kiːn] *adj* (*interest, desire*) vivo(-a); (*eye, intelligence*) acuto(-a); (*competition*) serrato(-a); (*edge*) affilato(-a); (*eager*) entusiasta; **to be ~ to do** *or* **on doing sth** avere una gran voglia di fare qc; **to be ~ on sth** essere appassionato(-a) di qc; **to be ~ on sb** avere un debole per qn

keep [kiːp] (*pt, pp* **kept**) *vt* tenere; (*hold back*) trattenere; (*feed: one's family etc*) mantenere, sostentare; (*a promise*) mantenere; (*chickens, bees, pigs etc*) allevare ▷ *vi* (*food*) mantenersi; (*remain: in a certain state or place*) restare ▷ *n* (*of castle*) maschio; (*food etc*): **enough for his ~** abbastanza per vitto e alloggio; (inf): **for ~s** per sempre; **to ~ doing sth** continuare a fare qc; fare qc di continuo; **to ~ sb from doing** impedire a qn di fare; **to ~ sb busy/a place away** tenere qn occupato(-a)/un luogo in ordine; **to ~ sth to o.s.** tenere qc per sé; **to ~ sth (back) from sb** celare qc a qn; **to ~ time** (clock) andar bene; **keep away** vt **to keep sth/sb away from sb** tenere qc/qn lontano da qn ▷ vi **to keep away (from)** stare lontano (da); **keep back** vt (crowds, tears, money) trattenere ▷ vi tenersi indietro; **keep off** vt (dog, person) tenere lontano da ▷ vi stare alla larga; **keep your hands off!** non toccare!, giù le mani!; **"keep off the grass"** "non calpestare l'erba"; **keep on** vi **to keep on doing** continuare a fare; **to keep on (about sth)** continuare a insistere (su qc); **keep out** vt tener fuori; **"keep out"** "vietato l'accesso"; **keep up** vt continuare, mantenere ▷ vi **to keep up with** tener dietro a, andare di pari passo con; (work etc) farcela a seguire; **keeper** n custode m/f, guardiano(-a); **keeping** n (care) custodia; **in keeping with** in armonia con; in accordo con

kennel ['kɛnl] n canile m; **kennels** npl canile m; **to put a dog in ~s** mettere un cane al canile

Kenya ['kɛnjə] n Kenia m

kept [kɛpt] pt, pp of **keep**

kerb [kə:b] (BRIT) n orlo del marciapiede

kerosene ['kɛrəsi:n] n cherosene m

ketchup ['kɛtʃəp] n ketchup m inv

kettle ['kɛtl] n bollitore m

key [ki:] n (gen, Mus) chiave f; (of piano, typewriter) tasto ▷ adj chiave inv ▷ vt (also: **~ in**) digitare; **can I have my ~?** posso avere la mia chiave?; **keyboard** n tastiera; **keyhole** n buco della serratura; **keyring** n portachiavi m inv

kg abbr (= kilogram) Kg

khaki ['kɑ:kɪ] adj cachi ▷ n cachi m

kick [kɪk] vt calciare, dare calci a; (inf: habit etc) liberarsi di ▷ vi (horse) tirar calci ▷ n calcio; (thrill): **he does it for ~s** lo fa giusto per il piacere di farlo; **kick off** vi (Sport) dare il primo calcio; **kick-off** n (Sport) calcio d'inizio

kid [kɪd] n (inf: child) ragazzino(-a); (animal, leather) capretto ▷ vi (inf) scherzare

kidnap ['kɪdnæp] vt rapire, sequestrare; **kidnapping** n sequestro (di persona)

kidney ['kɪdnɪ] n (Anat) rene m; (Culin) rognone m; **kidney bean** n fagiolo borlotto

kill [kɪl] vt uccidere, ammazzare ▷ n uccisione f; **killer** n uccisore m, killer m inv; assassino(-a); **killing** n assassinio; **to make a killing** (inf) fare un bel colpo

kiln [kɪln] n forno

kilo ['ki:ləu] n chilo; **kilobyte** n (Comput) kilobyte m inv; **kilogram(me)** ['kɪləugræm] n chilogrammo; **kilometre** ['kɪləmi:tər] (US **kilometer**) n chilometro; **kilowatt** ['kɪləuwɔt] n chilowatt m inv

kilt [kɪlt] n gonnellino scozzese

kin [kɪn] n see **next**; **kith**

kind [kaɪnd] adj gentile, buono(-a) ▷ n sorta, specie f; (species) genere m; **what ~ of ...?** che tipo di ...?; **to be two of a ~** essere molto simili; **in ~** (Comm) in natura

kindergarten ['kɪndəgɑ:tn] n giardino d'infanzia

kindly ['kaɪndlɪ] adj pieno(-a) di bontà, benevolo(-a) ▷ adv con bontà, gentilmente; **will you ~ ...** vuole ... per favore

kindness ['kaɪndnɪs] n bontà, gentilezza

king [kɪŋ] n re m inv; **kingdom** n regno, reame m; **kingfisher** n martin m inv pescatore; **king-size(d) bed** n letto king-size

kiosk ['ki:ɔsk] n edicola, chiosco; (BRIT Tel) cabina (telefonica)

kipper ['kɪpəʳ] n aringa affumicata

kiss [kɪs] n bacio ▷ vt baciare; **to ~ (each other)** baciarsi; **kiss of life** n respirazione f bocca a bocca

kit [kɪt] n equipaggiamento, corredo; (set of tools etc) attrezzi mpl; (for assembly) scatola di montaggio

kitchen ['kɪtʃɪn] n cucina

kite [kaɪt] n (toy) aquilone m

kitten ['kɪtn] n gattino(-a), micino(-a)

kiwi ['ki:wi:] n (also: ~ **fruit**) kiwi m inv

km abbr (= kilometre) km

km/h abbr (= kilometres per hour) km/h

knack [næk] n: **to have the ~ of** avere l'abilità di

knee [ni:] n ginocchio; **kneecap** n rotula

kneel [ni:l] (pt, pp knelt) vi (also: ~ **down**) inginocchiarsi

knelt [nɛlt] pt, pp of **kneel**

knew [nju:] pt of **know**

knickers ['nɪkəz] (BRIT) npl mutandine fpl

knife [naɪf] (pl knives) n coltello ▷ vt accoltellare, dare una coltellata a

knight [naɪt] n cavaliere m; (Chess) cavallo

knit [nɪt] vt fare a maglia ▷ vi lavorare a maglia; (broken bones) saldarsi; **to ~ one's brows** aggrottare le sopracciglia; **knitting** n lavoro a maglia; **knitting needle** n ferro (da calza); **knitwear** n maglieria

knives [naɪvz] npl of **knife**

knob [nɔb] n bottone m; manopola

knock [nɔk] vt colpire; urtare; (fig: inf) criticare ▷ vi (at door etc): **to ~ at/on** bussare a ▷ n bussata; colpo, botta; **knock down** vt abbattere; **knock off** vi (inf: finish) smettere (di lavorare) ▷ vt (from price) far abbassare; (inf: steal) sgraffignare; **knock out** vt stendere; (Boxing) mettere K.O.; (defeat) battere; **knock over** vt

(person) investire; (object) far cadere; **knockout** n (Boxing) knock out m inv ▷ cpd a eliminazione

knot [nɔt] n nodo ▷ vt annodare

know [nəu] (pt knew, pp known) vt sapere; (person, author, place) conoscere; **I don't ~** non lo so; **do you ~ where I can ...?** sa dove posso ...?; **to ~ how to do** sapere fare; **to ~ about** or **of sth/sb** conoscere qc/qn; **know-all** n sapientone(-a); **know-how** n tecnica; pratica; **knowing** adj (look etc) d'intesa; **knowingly** adv (purposely) consapevolmente; (smile, look) con aria d'intesa; **know-it-all** (US) n = **know-all**

knowledge ['nɔlɪdʒ] n consapevolezza; (learning) conoscenza, sapere m; **knowledgeable** adj ben informato(-a)

known [nəun] pp of **know**

knuckle ['nʌkl] n nocca

koala [kəu'ɑ:lə] n (also: ~ **bear**) koala m inv

Koran [kɔ'rɑ:n] n Corano

Korea [kə'rɪə] n Corea; **Korean** adj, n coreano(-a)

kosher ['kəuʃəʳ] adj kasher inv

Kosovar, Kosovan ['kɔsəvaʳ, 'kɔsəvən] adj kosovaro(-a)

Kosovo ['kusəvəu] n Kosovo

Kremlin ['krɛmlɪn] n **the ~** il Cremlino

Kuwait [ku'weɪt] n Kuwait m

lavorare duro (a); **L~, the L~ party**
(BRIT) il partito laburista, i laburisti;
hard ~ lavori mpl forzati; **labourer**
n manovale m; **farm labourer**
lavoratore m agricolo

lace [leɪs] n merletto, pizzo; (of shoe
etc) laccio ▷ vt (shoe: also: ~ **up**)
allacciare

lack [læk] n mancanza ▷ vt mancare
di; **through** or **for ~ of** per mancanza
di; **to be ~ing** mancare; **to be ~ing in**
mancare di

lacquer ['lækə^r] n lacca

lacy ['leɪsɪ] adj (like lace) che sembra
un pizzo

lad [læd] n ragazzo, giovanotto

ladder ['lædə^r] n scala; (BRIT: in tights)
smagliatura

ladle ['leɪdl] n mestolo

lady ['leɪdɪ] n signora; dama; **L~
Smith** lady Smith; **the ladies' (room)**
i gabinetti per signore; **ladybird** (US
ladybug) n coccinella

lag [læg] n (of time) lasso, intervallo
▷ vi (also: ~ **behind**) trascinarsi ▷ vt
(pipes) rivestire di materiale isolante

lager ['lɑːgə^r] n lager m inv

lagoon [lə'guːn] n laguna

laid [leɪd] pt, pp of **lay**; **laid back** (inf)
adj rilassato(-a), tranquillo(-a)

lain [leɪn] pp of **lie**

lake [leɪk] n lago

lamb [læm] n agnello

lame [leɪm] adj zoppo(-a); (excuse etc)
zoppicante

lament [lə'mɛnt] n lamento ▷ vt
lamentare, piangere

lamp [læmp] n lampada; **lamppost**
['læmppəʊst] (BRIT) n lampione m;
lampshade ['læmpʃeɪd] n paralume
m

land [lænd] n (as opposed to sea) terra
(ferma); (country) paese m; (soil)
terreno; suolo; (estate) terreni mpl,
terre fpl ▷ vi (from ship) sbarcare;
(Aviat) atterrare; (fig: fall) cadere
▷ vt (passengers) sbarcare; (goods)

L (BRIT) abbr = **learner driver**

l. abbr (= litre) l

lab [læb] n abbr (= laboratory)
laboratorio

label ['leɪbl] n etichetta, cartellino;
(brand: of record) casa ▷ vt etichettare

labor etc ['leɪbə^r] (US) = **labour** etc

laboratory [lə'bɔrətərɪ] n laboratorio

Labor Day (US) n festa del lavoro

● **LABOR DAY**
●
● Negli Stati Uniti e nel Canada il
● **Labor Day**, la festa del lavoro,
● cade il primo lunedì di settembre,
● contrariamente a quanto accade
● nella maggior parte dei paesi
● europei dove tale celebrazione ha
● luogo il primo maggio.

labor union (US) n sindacato

labour ['leɪbə^r] (US **labor**) n (task)
lavoro; (workmen) manodopera; (Med):
to be in ~ avere le doglie ▷ vi **to ~ (at)**

scaricare; **to ~ sb with sth** affibbiare qc a qn; **landing** n atterraggio; (of staircase) pianerottolo; **landing card** n carta di sbarco; **landlady** n padrona or proprietaria di casa; **landlord** n padrone m or proprietario di casa; (of pub etc) padrone m; **landmark** n punto di riferimento; (fig) pietra miliare; **landowner** n proprietario(-a) terriero(-a); **landscape** n paesaggio; **landslide** n (Geo) frana; (fig: Pol) valanga

lane [leɪn] n stradina; (Aut, in race) corsia; **"get in ~"** "immettersi in corsia"

language ['læŋgwɪdʒ] n lingua; (way one speaks) linguaggio; **what ~s do you speak?** che lingue parla?; **bad ~** linguaggio volgare; **language laboratory** n laboratorio linguistico

lantern ['læntn] n lanterna

lap [læp] n (of track) giro; (of body): **in** or **on one's ~** in grembo ▷ vt (also: **~ up**) papparsi, leccare ▷ vi (waves) sciabordare

lapel [lə'pɛl] n risvolto

lapse [læps] n lapsus m inv; (longer) caduta ▷ vi (law) cadere; (membership, contract) scadere; **to ~ into bad habits** pigliare cattive abitudini; **~ of time** spazio di tempo

laptop (computer) ['læptɔp-] n laptop m inv

lard [lɑːd] n lardo

larder ['lɑːdər] n dispensa

large [lɑːdʒ] adj grande; (person, animal) grosso(-a); **at ~** (free) in libertà; (generally) in generale; nell'insieme; **largely** adv in gran parte; **large-scale** adj (map, drawing etc) in grande scala; (reforms, business activities) su vasta scala

lark [lɑːk] n (bird) allodola; (joke) scherzo, gioco

laryngitis [lærɪn'dʒaɪtɪs] n laringite f

lasagne [lə'zænjə] n lasagne fpl

laser ['leɪzər] n laser m; **laser printer** n stampante f laser inv

lash [læʃ] n frustata; (also: **eye~**) ciglio ▷ vt frustare; (tie): **to ~ to/together** legare a insieme; **lash out** vi: **to lash out (at** or **against sb)** attaccare violentemente (qn)

lass [læs] n ragazza

last [lɑːst] adj ultimo(-a); (week, month, year) scorso(-a), passato(-a) ▷ adv per ultimo ▷ vi durare; **~ week** la settimana scorsa; **~ night** ieri sera, la notte scorsa; **at ~** finalmente, alla fine; **~ but one** penultimo(-a); **lastly** adv infine, per finire; **last-minute** adj fatto(-a) (or preso(-a) etc) all'ultimo momento

latch [lætʃ] n chiavistello; **latch onto** vt fus (cling to: person) attaccarsi a, appiccicarsi a; (: idea) afferrare, capire

late [leɪt] adj (not on time) in ritardo; (far on in day etc) tardi inv; tardo(-a); (former) ex; (dead) defunto(-a) ▷ adv tardi; (behind time, schedule) in ritardo; **sorry I'm ~** scusi il ritardo; **the flight is two hours ~** il volo ha due ore di ritardo; **it's too ~** è troppo tardi; **of ~** di recente; **in the ~ afternoon** nel tardo pomeriggio; **in ~ May** verso la fine di maggio; **latecomer** n ritardatario(-a); **lately** adv recentemente; **later** ['leɪtər] adj (date etc) posteriore; (version etc) successivo(-a) ▷ adv più tardi; **later on** più avanti; **latest** ['leɪtɪst] adj ultimo(-a), più recente; **at the latest** al più tardi

lather ['lɑːðər] n schiuma di sapone ▷ vt insaponare

Latin ['lætɪn] n latino ▷ adj latino(-a); **Latin America** n America Latina; **Latin American** adj sudamericano(-a)

latitude ['lætɪtjuːd] n latitudine f; (fig) libertà d'azione

latter ['lætər] adj secondo(-a), più recente ▷ n **the ~** quest'ultimo, il secondo

laugh [lɑːf] *n* risata ▷ *vi* ridere; **laugh at** *vt fus* (*misfortune etc*) ridere di; **laughter** *n* riso; risate *fpl*

launch [lɔːntʃ] *n* (*of rocket, Comm*) lancio; (*of new ship*) varo; (*also*: **motor ~**) lancia ▷ *vt* (*rocket, Comm*) lanciare; (*ship, plan*) varare; **launch into** *vt fus* lanciarsi in

launder ['lɔːndər] *vt* lavare e stirare

Launderette® [lɔːn'drɛt] (*BRIT*) *n* lavanderia (automatica)

Laundromat® ['lɔːndrəmæt] (*US*) *n* lavanderia automatica

laundry ['lɔːndrɪ] *n* lavanderia; (*clothes*) biancheria; (: *dirty*) panni *mpl* da lavare

lava ['lɑːvə] *n* lava

lavatory ['lævətərɪ] *n* gabinetto

lavender ['lævəndər] *n* lavanda

lavish ['lævɪʃ] *adj* copioso(-a), abbondante; (*giving freely*): **~ with** prodigo(-a) di, largo(-a) in ▷ *vt* **to ~ sth on sb** colmare qn di qc

law [lɔː] *n* legge *f*; **civil/criminal ~** diritto civile/penale; **lawful** *adj* legale, lecito(-a); **lawless** *adj* che non conosce nessuna legge

lawn [lɔːn] *n* tappeto erboso; **lawnmower** *n* tosaerba *m or f inv*

lawsuit ['lɔːsuːt] *n* processo, causa

lawyer ['lɔːjər] *n* (*for sales, wills etc*) ≈ notaio; (*partner, in court*) ≈ avvocato(-essa)

lax [læks] *adj* rilassato(-a), negligente

laxative ['læksətɪv] *n* lassativo

lay [leɪ] (*pt, pp* **laid**) *pt of* **lie** ▷ *adj* laico(-a); (*not expert*) profano(-a) ▷ *vt* posare, mettere; (*eggs*) fare; (*trap*) tendere; (*plans*) fare, elaborare; **to ~ the table** apparecchiare la tavola; **lay down** *vt* mettere giù; (*rules etc*) formulare, fissare; **to lay down the law** dettar legge; **to lay down one's life** dare la propria vita; **lay off** *vt* (*workers*) licenziare; **lay on** *vt* (*provide*) fornire; **lay out** *vt* (*display*) presentare, disporre; **lay-by** (*BRIT*) *n*

piazzola (di sosta)

layer ['leɪər] *n* strato

layman ['leɪmən] (*irreg*) *n* laico; profano

layout ['leɪaut] *n* lay-out *m inv*, disposizione *f*; (*Press*) impaginazione *f*

lazy ['leɪzɪ] *adj* pigro(-a)

lb. *abbr* = **pound** (*weight*)

lead[1] [liːd] (*pt, pp* **led**) *n* (*front position*) posizione *f* di testa; (*distance, time ahead*) vantaggio; (*clue*) indizio; (*Elec*) filo (elettrico); (*for dog*) guinzaglio; (*Theatre*) parte *f* principale ▷ *vt* guidare, condurre; (*induce*) indurre; (*be leader of*) essere a capo di ▷ *vi* condurre; (*Sport*) essere in testa; **in the ~** in testa; **to ~ the way** fare strada; **lead up to** *vt fus* portare a

lead[2] [lɛd] *n* (*metal*) piombo; (*in pencil*) mina

leader ['liːdər] *n* capo; leader *m inv*; (*in newspaper*) articolo di fondo; (*Sport*) chi è in testa; **leadership** *n* direzione *f*; capacità di comando

lead-free ['lɛdfriː] *adj* senza piombo

leading ['liːdɪŋ] *adj* primo(-a), principale

lead singer *n* cantante alla testa di un gruppo

leaf [liːf] (*pl* **leaves**) *n* foglia ▷ *vi* **to ~ through sth** sfogliare qc; **to turn over a new ~** cambiar vita

leaflet ['liːflɪt] *n* dépliant *m inv*; (*Pol, Rel*) volantino

league [liːg] *n* lega; (*Football*) campionato; **to be in ~ with** essere in lega con

leak [liːk] *n* (*out*) fuga; (*in*) infiltrazione *f*; (*security leak*) fuga d'informazioni ▷ *vi* (*roof, bucket*) perdere; (*liquid*) uscire; (*shoes*) lasciar passare l'acqua ▷ *vt* (*information*) divulgare

lean [liːn] (*pt, pp* **leaned** *or* **leant**) *adj* magro(-a) ▷ *vt* **to ~ sth on sth** appoggiare qc su qc ▷ *vi* (*slope*) pendere; (*rest*): **to ~ against** appoggiarsi contro; essere

appoggiato(-a) a; **to ~ on** appoggiarsi
a; **lean forward** vi sporgersi in avanti;
lean over vi inclinarsi; **leaning** n
leaning (towards) propensione f
(per)
leant [lɛnt] pt, pp of **lean**
leap [liːp] (pt, pp **leaped** or **leapt**) n
salto, balzo ▷ vi saltare, balzare
leapt [lɛpt] pt, pp of **leap**
leap year n anno bisestile
learn [ləːn] (pt, pp **learned** or **learnt**)
vt, vi imparare; **to ~ about sth**
(hear, read) apprendere qc; **to ~ to
do sth** imparare a fare qc; **learner**
n principiante m/f; apprendista
m/f; (BRIT: also: **learner driver**)
guidatore(-a) principiante; **learning**
n erudizione f, sapienza
learnt [ləːnt] pt, pp of **learn**
lease [liːs] n contratto d'affitto ▷ vt
affittare
leash [liːʃ] n guinzaglio
least [liːst] adj: **the ~** (+ noun) il (la)
più piccolo(-a), il (la) minimo(-a);
(smallest amount of) il (la) meno ▷ adv
(+ verb) meno; **the ~** (+ adjective): **the
~ beautiful girl** la ragazza meno
bella; **the ~ possible effort** il minimo
sforzo possibile; **I have the ~ money**
ho meno denaro di tutti; **at ~** almeno;
not in the ~ affatto, per nulla
leather ['lɛðər] n cuoio
leave [liːv] (pt, pp **left**) vt lasciare;
(go away from) partire da ▷ vi
partire, andarsene; (bus, train)
partire ▷ n (time off) congedo; (Mil,
consent) licenza; **what time does
the train/bus ~?** a che ora parte il
treno/l'autobus?; **to be left** rimanere;
there's some milk left over c'è
rimasto del latte; **on ~** in congedo;
leave behind vt (person, object)
lasciare; (: forget) dimenticare; **leave
out** vt omettere, tralasciare
leaves [liːvz] npl of **leaf**
Lebanon ['lɛbənən] n Libano
lecture ['lɛktʃər] n conferenza; (Scol)

lezione f ▷ vi fare conferenze; fare
lezioni ▷ vt (scold): **to ~ sb on** or
about sth rimproverare qn or fare
una ramanzina a qn per qc; **to give
a ~ on** tenere una conferenza su;
lecture hall n aula magna; **lecturer**
['lɛktʃərər] (BRIT) n (at university)
professore(-essa), docente m/f;
lecture theatre n = **lecture hall**
led [lɛd] pt, pp of **lead**
ledge [lɛdʒ] n (of window) davanzale m;
(on wall etc) sporgenza; (of mountain)
cornice f, cengia
leek [liːk] n porro
left [lɛft] pt, pp of **leave** ▷ adj
sinistro(-a) ▷ adv a sinistra ▷ n
sinistra; **on the ~, to the ~** a sinistra;
the L~ (Pol) la sinistra; **left-hand** adj
the left-hand side il lato sinistro;
left-hand drive adj guida a sinistra;
left-handed adj mancino(-a);
left-luggage locker n armadietto
per deposito bagagli; **left-luggage
(office)** (BRIT) n deposito m bagagli
inv; **left-overs** npl avanzi mpl, resti
mpl; **left-wing** adj (Pol) di sinistra
leg [lɛg] n gamba; (of animal) zampa;
(of furniture) piede m; (Culin: of chicken)
coscia; (of journey) tappa; **1st/2nd ~**
(Sport) partita di andata/ritorno
legacy ['lɛgəsɪ] n eredità f inv
legal ['liːgl] adj legale; **legal holiday**
(US) n giorno festivo, festa nazionale;
legalize vt legalizzare; **legally**
adv legalmente; **legally binding**
legalmente vincolante
legend ['lɛdʒənd] n leggenda;
legendary ['lɛdʒəndərɪ] adj
leggendario(-a)
leggings ['lɛgɪnz] npl ghette fpl
legible ['lɛdʒəbl] adj leggibile
legislation [lɛdʒɪs'leɪʃən] n
legislazione f
legislative ['lɛdʒɪslətɪv] adj
legislativo(-a)
legitimate [lɪ'dʒɪtɪmət] adj
legittimo(-a)

leisure ['lɛʒəʳ] n agio, tempo libero; ricreazioni fpl; **at ~** con comodo; **leisure centre** n centro di ricreazione; **leisurely** adj tranquillo(-a), fatto(-a) con comodo or senza fretta

lemon ['lɛmən] n limone m; **lemonade** [-'neɪd] n limonata; **lemon tea** n tè m inv al limone

lend [lɛnd] (pt, pp **lent**) vt **to ~ sth (to sb)** prestare qc a qn; **could you ~ me some money?** mi può prestare dei soldi?

length [lɛŋθ] n lunghezza; (distance) distanza; (section: of road, pipe etc) pezzo, tratto; (of time) periodo; **at ~** (at last) finalmente, alla fine; (lengthily) a lungo; **lengthen** vt allungare, prolungare ▷ vi allungarsi; **lengthways** adv per il lungo; **lengthy** adj molto lungo(-a)

lens [lɛnz] n lente f; (of camera) obiettivo

Lent [lɛnt] n Quaresima

lent [lɛnt] pt, pp of **lend**

lentil ['lɛntl] n lenticchia

Leo ['li:əu] n Leone m

leopard ['lɛpəd] n leopardo

leotard ['li:ətɑ:d] n calzamaglia

leprosy ['lɛprəsɪ] n lebbra

lesbian ['lɛzbɪən] n lesbica

less [lɛs] adj, pron, adv meno ▷ prep ~ **tax/10% discount** meno tasse/il 10% di sconto; **~ than ever** meno che mai; **~ than half** meno della metà; **~ and ~** sempre meno; **the ~ he works ...** meno lavora ...; **lessen** ['lɛsn] vi diminuire, attenuarsi ▷ vt diminuire, ridurre; **lesser** ['lɛsəʳ] adj minore, più piccolo(-a); **to a lesser extent** in grado or misura minore

lesson ['lɛsn] n lezione f; **to teach sb a ~** dare una lezione a qn

let [lɛt] (pt, pp **let**) vt lasciare; (BRIT: lease) dare in affitto; **to ~ sb do sth** lasciare fare qc a qn, lasciare che qn faccia qc; **to ~ sb know sth** far sapere

qc a qn; **~'s go** andiamo; **~ him come** lo lasci venire; **"to ~"** "affittasi"; **let down** vt (lower) abbassare; (dress) allungare; (hair) sciogliere; (tyre) sgonfiare; (disappoint) deludere; **let in** vt lasciare entrare; (visitor etc) far entrare; **let off** vt (allow to go) lasciare andare; (firework etc) far partire; **let out** vt lasciare uscire; (scream) emettere

lethal ['li:θl] adj letale, mortale

letter ['lɛtəʳ] n lettera; **letterbox** (BRIT) n buca delle lettere

lettuce ['lɛtɪs] n lattuga, insalata

leukaemia [lu:'ki:mɪə] (US **leukemia**) n leucemia

level ['lɛvl] adj piatto(-a), piano(-a); orizzontale ▷ adv **to draw ~ with** mettersi alla pari di ▷ n livello ▷ vt livellare, spianare; **to be ~ with** essere alla pari di; **level crossing** (BRIT) n passaggio a livello

lever ['li:vəʳ] n leva; **leverage** n: **leverage (on** or **with)** forza (su); (fig) ascendente m (su)

levy ['lɛvɪ] n tassa, imposta ▷ vt imporre

liability [laɪə'bɪlətɪ] n responsabilità f inv; (handicap) peso

liable ['laɪəbl] adj (subject): ~ **to** soggetto(-a) a; passibile di; (responsible): ~ **for** responsabile (di); (likely): ~ **to do** propenso(-a) a fare

liaise [li:'eɪz] vi **to ~ (with)** mantenere i contatti (con)

liar ['laɪəʳ] n bugiardo(-a)

liberal ['lɪbərl] adj liberale; (generous): **to be ~ with** distribuire liberalmente; **Liberal Democrat** n liberaldemocratico(-a)

liberate ['lɪbəreɪt] vt liberare

liberation [lɪbə'reɪʃən] n liberazione f

liberty ['lɪbətɪ] n libertà f inv; **at ~** (criminal) in libertà; **at ~ to do** libero(-a) di fare

Libra ['li:brə] n Bilancia

librarian [laɪ'brɛərɪən] n

bibliotecario(-a)
library ['laɪbrərɪ] n biblioteca
Libya ['lɪbɪə] n Libia
lice [laɪs] npl of **louse**
licence ['laɪsns] (us **license**) n
autorizzazione f, permesso; (Comm)
licenza; (Radio, TV) canone m,
abbonamento; (also: **driving ~**: us:
also: **driver's license**) patente f di
guida; (excessive freedom) licenza
license ['laɪsns] n (us) = **licence** ▷ vt
dare una licenza a; **licensed** adj (for
alcohol) che ha la licenza di vendere
bibite alcoliche; **license plate** (esp
us) n (Aut) targa (automobilistica);
licensing hours (brɪt) npl orario
d'apertura (di un pub)
lick [lɪk] vt leccare; (inf: defeat)
stracciare; **to ~ one's lips** (fig) leccarsi
i baffi
lid [lɪd] n coperchio; (eyelid) palpebra
lie [laɪ] (pt **lay**, pp **lain**) vi (rest)
giacere, star disteso(-a); (of object: be
situated) trovarsi, essere; (tell lies: pt,
pp lied) mentire, dire bugie ▷ n bugia,
menzogna; **to ~ low** (fig) latitare; **lie
about** or **around** vi (things) essere in
giro; (person) bighellonare; **lie down**
vi stendersi, sdraiarsi
Liechtenstein ['lɪktənstaɪn] n
Liechtenstein m
lie-in ['laɪɪn] (brɪt) n: **to have a ~**
rimanere a letto
lieutenant [lɛf'tɛnənt, (us)
luː'tɛnənt] n tenente m
life [laɪf] (pl **lives**) n vita ▷ cpd di
vita; della vita; a vita; **to come to ~**
rianimarsi; **life assurance** (brɪt) n
= **life insurance**; **lifeboat** n scialuppa
di salvataggio; **lifeguard** n bagnino;
life insurance n assicurazione f
sulla vita; **life jacket** n giubbotto di
salvataggio; **lifelike** adj verosimile;
rassomigliante; **life preserver**
[-prɪ'zəːvəᵊ] (us) n salvagente
m; giubbotto di salvataggio; **life
sentence** n ergastolo; **lifestyle**

n stile m di vita; **lifetime** n: **in his
lifetime** durante la sua vita; **once in a
lifetime** una volta nella vita
lift [lɪft] vt sollevare; (ban, rule) levare
▷ vi (fog) alzarsi ▷ n (brɪt: elevator)
ascensore m; **to give sb a ~** (brɪt)
dare un passaggio a qn; **can you give
me a ~ to the station?** può darmi un
passaggio fino alla stazione?; **lift up**
vt sollevare, alzare; **lift-off** n decollo
light [laɪt] (pt, pp **lighted** or **lit**) n luce
f, lume m; (daylight) luce f, giorno;
(lamp) lampada; (Aut: rear light) luce
f di posizione; (: headlamp) fanale m;
(for cigarette etc): **have you got a ~?**
ha da accendere?; **lights** npl (Aut:
traffic lights) semaforo vt (candle,
cigarette, fire) accendere; (room): **to
be lit by** essere illuminato(-a) da adj
(room, colour) chiaro(-a); (not heavy,
also fig) leggero(-a); **to come to ~**
venire alla luce, emergere; **light up**
vi illuminarsi ▷ vt illuminare; **light
bulb** n lampadina; **lighten** vt (make
less heavy) alleggerire; **lighter** n
(also: **cigarette lighter**) accendino;
light-hearted adj gioioso(-a),
gaio(-a); **lighthouse** n faro;
lighting n illuminazione f; **lightly**
adv leggermente; **to get off lightly**
cavarsela a buon mercato
lightning ['laɪtnɪŋ] n lampo,
fulmine m
lightweight ['laɪtweɪt] adj (suit)
leggero(-a) ▷ n (Boxing) peso leggero
like [laɪk] vt (person) volere bene a;
(activity, object, food): **I ~ swimming/
that book/chocolate** mi piace
nuotare/quel libro/il cioccolato ▷ prep
come ▷ adj simile, uguale ▷ n the ~
uno(-a) uguale; **his ~s and dis~s** i suoi
gusti; **I would ~, I'd ~** mi piacerebbe,
vorrei; **would you ~ a coffee?**
gradirebbe un caffè?; **to be/look ~ sb/
sth** somigliare a qn/qc; **what does it
look/taste ~?** che aspetto/gusto
ha?; **what does it sound ~?** come fa?;

that's just ~ him è proprio da lui; **do it ~ this** fallo così; **it is nothing ~ ...** non è affatto come ...; **likeable** adj simpatico(-a)

likelihood ['laɪklɪhud] n probabilità

likely ['laɪklɪ] adj probabile; plausibile; **he's ~ to leave** probabilmente partirà; è probabile che parta; **not ~!** neanche per sogno!

likewise ['laɪkwaɪz] adv similmente, nello stesso modo

liking ['laɪkɪŋ] n: **~ (for)** debole m (per); **to be to sb's ~** piacere a qn

lilac ['laɪlək] n lilla m inv

Lilo® ['laɪləʊ] n materassino gonfiabile

lily ['lɪlɪ] n giglio

limb [lɪm] n arto

limbo ['lɪmbəʊ] n: **to be in ~** (fig) essere lasciato(-a) nel dimenticatoio

lime [laɪm] n (tree) tiglio; (fruit) limetta; (Geo) calce f

limelight ['laɪmlaɪt] n: **in the ~** (fig) alla ribalta, in vista

limestone ['laɪmstəʊn] n pietra calcarea; (Geo) calcare m

limit ['lɪmɪt] n limite m ▷ vt limitare; **limited** adj limitato(-a), ristretto(-a); **to be limited to** limitarsi a

limousine ['lɪməziːn] n limousine f inv

limp [lɪmp] n: **to have a ~** zoppicare ▷ vi zoppicare ▷ adj floscio(-a), flaccido(-a)

line [laɪn] n linea; (rope) corda; (for fishing) lenza; (wire) filo; (of poem) verso; (row, series) fila, riga; coda; (on face) ruga ▷ vt (clothes): **to ~ (with)** foderare (di); (box): **to ~ (with)** rivestire or foderare (di); (trees, crowd) fiancheggiare; **~ of business** settore m or ramo d'attività; **in ~ with** in linea con; **line up** vi allinearsi, mettersi in fila ▷ vt mettere in fila; (event, celebration) preparare

linear ['lɪnɪər] adj lineare

linen ['lɪnɪn] n biancheria, panni mpl; (cloth) tela di lino

liner ['laɪnər] n nave f di linea; (for bin) sacchetto

line-up ['laɪnʌp] n allineamento, fila; (Sport) formazione f di gioco

linger ['lɪŋgər] vi attardarsi; indugiare; (smell, tradition) persistere

lingerie ['lænʒəriː] n biancheria intima femminile

linguist ['lɪŋgwɪst] n linguista m/f; poliglotta m/f; **linguistic** adj linguistico(-a)

lining ['laɪnɪŋ] n fodera

link [lɪŋk] n (of a chain) anello; (relationship) legame m; (connection) collegamento ▷ vt collegare, unire, congiungere; (associate): **to ~ with** or **to** collegare a; **links** npl (Golf) pista or terreno da golf; **link up** vt collegare, unire ▷ vi riunirsi; associarsi

lion ['laɪən] n leone m; **lioness** n leonessa

lip [lɪp] n labbro; (of cup etc) orlo; **lip-read** vi leggere sulle labbra; **lip salve** [-sælv] n burro di cacao; **lipstick** n rossetto

liqueur [lɪˈkjuər] n liquore m

liquid ['lɪkwɪd] n liquido ▷ adj liquido(-a); **liquidizer** n frullatore m (a brocca)

liquor ['lɪkər] n alcool m; **liquor store** (US) n negozio di liquori

Lisbon ['lɪzbən] n Lisbona

lisp [lɪsp] n pronuncia blesa della "s"

list [lɪst] n lista, elenco ▷ vt (write down) mettere in lista; fare una lista di; (enumerate) elencare

listen ['lɪsn] vi ascoltare; **to ~ to** ascoltare; **listener** n ascoltatore(-trice)

lit [lɪt] pt, pp of **light**

liter ['liːtər] (US) n = **litre**

literacy ['lɪtərəsɪ] n il sapere leggere e scrivere

literal ['lɪtərl] adj letterale; **literally** adv alla lettera, letteralmente

literary ['lɪtərərɪ] adj letterario(-a)

literate ['lɪtərət] adj che sa leggere e scrivere

literature ['lɪtərɪtʃəʳ] n letteratura; (brochures etc) materiale m

litre ['liːtəʳ] (US **liter**) n litro

litter ['lɪtəʳ] n (rubbish) rifiuti mpl; (young animals) figliata; **litter bin** (BRIT) n cestino per rifiuti; **littered** adj **littered with** coperto(-a) di

little ['lɪtl] adj (small) piccolo(-a); (not much) poco(-a) ▷ adv poco; **a ~** un po' (di); **a ~ bit** un pochino; **~ by ~** a poco a poco; **little finger** n mignolo

live¹ [lɪv] vi vivere; (reside) vivere, abitare; **where do you ~?** dove abita?; **live together** vi vivere insieme, convivere; **live up to** vt fus tener fede a, non venir meno a

live² [laɪv] adj (animal) vivo(-a); (wire) sotto tensione; (bullet, missile) inesploso(-a); (broadcast) diretto(-a); (performance) dal vivo

livelihood ['laɪvlɪhud] n mezzi mpl di sostentamento

lively ['laɪvlɪ] adj vivace, vivo(-a)

liven up ['laɪvn'ʌp] vt (discussion, evening) animare ▷ vi ravvivarsi

liver ['lɪvəʳ] n fegato

lives [laɪvz] npl of **life**

livestock ['laɪvstɔk] n bestiame m

living ['lɪvɪŋ] adj vivo(-a), vivente ▷ n **to earn** or **make a ~** guadagnarsi la vita; **living room** n soggiorno

lizard ['lɪzəd] n lucertola

load [ləud] n (weight) peso; (thing carried) carico ▷ vt (also: **~ up**): **to ~ (with)** (lorry, ship) caricare (di); (gun, camera, Comput) caricare (con); **a ~ of, ~s of** (fig) un sacco di; **loaded** adj (vehicle): **loaded (with)** carico(-a) (di); (question) capzioso(-a); (inf: rich) carico(-a) di soldi

loaf [ləuf] (pl **loaves**) n pane m, pagnotta

loan [ləun] n prestito ▷ vt dare in prestito; **on ~** in prestito

loathe [ləuð] vt detestare, aborrire

loaves [ləuvz] npl of **loaf**

lobby ['lɔbɪ] n atrio, vestibolo; (Pol: pressure group) gruppo di pressione ▷ vt fare pressione su

lobster ['lɔbstəʳ] n aragosta

local ['ləukl] adj locale ▷ n (BRIT: pub) ≈ bar m inv all'angolo; **the locals** npl (local inhabitants) la gente della zona; **local anaesthetic** n anestesia locale; **local authority** n ente m locale; **local government** n amministrazione f locale; **locally** ['ləukəlɪ] adv da queste parti; nel vicinato

locate [ləu'keɪt] vt (find) trovare; (situate) collocare; situare

location [ləu'keɪʃən] n posizione f; **on ~** (Cinema) all'esterno

loch [lɔx] n lago

lock [lɔk] n (of door, box) serratura; (of canal) chiusa; (of hair) ciocca, riccio ▷ vt (with key) chiudere a chiave ▷ vi (door etc) chiudersi; (wheels) bloccarsi, incepparsi; **lock in** vt chiudere dentro (a chiave); **lock out** vt chiudere fuori; **lock up** vt (criminal, mental patient) rinchiudere; (house) chiudere (a chiave) ▷ vi chiudere tutto (a chiave)

locker ['lɔkəʳ] n armadietto; **locker-room** (US) n (Sport) spogliatoio

locksmith ['lɔksmɪθ] n magnano

locomotive [ləukə'məutɪv] n locomotiva

lodge [lɔdʒ] n casetta, portineria; (hunting lodge) casino di caccia ▷ vi (person): **to ~ (with)** essere a pensione (presso or da); (bullet etc) conficcarsi ▷ vt (appeal etc) presentare, fare; **to ~ a complaint** presentare un reclamo; **lodger** n affittuario(-a); (with room and meals) pensionante m/f

lodging ['lɔdʒɪŋ] n alloggio; see also **board**

loft [lɔft] n solaio, soffitta

log [lɔg] n (of wood) ceppo; (also: **~book**: Naut, Aviat) diario di bordo; (Aut) libretto di circolazione ▷ vt registrare; **log in** vi (Comput) aprire una sessione (*con codice di riconoscimento*); **log off** *vi* (*Comput*) terminare una sessione

logic ['lɔdʒɪk] *n* logica; **logical** *adj* logico(-a)

logo ['ləʊgəʊ] *n* logo *m inv*

lollipop ['lɔlɪpɔp] *n* lecca lecca *m inv*

lolly ['lɔlɪ] (*inf*) *n* lecca lecca *m inv*; (*also:* **ice ~**) ghiacciolo; (*money*) grana

London ['lʌndən] *n* Londra; **Londoner** *n* londinese *m/f*

lone [ləʊn] *adj* solitario(-a)

loneliness ['ləʊnlɪnɪs] *n* solitudine *f*, isolamento

lonely ['ləʊnlɪ] *adj* solo(-a); solitario(-a), isolato(-a)

long [lɔŋ] *adj* lungo(-a) ▷ *adv* a lungo, per molto tempo ▷ *vi* **to ~ for sth/to do** desiderare qc/di fare, non veder l'ora di aver qc/di fare; **so** *or* **as ~ as** (*while*) finché; (*provided that*) sempre che + *sub*; **don't be ~!** fai presto!; **how ~ is this river/course?** quanto è lungo questo fiume/corso?; **6 metres ~** lungo 6 metri; **6 months ~** che dura 6 mesi, di 6 mesi; **all night ~** tutta la notte; **he no ~er comes** non viene più; **~ before** molto tempo prima; **before ~** (+ *future*) presto, fra poco; (+ *past*) poco tempo dopo; **at ~ last** finalmente; **long-distance** *adj* (*race*) di fondo; (*call*) interurbano(-a); **long-haul** ['lɔŋhɔːl] *adj* (*flight*) a lunga percorrenza *inv*; **longing** *n* desiderio, voglia, brama

longitude ['lɔŋgɪtjuːd] *n* longitudine *f*

long: **long jump** *n* salto in lungo; **long-life** *adj* (*milk*) a lunga conservazione; (*batteries*) di lunga durata; **long-sighted** *adj* presbite; **long-standing** *adj* di vecchia data; **long-term** *adj* a lungo termine

loo [luː] (*BRIT: inf*) *n* W.C. *m inv*, cesso

look [lʊk] *vi* guardare; (*seem*) sembrare, parere; (*building etc*) **to ~ south/on to the sea** dare a sud/sul mare ▷ *n* sguardo; (*appearance*) aspetto, aria; **looks** *npl* (*good looks*) bellezza; **look after** *vt fus* occuparsi di, prendere cura di; (*keep an eye on*) guardare, badare a; **look around** *vi* guardarsi intorno; **look at** *vt fus* guardare; **look back** *vi*: **to look back on** (*event etc*) ripensare a; **look down on** *vt fus* (*fig*) guardare dall'alto, disprezzare; **look for** *vt fus* cercare; **we're looking for a hotel/restaurant** stiamo cercando un albergo/ristorante; **look forward to** *vt fus* non veder l'ora di; (*in letters*): **we look forward to hearing from you** in attesa di una vostra gentile risposta; **look into** *vt fus* esaminare; **look out** *vi* (*beware*): **to look out (for)** stare in guardia (per); **look out for** *vt fus* cercare; **look round** *vi* (*turn*) girarsi, voltarsi; (*in shop*) dare un'occhiata; **look through** *vt fus* (*papers, book*) scorrere; (*telescope*) guardare attraverso; **look up** *vi* alzare gli occhi; (*improve*) migliorare ▷ *vt* (*word*) cercare; (*friend*) andare a trovare; **look up to** *vt fus* avere rispetto per; **lookout** *n* posto d'osservazione; guardia; **to be on the lookout (for)** stare in guardia (per)

loom [luːm] *n* telaio ▷ *vi* (*also:* **~ up**) apparire minaccioso(-a); (*event*) essere imminente

loony ['luːnɪ] (*inf*) *n* pazzo(-a)

loop [luːp] *n* cappio ▷ *vt* **to ~ sth round sth** passare qc intorno a qc; **loophole** *n* via d'uscita; scappatoia

loose [luːs] *adj* (*knot*) sciolto(-a); (*screw*) allentato(-a); (*stone*) cadente; (*clothes*) ampio(-a), largo(-a); (*animal*) in libertà, scappato(-a); (*life, morals*) dissoluto(-a) ▷ *n* **to be on the ~** essere in libertà; **loosely** *adv* senza stringere; approssimativamente; **loosen** *vt* sciogliere; (*belt etc*) allentare

loot [luːt] *n* bottino ▷ *vt* saccheggiare

lop-sided ['lɔp'saɪdɪd] adj non equilibrato(-a), asimmetrico(-a)

lord [lɔːd] n signore m; **L~ Smith** lord Smith; **the L~** il Signore; **good L~!** buon Dio!; **the (House of) L~s** (BRIT) la Camera dei Lord

lorry ['lɔrɪ] (BRIT) n camion m inv; **lorry driver** (BRIT) n camionista m

lose [luːz] (pt, pp **lost**) vt perdere ▷ vi perdere; **I've lost my wallet/ passport** ho perso il portafoglio/ passaporto; **to ~ (time)** (clock) ritardare; **lose out** vi rimetterci; **loser** n perdente m/f

loss [lɔs] n perdita; **to be at a ~** essere perplesso(-a)

lost [lɔst] pt, pp of **lose** ▷ adj perduto(-a); **I'm ~** mi sono perso; **lost property** (US **lost and found**) n oggetti mpl smarriti

lot [lɔt] n (at auctions) lotto; (destiny) destino, sorte f; **the ~** tutto(-a) quanto(-a); tutti(-e) quanti(-e); **a ~** molto; **a ~ of** una gran quantità di, un sacco di; **~s of** molto(-a); **to draw ~s (for sth)** tirare a sorte (per qc)

lotion ['ləʊʃən] n lozione f

lottery ['lɔtərɪ] n lotteria

loud [laʊd] adj forte, alto(-a); (gaudy) vistoso(-a), sgargiante ▷ adv (speak etc) forte; **out ~** (read etc) ad alta voce; **loudly** adv fortemente, ad alta voce; **loudspeaker** n altoparlante m

lounge [laʊndʒ] n salotto, soggiorno; (at airport, station) sala d'attesa; (BRIT: also: **~ bar**) bar m inv con servizio a tavolino ▷ vi oziare

louse [laʊs] (pl **lice**) n pidocchio

lousy ['laʊzɪ] (inf) adj orrendo(-a), schifoso(-a); **to feel ~** stare da cani

love [lʌv] n amore m ▷ vt amare; voler bene a; **to ~ to do: I ~ to do** mi piace fare; **to be/fall in ~ with** essere innamorato(-a)/innamorarsi di; **to make ~** fare l'amore; "**15 ~**" (Tennis) "15 a zero"; **love affair** n relazione f; **love life** n vita sentimentale

lovely ['lʌvlɪ] adj bello(-a); (delicious: smell, meal) buono(-a)

lover ['lʌvə'] n amante m/f; (person in love) innamorato(-a); (amateur): **a ~ of** un(-un') amante di; un(-un') appassionato(-a) di

loving ['lʌvɪŋ] adj affettuoso(-a)

low [ləʊ] adj basso(-a) ▷ adv in basso ▷ n (Meteor) depressione f; **to be ~ on** (supplies etc) avere scarsità di; **to feel ~** sentirsi giù; **low-alcohol** adj a basso contenuto alcolico; **low-calorie** adj a basso contenuto calorico

lower ['ləʊə'] adj (bottom: of 2 things) più basso; (less important) meno importante ▷ vt calare; (prices, eyes, voice) abbassare

low-fat ['ləʊ'fæt] adj magro(-a)

loyal ['lɔɪəl] adj fedele, leale; **loyalty** n fedeltà, lealtà; **loyalty card** n carta che offre sconti a clienti abituali

L.P. n abbr = **long-playing record**

L-plates ['ɛlpleɪts] (BRIT) npl contrassegno P principiante

Lt abbr (= lieutenant) Ten.

Ltd abbr (= limited) ≈ S.r.l.

luck [lʌk] n fortuna, sorte f; **bad ~** sfortuna, mala sorte; **good ~!** buona fortuna!; **luckily** adv fortunatamente, per fortuna; **lucky** adj fortunato(-a); (number etc) che porta fortuna

lucrative ['luːkrətɪv] adj lucrativo(-a), lucroso(-a), profittevole

ludicrous ['luːdɪkrəs] adj ridicolo(-a)

luggage ['lʌgɪdʒ] n bagagli mpl; **our ~ hasn't arrived** i nostri bagagli non sono arrivati; **luggage rack** n portabagagli m inv

lukewarm ['luːkwɔːm] adj tiepido(-a)

lull [lʌl] n intervallo di calma ▷ vt **to ~ sb to sleep** cullare qn finché si addormenta

lullaby ['lʌləbaɪ] n ninnananna

lumber ['lʌmbə'] n (wood) legname m; (junk) roba vecchia

luminous ['luːmɪnəs] adj

luminoso(-a)

lump [lʌmp] *n* pezzo; (*in sauce*) grumo; (*swelling*) gonfiore *m*; (*also:* **sugar ~**) zolletta ▷ *vt* (*also:* **~ together**) riunire, mettere insieme; **lump sum** *n* somma globale; **lumpy** *adj* (*sauce*) pieno(-a) di grumi; (*bed*) bitorzoluto(-a)

lunatic ['luːnətɪk] *adj* pazzo(-a), matto(-a)

lunch [lʌntʃ] *n* pranzo, colazione *f*; **lunch break** *n* intervallo del pranzo; **lunch time** *n* ora di pranzo

lung [lʌŋ] *n* polmone *m*

lure [luəʳ] *n* richiamo; lusinga ▷ *vt* attirare (con l'inganno)

lurk [ləːk] *vi* stare in agguato

lush [lʌʃ] *adj* lussureggiante

lust [lʌst] *n* lussuria; cupidigia; desiderio; (*fig*): **~ for** sete *f* di

Luxembourg ['lʌksəmbəːg] *n* (*state*) Lussemburgo *m*; (*city*) Lussemburgo *f*

luxurious [lʌg'zjuərɪəs] *adj* sontuoso(-a), di lusso

luxury ['lʌkʃərɪ] *n* lusso ▷ *cpd* di lusso
 Be careful not to translate *luxury* by the Italian word *lussuria*.

Lycra® ['laɪkrə] *n* lycra® *f inv*

lying ['laɪɪŋ] *n* bugie *fpl*, menzogne *fpl* ▷ *adj* bugiardo(-a)

lyrics ['lɪrɪks] *npl* (*of song*) parole *fpl*

m. *abbr* = **metre**; **mile**; **million**

M.A. *abbr* = **Master of Arts**

ma (*inf*) [maː] *n* mamma

mac [mæk] (*BRIT*) *n* impermeabile *m*

macaroni [mækə'rəʊnɪ] *n* maccheroni *mpl*

Macedonia [mæsɪ'dəʊnɪə] *n* Macedonia; **Macedonian** [mæsɪ'dəʊnɪən] *adj* macedone ▷ *n* macedone *m/f*; (*Ling*) macedone *m*

machine [mə'ʃiːn] *n* macchina ▷ *vt* (*Tech*) lavorare a macchina; (*dress etc*) cucire a macchina; **machine gun** *n* mitragliatrice *f*; **machinery** *n* macchinario, macchine *fpl*; (*fig*) macchina; **machine washable** *adj* lavabile in lavatrice

macho ['mætʃəʊ] *adj* macho *inv*

mackerel ['mækrl] *n inv* sgombro

mackintosh ['mækɪntɔʃ] (*BRIT*) *n* impermeabile *m*

mad [mæd] *adj* matto(-a), pazzo(-a); (*foolish*) sciocco(-a); (*angry*) furioso(-a); **to be ~ about** (*keen*)

andare pazzo(-a) per
Madagascar [mædəˈɡæskəʳ] n
Madagascar m
madam [ˈmædəm] n signora
mad cow disease n encefalite f
bovina spongiforme
made [meɪd] pt, pp of **make**; **made-
to-measure** (BRIT) adj fatto(-a) su
misura; **made-up** [ˈmeɪdʌp] adj
(story) inventato(-a)
madly [ˈmædlɪ] adv follemente
madman [ˈmædmən] (irreg) n pazzo,
alienato
madness [ˈmædnɪs] n pazzia
Madrid [məˈdrɪd] n Madrid f
Mafia [ˈmæfɪə] n mafia f
mag [mæɡ] n abbr (BRIT inf)
= **magazine** (Press)
magazine [mæɡəˈziːn] n (Press)
rivista; (Radio, TV) rubrica

> Be careful not to translate
> *magazine* by the Italian word
> *magazzino*.

maggot [ˈmæɡət] n baco, verme m
magic [ˈmædʒɪk] n magia ▷ adj
magico(-a); **magical** adj magico(-a);
magician [məˈdʒɪʃən] n mago(-a)
magistrate [ˈmædʒɪstreɪt] n
magistrato; giudice m/f
magnet [ˈmæɡnɪt] n magnete m,
calamita; **magnetic** [-ˈnɛtɪk] adj
magnetico(-a)
magnificent [mæɡˈnɪfɪsnt] adj
magnifico(-a)
magnify [ˈmæɡnɪfaɪ] vt ingrandire;
magnifying glass n lente f
d'ingrandimento
magpie [ˈmæɡpaɪ] n gazza
mahogany [məˈhɔɡənɪ] n mogano
maid [meɪd] n domestica; (in hotel)
cameriera
maiden name [ˈmeɪdn-] n nome m
da nubile or da ragazza
mail [meɪl] n posta ▷ vt spedire (per
posta); **mailbox** (US) n cassetta
delle lettere; **mailing list** n elenco
d'indirizzi; **mailman** (irreg: US) n

portalettere m inv, postino; **mail-
order** n vendita (or acquisto) per
corrispondenza
main [meɪn] adj principale ▷ n
(pipe) conduttura principale; **main
course** n (Culin) piatto principale,
piatto forte; **mainland** n continente
m; **mainly** adv principalmente,
soprattutto; **main road** n strada
principale; **mainstream** n (fig)
corrente f principale; **main street** n
strada principale
maintain [meɪnˈteɪn] vt mantenere;
(affirm) sostenere; **maintenance**
[ˈmeɪntənəns] n manutenzione f;
(alimony) alimenti mpl
maisonette [meɪzəˈnɛt] n (BRIT)
appartamento a due piani
maize [meɪz] n granturco, mais m
majesty [ˈmædʒɪstɪ] n maestà f inv
major [ˈmeɪdʒəʳ] n (Mil) maggiore
m ▷ adj (greater, Mus) maggiore; (in
importance) principale, importante
Majorca [məˈjɔːkə] n Maiorca
majority [məˈdʒɔrɪtɪ] n maggioranza
make [meɪk] (pt, pp **made**) vt fare;
(manufacture) fare, fabbricare; (cause
to be): **to ~ sb sad** etc rendere qn triste
etc; (force): **to ~ sb do sth** costringere
qn a fare qc, far fare qc a qn; (equal): **2
and 2 ~ 4** 2 più 2 fa 4 ▷ n fabbricazione
f; (brand) marca; **to ~ a fool of sb** far
fare a qn la figura dello scemo; **to ~
a profit** realizzare un profitto; **to ~ a
loss** subire una perdita; **to ~ it** (arrive)
arrivare; (achieve sth) farcela; **what
time do you ~ it?** che ora fai?; **to ~
do with** arrangiarsi con; **make off**
vi svignarsela; **make out** vt (write
out) scrivere; (: cheque) emettere;
(understand) capire; (see) distinguere;
(: numbers) decifrare; **make up**
vt (constitute) formare; (invent)
inventare; (parcel) fare ▷ vi conciliarsi;
(with cosmetics) truccarsi; **make up
for** vt fus compensare; ricuperare;
makeover [ˈmeɪkəʊvəʳ] n (change of

image) cambiamento di immagine; (*of room, house*) trasformazione *f*; **maker** *n* (*of programme etc*) creatore(-trice); (*manufacturer*) fabbricante *m*; **makeshift** *adj* improvvisato(-a); **make-up** *n* trucco

making ['meɪkɪŋ] *n* (*fig*): **in the ~** in formazione; **to have the ~s of** (*actor, athlete etc*) avere la stoffa di

malaria [mə'lɛərɪə] *n* malaria

Malaysia [mə'leɪzɪə] *n* Malaysia

male [meɪl] *n* (*Biol*) maschio ▷ *adj* maschile; maschio(-a)

malicious [mə'lɪʃəs] *adj* malevolo(-a); (*Law*) doloso(-a)

malignant [mə'lɪgnənt] *adj* (*Med*) maligno(-a)

mall [mɔːl] *n* (*also*: **shopping ~**) centro commerciale

mallet ['mælɪt] *n* maglio

malnutrition [mælnjuː'trɪʃən] *n* denutrizione *f*

malpractice [mæl'præktɪs] *n* prevaricazione *f*; negligenza

malt [mɔːlt] *n* malto

Malta ['mɔːltə] *n* Malta; **Maltese** [mɔːl'tiːz] *adj*, *n* (*pl inv*) maltese (*m/f*); (*Ling*) maltese *m*

mammal ['mæml] *n* mammifero

mammoth ['mæməθ] *adj* enorme, gigantesco(-a)

man [mæn] (*pl* **men**) *n* uomo ▷ *vt* fornire d'uomini; stare a; **an old ~** un vecchio; **~ and wife** marito e moglie

manage ['mænɪdʒ] *vi* farcela ▷ *vt* (*be in charge of*) occuparsi di; gestire; **to ~ to do sth** riuscire a far qc; **manageable** *adj* maneggevole; fattibile; **management** *n* amministrazione *f*, direzione *f*; **manager** *n* direttore *m*; (*of shop, restaurant*) gerente *m*; (*of artist, Sport*) manager *m inv*; **manageress** [-ə'rɛs] *n* direttrice *f*; gerente *f*; **managerial** [-ə'dʒɪərɪəl] *adj* dirigenziale; **managing director** *n* amministratore *m* delegato

mandarin ['mændərɪn] *n* (*person, fruit*) mandarino

mandate ['mændeɪt] *n* mandato

mandatory ['mændətərɪ] *adj* obbligatorio(-a), ingiuntivo(-a)

mane [meɪn] *n* criniera

mangetout ['mɔnʒ'tuː] *n* pisello dolce, taccola

mango ['mæŋgəu] (*pl* **mangoes**) *n* mango

man: **manhole** ['mænhəul] *n* botola stradale; **manhood** ['mænhud] *n* età virile; virilità

mania ['meɪnɪə] *n* mania; **maniac** ['meɪnɪæk] *n* maniaco(-a)

manic ['mænɪk] *adj* (*behaviour, activity*) maniacale

manicure ['mænɪkjuər] *n* manicure *f inv*

manifest ['mænɪfɛst] *vt* manifestare ▷ *adj* manifesto(-a), palese

manifesto [mænɪ'fɛstəu] *n* manifesto

manipulate [mə'nɪpjuleɪt] *vt* manipolare

man: **mankind** [mæn'kaɪnd] *n* umanità, genere umano, **manly** ['mænlɪ] *adj* virile; coraggioso(-a); **man-made** *adj* sintetico(-a); artificiale

manner ['mænər] *n* maniera, modo; (*behaviour*) modo di fare; (*type, sort*): **all ~ of things** ogni genere di cosa; **manners** *npl* (*conduct*) maniere *fpl*; **bad ~s** maleducazione *f*

manoeuvre [mə'nuːvər] (*us* **maneuver**) *vt* manovrare ▷ *vi* far manovre ▷ *n* manovra

manpower ['mænpauər] *n* manodopera

mansion ['mænʃən] *n* casa signorile

manslaughter ['mænslɔːtər] *n* omicidio preterintenzionale

mantelpiece ['mæntlpiːs] *n* mensola del caminetto

manual ['mænjuəl] *adj* manuale ▷ *n* manuale *m*

manufacture [mænju'fæktʃəʳ]
vt fabbricare ▷ n fabbricazione
f, manifattura; **manufacturer** n
fabbricante m

manure [mə'njuəʳ] n concime m

manuscript ['mænjuskrɪpt] n
manoscritto

many ['mɛnɪ] adj molti(-e) ▷ pron
molti(-e); **a great ~** moltissimi(-e), un
gran numero (di); **~ a time** molte volte

map [mæp] n carta (geografica); (of
city) cartina; **can you show it to
me on the ~?** può indicarmelo sulla
cartina?

maple ['meɪpl] n acero

mar [mɑːʳ] vt sciupare

Mar. abbr (= March) mar.

marathon ['mærəθən] n maratona

marble ['mɑːbl] n marmo; (toy)
pallina, bilia

March [mɑːtʃ] n marzo

march [mɑːtʃ] vi marciare; sfilare ▷ n
marcia

mare [mɛəʳ] n giumenta

margarine [mɑːdʒə'riːn] n
margarina

margin ['mɑːdʒɪn] n margine m;
marginal adj marginale; **marginal
seat** (Pol) seggio elettorale ottenuto con
una stretta maggioranza; **marginally**
adv (bigger, better) lievemente, di poco;
(different) un po'

marigold ['mærɪɡəuld] n calendola

marijuana [mærɪ'wɑːnə] n
marijuana

marina [mə'riːnə] n marina

marinade n [mærɪ'neɪd] marinata
▷ vt ['mærɪneɪd] = **marinate**

marinate ['mærɪneɪt] vt marinare

marine [mə'riːn] adj (animal, plant)
marino(-a); (forces, engineering)
marittimo(-a) ▷ n (BRIT) fante m di
marina; (US) marine m inv

marital ['mærɪtl] adj maritale,
coniugale; **marital status** n stato
civile

maritime ['mærɪtaɪm] adj

marittimo(-a)

marjoram ['mɑːdʒərəm] n
maggiorana

mark [mɑːk] n segno; (stain) macchia;
(of skid etc) traccia; (BRIT Scol) voto;
(Sport) bersaglio; (currency) marco
▷ vt segnare; (stain) macchiare;
(indicate) indicare; (BRIT Scol) dare un
voto a; correggere; **to ~ time** segnare
il passo; **marked** adj spiccato(-a),
chiaro(-a); **marker** n (sign) segno;
(bookmark) segnalibro

market ['mɑːkɪt] n mercato
▷ vt (Comm) mettere in vendita;
marketing n marketing m;
marketplace n (piazza del) mercato;
(world of trade) piazza, mercato;
market research n indagine f or
ricerca di mercato

marmalade ['mɑːməleɪd] n
marmellata d'arance

maroon [mə'ruːn] vt (also fig): **to be
~ed (in** or **at)** essere abbandonato(-a)
(in) ▷ adj bordeaux inv

marquee [mɑː'kiː] n padiglione m

marriage ['mærɪdʒ] n matrimonio;
marriage certificate n certificato di
matrimonio

married ['mærɪd] adj sposato(-a);
(life, love) coniugale, matrimoniale

marrow ['mærəu] n midollo;
(vegetable) zucca

marry ['mærɪ] vt sposare, sposarsi
con; (vicar, priest etc) dare in
matrimonio ▷ vi (also: **get married**)
sposarsi

Mars [mɑːz] n (planet) Marte m

marsh [mɑːʃ] n palude f

marshal ['mɑːʃl] n maresciallo; (US:
fire) capo; (: police) capitano ▷ vt
(thoughts, support) ordinare; (soldiers)
adunare

martyr ['mɑːtəʳ] n martire m/f

marvel ['mɑːvl] n meraviglia ▷ vi **to ~
(at)** meravigliarsi (di); **marvellous** (US
marvelous) adj meraviglioso(-a)

Marxism ['mɑːksɪzəm] n marxismo

Marxist ['mɑːksɪst] *adj, n* marxista *m/f*
marzipan ['mɑːzɪpæn] *n* marzapane
m
mascara [mæs'kɑːrə] *n* mascara *m*
mascot ['mæskət] *n* mascotte *f inv*
masculine ['mæskjulɪn] *adj*
maschile; (*woman*) mascolino(-a)
mash [mæʃ] *vt* passare, schiacciare;
mashed potatoes *npl* purè *m* di
patate
mask [mɑːsk] *n* maschera ▷ *vt*
mascherare
mason ['meɪsn] *n* (*also*: **stone~**)
scalpellino; (*also*: **free~**) massone *m*;
masonry *n* muratura
mass [mæs] *n* moltitudine *f*, massa;
(*Physics*) massa; (*Rel*) messa ▷ *cpd* di
massa ▷ *vi* ammassarsi; **the masses**
npl (*ordinary people*) le masse; **~es of**
(*inf*) una montagna di
massacre ['mæsəkər] *n* massacro
massage ['mæsɑːʒ] *n* massaggio
massive ['mæsɪv] *adj* enorme,
massiccio(-a)
mass media *npl* mass media *mpl*
mass-produce ['mæsprə'djuːs] *vt*
produrre in serie
mast [mɑːst] *n* albero
master ['mɑːstər] *n* padrone *m*; (*Art
etc, teacher: in primary school*) maestro;
(: *in secondary school*) professore *m*;
(*title for boys*): **M~ X** Signorino X ▷ *vt*
domare; (*learn*) imparare a fondo;
(*understand*) conoscere a fondo;
mastermind *n* mente *f* superiore
▷ *vt* essere il cervello di; **Master of
Arts/Science** *n* Master *m inv* in
lettere/scienze; **masterpiece** *n*
capolavoro
masturbate ['mæstəbeɪt] *vi*
masturbare
mat [mæt] *n* stuoia; (*also*: **door~**)
stoino, zerbino; (*also*: **table ~**)
sottopiatto ▷ *adj* = **matt**
match [mætʃ] *n* fiammifero; (*game*)
partita, incontro; (*fig*) uguale *m/f*;
matrimonio; partito ▷ *vt* intonare;

(*go well with*) andare benissimo con;
(*equal*) uguagliare; (*correspond to*)
corrispondere a; (*pair: also:* **~ up**)
accoppiare ▷ *vi* combaciare; **to be
a good ~** andare bene; **matchbox** *n*
scatola per fiammiferi; **matching** *adj*
ben assortito(-a)
mate [meɪt] *n* compagno(-a) di
lavoro; (*inf: friend*) amico(-a); (*animal*)
compagno(-a); (*in merchant navy*)
secondo ▷ *vi* accoppiarsi
material [mə'tɪərɪəl] *n* (*substance*)
materiale *m*, materia; (*cloth*) stoffa
▷ *adj* materiale; **materials** *npl*
(*equipment*) materiali *mpl*
materialize [mə'tɪərɪəlaɪz] *vi*
materializzarsi, realizzarsi
maternal [mə'təːnl] *adj* materno(-a)
maternity [mə'təːnɪtɪ] *n* maternità;
maternity hospital *n* ≈ clinica
ostetrica; **maternity leave** *n*
congedo di maternità
math [mæθ] (*us*) *n* = **maths**
mathematical [mæθə'mætɪkl] *adj*
matematico(-a)
mathematician [mæθəmə'tɪʃən] *n*
matematico(-a)
mathematics [mæθə'mætɪks] *n*
matematica
maths [mæθs] (*us* **math**) *n*
matematica
matinée ['mætɪneɪ] *n* matinée *f inv*
matron ['meɪtrən] *n* (*in hospital*)
capoinfermiera; (*in school*) infermiera
matt [mæt] *adj* opaco(-a)
matter ['mætər] *n* questione *f*;
(*Physics*) materia, sostanza; (*content*)
contenuto; (*Med: pus*) pus *m* ▷ *vi*
importare; **it doesn't ~** non importa;
(*I don't mind*) non fa niente; **what's
the ~?** che cosa c'è?; **no ~ what**
qualsiasi cosa accada; **as a ~ of
course** come cosa naturale; **as a ~ of
fact** in verità; **matters** *npl* (*affairs*)
questioni
mattress ['mætrɪs] *n* materasso
mature [mə'tjuər] *adj* maturo(-a);

(*cheese*) stagionato(-a) ▷ *vi* maturare;
stagionare; **mature student** *n*
*studente universitario che ha più di 25
anni*; **maturity** *n* maturità

maul [mɔːl] *vt* lacerare

mauve [məʊv] *adj* malva *inv*

max *abbr* = **maximum**

maximize ['mæksɪmaɪz] *vt*
(*profits etc*) massimizzare; (*chances*)
aumentare al massimo

maximum ['mæksɪməm] (*pl*
maxima) *adj* massimo(-a) ▷ *n*
massimo

May [meɪ] *n* maggio

may [meɪ] (*conditional* **might**) *vi*
(*indicating possibility*): **he ~ come**
può darsi che venga; (*be allowed to*):
~ I smoke? posso fumare?; (*wishes*):
~ God bless you! Dio la benedica!;
you ~ as well go tanto vale che tu te
ne vada

maybe ['meɪbiː] *adv* forse, può darsi;
~ he'll ... può darsi che lui ... + *sub*,
forse lui ...

May Day *n* il primo maggio

mayhem ['meɪhɛm] *n* cagnara

mayonnaise [meɪə'neɪz] *n*
maionese *f*

mayor [mɛəʳ] *n* sindaco; **mayoress** *n*
sindaco (*donna*); moglie *f* del sindaco

maze [meɪz] *n* labirinto, dedalo

MD *n abbr* (= *Doctor of Medicine*) titolo di
studio; (*Comm*) see **managing director**

me [miː] *pron* mi, m' + *vowel or silent* "h";
(*stressed, after prep*) me; **he heard me**
mi ha *or* m'ha sentito; **give me a book**
dammi (*or* mi dia) un libro; **it's me**
sono io; **with me** con me; **without
me** senza di me

meadow ['mɛdəʊ] *n* prato

meagre ['miːgəʳ] (*US* **meager**) *adj*
magro(-a)

meal [miːl] *n* pasto; (*flour*) farina;
mealtime *n* l'ora di mangiare

mean [miːn] (*pt, pp* **meant**) *adj* (*with
money*) avaro(-a), gretto(-a); (*unkind*)
meschino(-a), maligno(-a); (*shabby*)

misero(-a); (*average*) medio(-a) ▷ *vt*
(*signify*) significare, voler dire; (*intend*):
to ~ to do aver l'intenzione di fare
▷ *n* mezzo; (*Math*) media; **means** *npl*
(*way, money*) mezzi *mpl*; **by ~s of** per
mezzo di; **by all ~s** ma certo, prego;
to be ~t for essere destinato(-a) a; **do
you ~ it?** dice sul serio?; **what do you
~?** che cosa vuol dire?

meaning ['miːnɪŋ] *n* significato,
senso; **meaningful** *adj*
significativo(-a); **meaningless** *adj*
senza senso

meant [mɛnt] *pt, pp of* **mean**

meantime ['miːntaɪm] *adv* (*also:* **in
the ~**) nel frattempo

meanwhile ['miːnwaɪl] *adv* nel
frattempo

measles ['miːzlz] *n* morbillo

measure ['mɛʒəʳ] *vt, vi* misurare ▷ *n*
misura; (*also:* **tape ~**) metro

measurement ['mɛʒəmənt] *n* (*act*)
misurazione *f*; (*measure*) misura;
chest/hip ~ giro petto/fianchi; **to
take sb's ~s** prendere le misure di qn

meat [miːt] *n* carne *f*; **I don't eat ~**
non mangio carne; **cold ~** affettato;
meatball *n* polpetta di carne

Mecca ['mɛkə] *n* (*also fig*) la Mecca

mechanic [mɪ'kænɪk] *n* meccanico;
can you send a ~? può mandare
un meccanico?; **mechanical** *adj*
meccanico(-a)

mechanism ['mɛkənɪzəm] *n*
meccanismo

medal ['mɛdl] *n* medaglia; **medallist**
(*US* **medalist**) *n* (*Sport*): **to be a gold
medallist** essere medaglia d'oro

meddle ['mɛdl] *vi* **to ~ in** immischiarsi
in, mettere le mani in; **to ~ with**
toccare

media ['miːdɪə] *npl* media *mpl*

mediaeval [mɛdɪ'iːvl] *adj*
= **medieval**

mediate ['miːdɪeɪt] *vi* fare da
mediatore(-trice)

medical ['mɛdɪkl] *adj* medico(-a) ▷ *n*

visita medica; **medical certificate** n
certificato medico

medicated['mɛdɪkeɪtɪd] adj
medicato(-a)

medication[mɛdɪ'keɪʃən] n
medicinali mpl, farmaci mpl

medicine['mɛdsɪn] n medicina

medieval[mɛdɪ'iːvl] adj medievale

mediocre[miːdɪ'əukər] adj mediocre

meditate['mɛdɪteɪt] vi **to ~ (on)**
meditare (su)

meditation[mɛdɪ'teɪʃən] n
meditazione f

Mediterranean[mɛdɪtə'reɪnɪən]
adj mediterraneo(-a); **the ~ (Sea)** il
(mare) Mediterraneo

medium['miːdɪəm] (pl **media**)
adj medio(-a) ▷ n (means) mezzo;
(pl mediums: person) medium m
inv; **medium-sized** adj (tin etc) di
grandezza media; (clothes) di taglia
media; **medium wave** n onde fpl
medie

meek[miːk] adj dolce, umile

meet[miːt] (pt, pp **met**) vt incontrare;
(for the first time) fare la conoscenza di;
(go and fetch) andare a prendere; (fig)
affrontare; soddisfare; raggiungere
▷ vi incontrarsi; (in session) riunirsi;
(join: objects) unirsi; **nice to ~ you**
piacere (di conoscerla); **meet up** vi **to
meet up with sb** incontrare qn; **meet
with** vt fus incontrare; **meeting** n
incontro; (session: of club etc) riunione
f; (interview) intervista; **she's at
a meeting** (Comm) è in riunione;
meeting place n luogo d'incontro

megabyte['mɛgəbaɪt] n (Comput)
megabyte m inv

megaphone['mɛgəfəun] n
megafono

megapixel['mɛgəpɪksl] n
megapixel m inv

melancholy['mɛlənkəlɪ] n
malinconia ▷ adj malinconico(-a)

melody['mɛlədɪ] n melodia

melon['mɛlən] n melone m

melt[mɛlt] vi (gen) sciogliersi,
struggersi; (metals) fondersi ▷ vt
sciogliere, struggere; fondere

member['mɛmbər] n membro;
Member of Congress(us)
n membro del Congresso;
Member of Parliament(brit)
n deputato(-a); **Member of the
European Parliament**(brit) n
eurodeputato(-a); **Member of
the Scottish Parliament**(brit)
n deputato(-a) del Parlamento
scozzese; **membership** n iscrizione
f, (numero d')iscritti mpl, membri
mpl; **membership card** n tessera (di
iscrizione)

memento[mə'mɛntəu] n ricordo,
souvenir m inv

memo['mɛməu] n appunto; (Comm
etc) comunicazione f di servizio

memorable['mɛmərəbl] adj
memorabile

memorandum[mɛmə'rændəm] (pl
memoranda) n appunto; (Comm etc)
comunicazione f di servizio

memorial[mɪ'mɔːrɪəl] n
monumento commemorativo ▷ adj
commemorativo(-a)

memorize['mɛməraɪz] vt
memorizzare

memory['mɛmərɪ] n (also Comput)
memoria; (recollection) ricordo;
memory card n (for digital camera)
scheda di memoria

men[mɛn] npl of **man**

menace['mɛnəs] n minaccia ▷ vt
minacciare

mend[mɛnd] vt aggiustare, riparare;
(darn) rammendare ▷ n **on the ~** in via
di guarigione

meningitis[mɛnɪn'dʒaɪtɪs] n
meningite f

menopause['mɛnəupɔːz] n
menopausa

men's room n: **the men's room** (esp
us) la toilette degli uomini

menstruation[mɛnstru'eɪʃən] n

mestruazione f

menswear ['mɛnzweəʳ] n
abbigliamento maschile

mental ['mɛntl] adj mentale; **mental
hospital** n ospedale m psichiatrico;
mentality [mɛn'tælɪtɪ] n mentalità
f inv; **mentally** adv: **to be mentally
handicapped** essere minorato
psichico

menthol ['mɛnθɔl] n mentolo

mention ['mɛnʃən] n menzione f ▷ vt
menzionare, far menzione di; **don't ~
it!** non c'è di che!, prego!

menu ['mɛnjuː] n (set menu, Comput)
menù m inv; (printed) carta; **could we
see the ~?** ci può portare il menù?

MEP n abbr = **Member of the
European Parliament**

mercenary ['məːsɪnərɪ] adj venale
▷ n mercenario

merchandise ['məːtʃəndaɪz] n
merci fpl

merchant ['məːtʃənt] n mercante m,
commerciante m; **merchant navy**
(US **merchant marine**) n marina
mercantile

merciless ['məːsɪlɪs] adj spietato(-a)

mercury ['məːkjʊrɪ] n mercurio

mercy ['məːsɪ] n pietà f; (Rel)
misericordia; **at the ~ of** alla mercè di

mere [mɪəʳ] adj semplice; **by a ~
chance** per mero caso; **merely** adv
semplicemente, non ... che

merge [məːdʒ] vt unire ▷ vi fondersi,
unirsi; (Comm) fondersi; **merger** n
(Comm) fusione f

meringue [mə'ræŋ] n meringa

merit ['mɛrɪt] n merito, valore m ▷ vt
meritare

mermaid ['məːmeɪd] n sirena

merry ['mɛrɪ] adj gaio(-a), allegro(-a);
M~ Christmas! Buon Natale!; **merry-
go-round** n carosello

mesh [mɛʃ] n maglia; rete f

mess [mɛs] n confusione f, disordine
m; (fig) pasticcio m; (dirt) sporcizia; (Mil)
mensa; **mess about** or **around** (inf)
vi trastullarsi; **mess with** (inf) vt
fus (challenge, confront) litigare con;
(drugs, drinks) abusare di; **mess up** vt
sporcare; fare un pasticcio di; rovinare

message ['mɛsɪdʒ] n messaggio;
can I leave a ~? posso lasciare un
messaggio?; **are there any ~s for
me?** ci sono messaggi per me?;
message board n (Comput) bacheca
elettronica

messenger ['mɛsɪndʒəʳ] n
messaggero(-a)

Messrs ['mɛsəz] abbr (on letters) Spett.

messy ['mɛsɪ] adj sporco(-a),
disordinato(-a)

met [mɛt] pt, pp of **meet**

metabolism [mɛ'tæbəlɪzəm] n
metabolismo

metal ['mɛtl] n metallo; **metallic**
[-'tælɪk] adj metallico(-a)

metaphor ['mɛtəfəʳ] n metafora

meteor ['miːtɪəʳ] n meteora;
meteorite ['miːtɪəraɪt] n meteorite m

meteorology [miːtɪə'rɔlədʒɪ] n
meteorologia

meter ['miːtəʳ] n (instrument)
contatore m; (parking meter)
parchimetro; (US: unit) = **metre**

method ['mɛθəd] n metodo;
methodical [mɪ'θɔdɪkl] adj
metodico(-a)

meths [mɛθs] (BRIT) n alcool m
denaturato

meticulous [mɛ'tɪkjʊləs] adj
meticoloso(-a)

metre ['miːtəʳ] (US **meter**) n metro

metric ['mɛtrɪk] adj metrico(-a)

metro ['mɛtrəu] n metro m inv

metropolitan [mɛtrə'pɔlɪtən] adj
metropolitano(-a)

Mexican ['mɛksɪkən] adj, n
messicano(-a)

Mexico ['mɛksɪkəu] n Messico

mg abbr (= milligram) mg

mice [maɪs] npl of **mouse**

micro... ['maɪkrəu] prefix micro...;
microchip n microcircuito

integrato; **microphone** n microfono; **microscope** n microscopio; **microwave** n (also: **microwave oven**) forno a microonde

mid [mɪd] adj ▷ **~ May** metà maggio; **~ afternoon** metà pomeriggio; **in ~ air** a mezz'aria; **midday** n mezzogiorno

middle ['mɪdl] n mezzo; centro; (waist) vita ▷ adj di mezzo; **in the ~ of the night** nel bel mezzo della notte; **middle-aged** adj di mezza età; **Middle Ages** npl: **the Middle Ages** il Medioevo; **middle-class** adj ≈ borghese; **Middle East** n Medio Oriente m; **middle name** n secondo nome m; **middle school** n (US) scuola media per ragazzi dagli 11 ai 14 anni; (BRIT) scuola media per ragazzi dagli 8 o 9 ai 12 o 13 anni

midge [mɪdʒ] n moscerino

midget ['mɪdʒɪt] n nano(-a)

midnight ['mɪdnaɪt] n mezzanotte f

midst [mɪdst] n: **in the ~ of** in mezzo a

midsummer [mɪd'sʌmər] n mezza or piena estate f

midway [mɪd'weɪ] adj, adv: **~ (between)** a mezza strada (fra); **~ (through)** a metà (di)

midweek [mɪd'wiːk] adv a metà settimana

midwife ['mɪdwaɪf] (pl **midwives**) n levatrice f

midwinter [mɪd'wɪntər] n pieno inverno

might [maɪt] vb see **may** ▷ n potere m, forza; **mighty** adj forte, potente

migraine ['miːgreɪn] n emicrania

migrant ['maɪgrənt] adj (bird) migratore(-trice); (worker) emigrato(-a)

migrate [maɪ'greɪt] vi (bird) migrare; (person) emigrare

migration [maɪ'greɪʃən] n migrazione f

mike [maɪk] n abbr (= microphone) microfono

Milan [mɪ'læn] n Milano f

mild [maɪld] adj mite; (person, voice) dolce; (flavour) delicato(-a); (illness) leggero(-a); (interest) blando(-a) ▷ n (beer) birra leggera; **mildly** ['maɪldlɪ] adv mitemente; dolcemente; delicatamente; leggermente; blandamente; **to put it mildly** a dire poco

mile [maɪl] n miglio; **mileage** n distanza in miglia, ≈ chilometraggio; **mileometer** [maɪ'lɔmɪtər] n ≈ contachilometri m inv; **milestone** ['maɪlstəun] n pietra miliare

military ['mɪlɪtərɪ] adj militare

militia [mɪ'lɪʃə] n milizia

milk [mɪlk] n latte m ▷ vt (cow) mungere; (fig) sfruttare; **milk chocolate** n cioccolato al latte; **milkman** (irreg) n lattaio; **milky** adj lattiginoso(-a); (colour) latteo(-a)

mill [mɪl] n mulino; (small: for coffee, pepper etc) macinino; (factory) fabbrica; (spinning mill) filatura ▷ vt macinare ▷ vi (also: **~ about**) brulicare

millennium [mɪ'lenɪəm] (pl **millenniums** or **millennia**) n millennio

milli... ['mɪlɪ] prefix: **milligram(me)** n milligrammo; **millilitre** ['mɪlɪliːtər] (US **milliliter**) n millilitro; **millimetre** (US **millimeter**) n millimetro

million ['mɪljən] num milione m; **millionaire** n milionario, ≈ miliardario; **millionth** num milionesimo(-a)

milometer [maɪ'lɔmɪtər] n = **mileometer**

mime [maɪm] n mimo ▷ vt, vi mimare

mimic ['mɪmɪk] n imitatore(-trice) ▷ vt fare la mimica di

min. abbr = **minute(s)**; **minimum**

mince [mɪns] vt tritare, macinare ▷ n (BRIT Culin) carne f tritata or macinata; **mincemeat** n frutta secca tritata per uso in pasticceria; (US) carne f tritata or macinata; **mince pie** n specie di torta con frutta secca

mind [maɪnd] *n* mente *f* ▷ *vt* (*attend to, look after*) badare a, occuparsi di; (*be careful*) fare attenzione a, stare attento(-a) a; (*object to*): **I don't ~ the noise** il rumore non mi dà alcun fastidio; **I don't ~** non m'importa; **do you ~ if ...?** le dispiace se...?; **it is on my ~** mi preoccupa; **to my ~** secondo me, a mio parere; **to be out of one's ~** essere uscito(-a) di mente; **to keep** or **bear sth in ~** non dimenticare qc; **to make up one's ~** decidersi; **~ you, ...** sì, però va detto che ...; **never ~** non importa, non fa niente; (*don't worry*) non preoccuparti; **"~ the step"** "attenzione allo scalino"; **mindless** *adj* idiota

mine[1] [maɪn] *pron* il (la) mio(-a); (*pl*) i (le) miei (mei); **that book is ~** quel libro è mio; **yours is red, ~ is green** il tuo è rosso, il mio è verde; **a friend of ~** un mio amico

mine[2] [maɪn] *n* miniera; (*explosive*) mina ▷ *vt* (*coal*) estrarre; (*ship, beach*) minare; **minefield** *n* (*also fig*) campo minato; **miner** [maɪnəʳ] *n* minatore *m*

mineral [mɪnərəl] *adj* minerale ▷ *n* minerale *m*; **mineral water** *n* acqua minerale

mingle [mɪŋgl] *vi* **to ~ with** mescolarsi a, mischiarsi con

miniature [mɪnətʃəʳ] *adj* in miniatura ▷ *n* miniatura

minibar [mɪnɪbɑːʳ] *n* minibar *m inv*

minibus [mɪnɪbʌs] *n* minibus *m inv*

minicab [mɪnɪkæb] *n* (*BRIT*) ≈ taxi *m inv*

minimal [mɪnɪml] *adj* minimo(-a)

minimize [mɪnɪmaɪz] *vt* minimizzare

minimum [mɪnɪməm] (*pl* **minima**) *n* minimo ▷ *adj* minimo(-a)

mining [maɪnɪŋ] *n* industria mineraria

miniskirt [mɪnɪskəːt] *n* minigonna

minister [mɪnɪstəʳ] *n* (*BRIT Pol*) ministro; (*Rel*) pastore *m*

ministry [mɪnɪstrɪ] *n* ministero

minor [maɪnəʳ] *adj* minore, di poca importanza; (*Mus*) minore ▷ *n* (*Law*) minorenne *m/f*

Minorca [mɪˈnɔːkə] *n* Minorca

minority [maɪˈnɔrɪtɪ] *n* minoranza

mint [mɪnt] *n* (*plant*) menta; (*sweet*) pasticca di menta ▷ *vt* (*coins*) battere; **the (Royal) M~** (*BRIT*), **the (US) M~** (*US*) la Zecca; **in ~ condition** come nuovo(-a) di zecca

minus [maɪnəs] *n* (*also*: **~ sign**) segno meno ▷ *prep* meno

minute [*adj* maɪˈnjuːt, *n* mɪnɪt] *adj* minuscolo(-a); (*detail*) minuzioso(-a) ▷ *n* minuto; **minutes** *npl* (*of meeting*) verbale *m*

miracle [mɪrəkl] *n* miracolo

miraculous [mɪˈrækjuləs] *adj* miracoloso(-a)

mirage [mɪrɑːʒ] *n* miraggio

mirror [mɪrəʳ] *n* specchio; (*in car*) specchietto

misbehave [mɪsbɪˈheɪv] *vi* comportarsi male

misc. *abbr* = **miscellaneous**

miscarriage [mɪsˈkærɪdʒ] *n* (*Med*) aborto spontaneo; **miscarriage of justice** errore *m* giudiziario

miscellaneous [mɪsɪˈleɪnɪəs] *adj* (*items*) vario(-a); (*selection*) misto(-a)

mischief [mɪstʃɪf] *n* (*naughtiness*) birichineria; (*maliciousness*) malizia; **mischievous** *adj* birichino(-a)

misconception [mɪskənˈsɛpʃən] *n* idea sbagliata

misconduct [mɪsˈkɔndʌkt] *n* cattiva condotta; **professional ~** reato professionale

miser [maɪzəʳ] *n* avaro

miserable [mɪzərəbl] *adj* infelice; (*wretched*) miserabile; (*weather*) deprimente; (*offer, failure*) misero(-a)

misery [mɪzərɪ] *n* (*unhappiness*) tristezza; (*wretchedness*) miseria

misfortune [mɪsˈfɔːtʃən] *n* sfortuna

misgiving [mɪsˈgɪvɪŋ] *n* apprensione *f*; **to have ~s about** avere dei dubbi per quanto riguarda

misguided [mɪs'gaɪdɪd] adj sbagliato(-a), poco giudizioso(-a)

mishap ['mɪshæp] n disgrazia

misinterpret [mɪsɪn'təːprɪt] vt interpretare male

misjudge [mɪs'dʒʌdʒ] vt giudicare male

mislay [mɪs'leɪ] (irreg) vt smarrire

mislead [mɪs'liːd] (irreg) vt sviare; **misleading** adj ingannevole

misplace [mɪs'pleɪs] vt smarrire

misprint ['mɪsprɪnt] n errore m di stampa

misrepresent [mɪsreprɪ'zent] vt travisare

Miss [mɪs] n Signorina

miss [mɪs] vt (fail to get) perdere; (fail to hit) mancare; (fail to see): **you can't ~ it** non puoi non vederlo; (regret the absence of): **I ~ him** sento la sua mancanza ▷ vi mancare ▷ n (shot) colpo mancato; **we ~ed our train** abbiamo perso il treno; **miss out** (BRIT) vt omettere; **miss out on** vt fus (fun, party) perdersi; (chance, bargain) lasciarsi sfuggire

missile ['mɪsaɪl] n (Mil) missile m; (object thrown) proiettile m

missing ['mɪsɪŋ] adj perso(-a), smarrito(-a); (person) scomparso(-a); (: after disaster, Mil) disperso(-a); (removed) mancante; **to be ~** mancare

mission ['mɪʃən] n missione f; **missionary** n missionario(-a)

misspell [mɪs'spel] vt (irreg: like spell) sbagliare l'ortografia di

mist [mɪst] n nebbia, foschia ▷ vi (also: **~ over, ~ up**) annebbiarsi; (: BRIT: windows) appannarsi

mistake [mɪs'teɪk] (irreg: like take) n sbaglio, errore m ▷ vt sbagliarsi di; fraintendere; **to make a ~** fare uno sbaglio, sbagliare; **there must be some ~** ci dev'essere un errore; **by ~** per sbaglio; **to ~ for** prendere per; **mistaken** pp of **mistake** ▷ adj (idea

etc) sbagliato(-a); **to be mistaken** sbagliarsi

mister ['mɪstəʳ] (inf) n signore m; see **Mr**

mistletoe ['mɪsltəu] n vischio

mistook [mɪs'tuk] pt of **mistake**

mistress ['mɪstrɪs] n padrona; (lover) amante f; (BRIT Scol) insegnante f

mistrust [mɪs'trʌst] vt diffidare di

misty ['mɪstɪ] adj nebbioso(-a), brumoso(-a)

misunderstand [mɪsʌndə'stænd] (irreg) vt, vi capire male, fraintendere; **misunderstanding** n malinteso, equivoco; **there's been a misunderstanding** c'è stato un malinteso

misunderstood [mɪsʌndə'stud] pt, pp of **misunderstand**

misuse [n mɪs'juːs, vb mɪs'juːz] n cattivo uso; (of power) abuso ▷ vt far cattivo uso di; abusare di

mitt(en) ['mɪt(n)] n mezzo guanto; manopola

mix [mɪks] vt mescolare ▷ vi (people): **to ~ with** avere a che fare con ▷ n mescolanza; preparato; **mix up** vt mescolare; (confuse) confondere; **mixed** adj misto(-a); **mixed grill** n (BRIT) misto alla griglia; **mixed salad** n insalata mista; **mixed-up** adj (confused) confuso(-a); **mixer** n (for food: electric) frullatore m; (: hand) frullino; (person): **he is a good mixer** è molto socievole; **mixture** n mescolanza; (blend: of tobacco etc) miscela; (Med) sciroppo; **mix-up** n confusione f

ml abbr (= millilitre(s)) ml

mm abbr (= millimetre) mm

moan [məun] n gemito ▷ vi (inf: complain): **to ~ (about)** lamentarsi (di)

moat [məut] n fossato

mob [mɔb] n calca ▷ vt accalcarsi intorno a

mobile ['məubaɪl] adj mobile ▷ n (decoration) mobile m; **mobile home** n grande roulotte f inv (utilizzata come domicilio); **mobile phone** n telefono portatile, telefonino

mobility [məu'bɪlɪtɪ] n mobilità; (of applicant) disponibilità a viaggiare

mobilize ['məubɪlaɪz] vt mobilitare ▷ vi mobilitarsi

mock [mɔk] vt deridere, burlarsi di ▷ adj falso(-a); **mocks** npl (BRIT: Scol: inf) simulazione f degli esami; **mockery** n derisione f; **to make a mockery of** burlarsi di; (exam) rendere una farsa

mod cons ['mɔd'kɔnz] npl abbr (BRIT) = **modern conveniences**; see **convenience**

mode [məud] n modo

model ['mɔdl] n modello; (person: for fashion) indossatore(-trice); (: for artist) modello(-a) ▷ adj (small-scale: railway etc) in miniatura; (child, factory) modello inv ▷ vt modellare ▷ vi fare l'indossatore (or l'indossatrice); **to ~ clothes** presentare degli abiti

modem ['məudɛm] n modem m inv

moderate [adj 'mɔdərət, vb 'mɔdəreɪt] adj moderato(-a) ▷ vi moderarsi, placarsi ▷ vt moderare

moderation [mɔdə'reɪʃən] n moderazione f, misura; **in ~** in quantità moderata, con moderazione

modern ['mɔdən] adj moderno(-a); **mod cons** comodità fpl moderne; **modernize** vt modernizzare; **modern languages** npl lingue fpl moderne

modest ['mɔdɪst] adj modesto(-a); **modesty** n modestia

modification [mɔdɪfɪ'keɪʃən] n modificazione f; **to make ~s** fare or apportare delle modifiche

modify ['mɔdɪfaɪ] vt modificare

module ['mɔdjuːl] n modulo

mohair ['məuhɛər] n mohair m

Mohammed [məu'hæmɪd] n Maometto

moist [mɔɪst] adj umido(-a); **moisture** ['mɔɪstʃər] n umidità;

(on glass) goccioline fpl di vapore; **moisturizer** ['mɔɪstʃəraɪzər] n idratante f

mold etc [məuld] (US) n, vt = **mould**

mole [məul] n (animal, fig) talpa; (spot) neo

molecule ['mɔlɪkjuːl] n molecola

molest [məu'lɛst] vt molestare

molten ['məultən] adj fuso(-a)

mom [mɔm] (US) n = **mum**

moment ['məumənt] n momento, istante m; **at that ~** in quel momento; **at the ~** al momento, in questo momento; **momentarily** ['məuməntərɪlɪ] adv per un momento; (US: very soon) da un momento all'altro; **momentary** adj momentaneo(-a), passeggero(-a); **momentous** [-'mɛntəs] adj di grande importanza

momentum [məu'mɛntəm] n (Physics) momento; (fig) impeto; **to gather ~** aumentare di velocità

mommy ['mɔmɪ] (US) n = **mummy**

Mon. abbr (= Monday) lun.

Monaco ['mɔnəkəu] n Principato di Monaco

monarch ['mɔnək] n monarca m; **monarchy** n monarchia

monastery ['mɔnəstərɪ] n monastero

Monday ['mʌndɪ] n lunedì m inv

monetary ['mʌnɪtərɪ] adj monetario(-a)

money ['mʌnɪ] n denaro, soldi mpl; **I haven't got any ~** non ho soldi; **money belt** n marsupio (per soldi); **money order** n vaglia m inv

mongrel ['mʌŋgrəl] n (dog) cane m bastardo

monitor ['mɔnɪtər] n (TV, Comput) monitor m inv ▷ vt controllare

monk [mʌŋk] n monaco

monkey ['mʌŋkɪ] n scimmia

monologue ['mɔnəlɔg] n monologo

monopoly [mə'nɔpəlɪ] n monopolio

monosodium glutamate [mɔnə'səudɪəm'gluːtəmeɪt] n

glutammato di sodio

monotonous [məˈnɔtənəs] *adj* monotono(-a)

monsoon [mɔnˈsuːn] *n* monsone *m*

monster [ˈmɔnstəʳ] *n* mostro

month [mʌnθ] *n* mese *m*; **monthly** *adj* mensile ▷ *adv* al mese; ogni mese

monument [ˈmɔnjumənt] *n* monumento

mood [muːd] *n* umore *m*; **to be in a good/bad ~** essere di buon/cattivo umore; **moody** *adj* (*variable*) capriccioso(-a), lunatico(-a); (*sullen*) imbronciato(-a)

moon [muːn] *n* luna; **moonlight** *n* chiaro di luna

moor [muəʳ] *n* brughiera ▷ *vt* (*ship*) ormeggiare ▷ *vi* ormeggiarsi

moose [muːs] *n inv* alce *m*

mop [mɔp] *n* lavapavimenti *m inv*; (*also:* **~ of hair**) zazzera ▷ *vt* lavare con lo straccio; (*face*) asciugare; **mop up** *vt* asciugare con uno straccio

mope [məup] *vi* fare il broncio

moped [ˈməupɛd] *n* (BRIT) ciclomotore *m*

moral [ˈmɔrl] *adj* morale ▷ *n* morale *f*; **morals** *npl* (*principles*) moralità

morale [mɔˈrɑːl] *n* morale *m*

morality [məˈrælɪtɪ] *n* moralità

morbid [ˈmɔːbɪd] *adj* morboso(-a)

 KEYWORD

more [mɔːʳ] *adj* 1 (*greater in number etc*) più; **more people/letters than we expected** più persone/lettere di quante ne aspettavamo; **I have more wine/money than you** ho più vino/soldi di te; **I have more wine than beer** ho più vino che birra
2 (*additional*) altro(-a), ancora; **do you want (some) more tea?** vuole dell'altro tè?, vuole ancora del tè?; **I have no** *or* **I don't have any more money** non ho più soldi

▷ *pron* 1 (*greater amount*) più; **more than 10** più di 10; **it cost more than we expected** ha costato più di quanto ci aspettavamo
2 (*further or additional amount*) ancora; **is there any more?** ce n'è ancora?; **there's no more** non ce n'è più; **a little more** ancora un po'; **many/much more** molti(-e)/molto(-a) di più

▷ *adv* **more dangerous/easily (than)** più pericoloso/facilmente (di); **more and more** sempre di più; **more and more difficult** sempre più difficile; **more or less** più o meno; **more than ever** più che mai

moreover [mɔːˈrəuvəʳ] *adv* inoltre, di più

morgue [mɔːg] *n* obitorio

morning [ˈmɔːnɪŋ] *n* mattina, mattino; (*duration*) mattinata ▷ *cpd* del mattino; **in the ~** la mattina; **7 o'clock in the ~** le 7 di *or* della mattina; **morning sickness** *n* nausee *fpl* mattutine

Moroccan [məˈrɔkən] *adj*, *n* marocchino(-a)

Morocco [məˈrɔkəu] *n* Marocco

moron [ˈmɔːrɔn] (*inf*) *n* deficiente *m/f*

morphine [ˈmɔːfiːn] *n* morfina

morris dancing *n* vedi nota nel riquadro

● **MORRIS DANCING**
●
● Il **morris dancing** è una
● danza folcloristica inglese
● tradizionalmente riservata agli
● uomini. Vestiti di bianco e con dei
● campanelli attaccati alle caviglie,
● i ballerini eseguono una danza
● tenendo in mano dei fazzoletti
● bianchi e lunghi bastoni. Questa
● danza è molto popolare nelle feste
● paesane.

Morse [mɔːs] *n* (*also:* **~ code**) alfabeto

Morse
mortal ['mɔːtl] *adj* mortale ▷ *n*
mortale *m*
mortar ['mɔːtəʳ] *n* (*Constr*) malta;
(*dish*) mortaio
mortgage ['mɔːɡɪdʒ] *n* ipoteca; (*loan*)
prestito ipotecario ▷ *vt* ipotecare
mortician [mɔː'tɪʃən] (*us*) *n*
impresario di pompe funebri
mortified ['mɔːtɪfaɪd] *adj*
umiliato(-a)
mortuary ['mɔːtjuərɪ] *n* camera
mortuaria; obitorio
mosaic [məu'zeɪɪk] *n* mosaico
Moscow ['mɔskəu] *n* Mosca
Moslem ['mɔzləm] *adj*, *n* = **Muslim**
mosque [mɔsk] *n* moschea
mosquito [mɔs'kiːtəu] (*pl*
mosquitoes) *n* zanzara
moss [mɔs] *n* muschio
most [məust] *adj* (*almost all*) la
maggior parte di; (*largest, greatest*):
who has (the) ~ money? chi ha
più soldi di tutti? ▷ *pron* la maggior
parte ▷ *adv* più; (*work, sleep etc*) di
più; (*very*) molto, estremamente; **the
~** (*also: + adjective*) il(-la) più; **~ of** la
maggior parte di; **~ of them** quasi
tutti; **I saw (the) ~** ho visto più io; **at
the (very) ~** al massimo; **to make
the ~ of** trarre il massimo vantaggio
da; **a ~ interesting book** un libro
estremamente interessante; **mostly**
adv per lo più
MOT (*brit*) *n abbr* = **Ministry of
Transport**; **the ~ (test)** revisione
annuale obbligatoria degli autoveicoli
motel [məu'tɛl] *n* motel *m inv*
moth [mɔθ] *n* farfalla notturna; tarma
mother ['mʌðəʳ] *n* madre *f* ▷ *vt* (*care
for*) fare da madre a; **motherhood**
n maternità; **mother-in-law**
n suocera; **mother-of-pearl**
[mʌðərəv'pəːl] *n* madreperla;
Mother's Day *n* la festa della
mamma; **mother-to-be** [mʌðətə'biː]
n futura mamma; **mother tongue** *n*

madrelingua
motif [məu'tiːf] *n* motivo
motion ['məuʃən] *n* movimento,
moto; (*gesture*) gesto; (*at meeting*)
mozione *f* ▷ *vt*, *vi* **to ~ (to) sb to do**
fare cenno a qn di fare; **motionless**
adj immobile; **motion picture** *n* film
m inv
motivate ['məutɪveɪt] *vt* (*act,
decision*) dare origine a, motivare;
(*person*) spingere
motivation [məutɪ'veɪʃən] *n*
motivazione *f*
motive ['məutɪv] *n* motivo
motor ['məutəʳ] *n* motore *m*;
(*brit: inf: vehicle*) macchina ▷ *cpd*
automobilistico(-a); **motorbike** *n*
moto *f inv*; **motorboat** *n* motoscafo;
motorcar (*brit*) *n* automobile
f; **motorcycle** *n* motocicletta;
motorcyclist *n* motociclista
m/f; **motoring** (*brit*) *n* turismo
automobilistico; **motorist** *n*
automobilista *m/f*; **motor racing**
(*brit*) *n* corse *fpl* automobilistiche;
motorway (*brit*) *n* autostrada
motto ['mɔtəu] (*pl* **mottoes**) *n* motto
mould [məuld] (*us* **mold**) *n* forma,
stampo; (*mildew*) muffa ▷ *vt*
formare; (*fig*) foggiare; **mouldy** *adj*
ammuffito(-a); (*smell*) di muffa
mound [maund] *n* rialzo, collinetta;
(*heap*) mucchio
mount [maunt] *n* (*Geo*) monte *m*
▷ *vt* montare; (*horse*) montare a ▷ *vi*
(*increase*) aumentare; **mount up** *vi*
(*build up*) accumularsi
mountain ['mauntɪn] *n* montagna
▷ *cpd* di montagna; **mountain
bike** *n* mountain bike *f inv*;
mountaineer [-'nɪəʳ] *n* alpinista
m/f; **mountaineering** [-'nɪərɪŋ]
n alpinismo; **mountainous** *adj*
montagnoso(-a); **mountain range** *n*
catena montuosa
mourn [mɔːn] *vt* piangere, lamentare
▷ *vi* **to ~ (for sb)** piangere (la morte

di qn); **mourner** n parente m/f or amico(-a) del defunto; **mourning** n lutto; **in mourning** in lutto

mouse [maʊs] (pl **mice**) n topo; (Comput) mouse m inv; **mouse mat, mouse pad** n (Comput) tappetino del mouse

moussaka [mu'sɑːkə] n moussaka

mousse [muːs] n mousse f inv

moustache [məs'tɑːʃ] (US **mustache**) n baffi mpl

mouth [maʊθ, pl maʊðz] n bocca; (of river) bocca, foce f; (opening) orifizio; **mouthful** n boccata; **mouth organ** n armonica; **mouthpiece** n (Mus) imboccatura, bocchino; (spokesman) portavoce m/f inv; **mouthwash** n collutorio

move [muːv] n (movement) movimento; (in game) mossa; (: turn to play) turno; (change: of house) trasloco; (: of job) cambiamento ▷ vt muovere; (change position of) spostare; (emotionally) commuovere; (Pol: resolution etc) proporre ▷ vi (gen) muoversi, spostarsi; (also: ~ house) cambiar casa, traslocare; **to get a ~ on** affrettarsi, sbrigarsi; **can you ~ your car, please?** può spostare la macchina, per favore?; **to ~ sb to do sth** indurre or spingere qn a fare qc; **to ~ towards** andare verso; **move back** vi (return) ritornare; **move in** vi (to a house) entrare (in una nuova casa); (police etc) intervenire; **move off** vi partire; **move on** vi riprendere la strada; **move out** vi (of house) sgombrare; **move over** vi spostarsi; **move up** vi avanzare; **movement** ['muːvmənt] n (gen) movimento; (gesture) gesto; (of stars, water, physical) moto

movie ['muːvɪ] n film m inv; **the ~s** il cinema; **movie theater** (US) n cinema m inv

moving ['muːvɪŋ] adj mobile; (causing emotion) commovente

mow [məʊ] (pt **mowed**, pp **mowed** or **mown**) vt (grass) tagliare; (corn) mietere; **mower** n (also: **lawnmower**) tagliaerba m inv

Mozambique [məʊzəm'biːk] n Mozambico

MP n abbr = **Member of Parliament**

MP3 n abbr M3; **MP3 player** n lettore m MP3

mpg n abbr = **miles per gallon** (30 mpg = 9.4 l. per 100 km)

m.p.h. n abbr = **miles per hour** (60 m.p.h. = 96 km/h)

Mr ['mɪstər] (US **Mr.**) n **Mr X** Signor X, Sig. X

Mrs ['mɪsɪz] (US **Mrs.**) n **Mrs X** Signora X, Sig.ra X

Ms [mɪz] (US **Ms.**) n = **Miss** or **Mrs**; **Ms X** ≈ Signora X, ≈ Siq.ra X

● **Ms**
●
●
● In inglese si usa **Ms** al posto di "Mrs"
● (Signora) o "Miss" (Signorina) per
● evitare la distinzione tradizionale
● tra le donne sposate e quelle nubili.

MSP n abbr = **Member of the Scottish Parliament**

Mt abbr (Geo: = **mount**) M.

 KEYWORD

much [mʌtʃ] adj, pron molto(-a); **he's done so much work** ha lavorato così tanto; **I have as much money as you** ho tanti soldi quanti ne hai tu; **how much is it?** quant'è?; **it costs too much** costa troppo; **as much as you want** quanto vuoi

▷ adv **1** (greatly) molto, tanto; **thank you very much** molte grazie; **he's very much the gentleman** è il vero gentiluomo; **I read as much as I can** leggo quanto posso; **as much as you** tanto quanto te

2 (by far) molto; **it's much the**

biggest company in Europe è di gran lunga la più grossa società in Europa

3 (almost) grossomodo, praticamente; **they're much the same** sono praticamente uguali

muck [mʌk] n (dirt) sporcizia; **muck up** (inf) vt (ruin) rovinare; **mucky** adj (dirty) sporco(-a), lordo(-a)

mucus ['mjuːkəs] n muco

mud [mʌd] n fango

muddle ['mʌdl] n confusione f, disordine m; pasticcio ▷ vt (also: **~ up**) confondere

muddy ['mʌdɪ] adj fangoso(-a)

mudguard ['mʌdɡɑːd] n parafango

muesli ['mjuːzlɪ] n muesli m

muffin ['mʌfɪn] n specie di pasticcino soffice da tè

muffled ['mʌfld] adj smorzato(-a), attutito(-a)

muffler ['mʌfləʳ] (US) n (Aut) marmitta; (: on motorbike) silenziatore m

mug [mʌɡ] n (cup) tazzone m; (for beer) boccale m; (inf: face) muso; (: fool) scemo(-a) ▷ vt (assault) assalire; **mugger** ['mʌɡəʳ] n aggressore m; **mugging** n assalto

muggy ['mʌɡɪ] adj afoso(-a)

mule [mjuːl] n mulo

multicoloured ['mʌltɪkʌləd] (US **multicolored**) adj multicolore, variopinto(-a)

multimedia ['mʌltɪ'miːdɪə] adj multimedia inv

multinational [mʌltɪ'næʃənl] adj, n multinazionale f

multiple ['mʌltɪpl] adj multiplo(-a), molteplice ▷ n multiplo; **multiple choice (test)** n esercizi mpl a scelta multipla; **multiple sclerosis** [-sklɪ'rəʊsɪs] n sclerosi f a placche

multiplex cinema ['mʌltɪplɛks-] n cinema m inv multisala inv

multiplication [mʌltɪplɪ'keɪʃən] n moltiplicazione f

multiply ['mʌltɪplaɪ] vt moltiplicare ▷ vi moltiplicarsi

multistorey ['mʌltɪ'stɔːrɪ] (BRIT) adj (building, car park) a più piani

mum [mʌm] (BRIT: inf) n mamma ▷ adj **to keep ~** non aprire bocca

mumble ['mʌmbl] vt, vi borbottare

mummy ['mʌmɪ] n (BRIT: mother) mamma; (embalmed) mummia

mumps [mʌmps] n orecchioni mpl

munch [mʌntʃ] vt, vi sgranocchiare

municipal [mjuː'nɪsɪpl] adj municipale

mural ['mjuərl] n dipinto murale

murder ['məːdəʳ] n assassinio, omicidio ▷ vt assassinare; **murderer** n omicida m, assassino

murky ['məːkɪ] adj tenebroso(-a)

murmur ['məːməʳ] n mormorio ▷ vt, vi mormorare

muscle ['mʌsl] n muscolo; (fig) forza; **muscular** ['mʌskjuləʳ] adj muscolare; (person, arm) muscoloso(-a)

museum [mjuː'zɪəm] n museo

mushroom ['mʌʃrum] n fungo ▷ vi crescere in fretta

music ['mjuːzɪk] n musica; **musical** adj musicale; (person) portato(-a) per la musica ▷ n (show) commedia musicale; **musical instrument** n strumento musicale; **musician** [-'zɪʃən] n musicista m/f

Muslim ['mʌzlɪm] adj, n musulmano(-a)

muslin ['mʌzlɪn] n mussola

mussel ['mʌsl] n cozza

must [mʌst] aux vb (obligation): **I ~ do it** devo farlo; (probability): **he ~ be there by now** dovrebbe essere arrivato ormai; **I ~ have made a mistake** devo essermi sbagliato ▷ n **it's a ~** è d'obbligo

mustache ['mʌstæʃ] (US) n = **moustache**

mustard ['mʌstəd] n senape f,

mostarda

mustn't ['mʌsnt] = **must not**

mute [mjuːt] *adj, n* muto(-a)

mutilate ['mjuːtɪleɪt] *vt* mutilare

mutiny ['mjuːtɪnɪ] *n*
ammutinamento

mutter ['mʌtər] *vt, vi* borbottare,
brontolare

mutton ['mʌtn] *n* carne *f* di montone

mutual ['mjuːtʃuəl] *adj* mutuo(-a),
reciproco(-a)

muzzle ['mʌzl] *n* muso; (*protective
device*) museruola; (*of gun*) bocca ▷ *vt*
mettere la museruola a

my [maɪ] *adj* il (la) mio(-a); (*pl*) i (le)
miei (mie); **my house** la mia casa; **my
books** i miei libri; **my brother** mio
fratello; **I've washed my hair/cut
my finger** mi sono lavato i capelli/
tagliato il dito

myself [maɪ'sɛlf] *pron* (*reflexive*) mi;
(*emphatic*) io stesso(-a); (*after prep*) me;
see also **oneself**

mysterious [mɪs'tɪərɪəs] *adj*
misterioso(-a)

mystery ['mɪstərɪ] *n* mistero

mystical ['mɪstɪkəl] *adj* mistico(-a)

mystify ['mɪstɪfaɪ] *vt* mistificare;
(*puzzle*) confondere

myth [mɪθ] *n* mito; **mythology**
[mɪ'θɔlədʒɪ] *n* mitologia

n/a *abbr* = **not applicable**

nag [næg] *vt* tormentare ▷ *vi*
brontolare in continuazione

nail [neɪl] *n* (*human*) unghia; (*metal*)
chiodo ▷ *vt* inchiodare; **to ~ sb down
to (doing) sth** costringere qn a (fare)
qc; **nailbrush** *n* spazzolino da *or*
per unghie; **nailfile** *n* lima da *or* per
unghie; **nail polish** *n* smalto da *or*
per unghie; **nail polish remover** *n*
acetone *m*, solvente *m*; **nail scissors**
npl forbici *fpl* da *or* per unghie; **nail
varnish** (*BRIT*) *n* = **nail polish**

naïve [naɪ'iːv] *adj* ingenuo(-a)

naked ['neɪkɪd] *adj* nudo(-a)

name [neɪm] *n* nome *m*; (*reputation*)
nome, reputazione *f* ▷ *vt* (*baby etc*)
chiamare; (*plant, illness*) nominare;
(*person, object*) identificare; (*price,
date*) fissare; **what's your ~?** come si
chiama?; **by ~** di nome; **she knows
them all by ~** li conosce tutti per
nome; **namely** *adv* cioè

nanny ['nænɪ] *n* bambinaia

nap [næp] n (sleep) pisolino; (of cloth) peluria; **to be caught ~ping** essere preso alla sprovvista

napkin ['næpkɪn] n (also: **table ~**) tovagliolo

nappy ['næpɪ] (BRIT) n pannolino; **nappy rash** n arrossamento (causato dal pannolino)

narcotics [nɑː'kɔtɪkz] npl (drugs) narcotici, stupefacenti mpl

narrative ['nærətɪv] n narrativa

narrator [nə'reɪtə*] n narratore(-trice)

narrow ['nærəu] adj stretto(-a); (fig) limitato(-a), ristretto(-a) ▷ vi restringersi; **to have a ~ escape** farcela per un pelo; **narrow down** vt (search, investigation, possibilities) restringere; (list) ridurre; **narrowly** adv per un pelo; (time) per poco; **narrow-minded** adj meschino(-a)

nasal ['neɪzl] adj nasale

nasty ['nɑːstɪ] adj (person, remark: unpleasant) cattivo(-a); (: rude) villano(-a); (smell, wound, situation) brutto(-a)

nation ['neɪʃən] n nazione f

national ['næʃənl] adj nazionale ▷ n cittadino(-a); **national anthem** n inno nazionale; **national dress** n costume m nazionale; **National Health Service** (BRIT) n servizio nazionale di assistenza sanitaria, ≈ S. S.N. m; **National Insurance** (BRIT) n ≈ Previdenza Sociale; **nationalist** adj, n nazionalista (m/f); **nationality** [-'næliti] n nazionalità f inv; **nationalize** vt nazionalizzare; **national park** n parco nazionale; **National Trust** n sovrintendenza ai beni culturali e ambientali

● **NATIONAL TRUST**
●
● Fondato nel 1895, il **National**
● **Trust** è un'organizzazione che
● si occupa della tutela e della

● salvaguardia di luoghi di interesse
● storico o ambientale nel Regno
● Unito.

nationwide ['neɪʃənwaɪd] adj diffuso(-a) in tutto il paese ▷ adv in tutto il paese

native ['neɪtɪv] n abitante m/f del paese ▷ adj indigeno(-a); (country) natio(-a); (ability) innato(-a); **a ~ of Russia** un nativo della Russia; **a ~ speaker of French** una persona di madrelingua francese; **Native American** n discendente di tribù dell'America settentrionale

NATO ['neɪtəu] n abbr (= North Atlantic Treaty Organization) N.A.T.O. f

natural ['nætʃrəl] adj naturale; (ability) innato(-a); (manner) semplice; **natural gas** n gas m metano; **natural history** n storia naturale; **naturally** adv naturalmente; (by nature: gifted) di natura; **natural resources** npl risorse fpl naturali

nature ['neɪtʃə*] n natura; (character) natura, indole f; **by ~** di natura; **nature reserve** n (BRIT) parco naturale

naughty ['nɔːtɪ] adj (child) birichino(-a), cattivello(-a); (story, film) spinto(-a)

nausea ['nɔːsɪə] n (Med) nausea; (fig: disgust) schifo

naval ['neɪvl] adj navale

navel ['neɪvl] n ombelico

navigate ['nævɪgeɪt] vt percorrere navigando ▷ vi navigare; (Aut) fare da navigatore; **navigation** [-'geɪʃən] n navigazione f

navy ['neɪvɪ] n marina

Nazi ['nɑːtsɪ] n nazista m/f

NB abbr (= nota bene) N.B.

near [nɪə*] adj vicino(-a); (relation) prossimo(-a) ▷ adv vicino ▷ prep (also: **~ to**) vicino a, presso; (: time) verso ▷ vt avvicinarsi a; **nearby** [nɪə'baɪ] adj vicino(-a) ▷ adv vicino; **is there**

a bank nearby? c'è una banca qui vicino?; **nearly** adv quasi; **I nearly fell** per poco non sono caduto; **near-sighted** [nɪə'saɪtɪd] adj miope

neat [niːt] adj (person, room) ordinato(-a); (work) pulito(-a); (solution, plan) ben indovinato(-a), azzeccato(-a); (spirits) liscio(-a); **neatly** adv con ordine; (skilfully) abilmente

necessarily ['nɛsɪsrɪlɪ] adv necessariamente

necessary ['nɛsɪsrɪ] adj necessario(-a)

necessity [nɪ'sɛsɪtɪ] n necessità f inv

neck [nɛk] n collo; (of garment) colletto ▷ vi (inf) pomiciare, sbaciucchiarsi; **~ and ~** testa a testa; **necklace** ['nɛklɪs] n collana; **necktie** ['nɛktaɪ] n cravatta

nectarine ['nɛktərɪn] n nocepesca

need [niːd] n bisogno ▷ vt aver bisogno di; **do you ~ anything?** ha bisogno di qualcosa?; **to ~ to do** dover fare; aver bisogno di fare; **you don't ~ to go** non devi andare, non c'è bisogno che tu vada

needle ['niːdl] n ago; (on record player) puntina ▷ vt punzecchiare

needless ['niːdlɪs] adj inutile

needlework ['niːdlwəːk] n cucito

needn't ['niːdnt] = **need not**

needy ['niːdɪ] adj bisognoso(-a)

negative ['nɛgətɪv] n (Ling) negazione f; (Phot) negativo ▷ adj negativo(-a)

neglect [nɪ'glɛkt] vt trascurare ▷ n (of person, duty) negligenza; (of child, house etc) scarsa cura; **state of ~** stato di abbandono

negotiate [nɪ'gəuʃɪeɪt] vi **to ~ (with)** negoziare (con) ▷ vt (Comm) negoziare; (obstacle) superare; **negotiations** [nɪgəuʃɪ'eɪʃənz] pl n trattative fpl, negoziati mpl

negotiator [nɪ'gəuʃɪeɪtər] n negoziatore(-trice)

neighbour ['neɪbər] (US **neighbor**) n vicino(-a); **neighbourhood** n vicinato; **neighbouring** adj vicino(-a)

neither ['naɪðər] adj, pron né l'uno(-a) né l'altro(-a), nessuno(-a) dei (delle) due ▷ conj neanche, nemmeno, neppure ▷ adv **~ good nor bad** né buono né cattivo; **I didn't move and ~ did Claude** io non mi mossi e nemmeno Claude; **…, ~ did I refuse** …, ma non ho nemmeno rifiutato

neon ['niːɔn] n neon m

Nepal [nɪ'pɔːl] n Nepal m

nephew ['nɛvjuː] n nipote m

nerve [nəːv] n nervo; (fig) coraggio; (impudence) faccia tosta; **nerves** (nervousness) nervoso; **a fit of ~s** una crisi di nervi

nervous ['nəːvəs] adj nervoso(-a); (anxious) agitato(-a), in apprensione; **nervous breakdown** n esaurimento nervoso

nest [nɛst] n nido ▷ vi fare il nido, nidificare

net [nɛt] n rete f ▷ adj netto(-a) ▷ vt (fish etc) prendere con la rete; (profit) ricavare un utile netto di; **the N~** (Internet) Internet f; **netball** n specie di pallacanestro

Netherlands ['nɛðələndz] npl **the ~** i Paesi Bassi

nett [nɛt] adj = **net**

nettle ['nɛtl] n ortica

network ['nɛtwəːk] n rete f

neurotic [njuə'rɔtɪk] adj, n nevrotico(-a)

neuter ['njuːtər] adj neutro(-a) ▷ vt (cat etc) castrare

neutral ['njuːtrəl] adj neutro(-a); (person, nation) neutrale ▷ n (Aut): **in ~** in folle

never ['nɛvər] adv (non…) mai; **I've ~ been to Spain** non sono mai stato in Spagna; **~ again** mai più; **I'll ~ go there again** non ci vado più; **~ in my life** mai in vita mia; see also **mind**; **never-ending** adj interminabile;

nevertheless [nɛvəðə'lɛs] *adv* tuttavia, ciò nonostante, ciò nondimeno

new [njuː] *adj* nuovo(-a); (*brand new*) nuovo(-a) di zecca; **New Age** *n* New Age *f inv*; **newborn** *adj* neonato(-a); **newcomer** ['njuːˌkʌmə'] *n* nuovo(-a) venuto(-a); **newly** *adv* di recente

news [njuːz] *n* notizie *fpl*; (*Radio*) giornale *m* radio; (*TV*) telegiornale *m*; **a piece of ~** una notizia; **news agency** *n* agenzia di stampa; **newsagent** (*BRIT*) *n* giornalaio; **newscaster** *n* (*Radio, TV*) annunciatore(-trice); **news dealer** (*US*) *n* = **newsagent**; **newsletter** *n* bollettino; **newspaper** *n* giornale *m*; **newsreader** *n* = **newscaster**

newt [njuːt] *n* tritone *m*

New Year *n* Anno Nuovo; **New Year's Day** *n* il Capodanno; **New Year's Eve** *n* la vigilia di Capodanno

New York [-'jɔːk] *n* New York *f*

New Zealand [-'ziːlənd] *n* Nuova Zelanda; **New Zealander** *n* neozelandese *m/f*

next [nɛkst] *adj* prossimo(-a) ▷ *adv* accanto; (*in time*) dopo; **the ~ day** il giorno dopo, l'indomani; **~ time** la prossima volta; **~ year** l'anno prossimo; **when do we meet ~?** quando ci rincontriamo?; **~ to** accanto a; **~ to nothing** quasi niente; **~ please!** (avanti) il prossimo!; **next door** *adv, adj* accanto *inv*; **next-of-kin** *n* parente *m/f* prossimo(-a)

NHS *n abbr* = **National Health Service**

nibble ['nɪbl] *vt* mordicchiare

nice [naɪs] *adj* (*holiday, trip*) piacevole; (*flat, picture*) bello(-a); (*person*) simpatico(-a), gentile; **nicely** *adv* bene

niche [niːʃ] *n* (*Archit*) nicchia

nick [nɪk] *n* taglietto; tacca ▷ *vt* (*inf*) rubare; **in the ~ of time** appena in tempo

nickel ['nɪkl] *n* nichel *m*; (*US*) moneta da cinque centesimi di dollaro

nickname ['nɪkneɪm] *n* soprannome *m*

nicotine ['nɪkətiːn] *n* nicotina

niece [niːs] *n* nipote *f*

Nigeria [naɪ'dʒɪərɪə] *n* Nigeria

night [naɪt] *n* notte *f*; (*evening*) sera; **at ~** la sera; **by ~** di notte; **the ~ before last** l'altro ieri notte (*or* sera); **night club** *n* locale *m* notturno; **nightdress** *n* camicia da notte; **nightie** ['naɪtɪ] *n* = **nightdress**; **nightlife** ['naɪtlaɪf] *n* vita notturna; **nightly** ['naɪtlɪ] *adj* di ogni notte *or* sera; (*by night*) notturno(-a) ▷ *adv* ogni notte *or* sera; **nightmare** ['naɪtmɛə'] *n* incubo; **night school** *n* scuola serale; **night shift** *n* turno di notte; **night-time** *n* notte *f*

nil [nɪl] *n* nulla *m*; (*BRIT Sport*) zero

nine [naɪn] *num* nove; **nineteen** *num* diciannove; **nineteenth** [naɪn'tiːnθ] *num* diciannovesimo(-a); **ninetieth** ['naɪntɪɪθ] *num* novantesimo(-a); **ninety** *num* novanta; **ninth** [naɪnθ] *num* nono(-a)

nip [nɪp] *vt* pizzicare; (*bite*) mordere

nipple ['nɪpl] *n* (*Anat*) capezzolo

nitrogen ['naɪtrədʒən] *n* azoto

 KEYWORD

no [nəʊ] (*pl* **noes**) *adv* (*opposite of "yes"*) no; **are you coming? — no (I'm not)** viene? — no (non vengo); **would you like some more? — no thank you** ne vuole ancora un po'? — no, grazie ▷ *adj* (*not any*) nessuno(-a); **I have no money/time/books** non ho soldi/ tempo/libri; **no student would have done it** nessuno studente lo avrebbe fatto; **"no parking"** "divieto di sosta"; **"no smoking"** "vietato fumare" ▷ *n* no *m inv*

nobility [nəʊ'bɪlɪtɪ] *n* nobiltà

noble ['nəʊbl] *adj* nobile
nobody ['nəʊbədɪ] *pron* nessuno
nod [nɒd] *vi* accennare col capo, fare un cenno; (*in agreement*) annuire con un cenno del capo; (*sleep*) sonnecchiare ▷ *vt* **to ~ one's head** fare di sì col capo ▷ *n* cenno; **nod off** *vi* assopirsi
noise [nɔɪz] *n* rumore *m*; (*din, racket*) chiasso; **I can't sleep for the ~** non riesco a dormire a causa del rumore; **noisy** *adj* (*street, car*) rumoroso(-a); (*person*) chiassoso(-a)
nominal ['nɒmɪnl] *adj* nominale; (*rent*) simbolico(-a)
nominate ['nɒmɪneɪt] *vt* (*propose*) proporre come candidato; (*elect*) nominare; **nomination** [nɒmɪ'neɪʃən] *n* nomina; candidatura; **nominee** [nɒmɪ'niː] *n* persona nominata, candidato(-a)
none [nʌn] *pron* (*not one thing*) niente; (*not one person*) nessuno(-a); **~ of you** nessuno(-a) di voi; **I've ~ left** non ne ho più; **he's ~ the worse for it** non ne ha risentito
nonetheless [nʌnðə'lɛs] *adv* nondimeno
non-fiction [nɒn'fɪkʃən] *n* saggistica
nonsense ['nɒnsəns] *n* sciocchezze *fpl*
non: **non-smoker** *n* non fumatore(-trice); **non-smoking** *adj* (*person*) che non fuma; (*area, section*) per non fumatori; **non-stick** *adj* antiaderente, antiadesivo(-a)
noodles ['nuːdlz] *npl* taglierini *mpl*
noon [nuːn] *n* mezzogiorno
no-one ['nəʊwʌn] *pron* = **nobody**
nor [nɔːʳ] *conj* = **neither** ▷ *adv see* **neither**
norm [nɔːm] *n* norma
normal ['nɔːml] *adj* normale; **normally** *adv* normalmente
north [nɔːθ] *n* nord *m*, settentrione *m* ▷ *adj* nord *inv*, del nord, settentrionale ▷ *adv* verso nord;

North America *n* America del Nord; **North American** *adj, n* nordamericano(-a); **northbound** ['nɔːθbaʊnd] *adj* (*traffic*) diretto(-a) a nord; (*carriageway*) nord *inv*; **north-east** *n* nord-est *m*; **northeastern** *adj* nordorientale; **northern** ['nɔːðən] *adj* del nord, settentrionale; **Northern Ireland** *n* Irlanda del Nord; **North Korea** *n* Corea del Nord; **North Pole** *n* Polo Nord; **North Sea** *n* Mare *m* del Nord; **north-west** *n* nord-ovest *m*; **northwestern** *adj* nordoccidentale
Norway ['nɔːweɪ] *n* Norvegia; **Norwegian** [nɔː'wiːdʒən] *adj* norvegese ▷ *n* norvegese *m/f*; (*Ling*) norvegese *m*
nose [nəʊz] *n* naso; (*of animal*) muso ▷ *vi* **to ~ about** aggirarsi; **nosebleed** *n* emorragia nasale; **nosey** (*inf*) *adj* = **nosy**
nostalgia [nɒs'tældʒɪə] *n* nostalgia
nostalgic [nɒs'tældʒɪk] *adj* nostalgico(-a)
nostril ['nɒstrɪl] *n* narice *f*; (*of horse*) frogia
nosy ['nəʊzɪ] (*inf*) *adj* curioso(-a)
not [nɒt] *adv* non; **he is ~ or isn't here** non è qui, non c'è; **you must ~ or you mustn't do that** non devi fare quello; **it's too late, isn't it** *or* **is it ~?** è troppo tardi, vero?; **~ that I don't like him** non che (lui) non mi piaccia; **~ yet/now** non ancora/ora; *see also* **all**; **only**
notable ['nəʊtəbl] *adj* notevole; **notably** ['nəʊtəblɪ] *adv* (*markedly*) notevolmente; (*particularly*) in particolare
notch [nɒtʃ] *n* tacca; (*in saw*) dente *m*
note [nəʊt] *n* nota; (*letter, banknote*) biglietto ▷ *vt* (*also*: **~ down**) prendere nota di; **to take ~s** prendere appunti; **notebook** *n* taccuino; **noted** ['nəʊtɪd] *adj* celebre; **notepad** *n* bloc-notes *m inv*; **notepaper** *n* carta da lettere

nothing ['nʌθɪŋ] n nulla m, niente m; (zero) zero; **he does ~** non fa niente; **~ new/much** etc niente di nuovo/speciale etc; **for ~** per niente

notice ['nəʊtɪs] n avviso; (of leaving) preavviso ▷ vt notare, accorgersi di; **to take ~ of** fare attenzione a; **to bring sth to sb's ~** far notare qc a qn; **at short ~** con un breve preavviso; **until further ~** fino a nuovo avviso; **to hand in one's ~** licenziarsi; **noticeable** adj evidente

notify ['nəʊtɪfaɪ] vt **to ~ sth to sb** far sapere qc a qn; **to ~ sb of sth** avvisare qn di qc

notion ['nəʊʃən] n idea; (concept) nozione f; **notions** npl (US: haberdashery) merceria

notorious [nəʊ'tɔːrɪəs] adj famigerato(-a)

notwithstanding [nɔtwɪθ'stændɪŋ] adv nondimeno ▷ prep nonostante, malgrado

nought [nɔːt] n zero

noun [naun] n nome m, sostantivo

nourish ['nʌrɪʃ] vt nutrire; **nourishment** n nutrimento

Nov. abbr (= November) nov.

novel ['nɔvl] n romanzo ▷ adj nuovo(-a); **novelist** n romanziere(-a); **novelty** n novità f inv

November [nəʊ'vɛmbə^r] n novembre m

novice ['nɔvɪs] n principiante m/f; (Rel) novizio(-a)

now [nau] adv ora, adesso ▷ conj **~ (that)** adesso che, ora che; **by ~** ormai; **just ~** proprio ora; **right ~** subito, immediatamente; **~ and then, ~ and again** ogni tanto; **from ~ on** da ora in poi; **nowadays** ['nauədeɪz] adv oggidì

nowhere ['nəʊwɛə^r] adv in nessun luogo, da nessuna parte

nozzle ['nɔzl] n (of hose etc) boccaglio; (of fire extinguisher) lancia

nr abbr (BRIT) = **near**

nuclear ['njuːklɪə^r] adj nucleare

nucleus ['njuːklɪəs] (pl **nuclei**) n nucleo

nude [njuːd] adj nudo(-a) ▷ n (Art) nudo; **in the ~** tutto(-a) nudo(-a)

nudge [nʌdʒ] vt dare una gomitata a

nudist ['njuːdɪst] n nudista m/f

nudity ['njuːdɪtɪ] n nudità

nuisance ['njuːsns] n **it's a ~** è una seccatura; **he's a ~** è uno scocciatore

numb [nʌm] adj **~ (with)** intorpidito(-a) (da); (with fear) impietrito(-a) (da); **~ with cold** intirizzito(-a) (dal freddo)

number ['nʌmbə^r] n numero ▷ vt numerare; (include) contare; **a ~ of** un certo numero di; **to be ~ed among** venire annoverato(-a) tra; **they were 10 in ~** erano in tutto 10; **number plate** (BRIT) n (Aut) targa; **Number Ten** n (BRIT: = 10 Downing Street) residenza del Primo Ministro del Regno Unito

numerical [njuː'mɛrɪkl] adj numerico(-a)

numerous ['njuːmərəs] adj numeroso(-a)

nun [nʌn] n suora, monaca

nurse [nəːs] n infermiere(-a); (also: **~maid**) bambinaia ▷ vt (patient, cold) curare; (baby: BRIT) cullare; (: US) allattare, dare il latte a

nursery ['nəːsərɪ] n (room) camera dei bambini; (institution) asilo; (for plants) vivaio; **nursery rhyme** n filastrocca; **nursery school** n scuola materna; **nursery slope** (BRIT) n (Ski) pista per principianti

nursing ['nəːsɪŋ] n (profession) professione f di infermiere (or di infermiera); (care) cura; **nursing home** n casa di cura

nurture ['nəːtʃə^r] vt allevare; nutrire

nut [nʌt] n (of metal) dado; (fruit) noce f

nutmeg ['nʌtmɛg] n noce f moscata

nutrient ['njuːtrɪənt] adj nutriente ▷ n sostanza nutritiva

nutrition [nju:'trɪʃən] *n* nutrizione *f*
nutritious [nju:'trɪʃəs] *adj* nutriente
nuts [nʌts] (*inf*) *adj* matto(-a)
NVQ *n abbr* (*BRIT*) = **National Vocational Qualification**
nylon ['naɪlɔn] *n* nailon *m* ▷ *adj* di nailon

oak [əuk] *n* quercia ▷ *adj* di quercia
O.A.P. (*BRIT*) *n, abbr* = **old age pensioner**
oar [ɔːʳ] *n* remo
oasis [əu'eɪsɪs] (*pl* **oases**) *n* oasi *f inv*
oath [əuθ] *n* giuramento; (*swear word*) bestemmia
oatmeal ['əutmiːl] *n* farina d'avena
oats [əuts] *npl* avena
obedience [ə'biːdɪəns] *n* ubbidienza
obedient [ə'biːdɪənt] *adj* ubbidiente
obese [əu'biːs] *adj* obeso(-a)
obesity [əu'biːsɪtɪ] *n* obesità
obey [ə'beɪ] *vt* ubbidire a; (*instructions, regulations*) osservare
obituary [ə'bɪtjuərɪ] *n* necrologia
object [*n* 'ɔbdʒɪkt, *vb* əb'dʒɛkt] *n* oggetto; (*purpose*) scopo, intento; (*Ling*) complemento oggetto ▷ *vi* **to ~ to** (*attitude*) disapprovare; (*proposal*) protestare contro, sollevare delle obiezioni contro; **expense is no ~** non si bada a spese; **to ~ that** obiettare che; **objection** [əb'dʒɛkʃən] *n*

obiezione f; **objective** n obiettivo

obligation [ɔblɪˈgeɪʃən] n obbligo, dovere m; **without ~** senza impegno

obligatory [əˈblɪgətərɪ] adj obbligatorio(-a)

oblige [əˈblaɪdʒ] vt (force): **to ~ sb to do** costringere qn a fare; (do a favour) fare una cortesia a; **to be ~d to sb for sth** essere grato a qn per qc

oblique [əˈbliːk] adj obliquo(-a); (allusion) indiretto(-a)

obliterate [əˈblɪtəreɪt] vt cancellare

oblivious [əˈblɪvɪəs] adj **~ of** incurante di; inconscio(-a) di

oblong [ˈɔblɔŋ] adj oblungo(-a) ▷ n rettangolo

obnoxious [əbˈnɔkʃəs] adj odioso(-a); (smell) disgustoso(-a), ripugnante

oboe [ˈəubəu] n oboe m

obscene [əbˈsiːn] adj osceno(-a)

obscure [əbˈskjuəʳ] adj oscuro(-a) ▷ vt oscurare; (hide: sun) nascondere

observant [əbˈzəːvnt] adj attento(-a)

> Be careful not to translate *observant* by the Italian word *osservante*.

observation [ɔbzəˈveɪʃən] n osservazione f; (by police etc) sorveglianza

observatory [əbˈzəːvətrɪ] n osservatorio

observe [əbˈzəːv] vt osservare; (remark) fare osservare; **observer** n osservatore(-trice)

obsess [əbˈsɛs] vt ossessionare; **obsession** [əbˈsɛʃən] n ossessione f; **obsessive** adj ossessivo(-a)

obsolete [ˈɔbsəliːt] adj obsoleto(-a)

obstacle [ˈɔbstəkl] n ostacolo

obstinate [ˈɔbstɪnɪt] adj ostinato(-a)

obstruct [əbˈstrʌkt] vt (block) ostruire, ostacolare; (halt) fermare; (hinder) impedire; **obstruction** [əbˈstrʌkʃən] n ostruzione f; ostacolo

obtain [əbˈteɪn] vt ottenere

obvious [ˈɔbvɪəs] adj ovvio(-a), evidente; **obviously** adv ovviamente;

certo

occasion [əˈkeɪʒən] n occasione f; (event) avvenimento; **occasional** adj occasionale; **occasionally** adv ogni tanto

occult [ɔˈkʌlt] adj occulto(-a) ▷ n **the ~** l'occulto

occupant [ˈɔkjupənt] n occupante m/f; (of boat, car etc) persona a bordo

occupation [ɔkjuˈpeɪʃən] n occupazione f; (job) mestiere m, professione f

occupy [ˈɔkjupaɪ] vt occupare; **to ~ o.s. in doing** occuparsi a fare

occur [əˈkəːʳ] vi succedere, capitare; **to ~ to sb** venire in mente a qn; **occurrence** n caso, fatto; presenza

> Be careful not to translate *occur* by the Italian word *occorrere*.

ocean [ˈəuʃən] n oceano

o'clock [əˈklɔk] adv **it is 5 o'clock** sono le 5

Oct. abbr (= October) ott.

October [ɔkˈtəubəʳ] n ottobre m

octopus [ˈɔktəpəs] n polpo, piovra

odd [ɔd] adj (strange) strano(-a), bizzarro(-a); (number) dispari inv; (not of a set) spaiato(-a); **60-~** 60 e oltre; **at ~ times** di tanto in tanto; **the ~ one out** l'eccezione f; **oddly** adv stranamente; **odds** npl (in betting) quota

odometer [ɔˈdɔmɪtəʳ] n odometro

odour [ˈəudəʳ] (us **odor**) n odore m; (unpleasant) cattivo odore

 KEYWORD

of [ɔv, əv] prep 1 (gen) di; **a boy of 10** un ragazzo di 10 anni; **a friend of ours** un nostro amico; **that was kind of you** è stato molto gentile da parte sua

2 (expressing quantity, amount, dates etc) di; **a kilo of flour** un chilo di farina; **how much of this do you need?** quanto gliene serve?; **there were 3 of them** (people) erano in 3; (objects) ce

n'erano 3; **3 of us went** 3 di noi sono andati; **the 5th of July** il 5 luglio 3 (*from, out of*) di, in; *of* **made of wood** (fatto) di or in legno

KEYWORD

off [ɔf] *adv* **1** (*distance, time*): **it's a long way off** è lontano; **the game is 3 days off** la partita è tra 3 giorni **2** (*departure, removal*) via; **to go off to Paris** andarsene a Parigi; **I must be off** devo andare via; **to take off one's coat** togliersi il cappotto; **the button came off** il bottone è venuto via or si è staccato; **10% off** con lo sconto del 10%

3 (*not at work*): **to have a day off** avere un giorno libero; **to be off sick** essere assente per malattia ▷ *adj* (*engine*) spento(-a); (*tap*) chiuso(-a); (*cancelled*) sospeso(-a); (*BRIT: food*) andato(-a) a male; **on the off chance** nel caso; **to have an off day** non essere in forma ▷ *prep* **1** (*motion, removal etc*) da; (*distant from*) a poca distanza da; **a street off the square** una strada che parte dalla piazza

2: **to be off meat** non mangiare più la carne

offence [ə'fɛns] (*US* **offense**) *n* (*Law*) contravvenzione *f*; (: *more serious*) reato; **to take ~ at** offendersi per

offend [ə'fɛnd] *vt* (*person*) offendere; **offender** *n* delinquente *m/f*; (*against regulations*) contravventore(-trice)

offense [ə'fɛns] (*US*) *n* = **offence**

offensive [ə'fɛnsɪv] *adj* offensivo(-a); (*smell etc*) sgradevole, ripugnante ▷ *n* (*Mil*) offensiva

offer ['ɔfəʳ] *n* offerta, proposta ▷ *vt* offrire; **"on ~"** (*Comm*) "in offerta speciale"

offhand [ɔf'hænd] *adj* disinvolto(-a), noncurante ▷ *adv* su due piedi

office ['ɔfɪs] *n* (*place*) ufficio; (*position*) carica; **doctor's ~** (*US*) studio; **to take ~** entrare in carica; **office block** (*US* **office building**) *n* complesso di uffici; **office hours** *npl* orario d'ufficio; (*US Med*) orario di visite

officer ['ɔfɪsəʳ] *n* (*Mil etc*) ufficiale *m*; (*also*: **police ~**) agente *m* di polizia; (*of organization*) funzionario

office worker *n* impiegato(-a) d'ufficio

official [ə'fɪʃl] *adj* (*authorized*) ufficiale ▷ *n* ufficiale *m*; (*civil servant*) impiegato(-a) statale; funzionario

off: **off-licence** (*BRIT*) *n* (*shop*) spaccio di bevande alcoliche; **off-line** *adj*, *adv* (*Comput*) off-line *inv*, fuori linea; (: *switched off*) spento(-a); **off-peak** *adj* (*ticket, heating etc*) a tariffa ridotta; (*time*) non di punta; **off-putting** (*BRIT*) *adj* sgradevole, antipatico(-a); **off-season** *adj*, *adv* fuori stagione; **offset** ['ɔfsɛt] (*irreg*) *vt* (*counteract*) controbilanciare, compensare; **offshore** [ɔf'ʃɔːʳ] *adj* (*breeze*) di terra; (*island*) vicino alla costa; (*fishing*) costiero(-a); **offside** ['ɔf'saɪd] *adj* (*Sport*) fuori gioco; (*Aut*: *in Britain*) destro(-a); (: *in Italy etc*) sinistro(-a); **offspring** ['ɔfsprɪŋ] *n inv* prole *f*, discendenza

often ['ɔfn] *adv* spesso; **how ~ do you go?** quanto spesso ci vai?

oh [əu] *excl* oh!

oil [ɔɪl] *n* olio; (*petroleum*) petrolio; (*for central heating*) nafta ▷ *vt* (*machine*) lubrificare; **oil filter** *n* (*Aut*) filtro dell'olio; **oil painting** *n* quadro a olio; **oil refinery** *n* raffineria di petrolio; **oil rig** *n* derrick *m inv*; (*at sea*) piattaforma per trivellazioni subacquee; **oil slick** *n* chiazza d'olio; **oil tanker** *n* (*ship*) petroliera; (*truck*) autocisterna per petrolio; **oil well** *n* pozzo petrolifero; **oily** *adj* unto(-a), oleoso(-a); (*food*) grasso(-a)

ointment ['ɔɪntmənt] *n* unguento

O.K. ['əu'keɪ] *excl* d'accordo! ▷ *adj* non male *inv* ▷ *vt* approvare; **is it O.K.?, are you O.K.?** tutto bene?

old [əuld] *adj* vecchio(-a); (*ancient*) antico(-a), vecchio(-a); (*person*) vecchio(-a), anziano(-a); **how ~ are you?** quanti anni ha?; **he's 10 years ~** ha 10 anni; **~er brother** fratello maggiore; **old age** *n* vecchiaia; **old-age pension** ['əuldeɪdʒ-] *n* (*BRIT*) pensione *f* di vecchiaia; **old-age pensioner** (*BRIT*) *n* pensionato(-a); **old-fashioned** *adj* antiquato(-a), fuori moda; (*person*) all'antica; **old people's home** *n* ricovero per anziani

olive ['ɔlɪv] *n* (*fruit*) oliva; (*tree*) olivo ▷ *adj* (*also*: **~-green**) verde oliva *inv*; **olive oil** *n* olio d'oliva

Olympic [əu'lɪmpɪk] *adj* olimpico(-a); **the ~ Games, the ~s** i giochi olimpici, le Olimpiadi

omelet(te) ['ɔmlɪt] *n* omelette *f inv*

omen ['əumən] *n* presagio, augurio

ominous ['ɔmɪnəs] *adj* minaccioso(-a); (*event*) di malaugurio

omit [əu'mɪt] *vt* omettere

KEYWORD

on [ɔn] *prep* **1** (*indicating position*) su; **on the wall** sulla parete; **on the left** a *or* sulla sinistra

2 (*indicating means, method, condition etc*): **on foot** a piedi; **on the train/plane** in treno/aereo; **on the telephone** al telefono; **on the radio/television** alla radio/televisione; **to be on drugs** drogarsi; **on holiday** in vacanza

3 (*of time*): **on Friday** venerdì; **on Fridays** il *or* di venerdì; **on June 20th** il 20 giugno; **on Friday, June 20th** venerdì, 20 giugno; **a week on Friday** venerdì a otto; **on his arrival** al suo arrivo; **on seeing this** vedendo ciò

4 (*about, concerning*) su, di; **information on train services** informazioni sui collegamenti ferroviari; **a book on Goldoni/physics** un libro su Goldoni/di *or* sulla fisica

▷ *adv* **1** (*referring to dress, covering*): **to have one's coat on** avere indosso il cappotto; **to put one's coat on** mettersi il cappotto; **what's she got on?** cosa indossa?; **she put her boots/gloves/hat on** si mise gli stivali/i guanti/il cappello; **screw the lid on tightly** avvita bene il coperchio

2 (*further, continuously*): **to walk on, go on** *etc* continuare, proseguire *etc*; **to read on** continuare a leggere; **on and off** ogni tanto

▷ *adj* **1** (*in operation: machine, TV, light*) acceso(-a); (: *tap*) aperto(-a); (: *brake*) inserito(-a); **is the meeting still on?** (*in progress*) la riunione è ancora in corso?; (*not cancelled*) è confermato l'incontro?; **there's a good film on at the cinema** danno un buon film al cinema

2 (*inf*): **that's not on!** (*not acceptable*) non si fa così!; (*not possible*) non se ne parla neanche!

once [wʌns] *adv* una volta ▷ *conj* non appena, quando; **~ he had left/it was done** dopo che se n'era andato/fu fatto; **at ~** subito; (*simultaneously*) a un tempo; **~ a week** una volta per settimana; **~ more** ancora una volta; **~ and for all** una volta per sempre; **~ upon a time** c'era una volta

oncoming ['ɔnkʌmɪŋ] *adj* (*traffic*) che viene in senso opposto

KEYWORD

one [wʌn] *num* uno(-a); **one hundred and fifty** centocinquanta; **one day** un giorno

▷ *adj* **1** (*sole*) unico(-a); **the one book which** l'unico libro che; **the one man**

who l'unico che
2 (*same*) stesso(-a); **they came in the one car** sono venuti nella stessa macchina
▷ *pron* 1: **this one** questo(-a); **that one** quello(-a); **I've already got one/a red one** ne ho già uno/uno rosso; **one by one** uno per uno
2: **one another** l'un l'altro; **to look at one another** guardarsi; **to help one another** aiutarsi l'un l'altro *or* a vicenda
3 (*impersonal*) si; **one never knows** non si sa mai; **to cut one's finger** tagliarsi un dito; **one needs to eat** bisogna mangiare

one-off (BRIT: *inf*) *n* fatto eccezionale
oneself [wʌn'sɛlf] *pron* (*reflexive*) si; (*after prep*) se stesso(-a), sé; **to do sth (by) ~** fare qc da sé; **to hurt ~** farsi male; **to keep sth for ~** tenere qc per sé; **to talk to ~** parlare da solo
one-shot [wʌn'ʃɔt] (US) *n* = **one-off**; **one-sided** *adj* (*argument*) unilaterale; **one-to-one** *adj* (*relationship*) univoco(-a); **one-way** *adj* (*street, traffic*) a senso unico
ongoing ['ɔngəʊɪŋ] *adj* in corso; in attuazione
onion ['ʌnjən] *n* cipolla
on-line ['ɔnlaɪn] *adj, adv* (*Comput*) on-line *inv*
onlooker ['ɔnlʊkə'] *n* spettatore(-trice)
only ['əʊnlɪ] *adv* solo, soltanto ▷ *adj* solo(-a), unico(-a) ▷ *conj* solo che, ma; **an ~ child** un figlio unico; **not ~ ... but also** non solo ... ma anche
on-screen [ɔn'skriːn] *adj* sullo schermo *inv*
onset ['ɔnsɛt] *n* inizio
onto ['ɔntu] *prep* = **on to**
onward(s) ['ɔnwəd(z)] *adv* (*move*) in avanti; **from that time onward(s)** da quella volta in poi

oops [ups] *excl* ops! (*esprime rincrescimento per un piccolo contrattempo*); **~-a-daisy!** oplà!
ooze [uːz] *vi* stillare
opaque [əʊ'peɪk] *adj* opaco(-a)
open ['əʊpn] *adj* aperto(-a); (*road*) libero(-a); (*meeting*) pubblico(-a)
▷ *vt* aprire ▷ *vi* (*eyes, door, debate*) aprirsi; (*flower*) sbocciare; (*shop, bank, museum*) aprire; (*book etc: commence*) cominciare; **is it ~ to the public?** è aperto al pubblico?; **in the ~ (air)** all'aperto; **what time do you ~?** a che ora aprite?; **open up** *vt* aprire; (*blocked road*) sgombrare ▷ *vi* (*shop, business*) aprire; **open-air** *adj* all'aperto; **opening** *adj* (*speech*) di apertura ▷ *n* apertura; (*opportunity*) occasione *f*, opportunità *f inv*; sbocco; **opening hours** *npl* orario d'apertura; **open learning** *n* sistema educativo secondo il quale lo studente ha maggior controllo e gestione delle modalità di apprendimento; **openly** *adv* apertamente; **open-minded** *adj* che ha la mente aperta; **open-necked** *adj* col collo slacciato; **open-plan** *adj* senza pareti divisorie; **Open University** *n* (BRIT) *vedi nota nel riquadro*

● **OPEN UNIVERSITY**
●
● La **Open University**, fondata in
● Gran Bretagna nel 1969, organizza
● corsi di laurea per corrispondenza o
● via Internet. Alcune lezioni possono
● venir seguite per radio o alla
● televisione e vengono organizzati
● regolari corsi estivi.

opera ['ɔpərə] *n* opera; **opera house** *n* opera; **opera singer** *n* cantante *m/f* d'opera *or* lirico(-a)
operate ['ɔpəreɪt] *vt* (*machine*) azionare, far funzionare; (*system*) usare ▷ *vi* funzionare; (*drug*) essere

efficace; **to ~ on sb (for)** (*Med*) operare qn (di)

operating room (*us*) *n* = **operating theatre**

operating theatre *n* (*Med*) sala operatoria

operation [ɔpəˈreɪʃən] *n* operazione *f*; **to be in ~** (*machine*) essere in azione *or* funzionamento; (*system*) essere in vigore; **to have an ~** (*Med*) subire un'operazione; **operational** *adj* in funzione; d'esercizio

operative [ˈɔpərətɪv] *adj* (*measure*) operativo(-a)

operator [ˈɔpəreɪtəʳ] *n* (*of machine*) operatore(-trice); (*Tel*) centralinista *m/f*

opinion [əˈpɪnɪən] *n* opinione *f*, parere *m*; **in my ~** secondo me, a mio avviso; **opinion poll** *n* sondaggio di opinioni

opponent [əˈpəunənt] *n* avversario(-a)

opportunity [ɔpəˈtjuːnɪtɪ] *n* opportunità *f inv*, occasione *f*; **to take the ~ of doing** cogliere l'occasione per fare

oppose [əˈpəuz] *vt* opporsi a; **~d to** contrario(-a) a; **as ~d to** in contrasto con

opposite [ˈɔpəzɪt] *adj* opposto(-a); (*house etc*) di fronte ▷ *adv* di fronte, dirimpetto ▷ *prep* di fronte a ▷ *n* **the ~** il contrario, l'opposto; **the ~ sex** l'altro sesso

opposition [ɔpəˈzɪʃən] *n* opposizione *f*

oppress [əˈprɛs] *vt* opprimere

opt [ɔpt] *vi* **to ~ for** optare per; **to ~ to do** scegliere di fare; **opt out** *vi* **to opt out of** ritirarsi da

optician [ɔpˈtɪʃən] *n* ottico

optimism [ˈɔptɪmɪzəm] *n* ottimismo

optimist [ˈɔptɪmɪst] *n* ottimista *m/f*; **optimistic** [-ˈmɪstɪk] *adj* ottimistico(-a)

optimum [ˈɔptɪməm] *adj* ottimale

option [ˈɔpʃən] *n* scelta; (*Scol*) materia facoltativa; (*Comm*) opzione *f*; **optional** *adj* facoltativo(-a); (*Comm*) a scelta

or [ɔːʳ] *conj* o, oppure; (*with negative*): **he hasn't seen or heard anything** non ha visto né sentito niente; **or else** se no, altrimenti; oppure

oral [ˈɔːrəl] *adj* orale ▷ *n* esame *m* orale

orange [ˈɔrɪndʒ] *n* (*fruit*) arancia ▷ *adj* arancione; **orange juice** *n* succo d'arancia; **orange squash** *n* succo d'arancia (*da diluire con l'acqua*)

orbit [ˈɔːbɪt] *n* orbita ▷ *vt* orbitare intorno a

orchard [ˈɔːtʃəd] *n* frutteto

orchestra [ˈɔːkɪstrə] *n* orchestra; (*us: seating*) platea

orchid [ˈɔːkɪd] *n* orchidea

ordeal [ɔːˈdiːl] *n* prova, travaglio

order [ˈɔːdəʳ] *n* ordine *m*; (*Comm*) ordinazione *f* ▷ *vt* ordinare; **can I ~ now, please?** posso ordinare, per favore?; **in ~** in ordine; (*of document*) in regola; **in (working) ~** funzionante; **in ~ to do** per fare; **in ~ that** affinché + *sub*; **on ~** (*Comm*) in ordinazione; **out of ~** non in ordine; (*not working*) guasto; **to ~ sb to do** ordinare a qn di fare; **order form** *n* modulo d'ordinazione; **orderly** *n* (*Mil*) attendente *m*; (*Med*) inserviente *m* ▷ *adj* (*room*) ordinato(-a); (*mind*) metodico(-a); (*person*) ordinato(-a), metodico(-a)

ordinary [ˈɔːdnrɪ] *adj* normale, comune; (*pej*) mediocre; **out of the ~** diverso dal solito, fuori dell'ordinario

ore [ɔːʳ] *n* minerale *m* grezzo

oregano [ɔrɪˈɡɑːnəu] *n* origano

organ [ˈɔːɡən] *n* organo; **organic** [ɔːˈɡænɪk] *adj* organico(-a); (*of food*) biologico(-a); **organism** *n* organismo

organization [ɔːɡənaɪˈzeɪʃən] *n* organizzazione *f*

organize [ˈɔːɡənaɪz] *vt* organizzare; **to get ~d** organizzarsi; **organized**

['ɔ:gənaizd] adj organizzato(-a);
organizer n organizzatore(-trice)

orgasm ['ɔ:gæzəm] n orgasmo

orgy ['ɔ:dʒɪ] n orgia

oriental [ɔːrɪ'entl] adj, n orientale m/f

orientation [ɔːrɪen'teɪʃən] n
orientamento

origin ['ɔrɪdʒɪn] n origine f

original [ə'rɪdʒɪnl] adj originale;
(earliest) originario(-a) ▷ n originale m;
originally adv (at first) all'inizio

originate [ə'rɪdʒɪneɪt] vi **to ~ from**
essere originario(-a) di; (suggestion)
provenire da; **to ~ in** avere origine in

Orkneys ['ɔ:knɪz] npl: **the ~** (also: **the
Orkney Islands**) le Orcadi

ornament ['ɔ:nəmənt] n ornamento;
(trinket) ninnolo; **ornamental**
[-'mentl] adj ornamentale

ornate [ɔ:'neɪt] adj molto ornato(-a)

orphan ['ɔ:fn] n orfano(-a)

orthodox ['ɔ:θədɔks] adj
ortodosso(-a)

orthopaedic [ɔ:θə'pi:dɪk] (US
orthopedic) adj ortopedico(-a)

osteopath ['ɔstɪəpæθ] n specialista
m/f di osteopatia

ostrich ['ɔstrɪtʃ] n struzzo

other ['ʌðər] adj altro(-a) ▷ pron **the
~ (one)** l'altro(-a); **~s** (other people)
altri mpl; **~ than** altro che; a parte;
otherwise adv, conj altrimenti

otter ['ɔtər] n lontra

ouch [autʃ] excl ohi!, ahi!

ought [ɔːt] (pt **ought**) aux vb **I ~ to do
it** dovrei farlo; **this ~ to have been
corrected** questo avrebbe dovuto
essere corretto; **he ~ to win** dovrebbe
vincere

ounce [auns] n oncia (= 28.35 g, 16 in
a pound)

our ['auər] adj il (la) nostro(-a); (pl) i (le)
nostri(-e); see also **my**; **ours** pron il (la)
nostro(-a); (pl) i (le) nostri(-e); see also
mine; **ourselves** pron pl (reflexive) ci;
(after preposition) noi; (emphatic) noi
stessi(-e); see also **oneself**

oust [aust] vt cacciare, espellere

out [aut] adv (gen) fuori; **~ here/there**
qui/là fuori; **to speak ~ loud** parlare
forte; **to have a night ~** uscire una
sera; **the boat was 10 km ~** la barca
era a 10 km dalla costa; **3 days ~ from
Plymouth** a 3 giorni da Plymouth; **~
of** (outside) fuori di; (because of) per; **~
of 10** su 10; **~ of petrol** senza benzina;
outback ['autbæk] n (in Australia)
interno, entroterra; **outbound** adj
outbound (for or **from)** in partenza
(per or da); **outbreak** ['autbreɪk]
n scoppio; epidemia; **outburst**
['autbə:st] n scoppio; **outcast**
['autkɑ:st] n esule m/f; (socially)
paria m inv; **outcome** ['autkʌm] n
esito, risultato; **outcry** ['autkraɪ]
n protesta, clamore m; **outdated**
[aut'deɪtɪd] adj (custom, clothes) fuori
moda; (idea) sorpassato(-a); **outdoor**
[aut'dɔ:r] adj all'aperto; **outdoors**
adv fuori; all'aria aperta

outer ['autər] adj esteriore; **outer
space** n spazio cosmico

outfit ['autfɪt] n (clothes) completo;
(: for sport) tenuta

out: **outgoing** ['autgəuɪŋ] adj
(character) socievole; **outgoings** (BRIT)
npl (expenses) spese fpl, uscite fpl;
outhouse ['authaus] n costruzione
f annessa

outing ['autɪŋ] n gita; escursione f

out: **outlaw** ['autlɔ:] n fuorilegge
m/f ▷ vt bandire; **outlay** ['autleɪ]
n spese fpl; (investment) sborsa,
spesa; **outlet** ['autlet] n (for liquid
etc) sbocco, scarico; (US Elec) presa di
corrente; (also: **retail outlet**) punto
di vendita; **outline** ['autlaɪn] n
contorno, profilo; (summary) abbozzo,
grandi linee fpl ▷ vt (fig) descrivere
a grandi linee; **outlook** ['autluk]
n prospettiva, vista; **outnumber**
[aut'nʌmbər] vt superare in
numero; **out-of-date** adj (passport)
scaduto(-a); (clothes) fuori moda

inv; **out-of-doors** [autəv'dɔːz] adv
all'aperto; **out-of-the-way** adj
(place) fuori mano inv; **out-of-town**
[autə'taun] adj (shopping centre etc)
fuori città; **outpatient** ['autpeɪʃənt]
n paziente m/f esterno(-a); **outpost**
['autpəust] n avamposto; **output**
['autput] n produzione f; (Comput)
output m inv

outrage ['autreɪdʒ] n oltraggio;
scandalo ▷ vt oltraggiare;
outrageous [-'reɪdʒəs] adj
oltraggioso(-a), scandaloso(-a)

outright [adv aut'raɪt, adj 'autraɪt]
adv completamente; schiettamente;
apertamente; sul colpo ▷ adj
completo(-a), schietto(-a) e netto(-a)

outset ['autsɛt] n inizio

outside [aut'saɪd] n esterno,
esteriore m ▷ adj esterno(-a),
esteriore ▷ adv fuori, all'esterno
▷ prep fuori di, all'esterno di; **at the ~**
(fig) al massimo; **outside lane** n (Aut)
corsia di sorpasso; **outside line** n (Tel)
linea esterna; **outsider** n (in race etc)
outsider m inv; (stranger) estraneo(-a)

out: **outsize** ['autsaɪz] adj (clothes) per
taglie forti; **outskirts** ['autskəːts]
npl sobborghi mpl; **outspoken**
[aut'spəukən] adj molto franco(-a);
outstanding [aut'stændɪŋ] adj
eccezionale, di rilievo; (unfinished)
non completo(-a); non evaso(-a); non
regolato(-a)

outward ['autwəd] adj (sign,
appearances) esteriore; (journey)
d'andata; **outwards** ['autwədz] adv
(esp BRIT) = **outward**

outweigh [aut'weɪ] vt avere maggior
peso di

oval ['əuvl] adj ovale ▷ n ovale m

ovary ['əuvərɪ] n ovaia

oven ['ʌvn] n forno; **oven glove** n
guanto da forno; **ovenproof** adj da
forno; **oven-ready** adj pronto(-a) da
infornare

over ['əuvəʳ] adv al di sopra ▷ adj (or
adv) (finished) finito(-a), terminato(-a);
(too) troppo; (remaining) che avanza
▷ prep su; sopra; (above) al di sopra
di; (on the other side of) di là di; (more
than) più di; (during) durante; **~ here**
qui; **~ there** là; **all ~** (everywhere)
dappertutto; (finished) tutto(-a)
finito(-a); **~ and ~ (again)** più e più
volte; **~ and above** oltre (a); **to ask sb
~** invitare qn (a passare)

overall [adj, n 'əuvərɔːl, adv
əuvər'ɔːl] adj totale ▷ n (BRIT)
grembiule m ▷ adv nell'insieme,
complessivamente; **overalls** npl
(worker's overalls) tuta (da lavoro)

overboard ['əuvəbɔːd] adv (Naut)
fuori bordo, in mare

overcame [əuvə'keɪm] pt of
overcome

overcast ['əuvəkɑːst] adj (sky)
coperto(-a)

overcharge [əuvə'tʃɑːdʒ] vt **to ~ sb
for sth** far pagare troppo caro a qn
per qc

overcoat ['əuvəkəut] n soprabito,
cappotto

overcome [əuvə'kʌm] (irreg) vt
superare; sopraffare

over: **overcrowded** [əuvə'kraudɪd]
adj sovraffollato(-a); **overdo**
[əuvə'duː] (irreg) vt esagerare;
(overcook) cuocere troppo; **overdone**
[əuvə'dʌn] adj troppo cotto(-a);
overdose ['əuvədəus] n dose f
eccessiva; **overdraft** ['əuvədrɑːft]
n scoperto (di conto); **overdrawn**
[əuvə'drɔːn] adj (account)
scoperto(-a); **overdue** [əuvə'djuː]
adj in ritardo; **overestimate**
[əuvər'ɛstɪmeɪt] vt sopravvalutare

overflow [vb əuvə'fləu, n 'əuvəfləu]
vi traboccare ▷ n (also: **~ pipe**)
troppopieno

overgrown [əuvə'grəun] adj (garden)
ricoperto(-a) di vegetazione

overhaul [vb əuvə'hɔːl, n 'əuvəhɔːl] vt
revisionare ▷ n revisione f

overhead [adv əuvə'hɛd, adj, n 'əuvəhɛd] adv di sopra ▷ adj aereo(-a); (lighting) verticale ▷ n (US) = **overheads; overhead projector** n lavagna luminosa; **overheads** npl spese fpl generali

over: overhear [əuvə'hɪəʳ] (irreg) vt sentire (per caso); **overheat** [əuvə'hi:t] vi (engine) surriscaldare; **overland** adj, adv per via di terra; **overlap** [əuvə'læp] vi sovrapporsi; **overleaf** [əuvə'li:f] adv a tergo; **overload** [əuvə'ləud] vt sovraccaricare; **overlook** [əuvə'luk] vt (have view of) dare su; (miss) trascurare; (forgive) passare sopra a

overnight [əuvə'naɪt] adv (happen) durante la notte; (fig) tutto ad un tratto ▷ adj di notte; **he stayed there ~** ci ha passato la notte; **overnight bag** n borsa da viaggio

overpass ['əuvəpɑːs] n cavalcavia m inv

overpower [əuvə'pauəʳ] vt sopraffare; **overpowering** adj irresistibile; (heat, stench) soffocante

over: overreact [əuvəri:'ækt] vi reagire in modo esagerato; **overrule** [əuvə'ruːl] vt (decision) annullare; (claim) respingere; **overrun** [əuvə'rʌn] (irreg: like run) vt (country) invadere; (time limit) superare

overseas [əuvə'siːz] adv oltremare; (abroad) all'estero ▷ adj (trade) estero(-a); (visitor) straniero(-a)

oversee [əuvə'siː] vt irreg sorvegliare

overshadow [əuvə'ʃædəu] vt far ombra su; (fig) eclissare

oversight ['əuvəsaɪt] n omissione f, svista

oversleep [əuvə'sliːp] (irreg) vt dormire troppo a lungo

overspend [əuvə'spɛnd] vi irreg spendere troppo; **we have overspent by 5000 dollars** abbiamo speso 5000 dollari di troppo

overt [əu'vəːt] adj palese

overtake [əuvə'teɪk] (irreg) vt sorpassare

over: overthrow [əuvə'θrəu] (irreg) vt (government) rovesciare; **overtime** ['əuvətaɪm] n (lavoro) straordinario

overtook [əuvə'tuk] pt of **overtake**

over: overturn [əuvə'təːn] vt rovesciare ▷ vi rovesciarsi; **overweight** [əuvə'weɪt] adj (person) troppo grasso(-a); **overwhelm** [əuvə'wɛlm] vt sopraffare; sommergere; schiacciare; **overwhelming** adj (victory, defeat) schiacciante; (heat, desire) intenso(-a)

ow [au] excl ahi!

owe [əu] vt **to ~ sb sth, to ~ sth to sb** dovere qc a qn; **how much do I ~ you?** quanto le devo?; **owing to** prep a causa di

owl [aul] n gufo

own [əun] vt possedere ▷ adj proprio(-a); **a room of my ~** la mia propria camera; **to get one's ~ back** vendicarsi; **on one's ~** tutto(-a) solo(-a); **own up** vi confessare; **owner** n proprietario(-a); **ownership** n possesso

ox [ɔks] (pl **oxen**) n bue m

Oxbridge ['ɔksbrɪdʒ] n le università di Oxford e/o Cambridge

oxen ['ɔksn] npl of **ox**

oxygen ['ɔksɪdʒən] n ossigeno

oyster ['ɔɪstəʳ] n ostrica

oz. abbr = **ounce(s)**

ozone ['əuzəun] n ozono; **ozone friendly** adj che non danneggia l'ozono; **ozone layer** n fascia d'ozono

p

p [piː] *abbr* = **penny**; **pence**
P.A. *n abbr* = **personal assistant**; **public address system**
p.a. *abbr* = **per annum**
pace [peɪs] *n* passo; (*speed*) passo; velocità ▷ *vi* **to ~ up and down** camminare su e giù; **to keep ~ with** camminare di pari passo a; (*events*) tenersi al corrente di; **pacemaker** *n* (*Med*) segnapasso; (*Sport: also:* **pace setter**) battistrada *m inv*
Pacific [pə'sɪfɪk] *n* **the ~ (Ocean)** il Pacifico, l'Oceano Pacifico
pacifier ['pæsɪfaɪəʳ] (*US*) *n* (*dummy*) succhiotto, ciuccio (*col*)
pack [pæk] *n* pacco; (*US: of cigarettes*) pacchetto; (*backpack*) zaino; (*of hounds*) muta; (*of thieves etc*) banda; (*of cards*) mazzo ▷ *vt* (*in suitcase etc*) mettere; (*box*) riempire; (*cram*) stipare, pigiare; **to ~ (one's bags)** fare la valigia; **to ~ sb off** spedire via qn; **~ it in!** (*inf*) dacci un taglio!; **pack in** (*BRIT inf*) *vi* (*watch, car*) guastarsi ▷ *vt* mollare, piantare; **pack it in!** piantala!; **pack up** *vi* (*BRIT inf: machine*) guastarsi; (: *person*) far fagotto ▷ *vt* (*belongings, clothes*) mettere in una valigia; (*goods, presents*) imballare
package ['pækɪdʒ] *n* pacco; balla; (*also:* **~ deal**) pacchetto; forfait *m inv*; **package holiday** *n* vacanza organizzata; **package tour** *n* viaggio organizzato
packaging ['pækɪdʒɪŋ] *n* confezione *f*, imballo
packed [pækt] *adj* (*crowded*) affollato(-a); **packed lunch** *n* pranzo al sacco
packet ['pækɪt] *n* pacchetto
packing ['pækɪŋ] *n* imballaggio
pact [pækt] *n* patto, accordo; trattato
pad [pæd] *n* blocco; (*to prevent friction*) cuscinetto; (*inf: flat*) appartamentino ▷ *vt* imbottire; **padded** *adj* imbottito(-a)
paddle ['pædl] *n* (*oar*) pagaia; (*US: for table tennis*) racchetta da ping-pong ▷ *vi* sguazzare ▷ *vt* **to ~ a canoe** *etc* vogare con la pagaia; **paddling pool** (*BRIT*) *n* piscina per bambini
paddock ['pædək] *n* prato recintato; (*at racecourse*) paddock *m inv*
padlock ['pædlɔk] *n* lucchetto
paedophile ['piːdəufaɪl] (*US* **pedophile**) *adj, n* pedofilo(-a)
page [peɪdʒ] *n* pagina; (*also:* **~ boy**) paggio ▷ *vt* (*in hotel etc*) (far) chiamare
pager ['peɪdʒəʳ] *n* (*Tel*) cercapersone *m inv*
paid [peɪd] *pt, pp of* **pay** ▷ *adj* (*work, official*) rimunerato(-a); **to put ~ to** (*BRIT*) mettere fine a
pain [peɪn] *n* dolore *m*; **to be in ~** soffrire, aver male; **to take ~s to do** mettercela tutta per fare; **painful** *adj* doloroso(-a), che fa male; difficile, penoso(-a); **painkiller** *n* antalgico, antidolorifico; **painstaking** ['peɪnzteɪkɪŋ] *adj* (*person*)

sollecito(-a); (*work*) accurato(-a)

paint [peɪnt] *n* vernice *f*, colore *m* ▷ *vt* dipingere; (*walls, door etc*) verniciare; **to ~ the door blue** verniciare la porta di azzurro; **paintbrush** *n* pennello; **painter** *n* (*artist*) pittore *m*; (*decorator*) imbianchino; **painting** *n* pittura; verniciatura; (*picture*) dipinto, quadro

pair [pɛə^r] *n* (*of shoes, gloves etc*) paio; (*of people*) coppia; duo *m inv*; **a ~ of scissors/trousers** un paio di forbici/ pantaloni

pajamas [pɪˈdʒɑːməz] (*US*) *npl* pigiama *m*

Pakistan [pɑːkɪˈstɑːn] *n* Pakistan *m*; **Pakistani** *adj, n* pakistano(-a)

pal [pæl] (*inf*) *n* amico(-a), compagno(-a)

palace [ˈpæləs] *n* palazzo

pale [peɪl] *adj* pallido(-a) ▷ *n* **to be beyond the ~** aver oltrepassato ogni limite

Palestine [ˈpælɪstaɪn] *n* Palestina; **Palestinian** [-ˈtɪnɪən] *adj, n* palestinese *m/f*

palm [pɑːm] *n* (*Anat*) palma, palmo; (*also: ~ tree*) palma ▷ *vt* **to ~ sth off on sb** (*inf*) rifilare qc a qn

pamper [ˈpæmpə^r] *vt* viziare, coccolare

pamphlet [ˈpæmflət] *n* dépliant *m inv*

pan [pæn] *n* (*also:* **sauce~**) casseruola; (*also:* **frying ~**) padella

pancake [ˈpænkeɪk] *n* frittella

panda [ˈpændə] *n* panda *m inv*

pane [peɪn] *n* vetro

panel [ˈpænl] *n* (*of wood, cloth etc*) pannello; (*Radio, TV*) giuria

panhandler [ˈpænhændlə^r] (*US*) *n* (*inf*) accattone(-a)

panic [ˈpænɪk] *n* panico ▷ *vi* perdere il sangue freddo

panorama [pænəˈrɑːmə] *n* panorama *m*

pansy [ˈpænzɪ] *n* (*Bot*) viola del pensiero, pensée *f inv*; (*inf: pej*) femminuccia

pant [pænt] *vi* ansare

panther [ˈpænθə^r] *n* pantera

panties [ˈpæntɪz] *npl* slip *m*, mutandine *fpl*

pantomime [ˈpæntəmaɪm] (*BRIT*) *n* pantomima

● **PANTOMIME**
●
● In Gran Bretagna la **pantomime** è
● una sorta di libera interpretazione
● delle favole più conosciute, che
● vengono messe in scena a teatro
● durante il periodo natalizio. È uno
● spettacolo per tutta la famiglia
● che prevede la partecipazione del
● pubblico.

pants [pænts] *npl* mutande *fpl*, slip *m*; (*US: trousers*) pantaloni *mpl*

paper [ˈpeɪpə^r] *n* carta; (*also:* **wall~**) carta da parati, tappezzeria; (*also:* **news~**) giornale *m*; (*study, article*) saggio; (*exam*) prova scritta ▷ *adj* di carta ▷ *vt* tappezzare; **papers** *npl* (*also:* **identity ~s**) carte *fpl*, documenti *mpl*; **paperback** *n* tascabile *m*; edizione *f* economica; **paper bag** *n* sacchetto di carta; **paper clip** *n* graffetta, clip *f inv*; **paper shop** *n* (*BRIT*) giornalaio (*negozio*); **paperwork** *n* lavoro amministrativo

paprika [ˈpæprɪkə] *n* paprica

par [pɑː^r] *n* parità, pari *f*; (*Golf*) norma; **on a ~ with** alla pari con

paracetamol [pærəˈsiːtəmɔl] (*BRIT*) *n* paracetamolo

parachute [ˈpærəʃuːt] *n* paracadute *m inv*

parade [pəˈreɪd] *n* parata ▷ *vt* (*fig*) fare sfoggio di ▷ *vi* sfilare in parata

paradise [ˈpærədaɪs] *n* paradiso

paradox [ˈpærədɔks] *n* paradosso

paraffin [ˈpærəfɪn] (*BRIT*) *n* **~ (oil)** paraffina

paragraph [ˈpærəgrɑːf] *n* paragrafo

parallel [ˈpærəlɛl] *adj* parallelo(-a);

(*fig*) analogo(-a) ▷ *n* (*line*) parallela; (*fig*, *Geo*) parallelo

paralysed ['pærəlaɪzd] *adj* paralizzato(-a)

paralysis [pə'rælɪsɪs] *n* paralisi *f inv*

paramedic [pærə'mɛdɪk] *n* paramedico

paranoid ['pærənɔɪd] *adj* paranoico(-a)

parasite ['pærəsaɪt] *n* parassita *m*

parcel ['pɑːsl] *n* pacco, pacchetto ▷ *vt* (*also*: ~ **up**) impaccare

pardon ['pɑːdn] *n* perdono; grazia ▷ *vt* perdonare; (*Law*) graziare; ~ **me!** mi scusi!; **I beg your ~!** scusi!; **I beg your ~?** (*BRIT*), ~ **me?** (*US*) prego?

parent ['pɛərənt] *n* genitore *m*; **parents** *npl* (*mother and father*) genitori *mpl*; **parental** [pə'rɛntl] *adj* dei genitori

> Be careful not to translate *parent* by the Italian word *parente*.

Paris ['pærɪs] *n* Parigi *f*

parish ['pærɪʃ] *n* parrocchia; (*BRIT: civil*) ≈ municipio

Parisian [pə'rɪzɪən] *adj*, *n* parigino(-a)

park [pɑːk] *n* parco ▷ *vt*, *vi* parcheggiare; **can I ~ here?** posso parcheggiare qui?

parking ['pɑːkɪŋ] *n* parcheggio; **"no ~"** "sosta vietata"; **parking lot** (*US*) *n* posteggio, parcheggio; **parking meter** *n* parchimetro; **parking ticket** *n* multa per sosta vietata

parkway ['pɑːkweɪ] (*US*) *n* viale *m*

parliament ['pɑːləmənt] *n* parlamento; **parliamentary** [pɑːlə'mɛntərɪ] *adj* parlamentare

Parmesan [pɑːmɪ'zæn] *n* (*also*: ~ **cheese**) parmigiano

parole [pə'rəul] *n* **on ~** in libertà per buona condotta

parrot ['pærət] *n* pappagallo

parsley ['pɑːslɪ] *n* prezzemolo

parsnip ['pɑːsnɪp] *n* pastinaca

parson ['pɑːsn] *n* prete *m*; (*Church of England*) parroco

part [pɑːt] *n* parte *f*; (*of machine*) pezzo; (*US: in hair*) scriminatura ▷ *adj* in parte ▷ *adv* = **partly** ▷ *vt* separare ▷ *vi* (*people*) separarsi; **to take ~ in** prendere parte a; **for my ~** per parte mia; **to take sth in good ~** prendere bene qc; **to take sb's ~** parteggiare per *or* prendere le parti di qn; **for the most ~** in generale; nella maggior parte dei casi; **part with** *vt fus* separarsi da; rinunciare a

partial ['pɑːʃl] *adj* parziale; **to be ~ to** avere un debole per

participant [pɑː'tɪsɪpənt] *n* ~ **(in)** partecipante *m/f* (a)

participate [pɑː'tɪsɪpeɪt] *vi* **to ~ (in)** prendere parte (a), partecipare (a)

particle ['pɑːtɪkl] *n* particella

particular [pə'tɪkjuləʳ] *adj* particolare; speciale; (*fussy*) difficile; meticoloso(-a); **in ~** in particolare, particolarmente; **particularly** *adv* particolarmente; in particolare; **particulars** *npl* particolari *mpl*, dettagli *mpl*; (*information*) informazioni *fpl*

parting ['pɑːtɪŋ] *n* separazione *f*; (*BRIT: in hair*) scriminatura ▷ *adj* d'addio

partition [pɑː'tɪʃən] *n* (*Pol*) partizione *f*; (*wall*) tramezzo

partly ['pɑːtlɪ] *adv* parzialmente; in parte

partner ['pɑːtnəʳ] *n* (*Comm*) socio(-a); (*wife, husband etc, Sport*) compagno(-a); (*at dance*) cavaliere/dama; **partnership** *n* associazione *f*; (*Comm*) società *f inv*

part of speech *n* parte *f* del discorso

partridge ['pɑːtrɪdʒ] *n* pernice *f*

part-time ['pɑːt'taɪm] *adj*, *adv* a orario ridotto

party ['pɑːtɪ] *n* (*Pol*) partito; (*group*) gruppo; (*Law*) parte *f*; (*celebration*) ricevimento; serata; festa ▷ *cpd* (*Pol*) del partito, di partito

pass [pɑːs] *vt* (*gen*) passare; (*place*) passare davanti a; (*exam*) passare, superare; (*candidate*) promuovere; (*overtake, surpass*) sorpassare, superare; (*approve*) approvare ▷ *vi* passare ▷ *n* (*permit*) lasciapassare *m inv*; permesso; (*in mountains*) passo, gola; (*Sport*) passaggio; (*Scol*) **to get a ~** prendere la sufficienza; **could you ~ the salt/oil, please?** mi passa il sale/l'olio, per favore?; **to ~ sth through a hole** *etc* far passare qc attraverso un buco *etc*; **to make a ~ at sb** (*inf*) fare delle proposte *or* delle avances a qn; **pass away** *vi* morire; **pass by** *vi* passare ▷ *vt* trascurare; **pass on** *vt* passare; **pass out** *vi* svenire; **pass over** *vi* (*die*) spirare ▷ *vt* lasciare da parte; **pass up** *vt* (*opportunity*) lasciarsi sfuggire, perdere; **passable** *adj* (*road*) praticabile; (*work*) accettabile

passage ['pæsɪdʒ] *n* (*gen*) passaggio; (*also:* **~way**) corridoio; (*in book*) brano, passo; (*by boat*) traversata

passenger ['pæsɪndʒəʳ] *n* passeggero(-a)

passer-by [pɑːsə'baɪ] *n* passante *m/f*

passing place *n* (*Aut*) piazzola di sosta

passion ['pæʃən] *n* passione *f*; amore *m*; **passionate** *adj* appassionato(-a); **passion fruit** *n* frutto della passione

passive ['pæsɪv] *adj* (*also Ling*) passivo(-a)

passport ['pɑːspɔːt] *n* passaporto; **passport control** *n* controllo *m* passaporti *inv*; **passport office** *n* ufficio *m* passaporti *inv*

password ['pɑːswɜːd] *n* parola d'ordine

past [pɑːst] *prep* (*further than*) oltre, di là di; dopo; (*later than*) dopo ▷ *adj* passato(-a); (*president etc*) ex *inv* ▷ *n* passato; **he's ~ forty** ha più di quarant'anni; **ten ~ eight** le otto e dieci; **for the ~ few days** da qualche

giorno; in questi ultimi giorni; **to run ~** passare di corsa

pasta ['pæstə] *n* pasta

paste [peɪst] *n* (*glue*) colla; (*Culin*) pâté *m inv*; pasta ▷ *vt* collare

pastel ['pæstl] *adj* pastello *inv*

pasteurized ['pæstəraɪzd] *adj* pastorizzato(-a)

pastime ['pɑːstaɪm] *n* passatempo

pastor ['pɑːstəʳ] *n* pastore *m*

past participle [-'pɑːtɪsɪpl] *n* (*Ling*) participio passato

pastry ['peɪstrɪ] *n* pasta

pasture ['pɑːstʃəʳ] *n* pascolo

pasty¹ ['pæstɪ] *n* pasticcio di carne

pasty² ['peɪstɪ] *adj* (*face etc*) smorto(-a)

pat [pæt] *vt* accarezzare, dare un colpetto (affettuoso) a

patch [pætʃ] *n* (*of material, on tyre*) toppa; (*eye patch*) benda; (*spot*) macchia ▷ *vt* (*clothes*) rattoppare; **(to go through) a bad ~** (attraversare) un brutto periodo; **patchy** *adj* irregolare

pâté ['pæteɪ] *n* pâté *m inv*

patent ['peɪtnt] *n* brevetto ▷ *vt* brevettare ▷ *adj* patente, manifesto(-a)

paternal [pə'tɜːnl] *adj* paterno(-a)

paternity leave [pə'tɜːnɪtɪ-] *n* congedo di paternità

path [pɑːθ] *n* sentiero, viottolo; viale *m*; (*fig*) via, strada; (*of planet, missile*) traiettoria

pathetic [pə'θɛtɪk] *adj* (*pitiful*) patetico(-a); (*very bad*) penoso(-a)

pathway ['pɑːθweɪ] *n* sentiero

patience ['peɪʃns] *n* pazienza; (BRIT *Cards*) solitario

patient ['peɪʃnt] *n* paziente *m/f*, malato(-a) ▷ *adj* paziente

patio ['pætɪəu] *n* terrazza

patriotic [pætrɪ'ɔtɪk] *adj* patriottico(-a)

patrol [pə'trəul] *n* pattuglia ▷ *vt* pattugliare; **patrol car** *n* autoradio *f*

inv (della polizia)
patron ['peɪtrən] *n* (*in shop*) cliente
m/f; (*of charity*) benefattore(-trice); **~
of the arts** mecenate *m/f*
patronizing ['pætrənaɪzɪŋ] *adj*
condiscendente
pattern ['pætən] *n* modello; (*design*)
disegno, motivo; **patterned** *adj* a
disegni, a motivi; (*material*) fantasia *inv*
pause [pɔːz] *n* pausa ▷ *vi* fare una
pausa, arrestarsi
pave [peɪv] *vt* pavimentare; **to ~ the
way for** aprire la via a
pavement ['peɪvmənt] (*BRIT*) *n*
marciapiede *m*

> Be careful not to translate
> *pavement* by the Italian word
> *pavimento*.

pavilion [pə'vɪlɪən] *n* (*Sport*) edificio
annesso a campo sportivo
paving ['peɪvɪŋ] *n* pavimentazione *f*
paw [pɔː] *n* zampa
pawn [pɔːn] *n* (*Chess*) pedone *m*; (*fig*)
pedina ▷ *vt* dare in pegno; **pawn
broker** *n* prestatore *m* su pegno
pay [peɪ] (*pt, pp* **paid**) *n* stipendio;
paga ▷ *vt* pagare ▷ *vi* (*be profitable*)
rendere; **can I ~ by credit card?** posso
pagare con la carta di credito?; **to ~
attention (to)** fare attenzione (a); **to
~ sb a visit** far visita a qn; **to ~ one's
respects to sb** porgere i propri rispetti
a qn; **pay back** *vt* rimborsare; **pay for**
vt fus pagare; **pay in** *vt* versare; **pay
off** *vt* (*debt*) saldare; (*person*) pagare;
(*employee*) pagare e licenziare ▷ *vi*
(*scheme, decision*) dare dei frutti; **pay
out** *vt* (*money*) sborsare, tirar fuori;
(*rope*) far allentare; **pay up** *vt* saldare;
payable *adj* pagabile
pay-as-you-go ['peɪəzjuːgəʊ] *adj*
(*mobile phone*) con scheda prepagata
pay: **pay day** *n* giorno di paga;
pay envelope (*US*) *n* = **pay
packet**; **payment** *n* pagamento;
versamento; saldo; **payout** *n*
pagamento; (*in competition*) premio;

pay packet (*BRIT*) *n* busta *f* paga
inv; **pay phone** *n* cabina telefonica;
payroll *n* ruolo (organico); **pay slip**
n foglio *m* paga *inv*; **pay television** *n*
televisione *f* a pagamento, pay-tv *f inv*
PC *n abbr* = **personal computer** ▷ *adv*
abbr = **politically correct**
p.c. *abbr* = **per cent**
PDA *n abbr* (= *personal digital assistant*)
PDA *m inv*
PE *n abbr* (= *physical education*) ed. fisica
pea [piː] *n* pisello
peace [piːs] *n* pace *f*; **peaceful** *adj*
pacifico(-a), calmo(-a)
peach [piːtʃ] *n* pesca
peacock ['piːkɔk] *n* pavone *m*
peak [piːk] *n* (*of mountain*) cima, vetta;
(*mountain itself*) picco; (*of cap*) visiera;
(*fig*) apice *m*, culmine *m*; **peak hours**
npl ore *fpl* di punta
peanut ['piːnʌt] *n* arachide *f*,
nocciolina americana; **peanut butter**
n burro di arachidi
pear [pɛəʳ] *n* pera
pearl [pəːl] *n* perla
peasant ['pɛznt] *n* contadino(-a)
peat [piːt] *n* torba
pebble ['pɛbl] *n* ciottolo
peck [pɛk] *vt* (*also*: **~ at**) beccare ▷ *n*
colpo di becco; (*kiss*) bacetto; **peckish**
(*BRIT*: *inf*) *adj* **I feel peckish** ho un
languorino
peculiar [pɪ'kjuːlɪəʳ] *adj* strano(-a),
bizzarro(-a); peculiare; **~ to** peculiare di
pedal ['pɛdl] *n* pedale *m* ▷ *vi* pedalare
pedalo ['pɛdələu] *n* pedalò *m inv*
pedestal ['pɛdəstl] *n* piedestallo
pedestrian [pɪ'dɛstrɪən] *n*
pedone(-a) ▷ *adj* pedonale; (*fig*)
prosaico(-a), pedestre; **pedestrian
crossing** (*BRIT*) *n* passaggio
pedonale; **pedestrianized** *adj*: **a
pedestrianized street** una zona
pedonalizzata; **pedestrian precinct**
(*BRIT*), **pedestrian zone** (*US*) *n* zona
pedonale
pedigree ['pɛdɪgriː] *n* (*of animal*)

pedigree m inv; (fig) background m inv
▷ cpd (animal) di razza

pedophile ['pi:dəufaɪl] (US) n
= **paedophile**

pee [pi:] (inf) vi pisciare

peek [pi:k] vi guardare furtivamente

peel [pi:l] n buccia; (of orange, lemon)
scorza ▷ vt sbucciare ▷ vi (paint etc)
staccarsi

peep [pi:p] n (BRIT: look) sguardo
furtivo, sbirciata; (sound) pigolio ▷ vi
(BRIT) guardare furtivamente

peer [pɪəʳ] vi **to ~ at** scrutare
▷ n (noble) pari m inv; (equal) pari
m/f inv, uguale m/f; (contemporary)
contemporaneo(-a)

peg [pɛg] n caviglia; (for coat etc)
attaccapanni m inv; (BRIT: also:
clothes ~) molletta

pelican ['pɛlɪkən] n pellicano;
pelican crossing (BRIT) n (Aut)
attraversamento pedonale con semaforo a
controllo manuale

pelt [pɛlt] vt **to ~ sb (with)**
bombardare qn (con) ▷ vi (rain)
piovere a dirotto; (inf: run) filare ▷ n
pelle f

pelvis ['pɛlvɪs] n pelvi f inv, bacino

pen [pɛn] n penna; (for sheep) recinto

penalty ['pɛnltɪ] n penalità f inv;
sanzione f penale; (fine) ammenda;
(Sport) penalizzazione f

pence [pɛns] (BRIT) npl of **penny**

pencil ['pɛnsl] n matita; **pencil
in** vt scrivere a matita; **pencil
case** n astuccio per matite; **pencil
sharpener** n temperamatite m inv

pendant ['pɛndnt] n pendaglio

pending ['pɛndɪŋ] prep in attesa di
▷ adj in sospeso

penetrate ['pɛnɪtreɪt] vt penetrare

penfriend ['pɛnfrɛnd] (BRIT) n
corrispondente m/f

penguin ['pɛŋgwɪn] n pinguino

penicillin [pɛnɪ'sɪlɪn] n penicillina

peninsula [pə'nɪnsjulə] n penisola

penis ['pi:nɪs] n pene m

penitentiary [pɛnɪ'tɛnʃərɪ] (US) n
carcere m

penknife ['pɛnnaɪf] n temperino

penniless ['pɛnɪlɪs] adj senza un
soldo

penny ['pɛnɪ] (pl **pennies** or **pence**)
(BRIT) n penny m; (US) centesimo

penpal ['pɛnpæl] n corrispondente
m/f

pension ['pɛnʃən] n pensione f;
pensioner (BRIT) n pensionato(-a)

pentagon ['pɛntəgən] n pentagono;
the P~ (US Pol) il Pentagono

penthouse ['pɛnthaus] n
appartamento (di lusso) nell'attico

penultimate [pɪ'nʌltɪmət] adj
penultimo(-a)

people ['pi:pl] npl gente f; persone
fpl; (citizens) popolo ▷ n (nation,
race) popolo; **4/several ~ came**
4/parecchie persone sono venute; **~
say that ...** si dice che ...

pepper ['pɛpəʳ] n pepe m; (vegetable)
peperone m ▷ vt (fig): **to ~ with**
spruzzare di; **peppermint** n (sweet)
pasticca di menta

per [pəːʳ] prep per; a; **~ hour** all'ora; **~
kilo** etc il chilo etc; **~ day** al giorno

perceive [pə'si:v] vt percepire; (notice)
accorgersi di

per cent adv per cento

percentage [pə'sɛntɪdʒ] n
percentuale f

perception [pə'sɛpʃən] n percezione
f; sensibilità; perspicacia

perch [pəːtʃ] n (fish) pesce m persico;
(for bird) sostegno, ramo ▷ vi
appollaiarsi

percussion [pə'kʌʃən] n percussione
f; (Mus) strumenti mpl a percussione

perfect [adj, n 'pəːfɪkt, vb pə'fɛkt]
adj perfetto(-a) ▷ n (also: **~ tense**)
perfetto, passato prossimo ▷ vt
perfezionare; mettere a punto;
perfection [pə'fɛkʃən] n perfezione
f; **perfectly** adv perfettamente, alla
perfezione

perform [pə'fɔ:m] vt (carry out) eseguire, fare; (symphony etc) suonare; (play, ballet) dare; (opera) fare ▷ vi suonare; recitare; **performance** n esecuzione f; (at theatre etc) rappresentazione f, spettacolo; (of an artist) interpretazione f; (of player etc) performance f; (of car, engine) prestazione f; **performer** n artista m/f

perfume ['pə:fju:m] n profumo
perhaps [pə'hæps] adv forse
perimeter [pə'rɪmɪtə'] n perimetro
period ['pɪərɪəd] n periodo; (History) epoca; (Scol) lezione f; (full stop) punto; (Med) mestruazioni fpl ▷ adj (costume, furniture) d'epoca; **periodical** [-'ɔdɪkl] n periodico; **periodically** adv periodicamente
perish ['pɛrɪʃ] vi perire, morire; (decay) deteriorarsi
perjury ['pə:dʒərɪ] n spergiuro
perk [pə:k] (inf) n vantaggio
perm [pə:m] n (for hair) permanente f
permanent ['pə:mənənt] adj permanente; **permanently** adv definitivamente
permission [pə'mɪʃən] n permesso
permit [n 'pə:mɪt, vb pə'mɪt] n permesso ▷ vt permettere; **to ~ sb to do** permettere a qn di fare
perplex [pə'plɛks] vt lasciare perplesso/a
persecute ['pə:sɪkju:t] vt perseguitare
persecution [pə:sɪ'kju:ʃən] n persecuzione f
persevere [pə:sɪ'vɪə'] vi perseverare
Persian ['pə:ʃən] adj persiano(-a) ▷ n (Ling) persiano; **the (~) Gulf** n il Golfo Persico
persist [pə'sɪst] vi **to ~ (in doing)** persistere (nel fare); ostinarsi (a fare); **persistent** adj persistente; ostinato(-a)
person ['pə:sn] n persona; **in ~** di or in persona, personalmente;

personal adj personale; individuale; **personal assistant** n segretaria personale; **personal computer** n personal computer m inv; **personality** [-'nælɪtɪ] n personalità f inv; **personally** adv personalmente; **to take sth personally** prendere qc come una critica personale; **personal organizer** n (Filofax®) Fulltime®; (electronic) agenda elettronica; **personal stereo** n Walkman® m inv
personnel [pə:sə'nɛl] n personale m
perspective [pə'spɛktɪv] n prospettiva
perspiration [pə:spɪ'reɪʃən] n traspirazione f, sudore m
persuade [pə'sweɪd] vt **to ~ sb to do sth** persuadere qn a fare qc
persuasion [pə'sweɪʒən] n persuasione f; (creed) convinzione f, credo
persuasive [pə'sweɪsɪv] adj persuasivo(-a)
perverse [pə'və:s] adj perverso(-a)
pervert [n 'pə:və:t, vb pə'və:t] n pervertito(-a) ▷ vt pervertire
pessimism ['pɛsɪmɪzəm] n pessimismo
pessimist ['pɛsɪmɪst] n pessimista m/f; **pessimistic** [-'mɪstɪk] adj pessimistico(-a)
pest [pɛst] n animale m (or insetto) pestifero; (fig) peste f
pester ['pɛstə'] vt tormentare, molestare
pesticide ['pɛstɪsaɪd] n pesticida m
pet [pɛt] n animale m domestico ▷ cpd favorito(-a) ▷ vt accarezzare; **teacher's ~** favorito(-a) del maestro
petal ['pɛtl] n petalo
petite [pə'ti:t] adj piccolo(-a) e aggraziato(-a)
petition [pə'tɪʃən] n petizione f
petrified ['pɛtrɪfaɪd] adj (fig) morto(-a) di paura
petrol ['pɛtrəl] n (BRIT) benzina; **two/four-star ~** ≈ benzina normale/super;

I've run out of ~ sono rimasto senza benzina

Be careful not to translate *petrol* by the Italian word *petrolio*.

petroleum [pə'trəʊlɪəm] n petrolio
petrol: **petrol pump** (BRIT) n (in car, at garage) pompa di benzina; **petrol station** (BRIT) n stazione f di rifornimento; **petrol tank** (BRIT) n serbatoio della benzina
petticoat ['petɪkəʊt] n sottana
petty ['petɪ] adj (mean) meschino(-a); (unimportant) insignificante
pew [pju:] n panca (di chiesa)
pewter ['pju:tər] n peltro
phantom ['fæntəm] n fantasma m
pharmacist ['fɑ:məsɪst] n farmacista m/f
pharmacy ['fɑ:məsɪ] n farmacia
phase [feɪz] n fase f, periodo; **phase in** vt introdurre gradualmente; **phase out** vt (machinery) eliminare gradualmente; (product) ritirare gradualmente; (job, subsidy) abolire gradualmente
Ph.D. n abbr = **Doctor of Philosophy**
pheasant ['feznt] n fagiano
phenomena [fə'nɒmɪnə] npl of **phenomenon**
phenomenal [fɪ'nɒmɪnl] adj fenomenale
phenomenon [fə'nɒmɪnən] (pl **phenomena**) n fenomeno
Philippines ['fɪlɪpi:nz] npl **the ~** le Filippine
philosopher [fɪ'lɒsəfər] n filosofo(-a)
philosophical [fɪlə'sɒfɪkl] adj filosofico(-a)
philosophy [fɪ'lɒsəfɪ] n filosofia
phlegm [flɛm] n flemma
phobia ['fəʊbjə] n fobia
phone [fəʊn] n telefono ▷ vt telefonare; **to be on the ~** avere il telefono; (be calling) essere al telefono; **phone back** vt, vi richiamare; **phone up** vt telefonare a ▷ vi telefonare; **phone book** n guida del telefono,

elenco telefonico; **phone booth** n = **phone box**; **phone box** n cabina telefonica; **phone call** n telefonata; **phonecard** n scheda telefonica; **phone number** n numero di telefono
phonetics [fə'nɛtɪks] n fonetica
phoney ['fəʊnɪ] adj falso(-a), fasullo(-a)
photo ['fəʊtəʊ] n foto f inv
photo... ['fəʊtəʊ] prefix: **photo album** n (new) album m inv per fotografie; (containing photos) album m inv delle fotografie; **photocopier** n fotocopiatrice f; **photocopy** n fotocopia ▷ vt fotocopiare
photograph ['fəʊtəgræf] n fotografia ▷ vt fotografare; **photographer** [fə'tɒgrəfər] n fotografo; **photography** [fə'tɒgrəfɪ] n fotografia
phrase [freɪz] n espressione f; (Ling) locuzione f; (Mus) frase f ▷ vt esprimere; **phrase book** n vocabolarietto
physical ['fɪzɪkl] adj fisico(-a); **physical education** n educazione f fisica; **physically** adv fisicamente
physician [fɪ'zɪʃən] n medico
physicist ['fɪzɪsɪst] n fisico
physics ['fɪzɪks] n fisica
physiotherapist [fɪzɪəʊ'θerəpɪst] n fisioterapista m/f
physiotherapy [fɪzɪəʊ'θerəpɪ] n fisioterapia
physique [fɪ'zi:k] n fisico; costituzione f
pianist ['pi:ənɪst] n pianista m/f
piano [pɪ'ænəʊ] n pianoforte m
pick [pɪk] n (tool: also: **~-axe**) piccone m ▷ vt scegliere; (gather) cogliere; (remove) togliere; (lock) far scattare; **take your ~** scelga; **the ~ of** il fior fiore di; **to ~ one's nose** mettersi le dita nel naso; **to ~ one's teeth** pulirsi i denti con lo stuzzicadenti; **to ~ a quarrel** attaccar briga; **pick on** vt fus (person) avercela con; **pick out** vt scegliere;

(distinguish) distinguere; **pick up** vi
(improve) migliorarsi ▷ vt raccogliere;
(Police, Radio) prendere; (collect)
passare a prendere; (Aut: give lift to)
far salire; (person: for sexual encounter)
rimorchiare; (learn) imparare; **to pick
up speed** acquistare velocità; **to pick
o.s. up** rialzarsi

pickle ['pɪkl] n (also: **~s**: as condiment)
sottaceti mpl; (fig: mess) pasticcio
▷ vt mettere sottaceto; mettere in
salamoia

pickpocket ['pɪkpɔkɪt] n borsaiolo

pick-up ['pɪkʌp] n (BRIT: on record
player) pick-up m inv; (small truck: also:
~ truck, **~ van**) camioncino

picnic ['pɪknɪk] n picnic m inv; **picnic
area** n area per il picnic

picture ['pɪktʃər] n quadro; (painting)
pittura; (photograph) foto(grafia);
(drawing) disegno; (film) film m inv
▷ vt raffigurarsi; **pictures** (BRIT) npl
(cinema): **the ~s** il cinema; **would you
take a ~ of us, please?** può farci una
foto, per favore?; **picture frame** n
cornice m inv; **picture messaging**
n picture messaging m, invio di
messaggini con disegni

picturesque [pɪktʃə'rɛsk] adj
pittoresco(-a)

pie [paɪ] n torta; (of meat) pasticcio

piece [piːs] n pezzo; (of land)
appezzamento; (item): **a ~ of
furniture/advice** un mobile/
consiglio ▷ vt **to ~ together** mettere
insieme; **to take to ~s** smontare

pie chart n grafico a torta

pier [pɪər] n molo; (of bridge etc) pila

pierce [pɪəs] vt forare; (with arrow
etc) trafiggere; **pierced** adj: **I've
got pierced ears** ho i buchi per gli
orecchini

pig [pɪg] n maiale m, porco

pigeon ['pɪdʒən] n piccione m

piggy bank ['pɪgɪ-] n salvadanaro

pigsty ['pɪgstaɪ] n porcile m

pigtail ['pɪgteɪl] n treccina

pike [paɪk] n (fish) luccio

pilchard ['pɪltʃəd] n specie di sardina

pile [paɪl] n (pillar, of books) pila;
(heap) mucchio; (of carpet) pelo; **to ~
into** (car) stiparsi or ammucchiarsi
in; **pile up** vt ammucchiare ▷ vi
ammucchiarsi; **piles** [paɪlz] npl
emorroidi fpl; **pile-up** ['paɪlʌp] n (Aut)
tamponamento a catena

pilgrimage ['pɪlgrɪmɪdʒ] n
pellegrinaggio

pill [pɪl] n pillola; **the ~** la pillola

pillar ['pɪlər] n colonna

pillow ['pɪləu] n guanciale m;
pillowcase n federa

pilot ['paɪlət] n pilota m/f ▷ cpd
(scheme etc) pilota inv ▷ vt pilotare;
pilot light n fiamma pilota

pimple ['pɪmpl] n foruncolo

pin [pɪn] n spillo; (Tech) perno ▷ vt
attaccare con uno spillo; **~s and
needles** formicolio; **to ~ sb down** (fig)
obbligare qn a pronunziarsi; **to ~ sth
on sb** (fig) addossare la colpa di qc a qn

PIN n abbr (= personal identification
number) codice m segreto

pinafore ['pɪnəfɔːr] n (also: **~ dress**)
grembiule m (senza maniche)

pinch [pɪntʃ] n pizzicotto, pizzico ▷ vt
pizzicare; (inf: steal) grattare; **at a ~** in
caso di bisogno

pine [paɪn] n (also: **~ tree**) pino ▷ vi **to
~ for** struggersi dal desiderio di

pineapple ['paɪnæpl] n ananas m inv

ping [pɪŋ] n (noise) tintinnio; **ping-
pong®** n ping-pong® m

pink [pɪŋk] adj rosa inv ▷ n (colour)
rosa m inv; (Bot) garofano

pinpoint ['pɪnpɔɪnt] vt indicare con
precisione

pint [paɪnt] n pinta (BRIT = 0.57l; US =
0.47l); (BRIT: inf) ≈ birra da mezzo

pioneer [paɪə'nɪər] n pioniere(-a)

pious ['paɪəs] adj pio(-a)

pip [pɪp] n (seed) seme m; (BRIT: time
signal on radio) segnale m orario

pipe [paɪp] n tubo; (for smoking)

pipa ▷ vt portare per mezzo di
tubazione; **pipeline** n conduttura;
(for oil) oleodotto; **piper** n piffero;
suonatore(-trice) di cornamusa
pirate ['paɪərət] n pirata m ▷ vt
riprodurre abusivamente
Pisces ['paɪsiːz] n Pesci mpl
piss [pɪs] (inf) vi pisciare; **pissed** (inf)
adj (drunk) ubriaco(-a) fradicio(-a)
pistol ['pɪstl] n pistola
piston ['pɪstən] n pistone m
pit [pɪt] n buca, fossa; (also: **coal ~**)
miniera; (quarry) cava ▷ vt **to ~ sb
against sb** opporre qn a qn
pitch [pɪtʃ] n (BRIT Sport) campo; (Mus)
tono; (tar) pece f; (fig) grado, punto
▷ vt (throw) lanciare ▷ vi (fall) cascare;
to ~ a tent piantare una tenda; **pitch-
black** adj nero(-a) come la pece
pitfall ['pɪtfɔːl] n trappola
pith [pɪθ] n (of plant) midollo; (of
orange) parte f interna della scorza;
(fig) essenza, succo; vigore m
pitiful ['pɪtɪful] adj (touching)
pietoso(-a)
pity ['pɪtɪ] n pietà ▷ vt aver pietà di;
what a ~! che peccato!
pizza ['piːtsə] n pizza
placard ['plækɑːd] n affisso
place [pleɪs] n posto, luogo; (proper
position, rank, seat) posto; (house) casa,
alloggio; (home): **at/to his ~** a casa
sua ▷ vt (object) posare, mettere;
(identify) riconoscere; individuare;
to take ~ aver luogo; succedere;
to change ~s with sb scambiare il
posto con qn; **out of ~** (not suitable)
inopportuno(-a); **in the first ~** in
primo luogo; **to ~ an order** dare
un'ordinazione; **to be ~d** (in race,
exam) classificarsi; **place mat** n
sottopiatto; (in linen etc) tovaglietta;
placement n collocamento; (job)
lavoro
placid ['plæsɪd] adj placido(-a),
calmo(-a)
plague [pleɪg] n peste f ▷ vt

tormentare
plaice [pleɪs] n inv pianuzza
plain [pleɪn] adj (clear) chiaro(-a),
palese; (simple) semplice; (frank)
franco(-a), aperto(-a); (not handsome)
bruttino(-a); (without seasoning etc)
scondito(-a); naturale; (in one colour)
tinta unita inv ▷ adv francamente,
chiaramente ▷ n pianura; **plain
chocolate** n cioccolato fondente;
plainly adv chiaramente; (frankly)
francamente
plaintiff ['pleɪntɪf] n attore(-trice)
plait [plæt] n treccia
plan [plæn] n pianta; (scheme)
progetto, piano ▷ vt (think in advance)
progettare; (prepare) organizzare
▷ vi far piani or progetti; **to ~ to do**
progettare di fare
plane [pleɪn] n (Aviat) aereo; (tree)
platano; (tool) pialla; (Art, Math etc)
piano ▷ adj piano(-a), piatto(-a) ▷ vt
(with tool) piallare
planet ['plænɪt] n pianeta m
plank [plæŋk] n tavola, asse f
planning ['plænɪŋ] n progettazione f;
family ~ pianificazione f delle nascite
plant [plɑːnt] n pianta; (machinery)
impianto; (factory) fabbrica ▷ vt
piantare; (bomb) mettere
plantation [plæn'teɪʃən] n
piantagione f
plaque [plæk] n placca
plasma TV ['plæzmə-] n TV f inv al
plasma
plaster ['plɑːstəʳ] n intonaco; (also: ~
of Paris) gesso; (BRIT: also: **sticking
~**) cerotto ▷ vt intonacare; ingessare;
(cover): **to ~ with** coprire di; **plaster
cast** n (Med) ingessatura, gesso;
(model, statue) modello in gesso
plastic ['plæstɪk] n plastica ▷ adj
(made of plastic) di or in plastica;
plastic bag n sacchetto di plastica;
plastic surgery n chirurgia plastica
plate [pleɪt] n (dish) piatto; (in book)
tavola; (dental plate) dentiera; **gold/**

silver ~ vasellame *m* d'oro/d'argento
plateau ['plætəu] (*pl* **plateaus** or
plateaux) *n* altipiano
platform ['plætfɔːm] *n* (*stage, at
meeting*) palco; (*Rail*) marciapiede *m*;
(*BRIT: of bus*) piattaforma; **which ~
does the train for Rome go from?**
da che binario parte il treno per Roma?
platinum ['plætɪnəm] *n* platino
platoon [plə'tuːn] *n* plotone *m*
platter ['plætə'] *n* piatto
plausible ['plɔːzɪbl] *adj* plausibile,
credibile; (*person*) convincente
play [pleɪ] *n* gioco; (*Theatre*)
commedia ▷ *vt* (*game*) giocare a;
(*team, opponent*) giocare contro;
(*instrument, piece of music*) suonare;
(*record, tape*) ascoltare; (*role, part*)
interpretare ▷ *vi* giocare; suonare;
recitare; **to ~ safe** giocare sul sicuro;
play back *vt* riascoltare, risentire;
play up *vi* (*cause trouble*) fare i
capricci; **player** *n* giocatore(-trice);
(*Theatre*) attore(-trice); (*Mus*)
musicista *m/f*; **playful** *adj*
giocoso(-a); **playground** *n* (*in school*)
cortile *m* per la ricreazione; (*in park*)
parco *m* giochi *inv*; **playgroup** *n*
giardino d'infanzia; **playing card** *n*
carta da gioco; **playing field** *n* campo
sportivo; **playschool** *n* = **playgroup**;
playtime *n* (*Scol*) ricreazione *f*;
playwright *n* drammaturgo(-a)
plc *abbr* (= *public limited company*)
società per azioni a responsabilità
limitata quotata in borsa
plea [pliː] *n* (*request*) preghiera,
domanda; (*Law*) (argomento di) difesa
plead [pliːd] *vt* patrocinare; (*give as
excuse*) addurre a pretesto ▷ *vi* (*Law*)
perorare la causa; (*beg*): **to ~ with sb**
implorare qn
pleasant ['plɛznt] *adj* piacevole,
gradevole
please [pliːz] *excl* per piacere!, per
favore!; (*acceptance*): **yes, ~** sì, grazie
▷ *vt* piacere a ▷ *vi* piacere; (*think fit*):

do as you ~ faccia come le pare; **~
yourself!** come ti (*or* le) pare!; **pleased**
adj **pleased (with)** contento(-a) (di);
pleased to meet you! piacere!
pleasure ['plɛʒə'] *n* piacere *m*; **"it's a
~"** "prego"
pleat [pliːt] *n* piega
pledge [plɛdʒ] *n* pegno; (*promise*)
promessa ▷ *vt* impegnare;
promettere
plentiful ['plɛntɪful] *adj* abbondante,
copioso(-a)
plenty ['plɛntɪ] *n* **~ of** tanto(-a),
molto(-a); un'abbondanza di
pliers ['plaɪəz] *npl* pinza
plight [plaɪt] *n* situazione *f* critica
plod [plɔd] *vi* camminare a stento;
(*fig*) sgobbare
plonk [plɔŋk] (*inf*) *n* (*BRIT: wine*) vino
da poco ▷ *vt* **to ~ sth down** buttare
giù qc bruscamente
plot [plɔt] *n* congiura, cospirazione *f*;
(*of story, play*) trama; (*of land*) lotto ▷ *vt*
(*mark out*) fare la pianta di; rilevare;
(: *diagram etc*) tracciare; (*conspire*)
congiurare, cospirare ▷ *vi* congiurare
plough [plau] (*US* **plow**) *n* aratro
▷ *vt* (*earth*) arare; **to ~ money into**
(*company etc*) investire danaro in;
ploughman's lunch ['plaumənz-]
(*BRIT*) *n* pasto a base di pane, formaggio
e birra
plow [plau] (*US*) = **plough**
ploy [plɔɪ] *n* stratagemma *m*
pluck [plʌk] *vt* (*fruit*) cogliere; (*musical
instrument*) pizzicare; (*bird*) spennare;
(*hairs*) togliere ▷ *n* coraggio, fegato;
to ~ up courage farsi coraggio
plug [plʌg] *n* tappo; (*Elec*) spina; (*Aut:
also:* **spark(ing) ~**) candela ▷ *vt* (*hole*)
tappare; (*inf: advertise*) spingere; **plug
in** *vt* (*Elec*) attaccare a una presa;
plughole *n* (*BRIT*) scarico
plum [plʌm] *n* (*fruit*) susina
plumber ['plʌmə'] *n* idraulico
plumbing ['plʌmɪŋ] *n* (*trade*) lavoro di
idraulico; (*piping*) tubature *fpl*

plummet ['plʌmɪt] vi: **to ~ (down)** cadere a piombo

plump [plʌmp] adj grassoccio(-a) ▷ vi **to ~ for** (inf: choose) decidersi per

plunge [plʌndʒ] n tuffo; (fig) caduta ▷ vt immergere ▷ vi (fall) cadere, precipitare; (dive) tuffarsi; **to take the ~** saltare il fosso

plural ['pluərl] adj plurale ▷ n plurale m

plus [plʌs] n (also: **~ sign**) segno più ▷ prep più; **ten/twenty ~** più di dieci/venti

ply [plaɪ] vt (a trade) esercitare ▷ vi (ship) fare il servizio ▷ n (of wool, rope) capo; **to ~ sb with drink** dare di bere continuamente a qn; **plywood** n legno compensato

P.M. n abbr = **prime minister**

p.m. adv abbr (= post meridiem) del pomeriggio

PMS n abbr (= premenstrual syndrome) sindrome f premestruale

PMT n abbr (= premenstrual tension) sindrome f premestruale

pneumatic drill [nju:'mætɪk-] n martello pneumatico

pneumonia [nju:'məunɪə] n polmonite f

poach [pəutʃ] vt (cook: egg) affogare; (: fish) cuocere in bianco; (steal) cacciare (or pescare) di frodo ▷ vi fare il bracconiere; **poached** adj (egg) affogato(-a)

P.O. Box n abbr = **Post Office Box**

pocket ['pɔkɪt] n tasca ▷ vt intascare; **to be out of ~** (BRIT) rimetterci; **pocketbook** (US) n (wallet) portafoglio; **pocket money** n paghetta, settimana

pod [pɔd] n guscio

podcast ['pɔdkɑ:st] n podcast m inv

podiatrist [pɔ'di:ətrɪst] (US) n callista m/f, pedicure m/f

podium ['pəudɪəm] n podio

poem ['pəuɪm] n poesia

poet ['pəuɪt] n poeta/essa; **poetic** [-'ɛtɪk] adj poetico(-a); **poetry** n poesia

poignant ['pɔɪnjənt] adj struggente

point [pɔɪnt] n (gen) punto; (tip: of needle etc) punta; (in time) punto, momento; (Scol) voto; (main idea, important part) nocciolo; (Elec) presa (di corrente); (also: **decimal ~**): **2 ~ 3 (2.3)** 2 virgola 3 (2,3) ▷ vt (show) indicare; (gun etc): **to ~ sth at** puntare qc contro ▷ vi **to ~ at** mostrare a dito; **points** npl (Aut) puntine fpl; (Rail) scambio; **to be on the ~ of doing sth** essere sul punto di or stare per fare qc; **to make a ~** fare un'osservazione; **to get/miss the ~** capire/non capire; **to come to the ~** venire al fatto; **there's no ~ in doing** è inutile (fare); **point out** vt far notare; **point-blank** adv (also: **at point-blank range**) a bruciapelo; (fig) categoricamente; **pointed** adj (shape) aguzzo(-a), appuntito(-a); (remark) specifico(-a); **pointer** n (needle) lancetta; (fig) indicazione f, consiglio; **pointless** adj inutile, vano(-a); **point of view** n punto di vista

poison ['pɔɪzn] n veleno ▷ vt avvelenare; **poisonous** adj velenoso(-a)

poke [pəuk] vt (fire) attizzare; (jab with finger, stick etc) punzecchiare; (put): **to ~ sth in(to)** spingere qc dentro; **poke about** or **around** vi frugare; **poke out** vi (stick out) sporger fuori

poker ['pəukə^r] n attizzatoio; (Cards) poker m

Poland ['pəulənd] n Polonia

polar ['pəulə^r] adj polare; **polar bear** n orso bianco

Pole [pəul] n polacco(-a)

pole [pəul] n (of wood) palo; (Elec, Geo) polo; **pole bean** (US) n (runner bean) fagiolino; **pole vault** n salto con l'asta

police [pə'li:s] n polizia ▷ vt mantenere l'ordine in; **police car** n macchina della polizia; **police**

constable (BRIT) n agente m di
polizia; **police force** n corpo di
polizia, polizia; **policeman** (irreg)
n poliziotto, agente m di polizia;
police officer n = **police constable**;
police station n posto di polizia;
policewoman (irreg) n donna f
poliziotto inv

policy ['pɒlɪsɪ] n politica; (also:
insurance ~) polizza (d'assicurazione)

polio ['pəʊlɪəʊ] n polio f

Polish ['pəʊlɪʃ] adj polacco(-a) ▷ n
(Ling) polacco

polish ['pɒlɪʃ] n (for shoes) lucido; (for
floor) cera; (for nails) smalto; (shine)
lucentezza, lustro; (fig: refinement)
raffinatezza ▷ vt lucidare; (fig:
improve) raffinare; **polish off** vt
(food) mangiarsi; **polished** adj (fig)
raffinato(-a)

polite [pə'laɪt] adj cortese; **politeness**
n cortesia

political [pə'lɪtɪkl] adj politico(-a);
politically adv politicamente;
politically correct politicamente
corretto(-a)

politician [pɒlɪ'tɪʃən] n politico

politics ['pɒlɪtɪks] n politica ▷ npl
(views, policies) idee fpl politiche

poll [pəʊl] n scrutinio; (votes cast)
voti mpl; (also: **opinion ~**) sondaggio
(d'opinioni) ▷ vt ottenere

pollen ['pɒlən] n polline m

polling station ['pəʊlɪŋ-] (BRIT) n
sezione f elettorale

pollute [pə'lu:t] vt inquinare

pollution [pə'lu:ʃən] n inquinamento

polo ['pəʊləʊ] n polo; **polo-neck** n
collo alto; (also: **polo-neck sweater**)
dolcevita ▷ adj a collo alto; **polo shirt**
n polo f inv

polyester [pɒlɪ'ɛstəʳ] n poliestere m

polystyrene [pɒlɪ'staɪri:n] n
polistirolo

polythene ['pɒlɪθi:n] n politene m;
polythene bag n sacco di plastica

pomegranate ['pɒmɪɡrænɪt] n

melagrana

pompous ['pɒmpəs] adj pomposo(-a)

pond [pɒnd] n pozza; stagno

ponder ['pɒndəʳ] vt ponderare,
riflettere su

pony ['pəʊnɪ] n pony m inv; **ponytail**
n coda di cavallo; **pony trekking**
[-trɛkɪŋ] (BRIT) n escursione f a cavallo

poodle ['pu:dl] n barboncino,
barbone m

pool [pu:l] n (puddle) pozza; (pond)
stagno; (also: **swimming ~**) piscina;
(fig: of light) cerchio; (billiards) specie di
biliardo a buca ▷ vt mettere in comune;
pools npl (football pools) ≈ totocalcio;
typing ~ servizio comune di
dattilografia

poor [pʊəʳ] adj povero(-a); (mediocre)
mediocre, cattivo(-a) ▷ npl **the ~**
i poveri; **~ in** povero(-a) di; **poorly**
adv poveramente; male ▷ adj
indisposto(-a), malato(-a)

pop [pɒp] n (noise) schiocco; (Mus)
musica pop; (drink) bibita gasata; (US:
inf: father) babbo ▷ vt (put) mettere
(in fretta) ▷ vi scoppiare; (cork)
schioccare; **pop in** vi passare; **pop
out** vi fare un salto fuori; **popcorn** n
pop-corn m

poplar ['pɒpləʳ] n pioppo

popper ['pɒpəʳ] n bottone m a
pressione

poppy ['pɒpɪ] n papavero

Popsicle® ['pɒpsɪkl] (US) n (ice lolly)
ghiacciolo

pop star n pop star f inv

popular ['pɒpjʊləʳ] adj popolare;
(fashionable) in voga; **popularity**
[-'lærɪtɪ] n popolarità

population [pɒpjʊ'leɪʃən] n
popolazione f

pop-up adj (Comput: menu, window) a
comparsa

porcelain ['pɔ:slɪn] n porcellana

porch [pɔ:tʃ] n veranda

pore [pɔ:ʳ] n poro ▷ vi **to ~ over** essere
immerso(-a) in

pork [pɔːk] n carne f di maiale; **pork chop** n braciola or costoletta di maiale; **pork pie** n (BRIT: Culin) pasticcio di maiale in crosta

porn [pɔːn] (inf) n pornografia ▷ adj porno inv; **pornographic** [pɔːnəˈɡræfɪk] adj pornografico(-a); **pornography** [pɔːˈnɔɡrəfɪ] n pornografia

porridge [ˈpɔrɪdʒ] n porridge m

port [pɔːt] n (gen, wine) porto; (Naut: left side) babordo

portable [ˈpɔːtəbl] adj portatile

porter [ˈpɔːtəʳ] n (for luggage) facchino, portabagagli m inv; (doorkeeper) portiere m, portinaio

portfolio [pɔːtˈfəʊlɪəʊ] n (case) cartella; (Pol, Finance) portafoglio; (of artist) raccolta dei propri lavori

portion [ˈpɔːʃən] n porzione f

port of call n (porto di) scalo

portrait [ˈpɔːtreɪt] n ritratto

portray [pɔːˈtreɪ] vt fare il ritratto di; (character on stage) rappresentare; (in writing) ritrarre

Portugal [ˈpɔːtjuɡl] n Portogallo

Portuguese [pɔːtjuˈɡiːz] adj portoghese ▷ n inv portoghese m/f; (Ling) portoghese m

pose [pəʊz] n posa ▷ vi posare; (pretend): **to ~ as** atteggiarsi a, posare a ▷ vt porre

posh [pɔʃ] (inf) adj elegante; (family) per bene

position [pəˈzɪʃən] n posizione f; (job) posto ▷ vt sistemare

positive [ˈpɔzɪtɪv] adj positivo(-a); (certain) sicuro(-a), certo(-a); (definite) preciso(-a), definitivo(-a); **positively** adv (affirmatively, enthusiastically) positivamente; (decisively) decisamente; (really) assolutamente

possess [pəˈzɛs] vt possedere; **possession** [pəˈzɛʃən] n possesso; **possessions** npl (belongings) beni mpl; **possessive** adj possessivo(-a)

possibility [pɔsɪˈbɪlɪtɪ] n

possibilità f inv

possible [ˈpɔsɪbl] adj possibile; **as big as ~** il più grande possibile; **possibly** [ˈpɔsɪblɪ] adv (perhaps) forse; **if you possibly can** se le è possibile; **I cannot possibly come** proprio non posso venire

post [pəʊst] n (BRIT) posta; (: collection) levata; (job, situation) posto; (Mil) postazione f; (pole) palo ▷ vt (BRIT: send by post) imbucare; (: appoint): **to ~ to** assegnare a; **where can I ~ these cards?** dove posso imbucare queste cartoline?; **postage** n affrancatura; **postal** adj postale; **postal order** n vaglia m inv postale; **postbox** (BRIT) n cassetta postale; **postcard** n cartolina; **postcode** n (BRIT) codice m (di avviamento) postale

poster [ˈpəʊstəʳ] n manifesto, affisso

postgraduate [ˈpəʊstˈɡrædjuət] n laureato/a che continua gli studi

postman [ˈpəʊstmən] (irreg) n postino

postmark [ˈpəʊstmɑːk] n bollo or timbro postale

post-mortem [-ˈmɔːtəm] n autopsia

post office n (building) ufficio postale; (organization): **the Post Office** ≈ le Poste e Telecomunicazioni

postpone [pəsˈpəʊn] vt rinviare

posture [ˈpɔstʃəʳ] n portamento; (pose) posa, atteggiamento

postwoman [ˈpəʊstwumən] (BRIT: irreg) n postina

pot [pɔt] n (for cooking) pentola; casseruola; (teapot) teiera; (coffeepot) caffettiera; (for plants, jam) vaso; (inf: marijuana) erba ▷ vt (plant) piantare in vaso; **a ~ of tea for two** tè per due; **to go to ~** (inf: work, performance) andare in malora

potato [pəˈteɪtəʊ] (pl **potatoes**) n patata; **potato peeler** n sbucciapatate m inv

potent [ˈpəʊtnt] adj potente, forte

potential [pə'tɛnʃl] *adj* potenziale ▷ *n* possibilità *fpl*

pothole ['pɔthəul] *n* (*in road*) buca; (*BRIT: underground*) caverna

pot plant *n* pianta in vaso

potter ['pɔtə^r] *n* vasaio ▷ *vi* **to ~ around, ~ about** (*BRIT*) lavoracchiare; **pottery** *n* ceramiche *fpl*; (*factory*) fabbrica di ceramiche

potty ['pɔtɪ] *adj* (*inf: mad*) tocco(-a) ▷ *n* (*child's*) vasino

pouch [pautʃ] *n* borsa; (*Zool*) marsupio

poultry ['pəultrɪ] *n* pollame *m*

pounce [pauns] *vi* **to ~ (on)** piombare (su)

pound [paund] *n* (*weight*) libbra; (*money*) (*lira*) sterlina ▷ *vt* (*beat*) battere; (*crush*) pestare, polverizzare ▷ *vi* (*beat*) battere, martellare; **pound sterling** *n* sterlina (inglese)

pour [pɔ:^r] *vt* versare ▷ *vi* riversarsi; (*rain*) piovere a dirotto; **pour in** *vi* affluire in gran quantità; **pour out** *vi* (*people*) uscire a fiumi ▷ *vt* vuotare; versare; (*fig*) sfogare; **pouring** *adj*: **pouring rain** pioggia torrenziale

pout [paut] *vi* sporgere le labbra; fare il broncio

poverty ['pɔvətɪ] *n* povertà, miseria

powder ['paudə^r] *n* polvere *f* ▷ *vt* **to ~ one's face** incipriarsi il viso; **powdered milk** *n* latte *m* in polvere

power ['pauə^r] *n* (*strength*) potenza, forza; (*ability, Pol: of party, leader*) potere *m*; (*Elec*) corrente *f*; **to be in ~** (*Pol etc*) essere al potere; **power cut** (*BRIT*) *n* interruzione *f* or mancanza di corrente; **power failure** *n* interruzione *f* della corrente elettrica; **powerful** *adj* potente, forte; **powerless** *adj* impotente; **powerless to do** impossibilitato(-a) a fare; **power point** (*BRIT*) *n* presa di corrente; **power station** *n* centrale *f* elettrica

p.p. *abbr* = **per procurationem**; **p.p. J. Smith** per J. Smith; (= *pages*) p.p.

PR *abbr* = **public relations**

practical ['præktɪkl] *adj* pratico(-a); **practical joke** *n* beffa; **practically** *adv* praticamente

practice ['præktɪs] *n* pratica; (*of profession*) esercizio; (*at football etc*) allenamento; (*business*) gabinetto; clientela ▷ *vt, vi* (*US*) = **practise**; **in ~** (*in reality*) in pratica; **out of ~** fuori esercizio

practise ['præktɪs] (*US* **practice**) *vt* (*work at: piano, one's backhand etc*) esercitarsi a; (*train for: skiing, running etc*) allenarsi a; (*a sport, religion*) praticare; (*method*) usare; (*profession*) esercitare ▷ *vi* esercitarsi; (*train*) allenarsi; (*lawyer, doctor*) esercitare; **practising** *adj* (*Christian etc*) praticante; (*lawyer*) che esercita la professione

practitioner [præk'tɪʃənə^r] *n* professionista *m/f*

pragmatic [præg'mætɪk] *adj* pragmatico(-a)

prairie ['prɛərɪ] *n* prateria

praise [preɪz] *n* elogio, lode *f* ▷ *vt* elogiare, lodare

pram [præm] (*BRIT*) *n* carrozzina

prank [præŋk] *n* burla

prawn [prɔ:n] *n* gamberetto; **prawn cocktail** *n* cocktail *m inv* di gamberetti

pray [preɪ] *vi* pregare; **prayer** [prɛə^r] *n* preghiera

preach [pri:tʃ] *vt, vi* predicare; **preacher** *n* predicatore(-trice); (*US: minister*) pastore *m*

precarious [prɪ'kɛərɪəs] *adj* precario(-a)

precaution [prɪ'kɔːʃən] *n* precauzione *f*

precede [prɪ'siːd] *vt* precedere; **precedent** ['prɛsɪdənt] *n* precedente *m*; **preceding** [prɪ'siːdɪŋ] *adj* precedente

precinct ['priːsɪŋkt] (*US*) *n* circoscrizione *f*

precious ['prɛʃəs] *adj* prezioso(-a)
precise [prɪ'saɪs] *adj* preciso(-a);
  precisely *adv* precisamente
precision [prɪ'sɪʒən] *n* precisione *f*
predator ['prɛdətər] *n* predatore *m*
predecessor ['priːdɪsɛsər] *n*
  predecessore(-a)
predicament [prɪ'dɪkəmənt] *n*
  situazione *f* difficile
predict [prɪ'dɪkt] *vt* predire;
  predictable *adj* prevedibile;
  prediction [prɪ'dɪkʃən] *n* predizione *f*
predominantly [prɪ'dɔmɪnəntlɪ]
  adv in maggior parte; soprattutto
preface ['prɛfəs] *n* prefazione *f*
prefect ['priːfɛkt] *n* (BRIT: in school)
  studente(-essa) con funzioni
  disciplinari; (French etc, Admin)
  prefetto
prefer [prɪ'fəːr] *vt* preferire; **to ~ doing**
  or **to do** preferire fare; **preferable**
  ['prɛfrəbl] *adj* preferibile; **preferably**
  ['prɛfrəblɪ] *adv* preferibilmente;
  preference ['prɛfrəns] *n* preferenza
prefix ['priːfɪks] *n* prefisso
pregnancy ['prɛgnənsɪ] *n* gravidanza
pregnant ['prɛgnənt] *adj* incinta *ag*
prehistoric ['priːhɪs'tɔrɪk] *adj*
  preistorico(-a)
prejudice ['prɛdʒudɪs] *n* pregiudizio;
  (harm) torto, danno; **prejudiced** *adj*
  prejudiced (against) prevenuto(-a)
  (contro); **prejudiced (in favour of)**
  ben disposto(-a) (verso)
preliminary [prɪ'lɪmɪnərɪ] *adj*
  preliminare
prelude ['prɛljuːd] *n* preludio
premature ['prɛmətʃuər] *adj*
  prematuro(-a)
premier ['prɛmɪər] *adj* primo(-a) ▷ *n*
  (Pol) primo ministro
première ['prɛmɪɛər] *n* prima
Premier League *n* ≈ serie A
premises ['prɛmɪsɪz] *npl* locale *m*;
  on the ~ sul posto; **business ~** locali
  commerciali
premium ['priːmɪəm] *n* premio; **to**

be at a ~ essere ricercatissimo
premonition [prɛmə'nɪʃən] *n*
  premonizione *f*
preoccupied [priː'ɔkjupaɪd] *adj*
  preoccupato(-a)
prepaid [priː'peɪd] *adj* pagato(-a) in
  anticipo
preparation [prɛpə'reɪʃən] *n*
  preparazione *f*; **preparations** *npl* (for
  trip, war) preparativi *mpl*
preparatory school [prɪ'pærətərɪ-]
  n scuola elementare privata
prepare [prɪ'pɛər] *vt* preparare ▷ *vi* **to**
  ~ for prepararsi a; **~d to** pronto(-a) a
preposition [prɛpə'zɪʃən] *n*
  preposizione *f*
prep school *n* = **preparatory school**
preschool ['priː'skuːl] *adj* (age)
  prescolastico(-a); (child) in età
  prescolastica
prescribe [prɪ'skraɪb] *vt* (Med)
  prescrivere
prescription [prɪ'skrɪpʃən] *n*
  prescrizione *f*; (Med) ricetta; **could**
  you write me a ~? mi può fare una
  ricetta medica?
presence ['prɛzns] *n* presenza; **~ of**
  mind presenza di spirito
present [adj, n 'prɛznt, vb prɪ'zɛnt] *adj*
  presente; (wife, residence, job) attuale
  ▷ *n* (actuality): **the ~** il presente; (gift)
  regalo ▷ *vt* presentare; (give): **to ~**
  sb with sth offrire qc a qn; **to give**
  sb a ~ fare un regalo a qn; **at ~** al
  momento; **presentable** [prɪ'zɛntəbl]
  adj presentabile; **presentation**
  [-'teɪʃən] *n* presentazione *f*; (ceremony)
  consegna ufficiale; **present-day** *adj*
  attuale, d'oggigiorno; **presenter**
  n (Radio, TV) presentatore(-trice);
  presently *adv* (soon) fra poco, presto;
  (at present) al momento; **present**
  participle *n* participio presente
preservation [prɛzə'veɪʃən] *n*
  preservazione *f*, conservazione *f*

preservative [prɪˈzəːvətɪv] n
conservante m
preserve [prɪˈzəːv] vt (keep safe)
preservare, proteggere; (maintain)
conservare; (food) mettere in conserva
▷ n (often pl: jam) marmellata; (: fruit)
frutta sciroppata
preside [prɪˈzaɪd] vi **to ~ (over)**
presiedere (a)
president [ˈprɛzɪdənt] n presidente
m; **presidential** [-ˈdɛnʃl] adj
presidenziale
press [prɛs] n (newspapers etc): **the
P~** la stampa; (tool, machine) pressa;
(for wine) torchio ▷ vt (push) premere,
pigiare; (squeeze) spremere; (: hand)
stringere; (clothes: iron) stirare;
(pursue) incalzare; (insist): **to ~ sth on
sb** far accettare qc da qn ▷ vi premere;
accalcare; **we are ~ed for time** ci
manca il tempo; **to ~ for sth** insistere
per avere qc; **press conference** n
conferenza f stampa inv; **pressing** adj
urgente; **press stud** (BRIT) n bottone
m a pressione; **press-up** (BRIT) n
flessione f sulle braccia
pressure [ˈprɛʃəʳ] n pressione f;
to put ~ on sb (to do) mettere qn
sotto pressione (affinché faccia);
pressure cooker n pentola a
pressione; **pressure group** n gruppo
di pressione
prestige [prɛsˈtiːʒ] n prestigio
prestigious [prɛsˈtɪdʒəs] adj
prestigioso(-a)
presumably [prɪˈzjuːməblɪ] adv
presumibilmente
presume [prɪˈzjuːm] vt supporre
pretence [prɪˈtɛns] (US **pretense**) n
(claim) pretesa; **to make a ~ of doing**
far finta di fare; **under false ~s** con
l'inganno
pretend [prɪˈtɛnd] vt (feign) fingere
▷ vi far finta; **to ~ to do** far finta di fare
pretense [prɪˈtɛns] (US) n = **pretence**
pretentious [prɪˈtɛnʃəs] adj
pretenzioso(-a)

pretext [ˈpriːtɛkst] n pretesto
pretty [ˈprɪtɪ] adj grazioso(-a),
carino(-a) ▷ adv abbastanza, assai
prevail [prɪˈveɪl] vi (win, be usual)
prevalere; (persuade): **to ~ (up)on sb
to do** persuadere qn a fare; **prevailing**
adj dominante
prevalent [ˈprɛvələnt] adj (belief)
predominante; (customs) diffuso(-a);
(fashion) corrente; (disease) comune
prevent [prɪˈvɛnt] vt **to ~ sb from
doing** impedire a qn di fare; **to ~
sth from happening** impedire che
qc succeda; **prevention** [-ˈvɛnʃən]
n prevenzione f; **preventive** adj
preventivo(-a)
preview [ˈpriːvjuː] n (of film)
anteprima
previous [ˈpriːvɪəs] adj precedente;
anteriore; **previously** adv prima
prey [preɪ] n preda ▷ vi **to ~ on** far
preda di; **it was ~ing on his mind** lo
stava ossessionando
price [praɪs] n prezzo ▷ vt (goods)
fissare il prezzo di; valutare; **priceless**
adj inapprezzabile; **price list** n listino
(dei) prezzi
prick [prɪk] n puntura ▷ vt pungere;
to ~ up one's ears drizzare gli orecchi
prickly [ˈprɪklɪ] adj spinoso(-a)
pride [praɪd] n orgoglio; superbia ▷ vt
to ~ o.s. on essere orgoglioso(-a) di,
vantarsi di
priest [priːst] n prete m, sacerdote m
primarily [ˈpraɪmərɪlɪ] adv
principalmente, essenzialmente
primary [ˈpraɪmərɪ] adj primario(-a);
(first in importance) primo(-a) ▷ n (US:
election) primarie fpl; **primary school**
(BRIT) n scuola elementare
prime [praɪm] adj primario(-a),
fondamentale; (excellent) di prima
qualità ▷ vt (wood) preparare; (fig)
mettere al corrente ▷ n **in the ~ of life**
nel fiore della vita; **Prime Minister** n
primo ministro
primitive [ˈprɪmɪtɪv] adj primitivo(-a)

primrose ['prɪmrəuz] n primavera

prince [prɪns] n principe m

princess [prɪn'sɛs] n principessa

principal ['prɪnsɪpl] adj principale ▷ n (headmaster) preside m; **principally** adv principalmente

principle ['prɪnsɪpl] n principio; **in ~** in linea di principio; **on ~** per principio

print [prɪnt] n (mark) impronta; (letters) caratteri mpl; (fabric) tessuto stampato; (Art, Phot) stampa ▷ vt imprimere; (publish) stampare, pubblicare; (write in capitals) scrivere in stampatello; **out of ~** esaurito(-a); **print out** vt (Comput) stampare; **printer** n tipografo; (machine) stampante f; **printout** n tabulato

prior ['praɪəʳ] adj precedente; (claim etc) più importante; **~ to doing** prima di fare

priority [praɪ'ɔrɪtɪ] n priorità f inv; precedenza

prison ['prɪzn] n prigione f ▷ cpd (system) carcerario(-a); (conditions, food) nelle o delle prigioni; **prisoner** n prigioniero(-a); **prisoner-of-war** n prigioniero(-a) di guerra

pristine ['prɪstiːn] adj immacolato(-a)

privacy ['prɪvəsɪ] n solitudine f, intimità

private ['praɪvɪt] adj privato(-a); personale ▷ n soldato semplice; **"~"** (on envelope) "riservata"; (on door) "privato"; **in ~** in privato; **privately** adv in privato; (within oneself) dentro di sé; **private property** n proprietà privata; **private school** n scuola privata

privatize ['praɪvɪtaɪz] vt privatizzare

privilege ['prɪvɪlɪdʒ] n privilegio

prize [praɪz] n premio ▷ adj (example, idiot) perfetto(-a); (bull, novel) premiato(-a) ▷ vt apprezzare, pregiare; **prize-giving** n premiazione f; **prizewinner** n premiato(-a)

pro [prəu] n (Sport) professionista m/f ▷ prep pro; **the ~s and cons** il pro e il contro

probability [prɔbə'bɪlɪtɪ] n probabilità f inv; **in all ~** con tutta probabilità

probable ['prɔbəbl] adj probabile

probably ['prɔbəblɪ] adv probabilmente

probation [prə'beɪʃən] n **on ~** (employee) in prova; (Law) in libertà vigilata

probe [prəub] n (Med, Space) sonda; (enquiry) indagine f, investigazione f ▷ vt sondare, esplorare; indagare

problem ['prɔbləm] n problema m

procedure [prə'siːdʒəʳ] n (Admin, Law) procedura; (method) metodo, procedimento

proceed [prə'siːd] vi (go forward) avanzare, andare avanti; (go about it) procedere; (continue): **to ~ (with)** continuare; **to ~ to** andare a; passare a; **to ~ to do** mettersi a fare; **proceedings** npl misure fpl; (Law) procedimento; (meeting) riunione f; (records) rendiconti mpl; atti mpl; **proceeds** ['prəusiːdz] npl profitto, incasso

process ['prəusɛs] n processo; (method) metodo, sistema m ▷ vt trattare; (information) elaborare

procession [prə'sɛʃən] n processione f, corteo; **funeral ~** corteo funebre

proclaim [prə'kleɪm] vt proclamare, dichiarare

prod [prɔd] vt dare un colpetto a; pungolare ▷ n colpetto

produce [n 'prɔdjuːs, vb prə'djuːs] n (Agr) prodotto, prodotti mpl ▷ vt produrre; (show) esibire, mostrare; (cause) cagionare, causare; **producer** n (Theatre) regista m/f; (Agr, Cinema) produttore m

product ['prɔdʌkt] n prodotto; **production** [prə'dʌkʃən] n produzione f; **productive** [prə'dʌktɪv] adj produttivo(-a); **productivity** [prɔdʌk'tɪvɪtɪ] n produttività

Prof. *abbr* (= *professor*) Prof.
profession [prə'fɛʃən] *n* professione
f; **professional** *n* professionista
m/f ▷ *adj* professionale; (*work*) da
professionista
professor [prə'fɛsə^r] *n* professore
m (*titolare di una cattedra*); (*US*)
professore(-essa)
profile ['prəufaɪl] *n* profilo
profit ['prɔfɪt] *n* profitto; beneficio
▷ *vi* **to ~ (by** *or* **from)** approfittare (di);
profitable *adj* redditizio(-a)
profound [prə'faund] *adj*
profondo(-a)
programme ['prəugræm]
(*US* **program**) *n* programma
m ▷ *vt* programmare;
programmer (*US* **programer**)
n programmatore(-trice);
programming (*US* **programing**) *n*
programmazione f
progress [*n* 'prəugrɛs, *vb* prə'grɛs] *n*
progresso ▷ *vi* avanzare, procedere;
in ~ in corso; **to make ~** far
progressi; **progressive** [-'grɛsɪv] *adj*
progressivo(-a); (*person*) progressista
prohibit [prə'hɪbɪt] *vt* proibire,
vietare
project [*n* 'prɔdʒɛkt, *vb* prə'dʒɛkt] *n*
(*plan*) piano; (*venture*) progetto; (*Scol*)
studio ▷ *vt* proiettare ▷ *vi* (*stick out*)
sporgere; **projection** [prə'dʒɛkʃən]
n proiezione f; sporgenza; **projector**
[prə'dʒɛktə^r] *n* proiettore *m*
prolific [prə'lɪfɪk] *adj* (*artist etc*)
fecondo(-a)
prolong [prə'lɔŋ] *vt* prolungare
prom [prɔm] *n abbr* = **promenade**;
(*US: ball*) ballo studentesco

● **PROM**
●
● In Gran Bretagna i **Proms**, o
● "promenade concerts", sono
● concerti di musica classica, i più
● noti dei quali sono eseguiti nella
● prestigiosa **Royal Albert Hall** a
● Londra. Si chiamano così perché
● un tempo il pubblico seguiva i
● concerti in piedi, passeggiando
● (in inglese "promenade" voleva
● dire, appunto, passeggiata). Negli
● Stati Uniti, invece, con **prom**, si
● intende l'annuale ballo studentesco
● di un'università o di una scuola
● secondaria.

promenade [prɔmə'nɑːd] *n* (*by sea*)
lungomare *m*
prominent ['prɔmɪnənt] *adj*
(*standing out*) prominente; (*important*)
importante
promiscuous [prə'mɪskjuəs] *adj*
(*sexually*) di facili costumi
promise ['prɔmɪs] *n* promessa ▷ *vt*,
vi promettere; **to ~ sb sth, ~ sth to sb**
promettere qc a qn; **to ~ (sb) that/to
do sth** promettere (a qn) che/di fare
qc; **promising** *adj* promettente
promote [prə'məut] *vt* promuovere;
(*venture, event*) organizzare;
promotion [-'məuʃən] *n*
promozione f
prompt [prɔmpt] *adj* rapido(-a),
svelto(-a); puntuale; (*reply*)
sollecito(-a) ▷ *adv* (*punctually*)
in punto ▷ *n* (*Comput*) prompt *m*
▷ *vt* incitare; provocare; (*Theatre*)
suggerire a; **to ~ sb to do** incitare qn
a fare; **promptly** *adv* prontamente;
puntualmente
prone [prəun] *adj* (*lying*) prono(-a); **~
to** propenso(-a) a, incline a
prong [prɔŋ] *n* rebbio, punta
pronoun ['prəunaun] *n* pronome *m*
pronounce [prə'nauns] *vt*
pronunciare; **how do you ~ it?** come
si pronuncia?
pronunciation [prənʌnsɪ'eɪʃən] *n*
pronuncia
proof [pruːf] *n* prova; (*of book*) bozza;
(*Phot*) provino ▷ *adj* **~ against** a
prova di
prop [prɔp] *n* sostegno, appoggio ▷ *vt*

(also: **~ up**) sostenere, appoggiare; (lean): **to ~ sth against** appoggiare qc contro or a; **props** oggetti *m inv* di scena; **prop up** *vt* sostenere, appoggiare

propaganda [prɔpə'gændə] *n* propaganda

propeller [prə'pɛləʳ] *n* elica

proper ['prɔpəʳ] *adj (suited, right)* adatto(-a), appropriato(-a); *(seemly)* decente; *(authentic)* vero(-a); *(inf: real: noun)* + vero(-a) e proprio(-a); **properly** ['prɔpəlɪ] *adv (eat, study)* bene; *(behave)* come si deve; **proper noun** *n* nome *m* proprio

property ['prɔpətɪ] *n (things owned)* beni *mpl*; *(land, building)* proprietà *finv*; *(Chem etc: quality)* proprietà

prophecy ['prɔfɪsɪ] *n* profezia

prophet ['prɔfɪt] *n* profeta *m*

proportion [prə'pɔːʃən] *n* proporzione *f*; *(share)* parte *f*; **proportions** *npl (size)* proporzioni *fpl*; **proportional** *adj* proporzionale

proposal [prə'pəuzl] *n* proposta; *(plan)* progetto; *(of marriage)* proposta di matrimonio

propose [prə'pəuz] *vt* proporre, suggerire ▷ *vi* fare una proposta di matrimonio; **to ~ to do** proporsi di fare, aver l'intenzione di fare

proposition [prɔpə'zɪʃən] *n* proposizione *f*; *(offer)* proposta

proprietor [prə'praɪətəʳ] *n* proprietario(-a)

prose [prəuz] *n* prosa

prosecute ['prɔsɪkjuːt] *vt* processare; **prosecution** [-'kjuːʃən] *n* processo; *(accusing side)* accusa; **prosecutor** *n (also:* **public prosecutor)** ≈ procuratore *m* della Repubblica

prospect [*n* 'prɔspɛkt, *vb* prə'spɛkt] *n* prospettiva; *(hope)* speranza ▷ *vi* **to ~ for** cercare; **prospects** *npl (for work etc)* prospettive *fpl*; **prospective** [-'spɛktɪv] *adj* possibile; futuro(-a)

prospectus [prə'spɛktəs] *n*

prospetto, programma *m*

prosper ['prɔspəʳ] *vi* prosperare; **prosperity** [prɔ'spɛrɪtɪ] *n* prosperità; **prosperous** *adj* prospero(-a)

prostitute ['prɔstɪtjuːt] *n* prostituta; **male ~** uomo che si prostituisce

protect [prə'tɛkt] *vt* proteggere, salvaguardare; **protection** *n* protezione *f*; **protective** *adj* protettivo(-a)

protein ['prəutiːn] *n* proteina

protest [*n* 'prəutɛst, *vb* prə'tɛst] *n* protesta ▷ *vt, vi* protestare

Protestant ['prɔtɪstənt] *adj, n* protestante *m/f*

protester [prə'tɛstəʳ] *n* dimostrante *m/f*

protractor [prə'træktəʳ] *n (Geom)* goniometro

proud [praud] *adj* fiero(-a), orgoglioso(-a); *(pej)* superbo(-a)

prove [pruːv] *vt* provare, dimostrare ▷ *vi* **to ~ (to be) correct** *etc* risultare vero(-a) *etc*; **to ~ o.s.** mostrare le proprie capacità

proverb ['prɔvəːb] *n* proverbio

provide [prə'vaɪd] *vt* fornire, provvedere; **to ~ sb with sth** fornire or provvedere qn di qc; **provide for** *vt fus* provvedere a; *(future event)* prevedere; **provided** *conj* **provided (that)** purché + *sub*, a condizione che + *sub*; **providing** [prə'vaɪdɪŋ] *conj* purché +*sub*, a condizione che +*sub*

province ['prɔvɪns] *n* provincia; **provincial** [prə'vɪnʃəl] *adj* provinciale

provision [prə'vɪʒən] *n (supply)* riserva; *(supplying)* provvista; rifornimento; *(stipulation)* condizione *f*; **provisions** *npl (food)* provviste *fpl*; **provisional** *adj* provvisorio(-a)

provocative [prə'vɔkətɪv] *adj (aggressive)* provocatorio(-a); *(thought-provoking)* stimolante; *(seductive)* provocante

provoke [prə'vəuk] *vt* provocare; incitare

prowl [praul] vi (also: **~ about, ~ around**) aggirarsi ▷ n **to be on the ~** aggirarsi

proximity [prɔk'sɪmɪtɪ] n prossimità

proxy ['prɔksɪ] n **by ~** per procura

prudent ['pruːdnt] adj prudente

prune [pruːn] n prugna secca ▷ vt potare

pry [praɪ] vi **to ~ into** ficcare il naso in

PS abbr (= postscript) P.S.

pseudonym ['sjuːdənɪm] n pseudonimo

psychiatric [saɪkɪ'ætrɪk] adj psichiatrico(-a)

psychiatrist [saɪ'kaɪətrɪst] n psichiatra m/f

psychic ['saɪkɪk] adj (also: **~al**) psichico(-a); (person) dotato(-a) di qualità telepatiche

psychoanalysis (pl **-ses**) [saɪkəuə'nælɪsɪs, -siːz] n psicanalisi f inv

psychological [saɪkə'lɔdʒɪkl] adj psicologico(-a)

psychologist [saɪ'kɔlədʒɪst] n psicologo(-a)

psychology [saɪ'kɔlədʒɪ] n psicologia

psychotherapy [saɪkəu'θɛrəpɪ] n psicoterapia

pt abbr (= pint; point) pt.

PTO abbr (= please turn over) v.r.

pub [pʌb] n abbr (= public house) pub m inv

puberty ['pjuːbətɪ] n pubertà

public ['pʌblɪk] adj pubblico(-a) ▷ n pubblico; **in ~** in pubblico

publication [pʌblɪ'keɪʃən] n pubblicazione f

public: **public company** n società f inv per azioni (costituita tramite pubblica sottoscrizione); **public convenience** (BRIT) n gabinetti mpl; **public holiday** n giorno festivo, festa nazionale; **public house** (BRIT) n pub m inv

publicity [pʌb'lɪsɪtɪ] n pubblicità

publicize ['pʌblɪsaɪz] vt rendere pubblico(-a)

public: **public limited company** n ≈ società per azioni a responsabilità limitata (quotata in Borsa); **publicly** ['pʌblɪklɪ] adv pubblicamente; **public opinion** n opinione f pubblica; **public relations** n pubbliche relazioni fpl; **public school** n (BRIT) scuola privata; (US) scuola statale; **public transport** n mezzi mpl pubblici

publish ['pʌblɪʃ] vt pubblicare; **publisher** n editore m; **publishing** n (industry) editoria; (of a book) pubblicazione f

pub lunch n pranzo semplice ed economico servito nei pub

pudding ['pudɪŋ] n budino; (BRIT: dessert) dolce m; **black ~, (US) blood ~** sanguinaccio

puddle ['pʌdl] n pozza, pozzanghera

Puerto Rico ['pwɜː'təu'riː'kəu] n Portorico

puff [pʌf] n sbuffo ▷ vt **to ~ one's pipe** tirare sboccate di fumo ▷ vi (pant) ansare; **puff pastry** n pasta sfoglia

pull [pul] n (tug): **to give sth a ~** tirare su qc ▷ vt tirare; (muscle) strappare; (trigger) premere ▷ vi tirare; **to ~ to pieces** fare a pezzi; **to ~ one's punches** (Boxing) risparmiare l'avversario; **to ~ one's weight** dare il proprio contributo; **to ~ o.s. together** ricomporsi, riprendersi; **to ~ sb's leg** prendere in giro qn; **pull apart** vt (break) fare a pezzi; **pull away** vi (move off: vehicle) muoversi, partire; (boat) staccarsi dal molo, salpare; (draw back: person) indietreggiare; **pull back** vt (lever etc) tirare indietro; (curtains) aprire ▷ vi (from confrontation etc) tirarsi indietro; (Mil: withdraw) ritirarsi; **pull down** vt (house) demolire; (tree) abbattere; **pull in** vi (Aut: at the kerb) accostarsi; (Rail) entrare in stazione; **pull off** vt (clothes) togliere; (deal etc) portare a compimento; **pull out** vi partire; (Aut: come out of line) spostarsi sulla mezzeria ▷ vt staccare; far

uscire; (*withdraw*) ritirare; **pull over**
vi (*Aut*) accostare; **pull up** *vi* (*stop*)
fermarsi ▷ *vt* (*raise*) sollevare; (*uproot*)
sradicare
pulley ['pulɪ] *n* puleggia, carrucola
pullover ['puləuvəʳ] *n* pullover *m inv*
pulp [pʌlp] *n* (*of fruit*) polpa
pulpit ['pulpɪt] *n* pulpito
pulse [pʌls] *n* polso; (*Bot*) legume *m*;
pulses *npl* (*Culin*) legumi *mpl*
puma ['pju:mə] *n* puma *m inv*
pump [pʌmp] *n* pompa; (*shoe*)
scarpetta ▷ *vt* pompare; **pump up** *vt*
gonfiare
pumpkin ['pʌmpkɪn] *n* zucca
pun [pʌn] *n* gioco di parole
punch [pʌntʃ] *n* (*blow*) pugno; (*tool*)
punzone *m*; (*drink*) ponce *m* ▷ *vt* (*hit*):
to ~ sb/sth dare un pugno a qn/qc;
punch-up (*BRIT: inf*) *n* rissa
punctual ['pʌŋktjuəl] *adj* puntuale
punctuation [pʌŋktju'eɪʃən] *n*
interpunzione *f*, punteggiatura
puncture ['pʌŋktʃəʳ] *n* foratura ▷ *vt*
forare

> Be careful not to translate
> *puncture* by the Italian word
> *puntura*.

punish ['pʌnɪʃ] *vt* punire;
punishment *n* punizione *f*
punk [pʌŋk] *n* (*also:* **~ rocker**) punk *m/
f inv*; (*also:* **~ rock**) musica punk, punk
rock *m*; (*us: inf: hoodlum*) teppista *m*
pup [pʌp] *n* cucciolo(-a)
pupil ['pju:pl] *n* allievo(-a); (*Anat*)
pupilla
puppet ['pʌpɪt] *n* burattino
puppy ['pʌpɪ] *n* cucciolo(-a),
cagnolino(-a)
purchase ['pə:tʃɪs] *n* acquisto,
compera ▷ *vt* comprare
pure [pjuəʳ] *adj* puro(-a); **purely**
['pjuəlɪ] *adv* puramente
purify ['pjuərɪfaɪ] *vt* purificare
purity ['pjuərɪtɪ] *n* purezza
purple ['pə:pl] *adj* di porpora; viola *inv*
purpose ['pə:pəs] *n* intenzione *f*,

scopo; **on ~** apposta
purr [pə:ʳ] *vi* fare le fusa
purse [pə:s] *n* (*BRIT*) borsellino; (*US*)
borsetta ▷ *vt* contrarre
pursue [pə'sju:] *vt* inseguire; (*fig:
activity etc*) continuare con; (: *aim etc*)
perseguire
pursuit [pə'sju:t] *n* inseguimento;
(*fig*) ricerca; (*pastime*) passatempo
pus [pʌs] *n* pus *m*
push [puʃ] *n* spinta; (*effort*) grande
sforzo; (*drive*) energia ▷ *vt* spingere;
(*button*) premere; (*thrust*): **to ~
sth (into)** ficcare qc (in); (*fig*) fare
pubblicità a ▷ *vi* spingere; premere;
to ~ for (*fig*) insistere per; **push
in** *vi* introdursi a forza; **push off**
(*inf*) *vi* filare; **push on** *vi* (*continue*)
continuare; **push over** *vt* far
cadere; **push through** *vi* farsi
largo spingendo ▷ *vt* (*measure*)
far approvare; **pushchair** (*BRIT*) *n*
passeggino; **pusher** *n* (*drug pusher*)
spacciatore(-trice); **push-up** (*US*) *n*
(*press-up*) flessione *f* sulle braccia
pussy(-cat) ['pusɪ(-)] (*inf*) *n* micio
put [put] (*pt, pp* **put**) *vt* mettere, porre;
(*say*) dire, esprimere; (*a question*)
fare; (*estimate*) stimare; **put away** *vt*
(*return*) mettere a posto; **put back** *vt*
(*replace*) rimettere (a posto); (*postpone*)
rinviare; (*delay*) ritardare; **put by** *vt*
(*money*) mettere da parte; **put down**
vt (*parcel etc*) posare, mettere giù;
(*pay*) versare; (*in writing*) mettere per
iscritto; (*revolt, animal*) sopprimere;
(*attribute*) attribuire; **put forward** *vt*
(*ideas*) avanzare, proporre; **put in** *vt*
(*application, complaint*) presentare;
(*time, effort*) mettere; **put off** *vt*
(*postpone*) rimandare, rinviare;
(*discourage*) dissuadere; **put on** *vt*
(*clothes, lipstick etc*) mettere; (*light
etc*) accendere; (*play etc*) mettere
in scena; (*food, meal*) mettere su;
(*brake*) mettere; **to put on weight**
ingrassare; **to put on airs** darsi delle

arie; **put out** vt mettere fuori; (*one's hand*) porgere; (*light etc*) spegnere; (*person: inconvenience*) scomodare; **put through** vt (*Tel: call*) passare; (: *person*) mettere in comunicazione; (*plan*) far approvare; **put up** vt (*raise*) sollevare, alzare; (: *umbrella*) aprire; (: *tent*) montare; (*pin up*) affiggere; (*hang*) appendere; (*build*) costruire, erigere; (*increase*) aumentare; (*accommodate*) alloggiare; **put aside** vt (*lay down: book etc*) mettere da una parte, posare; (*save*) mettere da parte, (*in shop*) tenere da parte; **put together** vt mettere insieme, riunire; (*assemble: furniture*) montare; (: *meal*) improvvisare; **put up with** vt fus sopportare

putt [pʌt] n colpo leggero; **putting green** n green m inv; campo da putting

puzzle ['pʌzl] n enigma m, mistero; (*jigsaw*) puzzle m; (*also:* **crossword ~**) parole fpl incrociate, cruciverba m inv ▷ vt confondere, rendere perplesso(-a) ▷ vi scervellarsi; **puzzled** adj perplesso(-a); **puzzling** adj (*question*) poco chiaro(-a); (*attitude, set of instructions*) incomprensibile

pyjamas [pɪ'dʒɑːməz] (BRIT) npl pigiama m

pylon ['paɪlən] n pilone m

pyramid ['pɪrəmɪd] n piramide f

Pyrenees [pɪrɪ'niːz] npl **the ~** i Pirenei

quack [kwæk] n (*of duck*) qua qua m inv; (*pej: doctor*) dottoruccio(-a)

quadruple [kwɔ'drupl] vt quadruplicare ▷ vi quadruplicarsi

quail [kweɪl] n (*Zool*) quaglia ▷ vi (*person*): **to ~ at** or **before** perdersi d'animo davanti a

quaint [kweɪnt] adj bizzarro(-a); (*old-fashioned*) antiquato(-a); grazioso(-a), pittoresco(-a)

quake [kweɪk] vi tremare ▷ n abbr = **earthquake**

qualification [kwɔlɪfɪ'keɪʃən] n (*degree etc*) qualifica, titolo; (*ability*) competenza, qualificazione f; (*limitation*) riserva, restrizione f

qualified ['kwɔlɪfaɪd] adj qualificato(-a); (*able*): **~ to** competente in, qualificato(-a) a; (*limited*) condizionato(-a)

qualify ['kwɔlɪfaɪ] vt abilitare; (*limit: statement*) modificare, precisare ▷ vi **to ~ (as)** qualificarsi (come); **to ~ (for)** acquistare i requisiti necessari (per);

(*Sport*) qualificarsi (per *or* a)

quality ['kwɔlɪtɪ] *n* qualità *f inv*

qualm [kwɑ:m] *n* dubbio; scrupolo

quantify ['kwɔntɪfaɪ] *vt* quantificare

quantity ['kwɔntɪtɪ] *n* quantità *f inv*

quarantine ['kwɔrnti:n] *n* quarantena

quarrel ['kwɔrl] *n* lite *f*, disputa ▷ *vi* litigare

quarry ['kwɔrɪ] *n* (*for stone*) cava; (*animal*) preda

quart [kwɔ:t] *n* ≈ litro

quarter ['kwɔ:tə'] *n* quarto; (*us: coin*) quarto di dollaro; (*of year*) trimestre *m*; (*district*) quartiere *m* ▷ *vt* dividere in quattro; (*Mil*) alloggiare; **quarters** *npl* (*living quarters*) alloggio; (*Mil*) alloggi *mpl*, quadrato; **a ~ of an hour** un quarto d'ora; **quarter final** *n* quarto di finale; **quarterly** *adj* trimestrale ▷ *adv* trimestralmente

quartet(te) [kwɔ:'tɛt] *n* quartetto

quartz [kwɔ:ts] *n* quarzo

quay [ki:] *n* (*also*: **~side**) banchina

queasy ['kwi:zɪ] *adj* (*stomach*) delicato(-a); **to feel ~** aver la nausea

queen [kwi:n] *n* (*gen*) regina; (*Cards etc*) regina, donna

queer [kwɪə'] *adj* strano(-a), curioso(-a) ▷ *n* (*inf*) finocchio

quench [kwɛntʃ] *vt* **to ~ one's thirst** dissetarsi

query ['kwɪərɪ] *n* domanda, questione *f* ▷ *vt* mettere in questione

quest [kwɛst] *n* cerca, ricerca

question ['kwɛstʃən] *n* domanda, questione *f* ▷ *vt* (*person*) interrogare; (*plan, idea*) mettere in questione *or* in dubbio; **it's a ~ of doing** si tratta di fare; **beyond ~** fuori di dubbio; **out of the ~** fuori discussione, impossibile; **questionable** *adj* discutibile; **question mark** *n* punto interrogativo; **questionnaire** [kwɛstʃə'nɛə'] *n* questionario

queue [kju:] (*BRIT*) *n* coda, fila ▷ *vi* fare la coda

quiche [ki:ʃ] *n* torta salata a base di uova, formaggio, prosciutto o altro

quick [kwɪk] *adj* rapido(-a), veloce; (*reply*) pronto(-a); (*mind*) pronto(-a), acuto(-a) ▷ *n* **cut to the ~** (*fig*) toccato(-a) sul vivo; **be ~!** fa presto!; **quickly** *adv* rapidamente, velocemente

quid [kwɪd] (*BRIT: inf*) *n inv* sterlina

quiet ['kwaɪət] *adj* tranquillo(-a), quieto(-a); (*ceremony*) semplice ▷ *n* tranquillità, calma ▷ *vt*, *vi* (*us*) = **quieten**; **keep ~!** sta zitto!; **quieten** (*also*: **quieten down**) *vi* calmarsi, chetarsi ▷ *vt* calmare, chetare; **quietly** *adv* tranquillamente, calmamente; sommessamente

quilt [kwɪlt] *n* trapunta; (*continental quilt*) piumino

quirky ['kwə:kɪ] *adj* stravagante

quit [kwɪt] (*pt*, *pp* **quit** *or* **quitted**) *vt* mollare; (*premises*) lasciare, partire da ▷ *vi* (*give up*) mollare; (*resign*) dimettersi

quite [kwaɪt] *adv* (*rather*) assai; (*entirely*) completamente, del tutto; **I ~ understand** capisco perfettamente; **that's not ~ big enough** non è proprio sufficiente; **~ a few of them** non pochi di loro; **~ (so)!** esatto!

quits [kwɪts] *adj* **~ (with)** pari (con); **let's call it ~** adesso siamo pari

quiver ['kwɪvə'] *vi* tremare, fremere

quiz [kwɪz] *n* (*game*) quiz *m inv*; indovinello ▷ *vt* interrogare

quota ['kwəʊtə] *n* quota

quotation [kwəʊ'teɪʃən] *n* citazione *f*; (*of shares etc*) quotazione *f*; (*estimate*) preventivo; **quotation marks** *npl* virgolette *fpl*

quote [kwəʊt] *n* citazione *f* ▷ *vt* (*sentence*) citare; (*price*) dare, fissare; (*shares*) quotare ▷ *vi* **to ~ from** citare; **quotes** *npl* = **quotation marks**

r

rabbi ['ræbaɪ] n rabbino
rabbit ['ræbɪt] n coniglio
rabies ['reɪbiːz] n rabbia
RAC (BRIT) n abbr = **Royal Automobile Club**
rac(c)oon [rə'kuːn] n procione m
race [reɪs] n razza; (competition, rush) corsa ▷ vt (horse) far correre ▷ vi correre; (engine) imballarsi; **race car** (US) n = **racing car**; **racecourse** n campo di corse, ippodromo; **racehorse** n cavallo da corsa; **racetrack** n pista
racial ['reɪʃl] adj razziale
racing ['reɪsɪŋ] n corsa; **racing car** (BRIT) n macchina da corsa; **racing driver** (BRIT) n corridore m automobilista
racism ['reɪsɪzəm] n razzismo; **racist** adj, n razzista m/f
rack [ræk] n rastrelliera; (also: **luggage ~**) rete f, portabagagli m inv; (also: **roof ~**) portabagagli m inv; (dish rack) scolapiatti m inv ▷ vt **~ed by**

torturato(-a) da; **to ~ one's brains** scervellarsi
racket ['rækɪt] n (for tennis) racchetta; (noise) fracasso; baccano; (swindle) imbroglio, truffa; (organized crime) racket m inv
racquet ['rækɪt] n racchetta
radar ['reɪdɑːʳ] n radar m
radiation [reɪdɪ'eɪʃən] n irradiamento; (radioactive) radiazione f
radiator ['reɪdɪeɪtəʳ] n radiatore m
radical ['rædɪkl] adj radicale
radio ['reɪdɪəu] n radio f inv; **on the ~** alla radio; **radioactive** [reɪdɪəu'æktɪv] adj radioattivo(-a); **radio station** n stazione f radio inv
radish ['rædɪʃ] n ravanello
RAF n abbr = **Royal Air Force**
raffle ['ræfl] n lotteria
raft [rɑːft] n zattera; (also: **life ~**) zattera di salvataggio
rag [ræg] n straccio, cencio; (pej: newspaper) giornalaccio, bandiera; (for charity) iniziativa studentesca a scopo benefico; **rags** npl (torn clothes) stracci mpl, brandelli mpl
rage [reɪdʒ] n (fury) collera, furia ▷ vi (person) andare su tutte le furie; (storm) infuriare; **it's all the ~** fa furore
ragged ['rægɪd] adj (edge) irregolare; (clothes) logoro(-a); (appearance) pezzente
raid [reɪd] n (Mil) incursione f; (criminal) rapina; (by police) irruzione f ▷ vt fare un'incursione in; rapinare; fare irruzione in
rail [reɪl] n (on stair) ringhiera; (on bridge, balcony) parapetto; (of ship) battagliola; **railcard** n (BRIT) tessera di riduzione ferroviaria; **railing(s)** n(pl) ringhiere fpl; **railroad** (US) n = **railway**; **railway** (BRIT: irreg) n ferrovia; **railway line** (BRIT) n linea ferroviaria; **railway station** (BRIT) n stazione f ferroviaria
rain [reɪn] n pioggia ▷ vi piovere; **in the ~** sotto la pioggia; **it's ~ing** piove;

rainbow n arcobaleno; **raincoat** n impermeabile m; **raindrop** n goccia di pioggia; **rainfall** n pioggia; (*measurement*) piovosità; **rainforest** n foresta pluviale; **rainy** adj piovoso(-a)

raise [reɪz] n aumento ▷ vt (*lift*) alzare; sollevare; (*increase*) aumentare; (*a protest, doubt, question*) sollevare; (*cattle, family*) allevare; (*crop*) coltivare; (*army, funds*) raccogliere; (*loan*) ottenere; **to ~ one's voice** alzare la voce

raisin ['reɪzn] n uva secca

rake [reɪk] n (*tool*) rastrello ▷ vt (*garden*) rastrellare

rally ['rælɪ] n (*Pol etc*) riunione f; (*Aut*) rally m inv; (*Tennis*) scambio ▷ vt riunire, radunare ▷ vi (*sick person, Stock Exchange*) riprendersi

RAM [ræm] n abbr (= *random access memory*) memoria ad accesso casuale

ram [ræm] n montone m, ariete m ▷ vt conficcare; (*crash into*) cozzare, sbattere contro, percuotere; speronare

Ramadan [ræmə'dæn] n Ramadan m inv

ramble ['ræmbl] n escursione f ▷ vi (*pej: also: ~ on*) divagare; **rambler** n escursionista m/f; (*Bot*) rosa rampicante; **rambling** adj (*speech*) sconnesso(-a); (*house*) tutto(-a) a nicchie e corridoi; (*Bot*) rampicante

ramp [ræmp] n rampa; **on/off ~** (*US Aut*) raccordo di entrata/uscita

rampage [ræm'peɪdʒ] n **to go on the ~** scatenarsi in modo violento

ran [ræn] pt of **run**

ranch [rɑːntʃ] n ranch m inv

random ['rændəm] adj fatto(-a) or detto(-a) per caso; (*Comput, Math*) casuale ▷ n **at ~** a casaccio

rang [ræŋ] pt of **ring**

range [reɪndʒ] n (*of mountains*) catena; (*of missile, voice*) portata; (*of proposals, products*) gamma; (*Mil: also:* **shooting ~**) campo di tiro; (*also:*

kitchen ~) fornello, cucina economica ▷ vt disporre ▷ vi **to ~ over** coprire; **to ~ from ... to** andare da ... a

ranger ['reɪndʒəʳ] n guardia forestale

rank [ræŋk] n fila; (*status, Mil*) grado; (*BRIT: also:* **taxi ~**) posteggio di taxi ▷ vi **to ~ among** essere tra ▷ adj puzzolente; vero(-a) e proprio(-a); **the ~ and file** (*fig*) la gran massa

ransom ['rænsəm] n riscatto; **to hold sb to ~** (*fig*) esercitare pressione su qn

rant [rænt] vi vociare

rap [ræp] vt bussare a; picchiare su ▷ n (*music*) rap m inv

rape [reɪp] n violenza carnale, stupro; (*Bot*) ravizzone m ▷ vt violentare

rapid ['ræpɪd] adj rapido(-a); **rapidly** adv rapidamente; **rapids** npl (*Geo*) rapida

rapist ['reɪpɪst] n violentatore m

rapport [ræ'pɔːʳ] n rapporto

rare [rɛəʳ] adj raro(-a); (*Culin: steak*) al sangue; **rarely** ['rɛəlɪ] adv raramente

rash [ræʃ] adj imprudente, sconsiderato(-a) ▷ n (*Med*) eruzione f; (*of events etc*) scoppio

rasher ['ræʃəʳ] n fetta sottile (di lardo or prosciutto)

raspberry ['rɑːzbərɪ] n lampone m

rat [ræt] n ratto

rate [reɪt] n (*proportion*) tasso, percentuale f; (*speed*) velocità f inv; (*price*) tariffa ▷ vt giudicare; stimare; **rates** npl (*BRIT: property tax*) imposte fpl comunali; (*fees*) tariffe fpl; **to ~ sb/sth as** valutare qn/qc come

rather ['rɑːðəʳ] adv piuttosto; **it's ~ expensive** è piuttosto caro; (*too*) è un po' caro; **there's ~ a lot** ce n'è parecchio; **I would** or **I'd ~ go** preferirei andare

rating ['reɪtɪŋ] n (*assessment*) valutazione f; (*score*) punteggio di merito; **ratings** npl (*Radio, TV*) indice m di ascolto

ratio ['reɪʃɪəu] n proporzione f, rapporto

ration ['ræʃən] n (gen pl) razioni fpl
▷ vt razionare; **rations** npl razioni fpl

rational ['ræʃənl] adj razionale,
ragionevole; (solution, reasoning)
logico(-a)

rattle ['rætl] n tintinnio; (louder)
strepito; (for baby) sonaglino ▷ vi
risuonare, tintinnare; fare un rumore
di ferraglia ▷ vt scuotere (con
strepito)

rave [reɪv] vi (in anger) infuriarsi; (with
enthusiasm) andare in estasi; (Med)
delirare ▷ n (BRIT: inf: party) rave m inv

raven ['reɪvən] n corvo

ravine [rə'viːn] n burrone m

raw [rɔː] adj (uncooked) crudo(-a); (not
processed) greggio(-a); (sore) vivo(-a);
(inexperienced) inesperto(-a); (weather,
day) gelido(-a)

ray [reɪ] n raggio; **a ~ of hope** un
barlume di speranza

razor ['reɪzər] n rasoio; **razor blade** n
lama di rasoio

Rd abbr = **road**

re [riː] prep con riferimento a

RE n abbr (BRIT Mil: = Royal Engineers)
≈ G.M. (Genio Militare); (BRIT)
= **religious education**

reach [riːtʃ] n portata; (of river etc)
tratto ▷ vt raggiungere; arrivare
a ▷ vi stendersi; **out of/within ~**
fuori/a portata di mano; **within
~ of the shops/station** vicino ai
negozi/alla stazione; **reach out** vt
(hand) allungare ▷ vi **to reach out for**
stendere la mano per prendere

react [riː'ækt] vi reagire; **reaction**
[-'ækʃən] n reazione f; **reactor**
[riː'æktər] n reattore m

read [riːd, pt, pp rɛd] (pt, pp **read**) vi
leggere ▷ vt leggere; (understand)
intendere, interpretare; (study)
studiare; **read out** vt leggere ad alta
voce; **reader** n lettore(-trice); (BRIT:
at university) professore con funzioni
preminenti di ricerca

readily ['rɛdɪlɪ] adv volentieri; (easily)

facilmente; (quickly) prontamente

reading ['riːdɪŋ] n lettura;
(understanding) interpretazione f; (on
instrument) indicazione f

ready ['rɛdɪ] adj pronto(-a); (willing)
pronto(-a), disposto(-a); (available)
disponibile ▷ n **at the ~** (Mil) pronto a
sparare; **when will my photos be ~?**
quando saranno pronte le mie foto?;
to get ~ vi prepararsi ▷ vt preparare;
ready-made n prefabbricato(-a);
(clothes) confezionato(-a)

real [rɪəl] adj reale; vero(-a); **in ~
terms** in realtà; **real ale** n birra ad
effervescenza naturale; **real estate** n
beni mpl immobili; **realistic** [-'lɪstɪk]
adj realistico(-a); **reality** [riː'ælɪtɪ] n
realtà f inv; **reality TV** n reality TV f inv

realization [rɪəlaɪ'zeɪʃən] n presa di
coscienza; realizzazione f

realize ['rɪəlaɪz] vt (understand)
rendersi conto di

really ['rɪəlɪ] adv veramente, davvero;
~! (indicating annoyance) oh, insomma!

realm [rɛlm] n reame m, regno

Realtor® ['rɪəltɔːr] (us) n agente m
immobiliare

reappear [riːə'pɪər] vi ricomparire,
riapparire

rear [rɪər] adj di dietro; (Aut: wheel
etc) posteriore ▷ n didietro, parte f
posteriore ▷ vt (cattle, family) allevare
▷ vi (also: ~ up: animal) impennarsi

rearrange [riːə'reɪndʒ] vt riordinare

rear: rear-view mirror ['rɪəvjuː-]
n (Aut) specchio retrovisore; **rear-
wheel drive** n trazione fpl posteriore

reason ['riːzn] n ragione f; (cause,
motive) ragione, motivo ▷ vi **to ~
with sb** far ragionare qn; **it stands
to ~ that** è ovvio che; **reasonable**
adj ragionevole; (not bad) accettabile;
reasonably adv ragionevolmente;
reasoning n ragionamento

reassurance [riːə'ʃuərəns] n
rassicurazione f

reassure [riːə'ʃuər] vt rassicurare; **to ~**

sb of rassicurare qn di or su

rebate ['riːbeɪt] n (on tax etc) sgravio

rebel [n 'rɛbl, vb rɪ'bɛl] n ribelle m/f ▷ vi ribellarsi; **rebellion** n ribellione f; **rebellious** adj ribelle

rebuild [riː'bɪld] vt irreg ricostruire

recall [rɪ'kɔːl] vt richiamare; (remember) ricordare, richiamare alla mente ▷ n richiamo

rec'd abbr = **received**

receipt [rɪ'siːt] n (document) ricevuta; (act of receiving) ricevimento; **receipts** npl (Comm) introiti mpl; **can I have a ~, please?** posso avere una ricevuta, per favore?

receive [rɪ'siːv] vt ricevere; (guest) ricevere, accogliere; **receiver** [rɪ'siːvəʳ] n (Tel) ricevitore m; (Radio, TV) apparecchio ricevente; (of stolen goods) ricettatore(-trice); (Comm) curatore m fallimentare

recent ['riːsnt] adj recente; **recently** adv recentemente

reception [rɪ'sɛpʃən] n ricevimento; (welcome) accoglienza; (TV etc) ricezione f; **reception desk** n (in hotel) reception f inv; (in hospital, at doctor's) accettazione f; (in offices etc) portineria; **receptionist** n receptionist m/f inv

recession [rɪ'sɛʃən] n recessione f

recharge [riː'tʃɑːdʒ] vt (battery) ricaricare

recipe ['rɛsɪpɪ] n ricetta

recipient [rɪ'sɪpɪənt] n beneficiario(-a); (of letter) destinatario(-a)

recital [rɪ'saɪtl] n recital m inv

recite [rɪ'saɪt] vt (poem) recitare

reckless ['rɛkləs] adj (driver etc) spericolato(-a); (spending) folle

reckon ['rɛkən] vt (count) calcolare; (think): **I ~ that ...** penso che ...

reclaim [rɪ'kleɪm] vt (demand back) richiedere, reclamare; (land) bonificare; (materials) recuperare

recline [rɪ'klaɪn] vi stare sdraiato(-a)

recognition [rɛkəg'nɪʃən] n riconoscimento; **transformed beyond ~** irriconoscibile

recognize ['rɛkəgnaɪz] vt **to ~ (by/ as)** riconoscere (a or da/come)

recollection [rɛkə'lɛkʃən] n ricordo

recommend [rɛkə'mɛnd] vt raccomandare; (advise) consigliare; **can you ~ a good restaurant?** mi può consigliare un buon ristorante?; **recommendation** [rɛkəmɛn'deɪʃən] n raccomandazione f; consiglio

reconcile ['rɛkənsaɪl] vt (two people) riconciliare; (two facts) conciliare, quadrare; **to ~ o.s. to** rassegnarsi a

reconsider [riːkən'sɪdəʳ] vt riconsiderare

reconstruct [riːkən'strʌkt] vt ricostruire

record [n 'rɛkɔːd, vb rɪ'kɔːd] n ricordo, documento; (of meeting etc) nota, verbale m; (register) registro; (file) pratica, dossier m inv; (Comput) record m inv; (also: **criminal ~**) fedina penale sporca; (Mus: disc) disco; (Sport) record m inv, primato ▷ vt (set down) prendere nota di, registrare; (Mus: song etc) registrare; **in ~ time** a tempo di record; **off the ~** adj ufficioso(-a) ▷ adv ufficiosamente; **recorded delivery** n (Brit) (Post): **recorded delivery letter** etc lettera etc raccomandata; **recorder** n (Mus) flauto diritto; **recording** n (Mus) registrazione f; **record player** n giradischi m inv

recount [rɪ'kaunt] vt raccontare, narrare

recover [rɪ'kʌvəʳ] vt ricuperare ▷ vi **to ~ (from)** riprendersi (da); **recovery** [rɪ'kʌvərɪ] n ricupero; ristabilimento; ripresa

> Be careful not to translate *recover* by the Italian word *ricoverare*.

recreate [riːkrɪ'eɪt] vt ricreare

recreation [rɛkrɪ'eɪʃən] n ricreazione

f; svago; **recreational drug**
[rɛkrɪ'eɪʃənl-] n sostanza stupefacente
usata a scopo ricreativo; **recreational**
vehicle (us) n camper m inv
recruit [rɪ'kru:t] n recluta; (in
company) nuovo(-a) assunto(-a)
▷ vt reclutare; **recruitment** n
reclutamento
rectangle ['rɛktæŋgl] n rettangolo;
rectangular [-'tæŋgjuləʳ] adj
rettangolare
rectify ['rɛktɪfaɪ] vt (error) rettificare;
(omission) riparare
rector ['rɛktəʳ] n (Rel) parroco
(anglicano)
recur [rɪ'kə:ʳ] vi riaccadere; (symptoms)
ripresentarsi; **recurring** adj (Math)
periodico(-a)
recyclable [ri:'saɪkləbl] adj riciclabile
recycle [ri:'saɪkl] vt riciclare
recycling [ri:'saɪklɪŋ] n riciclaggio
red [rɛd] n rosso; (Pol: pej) rosso(-a)
▷ adj rosso(-a); **in the ~** (account)
scoperto; (business) in deficit; **Red**
Cross n Croce f Rossa; **redcurrant** n
ribes m inv
redeem [rɪ'di:m] vt (debt) riscattare;
(sth in pawn) ritirare; (fig, also Rel)
redimere
red: red-haired [-'hɛəd] adj dai capelli
rossi; **redhead** ['rɛdhɛd] n rosso(-a);
red-hot adj arroventato(-a); **red**
light n **to go through a red light**
(Aut) passare col rosso; **red-light**
district ['rɛdlaɪt-] n quartiere m a luci
rosse; **red meat** n carne f rossa
reduce [rɪ'dju:s] vt ridurre; (lower)
ridurre, abbassare; **"~ speed now"**
(Aut) "rallentare"; **at a ~d price**
scontato(-a); **reduced** adj (decreased)
ridotto(-a); **at a reduced price** a
prezzo ribassato or ridotto; **"greatly**
reduced prices" "grandi ribassi";
reduction [rɪ'dʌkʃən] n riduzione f;
(of price) ribasso; (discount) sconto;
is there a reduction for children/
students? ci sono riduzioni per i

bambini/gli studenti?
redundancy [rɪ'dʌndənsɪ] n
licenziamento
redundant [rɪ'dʌndnt] adj (worker)
licenziato(-a); (detail, object)
superfluo(-a); **to be made ~** essere
licenziato (per eccesso di personale)
reed [ri:d] n (Bot) canna; (Mus: of
clarinet etc) ancia
reef [ri:f] n (at sea) scogliera
reel [ri:l] n bobina, rocchetto; (Fishing)
mulinello; (Cinema) rotolo; (dance)
danza veloce scozzese ▷ vi (sway)
barcollare
ref [rɛf] (inf) n abbr (= referee) arbitro
refectory [rɪ'fɛktərɪ] n refettorio
refer [rɪ'fə:ʳ] vt **to ~ sth to** (dispute,
decision) deferire qc a; **to ~ sb to**
(inquirer, Med: patient) indirizzare qn
a; (reader: to text) rimandare qn a ▷ vi
~ to (allude to) accennare a; (consult)
rivolgersi a
referee [rɛfə'ri:] n arbitro; (BRIT: for
job application) referenza ▷ vt
arbitrare
reference ['rɛfrəns] n riferimento;
(mention) menzione f, allusione f; (for
job application) referenza; **with ~ to**
(Comm: in letter) in or con riferimento
a; **reference number** n numero di
riferimento
refill [vb ri:'fɪl, n 'ri:fɪl] vt riempire di
nuovo; (pen, lighter etc) ricaricare ▷ n
(for pen etc) ricambio
refine [rɪ'faɪn] vt raffinare; **refined**
adj (person, taste) raffinato(-a);
refinery n raffineria
reflect [rɪ'flɛkt] vt (light, image)
riflettere; (fig) rispecchiare ▷ vi (think)
riflettere, considerare; **it ~s badly/**
well on him si ripercuote su di lui in
senso negativo/positivo; **reflection**
[-'flɛkʃən] n riflessione f; (image)
riflesso; (criticism): **reflection on**
giudizio su; attacco a; **on reflection**
pensandoci sopra
reflex ['ri:flɛks] adj riflesso(-a) ▷ n

riflesso

reform [rɪ'fɔːm] n (of sinner etc)
correzione f; (of law etc) riforma ▷ vt
correggere; riformare

refrain [rɪ'freɪn] vi **to ~ from doing**
trattenersi dal fare ▷ n ritornello

refresh [rɪ'frɛʃ] vt rinfrescare; (food,
sleep) ristorare; **refreshing** adj
(drink) rinfrescante; (sleep) riposante,
ristoratore(-trice); **refreshments** npl
rinfreschi mpl

refrigerator [rɪ'frɪdʒəreɪtəʳ] n
frigorifero

refuel [riː'fjuəl] vi far rifornimento (di
carburante)

refuge ['rɛfjuːdʒ] n rifugio; **to take ~
in** rifugiarsi in; **refugee** [rɛfju'dʒiː] n
rifugiato(-a), profugo(-a)

refund [n 'riːfʌnd, vb rɪ'fʌnd] n
rimborso ▷ vt rimborsare

refurbish [riː'fəːbɪʃ] vt rimettere a
nuovo

refusal [rɪ'fjuːzəl] n rifiuto; **to have
first ~ on** avere il diritto d'opzione su

refuse [n 'rɛfjuːs, vb rɪ'fjuːz] n rifiuti
mpl ▷ vt, vi rifiutare; **to ~ to do**
rifiutare di fare

regain [rɪ'geɪn] vt riguadagnare;
riacquistare, ricuperare

regard [rɪ'gaːd] n riguardo, stima
▷ vt considerare, stimare; **to give
one's ~s to** porgere i suoi saluti a;
"with kindest ~s" "cordiali saluti";
regarding prep riguardo a, per
quanto riguarda; **regardless** adv lo
stesso; **regardless of** a dispetto di,
nonostante

regenerate [rɪ'dʒɛnəreɪt] vt
rigenerare

reggae ['rɛgeɪ] n reggae m

regiment ['rɛdʒɪmənt] n reggimento

region ['riːdʒən] n regione f; **in the
~ of** (fig) all'incirca di; **regional** adj
regionale

register ['rɛdʒɪstəʳ] n registro; (also:
electoral ~) lista elettorale ▷ vt
registrare; (vehicle) immatricolare;

(letter) assicurare; (instrument) segnare
▷ vi iscriversi; (at hotel) firmare il
registro; (make impression) entrare in
testa; **registered** (BRIT) adj (letter)
assicurato(-a)

registrar ['rɛdʒɪstraːʳ] n ufficiale m di
stato civile; segretario

registration [rɛdʒɪs'treɪʃən] n (act)
registrazione f; iscrizione f; (Aut: also: ~
number) numero di targa

registry office (BRIT) n anagrafe f;
to get married in a ~ ≈ sposarsi in
municipio

regret [rɪ'grɛt] n rimpianto,
rincrescimento ▷ vt rimpiangere;
regrettable adj deplorevole

regular ['rɛgjuləʳ] adj regolare;
(usual) abituale, normale; (soldier)
dell'esercito regolare ▷ n (client etc)
cliente m/f abituale; **regularly** adv
regolarmente

regulate ['rɛgjuleɪt] vt regolare;
regulation [-'leɪʃən] n regolazione f;
(rule) regola, regolamento

rehabilitation ['riːhəbɪlɪ'teɪʃən] n (of
offender) riabilitazione f; (of disabled)
riadattamento

rehearsal [rɪ'həːsəl] n prova

rehearse [rɪ'həːs] vt provare

reign [reɪn] n regno ▷ vi regnare

reimburse [riːɪm'bəːs] vt rimborsare

rein [reɪn] n (for horse) briglia

reincarnation [riːɪnkaː'neɪʃən] n
reincarnazione f

reindeer ['reɪndɪəʳ] n inv renna

reinforce [riːɪn'fɔːs] vt rinforzare;
reinforcements npl (Mil) rinforzi mpl

reinstate [riːɪn'steɪt] vt reintegrare

reject [n 'riːdʒɛkt, vb rɪ'dʒɛkt]
n (Comm) scarto ▷ vt rifiutare,
respingere; (Comm: goods) scartare;
rejection [rɪ'dʒɛkʃən] n rifiuto

rejoice [rɪ'dʒɔɪs] vi **to ~ (at or over)**
provare diletto in

relate [rɪ'leɪt] vt (tell) raccontare;
(connect) collegare ▷ vi **to ~ to**
(connect) riferirsi a; (get on with)

stabilire un rapporto con; **relating to** che riguarda, rispetto a; **related** adj **related (to)** imparentato(-a) (con); collegato(-a) or connesso(-a) (a)

relation [rɪˈleɪʃən] n (person) parente m/f; (link) rapporto, relazione f; **relations** npl (relatives) parenti mpl; **relationship** n rapporto; (personal ties) rapporti mpl, relazioni fpl; (also: **family relationship**) legami mpl di parentela

relative [ˈrɛlətɪv] n parente m/f ▷ adj relativo(-a); (respective) rispettivo(-a); **relatively** adv relativamente; (fairly, rather) abbastanza

relax [rɪˈlæks] vi rilasciarsi; (person: unwind) rilassarsi ▷ vt rilasciare; (mind, person) rilassare; **relaxation** [riːlækˈseɪʃən] n rilasciamento; rilassamento; (entertainment) ricreazione f, svago; **relaxed** adj rilassato(-a); **relaxing** adj rilassante

relay [ˈriːleɪ] n (Sport) corsa a staffetta ▷ vt (message) trasmettere

release [rɪˈliːs] n (from prison) rilascio; (from obligation) liberazione f; (of gas etc) emissione f; (of film etc) distribuzione f; (record) disco; (device) disinnesto ▷ vt (prisoner) rilasciare; (from obligation, wreckage etc) liberare; (book, film) fare uscire; (news) rendere pubblico(-a); (gas etc) emettere; (Tech: catch, spring etc) disinnestare

relegate [ˈrɛləgeɪt] vt relegare; (BRIT Sport): **to be ~d** essere retrocesso(-a)

relent [rɪˈlɛnt] vi cedere; **relentless** adj implacabile

relevant [ˈrɛləvənt] adj pertinente; (chapter) in questione; **~ to** pertinente a

> Be careful not to translate **relevant** by the Italian word **rilevante**.

reliable [rɪˈlaɪəbl] adj (person, firm) fidato(-a), che dà affidamento; (method) sicuro(-a); (machine) affidabile

relic [ˈrɛlɪk] n (Rel) reliquia; (of the past) resto

relief [rɪˈliːf] n (from pain, anxiety) sollievo; (help, supplies) soccorsi mpl; (Art, Geo) rilievo

relieve [rɪˈliːv] vt (pain, patient) sollevare; (bring help) soccorrere; (take over from: gen) sostituire; (: guard) rilevare; **to ~ sb of sth** (load) alleggerire qn di qc; **to ~ o.s.** fare i propri bisogni; **relieved** adj sollevato(-a); **to be relieved that ...** essere sollevato(-a) (dal fatto) che ...; **i'm relieved to hear it** mi hai tolto un peso con questa notizia

religion [rɪˈlɪdʒən] n religione f

religious [rɪˈlɪdʒəs] adj religioso(-a); **religious education** n religione f

relish [ˈrɛlɪʃ] n (Culin) condimento; (enjoyment) gran piacere m ▷ vt (food etc) godere; **to ~ doing** adorare fare

relocate [riːləʊˈkeɪt] vt trasferire ▷ vi trasferirsi

reluctance [rɪˈlʌktəns] n riluttanza

reluctant [rɪˈlʌktənt] adj riluttante, mal disposto(-a); **reluctantly** adv di mala voglia, a malincuore

rely [rɪˈlaɪ]: **to ~ on** vt fus contare su; (be dependent) dipendere da

remain [rɪˈmeɪn] vi restare, rimanere; **remainder** n resto; (Comm) rimanenza; **remaining** adj che rimane; **remains** npl resti mpl

remand [rɪˈmɑːnd] n **on ~** in detenzione preventiva ▷ vt **to ~ in custody** rinviare in carcere; trattenere a disposizione della legge

remark [rɪˈmɑːk] n osservazione f ▷ vt osservare, dire; **remarkable** adj notevole; eccezionale

remarry [riːˈmærɪ] vi risposarsi

remedy [ˈrɛmədɪ] n **~ (for)** rimedio (per) ▷ vt rimediare a

remember [rɪˈmɛmbəʳ] vt ricordare, ricordarsi di; **~ me to him** salutalo da parte mia; **Remembrance Day** [rɪˈmɛmbrəns-] n 11 novembre, giorno *della commemorazione dei caduti in guerra*

- ● **REMEMBRANCE DAY**
- ●
- ● In Gran Bretagna, il
- ● **Remembrance Day** è un giorno
- ● di commemorazione dei caduti
- ● in guerra. Si celebra ogni anno
- ● la domenica più vicina all'11
- ● novembre, anniversario della firma
- ● dell'armistizio con la Germania
- ● nel 1918.

remind [rɪ'maɪnd] *vt* **to ~ sb of sth** ricordare qc a qn; **to ~ sb to do** ricordare a qn di fare; **reminder** *n* richiamo; *(note etc)* promemoria *m inv*
reminiscent [rɛmɪ'nɪsnt] *adj* **~ of** che fa pensare a, che richiama
remnant ['rɛmnənt] *n* resto, avanzo
remorse [rɪ'mɔːs] *n* rimorso
remote [rɪ'məut] *adj* remoto(-a), lontano(-a); *(person)* distaccato(-a); **remote control** *n* telecomando; **remotely** *adv* remotamente; *(slightly)* vagamente
removal [rɪ'muːvəl] *n (taking away)* rimozione *f*; soppressione *f*; (BRIT: *from house)* trasloco; *(from office: dismissal)* destituzione *f*; *(Med)* ablazione *f*; **removal man** *(irreg)* *n* (BRIT) addetto ai traslochi; **removal van** (BRIT) *n* furgone *m* per traslochi
remove [rɪ'muːv] *vt* togliere, rimuovere; *(employee)* destituire; *(stain)* far sparire; *(doubt, abuse)* sopprimere, eliminare
Renaissance [rɪ'neɪsɑ̃:ns] *n* **the ~** il Rinascimento
rename [riː'neɪm] *vt* ribattezzare
render ['rɛndəʳ] *vt* rendere
rendezvous ['rɔndɪvuː] *n* appuntamento; *(place)* luogo d'incontro; *(meeting)* incontro
renew [rɪ'njuː] *vt* rinnovare; *(negotiations)* riprendere

renovate ['rɛnəveɪt] *vt* rinnovare; *(art work)* restaurare
renowned [rɪ'naund] *adj* rinomato(-a)
rent [rɛnt] *n* affitto ▷ *vt (take for rent)* prendere in affitto; *(also: ~ out)* dare in affitto; **rental** *n (for television, car)* fitto
reorganize [riː'ɔːgənaɪz] *vt* riorganizzare
rep [rɛp] *n abbr (Comm: = representative)* rappresentante *m/f*; *(Theatre: = repertory)* teatro di repertorio
repair [rɪ'pɛəʳ] *n* riparazione *f* ▷ *vt* riparare; **in good/bad ~** in buone/ cattive condizioni; **where can I get this ~ed?** dove lo posso far riparare?; **repair kit** *n* corredo per riparazioni
repay [riː'peɪ] *(irreg)* *vt (money, creditor)* rimborsare, ripagare; *(sb's efforts)* ricompensare; *(favour)* ricambiare; **repayment** *n* pagamento; rimborso
repeat [rɪ'piːt] *n (Radio, TV)* replica ▷ *vt* ripetere; *(pattern)* riprodurre; *(promise, attack, also Comm: order)* rinnovare ▷ *vi* ripetere; **can you ~ that, please?** può ripetere, per favore?; **repeatedly** *adv* ripetutamente, spesso; **repeat prescription** *n* (BRIT) ricetta ripetibile
repellent [rɪ'pɛlənt] *adj* repellente ▷ *n* **insect ~** prodotto *m* anti-insetti *inv*
repercussions [riːpə'kʌʃənz] *npl* ripercussioni *fpl*
repetition [rɛpɪ'tɪʃən] *n* ripetizione *f*
repetitive [rɪ'pɛtɪtɪv] *adj (movement)* che si ripete; *(work)* monotono(-a); *(speech)* pieno(-a) di ripetizioni
replace [rɪ'pleɪs] *vt (put back)* rimettere a posto; *(take the place of)* sostituire; **replacement** *n* rimessa; *(person)* sostituto(-a)
replay ['riːpleɪ] *n (of match)* partita ripetuta; *(of tape, film)* replay *m inv*
replica ['rɛplɪkə] *n* replica, copia
reply [rɪ'plaɪ] *n* risposta ▷ *vi*

rispondere

report [rɪ'pɔːt] n rapporto; (Press etc) cronaca; (BRIT: also: **school ~**) pagella; (of gun) sparo ▷ vt riportare; (Press etc) fare una cronaca su; (bring to notice: occurrence) segnalare; (: person) denunciare ▷ vi (make a report) fare un rapporto (or una cronaca); (present o.s.): **to ~ (to sb)** presentarsi (a qn); **I'd like to ~ a theft** vorrei denunciare un furto; **report card** (US, Scottish) n pagella; **reportedly** adv stando a quanto si dice; **he reportedly told them to ...** avrebbe detto loro di ...; **reporter** n reporter m inv

represent [rɛprɪ'zɛnt] vt rappresentare; **representation** [-'teɪʃən] n rappresentazione f; (petition) rappresentanza; **representative** n rappresentante m/f; (US Pol) deputato(-a) ▷ adj rappresentativo(-a)

repress [rɪ'prɛs] vt reprimere; **repression** [-'prɛʃən] n repressione f

reprimand ['rɛprɪmɑːnd] n rimprovero ▷ vt rimproverare

reproduce [riːprə'djuːs] vt riprodurre ▷ vi riprodursi; **reproduction** [-'dʌkʃən] n riproduzione f

reptile ['rɛptaɪl] n rettile m

republic [rɪ'pʌblɪk] n repubblica; **republican** adj, n repubblicano(-a)

reputable ['rɛpjutəbl] adj di buona reputazione; (occupation) rispettabile

reputation [rɛpju'teɪʃən] n reputazione f

request [rɪ'kwɛst] n domanda; (formal) richiesta ▷ vt: **to ~ (of or from sb)** chiedere (a qn); **request stop** (BRIT) n (for bus) fermata facoltativa or a richiesta

require [rɪ'kwaɪəʳ] vt (need: person) aver bisogno di; (: thing, situation) richiedere; (want) volere, esigere; (order): **to ~ sb to do sth** ordinare a qn di fare qc; **requirement** n esigenza; bisogno; requisito

resat [riː'sæt] pt, pp of **resit**

rescue ['rɛskjuː] n salvataggio; (help) soccorso ▷ vt salvare

research [rɪ'səːtʃ] n ricerca, ricerche fpl ▷ vt fare ricerche su

resemblance [rɪ'zɛmbləns] n somiglianza

resemble [rɪ'zɛmbl] vt assomigliare a

resent [rɪ'zɛnt] vt risentirsi di; **resentful** adj pieno(-a) di risentimento; **resentment** n risentimento

reservation [rɛzə'veɪʃən] n (booking) prenotazione f; (doubt) dubbio; (protected area) riserva; (BRIT: on road: also: **central ~**) spartitraffico m inv; **reservation desk** (US) n (in hotel) reception f inv

reserve [rɪ'zəːv] n riserva ▷ vt (seats etc) prenotare; **reserved** adj (shy) riservato(-a)

reservoir ['rɛzəvwɑːʳ] n serbatoio

residence ['rɛzɪdəns] n residenza; **residence permit** (BRIT) n permesso di soggiorno

resident ['rɛzɪdənt] n residente m/f; (in hotel) cliente m/f fisso(-a) ▷ adj residente; (doctor) fisso(-a); (course, college) a tempo pieno con pernottamento; **residential** [-'dɛnʃəl] adj di residenza; (area) residenziale

residue ['rɛzɪdjuː] n resto; (Chem, Physics) residuo

resign [rɪ'zaɪn] vt (one's post) dimettersi da ▷ vi dimettersi; **to ~ o.s. to** rassegnarsi a; **resignation** [rɛzɪg'neɪʃən] n dimissioni fpl; rassegnazione f

resin ['rɛzɪn] n resina

resist [rɪ'zɪst] vt resistere a; **resistance** n resistenza

resit ['riːsɪt] (BRIT) (pt, pp **resat**) vt (exam) ripresentarsi a; (subject) ridare l'esame di ▷ n: **he's got his French ~ on Friday** deve ridare l'esame di francese venerdì

resolution [rɛzə'luːʃən] n risoluzione f

resolve [rɪ'zɔlv] *n* risoluzione *f* ▷ *vi* (*decide*): **to ~ to do** decidere di fare ▷ *vt* (*problem*) risolvere

resort [rɪ'zɔːt] *n* (*town*) stazione *f*; (*recourse*) ricorso ▷ *vi* **to ~ to** aver ricorso a; **in the last ~** come ultima risorsa

resource [rɪ'sɔːs] *n* risorsa; **resourceful** *adj* pieno(-a) di risorse, intraprendente

respect [rɪs'pɛkt] *n* rispetto ▷ *vt* rispettare; **respectable** *adj* rispettabile; **respectful** *adj* rispettoso(-a); **respective** [rɪs'pɛktɪv] *adj* rispettivo(-a); **respectively** *adv* rispettivamente

respite ['rɛspaɪt] *n* respiro, tregua

respond [rɪs'pɔnd] *vi* rispondere, **response** [rɪs'pɔns] *n* risposta

responsibility [rɪspɔnsɪ'bɪlɪtɪ] *n* responsabilità *f inv*

responsible [rɪs'pɔnsɪbl] *adj* (*trustworthy*) fidato(-a); (*job*) di (grande) responsabilità; **~ (for)** responsabile (di); **responsibly** *adv* responsabilmente

responsive [rɪs'pɔnsɪv] *adj* che reagisce

rest [rɛst] *n* riposo; (*stop*) sosta, pausa; (*Mus*) pausa; (*object: to support sth*) appoggio, sostegno; (*remainder*) resto, avanzi *mpl* ▷ *vi* riposarsi; (*remain*) rimanere, restare; (*be supported*): **to ~ on** appoggiarsi su ▷ *vt* (*far*) riposare; (*lean*): **to ~ sth on/against** appoggiare qc su/contro; **the ~ of them** gli altri; **it ~s with him to decide** sta a lui decidere

restaurant ['rɛstərɔn] *n* ristorante *m*; **restaurant car** (*BRIT*) *n* vagone *m* ristorante

restless ['rɛstlɪs] *adj* agitato(-a), irrequieto(-a)

restoration [rɛstə'reɪʃən] *n* restauro, restituzione *f*

restore [rɪ'stɔː'] *vt* (*building, to power*) restaurare; (*sth stolen*) restituire; (*peace, health*) ristorare

restrain [rɪs'treɪn] *vt* (*feeling, growth*) contenere, frenare; (*person*): **to ~ (from doing)** trattenere (dal fare); **restraint** *n* (*restriction*) limitazione *f*; (*moderation*) ritegno; (*of style*) contenutezza

restrict [rɪs'trɪkt] *vt* restringere, limitare; **restriction** [-kʃən] *n* **restriction (on)** restrizione *f* (di), limitazione *f*

rest room (*US*) *n* toletta

restructure [riː'strʌktʃə'] *vt* ristrutturare

result [rɪ'zʌlt] *n* risultato ▷ *vi* **to ~ in** avere per risultato; **as a ~ of** in or di conseguenza a, in seguito a

resume [rɪ'zjuːm] *vt, vi* (*work, journey*) riprendere

résumé ['reɪzjumeɪ] *n* riassunto; (*US*) curriculum *m inv* vitae

resuscitate [rɪ'sʌsɪteɪt] *vt* (*Med*) risuscitare

retail ['riːteɪl] *adj, adv* al minuto ▷ *vt* vendere al minuto; **retailer** n commerciante *m/f* al minuto, dettagliante *m/f*

retain [rɪ'teɪn] *vt* (*keep*) tenere, serbare

retaliation [rɪtælɪ'eɪʃən] *n* rappresaglie *fpl*

retarded [rɪ'tɑːdɪd] *adj* ritardato(-a)

retire [rɪ'taɪə'] *vi* (*give up work*) andare in pensione; (*withdraw*) ritirarsi, andarsene; (*go to bed*) andare a letto, ritirarsi; **retired** *adj* (*person*) pensionato(-a); **retirement** *n* pensione *f*; (*act*) pensionamento

retort [rɪ'tɔːt] *vi* rimbeccare

retreat [rɪ'triːt] *n* ritirata; (*place*) rifugio ▷ *vi* battere in ritirata

retrieve [rɪ'triːv] *vt* (*sth lost*) ricuperare, ritrovare; (*situation, honour*) salvare; (*error, loss*) rimediare a

retrospect ['rɛtrəspɛkt] *n* **in ~** guardando indietro; **retrospective**

[-'spɛktɪv] *adj* retrospettivo(-a); *(law)* retroattivo(-a)

return [rɪ'tə:n] *n (going or coming back)* ritorno; *(of sth stolen etc)* restituzione f; *(Finance: from land, shares)* profitto, reddito ▷ *cpd (journey, match)* di ritorno; *(BRIT: ticket)* di andata e ritorno ▷ *vi* tornare, ritornare ▷ *vt* rendere, restituire; *(bring back)* riportare; *(send back)* mandare indietro; *(put back)* rimettere; *(Pol: candidate)* eleggere; **returns** *npl (Comm)* incassi *mpl*; profitti *mpl*, **in ~ (for)** in cambio (di); **by ~ of post** a stretto giro di posta; **many happy ~s (of the day)!** cento di questi giorni!; **return ticket** *n (esp BRIT)* biglietto di andata e ritorno

reunion [ri:'ju:nɪən] *n* riunione f

reunite [ri:ju:'naɪt] *vt* riunire

revamp ['ri:'væmp] *vt (firm)* riorganizzare

reveal [rɪ'vi:l] *vt (make known)* rivelare, svelare; *(display)* rivelare, mostrare; **revealing** *adj* rivelatore(-trice); *(dress)* scollato(-a)

revel ['rɛvl] *vi* **to ~ in sth/in doing** dilettarsi di qc/a fare

revelation [rɛvə'leɪʃən] *n* rivelazione f

revenge [rɪ'vɛndʒ] *n* vendetta ▷ *vt* vendicare; **to take ~ on** vendicarsi di

revenue ['rɛvənju:] *n* reddito

Reverend ['rɛvərənd] *adj (in titles)* reverendo(-a)

reversal [rɪ'və:sl] *n* capovolgimento

reverse [rɪ'və:s] *n* contrario, opposto; *(back, defeat)* rovescio; *(Aut: also: ~ gear)* marcia indietro ▷ *adj (order, direction)* contrario(-a), opposto(-a) ▷ *vt (turn)* invertire, rivoltare; *(change)* capovolgere, rovesciare; *(Law: judgment)* cassare; *(car)* fare marcia indietro con ▷ *vi (BRIT Aut, person etc)* fare marcia indietro; **reverse-charge call** [rɪ'və:stʃɑ:dʒ-] *(BRIT) n (Tel)* telefonata con addebito al ricevente;

reversing lights *(BRIT) npl (Aut)* luci *fpl* per la retromarcia

revert [rɪ'və:t] *vi* **to ~ to** tornare a

review [rɪ'vju:] *n* rivista; *(of book, film)* recensione f; *(of situation)* esame *m* ▷ *vt* passare in rivista; fare la recensione di; fare il punto di

revise [rɪ'vaɪz] *vt (manuscript)* rivedere, correggere; *(opinion)* emendare, modificare; *(study: subject, notes)* ripassare; **revision** [rɪ'vɪʒən] *n* revisione f; ripasso

revival [rɪ'vaɪvəl] *n* ripresa; ristabilimento; *(of faith)* risveglio

revive [rɪ'vaɪv] *vt (person)* rianimare; *(custom)* far rivivere; *(hope, courage, economy)* ravvivare; *(play, fashion)* riesumare ▷ *vi (person)* rianimarsi; *(hope)* ravvivarsi; *(activity)* riprendersi

revolt [rɪ'vəult] *n* rivolta, ribellione f ▷ *vi* rivoltarsi, ribellarsi ▷ *vt (far)* rivoltare; **revolting** *adj* ripugnante

revolution [rɛvə'lu:ʃən] *n* rivoluzione f; *(of wheel etc)* rivoluzione, giro; **revolutionary** *adj, n* rivoluzionario(-a)

revolve [rɪ'vɔlv] *vi* girare

revolver [rɪ'vɔlvə*] *n* rivoltella

reward [rɪ'wɔ:d] *n* ricompensa, premio ▷ *vt* **to ~ (for)** ricompensare (per); **rewarding** *adj (fig)* gratificante

rewind [ri:'waɪnd] *(irreg) vt (watch)* ricaricare; *(ribbon etc)* riavvolgere

rewrite [ri:'raɪt] *vt irreg* riscrivere

rheumatism ['ru:mətɪzəm] *n* reumatismo

rhinoceros [raɪ'nɔsərəs] *n* rinoceronte *m*

rhubarb ['ru:bɑ:b] *n* rabarbaro

rhyme [raɪm] *n* rima; *(verse)* poesia

rhythm ['rɪðm] *n* ritmo

rib [rɪb] *n (Anat)* costola ▷ *vt (tease)* punzecchiare

ribbon ['rɪbən] *n* nastro; **in ~s** *(torn)* a brandelli

rice [raɪs] *n* riso; **rice pudding** *n* budino di riso

rich [rɪtʃ] *adj* ricco(-a); (*clothes*) sontuoso(-a); (*abundant*): **~ in** ricco(-a) di

rid [rɪd] (*pt, pp* **rid**) *vt* **to ~ sb of** sbarazzare *or* liberare qn di; **to get ~ of** sbarazzarsi di

riddle ['rɪdl] *n* (*puzzle*) indovinello ▷ *vt* **to be ~d with** (*holes*) essere crivellato(-a) di; (*doubts*) essere pieno(-a) di

ride [raɪd] (*pt* **rode**, *pp* **ridden**) *n* (*on horse*) cavalcata; (*outing*) passeggiata; (*distance covered*) cavalcata; corsa ▷ *vi* (*as sport*) cavalcare; (*go somewhere: on horse, bicycle*) andare (a cavallo *or* in bicicletta *etc*); (*journey: on bicycle, motorcycle, bus*) andare, viaggiare ▷ *vt* (*a horse*) montare, cavalcare; **to take sb for a ~** (*fig*) prendere in giro qn; fregare qn; **to ~ a horse/ bicycle/camel** montare a cavallo/in bicicletta/in groppa a un cammello; **rider** *n* cavalcatore(-trice); (*in race*) fantino; (*on bicycle*) ciclista *m/f*; (*on motorcycle*) motociclista *m/f*

ridge [rɪdʒ] *n* (*of hill*) cresta; (*of roof*) colmo; (*on object*) riga (in rilievo)

ridicule ['rɪdɪkjuːl] *n* ridicolo; scherno ▷ *vt* mettere in ridicolo; **ridiculous** [rɪ'dɪkjuləs] *adj* ridicolo(-a)

riding ['raɪdɪŋ] *n* equitazione *f*; **riding school** *n* scuola d'equitazione

rife [raɪf] *adj* diffuso(-a); **to be ~ with** abbondare di

rifle ['raɪfl] *n* carabina ▷ *vt* vuotare

rift [rɪft] *n* fessura, crepatura; (*fig: disagreement*) incrinatura, disaccordo

rig [rɪg] *n* (*also:* **oil ~**: *on land*) derrick *m inv*; (*: at sea*) piattaforma di trivellazione ▷ *vt* (*election etc*) truccare

right [raɪt] *adj* giusto(-a); (*suitable*) appropriato(-a); (*not left*) destro(-a) ▷ *n* giusto; (*title, claim*) diritto; (*not left*) destra ▷ *adv* (*answer*) correttamente; (*not on the left*) a destra ▷ *vt* raddrizzare; (*fig*) riparare ▷ *excl* bene!; **to be ~** (*person*) aver ragione; (*answer*) essere giusto(-a) *or* corretto(-a); **by ~s** di diritto; **on the ~** a destra; **to be in the ~** aver ragione, essere nel giusto; **~ now** proprio adesso; subito; **~ away** subito; **right angle** *n* angolo retto; **rightful** *adj* (*heir*) legittimo(-a); **right-hand** *adj* **right-hand drive** guida a destra; **the right-hand side** il lato destro; **right-handed** *adj* (*person*) che adopera la mano destra; **rightly** *adv* bene, correttamente; (*with reason*) a ragione; **right of way** *n* diritto di passaggio; (*Aut*) precedenza; **right-wing** *adj* (*Pol*) di destra

rigid ['rɪdʒɪd] *adj* rigido(-a); (*principle*) rigoroso(-a)

rigorous ['rɪgərəs] *adj* rigoroso(-a)

rim [rɪm] *n* orlo; (*of spectacles*) montatura; (*of wheel*) cerchione *m*

rind [raɪnd] *n* (*of bacon*) cotenna; (*of lemon etc*) scorza

ring [rɪŋ] (*pt* **rang**, *pp* **rung**) *n* anello; (*of people, objects*) cerchio; (*of spies*) giro; (*of smoke etc*) spirale *m*; (*arena*) pista, arena; (*for boxing*) ring *m inv*; (*sound of bell*) scampanio ▷ *vi* (*person, bell, telephone*) suonare; (*also:* **~ out**: *voice, words*) risuonare; (*Tel*) telefonare; (*ears*) fischiare ▷ *vt* (BRIT Tel) telefonare a; (*: bell, doorbell*) suonare; **to give sb a ~** (BRIT Tel) dare un colpo di telefono a qn; **ring back** *vt, vi* (Tel) richiamare; **ring off** (BRIT) *vi* (Tel) mettere giù, riattaccare; **ring up** (BRIT) *vt* (Tel) telefonare a; **ringing tone** (BRIT) *n* (Tel) segnale *m* di libero; **ringleader** *n* (*of gang*) capobanda *m*; **ring road** (BRIT) *n* raccordo anulare

ring tone *n* suoneria

rink [rɪŋk] *n* (*also:* **ice ~**) pista di pattinaggio

rinse [rɪns] *n* risciacquatura; (*hair tint*) cachet *m inv* ▷ *vt* sciacquare

riot ['raɪət] *n* sommossa, tumulto; (*of colours*) orgia ▷ *vi* tumultuare; **to run ~** creare disordine

rip [rɪp] *n* strappo ▷ *vt* strappare

▷ vi strapparsi; **rip off** vt (inf: cheat) fregare; **rip up** vt stracciare

ripe [raɪp] adj (fruit, grain) maturo(-a); (cheese) stagionato(-a)

rip-off ['rɪpɔf] n (inf): **it's a ~!** è un furto!

ripple ['rɪpl] n increspamento, ondulazione f; mormorio ▷ vi incresparsi

rise [raɪz] (pt **rose**, pp **risen**) n (slope) salita, pendio; (hill) altura; (increase: in wages: BRIT) aumento; (: in prices, temperature) rialzo, aumento; (fig: to power etc) ascesa ▷ vi alzarsi, levarsi; (prices) aumentare; (waters, river) crescere; (sun, wind, person: from chair, bed) levarsi; (also: **~ up**: building) ergersi; (: rebel) insorgere; ribellarsi; (in rank) salire; **to give ~ to** provocare, dare origine a; **to ~ to the occasion** essere all'altezza; **risen** ['rɪzn] pp of **rise**; **rising** adj (increasing: number) sempre crescente; (: prices) in aumento; (tide) montante; (sun, moon) nascente, che sorge

risk [rɪsk] n rischio; pericolo ▷ vt rischiare; **to take** or **run the ~ of doing** correre il rischio di fare; **at ~ in** pericolo; **at one's own ~** a proprio rischio e pericolo; **risky** adj rischioso(-a)

rite [raɪt] n rito; **last ~s** l'estrema unzione

ritual ['rɪtjuəl] adj rituale ▷ n rituale m

rival ['raɪvl] n rivale m/f; (in business) concorrente m/f ▷ adj rivale; che fa concorrenza ▷ vt essere in concorrenza con; **to ~ sb/sth in** competere con qn/qc in; **rivalry** n rivalità; concorrenza

river ['rɪvə'] n fiume m ▷ cpd (port, traffic) fluviale; **up/down ~** a monte/valle; **riverbank** n argine m

rivet ['rɪvɪt] n ribattino, rivetto ▷ vt (fig) concentrare, fissare

Riviera [rɪvɪ'ɛərə] n **the (French) ~** la Costa Azzurra; **the Italian ~** la Riviera

road [rəud] n strada, via; (small) cammino; (in town) via ▷ cpd stradale; **major/minor ~** strada con/senza diritto di precedenza; **which ~ do I take for ...?** che strada devo prendere per andare a...?; **roadblock** n blocco stradale; **road map** n carta stradale; **road rage** n comportamento aggressivo al volante; **road safety** n sicurezza sulle strade; **roadside** n margine m della strada; **roadsign** n cartello stradale; **road tax** n (BRIT) tassa di circolazione; **roadworks** npl lavori mpl stradali

roam [rəum] vi errare, vagabondare

roar [rɔː'] n ruggito; (of crowd) tumulto; (of thunder, storm) muggito; (of laughter) scoppio ▷ vi ruggire; tumultuare; muggire; **to ~ with laughter** scoppiare dalle risa; **to do a ~ing trade** fare affari d'oro

roast [rəust] n arrosto ▷ vt arrostire; (coffee) tostare, torrefare; **roast beef** n arrosto di manzo

rob [rɔb] vt (person) rubare; (bank) svaligiare; **to ~ sb of sth** derubare qn di qc; (fig: deprive) privare qn di qc; **robber** n ladro; (armed) rapinatore m; **robbery** n furto; rapina

robe [rəub] n (for ceremony etc) abito; (also: **bath ~**) accappatoio; (US: also: **lap ~**) coperta

robin ['rɔbɪn] n pettirosso

robot ['rəubɔt] n robot m inv

robust [rəu'bʌst] adj robusto(-a); (economy) solido(-a)

rock [rɔk] n (substance) roccia; (boulder) masso; roccia; (in sea) scoglio; (US: pebble) ciottolo; (BRIT: sweet) zucchero candito ▷ vt (swing gently: cradle) dondolare; (: child) cullare; (shake) scrollare, far tremare ▷ vi dondolarsi; scrollarsi, tremare; **on the ~s** (drink) col ghiaccio; (marriage etc) in crisi; **rock and roll** n rock and roll m; **rock climbing** n roccia

rocket [ˈrɒkɪt] n razzo
rocking chair n sedia a dondolo
rocky [ˈrɒkɪ] adj (hill) roccioso(-a); (path) sassoso(-a); (marriage etc) instabile
rod [rɒd] n (metallic, Tech) asta; (wooden) bacchetta; (also: **fishing ~**) canna da pesca
rode [rəud] pt of **ride**
rodent [ˈrəudnt] n roditore m
rogue [rəug] n mascalzone m
role [rəul] n ruolo; **role-model** n modello (di comportamento)
roll [rəul] n rotolo; (of banknotes) mazzo; (also: **bread ~**) panino; (register) lista; (sound: of drums etc) rullo ▷ vt rotolare; (also: **~ up**: string) aggomitolare; (: sleeves) rimboccare; (cigarettes) arrotolare; (eyes) roteare; (also: **~ out**: pastry) stendere; (lawn, road etc) spianare ▷ vi rotolare; (wheel) girare; (drum) rullare; (vehicle: also: **~ along**) avanzare; (ship) rollare; **roll over** vi rivoltarsi; **roll up** (inf) vi (arrive) arrivare ▷ vt (carpet) arrotolare; **roller** n rullo; (wheel) rotella; (for hair) bigodino; **Rollerblades®** npl pattini mpl in linea; **roller coaster** [-ˈkəustəʳ] n montagne fpl russe; **roller skates** npl pattini mpl a rotelle; **roller-skating** n pattinaggio a rotelle; **to go roller-skating** andare a pattinare (con i pattini a rotelle); **rolling pin** n matterello
ROM [rɒm] n abbr (= read only memory) memoria di sola lettura
Roman [ˈrəumən] adj, n romano(-a); **Roman Catholic** adj, n cattolico(-a)
romance [rəˈmæns] n storia (or avventura or film m inv) romantico(-a); (charm) poesia; (love affair) idillio
Romania [rəuˈmeɪnɪə] n Romania
Romanian [rəuˈmeɪnɪən] adj romeno(-a) ▷ n romeno; (Ling) romeno
Roman numeral n numero romano

romantic [rəˈmæntɪk] adj romantico(-a); sentimentale
Rome [rəum] n Roma
roof [ruːf] n tetto; (of tunnel, cave) volta ▷ vt coprire (con un tetto); **~ of the mouth** palato; **roof rack** n (Aut) portabagagli m inv
rook [ruk] n (bird) corvo nero; (Chess) torre f
room [ruːm] n (in house) stanza; (bedroom, in hotel) camera; (in school etc) sala; (space) posto, spazio; **roommate** n compagno(-a) di stanza; **room service** n servizio da camera; **roomy** adj spazioso(-a); (garment) ampio(-a)
rooster [ˈruːstəʳ] n gallo
root [ruːt] n radice f ▷ vi (plant, belief) attecchire
rope [rəup] n corda, fune f; (Naut) cavo ▷ vt (box) legare; (climbers) legare in cordata; (area: also: **~ off**) isolare cingendo con cordoni; **to know the ~s** (fig) conoscere i trucchi del mestiere
rose [rəuz] pt of **rise** ▷ n rosa; (also: **~ bush**) rosaio; (on watering can) rosetta
rosé [ˈrəuzeɪ] n vino rosato
rosemary [ˈrəuzmərɪ] n rosmarino
rosy [ˈrəuzɪ] adj roseo(-a)
rot [rɒt] n (decay) putrefazione f; (inf: nonsense) stupidaggini fpl ▷ vt, vi imputridire, marcire
rota [ˈrəutə] n tabella dei turni
rotate [rəuˈteɪt] vt (revolve) far girare; (change round: jobs) fare a turno ▷ vi (revolve) girare
rotten [ˈrɒtn] adj (decayed) putrido(-a), marcio(-a); (dishonest) corrotto(-a); (inf: bad) brutto(-a); (: action) vigliacco(-a); **to feel ~** (ill) sentirsi da cani
rough [rʌf] adj (skin, surface) ruvido(-a); (terrain, road) accidentato(-a); (voice) rauco(-a); (person, manner: coarse) rozzo(-a), aspro(-a); (: violent) brutale; (district)

malfamato(-a); (*weather*) cattivo(-a); (*sea*) mosso(-a); (*plan*) abbozzato(-a); (*guess*) approssimativo(-a) ▷ *n* (*Golf*) macchia; **to ~ it** far vita dura; **to sleep ~** (BRIT) dormire all'addiaccio; **roughly** *adv* (*handle*) rudemente, brutalmente; (*make*) grossolanamente; (*speak*) bruscamente; (*approximately*) approssimativamente

roulette [ruːˈlɛt] *n* roulette *f*

round [raund] *adj* rotondo(-a); (*figures*) tondo(-a) ▷ *n* (BRIT: *of toast*) fetta; (*duty: of policeman, milkman etc*) giro; (: *of doctor*) visite *fpl*; (*game: of cards, golf, in competition*) partita; (*of ammunition*) cartuccia; (*Boxing*) round *m inv*; (*of talks*) serie *f inv* ▷ *vt* (*corner*) girare; (*bend*) prendere ▷ *prep* intorno a ▷ *adv* **all ~** tutt'attorno; **to go the long way ~** fare il giro più lungo; **all the year ~** tutto l'anno; **it's just ~ the corner** (*also fig*) è dietro l'angolo; **~ the clock** ininterrottamente; **to go ~ to sb's house** andare da qn; **go ~ the back** passi dietro; **enough to go ~** abbastanza per tutti; **~ of applause** applausi *mpl*; **~ of drinks** giro di bibite; **~ of sandwiches** sandwich *m inv*; **round off** *vt* (*speech etc*) finire; **round up** *vt* radunare; (*criminals*) fare una retata di; (*prices*) arrotondare; **roundabout** *n* (BRIT Aut) rotatoria; (: *at fair*) giostra ▷ *adj* (*route, means*) indiretto(-a); **round trip** *n* (*viaggio di*) andata e ritorno; **roundup** *n* raduno; (*of criminals*) retata

rouse [rauz] *vt* (*wake up*) svegliare; (*stir up*) destare; provocare; risvegliare

route [ruːt] *n* itinerario; (*of bus*) percorso

routine [ruːˈtiːn] *adj* (*work*) corrente, abituale; (*procedure*) solito(-a) ▷ *n* (*pej*) routine *f*, tran tran *m*; (*Theatre*) numero

row¹ [rəu] *n* (*line*) riga, fila; (*Knitting*) ferro; (*behind one another: of cars, people*) fila; (*in boat*) remata ▷ *vi* (*in boat*) remare; (*as sport*) vogare ▷ *vt* (*boat*) manovrare a remi; **in a ~** (*fig*) di fila

row² [rau] *n* (*racket*) baccano, chiasso; (*dispute*) lite *f*; (*scolding*) sgridata ▷ *vi* (*argue*) litigare

rowboat [ˈrəubəut] (US) *n* barca a remi

rowing [ˈrəuɪŋ] *n* canottaggio; **rowing boat** (BRIT) *n* barca a remi

royal [ˈrɔɪəl] *adj* reale; **royalty** [ˈrɔɪəltɪ] *n* (*royal persons*) (membri *mpl* della) famiglia reale; (*payment: to author*) diritti *mpl* d'autore

rpm *abbr* (= revolutions per minute) giri/min.

R.S.V.P. *abbr* (= répondez s'il vous plaît) R.S.V.P.

Rt. Hon. (BRIT) *abbr* (= Right Honourable) ≈ Onorevole

rub [rʌb] *n* **to give sth a ~** strofinare qc; (*sore place*) massaggiare qc ▷ *vt* strofinare; massaggiare; (*hands: also: ~ together*) sfregarsi; **rub off** *vi* andare via; **rub out** *vt* cancellare

rubber [ˈrʌbəʳ] *n* gomma; **rubber band** *n* elastico; **rubber gloves** *npl* guanti *mpl* di gomma

rubbish [ˈrʌbɪʃ] *n* (*from household*) immondizie *fpl*, rifiuti *mpl*; (*fig, pej*) cose *fpl* senza valore; robaccia; sciocchezze *fpl*; **rubbish bin** (BRIT) *n* pattumiera; **rubbish dump** *n* (*in town*) immondezzaio

rubble [ˈrʌbl] *n* macerie *fpl*; (*smaller*) pietrisco

ruby [ˈruːbɪ] *n* rubino

rucksack [ˈrʌksæk] *n* zaino

rudder [ˈrʌdəʳ] *n* timone *m*

rude [ruːd] *adj* (*impolite: person*) scortese, rozzo(-a); (: *word, manners*) grossolano(-a), rozzo(-a); (*shocking*) indecente

ruffle['rʌfl] vt (hair) scompigliare; (clothes, water) increspare; (fig: person) turbare

rug[rʌg] n tappeto; (BRIT: for knees) coperta

rugby['rʌgbɪ] n (also: **~ football**) rugby m

rugged['rʌgɪd] adj (landscape) aspro(-a); (features, determination) duro(-a); (character) brusco(-a)

ruin['ruːɪn] n rovina ▷ vt rovinare; **ruins** npl (of building, castle etc) rovine fpl, ruderi mpl

rule[ruːl] n regola; (regulation) regolamento, regola; (government) governo; (ruler) riga ▷ vt (country) governare; (person) dominare ▷ vi regnare; decidere; (Law) dichiarare; **as a ~** normalmente; **rule out** vt escludere; **ruler** n (sovereign) sovrano(-a); (for measuring) regolo, riga; **ruling** adj (party) al potere; (class) dirigente ▷ n (Law) decisione f

rum[rʌm] n rum m

Rumania etc [ruː'meɪnɪə] n = **Romania** etc

rumble['rʌmbl] n rimbombo; brontolio ▷ vi rimbombare; (stomach, pipe) brontolare

rumour['ruːməʳ] (US **rumor**) n voce f ▷ vt **it is ~ed that** corre voce che
> Be careful not to translate **rumour** by the Italian word **rumore**.

rump steak [rʌmp-] n bistecca di girello

run[rʌn] (pt **ran**, pp **run**) n corsa; (outing) gita (in macchina); (distance travelled) percorso, tragitto; (Ski) pista; (Cricket, Baseball) meta; (series) serie f; (Theatre) periodo di rappresentazione; (in tights, stockings) smagliatura ▷ vt (distance) correre; (operate: business) gestire, dirigere; (: competition, course) organizzare; (: hotel) gestire; (: house) governare; (Comput) eseguire; (water, bath) far scorrere; (force through: rope,

pipe): **to ~ sth through** far passare qc attraverso; (pass: hand, finger): **to ~ sth over** passare qc su; (Press: feature) presentare ▷ vi correre; (flee) scappare; (pass: road etc) passare; (work: machine, factory) funzionare, andare; (bus, train: operate) far servizio; (: travel) circolare; (continue: play, contract) durare; (slide: drawer; flow: river, bath) scorrere; (colours, washing) stemperarsi; (in election) presentarsi candidato; (nose) colare; **there was a ~ on ...** c'era una corsa a ...; **in the long ~** a lungo andare; **on the ~** in fuga; **to ~ a race** partecipare ad una gara; **I'll ~ you to the station** la porto alla stazione; **to ~ a risk** correre un rischio; **run after** vt fus (to catch up) rincorrere; (chase) correre dietro a; **run away** vi fuggire; **run down** vt (production) ridurre gradualmente; (factory) rallentare l'attività di; (Aut) investire; (criticize) criticare; **to be run down** (person: tired) essere esausto(-a); **run into** vt fus (meet: person) incontrare per caso; (: trouble) incontrare, trovare; (collide with) andare a sbattere contro; **run off** vi fuggire ▷ vt (water) far scolare; (copies) fare; **run out** vi (person) uscire di corsa; (liquid) colare; (lease) scadere; (money) esaurirsi; **run out of** vt fus rimanere a corto di; **run over** vt (Aut) investire, mettere sotto ▷ vt fus (revise) rivedere; **run through** vt fus (instructions) dare una scorsa a; (rehearse: play) riprovare, ripetere; **run up** vt (debt) lasciar accumulare; **to run up against** (difficulties) incontrare; **runaway** adj (person) fuggiasco(-a); (horse) in libertà; (truck) fuori controllo

rung[rʌŋ] pp of **ring** ▷ n (of ladder) piolo

runner['rʌnəʳ] n (in race) corridore m; (: horse) partente m/f; (on sledge) pattino; (for drawer etc) guida; **runner**

bean (BRIT) n fagiolo rampicante;
runner-up n secondo(-a) arrivato(-a)
running ['rʌnɪŋ] n corsa; direzione
f; organizzazione f; funzionamento
▷ adj (water) corrente; (commentary)
simultaneo(-a); **to be in/out of the ~
for sth** essere/non essere più in lizza
per qc; **6 days ~** 6 giorni di seguito
runny ['rʌnɪ] adj che cola
run-up ['rʌnʌp] n **~ to** (election etc)
periodo che precede
runway ['rʌnweɪ] n (Aviat) pista (di
decollo)
rupture ['rʌptʃər] n (Med) ernia
rural ['rʊərəl] adj rurale
rush [rʌʃ] n corsa precipitosa; (hurry)
furia, fretta; (sudden demand): **~ for**
corsa a; (current) flusso; (of emotion)
impeto; (Bot) giunco ▷ vt mandare or
spedire velocemente; (attack: town etc)
prendere d'assalto ▷ vi precipitarsi;
rush hour n ora di punta
Russia ['rʌʃə] n Russia; **Russian** adj
russo(-a) ▷ n russo(-a); (Ling) russo
rust [rʌst] n ruggine f ▷ vi arrugginirsi
rusty ['rʌstɪ] adj arrugginito(-a)
ruthless ['ruːθlɪs] adj spietato(-a)
RV abbr (= revised version) versione
riveduta della Bibbia ▷ n abbr (US) see
recreational vehicle
rye [raɪ] n segale f

S

Sabbath ['sæbəθ] n (Jewish) sabato;
(Christian) domenica
sabotage ['sæbətɑːʒ] n sabotaggio
▷ vt sabotare
saccharin(e) ['sækərɪn] n saccarina
sachet ['sæʃeɪ] n bustina
sack [sæk] n (bag) sacco ▷ vt (dismiss)
licenziare, mandare a spasso; (plunder)
saccheggiare; **to get the ~** essere
mandato a spasso
sacred ['seɪkrɪd] adj sacro(-a)
sacrifice ['sækrɪfaɪs] n sacrificio ▷ vt
sacrificare
sad [sæd] adj triste
saddle ['sædl] n sella ▷ vt (horse)
sellare; **to be ~d with sth** (inf) avere
qc sulle spalle
sadistic [sə'dɪstɪk] adj sadico(-a)
sadly ['sædlɪ] adv tristemente;
(regrettably) sfortunatamente; **~
lacking in** penosamente privo di
sadness ['sædnɪs] n tristezza
s.a.e. n abbr (= stamped addressed
envelope) busta affrancata e con indirizzo

safari [sə'fɑːrɪ] n safari m inv
safe [seɪf] adj sicuro(-a); (out of danger)
salvo(-a), al sicuro; (cautious) prudente
▷ n cassaforte f; **~ from** al sicuro da;
~ and sound sano(-a) e salvo(-a);
(just) to be on the ~ side per non
correre rischi; **could you put this in
the ~, please?** lo potrebbe mettere
nella cassaforte, per favore?; **safely**
adv sicuramente; sano(-a) e salvo(-a);
prudentemente; **safe sex** n sesso
sicuro
safety ['seɪftɪ] n sicurezza; **safety
belt** n cintura di sicurezza; **safety pin**
n spilla di sicurezza
saffron ['sæfrən] n zafferano
sag [sæg] vi incurvarsi; afflosciarsi
sage [seɪdʒ] n (herb) salvia; (man)
saggio
Sagittarius [sædʒɪ'tɛərɪəs] n
Sagittario
Sahara [sə'hɑːrə] n **the ~ (Desert)** il
(deserto del) Sahara
said [sɛd] pt, pp of **say**
sail [seɪl] n (on boat) vela; (trip): **to
go for a ~** fare un giro in barca a vela
▷ vt (boat) condurre, governare ▷ vi
(travel: ship) navigare; (: passenger)
viaggiare per mare; (set off) salpare;
(sport) fare della vela; **they ~ed into
Genoa** entrarono nel porto di Genova;
sailboat (us) n barca a vela; **sailing**
n (sport) vela; **to go sailing** fare della
vela; **sailing boat** n barca a vela;
sailor n marinaio
saint [seɪnt] n santo(-a)
sake [seɪk] n **for the ~ of** per, per
amore di
salad ['sæləd] n insalata; **salad
cream** (BRIT) n (tipo di) maionese f;
salad dressing n condimento per
insalata
salami [sə'lɑːmɪ] n salame m
salary ['sælərɪ] n stipendio
sale [seɪl] n vendita; (at reduced
prices) svendita, liquidazione f;
(auction) vendita all'asta; **"for ~"**
"in vendita"; **on ~** in vendita; **on ~
or return** da vendere o rimandare;
sales npl (total amount sold) vendite
fpl; **sales assistant** (us **sales clerk**)
n commesso(-a); **salesman/
woman** (irreg) n commesso(-a);
(representative) rappresentante
m/f; **salesperson** (irreg) n (in
shop) commesso; (representative)
rappresentante m/f di commercio;
sales rep n rappresentante m/f di
commercio
saline ['seɪlaɪn] adj salino(-a)
saliva [sə'laɪvə] n saliva
salmon ['sæmən] n inv salmone m
salon ['sælɔn] n (hairdressing salon)
parrucchiere(-a); (beauty salon) salone
m di bellezza
saloon [sə'luːn] n (us) saloon m inv,
bar m inv; (BRIT: Aut) berlina; (ship's
lounge) salone m
salt [sɔlt] n sale m ▷ vt salare;
saltwater adj di mare; **salty** adj
salato(-a)
salute [sə'luːt] n saluto ▷ vt salutare
salvage ['sælvɪdʒ] n (saving)
salvataggio; (things saved) beni mpl
salvati or recuperati ▷ vt salvare,
mettere in salvo
Salvation Army [sæl'veɪʃən-] n
Esercito della Salvezza
same [seɪm] adj stesso(-a),
medesimo(-a) ▷ pron **the ~** lo (la)
stesso(-a), gli (le) stessi(-e); **the ~
book as** lo stesso libro di (o che); **at
the ~ time** allo stesso tempo; **all
or just the ~** tuttavia; **to do the ~
as sb** fare come qn; **the ~ to you!**
altrettanto a te!
sample ['sɑːmpl] n campione m ▷ vt
(food) assaggiare; (wine) degustare
sanction ['sæŋkʃən] n sanzione f ▷ vt
sancire, sanzionare; **sanctions** npl
(Pol) sanzioni fpl
sanctuary ['sæŋktjuərɪ] n (holy place)
santuario; (refuge) rifugio; (for wildlife)
riserva

sand [sænd] n sabbia ▷ vt (also: **~ down**) cartavetrare

sandal ['sændl] n sandalo

sand: **sandbox** ['sændbɔks] (US) n = **sandpit**; **sandcastle** ['sændkɑːsl] n castello di sabbia; **sand dune** n duna di sabbia; **sandpaper** ['sændpeɪpəʳ] n carta vetrata; **sandpit** ['sændpɪt] n (for children) buca di sabbia; **sands** npl spiaggia; **sandstone** ['sændstəʊn] n arenaria

sandwich ['sændwɪtʃ] n tramezzino, panino, sandwich m inv ▷ vt **~ed between** incastrato(-a) fra; **cheese/ ham ~** sandwich al formaggio/ prosciutto

sandy ['sændɪ] adj sabbioso(-a); (colour) color sabbia inv, biondo(-a) rossiccio(-a)

sane [seɪn] adj (person) sano(-a) di mente; (outlook) sensato(-a)

sang [sæŋ] pt of **sing**

sanitary towel ['sænɪtərɪ-] (US **sanitary napkin**) n assorbente m (igienico)

sanity ['sænɪtɪ] n sanità mentale; (common sense) buon senso

sank [sæŋk] pt of **sink**

Santa Claus [sæntə'klɔːz] n Babbo Natale

sap [sæp] n (of plants) linfa ▷ vt (strength) fiaccare

sapphire ['sæfaɪəʳ] n zaffiro

sarcasm ['sɑːkæzm] n sarcasmo

sarcastic [sɑː'kæstɪk] adj sarcastico(-a); **to be ~** fare del sarcasmo

sardine [sɑː'diːn] n sardina

Sardinia [sɑː'dɪnɪə] n Sardegna

SASE (US) n abbr (= self-addressed stamped envelope) busta affrancata e con indirizzo

sat [sæt] pt, pp of **sit**

Sat. abbr (= Saturday) sab.

satchel ['sætʃl] n cartella

satellite ['sætəlaɪt] adj satellite ▷ n satellite m; **satellite dish** n antenna parabolica; **satellite television** n televisione f via satellite

satin ['sætɪn] n raso ▷ adj di raso

satire ['sætaɪəʳ] n satira

satisfaction [sætɪs'fækʃən] n soddisfazione f

satisfactory [sætɪs'fæktərɪ] adj soddisfacente

satisfied ['sætɪsfaɪd] adj (customer) soddisfatto(-a); **to be ~ (with sth)** essere soddisfatto(-a) (di qc)

satisfy ['sætɪsfaɪ] vt soddisfare; (convince) convincere

Saturday ['sætədɪ] n sabato

sauce [sɔːs] n salsa; (containing meat, fish) sugo; **saucepan** n casseruola

saucer ['sɔːsəʳ] n sottocoppa m, piattino

Saudi Arabia ['saʊdɪ-] n Arabia Saudita

sauna ['sɔːnə] n sauna

sausage ['sɔsɪdʒ] n salsiccia; **sausage roll** n rotolo di pasta sfoglia ripieno di salsiccia

sautéed ['səʊteɪd] adj saltato(-a)

savage ['sævɪdʒ] adj (cruel, fierce) selvaggio(-a), feroce; (primitive) primitivo(-a) ▷ n selvaggio(-a) ▷ vt attaccare selvaggiamente

save [seɪv] vt (person, belongings, Comput) salvare; (money) risparmiare, mettere da parte; (time) risparmiare; (food) conservare; (avoid: trouble) evitare; (Sport) parare ▷ vi (also: **~ up**) economizzare ▷ n (Sport) parata ▷ prep salvo, a eccezione di

savings ['seɪvɪŋz] npl (money) risparmi mpl; **savings account** n libretto di risparmio; **savings and loan association** (US) n ≈ società di credito immobiliare

savoury ['seɪvərɪ] (US **savory**) adj (dish: not sweet) salato(-a)

saw [sɔː] (pt **sawed**, pp **sawed** or **sawn**) pt of **see** ▷ n (tool) sega ▷ vt segare; **sawdust** n segatura

sawn [sɔːn] pp of **saw**

saxophone ['sæksəfəun] *n*
sassofono

say [seɪ] (*pt, pp* **said**) *n* **to have one's ~**
fare sentire il proprio parere; **to have
a** *or* **some ~** avere voce in capitolo
▷ *vt* dire; **could you ~ that again?**
potrebbe ripeterlo?; **that goes
without ~ing** va da sé; **saying** *n*
proverbio, detto

scab [skæb] *n* crosta; (*pej*) crumiro(-a)

scaffolding ['skæfəldɪŋ] *n*
impalcatura

scald [skɔːld] *n* scottatura ▷ *vt*
scottare

scale [skeɪl] *n* scala; (*of fish*) squama
▷ *vt* (*mountain*) scalare; **scales** *npl*
(*for weighing*) bilancia; **on a large ~** su
vasta scala; **~ of charges** tariffa

scallion ['skæljən] *n* cipolla; (*us:
shallot*) scalogna; (*: leek*) porro

scallop ['skɔləp] *n* (*Zool*) pettine *m*;
(*Sewing*) smerlo

scalp [skælp] *n* cuoio capelluto ▷ *vt*
scotennare

scalpel ['skælpl] *n* bisturi *m inv*

scam [skæm] *n* (*inf*) truffa

scampi ['skæmpɪ] *npl* scampi *mpl*

scan [skæn] *vt* scrutare; (*glance at
quickly*) scorrere, dare un'occhiata a;
(*TV*) analizzare; (*Radar*) esplorare ▷ *n*
(*Med*) ecografia

scandal ['skændl] *n* scandalo; (*gossip*)
pettegolezzi *mpl*

Scandinavia [skændɪ'neɪvɪə] *n*
Scandinavia; **Scandinavian** *adj, n*
scandinavo(-a)

scanner ['skænər] *n* (*Radar, Med*)
scanner *m inv*

scapegoat ['skeɪpgəut] *n* capro
espiatorio

scar [skɑː] *n* cicatrice *f* ▷ *vt* sfregiare

scarce [skeəs] *adj* scarso(-a); (*copy,
edition*) raro(-a); **to make o.s. ~** (*inf*)
squagliarsela; **scarcely** *adv* appena

scare [skeər] *n* spavento; panico
▷ *vt* spaventare, atterrire; **there
was a bomb ~ at the bank** hanno
evacuato la banca per paura di un
attentato dinamitardo; **to ~ sb stiff**
spaventare a morte qn; **scarecrow** *n*
spaventapasseri *m inv*; **scared** *adj* **to
be scared** aver paura

scarf [skɑːf] (*pl* **scarves** *or* **scarfs**) *n*
(*long*) sciarpa; (*square*) fazzoletto da
testa, foulard *m inv*

scarlet ['skɑːlɪt] *adj* scarlatto(-a)

scarves [skɑːvz] *npl of* **scarf**

scary ['skɛərɪ] *adj* che spaventa

scatter ['skætər] *vt* spargere; (*crowd*)
disperdere ▷ *vi* disperdersi

scenario [sɪ'nɑːrɪəu] *n* (*Theatre,
Cinema*) copione *m*; (*fig*) situazione *f*

scene [siːn] *n* (*Theatre, fig etc*) scena;
(*of crime, accident*) scena, luogo;
(*sight, view*) vista, veduta; **scenery**
n (*Theatre*) scenario; (*landscape*)
panorama *m*; **scenic** *adj* scenico(-a);
panoramico(-a)

scent [sɛnt] *n* profumo; (*sense of smell*)
olfatto, odorato; (*fig: track*) pista

sceptical ['skɛptɪkəl] (*us* **skeptical**)
adj scettico(-a)

schedule ['ʃɛdjuːl, *us* 'skɛdjuːl]
n programma *m*, piano; (*of trains*)
orario; (*of prices etc*) lista, tabella ▷ *vt*
fissare; **on ~** in orario; **to be ahead
of/behind ~** essere in anticipo/ritardo
sul previsto; **scheduled flight** *n* volo
di linea

scheme [skiːm] *n* piano, progetto;
(*method*) sistema *m*; (*dishonest plan,
plot*) intrigo, trama; (*arrangement*)
disposizione *f*, sistemazione *f*; (*pension
scheme etc*) programma *m* ▷ *vi* fare
progetti; (*intrigue*) complottare

schizophrenic [skɪtsə'frɛnɪk] *adj, n*
schizofrenico(-a)

scholar ['skɔlər] *n* (*expert*)
studioso(-a); **scholarship** *n*
erudizione *f*; (*grant*) borsa di studio

school [skuːl] *n* (*primary, secondary*)
scuola; (*university: us*) università *f
inv* ▷ *cpd* scolare, scolastico(-a) ▷ *vt*
(*animal*) addestrare; **schoolbook** *n*

libro scolastico; **schoolboy** n scolaro;
school children npl scolari mpl;
schoolgirl n scolara; **schooling**
n istruzione f; **schoolteacher** n
insegnante m/f, docente m/f; (primary)
maestro(-a)

science ['saɪəns] n scienza; **science
fiction** n fantascienza; **scientific**
[-'tɪfɪk] adj scientifico(-a); **scientist** n
scienziato(-a)

sci-fi ['saɪfaɪ] n abbr (inf) = **science
fiction**

scissors ['sɪzəz] npl forbici fpl

scold [skəuld] vt rimproverare

scone [skɒn] n focaccina da tè

scoop [sku:p] n mestolo; (for ice cream)
cucchiaio dosatore; (Press) colpo
giornalistico, notizia (in) esclusiva

scooter ['sku:tə*] n (motor cycle)
motoretta, scooter m inv; (toy)
monopattino

scope [skəup] n (capacity: of plan,
undertaking) portata; (: of person)
capacità fpl; (opportunity) possibilità
fpl

scorching ['skɔ:tʃɪŋ] adj cocente,
scottante

score [skɔ:*] n punti mpl, punteggio;
(Mus) partitura, spartito; (twenty)
venti ▷ vt (goal, point) segnare, fare;
(success) ottenere ▷ vi segnare;
(Football) fare un goal; (keep score)
segnare i punti; **~s of** (very many)
un sacco di; **on that ~** a questo
riguardo; **to ~ 6 out of 10** prendere
6 su 10; **score out** vt cancellare
con un segno; **scoreboard** n
tabellone m segnapunti; **scorer** n
marcatore(-trice); (keeping score)
segnapunti m inv

scorn [skɔ:n] n disprezzo ▷ vt
disprezzare

Scorpio ['skɔ:pɪəu] n Scorpione m

scorpion ['skɔ:pɪən] n scorpione m

Scot [skɒt] n scozzese m/f

Scotch tape® n scotch® m

Scotland ['skɒtlənd] n Scozia

Scots [skɒts] adj scozzese; **Scotsman**
(irreg) n scozzese m; **Scotswoman**
(irreg) n scozzese f; **Scottish** ['skɒtɪʃ]
adj scozzese; **Scottish Parliament** n
Parlamento scozzese

scout [skaut] n (Mil) esploratore m;
(also: **boy ~**) giovane esploratore,
scout m inv

scowl [skaul] vi accigliarsi, aggrottare
le sopracciglia; **to ~ at** guardare torvo

scramble ['skræmbl] n arrampicata
▷ vi inerpicarsi; **to ~ out** etc uscire
etc in fretta; **to ~ for** azzuffarsi
per; **scrambled eggs** npl uova fpl
strapazzate

scrap [skræp] n pezzo, pezzetto;
(fight) zuffa; (also: **~ iron**) rottami
mpl di ferro, ferraglia ▷ vt demolire;
(fig) scartare ▷ vi **to ~ (with sb)** fare
a botte (con qn); **scraps** npl (waste)
scarti mpl; **scrapbook** n album m inv
di ritagli

scrape [skreɪp] vt, vi raschiare,
grattare ▷ n **to get into a ~** cacciarsi
in un guaio

scrap paper n cartaccia

scratch [skrætʃ] n graffio ▷ cpd **~
team** squadra raccogliticcia ▷ vt
graffiare, rigare ▷ vi grattare;
(paint, car) graffiare; **to start from ~**
cominciare or partire da zero; **to be up
to ~** essere all'altezza; **scratch card** n
(BRIT) cartolina f gratta e vinci

scream [skri:m] n grido, urlo ▷ vi
urlare, gridare

screen [skri:n] n schermo; (fig) muro,
cortina, velo ▷ vt schermare, fare
schermo a; (from the wind etc) riparare;
(film) proiettare; (book) adattare per lo
schermo; (candidates etc) selezionare;
screening n (Med) dépistage m inv;
screenplay n sceneggiatura; **screen
saver** n (Comput) screen saver m inv

screw [skru:] n vite f ▷ vt avvitare;
screw up vt (paper etc) spiegazzare;
(inf: ruin) rovinare; **to screw up one's
eyes** strizzare gli occhi; **screwdriver**

n cacciavite *m*

scribble ['skrɪbl] *n* scarabocchio ▷ *vt* scribacchiare in fretta ▷ *vi* scarabocchiare

script [skrɪpt] *n* (*Cinema etc*) copione *m*; (*in exam*) elaborato *or* compito d'esame

scroll [skrəul] *n* rotolo di carta

scrub [skrʌb] *n* (*land*) boscaglia ▷ *vt* pulire strofinando; (*reject*) annullare

scruffy ['skrʌfɪ] *adj* sciatto(-a)

scrum(mage) ['skrʌm(ɪdʒ)] *n* mischia

scrutiny ['skru:tɪnɪ] *n* esame *m* accurato

scuba diving ['sku:bə-] *n* immersioni *fpl* subacquee

sculptor ['skʌlptəʳ] *n* scultore *m*

sculpture ['skʌlptʃəʳ] *n* scultura

scum [skʌm] *n* schiuma; (*pej: people*) feccia

scurry ['skʌrɪ] *vi* sgambare, affrettarsi

sea [si:] *n* mare *m* ▷ *cpd* marino(-a), del mare; (*bird, fish*) di mare; (*route, transport*) marittimo(-a); **by ~** (*travel*) per mare; **on the ~** (*boat*) in mare; (*town*) di mare; **to be all at ~** (*fig*) non sapere che pesci pigliare; **out to ~** al largo; **(out) at ~** in mare; **seafood** *n* frutti *mpl* di mare; **sea front** *n* lungomare *m*; **seagull** *n* gabbiano

seal [si:l] *n* (*animal*) foca; (*stamp*) sigillo; (*impression*) impronta del sigillo ▷ *vt* sigillare; **seal off** *vt* (*close*) sigillare; (*forbid entry to*) bloccare l'accesso a

sea level *n* livello del mare

seam [si:m] *n* cucitura; (*of coal*) filone *m*

search [sə:tʃ] *n* ricerca; (*Law: at sb's home*) perquisizione *f* ▷ *vt* frugare ▷ *vi* **to ~ for** ricercare; **in ~ of** alla ricerca di; **search engine** *n* (*Comput*) motore *m* di ricerca; **search party** *n* squadra di soccorso

sea: **seashore** ['si:ʃɔ:ʳ] *n* spiaggia; **seasick** ['si:sɪk] *adj* che soffre il mal

di mare; **seaside** ['si:saɪd] *n* spiaggia; **seaside resort** *n* stazione *f* balneare

season ['si:zn] *n* stagione *f* ▷ *vt* condire, insaporire; **seasonal** *adj* stagionale; **seasoning** *n* condimento; **season ticket** *n* abbonamento

seat [si:t] *n* sedile *m*; (*in bus, train: place*) posto; (*Parliament*) seggio; (*buttocks*) didietro; (*of trousers*) fondo ▷ *vt* far sedere; (*have room for*) avere *or* essere fornito(-a) di posti a sedere per; **I'd like to book two ~s** vorrei prenotare due posti; **to be ~ed** essere seduto(-a); **seat belt** *n* cintura di sicurezza; **seating** *n* posti *mpl* a sedere

sea: **sea water** *n* acqua di mare; **seaweed** ['si:wi:d] *n* alghe *fpl*

sec. *abbr* = **second(s)**

secluded [sɪ'klu:dɪd] *adj* isolato(-a), appartato(-a)

second ['sɛkənd] *num* secondo(-a) ▷ *adv* (*in race etc*) al secondo posto ▷ *n* (*unit of time*) secondo; (*Aut: also:* **~ gear**) seconda; (*Comm: imperfect*) scarto; (*BRIT: Scol: degree*) laurea con punteggio discreto ▷ *vt* (*motion*) appoggiare; **secondary** *adj* secondario(-a); **secondary school** *n* scuola secondaria; **second-class** *adj* di seconda classe ▷ *adv* in seconda classe; **secondhand** *adj* di seconda mano, usato(-a); **secondly** *adv* in secondo luogo; **second-rate** *adj* scadente; **second thoughts** *npl* ripensamenti *mpl*; **on second thoughts** (*BRIT*) *or* **thought** (*US*) ripensandoci bene

secrecy ['si:krəsɪ] *n* segretezza

secret ['si:krɪt] *adj* segreto(-a) ▷ *n* segreto; **in ~** in segreto

secretary ['sɛkrətrɪ] *n* segretario(-a); **S~ of State (for)** (*BRIT: Pol*) ministro (di)

secretive ['si:krətɪv] *adj* riservato(-a)

secret service *n* servizi *mpl* segreti

sect [sɛkt] n setta

section ['sɛkʃən] n sezione f

sector ['sɛktər] n settore m

secular ['sɛkjulər] adj secolare

secure [sɪ'kjuər] adj sicuro(-a); (firmly fixed) assicurato(-a), ben fermato(-a); (in safe place) al sicuro ▷ vt (fix) fissare, assicurare; (get) ottenere, assicurarsi; **securities** npl (Stock Exchange) titoli mpl

security [sɪ'kjuərɪtɪ] n sicurezza; (for loan) garanzia; **security guard** n guardia giurata

sedan [sə'dæn] (US) n (Aut) berlina

sedate [sɪ'deɪt] adj posato(-a), calmo(-a) ▷ vt calmare

sedative ['sɛdɪtɪv] n sedativo, calmante m

seduce [sɪ'djuːs] vt sedurre; **seductive** [-'dʌktɪv] adj seducente

see [siː] (pt **saw**, pp **seen**) vt vedere; (accompany): **to ~ sb to the door** accompagnare qn alla porta ▷ vi vedere; (understand) capire ▷ n sede f vescovile; **to ~ that** (ensure) badare che + sub, fare in modo che + sub; **~ you soon!** a presto!; **see off** vt salutare alla partenza; **see out** vt (take to the door) accompagnare alla porta; **see through** vt portare a termine ▷ vt fus non lasciarsi ingannare da; **see to** vt fus occuparsi di

seed [siːd] n seme m; (fig) germe m; (Tennis etc) testa di serie; **to go to ~** fare seme; (fig) scadere

seeing ['siːɪŋ] conj **~ (that)** visto che

seek [siːk] (pt, pp **sought**) vt cercare

seem [siːm] vi sembrare, parere; **there ~s to be ...** sembra che ci sia ...; **seemingly** adv apparentemente

seen [siːn] pp of **see**

seesaw ['siːsɔː] n altalena a bilico

segment ['sɛgmənt] n segmento

segregate ['sɛgrɪgeɪt] vt segregare, isolare

seize [siːz] vt (grasp) afferrare; (take possession of) impadronirsi di; (Law) sequestrare

seizure ['siːʒər] n (Med) attacco; (Law) confisca, sequestro

seldom ['sɛldəm] adv raramente

select [sɪ'lɛkt] adj scelto(-a) ▷ vt scegliere, selezionare; **selection** [-'lɛkʃən] n selezione f, scelta; **selective** adj selettivo(-a)

self [sɛlf] n **the ~** l'io m ▷ prefix auto...; **self-assured** adj sicuro(-a) di sé; **self-catering** (BRIT) adj in cui ci si cucina da sé; **self-centred** (US **self-centered**) adj egocentrico(-a); **self-confidence** n sicurezza di sé; **self-confident** adj sicuro(-a) di sé; **self-conscious** adj timido(-a); **self-contained** (BRIT) adj (flat) indipendente; **self-control** n autocontrollo; **self-defence** (US **self-defense**) n autodifesa; (Law) legittima difesa; **self-drive** adj (BRIT: rented car) senza autista; **self-employed** adj che lavora in proprio; **self-esteem** n amor proprio m; **self-indulgent** adj indulgente verso se stesso(-a); **self-interest** n interesse m personale; **selfish** adj egoista; **self-pity** n autocommiserazione f; **self-raising** (US **self-rising**) adj **self-raising flour** miscela di farina e lievito; **self-respect** n rispetto di sé, amor proprio; **self-service** n autoservizio, self-service m

sell [sɛl] (pt, pp **sold**) vt vendere ▷ vi vendersi; **to ~ at** or **for 1000 euros** essere in vendita a 1000 euro; **sell off** vt svendere, liquidare; **sell out** vi **to sell out (of sth)** esaurire (qc); **the tickets are all sold out** i biglietti sono esauriti; **sell-by date** ['sɛlbaɪ-] n data di scadenza; **seller** n venditore(-trice)

Sellotape® ['sɛləuteɪp] (BRIT) n nastro adesivo, scotch® m

selves [sɛlvz] npl of **self**

semester [sɪ'mɛstər] (US) n semestre m

semi... ['sɛmɪ] prefix semi...;

semicircle n semicerchio;
semidetached (house)
[sɛmɪdɪ'tætʃt-] (BRIT) n casa gemella;
semi-final n semifinale f
seminar ['sɛmɪnɑːʳ] n seminario
semi-skimmed ['sɛmɪ'skɪmd] adj
(milk) parzialmente scremato(-a)
senate ['sɛnɪt] n senato; **senator** n
senatore(-trice)
send [sɛnd] (pt, pp **sent**) vt mandare;
send back vt rimandare; **send
for** vt fus mandare a chiamare,
far venire; **send in** vt (report,
application, resignation) presentare;
send off vt (goods) spedire; (BRIT:
Sport: player) espellere; **send on** vt
(BRIT: letter) inoltrare; (luggage etc:
in advance) spedire in anticipo; **send
out** vt (invitation) diramare; **send
up** vt (person, price) far salire; (BRIT:
parody) mettere in ridicolo; **sender**
n mittente m/f; **send-off** n **to give
sb a good send-off** festeggiare la
partenza di qn
senile ['siːnaɪl] adj senile
senior ['siːnɪəʳ] adj (older) più
vecchio(-a); (of higher rank) di grado
più elevato; **senior citizen** n persona
anziana; **senior high school** (US) n
≈ liceo
sensation [sɛn'seɪʃən] n sensazione
f; **sensational** adj sensazionale;
(marvellous) eccezionale
sense [sɛns] n senso; (feeling)
sensazione f, senso; (meaning) senso,
significato; (wisdom) buonsenso ▷ vt
sentire, percepire; **it makes ~** ha
senso; **senseless** adj sciocco(-a);
(unconscious) privo(-a) di sensi;
sense of humour (BRIT) n senso
dell'umorismo
sensible ['sɛnsɪbl] adj sensato(-a),
ragionevole

Be careful not to translate
sensible by the Italian word
sensibile.

sensitive ['sɛnsɪtɪv] adj sensibile;
(skin, question) delicato(-a)
sensual ['sɛnsjuəl] adj sensuale
sensuous ['sɛnsjuəs] adj sensuale
sent [sɛnt] pt, pp of **send**
sentence ['sɛntns] n (Ling) frase
f; (Law: judgment) sentenza;
(: punishment) condanna ▷ vt **to ~ sb
to death/to 5 years** condannare qn a
morte/a 5 anni
sentiment ['sɛntɪmənt] n
sentimento; (opinion) opinione
f; **sentimental** [-'mɛntl] adj
sentimentale
Sep. abbr (= September) Sett.
separate [adj 'sɛprɪt, vb 'sɛpəreɪt]
adj separato(-a) ▷ vt separare
▷ vi separarsi; **separately** adv
separatamente; **separates** npl
(clothes) coordinati mpl; **separation**
[-'reɪʃən] n separazione f
September [sɛp'tɛmbəʳ] n
settembre m
septic ['sɛptɪk] adj settico(-a); (wound)
infettato(-a); **septic tank** n fossa
settica
sequel ['siːkwl] n conseguenza; (of
story) seguito; (of film) sequenza
sequence ['siːkwəns] n (series) serie f;
(order) ordine m
sequin ['siːkwɪn] n lustrino, paillette
f inv
Serb [sɜːb] adj, n = **Serbian**
Serbia ['sɜːbɪə] n Serbia
Serbian ['sɜːbɪən] adj serbo(-a) ▷ n
serbo(-a); (Ling) serbo
sergeant ['sɑːdʒənt] n sergente m;
(Police) brigadiere m
serial ['sɪərɪəl] n (Press) romanzo a
puntate; (Radio, TV) trasmissione f a
puntate, serial m inv; **serial killer** n
serial-killer m/f inv; **serial number** n
numero di serie
series ['sɪəriːz] n inv serie f inv;
(Publishing) collana
serious ['sɪərɪəs] adj serio(-a), grave;
seriously adv seriamente
sermon ['sɜːmən] n sermone m

servant ['sə:vənt] n domestico(-a)
serve [sə:v] vt (employer etc) servire,
essere a servizio di; (purpose) servire
a; (customer, food, meal) servire;
(apprenticeship) fare; (prison term)
scontare ▷ vi (also Tennis) servire; (be
useful): **to ~ as/for/to do** servire da/
per/per fare ▷ n (Tennis) servizio; **it ~s
him right** ben gli sta, se l'è meritata;
server n (Comput) server m inv
service ['sə:vɪs] n servizio; (Aut:
maintenance) assistenza, revisione f
▷ vt (car, washing machine) revisionare;
to be of ~ to sb essere d'aiuto a qn;
~ included/not included servizio
compreso/escluso; **services** (BRIT:
on motorway) stazione f di servizio;
(Mil): **the S~s** le Forze Armate;
service area n (on motorway) area
di servizio; **service charge** (BRIT) n
servizio; **serviceman** (irreg) n militare
m; **service station** n stazione f di
servizio
serviette [sə:vɪ'ɛt] (BRIT) n tovagliolo
session ['sɛʃən] n (sitting) seduta,
sessione f; (Scol) anno scolastico (or
accademico)
set [sɛt] (pt, pp set) n serie f inv;
(of cutlery etc) servizio; (Radio, TV)
apparecchio; (Tennis) set m inv;
(group of people) mondo, ambiente
m; (Cinema) scenario; (Theatre: stage)
scene fpl; (: scenery) scenario; (Math)
insieme m; (Hairdressing) messa
in piega ▷ adj (fixed) stabilito(-a),
determinato(-a); (ready) pronto(-a)
▷ vt (place) posare, mettere; (arrange)
sistemare; (fix) fissare; (adjust)
regolare; (decide: rules etc) stabilire,
fissare ▷ vi (sun) tramontare; (jam,
jelly) rapprendersi; (concrete) fare
presa; **to be ~ on doing** essere deciso
a fare; **to ~ to music** mettere in
musica; **to ~ on fire** dare fuoco a; **to ~
free** liberare; **to ~ sth going** mettere
in moto qc; **to ~ sail** prendere il mare;
set aside vt mettere da parte; **set

down** vt (bus, train) lasciare; **set in** vi
(infection) svilupparsi; (complications)
intervenire; **the rain has set in for
the day** ormai pioverà tutto il giorno;
set off vi partire ▷ vt (bomb) far
scoppiare; (cause to start) mettere in
moto; (show up well) dare risalto a; **set
out** vi partire ▷ vt (arrange) disporre;
(state) esporre, presentare; **to set
out to do** proporsi di fare; **set up** vt
(organization) fondare, costituire;
setback n (hitch) contrattempo,
inconveniente m; **set menu** n menù
m inv fisso
settee [sɛ'ti:] n divano, sofà m inv
setting ['sɛtɪŋ] n (background)
ambiente m; (of controls) posizione f;
(of sun) tramonto; (of jewel) montatura
settle ['sɛtl] vt (argument, matter)
appianare; (accounts) regolare; (Med:
calm) calmare ▷ vi (bird, dust etc)
posarsi; (sediment) depositarsi; **to ~
for sth** accontentarsi di qc; **to ~ on
sth** decidersi per qc; **settle down**
vi (get comfortable) sistemarsi; (calm
down) calmarsi; (get back to normal:
situation) tornare alla normalità;
settle in vi sistemarsi; **settle up** vi
to settle up with sb regolare i conti
con qn; **settlement** n (payment)
pagamento, saldo; (agreement)
accordo; (colony) colonia; (village etc)
villaggio, comunità f inv
setup ['sɛtʌp] n (arrangement)
sistemazione f; (situation) situazione f
seven ['sɛvn] num sette; **seventeen**
num diciassette; **seventeenth**
[sɛvn'ti:nθ] num diciassettesimo(-a);
seventh num settimo(-a);
seventieth ['sɛvntɪɪθ] num
settantesimo(-a); **seventy** num
settanta
sever ['sɛvər] vt recidere, tagliare;
(relations) troncare
several ['sɛvərl] adj, pron alcuni(-e),
diversi(-e); **~ of us** alcuni di noi
severe [sɪ'vɪər] adj severo(-a); (serious)

serio(-a), grave; (*hard*) duro(-a); (*plain*)
semplice, sobrio(-a)

sew [səʊ] (*pt* **sewed**, *pp* **sewn**) *vt, vi*
cucire

sewage ['suːɪdʒ] *n* acque *fpl* di scolo

sewer ['suːəʳ] *n* fogna

sewing ['səʊɪŋ] *n* cucitura; cucito;
sewing machine *n* macchina da
cucire

sewn [səʊn] *pp of* **sew**

sex [sɛks] *n* sesso; **to have ~ with**
avere rapporti sessuali con; **sexism**
['sɛksɪzəm] *n* sessismo; **sexist** *adj,
n* sessista *m/f*; **sexual** ['sɛksjuəl]
adj sessuale; **sexual intercourse**
n rapporti *mpl* sessuali; **sexuality**
[sɛksju'ælɪtɪ] *n* sessualità; **sexy**
['sɛksɪ] *adj* provocante, sexy *inv*

shabby ['ʃæbɪ] *adj* malandato(-a);
(*behaviour*) vergognoso(-a)

shack [ʃæk] *n* baracca, capanna

shade [ʃeɪd] *n* ombra; (*for lamp*)
paralume *m*; (*of colour*) tonalità *f inv*;
(*small quantity*): **a ~ (more/too large)**
un po' (di più/troppo grande) ▷ *vt*
ombreggiare, fare ombra a; **in the ~**
all'ombra; **shades** (*US*) *npl* (*sunglasses*)
occhiali *mpl* da sole

shadow ['ʃædəʊ] *n* ombra ▷ *vt*
(*follow*) pedinare; **shadow cabinet**
(*BRIT*) *n* (*Pol*) governo *m* ombra *inv*

shady ['ʃeɪdɪ] *adj* ombroso(-a); (*fig:
dishonest*) losco(-a), equivoco(-a)

shaft [ʃɑːft] *n* (*of arrow, spear*) asta;
(*Aut, Tech*) albero; (*of mine*) pozzo; (*of
lift*) tromba; (*of light*) raggio

shake [ʃeɪk] (*pt* **shook**, *pp* **shaken**) *vt*
scuotere; (*bottle, cocktail*) agitare ▷ *vi*
tremare; **to ~ one's head** (*in refusal,
dismay*) scuotere la testa; **to ~ hands
with sb** stringere *or* dare la mano a
qn; **shake off** *vt* scrollare (via); (*fig*)
sbarazzarsi di; **shake up** *vt* scuotere;
shaky *adj* (*hand, voice*) tremante;
(*building*) traballante

shall [ʃæl] *aux vb* **I ~ go** andrò; **~ I open
the door?** apro io la porta?; **I'll get**

some, ~ I? ne prendo un po', va bene?

shallow ['ʃæləʊ] *adj* poco
profondo(-a); (*fig*) superficiale

sham [ʃæm] *n* finzione *f*, messinscena;
(*jewellery, furniture*) imitazione *f*

shambles ['ʃæmblz] *n* confusione *f*,
baraonda, scompiglio

shame [ʃeɪm] *n* vergogna ▷ *vt* far
vergognare; **it is a ~ (that/to
do)** è un peccato (che + *sub*/fare);
what a ~! che peccato!; **shameful**
adj vergognoso(-a); **shameless**
adj sfrontato(-a); (*immodest*)
spudorato(-a)

shampoo [ʃæm'puː] *n* shampoo *m inv*
▷ *vt* fare lo shampoo a

shandy ['ʃændɪ] *n* birra con gassosa

shan't [ʃɑːnt] = **shall not**

shape [ʃeɪp] *n* forma ▷ *vt* formare;
(*statement*) formulare; (*sb's ideas*)
condizionare; **to take ~** prendere
forma

share [ʃɛəʳ] *n* (*thing received,
contribution*) parte *f*; (*Comm*) azione
f ▷ *vt* dividere; (*have in common*)
condividere, avere in comune;
shareholder *n* azionista *m/f*

shark [ʃɑːk] *n* squalo, pescecane *m*

sharp [ʃɑːp] *adj* (*razor, knife*)
affilato(-a); (*point*) acuto(-a),
acuminato(-a); (*nose, chin*) aguzzo(-a);
(*outline, contrast*) netto(-a); (*cold,
pain*) pungente; (*voice*) stridulo(-a);
(*person: quick-witted*) sveglio(-a);
(: *unscrupulous*) disonesto(-a); (*Mus*):
C ~ do diesis ▷ *n* (*Mus*) diesis *m inv*
▷ *adv* **at 2 o'clock ~** alle due in punto;
sharpen *vt* affilare; (*pencil*) fare
la punta a; (*fig*) aguzzare; **sharpener**
n (*also:* **pencil sharpener**)
temperamatite *m inv*; **sharply** *adv*
(*turn, stop*) bruscamente; (*stand out,
contrast*) nettamente; (*criticize, retort*)
duramente, aspramente

shatter ['ʃætəʳ] *vt* mandare in
frantumi, frantumare; (*fig: upset*)
distruggere; (: *ruin*) rovinare ▷ *vi*

frantumarsi, andare in pezzi; **shattered** adj (grief-stricken) sconvolto(-a); (exhausted) a pezzi, distrutto(-a)

shave [ʃeɪv] vt radere, rasare ▷ vi radersi, farsi la barba ▷ n **to have a ~** farsi la barba; **shaver** n (also: **electric shaver**) rasoio elettrico

shaving cream n crema da barba

shaving foam n = **shaving cream**

shavings ['ʃeɪvɪŋz] npl (of wood etc) trucioli mpl

shawl [ʃɔːl] n scialle m

she [ʃiː] pron ella, lei; **~-cat** gatta; **~-elephant** elefantessa

sheath [ʃiːθ] n fodero, guaina; (contraceptive) preservativo

shed [ʃɛd] (pt, pp **shed**) n capannone m ▷ vt (leaves, fur etc) perdere; (tears, blood) versare; (workers) liberarsi di

she'd [ʃiːd] = **she had; she would**

sheep [ʃiːp] n inv pecora; **sheepdog** n cane m da pastore; **sheepskin** n pelle f di pecora

sheer [ʃɪəʳ] adj (utter) vero(-a) (e proprio(-a)); (steep) a picco, perpendicolare; (almost transparent) sottile ▷ adv a picco

sheet [ʃiːt] n (on bed) lenzuolo; (of paper) foglio; (of glass, ice) lastra; (of metal) foglio, lamina

sheik(h) [ʃeɪk] n sceicco

shelf [ʃɛlf] (pl **shelves**) n scaffale m, mensola

shell [ʃɛl] n (on beach) conchiglia; (of egg, nut etc) guscio; (explosive) granata; (of building) scheletro ▷ vt (peas) sgranare; (Mil) bombardare

she'll [ʃiːl] = **she will; she shall**

shellfish ['ʃɛlfɪʃ] n inv (crab etc) crostaceo; (scallop etc) mollusco; (as food) crostacei; molluschi

shelter ['ʃɛltəʳ] n riparo, rifugio ▷ vt riparare, proteggere; (give lodging to) dare rifugio or asilo a ▷ vi ripararsi, mettersi al riparo; **sheltered** adj riparato(-a)

shelves ['ʃɛlvz] npl of **shelf**

shelving ['ʃɛlvɪŋ] n scaffalature fpl

shepherd ['ʃɛpəd] n pastore m ▷ vt (guide) guidare; **shepherd's pie** (BRIT) n timballo di carne macinata e purè di patate

sheriff ['ʃɛrɪf] (US) n sceriffo

sherry ['ʃɛrɪ] n sherry m inv

she's [ʃiːz] = **she is; she has**

Shetland ['ʃɛtlənd] n (also: **the ~s, the ~ Isles**) le isole Shetland, le Shetland

shield [ʃiːld] n scudo; (trophy) scudetto; (protection) schermo ▷ vt **to ~ (from)** riparare (da), proteggere (da or contro)

shift [ʃɪft] n (change) cambiamento; (of workers) turno ▷ vt spostare, muovere; (remove) rimuovere ▷ vi spostarsi, muoversi

shin [ʃɪn] n tibia

shine [ʃaɪn] (pt, pp **shone**) n splendore m, lucentezza ▷ vi (ri)splendere, brillare ▷ vt far brillare, far risplendere; (torch): **to ~ sth on** puntare qc verso

shingles ['ʃɪŋglz] n (Med) herpes zoster m

shiny ['ʃaɪnɪ] adj lucente, lucido(-a)

ship [ʃɪp] n nave f ▷ vt trasportare (via mare); (send) spedire (via mare); **shipment** n carico; **shipping** n (ships) naviglio; (traffic) navigazione f; **shipwreck** n relitto; (event) naufragio ▷ vt **to be shipwrecked** naufragare, fare naufragio; **shipyard** n cantiere m navale

shirt [ʃəːt] n camicia; **in ~ sleeves** in maniche di camicia

shit [ʃɪt] (infl) excl merda (!)

shiver ['ʃɪvəʳ] n brivido ▷ vi rabbrividire, tremare

shock [ʃɔk] n (impact) urto, colpo; (Elec) scossa; (emotional) colpo, shock m inv; (Med) shock ▷ vt colpire, scioccare; scandalizzare; **shocking** adj scioccante, traumatizzante;

scandaloso(-a)

shoe [ʃuː] (pt, pp **shod**) n scarpa; (also: **horse~**) ferro di cavallo ▷ vt (horse) ferrare; **shoelace** n stringa; **shoe polish** n lucido per scarpe; **shoeshop** n calzoleria

shone [ʃɔn] pt, pp of **shine**

shook [ʃuk] pt of **shake**

shoot [ʃuːt] (pt, pp **shot**) n (on branch, seedling) germoglio ▷ vt (game) cacciare, andare a caccia di; (person) sparare a; (execute) fucilare; (film) girare ▷ vi (with gun): **to ~ (at)** sparare (a), fare fuoco (su); (with bow): **to ~ (at)** tirare (su); (Football) sparare, tirare (forte); **shoot down** vt (plane) abbattere; **shoot up** vi (fig) salire alle stelle; **shooting** n (shots) sparatoria; (Hunting) caccia

shop [ʃɔp] n negozio; (workshop) officina ▷ vi (also: **go ~ping**) fare spese; **shop assistant** (BRIT) n commesso(-a); **shopkeeper** n negoziante m/f, bottegaio(-a); **shoplifting** n taccheggio; **shopping** n (goods) spesa, acquisti mpl; **shopping bag** n borsa per la spesa; **shopping centre** (US **shopping center**) n centro commerciale; **shopping mall** n centro commerciale; **shopping trolley** n (BRIT) carrello del supermercato; **shop window** n vetrina

shore [ʃɔːʳ] n (of sea) riva, spiaggia; (of lake) riva ▷ vt **to ~ (up)** puntellare; **on ~** a riva

short [ʃɔːt] adj (not long) corto(-a); (soon finished) breve; (person) basso(-a); (curt) brusco(-a), secco(-a); (insufficient) insufficiente ▷ n (also: **~ film**) cortometraggio; **to be ~ of sth** essere a corto di or mancare di qc; **in ~** in breve; **~ of doing** a meno che non si faccia; **everything ~ of** tutto fuorché; **it is ~ for** è l'abbreviazione or il diminutivo di; **to cut ~** (speech, visit) accorciare, abbreviare; **to fall**

~ of venir meno a; non soddisfare; **to run ~** rimanere senza; **to stop ~** fermarsi di colpo; **to stop ~ of** non arrivare fino a; **shortage** n scarsezza, carenza; **shortbread** n biscotto di pasta frolla; **shortcoming** n difetto; **short(crust) pastry** (BRIT) n pasta frolla; **shortcut** n scorciatoia; **shorten** vt accorciare, ridurre; **shortfall** n deficit m; **shorthand** (BRIT) n stenografia; **short-lived** adj di breve durata; **shortly** adv fra poco; **shorts** npl (also: **a pair of shorts**) i calzoncini; **short-sighted** (BRIT) adj miope; **short-sleeved** [ˈʃɔːtsliːvd] adj a maniche corte; **short story** n racconto, novella; **short-tempered** adj irascibile; **short-term** adj (effect) di or a breve durata; (borrowing) a breve scadenza

shot [ʃɔt] pt, pp of **shoot** ▷ n sparo, colpo; (try) prova; (Football) tiro; (injection) iniezione f; (Phot) foto f inv; **like a ~** come un razzo; (very readily) immediatamente; **shotgun** n fucile m da caccia

should [ʃud] aux vb **I ~ go now** dovrei andare ora; **he ~ be there now** dovrebbe essere arrivato ora; **I ~ go if I were you** se fossi in te andrei; **I ~ like to** mi piacerebbe

shoulder [ˈʃəuldəʳ] n spalla; (BRIT: of road): **hard ~** banchina ▷ vt (fig) addossarsi, prendere sulle proprie spalle; **shoulder blade** n scapola

shouldn't [ˈʃudnt] = **should not**

shout [ʃaut] n urlo, grido ▷ vt gridare ▷ vi (also: **~ out**) urlare, gridare

shove [ʃʌv] vt spingere; (inf: put): **to ~ sth in** ficcare qc in

shovel [ˈʃʌvl] n pala ▷ vt spalare

show [ʃəu] (pt **showed**, pp **shown**) n (of emotion) dimostrazione f, manifestazione f; (semblance) apparenza; (exhibition) mostra, esposizione f; (Theatre, Cinema) spettacolo ▷ vt far vedere, mostrare;

(*courage etc*) dimostrare, dar prova di; (*exhibit*) esporre ▷ vi vedersi, essere visibile; **for ~** per fare scena; **on ~** (*exhibits etc*) esposto(-a); **can you ~ me where it is, please?** può mostrarmi dov'è, per favore?; **show in** vt (*person*) far entrare; **show off** vi (*pej*) esibirsi, mettersi in mostra ▷ vt (*display*) mettere in risalto; (*pej*) mettere in mostra; **show out** vt (*person*) accompagnare alla porta; **show up** vi (*stand out*) essere ben visibile; (*inf: turn up*) farsi vedere ▷ vt mettere in risalto; **show business** n industria dello spettacolo

shower ['ʃauəʳ] n (*rain*) acquazzone m; (*of stones etc*) pioggia; (*also:* **~bath**) doccia ▷ vi fare la doccia ▷ vt **to ~ sb with** (*gifts, abuse etc*) coprire qn di; (*missiles*) lanciare contro qn una pioggia di; **to have a ~** fare la doccia; **shower cap** n cuffia da doccia; **shower gel** n gel m doccia inv

showing ['ʃəuɪŋ] n (*of film*) proiezione f

show jumping n concorso ippico (di salto ad ostacoli)

shown [ʃəun] pp of **show**

show: **show-off** (*inf*) n (*person*) esibizionista m/f; **showroom** n sala d'esposizione

shrank [ʃræŋk] pt of **shrink**

shred [ʃrɛd] n (*gen pl*) brandello ▷ vt fare a brandelli; (*Culin*) sminuzzare, tagliuzzare

shrewd [ʃruːd] adj astuto(-a), scaltro(-a)

shriek [ʃriːk] n strillo ▷ vi strillare

shrimp [ʃrɪmp] n gamberetto

shrine [ʃraɪn] n reliquario; (*place*) santuario

shrink [ʃrɪŋk] (pt **shrank**, pp **shrunk**) vi restringersi; (*fig*) ridursi; (*also:* **~ away**) ritrarsi ▷ vt (*wool*) far restringere ▷ n (*inf: pej*) psicanalista m/f; **to ~ from doing sth** rifuggire dal fare qc

shrivel ['ʃrɪvl] (*also:* **~ up**) vt raggrinzire, avvizzire ▷ vi raggrinzirsi, avvizzire

shroud [ʃraud] n lenzuolo funebre ▷ vt **~ed in mystery** avvolto(-a) nel mistero

Shrove Tuesday ['ʃrəuv-] n martedì m grasso

shrub [ʃrʌb] n arbusto

shrug [ʃrʌg] n scrollata di spalle ▷ vt, vi **to ~ (one's shoulders)** alzare le spalle, fare spallucce; **shrug off** vt passare sopra a

shrunk [ʃrʌŋk] pp of **shrink**

shudder ['ʃʌdəʳ] n brivido ▷ vi rabbrividire

shuffle ['ʃʌfl] vt (*cards*) mescolare; **to ~ (one's feet)** strascicare i piedi

shun [ʃʌn] vt sfuggire, evitare

shut [ʃʌt] (pt, pp **shut**) vt chiudere ▷ vi chiudersi, chiudere; **shut down** vt, vi chiudere definitivamente; **shut up** vi (*inf: keep quiet*) stare zitto(-a), fare silenzio ▷ vt (*close*) chiudere; (*silence*) far tacere; **shutter** n imposta; (*Phot*) otturatore m

shuttle ['ʃʌtl] n spola, navetta; (*space shuttle*) navetta (spaziale); (*also:* **~ service**) servizio m navetta inv; **shuttlecock** ['ʃʌtlkɔk] n volano

shy [ʃaɪ] adj timido(-a)

sibling ['sɪblɪŋ] n (*formal*) fratello/sorella

Sicily ['sɪsɪlɪ] n Sicilia

sick [sɪk] adj (*ill*) malato(-a); (*vomiting*): **to be ~** vomitare; (*humour*) macabro(-a); **to feel ~** avere la nausea; **to be ~ of** (*fig*) averne abbastanza di; **sickening** adj (*fig*) disgustoso(-a), rivoltante; **sick leave** n congedo per malattia; **sickly** adj malaticcio(-a); (*causing nausea*) nauseante; **sickness** n malattia; (*vomiting*) vomito

side [saɪd] n lato; (*of lake*) riva; (*team*) squadra ▷ cpd (*door, entrance*) laterale ▷ vi **to ~ with sb** parteggiare per qn, prendere le parti di qn; **by the ~ of** a fianco di; (*road*) sul ciglio di; **~ by ~** fianco a fianco; **from ~ to ~** da una parte all'altra; **to take ~s (with)** schierarsi (con); **sideboard** n credenza; **sideboards** (*BRIT*), **sideburns** ['saɪdbə:nz] npl (*whiskers*) basette fpl; **sidelight** n (*Aut*) luce f di posizione; **sideline** n (*Sport*) linea laterale; (*fig*) attività secondaria; **side order** n contorno (*pietanza*); **side road** n strada secondaria; **side street** n traversa; **sidetrack** vt (*fig*) distrarre; **sidewalk** (*US*) n marciapiede m; **sideways** adv (*move*) di lato, di fianco

siege [si:dʒ] n assedio

sieve [sɪv] n setaccio ▷ vt setacciare

sift [sɪft] vt passare al crivello; (*fig*) vagliare

sigh [saɪ] n sospiro ▷ vi sospirare

sight [saɪt] n (*faculty*) vista; (*spectacle*) spettacolo; (*on gun*) mira ▷ vt avvistare; **in ~** in vista; **on ~** a vista; **out of ~** non visibile; **sightseeing** n giro turistico; **to go sightseeing** visitare una località

sign [saɪn] n segno; (*with hand etc*) segno, gesto; (*notice*) insegna, cartello ▷ vt firmare; (*player*) ingaggiare; **where do I ~?** dove devo firmare?; **sign for** vt fus (*item*) firmare per l'accettazione di; **sign in** vi firmare il registro (all'arrivo); **sign on** vi (*Mil*) arruolarsi; (*as unemployed*) iscriversi sulla lista (dell'ufficio di collocamento) ▷ vt (*Mil*) arruolare; (*employee*) assumere; **sign up** vi (*Mil*) arruolarsi; (*for course*) iscriversi ▷ vt (*player*) ingaggiare; (*recruits*) reclutare

signal ['sɪgnl] n segnale m ▷ vi (*Aut*) segnalare, mettere la freccia ▷ vt (*person*) fare segno a; (*message*) comunicare per mezzo di segnali

signature ['sɪgnətʃər] n firma

significance [sɪg'nɪfɪkəns] n significato; importanza

significant [sɪg'nɪfɪkənt] adj significativo(-a)

signify ['sɪgnɪfaɪ] vt significare

sign language n linguaggio dei muti

signpost ['saɪnpəust] n cartello indicatore

Sikh [si:k] adj, n sikh (*m/f*) inv

silence ['saɪlns] n silenzio ▷ vt tacere, ridurre al silenzio

silent ['saɪlnt] adj silenzioso(-a); (*film*) muto(-a); **to remain ~** tacere, stare zitto

silhouette [sɪlu:'ɛt] n silhouette f inv

silicon chip ['sɪlɪkən-] n piastrina di silicio

silk [sɪlk] n seta ▷ adj di seta

silly ['sɪlɪ] adj stupido(-a), sciocco(-a)

silver ['sɪlvər] n argento; (*money*) monete da 5, 10, 20 or 50 pence; (*also:* **~ware**) argenteria ▷ adj d'argento; **silver-plated** adj argentato(-a)

similar ['sɪmɪlər] adj **~ (to)** simile (a); **similarity** [sɪmɪ'lærɪtɪ] n somiglianza, rassomiglianza; **similarly** adv allo stesso modo; così pure

simmer ['sɪmər] vi cuocere a fuoco lento

simple ['sɪmpl] adj semplice; **simplicity** [-'plɪsɪtɪ] n semplicità; **simplify** vt semplificare; **simply** adv semplicemente

simulate ['sɪmjuleɪt] vt fingere, simulare

simultaneous [sɪməl'teɪnɪəs] adj simultaneo(-a); **simultaneously** adv simultaneamente, contemporaneamente

sin [sɪn] n peccato ▷ vi peccare

since [sɪns] adv da allora ▷ prep da ▷ conj (*time*) da quando; (*because*) poiché, dato che; **~ then, ever ~** da allora

sincere [sɪn'sɪər] adj sincero(-a); **sincerely** adv **yours sincerely** (*in letters*) distinti saluti

sing [sɪŋ] (*pt* **sang**, *pp* **sung**) vt, vi

cantare

Singapore [sɪŋɡə'pɔːʳ] n Singapore f

singer ['sɪŋəʳ] n cantante m/f

singing ['sɪŋɪŋ] n canto

single ['sɪŋɡl] adj solo(-a), unico(-a); (unmarried: man) celibe; (: woman) nubile; (not double) semplice ▷ n (BRIT: also: **~ ticket**) biglietto di (sola) andata; (record) 45 giri m; **singles** n (Tennis) singolo; **single out** vt scegliere; (distinguish) distinguere; **single bed** n letto singolo; **single file** n **in single file** in fila indiana; **single-handed** adv senza aiuto, da solo(-a); **single-minded** adj tenace, risoluto(-a); **single parent** n (mother) ragazza f madre inv; (father) ragazzo m padre inv; **single-parent family** famiglia monoparentale; **single room** n camera singola

singular ['sɪŋɡjʊləʳ] adj (exceptional, Ling) singolare ▷ n (Ling) singolare m

sinister ['sɪnɪstəʳ] adj sinistro(-a)

sink [sɪŋk] (pt **sank**, pp **sunk**) n lavandino, acquaio ▷ vt (ship) (fare) affondare, colare a picco; (foundations) scavare; (piles etc): **to ~ sth into** conficcare qc in ▷ vi affondare, andare a fondo; (ground etc) cedere, avvallarsi; **my heart sank** mi sentii venir meno; **sink in** vi penetrare

sinus ['saɪnəs] n (Anat) seno

sip [sɪp] n sorso ▷ vt sorseggiare

sir [səʳ] n signore m; **S~ John Smith** Sir John Smith; **yes ~** sì, signore

siren ['saɪərn] n sirena

sirloin ['səːlɔɪn] n controfiletto

sister ['sɪstəʳ] n sorella; (nun) suora; (BRIT: nurse) infermiera f caposala inv; **sister-in-law** n cognata

sit [sɪt] (pt, pp **sat**) vi sedere, sedersi; (assembly) essere in seduta; (for painter) posare ▷ vt (exam) sostenere, dare; **sit back** vi (in seat) appoggiarsi allo schienale; **sit down** vi sedersi; **sit on** vt fus (jury, committee) far parte di; **sit up** vi tirarsi su a sedere; (not go to

bed) stare alzato(-a) fino a tardi

sitcom ['sɪtkɔm] n abbr (= situation comedy) commedia di situazione; (TV) telefilm m inv comico d'interni

site [saɪt] n posto; (also: **building ~**) cantiere m ▷ vt situare

sitting ['sɪtɪŋ] n (of assembly etc) seduta; (in canteen) turno; **sitting room** n soggiorno

situated ['sɪtjʊeɪtɪd] adj situato(-a)

situation [sɪtjʊ'eɪʃən] n situazione f; (job) lavoro; (location) posizione f; **"~s vacant"** (BRIT) "offerte fpl di impiego"

six [sɪks] num sei; **sixteen** num sedici; **sixteenth** [sɪks'tiːnθ] num sedicesimo(-a); **sixth** num sesto(-a); **sixth form** n (BRIT) ultimo biennio delle scuole superiori; **sixth-form college** n istituto che offre corsi di preparazione all'esame di maturità per ragazzi dai 16 ai 18 anni; **sixtieth** ['sɪkstɪɪθ] num sessantesimo(-a) ▷ pron (in series) sessantesimo(-a); (fraction) sessantesimo; **sixty** num sessanta

size [saɪz] n dimensioni fpl; (of clothing) taglia, misura; (of shoes) numero; (glue) colla; **sizeable** adj considerevole

sizzle ['sɪzl] vi sfrigolare

skate [skeɪt] n pattino; (fish: pl inv) razza ▷ vi pattinare; **skateboard** n skateboard m inv; **skateboarding** n skateboard m inv; **skater** n pattinatore(-trice); **skating** n pattinaggio; **skating rink** n pista di pattinaggio

skeleton ['skɛlɪtn] n scheletro

skeptical ['skɛptɪkl] (us) adj = **sceptical**

sketch [skɛtʃ] n (drawing) schizzo, abbozzo; (Theatre) scenetta comica, sketch m inv ▷ vt abbozzare, schizzare

skewer ['skjuːəʳ] n spiedo

ski [skiː] n sci m inv ▷ vi sciare; **ski boot** n scarpone m da sci

skid [skɪd] n slittamento ▷ vi slittare

ski: **skier** ['skiːəʳ] n sciatore(-trice);

skiing ['ski:ɪŋ] *n* sci *m*

skilful ['skɪlful] (*us* **skillful**) *adj* abile

ski lift *n* sciovia

skill [skɪl] *n* abilità *f* inv, capacità *f* inv; **skilled** *adj* esperto(-a); (*worker*) qualificato(-a), specializzato(-a)

skim [skɪm] *vt* (*milk*) scremare; (*glide over*) sfiorare ▷ *vi* **to ~ through** (*fig*) scorrere, dare una scorsa a; **skimmed milk** (*us* **skim milk**) *n* latte *m* scremato

skin [skɪn] *n* pelle *f* ▷ *vt* (*fruit etc*) sbucciare; (*animal*) scuoiare, spellare; **skinhead** *n* skinhead *m/f* inv; **skinny** *adj* molto magro(-a), pelle e ossa *inv*

skip [skɪp] *n* saltello, balzo; (*BRIT: container*) benna ▷ *vi* saltare; (*with rope*) saltare la corda ▷ *vt* saltare

ski: **ski pass** *n* ski pass *m*; **ski pole** *n* racchetta (da sci)

skipper ['skɪpəʳ] *n* (*Naut, Sport*) capitano

skipping rope ['skɪpɪŋ-] (*us* **skip rope**) *n* corda per saltare

skirt [skə:t] *n* gonna, sottana ▷ *vt* fiancheggiare, costeggiare

skirting board (*BRIT*) *n* zoccolo

ski slope *n* pista da sci

ski suit *n* tuta da sci

skull [skʌl] *n* cranio, teschio

skunk [skʌŋk] *n* moffetta

sky [skaɪ] *n* cielo; **skyscraper** *n* grattacielo

slab [slæb] *n* lastra; (*of cake, cheese*) fetta

slack [slæk] *adj* (*loose*) allentato(-a); (*slow*) lento(-a); (*careless*) negligente; **slacks** *npl* (*trousers*) pantaloni *mpl*

slain [sleɪn] *pp of* **slay**

slam [slæm] *vt* (*door*) sbattere; (*throw*) scaraventare; (*criticize*) stroncare ▷ *vi* sbattere

slander ['slɑ:ndəʳ] *n* calunnia; diffamazione *f*

slang [slæŋ] *n* gergo, slang *m*

slant [slɑ:nt] *n* pendenza, inclinazione *f*; (*fig*) angolazione *f*, punto di vista

slap [slæp] *n* manata, pacca; (*on face*) schiaffo ▷ *vt* dare una manata a; schiaffeggiare ▷ *adv* (*directly*) in pieno; **~ a coat of paint on it** dagli una mano di vernice

slash [slæʃ] *vt* tagliare; (*face*) sfregiare; (*fig: prices*) ridurre drasticamente, tagliare

slate [sleɪt] *n* ardesia; (*piece*) lastra di ardesia ▷ *vt* (*fig: criticize*) stroncare, distruggere

slaughter ['slɔ:təʳ] *n* strage *f*, massacro ▷ *vt* (*animal*) macellare; (*people*) trucidare, massacrare; **slaughterhouse** *n* macello, mattatoio

Slav [slɑ:v] *adj, n* slavo(-a)

slave [sleɪv] *n* schiavo(-a) ▷ *vi* (*also: ~ away*) lavorare come uno schiavo; **slavery** *n* schiavitù *f*

slay [sleɪ] (*pt* **slew**, *pp* **slain**) *vt* (*formal*) uccidere

sleazy ['sli:zɪ] *adj* trasandato(-a)

sled [slɛd] (*us*) = **sledge**

sledge [slɛdʒ] *n* slitta

sleek [sli:k] *adj* (*hair, fur*) lucido(-a), lucente; (*car, boat*) slanciato(-a), affusolato(-a)

sleep [sli:p] (*pt, pp* **slept**) *n* sonno ▷ *vi* dormire; **to go to ~** addormentarsi; **sleep in** *vi* (*oversleep*) dormire fino a tardi; **sleep together** *vi* (*have sex*) andare a letto insieme; **sleeper** (*BRIT*) *n* (*Rail: on track*) traversina; (*: train*) treno di vagoni letto; **sleeping bag** *n* sacco a pelo; **sleeping car** *n* vagone *m* letto *inv*, carrozza *f* letto *inv*; **sleeping pill** *n* sonnifero; **sleepover** *n* notte *f* che un ragazzino passa da amici; **sleepwalk** *vi* camminare nel sonno; (*as a habit*) essere sonnambulo(-a); **sleepy** *adj* assonnato(-a), sonnolento(-a); (*fig*) addormentato(-a)

sleet [sli:t] *n* nevischio

sleeve [sli:v] *n* manica; (*of record*)

copertina; **sleeveless** *adj* (*garment*) senza maniche

sleigh [sleɪ] *n* slitta

slender ['slendəʳ] *adj* snello(-a), sottile; (*not enough*) scarso(-a), esiguo(-a)

slept [slept] *pt, pp of* **sleep**

slew [sluː] *pt of* **slay** ▷ *vi* (BRIT) girare

slice [slaɪs] *n* fetta ▷ *vt* affettare, tagliare a fette

slick [slɪk] *adj* (*skilful*) brillante; (*clever*) furbo(-a) ▷ *n* (*also*: **oil ~**) chiazza di petrolio

slide [slaɪd] (*pt, pp* **slid**) *n* scivolone *m*; (*in playground*) scivolo; (*Phot*) diapositiva; (BRIT: *also*: **hair ~**) fermaglio (per capelli) ▷ *vt* far scivolare ▷ *vi* scivolare; **sliding** *adj* (*door*) scorrevole

slight [slaɪt] *adj* (*slim*) snello(-a), sottile; (*frail*) delicato(-a), fragile; (*trivial*) insignificante; (*small*) piccolo(-a) ▷ *n* offesa, affronto; **not in the ~est** affatto, neppure per sogno; **slightly** *adv* lievemente, un po'

slim [slɪm] *adj* magro(-a), snello(-a) ▷ *vi* dimagrire; fare (*or* seguire) una dieta dimagrante; **slimming** ['slɪmɪŋ] *adj* (*diet*) dimagrante; (*food*) ipocalorico(-a)

slimy ['slaɪmɪ] *adj* (*also fig: person*) viscido(-a); (*covered with mud*) melmoso(-a)

sling [slɪŋ] (*pt, pp* **slung**) *n* (*Med*) fascia al collo; (*for baby*) marsupio ▷ *vt* lanciare, tirare

slip [slɪp] *n* scivolata, scivolone *m*; (*mistake*) errore *m*, sbaglio; (*underskirt*) sottoveste *f*; (*of paper*) striscia di carta; tagliando, scontrino ▷ *vt* (*slide*) far scivolare ▷ *vi* (*slide*) scivolare; (*move smoothly*): **to ~ into/out of** scivolare in/fuori da; (*decline*) declinare; **to ~ sth on/off** infilarsi/togliersi qc; **to give sb the ~** sfuggire qn; **a ~ of the tongue** un lapsus linguae; **slip up** *vi* sbagliarsi

slipper ['slɪpəʳ] *n* pantofola

slippery ['slɪpərɪ] *adj* scivoloso(-a)

slip road (BRIT) *n* (*to motorway*) rampa di accesso

slit [slɪt] *n* (*pt, pp* **slit**) *n* fessura, fenditura; (*cut*) taglio ▷ *vt* fendere; tagliare

slog [slɒg] (BRIT) *n* faticata ▷ *vi* lavorare con accanimento, sgobbare

slogan ['sləʊgən] *n* motto, slogan *m inv*

slope [sləʊp] *n* pendio; (*side of mountain*) versante *m*; (*ski slope*) pista; (*of roof*) pendenza; (*of floor*) inclinazione *f* ▷ *vi* **to ~ down** declinare; **to ~ up** essere in salita; **sloping** *adj* inclinato(-a)

sloppy ['slɒpɪ] *adj* (*work*) tirato(-a) via; (*appearance*) sciatto(-a)

slot [slɒt] *n* fessura ▷ *vt* **to ~ sth into** infilare qc in; **slot machine** *n* (BRIT: *vending machine*) distributore *m* automatico; (*for gambling*) slot-machine *f inv*

Slovakia [sləʊˈvækɪə] *n* Slovacchia

Slovene [ˈsləʊviːn] *adj* sloveno(-a) ▷ *n* sloveno(-a); (*Ling*) sloveno

Slovenia [sləʊˈviːnɪə] *n* Slovenia; **Slovenian** *adj, n* = **Slovene**

slow [sləʊ] *adj* lento(-a); (*watch*): **to be ~** essere indietro ▷ *adv* lentamente ▷ *vt, vi* (*also*: **~ down, ~ up**) rallentare; **"~"** (*road sign*) "rallentare"; **slow down** *vi* rallentare; **slowly** *adv* lentamente; **slow motion** *n* **in slow motion** al rallentatore

slug [slʌg] *n* lumaca; (*bullet*) pallottola; **sluggish** *adj* lento(-a); (*trading*) stagnante

slum [slʌm] *n* catapecchia

slump [slʌmp] *n* crollo, caduta; (*economic*) depressione *f*, crisi *f inv* ▷ *vi* crollare

slung [slʌŋ] *pt, pp of* **sling**

slur [slɜːʳ] *n* (*fig*): **~ (on)** calunnia (su) ▷ *vt* pronunciare in modo indistinto

sly [slaɪ] *adj* (*smile, remark*)

sornione(-a); (*person*) furbo(-a)

smack [smæk] *n* (*slap*) pacca; (*on face*) schiaffo ▷ *vt* schiaffeggiare; (*child*) picchiare ▷ *vi* **to ~ of** puzzare di

small [smɔːl] *adj* piccolo(-a); **small ads** (BRIT) *npl* piccola pubblicità; **small change** *n* moneta, spiccioli *mpl*

smart [smɑːt] *adj* elegante; (*fashionable*) alla moda; (*clever*) intelligente; (*quick*) sveglio(-a) ▷ *vi* bruciare; **smartcard** ['smɑːtkɑːd] *n* smartcard *f inv*, carta intelligente

smash [smæʃ] *n* (*also*: **~-up**) scontro, collisione *f*; (*smash hit*) successone *m* ▷ *vt* frantumare, fracassare; (*Sport: record*) battere ▷ *vi* frantumarsi, andare in pezzi; **smashing** (*inf*) *adj* favoloso(-a), formidabile

smear [smɪəʳ] *n* macchia; (*Med*) striscio ▷ *vt* spalmare; (*make dirty*) sporcare; **smear test** *n* (BRIT Med) Pap-test *m inv*

smell [smɛl] (*pt* **smelt** *or* **smelled**) *n* odore *m*; (*sense*) olfatto, odorato ▷ *vt* sentire (l')odore di ▷ *vi* (*food etc*): **to ~ (of)** avere odore (di); (*pej*) puzzare, avere un cattivo odore; **smelly** *adj* puzzolente

smelt [smɛlt] *pt, pp of* **smell** ▷ *vt* (*ore*) fondere

smile [smaɪl] *n* sorriso ▷ *vi* sorridere

smirk [sməːk] *n* sorriso furbo; sorriso compiaciuto

smog [smɔg] *n* smog *m*

smoke [sməʊk] *n* fumo ▷ *vt, vi* fumare; **do you mind if I ~?** le dà fastidio se fumo?; **smoke alarm** *n* rivelatore *f* di fumo; **smoked** *adj* (*bacon, glass*) affumicato(-a); **smoker** *n* (*person*) fumatore(-trice); (*Rail*) carrozza per fumatori; **smoking** *n* fumo; **"no smoking"** (*sign*) "vietato fumare"; **smoky** *adj* fumoso(-a); (*taste*) affumicato(-a)

smooth [smuːð] *adj* liscio(-a); (*sauce*) omogeneo(-a); (*flavour, whisky*) amabile; (*movement*) regolare; (*person*)

mellifluo(-a) ▷ *vt* (*also*: **~ out**) lisciare, spianare; (: *difficulties*) appianare

smother ['smʌðəʳ] *vt* soffocare

SMS *abbr* (= *short message service*) SMS; **SMS message** *n* SMS *m inv*, messaggino

smudge [smʌdʒ] *n* macchia; sbavatura ▷ *vt* imbrattare, sporcare

smug [smʌg] *adj* soddisfatto(-a), compiaciuto(-a)

smuggle ['smʌgl] *vt* contrabbandare; **smuggling** *n* contrabbando

snack [snæk] *n* spuntino; **snack bar** *n* tavola calda, snack bar *m inv*

snag [snæg] *n* intoppo, ostacolo imprevisto

snail [sneɪl] *n* chiocciola

snake [sneɪk] *n* serpente *m*

snap [snæp] *n* (*sound*) schianto, colpo secco; (*photograph*) istantanea ▷ *adj* improvviso(-a) ▷ *vt* (*far*) schioccare; (*break*) spezzare di netto ▷ *vi* spezzarsi con un rumore secco; (*fig: person*) parlare con tono secco; **to ~ shut** chiudersi di scatto; **snap at** *vt fus* (*dog*) cercare di mordere; **snap up** *vt* afferrare; **snapshot** *n* istantanea

snarl [snɑːl] *vi* ringhiare

snatch [snætʃ] *n* (*small amount*) frammento ▷ *vt* strappare (con violenza); (*fig*) rubare

sneak [sniːk] (*pt* (US) **snuck**) *vi* **to ~ in/out** entrare/uscire di nascosto ▷ *n* spione(-a); **to ~ up on sb** avvicinarsi quatto quatto a qn; **sneakers** *npl* scarpe *fpl* da ginnastica

sneer [snɪəʳ] *vi* sogghignare; **to ~ at** farsi beffe di

sneeze [sniːz] *n* starnuto ▷ *vi* starnutire

sniff [snɪf] *n* fiutata, annusata ▷ *vi* tirare su col naso ▷ *vt* fiutare, annusare

snigger ['snɪgəʳ] *vi* ridacchiare, ridere sotto i baffi

snip [snɪp] *n* pezzetto; (*bargain*) (buon) affare *m*, occasione *f* ▷ *vt* tagliare

sniper ['snaɪpə^r] n (marksman) franco
tiratore m, cecchino

snob [snɔb] n snob m/f inv

snooker ['snu:kə^r] n tipo di gioco del
biliardo

snoop ['snu:p] vi **to ~ about** curiosare

snooze [snu:z] n sonnellino, pisolino
▷ vi fare un sonnellino

snore [snɔ:^r] vi russare

snorkel ['snɔ:kl] n (of swimmer)
respiratore m a tubo

snort [snɔ:t] n sbuffo ▷ vi sbuffare

snow [snəu] n neve f ▷ vi nevicare;
snowball n palla di neve ▷ vi (fig)
crescere a vista d'occhio; **snowstorm**
n tormenta

snub [snʌb] vt snobbare ▷ n offesa,
affronto

snug [snʌg] adj comodo(-a); (room,
house) accogliente, comodo(-a)

⭕ **KEYWORD**

so [səu] adv **1** (thus, likewise) così; **if so**
se è così, quand'è così; **I didn't do it
— you did so!** non l'ho fatto io — sì
che l'hai fatto!; **so do I, so am I** etc
anch'io; **it's 5 o'clock — so it is!** sono
le 5 — davvero!; **I hope so** lo spero; **I
think so** penso di sì; **so far** finora, fin
qui; (in past) fino ad allora

2 (in comparisons etc: to such a degree)
così; **so big (that)** così grande (che);
she's not so clever as her brother
lei non è (così) intelligente come suo
fratello

3: **so much** adj tanto(-a)
▷ adv tanto; **I've got so much work/
money** ho tanto lavoro/tanti soldi;
I love you so much ti amo tanto; **so
many** tanti(-e)

4 (phrases): **10 or so** circa 10; **so long!**
(inf: goodbye) ciao!, ci vediamo!
▷ conj **1** (expressing purpose): **so as to
do** in modo or così da fare; **we hurried
so as not to be late** ci affrettammo

per non fare tardi; **so (that)** affinché +
sub, perché + sub

2 (expressing result): **he didn't arrive
so I left** non è venuto così me ne sono
andata; **so you see, I could have
gone** vedi, sarei potuto andare

soak [səuk] vt inzuppare; (clothes)
mettere a mollo ▷ vi (clothes etc)
essere a mollo; **soak up** vt assorbire;
soaking adj (also: **soaking wet**)
fradicio(-a)

so-and-so ['səuənsəu] n (somebody)
un tale; **Mr/Mrs ~** signor/signora tal
dei tali

soap [səup] n sapone m; **soap opera**
n soap opera f inv; **soap powder** n
detersivo

soar [sɔ:^r] vi volare in alto; (price etc)
salire alle stelle; (building) ergersi

sob [sɔb] n singhiozzo ▷ vi
singhiozzare

sober ['səubə^r] adj sobrio(-a); (not
drunk) non ubriaco(-a); (moderate)
moderato(-a); **sober up** vt far
passare la sbornia ▷ vi farsi passare
la sbornia

so-called ['səu'kɔ:ld] adj
cosiddetto(-a)

soccer ['sɔkə^r] n calcio

sociable ['səuʃəbl] adj socievole

social ['səuʃl] adj sociale ▷ n festa,
serata; **socialism** n socialismo;
socialist adj, n socialista m/f;
socialize vi **to socialize (with)**
socializzare (con); **social life** n vita
sociale; **socially** adv socialmente,
in società; **social security** (BRIT) n
previdenza sociale; **social services**
npl servizi mpl sociali; **social work**
n servizio sociale; **social worker** n
assistente m/f sociale

society [sə'saɪətɪ] n società f inv; (club)
società, associazione f; (also: **high ~**)
alta società

sociology [səusɪ'ɔlədʒɪ] n sociologia

sock [sɔk] n calzino

socket ['sɔkɪt] n cavità f inv; (of eye) orbita; (BRIT: Elec: also: **wall ~**) presa di corrente

soda ['səudə] n (Chem) soda; (also: **~ water**) acqua di seltz; (US: also: **~ pop**) gassosa

sodium ['səudɪəm] n sodio

sofa ['səufə] n sofà m inv; **sofa bed** n divano m letto inv

soft [sɔft] adj (not rough) morbido(-a); (not hard) soffice; (not loud) sommesso(-a); (not bright) tenue; (kind) gentile; **soft drink** n analcolico; **soft drugs** npl droghe fpl leggere; **soften** ['sɔfn] vt ammorbidire; addolcire; attenuare ▷ vi ammorbidirsi; addolcirsi; attenuarsi; **softly** adv dolcemente; morbidamente; **software** ['sɔftwɛər] n (Comput) software m

soggy ['sɔgɪ] adj inzuppato(-a)

soil [sɔɪl] n terreno ▷ vt sporcare

solar ['səulər] adj solare; **solar power** n energie solare; **solar system** n sistema m solare

sold [səuld] pt, pp of **sell**

soldier ['səuldʒər] n soldato, militare m

sold out adj (Comm) esaurito(-a)

sole [səul] n (of foot) pianta (del piede); (of shoe) suola; (fish: pl inv) sogliola ▷ adj solo(-a), unico(-a); **solely** adv solamente, unicamente; **I will hold you solely responsible** la considererò il solo responsabile

solemn ['sɔləm] adj solenne

solicitor [sə'lɪsɪtər] (BRIT) n (for wills etc) ≈ notaio; (in court) ≈ avvocato

solid ['sɔlɪd] adj solido(-a); (not hollow) pieno(-a); (meal) sostanzioso(-a) ▷ n solido

solitary ['sɔlɪtərɪ] adj solitario(-a)

solitude ['sɔlɪtjuːd] n solitudine f

solo ['səuləu] n assolo; **soloist** n solista m/f

soluble ['sɔljubl] adj solubile

solution [sə'luːʃən] n soluzione f

solve [sɔlv] vt risolvere

solvent ['sɔlvənt] adj (Comm) solvibile ▷ n (Chem) solvente m

sombre ['sɔmbər] (US **somber**) adj scuro(-a); (mood, person) triste

 KEYWORD

some [sʌm] adj **1** (a certain amount or number of): **some tea/water/cream** del tè/dell'acqua/della panna; **some children/apples** dei bambini/delle mele

2 (certain: in contrasts) certo(-a); **some people say that ...** alcuni dicono che ..., certa gente dice che ...

3 (unspecified) un(a) certo(-a), qualche; **some woman was asking for you** una tale chiedeva di lei; **some day** un giorno; **some day next week** un giorno della prossima settimana ▷ pron **1** (a certain number) alcuni(-e), certi(-e); **I've got some** (books etc) ne ho alcuni; **some (of them) have been sold** alcuni sono stati venduti **2** (a certain amount) un po'; **I've got some** (money, milk) ne ho un po'; **I've read some of the book** ho letto parte del libro ▷ adv **some 10 people** circa 10 persone

some: **somebody** ['sʌmbədɪ] pron = **someone**; **somehow** ['sʌmhau] adv in un modo o nell'altro, in qualche modo; (for some reason) per qualche ragione; **someone** ['sʌmwʌn] pron qualcuno; **someplace** ['sʌmpleɪs] (US) adv = **somewhere**; **something** ['sʌmθɪŋ] pron qualcosa, qualche cosa; **something nice** qualcosa di bello; **something to do** qualcosa da fare; **sometime** ['sʌmtaɪm] adv (in future) una volta o l'altra; (in past): **sometime last month** durante il mese scorso; **sometimes** ['sʌmtaɪmz] adv qualche volta;

somewhat ['sʌmwɔt] adv piuttosto;
somewhere ['sʌmwɛəʳ] adv in or da
qualche parte
son [sʌn] n figlio
song [sɔŋ] n canzone f
son-in-law ['sʌnɪnlɔ:] n genero
soon [su:n] adv presto, fra poco; (early,
a short time after) presto; **~ afterwards**
poco dopo; see also **as; sooner** adv
(time) prima; (preference): **I would
sooner do** preferirei fare; **sooner or
later** prima o poi
soothe [su:ð] vt calmare
sophisticated [sə'fɪstɪkeɪtɪd]
adj sofisticato(-a); raffinato(-a);
complesso(-a)
sophomore ['sɔfəmɔ:ʳ] (US) n
studente(-essa) del secondo anno
soprano [sə'prɑ:nəu] n (voice)
soprano m; (singer) soprano m/f
sorbet ['sɔ:beɪ] n sorbetto
sordid ['sɔ:dɪd] adj sordido(-a)
sore [sɔ:ʳ] adj (painful) dolorante ▷ n
piaga
sorrow ['sɔrəu] n dolore m
sorry ['sɔrɪ] adj spiacente; (condition,
excuse) misero(-a); **~!** scusa! (or scusi! or
scusate!); **to feel ~ for sb** rincrescersi
per qn
sort [sɔ:t] n specie f, genere m; **sort
out** vt (papers) classificare; ordinare;
(: letters etc) smistare; (: problems)
risolvere; (Comput) ordinare
SOS n abbr (= save our souls) S.O.S. m inv
so-so ['səusəu] adv così così
sought [sɔ:t] pt, pp of **seek**
soul [səul] n anima
sound [saund] adj (healthy) sano(-a);
(safe, not damaged) solido(-a), in
buono stato; (reliable, not superficial)
solido(-a); (sensible) giudizioso(-a),
di buon senso ▷ adv **~ asleep**
profondamente addormentato
▷ n suono; (noise) rumore m; (Geo)
stretto ▷ vt (alarm) suonare ▷ vi
suonare; (fig: seem) sembrare; **to ~ like**
rassomigliare a; **soundtrack** n (of

film) colonna sonora
soup [su:p] n minestra; brodo; zuppa
sour ['sauəʳ] adj aspro(-a); (fruit)
acerbo(-a); (milk) acido(-a); (fig)
arcigno(-a); acido(-a); **it's ~ grapes** è
soltanto invidia
source [sɔ:s] n fonte f, sorgente f;
(fig) fonte
south [sauθ] n sud m, meridione
m, mezzogiorno ▷ adj del sud, sud
inv, meridionale ▷ adv verso sud;
South Africa n Sudafrica m; **South
African** adj, n sudafricano(-a);
South America n Sudamerica m,
America del sud; **South American**
adj, n sudamericano(-a); **southbound**
['sauθbaund] adj (gen) diretto(-a)
a sud; (carriageway) sud inv;
southeastern [sauθ'i:stən] adj
sudorientale; **southern** ['sʌðən] adj
del sud, meridionale; esposto(-a)
a sud; **South Korea** n Corea f
del Sud; **South Pole** n Polo Sud;
southward(s) adv verso sud; **south-
west** n sud-ovest m; **southwestern**
[sauθ'westən] adj sudoccidentale
souvenir [su:və'nɪəʳ] n ricordo,
souvenir m inv
sovereign ['sɔvrɪn] adj, n sovrano(-a)
sow[1] [səu] (pt **sowed**, pp **sown**) vt
seminare
sow[2] [sau] n scrofa
soya ['sɔɪə] (US **soy**) n **~ bean** n seme
m di soia; **soya sauce** n salsa di soia
spa [spɑ:] n (resort) stazione f termale;
(US: also: **health ~**) centro di cure
estetiche
space [speɪs] n spazio; (room) posto;
spazio; (length of time) intervallo ▷ cpd
spaziale ▷ vt (also: **~ out**) distanziare;
spacecraft n inv veicolo spaziale;
spaceship n = **spacecraft**
spacious ['speɪʃəs] adj spazioso(-a),
ampio(-a)
spade [speɪd] n (tool) vanga; pala;
(child's) paletta; **spades** npl (Cards)
picche fpl

spaghetti [spəˈgɛtɪ] n spaghetti mpl

Spain [speɪn] n Spagna

spam [spæm] (Comput) n spamming
▷ vt **to ~ sb** inviare a qn messaggi
pubblicitari non richiesti via email

span [spæn] n (of bird, plane) apertura
alare; (of arch) campata; (in time)
periodo; durata ▷ vt attraversare; (fig)
abbracciare

Spaniard [ˈspænjəd] n spagnolo(-a)

Spanish [ˈspænɪʃ] adj spagnolo(-a)
▷ n (Ling) spagnolo; **the Spanish** npl
gli Spagnoli

spank [spæŋk] vt sculacciare

spanner [ˈspænər] (BRIT) n chiave f
inglese

spare [spɛər] adj di riserva, di scorta;
(surplus) in più, d'avanzo ▷ n (part)
pezzo di ricambio ▷ vt (do without) fare
a meno di; (afford to give) concedere;
(refrain from hurting, using) risparmiare;
to ~ (surplus) d'avanzo; **spare part**
n pezzo di ricambio; **spare room** n
stanza degli ospiti; **spare time** n
tempo libero; **spare tyre** (US **spare
tire**) n (Aut) gomma di scorta; **spare
wheel** n (Aut) ruota di scorta

spark [spɑːk] n scintilla; **spark(ing)
plug** n candela

sparkle [ˈspɑːkl] n scintillio, sfavillio
▷ vi scintillare, sfavillare

sparrow [ˈspærəu] n passero

sparse [spɑːs] adj sparso(-a), rado(-a)

spasm [ˈspæzəm] n (Med) spasmo;
(fig) accesso, attacco

spat [spæt] pt, pp of **spit**

spate [speɪt] n (fig): **~ of** diluvio or
fiume m di

spatula [ˈspætjulə] n spatola

speak [spiːk] (pt **spoke**, pp **spoken**)
vt (language) parlare; (truth) dire ▷ vi
parlare; **I don't ~ Italian** non parlo
italiano; **do you ~ English?** parla
inglese?; **to ~ to sb/of about sth**
parlare a qn/di qc; **can I ~ to ...?** posso
parlare con...?; **~ up!** parla più forte!;
speaker n (in public) oratore(-trice);

(also: **loudspeaker**) altoparlante
m; (Pol): **the Speaker** il presidente
della Camera dei Comuni (BRIT) or dei
Rappresentanti (US)

spear [spɪər] n lancia ▷ vt infilzare

special [ˈspɛʃl] adj speciale; **special
delivery** n (Post): **by special
delivery** per espresso; **special
effects** npl (Cine) effetti mpl speciali;
specialist n specialista m/f;
speciality [spɛʃɪˈælɪtɪ] n specialità f
inv; **I'd like to try a local speciality**
vorrei assaggiare una specialità del
posto; **specialize** vi **to specialize
(in)** specializzarsi (in); **specially** adv
specialmente, particolarmente;
special needs adj **special needs
children** bambini mpl con difficoltà
di apprendimento; **special offer**
n (Comm) offerta speciale; **special
school** n (BRIT) scuola speciale (per
portatori di handicap); **specialty** (US) n
= **speciality**

species [ˈspiːʃiːz] n inv specie f inv

specific [spəˈsɪfɪk] adj specifico(-a);
preciso(-a); **specifically** adv
esplicitamente; (especially)
appositamente

specify [ˈspɛsɪfaɪ] vt specificare,
precisare; **unless otherwise
specified** salvo indicazioni contrarie

specimen [ˈspɛsɪmən] n esemplare
m, modello; (Med) campione m

speck [spɛk] n puntino, macchiolina;
(particle) granello

spectacle [ˈspɛktəkl] n spettacolo;
spectacles npl (glasses) occhiali
mpl; **spectacular** [-ˈtækjulər] adj
spettacolare

spectator [spɛkˈteɪtər] n spettatore m

spectrum [ˈspɛktrəm] (pl **spectra**)
n spettro

speculate [ˈspɛkjuleɪt] vi speculare;
(try to guess): **to ~ about** fare ipotesi su

sped [spɛd] pt, pp of **speed**

speech [spiːtʃ] n (faculty) parola;
(talk, Theatre) discorso; (manner of

speaking) parlata; **speechless** *adj* ammutolito(-a), muto(-a)

speed [spiːd] *n* velocità *f inv*; (*promptness*) prontezza; **at full** *or* **top ~** a tutta velocità; **speed up** *vi, vt* accelerare; **speedboat** *n* motoscafo; **speeding** *n* (*Aut*) eccesso di velocità; **speed limit** *n* limite *m* di velocità; **speedometer** [spɪˈdɔmɪtəʳ] *n* tachimetro; **speedy** *adj* veloce, rapido(-a); pronto(-a)

spell [spɛl] (*pt, pp* **spelt** (*BRIT*) *or* **spelled**) *n* (*also*: **magic ~**) incantesimo; (*period of time*) (breve) periodo ▷ *vt* (*in writing*) scrivere (lettera per lettera); (*aloud*) dire lettera per lettera; (*fig*) significare; **to cast a ~ on sb** fare un incantesimo a qn; **he can't ~** fa errori di ortografia; **spell out** *vt* (*letter by letter*) dettare lettera per lettera; (*explain*): **to spell sth out for sb** spiegare qc a qn per filo e per segno; **spellchecker** [ˈspɛltʃekəʳ] *n* correttore *m* ortografico; **spelling** *n* ortografia

spelt [spɛlt] (*BRIT*) *pt, pp of* **spell**

spend [spɛnd] (*pt, pp* **spent**) *vt* (*money*) spendere; (*time, life*) passare; **spending** *n* **government spending** spesa pubblica

spent [spɛnt] *pt, pp of* **spend**

sperm [spəːm] *n* sperma *m*

sphere [sfɪəʳ] *n* sfera

spice [spaɪs] *n* spezia ▷ *vt* aromatizzare

spicy [ˈspaɪsɪ] *adj* piccante

spider [ˈspaɪdəʳ] *n* ragno

spike [spaɪk] *n* punta

spill [spɪl] (*pt, pp* **spilt** *or* **spilled**) *vt* versare, rovesciare ▷ *vi* versarsi, rovesciarsi

spin [spɪn] (*pt, pp* **spun**) *n* (*revolution of wheel*) rotazione *f*; (*Aviat*) avvitamento; (*trip in car*) giretto ▷ *vt* (*wool etc*) filare; (*wheel*) far girare ▷ *vi* girare

spinach [ˈspɪnɪtʃ] *n* spinacio; (*as food*) spinaci *mpl*

spinal [ˈspaɪnl] *adj* spinale

spin doctor (*inf*) *n* esperto di comunicazioni responsabile dell'immagine di un partito politico

spin-dryer [spɪnˈdraɪəʳ] (*BRIT*) *n* centrifuga

spine [spaɪn] *n* spina dorsale; (*thorn*) spina

spiral [ˈspaɪərl] *n* spirale *f* ▷ *vi* (*fig*) salire a spirale

spire [ˈspaɪəʳ] *n* guglia

spirit [ˈspɪrɪt] *n* spirito; (*ghost*) spirito, fantasma *m*; (*mood*) stato d'animo, umore *m*; (*courage*) coraggio, **spirits** *npl* (*drink*) alcolici *mpl*; **in good ~s** di buon umore

spiritual [ˈspɪrɪtjuəl] *adj* spirituale

spit [spɪt] (*pt, pp* **spat**) *n* (*for roasting*) spiedo; (*saliva*) sputo; saliva ▷ *vi* sputare; (*fire, fat*) scoppiettare

spite [spaɪt] *n* dispetto ▷ *vt* contrariare, far dispetto a; **in ~ of** nonostante, malgrado; **spiteful** *adj* dispettoso(-a)

splash [splæʃ] *n* spruzzo; (*sound*) splash *m inv*; (*of colour*) schizzo ▷ *vt* spruzzare ▷ *vi* (*also*: **~ about**) sguazzare; **splash out** (*inf*) *vi* (*BRIT*) fare spese folli

splendid [ˈsplɛndɪd] *adj* splendido(-a), magnifico(-a)

splinter [ˈsplɪntəʳ] *n* scheggia ▷ *vi* scheggiarsi

split [splɪt] (*pt, pp* **split**) *n* spaccatura; (*fig: division, quarrel*) scissione *f* ▷ *vt* spaccare; (*party*) dividere; (*work, profits*) spartire, ripartire ▷ *vi* (*divide*) dividersi; **split up** *vi* (*couple*) separarsi, rompere; (*meeting*) sciogliersi

spoil [spɔɪl] (*pt, pp* **spoilt** *or* **spoiled**) *vt* (*damage*) rovinare, guastare; (*mar*) sciupare; (*child*) viziare

spoilt [spɔɪlt] *pt, pp of* **spoil**

spoke [spəuk] *pt of* **speak** ▷ *n* raggio

spoken [ˈspəukn] *pp of* **speak**

spokesman [ˈspəuksmən] (*irreg*) *n*

portavoce m inv

spokesperson ['spəukspə:sn] n
portavoce m/f

spokeswoman ['spəukswumən]
(irreg) n portavoce f inv

sponge [spʌndʒ] n spugna; (also: ~
cake) pan m di spagna ▷ vt spugnare,
pulire con una spugna ▷ vi **to ~ off** or
on scroccare a; **sponge bag** (BRIT) n
nécessaire m inv

sponsor ['sponsə'] n (Radio, TV,
Sport etc) sponsor m inv; (Pol: of bill)
promotore(-trice) ▷ vt sponsorizzare;
(bill) presentare; **sponsorship** n
sponsorizzazione f

spontaneous [spon'teiniəs] adj
spontaneo(-a)

spooky ['spu:ki] (inf) adj che fa
accapponare la pelle

spoon [spu:n] n cucchiaio; **spoonful**
n cucchiaiata

sport [spo:t] n sport m inv; (person)
persona di spirito ▷ vt sfoggiare;
sport jacket (US) n = **sports jacket**;
sports car n automobile f sportiva;
sports centre (BRIT) n centro
sportivo; **sports jacket** (BRIT) n
giacca sportiva; **sportsman** (irreg)
n sportivo; **sportswear** n abiti mpl
sportivi; **sportswoman** (irreg) n
sportiva; **sporty** adj sportivo(-a)

spot [spot] n punto; (mark) macchia;
(dot: on pattern) pallino; (pimple)
foruncolo; (place) posto; (Radio, TV)
spot m inv; (small amount): **a ~ of**
un po' di ▷ vt (notice) individuare,
distinguere; **on the ~** sul posto;
(immediately) su due piedi; (in
difficulty) nei guai; **spotless** adj
immacolato(-a); **spotlight** n
proiettore m; (Aut) faro ausiliario

spouse [spauz] n sposo(-a)

sprain [sprein] n storta, distorsione
f ▷ vt **to ~ one's ankle** storcersi una
caviglia

sprang [spræŋ] pt of **spring**

sprawl [spro:l] vi sdraiarsi (in modo

scomposto); (place) estendersi
(disordinatamente)

spray [sprei] n spruzzo; (container)
nebulizzatore m, spray m inv; (of
flowers) mazzetto ▷ vt spruzzare;
(crops) irrorare

spread [spred] (pt, pp **spread**) n
diffusione f; (distribution) distribuzione
f, (Culin) pasta (da spalmare); (inf:
food) banchetto ▷ vt (cloth) stendere,
distendere; (butter etc) spalmare;
(disease, knowledge) propagare,
diffondere ▷ vi stendersi, distendersi;
spalmarsi; propagarsi, diffondersi;
spread out vi (move apart) separarsi;
spreadsheet n foglio elettronico ad
espansione

spree [spri:] n **to go on a ~** fare
baldoria

spring [spriŋ] (pt **sprang**, pp **sprung**)
n (leap) salto, balzo; (coiled metal)
molla; (season) primavera; (of water)
sorgente f ▷ vi saltare, balzare; **spring
up** vi (problem) presentarsi; **spring
onion** n (BRIT) cipollina

sprinkle ['spriŋkl] vt spruzzare;
spargere; **to ~ water** etc **on**, ~ **with
water** etc spruzzare dell'acqua etc su

sprint [sprint] n scatto ▷ vi scattare

sprung [sprʌŋ] pp of **spring**

spun [spʌn] pt, pp of **spin**

spur [spə:'] n sperone m; (fig) sprone
m, incentivo ▷ vt (also: ~ **on**) spronare;
on the ~ of the moment lì per lì

spurt [spə:t] n (of water) getto; (of
energy) scatto ▷ vi sgorgare

spy [spai] n spia ▷ vi **to ~ on** spiare
▷ vt (see) scorgere

sq. abbr = **square**

squabble ['skwɔbl] vi bisticciarsi

squad [skwɔd] n (Mil) plotone m;
(Police) squadra

squadron ['skwɔdrən] n (Mil)
squadrone m; (Aviat, Naut) squadriglia

squander ['skwɔndə'] vt dissipare

square [skweə'] n quadrato; (in
town) piazza ▷ adj quadrato(-a); (inf:

ideas, person) di vecchio stampo ▷ *vt* (*arrange*) regolare; (*Math*) elevare al quadrato; (*reconcile*) conciliare; **all ~** pari; **a ~ meal** un pasto abbondante; **2 metres ~** di 2 metri per 2; **1 ~ metre** 1 metro quadrato; **square root** *n* radice *f* quadrata

squash [skwɔʃ] *n* (*Sport*) squash *m*; (*BRIT: drink*): **lemon/orange ~** sciroppo di limone/arancia; (*US*) zucca; (*Sport*) squash *m* ▷ *vt* schiacciare

squat [skwɔt] *adj* tarchiato(-a), tozzo(-a) ▷ *vi* (*also:* **~ down**) accovacciarsi; **squatter** *n* occupante *m/f* abusivo(-a)

squeak [skwi:k] *vi* squittire

squeal [skwi:l] *vi* strillare

squeeze [skwi:z] *n* pressione *f*; (*also Econ*) stretta ▷ *vt* premere; (*hand, arm*) stringere

squid [skwɪd] *n* calamaro

squint [skwɪnt] *vi* essere strabico(-a) ▷ *n* **he has a ~** è strabico

squirm [skwə:m] *vi* contorcersi

squirrel ['skwɪrəl] *n* scoiattolo

squirt [skwə:t] *vi* schizzare; zampillare ▷ *vt* spruzzare

Sr *abbr* = **senior**

Sri Lanka [srɪ'læŋkə] *n* Sri Lanka *m*

St *abbr* = **saint**; **street**

stab [stæb] *n* (*with knife etc*) pugnalata; (*of pain*) fitta; (*inf: try*): **to have a ~ at (doing) sth** provare (a fare) qc ▷ *vt* pugnalare

stability [stə'bɪlɪtɪ] *n* stabilità

stable ['steɪbl] *n* (*for horses*) scuderia; (*for cattle*) stalla ▷ *adj* stabile

stack [stæk] *n* catasta, pila ▷ *vt* accatastare, ammucchiare

stadium ['steɪdɪəm] *n* stadio

staff [stɑ:f] *n* (*work force: gen*) personale *m*; (: *BRIT: Scol*) personale insegnante ▷ *vt* fornire di personale

stag [stæg] *n* cervo

stage [steɪdʒ] *n* palcoscenico; (*profession*): **the ~** il teatro, la scena; (*point*) punto; (*platform*) palco ▷ *vt* (*play*) allestire, mettere in scena; (*demonstration*) organizzare; **in ~s** per gradi; a tappe

stagger ['stægə^r] *vi* barcollare ▷ *vt* (*person*) sbalordire; (*hours, holidays*) scaglionare; **staggering** *adj* (*amazing*) sbalorditivo(-a)

stagnant ['stægnənt] *adj* stagnante

stag night, stag party *n* festa di addio al celibato

stain [steɪn] *n* macchia; (*colouring*) colorante *m* ▷ *vt* macchiare; (*wood*) tingere; **stained glass** [steɪnd'glɑ:s] *n* vetro colorato; **stainless steel** *n* acciaio inossidabile

staircase ['stɛəkeɪs] *n* scale *fpl*, scala

stairs [stɛəz] *npl* (*flight of stairs*) scale *fpl*, scala

stairway ['stɛəweɪ] *n* = **staircase**

stake [steɪk] *n* palo, piolo; (*Comm*) interesse *m*; (*Betting*) puntata, scommessa ▷ *vt* (*bet*) scommettere; (*risk*) rischiare; **to be at ~** essere in gioco

stale [steɪl] *adj* (*bread*) raffermo(-a); (*food*) stantio(-a); (*air*) viziato(-a); (*beer*) svaporato(-a); (*smell*) di chiuso

stalk [stɔ:k] *n* gambo, stelo ▷ *vt* inseguire

stall [stɔ:l] *n* bancarella; (*in stable*) box *m inv* di stalla ▷ *vt* (*Aut*) far spegnere; (*fig*) bloccare ▷ *vi* (*Aut*) spegnersi, fermarsi; (*fig*) temporeggiare

stamina ['stæmɪnə] *n* vigore *m*, resistenza

stammer ['stæmə^r] *n* balbuzie *f* ▷ *vi* balbettare

stamp [stæmp] *n* (*postage stamp*) francobollo; (*implement*) timbro; (*mark, also fig*) marchio, impronta; (*on document*) bollo; timbro ▷ *vi* (*also:* **~ one's foot**) battere il piede ▷ *vt* battere; (*letter*) affrancare; (*mark with a stamp*) timbrare; **stamp out** *vt* (*fire*) estinguere; (*crime*) eliminare; (*opposition*) soffocare; **stamped**

addressed envelope n (BRIT) busta affrancata e indirizzata

■ Be careful not to translate *stamp* by the Italian word *stampa*.

stampede [stæm'pi:d] n fuggi fuggi m inv

stance [stæns] n posizione f

stand [stænd] (pt, pp **stood**) n (position) posizione f; (for taxis) posteggio; (structure) supporto, sostegno; (at exhibition) stand m inv; (in shop) banco; (at market) bancarella; (booth) chiosco; (Sport) tribuna ▷ vi stare in piedi; (rise) alzarsi in piedi; (be placed) trovarsi ▷ vt (place) mettere, porre; (tolerate, withstand) resistere, sopportare; (treat) offrire; **to make a ~** prendere posizione; **to ~ for parliament** (BRIT) presentarsi come candidato (per il parlamento); **stand back** vi prendere le distanze; **stand by** vi (be ready) tenersi pronto(-a) ▷ vt fus (opinion) sostenere; **stand down** vi (withdraw) ritirarsi; **stand for** vt fus (signify) rappresentare, significare; (tolerate) sopportare, tollerare; **stand in for** vt fus sostituire; **stand out** vi (be prominent) spiccare; **stand up** vi (rise) alzarsi in piedi; **stand up for** vt fus difendere; **stand up to** vt fus tener testa a, resistere a

standard ['stændəd] n modello, standard m inv; (level) livello; (flag) stendardo ▷ adj (size etc) normale, standard inv; **standards** npl (morals) principi mpl, valori mpl; **standard of living** n livello di vita

stand-by ['stændbaɪ] n riserva, sostituto; **to be on ~** (gen) tenersi pronto(-a); (doctor) essere di guardia; **stand-by ticket** n (Aviat) biglietto senza garanzia

standing ['stændɪŋ] adj diritto(-a), in piedi; (permanent) permanente ▷ n rango, condizione f, posizione f; **of many years' ~** che esiste da molti anni; **standing order** (BRIT)

n (at bank) ordine m di pagamento (permanente)

stand: **standpoint** ['stændpɔɪnt] n punto di vista; **standstill** ['stændstɪl] n **at a standstill** fermo(-a); (fig) a un punto morto; **to come to a standstill** fermarsi; giungere a un punto morto

stank [stæŋk] pt of **stink**

staple ['steɪpl] n (for papers) graffetta ▷ adj (food etc) di base ▷ vt cucire

star [stɑːʳ] n stella; (celebrity) divo(-a) ▷ vi **to ~ (in)** essere il (or la) protagonista (di) ▷ vt (Cinema) essere interpretato(-a) da; **the stars** npl (Astrology) le stelle

starboard ['stɑːbəd] n dritta

starch [stɑːtʃ] n amido

stardom ['stɑːdəm] n celebrità

stare [stɛəʳ] n sguardo fisso ▷ vi **to ~ at** fissare

stark [stɑːk] adj (bleak) desolato(-a) ▷ adv **~ naked** completamente nudo(-a)

start [stɑːt] n inizio; (of race) partenza; (sudden movement) sobbalzo; (advantage) vantaggio ▷ vt cominciare, iniziare; (car) mettere in moto ▷ vi cominciare; (on journey) partire, mettersi in cammino; (jump) sobbalzare; **when does the film ~?** a che ora comincia il film?; **to ~ doing** or **to do sth** (in)cominciare a fare qc; **start off** vi cominciare; (leave) partire; **start out** vi (begin) cominciare; (set out) partire; **start up** vi cominciare; (car) avviarsi ▷ vt iniziare; (car) avviare; **starter** n (Aut) motorino d'avviamento; (Sport: official) starter m inv; (BRIT: Culin) primo piatto; **starting point** n punto di partenza

startle ['stɑːtl] vt far trasalire; **startling** adj sorprendente

starvation [stɑː'veɪʃən] n fame f, inedia

starve [stɑːv] vi morire di fame; soffrire la fame ▷ vt far morire di fame, affamare

state [steɪt] n stato ▷ vt dichiarare, affermare; annunciare; **the S~s** (USA) gli Stati Uniti; **to be in a ~** essere agitato(-a); **statement** n dichiarazione f; **state school** n scuola statale; **statesman** (irreg) n statista m

static ['stætɪk] n (Radio) scariche fpl ▷ adj statico(-a)

station ['steɪʃən] n stazione f ▷ vt collocare, disporre

stationary ['steɪʃənərɪ] adj fermo(-a), immobile

stationer's (shop) n cartoleria

stationery ['steɪʃnərɪ] n articoli mpl di cancelleria

station wagon (US) n giardinetta

statistic [stə'tɪstɪk] n statistica; **statistics** n (science) statistica

statue ['stætjuː] n statua

stature ['stætʃəʳ] n statura

status ['steɪtəs] n posizione f, condizione f sociale; prestigio; stato; **status quo** [-'kwəu] n **the status quo** lo statu quo

statutory ['stætjutrɪ] adj stabilito(-a) dalla legge, statutario(-a)

staunch [stɔːntʃ] adj fidato(-a), leale

stay [steɪ] n (period of time) soggiorno, permanenza ▷ vi rimanere; (reside) alloggiare, stare; (spend some time) trattenersi, soggiornare; **to ~ put** non muoversi; **to ~ the night** fermarsi per la notte; **stay away** vi (from person, building) stare lontano (from event) non andare; **stay behind** vi restare indietro; **stay in** vi (at home) stare in casa; **stay on** vi restare, rimanere; **stay out** vi (of house) rimanere fuori (di casa); **stay up** vi (at night) rimanere alzato(-a)

steadily ['stɛdɪlɪ] adv (firmly) saldamente; (constantly) continuamente; (fixedly) fisso; (walk) con passo sicuro

steady ['stɛdɪ] adj (not wobbling)

fermo(-a); (regular) costante; (person, character) serio(-a); (: calm) calmo(-a), tranquillo(-a) ▷ vt stabilizzare; calmare

steak [steɪk] n (meat) bistecca; (fish) trancia

steal [stiːl] (pt stole, pp stolen) vt rubare ▷ vi rubare; (move) muoversi furtivamente; **my wallet has been stolen** mi hanno rubato il portafoglio

steam [stiːm] n vapore m ▷ vt (Culin) cuocere a vapore ▷ vi fumare; **steam up** vi (window) appannarsi; **to get steamed up about sth** (fig) andare in bestia per qc; **steamy** adj (room) pieno(-a) di vapore; (window) appannato(-a)

steel [stiːl] n acciaio ▷ adj di acciaio

steep [stiːp] adj ripido(-a), scosceso(-a); (price) eccessivo(-a) ▷ vt inzuppare; (washing) mettere a mollo

steeple ['stiːpl] n campanile m

steer [stɪəʳ] vt guidare ▷ vi (Naut: person) governare; (car) guidarsi; **steering** n (Aut) sterzo; **steering wheel** n volante m

stem [stɛm] n (of flower, plant) stelo; (of tree) fusto; (of glass) gambo; (of fruit, leaf) picciolo ▷ vt contenere, arginare; **stem cell** n cellula staminale

step [stɛp] n passo; (stair) gradino, scalino; (action) mossa, azione f ▷ vi **to ~ forward/back** fare un passo avanti/indietro; **steps** npl (BRIT) = **stepladder**; **to be in/out of ~ (with)** stare/non stare al passo (con); **step down** vi (fig) ritirarsi; **step in** vi fare il proprio ingresso; **step up** vt aumentare; intensificare; **stepbrother** n fratellastro; **stepchild** n figliastro(-a); **stepdaughter** n figliastra; **stepfather** n patrigno; **stepladder** n scala a libretto; **stepmother** n matrigna; **stepsister** n sorellastra; **stepson** n figliastro

stereo ['stɛrɪəu] n (system) sistema m stereofonico; (record player)

stereo *m inv* ▷ *adj* (*also:* **~phonic**) stereofonico(-a)

stereotype ['stɪərɪətaɪp] *n* stereotipo

sterile ['stɛraɪl] *adj* sterile; **sterilize** ['stɛrɪlaɪz] *vt* sterilizzare

sterling ['stə:lɪŋ] *adj* (*gold, silver*) di buona lega ▷ *n* (*Econ*) (lira) sterlina; **a pound ~** una lira sterlina

stern [stə:n] *adj* severo(-a) ▷ *n* (*Naut*) poppa

steroid ['stɛrɔɪd] *n* steroide *m*

stew [stju:] *n* stufato ▷ *vt* cuocere in umido

steward ['stju:əd] *n* (*Aviat, Naut, Rail*) steward *m inv*; (*in club etc*) dispensiere *m*; **stewardess** *n* assistente *f* di volo, hostess *f inv*

stick [stɪk] (*pt, pp* **stuck**) *n* bastone *m*; (*of rhubarb, celery*) gambo; (*of dynamite*) candelotto ▷ *vt* (*glue*) attaccare; (*thrust*): **to ~ sth into** conficcare *or* piantare *or* infiggere qc in; (*inf: put*) ficcare; (*inf: tolerate*) sopportare ▷ *vi* attaccarsi; (*remain*) restare, rimanere; **stick out** *vi* sporgere, spuntare; **stick up** *vi* sporgere, spuntare; **stick up for** *vt fus* difendere; **sticker** *n* cartellino adesivo; **sticking plaster** *n* cerotto adesivo; **stick insect** *n* insetto *m* stecco *inv*; **stick shift** (*US*) *n* (*Aut*) cambio manuale

sticky ['stɪkɪ] *adj* attaccaticcio(-a), vischioso(-a); (*label*) adesivo(-a); (*fig: situation*) difficile

stiff [stɪf] *adj* rigido(-a), duro(-a); (*muscle*) legato(-a), indolenzito(-a); (*difficult*) difficile, arduo(-a); (*cold*) freddo(-a), formale; (*strong*) forte; (*high: price*) molto alto(-a) ▷ *adv* **bored ~** annoiato(-a) a morte

stifling ['staɪflɪŋ] *adj* (*heat*) soffocante

stigma ['stɪgmə] *n* (*fig*) stigma *m*

stiletto [stɪ'lɛtəʊ] (*BRIT*) *n* (*also:* **~ heel**) tacco a spillo

still [stɪl] *adj* fermo(-a); silenzioso(-a) ▷ *adv* (*up to this time, even*) ancora; (*nonetheless*) tuttavia, ciò nonostante

stimulate ['stɪmjuleɪt] *vt* stimolare

stimulus ['stɪmjuləs] (*pl* **stimuli**) *n* stimolo

sting [stɪŋ] (*pt, pp* **stung**) *n* puntura; (*organ*) pungiglione *m* ▷ *vt* pungere

stink [stɪŋk] (*pt* **stank**, *pp* **stunk**) *n* fetore *m*, puzzo ▷ *vi* puzzare

stir [stə:ʳ] *n* agitazione *f*, clamore *m* ▷ *vt* mescolare; (*fig*) risvegliare ▷ *vi* muoversi; **stir up** *vt* provocare, suscitare; **stir-fry** *vt* saltare in padella ▷ *n* pietanza al salto

stitch [stɪtʃ] *n* (*Sewing*) punto; (*Knitting*) maglia; (*Med*) punto (di sutura); (*pain*) fitta ▷ *vt* cucire, attaccare; suturare

stock [stɔk] *n* riserva, provvista; (*Comm*) giacenza, stock *m inv*; (*Agr*) bestiame *m*; (*Culin*) brodo; (*descent*) stirpe *f*; (*Finance*) titoli *mpl*; azioni *fpl* ▷ *adj* (*fig: reply etc*) consueto(-a); classico(-a) ▷ *vt* (*have in stock*) avere, vendere; **~s and shares** valori *mpl* di borsa; **in ~** in magazzino; **out of ~** esaurito(-a); **stockbroker** ['stɔkbrəʊkəʳ] *n* agente *m* di cambio; **stock cube** (*BRIT*) *n* dado; **stock exchange** *n* Borsa (valori); **stockholder** ['stɔkhəʊldəʳ] *n* (*Finance*) azionista *m/f*

stocking ['stɔkɪŋ] *n* calza

stock market *n* Borsa, mercato finanziario

stole [stəʊl] *pt of* **steal** ▷ *n* stola

stolen ['stəʊln] *pp of* **steal**

stomach ['stʌmək] *n* stomaco; (*belly*) pancia ▷ *vt* sopportare, digerire; **stomachache** *n* mal *m* di stomaco

stone [stəʊn] *n* pietra; (*pebble*) sasso, ciottolo; (*in fruit*) nocciolo; (*Med*) calcolo; (*BRIT: weight*) = 6.348 kg; 14 libbre ▷ *adj* di pietra ▷ *vt* lapidare; (*fruit*) togliere il nocciolo a

stood [stud] *pt, pp of* **stand**

stool [stu:l] *n* sgabello

stoop [stu:p] *vi* (*also:* **have a ~**) avere una curvatura; (*also:* **~ down**) chinarsi, curvarsi

stop [stɔp] n arresto; (*stopping place*) fermata; (*in punctuation*) punto ▷ vt arrestare, fermare; (*break off*) interrompere; (*also:* **put a ~ to**) porre fine a ▷ vi fermarsi; (*rain, noise etc*) cessare, finire; **to ~ doing sth** cessare or finire di fare qc; **could you ~ here/at the corner?** può fermarsi qui/all'angolo?; **to ~ dead** fermarsi di colpo; **stop by** vi passare, fare un salto; **stop off** vi sostare brevemente; **stopover** n breve sosta; (*Aviat*) scalo; **stoppage** ['stɔpɪdʒ] n arresto, fermata; (*of pay*) trattenuta; (*strike*) interruzione f del lavoro

storage ['stɔːrɪdʒ] n immagazzinamento

store [stɔːʳ] n provvista, riserva; (*depot*) deposito; (BRIT: *department store*) grande magazzino; (US: *shop*) negozio ▷ vt immagazzinare; **stores** npl (*provisions*) rifornimenti mpl, scorte fpl; **in ~** di riserva; in serbo; **storekeeper** (US) n negoziante m/f

storey ['stɔːrɪ] (US **story**) n piano

storm [stɔːm] n tempesta, temporale m, burrasca; uragano ▷ vi (*fig*) infuriarsi ▷ vt prendere d'assalto; **stormy** adj tempestoso(-a), burrascoso(-a)

story ['stɔːrɪ] n storia; favola; racconto; (US) = **storey**

stout [staut] adj solido(-a), robusto(-a); (*friend, supporter*) tenace; (*fat*) corpulento(-a), grasso(-a) ▷ n birra scura

stove [stəuv] n (*for cooking*) fornello; (: *small*) fornelletto; (*for heating*) stufa

straight [streɪt] adj dritto(-a); (*frank*) onesto(-a), franco(-a); (*simple*) semplice ▷ adv diritto; (*drink*) liscio; **to put** or **get ~** mettere in ordine, mettere ordine in; **~ away, ~ off** (*at once*) immediatamente; **straighten** vt (*also:* **straighten out**) raddrizzare; **straightforward** adj semplice;

onesto(-a), franco(-a)

strain [streɪn] n (*Tech*) sollecitazione f; (*physical*) sforzo; (*mental*) tensione f; (*Med*) strappo; distorsione f; (*streak, trace*) tendenza; elemento ▷ vt tendere; (*muscle*) sforzare; (*ankle*) storcere; (*resources*) pesare su; (*food*) colare; passare; **strained** adj (*muscle*) stirato(-a) (*laugh etc*) forzato(-a); (*relations*) teso(-a); **strainer** n passino, colino

strait [streɪt] n (*Geo*) stretto; **straits** npl **to be in dire ~s** (*fig*) essere nei guai

strand [strænd] n (*of thread*) filo; **stranded** adj nei guai; senza mezzi di trasporto

strange [streɪndʒ] adj (*not known*) sconosciuto(-a); (*odd*) strano(-a), bizzarro(-a); **strangely** adv stranamente; **stranger** n sconosciuto(-a); estraneo(-a)

strangle ['stræŋgl] vt strangolare

strap [stræp] n cinghia; (*of slip, dress*) spallina, bretella

strategic [strə'tiːdʒɪk] adj strategico(-a)

strategy ['strætɪdʒɪ] n strategia

straw [strɔː] n paglia; (*drinking straw*) cannuccia; **that's the last ~!** è la goccia che fa traboccare il vaso!

strawberry ['strɔːbərɪ] n fragola

stray [streɪ] adj (*animal*) randagio(-a); (*bullet*) vagante; (*scattered*) sparso(-a) ▷ vi perdersi

streak [striːk] n striscia; (*of hair*) mèche f inv ▷ vt striare, screziare ▷ vi **to ~ past** passare come un fulmine

stream [striːm] n ruscello; corrente f; (*of people, smoke etc*) fiume m ▷ vt (*Scol*) dividere in livelli di rendimento ▷ vi scorrere; **to ~ in/out** entrare/uscire a fiotti

street [striːt] n strada, via; **streetcar** (US) n tram m inv; **street light** n lampione m; **street map** n pianta (di una città)

street plan n pianta (di una città)

strength [strεŋθ] n forza;
strengthen vt rinforzare; fortificare;
consolidare

strenuous ['strεnjuəs] adj
vigoroso(-a), energico(-a); (tiring)
duro(-a), pesante

stress [strεs] n (force, pressure)
pressione f; (mental strain) tensione
f; (accent) accento ▷ vt insistere su,
sottolineare; accentare; **stressed**
adj (tense: person) stressato(-a);
(Ling, Poetry: syllable) accentato(-a);
stressful adj (job) difficile, stressante

stretch [strεtʃ] n (of sand etc) distesa
▷ vi stirarsi; (extend): **to ~ to** or **as far
as** estendersi fino a ▷ vt tendere,
allungare; (spread) distendere; (fig)
spingere (al massimo); **stretch out**
vi allungarsi, estendersi ▷ vt (arm
etc) allungare, tendere; (to spread)
distendere

stretcher ['strεtʃə^r] n barella, lettiga

strict [strɪkt] adj (severe) rigido(-a),
severo(-a); (precise) preciso(-a),
stretto(-a); **strictly** adv severamente;
rigorosamente; strettamente

stride [straɪd] (pt **strode**, pp **stridden**)
n passo lungo ▷ vi camminare a
grandi passi

strike [straɪk] (pt, pp **struck**) n
sciopero; (of oil etc) scoperta; (attack)
attacco ▷ vt colpire; (oil etc) scoprire,
trovare; (bargain) fare; (fig): **the
thought** or **it ~s me that ...** mi viene
in mente che ... ▷ vi scioperare;
(attack) attaccare; (clock) suonare; **on
~** (workers) in sciopero; **to ~ a match**
accendere un fiammifero; **striker** n
scioperante m/f; (Sport) attaccante m;
striking adj che colpisce

string [strɪŋ] (pt, pp **strung**) n spago;
(row) fila; sequenza; catena; (Mus)
corda ▷ vt **to ~ out** disporre di
fianco; **to ~ together** (words, ideas)
mettere insieme; **the strings** npl
(Mus) gli archi; **to pull ~s for sb** (fig)
raccomandare qn

strip [strɪp] n striscia ▷ vt spogliare;
(paint) togliere; (also: **~ down**:
machine) smontare ▷ vi spogliarsi;
strip off vt (paint etc) staccare ▷ vi
(person) spogliarsi

stripe [straɪp] n striscia, riga; (Mil,
Police) gallone m; **striped** adj a strisce
or righe

stripper ['strɪpə^r] n spogliarellista m/f

strip-search ['strɪpsə:tʃ] vt **to ~ sb**
perquisire qn facendolo ▷ spogliare
▷ n perquisizione (facendo spogliare il
perquisto)

strive [straɪv] (pt **strove**, pp **striven**)
vi **to ~ to do** sforzarsi di fare

strode [strəud] pt of **stride**

stroke [strəuk] n colpo; (Swimming)
bracciata; (: style) stile m; (Med) colpo
apoplettico ▷ vt accarezzare; **at a ~**
in un attimo

stroll [strəul] n giretto, passeggiata
▷ vi andare a spasso; **stroller** (us) n
passeggino

strong [strɔŋ] adj (gen) forte; (sturdy:
table, fabric etc) robusto(-a); **they
are 50 ~** sono in 50; **stronghold**
n (also fig) roccaforte f; **strongly**
adv fortemente, con forza;
energicamente; vivamente

strove [strəuv] pt of **strive**

struck [strʌk] pt, pp of **strike**

structure ['strʌktʃə^r] n struttura;
(building) costruzione f, fabbricato

struggle ['strʌgl] n lotta ▷ vi lottare

strung [strʌŋ] pt, pp of **string**

stub [stʌb] n mozzicone m; (of ticket
etc) matrice f, talloncino ▷ vt **to ~
one's toe** urtare or sbattere il dito del
piede; **stub out** vt schiacciare

stubble ['stʌbl] n stoppia; (on chin)
barba ispida

stubborn ['stʌbən] adj testardo(-a),
ostinato(-a)

stuck [stʌk] pt, pp of **stick** ▷ adj
(jammed) bloccato(-a)

stud [stʌd] n bottoncino; borchia;
(also: **~ earring**) orecchino a

pressione; (*also:* **~ farm**) scuderia, allevamento di cavalli; (*also:* **~ horse**) stallone *m* ▷ *vt* (*fig*): **~ded with** tempestato(-a) di

student ['stju:dənt] *n* studente(-essa) ▷ *cpd* studentesco(-a); universitario(-a); degli studenti; **student driver** (*us*) *n* conducente *m/f* principiante; **students' union** *n* (*BRIT: association*) circolo universitario; (: *building*) sede *f* del circolo universitario

studio ['stju:dɪəu] *n* studio; **studio flat** (*us* **studio apartment**) *n* monolocale *m*

study ['stʌdɪ] *n* studio ▷ *vt* studiare; esaminare ▷ *vi* studiare

stuff [stʌf] *n* roba; (*substance*) sostanza, materiale *m* ▷ *vt* imbottire; (*Culin*) farcire; (*dead animal*) impagliare; (*inf: push*) ficcare; **stuffing** *n* imbottitura; (*Culin*) ripieno; **stuffy** *adj* (*room*) mal ventilato(-a), senz'aria; (*ideas*) antiquato(-a)

stumble ['stʌmbl] *vi* inciampare; **to ~ across** (*fig*) imbattersi in

stump [stʌmp] *n* ceppo; (*of limb*) moncone *m* ▷ *vt*: **to be ~ed** essere sconcertato(-a)

stun [stʌn] *vt* stordire; (*amaze*) sbalordire

stung [stʌŋ] *pt, pp of* **sting**

stunk [stʌŋk] *pp of* **stink**

stunned [stʌnd] *adj* (*from blow*) stordito(-a); (*amazed, shocked*) sbalordito(-a)

stunning ['stʌnɪŋ] *adj* sbalorditivo(-a); (*girl etc*) fantastico(-a)

stunt [stʌnt] *n* bravata; trucco pubblicitario

stupid ['stju:pɪd] *adj* stupido(-a); **stupidity** [-'pɪdɪtɪ] *n* stupidità *f inv*, stupidaggine *f*

sturdy ['stə:dɪ] *adj* robusto(-a), vigoroso(-a); solido(-a)

stutter ['stʌtər] *n* balbuzie *f* ▷ *vi* balbettare

style [staɪl] *n* stile *m*; (*distinction*) eleganza, classe *f*; **stylish** *adj* elegante; **stylist** *n* **hair stylist** parrucchiere(-a)

sub... [sʌb] *prefix* sub..., sotto...; **subconscious** *adj* subcosciente ▷ *n* subcosciente *m*

subdued [səb'dju:d] *adj* pacato(-a); (*light*) attenuato(-a)

subject [*n* 'sʌbdʒɪkt, *vb* səb'dʒɛkt] *n* soggetto; (*citizen etc*) cittadino(-a); (*Scol*) materia ▷ *vt* **to ~ to** sottomettere a; esporre a; **to be ~ to** (*law*) essere sottomesso(-a) a; (*disease*) essere soggetto(-a) a; **subjective** [-'dʒɛktɪv] *adj* soggettivo(-a); **subject matter** *n* argomento; contenuto

subjunctive [səb'dʒʌŋktɪv] *adj* congiuntivo(-a) ▷ *n* congiuntivo

submarine [sʌbmə'ri:n] *n* sommergibile *m*

submission [səb'mɪʃən] *n* sottomissione *f*; (*claim*) richiesta

submit [səb'mɪt] *vt* sottomettere ▷ *vi* sottomettersi

subordinate [sə'bɔ:dɪnət] *adj, n* subordinato(-a)

subscribe [səb'skraɪb] *vi* contribuire; **to ~ to** (*opinion*) approvare, condividere; (*fund*) sottoscrivere a; (*newspaper*) abbonarsi a; essere abbonato(-a) a

subscription [səb'skrɪpʃən] *n* sottoscrizione *f*; abbonamento

subsequent ['sʌbsɪkwənt] *adj* successivo(-a), seguente; conseguente; **subsequently** *adv* in seguito, successivamente

subside [səb'saɪd] *vi* cedere, abbassarsi; (*flood*) decrescere; (*wind*) calmarsi

subsidiary [səb'sɪdɪərɪ] *adj* sussidiario(-a); accessorio(-a) ▷ *n* filiale *f*

subsidize ['sʌbsɪdaɪz] *vt* sovvenzionare

subsidy ['sʌbsɪdɪ] n sovvenzione f
substance ['sʌbstəns] n sostanza
substantial [səb'stænʃl] adj
solido(-a); (amount, progress etc)
notevole; (meal) sostanzioso(-a)
substitute ['sʌbstɪtjuːt] n (person)
sostituto(-a); (thing) succedaneo,
surrogato ▷ vt **to ~ sth/sb for**
sostituire qc/qn a; **substitution**
[sʌbstɪ'tjuːʃən] n sostituzione f
subtle ['sʌtl] adj sottile
subtract [səb'trækt] vt sottrarre
suburb ['sʌbəːb] n sobborgo; **the ~s**
la periferia; **suburban** [sə'bəːbən] adj
suburbano(-a)
subway ['sʌbweɪ] n (US: underground)
metropolitana; (BRIT: underpass)
sottopassaggio
succeed [sək'siːd] vi riuscire; avere
successo ▷ vt succedere a; **to ~ in
doing** riuscire a fare
success [sək'sɛs] n successo;
successful adj (venture) coronato(-a)
da successo, riuscito(-a); **to be
successful (in doing)** riuscire (a fare);
successfully adv con successo
succession [sək'sɛʃən] n
successione f
successive [sək'sɛsɪv] adj
successivo(-a); consecutivo(-a)
successor [sək'sɛsər] n successore m
succumb [sə'kʌm] vi soccombere
such [sʌtʃ] adj (of that kind): **~ a
book** un tale libro, un libro del genere;
~ books tali libri, libri del genere; (so
much): **~ courage** tanto coraggio
▷ adv talmente, così; **~ a long trip** un
viaggio così lungo; **~ a lot of** talmente
or così tanto(-a); **~ as** (like) come; **as
~** come or in quanto tale; **such-and-
such** adj tale (after noun)
suck [sʌk] vt succhiare; (breast, bottle)
poppare
Sudan [suː'dɑːn] n Sudan m
sudden ['sʌdn] adj improvviso(-a);
all of a ~ improvvisamente,
all'improvviso; **suddenly** adv

bruscamente, improvvisamente, di
colpo
sudoku [sʊ'dəʊkuː] n sudoku m inv
sue [suː] vt citare in giudizio
suede [sweɪd] n pelle f scamosciata
suffer ['sʌfər] vt soffrire, patire; (bear)
sopportare, tollerare ▷ vi soffrire;
to ~ from soffrire di; **suffering** n
sofferenza
suffice [sə'faɪs] vi essere sufficiente,
bastare
sufficient [sə'fɪʃənt] adj sufficiente; **~
money** abbastanza soldi
suffocate ['sʌfəkeɪt] vi (have difficulty
breathing) soffocare; (die through lack of
air) asfissiare
sugar ['ʃʊgər] n zucchero ▷ vt
zuccherare
suggest [sə'dʒɛst] vt proporre,
suggerire; indicare; **suggestion**
[-'dʒɛstʃən] n suggerimento,
proposta; indicazione f
suicide ['suːɪsaɪd] n (person) suicida
m/f; (act) suicidio; see also **commit**;
suicide bomber n kamikaze m/f inv,
attentatore(-trice) suicida inv; **suicide
bombing** n attentato suicida
suit [suːt] n (man's) vestito; (woman's)
completo, tailleur m inv; (Law) causa;
(Cards) seme m, colore m ▷ vt andar
bene a or per; essere adatto(-a) a or
per; (adapt): **to ~ sth to** adattare qc a;
well ~ed ben assortito(-a); **suitable**
adj adatto(-a); appropriato(-a);
suitcase ['suːtkeɪs] n valigia
suite [swiːt] n (of rooms)
appartamento; (Mus) suite f inv;
(furniture): **bedroom/dining room
~** arredo or mobilia per la camera da
letto/sala da pranzo
sulfur ['sʌlfər] (US) n = **sulphur**
sulk [sʌlk] vi fare il broncio
sulphur ['sʌlfər] (US **sulfur**) n zolfo
sultana [sʌl'tɑːnə] n (fruit) uva (secca)
sultanina
sum [sʌm] n somma; (Scol etc)
addizione f; **sum up** vt, vi riassumere

summarize ['sʌməraɪz] vt
riassumere, riepilogare

summary ['sʌmərɪ] n riassunto

summer ['sʌməʳ] n estate f ▷ cpd
d'estate, estivo(-a); **summer
holidays** npl vacanze fpl estive;
summertime n (season) estate f

summit ['sʌmɪt] n cima, sommità;
(Pol) vertice m

summon ['sʌmən] vt chiamare,
convocare

Sun. abbr (= Sunday) dom.

sun [sʌn] n sole m; **sunbathe** vi
prendere un bagno di sole; **sunbed** n
lettino solare; **sunblock** n protezione
f solare totale; **sunburn** n (painful)
scottatura; **sunburned, sunburnt**
adj abbronzato(-a); (painfully)
scottato(-a)

Sunday ['sʌndɪ] n domenica

Sunday paper n giornale m della
domenica

● **SUNDAY PAPER**
●
● I **Sunday papers** sono i giornali
● che escono di domenica. Sono
● generalmente corredati da
● supplementi e riviste di argomento
● culturale, sportivo e di attualità.

sunflower ['sʌnflauəʳ] n girasole m

sung [sʌŋ] pp of **sing**

sunglasses ['sʌnglɑ:sɪz] npl occhiali
mpl da sole

sunk [sʌŋk] pp of **sink**

sun: **sunlight** n (luce f del) sole m;
sun lounger n sedia a sdraio; **sunny**
adj assolato(-a), soleggiato(-a); (fig)
allegro(-a), felice; **sunrise** n levata
del sole, alba; **sun roof** n (Aut)
tetto apribile; **sunscreen** n (cream)
crema solare protettiva; **sunset** n
tramonto; **sunshade** n parasole
m; **sunshine** n luce f (del) sole m;
sunstroke n insolazione f, colpo
di sole; **suntan** n abbronzatura;

suntan lotion n lozione f solare;
suntan oil n olio solare

super ['su:pəʳ] (inf) adj fantastico(-a)

superb [su:'pə:b] adj magnifico(-a)

superficial [su:pə'fɪʃəl] adj
superficiale

superintendent [su:pərɪn'tɛndənt]
n direttore(-trice); (Police)
≈ commissario (capo)

superior [su'pɪərɪəʳ] adj, n superiore
m/f

superlative [su'pə:lətɪv] adj
superlativo(-a), supremo(-a) ▷ n
(Ling) superlativo

supermarket ['su:pəmɑ:kɪt] n
supermercato

supernatural [su:pə'nætʃərəl] adj
soprannaturale ▷ n soprannaturale m

superpower ['su:pəpauəʳ] n (Pol)
superpotenza

superstition [su:pə'stɪʃən] n
superstizione f

superstitious [su:pə'stɪʃəs] adj
superstizioso(-a)

superstore ['su:pəstɔ:ʳ] n (BRIT)
grande supermercato

supervise ['su:pəvaɪz] vt (person
etc) sorvegliare; (organization)
soprintendere a; **supervision**
[-'vɪʒən] n sorveglianza; supervisione
f; **supervisor** n sorvegliante
m/f; soprintendente m/f; (in shop)
capocommesso(-a)

supper ['sʌpəʳ] n cena

supple ['sʌpl] adj flessibile; agile

supplement [n 'sʌplɪmənt, vb
sʌplɪ'mɛnt] n supplemento ▷ vt
completare, integrare

supplier [sə'plaɪəʳ] n fornitore m

supply [sə'plaɪ] vt (provide)
fornire; (equip): **to ~ (with)**
approvvigionare (di), attrezzare (con)
▷ n riserva, provvista; (supplying)
approvvigionamento; (Tech)
alimentazione f; **supplies** npl (food)
viveri mpl; (Mil) sussistenza

support [sə'pɔ:t] n (moral, financial

etc) sostegno, appoggio; (*Tech*) supporto ▷ *vt* sostenere; (*financially*) mantenere; (*uphold*) sostenere, difendere; **supporter** *n* (*Pol etc*) sostenitore(-trice), fautore(-trice); (*Sport*) tifoso(-a).

> Be careful not to translate **support** by the Italian word **sopportare**.

suppose [sə'pəuz] *vt* supporre; Immaginare; **to be ~d to do** essere tenuto(-a) a fare; **supposedly** [sə'pəuzɪdlɪ] *adv* presumibilmente; **supposing** *conj* se, ammesso che + *sub*

suppress [sə'prɛs] *vt* reprimere; sopprimere; occultare

supreme [su'priːm] *adj* supremo(-a)

surcharge ['səːtʃɑːdʒ] *n* supplemento

sure [ʃuə'] *adj* sicuro(-a); (*definite, convinced*) sicuro(-a), certo(-a); **~!** (*of course*) senz'altro!, certo!; **~ enough** infatti; **to make ~ of sth/that** assicurarsi di qc/che; **surely** *adv* sicuramente; certamente

surf [səːf] *n* (*waves*) cavalloni *mpl*; (*foam*) spuma

surface ['səːfɪs] *n* superficie *f* ▷ *vt* (*road*) asfaltare ▷ *vi* risalire alla superficie; (*fig: news, feeling*) venire a galla

surfboard ['səːfbɔːd] *n* tavola per surfing

surfer ['səːfə'] *n* (*in sea*) surfista *m/f*; (*on the Internet*) navigatore(-trice)

surfing ['səːfɪŋ] *n* surfing *m*

surge [səːdʒ] *n* (*strong movement*) ondata; (*of feeling*) impeto ▷ *vi* gonfiarsi; (*people*) riversarsi

surgeon ['səːdʒən] *n* chirurgo

surgery ['səːdʒərɪ] *n* chirurgia; (*BRIT: room*) studio *or* gabinetto medico, ambulatorio; (: *also:* **~ hours**) orario delle visite *or* di consultazione; **to undergo ~** subire un intervento chirurgico

surname ['səːneɪm] *n* cognome *m*

surpass [səː'pɑːs] *vt* superare

surplus ['səːpləs] *n* eccedenza; (*Econ*) surplus *m inv* ▷ *adj* eccedente, d'avanzo

surprise [sə'praɪz] *n* sorpresa; (*astonishment*) stupore *m* ▷ *vt* sorprendere; stupire; **surprised** [sə'praɪzd] *adj* (*look, smile*) sorpreso(-a); **to be surprised** essere sorpreso, sorprendersi; **surprising** *adj* sorprendente, stupefacente; **surprisingly** *adv* (*easy, helpful*) sorprendentemente

surrender [sə'rɛndə'] *n* resa, capitolazione *f* ▷ *vi* arrendersi

surround [sə'raund] *vt* circondare; (*Mil etc*) accerchiare; **surrounding** *adj* circostante; **surroundings** *npl* dintorni *mpl*; (*fig*) ambiente *m*

surveillance [səː'veɪləns] *n* sorveglianza, controllo

survey [*n* 'səːveɪ, *vb* səː'veɪ] *n* quadro generale; (*study*) esame *m*; (*in housebuying etc*) perizia; (*of land*) rilevamento, rilievo topografico ▷ *vt* osservare; esaminare; valutare; rilevare; **surveyor** *n* perito; geometra *m*; (*of land*) agrimensore *m*

survival [sə'vaɪvl] *n* sopravvivenza; (*relic*) reliquia, vestigio

survive [sə'vaɪv] *vi* sopravvivere ▷ *vt* sopravvivere a; **survivor** *n* superstite *m/f*, sopravvissuto(-a)

suspect [*adj, n* 'sʌspɛkt, *vb* səs'pɛkt] *adj* sospetto(-a) ▷ *n* persona sospetta ▷ *vt* sospettare; (*think likely*) supporre; (*doubt*) dubitare

suspend [səs'pɛnd] *vt* sospendere; **suspended sentence** *n* condanna con la condizionale; **suspenders** *npl* (*BRIT*) giarrettiere *fpl*; (*US*) bretelle *fpl*

suspense [səs'pɛns] *n* apprensione *f*; (*in film etc*) suspense *m*; **to keep sb in ~** tenere qn in sospeso

suspension [səs'pɛnʃən] *n* (*gen Aut*) sospensione *f*; (*of driving licence*) ritiro temporaneo; **suspension bridge** *n* ponte m sospeso

suspicion [səs'pɪʃən] n sospetto;
suspicious [səs'pɪʃəs] adj (suspecting)
sospettoso(-a); (causing suspicion)
sospetto(-a)

sustain [səs'teɪn] vt sostenere;
sopportare; (Law: charge) confermare;
(suffer) subire

SUV n abbr (= sports utility vehicle)
SUV m inv

swallow ['swɔləu] n (bird) rondine f
▷ vt inghiottire; (fig: story) bere

swam [swæm] pt of **swim**

swamp [swɔmp] n palude f ▷ vt
sommergere

swan [swɔn] n cigno

swap [swɔp] vt **to ~ (for)** scambiare
(con)

swarm [swɔ:m] n sciame m ▷ vi (bees)
sciamare; (people) brulicare; (place): **to
be ~ing with** brulicare di

sway [sweɪ] vi (tree) ondeggiare;
(person) barcollare ▷ vt (influence)
influenzare, dominare

swear [swɛəʳ] (pt **swore**, pp **sworn**)
vi (curse) bestemmiare, imprecare
▷ vt (promise) giurare; **swear in** vt
prestare giuramento a; **swearword**
n parolaccia

sweat [swɛt] n sudore m,
traspirazione f ▷ vi sudare

sweater ['swɛtəʳ] n maglione m

sweatshirt ['swɛtʃə:t] n felpa

sweaty ['swɛtɪ] adj sudato(-a),
bagnato(-a) di sudore

Swede [swi:d] n svedese m/f

swede [swi:d] (BRIT) n rapa svedese

Sweden ['swi:dn] n Svezia; **Swedish**
['swi:dɪʃ] adj svedese ▷ n (Ling)
svedese m

sweep [swi:p] (pt, pp **swept**)
n spazzata; (also: **chimney ~**)
spazzacamino ▷ vt spazzare, scopare;
(current) spazzare ▷ vi (hand) muoversi
con gesto ampio; (wind) infuriare

sweet [swi:t] n (BRIT: pudding) dolce
m; (candy) caramella ▷ adj dolce;

(fresh) fresco(-a); (fig) piacevole;
delicato(-a), grazioso(-a); gentile;
sweetcorn n granturco dolce;
sweetener ['swi:tnəʳ] n (Culin)
dolcificante m; **sweetheart** n
innamorato(-a); **sweetshop** n (BRIT)
≈ pasticceria

swell [swɛl] (pt **swelled**, pp **swollen**,
swelled) n (of sea) mare m lungo
▷ adj (US: inf: excellent) favoloso(-a)
▷ vt gonfiare, ingrossare; aumentare
▷ vi gonfiarsi, ingrossarsi; (sound)
crescere; (also: **~ up**) gonfiarsi;
swelling n (Med) tumefazione f,
gonfiore m

swept [swɛpt] pt, pp of **sweep**

swerve [swə:v] vi deviare; (driver)
sterzare; (boxer) scartare

swift [swɪft] n (bird) rondone m ▷ adj
rapido(-a), veloce

swim [swɪm] (pt **swam**, pp **swum**)
n **to go for a ~** andare a fare una
nuotata ▷ vi nuotare; (Sport) fare del
nuoto; (head, room) girare ▷ vt (river,
channel) attraversare o percorrere a
nuoto; (length) nuotare; **swimmer**
n nuotatore(-trice); **swimming** n
nuoto; **swimming costume** (BRIT)
n costume m da bagno; **swimming
pool** n piscina; **swimming trunks**
npl costume m da bagno (da uomo);
swimsuit n costume m da bagno

swing [swɪŋ] (pt, pp **swung**) n
altalena; (movement) oscillazione f;
(Mus) ritmo; swing m ▷ vt dondolare,
far oscillare; (also: **~ round**) far
girare ▷ vi oscillare, dondolare; (also:
~ round: object) roteare; (: person)
girarsi, voltarsi; **to be in full ~**
(activity) essere in piena attività; (party
etc) essere nel pieno

swipe card n tessera magnetica

swirl [swə:l] vi turbinare, far mulinello

Swiss [swɪs] adj, n inv svizzero(-a)

switch [swɪtʃ] n (for light, radio etc)
interruttore m; (change) cambiamento
▷ vt (change) cambiare; scambiare;

switch off vt spegnere; **could you switch off the light?** puoi spegnere la luce?; **switch on** vt accendere; (engine, machine) mettere in moto, avviare; **switchboard** n (Tel) centralino

Switzerland ['swɪtsələnd] n Svizzera

swivel ['swɪvl] vi (also: ~ **round**) girare

swollen ['swəulən] pp of **swell**

swoop [swuːp] n incursione f ▷ vi (also: ~ **down**) scendere in picchiata, piombare

swop [swɔp] n, vt = **swap**

sword [sɔːd] n spada; **swordfish** n pesce m spada inv

swore [swɔːr] pt of **swear**

sworn [swɔːn] pp of **swear** ▷ adj giurato(-a)

swum [swʌm] pp of **swim**

swung [swʌŋ] pt, pp of **swing**

syllable ['sɪləbl] n sillaba

syllabus ['sɪləbəs] n programma m

symbol ['sɪmbl] n simbolo; **symbolic(al)** [sɪm'bɔlɪk(l)] adj simbolico(-a); **to be symbolic(al) of sth** simboleggiare qc

symmetrical [sɪ'mɛtrɪkl] adj simmetrico(-a)

symmetry ['sɪmɪtrɪ] n simmetria

sympathetic [sɪmpə'θɛtɪk] adj (showing pity) compassionevole; (kind) comprensivo(-a); ~ **towards** ben disposto(-a) verso

  Be careful not to translate
  sympathetic by the Italian word
  simpatico.

sympathize ['sɪmpəθaɪz] vi **to ~ with** (person) compatire; partecipare al dolore di; (cause) simpatizzare per

sympathy ['sɪmpəθɪ] n compassione f

symphony ['sɪmfənɪ] n sinfonia

symptom ['sɪmptəm] n sintomo; indizio

synagogue ['sɪnəgɔg] n sinagoga

syndicate ['sɪndɪkɪt] n sindacato

syndrome ['sɪndrəum] n sindrome f

synonym ['sɪnənɪm] n sinonimo

synthetic [sɪn'θɛtɪk] adj sintetico(-a)

Syria ['sɪrɪə] n Siria

syringe [sɪ'rɪndʒ] n siringa

syrup ['sɪrəp] n sciroppo; (also: **golden** ~) melassa raffinata

system ['sɪstəm] n sistema m; (order) metodo; (Anat) organismo; **systematic** [-'mætɪk] adj sistematico(-a); metodico(-a); **systems analyst** n analista m di sistemi

ta [tɑː] (BRIT: inf) excl grazie!

tab [tæb] n (loop on coat etc) laccetto; (label) etichetta; **to keep ~s on** (fig) tenere d'occhio

table ['teɪbl] n tavolo, tavola; (Math, Chem etc) tavola ▷ vt (BRIT: motion etc) presentare; **a ~ for 4, please** un tavolo per 4, per favore; **to lay** or **set the ~** apparecchiare or preparare la tavola; **tablecloth** n tovaglia; **table d'hôte** [tɑːbl'dəut] adj (meal) a prezzo fisso; **table lamp** n lampada da tavolo; **tablemat** n sottopiatto; **tablespoon** n cucchiaio da tavola; (also: **tablespoonful**: as measurement) cucchiaiata

tablet ['tæblɪt] n (Med) compressa; (of stone) targa

table tennis n tennis m da tavolo, ping-pong® m

tabloid ['tæblɔɪd] n (newspaper) tabloid m inv (giornale illustrato di formato ridotto); **the ~s, the ~ press** i giornali popolari

taboo [təˈbuː] adj, n tabù m inv

tack [tæk] n (nail) bulletta; (fig) approccio ▷ vt imbullettare; imbastire ▷ vi bordeggiare

tackle ['tækl] n attrezzatura, equipaggiamento; (for lifting) paranco; (Football) contrasto; (Rugby) placcaggio ▷ vt (difficulty) affrontare; (Football) contrastare; (Rugby) placcare

tacky ['tækɪ] adj appiccicaticcio(-a); (pej) scadente

tact [tækt] n tatto: **tactful** adj delicato(-a), discreto(-a)

tactics ['tæktɪks] n, npl tattica

tactless ['tæktlɪs] adj che manca di tatto

tadpole ['tædpəul] n girino

taffy ['tæfɪ] (US) n caramella f mou inv

tag [tæg] n etichetta

tail [teɪl] n coda; (of shirt) falda ▷ vt (follow) seguire, pedinare; **~s** npl (formal suit) frac m inv

tailor ['teɪləʳ] n sarto

Taiwan [taɪˈwɑːn] n Taiwan m; **Taiwanese** [taɪwəˈniːz] adj, n taiwanese

take [teɪk] (pt **took**, pp **taken**) vt prendere; (gain: prize) ottenere, vincere; (require: effort, courage) occorrere, volerci; (tolerate) accettare, sopportare; (hold: passengers etc) contenere; (accompany) accompagnare; (bring, carry) portare; (exam) sostenere, presentarsi a; **to ~ a photo/a shower** fare una fotografia/ una doccia; **I ~ it that** suppongo che; **take after** vt fus assomigliare a; **take apart** vt smontare; **take away** vt portare via; togliere; **take back** vt (return) restituire; riportare; (one's words) ritirare; **take down** vt (building) demolire; (letter etc) scrivere; **take in** vt (deceive) imbrogliare, abbindolare; (understand) capire; (include) comprendere, includere; (lodger) prendere, ospitare; **take**

off *vi* (*Aviat*) decollare; (*go away*) andarsene ▷ *vt* (*remove*) togliere; **take on** *vt* (*work*) accettare, intraprendere; (*employee*) assumere; (*opponent*) sfidare, affrontare; **take out** *vt* portare fuori; (*remove*) togliere; (*licence*) prendere, ottenere; **to take sth out of sth** (*drawer, pocket etc*) tirare qc fuori da qc; estrarre qc da qc; **take over** *vt* (*business*) rilevare ▷ *vi* **to take over from sb** prendere le consegne *or* il controllo da qn; **take up** *vt* (*dress*) accorciare; (*occupy: time, space*) occupare; (*engage in: hobby etc*) mettersi a; **to take sb up on sth** accettare qc da qn; **takeaway** (*BRIT*) *n* (*shop etc*) ≈ rosticceria; (*food*) pasto per asporto; **taken** *pp of* **take**; **takeoff** *n* (*Aviat*) decollo; **takeout** (*US*) *n* = **takeaway**; **takeover** *n* (*Comm*) assorbimento; **takings** ['teɪkɪŋz] *npl* (*Comm*) incasso

talc [tælk] *n* (*also*: **~um powder**) talco

tale [teɪl] *n* racconto, storia; **to tell ~s** (*fig: to teacher, parent etc*) fare la spia

talent ['tælnt] *n* talento; **talented** *adj* di talento

talk [tɔːk] *n* discorso; (*gossip*) chiacchiere *fpl*; (*conversation*) conversazione *f*; (*interview*) discussione *f* ▷ *vi* parlare; **~s** *npl* (*Pol etc*) colloqui *mpl*; **to ~ about** parlare di; **to ~ sb out of/into doing** dissuadere qn da/convincere qn a fare; **to ~ shop** parlare di lavoro *or* di affari; **talk over** *vt* discutere; **talk show** *n* conversazione *f* televisiva, talk show *m inv*

tall [tɔːl] *adj* alto(-a); **to be 6 feet ~** ≈ essere alto 1 metro e 80

tambourine [tæmbə'riːn] *n* tamburello

tame [teɪm] *adj* addomesticato(-a); (*fig: story, style*) insipido(-a), scialbo(-a)

tamper ['tæmpəʳ] *vi* **to ~ with** manomettere

tampon ['tæmpɔn] *n* tampone *m*

tan [tæn] *n* (*also*: **sun~**) abbronzatura ▷ *vi* abbronzarsi ▷ *adj* (*colour*) marrone rossiccio *inv*

tandem ['tændəm] *n* tandem *m inv*

tangerine [tændʒə'riːn] *n* mandarino

tangle ['tæŋgl] *n* groviglio; **to get into a ~** aggrovigliarsi; (*fig*) combinare un pasticcio

tank [tæŋk] *n* serbatoio; (*for fish*) acquario; (*Mil*) carro armato

tanker ['tæŋkəʳ] *n* (*ship*) nave *f* cisterna *inv*; (*truck*) autobotte *f*, autocisterna

tanned [tænd] *adj* abbronzato(-a)

tantrum ['tæntrəm] *n* accesso di collera

Tanzania [tænzə'nɪə] *n* Tanzania

tap [tæp] *n* (*on sink etc*) rubinetto; (*gentle blow*) colpetto ▷ *vt* dare un colpetto a; (*resources*) sfruttare, utilizzare; (*telephone*) mettere sotto controllo; **on ~** (*fig: resources*) a disposizione; **tap dancing** *n* tip tap *m*

tape [teɪp] *n* nastro; (*also*: **magnetic ~**) nastro (magnetico); (*sticky tape*) nastro adesivo ▷ *vt* (*record*) registrare (su nastro); (*stick*) attaccare con nastro adesivo; **tape measure** *n* metro a nastro; **tape recorder** *n* registratore *m* (a nastro)

tapestry ['tæpɪstrɪ] *n* arazzo; tappezzeria

tar [tɑːʳ] *n* catrame *m*

target ['tɑːgɪt] *n* bersaglio; (*fig: objective*) obiettivo

tariff ['tærɪf] *n* tariffa

tarmac ['tɑːmæk] *n* (*BRIT: on road*) macadam *m* al catrame; (*Aviat*) pista di decollo

tarpaulin [tɑː'pɔːlɪn] *n* tela incatramata

tarragon ['tærəgən] *n* dragoncello

tart [tɑːt] *n* (*Culin*) crostata; (*BRIT: inf: pej: woman*) sgualdrina ▷ *adj* (*flavour*) aspro(-a), agro(-a)

tartan ['tɑːtn] *n* tartan *m inv*

tartar(e) sauce n salsa tartara
task [tɑːsk] n compito; **to take to ~**
rimproverare
taste [teɪst] n gusto; (*flavour*) sapore
m, gusto; (*sample*) assaggio; (*fig:
glimpse, idea*) idea ▷ vt gustare;
(*sample*) assaggiare ▷ vi **to ~ of** or **like**
(*fish etc*) sapere or avere sapore di; **in
good/bad ~** di buon/cattivo gusto;
can I have a ~? posso assaggiarlo?;
you can ~ the garlic (in it) (ci) si
sente il sapore dell'aglio; **tasteful** adj
di buon gusto; **tasteless** adj (*food*)
insipido(-a); (*remark*) di cattivo gusto;
tasty adj saporito(-a), gustoso(-a)
tatters ['tætəz] npl: **in ~** a brandelli
tattoo [tə'tuː] n tatuaggio; (*spectacle*)
parata militare ▷ vt tatuare
taught [tɔːt] pt, pp of **teach**
taunt [tɔːnt] n scherno ▷ vt schernire
Taurus ['tɔːrəs] n Toro
taut [tɔːt] adj teso(-a)
tax [tæks] n (*on goods*) imposta; (*on
services*) tassa; (*on income*) imposte
fpl, tasse fpl ▷ vt tassare; (*fig: strain:
patience etc*) mettere alla prova; **tax-
free** adj esente da imposte
taxi ['tæksɪ] n taxi m inv ▷ vi (*Aviat*)
rullare; **can you call me a ~, please?**
può chiamarmi un taxi, per favore?;
taxi driver n tassista m/f; **taxi rank**
(*BRIT*) n = **taxi stand**; **taxi stand** n
posteggio dei taxi
tax payer n contribuente m/f
TB n abbr = **tuberculosis**
tea [tiː] n tè m inv; (*BRIT: snack: for
children*) merenda; **high ~** (*BRIT*) cena
leggera (*presa nel tardo pomeriggio*); **tea
bag** n bustina di tè; **tea break** (*BRIT*)
n intervallo per il tè
teach [tiːtʃ] (pt, pp **taught**) vt **to ~ sb
sth, ~ sth to sb** insegnare qc a qn ▷ vi
insegnare; **teacher** n insegnante m/f;
(*in secondary school*) professore(-essa);
(*in primary school*) maestro(-a);
teaching n insegnamento
tea: **tea cloth** n (*for dishes*)

strofinaccio; (*BRIT: for trolley*)
tovaglietta da tè; **teacup** ['tiːkʌp] n
tazza da tè
tea leaves npl foglie fpl di tè
team [tiːm] n squadra; (*of animals*)
tiro; **team up** vi **to team up (with)**
mettersi insieme (a)
teapot ['tiːpɔt] n teiera
tear[1] [tɛər] (pt **tore**, pp **torn**) n strappo
▷ vt strappare ▷ vi strapparsi; **tear
apart** vt (*also fig*) distruggere; **tear
down** vt +adv (*building, statue*)
demolire; (*poster, flag*) tirare giù; **tear
off** vt (*sheet of paper etc*) strappare;
(*one's clothes*) togliersi di dosso; **tear
up** vt (*sheet of paper etc*) strappare
tear[2] [tɪər] n lacrima; **in ~s** in lacrime
tearful ['tɪəful] adj piangente,
lacrimoso(-a); **tear gas** n gas m
lacrimogeno
tearoom ['tiːruːm] n sala da tè
tease [tiːz] vt canzonare; (*unkindly*)
tormentare
tea: **teaspoon** n cucchiaino da tè;
(*also*: **teaspoonful**: *as measurement*)
cucchiaino; **teatime** n ora del tè;
tea towel (*BRIT*) n strofinaccio (per
i piatti)
technical ['tɛknɪkl] adj tecnico(-a)
technician [tɛk'nɪʃən] n tecnico(-a)
technique [tɛk'niːk] n tecnica
technology [tɛk'nɔlədʒɪ] n
tecnologia
teddy (bear) ['tɛdɪ-] n orsacchiotto
tedious ['tiːdɪəs] adj noioso(-a),
tedioso(-a)
tee [tiː] n (*Golf*) tee m inv
teen [tiːn] adj = **teenage** ▷ n (*US*)
= **teenager**
teenage ['tiːneɪdʒ] adj (*fashions
etc*) per giovani, per adolescenti;
teenager n adolescente m/f
teens [tiːnz] npl **to be in one's ~**
essere adolescente
teeth [tiːθ] npl of **tooth**
teetotal ['tiː'təutl] adj astemio(-a)
telecommunications ['tɛlɪkəm-

juːnɪ'keɪʃənz] n telecomunicazioni fpl
telegram ['tɛlɪgræm] n
telegramma m
telegraph pole n palo del telegrafo
telephone ['tɛlɪfəun] n telefono
▷ vt (person) telefonare a; (message)
comunicare per telefono; **telephone
book** n elenco telefonico; **telephone
booth** (BRIT), **telephone box** n
cabina telefonica; **telephone call**
n telefonata; **telephone directory**
n elenco telefonico; **telephone
number** n numero di telefono
telesales ['tɛlɪseɪlz] n vendita per
telefono
telescope ['tɛlɪskəup] n telescopio
televise ['tɛlɪvaɪz] vt teletrasmettere
television ['tɛlɪvɪʒən] n televisione
f; **on ~** alla televisione; **television
programme** n programma m
televisivo
tell [tɛl] (pt, pp **told**) vt dire; (relate:
story) raccontare; (distinguish): **to
~ sth from** distinguere qc da ▷ vi
(talk): **to ~ (of)** parlare (di); (have
effect) farsi sentire, avere effetto; **to
~ sb to do** dire a qn di fare; **tell off** vt
rimproverare, sgridare; **teller** n (in
bank) cassiere(-a)
telly ['tɛlɪ] (BRIT: inf) n abbr
(= television) tivù f inv
temp [tɛmp] n abbr (= temporary)
segretaria temporanea
temper ['tɛmpər] n (nature) carattere
m; (mood) umore m; (fit of anger) collera
▷ vt (moderate) moderare; **to be in
a ~** essere in collera; **to lose one's ~**
andare in collera
temperament ['tɛmprəmənt]
n (nature) temperamento;
temperamental [-'mɛntl] adj
capriccioso(-a)
temperature ['tɛmprətʃər] n
temperatura; **to have** or **run a ~** avere
la febbre
temple ['tɛmpl] n (building) tempio;
(Anat) tempia

temporary ['tɛmpərərɪ] adj
temporaneo(-a); (job, worker)
avventizio(-a), temporaneo(-a)
tempt [tɛmpt] vt tentare; **to ~ sb into
doing** indurre qn a fare; **temptation**
[-'teɪʃən] n tentazione f; **tempting**
adj allettante
ten [tɛn] num dieci
tenant ['tɛnənt] n inquilino(-a)
tend [tɛnd] vt badare a, occuparsi
di ▷ vi **to ~ to do** tendere a fare;
tendency ['tɛndənsɪ] n tendenza
tender ['tɛndər] adj tenero(-a); (sore)
dolorante ▷ n (Comm: offer) offerta;
(money): **legal ~** moneta in corso
legale ▷ vt offrire
tendon ['tɛndən] n tendine m
tenner ['tɛnər] n (BRIT inf) (banconota
da) dieci sterline fpl
tennis ['tɛnɪs] n tennis m; **tennis
ball** n palla da tennis; **tennis court**
n campo da tennis; **tennis match**
n partita di tennis; **tennis player**
n tennista m/f; **tennis racket** n
racchetta da tennis
tenor ['tɛnər] n (Mus) tenore m
tenpin bowling ['tɛnpɪn-] n
bowling m
tense [tɛns] adj teso(-a) ▷ n (Ling)
tempo
tension ['tɛnʃən] n tensione f
tent [tɛnt] n tenda
tentative ['tɛntətɪv] adj esitante,
incerto(-a); (conclusion) provvisorio(-a)
tenth [tɛnθ] num decimo(-a)
tent: **tent peg** n picchetto da tenda;
tent pole n palo da tenda, montante
m
tepid ['tɛpɪd] adj tiepido(-a)
term [təːm] n termine m; (Scol)
trimestre m; (Law) sessione f ▷ vt
chiamare, definire; **~s** npl (conditions)
condizioni fpl; (Comm) prezzi mpl,
tariffe fpl; **in the short/long ~** a
breve/lunga scadenza; **to be on good
~s with sb** essere in buoni rapporti
con qn; **to come to ~s with** (problem)

affrontare

terminal ['tə:mɪnl] *adj* finale, terminale; *(disease)* terminale ▷ *n* *(Elec)* morsetto; *(Comput)* terminale *m*; *(Aviat, for oil, ore etc)* terminal *m inv*; *(BRIT: also:* **coach ~**) capolinea *m*

terminate ['tə:mɪneɪt] *vt* mettere fine a

termini ['tə:mɪnaɪ] *npl of* **terminus**

terminology [tə:mɪ'nɔlədʒɪ] *n* terminologia

terminus ['tə:mɪnəs] (*pl* **termini**) *n* (*for buses*) capolinea *m*; (*for trains*) stazione *f* terminale

terrace ['tɛrəs] *n* terrazza; *(BRIT: row of houses)* fila di case a schiera; **terraced** *adj* (*garden*) a terrazze

terrain [tɛ'reɪn] *n* terreno

terrestrial [tɪ'rɛstrɪəl] *adj* (*life*) terrestre; (*BRIT: channel*) terrestre

terrible ['tɛrɪbl] *adj* terribile; **terribly** *adv* terribilmente; (*very badly*) malissimo

terrier ['tɛrɪər] *n* terrier *m inv*

terrific [tə'rɪfɪk] *adj* incredibile, fantastico(-a); (*wonderful*) formidabile, eccezionale

terrified ['tɛrɪfaɪd] *adj* atterrito(-a)

terrify ['tɛrɪfaɪ] *vt* terrorizzare; **terrifying** *adj* terrificante

territorial [tɛrɪ'tɔːrɪəl] *adj* territoriale

territory ['tɛrɪtərɪ] *n* territorio

terror ['tɛrər] *n* terrore *m*; **terrorism** *n* terrorismo; **terrorist** *n* terrorista *m/f*

test [tɛst] *n* (*trial, check: of courage etc*) prova; (*Med*) esame *m*; (*Chem*) analisi *f inv*; (*exam: of intelligence etc*) test *m inv*; (: *in school*) compito in classe; (*also:* **driving ~**) esame *m* di guida ▷ *vt* provare; esaminare; analizzare; sottoporre ad esame; **to ~ sb in history** esaminare qn in storia

testicle ['tɛstɪkl] *n* testicolo

testify ['tɛstɪfaɪ] *vi* (*Law*) testimoniare, deporre; **to ~ to sth** (*Law*) testimoniare qc; (*gen*)

comprovare *or* dimostrare qc

testimony ['tɛstɪmənɪ] *n* (*Law*) testimonianza, deposizione *f*

test: **test match** *n* (*Cricket, Rugby*) partita internazionale; **test tube** *n* provetta

tetanus ['tɛtənəs] *n* tetano

text [tɛkst] *n* testo; (*on mobile phone*) SMS *m inv*, messaggino ▷ *vt* **to ~ sb** (*inf*) mandare un SMS a qn; **textbook** *n* libro di testo

textile ['tɛkstaɪl] *n* tessile *m*

text message *n* (*Tel*) SMS *m inv*, messaggino

text messaging [-'mɛsɪdʒɪŋ] *n* il mandarsi SMS

texture ['tɛkstʃər] *n* tessitura; (*of skin, paper etc*) struttura

Thai [taɪ] *adj* tailandese ▷ *n* tailandese *m/f*; (*Ling*) tailandese *m*

Thailand ['taɪlænd] *n* Tailandia

Thames [tɛmz] *n*: **the ~** il Tamigi

than [ðæn, ðən] *conj* (*in comparisons*) che; (*with numerals, pronouns, proper names*) di; **more ~ 10/once** più di 10/una volta; **I have more/less ~ you** ne ho più/meno di te; **I have more pens ~ pencils** ho più penne che matite; **she is older ~ you think** è più vecchia di quanto tu (non) pensi

thank [θæŋk] *vt* ringraziare; **~ you (very much)** grazie (tante); **thanks** *npl* ringraziamenti *mpl*, grazie *fpl* ▷ *excl* grazie!; **~s to** grazie a; **thankfully** *adv* con riconoscenza; con sollievo; **thankfully there were few victims** grazie al cielo ci sono state poche vittime; **Thanksgiving (Day)** *n* giorno del ringraziamento

● **THANKSGIVING (DAY)**
●
● Negli Stati Uniti il quarto giovedì di
● novembre ricorre il **Thanksgiving**
● **(Day)**, festa che rievoca la
● celebrazione con cui i Padri
● Pellegrini, fondatori della colonia

di Plymouth in Massachusetts,
ringraziarono Dio del buon raccolto
del 1621.

 KEYWORD

that [ðæt] (pl **those**) adj
(demonstrative) quel (quell', quello) m;
quella (quell') f; **that man/woman/
book** quell'uomo/quella donna/quel
libro; (not "this") quell'uomo/quella
donna/quel libro là; **that one**
quello(-a) là
▷ pron 1 (demonstrative) ciò; (not "this
one") quello(-a); **who's that?** chi è?;
what's that? cos'è quello?; **is that
you?** sei tu?; **I prefer this to that**
preferisco questo a quello; **that's what
he said** questo è ciò che ha detto;
what happened after that? che è
successo dopo?; **that is (to say)** cioè
2 (relative: direct) che; (: indirect) cui;
the book (that) I read il libro che
ho letto; **the box (that) I put it in** la
scatola in cui l'ho messo; **the people
(that) I spoke to** le persone con cui or
con le quali ho parlato
3 (relative: of time) in cui; **the day
(that) he came** il giorno in cui è venuto
▷ conj che; **he thought that I was ill**
pensava che io fossi malato
▷ adv (demonstrative) **I can't
work that much** non posso lavorare
(così) tanto; **that high** così alto; **the
wall's about that high and that
thick** il muro è alto circa così e spesso
circa così

thatched [θætʃt] adj (roof) di paglia
thaw [θɔː] n disgelo ▷ vi (ice)
sciogliersi; (food) scongelarsi ▷ vt
(food: also: **~ out**) (fare) scongelare

 KEYWORD

the [ðiː, ðə] def art 1 (gen) il (lo, l') m; la
(l') f; i (gli) mpl; le fpl; **the boy/girl/ink**
il ragazzo/la ragazza/l'inchiostro;
the books/pencils i libri/le matite;
the history of the world la storia
del mondo; **give it to the postman**
dallo al postino; **I haven't the time/
money** non ho tempo/soldi; **the rich
and the poor** i ricchi e i poveri
2 (in titles): **Elizabeth the First**
Elisabetta prima; **Peter the Great**
Pietro il grande
3 (in comparisons): **the more he
works, the more he earns** più lavora
più guadagna

theatre ['θɪətə*] (US **theater**) n
teatro; (also: **lecture ~**) aula magna;
(also: **operating ~**) sala operatoria
theft [θɛft] n furto
their [ðɛə*] adj il (la) loro; (pl) i (le) loro;
theirs pron il (la) loro; (pl) i (le) loro;
see also **my**; **mine**
them [ðɛm, ðəm] pron (direct) li (le);
(indirect) gli (loro (after vb)); (stressed,
after prep: people) loro; (: people, things)
essi(-e); see also **me**
theme [θiːm] n tema m; **theme park**
n parco di divertimenti (intorno a un
tema centrale)
themselves [ðəm'sɛlvz] pl pron
(reflexive) si; (emphatic) loro stessi(-e);
(after prep) se stessi(-e)
then [ðɛn] adv (at that time) allora;
(next) poi, dopo; (and also) e poi ▷ conj
(therefore) perciò, dunque, quindi ▷ adj
the ~ president il presidente di allora;
by ~ allora; **from ~ on** da allora in poi
theology [θɪ'ɔlədʒɪ] n teologia
theory ['θɪərɪ] n teoria
therapist ['θɛrəpɪst] n terapista m/f
therapy ['θɛrəpɪ] n terapia

 KEYWORD

there [ðɛə*] adv 1: **there is, there
are** c'è, ci sono; **there are 3 of them**
(people) sono in 3; (things) ce ne sono 3;
there is no-one here non c'è nessuno

qui; **there has been an accident** c'è stato un incidente

2 (*referring to place*) là, lì; **up/in/down there** lassù/là dentro/laggiù; **he went there on Friday** ci è andato venerdì; **I want that book there** voglio quel libro là *or* lì; **there he is!** eccolo!

3: **there, there** (*esp to child*) su, su

there: **thereabouts** [ðɛərəˈbauts] *adv* (*place*) nei pressi, da quelle parti; (*amount*) giù di lì, all'incirca; **thereafter** [ðɛərˈɑːftəʳ] *adv* da allora in poi; **thereby** [ðɛəˈbaɪ] *adv* con ciò; **therefore** [ˈðɛəfɔːʳ] *adv* perciò, quindi; **there's** [ðɛəz] = **there is**; **there has**

thermal [ˈθəːml] *adj* termico(-a)

thermometer [θəˈmɔmɪtəʳ] *n* termometro

thermostat [ˈθəːməstæt] *n* termostato

these [ðiːz] *pl pron, adj* questi(-e)

thesis [ˈθiːsɪs] (*pl* **theses**) *n* tesi *f inv*

they [ðeɪ] *pl pron* essi (esse); (*people only*) loro; **~ say that ...** (*it is said that*) si dice che ...; **they'd** = **they had**; **they would**; **they'll** = **they shall**; **they will**; **they're** = **they are**; **they've** = **they have**

thick [θɪk] *adj* spesso(-a); (*crowd*) compatto(-a); (*stupid*) ottuso(-a), lento(-a) ▷ *n* **in the ~ of** nel folto di; **it's 20 cm ~** ha uno spessore di 20 cm; **thicken** *vi* ispessire ▷ *vt* (*sauce etc*) ispessire, rendere più denso(-a); **thickness** *n* spessore *m*

thief [θiːf] (*pl* **thieves**) *n* ladro(-a)

thigh [θaɪ] *n* coscia

thin [θɪn] *adj* sottile; (*person*) magro(-a); (*soup*) poco denso(-a) ▷ *vt* **to ~ (down)** (*sauce, paint*) diluire

thing [θɪŋ] *n* cosa; (*object*) oggetto; (*mania*): **to have a ~ about** essere fissato(-a) con; **~s** *npl* (*belongings*) cose *fpl*; **poor ~** poverino(-a); **the**

best ~ would be to la cosa migliore sarebbe di; **how are ~s?** come va?

think [θɪŋk] (*pt, pp* **thought**) *vi* pensare, riflettere ▷ *vt* pensare, credere; (*imagine*) immaginare; **to ~ of** pensare a; **what did you ~ of them?** cosa ne ha pensato?; **to ~ about sth/sb** pensare a qc/qn; **I'll ~ about it** ci penserò; **to ~ of doing** pensare di fare; **I ~ so/not** penso di sì/no; **to ~ well of** avere una buona opinione di; **think over** *vt* riflettere su; **think up** *vt* ideare

third [θəːd] *num* terzo(-a) ▷ *n* terzo(-a); (*fraction*) terzo, terza parte *f*; (*Aut*) terza; (*Brit: Scol*) laurea col minimo dei voti; **thirdly** *adv* in terzo luogo; **third party insurance** (*Brit*) *n* assicurazione *f* contro terzi; **Third World** *n*: **the Third World** il Terzo Mondo

thirst [θəːst] *n* sete *f*; **thirsty** *adj* (*person*) assetato(-a), che ha sete

thirteen [θəːˈtiːn] *num* tredici; **thirteenth** [-ˈtiːnθ] *num* tredicesmo(-a)

thirtieth [ˈθəːtɪɪθ] *num* trentesimo(-a)

thirty [ˈθəːtɪ] *num* trenta

○ KEYWORD

this [ðɪs] (*pl* **these**) *adj* (*demonstrative*) questo(-a); **this man/woman/book** quest'uomo/questa donna/questo libro; (*not* "that") quest'uomo/questa donna/questo libro qui; **this one** questo(-a) qui

▷ *pron* (*demonstrative*) questo(-a); (*not* "that one") questo(-a) qui; **who/ what is this?** chi è/che cos'è questo?; **I prefer this to that** preferisco questo a quello; **this is where I live** io abito qui; **this is what he said** questo è ciò che ha detto; **this is Mr Brown** (*in introductions, photo*) questo è il signor Brown; (*on telephone*) sono il

signor Brown
▷ adv (demonstrative): **this high/long**
etc alto/lungo etc così; **I didn't know
things were this bad** non sapevo
andasse così male

thistle ['θɪsl] n cardo
thorn [θɔːn] n spina
thorough ['θʌrə] adj (search)
minuzioso(-a); (knowledge, research)
approfondito(-a), profondo(-a);
(person) coscienzioso(-a); (cleaning)
a fondo; **thoroughly** adv (search)
minuziosamente; (wash, study) a
fondo; (very) assolutamente
those [ðəuz] pl pron quelli(-e) ▷ pl adj
quei (quegli) mpl; quelle fpl
though [ðəu] conj benché, sebbene
▷ adv comunque
thought [θɔːt] pt, pp of **think** ▷ n
pensiero; (opinion) opinione f;
thoughtful adj pensieroso(-a),
pensoso(-a); (considerate)
premuroso(-a); **thoughtless** adj
sconsiderato(-a); (behaviour) scortese
thousand ['θauzənd] num mille; **one
~ s** mille; **~s of** migliaia di; **thousandth**
num millesimo(-a)
thrash [θræʃ] vt picchiare; bastonare;
(defeat) battere
thread [θrɛd] n filo; (of screw) filetto
▷ vt (needle) infilare
threat [θrɛt] n minaccia; **threaten** vi
(storm) minacciare ▷ vt **to threaten
sb with/to do** minacciare qn con/di
fare; **threatening** adj minaccioso(-a)
three [θriː] num tre; **three-
dimensional** adj tridimensionale;
(film) stereoscopico(-a); **three-
piece suite** ['θriː-piːs-] n salotto
comprendente un divano e due
poltrone; **three-quarters** npl tre
quarti mpl; **three-quarters full** pieno
per tre quarti
threshold ['θrɛʃhəuld] n soglia
threw [θruː] pt of **throw**
thrill [θrɪl] n brivido ▷ vt (audience)

elettrizzare; **to be ~ed** (with gift etc)
essere elettrizzato(-a); **thrilled** adj **I
was thrilled to get your letter** la tua
lettera mi ha fatto veramente piacere;
thriller n thriller m inv; **thrilling** adj
(book) pieno(-a) di suspense; (news,
discovery) elettrizzante
thriving ['θraɪvɪŋ] adj fiorente
throat [θrəut] n gola; **to have a sore
~** avere (un or il) mal di gola
throb [θrɔb] vi palpitare; pulsare;
vibrare
throne [θrəun] n trono
through [θruː] prep attraverso;
(time) per, durante; (by means of) per
mezzo di; (owing to) a causa di ▷ adj
(ticket, train, passage) diretto(-a)
▷ adv attraverso; **to put sb ~ to sb**
(Tel) passare qn a qn; **to be ~** (Tel)
ottenere la comunicazione; (have
finished) essere finito(-a); **"no ~
road"** (BRIT) "strada senza sbocco";
throughout prep (place) dappertutto
in; (time) per or durante tutto(-a) ▷ adv
dappertutto; sempre
throw [θrəu] (pt **threw**, pp **thrown**)
n (Sport) lancio, tiro ▷ vt tirare,
gettare; (Sport) lanciare, tirare; (rider)
disarcionare; (fig) confondere; **to ~ a
party** dare una festa; **throw away**
vt gettare or buttare via; **throw in** vt
(Sport: ball) rimettere in gioco; (include)
aggiungere; **throw off** vt sbarazzarsi
di; **throw out** vt buttare fuori; (reject)
respingere; **throw up** vi vomitare
thru [θruː] (US) prep, adj, adv
= **through**
thrush [θrʌʃ] n tordo
thrust [θrʌst] (pt, pp **thrust**) vt
spingere con forza; (push in) conficcare
thud [θʌd] n tonfo
thug [θʌg] n delinquente m
thumb [θʌm] n (Anat) pollice m; **to ~ a
lift** fare l'autostop; **thumbtack** (US) n
puntina da disegno
thump [θʌmp] n colpo forte; (sound)
tonfo ▷ vt (person) picchiare; (object)

battere su ▷ vi picchiare; battere
thunder ['θʌndə^r] n tuono ▷ vi
tuonare; (train etc): **to ~ past** passare
con un rombo; **thunderstorm** n
temporale m
Thur(s). abbr (= Thursday) gio.
Thursday ['θəːzdɪ] n giovedì m inv
thus [ðʌs] adv così
thwart [θwɔːt] vt contrastare
thyme [taɪm] n timo
Tiber ['taɪbə^r] n: **the ~** il Tevere
Tibet [tɪ'bɛt] n Tibet m
tick [tɪk] n (sound: of clock) tic tac m inv;
(mark) segno; spunta; (Zool) zecca;
(BRIT: inf): **in a ~** in un attimo ▷ vi
fare tic tac ▷ vt spuntare; **tick off** vt
spuntare; (person) sgridare
ticket ['tɪkɪt] n biglietto; (in shop: on
goods) etichetta; (parking ticket) multa;
(for library) scheda; **a single/return
~ to ...** un biglietto di sola andata/di
andata e ritorno per...; **ticket barrier**
n (BRIT: Rail) cancelletto d'ingresso;
ticket collector n bigliettaio; **ticket
inspector** n controllore m; **ticket
machine** n distributore m di biglietti;
ticket office n biglietteria
tickle ['tɪkl] vt fare il solletico a; (fig)
solleticare ▷ vi **it ~s** mi (or gli etc) fa il
solletico; **ticklish** [-lɪʃ] adj che soffre il
solletico; (problem) delicato(-a)
tide [taɪd] n marea; (fig: of events)
corso; **high/low ~** alta/bassa marea
tidy ['taɪdɪ] adj (room) ordinato(-a),
lindo(-a); (dress, work) curato(-a), in
ordine; (person) ordinato(-a) ▷ vt (also:
~ up) riordinare, mettere in ordine
tie [taɪ] n (string etc) legaccio; (BRIT:
also: **neck~**) cravatta; (fig: link)
legame m; (Sport: draw) pareggio ▷ vt
(parcel) legare; (ribbon) annodare ▷ vi
(Sport) pareggiare; **to ~ sth in a bow**
annodare qc; **to ~ a knot in sth** fare
un nodo a qc; **tie down** vt legare; (to
price etc) costringere ad accettare;
tie up vt (parcel, dog) legare;
(boat) ormeggiare; (arrangements)

concludere; **to be tied up** (busy)
essere occupato(-a) or preso(-a)
tier [tɪə^r] n fila; (of cake) piano, strato
tiger ['taɪgə^r] n tigre f
tight [taɪt] adj (rope) teso(-a),
tirato(-a); (money) poco(-a);
(clothes, budget, bend etc) stretto(-a);
(control) severo(-a), fermo(-a); (inf:
drunk) sbronzo(-a) ▷ adv (squeeze)
fortemente; (shut) ermeticamente;
tighten vt (rope) tendere; (screw)
stringere; (control) rinforzare ▷ vi
tendersi; stringersi; **tightly** adv
(grasp) bene, saldamente; **tights**
(BRIT) npl collant m inv
tile [taɪl] n (on roof) tegola; (on wall or
floor) piastrella, mattonella
till [tɪl] n registratore m di cassa ▷ vt
(land) coltivare ▷ prep, conj = **until**
tilt [tɪlt] vt inclinare, far pendere ▷ vi
inclinarsi, pendere
timber ['tɪmbə^r] n (material)
legname m
time [taɪm] n tempo; (epoch: often pl)
epoca, tempo; (by clock) ora; (moment)
momento; (occasion) volta; (Mus)
tempo ▷ vt (race) cronometrare;
(programme) calcolare la durata di; (fix
moment for) programmare; (remark
etc) dire (or fare) al momento giusto;
a long ~ molto tempo; **what ~ does
the museum/shop open?** a che ora
apre il museo/negozio?; **for the ~
being** per il momento; **4 at a ~** 4 per
or alla volta; **from ~ to ~** ogni tanto;
at ~s a volte; **in ~** (soon enough) in
tempo; (after some time) col tempo;
(Mus) a tempo; **in a week's ~** fra una
settimana; **in no ~** in un attimo;
any ~ in qualsiasi momento; **on ~**
puntualmente; **5 ~s 5** 5 volte 5, 5 per 5;
what ~ is it? che ora è?, che ore sono?;
to have a good ~ divertirsi; **time
limit** n limite m di tempo; **timely**
adj opportuno(-a); **timer** n (time
switch) temporizzatore m; (in kitchen)
contaminuti m inv; **time-share**

adj **time-share apartment/villa** appartamento/villa in multiproprietà; **timetable** *n* orario; **time zone** *n* fuso orario

timid ['tɪmɪd] *adj* timido(-a); (*easily scared*) pauroso(-a)

timing ['taɪmɪŋ] *n* (*Sport*) cronometraggio; (*fig*) scelta del momento opportuno

tin [tɪn] *n* stagno; (*also:* ~ **plate**) latta; (*container*) scatola; (*BRIT: can*) barattolo (di latta), lattina; **tinfoil** *n* stagnola

tingle ['tɪŋgl] *vi* pizzicare

tinker ['tɪŋkə^r]: ~ **with** *vt fus* armeggiare intorno a; cercare di riparare

tinned [tɪnd] (*BRIT*) *adj* (*food*) in scatola

tin opener ['-əupnə^r] (*BRIT*) *n* apriscatole *m inv*

tint [tɪnt] *n* tinta; **tinted** *adj* (*hair*) tinto(-a); (*spectacles, glass*) colorato(-a)

tiny ['taɪnɪ] *adj* minuscolo(-a)

tip [tɪp] *n* (*end*) punta; (*gratuity*) mancia; (*BRIT: for rubbish*) immondezzaio; (*advice*) suggerimento ▷ *vt* (*waiter*) dare la mancia a; (*tilt*) inclinare; (*overturn: also:* ~ **over**) capovolgere; (*empty: also:* ~ **out**) scaricare; **how much should I ~?** quanto devo lasciare di mancia?; **tip off** *vt* fare una soffiata a

tiptoe ['tɪptəu] *n*: **on** ~ in punta di piedi

tire ['taɪə^r] *n* (*US*) = **tyre** ▷ *vt* stancare ▷ *vi* stancarsi; **tired** *adj* stanco(-a); **to be tired of** essere stanco *or* stufo di; **tire pressure** (*US*) *n* = **tyre pressure**; **tiring** *adj* faticoso(-a)

tissue ['tɪʃuː] *n* tessuto; (*paper handkerchief*) fazzoletto di carta; **tissue paper** *n* carta velina

tit [tɪt] *n* (*bird*) cinciallegra; **to give ~ for tat** rendere pan per focaccia

title ['taɪtl] *n* titolo

T-junction ['tiː'dʒʌŋkʃən] *n* incrocio a T

TM *abbr* = **trademark**

 KEYWORD

to [tuː, tə] *prep* **1** (*direction*) a; **to go to France/London/school** andare in Francia/a Londra/a scuola; **to go to Paul's/the doctor's** andare da Paul/ dal dottore; **the road to Edinburgh** la strada per Edimburgo; **to the left/ right** a sinistra/destra

2 (*as far as*) (fino) a; **from here to London** da qui a Londra; **to count to 10** contare fino a 10; **from 40 to 50 people** da 40 a 50 persone

3 (*with expressions of time*): **a quarter to 5** le 5 meno un quarto; **it's twenty to 3** sono le 3 meno venti

4 (*for, of*): **the key to the front door** la chiave della porta d'ingresso; **a letter to his wife** una lettera per la moglie

5 (*expressing indirect object*) a; **to give sth to sb** dare qc a qn; **to talk to sb** parlare a qn; **to be a danger to sb/sth** rappresentare un pericolo per qn/qc

6 (*in relation to*) a; **3 goals to 2** 3 goal a 2; **30 miles to the gallon** ≈ 11 chilometri con un litro

7 (*purpose, result*): **to come to sb's aid** venire in aiuto a qn; **to sentence sb to death** condannare a morte qn; **to my surprise** con mia sorpresa

▷ *with vb* **1** (*simple infinitive*): **to go/ eat** *etc* andare/mangiare *etc*

2 (*following another vb*): **to want/ try/start to do** volere/cercare di/cominciare a fare

3 (*with vb omitted*): **I don't want to** non voglio (farlo); **you ought to** devi (farlo)

4 (*purpose, result*) per; **I did it to help you** l'ho fatto per aiutarti

5 (*equivalent to relative clause*): **I have**

things to do ho da fare; **the main thing is to try** la cosa più importante è provare
6 (after adjective etc): **ready to go** pronto a partire; **too old/young to ...** troppo vecchio/giovane per ...
▷ adv **to push the door to** accostare la porta

toad [təud] n rospo; **toadstool** n fungo (velenoso)
toast [təust] n (Culin) pane m tostato; (drink, speech) brindisi m inv ▷ vt (Culin) tostare; (drink to) brindare a; **a piece** or **slice of ~** una fetta di pane tostato; **toaster** n tostapane m inv
tobacco [tə'bækəu] n tabacco
toboggan [tə'bɔgən] n toboga m inv
today [tə'deɪ] adv oggi ▷ n (also fig) oggi m
toddler ['tɔdlə^r] n bambino(-a) che impara a camminare
toe [təu] n dito del piede; (of shoe) punta; **to ~ the line** (fig) stare in riga, conformarsi; **toenail** n unghia del piede
toffee ['tɔfɪ] n caramella
together [tə'geðə^r] adv insieme; (at same time) allo stesso tempo; **~ with** insieme a
toilet ['tɔɪlət] n (BRIT: lavatory) gabinetto ▷ cpd (bag, soap etc) da toletta; **where's the ~?** dov'è il bagno?; **toilet bag** (BRIT) nécessaire m inv da toilette; **toilet paper** n carta igienica; **toiletries** npl articoli mpl da toletta; **toilet roll** n rotolo di carta igienica
token ['təukən] n (sign) segno; (substitute coin) gettone m; **book/ record/gift ~** (BRIT) buono-libro/ disco/regalo
Tokyo ['təukjəu] n Tokyo f
told [təuld] pt, pp of **tell**
tolerant ['tɔlərnt] adj **~ (of)** tollerante (nei confronti di)
tolerate ['tɔləreɪt] vt sopportare;

(Med, Tech) tollerare
toll [təul] n (tax, charge) pedaggio
▷ vi (bell) suonare; **the accident ~ on the roads** il numero delle vittime della strada; **toll call** (us) n (Tel) (telefonata) interurbana; **toll-free** (us) adj senza addebito, gratuito(-a)
▷ adv gratuitamente; **toll-free number** ≈ numero verde
tomato [tə'mɑ:təu] (pl **tomatoes**) n pomodoro; **tomato sauce** n salsa di pomodoro
tomb [tu:m] n tomba; **tombstone** ['tu:mstəun] n pietra tombale
tomorrow [tə'mɔrəu] adv domani
▷ n (also fig) domani m inv; **the day after ~** dopodomani; **~ morning** domani mattina
ton [tʌn] n tonnellata; (BRIT: 1016 kg: US: 907 kg: metric 1000 kg): **~s of** (inf) un mucchio or sacco di
tone [təun] n tono ▷ vi (also: **~ in**) intonarsi; **tone down** vt (colour, criticism, sound) attenuare
tongs [tɔŋz] npl tenaglie fpl; (for coal) molle fpl; (for hair) arricciacapelli m inv
tongue [tʌŋ] n lingua; **~ in cheek** (say, speak) ironicamente
tonic ['tɔnɪk] n (Med) tonico; (also: **~ water**) acqua tonica
tonight [tə'naɪt] adv stanotte; (this evening) stasera ▷ n questa notte; questa sera
tonne [tʌn] n (BRIT: metric ton) tonnellata
tonsil ['tɔnsl] n tonsilla; **tonsillitis** [-'laɪtɪs] n tonsillite f
too [tu:] adv (excessively) troppo; (also) anche; (also: **~ much**) ▷ adv troppo ▷ adj troppo(-a); **~ many** troppi(-e)
took [tuk] pt of **take**
tool [tu:l] n utensile m, attrezzo; **tool box** n cassetta f portautensili; **tool kit** n cassetta di attrezzi
tooth [tu:θ] (pl **teeth**) n (Anat, Tech) dente m; **toothache** n mal m di denti; **toothbrush** n spazzolino da denti;

toothpaste n dentifricio; **toothpick** n stuzzicadenti m inv

top [tɔp] n (of mountain, page, ladder) cima; (of box, cupboard, table) sopra m inv, parte f superiore; (lid: of box, jar) coperchio; (: of bottle) tappo; (blouse etc) sopra m inv; (toy) trottola ▷ adj più alto(-a); (in rank) primo(-a); (best) migliore ▷ vt (exceed) superare; (be first in) essere in testa a; **on ~ of** sopra, in cima a; (in addition to) oltre a; **from ~ to bottom** da cima a fondo; **top up** (us **top off**) vt riempire; (salary) integrare; **top floor** n ultimo piano; **top hat** n cilindro

topic ['tɔpɪk] n argomento; **topical** adj d'attualità

topless ['tɔplɪs] adj (bather etc) col seno scoperto

topping ['tɔpɪŋ] n (Culin) guarnizione f

topple ['tɔpl] vt rovesciare, far cadere ▷ vi cadere; traballare

top-up ['tɔpʌp] n (for mobile phone: also: **~ card**) ricarica

torch [tɔːtʃ] n torcia; (BRIT: electric) lampadina tascabile

tore [tɔːʳ] pt of **tear**[1]

torment [n 'tɔːmɛnt, vb tɔː'mɛnt] n tormento ▷ vt tormentare

torn [tɔːn] pp of **tear**[1]

tornado [tɔː'neɪdəu] (pl **tornadoes**) n tornado

torpedo [tɔː'piːdəu] (pl **torpedoes**) n siluro

torrent ['tɔrnt] n torrente m; **torrential** [tɔ'rɛnʃl] adj torrenziale

tortoise ['tɔːtəs] n tartaruga

torture ['tɔːtʃəʳ] n tortura ▷ vt torturare

Tory ['tɔːrɪ] (BRIT: Pol) adj dei tories, conservatore(-trice) ▷ n tory m/f inv, conservatore(-trice)

toss [tɔs] vt gettare, lanciare; (one's head) scuotere; **to ~ a coin** fare a testa o croce; **to ~ up for sth** fare a testa o croce per qc; **to ~ and turn** (in bed)

girarsi e rigirarsi

total ['təutl] adj totale ▷ n totale m ▷ vt (add up) sommare; (amount to) ammontare a

totalitarian [təutælɪ'tɛərɪən] adj totalitario(-a)

totally ['təutəlɪ] adv completamente

touch [tʌtʃ] n tocco; (sense) tatto; (contact) contatto ▷ vt toccare; **a ~ of** (fig) un tocco di; un pizzico di; **to get in ~ with** mettersi in contatto con; **to lose ~** (friends) perdersi di vista; **touch down** vi (on land) atterrare; **touchdown** n atterraggio; (on sea) ammaraggio; (US: Football) meta; **touched** adj commosso(-a); **touching** adj commovente; **touchline** n (Sport) linea laterale; **touch-sensitive** adj sensibile al tatto

tough [tʌf] adj duro(-a); (resistant) resistente

tour ['tuəʳ] n viaggio; (also: **package ~**) viaggio organizzato or tutto compreso; (of town, museum) visita; (by artist) tournée f inv ▷ vt visitare; **tour guide** n guida turistica

tourism ['tuərɪzəm] n turismo

tourist ['tuərɪst] n turista m/f ▷ adv (travel) in classe turistica ▷ cpd turistico(-a); **tourist office** n pro loco f inv

tournament ['tuənəmənt] n torneo

tour operator n (BRIT) operatore m turistico

tow [təu] vt rimorchiare; **"on ~"** (BRIT), **"in ~"** (US) "veicolo rimorchiato"; **tow away** vt rimorchiare

toward(s) [tə'wɔːd(z)] prep verso; (of attitude) nei confronti di; (of purpose) per

towel ['tauəl] n asciugamano; (also: **tea ~**) strofinaccio; **towelling** n (fabric) spugna

tower ['tauəʳ] n torre f; **tower block** (BRIT) n palazzone m

town [taun] n città f inv; **to go to ~** andare in città; (fig) mettercela tutta;

town centre n centro (città); **town hall** n ≈ municipio

tow truck (us) n carro m, attrezzi inv

toxic ['tɔksɪk] adj tossico(-a)

toy [tɔɪ] n giocattolo; **toy with** vt fus giocare con; (idea) accarezzare, trastullarsi con; **toyshop** n negozio di giocattoli

trace [treɪs] n traccia ▷ vt (draw) tracciare; (follow) seguire; (locate) rintracciare

track [træk] n (of person, animal) traccia; (on tape, Sport, path: gen) pista; (: of bullet etc) traiettoria; (: of suspect, animal) pista, tracce fpl; (Rail) binario, rotaie fpl ▷ vt seguire le tracce di; **to keep ~ of** seguire; **track down** vt (prey) scovare; snidare; (sth lost) rintracciare; **tracksuit** n tuta sportiva

tractor ['træktər] n trattore m

trade [treɪd] n commercio; (skill, job) mestiere m ▷ vi commerciare ▷ vt **to ~ sth (for sth)** barattare qc (con qc); **to ~ with/in** commerciare con/in; **trade in** vt (old car etc) dare come pagamento parziale; **trademark** n marchio di fabbrica; **trader** n commerciante m/f; **tradesman** (irreg) n fornitore m; (shopkeeper) negoziante m; **trade union** n sindacato

trading ['treɪdɪŋ] n commercio

tradition [trə'dɪʃən] n tradizione f; **traditional** adj tradizionale

traffic ['træfɪk] n traffico ▷ vi **to ~ in** (pej: liquor, drugs) trafficare in; **traffic circle** (us) n isola rotatoria; **traffic island** n salvagente m, isola f, spartitraffico inv; **traffic jam** n ingorgo (del traffico); **traffic lights** npl semaforo; **traffic warden** n addetto(-a) al controllo del traffico e del parcheggio

tragedy ['trædʒədɪ] n tragedia

tragic ['trædʒɪk] adj tragico(-a)

trail [treɪl] n (tracks) tracce fpl, pista; (path) sentiero; (of smoke etc) scia ▷ vt trascinare, strascicare; (follow) seguire ▷ vi essere al traino; (dress etc) strusciare; (plant) arrampicarsi; strisciare; (in game) essere in svantaggio; **trailer** n (Aut) rimorchio; (us) roulotte f inv; (Cinema) prossimamente m inv

train [treɪn] n treno; (of dress) coda, strascico ▷ vt (apprentice, doctor etc) formare; (sportsman) allenare; (dog) addestrare; (memory) esercitare; (point: gun etc): **to ~ sth on** puntare qc contro ▷ vi formarsi; allenarsi; **what time does the ~ from Rome get in?** a che ora arriva il treno da Roma?; **is this the ~ for …?** è questo il treno per…?; **one's ~ of thought** il filo dei propri pensieri; **trainee** [treɪ'niː] n (in trade) apprendista m/f; **trainer** n (Sport) allenatore(-trice); (: shoe) scarpa da ginnastica; (of dogs etc) addestratore(-trice); **trainers** npl (shoes) scarpe fpl da ginnastica; **training** n formazione f; allenamento; addestramento; **in training** (Sport) in allenamento; **training course** n corso di formazione professionale; **training shoes** npl scarpe fpl da ginnastica

trait [treɪt] n tratto

traitor ['treɪtər] n traditore m

tram [træm] (BRIT) n (also: **~car**) tram m inv

tramp [træmp] n (person) vagabondo(-a); (inf: pej: woman) sgualdrina

trample ['træmpl] vt: **to ~ (underfoot)** calpestare

trampoline ['træmpəliːn] n trampolino

tranquil ['træŋkwɪl] adj tranquillo(-a); **tranquillizer** (us **tranquilizer**) n (Med) tranquillante m

transaction [træn'zækʃən] n transazione f

transatlantic ['trænzət'læntɪk] adj transatlantico(-a)

transcript ['trænskrɪpt] n
trascrizione f
transfer [n 'trænsfəʳ, vb træns'fəʳ] n
(gen: also Sport) trasferimento; (Pol:
of power) passaggio; (picture, design)
decalcomania; (: stick-on) autoadesivo
▷ vt trasferire; passare; **to ~ the
charges** (BRIT: Tel) fare una chiamata
a carico del destinatario
transform [træns'fɔːm] vt
trasformare; **transformation** n
trasformazione f
transfusion [træns'fjuːʒən] n
trasfusione f
transit ['trænzɪt] n **in ~** in transito
transition [træn'zɪʃən] n passaggio,
transizione f
transitive ['trænzɪtɪv] adj (Ling)
transitivo(-a)
translate [trænz'leɪt] vt tradurre;
can you ~ this for me? me lo può
tradurre?; **translation** [-'leɪʃən]
n traduzione f; **translator** n
traduttore(-trice)
transmission [trænz'mɪʃən] n
trasmissione f
transmit [trænz'mɪt] vt trasmettere;
transmitter n trasmettitore m
transparent [træns'pærnt] adj
trasparente
transplant [vb træns'plɑːnt, n
'trænsplɑːnt] vt trapiantare ▷ n
(Med) trapianto
transport [n 'trænspɔːt, vb træns'pɔːt]
n trasporto ▷ vt trasportare;
transportation [-'teɪʃən] n (mezzo
di) trasporto
transvestite [trænz'vɛstaɪt] n
travestito(-a)
trap [træp] n (snare, trick) trappola;
(carriage) calesse m ▷ vt prendere in
trappola, intrappolare
trash [træʃ] (pej) n (goods) ciarpame m;
(nonsense) sciocchezze fpl; **trash can**
(US) n secchio della spazzatura
trauma ['trɔːmə] n trauma
m; **traumatic** [-'mætɪk] adj

traumatico(-a)
travel ['trævl] n viaggio; viaggi
mpl ▷ vi viaggiare ▷ vt (distance)
percorrere; **travel agency** n agenzia
(di) viaggi; **travel agent** n agente
m di viaggio; **travel insurance** n
assicurazione f di viaggio; **traveller**
(US **traveler**) n viaggiatore(-trice);
traveller's cheque (US **traveler's
check**) n assegno turistico;
travelling (US **traveling**) n viaggi
mpl; **travel-sick** adj **to get travel-
sick** (in vehicle) soffrire di mal d'auto;
(in aeroplane) soffrire di mal d'aria; (in
boat) soffrire di mal di mare; **travel
sickness** n mal m d'auto (or di mare
or d'aria)
tray [treɪ] n (for carrying) vassoio; (on
desk) vaschetta
treacherous ['trɛtʃərəs] adj infido(-a)
treacle ['triːkl] n melassa
tread [trɛd] (pt **trod**, pp **trodden**) n
passo; (sound) rumore m di passi; (of
stairs) pedata; (of tyre) battistrada m
inv ▷ vi camminare; **tread on** vt fus
calpestare
treasure ['trɛʒəʳ] n tesoro ▷ vt (value)
tenere in gran conto, apprezzare
molto; (store) custodire gelosamente;
treasurer ['trɛʒərəʳ] n tesoriere(-a)
treasury ['trɛʒərɪ] n **the T~** (BRIT),
the T~ Department (US) il ministero
del Tesoro
treat [triːt] n regalo ▷ vt trattare;
(Med) curare; **to ~ sb to sth** offrire
qc a qn; **treatment** ['triːtmənt] n
trattamento
treaty ['triːtɪ] n patto, trattato
treble ['trɛbl] adj triplo(-a), triplice
▷ vt triplicare ▷ vi triplicarsi
tree [triː] n albero
trek [trɛk] n escursione f a piedi;
escursione f in macchina; (tiring walk)
camminata sfiancante ▷ vi (as holiday)
fare dell'escursionismo
tremble ['trɛmbl] vi tremare
tremendous [trɪ'mɛndəs] adj

(*enormous*) enorme; (*excellent*) fantastico(-a), strepitoso(-a)

> Be careful not to translate *tremendous* by the Italian word *tremendo*.

trench [trɛntʃ] n trincea

trend [trɛnd] n (*tendency*) tendenza; (*of events*) corso; (*fashion*) moda; **trendy** adj (*idea*) di moda; (*clothes*) all'ultima moda

trespass ['trɛspəs] vi: **to ~ on** entrare abusivamente in; **"no ~ing"** "proprietà privata", "vietato l'accesso"

trial ['traɪəl] n (*Law*) processo; (*test: of machine etc*) collaudo; **on ~** (*Law*) sotto processo; **trial period** n periodo di prova

triangle ['traɪæŋgl] n (*Math, Mus*) triangolo

triangular [traɪ'æŋgjulər] adj triangolare

tribe [traɪb] n tribù f inv

tribunal [traɪ'bjuːnl] n tribunale m

tribute ['trɪbjuːt] n tributo, omaggio; **to pay ~ to** rendere omaggio a

trick [trɪk] n trucco; (*joke*) tiro; (*Cards*) presa ▷ vt imbrogliare, ingannare; **to play a ~ on sb** giocare un tiro a qn; **that should do the ~** vedrai che funziona

trickle ['trɪkl] n (*of water etc*) rivolo; gocciolio ▷ vi gocciolare

tricky ['trɪkɪ] adj difficile, delicato(-a)

tricycle ['traɪsɪkl] n triciclo

trifle ['traɪfl] n sciocchezza; (*BRIT: Culin*) ≈ zuppa inglese ▷ adv **a ~ long** un po' lungo

trigger ['trɪgər] n (*of gun*) grilletto

trim [trɪm] adj (*house, garden*) ben tenuto(-a); (*figure*) snello(-a) ▷ n (*haircut etc*) spuntata, regolata; (*embellishment*) finiture fpl; (*on car*) guarnizioni fpl ▷ vt spuntare; (*decorate*): **to ~ (with)** decorare (con); (*Naut: a sail*) orientare

trio ['triːəu] n trio

trip [trɪp] n viaggio; (*excursion*) gita,

escursione f; (*stumble*) passo falso ▷ vi inciampare; (*go lightly*) camminare con passo leggero; **on a ~** in viaggio; **trip up** vi inciampare ▷ vt fare lo sgambetto a

triple ['trɪpl] adj triplo(-a)

triplets ['trɪplɪts] npl bambini(-e) trigemini(-e)

tripod ['traɪpɔd] n treppiede m

triumph ['traɪʌmf] n trionfo ▷ vi **to ~ (over)** trionfare (su); **triumphant** [traɪ'ʌmfənt] adj trionfante

trivial ['trɪvɪəl] adj insignificante; (*commonplace*) banale

> Be careful not to translate *trivial* by the Italian word *triviale*.

trod [trɔd] pt of **tread**

trodden ['trɔdn] pp of **tread**

trolley ['trɔlɪ] n carrello

trombone [trɔm'bəun] n trombone m

troop [truːp] n gruppo; (*Mil*) squadrone m; **~s** npl (*Mil*) truppe fpl

trophy ['trəufɪ] n trofeo

tropical ['trɔpɪkl] adj tropicale

trot [trɔt] n trotto ▷ vi trottare; **on the ~** (*BRIT: fig*) di fila, uno(-a) dopo l'altro(-a)

trouble ['trʌbl] n difficoltà f inv, problema m; difficoltà fpl, problemi; (*worry*) preoccupazione f; (*bother, effort*) sforzo; (*Pol*) conflitti mpl, disordine m; (*Med*): **stomach** etc **~** disturbi mpl gastrici etc ▷ vt disturbare; (*worry*) preoccupare ▷ vi **to ~ to do** disturbarsi a fare; **~s** npl (*Pol etc*) disordini mpl; **to be in ~** avere dei problemi; **it's no ~!** di niente!; **what's the ~?** cosa c'è che non va?; **I'm sorry to ~ you** scusi il disturbo; **troubled** adj (*person*) preoccupato(-a), inquieto(-a); (*epoch, life*) agitato(-a), difficile; **troublemaker** n elemento disturbatore, agitatore(-trice); (*child*) disloco(-a); **troublesome** adj fastidioso(-a), seccante

trough [trɔf] n (drinking trough)
abbeveratoio; (also: **feeding ~**)
trogolo, mangiatoia; (channel)
canale m
trousers ['trauzəz] npl pantaloni mpl,
calzoni mpl; **short ~** calzoncini mpl
trout [traut] n inv trota
trowel ['trauəl] n cazzuola
truant ['truənt] (BRIT) n: **to play ~**
marinare la scuola
truce [truːs] n tregua
truck [trʌk] n autocarro, camion
m inv; (Rail) carro merci aperto; (for
luggage) carrello m portabagagli inv;
truck driver n camionista m/f
true [truː] adj vero(-a); (accurate)
accurato(-a), esatto(-a); (genuine)
reale; (faithful) fedele; **to come ~**
avverarsi
truly ['truːlɪ] adv veramente;
(truthfully) sinceramente; (faithfully):
yours ~ (in letter) distinti saluti
trumpet ['trʌmpɪt] n tromba
trunk [trʌŋk] n (of tree, person) tronco;
(of elephant) proboscide f; (case) baule
m; (us: Aut) bagagliaio; **~s** (also:
swimming ~s) calzoncini mpl da
bagno
trust [trʌst] n fiducia; (Law)
amministrazione f fiduciaria; (Comm)
trust m inv ▷ vt (rely on) contare
su; (hope) sperare; (entrust): **to ~
sth to sb** affidare qc a qn; **trusted**
adj fidato(-a); **trustworthy** adj
fidato(-a), degno(-a) di fiducia
truth [truːθ, pl truːðz] n verità f inv;
truthful adj (person) sincero(-a);
(description) veritiero(-a), esatto(-a)
try [traɪ] n prova, tentativo; (Rugby)
meta ▷ vt (Law) giudicare; (test:
also: **~ out**) provare; (strain) mettere
alla prova ▷ vi provare; **to have a ~**
fare un tentativo; **to ~ to do** (seek)
cercare di fare; **try on** vt (clothes)
provare; **trying** adj (day, experience)
logorante, pesante; (child) difficile,
insopportabile

T-shirt ['tiːʃəːt] n maglietta
tsunami [tsʊ'nɑːmɪ] n tsunami m inv
tub [tʌb] n tinozza; mastello; (bath)
bagno
tube [tjuːb] n tubo; (BRIT: underground)
metropolitana, metrò m inv; (for tyre)
camera d'aria
tuberculosis [tjubəːkjuˈləusɪs] n
tubercolosi f inv
tube station (BRIT) n stazione f della
metropolitana
tuck [tʌk] vt (put) mettere; **tuck away**
vt riporre; (building): **to be tucked
away** essere in un luogo isolato;
tuck in vt mettere dentro; (child)
rimboccare ▷ vi (eat) mangiare di
buon appetito; abbuffarsi; **tuck shop**
n negozio di pasticceria (in una scuola)
Tue(s). abbr (= Tuesday) mar.
Tuesday ['tjuːzdɪ] n martedì m inv
tug [tʌg] n (ship) rimorchiatore m ▷ vt
tirare con forza
tuition [tjuːˈɪʃən] n (BRIT) lezioni f pl;
(: private tuition) lezioni f pl private; (us:
school fees) tasse f pl scolastiche
tulip ['tjuːlɪp] n tulipano
tumble ['tʌmbl] n (fall) capitombolo
▷ vi capitombolare, ruzzolare; **to ~ to
sth** (inf) realizzare qc; **tumble dryer**
(BRIT) n asciugatrice f
tumbler ['tʌmblər] n bicchiere m
(senza stelo)
tummy ['tʌmɪ] (inf) n pancia
tumour ['tjuːmər] (US **tumor**) n
tumore m
tuna ['tjuːnə] n inv (also: **~ fish**) tonno
tune [tjuːn] n (melody) melodia,
aria ▷ vt (Mus) accordare; (Radio, TV,
Aut) regolare, mettere a punto; **to
be in/out of ~** (instrument) essere
accordato(-a)/scordato(-a); (singer)
essere intonato(-a)/stonato(-a);
tune in vi **to tune in (to)** (Radio,
TV) sintonizzarsi (su); **tune up** vi
(musician) accordare lo strumento
tunic ['tjuːnɪk] n tunica
Tunisia [tjuːˈnɪzɪə] n Tunisia

tunnel ['tʌnl] n galleria ▷ vi scavare una galleria
turbulence ['tə:bjuləns] n (Aviat) turbolenza
turf [tə:f] n terreno erboso; (clod) zolla ▷ vt coprire di zolle erbose
Turin [tjuə'rɪn] n Torino f
Turk [tə:k] n turco(-a)
Turkey ['tə:kɪ] n Turchia
turkey ['tə:kɪ] n tacchino
Turkish ['tə:kɪʃ] adj turco(-a) ▷ n (Ling) turco
turmoil ['tə:mɔɪl] n confusione f, tumulto
turn [tə:n] n giro; (change) cambiamento; (in road) curva; (tendency: of mind, events) tendenza; (performance) numero; (chance) turno; (Med) crisi f inv, attacco ▷ vt girare, voltare; (change): **to ~ sth into** trasformare qc in ▷ vi girare; (person: look back) girarsi, voltarsi; (reverse direction) girare; (change) cambiare; (milk) andare a male; (become) diventare; **a good ~** un buon servizio; **it gave me quite a ~** mi ha fatto prendere un bello spavento; **"no left ~"** (Aut) "divieto di svolta a sinistra"; **it's your ~** tocca a lei; **in ~** a sua volta; a turno; **to take ~s (at sth)** fare (qc) a turno; **~ left/right at the next junction** al prossimo incrocio, giri a sinistra/destra; **turn around** vi (person) girarsi; (rotate) girare ▷ vt (object) girare; **turn away** vi girarsi (dall'altra parte) ▷ vt mandare via; **turn back** vi ritornare, tornare indietro ▷ vt far tornare indietro; (clock) spostare indietro; **turn down** vt (refuse) rifiutare; (reduce) abbassare; (fold) ripiegare; **turn in** vi (inf: go to bed) andare a letto ▷ vt (fold) voltare in dentro; **turn off** vi (from road) girare, voltare ▷ vt (light, radio, engine etc) spegnere; **I can't turn the heating off** non riesco a spegnere il riscaldamento; **turn on** vt (light,

radio etc) accendere; **I can't turn the heating on** non riesco ad accendere il riscaldamento; **turn out** vt (light, gas) chiudere; spegnere ▷ vi (voters) presentarsi; **to turn out to be ...** rivelarsi ..., risultare ...; **turn over** vi (person) girarsi ▷ vt girare; **turn round** vi girare; (person) girarsi; **turn to** vt fus **to turn to sb** girarsi verso qn; **to turn to sb for help** rivolgersi a qn per aiuto; **turn up** vi (person) arrivare, presentarsi; (lost object) saltar fuori ▷ vt (collar, sound) alzare; **turning** n (in road) curva; **turning point** n (fig) svolta decisiva
turnip ['tə:nɪp] n rapa
turn: **turnout** ['tə:naut] n presenza, affluenza; **turnover** ['tə:nəuvə'] n (Comm) turnover m inv; (Culin): **apple etc turnover** sfogliatella alle melle ecc; **turnstile** ['tə:nstaɪl] n tornella; **turn-up** (BRIT) n (on trousers) risvolto
turquoise ['tə:kwɔɪz] n turchese m ▷ adj turchese
turtle ['tə:tl] n testuggine f; **turtleneck (sweater)** ['tə:tlnɛk-] n maglione m con il collo alto
Tuscany ['tʌskəni] n Toscana
tusk [tʌsk] n zanna
tutor ['tju:tə'] n (in college) docente m/f (responsabile di un gruppo di studenti); (private teacher) precettore m; **tutorial** [-'tɔ:rɪəl] n (Scol) lezione f con discussione (a un gruppo limitato)
tuxedo [tʌk'si:dəu] (US) n smoking m inv
TV [ti:'vi:] n abbr (= television) tivù f inv
tweed [twi:d] n tweed m inv
tweezers ['twi:zəz] npl pinzette fpl
twelfth [twelfθ] num dodicesimo(-a)
twelve [twelv] num dodici; **at ~ o'clock** alle dodici, a mezzogiorno; (midnight) a mezzanotte
twentieth ['twentɪɪθ] num ventesimo(-a)
twenty ['twentɪ] num venti
twice [twaɪs] adv due volte; **~ as**

much due volte tanto; **~ a week** due volte alla settimana

twig [twɪg] n ramoscello ▷ vt, vi (inf) capire

twilight ['twaɪlaɪt] n crepuscolo

twin [twɪn] adj, n gemello(-a) ▷ vt **to ~ one town with another** fare il gemellaggio di una città con un'altra; **twin(-bedded) room** n stanza con letti gemelli; **twin beds** npl letti mpl gemelli

twinkle ['twɪŋkl] vi scintillare; (eyes) brillare

twist [twɪst] n torsione f; (in wire, flex) piega; (in road) curva; (in story) colpo di scena ▷ vt attorcigliare; (ankle) slogare; (weave) intrecciare; (roll around) arrotolare; (fig) distorcere ▷ vi (road) serpeggiare

twit [twɪt] (inf) n cretino(-a)

twitch [twɪtʃ] n tiratina; (nervous) tic m inv ▷ vi contrarsi

two [tuː] num due; **to put ~ and ~ together** (fig) fare uno più uno

type [taɪp] n (category) genere m; (model) modello; (example) tipo; (Typ) tipo, carattere m ▷ vt (letter etc) battere (a macchina), dattilografare; **typewriter** n macchina da scrivere

typhoid ['taɪfɔɪd] n tifoidea

typhoon [taɪ'fuːn] n tifone m

typical ['tɪpɪkl] adj tipico(-a); **typically** adv tipicamente; **typically, he arrived late** come al solito è arrivato tardi

typing ['taɪpɪŋ] n dattilografia

typist ['taɪpɪst] n dattilografo(-a)

tyre ['taɪər] (us **tire**) n pneumatico, gomma; **I've got a flat ~** ho una gomma a terra; **tyre pressure** n pressione f (delle gomme)

UFO ['juːfəʊ] n abbr (= unidentified flying object) UFO m inv

Uganda [juː'gændə] n Uganda

ugly ['ʌglɪ] adj brutto(-a)

UHT abbr (= ultra heat treated) UHT inv, a lunga conservazione

UK n abbr = **United Kingdom**

ulcer ['ʌlsər] n ulcera; (also: **mouth ~**) afta

ultimate ['ʌltɪmət] adj ultimo(-a), finale; (authority) massimo(-a), supremo(-a); **ultimately** adv alla fine; in definitiva, in fin dei conti

ultimatum [ʌltɪ'meɪtəm, -tə] (pl **ultimatums** or **ultimata**) n ultimatum m inv

ultrasound [ʌltrə'saʊnd] n (Med) ultrasuono

ultraviolet ['ʌltrə'vaɪəlɪt] adj ultravioletto(-a)

umbrella [ʌm'brɛlə] n ombrello

umpire ['ʌmpaɪər] n arbitro

UN n abbr (= United Nations) ONU f

unable [ʌn'eɪbl] adj **to be ~ to** non

potere, essere nell'impossibilità di;
essere incapace di

unacceptable [ʌnək'sɛptəbl] adj
(proposal, behaviour) inaccettabile;
(price) impossibile

unanimous [juː'nænɪməs] adj
unanime

unarmed [ʌn'ɑːmd] adj (without
a weapon) disarmato(-a); (combat)
senz'armi

unattended [ʌnə'tɛndɪd] adj (car,
child, luggage) incustodito(-a)

unattractive [ʌnə'træktɪv] adj poco
attraente

unavailable [ʌnə'veɪləbl] adj (article,
room, book) non disponibile; (person)
impegnato(-a)

unavoidable [ʌnə'vɔɪdəbl] adj
inevitabile

unaware [ʌnə'wɛəʳ] adj **to be ~ of**
non sapere, ignorare; **unawares** adv
di sorpresa, alla sprovvista

unbearable [ʌn'bɛərəbl] adj
insopportabile

unbeatable [ʌn'biːtəbl] adj
imbattibile

unbelievable [ʌnbɪ'liːvəbl] adj
incredibile

unborn [ʌn'bɔːn] adj non ancora
nato(-a)

unbutton [ʌn'bʌtn] vt sbottonare

uncalled-for [ʌn'kɔːldfɔːʳ] adj
(remark) fuori luogo inv; (action)
ingiustificato(-a)

uncanny [ʌn'kænɪ] adj
misterioso(-a), strano(-a)

uncertain [ʌn'səːtn] adj incerto(-a);
dubbio(-a); **uncertainty** n incertezza

unchanged [ʌn'tʃeɪndʒd] adj
invariato(-a)

uncle ['ʌŋkl] n zio

unclear [ʌn'klɪəʳ] adj non chiaro(-a);
**I'm still ~ about what I'm supposed
to do** non ho ancora ben capito cosa
dovrei fare

uncomfortable [ʌn'kʌmfətəbl]
adj scomodo(-a); (uneasy) a disagio,

agitato(-a); (unpleasant) fastidioso(-a)

uncommon [ʌn'kɔmən] adj raro(-a),
insolito(-a), non comune

unconditional [ʌnkən'dɪʃənl] adj
incondizionato(-a), senza condizioni

unconscious [ʌn'kɔnʃəs] adj
privo(-a) di sensi, svenuto(-a);
(unaware) inconsapevole,
inconscio(-a) ▷ n **the ~** l'inconscio

uncontrollable [ʌnkən'trəuləbl] adj
incontrollabile; indisciplinato(-a)

unconventional [ʌnkən'vɛnʃənl]
adj poco convenzionale

uncover [ʌn'kʌvəʳ] vt scoprire

undecided [ʌndɪ'saɪdɪd] adj
indeciso(-a)

undeniable [ʌndɪ'naɪəbl] adj
innegabile, indiscutibile

under ['ʌndəʳ] prep sotto; (less than)
meno di; al disotto di; (according
to) secondo, in conformità a ▷ adv
(al) disotto; **~ there** là sotto; **~
repair** in riparazione; **undercover**
adj segreto(-a), clandestino(-a);
underdone adj (Culin) al sangue;
(pej) poco cotto(-a); **underestimate**
vt sottovalutare; **undergo** vt (irreg)
subire; (treatment) sottoporsi a;
undergraduate n studente(-essa)
universitario(-a); **underground**
n (BRIT: railway) metropolitana;
(Pol) movimento clandestino ▷ adj
sotterraneo(-a); (fig) clandestino(-a)
▷ adv sottoterra; **to go underground**
(fig) darsi alla macchia; **undergrowth**
n sottobosco; **underline** vt
sottolineare; **undermine** vt minare;
underneath [ʌndə'niːθ] adv sotto,
disotto ▷ prep sotto, al di sotto
di; **underpants** npl mutande
fpl, slip m inv; **underpass** (BRIT) n
sottopassaggio; **underprivileged**
adj non abbiente; meno favorito(-a);
underscore vt sottolineare;
undershirt (US) n maglietta;
underskirt (BRIT) n sottoveste f

understand [ʌndə'stænd] (irreg: like

stand) vt, vi capire, comprendere; **I don't ~** non capisco; **I ~ that ...** sento che ...; credo di capire che ...; **understandable** adj comprensibile; **understanding** adj comprensivo(-a) ▷ n comprensione f; (agreement) accordo

understatement [ʌndəˈsteɪtmənt] n **that's an ~!** a dire poco!

understood [ʌndəˈstud] pt, pp of **understand** ▷ adj inteso(-a); (implied) sottinteso(-a)

undertake [ʌndəˈteɪk] (irreg: like **take**) vt intraprendere; **to ~ to do sth** impegnarsi a fare qc

undertaker [ˈʌndəteɪkər] n impresario di pompe funebri

undertaking [ʌndəˈteɪkɪŋ] n impresa; (promise) promessa

under: **underwater** [ʌndəˈwɔːtər] adv sott'acqua ▷ adj subacqueo(-a); **underway** [ʌndəˈweɪ] adj **to be underway** essere in corso; **underwear** [ˈʌndəweər] n biancheria (intima); **underwent** [ʌndəˈwɛnt] vb see **undergo**; **underworld** [ˈʌndəwɔːld] n (of crime) malavita

undesirable [ʌndɪˈzaɪərəbl] adj sgradevole

undisputed [ʌndɪsˈpjuːtɪd] adj indiscusso(-a)

undo [ʌnˈduː] vt (irreg) disfare

undone [ʌnˈdʌn] pp of **undo**; **to come ~** slacciarsi

undoubtedly [ʌnˈdautɪdlɪ] adv senza alcun dubbio

undress [ʌnˈdrɛs] vi spogliarsi

unearth [ʌnˈəːθ] vt dissotterrare; (fig) scoprire

uneasy [ʌnˈiːzɪ] adj a disagio; (worried) preoccupato(-a); (peace) precario(-a)

unemployed [ʌnɪmˈplɔɪd] adj disoccupato(-a) ▷ npl **the ~** i disoccupati

unemployment [ʌnɪmˈplɔɪmənt] n disoccupazione f; **unemployment benefit** (US **unemployment compensation**) n sussidio di disoccupazione

unequal [ʌnˈiːkwəl] adj (length, objects) disuguale; (amounts) diverso(-a); (division of labour) ineguale

uneven [ʌnˈiːvn] adj ineguale; irregolare

unexpected [ʌnɪkˈspɛktɪd] adj inatteso(-a), imprevisto(-a); **unexpectedly** adv inaspettatamente

unfair [ʌnˈfɛər] adj **~ (to)** ingiusto(-a) (nei confronti di)

unfaithful [ʌnˈfeɪθful] adj infedele

unfamiliar [ʌnfəˈmɪlɪər] adj sconosciuto(-a), strano(-a); **to be ~ with** non avere familiarità con

unfashionable [ʌnˈfæʃnəbl] adj (clothes) fuori moda; (district) non alla moda

unfasten [ʌnˈfɑːsn] vt slacciare; sciogliere

unfavourable [ʌnˈfeɪvərəbl] (US **unfavorable**) adj sfavorevole

unfinished [ʌnˈfɪnɪʃt] adj incompleto(-a)

unfit [ʌnˈfɪt] adj (ill) malato(-a), in cattiva salute; (incompetent): **~ (for)** incompetente (in); (: work, Mil) inabile (a)

unfold [ʌnˈfəuld] vt spiegare ▷ vi (story, plot) svelarsi

unforgettable [ʌnfəˈgɛtəbl] adj indimenticabile

unfortunate [ʌnˈfɔːtʃnət] adj sfortunato(-a); (event, remark) infelice; **unfortunately** adv sfortunatamente, purtroppo

unfriendly [ʌnˈfrɛndlɪ] adj poco amichevole, freddo(-a)

unfurnished [ʌnˈfəːnɪʃt] adj non ammobiliato(-a)

unhappiness [ʌnˈhæpɪnɪs] n infelicità

unhappy [ʌnˈhæpɪ] adj infelice; **~ about/with** (arrangements etc) insoddisfatto(-a) di

unhealthy [ʌnˈhɛlθɪ] adj (gen)

malsano(-a); (*person*) malaticcio(-a)

unheard-of [ʌnˈhəːdɔv] *adj* inaudito(-a), senza precedenti

unhelpful [ʌnˈhɛlpful] *adj* poco disponibile

unhurt [ʌnˈhəːt] *adj* illeso(-a)

unidentified [ʌnaɪˈdɛntɪfaɪd] *adj* non identificato(-a)

uniform [ˈjuːnɪfɔːm] *n* uniforme *f*, divisa ▷ *adj* uniforme

unify [ˈjuːnɪfaɪ] *vt* unificare

unimportant [ʌnɪmˈpɔːtənt] *adj* senza importanza, di scarsa importanza

uninhabited [ʌnɪnˈhæbɪtɪd] *adj* disabitato(-a)

unintentional [ʌnɪnˈtɛnʃənəl] *adj* involontario(-a)

union [ˈjuːnjən] *n* unione *f*; (*also:* **trade ~**) sindacato ▷ *cpd* sindacale, dei sindacati; **Union Jack** *n* bandiera *nazionale britannica*

unique [juːˈniːk] *adj* unico(-a)

unisex [ˈjuːnɪsɛks] *adj* unisex *inv*

unit [ˈjuːnɪt] *n* unità *f inv*; (*section: of furniture etc*) elemento; (*team, squad*) reparto, squadra

unite [juːˈnaɪt] *vt* unire ▷ *vi* unirsi; **united** *adj* unito(-a); unificato(-a); (*efforts*) congiunto(-a); **United Kingdom** *n* Regno Unito; **United Nations (Organization)** *n* (Organizzazione *f* delle) Nazioni Unite; **United States (of America)** *n* Stati *mpl* Uniti (d'America)

unity [ˈjuːnɪtɪ] *n* unità

universal [juːnɪˈvəːsl] *adj* universale

universe [ˈjuːnɪvəːs] *n* universo

university [juːnɪˈvəːsɪtɪ] *n* università *f inv*

unjust [ʌnˈdʒʌst] *adj* ingiusto(-a)

unkind [ʌnˈkaɪnd] *adj* scortese; crudele

unknown [ʌnˈnəun] *adj* sconosciuto(-a)

unlawful [ʌnˈlɔːful] *adj* illecito(-a), illegale

unleaded [ʌnˈlɛdɪd] *adj* (*petrol, fuel*) verde, senza piombo

unleash [ʌnˈliːʃ] *vt* (*fig*) scatenare

unless [ʌnˈlɛs] *conj* a meno che (non) + *sub*

unlike [ʌnˈlaɪk] *adj* diverso(-a) ▷ *prep* a differenza di, contrariamente a

unlikely [ʌnˈlaɪklɪ] *adj* improbabile

unlimited [ʌnˈlɪmɪtɪd] *adj* illimitato(-a)

unlisted [ʌnˈlɪstɪd] (*us*) *adj* (*Tel*): **to be ~** non essere sull'elenco

unload [ʌnˈləud] *vt* scaricare

unlock [ʌnˈlɔk] *vt* aprire

unlucky [ʌnˈlʌkɪ] *adj* sfortunato(-a); (*object, number*) che porta sfortuna

unmarried [ʌnˈmærɪd] *adj* non sposato(-a); (*man only*) scapolo, celibe; (*woman only*) nubile

unmistak(e)able [ʌnmɪsˈteɪkəbl] *adj* inconfondibile

unnatural [ʌnˈnætʃrəl] *adj* innaturale; contro natura

unnecessary [ʌnˈnɛsəsərɪ] *adj* inutile, superfluo(-a)

UNO [ˈjuːnəu] *n abbr* (= *United Nations Organization*) ONU *f*

unofficial [ʌnəˈfɪʃl] *adj* non ufficiale; (*strike*) non dichiarato(-a) dal sindacato

unpack [ʌnˈpæk] *vi* disfare la valigia (*or* le valigie) ▷ *vt* disfare

unpaid [ʌnˈpeɪd] *adj* (*holiday*) non pagato(-a); (*work*) non retribuito(-a); (*bill, debt*) da pagare

unpleasant [ʌnˈplɛznt] *adj* spiacevole

unplug [ʌnˈplʌg] *vt* staccare

unpopular [ʌnˈpɔpjuləʳ] *adj* impopolare

unprecedented [ʌnˈprɛsɪdəntɪd] *adj* senza precedenti

unpredictable [ʌnprɪˈdɪktəbl] *adj* imprevedibile

unprotected [ˈʌnprəˈtɛktɪd] *adj* (*sex*) non protetto(-a)

unqualified [ʌnˈkwɔlɪfaɪd] *adj*

(*teacher*) non abilitato(-a); (*success*)
assoluto(-a), senza riserve

unravel [ʌn'rævl] *vt* dipanare,
districare

unreal [ʌn'rɪəl] *adj* irreale

unrealistic [ʌnrɪə'lɪstɪk] *adj* non
realistico(-a)

unreasonable [ʌn'ri:znəbl] *adj*
irragionevole

unrelated [ʌnrɪ'leɪtɪd] *adj* ~
(to) senza rapporto (con); non
imparentato(-a) (con)

unreliable [ʌnrɪ'laɪəbl] *adj* (*person*,
machine) che non dà affidamento;
(*news*, *source of information*)
inattendibile

unrest [ʌn'rɛst] *n* agitazione *f*

unroll [ʌn'rəʊl] *vt* srotolare

unruly [ʌn'ru:lɪ] *adj* indisciplinato(-a)

unsafe [ʌn'seɪf] *adj* pericoloso(-a),
rischioso(-a)

unsatisfactory ['ʌnsætɪs'fæktərɪ]
adj che lascia a desiderare,
insufficiente

unscrew [ʌn'skru:] *vt* svitare

unsettled [ʌn'sɛtld] *adj* (*person*)
turbato(-a); indeciso(-a); (*weather*)
instabile

unsettling [ʌn'sɛtlɪŋ] *adj*
inquietante

unsightly [ʌn'saɪtlɪ] *adj* brutto(-a),
sgradevole a vedersi

unskilled [ʌn'skɪld] *adj* non
specializzato(-a)

unspoiled ['ʌn'spɔɪld], **unspoilt**
['ʌn'spɔɪlt] *adj* (*place*) non
deturpato(-a)

unstable [ʌn'steɪbl] *adj* (*gen*)
instabile; (*mentally*) squilibrato(-a)

unsteady [ʌn'stɛdɪ] *adj* instabile,
malsicuro(-a)

unsuccessful [ʌnsək'sɛsful] *adj*
(*writer*, *proposal*) che non ha successo;
(*marriage*, *attempt*) mal riuscito(-a),
fallito(-a); **to be ~** (*in attempting sth*)
non avere successo

unsuitable [ʌn'su:təbl] *adj*

inadatto(-a); inopportuno(-a);
sconveniente

unsure [ʌn'ʃʊə] *adj* incerto(-a); **to be
~ of o.s** essere insicuro(-a)

untidy [ʌn'taɪdɪ] *adj* (*room*) in
disordine; (*appearance*) trascurato(-a);
(*person*) disordinato(-a)

untie [ʌn'taɪ] *vt* (*knot*, *parcel*) disfare;
(*prisoner*, *dog*) slegare

until [ʌn'tɪl] *prep* fino a; (*after negative*)
prima di ▷ *conj* finché, fino a quando;
(*in past*, *after negative*) prima che + *sub*,
prima di + *infinitive*; **~ he comes** finché
or fino a quando non arriva; **~ now**
finora; **~ then** fino ad allora

untrue [ʌn'tru:] *adj* (*statement*)
falso(-a), non vero(-a)

unused [ʌn'ju:zd] *adj* nuovo(-a)

unusual [ʌn'ju:ʒuəl] *adj* insolito(-a),
eccezionale, raro(-a); **unusually** *adv*
insolitamente

unveil [ʌn'veɪl] *vt* scoprire; svelare

unwanted [ʌn'wɒntɪd] *adj* (*clothing*)
smesso(-a); (*child*) non desiderato(-a)

unwell [ʌn'wɛl] *adj* indisposto(-a); **to
feel ~** non sentirsi bene

unwilling [ʌn'wɪlɪŋ] *adj*: **to be ~ to
do** non voler fare

unwind [ʌn'waɪnd] (*irreg: like* **wind**¹)
vt svolgere, srotolare ▷ *vi* (*relax*)
rilassarsi

unwise [ʌn'waɪz] *adj* poco saggio(-a)

unwittingly [ʌn'wɪtɪŋlɪ] *adv* senza
volerlo

unwrap [ʌn'ræp] *vt* disfare; aprire

unzip [ʌn'zɪp] *vt* aprire (la chiusura
lampo di); (*Comput*) dezippare

 KEYWORD

up [ʌp] *prep* **he went up the stairs/
the hill** è salito su per le scale/sulla
collina; **the cat was up a tree** il gatto
era su su un albero; **they live further up
the street** vivono un po' più su nella
stessa strada

▷ *adv* **1** (*upwards*, *higher*) su, in alto;

up in the sky/the mountains su nel cielo/in montagna; **up there** lassù; **up above** su in alto
2: **to be up** (out of bed) essere alzato(-a); (prices, level) essere salito(-a)
3: **up to** (as far as) fino a; **up to now** finora
4: **to be up to** (depending on): **it's up to you** sta a lei, dipende da lei; (equal to): **he's not up to it** (job, task etc) non ne è all'altezza; (inf: be doing): **what is he up to?** cosa sta combinando?
▷ n **ups and downs** alti e bassi mpl

up-and-coming ['ʌpənd'kʌmɪŋ] adj pieno(-a) di promesse, promettente
upbringing ['ʌpbrɪŋɪŋ] n educazione f
update [ʌp'deɪt] vt aggiornare
upfront [ʌp'frʌnt] adj (inf) franco(-a), aperto(-a) ▷ adv (pay) subito
upgrade [ʌp'greɪd] vt (house, job) migliorare; (employee) avanzare di grado
upheaval [ʌp'hiːvl] n sconvolgimento; tumulto
uphill [ʌp'hɪl] adj in salita; (fig: task) difficile ▷ adv **to go ~** andare in salita, salire
upholstery [ʌp'həulstəri] n tappezzeria
upmarket [ʌp'mɑːkɪt] adj (product) che si rivolge ad una fascia di mercato superiore
upon [ə'pɔn] prep su
upper ['ʌpəʳ] adj superiore ▷ n (of shoe) tomaia; **upper-class** adj dell'alta borghesia
upright ['ʌpraɪt] adj diritto(-a); verticale; (fig) diritto(-a), onesto(-a)
uprising ['ʌpraɪzɪŋ] n insurrezione f, rivolta
uproar ['ʌprɔːʳ] n tumulto, clamore m
upset [n 'ʌpsɛt, vb, adj ʌp'sɛt] (irreg: like **set**) n (to plan etc) contrattempo; (stomach upset) disturbo ▷ vt (glass

etc) rovesciare; (plan, stomach) scombussolare; (person: offend) contrariare; (: grieve) addolorare; sconvolgere ▷ adj contrariato(-a), addolorato(-a); (stomach) scombussolato(-a)
upside-down [ʌpsaɪd'daun] adv sottosopra
upstairs [ʌp'stɛəz] adv, adj di sopra, al piano superiore ▷ n piano di sopra
up-to-date ['ʌptə'deɪt] adj moderno(-a); aggiornato(-a)
uptown ['ʌptaun] (US) adv verso i quartieri residenziali ▷ adj dei quartieri residenziali
upward ['ʌpwəd] adj ascendente; verso l'alto; **upward(s)** adv in su, verso l'alto
uranium [juə'reɪnɪəm] n uranio
Uranus [juə'reɪnəs] n (planet) Urano
urban ['əːbən] adj urbano(-a)
urge [əːdʒ] n impulso; stimolo; forte desiderio ▷ vt **to ~ sb to do** esortare qn a fare, spingere qn a fare; raccomandare a qn di fare
urgency ['əːdʒənsɪ] n urgenza; (of tone) insistenza
urgent ['əːdʒənt] adj urgente; (voice) insistente
urinal ['juərɪnl] n (BRIT: building) vespasiano; (: vessel) orinale m, pappagallo
urinate ['juərɪneɪt] vi orinare
urine ['juərɪn] n orina
URL n abbr (= uniform resource locator) URL m inv, sito web
us [ʌs] pron ci; (stressed, after prep) noi; see also **me**
US(A) n abbr (= United States (of America)) USA mpl
use [n juːs, vb juːz] n uso; impiego, utilizzazione f ▷ vt usare, utilizzare, servirsi di; **in ~** in uso; **out of ~** fuori uso; **to be of ~** essere utile, servire; **it's no ~** non serve, è inutile; **she ~d to do it** lo faceva (una volta), era solita farlo; **to be ~d to** avere l'abitudine di; **use**

up vt consumare; esaurire; **used** adj
(object, car) usato(-a); **useful** adj utile;
useless adj inutile; (person) inetto(-a);
user n utente m/f; **user-friendly** adj
(computer) di facile uso
usual ['juːʒuəl] adj solito(-a); **as ~**
come al solito, come d'abitudine;
usually adv di solito
utensil [juːˈtɛnsl] n utensile m;
kitchen ~s utensili da cucina
utility [juːˈtɪlɪtɪ] n utilità; (also: **public**
~) servizio pubblico
utilize ['juːtɪlaɪz] vt utilizzare;
sfruttare
utmost ['ʌtməust] adj estremo(-a)
▷ n **to do one's ~** fare il possibile or
di tutto
utter ['ʌtəʳ] adj assoluto(-a), totale
▷ vt pronunciare, proferire; emettere;
utterly adv completamente, del
tutto
U-turn ['juːˈtəːn] n inversione f a U

v. abbr = **verse**; **versus**; **volt**; (= vide)
vedi, vedere
vacancy ['veɪkənsɪ] n (BRIT: job)
posto libero; (room) stanza libera; **"no**
vacancies" "completo"

> Be careful not to translate
> *vacancy* by the Italian word
> *vacanza*.

vacant ['veɪkənt] adj (job, seat etc)
libero(-a); (expression) assente
vacate [vəˈkeɪt] vt lasciare libero(-a)
vacation [vəˈkeɪʃən] (esp US)
n vacanze fpl; **vacationer** (US
vacationist) n vacanziere(-a)
vaccination [væksɪˈneɪʃən] n
vaccinazione f
vaccine ['væksiːn] n vaccino
vacuum ['vækjum] n vuoto; **vacuum**
cleaner n aspirapolvere m inv
vagina [vəˈdʒaɪnə] n vagina
vague [veɪg] adj vago(-a); (blurred:
photo, memory) sfocato(-a)
vain [veɪn] adj (useless) inutile,
vano(-a); (conceited) vanitoso(-a); **in ~**

inutilmente, invano

Valentine's Day ['væləntaɪnzdeɪ] *n*
San Valentino *m*

valid ['vælɪd] *adj* valido(-a), valevole;
(*excuse*) valido(-a)

valley ['vælɪ] *n* valle *f*

valuable ['væljuəbl] *adj* (*jewel*)
di (grande) valore; (*time, help*)
prezioso(-a); **valuables** *npl* oggetti
mpl di valore

value ['vælju:] *n* valore *m* ▷ *vt* (*fix price*) valutare, dare un prezzo a;
(*cherish*) apprezzare, tenere a; **~s** *npl*
(*principles*) valori *mpl*

valve [vælv] *n* valvola

vampire ['væmpaɪə'] *n* vampiro

van [væn] *n* (Aut) furgone *m*; (BRIT: Rail) vagone *m*

vandal ['vændl] *n* vandalo(-a);
vandalism *n* vandalismo; **vandalize**
vt vandalizzare

vanilla [və'nɪlə] *n* vaniglia ▷ *cpd* (*ice cream*) alla vaniglia

vanish ['vænɪʃ] *vi* svanire, scomparire

vanity ['vænɪtɪ] *n* vanità

vapour ['veɪpə'] (US **vapor**) *n*
vapore *m*

variable ['vɛərɪəbl] *adj* variabile;
(*mood*) mutevole

variant ['vɛərɪənt] *n* variante *f*

variation [vɛərɪ'eɪʃən] *n* variazione *f*;
(*in opinion*) cambiamento

varied ['vɛərɪd] *adj* vario(-a),
diverso(-a)

variety [və'raɪətɪ] *n* varietà *f inv*;
(*quantity*) quantità, numero

various ['vɛərɪəs] *adj* vario(-a),
diverso(-a); (*several*) parecchi(-e),
molti(-e)

varnish ['vɑːnɪʃ] *n* vernice *f*; (*nail varnish*) smalto ▷ *vt* verniciare;
mettere lo smalto su

vary ['vɛərɪ] *vt, vi* variare, mutare

vase [vɑːz] *n* vaso

Vaseline® ['væsɪliːn] *n* vaselina

vast [vɑːst] *adj* vasto(-a); (*amount, success*) enorme

VAT [væt] *n abbr* (= *value added tax*)
I.V.A. *f*

Vatican ['vætɪkən] *n*: **the ~** il Vaticano

vault [vɔːlt] *n* (*of roof*) volta; (*tomb*)
tomba; (*in bank*) camera blindata ▷ *vt*
(*also*: **~ over**) saltare (d'un balzo)

VCR *n abbr* = **video cassette recorder**

VDU *n abbr* = **visual display unit**

veal [viːl] *n* vitello

veer [vɪə'] *vi* girare; virare

vegan ['viːgən] *n* vegetaliano(-a)

vegetable ['vɛdʒtəbl] *n* verdura,
ortaggio ▷ *adj* vegetale

vegetarian [vɛdʒɪ'tɛərɪən] *adj, n*
vegetariano(-a); **do you have any ~
dishes?** avete piatti vegetariani?

vegetation [vɛdʒɪ'teɪʃən] *n*
vegetazione *f*

vehicle ['viːɪkl] *n* veicolo

veil [veɪl] *n* velo

vein [veɪn] *n* vena; (*on leaf*) nervatura

Velcro® ['vɛlkrəʊ] *n* velcro® *m inv*

velvet ['vɛlvɪt] *n* velluto ▷ *adj* di
velluto

vending machine ['vɛndɪŋ-] *n*
distributore *m* automatico

vendor ['vɛndə'] *n* venditore(-trice)

vengeance ['vɛndʒəns] *n* vendetta;
with a ~ (*fig*) davvero; furiosamente

Venice ['vɛnɪs] *n* Venezia

venison ['vɛnɪsn] *n* carne *f* di cervo

venom ['vɛnəm] *n* veleno

vent [vɛnt] *n* foro, apertura; (*in dress, jacket*) spacco ▷ *vt* (*fig: one's feelings*)
sfogare, dare sfogo a

ventilation [vɛntɪ'leɪʃən] *n*
ventilazione *f*

venture ['vɛntʃə'] *n* impresa
(rischiosa) ▷ *vt* rischiare, azzardare
▷ *vi* avventurarsi; **business ~**
iniziativa commerciale

venue ['vɛnjuː] *n* luogo (designato)
per l'incontro

Venus ['viːnəs] *n* (*planet*) Venere *m*

verb [vəːb] *n* verbo; **verbal** *adj*
verbale; (*translation*) orale

verdict ['vəːdɪkt] *n* verdetto

verge [vəːdʒ] (BRIT) n bordo, orlo; **"soft ~s"** (BRIT: Aut) banchine fpl cedevoli; **on the ~ of doing** sul punto di fare

verify ['vɛrɪfaɪ] vt verificare; (prove the truth of) confermare

versatile ['vəːsətaɪl] adj (person) versatile; (machine, tool etc) (che si presta) a molti usi

verse [vəːs] n versi mpl; (stanza) stanza, strofa; (in bible) versetto

version ['vəːʃən] n versione f

versus ['vəːsəs] prep contro

vertical ['vəːtɪkl] adj verticale ▷ n verticale m

very ['vɛrɪ] adv molto ▷ adj **the ~ book which** proprio il libro che; **the ~ last** proprio l'ultimo; **at the ~ least** almeno; **~ much** moltissimo

vessel ['vɛsl] n (Anat) vaso; (Naut) nave f; (container) recipiente m

vest [vɛst] n (BRIT) maglia; (: sleeveless) canottiera; (US: waistcoat) gilè m inv

vet [vɛt] n abbr (BRIT: = veterinary surgeon) veterinario ▷ vt esaminare minuziosamente

veteran ['vɛtərn] n (also: **war ~**) veterano

veterinary surgeon ['vɛtrɪnərɪ-] (US **veterinarian**) n veterinario

veto ['viːtəu] (pl **vetoes**) n veto ▷ vt opporre il veto a

via ['vaɪə] prep (by way of) via; (by means of) tramite

viable ['vaɪəbl] adj attuabile; vitale

vibrate [vaɪ'breɪt] vi **to ~ (with)** vibrare (di); (resound) risonare (di)

vibration [vaɪ'breɪʃən] n vibrazione f

vicar ['vɪkəʳ] n pastore m

vice [vaɪs] n (evil) vizio; (Tech) morsa; **vice-chairman** (irreg) n vicepresidente m

vice versa ['vaɪsɪ'vəːsə] adv viceversa

vicinity [vɪ'sɪnɪtɪ] n vicinanze fpl

vicious ['vɪʃəs] adj (remark, dog) cattivo(-a); (blow) violento(-a)

victim ['vɪktɪm] n vittima

victor ['vɪktəʳ] n vincitore m

Victorian [vɪk'tɔːrɪən] adj vittoriano(-a)

victorious [vɪk'tɔːrɪəs] adj vittorioso(-a)

victory ['vɪktərɪ] n vittoria

video ['vɪdɪəu] cpd video... ▷ n (video film) video m inv; (also: **~ cassette**) videocassetta; (also: **~ cassette recorder**) videoregistratore m; **video call** n videochiamata; **video camera** n videocamera; **video (cassette) recorder** n videoregistratore m; **video game** n videogioco; **videophone** ['vɪdɪəufəun] n videotelefono; **video shop** n videonoleggio; **video tape** n videotape m inv; **video wall** n schermo m multivideo inv

vie [vaɪ] vi: **to ~ with** competere con, rivaleggiare con

Vienna [vɪ'ɛnə] n Vienna

Vietnam [vjɛt'næm] n Vietnam m; **Vietnamese** adj, n inv vietnamita m/f

view [vjuː] n vista, veduta; (opinion) opinione f ▷ vt (look at: also fig) considerare; (house) visitare; **on ~** (in museum etc) esposto(-a); **in full ~ of** sotto gli occhi di; **in ~ of the weather/the fact that** considerato il tempo/che; **in my ~** a mio parere; **viewer** n spettatore(-trice); **viewpoint** n punto di vista; (place) posizione f

vigilant ['vɪdʒɪlənt] adj vigile

vigorous ['vɪgərəs] adj vigoroso(-a)

vile [vaɪl] adj (action) vile; (smell) disgustoso(-a), nauseante; (temper) pessimo(-a)

villa ['vɪlə] n villa

village ['vɪlɪdʒ] n villaggio; **villager** n abitante m/f di villaggio

villain ['vɪlən] n (scoundrel) canaglia; (BRIT: criminal) criminale m; (in novel etc) cattivo

vinaigrette [vɪneɪ'grɛt] n vinaigrette f inv

vine [vaɪn] n vite f; (climbing plant) rampicante m

vinegar ['vɪnɪgəʳ] n aceto

vineyard ['vɪnjɑːd] n vigna, vigneto

vintage ['vɪntɪdʒ] n (year) annata, produzione f ▷ cpd d'annata

vinyl ['vaɪnl] n vinile m

viola [vɪ'əulə] n viola

violate ['vaɪəleɪt] vt violare

violation [vaɪə'leɪʃən] n violazione f; **in ~ of sth** violando qc

violence ['vaɪələns] n violenza

violent ['vaɪələnt] adj violento(-a)

violet ['vaɪələt] adj (colour) viola inv, violetto(-a) ▷ n (plant) violetta; (colour) violetto

violin [vaɪə'lɪn] n violino

VIP n abbr (= very important person) V.I.P. m/f inv

virgin ['vəːdʒɪn] n vergine f ▷ adj vergine inv

Virgo ['vəːgəu] n (sign) Vergine f

virtual ['vəːtjuəl] adj effettivo(-a), vero(-a); (Comput, Physics) virtuale; (in effect): **it's a ~ impossibility** è praticamente impossibile; **the ~ leader** il capo all'atto pratico; **virtually** ['vəːtjuəlɪ] adv (almost) praticamente; **virtual reality** n (Comput) realtà virtuale

virtue ['vəːtjuː] n virtù f inv; (advantage) pregio, vantaggio; **by ~ of** grazie a

virus ['vaɪərəs] n (also Comput) virus m inv

visa ['viːzə] n visto

vise [vaɪs] (us) n (Tech) = **vice**

visibility [vɪzɪ'bɪlɪtɪ] n visibilità

visible ['vɪzəbl] adj visibile

vision ['vɪʒən] n (sight) vista; (foresight, in dream) visione f

visit ['vɪzɪt] n visita; (stay) soggiorno ▷ vt (person: us: also: **~ with**) andare a trovare; (place) visitare; **visiting hours** npl (in hospital etc) orario delle visite; **visitor** n visitatore(-trice); (guest) ospite m/f; **visitor centre** (us

visitor center) n centro informazioni per visitatori di museo, zoo, parco ecc

visual ['vɪzjuəl] adj visivo(-a); visuale; ottico(-a); **visualize** ['vɪzjuəlaɪz] vt immaginare, figurarsi; (foresee) prevedere

vital ['vaɪtl] adj vitale

vitality [vaɪ'tælɪtɪ] n vitalità

vitamin ['vɪtəmɪn] n vitamina

vivid ['vɪvɪd] adj vivido(-a)

V-neck ['viːnɛk] n maglione m con lo scollo a V

vocabulary [vəu'kæbjuləɪ] n vocabolario

vocal ['vəukl] adj (Mus) vocale; (communication) verbale

vocational [vəu'keɪʃənl] adj professionale

vodka ['vɔdkə] n vodka f inv

vogue [vəug] n moda; (popularity) popolarità, voga

voice [vɔɪs] n voce f ▷ vt (opinion) esprimere; **voice mail** n servizio di segretaria telefonica

void [vɔɪd] n vuoto ▷ adj (invalid) nullo(-a); (empty): **~ of** privo(-a) di

volatile ['vɔlətaɪl] adj volatile; (fig) volubile

volcano [vɔl'keɪnəu] (pl **volcanoes**) n vulcano

volleyball ['vɔlɪbɔːl] n pallavolo f

volt [vəult] n volt m inv; **voltage** n tensione f, voltaggio

volume ['vɔljuːm] n volume m

voluntarily ['vɔləntrɪlɪ] adv volontariamente; gratuitamente

voluntary ['vɔləntərɪ] adj volontario(-a); (unpaid) gratuito(-a), non retribuito(-a)

volunteer [vɔlən'tɪəʳ] n volontario(-a) ▷ vt offrire volontariamente ▷ vi (Mil) arruolarsi volontario; **to ~ to do** offrire (volontariamente) di fare

vomit ['vɔmɪt] n vomito ▷ vt, vi vomitare

vote [vəut] n voto, suffragio; (cast)

voto; (*franchise*) diritto di voto
▷ *vt* **to be ~d chairman** *etc* venir
eletto presidente *etc*; (*propose*): **to
~ that** approvare la proposta che
▷ *vi* votare; **~ of thanks** discorso
di ringraziamento; **voter** *n*
elettore(-trice); **voting** *n* scrutinio
voucher ['vautʃəʳ] *n* (*for meal, petrol
etc*) buono
vow [vau] *n* voto, promessa solenne
▷ *vt* **to ~ to do/that** giurare di
fare/che
vowel ['vauəl] *n* vocale *f*
voyage ['vɔɪɪdʒ] *n* viaggio per mare,
traversata
vulgar ['vʌlgəʳ] *adj* volgare
vulnerable ['vʌlnərəbl] *adj*
vulnerabile
vulture ['vʌltʃəʳ] *n* avvoltoio

waddle ['wɔdl] *vi* camminare come
una papera
wade [weɪd] *vi*: **to ~ through**
camminare a stento in; (*fig: book*)
leggere con fatica
wafer ['weɪfəʳ] *n* (*Culin*) cialda
waffle ['wɔfl] *n* (*Culin*) cialda; (*inf*)
ciance *fpl* ▷ *vi* cianciare
wag [wæg] *vt* agitare, muovere ▷ *vi*
agitarsi
wage [weɪdʒ] *n* (*also: ~s*) salario, paga
▷ *vt* **to ~ war** fare la guerra
wag(g)on ['wægən] *n* (*horse-drawn*)
carro; (BRIT: *Rail*) vagone *m* (merci)
wail [weɪl] *n* gemito; (*of siren*) urlo ▷ *vi*
gemere; urlare
waist [weɪst] *n* vita, cintola;
waistcoat (BRIT) *n* panciotto, gilè
m inv
wait [weɪt] *n* attesa ▷ *vi* aspettare,
attendere; **to lie in ~ for** stare in
agguato a; **to ~ for** aspettare; **~ for
me, please** aspettami, per favore; **I
can't ~ to** (*fig*) non vedo l'ora di; **wait**

on vt fus servire; **waiter** n cameriere m; **waiting list** n lista di attesa; **waiting room** n sala d'aspetto or d'attesa; **waitress** n cameriera

waive [weɪv] vt rinunciare a, abbandonare

wake [weɪk] (pt **woke, waked**, pp **woken, waked**) vt (also: ~ **up**) svegliare ▷ vi (also: ~ **up**) svegliarsi ▷ n (for dead person) veglia funebre; (Naut) scia

Wales [weɪlz] n Galles m

walk [wɔːk] n passeggiata; (short) giretto; (gait) passo, andatura; (path) sentiero; (in park etc) sentiero, vialetto ▷ vi camminare; (for pleasure, exercise) passeggiare ▷ vt (distance) fare or percorrere a piedi; (dog) accompagnare, portare a passeggiare; **10 minutes' ~ from** 10 minuti di cammino or a piedi da; **from all ~s of life** di tutte le condizioni sociali; **walk out** vi (audience) andarsene; (workers) scendere in sciopero; **walker** n (person) camminatore(-trice); **walkie-talkie** ['wɔːkɪ'tɔːkɪ] n walkie-talkie m inv; **walking** n camminare m; **walking shoes** npl pedule fpl; **walking stick** n bastone m da passeggio; **Walkman®** ['wɔːkmən] n Walkman® m inv; **walkway** n passaggio pedonale

wall [wɔːl] n muro; (internal, of tunnel, cave) parete f

wallet ['wɒlɪt] n portafoglio; **I can't find my ~** non trovo il portafoglio

wallpaper ['wɔːlpeɪpəʳ] n carta da parati ▷ vt (room) mettere la carta da parati in

walnut ['wɔːlnʌt] n noce f; (tree, wood) noce m

walrus ['wɔːlrəs] (pl **walrus** or **walruses**) n tricheco

waltz [wɔːlts] n valzer m inv ▷ vi ballare il valzer

wand [wɒnd] n (also: **magic ~**) bacchetta (magica)

wander ['wɒndəʳ] vi (person) girare senza meta, girovagare; (thoughts) vagare ▷ vt girovagare per

want [wɒnt] vt volere; (need) aver bisogno di ▷ n **for ~ of** per mancanza di; **wanted** adj (criminal) ricercato(-a); **"wanted"** (in adverts) "cercasi"

war [wɔːʳ] n guerra; **to make ~ (on)** far guerra (a)

ward [wɔːd] n (in hospital: room) corsia; (: section) reparto; (Pol) circoscrizione f; (Law: child: also: ~ **of court**) pupillo(-a)

warden ['wɔːdn] n (of park, game reserve, youth hostel) guardiano(-a); (BRIT: of institution) direttore(-trice); (BRIT: also: **traffic ~**) addetto(-a) al controllo del traffico e del parcheggio

wardrobe ['wɔːdrəub] n (cupboard) guardaroba m inv, armadio; (clothes) guardaroba; (Cinema, Theatre) costumi mpl

warehouse ['wɛəhaus] n magazzino

warfare ['wɔːfɛəʳ] n guerra

warhead ['wɔːhɛd] n (Mil) testata

warm [wɔːm] adj caldo(-a); (thanks, welcome, applause) caloroso(-a); (person) cordiale; **it's ~** fa caldo; **I'm ~** ho caldo; **warm up** vi scaldarsi, riscaldarsi ▷ vt scaldare, riscaldare; (engine) far scaldare; **warmly** adv (applaud, welcome) calorosamente; (dress) con abiti pesanti; **warmth** n calore m

warn [wɔːn] vt: **to ~ sb that/(not) to do/of** avvertire or avvisare qn che/di (non) fare/di; **warning** n avvertimento; (notice) avviso; (signal) segnalazione f; **warning light** n spia luminosa

warrant ['wɒrnt] n (voucher) buono; (Law: to arrest) mandato di cattura; (: to search) mandato di perquisizione

warranty ['wɒrəntɪ] n garanzia

warrior ['wɒrɪəʳ] n guerriero(-a)

Warsaw ['wɔːsɔː] n Varsavia

warship ['wɔːʃɪp] n nave f da guerra
wart [wɔːt] n verruca
wartime ['wɔːtaɪm] n **in ~** in tempo di guerra
wary ['wɛərɪ] adj prudente
was [wɔz] pt of **be**
wash [wɔʃ] vt lavare ▷ vi lavarsi; (sea):
  to ~ over/against sth infrangersi su/contro qc ▷ n lavaggio; (of ship) scia; **to give sth a ~** lavare qc, dare una lavata a qc; **to have a ~** lavarsi;
  wash up vi (BRIT) lavare i piatti; (US) darsi una lavata; **washbasin** (US **washbowl**) n lavabo; **wash cloth** (US) n pezzuola (per lavarsi); **washer** n (Tech) rondella; **washing** n (linen etc) bucato; **washing line** n (BRIT) corda del bucato; **washing machine** n lavatrice f; **washing powder** (BRIT) n detersivo (in polvere)
Washington ['wɔʃɪŋtən] n Washington f
wash: **washing-up** n rigovernatura, lavatura dei piatti; **washing-up liquid** n detersivo liquido (per stoviglie);
  washroom n gabinetto
wasn't ['wɔznt] = **was not**
wasp [wɔsp] n vespa
waste [weɪst] n spreco; (of time) perdita; (rubbish) rifiuti mpl; (also: **household ~**) immondizie fpl ▷ adj (material) di scarto; (food) avanzato(-a); (land) incolto(-a) ▷ vt sprecare; **waste ground** (BRIT) n terreno incolto or abbandonato; **wastepaper basket** ['weɪstpeɪpə-] n cestino per la carta straccia
watch [wɔtʃ] n (also: **wrist ~**) orologio (da polso); (act of watching, vigilance) sorveglianza; (guard: Mil, Naut) guardia; (Naut: spell of duty) quarto ▷ vt (look at) osservare; (: match, programme) guardare; (spy on, guard) sorvegliare, tenere d'occhio; (be careful of) fare attenzione a ▷ vi osservare, guardare; (keep guard) fare or montare la guardia; **watch out** vi

fare attenzione; **watchdog** n (also fig) cane m da guardia; **watch strap** n cinturino da orologio
water ['wɔːtər] n acqua ▷ vt (plant) annaffiare ▷ vi (eyes) lacrimare; (mouth): **to make sb's mouth ~** far venire l'acquolina in bocca a qn; **in British ~s** nelle acque territoriali britanniche; **water down** vt (milk) diluire; (fig: story) edulcorare;
  watercolour (US **watercolor**) n acquerello; **watercress** n crescione m; **waterfall** n cascata; **watering can** n annaffiatoio; **watermelon** n anguria, cocomero; **waterproof** adj impermeabile; **water-skiing** n sci m acquatico
watt [wɔt] n watt m inv
wave [weɪv] n onda; (of hand) gesto, segno; (in hair) ondulazione f; (fig: surge) ondata ▷ vi fare un cenno con la mano; (branches, grass) ondeggiare; (flag) sventolare ▷ vt (hand) fare un gesto con; (handkerchief) sventolare; (stick) brandire; **wavelength** n lunghezza d'onda
waver ['weɪvər] vi esitare; (voice) tremolare
wavy ['weɪvɪ] adj ondulato(-a); ondeggiante
wax [wæks] n cera ▷ vt dare la cera a; (car) lucidare ▷ vi (moon) crescere
way [weɪ] n via, strada; (path, access) passaggio; (distance) distanza; (direction) parte f, direzione f; (manner) modo, stile m; (habit) abitudine f; **which ~? — this ~** da che parte or in quale direzione? — da questa parte or per di qua; **on the ~** (en route) per strada; **to be on one's ~** essere in cammino or sulla strada; **to be in the ~** bloccare il passaggio; (fig) essere tra i piedi or d'impiccio; **to go out of one's ~ to do** (fig) mettercela tutta or fare di tutto per fare; **under ~** (project) in corso; **to lose one's ~** perdere la strada; **in a ~** in un certo senso; **in**

some ~s sotto certi aspetti; **no ~!**
(*inf*) neanche per idea!; **by the ~** a
proposito ...; **"~ in"** (*BRIT*) "entrata",
"ingresso"; **"~ out"** (*BRIT*) "uscita"; **the
~ back** la strada del ritorno; **"give ~"**
(*BRIT: Aut*) "dare la precedenza"

W.C. [ˈdʌbljuːsiː] (*BRIT*) *n* W.C. *m inv*,
gabinetto

we [wiː] *pl pron* noi

weak [wiːk] *adj* debole; (*health*)
precario(-a); (*beam etc*) fragile; (*tea*)
leggero(-a); **weaken** *vi* indebolirsi
▷ *vt* indebolire; **weakness** *n*
debolezza; (*fault*) punto debole,
difetto; **to have a weakness for**
avere un debole per

wealth [wɛlθ] *n* (*money, resources*)
ricchezza, ricchezze *fpl*; (*of details*)
abbondanza, profusione *f*; **wealthy**
adj ricco(-a)

weapon [ˈwɛpən] *n* arma; **~s of mass
destruction** armi *mpl* di distruzione
di massa

wear [wɛəʳ] (*pt* **wore**, *pp* **worn**)
n (*use*) uso; (*damage through use*)
logorio, usura; (*clothing*): **sports/
baby ~** abbigliamento sportivo/per
neonati ▷ *vt* (*clothes*) portare; (*put
on*) mettersi; (*damage: through use*)
consumare ▷ *vi* (*last*) durare; (*rub
etc through*) consumarsi; **evening ~**
abiti *mpl or* tenuta da sera; **wear off**
vi sparire lentamente; **wear out**
vt consumare; (*person, strength*) esaurire

weary [ˈwɪərɪ] *adj* stanco(-a) ▷ *vi* **to ~
of** stancarsi di

weasel [ˈwiːzl] *n* (*Zool*) donnola

weather [ˈwɛðəʳ] *n* tempo ▷ *vt*
(*storm, crisis*) superare; **what's the ~
like?** che tempo fa?; **under the ~** (*fig:
ill*) poco bene; **weather forecast** *n*
previsioni *fpl* del tempo, bollettino
meteorologico

weave [wiːv] (*pt* **wove**, *pp* **woven**) *vt*
(*cloth*) tessere; (*basket*) intrecciare

web [wɛb] *n* (*of spider*) ragnatela; (*on
foot*) palma; (*fabric, also fig*) tessuto;

the (World Wide) W~ la Rete;
webcam [ˈwɛbkæm] *n* webcam *f
inv*; **web page** *n* (*Comput*) pagina
f web *inv*; **website** *n* (*Comput*) sito
(Internet)

wed [wɛd] (*pt, pp* **wedded**) *vt* sposare
▷ *vi* sposarsi

we'd [wiːd] = **we had**; **we would**

Wed. *abbr* (= *Wednesday*) mer.

wedding [ˈwɛdɪŋ] *n* matrimonio;
wedding anniversary *n*
anniversario di matrimonio; **wedding
day** *n* giorno delle nozze *or* del
matrimonio; **wedding dress** *n* abito
nuziale; **wedding ring** *n* fede *f*

wedge [wɛdʒ] *n* (*of wood etc*) zeppa; (*of
cake*) fetta ▷ *vt* (*fix*) fissare con zeppe;
(*pack tightly*) incastrare

Wednesday [ˈwɛdnzdɪ] *n* mercoledì
m inv

wee [wiː] (*Scottish*) *adj* piccolo(-a)

weed [wiːd] *n* erbaccia ▷ *vt* diserbare;
weedkiller *n* diserbante *m*

week [wiːk] *n* settimana; **a ~
today/on Friday** oggi/venerdì a otto;
weekday *n* giorno feriale; (*Comm*)
giornata lavorativa; **weekend** *n*
fine settimana *m or f inv*, weekend
m inv; **weekly** *adv* ogni settimana,
settimanalmente ▷ *adj* settimanale
▷ *n* settimanale *m*

weep [wiːp] (*pt, pp* **wept**) *vi* (*person*)
piangere

weigh [weɪ] *vt, vi* pesare; **to ~ anchor**
salpare l'ancora; **weigh up** *vt*
valutare

weight [weɪt] *n* peso; **to lose/
put on ~** dimagrire/ingrassare;
weightlifting *n* sollevamento pesi

weir [wɪəʳ] *n* diga

weird [wɪəd] *adj* strano(-a),
bizzarro(-a); (*eerie*) soprannaturale

welcome [ˈwɛlkəm] *adj*
benvenuto(-a) ▷ *n* accoglienza,
benvenuto ▷ *vt* dare il benvenuto a;
(*be glad of*) rallegrarsi di; **thank you
— you're ~!** grazie — prego!

weld [wɛld] n saldatura ▷ vt saldare
welfare ['wɛlfɛəʳ] n benessere m;
 welfare state n stato assistenziale
well [wɛl] n pozzo ▷ adv bene ▷ adj **to
 be ~** (person) stare bene ▷ excl allora!;
 ma!; ebbene!; **as ~** anche; **as ~ as** così
 come; oltre a; **~ done!** bravo(-a)!;
 get ~ soon! guarisci presto!; **to do ~**
 andare bene
we'll [wiːl] = **we will**; **we shall**
well: **well-behaved** adj ubbidiente;
 well-built adj (person) ben fatto(-a);
 well-dressed adj ben vestito(-a),
 vestito(-a) bene
wellies (inf) ['wɛlɪz] npl (BRIT) stivali
 mpl di gomma
well: **well-known** adj noto(-a),
 famoso(-a); **well-off** adj benestante,
 danaroso(-a); **well-paid** [wɛl'peɪd]
 adj ben pagato(-a)
Welsh [wɛlʃ] adj gallese ▷ n (Ling)
 gallese m; **Welshman** (irreg) n gallese
 m; **Welshwoman** (irreg) n gallese f
went [wɛnt] pt of **go**
wept [wɛpt] pt, pp of **weep**
were [wəːʳ] pt of **be**
we're [wɪəʳ] = **we are**
weren't [wəːnt] = **were not**
west [wɛst] n ovest m, occidente
 m, ponente m ▷ adj (a) ovest inv,
 occidentale ▷ adv verso ovest; **the
 W~** l'Occidente m; **westbound**
 ['wɛstbaʊnd] adj (traffic) diretto(-a)
 a ovest; (carriageway) ovest inv;
 western adj occidentale, dell'ovest
 ▷ n (Cinema) western m inv; **West
 Indian** adj delle Indie Occidentali ▷ n
 abitante m/f delle Indie Occidentali;
 West Indies [-'ɪndɪz] npl Indie fpl
 Occidentali
wet [wɛt] adj umido(-a), bagnato(-a);
 (soaked) fradicio(-a); (rainy)
 piovoso(-a) ▷ n (BRIT: Pol) politico
 moderato; **to get ~** bagnarsi; **"~
 paint"** "vernice fresca"; **wetsuit** n
 tuta da sub
we've [wiːv] = **we have**

whack [wæk] vt picchiare, battere
whale [weɪl] n (Zool) balena
wharf [wɔːf] (pl **wharves**) n
 banchina

O KEYWORD

what [wɔt] adj **1** (in direct/indirect
 questions) che; quale; **what size is it?**
 che taglia è?; **what colour is it?** di che
 colore è?; **what books do you want?**
 quali or che libri vuole?
 2 (in exclamations) che; **what a mess!**
 che disordine!
 ▷ pron **1** (interrogative) che cosa, cosa,
 che; **what are you doing?** che or
 (che) cosa fai?; **what you talking
 about?** di che cosa parli?; **what is it
 called?** come si chiama?; **what about
 me?** e io?; **what about doing …?** e se
 facessimo …?
 2 (relative) ciò che, quello che; **I saw
 what you did/was on the table** ho
 visto quello che hai fatto/quello che
 era sul tavolo
 3 (indirect use) (che) cosa; **he asked
 me what she had said** mi ha chiesto
 che cosa avesse detto; **tell me what
 you're thinking about** dimmi a cosa
 stai pensando
 ▷ excl (disbelieving) cosa!, come!

whatever [wɔt'ɛvə] adj **~ book**
 qualunque or qualsiasi libro + sub
 ▷ pron **do ~ is necessary/you want**
 faccia qualunque or qualsiasi cosa
 sia necessaria/lei voglia; **~ happens**
 qualunque cosa accada; **no reason
 ~ or whatsoever** nessuna ragione
 affatto or al mondo; **nothing ~**
 proprio niente
whatsoever [wɔtsəʊ'ɛvə] adj
 = **whatever**
wheat [wiːt] n grano, frumento
wheel [wiːl] n ruota; (Aut: also:
 steering ~) volante m; (Naut) (ruota
 del) timone m ▷ vt spingere ▷ vi

(birds) roteare; (also: **~ round**) girare;
wheelbarrow n carriola; **wheelchair**
n sedia a rotelle; **wheel clamp** n (Aut)
morsa che blocca la ruota di una vettura in
sosta vietata
wheeze [wiːz] vi ansimare

 KEYWORD

when [wɛn] adv quando; **when did it
happen?** quando è successo?
▷ conj **1** (at, during, after the time that)
quando; **she was reading when
I came in** quando sono entrato lei
leggeva; **that was when I needed
you** era allora che avevo bisogno di te
2 (on, at which): **on the day when
I met him** il giorno in cui l'ho
incontrato; **one day when it was
raining** un giorno che pioveva
3 (whereas) quando, mentre; **you said
I was wrong when in fact I was
right** mi hai detto che avevo torto,
quando in realtà avevo ragione

whenever [wɛn'ɛvə] adv quando mai
▷ conj quando; (every time that) ogni
volta che
where [wɛəʳ] adv, conj dove; **this is ~**
è qui che; **whereabouts** adv dove
▷ n sb's whereabouts luogo dove
qn si trova; **whereas** conj mentre;
whereby pron per cui; **wherever**
[-'ɛvəʳ] conj dovunque + sub;
(interrogative) dove mai
whether ['wɛðəʳ] conj se; **I don't
know ~ to accept or not** non so se
accettare o no; **it's doubtful ~** è poco
probabile che; **~ you go or not** che lei
vada o no

 KEYWORD

which [wɪtʃ] adj **1** (interrogative: direct,
indirect) quale; **which picture do you
want?** quale quadro vuole?; **which
one?** quale?; **which one of you did it?**

chi di voi lo ha fatto?
2: **in which case** nel qual caso
▷ pron **1** (interrogative) quale; **which
(of these) are yours?** quali di
questi sono suoi?; **which of you are
coming?** chi di voi viene?
2 (relative) che; (: indirect) cui, il (la)
quale; **the apple which you ate/
which is on the table** la mela che hai
mangiato/che è sul tavolo; **the chair
on which you are sitting** la sedia
sulla quale or su cui sei seduto; **he said
he knew, which is true** ha detto che
lo sapeva, il che è vero; **after which**
dopo di che

whichever [wɪtʃ'ɛvə] adj take **~ book
you prefer** prenda qualsiasi libro che
preferisce; **~ book you take** qualsiasi
libro prenda
while [waɪl] n momento ▷ conj
mentre; (as long as) finché; (although)
sebbene + sub; per quanto + sub; **for a
~** per un po'
whilst [waɪlst] conj = **while**
whim [wɪm] n capriccio
whine [waɪn] n gemito ▷ vi gemere;
uggiolare; piagnucolare
whip [wɪp] n frusta; (for riding)
frustino; (Pol: person) capogruppo (che
sovrintende alla disciplina dei colleghi
di partito) ▷ vt frustare; (cream, eggs)
sbattere; **whipped cream** n panna
montata
whirl [wəːl] vt (far) girare
rapidamente, (far) turbinare ▷ vi
(dancers) volteggiare; (leaves, water)
sollevarsi in vortice
whisk [wɪsk] n (Culin) frusta; frullino
▷ vt sbattere, frullare; **to ~ sb away** or
off portar via qn a tutta velocità
whiskers ['wɪskəz] npl (of animal)
baffi mpl; (of man) favoriti mpl
whisky ['wɪskɪ] (US, Ireland **whiskey**)
n whisky m inv
whisper ['wɪspəʳ] n sussurro ▷ vt, vi
sussurrare

whistle ['wɪsl] *n* (*sound*) fischio; (*object*) fischietto ▷ *vi* fischiare

white [waɪt] *adj* bianco(-a); (*with fear*) pallido(-a) ▷ *n* bianco; (*person*) bianco(-a); **whiteboard** ['waɪtbɔ:d] *n* lavagna bianca; **White House** *n* Casa Bianca; **whitewash** *n* (*paint*) bianco di calce ▷ *vt* imbiancare; (*fig*) coprire

whiting ['waɪtɪŋ] *n inv* (*fish*) merlango

Whitsun ['wɪtsn] *n* Pentecoste *f*

whittle ['wɪtl] *vt*: **to ~ away, ~ down** ridurre, tagliare

whizz [wɪz] *vi*: **to ~ past** *or* **by** passare sfrecciando

KEYWORD

who [hu:] *pron* **1** (*interrogative*) chi; **who is it?, who's there?** chi è? **2** (*relative*) che; **the man who spoke to me** l'uomo che ha parlato con me; **those who can swim** quelli che sanno nuotare

whoever [hu:'ɛvə] *pron*: **~ finds it** chiunque lo trovi; **ask ~ you like** lo chieda a chiunque vuole; **~ she marries** chiunque sposerà, non importa chi sposerà; **~ told you that?** chi mai gliel'ha detto?

whole [həul] *adj* (*complete*) tutto(-a), completo(-a); (*not broken*) intero(-a), intatto(-a) ▷ *n* (*all*): **the ~ of** tutto(-a) il (la); (*entire unit*) tutto; (*not broken*) tutto; **the ~ of the town** tutta la città, la città intera; **on the ~, as a ~** nel complesso, nell'insieme; **wholefood(s)** *n(pl)* cibo integrale; **wholeheartedly** [həul'hɑ:tɪdlɪ] *adv* sentitamente, di tutto cuore; **wholemeal** *adj* (*bread, flour*) integrale; **wholesale** *n* commercio *or* vendita all'ingrosso ▷ *adj* all'ingrosso; (*destruction*) totale; **wholewheat** *adj* = **wholemeal**;

wholly *adv* completamente, del tutto

KEYWORD

whom [hu:m] *pron* **1** (*interrogative*) chi; **whom did you see?** chi hai visto?; **to whom did you give it?** a chi lo hai dato? **2** (*relative*) che, *prep* + il (la) quale (*check syntax of Italian verb used*); **the man whom I saw/to whom I spoke** l'uomo che ho visto/al quale ho parlato

whore [hɔ:] (*inf: pej*) *n* puttana

KEYWORD

whose [hu:z] *adj* **1** (*possessive: interrogative*) di chi; **whose book is this?, whose is this book?** di chi è questo libro?; **whose daughter are you?** di chi sei figlia? **2** (*possessive: relative*): **the man whose son you rescued** l'uomo il cui figlio hai salvato; **the girl whose sister you were speaking to** la ragazza alla cui sorella stavi parlando ▷ *pron* di chi; **whose is this?** di chi è questo?; **I know whose it is** so di chi è

KEYWORD

why [waɪ] *adv* perché; **why not?** perché no?; **why not do it now?** perché non farlo adesso? ▷ *conj* **I wonder why he said that** mi chiedo perché l'abbia detto; **that's not why I'm here** non è questo il motivo per cui sono qui; **the reason why** il motivo per cui ▷ *excl* (*surprise*) ma guarda un po'l; (*remonstrating*) ma (via)!; (*explaining*) ebbene!

wicked ['wɪkɪd] *adj* cattivo(-a),

malvagio(-a); maligno(-a); perfido(-a)
wicket ['wɪkɪt] n (Cricket) porta; area tra le due porte
wide [waɪd] adj largo(-a); (area, knowledge) vasto(-a); (choice) ampio(-a) ▷ adv **to open ~** spalancare; **to shoot ~** tirare a vuoto or fuori bersaglio; **widely** adv (differing) molto, completamente; (travelled, spaced) molto; (believed) generalmente; **widen** vt allargare, ampliare; **wide open** adj spalancato(-a); **widespread** adj (belief etc) molto or assai diffuso(-a)
widow ['wɪdəu] n vedova; **widower** n vedovo
width [wɪdθ] n larghezza
wield [wi:ld] vt (sword) maneggiare; (power) esercitare
wife [waɪf] (pl **wives**) n moglie f
WiFi ['waɪfaɪ] n WiFi m
wig [wɪg] n parrucca
wild [waɪld] adj selvatico(-a); selvaggio(-a); (sea, weather) tempestoso(-a); (idea, life) folle; stravagante; (applause) frenetico(-a); **wilderness** ['wɪldənɪs] n deserto; **wildlife** n natura; **wildly** adv selvaggiamente; (applaud) freneticamente; (hit, guess) a casaccio; (happy) follemente

 KEYWORD

will [wɪl] (pt, pp **willed**) aux vb **1** (forming future tense): **I will finish it tomorrow** lo finirò domani; **I will have finished it by tomorrow** lo finirò entro domani; **will you do it? — yes I will/no I won't** lo farai? — sì (lo farò)/no (non lo farò)
2 (in conjectures, predictions): **he will** or **he'll be there by now** dovrebbe essere arrivato ora; **that will be the postman** sarà il postino
3 (in commands, requests, offers): **will you be quiet!** vuoi stare zitto?; **will**

you come? vieni anche tu?; **will you help me?** mi aiuti?, mi puoi aiutare?; **will you have a cup of tea?** vorrebbe una tazza di tè?; **I won't put up with it!** non lo accetterò!
▷ vt **to will sb to do** volere che qn faccia; **he willed himself to go on** continuò grazie a un grande sforzo di volontà
▷ n volontà; testamento

willing ['wɪlɪŋ] adj volonteroso(-a); **~ to do** disposto(-a) a fare; **willingly** adv volentieri
willow ['wɪləu] n salice m
willpower ['wɪlpauə'] n forza di volontà
wilt [wɪlt] vi appassire
win [wɪn] (pt, pp **won**) n (in sports etc) vittoria ▷ vt (battle, prize, money) vincere; (popularity) conquistare ▷ vi vincere; **win over** vt convincere
wince [wɪns] vi trasalire
wind¹ [waɪnd] (pt, pp **wound**) vt attorcigliare; (wrap) avvolgere; (clock, toy) caricare ▷ vi (road, river) serpeggiare; **wind down** vt (car window) abbassare; (fig: production, business) diminuire; **wind up** vt (clock) caricare; (debate) concludere
wind² [wɪnd] n vento; (Med) flatulenza; (breath) respiro, fiato ▷ vt (take breath away) far restare senza fiato; **~ power** energia eolica
windfall ['wɪndfɔ:l] n (money) guadagno insperato
winding ['waɪndɪŋ] adj (road) serpeggiante; (staircase) a chiocciola
windmill ['wɪndmɪl] n mulino a vento
window ['wɪndəu] n finestra; (in car, train, plane) finestrino; (in shop etc) vetrina; (also: ~ **pane**) vetro; **I'd like a ~ seat** vorrei un posto vicino al finestrino; **window box** n cassetta da fiori; **window cleaner** n (person) pulitore m di finestre; **window pane**

n vetro; **window seat** *n* posto finestrino; **windowsill** *n* davanzale *m*

windscreen ['wɪndskriːn] (*US* **windshield**) *n* parabrezza *m inv*; **windscreen wiper** (*US* **windshield wiper**) *n* tergicristallo

windsurfing ['wɪndsəːfɪŋ] *n* windsurf *m inv*

windy ['wɪndɪ] *adj* ventoso(-a); **it's ~** c'è vento

wine [waɪn] *n* vino; **wine bar** *n* enoteca (*per degustazione*); **wine glass** *n* bicchiere *m* da vino; **wine list** *n* lista dei vini; **wine tasting** *n* degustazione *f* dei vini

wing [wɪŋ] *n* ala; (*Aut*) fiancata; **wing mirror** *n* (*BRIT*) specchietto retrovisore esterno

wink [wɪŋk] *n* ammiccamento ▷ *vi* ammiccare, fare l'occhiolino; (*light*) baluginare

winner ['wɪnəʳ] *n* vincitore(-trice)

winning ['wɪnɪŋ] *adj* (*team, goal*) vincente; (*smile*) affascinante

winter ['wɪntəʳ] *n* inverno; **winter sports** *npl* sport *mpl* invernali; **wintertime** *n* inverno, stagione *f* invernale

wipe [waɪp] *n* pulita, passata ▷ *vt* pulire (strofinando); (*erase: tape*) cancellare; **wipe out** *vt* (*debt*) pagare, liquidare; (*memory*) cancellare; (*destroy*) annientare; **wipe up** *vt* asciugare

wire ['waɪəʳ] *n* filo; (*Elec*) filo elettrico; (*Tel*) telegramma *m* ▷ *vt* (*house*) fare l'impianto elettrico di; (*also: ~ up*) collegare, allacciare; (*person*) telegrafare

wiring ['waɪərɪŋ] *n* impianto elettrico

wisdom ['wɪzdəm] *n* saggezza; (*of action*) prudenza; **wisdom tooth** *n* dente *m* del giudizio

wise [waɪz] *adj* saggio(-a); prudente; giudizioso(-a)

wish [wɪʃ] *n* (*desire*) desiderio; (*specific desire*) richiesta ▷ *vt* desiderare,

volere; **best ~es** (*on birthday etc*) i migliori auguri; **with best ~es** (*in letter*) cordiali saluti, con i migliori saluti; **to ~ sb goodbye** dire arrivederci a qn; **he ~ed me well** mi augurò di riuscire; **to ~ to do/sb to do** desiderare *or* volere fare/che qn faccia; **to ~ for** desiderare

wistful ['wɪstful] *adj* malinconico(-a)

wit [wɪt] *n* (*also*: **~s**) intelligenza; presenza di spirito; (*wittiness*) spirito, arguzia; (*person*) bello spirito

witch [wɪtʃ] *n* strega

⬤ **KEYWORD**

with [wɪð, wɪθ] *prep* **1** (*in the company of*) con; **I was with him** ero con lui; **we stayed with friends** siamo stati da amici; **I'll be with you in a minute** vengo subito

2 (*descriptive*) con; **a room with a view** una stanza con vista sul mare (*or* sulle montagne *etc*); **the man with the grey hat/blue eyes** l'uomo con il cappello grigio/gli occhi blu

3 (*indicating manner, means, cause*): **with tears in her eyes** con le lacrime agli occhi; **red with anger** rosso dalla rabbia; **to shake with fear** tremare di paura

4 : **I'm with you** (*I understand*) la seguo; **to be with it** (*inf: up-to-date*) essere alla moda; (: *alert*) essere sveglio(-a)

withdraw [wɪθ'drɔː] (*irreg: like draw*) *vt* ritirare; (*money from bank*) ritirare; prelevare ▷ *vi* ritirarsi; **withdrawal** *n* ritiro; prelievo; (*of army*) ritirata; **withdrawal symptoms** *n* (*Med*) crisi *f* di astinenza; **withdrawn** *adj* (*person*) distaccato(-a)

withdrew [wɪθ'druː] *pt of* **withdraw**

wither ['wɪðəʳ] *vi* appassire

withhold [wɪθ'həuld] (*irreg: like hold*) *vt* (*money*) trattenere; (*permission*): **to**

~ (from) rifiutare (a); (*information*): **to ~ (from)** nascondere (a)
within [wɪð'ɪn] *prep* all'interno; (*in time, distances*) entro ▷ *adv* all'interno, dentro; **~ reach (of)** alla portata (di); **~ sight (of)** in vista (di); **~ a mile of** entro un miglio da; **~ the week** prima della fine della settimana
without [wɪð'aut] *prep* senza; **to go ~ sth** fare a meno di qc
withstand [wɪð'stænd] (*irreg: like* **stand**) *vt* resistere a
witness ['wɪtnɪs] *n* (*person, also Law*) testimone *m/f* ▷ *vt* (*event*) essere testimone di; (*document*) attestare l'autenticità di
witty ['wɪtɪ] *adj* spiritoso(-a)
wives [waɪvz] *npl of* **wife**
wizard ['wɪzəd] *n* mago
wk *abbr* = **week**
wobble ['wɔbl] *vi* tremare; (*chair*) traballare
woe [wəu] *n* dolore *m*; disgrazia
woke [wəuk] *pt of* **wake**
woken ['wəukn] *pp of* **wake**
wolf [wulf] (*pl* **wolves**) *n* lupo
woman ['wumən] (*pl* **women**) *n* donna
womb [wu:m] *n* (*Anat*) utero
women ['wɪmɪn] *npl of* **woman**
won [wʌn] *pt, pp of* **win**
wonder ['wʌndə'] *n* meraviglia ▷ *vi* **to ~ whether/why** domandarsi se/perché; **to ~ at** essere sorpreso(-a) di; meravigliarsi di; **to ~ about** domandarsi di; pensare a; **it's no ~ that** c'è poco *or* non c'è da meravigliarsi che + *sub*; **wonderful** *adj* meraviglioso(-a)
won't [wəunt] = **will not**
wood [wud] *n* legno; (*timber*) legname *m*; (*forest*) bosco; **wooden** *adj* di legno; (*fig*) rigido(-a); inespressivo(-a); **woodwind** *npl* (*Mus*): **the woodwind** i legni; **woodwork** *n* (*craft, subject*) falegnameria
wool [wul] *n* lana; **to pull the ~**

over sb's eyes (*fig*) imbrogliare qn; **woollen** (*us* **woolen**) *adj* di lana; (*industry*) laniero(-a); **woolly** (*us* **wooly**) *adj* di lana; (*fig: ideas*) confuso(-a)
word [wə:d] *n* parola; (*news*) notizie *fpl* ▷ *vt* esprimere, formulare; **in other ~s** in altre parole; **to break/keep one's ~** non mantenere/mantenere la propria parola; **to have ~s with sb** avere un diverbio con qn; **wording** *n* formulazione *f*; **word processing** *n* elaborazione *f* di testi, word processing *m*; **word processor** *n* word processor *m inv*
wore [wɔ:'] *pt of* **wear**
work [wə:k] *n* lavoro; (*Art, Literature*) opera ▷ *vi* lavorare; (*mechanism, plan etc*) funzionare; (*medicine*) essere efficace ▷ *vt* (*clay, wood etc*) lavorare; (*mine etc*) sfruttare; (*machine*) far funzionare; (*cause: effect, miracle*) fare; **to be out of ~** essere disoccupato(-a); **~s** *n* (*BRIT: factory*) fabbrica *npl* (*of clock, machine*) meccanismo; **how does this ~?** come funziona?; **the TV isn't ~ing** la TV non funziona; **to ~ loose** *vi* (*plans etc*) riuscire, andare bene ▷ *vt* (*problem*) risolvere; (*plan*) elaborare; **it works out at £100** fa 100 sterline; **worker** *n* lavoratore(-trice), operaio(-a); **work experience** *n* (*previous jobs*) esperienze *fpl* lavorative; (*student training placement*) tirocinio; **workforce** *n* forza lavoro; **working class** *n* classe *f* operaia; **working week** *n* settimana lavorativa; **workman** (*irreg*) *n* operaio; **work of art** *n* opera d'arte; **workout** *n* (*Sport*) allenamento; **work permit** *n* permesso di lavoro; **workplace** *n* posto di lavoro; **workshop** *n* officina; (*practical session*) gruppo di lavoro; **work station** *n* stazione *f* di lavoro; **work surface** *n* piano di lavoro; **worktop** *n* piano di lavoro

world [wəːld] n mondo ▷ cpd (champion) del mondo; (power, war) mondiale; **to think the ~ of sb** (fig) pensare un gran bene di qn; **World Cup** n (Football) Coppa del Mondo; **world-wide** adj universale; **World-Wide Web** n World Wide Web m

worm [wəːm] n (also: **earth~**) verme m

worn [wɔːn] pp of **wear** ▷ adj usato(-a); **worn-out** adj (object) consumato(-a), logoro(-a); (person) sfinito(-a)

worried ['wʌrɪd] adj preoccupato(-a)

worry ['wʌrɪ] n preoccupazione f ▷ vt preoccupare ▷ vi preoccuparsi; **worrying** adj preoccupante

worse [wəːs] adj peggiore ▷ adv, n peggio; **a change for the ~** un peggioramento; **worsen** vt, vi peggiorare; **worse off** adj in condizioni (economiche) peggiori

worship ['wəːʃɪp] n culto ▷ vt (God) adorare, venerare; (person) adorare; **Your W~** (BRIT: to mayor) signor sindaco; (: to judge) signor giudice

worst [wəːst] adj il (la) peggiore ▷ adv, n peggio; **at ~** al peggio, per male che vada

worth [wəːθ] n valore m ▷ adj **to be ~** valere; **it's ~ it** ne vale la pena; **it is ~ one's while (to do)** vale la pena (fare); **worthless** adj di nessun valore; **worthwhile** adj (activity) utile; (cause) lodevole

worthy ['wəːðɪ] adj (person) degno(-a); (motive) lodevole; **~ of** degno di

 KEYWORD

would [wud] aux vb **1** (conditional tense): **if you asked him he would do it** se glielo chiedesse lo farebbe; **if you had asked him he would have done it** se glielo avesse chiesto lo avrebbe fatto

2 (in offers, invitations, requests): **would you like a biscuit?** vorrebbe or vuole un biscotto?; **would you ask him to come in?** lo faccia entrare, per cortesia; **would you open the window please?** apra la finestra, per favore

3 (in indirect speech): **I said I would do it** ho detto che l'avrei fatto

4 (emphatic): **it WOULD have to snow today!** doveva proprio nevicare oggi!

5 (insistence): **she wouldn't do it** non ha voluto farlo

6 (conjecture): **it would have been midnight** sarà stato mezzanotte; **it would seem so** sembrerebbe proprio di sì

7 (indicating habit): **he would go there on Mondays** andava lì ogni lunedì

wouldn't ['wudnt] = **would not**

wound¹ [waund] pt, pp of **wind¹**

wound² [wuːnd] n ferita ▷ vt ferire

wove [wəuv] pt of **weave**

woven ['wəuvn] pp of **weave**

wrap [ræp] vt avvolgere; (pack: also: **~ up**) incartare; **wrapper** n (on chocolate) carta; (BRIT: of book) copertina; **wrapping** ['ræpɪŋ] n carta; **wrapping paper** n carta da pacchi; (for gift) carta da regali

wreath [riːθ, pl riːðz] n corona

wreck [rɛk] n (sea disaster) naufragio; (ship) relitto; (pej: person) rottame m ▷ vt demolire; (ship) far naufragare; (fig) rovinare; **wreckage** n rottami mpl; (of building) macerie fpl; (of ship) relitti mpl

wren [rɛn] n (Zool) scricciolo

wrench [rɛntʃ] n (Tech) chiave f; (tug) torsione f brusca; (fig) strazio ▷ vt strappare; storcere; **to ~ sth from** strappare qc a or da

wrestle ['rɛsl] vi **to ~ (with sb)** lottare (con qn); **wrestler** n lottatore(-trice); **wrestling** n lotta

wretched ['rɛtʃɪd] *adj* disgraziato(-a); (*inf: weather, holiday*) orrendo(-a), orribile; (: *child, dog*) pestifero(-a)

wriggle ['rɪgl] *vi* (*also:* **~ about**) dimenarsi; (: *snake, worm*) serpeggiare, muoversi serpeggiando

wring [rɪŋ] (*pt, pp* **wrung**) *vt* torcere; (*wet clothes*) strizzare; (*fig*): **to ~ sth out of** strappare qc a

wrinkle ['rɪŋkl] *n* (*on skin*) ruga; (*on paper etc*) grinza ▷ *vt* (*nose*) torcere; (*forehead*) corrugare ▷ *vi* (*skin, paint*) raggrinzirsi

wrist [rɪst] *n* polso

write [raɪt] (*pt* **wrote**, *pp* **written**) *vt, vi* scrivere; **write down** *vt* annotare; (*put in writing*) mettere per iscritto; **write off** *vt* (*debt, plan*) cancellare; **write out** *vt* mettere per iscritto; (*cheque, receipt*) scrivere; **write-off** *n* perdita completa; **writer** *n* autore(-trice), scrittore(-trice)

writing ['raɪtɪŋ] *n* scrittura; (*of author*) scritto, opera; **in ~** per iscritto; **writing paper** *n* carta da lettere

written ['rɪtn] *pp of* **write**

wrong [rɔŋ] *adj* sbagliato(-a); (*not suitable*) inadatto(-a); (*wicked*) cattivo(-a); (*unfair*) ingiusto(-a) ▷ *adv* in modo sbagliato, erroneamente ▷ *n* (*injustice*) torto ▷ *vt* fare torto a; **I took a ~ turning** ho sbagliato strada; **you are ~ to do it** ha torto a farlo; **you are ~ about that, you've got it ~** si sbaglia; **to be in the ~** avere torto; **what's ~?** cosa c'è che non va?; **to go ~** (*person*) sbagliarsi; (*plan*) fallire, non riuscire; (*machine*) guastarsi; **wrongly** *adv* (*incorrectly, by mistake*) in modo sbagliato; **wrong number** *n* (*Tel*): **you've got the wrong number** ha sbagliato numero

wrote [rəut] *pt of* **write**

wrung [rʌŋ] *pt, pp of* **wring**

WWW *n abbr* = **World Wide Web**; **the ~** la Rete

XL *abbr* = **extra large**

Xmas ['ɛksməs] *n abbr* = **Christmas**

X-ray ['ɛksreɪ] *n* raggio X; (*photograph*) radiografia ▷ *vt* radiografare

xylophone ['zaɪləfəun] *n* xilofono

yacht [jɔt] *n* panfilo, yacht *m inv*;
yachting *n* yachting *m*, sport *m*
della vela
yard [jɑːd] *n* (*of house etc*) cortile *m*;
(*measure*) iarda (= 914 mm; 3 feet); **yard
sale** (*US*) *n* vendita di oggetti usati nel
cortile di una casa privata
yarn [jɑːn] *n* filato; (*tale*) lunga storia
yawn [jɔːn] *n* sbadiglio ▷ *vi*
sbadigliare
yd. *abbr* = **yard(s)**
yeah [jɛə] *n* (*inf*) *adv* sì
year [jɪəʳ] *n* anno; (*referring to harvest,
wine etc*) annata; **he is 8 ~s old** ha
8 anni; **an eight-~-old child** un(a)
bambino(-a) di otto anni; **yearly** *adj*
annuale ▷ *adv* annualmente
yearn [jəːn] *vi*: **to ~ for sth/to do**
desiderare ardentemente qc/di fare
yeast [jiːst] *n* lievito
yell [jɛl] *n* urlo ▷ *vi* urlare
yellow ['jɛləʊ] *adj* giallo(-a); **Yellow
Pages**® *npl* pagine *fpl* gialle
yes [jɛs] *adv* sì ▷ *n* sì *m inv*; **to say/**

answer ~ dire/rispondere di sì
yesterday ['jɛstədɪ] *adv* ieri ▷ *n* ieri *m
inv*; **~ morning/evening** ieri mattina/
sera; **all day ~** ieri per tutta la giornata
yet [jɛt] *adv* ancora; già ▷ *conj* ma,
tuttavia; **it is not finished ~** non
è ancora finito; **the best ~** finora il
migliore; **as ~** finora
yew [juː] *n* tasso (*albero*)
Yiddish ['jɪdɪʃ] *n* yiddish *m*
yield [jiːld] *n* produzione *f*, resa;
reddito ▷ *vt* produrre, rendere;
(*surrender*) cedere ▷ *vi* cedere; (*US: Aut*)
dare la precedenza
yob(bo) ['jɔb(əʊ)] *n* (*BRIT inf*) bullo
yoga ['jəʊgə] *n* yoga *m*
yog(h)urt ['jəʊgət] *n* iogurt *m inv*
yolk [jəʊk] *n* tuorlo, rosso d'uovo

 KEYWORD

you [juː] *pron* **1** (*subject*) tu; (: *polite
form*) lei; (: *pl*) voi; (: *very formal*) loro;
you Italians enjoy your food a voi
Italiani piace mangiare bene; **you and
I will go** tu ed io *or* lei ed io andiamo
2 (*object: direct*) ti; la; vi; loro (*after
vb*); (: *indirect*) ti; le; vi; loro (*after vb*); **I
know you** ti *or* la *or* vi conosco; **I gave
it to you** te l'ho dato; gliel'ho dato; ve
l'ho dato; l'ho dato loro
3 (*stressed, after prep, in comparisons*)
te; lei; voi; loro; **I told you to do it** ho
detto a TE (*or* a LEI *etc*) di farlo; **she's
younger than you** è più giovane di
te (*or* lei *etc*)
4 (*impers: one*) si; **fresh air does you
good** l'aria fresca fa bene; **you never
know** non si sa mai

you'd [juːd] = **you had**; **you would**
you'll [juːl] = **you will**; **you shall**
young [jʌŋ] *adj* giovane ▷ *npl* (*of
animal*) piccoli *mpl*; (*people*): **the ~**
i giovani, la gioventù; **youngster**
n giovanotto, ragazzo; (*child*)
bambino(-a)

your [jɔːʳ] *adj* il (la) tuo(-a) *pl*, i (le) tuoi (tue); il (la) suo(-a); (*pl*) i (le) suoi (sue); il (la) vostro(-a); (*pl*) i (le) vostri(-e); il (la) loro; (*pl*) i (le) loro; *see also* **my**

you're [juəʳ] = **you are**

yours [jɔːz] *pron* il (la) tuo(-a); (*pl*) i (le) tuoi (tue); (*polite form*) il (la) suo(-a); (*pl*) i (le) suoi (sue); (*pl*) il (la) vostro(-a); (*pl*) i (le) vostri(-e); (: *very formal*) il (la) loro; (*pl*) i (le) loro; *see also* **mine**; **faithfully**; **sincerely**

yourself [jɔːˈsɛlf] *pron* (*reflexive*) ti; si; (*after prep*) te; sé; (*emphatic*) tu stesso(-a); lei stesso(-a); **yourselves** *pl pron* (*reflexive*) vi; si; (*after prep*) voi; loro; (*emphatic*) voi stessi(-e); loro stessi(-e); *see also* **oneself**

youth [juːθ, *pl* juːðz] *n* gioventù *f*; (*young man*) giovane *m*, ragazzo; **youth club** *n* centro giovanile; **youthful** *adj* giovane; da giovane; giovanile; **youth hostel** *n* ostello della gioventù

you've [juːv] = **you have**

Yugoslavia [ˈjuːgəuˈslaːvɪə] *n* (*Hist*) Jugoslavia

Z

zeal [ziːl] *n* zelo; entusiasmo

zebra [ˈziːbrə] *n* zebra; **zebra crossing** (*BRIT*) *n* (passaggio pedonale a) strisce *fpl*, zebre *fpl*

zero [ˈzɪərəu] *n* zero

zest [zɛst] *n* gusto; (*Culin*) buccia

zigzag [ˈzɪgzæg] *n* zigzag *m inv* ▷ *vi* zigzagare

Zimbabwe [zɪmˈbɑːbwɪ] *n* Zimbabwe *m*

zinc [zɪŋk] *n* zinco

zip [zɪp] *n* (*also:* ~ **fastener**, (*US*) **zipper**) chiusura *f* or cerniera *f* lampo *inv* ▷ *vt* (*also:* ~ **up**) chiudere con una cerniera lampo; **zip code** (*US*) *n* codice *m* di avviamento postale; **zipper** (*US*) *n* cerniera *f* lampo *inv*

zit [zɪt] *n* brufolo

zodiac [ˈzəudɪæk] *n* zodiaco

zone [zəun] *n* (*also Mil*) zona

zoo [zuː] *n* zoo *m inv*

zoology [zuːˈɔlədʒɪ] *n* zoologia

zoom [zuːm] *vi*: **to ~ past** sfrecciare; **zoom lens** *n* zoom *m inv*, obiettivo a

focale variabile
zucchini [zuːˈkiːnɪ] (*us*) *npl*
   (*courgettes*) zucchine *fpl*

VERB TABLES

Introduction

The **Verb Tables** in the following section contain 32 tables of the most common Italian verbs (some regular and some irregular) in alphabetical order. Each table shows you the following forms: **Present**, **Perfect**, **Imperfect**, **Future**, **Conditional**, **Present Subjunctive**, **Imperative** and the **Past Participle** and **Gerund**.

In order to help you use the verbs shown in Verb Tables correctly, there are also a number of example phrases at the bottom of each page to show the verb as it is used in context.

In Italian there are **regular** verbs (their forms follow the regular patterns of -**are**, -**ere** or -**ire** verbs), and **irregular** verbs (their forms do not follow the normal rules). Examples of regular verbs in these tables are:

> **parlare** (regular -**are** verb, Verb Table 16)
> **credere** (regular -**ere** verb, Verb Table 7)
> **capire** (regular -**ire** verb, Verb Table 6)

Some irregular verbs are irregular in most of their forms, while others may only have a couple of irregular forms.

▶ **addormentarsi** (to go to sleep)

PRESENT

(io)	mi addormento
(tu)	ti addormenti
(lui/lei) (lei/Lei)	si addormenta
(noi)	ci addormentiamo
(voi)	vi addormentate
(loro)	si addormentano

PERFECT

(io)	mi sono addormentato/a
(tu)	ti sei addormentato/a
(lui/lei) (lei/Lei)	si è addormentato/a
(noi)	ci siamo addormentati/e
(voi)	vi siete addormentati/e
(loro)	si sono addormentati/e

IMPERFECT

(io)	mi addormentavo
(tu)	ti addormentavi
(lui/lei) (lei/Lei)	si addormentava
(noi)	ci addormentavamo
(voi)	vi addormentavate
(loro)	si addormentavano

IMPERATIVE

addormentati
addormentiamoci
addormentatevi

FUTURE

(io)	mi addormenterò
(tu)	ti addormenterai
(lui/lei) (lei/Lei)	si addormenterà
(noi)	ci addormenteremo
(voi)	vi addormenterete
(loro)	si addormenteranno

CONDITIONAL

(io)	mi addormenterei
(tu)	ti addormenteresti
(lui/lei) (lei/Lei)	si addormenterebbe
(noi)	ci addormenteremmo
(voi)	vi addormentereste
(loro)	si addormenterebbero

PRESENT SUBJUNCTIVE

(io)	mi addormenti
(tu)	ti addormenti
(lui/lei) (lei/Lei)	si addormenti
(noi)	ci addormentiamo
(voi)	vi addormentiate
(loro)	si addormentino

PAST PARTICIPLE

addormentato

GERUND

addormentando

EXAMPLE PHRASES

Non voleva **addormentarsi**. *He didn't want to go to sleep.*
Mi si **è addormentato** un piede. *My foot has gone to sleep.*
Sono stanco: stasera **mi addormenterò** subito. *I'm tired: I'll go to sleep immediately tonight.*

Italic letters in Italian words show where stress does not follow the usual rules.

▶ andare (to go)

	PRESENT		FUTURE
(io)	vado	(io)	andrò
(tu)	vai	(tu)	andrai
(lui/lei) (lei/Lei)	va	(lui/lei) (lei/Lei)	andrà
(noi)	andiamo	(noi)	andremo
(voi)	andate	(voi)	andrete
(loro)	vanno	(loro)	andranno

	PERFECT		CONDITIONAL
(io)	sono andato/a	(io)	andrei
(tu)	sei andato/a	(tu)	andresti
(lui/lei) (lei/Lei)	è andato/a	(lui/lei) (lei/Lei)	andrebbe
(noi)	siamo andati/e	(noi)	andremmo
(voi)	siete andati/e	(voi)	andreste
(loro)	sono andati/e	(loro)	andrebbero

	IMPERFECT		PRESENT SUBJUNCTIVE
(io)	andavo	(io)	vada
(tu)	andavi	(tu)	vada
(lui/lei) (lei/Lei)	andava	(lui/lei) (lei/Lei)	vada
(noi)	andavamo	(noi)	andiamo
(voi)	andavate	(voi)	andiate
(loro)	andavano	(loro)	vadano

IMPERATIVE
vai
andiamo
andate

PAST PARTICIPLE
andato

GERUND
andando

EXAMPLE PHRASES

Andremo in Grecia quest'estate. *We're going to Greece this summer.*
Su, **andiamo**! *Come on, let's go!*
Com'è **andata**? *How did it go?*
Come **va**? – bene, grazie! *How are you? – fine thanks!*
Stasera **andrei** volentieri al ristorante. *I'd like to go to a restaurant this evening.*

Remember that subject pronouns are not used very often in Italian.

▶ **avere** (to have)

PRESENT

(io)	ho
(tu)	hai
(lui/lei) (lei/Lei)	ha
(noi)	abbiamo
(voi)	avete
(loro)	hanno

PERFECT

(io)	ho avuto
(tu)	hai avuto
(lui/lei) (lei/Lei)	ha avuto
(noi)	abbiamo avuto
(voi)	avete avuto
(loro)	hanno avuto

IMPERFECT

(io)	avevo
(tu)	avevi
(lui/lei) (lei/Lei)	aveva
(noi)	avevamo
(voi)	avevate
(loro)	avevano

IMPERATIVE

abbi
abbiamo
abbiate

FUTURE

(io)	avrò
(tu)	avrai
(lui/lei) (lei/Lei)	avrà
(noi)	avremo
(voi)	avrete
(loro)	avranno

CONDITIONAL

(io)	avrei
(tu)	avresti
(lui/lei) (lei/Lei)	avrebbe
(noi)	avremmo
(voi)	avreste
(loro)	avrebbero

PRESENT SUBJUNCTIVE

(io)	abbia
(tu)	abbia
(lui/lei) (lei/Lei)	abbia
(noi)	abbiamo
(voi)	abbiate
(loro)	abbiano

PAST PARTICIPLE

avuto

GERUND

avendo

EXAMPLE PHRASES

All'inizio **ha avuto** un sacco di problemi. *He had a lot of problems at first.*
Ho già **mangiato**. *I've already eaten.*
Ha la macchina nuova. *She's got a new car.*
Aveva la mia età. *He was the same age as me.*
Quanti ne **abbiamo** oggi? *What's the date today?*

Italic letters in Italian words show where stress does not follow the usual rules.

▶ **bere** (to drink)

PRESENT

(io)	bevo
(tu)	bevi
(lui/lei) (lei/Lei)	beve
(noi)	beviamo
(voi)	bevete
(loro)	bevono

PERFECT

(io)	ho bevuto
(tu)	hai bevuto
(lui/lei) (lei/Lei)	ha bevuto
(noi)	abbiamo bevuto
(voi)	avete bevuto
(loro)	hanno bevuto

IMPERFECT

(io)	bevevo
(tu)	bevevi
(lui/lei) (lei/Lei)	beveva
(noi)	bevevamo
(voi)	bevevate
(loro)	bevevano

IMPERATIVE

bevi
beviamo
bevete

FUTURE

(io)	berrò
(tu)	berrai
(lui/lei) (lei/Lei)	berrà
(noi)	berremo
(voi)	berrete
(loro)	berranno

CONDITIONAL

(io)	berrei
(tu)	berresti
(lui/lei) (lei/Lei)	berrebbe
(noi)	berremmo
(voi)	berreste
(loro)	berrebbero

PRESENT SUBJUNCTIVE

(io)	beva
(tu)	beva
(lui/lei) (lei/Lei)	beva
(noi)	beviamo
(voi)	beviate
(loro)	bevano

PAST PARTICIPLE

bevuto

GERUND

bevendo

EXAMPLE PHRASES

Vuoi **bere** qualcosa? *Would you like something to drink?*
Berrei volentieri un bicchiere di vino bianco. *I'd love a glass of white wine.*
Beveva sei caffè al giorno, ma ora ha smesso. *He used to drink six cups of coffee a day, but he's stopped now.*

Remember that subject pronouns are not used very often in Italian.

▶ cadere (to fall)

PRESENT

(io)	cado
(tu)	cadi
(lui/lei)(lei/Lei)	cade
(noi)	cadiamo
(voi)	cadete
(loro)	cadono

PERFECT

(io)	sono caduto/a
(tu)	sei caduto/a
(lui/lei)(lei/Lei)	è caduto/a
(noi)	siamo caduti/e
(voi)	siete caduti/e
(loro)	sono caduti/e

IMPERFECT

(io)	cadevo
(tu)	cadevi
(lui/lei)(lei/Lei)	cadeva
(noi)	cadevamo
(voi)	cadevate
(loro)	cadevano

IMPERATIVE

cadi
cadiamo
cadete

FUTURE

(io)	cadrò
(tu)	cadrai
(lui/lei)(lei/Lei)	cadrà
(noi)	cadremo
(voi)	cadrete
(loro)	cadranno

CONDITIONAL

(io)	cadrei
(tu)	cadresti
(lui/lei)(lei/Lei)	cadrebbe
(noi)	cadremmo
(voi)	cadreste
(loro)	cadrebbero

PRESENT SUBJUNCTIVE

(io)	cada
(tu)	cada
(lui/lei)(lei/Lei)	cada
(noi)	cadiamo
(voi)	cadiate
(loro)	cadano

PAST PARTICIPLE

caduto

GERUND

cadendo

EXAMPLE PHRASES

Ho inciampato e **sono caduta**. *I tripped and fell.*
Il mio compleanno **cade** di lunedì. *My birthday is on a Monday.*
Ti **è caduta** la sciarpa. *You've dropped your scarf.*
Attento che fai **cadere** il bicchiere. *Mind you don't knock over your glass.*

Italic letters in Italian words show where stress does not follow the usual rules.

▶ capire (to understand)

PRESENT

(io)	capisco
(tu)	capisci
(lui/lei) (lei/Lei)	capisce
(noi)	capiamo
(voi)	capite
(loro)	capiscono

PERFECT

(io)	ho capito
(tu)	hai capito
(lui/lei) (lei/Lei)	ha capito
(noi)	abbiamo capito
(voi)	avete capito
(loro)	hanno capito

IMPERFECT

(io)	capivo
(tu)	capivi
(lui/lei) (lei/Lei)	capiva
(noi)	capivamo
(voi)	capivate
(loro)	capivano

IMPERATIVE

capisci
capiamo
capite

FUTURE

(io)	capirò
(tu)	capirai
(lui/lei) (lei/Lei)	capirà
(noi)	capiremo
(voi)	capirete
(loro)	capiranno

CONDITIONAL

(io)	capirei
(tu)	capiresti
(lui/lei) (lei/Lei)	capirebbe
(noi)	capiremmo
(voi)	capireste
(loro)	capirebbero

PRESENT SUBJUNCTIVE

(io)	capisca
(tu)	capisca
(lui/lei) (lei/Lei)	capisca
(noi)	capiamo
(voi)	capiate
(loro)	capiscano

PAST PARTICIPLE

capito

GERUND

capendo

EXAMPLE PHRASES

Va bene, **capisco**. *OK, I understand.*
Non **ho capito** una parola. *I didn't understand a word.*
Fammi **capire**... *Let me get this straight...*
Non ti **capirò** mai. *I'll never understand you.*

Italic letters in Italian words show where stress does not follow the usual rules.

▶ **credere** (to believe)

PRESENT

(io)	credo
(tu)	credi
(lui/lei) (lei/Lei)	crede
(noi)	crediamo
(voi)	credete
(loro)	credono

PERFECT

(io)	ho creduto
(tu)	hai creduto
(lui/lei) (lei/Lei)	ha creduto
(noi)	abbiamo creduto
(voi)	avete creduto
(loro)	hanno creduto

IMPERFECT

(io)	credevo
(tu)	credevi
(lui/lei) (lei/Lei)	credeva
(noi)	credevamo
(voi)	credevate
(loro)	credevano

IMPERATIVE

credi
crediamo
credete

FUTURE

(io)	crederò
(tu)	crederai
(lui/lei) (lei/Lei)	crederà
(noi)	crederemo
(voi)	crederete
(loro)	crederanno

CONDITIONAL

(io)	crederei
(tu)	crederesti
(lui/lei) (lei/Lei)	crederebbe
(noi)	crederemmo
(voi)	credereste
(loro)	crederebbero

PRESENT SUBJUNCTIVE

(io)	creda
(tu)	creda
(lui/lei) (lei/Lei)	creda
(noi)	crediamo
(voi)	crediate
(loro)	credano

PAST PARTICIPLE

creduto

GERUND

credendo

EXAMPLE PHRASES

Non dirmi che **credi** ai fantasmi! *Don't tell me you believe in ghosts!*
Non **credeva** ai suoi occhi. *She couldn't believe her eyes.*
Non ti **crederò** mai. *I'll never believe you.*

Remember that subject pronouns are not used very often in Italian.

▶ **dare** (to give)

PRESENT

(io)	do
(tu)	dai
(lui/lei) (lei/Lei)	dà
(noi)	diamo
(voi)	date
(loro)	danno

PERFECT

(io)	ho dato
(tu)	hai dato
(lui/lei) (lei/Lei)	ha dato
(noi)	abbiamo dato
(voi)	avete dato
(loro)	hanno dato

IMPERFECT

(io)	davo
(tu)	davi
(lui/lei) (lei/Lei)	dava
(noi)	davamo
(voi)	davate
(loro)	davano

IMPERATIVE

dai
diamo
date

FUTURE

(io)	darò
(tu)	darai
(lui/lei) (lei/Lei)	darà
(noi)	daremo
(voi)	darete
(loro)	daranno

CONDITIONAL

(io)	darei
(tu)	daresti
(lui/lei) (lei/Lei)	darebbe
(noi)	daremmo
(voi)	dareste
(loro)	darebbero

PRESENT SUBJUNCTIVE

(io)	dia
(tu)	dia
(lui/lei) (lei/Lei)	dia
(noi)	diamo
(voi)	diate
(loro)	diano

PAST PARTICIPLE

dato

GERUND

dando

EXAMPLE PHRASES

Gli **ho dato** un libro. *I gave him a book.*
Dammelo. *Give it to me.*
La mia finestra **dà** sul giardino. *My window looks onto the garden.*
Domani sera **daranno** un bel film in tv. *There's a good film on TV tomorrow evening.*
Dandoti da fare, potresti ottenere molto di più. *If you exerted yourself you could achieve a lot more.*

Remember that subject pronouns are not used very often in Italian.

▶ dire (to say)

PRESENT

(io)	dico
(tu)	dici
(lui/lei) (lei/Lei)	dice
(noi)	diciamo
(voi)	dite
(loro)	dicono

FUTURE

(io)	dirò
(tu)	dirai
(lui/lei) (lei/Lei)	dirà
(noi)	diremo
(voi)	direte
(loro)	diranno

PERFECT

(io)	ho detto
(tu)	hai detto
(lui/lei) (lei/Lei)	ha detto
(noi)	abbiamo detto
(voi)	avete detto
(loro)	hanno detto

CONDITIONAL

(io)	direi
(tu)	diresti
(lui/lei) (lei/Lei)	direbbe
(noi)	diremmo
(voi)	direste
(loro)	direbbero

IMPERFECT

(io)	dicevo
(tu)	dicevi
(lui/lei) (lei/Lei)	diceva
(noi)	dicevamo
(voi)	dicevate
(loro)	dicevano

PRESENT SUBJUNCTIVE

(io)	dica
(tu)	dica
(lui/lei) (lei/Lei)	dica
(noi)	diciamo
(voi)	diciate
(loro)	dicano

IMPERATIVE

di'
diciamo
dite

PAST PARTICIPLE

detto

GERUND

dicendo

EXAMPLE PHRASES

Ha detto che verrà. *He said he'll come.*
Come si **dice** "quadro" in inglese? *How do you say "quadro" in English?*
Che ne **diresti** di andarcene? *Shall we leave?*
Ti **dirò** un segreto. *I'll tell you a secret.*
Dimmi dov'è. *Tell me where it is.*

Italic letters in Italian words show where stress does not follow the usual rules.

▶ dormire (to sleep)

PRESENT

(io)	dormo
(tu)	dormi
(lui/lei) (lei/Lei)	dorme
(noi)	dormiamo
(voi)	dormite
(loro)	dormono

FUTURE

(io)	dormirò
(tu)	dormirai
(lui/lei) (lei/Lei)	dormirà
(noi)	dormiremo
(voi)	dormirete
(loro)	dormiranno

PERFECT

(io)	ho dormito
(tu)	hai dormito
(lui/lei) (lei/Lei)	ha dormito
(noi)	abbiamo dormito
(voi)	avete dormito
(loro)	hanno dormito

CONDITIONAL

(io)	dormirei
(tu)	dormiresti
(lui/lei) (lei/Lei)	dormirebbe
(noi)	dormiremmo
(voi)	dormireste
(loro)	dormirebbero

IMPERFECT

(io)	dormivo
(tu)	dormivi
(lui/lei) (lei/Lei)	dormiva
(noi)	dormivamo
(voi)	dormivate
(loro)	dormivano

PRESENT SUBJUNCTIVE

(io)	dorma
(tu)	dorma
(lui/lei) (lei/Lei)	dorma
(noi)	dormiamo
(voi)	dormiate
(loro)	dormano

IMPERATIVE

dormi
dormiamo
dormite

PAST PARTICIPLE

dormito

GERUND

dormendo

EXAMPLE PHRASES

Sta dormendo. *She's sleeping.*
Vado a **dormire**. *I'm going to bed.*
Stanotte **dormirò** come un ghiro. *I'll sleep like a log tonight.*

Italic letters in Italian words show where stress does not follow the usual rules.

▶ **dovere** (to have to)

PRESENT

(io)	devo
(tu)	devi
(lui/lei)(lei/Lei)	deve
(noi)	dobbiamo
(voi)	dovete
(loro)	devono

PERFECT

(io)	ho dovuto
(tu)	hai dovuto
(lui/lei)(lei/Lei)	ha dovuto
(noi)	abbiamo dovuto
(voi)	avete dovuto
(loro)	hanno dovuto

IMPERFECT

(io)	dovevo
(tu)	dovevi
(lui/lei)(lei/Lei)	doveva
(noi)	dovevamo
(voi)	dovevate
(loro)	dovevano

IMPERATIVE

–

FUTURE

(io)	dovrò
(tu)	dovrai
(lui/lei)(lei/Lei)	dovrà
(noi)	dovremo
(voi)	dovrete
(loro)	dovranno

CONDITIONAL

(io)	dovrei
(tu)	dovresti
(lui/lei)(lei/Lei)	dovrebbe
(noi)	dovremmo
(voi)	dovreste
(loro)	dovrebbero

PRESENT SUBJUNCTIVE

(io)	debba
(tu)	debba
(lui/lei)(lei/Lei)	debba
(noi)	dobbiamo
(voi)	dobbiate
(loro)	debbano

PAST PARTICIPLE

dovuto

GERUND

dovendo

EXAMPLE PHRASES

È **dovuto** partire. *He had to leave.*
Devi finire i compiti prima di uscire. *You must finish your homework before you go out.*
Dev'essere tardi. *It must be late.*
Dovrebbe arrivare alle dieci. *He should arrive at ten.*
Gli **dovevo** 30 euro e così l'ho invitato a cena. *I owed him 30 euros so I took him out to dinner.*

Remember that subject pronouns are not used very often in Italian.

▶ essere (to be)

PRESENT

(io)	sono
(tu)	sei
(lui/lei) (lei/Lei)	è
(noi)	siamo
(voi)	siete
(loro)	sono

PERFECT

(io)	sono stato/a
(tu)	sei stato/a
(lui/lei) (lei/Lei)	è stato/a
(noi)	siamo stati/e
(voi)	siete stati/e
(loro)	sono stati/e

IMPERFECT

(io)	ero
(tu)	eri
(lui/lei) (lei/Lei)	era
(noi)	eravamo
(voi)	eravate
(loro)	erano

IMPERATIVE

sii
siamo
siate

FUTURE

(io)	sarò
(tu)	sarai
(lui/lei) (lei/Lei)	sarà
(noi)	saremo
(voi)	sarete
(loro)	saranno

CONDITIONAL

(io)	sarei
(tu)	saresti
(lui/lei) (lei/Lei)	sarebbe
(noi)	saremmo
(voi)	sareste
(loro)	sarebbero

PRESENT SUBJUNCTIVE

(io)	sia
(tu)	sia
(lui/lei) (lei/Lei)	sia
(noi)	siamo
(voi)	siate
(loro)	siano

PAST PARTICIPLE

stato

GERUND

essendo

EXAMPLE PHRASES

Sono italiana. *I'm Italian.*
Mario **è** appena partito. *Mario has just left.*
Siete mai **stati** in Africa? *Have you ever been to Africa?*
Quando **è** arrivato erano le quattro in punto. *It was exactly four o'clock when he arrived.*
Alla festa ci **saranno** tutti i miei amici. *All my friends will be at the party.*

Italic letters in Italian words show where stress does not follow the usual rules.

▶ **fare** (to do; make)

PRESENT

(io)	faccio
(tu)	fai
(lui/lei) (lei/Lei)	fa
(noi)	facciamo
(voi)	fate
(loro)	fanno

FUTURE

(io)	farò
(tu)	farai
(lui/lei) (lei/Lei)	farà
(noi)	faremo
(voi)	farete
(loro)	faranno

PERFECT

(io)	ho fatto
(tu)	hai fatto
(lui/lei) (lei/Lei)	ha fatto
(noi)	abbiamo fatto
(voi)	avete fatto
(loro)	hanno fatto

CONDITIONAL

(io)	farei
(tu)	faresti
(lui/lei) (lei/Lei)	farebbe
(noi)	faremmo
(voi)	fareste
(loro)	farebbero

IMPERFECT

(io)	facevo
(tu)	facevi
(lui/lei) (lei/Lei)	faceva
(noi)	facevamo
(voi)	facevate
(loro)	facevano

PRESENT SUBJUNCTIVE

(io)	faccia
(tu)	faccia
(lui/lei) (lei/Lei)	faccia
(noi)	facciamo
(voi)	facciate
(loro)	facciano

IMPERATIVE

fai
facciamo
fate

PAST PARTICIPLE

fatto

GERUND

facendo

EXAMPLE PHRASES

Ho fatto un errore. *I made a mistake.*
Due più due **fa** quattro. *Two and two makes four.*
Cosa **stai facendo**? *What are you doing?*
Fa il medico. *He is a doctor.*
Fa caldo. *It's hot.*

Remember that subject pronouns are not used very often in Italian.

▶ **mettere** (to put)

PRESENT

(io)	metto
(tu)	metti
(lui/lei)(lei/Lei)	mette
(noi)	mettiamo
(voi)	mettete
(loro)	mettono

PERFECT

(io)	ho messo
(tu)	hai messo
(lui/lei)(lei/Lei)	ha messo
(noi)	abbiamo messo
(voi)	avete messo
(loro)	hanno messo

IMPERFECT

(io)	mettevo
(tu)	mettevi
(lui/lei)(lei/Lei)	metteva
(noi)	mettevamo
(voi)	mettevate
(loro)	mettevano

IMPERATIVE

metti
mettiamo
mettete

FUTURE

(io)	metterò
(tu)	metterai
(lui/lei)(lei/Lei)	metterà
(noi)	metteremo
(voi)	metterete
(loro)	metteranno

CONDITIONAL

(io)	metterei
(tu)	metteresti
(lui/lei)(lei/Lei)	metterebbe
(noi)	metteremmo
(voi)	mettereste
(loro)	metterebbero

PRESENT SUBJUNCTIVE

(io)	metta
(tu)	metta
(lui/lei)(lei/Lei)	metta
(noi)	mettiamo
(voi)	mettiate
(loro)	mettano

PAST PARTICIPLE

messo

GERUND

mettendo

EXAMPLE PHRASES

Hai messo i bambini a letto? *Have you put the children to bed?*
Metterò un annuncio sul giornale. *I'll put an advert in the paper.*
Mettiti là e aspetta. *Wait there.*
Quanto tempo ci **hai messo**? *How long did it take you?*
Non **metto** più quelle scarpe. *I don't wear those shoes any more.*

Remember that subject pronouns are not used very often in Italian.

▶ **parere** (to appear)

PRESENT

(io)	paio
(tu)	pari
(lui/lei) (lei/Lei)	pare
(noi)	pariamo
(voi)	parete
(loro)	paiono

PERFECT

(io)	sono parso/a
(tu)	sei parso/a
(lui/lei) (lei/Lei)	è parso/a
(noi)	siamo parsi/e
(voi)	siete parsi/e
(loro)	sono parsi/e

IMPERFECT

(io)	parevo
(tu)	parevi
(lui/lei) (lei/Lei)	pareva
(noi)	parevamo
(voi)	parevate
(loro)	parevano

IMPERATIVE

pari
pariamo
parete

FUTURE

(io)	parrò
(tu)	parrai
(lui/lei) (lei/Lei)	parrà
(noi)	parremo
(voi)	parrete
(loro)	parranno

CONDITIONAL

(io)	parrei
(tu)	parresti
(lui/lei) (lei/Lei)	parrebbe
(noi)	parremmo
(voi)	parreste
(loro)	parrebbero

PRESENT SUBJUNCTIVE

(io)	paia
(tu)	paia
(lui/lei) (lei/Lei)	paia
(noi)	paiamo
(voi)	paiate
(loro)	paiano

PAST PARTICIPLE

parso

GERUND

parendo

EXAMPLE PHRASES

Mi **pare** che sia già arrivato. *I think he's already here.*
Ci **è parso** che foste stanchi. *We thought you were tired.*
Faceva solo ciò che gli **pareva**. *He did just what he wanted.*

Italic letters in Italian words show where stress does not follow the usual rules.

▶ parlare (to speak)

PRESENT		FUTURE	
(io)	parlo	(io)	parlerò
(tu)	parli	(tu)	parlerai
(lui/lei)(lei/Lei)	parla	(lui/lei)(lei/Lei)	parlerà
(noi)	parliamo	(noi)	parleremo
(voi)	parlate	(voi)	parlerete
(loro)	parlano	(loro)	parleranno

PERFECT		CONDITIONAL	
(io)	ho parlato	(io)	parlerei
(tu)	hai parlato	(tu)	parleresti
(lui/lei)(lei/Lei)	ha parlato	(lui/lei)(lei/Lei)	parlerebbe
(noi)	abbiamo parlato	(noi)	parleremmo
(voi)	avete parlato	(voi)	parlereste
(loro)	hanno parlato	(loro)	parlerebbero

IMPERFECT		PRESENT SUBJUNCTIVE	
(io)	parlavo	(io)	parli
(tu)	parlavi	(tu)	parli
(lui/lei)(lei/Lei)	parlava	(lui/lei)(lei/Lei)	parli
(noi)	parlavamo	(noi)	parliamo
(voi)	parlavate	(voi)	parliate
(loro)	parlavano	(loro)	parlino

IMPERATIVE

parla
parliamo
parlate

PAST PARTICIPLE

parlato

GERUND

parlando

EXAMPLE PHRASES

Pronto, chi **parla**? *Hello, who's speaking?*
Non **parliamone** più. *Let's just forget about it.*
Abbiamo parlato per ore. *We talked for hours.*
Gli **parlerò** di te. *I'll talk to him about you.*
Di cosa **parla** quel libro? *What is that book about?*

Remember that subject pronouns are not used very often in Italian.

▶ **piacere** (to be pleasing)

PRESENT

(io)	piaccio
(tu)	piaci
(lui/lei) (lei/Lei)	piace
(noi)	piacciamo
(voi)	piacete
(loro)	piacciono

PERFECT

(io)	sono piaciuto/a
(tu)	sei piaciuto/a
(lui/lei) (lei/Lei)	è piaciuto/a
(noi)	siamo piaciuti/e
(voi)	siete piaciuti/e
(loro)	sono piaciuti/e

IMPERFECT

(io)	piacevo
(tu)	piacevi
(lui/lei) (lei/Lei)	piaceva
(noi)	piacevamo
(voi)	piacevate
(loro)	piacevano

IMPERATIVE

piaci
piacciamo
piacciate

FUTURE

(io)	piacerò
(tu)	piacerai
(lui/lei) (lei/Lei)	piacerà
(noi)	piaceremo
(voi)	piacerete
(loro)	piaceranno

CONDITIONAL

(io)	piacerei
(tu)	piaceresti
(lui/lei) (lei/Lei)	piacerebbe
(noi)	piaceremmo
(voi)	piacereste
(loro)	piacerebbero

PRESENT SUBJUNCTIVE

(io)	piaccia
(tu)	piaccia
(lui/lei) (lei/Lei)	piaccia
(noi)	piacciamo
(voi)	piacciate
(loro)	piacciano

PAST PARTICIPLE

piaciuto

GERUND

piacendo

EXAMPLE PHRASES

Questa musica non **mi piace**. *I don't like this music.*
Cosa **ti piacerebbe** fare? *What would you like to do?*
Da piccola non **mi piacevano** i ragni. *When I was little I didn't like spiders.*

Remember that subject pronouns are not used very often in Italian.

▶ **potere** (to be able)

PRESENT

(io)	posso
(tu)	puoi
(lui/lei) (lei/Lei)	può
(noi)	possiamo
(voi)	potete
(loro)	possono

PERFECT

(io)	ho potuto
(tu)	hai potuto
(lui/lei) (lei/Lei)	ha potuto
(noi)	abbiamo potuto
(voi)	avete potuto
(loro)	hanno potuto

IMPERFECT

(io)	potevo
(tu)	potevi
(lui/lei) (lei/Lei)	poteva
(noi)	potevamo
(voi)	potevate
(loro)	potevano

IMPERATIVE

–

FUTURE

(io)	potrò
(tu)	potrai
(lui/lei) (lei/Lei)	potrà
(noi)	potremo
(voi)	potrete
(loro)	potranno

CONDITIONAL

(io)	potrei
(tu)	potresti
(lui/lei) (lei/Lei)	potrebbe
(noi)	potremmo
(voi)	potreste
(loro)	potrebbero

PRESENT SUBJUNCTIVE

(io)	possa
(tu)	possa
(lui/lei) (lei/Lei)	possa
(noi)	possiamo
(voi)	possiate
(loro)	possano

PAST PARTICIPLE

potuto

GERUND

potendo

EXAMPLE PHRASES

Si **può** visitare il castello tutti i giorni dell'anno. *You can visit the castle any day of the year.*
Non **è potuto** venire. *He couldn't come.*
Non **potrò** venire domani. *I won't be able to come tomorrow.*
Può aver avuto un incidente. *He may have had an accident.*
Potrebbe essere vero. *It could be true.*

Remember that subject pronouns are not used very often in Italian.

▶ prendere (to take)

PRESENT

(io)	prendo
(tu)	prendi
(lui/lei) (lei/Lei)	prende
(noi)	prendiamo
(voi)	prendete
(loro)	prendono

PERFECT

(io)	ho preso
(tu)	hai preso
(lui/lei) (lei/Lei)	ha preso
(noi)	abbiamo preso
(voi)	avete preso
(loro)	hanno preso

IMPERFECT

(io)	prendevo
(tu)	prendevi
(lui/lei) (lei/Lei)	prendeva
(noi)	prendevamo
(voi)	prendevate
(loro)	prendevano

IMPERATIVE

prendi
prendiamo
prendete

FUTURE

(io)	prenderò
(tu)	prenderai
(lui/lei) (lei/Lei)	prenderà
(noi)	prenderemo
(voi)	prenderete
(loro)	prenderanno

CONDITIONAL

(io)	prenderei
(tu)	prenderesti
(lui/lei) (lei/Lei)	prenderebbe
(noi)	prenderemmo
(voi)	prendereste
(loro)	prenderebbero

PRESENT SUBJUNCTIVE

(io)	prenda
(tu)	prenda
(lui/lei) (lei/Lei)	prenda
(noi)	prendiamo
(voi)	prendiate
(loro)	prendano

PAST PARTICIPLE

preso

GERUND

prendendo

EXAMPLE PHRASES

Prendi quella borsa. *Take that bag.*
Ho preso un bel voto. *I got a good mark.*
Prende qualcosa da bere? *Would you like something to drink?*
Per chi mi **prendi**? *Who do you think I am?*

Italic letters in Italian words show where stress does not follow the usual rules.

▶ rimanere (to stay)

PRESENT

(io)	rimango
(tu)	rimani
(lui/lei) (lei/Lei)	rimane
(noi)	rimaniamo
(voi)	rimanete
(loro)	rimangono

PERFECT

(io)	sono rimasto/a
(tu)	sei rimasto/a
(lui/lei) (lei/Lei)	è rimasto/a
(noi)	siamo rimasti/e
(voi)	siete rimasti/e
(loro)	sono rimasti/e

IMPERFECT

(io)	rimanevo
(tu)	rimanevi
(lui/lei) (lei/Lei)	rimaneva
(noi)	rimanevamo
(voi)	rimanevate
(loro)	rimanevano

IMPERATIVE

rimani
rimaniamo
rimanete

FUTURE

(io)	rimarrò
(tu)	rimarrai
(lui/lei) (lei/Lei)	rimarrà
(noi)	rimarremo
(voi)	rimarrete
(loro)	rimarranno

CONDITIONAL

(io)	rimarrei
(tu)	rimarresti
(lui/lei) (lei/Lei)	rimarrebbe
(noi)	rimarremmo
(voi)	rimarreste
(loro)	rimarrebbero

PRESENT SUBJUNCTIVE

(io)	rimanga
(tu)	rimanga
(lui/lei) (lei/Lei)	rimanga
(noi)	rimaniamo
(voi)	rimaniate
(loro)	rimangano

PAST PARTICIPLE

rimasto

GERUND

rimanendo

EXAMPLE PHRASES

Sono rimasto a casa tutto il giorno. *I stayed at home all day.*
Mi piacerebbe **rimanere** qualche altro giorno. *I'd like to stay a few more days.*
Ci **rimarrebbero** molto male. *They'd be very upset.*

Italic letters in Italian words show where stress does not follow the usual rules.

► **sapere** (to know)

PRESENT

(io)	so
(tu)	sai
(lui/lei) (lei/Lei)	sa
(noi)	sappiamo
(voi)	sapete
(loro)	sanno

PERFECT

(io)	hai saputo
(tu)	ha saputo
(lui/lei) (lei/Lei)	abbiamo saputo
(noi)	avete saputo
(voi)	hanno saputo
(loro)	ho saputo

IMPERFECT

(io)	sapevo
(tu)	sapevi
(lui/lei) (lei/Lei)	sapeva
(noi)	sapevamo
(voi)	sapevate
(loro)	sapevano

IMPERATIVE

sappi
sappiamo
sappiate

FUTURE

(io)	saprò
(tu)	saprai
(lui/lei) (lei/Lei)	saprà
(noi)	sapremo
(voi)	saprete
(loro)	sapranno

CONDITIONAL

(io)	saprei
(tu)	sapresti
(lui/lei) (lei/Lei)	saprebbe
(noi)	sapremmo
(voi)	sapreste
(loro)	saprebbero

PRESENT SUBJUNCTIVE

(io)	sappia
(tu)	sappia
(lui/lei) (lei/Lei)	sappia
(noi)	sappiamo
(voi)	sappiate
(loro)	sappiano

PAST PARTICIPLE

saputo

GERUND

sapendo

EXAMPLE PHRASES

Sai dove abita? *Do you know where he lives?*
Non **sapeva** andare in bicicletta. *He couldn't ride a bike.*
Sa di fragola. *It tastes of strawberries.*

Remember that subject pronouns are not used very often in Italian.

▶ **scegliere** (to choose)

PRESENT

(io)	scelgo
(tu)	scegli
(lui/lei) (lei/Lei)	sceglie
(noi)	scegliamo
(voi)	scegliete
(loro)	scelgono

PERFECT

(io)	ho scelto
(tu)	hai scelto
(lui/lei) (lei/Lei)	ha scelto
(noi)	abbiamo scelto
(voi)	avete scelto
(loro)	hanno scelto

IMPERFECT

(io)	sceglievo
(tu)	sceglievi
(lui/lei) (lei/Lei)	sceglieva
(noi)	sceglievamo
(voi)	sceglievate
(loro)	sceglievano

IMPERATIVE

scegli
scegliamo
scegliete

FUTURE

(io)	sceglierò
(tu)	sceglierai
(lui/lei) (lei/Lei)	sceglierà
(noi)	sceglieremo
(voi)	sceglierete
(loro)	sceglieranno

CONDITIONAL

(io)	sceglierei
(tu)	sceglieresti
(lui/lei) (lei/Lei)	sceglierebbe
(noi)	sceglieremmo
(voi)	scegliereste
(loro)	sceglierebbero

PRESENT SUBJUNCTIVE

(io)	scelga
(tu)	scelga
(lui/lei) (lei/Lei)	scelga
(noi)	scegliamo
(voi)	scegliate
(loro)	scelgano

PAST PARTICIPLE

scelto

GERUND

scegliendo

EXAMPLE PHRASES

Chi **sceglie** il vino? *Who's going to choose the wine?*
Hai scelto il regalo per lei? *Have you chosen her present?*
Sceglievano sempre il vino più costoso. *They always chose the most expensive wine.*
Scegli la pizza che vuoi. *Choose which pizza you want.*
Non sa ancora quale abito **sceglierà**. *She hasn't decided yet which dress she'll choose.*
Stavo **scegliendo** le pesche più mature. *I was choosing the ripest peaches.*

Remember that subject pronouns are not used very often in Italian.

▶ sedere (to sit)

PRESENT

(io)	siedo
(tu)	siedi
(lui/lei) (lei/Lei)	siede
(noi)	sediamo
(voi)	sedete
(loro)	siedono

FUTURE

(io)	sederò
(tu)	sederai
(lui/lei) (lei/Lei)	sederà
(noi)	sederemo
(voi)	sederete
(loro)	sederanno

PERFECT

(io)	sono seduto/a
(tu)	sei seduto/a
(lui/lei) (lei/Lei)	è seduto/a
(noi)	siamo seduti/e
(voi)	siete seduti/e
(loro)	sono seduti/e

CONDITIONAL

(io)	sederei
(tu)	sederei
(lui/lei) (lei/Lei)	sederesti
(noi)	sederebbe
(voi)	sederemmo
(loro)	sedereste

IMPERFECT

(io)	sedevo
(tu)	sedevi
(lui/lei) (lei/Lei)	sedeva
(noi)	sedevamo
(voi)	sedevate
(loro)	sedevano

PRESENT SUBJUNCTIVE

(io)	sieda
(tu)	sieda
(lui/lei) (lei/Lei)	sieda
(noi)	sediamo
(voi)	sediate
(loro)	siedano

IMPERATIVE

siedi
sediamo
sedete

PAST PARTICIPLE

seduto

GERUND

sedendo

EXAMPLE PHRASES

Era seduta accanto a me. *She was sitting beside me.*
Si **è seduto** per terra. *He sat on the floor.*
Siediti qui! *Sit here!*

Italic letters in Italian words show where stress does not follow the usual rules.

▶ **spegnere** (to put out)

PRESENT

(io)	spengo
(tu)	spegni
(lui/lei) (lei/Lei)	spegne
(noi)	spegniamo
(voi)	spegnete
(loro)	spengono

FUTURE

(io)	spegnerò
(tu)	spegnerai
(lui/lei) (lei/Lei)	spegnerà
(noi)	spegneremo
(voi)	spegnerete
(loro)	spegneranno

PERFECT

(io)	ho spento
(tu)	hai spento
(lui/lei) (lei/Lei)	ha spento
(noi)	abbiamo spento
(voi)	avete spento
(loro)	hanno spento

CONDITIONAL

(io)	spegnerei
(tu)	spegneresti
(lui/lei) (lei/Lei)	spegnerebbe
(noi)	spegneremmo
(voi)	spegnereste
(loro)	spegnerebbero

IMPERFECT

(io)	spegnevo
(tu)	spegnevi
(lui/lei) (lei/Lei)	spegneva
(noi)	spegnevamo
(voi)	spegnevate
(loro)	spegnevano

PRESENT SUBJUNCTIVE

(io)	spenga
(tu)	spenga
(lui/lei) (lei/Lei)	spenga
(noi)	spegniamo
(voi)	spegniate
(loro)	spengano

IMPERATIVE

spegni
spegniamo
spegnete

PAST PARTICIPLE

spento

GERUND

spegnendo

EXAMPLE PHRASES

Hai spento la sigaretta? *Have you put your cigarette out?*
Spegnete le luci che guardiamo il film. *Turn off the lights and we'll watch the film.*
La luce si **è spenta** all'improvviso. *The light went off suddenly.*

Italic letters in Italian words show where stress does not follow the usual rules.

▶ **stare** (to be)

PRESENT

(io)	sto
(tu)	stai
(lui/lei) (lei/Lei)	sta
(noi)	stiamo
(voi)	state
(loro)	stanno

FUTURE

(io)	starò
(tu)	starai
(lui/lei) (lei/Lei)	starà
(noi)	staremo
(voi)	starete
(loro)	staranno

PERFECT

(io)	sono stato/a
(tu)	sei stato/a
(lui/lei) (lei/Lei)	è stato/a
(noi)	siamo stati/e
(voi)	siete stati/e
(loro)	sono stati/e

CONDITIONAL

(io)	starei
(tu)	staresti
(lui/lei) (lei/Lei)	starebbe
(noi)	staremmo
(voi)	stareste
(loro)	starebbero

IMPERFECT

(io)	stavo
(tu)	stavi
(lui/lei) (lei/Lei)	stava
(noi)	stavamo
(voi)	stavate
(loro)	stavano

PRESENT SUBJUNCTIVE

(io)	stia
(tu)	stia
(lui/lei) (lei/Lei)	stia
(noi)	stiamo
(voi)	stiate
(loro)	stiano

IMPERATIVE

stai
stiamo
state

PAST PARTICIPLE

stato

GERUND

stando

EXAMPLE PHRASES

Sei mai **stato** in Francia? *Have you ever been to France?*
Come **stai**? *How are you?*
Stavo andando a casa. *I was going home.*
A Londra **starò** da amici. *I'll be staying with friends in London.*
Stavo per uscire quando ha squillato il telefono. *I was about to go out when the phone rang.*

Italic letters in Italian words show where stress does not follow the usual rules.

▶ **tenere** (to hold)

PRESENT		FUTURE	
(io)	tengo	(io)	terrò
(tu)	tieni	(tu)	terrai
(lui/lei) (lei/Lei)	tiene	(lui/lei) (lei/Lei)	terrà
(noi)	teniamo	(noi)	terremo
(voi)	tenete	(voi)	terrete
(loro)	tengono	(loro)	terranno

PERFECT		CONDITIONAL	
(io)	ho tenuto	(io)	terrei
(tu)	hai tenuto	(tu)	terresti
(lui/lei) (lei/Lei)	ha tenuto	(lui/lei) (lei/Lei)	terrebbe
(noi)	abbiamo tenuto	(noi)	terremmo
(voi)	avete tenuto	(voi)	terreste
(loro)	hanno tenuto	(loro)	terrebbero

IMPERFECT		PRESENT SUBJUNCTIVE	
(io)	tenevo	(io)	tenga
(tu)	tenevi	(tu)	tenga
(lui/lei) (lei/Lei)	teneva	(lui/lei) (lei/Lei)	tenga
(noi)	tenevamo	(noi)	teniamo
(voi)	tenevate	(voi)	teniate
(loro)	tenevano	(loro)	tengano

IMPERATIVE	PAST PARTICIPLE
tieni	tenuto
teniamo	
tenete	

GERUND

tenendo

EXAMPLE PHRASES

Tiene la racchetta con la sinistra. *He holds the racket with his left hand.*
Tieniti forte! *Hold on tight!*
Si **tenevano** per mano. *They were holding hands.*
Tieniti pronta per le cinque. *Be ready by five.*
Tieni, questo è per te. *Here, this is for you*

Remember that subject pronouns are not used very often in Italian.

▶ **togliere** (to take off)

PRESENT

(io)	tolgo
(tu)	togli
(lui/lei) (lei/Lei)	toglie
(noi)	togliamo
(voi)	togliete
(loro)	tolgono

FUTURE

(io)	toglierò
(tu)	toglierai
(lui/lei) (lei/Lei)	toglierà
(noi)	toglieremo
(voi)	toglierete
(loro)	toglieranno

PERFECT

(io)	ho tolto
(tu)	hai tolto
(lui/lei) (lei/Lei)	ha tolto
(noi)	abbiamo tolto
(voi)	avete tolto
(loro)	hanno tolto

CONDITIONAL

(io)	toglierei
(tu)	toglieresti
(lui/lei) (lei/Lei)	toglierebbe
(noi)	toglieremmo
(voi)	togliereste
(loro)	toglierebbero

IMPERFECT

(io)	toglievo
(tu)	toglievi
(lui/lei) (lei/Lei)	toglieva
(noi)	toglievamo
(voi)	toglievate
(loro)	toglievano

PRESENT SUBJUNCTIVE

(io)	tolga
(tu)	tolga
(lui/lei) (lei/Lei)	tolga
(noi)	togliamo
(voi)	togliate
(loro)	tolgano

IMPERATIVE

togli
togliamo
togliete

PAST PARTICIPLE

tolto

GERUND

togliendo

EXAMPLE PHRASES

Togliti il cappotto. *Take off your coat.*
Ho tolto il poster dalla parete. *I took the poster off the wall.*
Mi **toglieranno** due denti. *I'm going to have two teeth out.*

Italic letters in Italian words show where stress does not follow the usual rules.

▶ uscire (to go out)

PRESENT

(io)	esco
(tu)	esci
(lui/lei) (lei/Lei)	esce
(noi)	usciamo
(voi)	uscite
(loro)	escono

PERFECT

(io)	sono uscito/a
(tu)	sei uscito/a
(lui/lei) (lei/Lei)	è uscito/a
(noi)	siamo usciti/e
(voi)	siete usciti/e
(loro)	sono usciti/e

IMPERFECT

(io)	uscivo
(tu)	uscivi
(lui/lei) (lei/Lei)	usciva
(noi)	uscivamo
(voi)	uscivate
(loro)	uscivano

IMPERATIVE

esci
usciamo
uscite

FUTURE

(io)	uscirò
(tu)	uscirai
(lui/lei) (lei/Lei)	uscirà
(noi)	usciremo
(voi)	uscirete
(loro)	usciranno

CONDITIONAL

(io)	uscirei
(tu)	usciresti
(lui/lei) (lei/Lei)	uscirebbe
(noi)	usciremmo
(voi)	uscireste
(loro)	uscirebbero

PRESENT SUBJUNCTIVE

(io)	esca
(tu)	esca
(lui/lei) (lei/Lei)	esca
(noi)	usciamo
(voi)	usciate
(loro)	escano

PAST PARTICIPLE

uscito

GERUND

uscendo

EXAMPLE PHRASES

È uscita a comprare il giornale. *She's gone out to buy a newspaper.*
Uscirà dall'ospedale domani. *He's coming out of hospital tomorrow.*
L'ho incontrata che **usciva** dalla farmacia. *I met her coming out of the chemist's.*
La rivista **esce** di lunedì. *The magazine comes out on Mondays.*

Italic letters in Italian words show where stress does not follow the usual rules.

▶ **valere** (to be worth)

PRESENT

(io)	valgo
(tu)	vali
(lui/lei) (lei/Lei)	vale
(noi)	valiamo
(voi)	valete
(loro)	valgono

PERFECT

(io)	sono valso/a
(tu)	sei valso/a
(lui/lei) (lei/Lei)	è valso/a
(noi)	siamo valsi/e
(voi)	siete valsi/e
(loro)	sono valsi/e

IMPERFECT

(io)	valevo
(tu)	valevi
(lui/lei) (lei/Lei)	valeva
(noi)	valevamo
(voi)	valevate
(loro)	valevano

IMPERATIVE

vali
valiamo
valete

FUTURE

(io)	varrò
(tu)	varrai
(lui/lei) (lei/Lei)	varrà
(noi)	varremo
(voi)	varrete
(loro)	varranno

CONDITIONAL

(io)	varrei
(tu)	varresti
(lui/lei) (lei/Lei)	varrebbe
(noi)	varremmo
(voi)	varreste
(loro)	varrebbero

PRESENT SUBJUNCTIVE

(io)	valga
(tu)	valga
(lui/lei) (lei/Lei)	valga
(noi)	valiamo
(voi)	valiate
(loro)	valgano

PAST PARTICIPLE

valso

GERUND

valendo

EXAMPLE PHRASES

L'auto **vale** tremila euro. *The car is worth three thousand euros.*
Non ne **vale** la pena. *It's not worth it.*
Senza il giardino, la casa non **varrebbe** niente. *Without the garden the house wouldn't be worth anything.*

Remember that subject pronouns are not used very often in Italian.

▶ vedere (to see)

PRESENT

(io)	vedo
(tu)	vedi
(lui/lei) (lei/Lei)	vede
(noi)	vediamo
(voi)	vedete
(loro)	vedono

FUTURE

(io)	vedrò
(tu)	vedrai
(lui/lei) (lei/Lei)	vedrà
(noi)	vedremo
(voi)	vedrete
(loro)	vedranno

PERFECT

(io)	ho visto
(tu)	hai visto
(lui/lei) (lei/Lei)	ha visto
(noi)	abbiamo visto
(voi)	avete visto
(loro)	hanno visto

CONDITIONAL

(io)	vedrei
(tu)	vedresti
(lui/lei) (lei/Lei)	vedrebbe
(noi)	vedremmo
(voi)	vedreste
(loro)	vedrebbero

IMPERFECT

(io)	vedevo
(tu)	vedevi
(lui/lei) (lei/Lei)	vedeva
(noi)	vedevamo
(voi)	vedevate
(loro)	vedevano

PRESENT SUBJUNCTIVE

(io)	veda
(tu)	veda
(lui/lei) (lei/Lei)	veda
(noi)	vediamo
(voi)	vediate
(loro)	vedano

IMPERATIVE

vedi
vediamo
vedete

PAST PARTICIPLE

visto

GERUND

vedendo

EXAMPLE PHRASES

Non ci **vedo** senza occhiali. *I can't see without my glasses.*
Ci **vediamo** domani! *See you tomorrow!*
Non **vedevo** l'ora di conoscerlo. *I couldn't wait to meet him.*

Italic letters in Italian words show where stress does not follow the usual rules.

▶ venire (to come)

PRESENT

(io)	vengo
(tu)	vieni
(lui/lei) (lei/Lei)	viene
(noi)	veniamo
(voi)	venite
(loro)	vengono

PERFECT

(io)	sono venuto/a
(tu)	sei venuto/a
(lui/lei) (lei/Lei)	è venuto/a
(noi)	siamo venuti/e
(voi)	siete venuti/e
(loro)	sono venuti/e

IMPERFECT

(io)	venivo
(tu)	venivi
(lui/lei) (lei/Lei)	veniva
(noi)	venivamo
(voi)	venivate
(loro)	venivano

IMPERATIVE

vieni
veniamo
venite

FUTURE

(io)	verrò
(tu)	verrai
(lui/lei) (lei/Lei)	verrà
(noi)	verremo
(voi)	verrete
(loro)	verranno

CONDITIONAL

(io)	verrei
(tu)	verresti
(lui/lei) (lei/Lei)	verrebbe
(noi)	verremmo
(voi)	verreste
(loro)	verrebbero

PRESENT SUBJUNCTIVE

(io)	venga
(tu)	venga
(lui/lei) (lei/Lei)	venga
(noi)	veniamo
(voi)	veniate
(loro)	vengano

PAST PARTICIPLE

venuto

GERUND

venendo

EXAMPLE PHRASES

È venuto in macchina. *He came by car.*
Da dove **vieni**? *Where do you come from?*
Vieni a trovarci. *Come and see us!*
Quanto **viene**? *How much is it?*

Remember that subject pronouns are not used very often in Italian.

volere (to want)

PRESENT

(io)	voglio
(tu)	vuoi
(lui/lei) (lei/Lei)	vuole
(noi)	vogliamo
(voi)	volete
(loro)	vogliono

FUTURE

(io)	vorrò
(tu)	vorrai
(lui/lei) (lei/Lei)	vorrà
(noi)	vorremo
(voi)	vorrete
(loro)	vorranno

PERFECT

(io)	ho voluto
(tu)	hai voluto
(lui/lei) (lei/Lei)	ha voluto
(noi)	abbiamo voluto
(voi)	avete voluto
(loro)	hanno voluto

CONDITIONAL

(io)	vorrei
(tu)	vorresti
(lui/lei) (lei/Lei)	vorrebbe
(noi)	vorremmo
(voi)	vorreste
(loro)	vorrebbero

IMPERFECT

(io)	volevo
(tu)	volevi
(lui/lei) (lei/Lei)	voleva
(noi)	volevamo
(voi)	volevate
(loro)	volevano

PRESENT SUBJUNCTIVE

(io)	voglia
(tu)	voglia
(lui/lei) (lei/Lei)	voglia
(noi)	vogliamo
(voi)	vogliate
(loro)	vogliano

IMPERATIVE

PAST PARTICIPLE

voluto

GERUND

volendo

SAMPLE PHRASES

Voglio comprare una macchina nuova. *I want to buy a new car.*

Devo pagare subito o posso pagare domani? – Come **vuole**. *Do I have to pay now or can I pay tomorrow? – As you prefer.*

Quanto ci **vorrà** prima che finiate? *How long will it take you to finish?*

La campanella **voleva** dire che la lezione era finita. *The bell meant that the lesson was over.*

Vorrei **volendo** non posso invitarti: la festa è sua. *I'd like to, but I can't invite you: it's his party.*

Italic letters in Italian words show where stress does not follow the usual rules.